Collins

LONDON
STREETFINDER

CONTENTS

Key to Map Pages	2-3
Key to Central London Map Symbols	4
Key to Outer London Map Symbols	5
Central London Maps	6-37
Outer London Maps	38-203
West End Theatres and Cinemas	204
West End Shopping	205
London Information	206-207
Index to Place Names	208-209
Index to Railway Stations	210-211
Index to Hospitals	212
Index to Street Names	213-368

Published by Collins
An imprint of HarperCollins*Publishers*
77-85 Fulham Palace Road, Hammersmith,
London W6 8JB

The HarperCollins website address is:
www.**fire**and**water**.com

Copyright © HarperCollins*Publishers* Ltd 2001
Mapping © Bartholomew Ltd 2001

Collins® is a registered trademark of
HarperCollins*Publishers* Limited

Mapping generated from Bartholomew digital
databases

Bartholomew website address is:
www.bartholomewmaps.com

London Underground Map by permission of London
Regional Transport
LRT Registered User No. 00/3264

Printed in Hong Kong

ISBN 0 00 449026 6 paperback   NM10571   ADD
ISBN 0 00 449027 4 spiral bound   NM10570

e-mail: roadcheck@harpercollins.co.uk

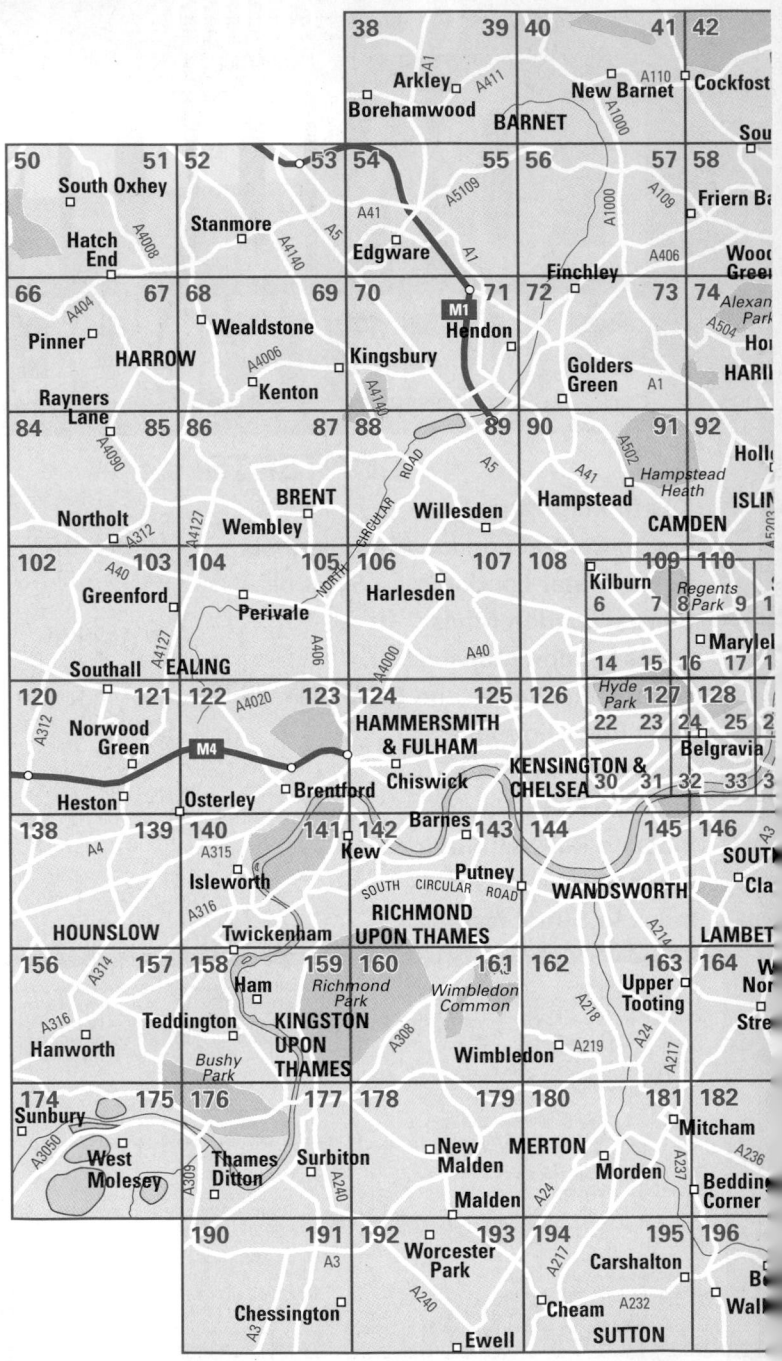

38	39	40	41	42
Arkley Borehamwood	A411 A1	BARNET	A110 New Barnet A1000	Cockfost Sou
50 South Oxhey Hatch End A4008	51	52 Stanmore A4140	53 A5	54 A41 Edgware A5109 A1	55	56 Finchley A1000	57 A109 A406	58 Friern B Wood Gree
66 A404 Pinner HARROW Rayners Lane	67	68 Wealdstone A4006 Kenton	69	70 Kingsbury A4140	71 M1 Hendon	72	73 Golders Green A1	74 Alexan Park A504 Hor HARII
84 A4090 Northolt	85	86 BRENT A4127 Wembley	87	88 A5 Willesden	89 NORTH CIRCULAR ROAD	90 Hampstead A41	91 A502 Hampstead Heath CAMDEN	92 Holl ISLIN
102 A40 Greenford Southall	103 EALING A4127	104 Perivale	105 NORTH	106 Harlesden A4000	107 A40	108	109 Kilburn 6 7 14 15	110 Regents 8 Park 9 1 Marylel 16 17 1
120 A312 Norwood Green Heston	121	122 M4 Osterley A4020	123 Brentford	124 HAMMERSMITH & FULHAM Chiswick	125	126 KENSINGTON & CHELSEA	127 Hyde Park 22 23 30 31	128 24 25 2 Belgravia 32 33 3
138 A4 HOUNSLOW	139	140 A315 Isleworth A316 Twickenham	141 Kew	142 Barnes SOUTH CIRCULAR ROAD RICHMOND UPON THAMES	143 Putney	144 WANDSWORTH A214	145	146 A3 SOUT Cla LAMBET
156 A314 A316 Hanworth	157 Teddington	158 Ham Bushy Park	159 Richmond Park KINGSTON UPON THAMES	160 Wimbledon Common A308	161	162 A218 Wimbledon A219	163 Upper Tooting A24	164 W Nor Stre A217
174 Sunbury A3050 West Molesey	175	176 A309 Thames Ditton	177 Surbiton A240	178 New Malden Malden A24	179	180 MERTON	181 Morden A237 Mitcham	182 A236 Beddin Corner
190	191 Chessington A3	192 Worcester Park A240	193 Ewell	194 A217 Cheam	195 Carshalton A232 SUTTON	196 B Wall

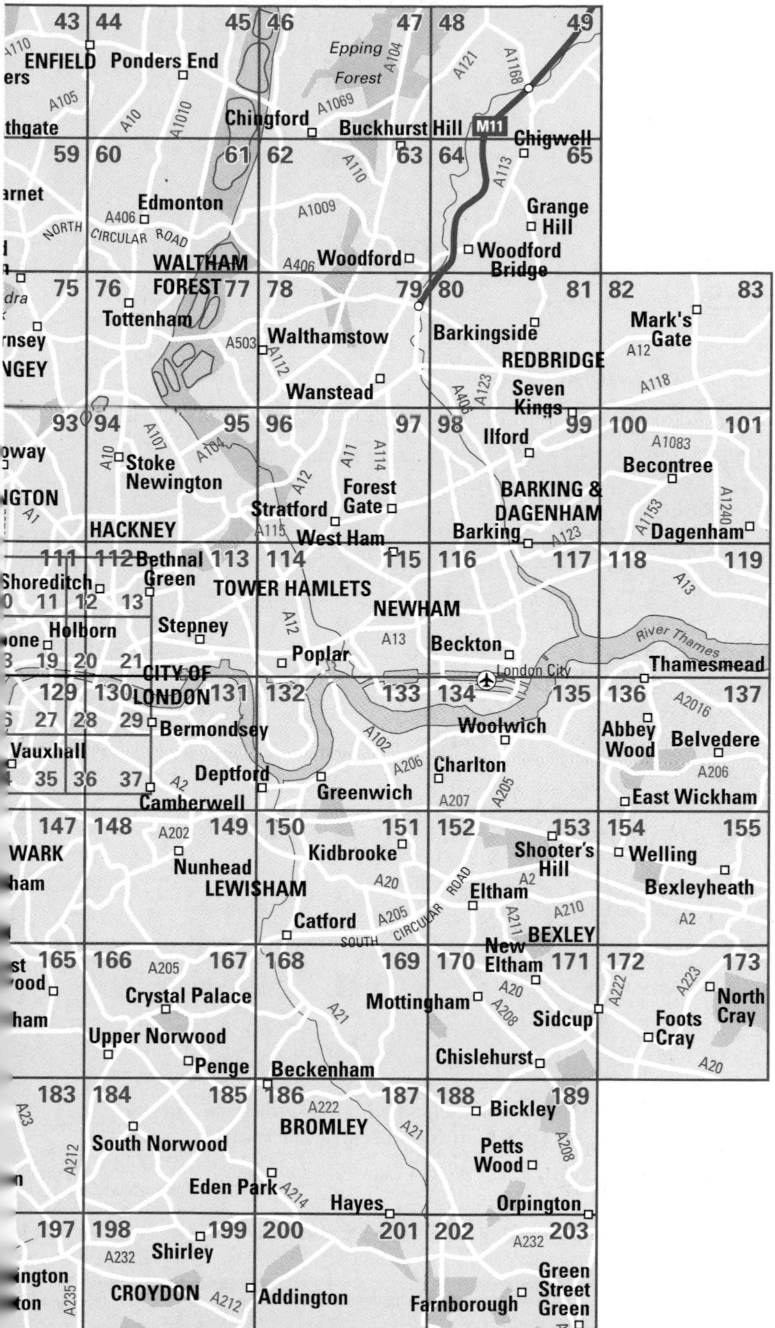

43	**44**	**45/46**	Epping	**47**	**48**	**49**	

A1110
ENFIELD **Ponders End**
ers
A105
thgate

43 **44** **45 46** Epping **47** **48** **49**
Forest
A104
A121 A1168
Chingford Buckhurst Hill **M11** Chigwell
A1069
A10 A1010

59 **60** **61** **62** A110 **63** **64** **65**
Edmonton Grange
arnet A1009 Hill
NORTH CIRCULAR ROAD A406 A113 Woodford
WALTHAM A406 Woodford Bridge

75 **76** FOREST **77** **78** **79** **80** **81** **82** **83**
dra Tottenham Mark's
A503 Walthamstow Barkingside A12 Gate
rnsey A112 REDBRIDGE A118
NGEY Wanstead Seven A123
Kings

93 **94** **95** **96** **97** **98** Ilford **99** **100** **101**
oway A107 Stoke A11 A1083
A104 Newington A12 A114 Forest Becontree
NGTON Stratford Gate A153 A1240
A1 HACKNEY West Ham Barking A123 Dagenham
BARKING &
DAGENHAM

111 **112** Bethnal **113** **114** **115** **116** **117** **118** **119**
Shoreditch Green A13
0 11 12 13 TOWER HAMLETS River Thames
one Holborn Stepney NEWHAM
3 19 20 21 A12 A13 Beckton
CITY OF Poplar London City Thamesmead
LONDON

129 **130** **131** **132** **133** **134** **135** **136** **137**
27 28 29 Bermondsey A102 Woolwich Abbey A2016
Vauxhall Deptford A206 Charlton Wood Belvedere
35 36 37 A2 A205 A206
Camberwell Greenwich A207 A205 East Wickham

147 **148** A202 **149** **150** **151** **152** **153** **154** **155**
WARK Nunhead Kidbrooke Shooter's Welling
ham LEWISHAM A20 Hill
Eltham A2 Bexleyheath
Catford A205 A210 A2
SOUTH CIRCULAR BEXLEY
New
165 **166** A205 **167** **168** **169** **170** Eltham **171** **172** **173**
st Crystal Palace Mottingham A20 North
ood A21 A208 Sidcup A222 A223 Cray
ham Upper Norwood Foots
Penge Beckenham Chislehurst Cray A20

183 **184** **185** **186** **187** **188** **189**
A23 A222 Bickley
South Norwood BROMLEY A21 Petts A208
A212 Wood
Eden Park A214 Orpington
Hayes

197 **198** **199** **200** **201** **202** **203**
ington A232 Shirley A232 Green
ton CROYDON A212 Addington Farnborough Street
A235 Green
A21

KEY TO CENTRAL LONDON MAP SYMBOLS

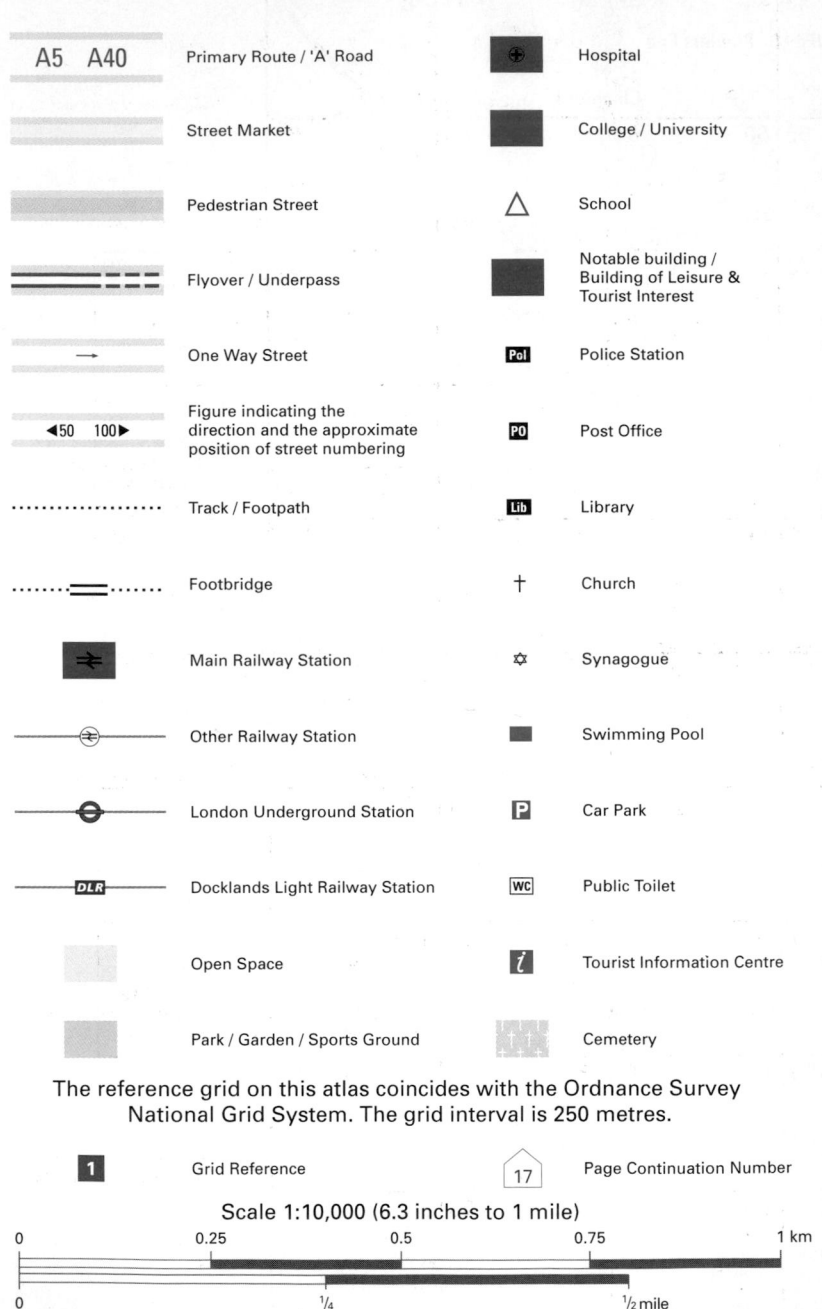

A5 A40	Primary Route / 'A' Road
	Street Market
	Pedestrian Street
	Flyover / Underpass
→	One Way Street
◀50 100▶	Figure indicating the direction and the approximate position of street numbering
····················	Track / Footpath
·······╍═══╍·······	Footbridge
⇌	Main Railway Station
✦	Other Railway Station
⊖	London Underground Station
DLR	Docklands Light Railway Station
	Open Space
	Park / Garden / Sports Ground

✛	Hospital
	College / University
△	School
	Notable building / Building of Leisure & Tourist Interest
Pol	Police Station
PO	Post Office
Lib	Library
†	Church
✡	Synagogue
■	Swimming Pool
P	Car Park
WC	Public Toilet
i	Tourist Information Centre
	Cemetery

The reference grid on this atlas coincides with the Ordnance Survey National Grid System. The grid interval is 250 metres.

1	Grid Reference	17	Page Continuation Number

Scale 1:10,000 (6.3 inches to 1 mile)

0	0.25	0.5	0.75	1 km

0		¹/₄		¹/₂ mile

KEY TO OUTER LONDON MAP SYMBOLS

M11 — Motorway	⊕ Hospital
A5 A40 — Primary Route / 'A' Road	▲ College / University
Toll — Toll	△ School
Flyover / Underpass	**Pol** Police Station
Street Market	**PO** Post Office / Sorting Office
Pedestrian Street	**Lib** Library
→ One Way Street (only shown on classified roads)	† Church
◄50 100► Figure indicating the direction and the approximate position of street numbering	🏛 Building of Leisure & Tourist Interest
·········· Track / Footpath	Other Buildings
⇌ Main Railway Station	Sports Stadium
⊛ Other Railway Station	Swimming Pool
⊖ London Underground Station	**P** Car Park
DLR Docklands Light Railway Station	**i** Tourist Information Centre
⊖ Tramway Station	Golf Course
Open Space / Allotments	Cemetery
Park / Garden / Sports Ground	Wood / Forest

The reference grid on this atlas coincides with the Ordnance Survey National Grid System. The grid interval is 500 metres.

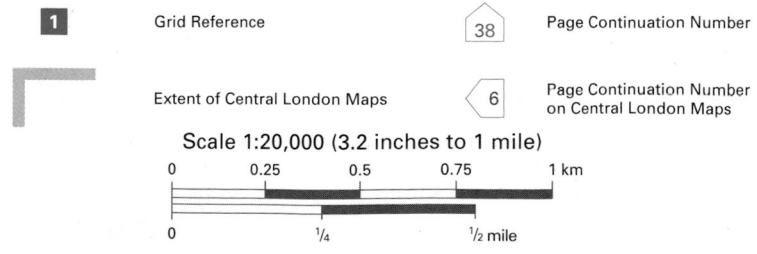

1 Grid Reference	38 Page Continuation Number
Extent of Central London Maps	6 Page Continuation Number on Central London Maps

Scale 1:20,000 (3.2 inches to 1 mile)

0   0.25   0.5   0.75   1 km

0   ¼   ½ mile

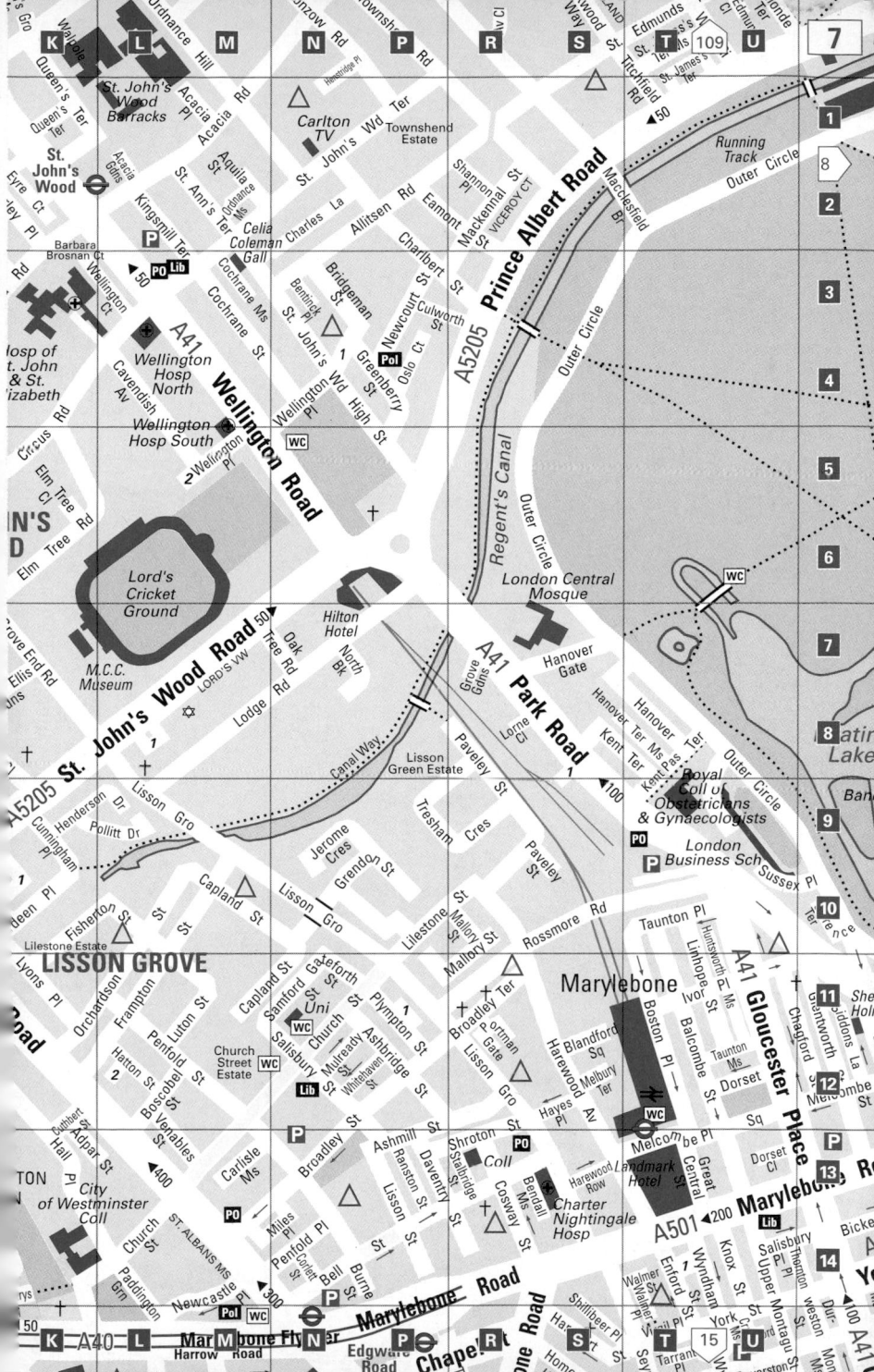

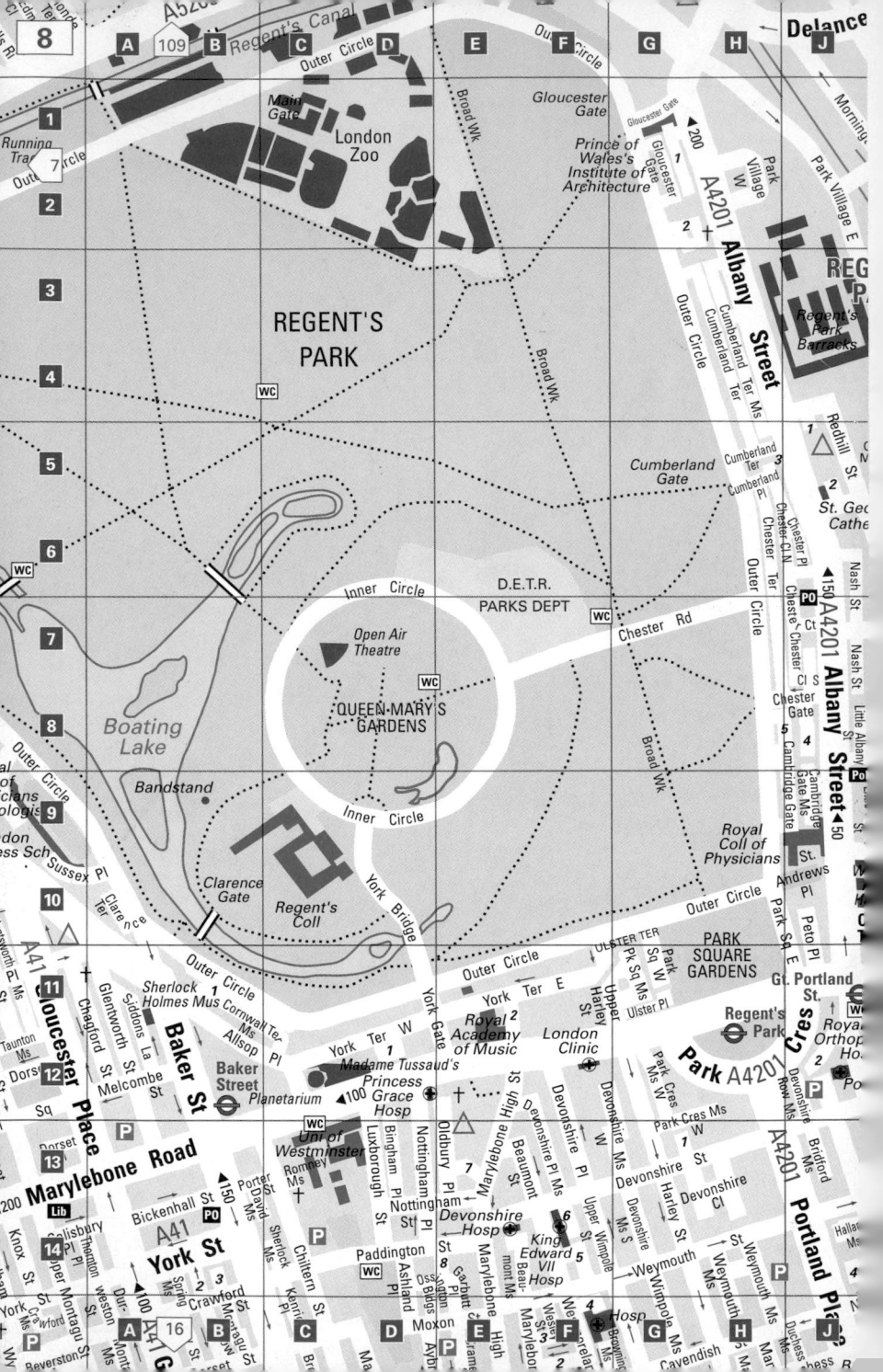

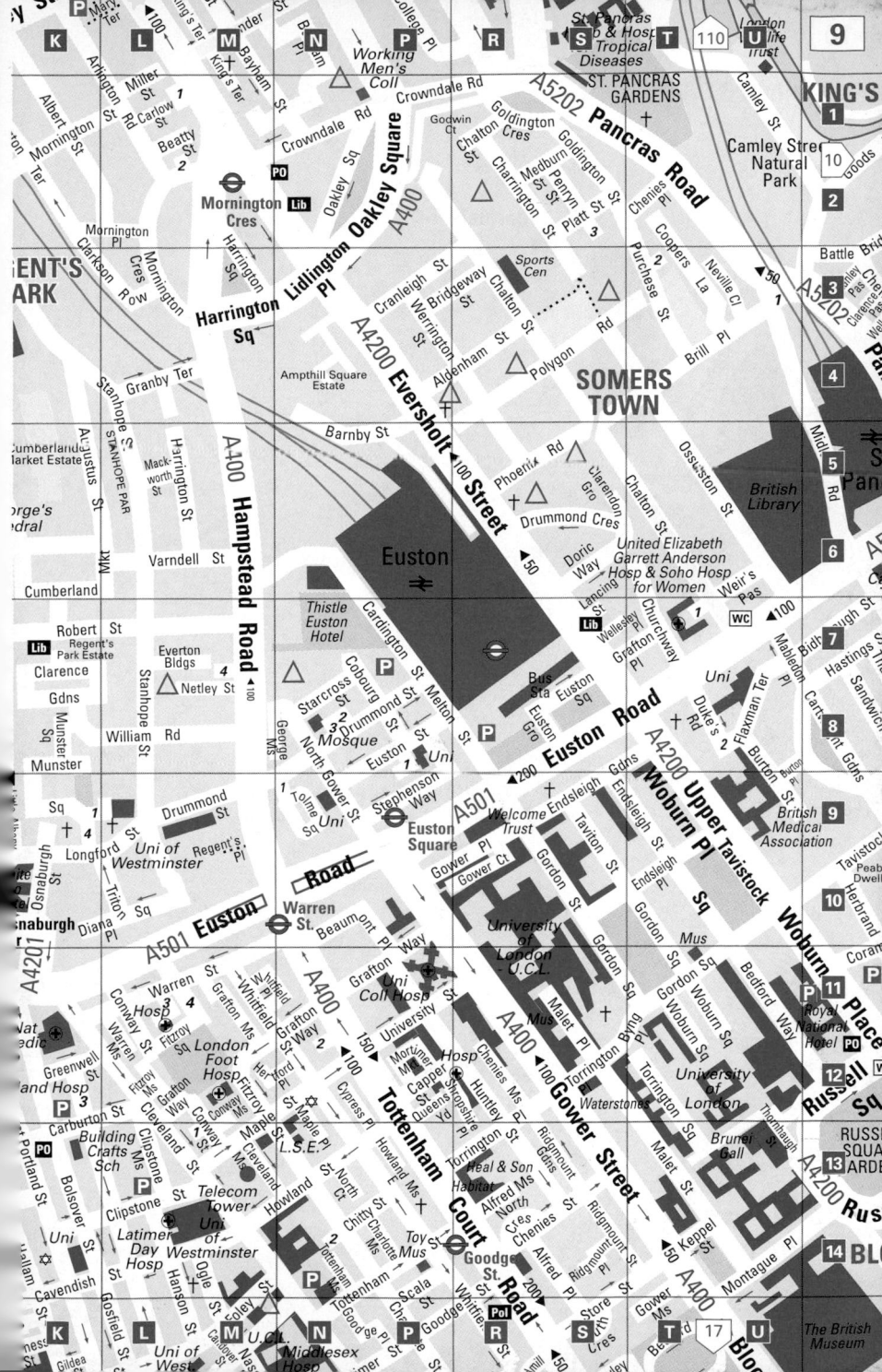

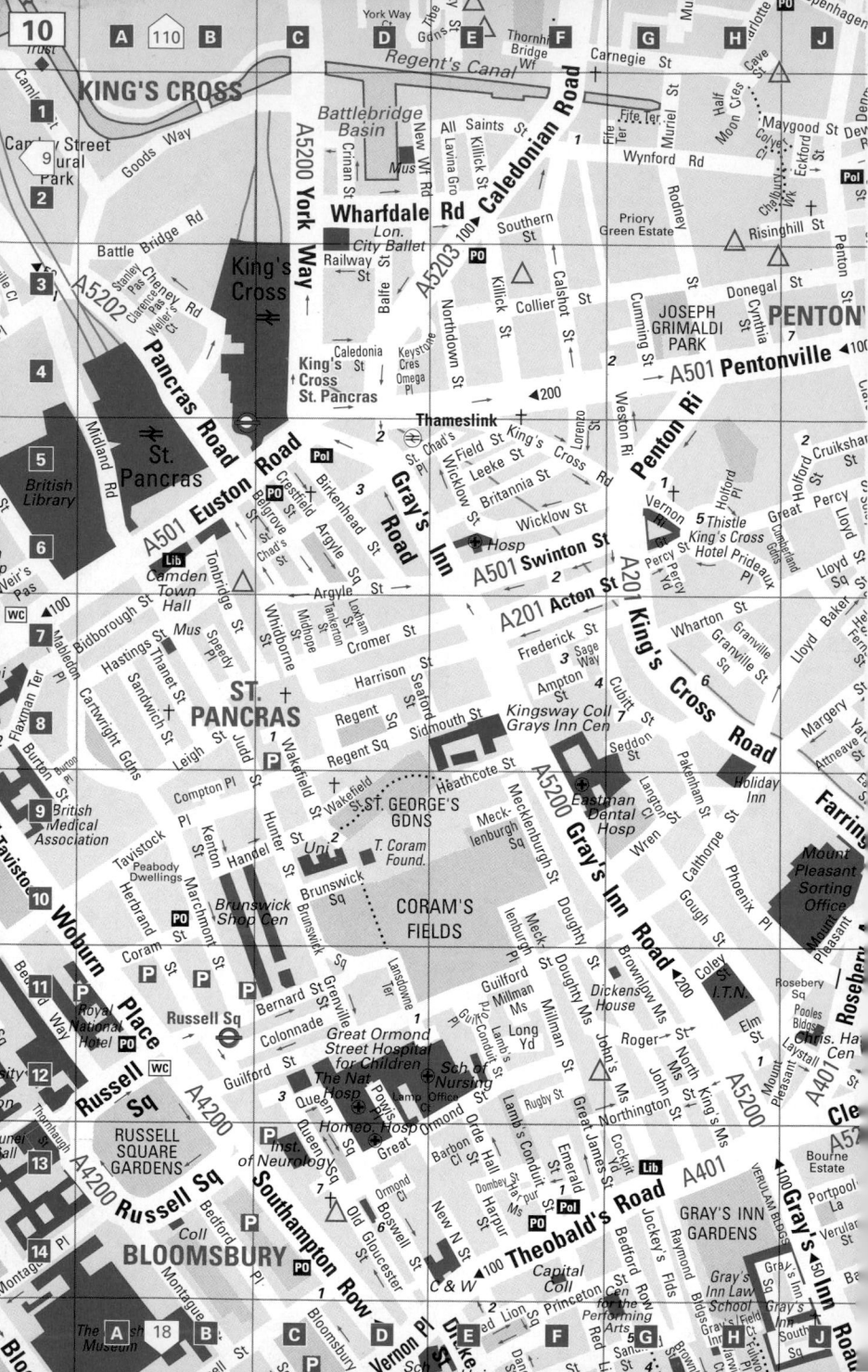

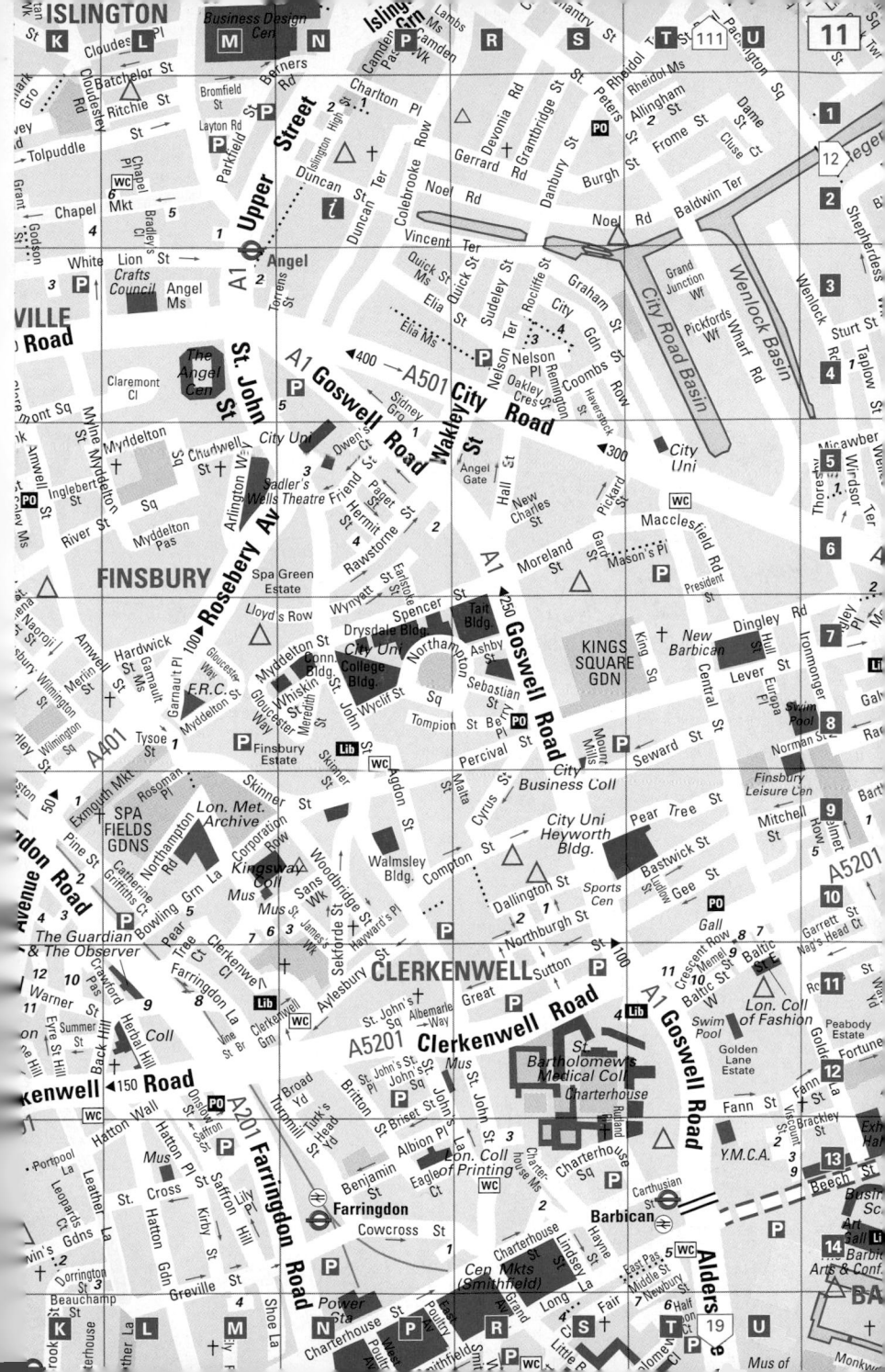

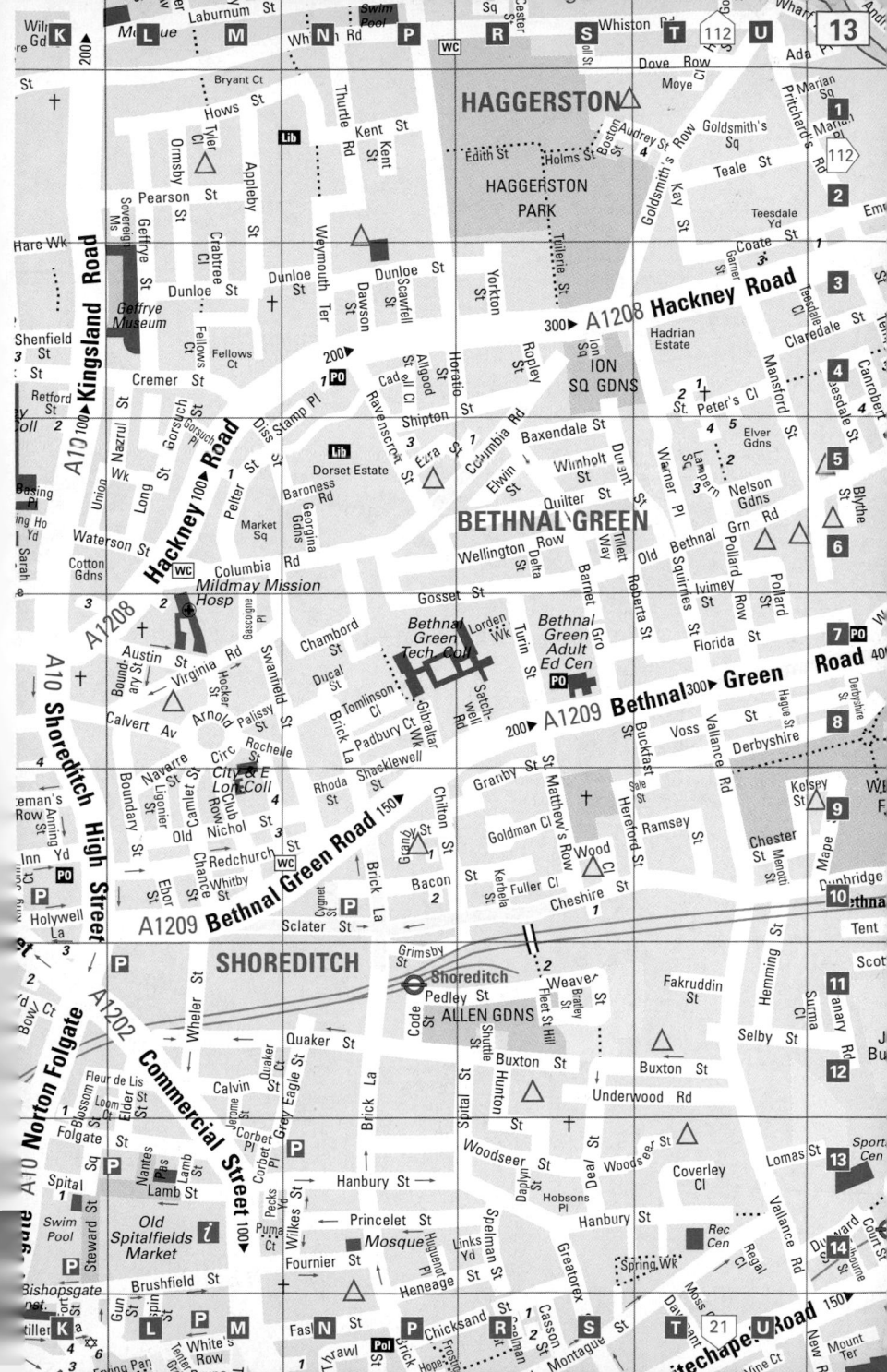

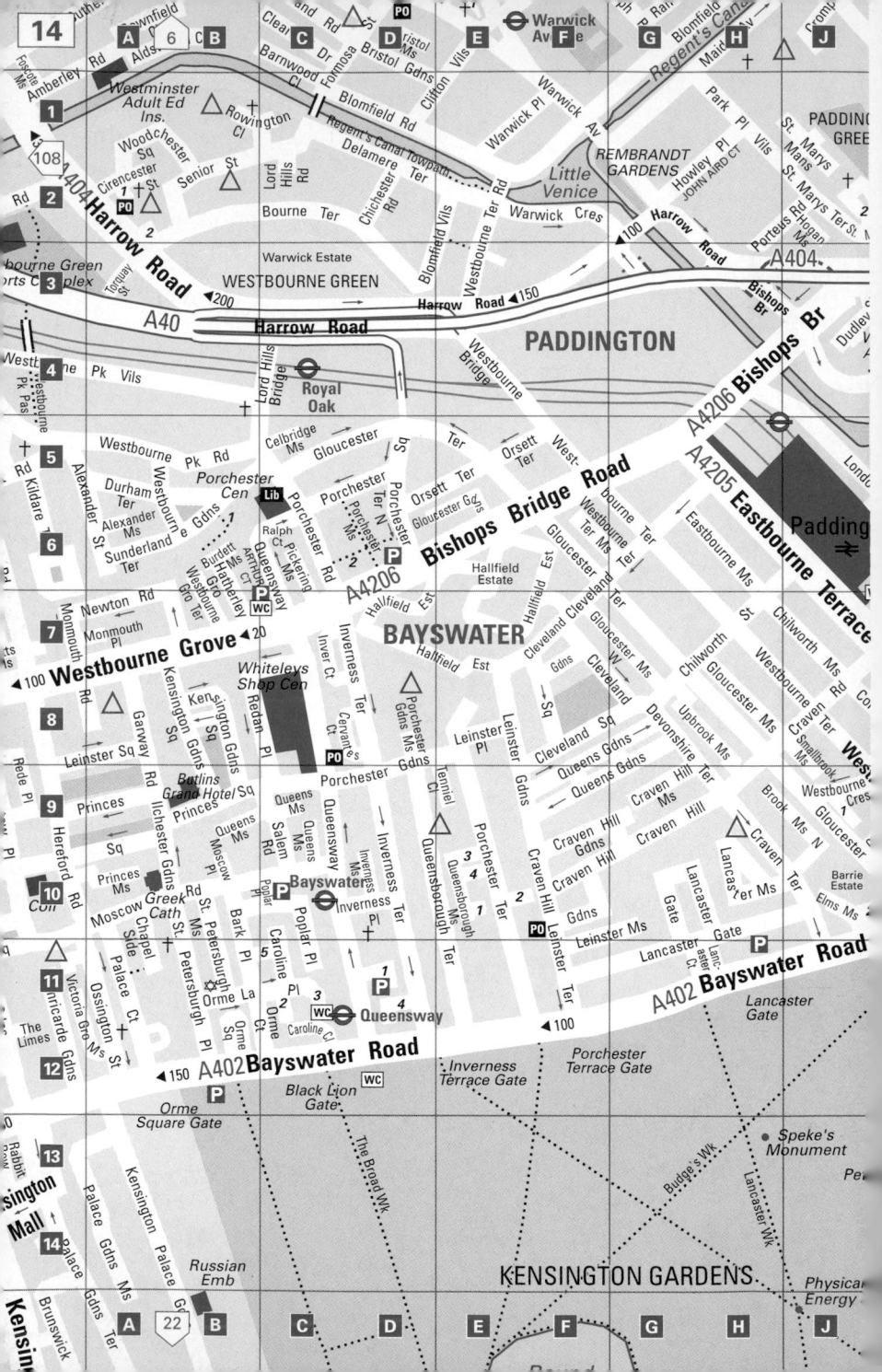

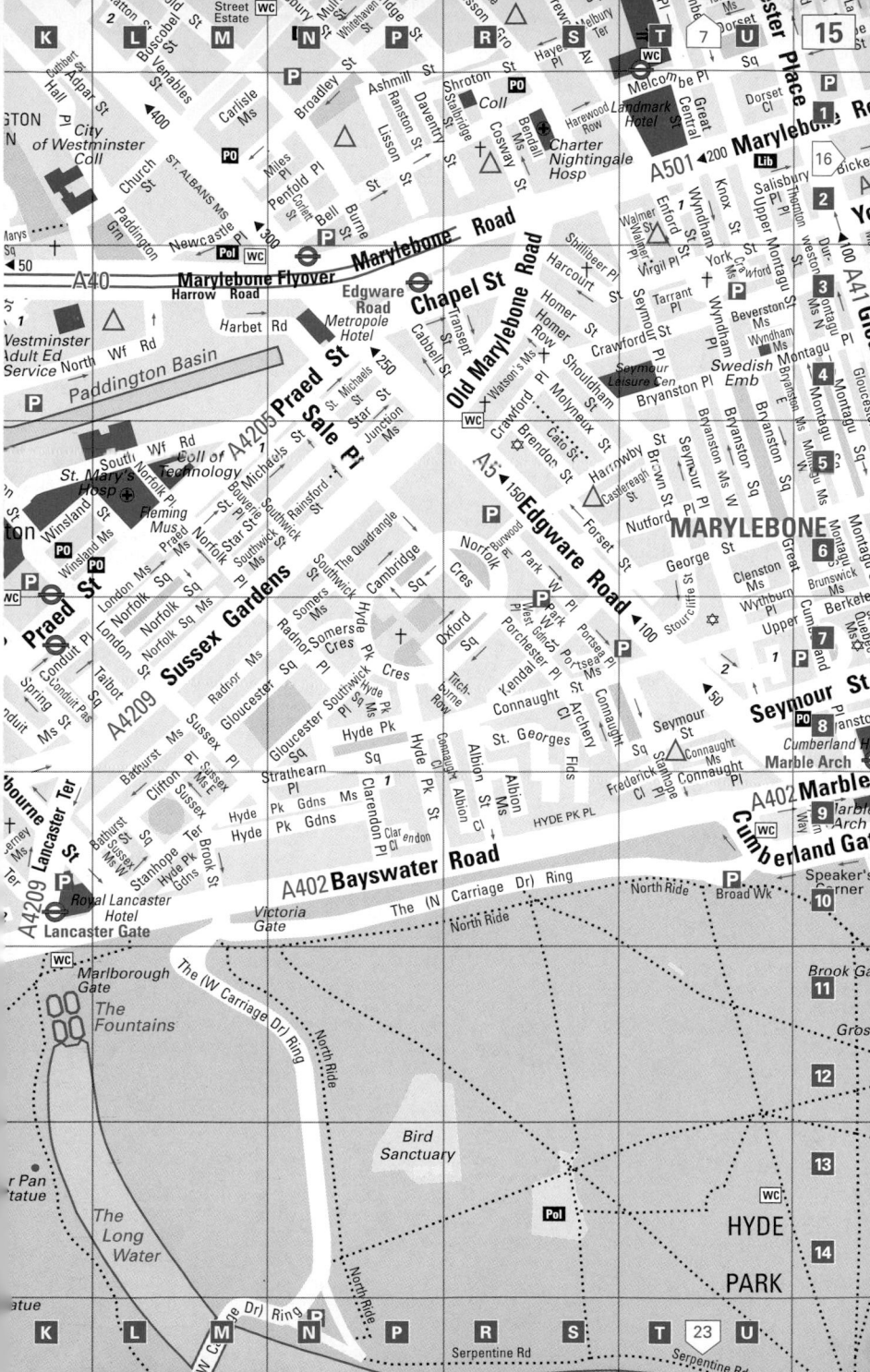

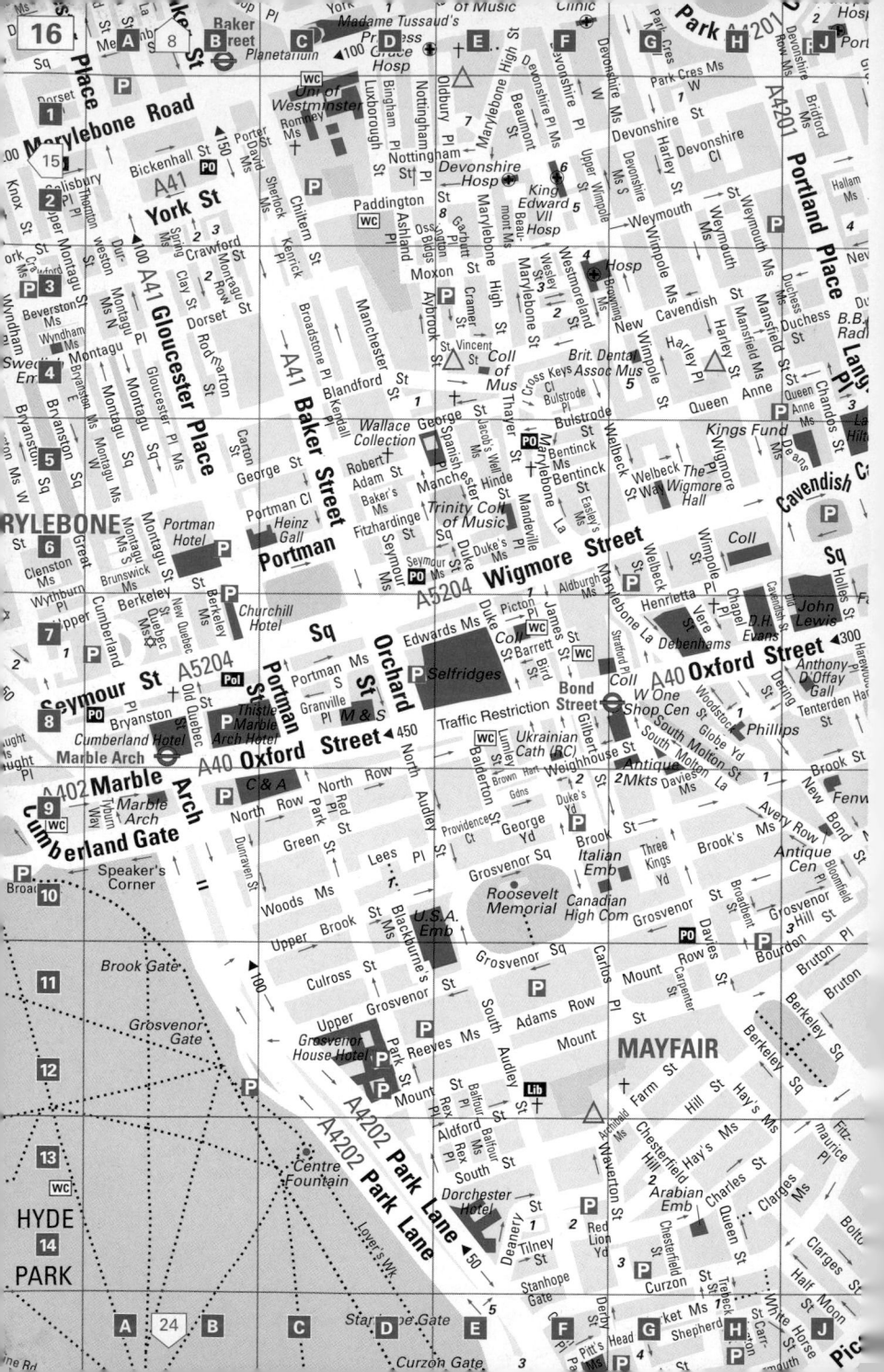

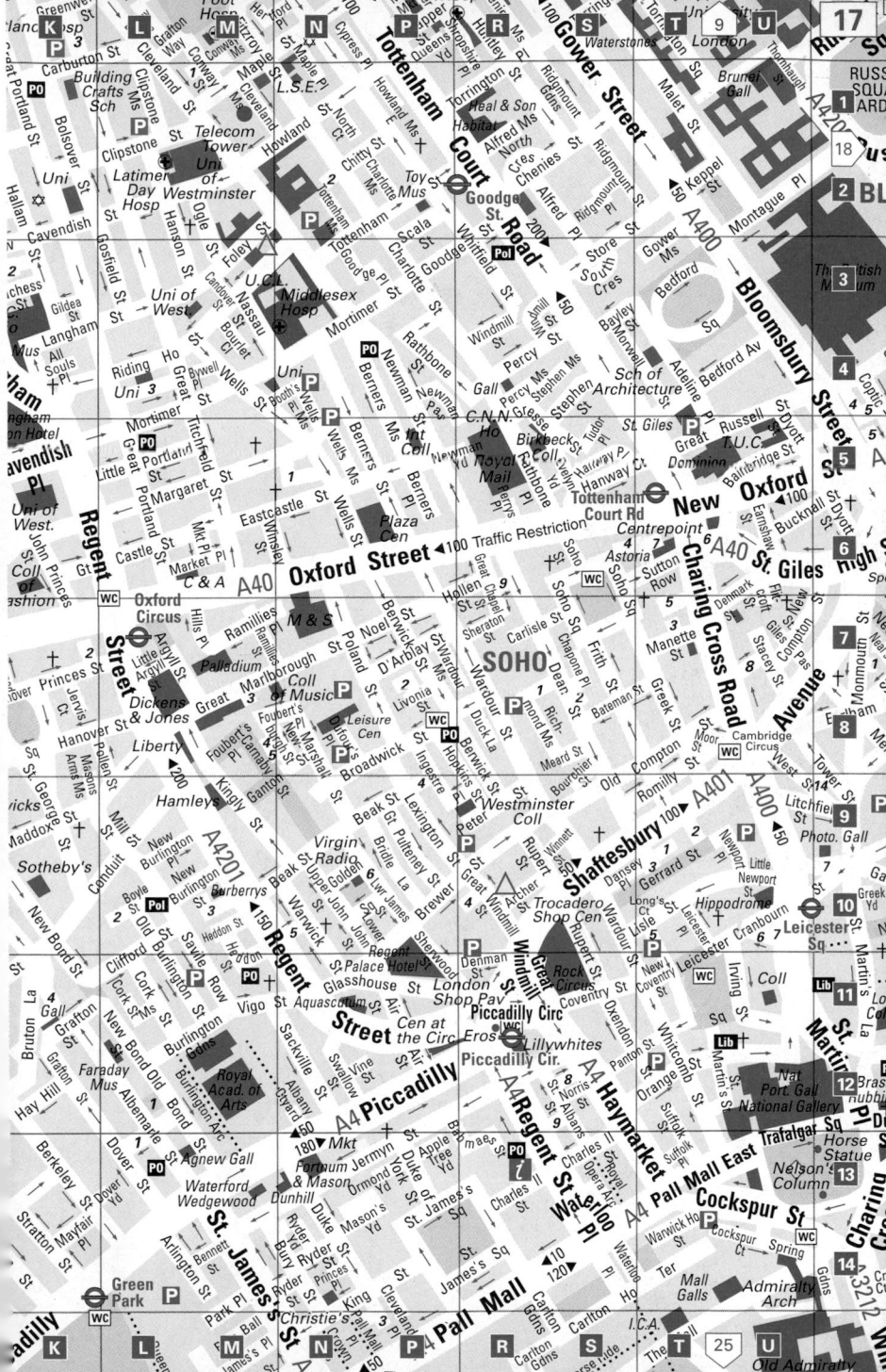

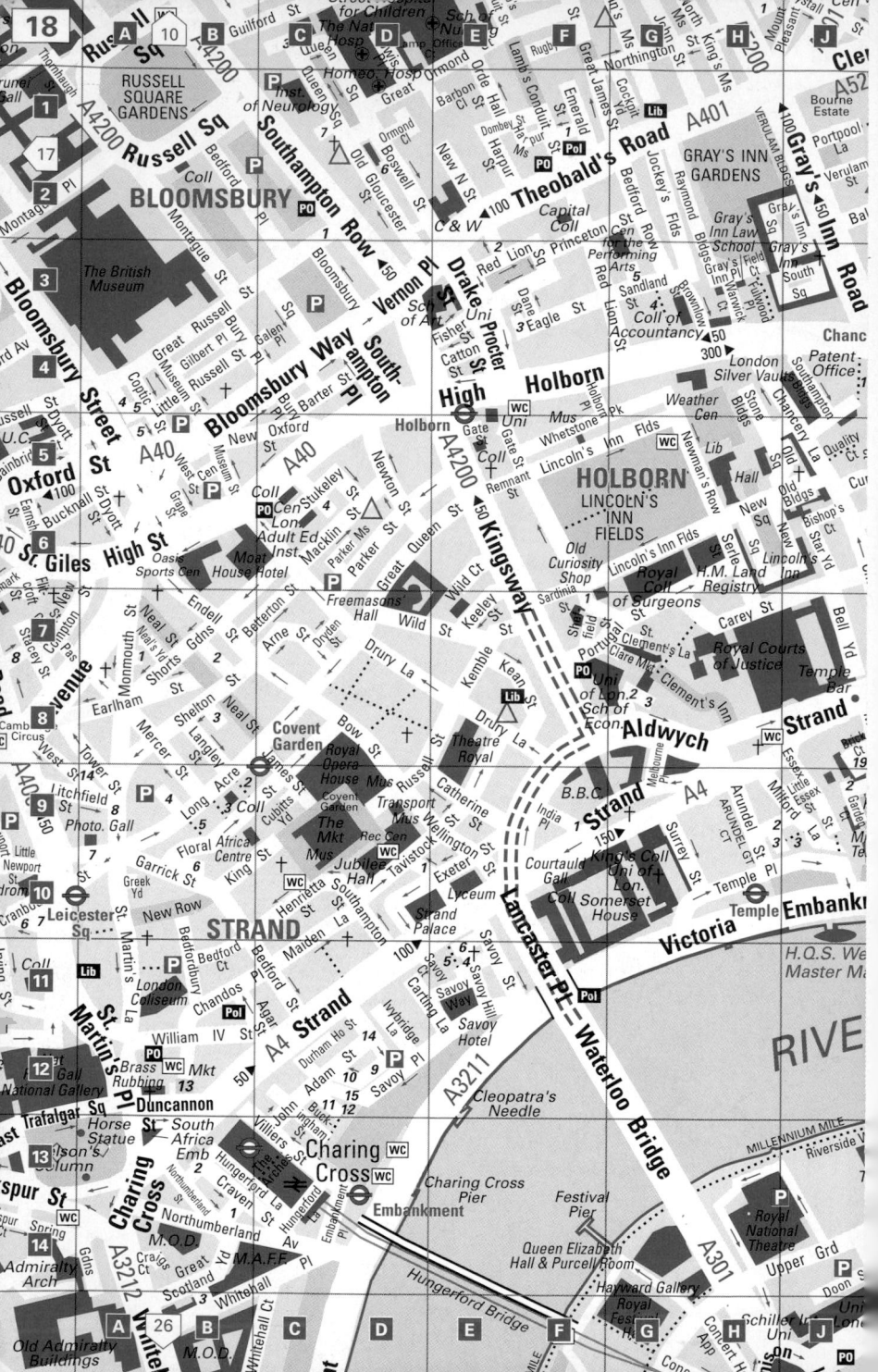

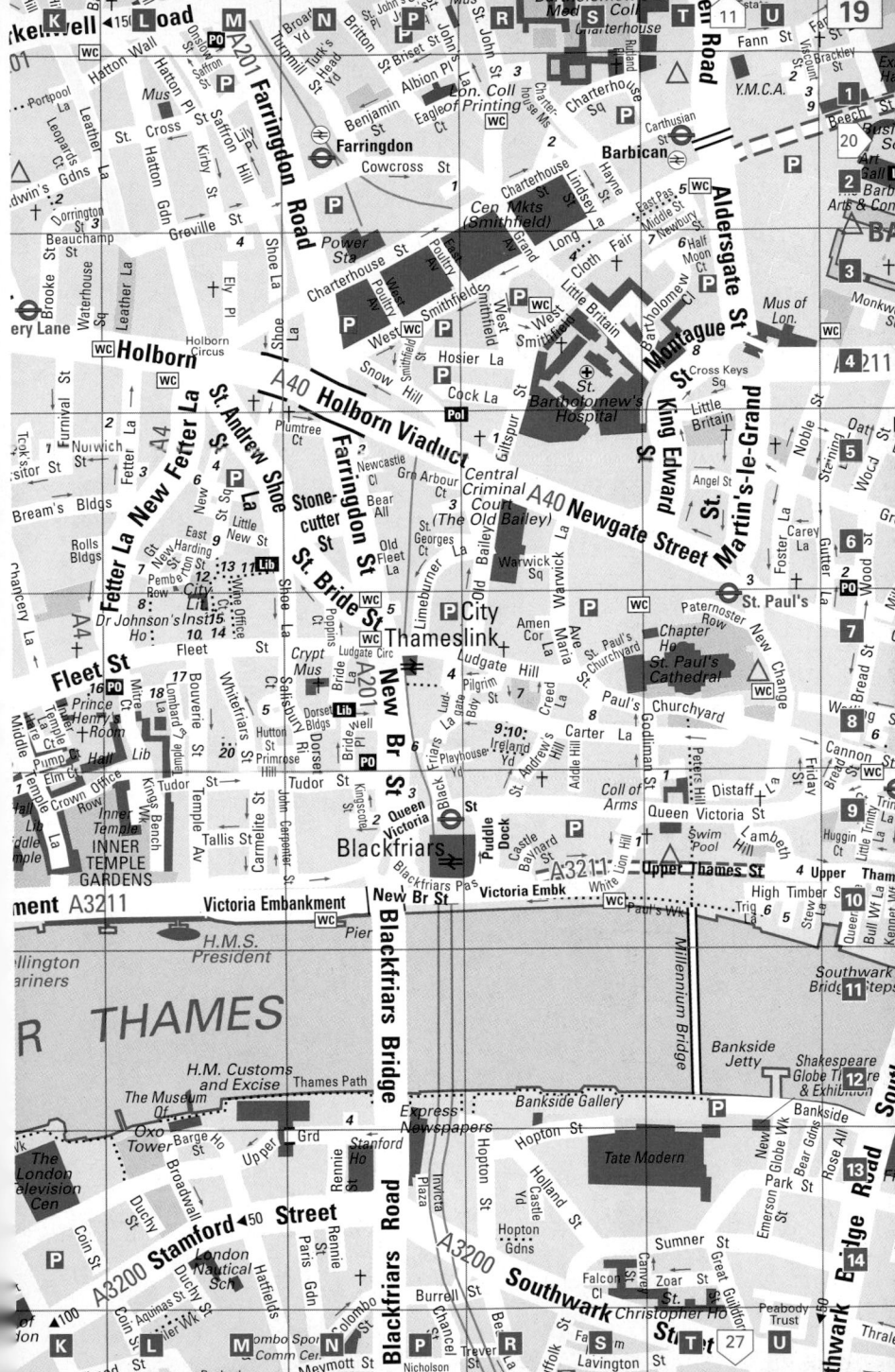

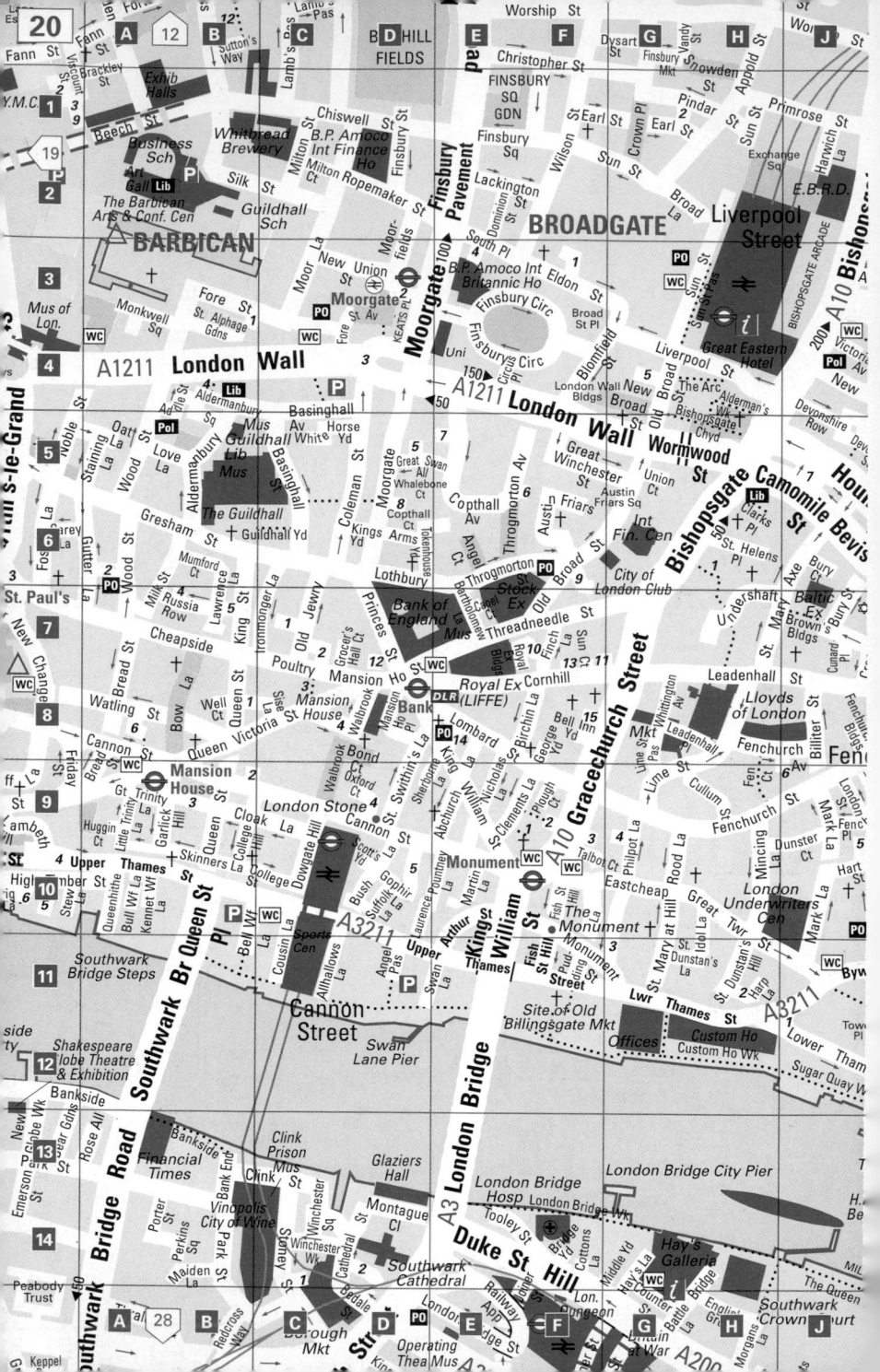

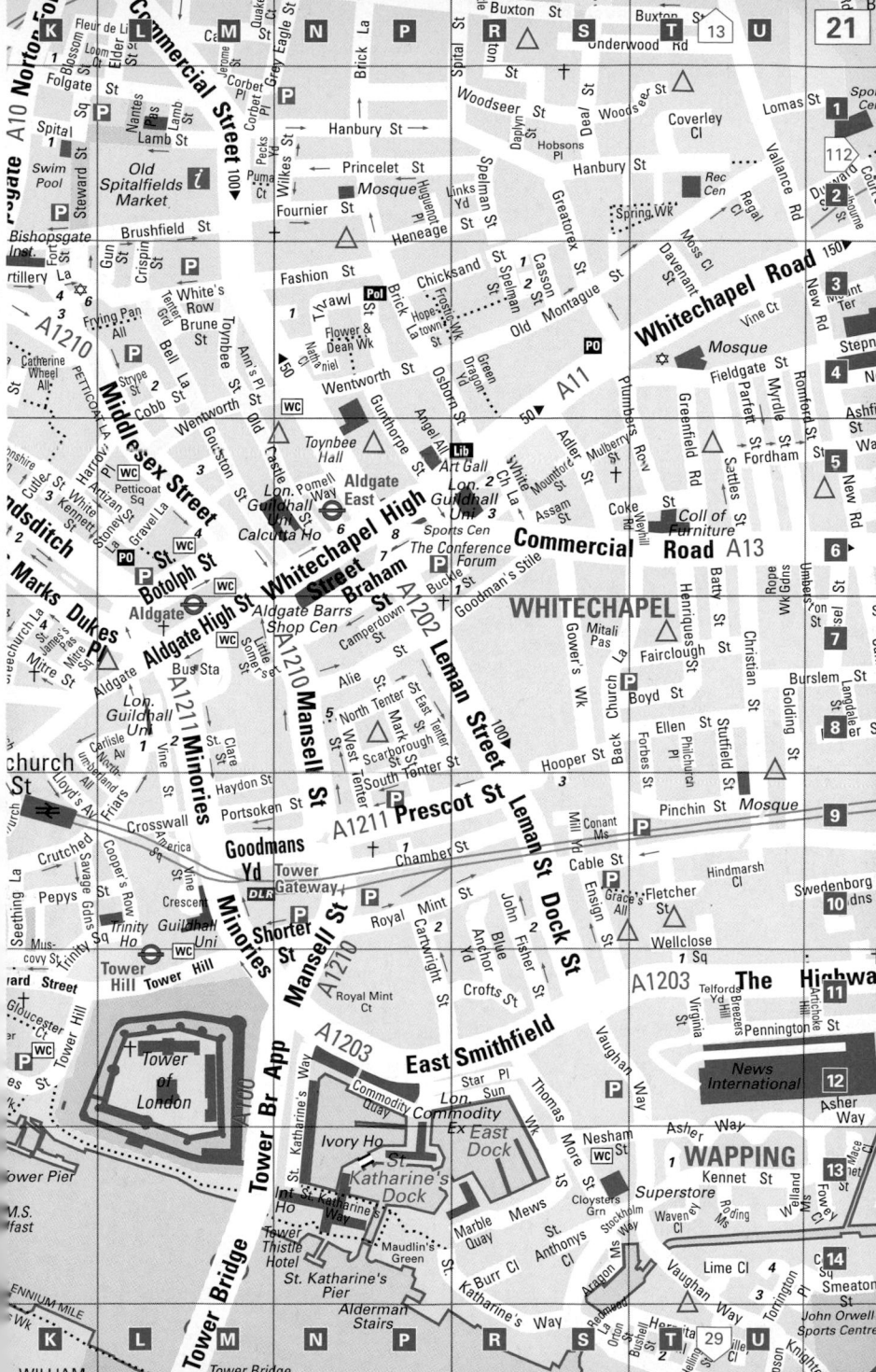

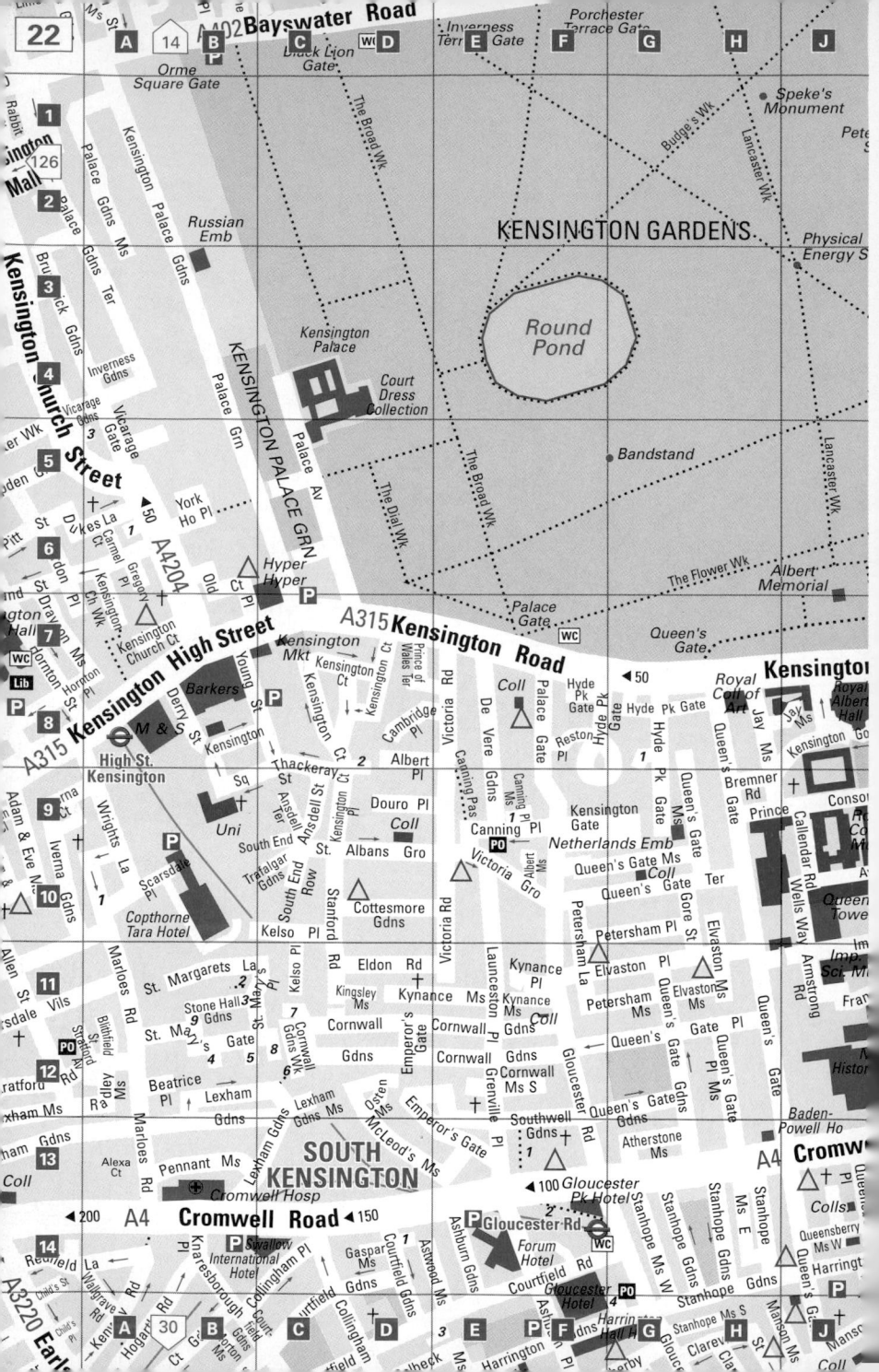

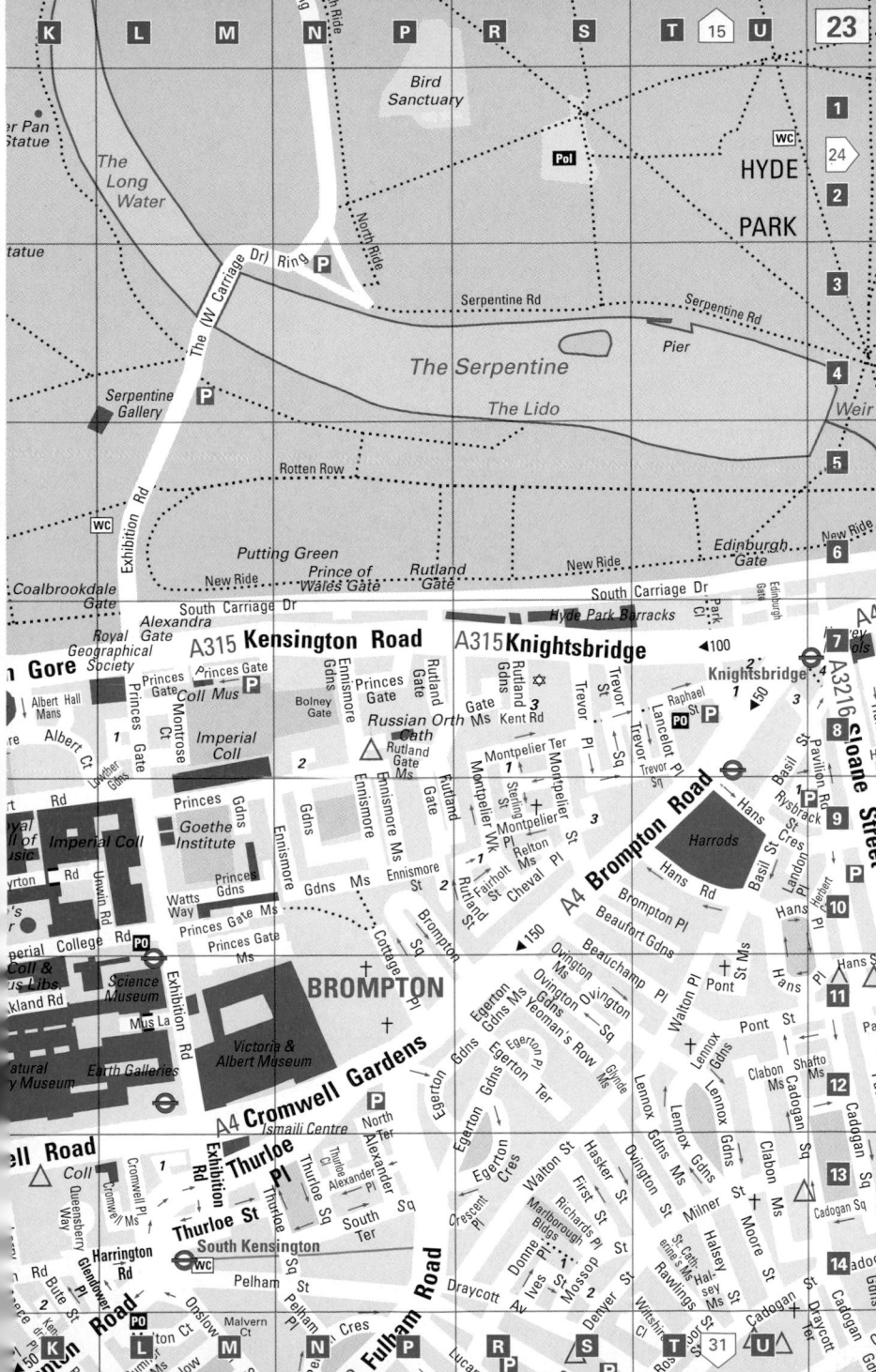

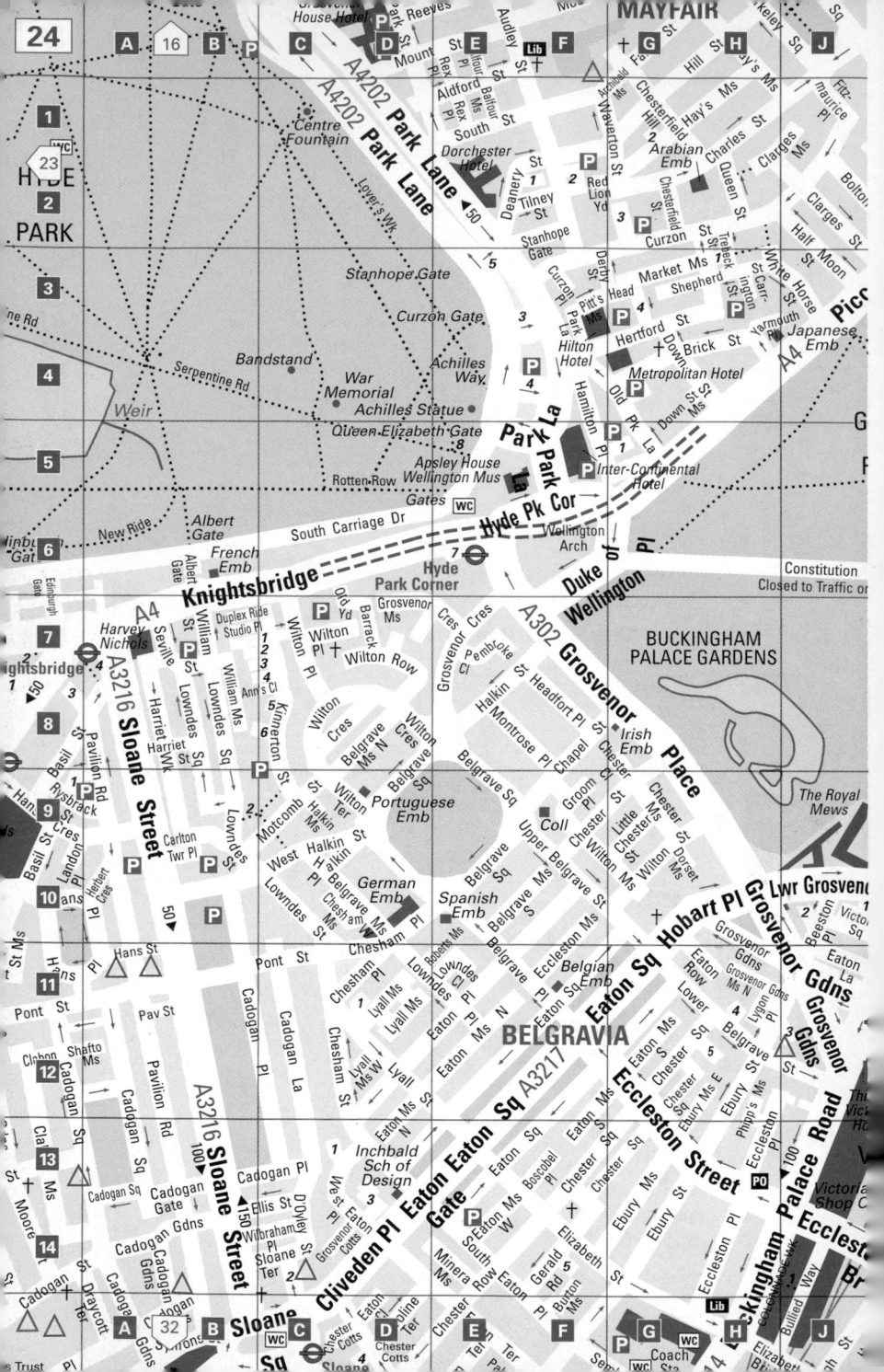

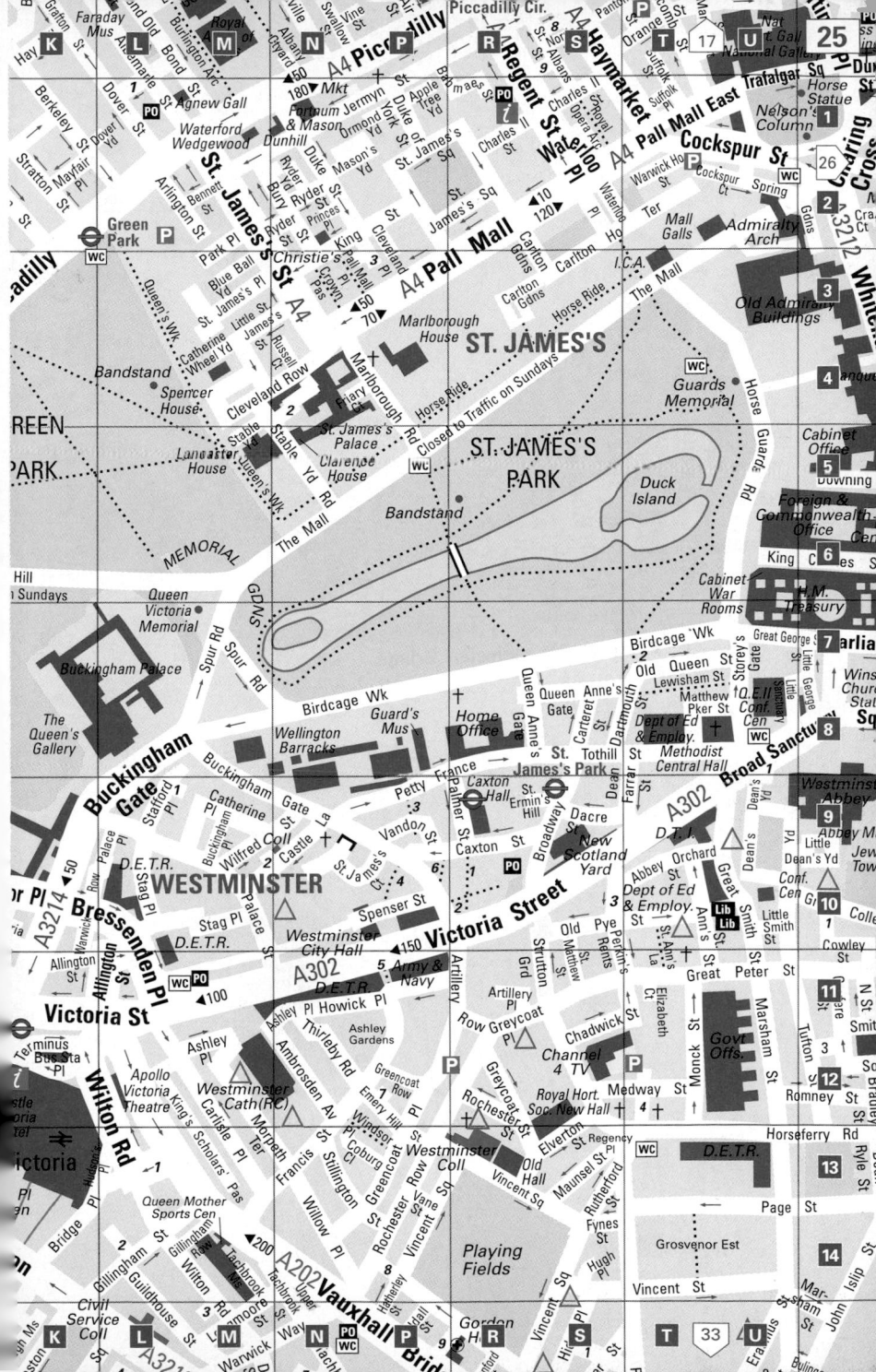

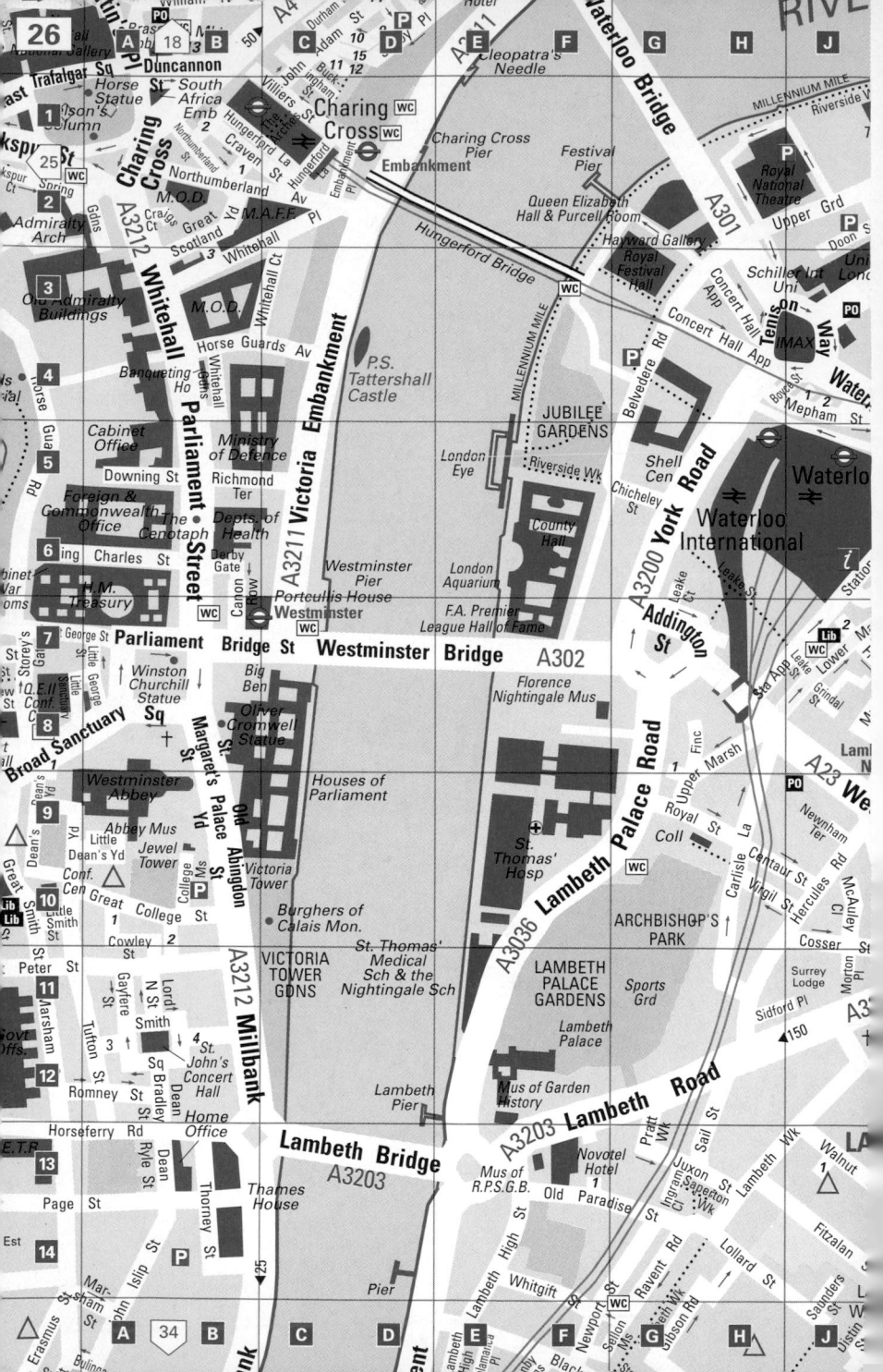

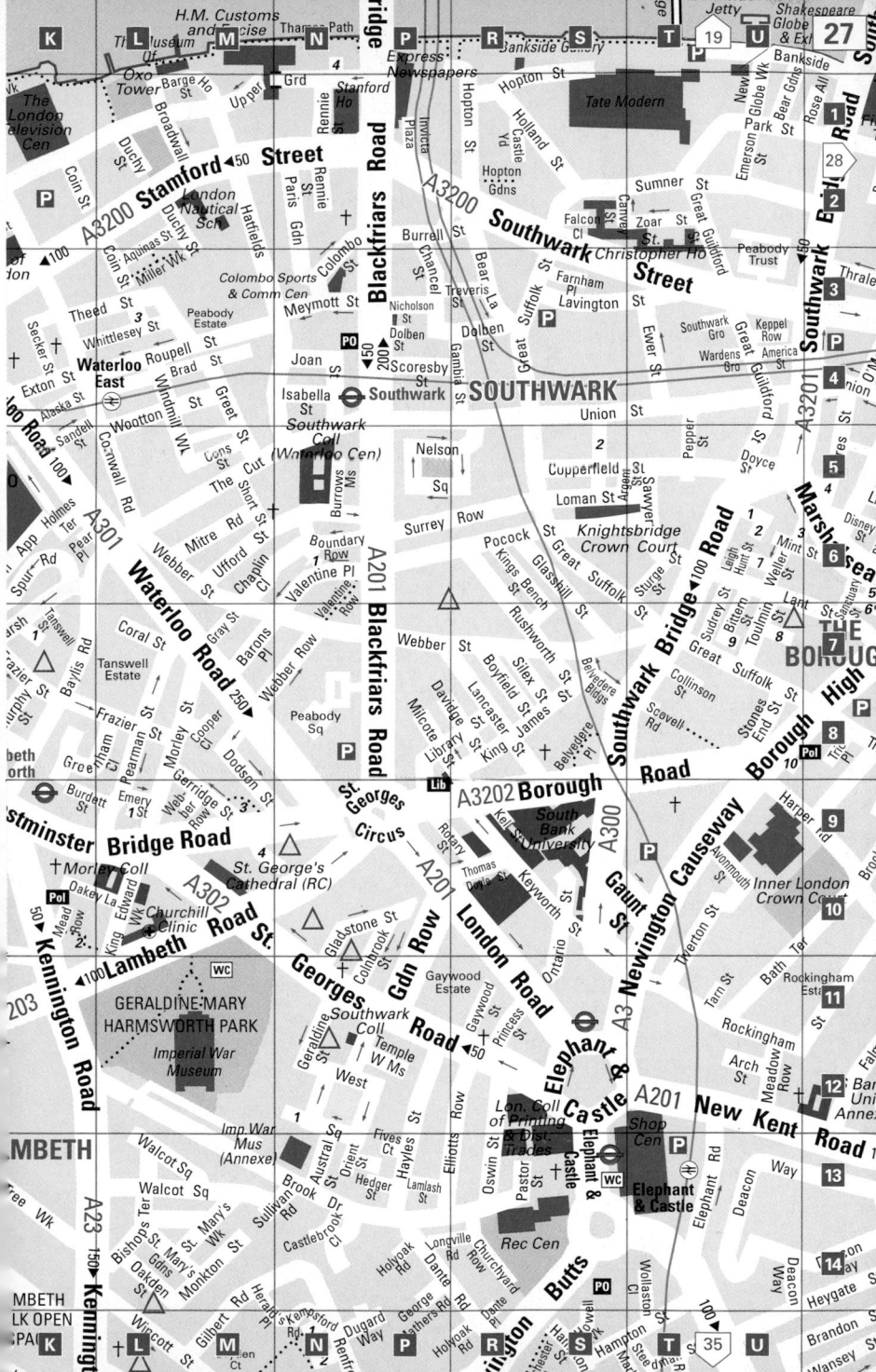

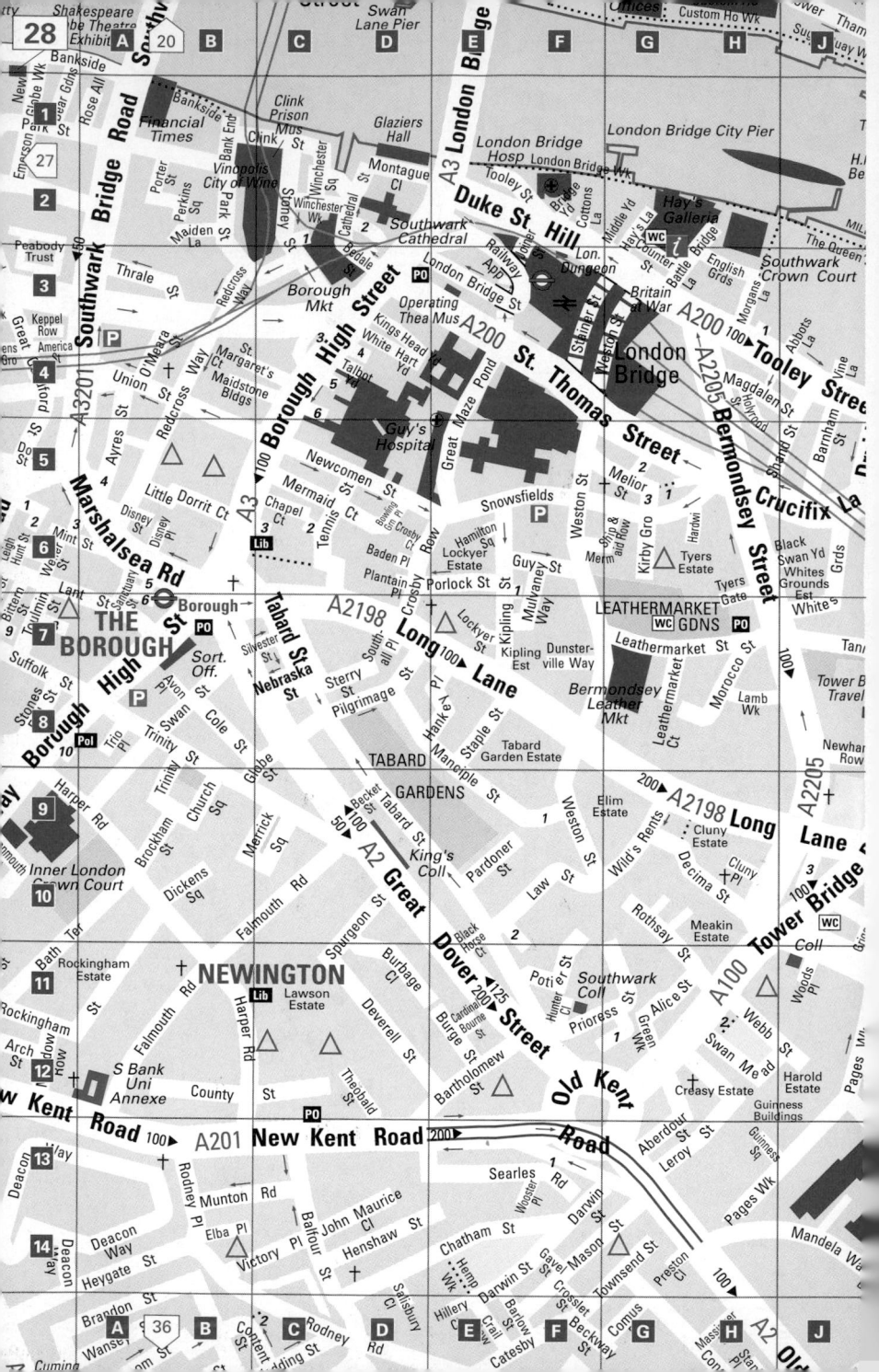

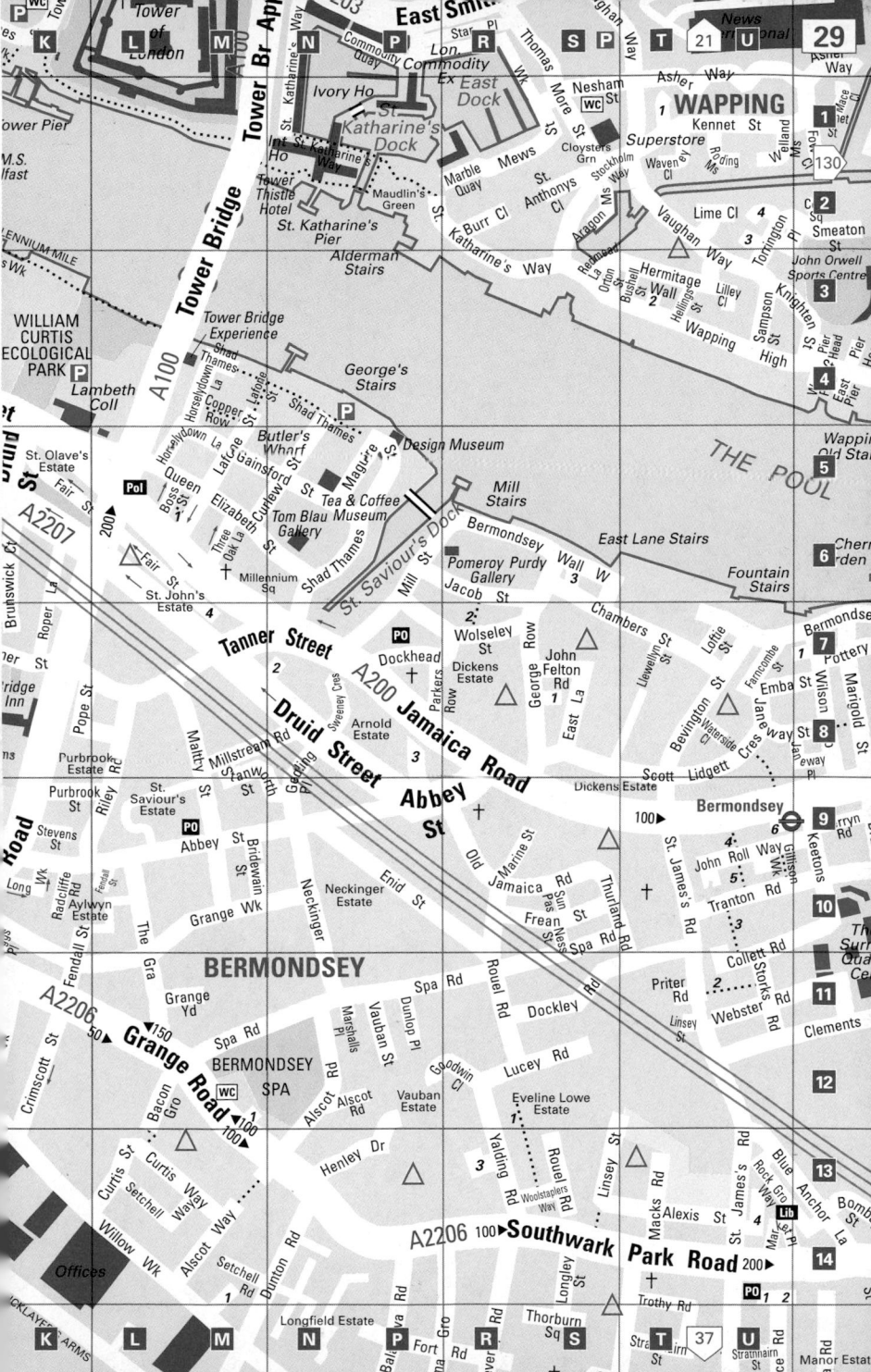

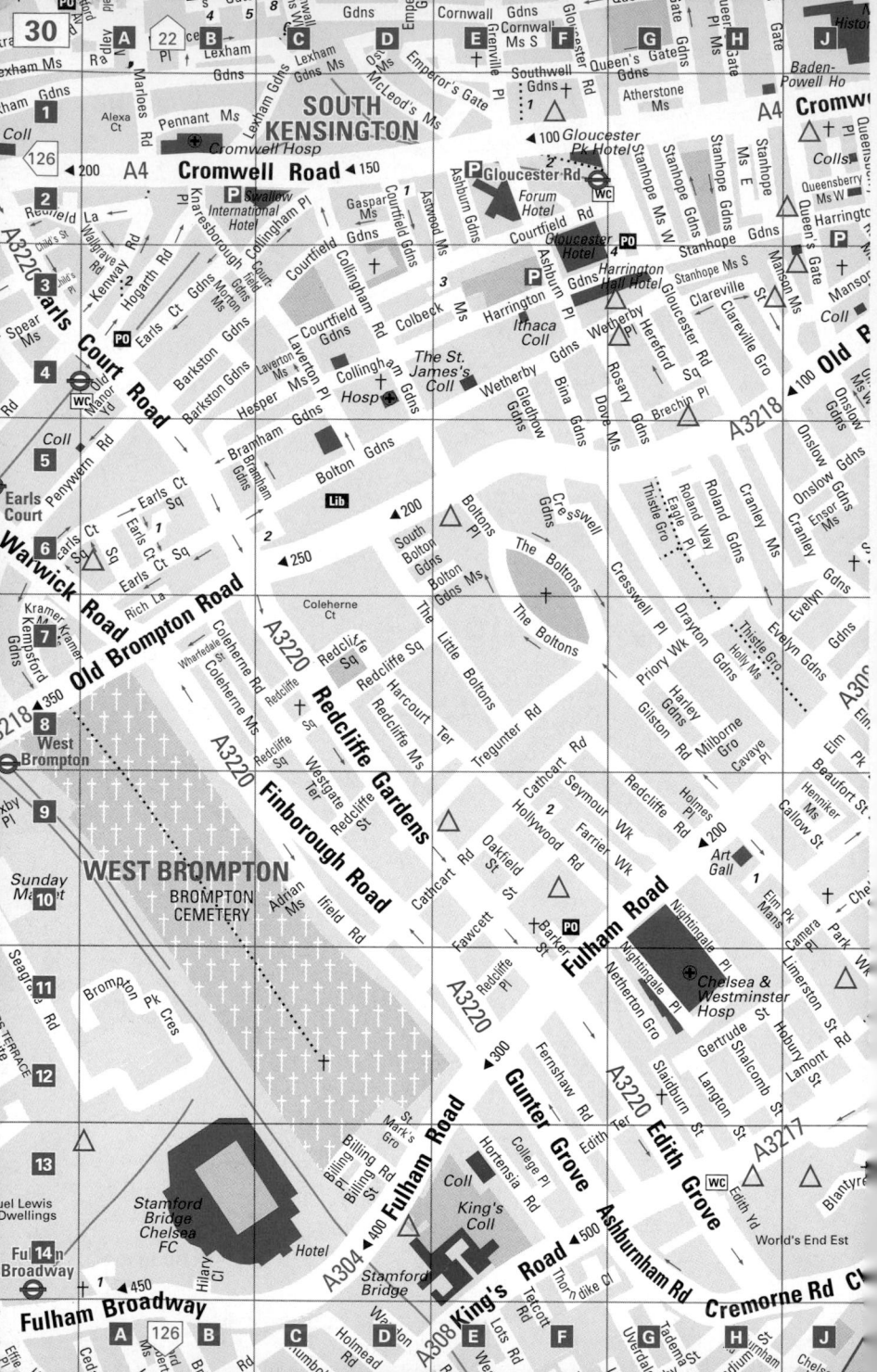

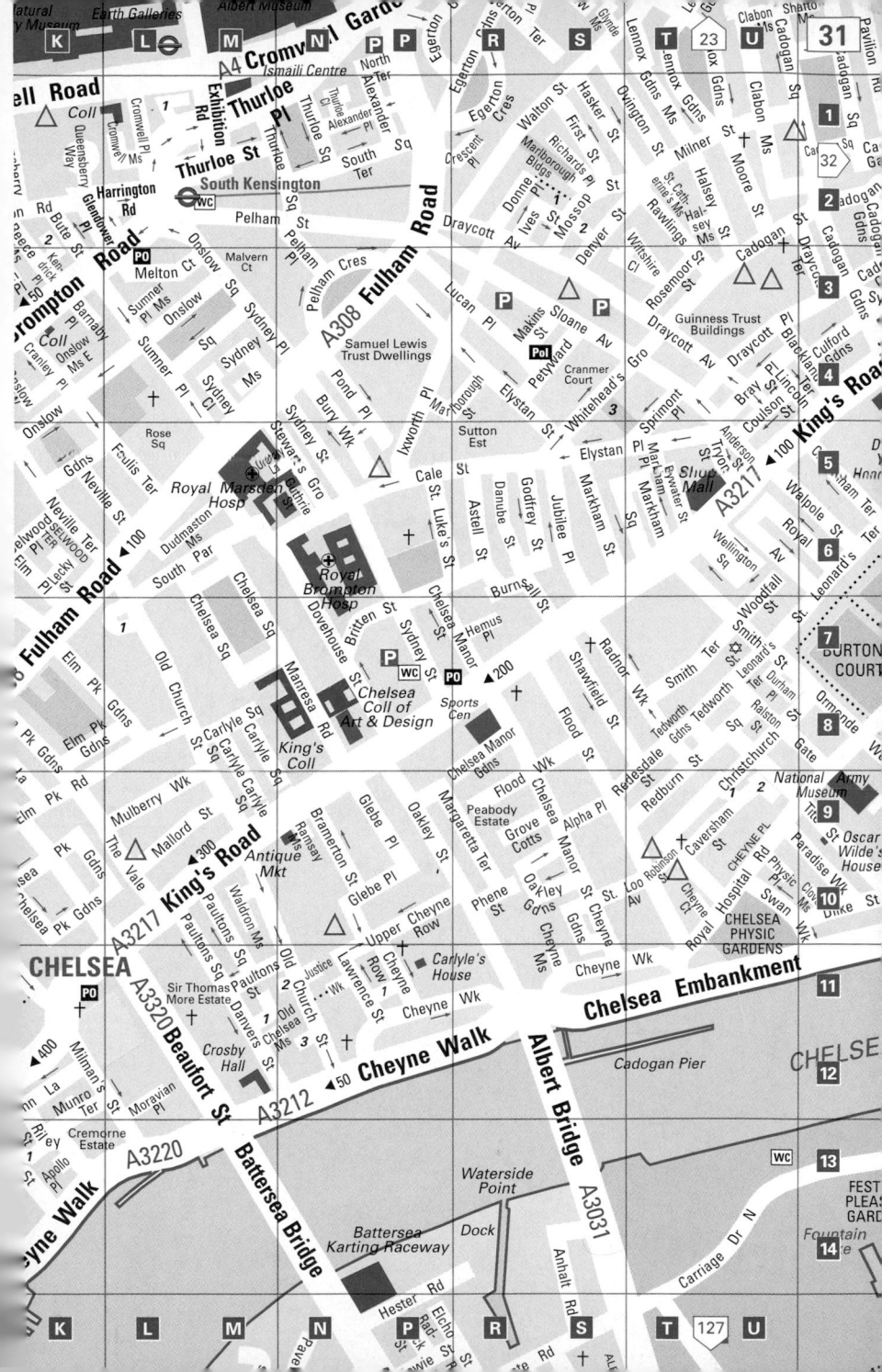

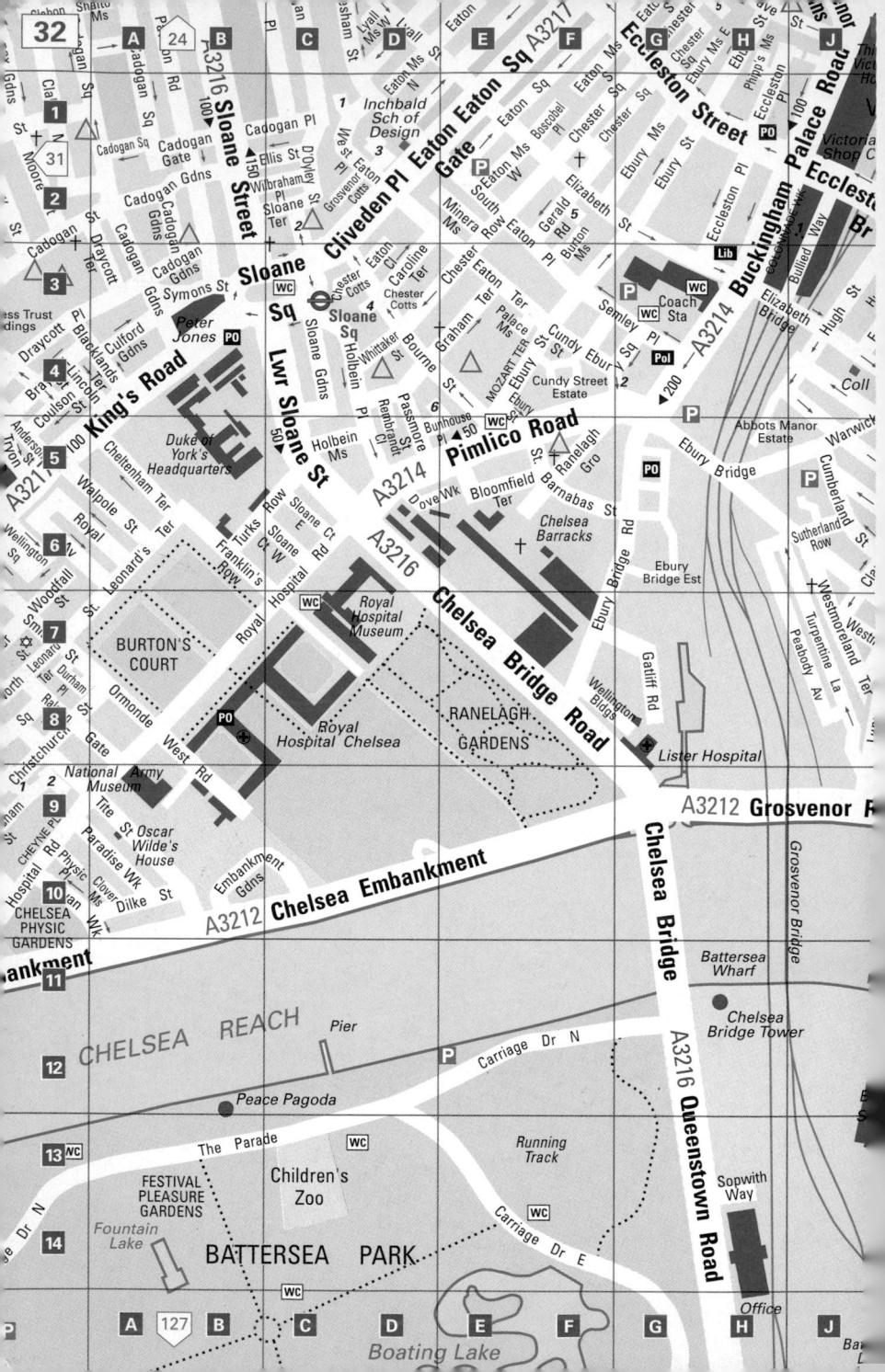

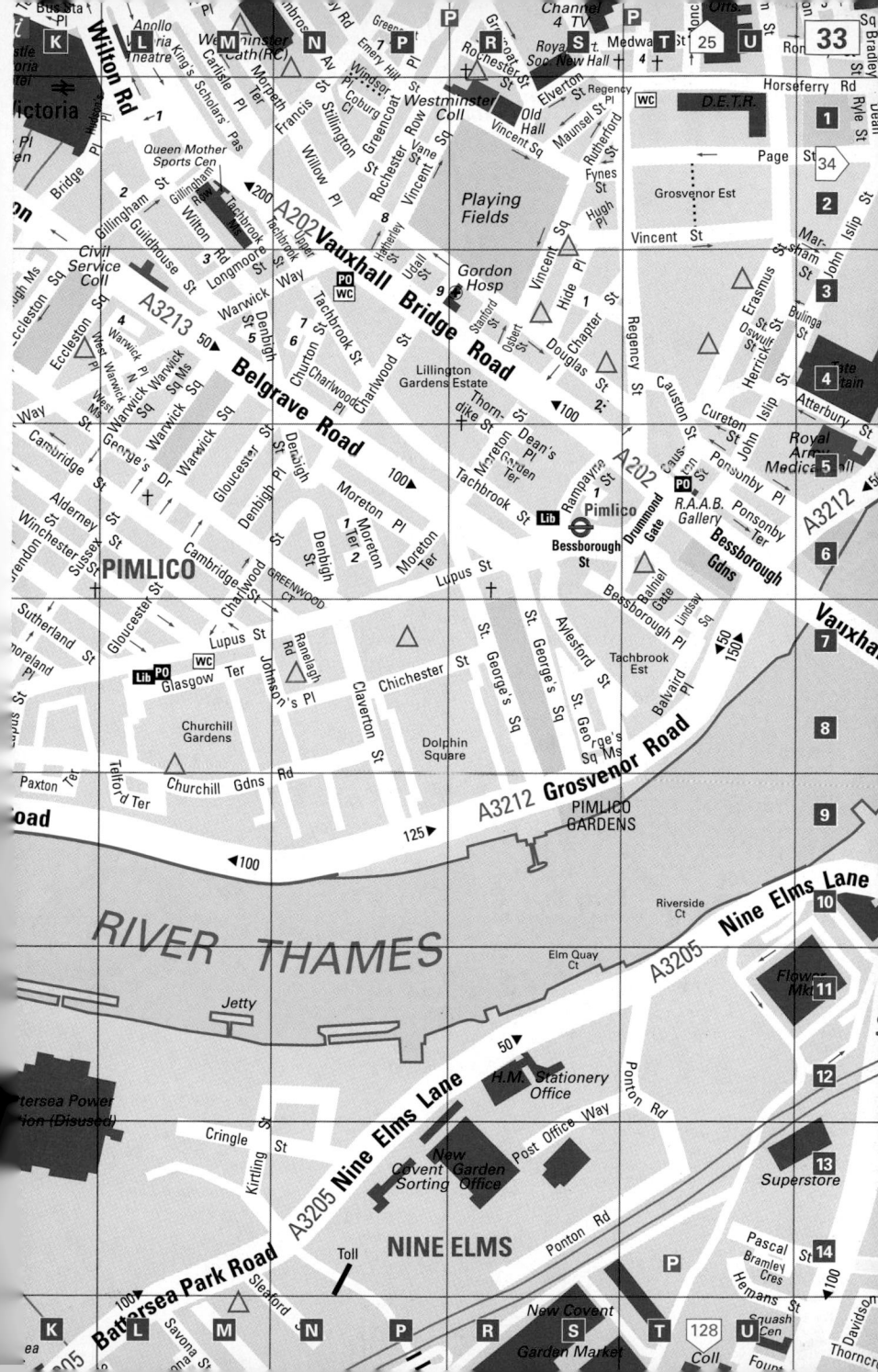

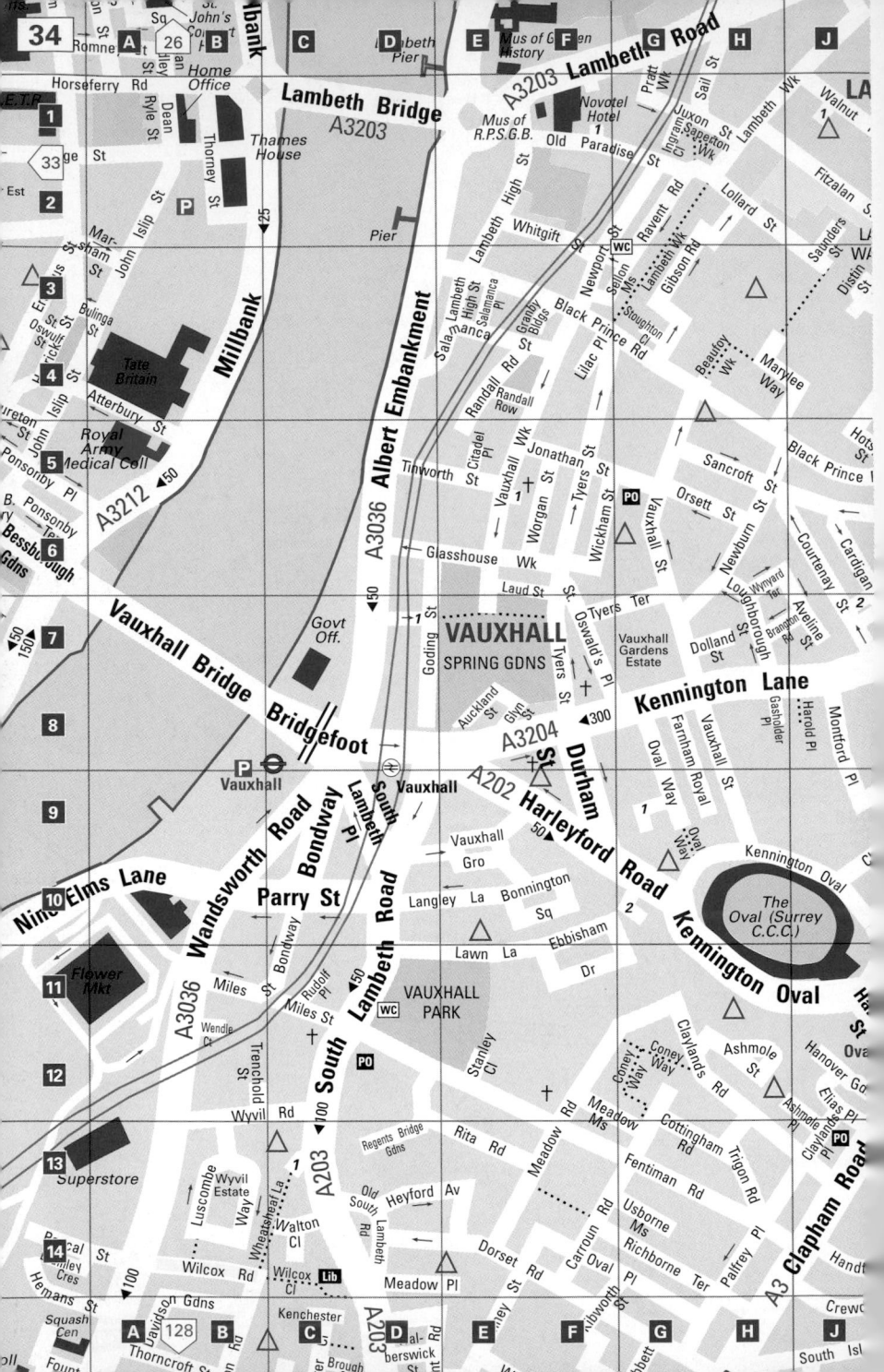

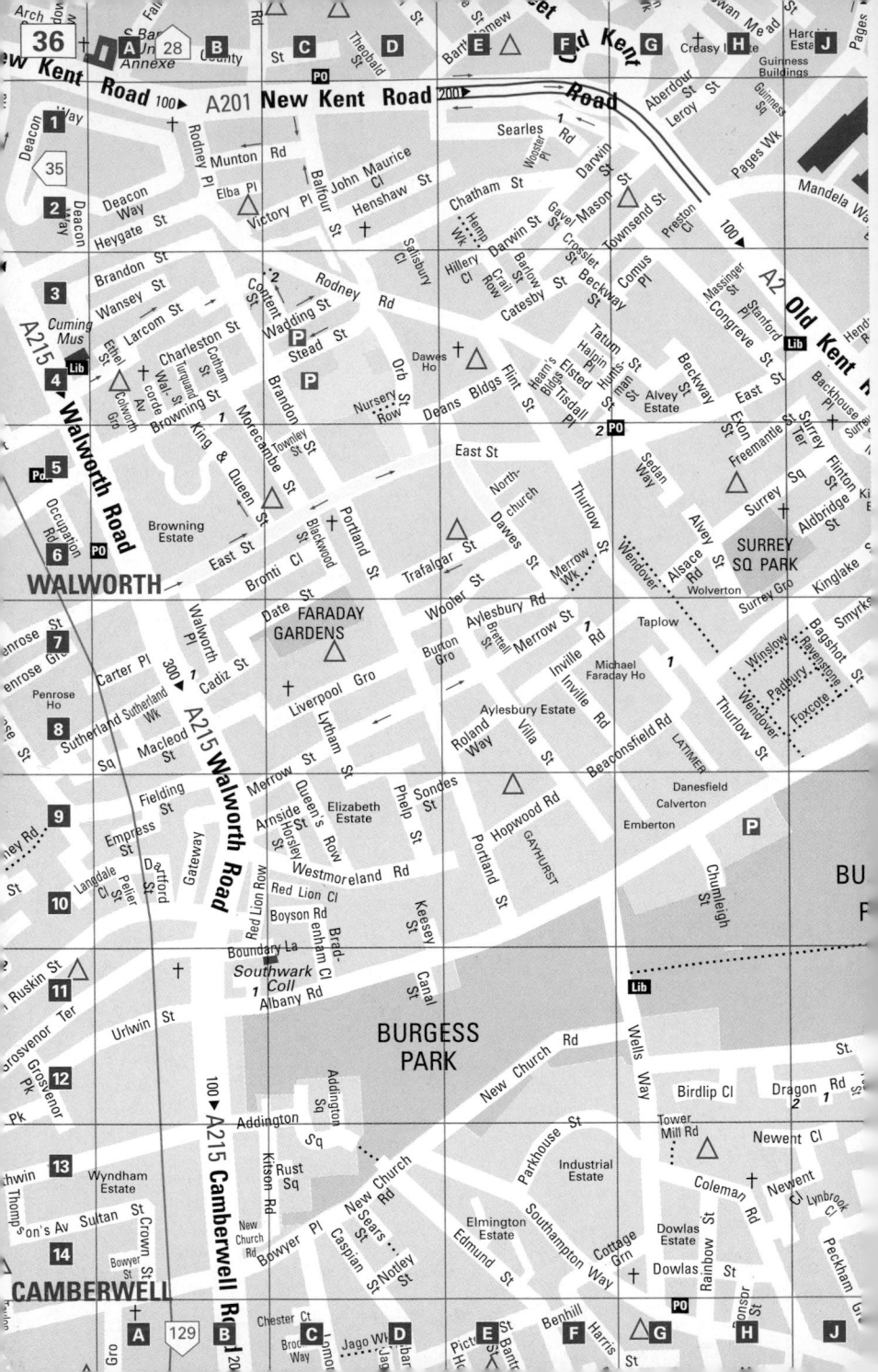

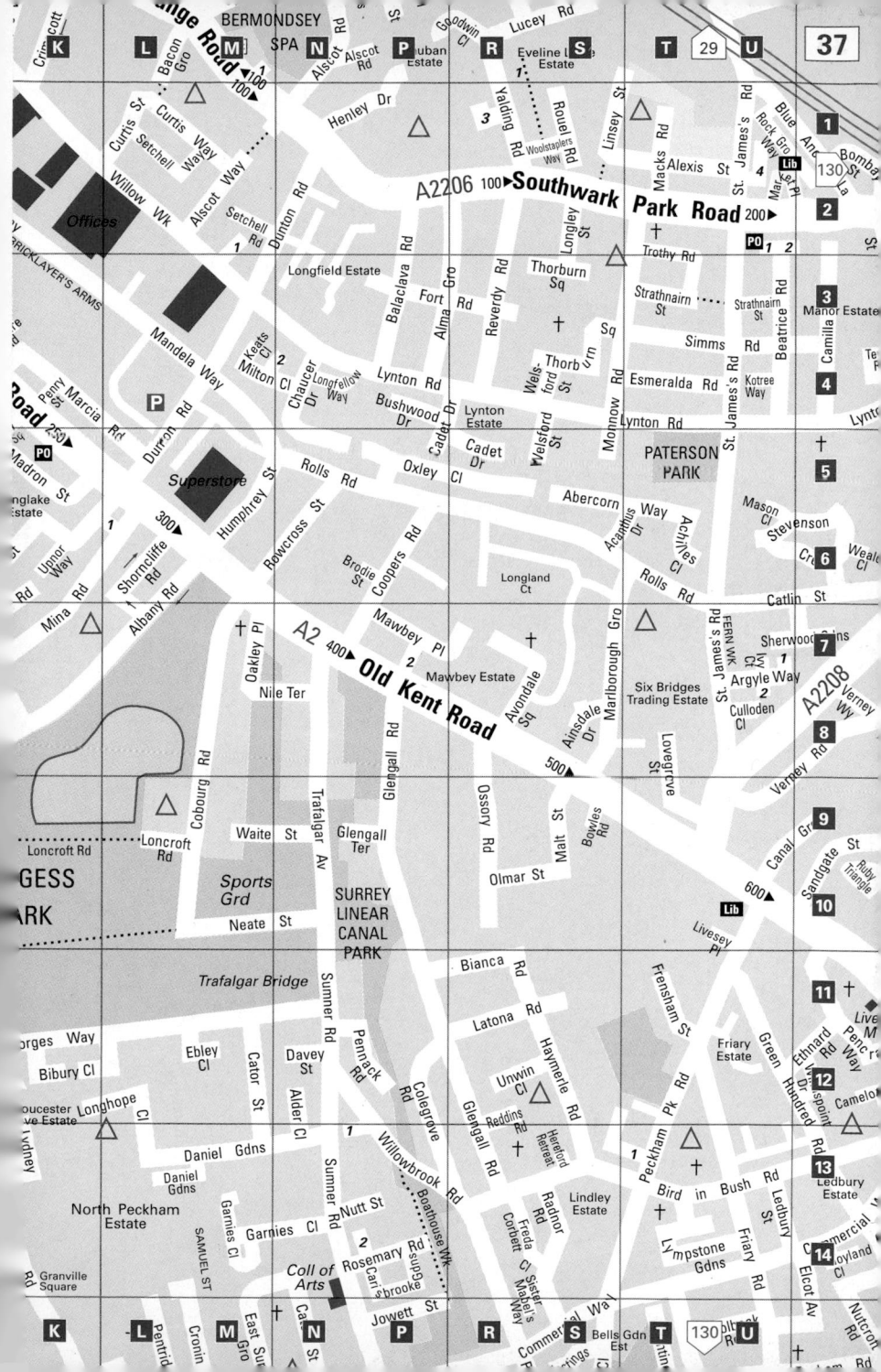

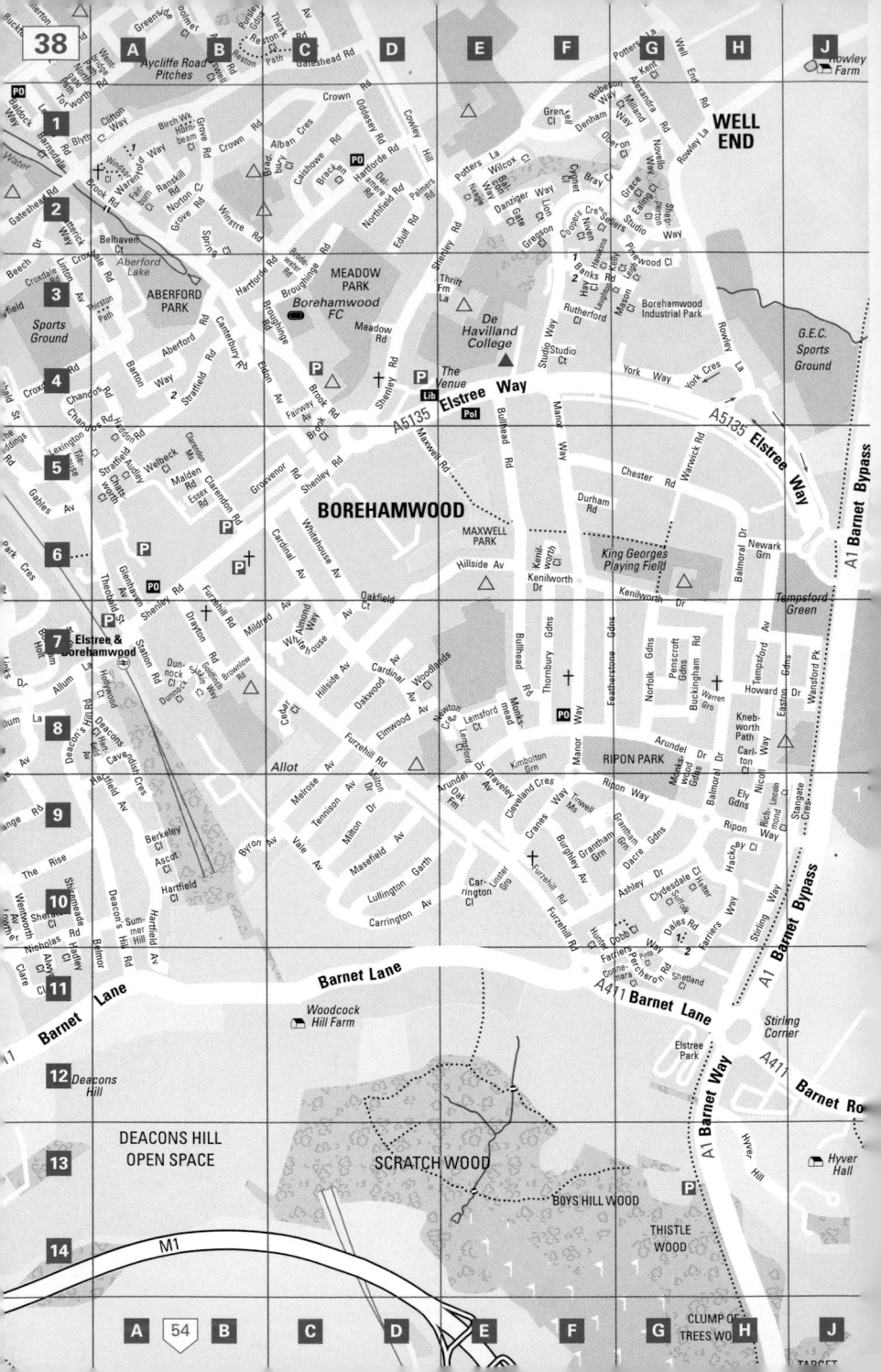

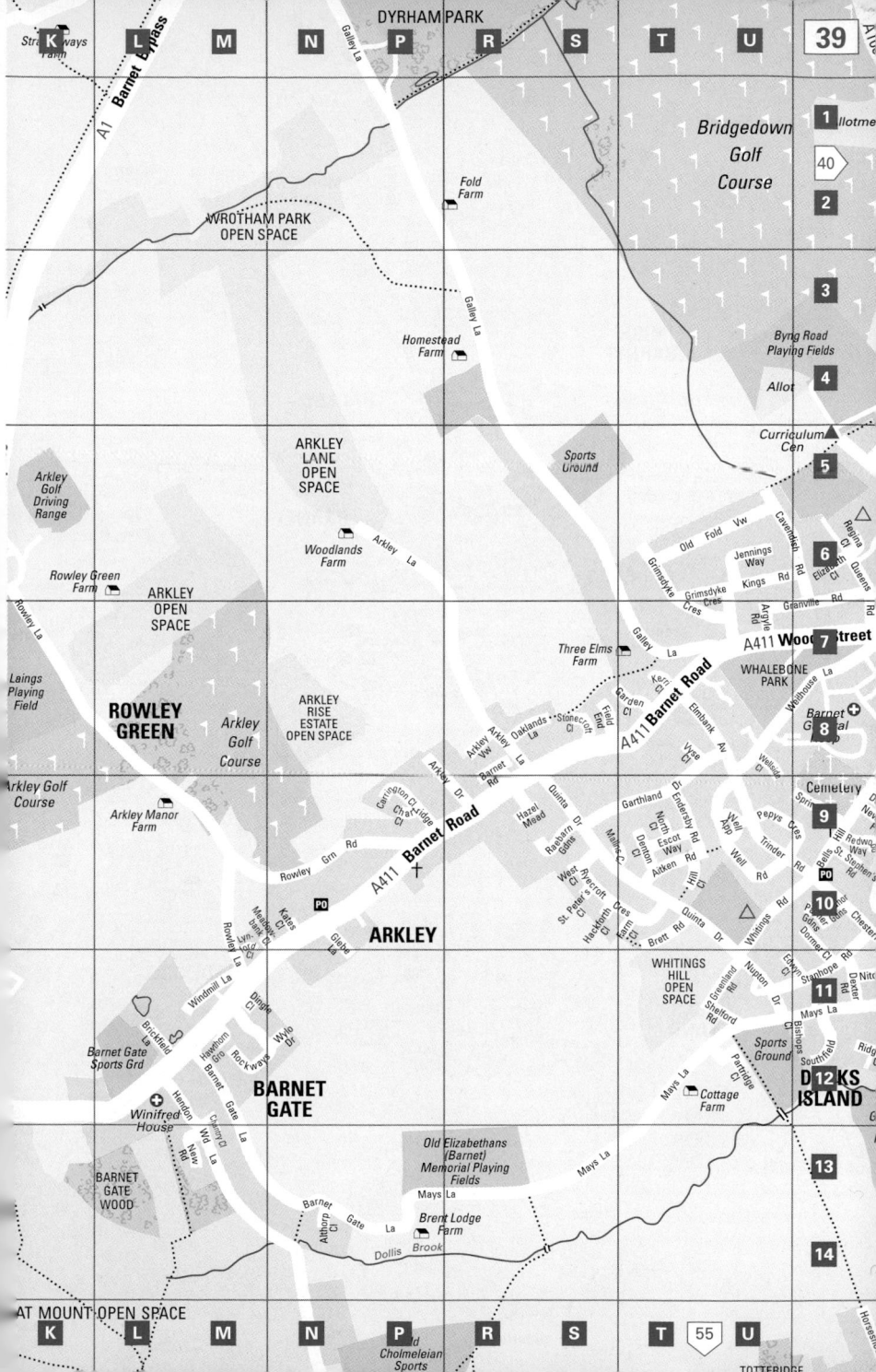

DYRHAM PARK

39

| K | L | M | N | P | R | S | T | U | **39** |

Bridgedown
Golf
Course

1 Ilotme

40

2

3

Byng Road
Playing Fields

Allot 4

Fold
Farm

WROTHAM PARK
OPEN SPACE

Curriculum
Cen

Homestead
Farm

5

ARKLEY
LANE
OPEN
SPACE

Sports
Ground

Old Fold Vw

Cavendish Rd

Regina

6

Arkley
Golf
Driving
Range

Jennings
Way

Elizabeth

Queens

Grimsdyke
Cres

Kings Rd

Woodlands
Farm

Arkley La

Grimsdyke
Cres

Argyle Rd

Granville

Rowley Green
Farm

ARKLEY
OPEN
SPACE

Three Elms
Farm

Galley La

A411 Wood Street

7

WHALEBONE
PARK

Webhouse La

Laings
Playing
Field

Garden La

Kent

A411 Barnet Road

Barnet
General

8

**ROWLEY
GREEN**

ARKLEY
RISE
ESTATE
OPEN SPACE

Arkley
Golf
Course

Arkley
Vw

Oaklands La

Stonecroft

Field
End

Elmbank

Vyse

Wellway

Cemetery

9

Arkley Golf
Course

Carrington Cl

Charldge
Cl

Barnet
Rd

Hazel
Mead

Quinta Dr

Garthland Dr

North
Denton
Rd

Enderley Rd

Escot
Way

Well
App

Well
Rd

Pepys Cres

Trinder Rd

New

Redwig

St. Stephen's

Arkley Manor
Farm

Rowley Grn Rd

A411 Barnet Road

Rasharn Dr
Gdns

Mallus Cl

Aitken Rd

Hill

PO

10

Pawlett

Dormer Cl

Chester

Rowley La

Kates Cl

Meadway Cl

Glebe La

PO

ARKLEY

West
Riscroft
Hacklmrb Cres

St. Peter's La

Brett Rd

Quinta Dr

Whitings Rd

11

Windmill La

Dingle Cl

Wylo Dr

WHITINGS
HILL
OPEN
SPACE

Greenfield Rd

Shefford Rd

Nupton Dr

Partridge Dr

Stanhope

Mays La

Hawthorn Gro

Barnet Gate

Rockways

Sports
Ground

Bishops

Southfield

Ridg

**BARNET
GATE**

Cottage
Farm

D 12 KS
ISLAND

Winifred
House

Hendon Wd La

Cherry Cl

New Rd

13

Barnet Gate
Sports Grd

Brickfield

Old Elizabethans
(Barnet)
Memorial Playing
Fields

Mays La

14

BARNET
GATE
WOOD

Barnet Gate La

Althorp Cl

Mays La

Brent Lodge
Farm

Dollis Brook

AT MOUNT OPEN SPACE

| K | L | M | N | P | R | S | T | **55** | U |

d
Cholmeleian
Sports

TOTTERIDGE

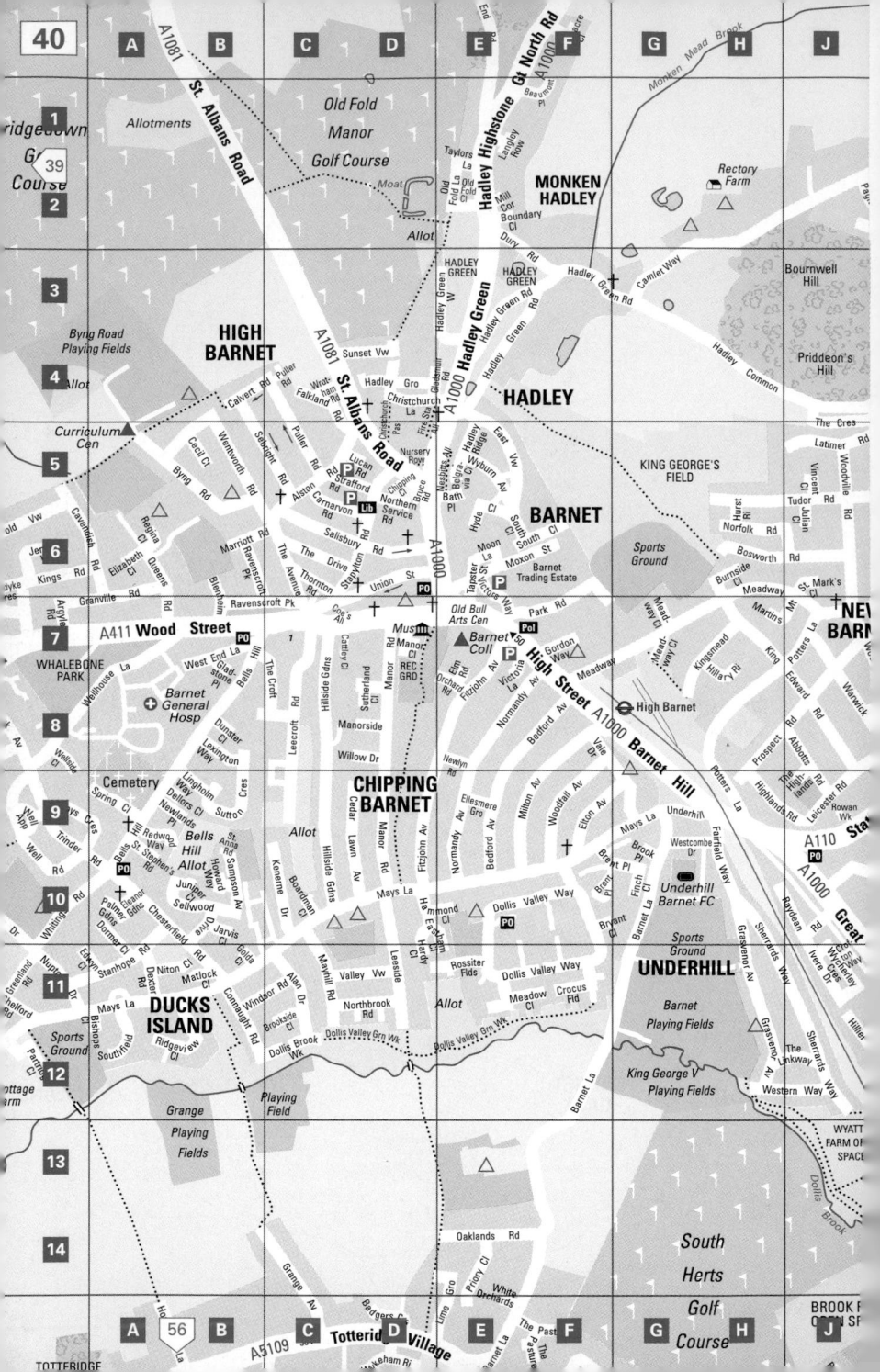

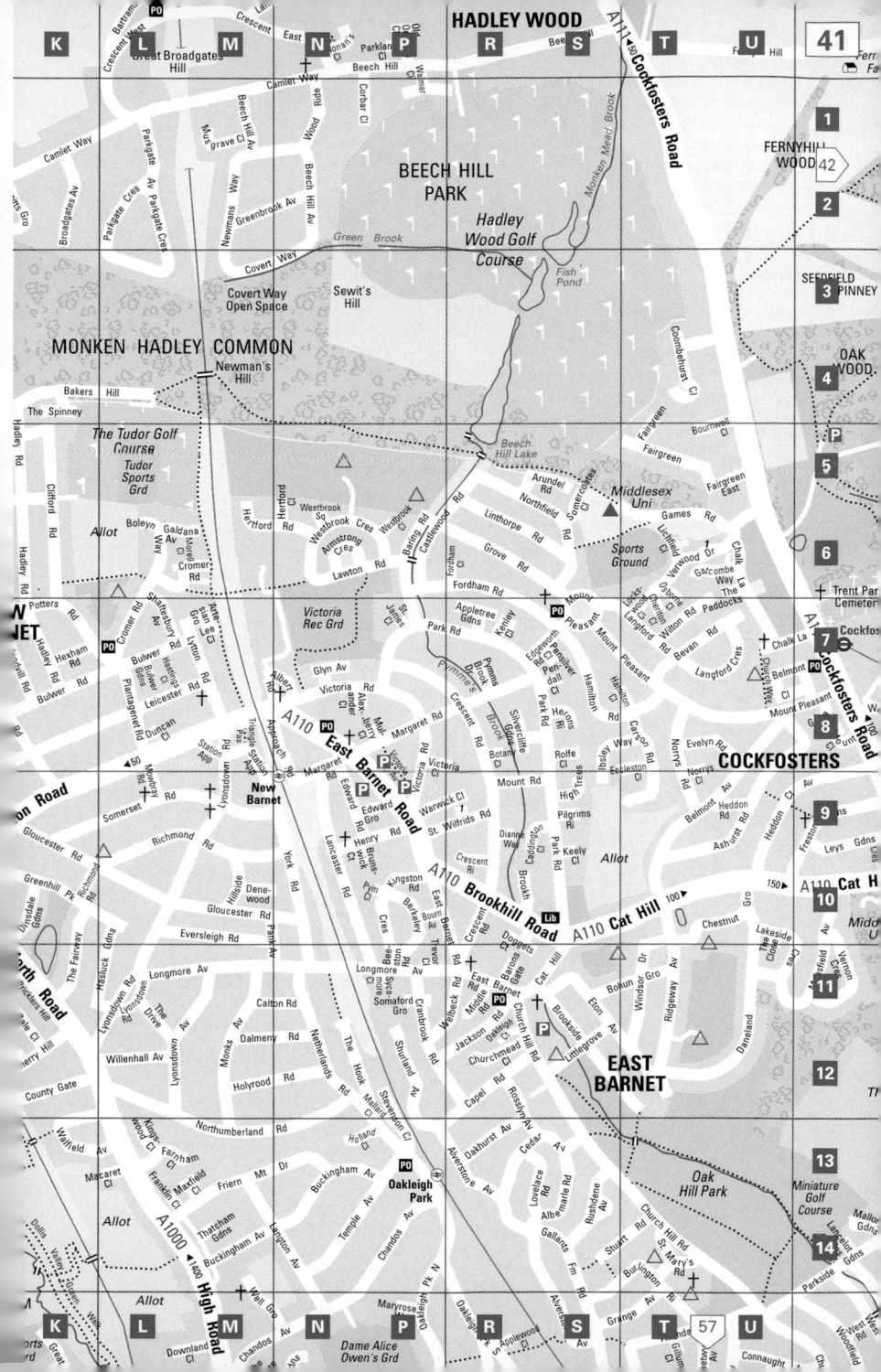

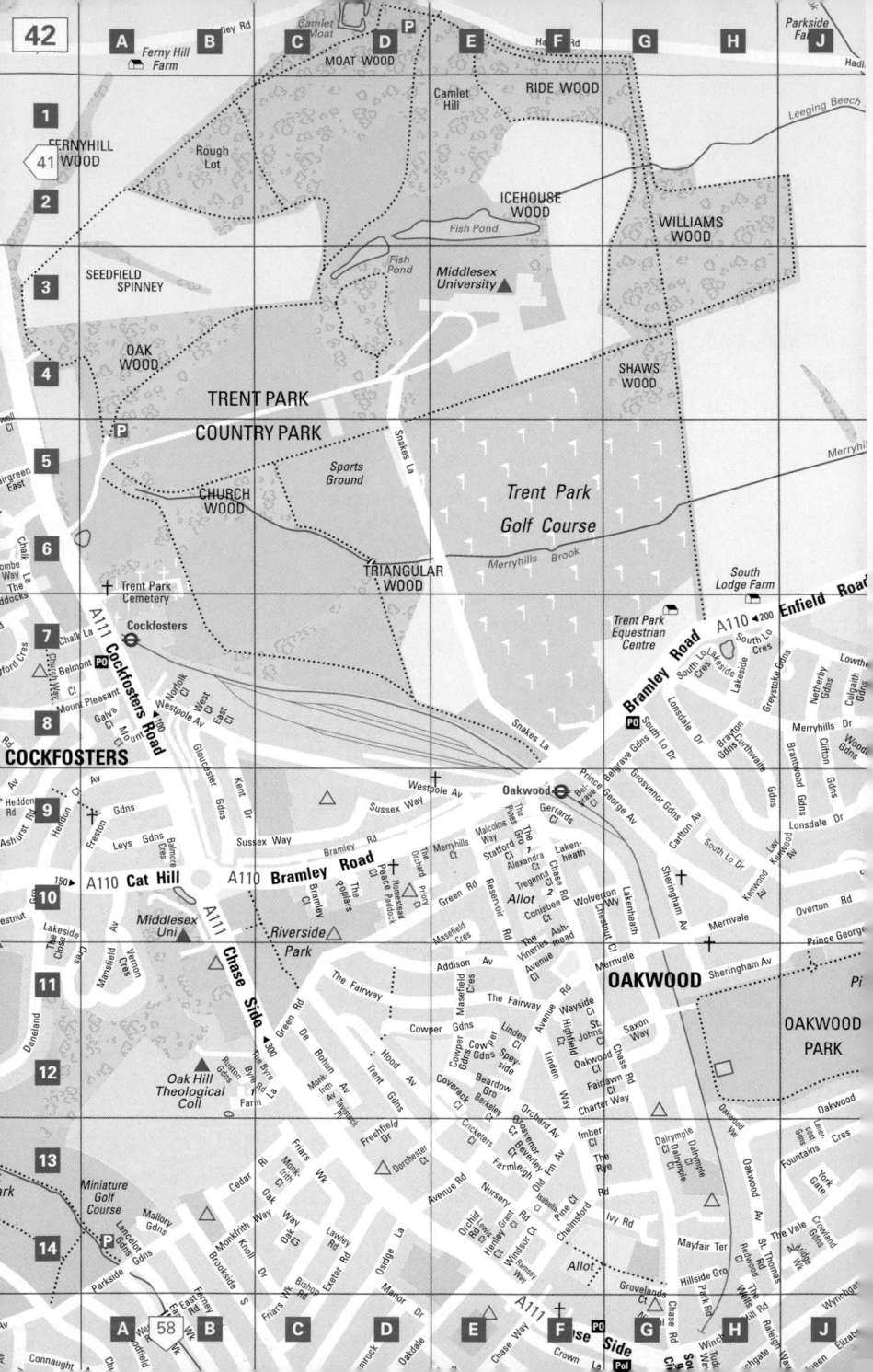

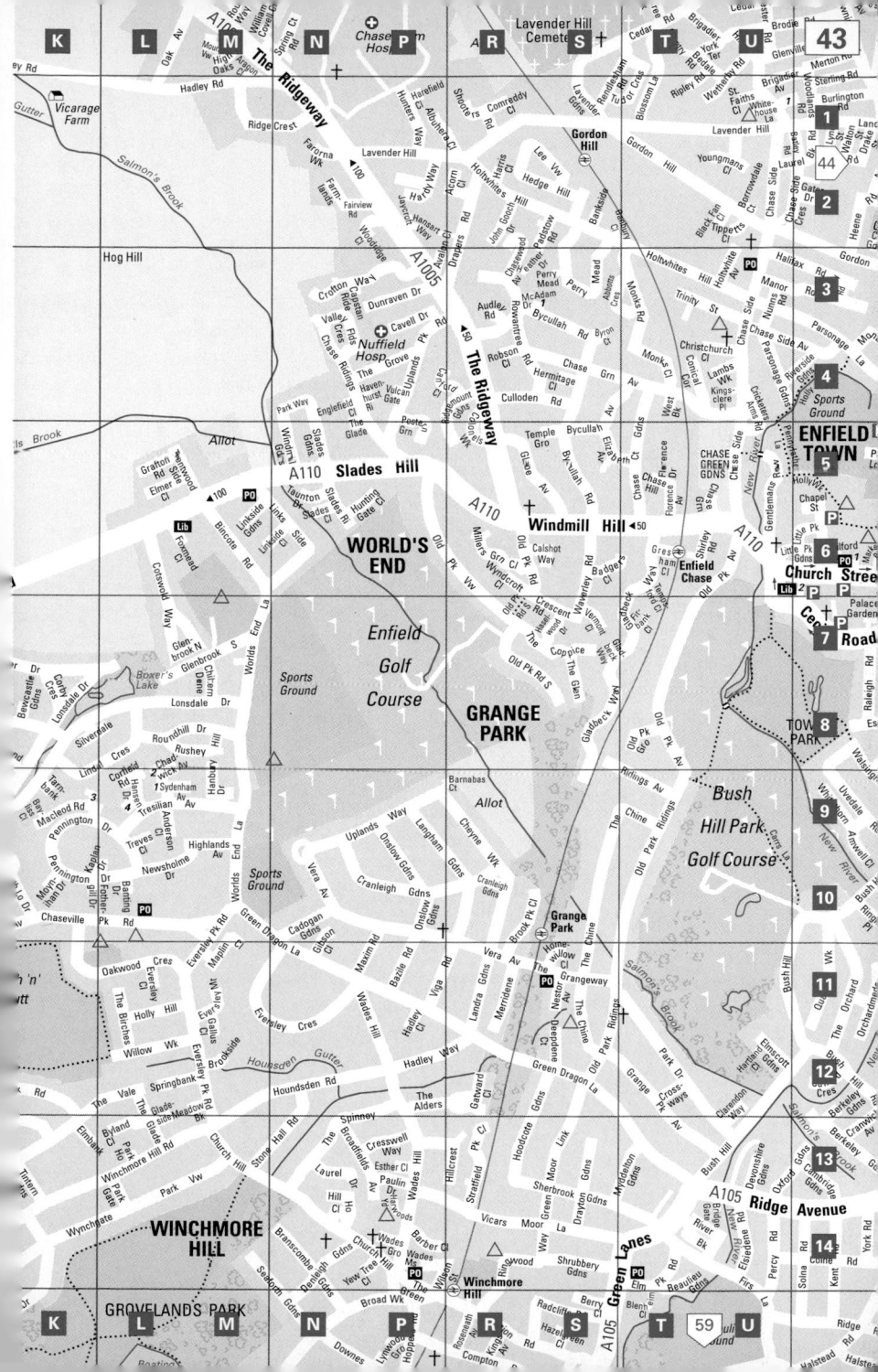

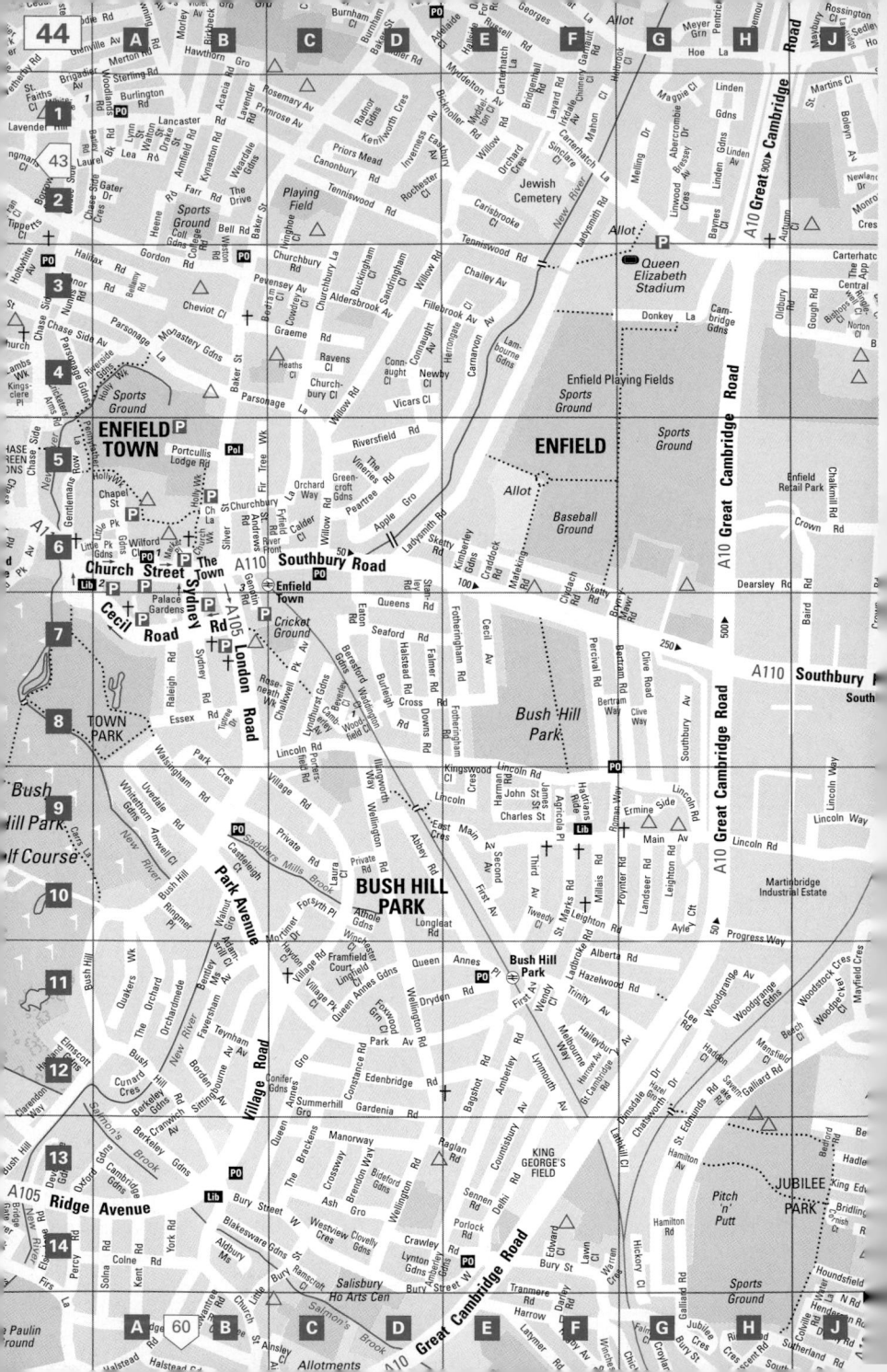

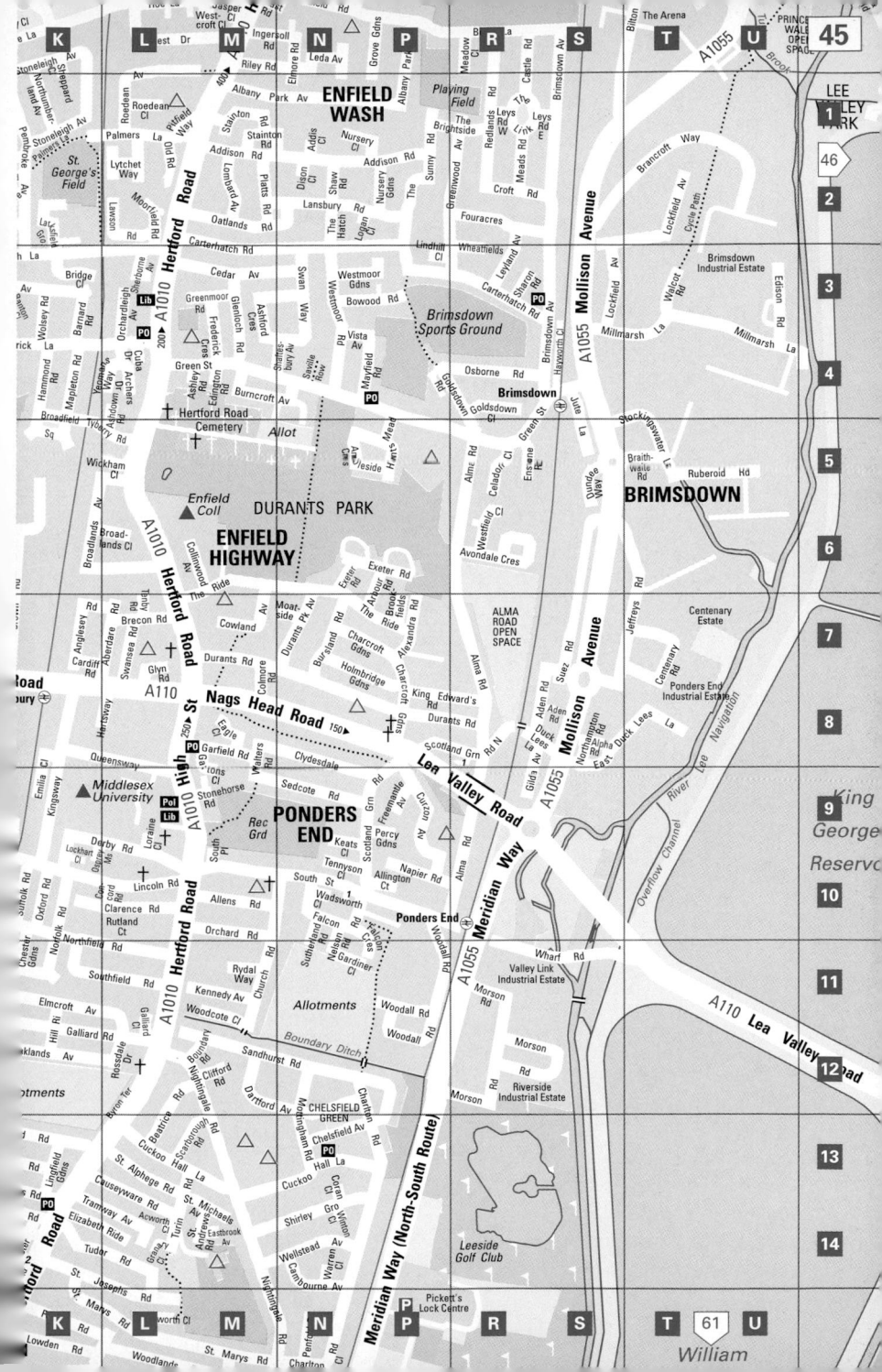

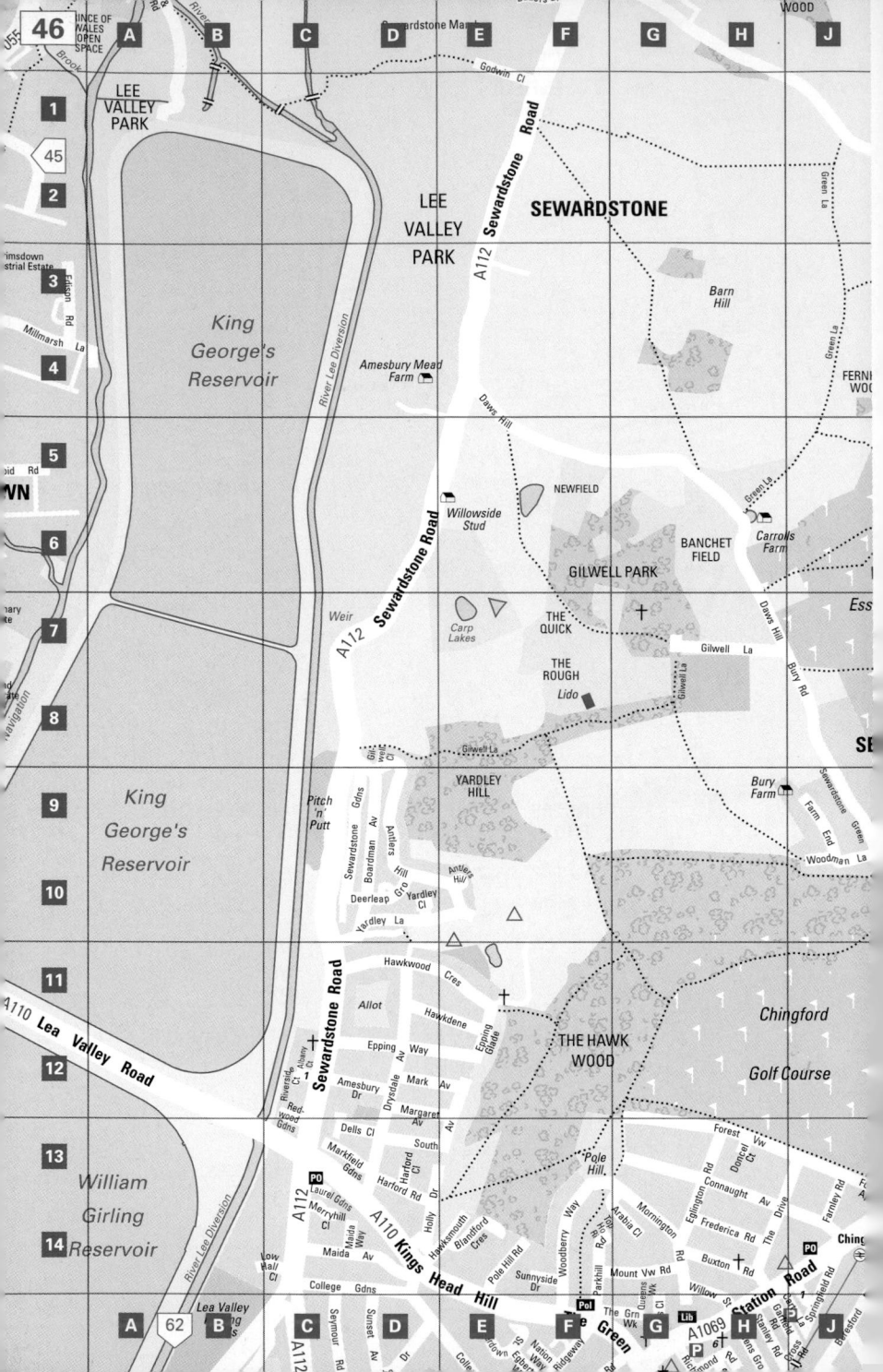

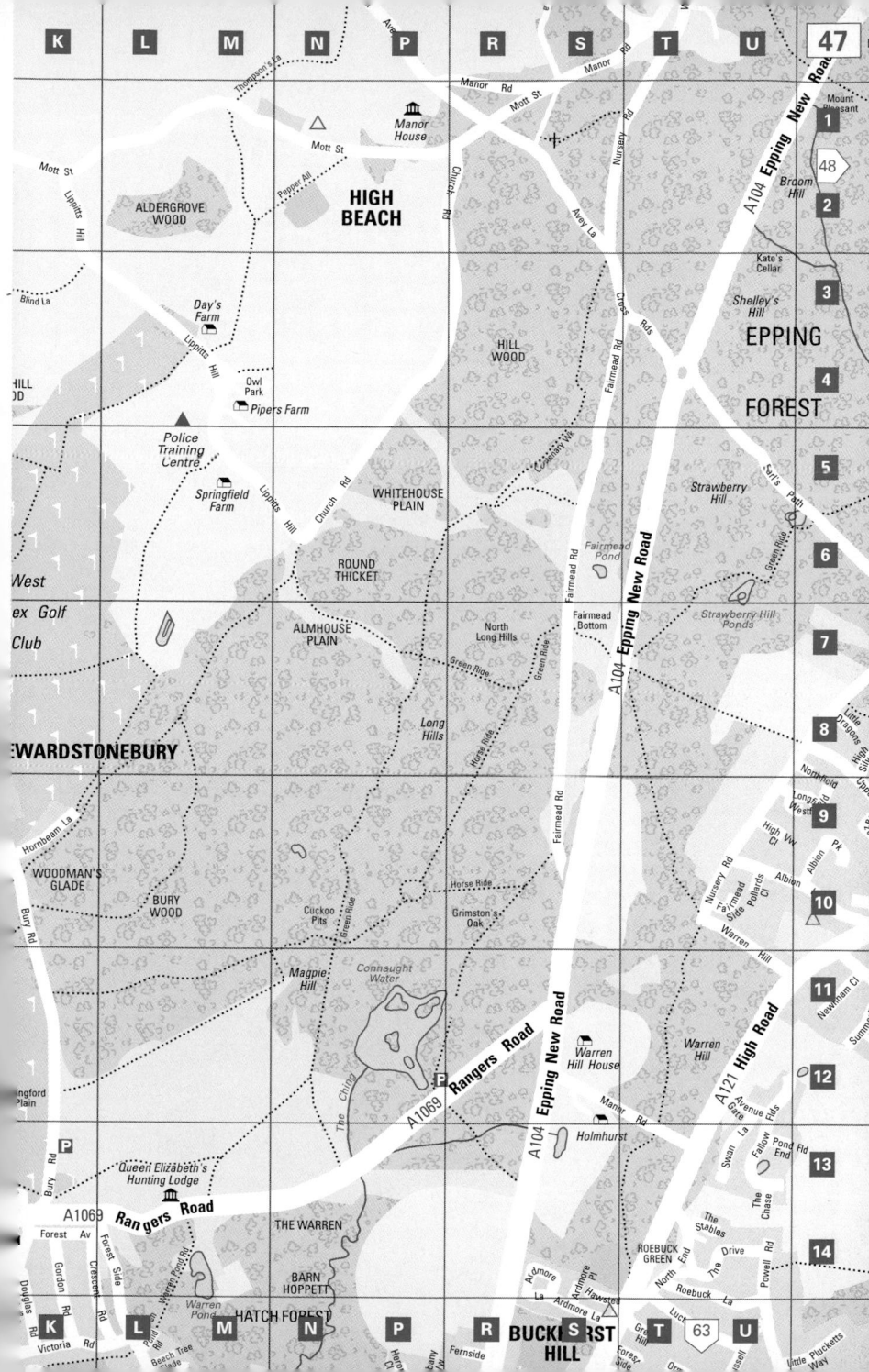

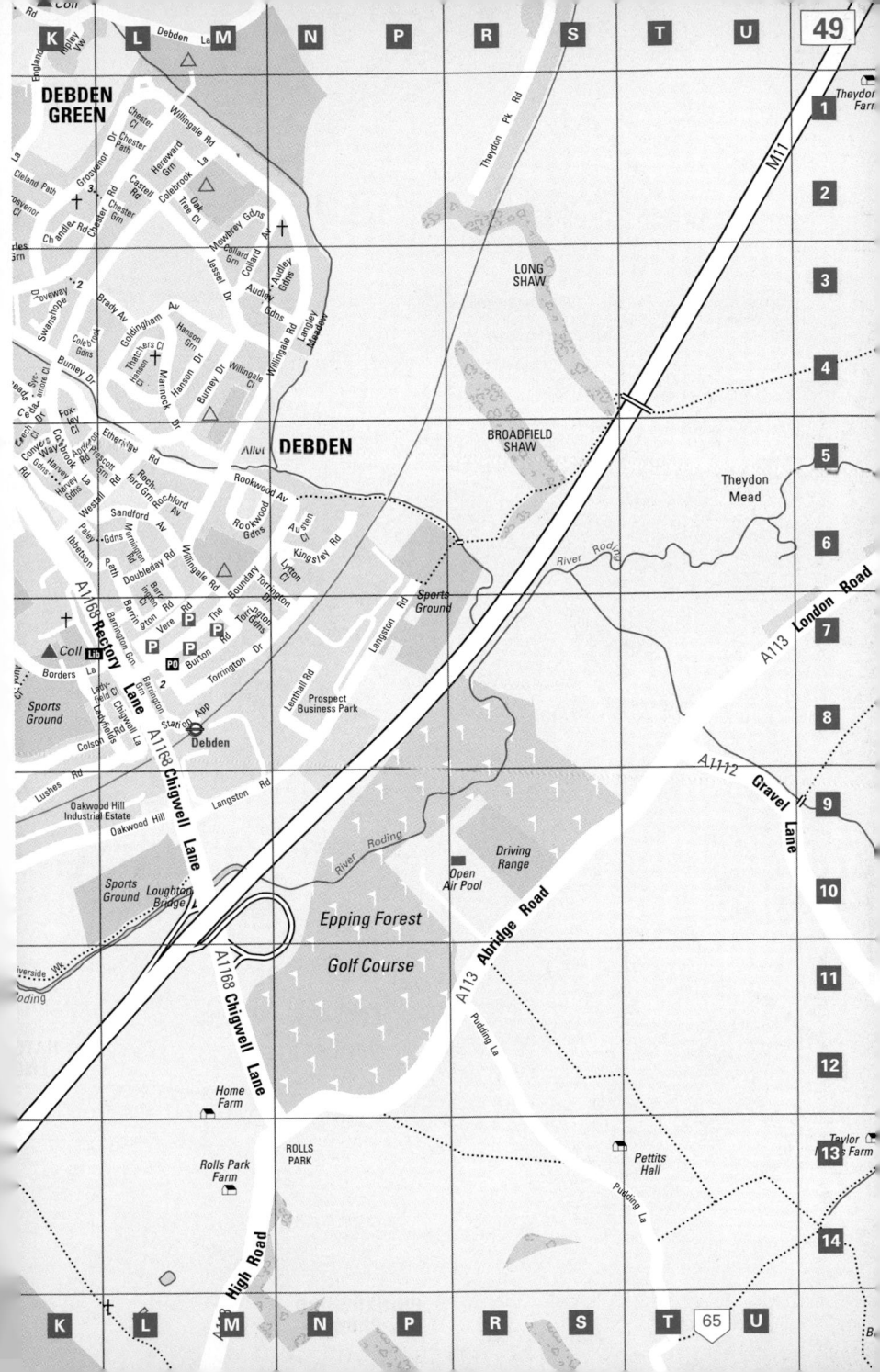

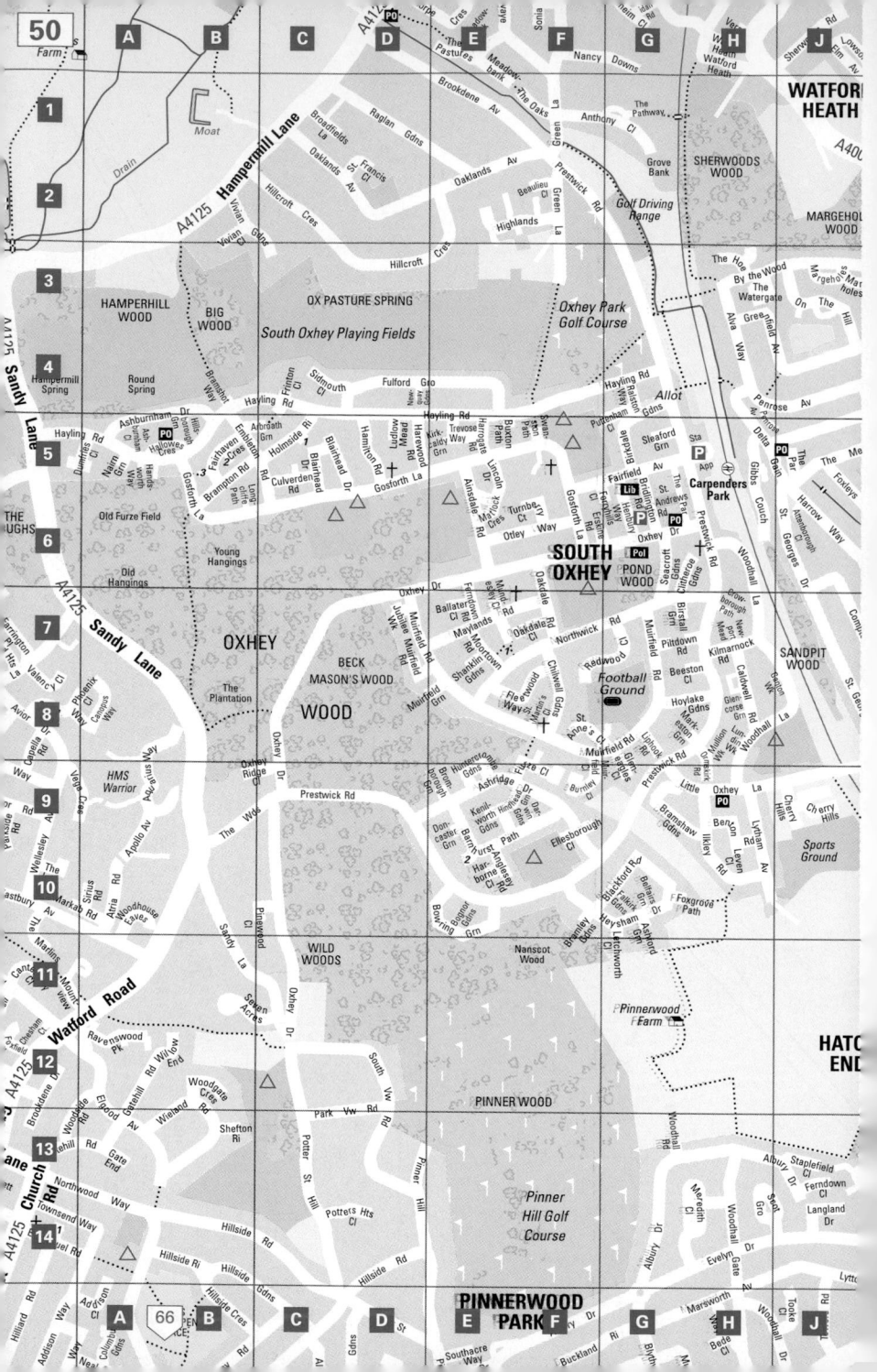

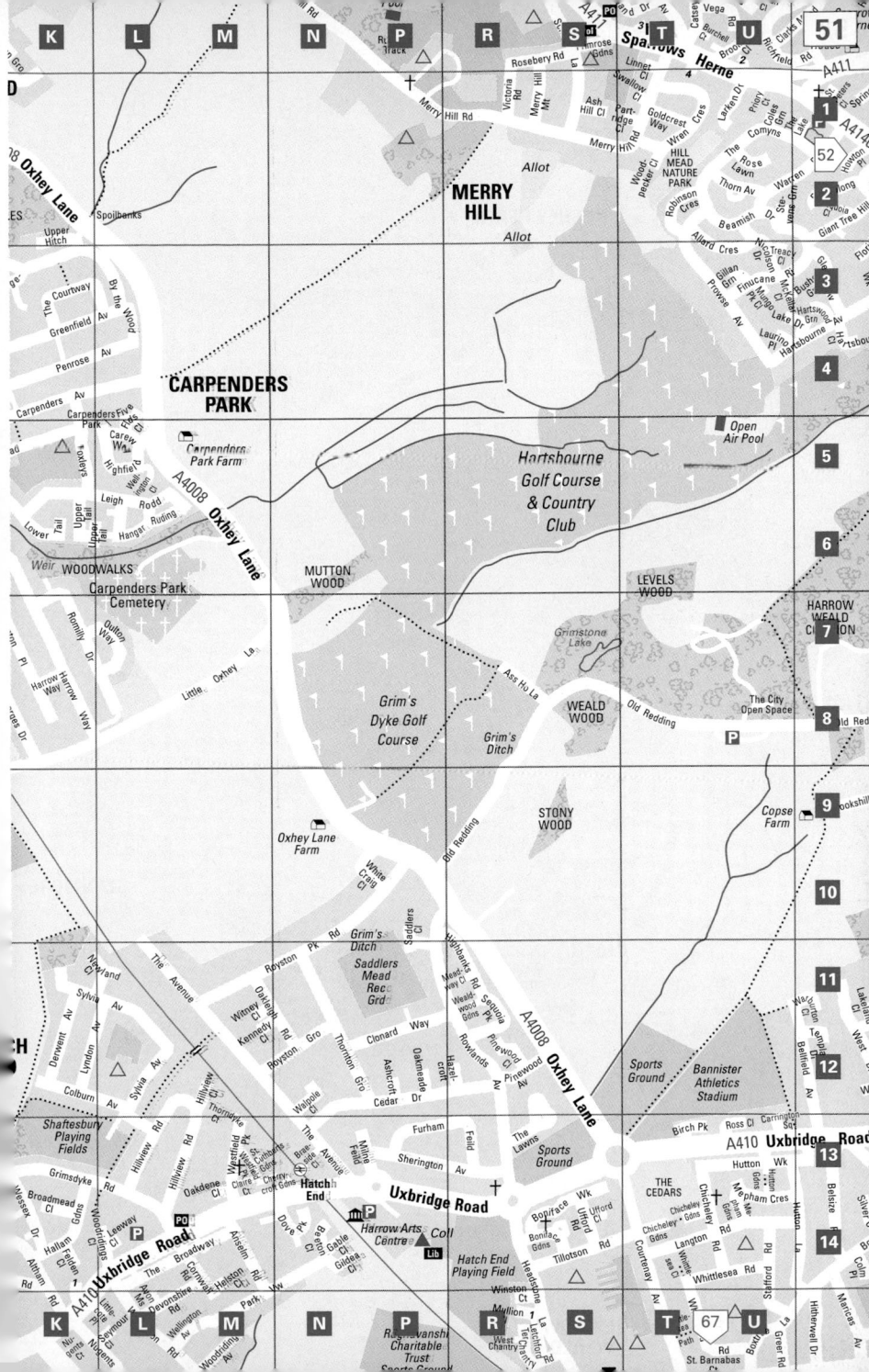

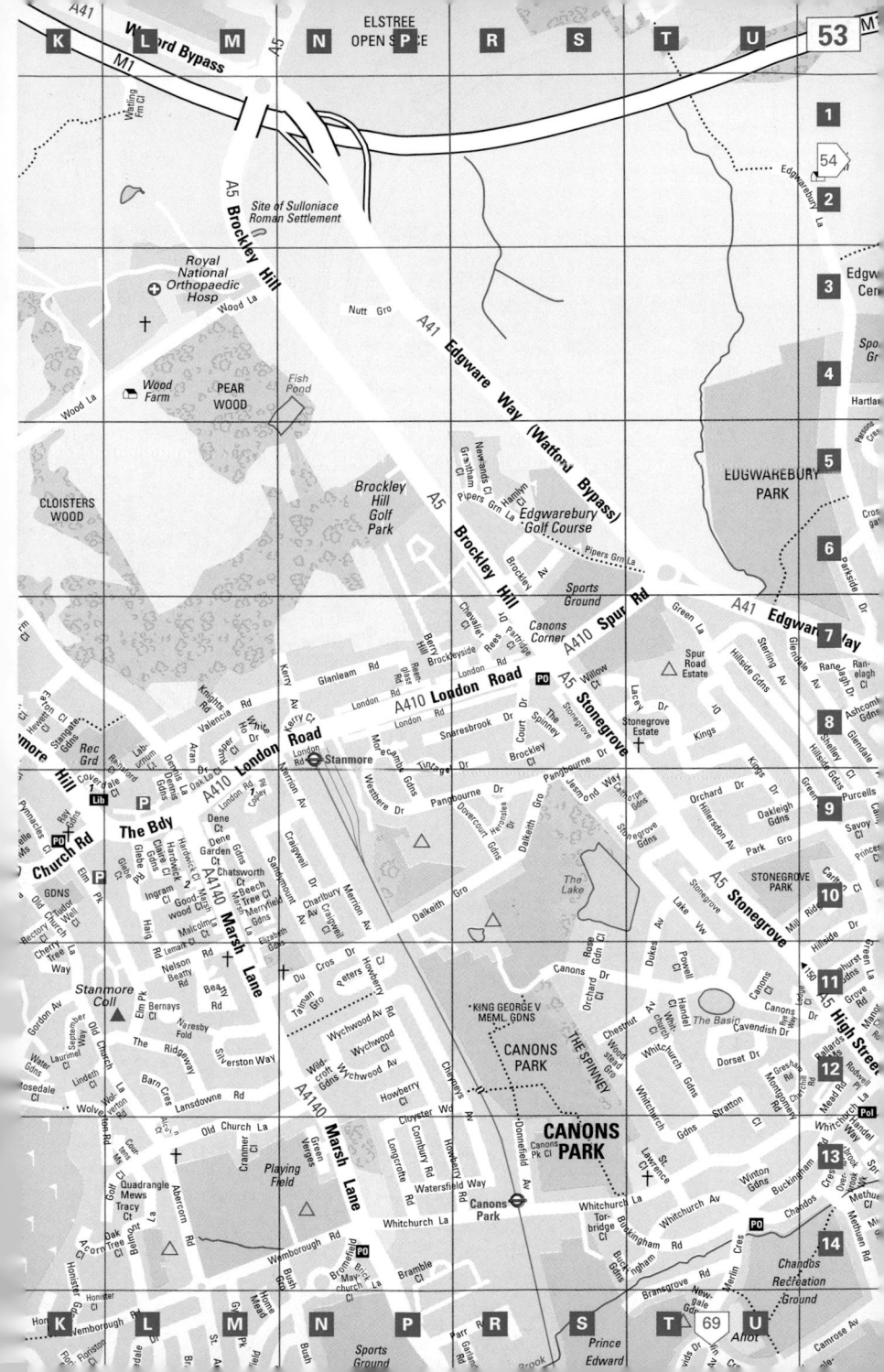

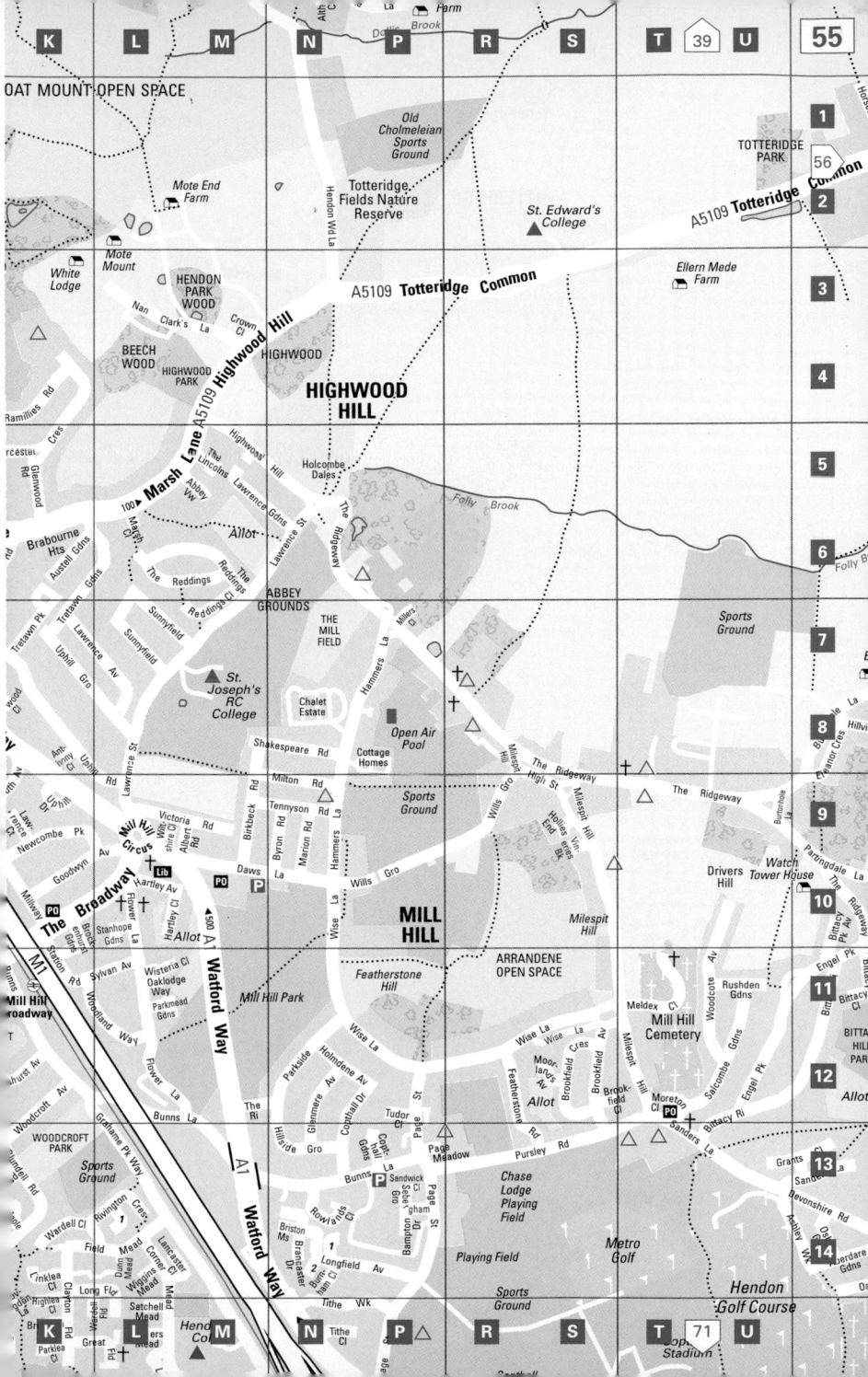

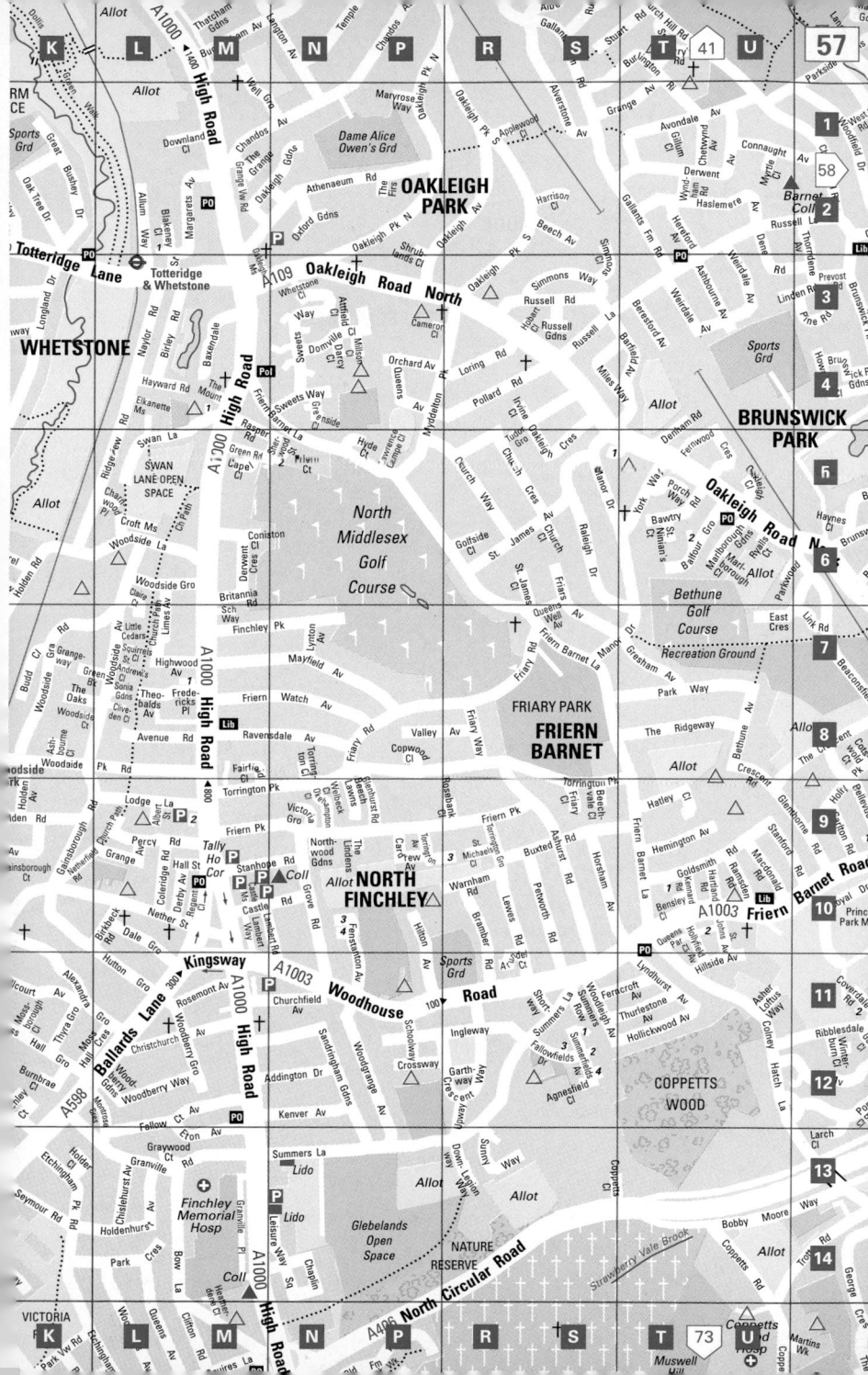

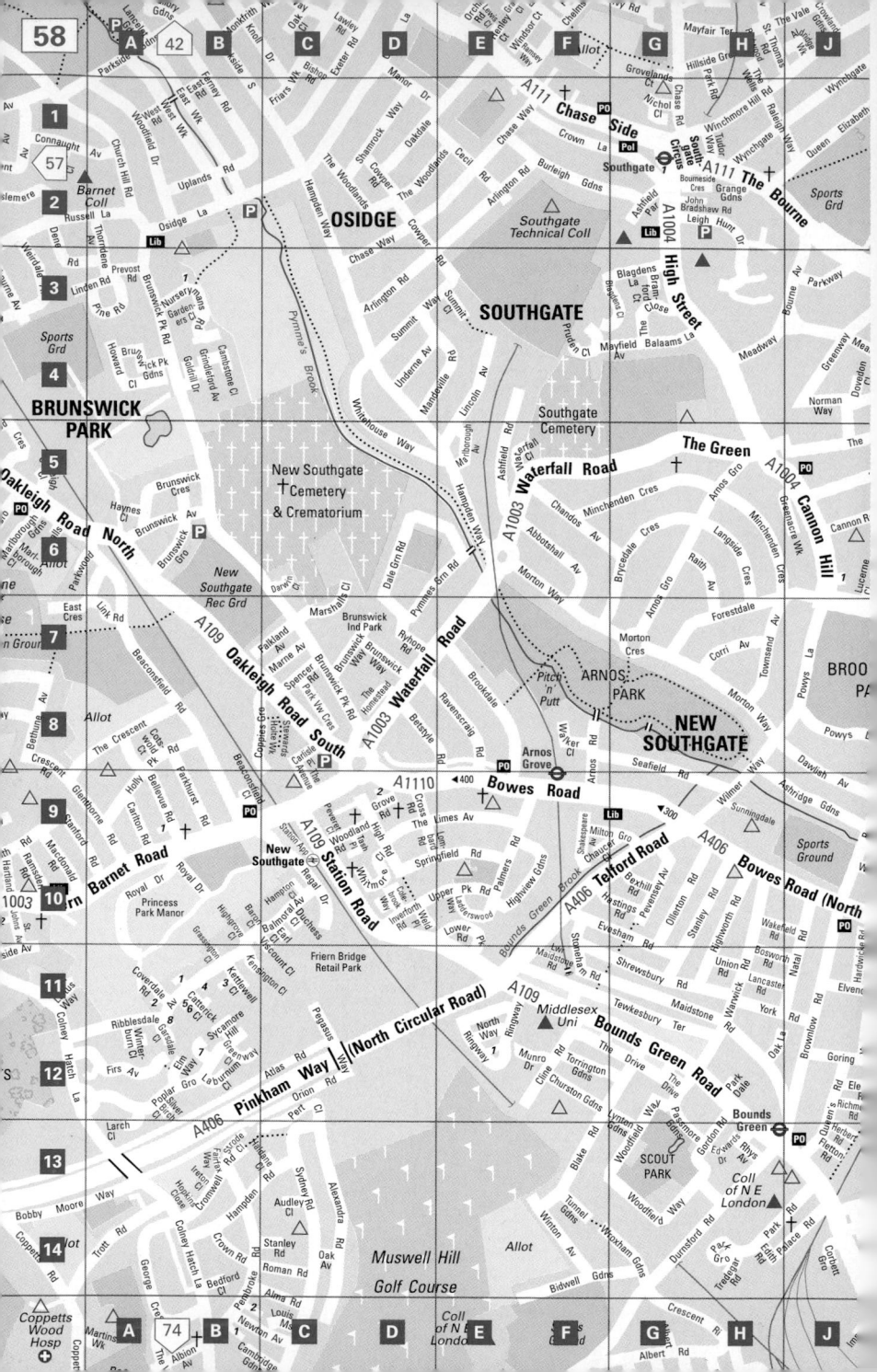

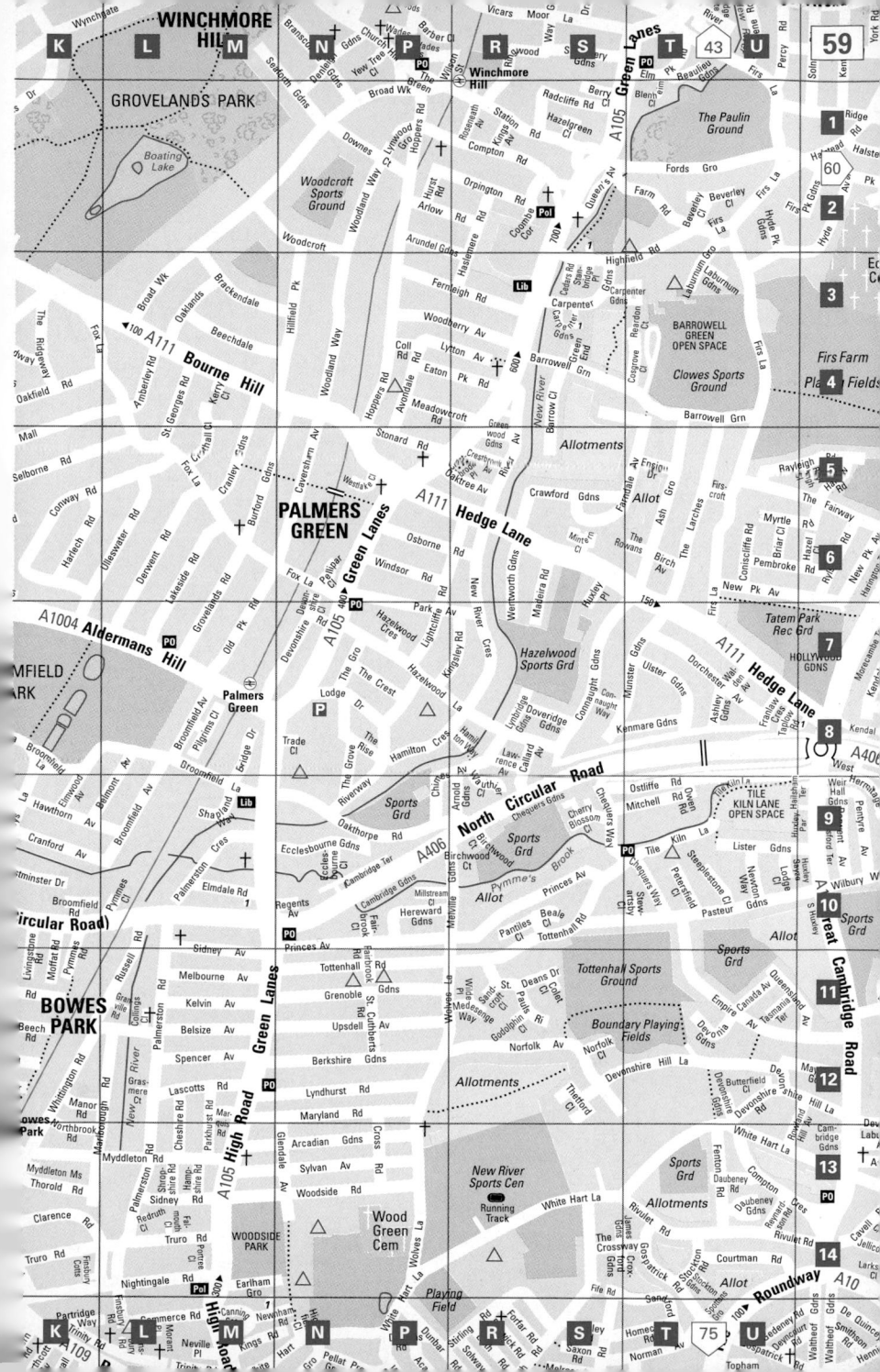

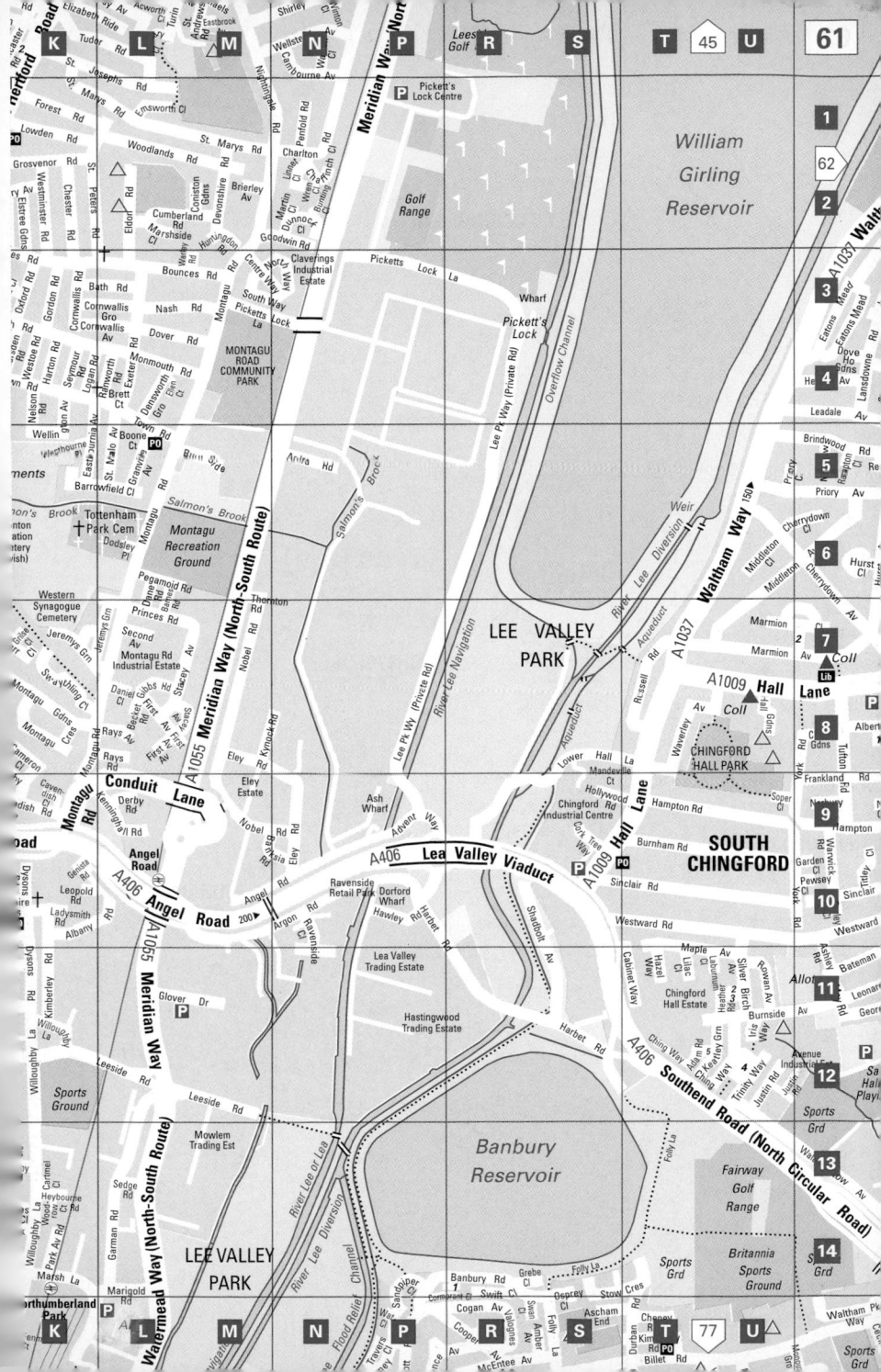

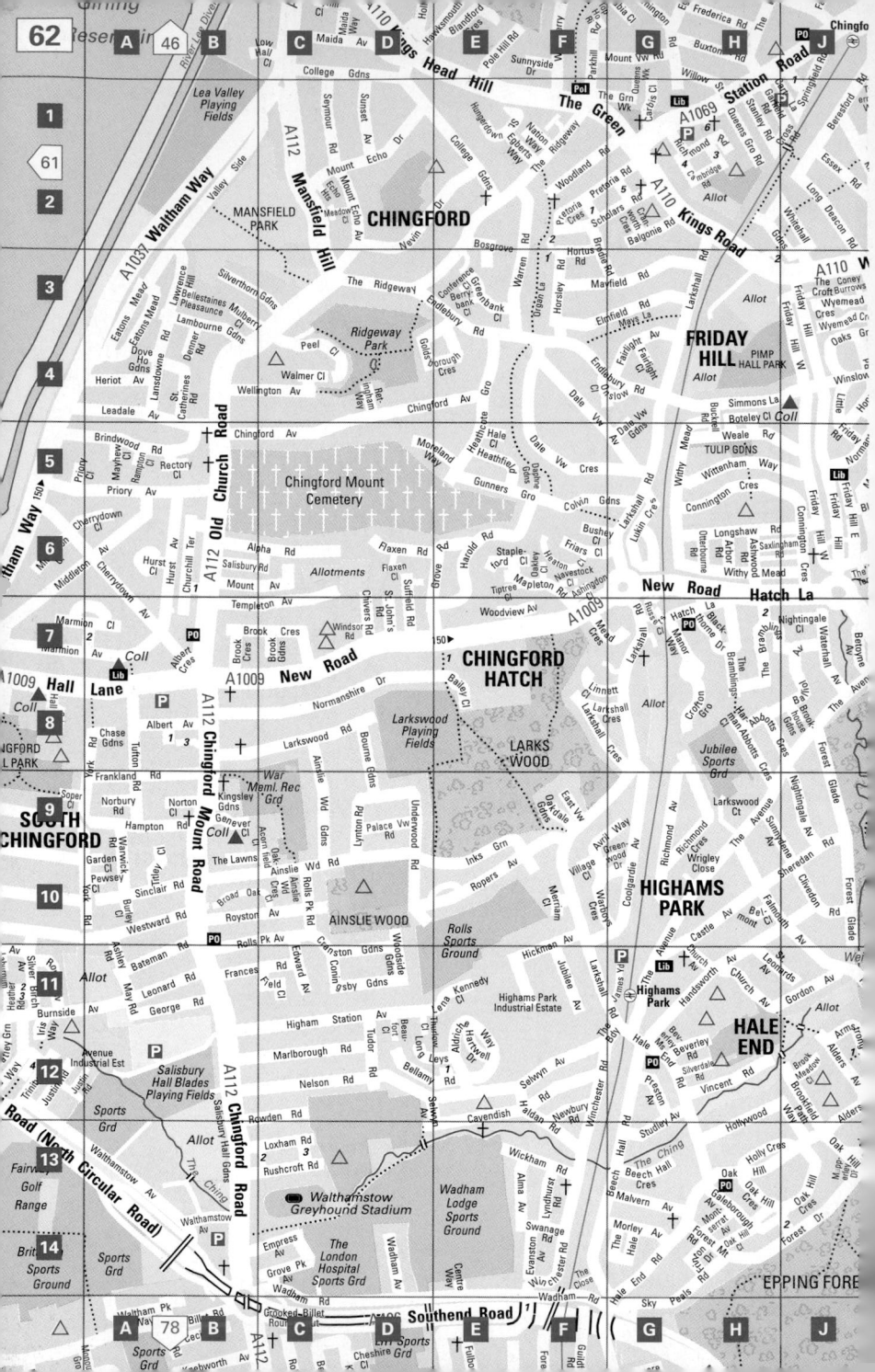

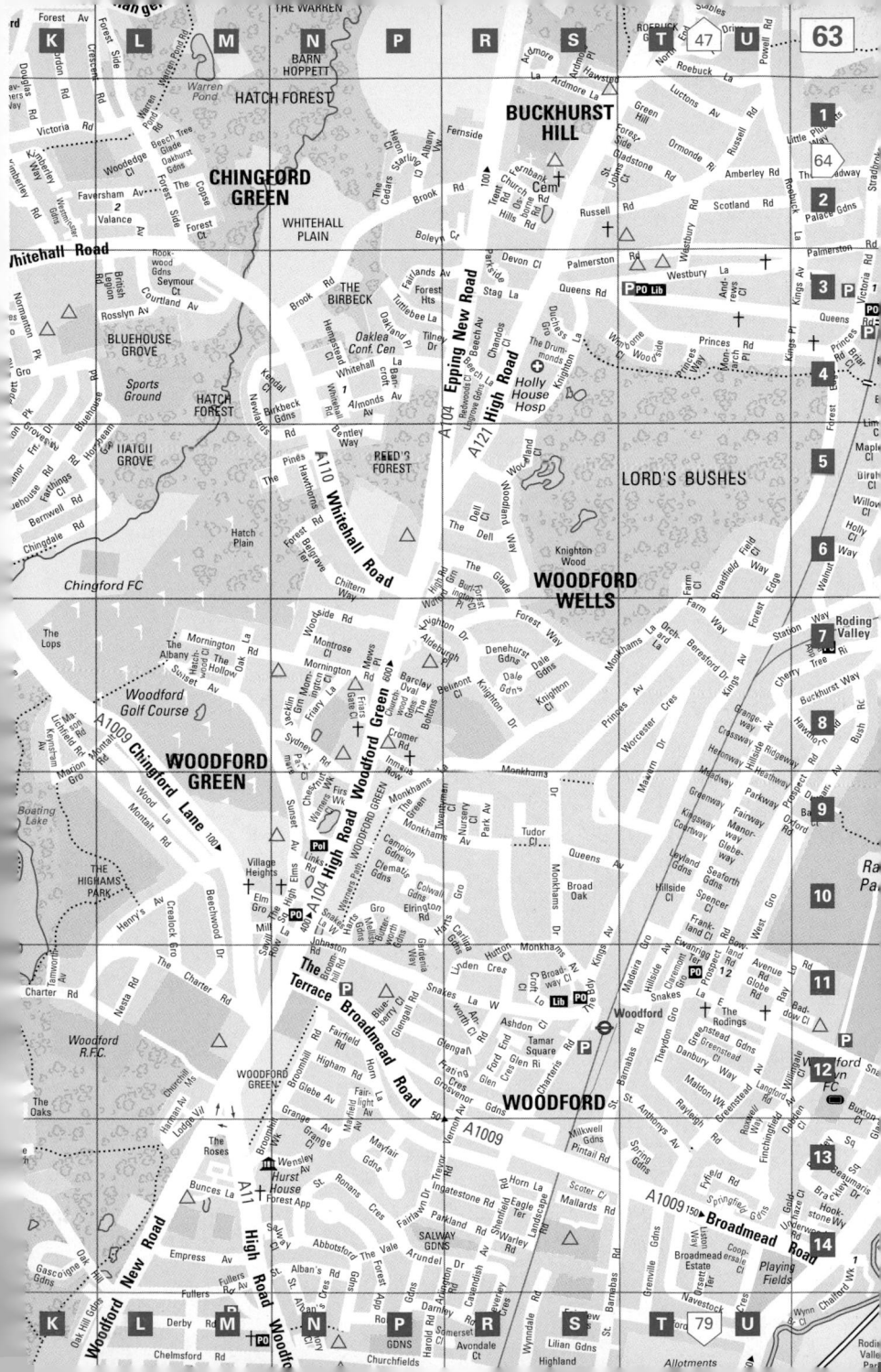

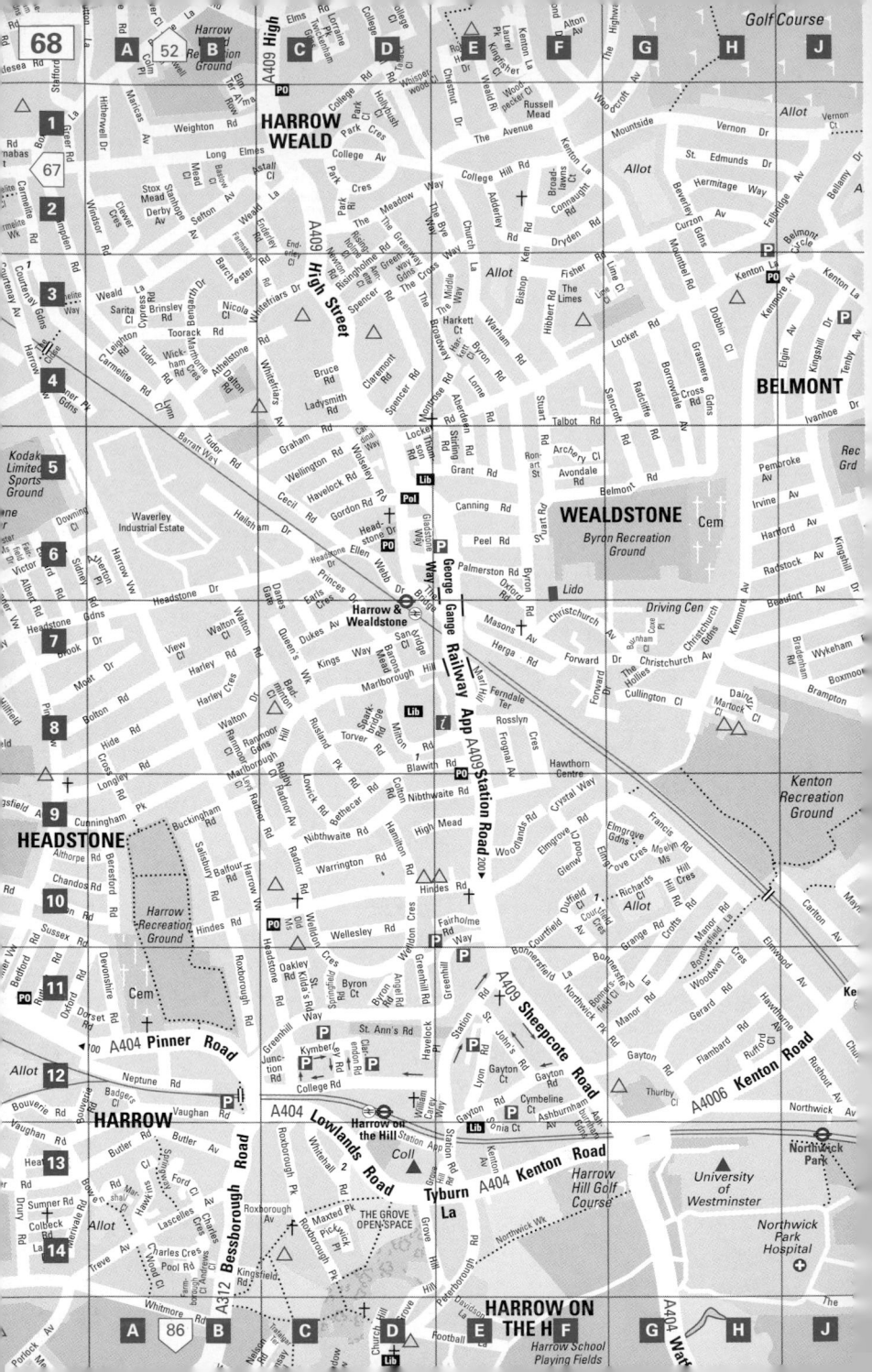

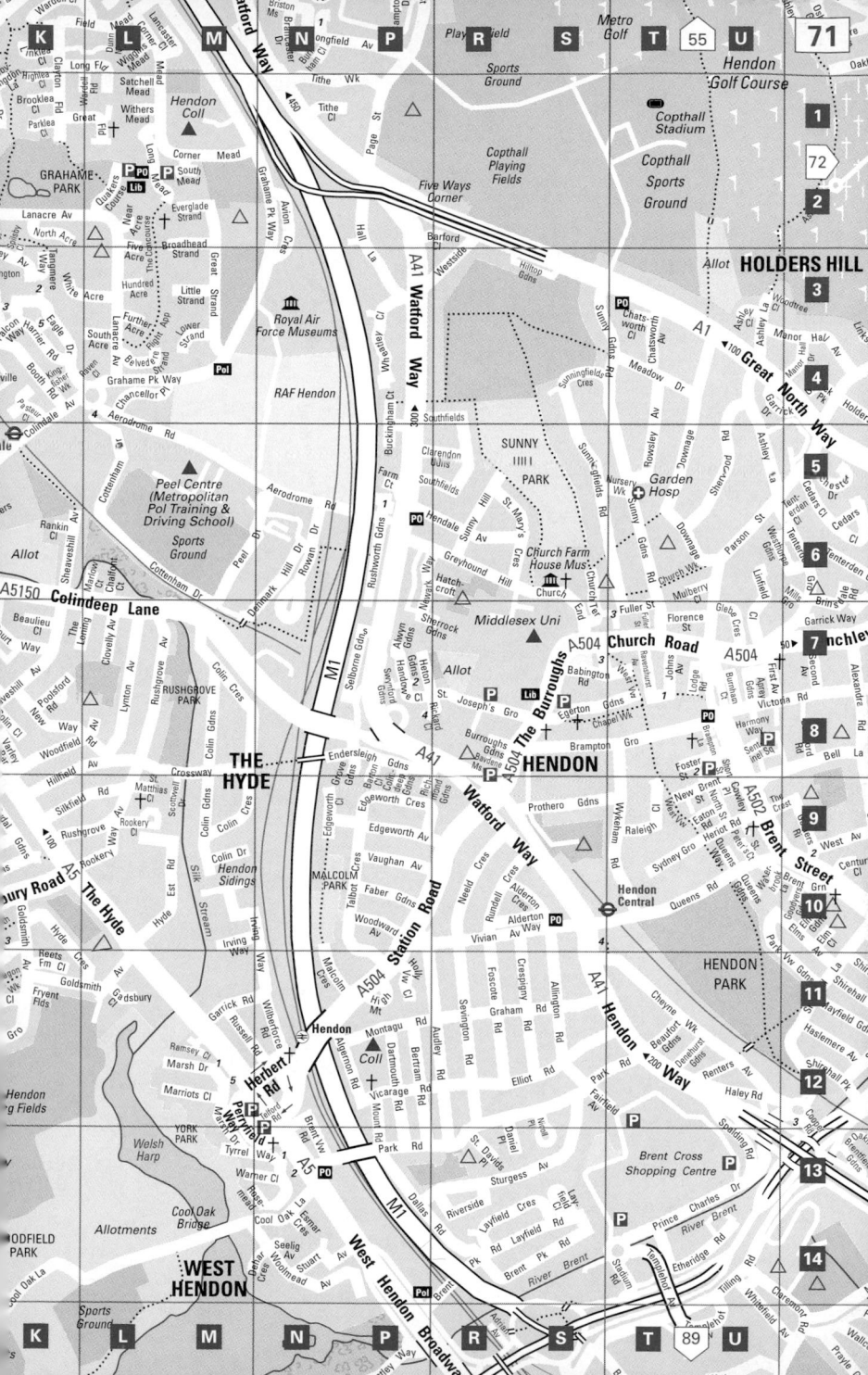

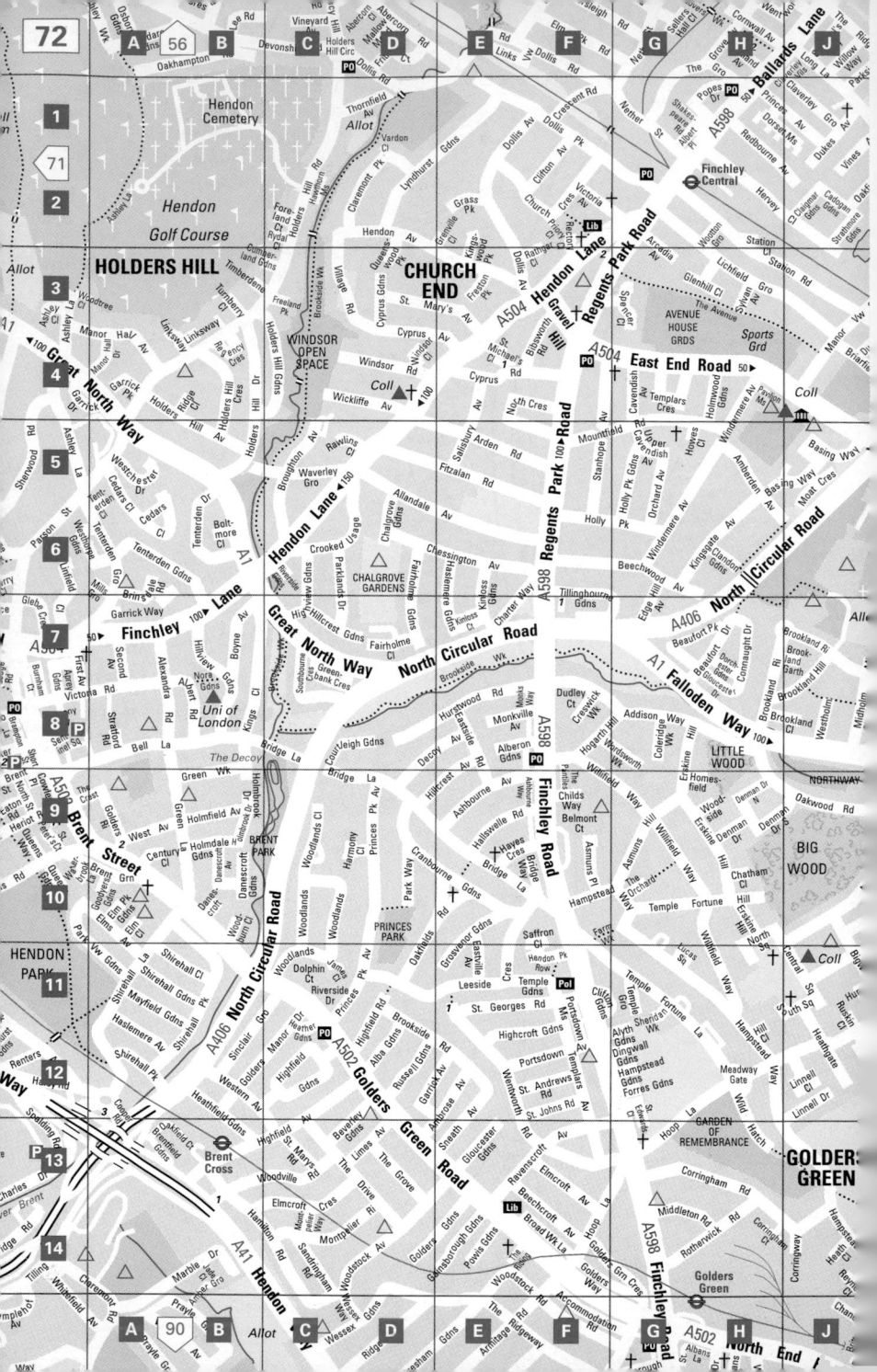

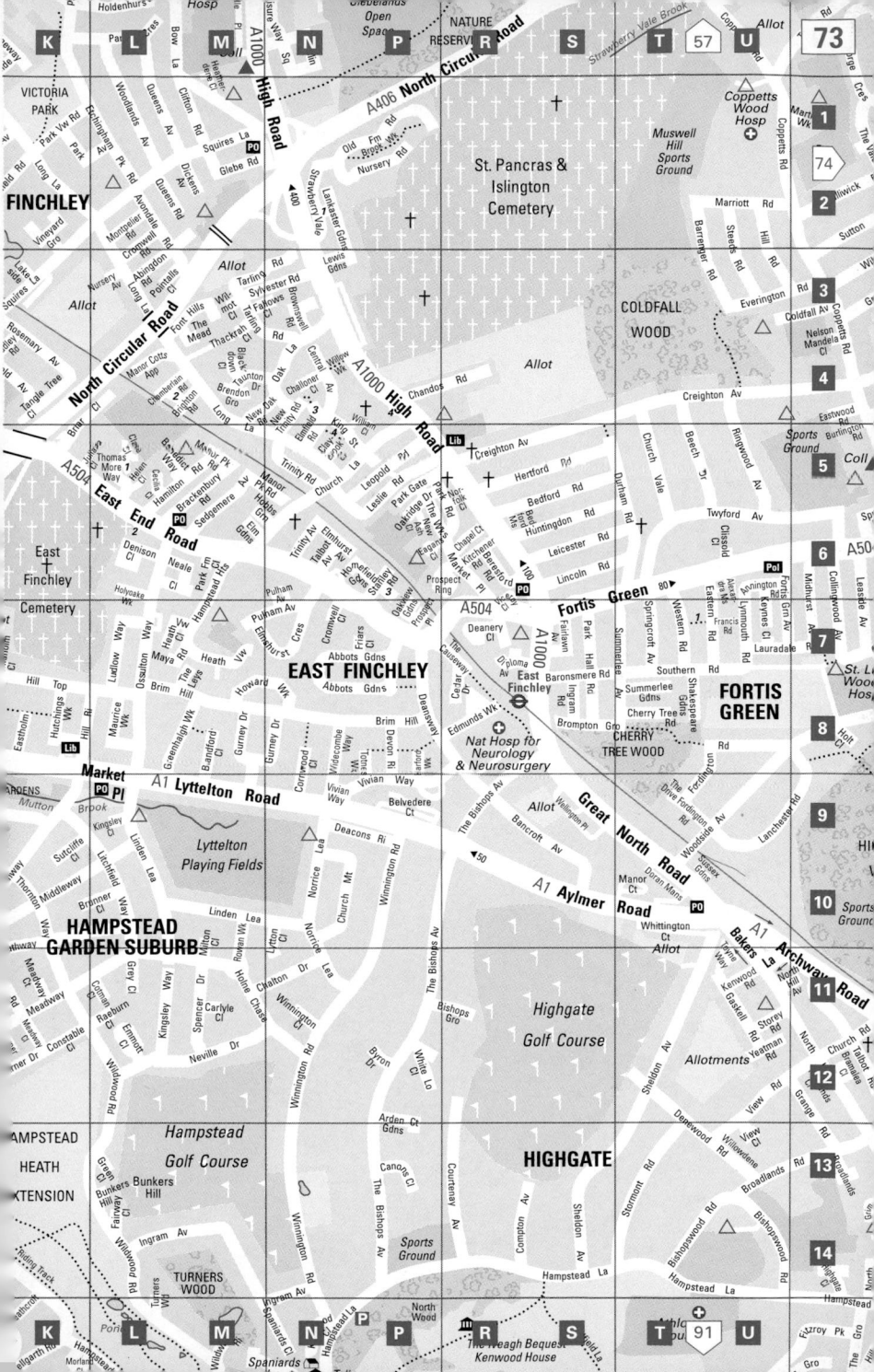

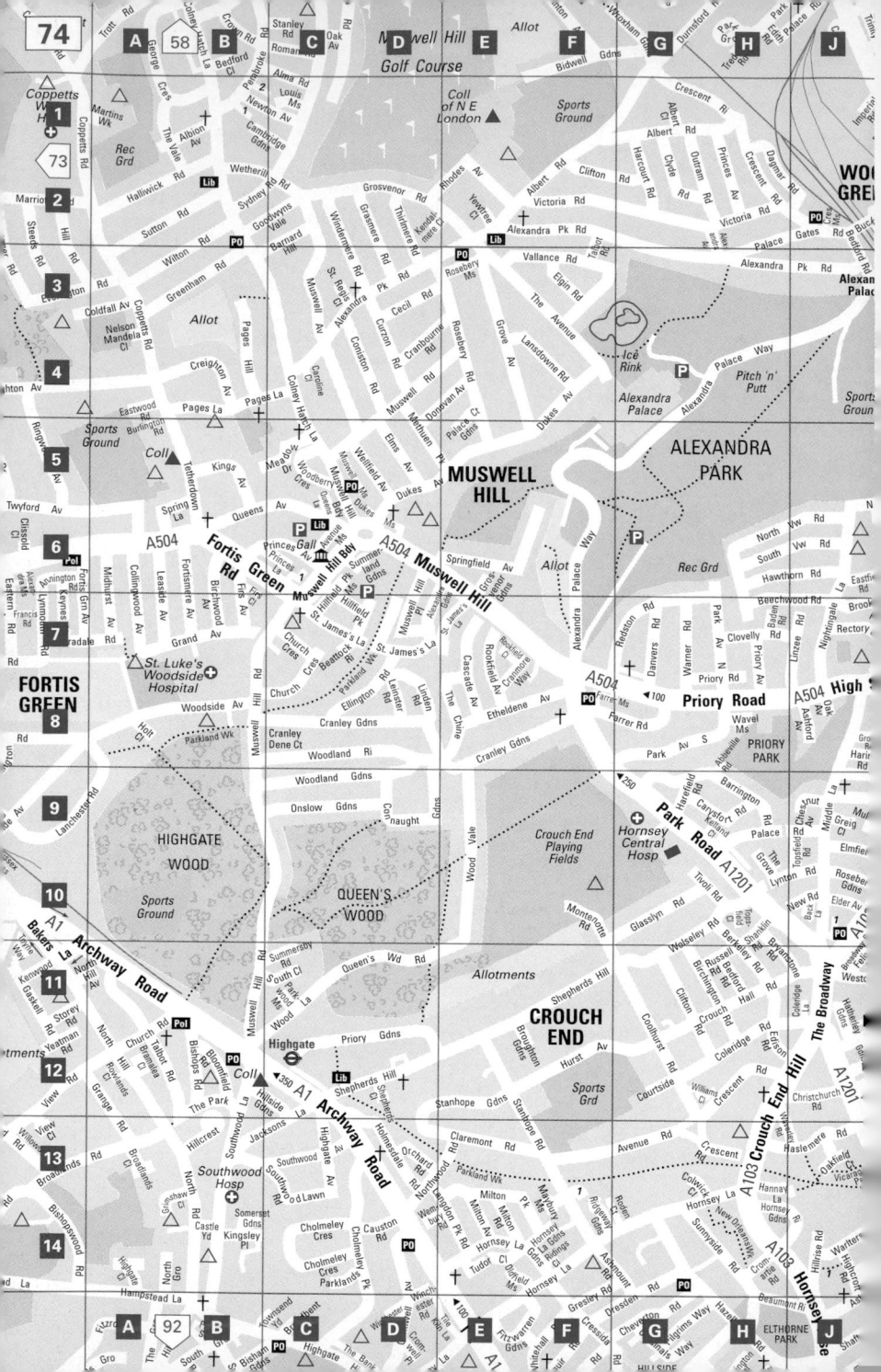

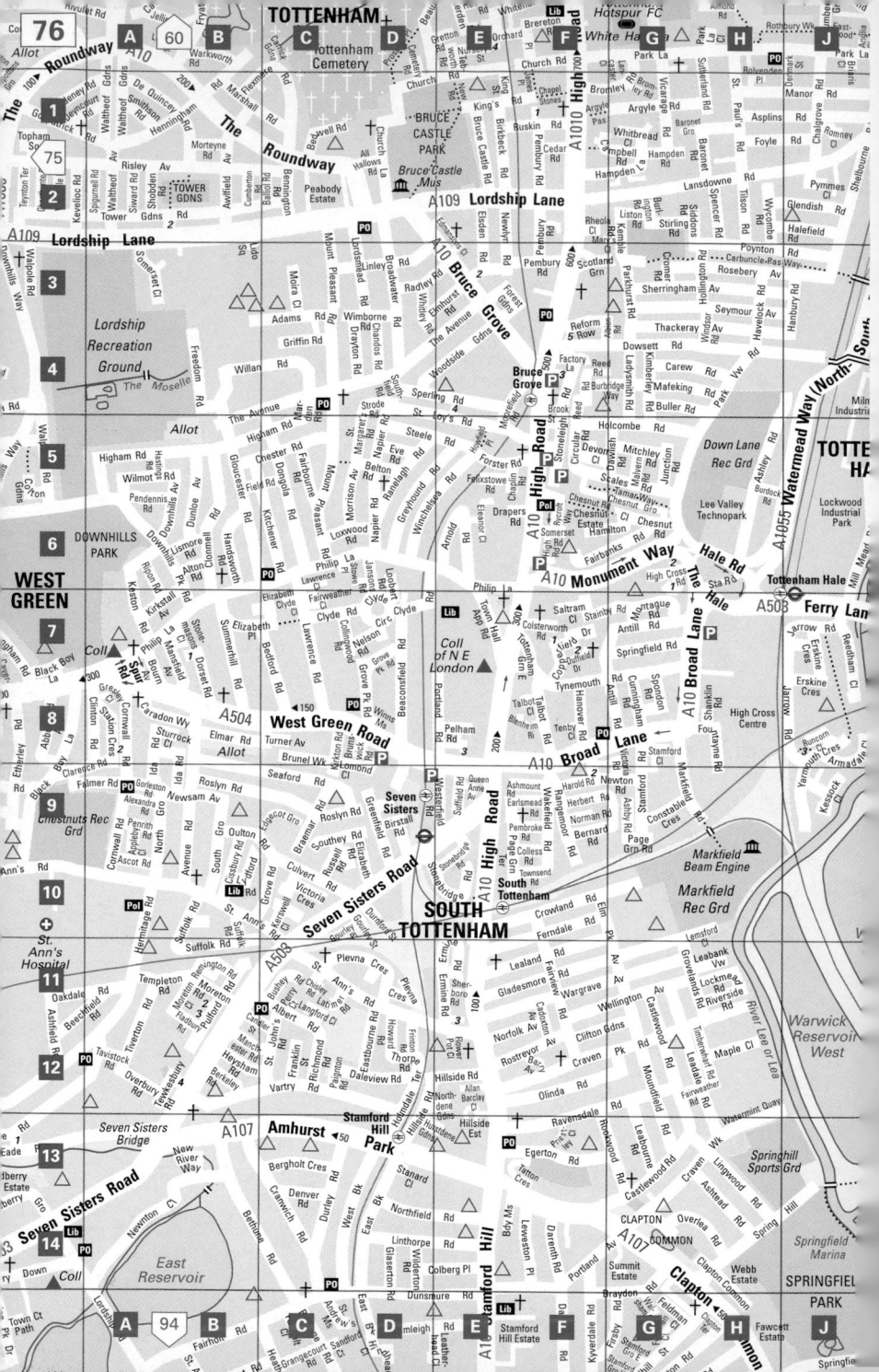

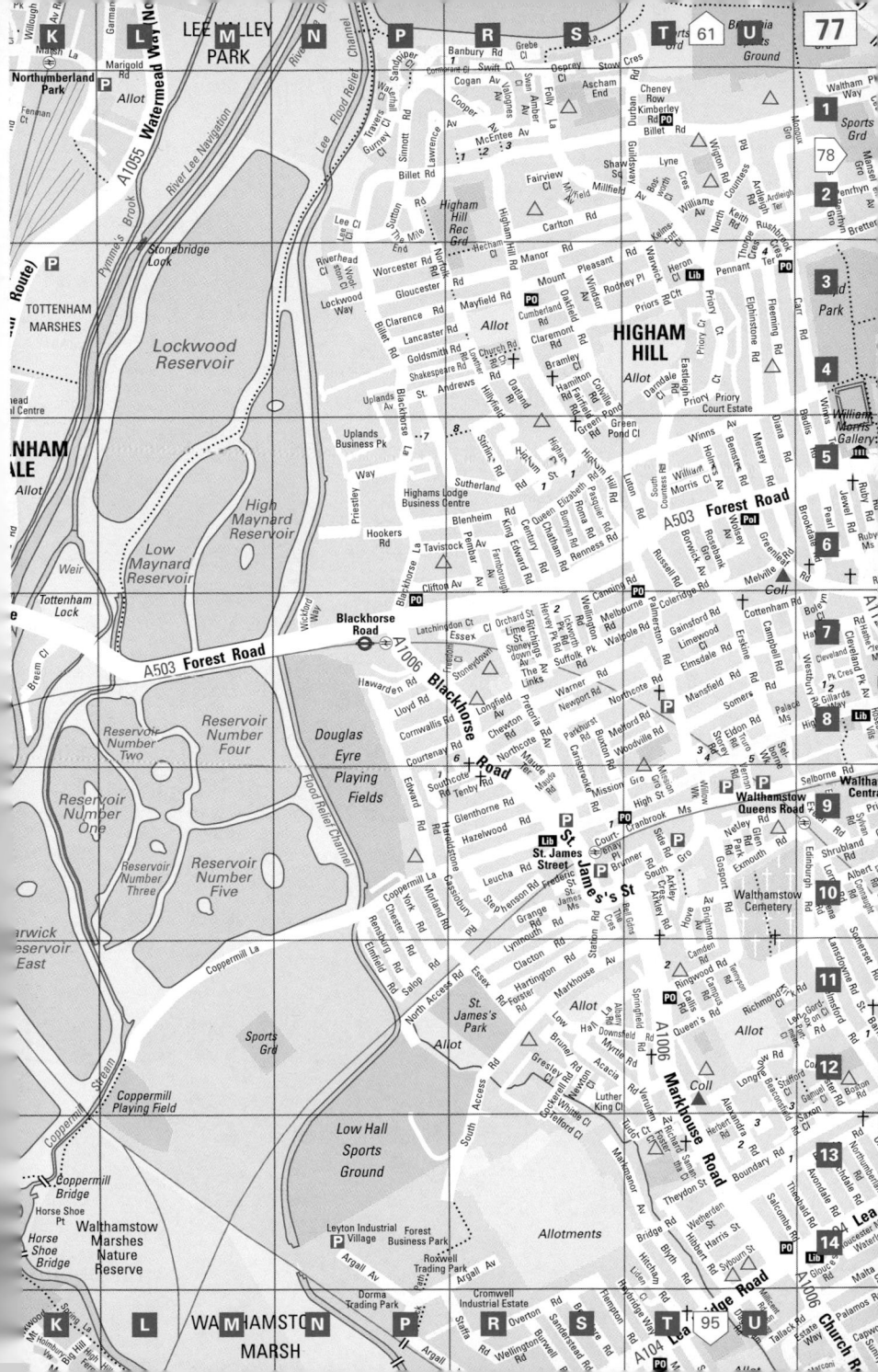

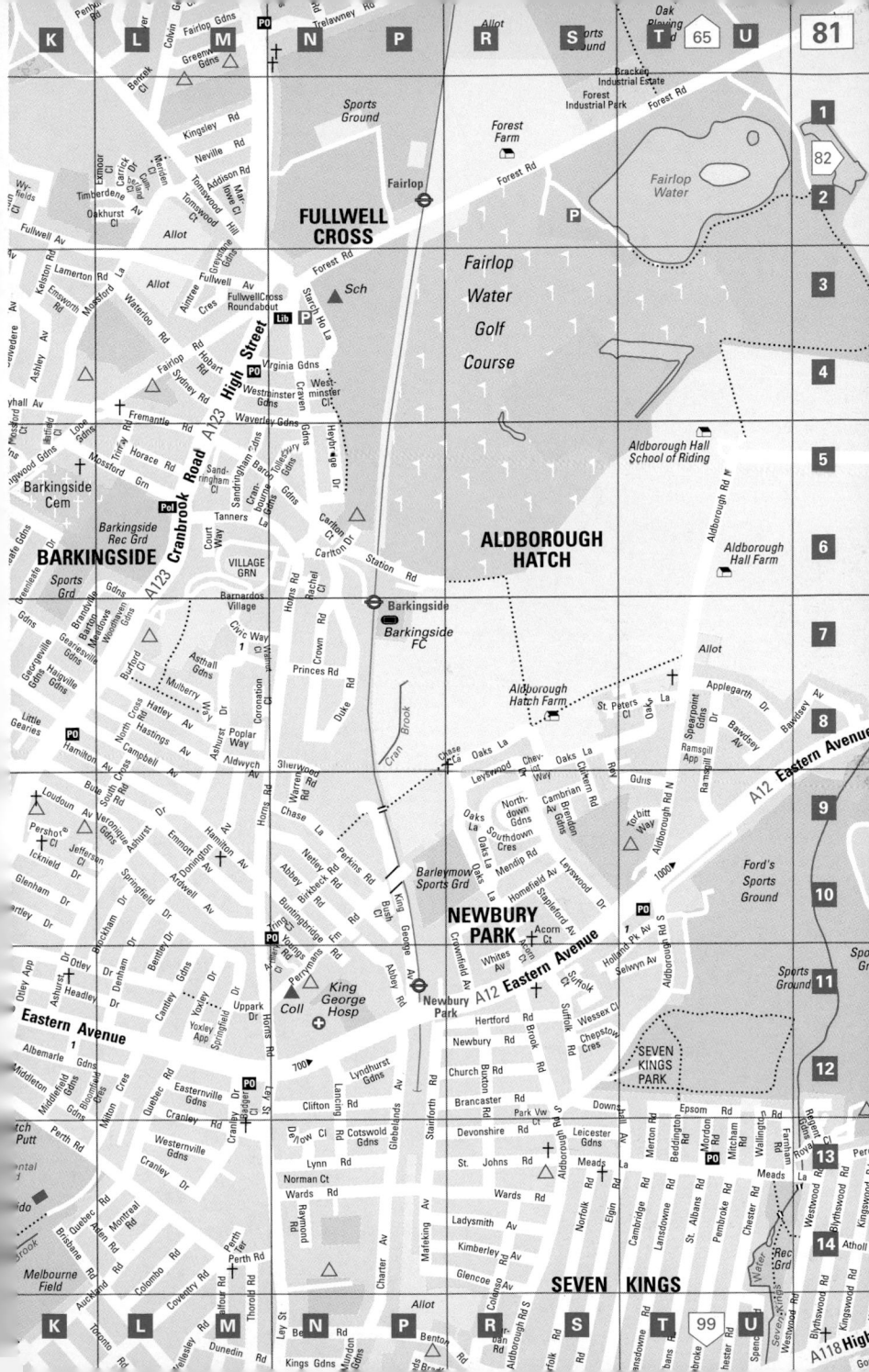

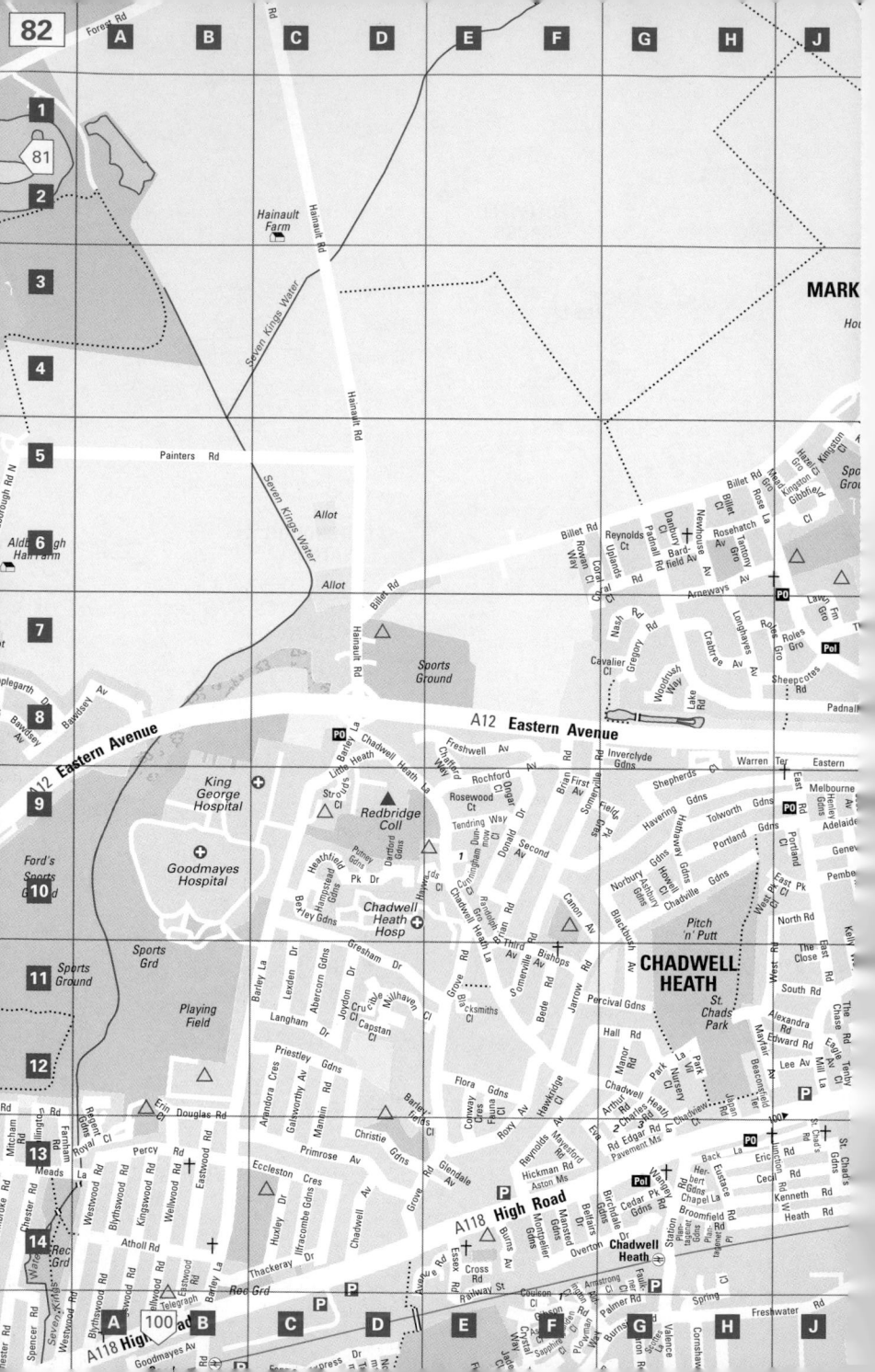

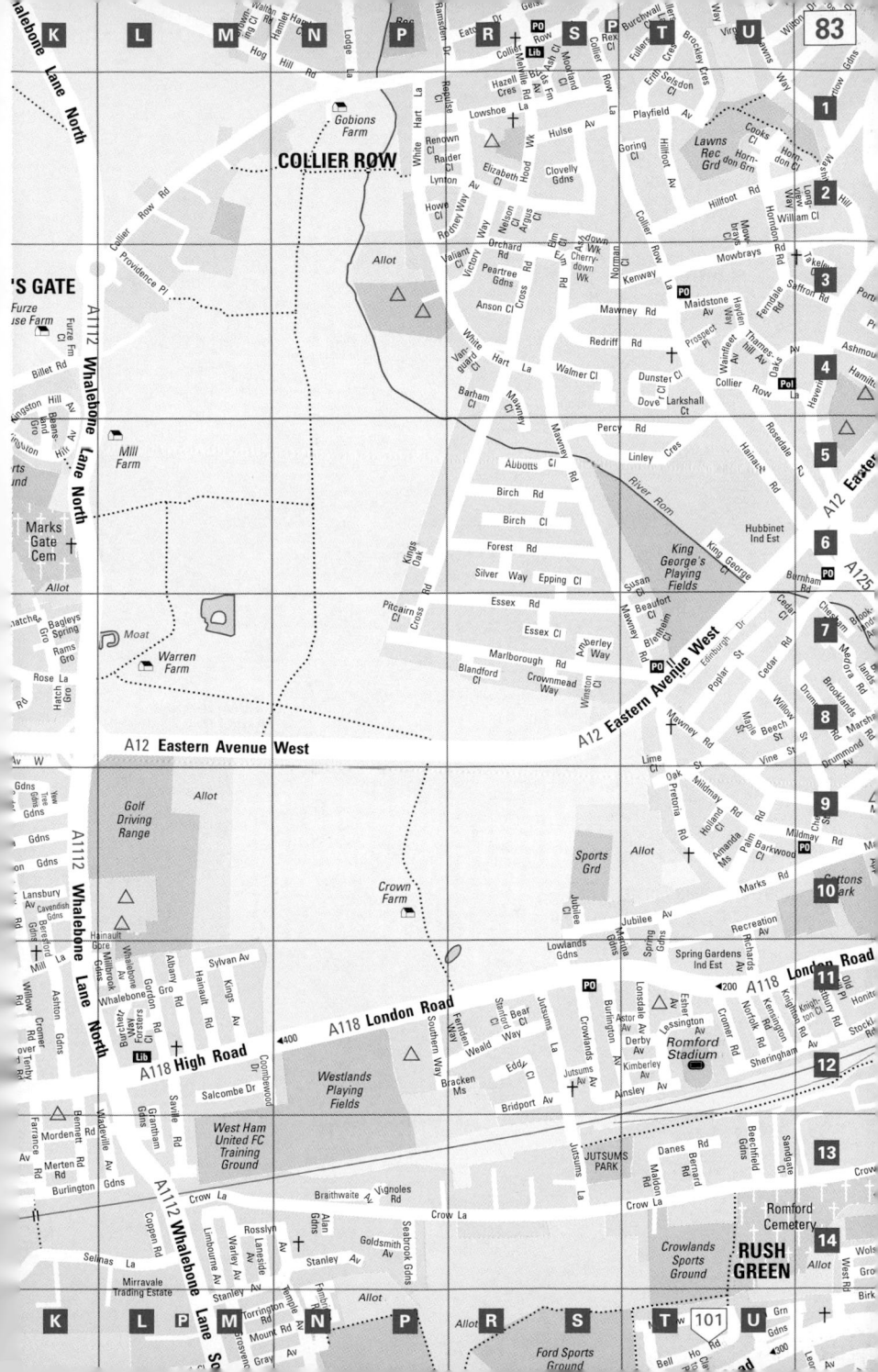

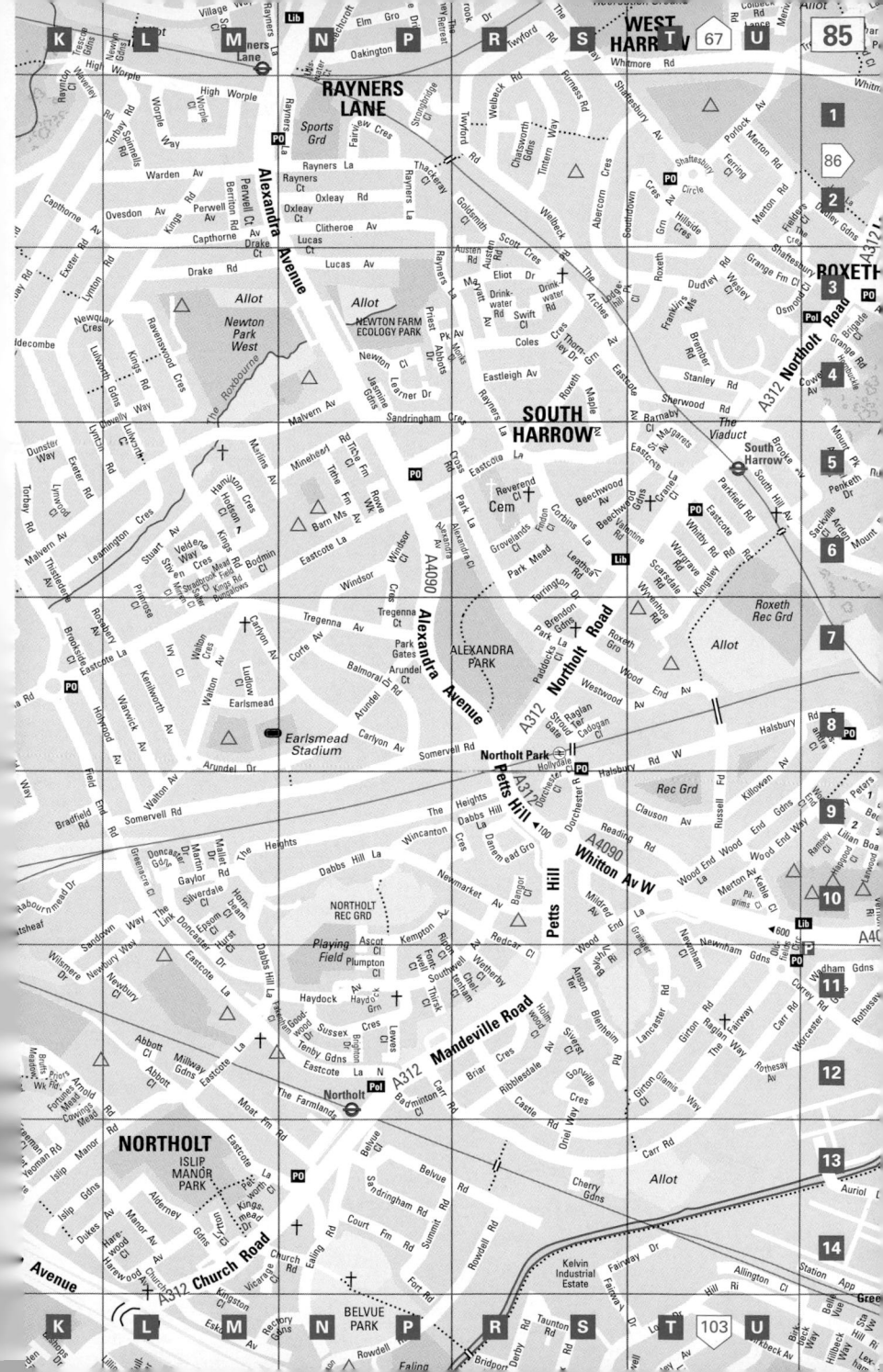

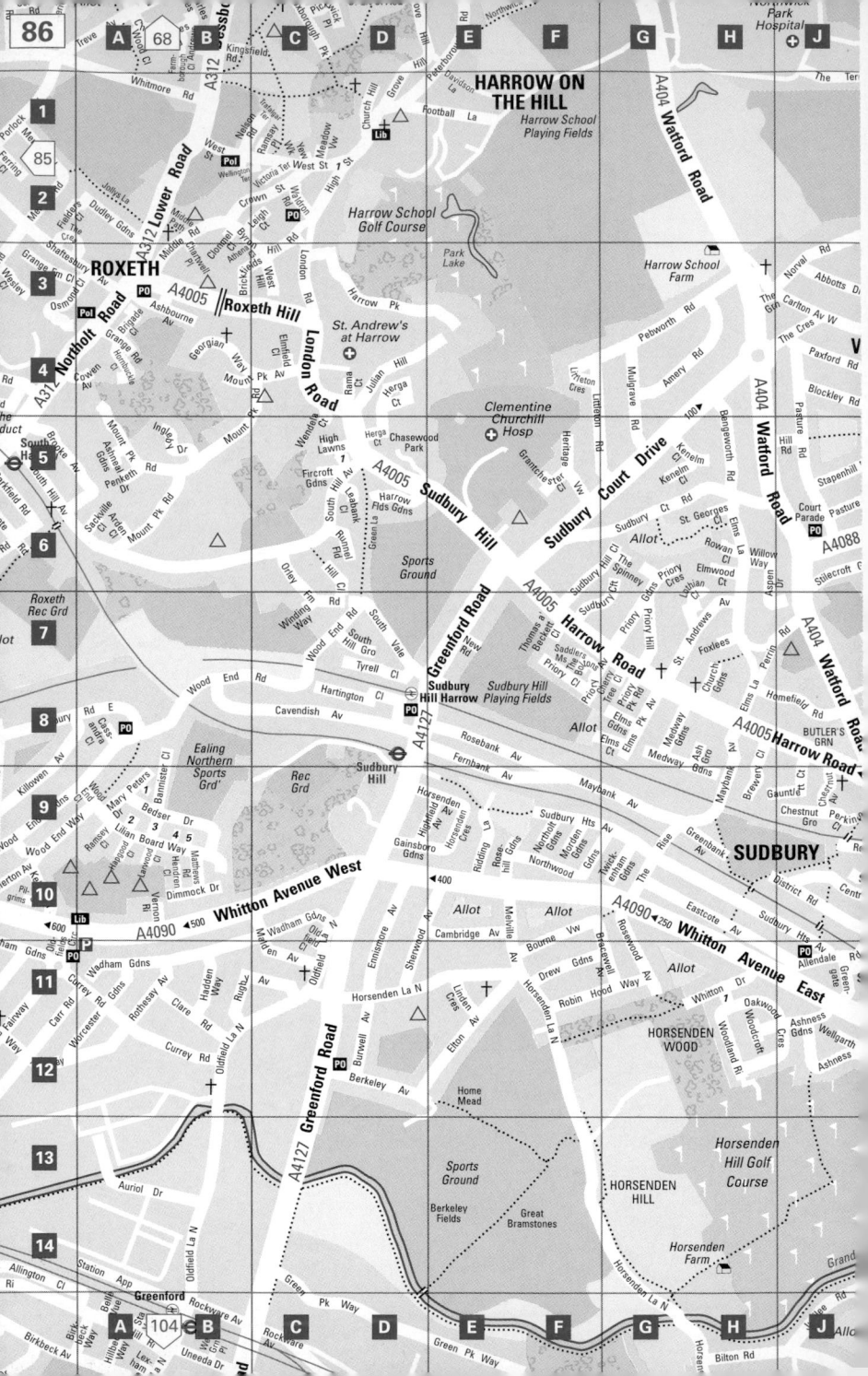

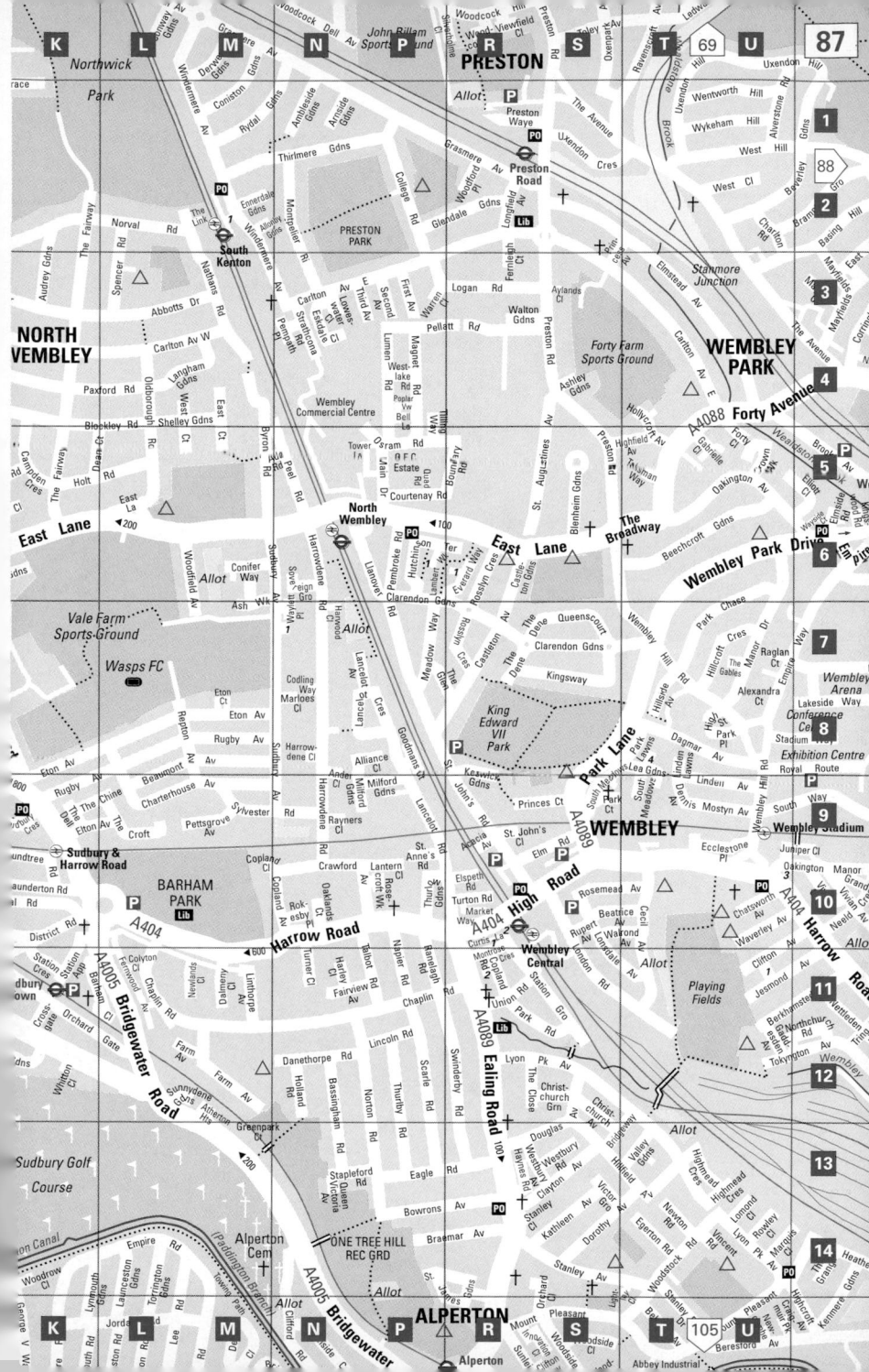

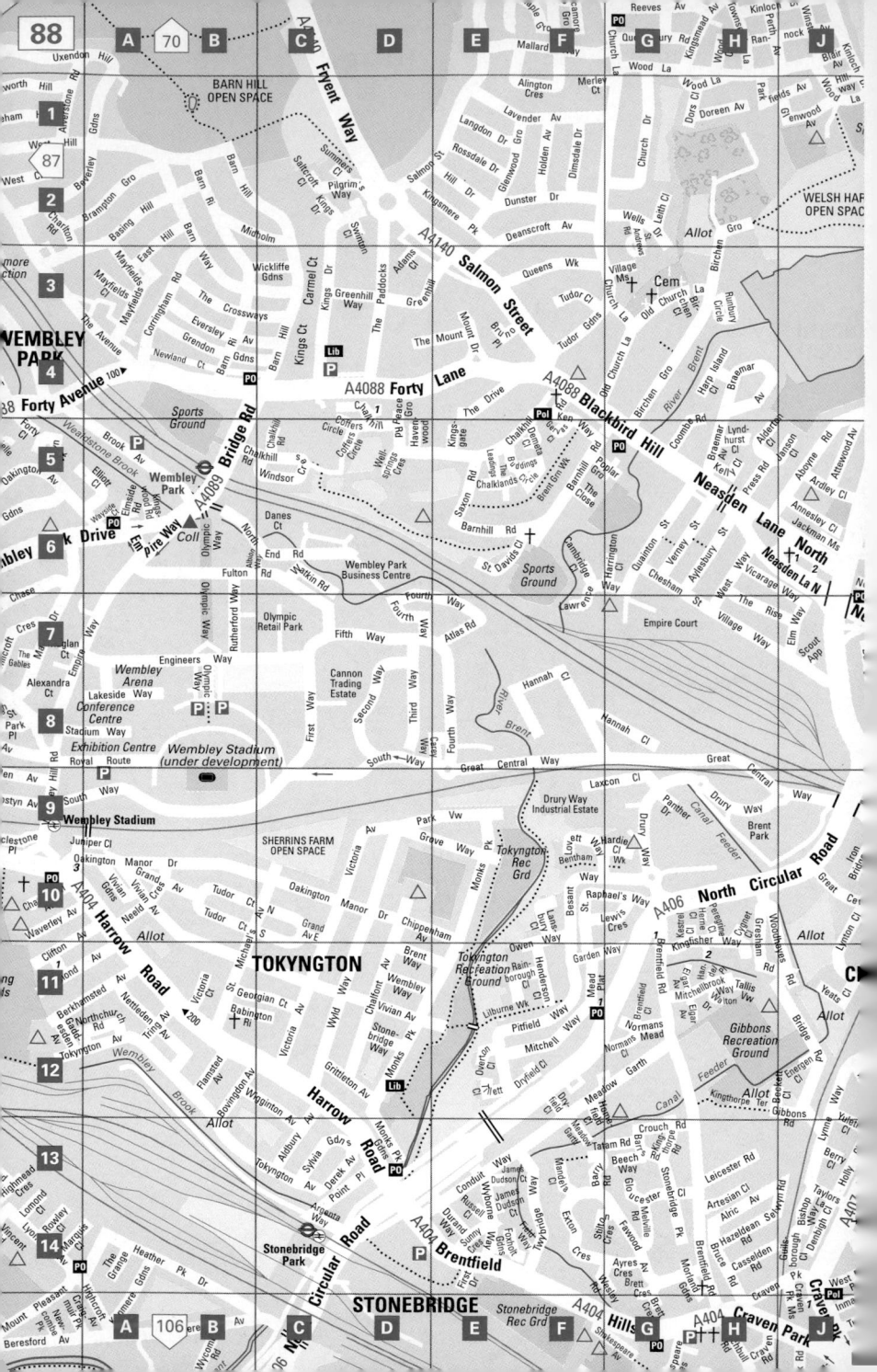

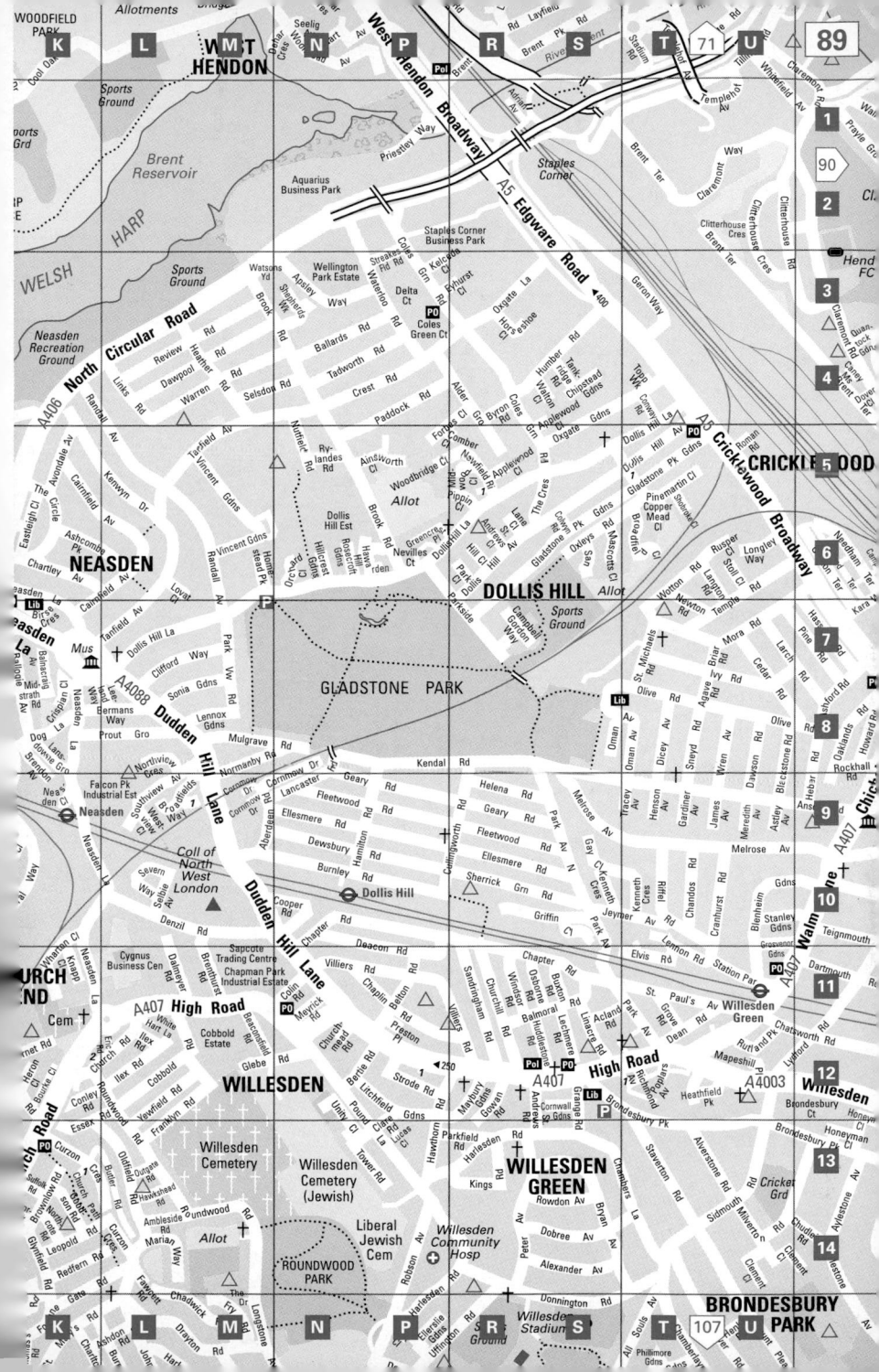

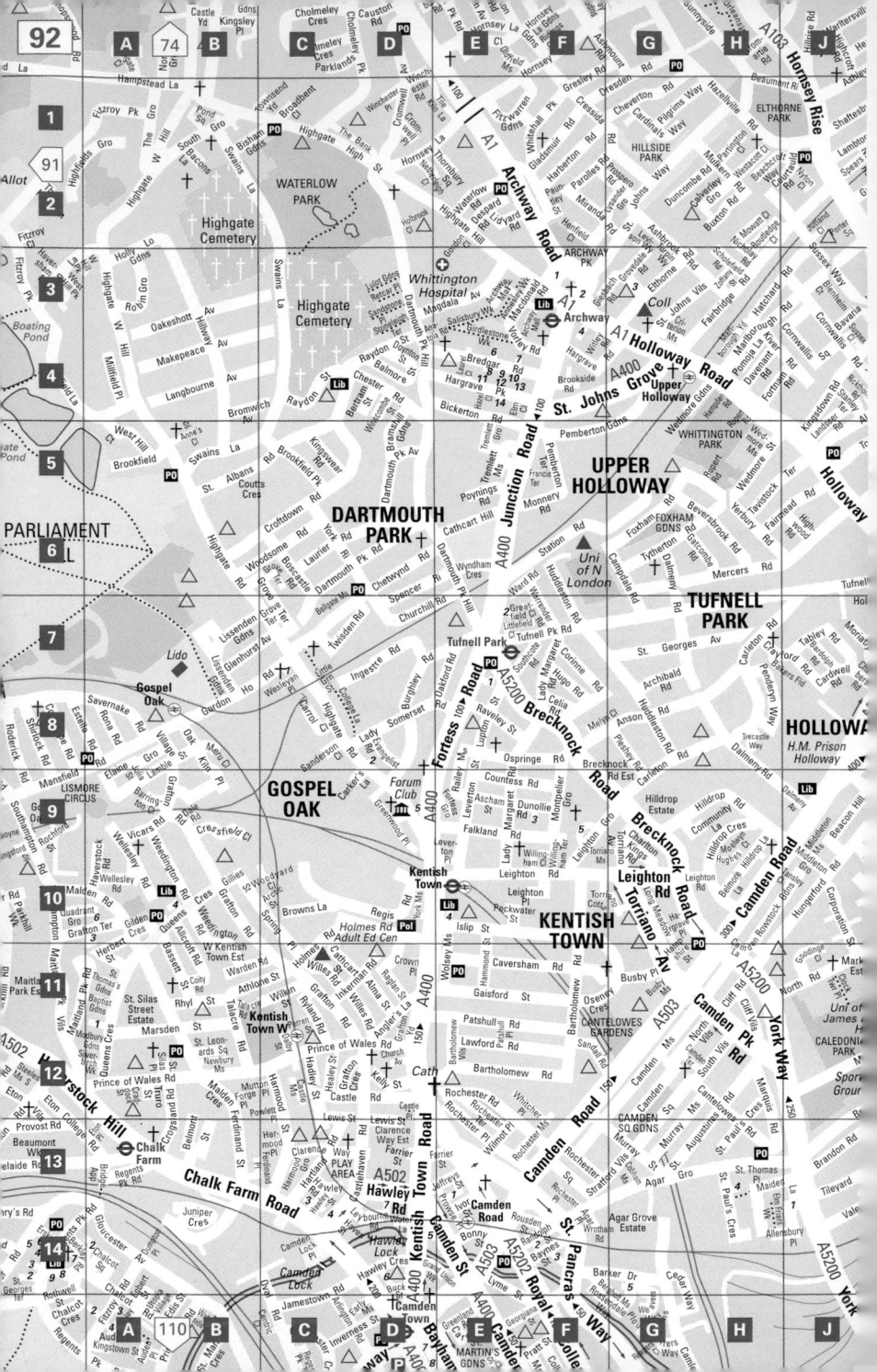

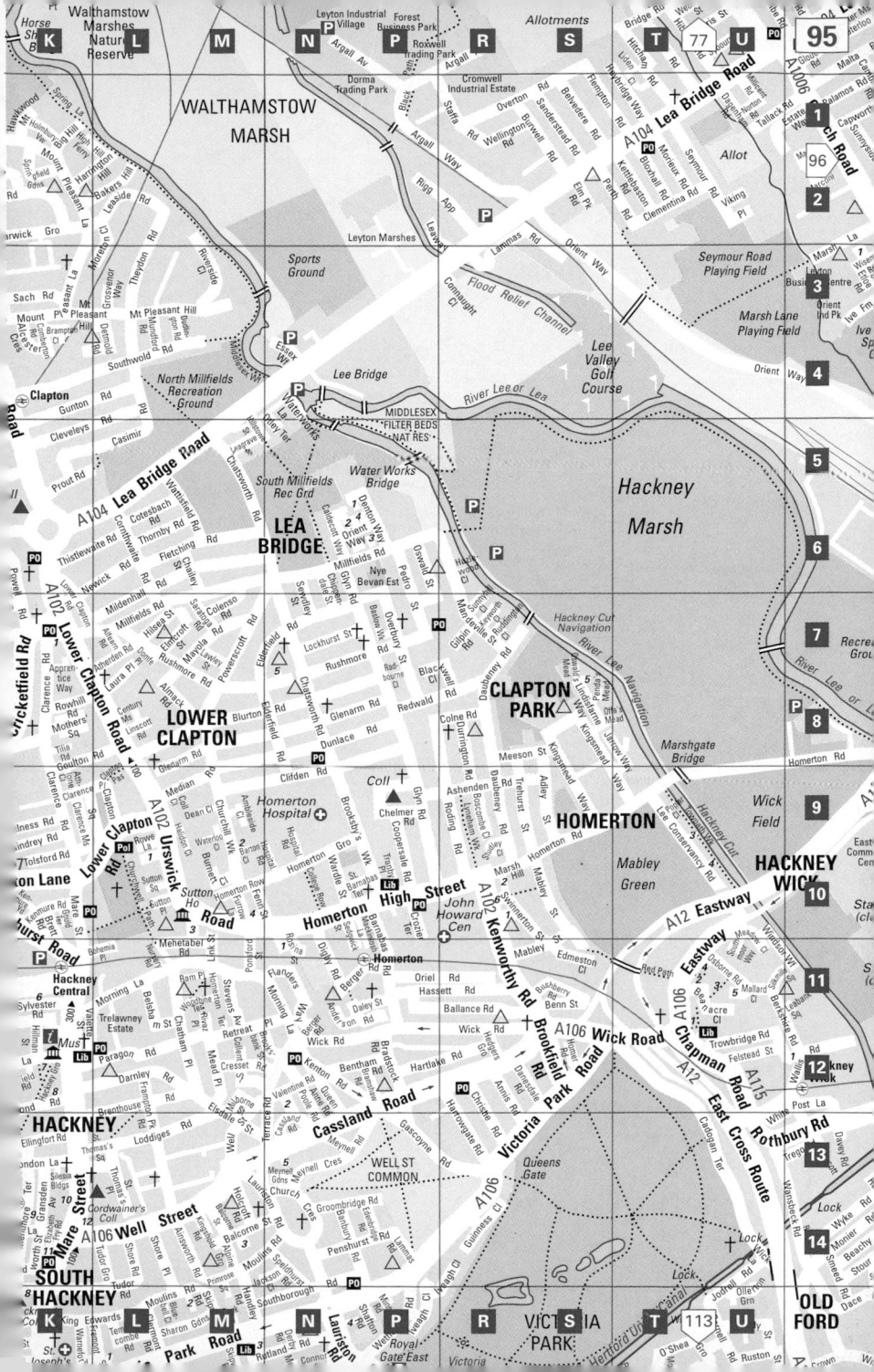

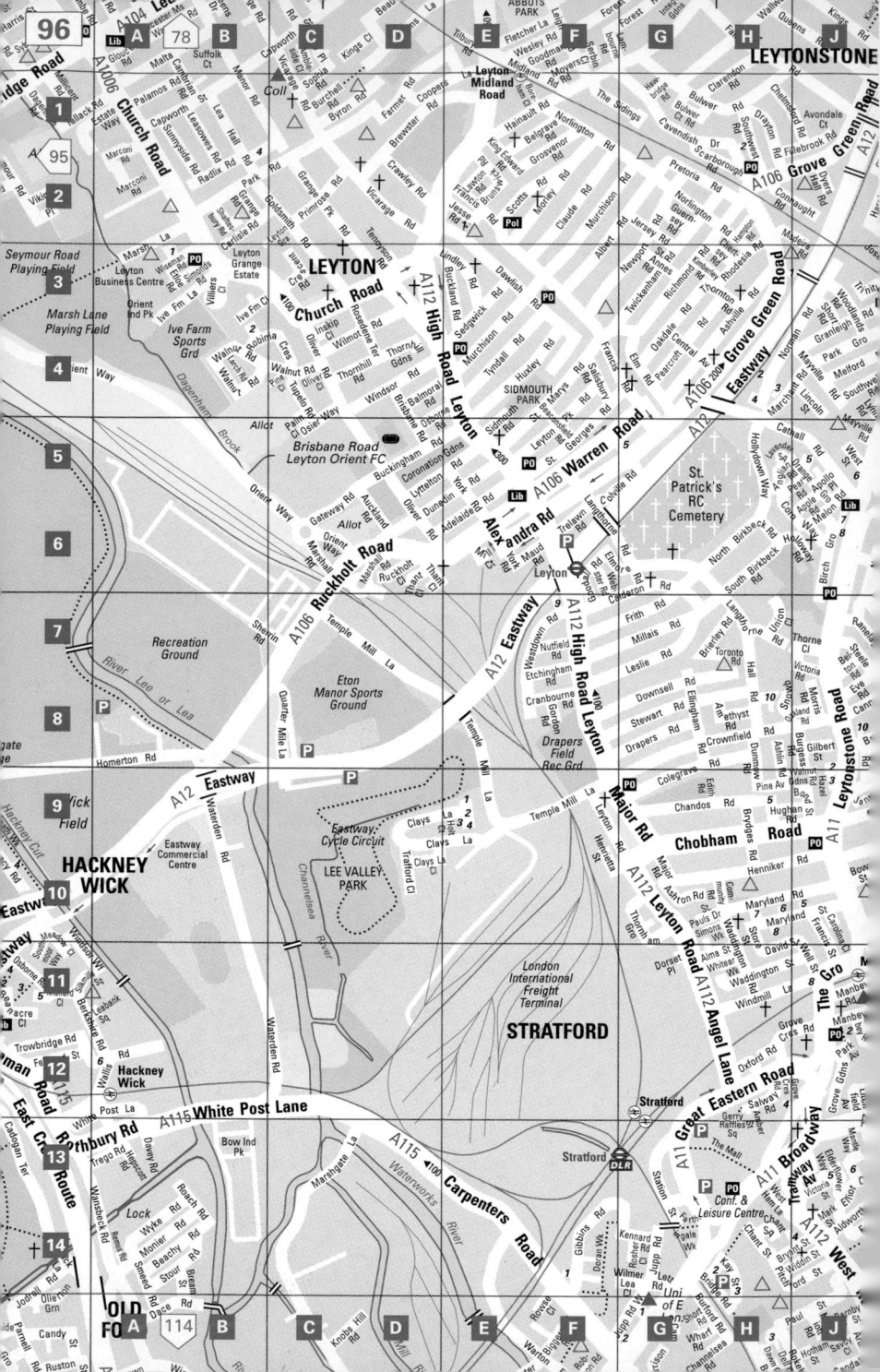

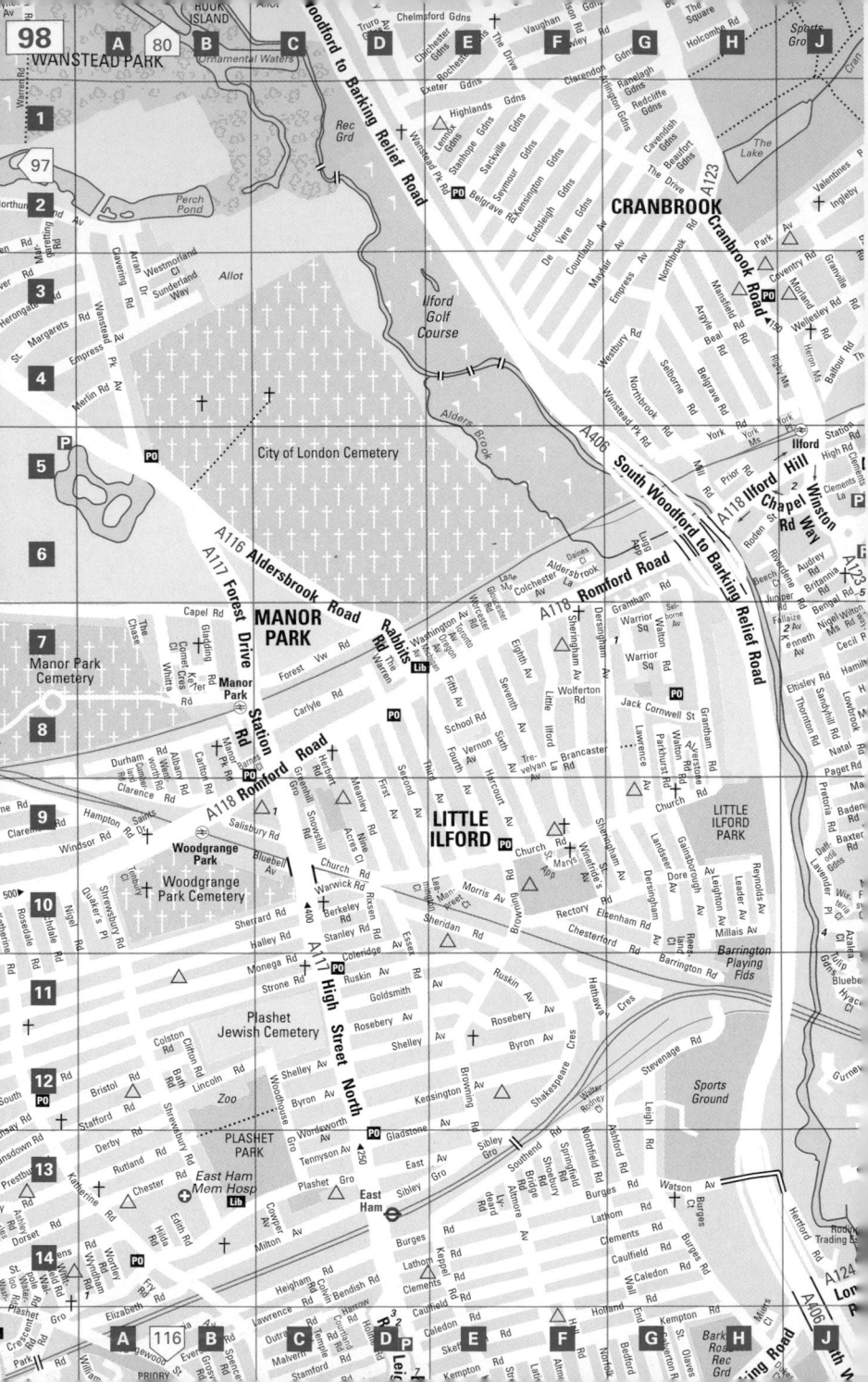

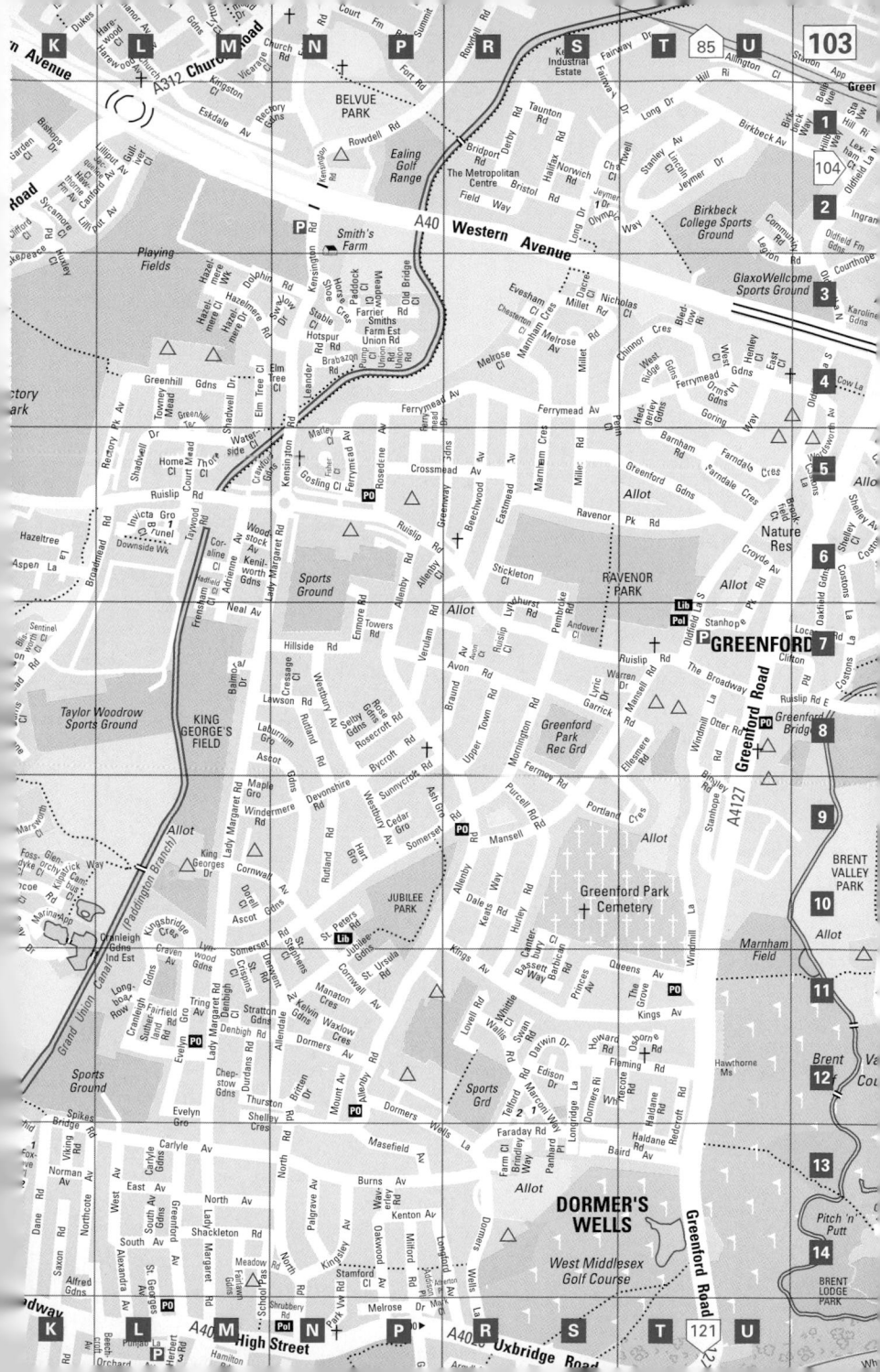

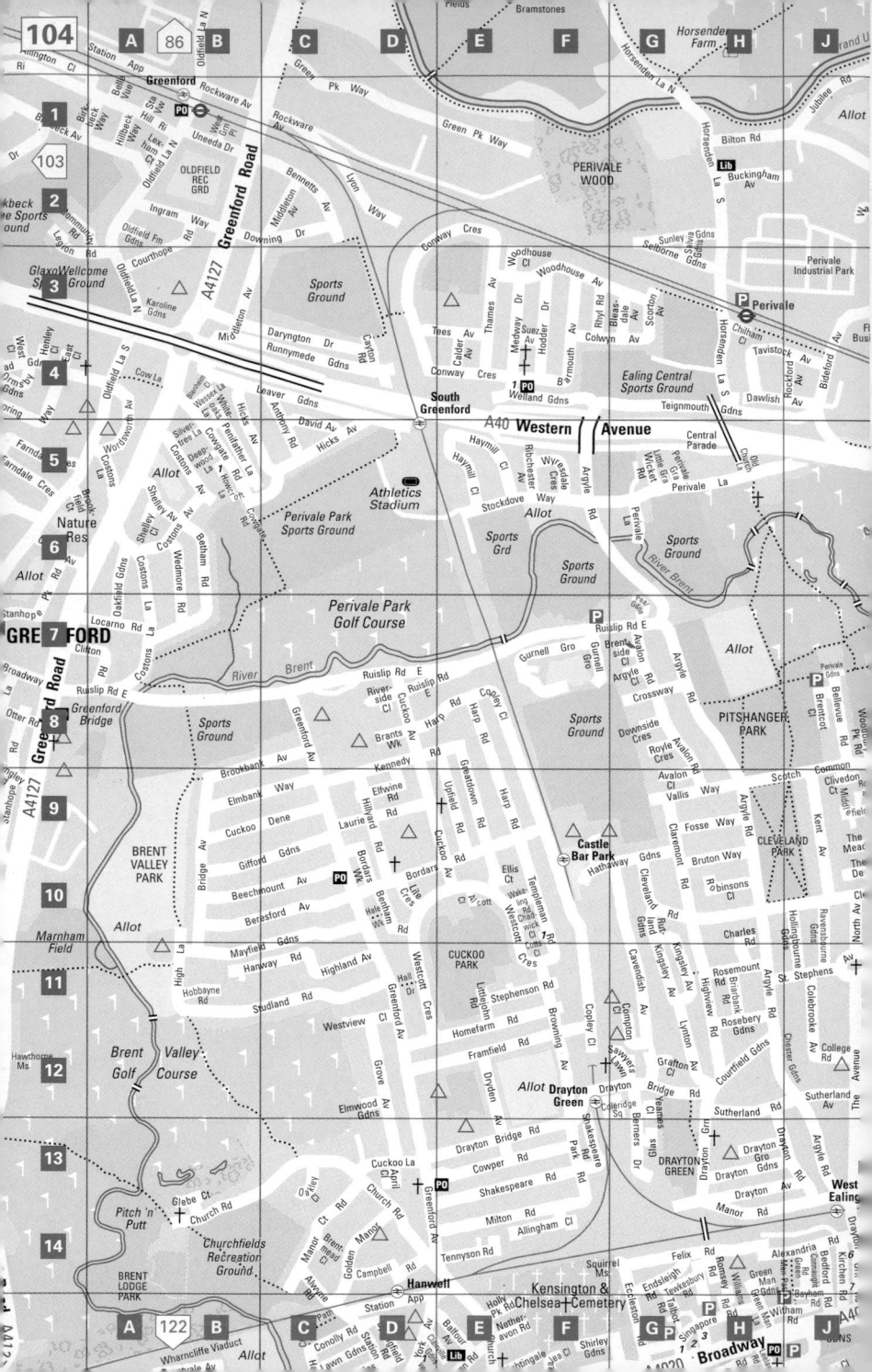

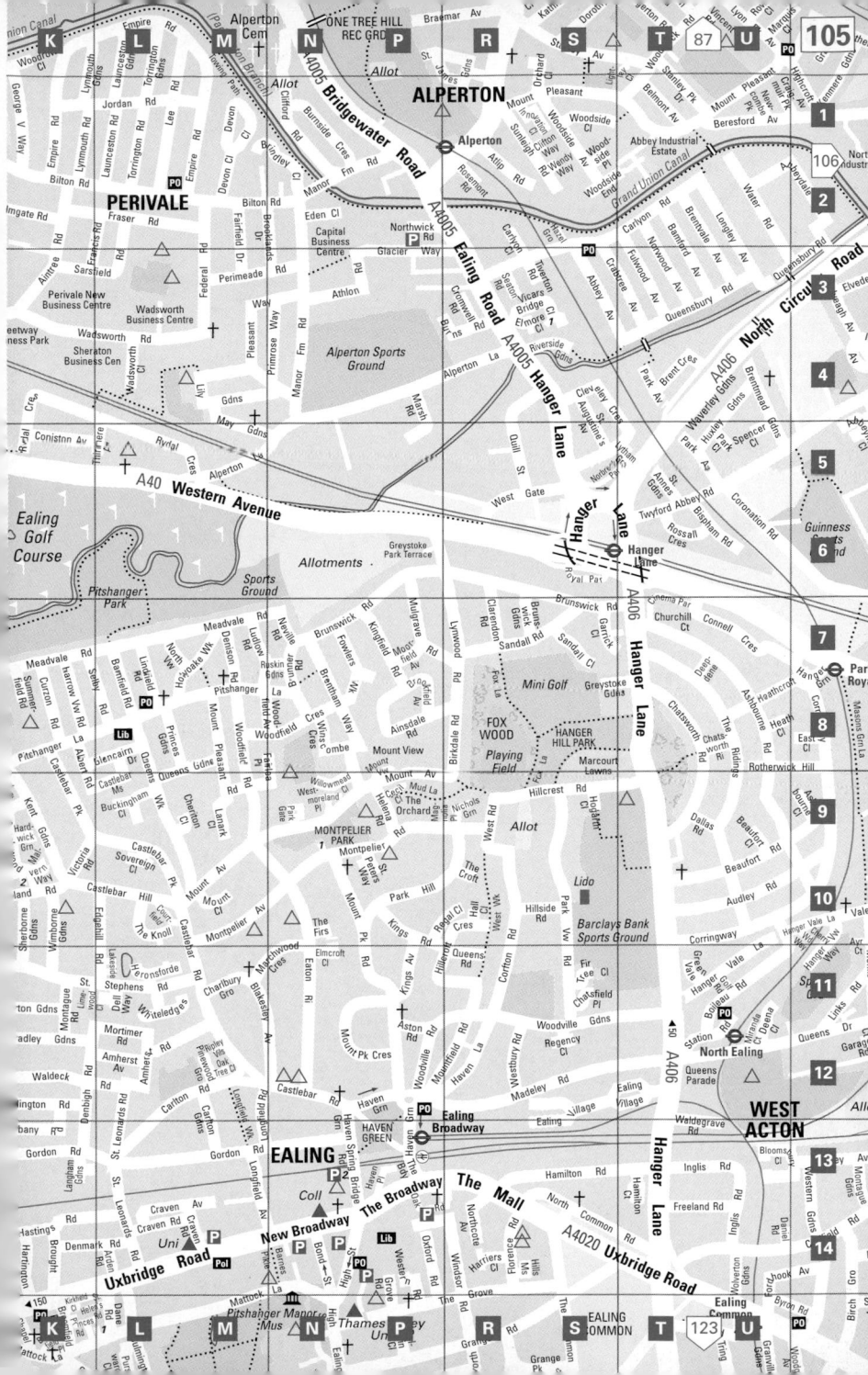

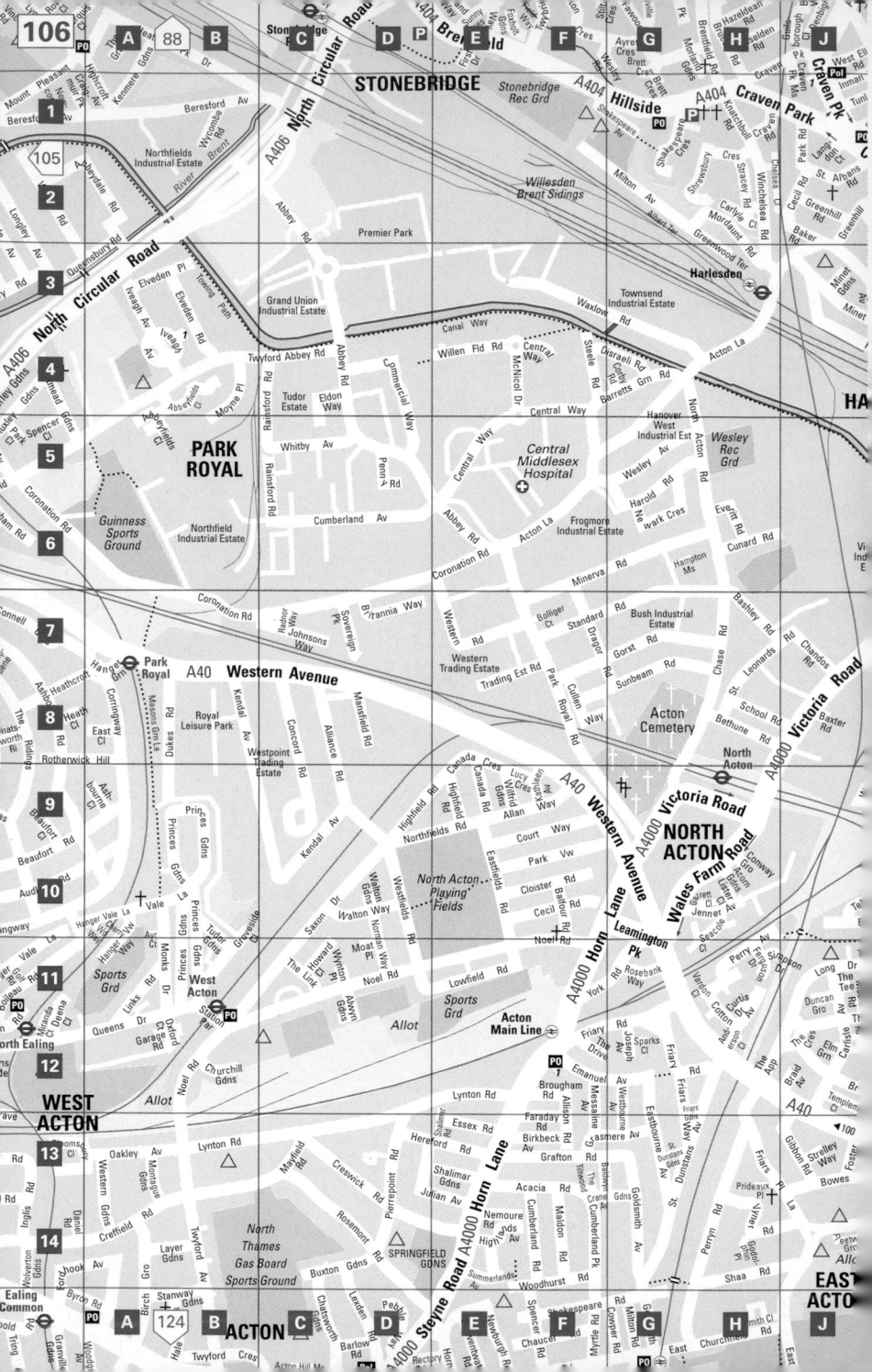

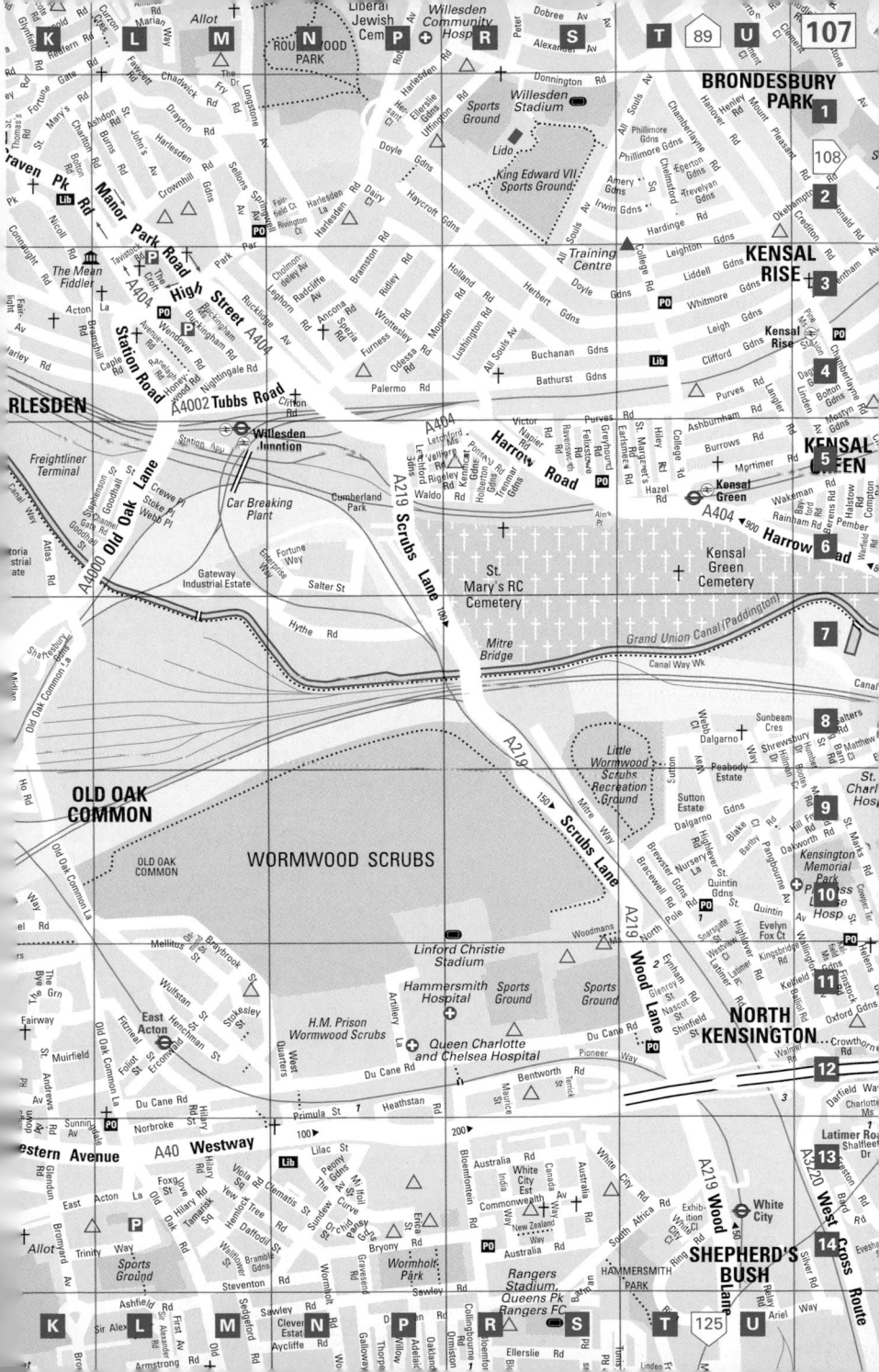

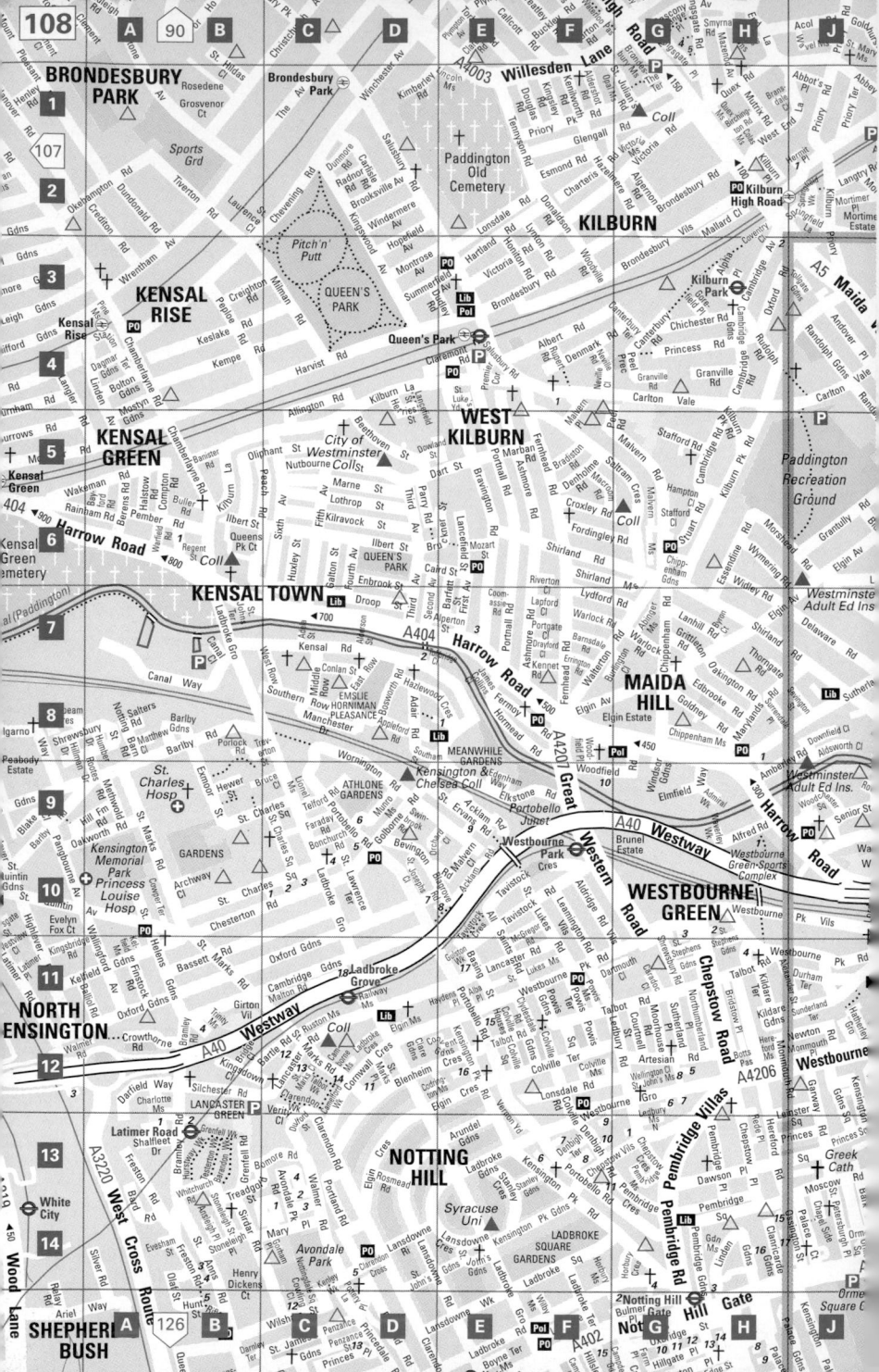

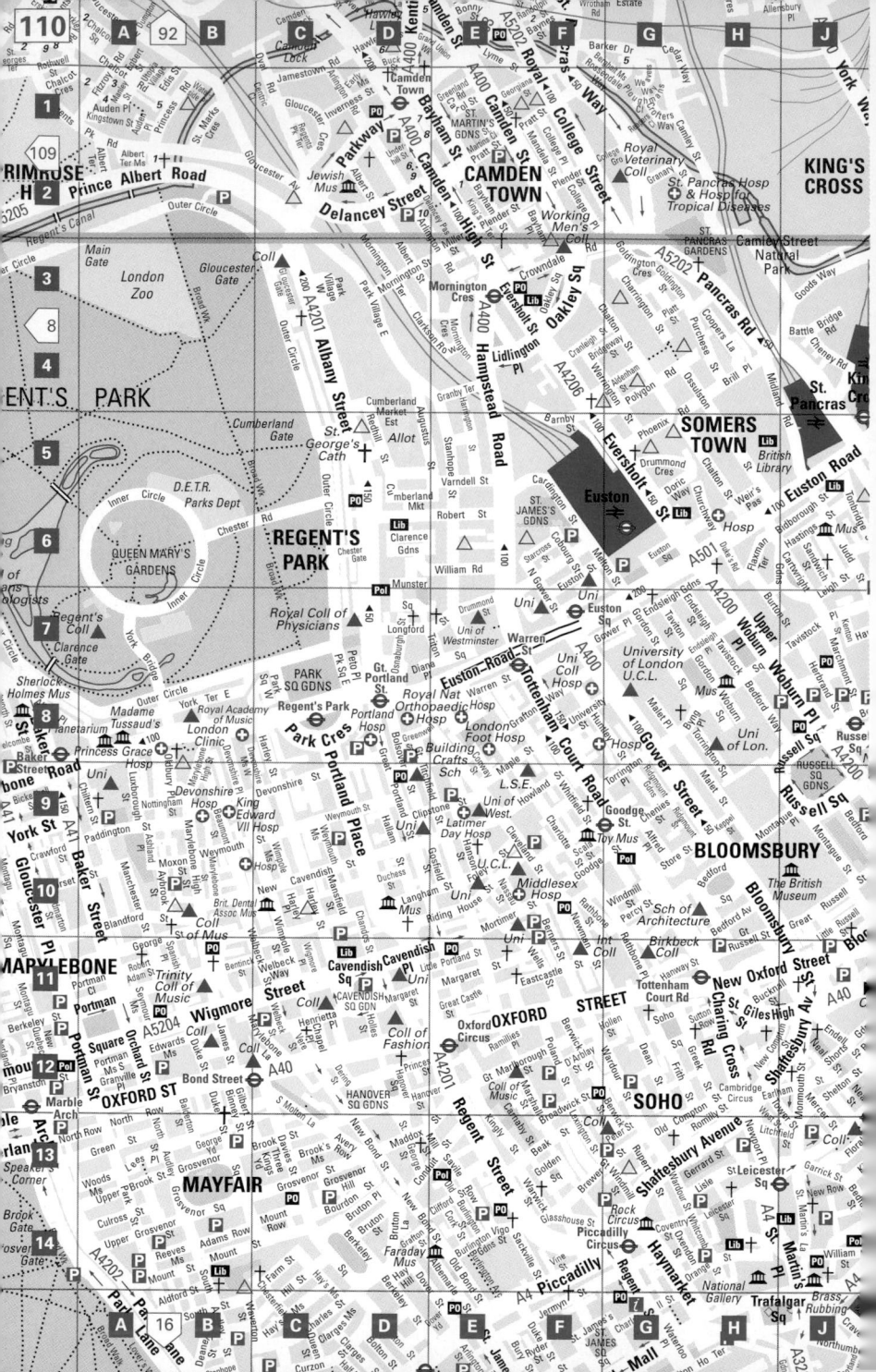

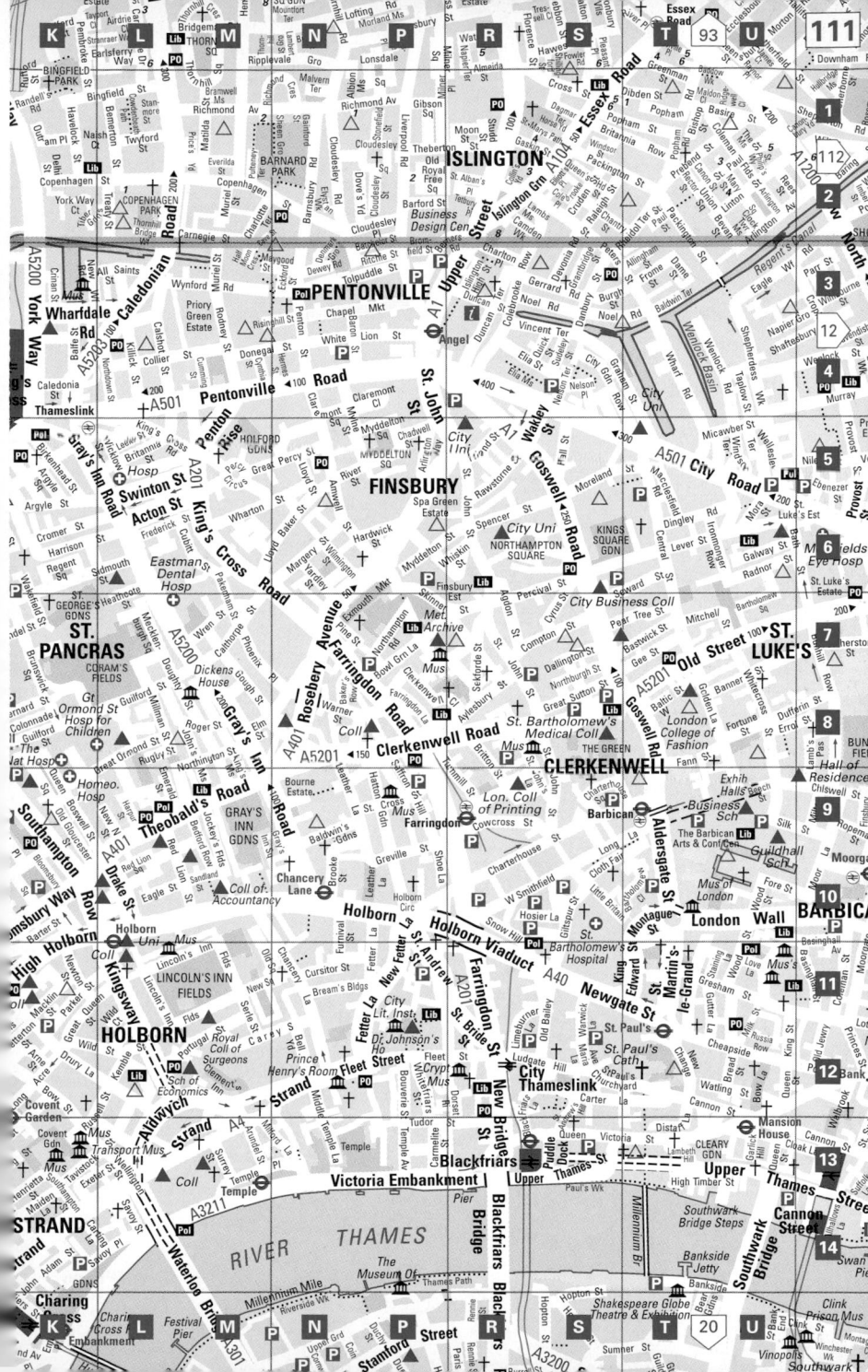

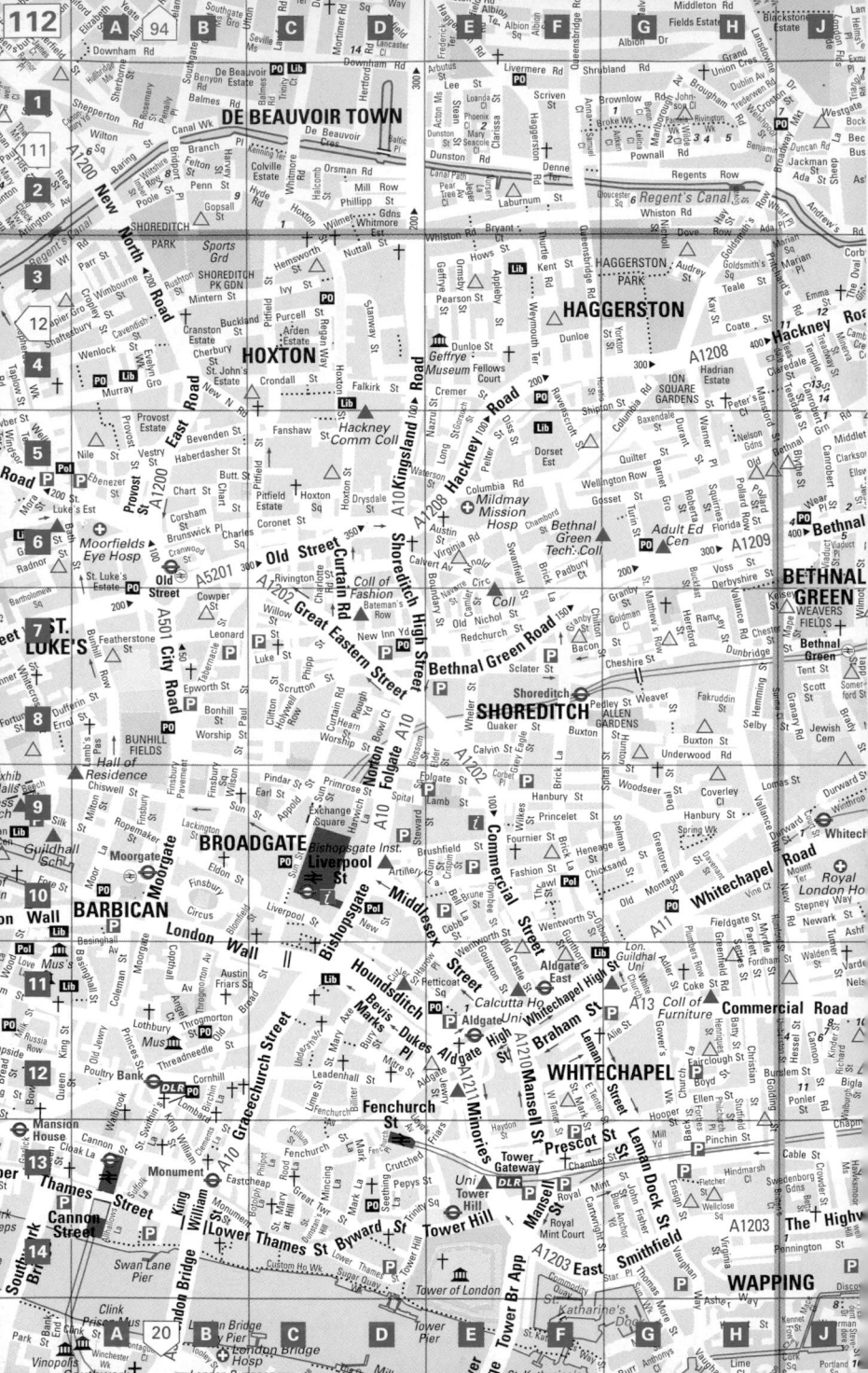

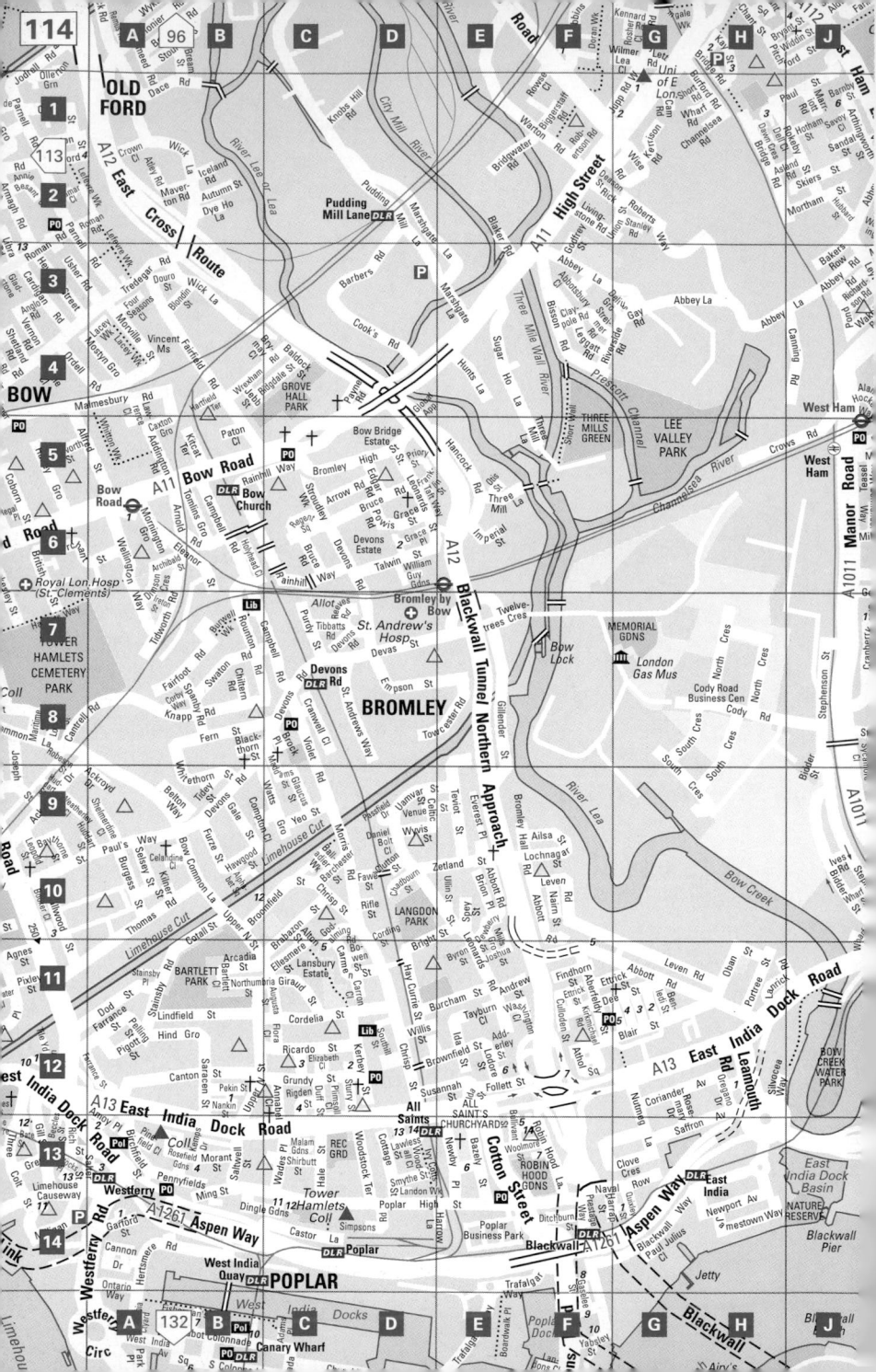

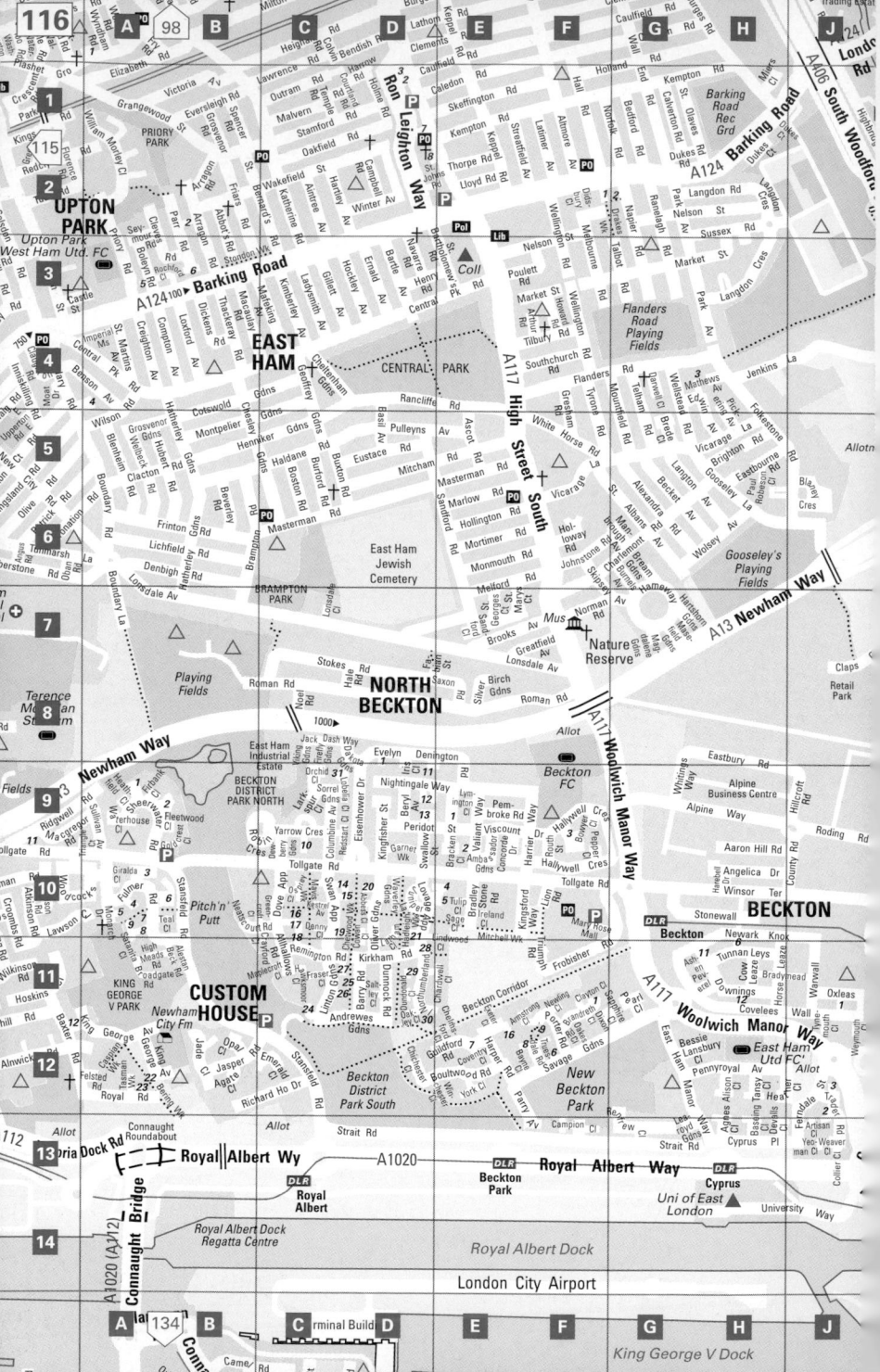

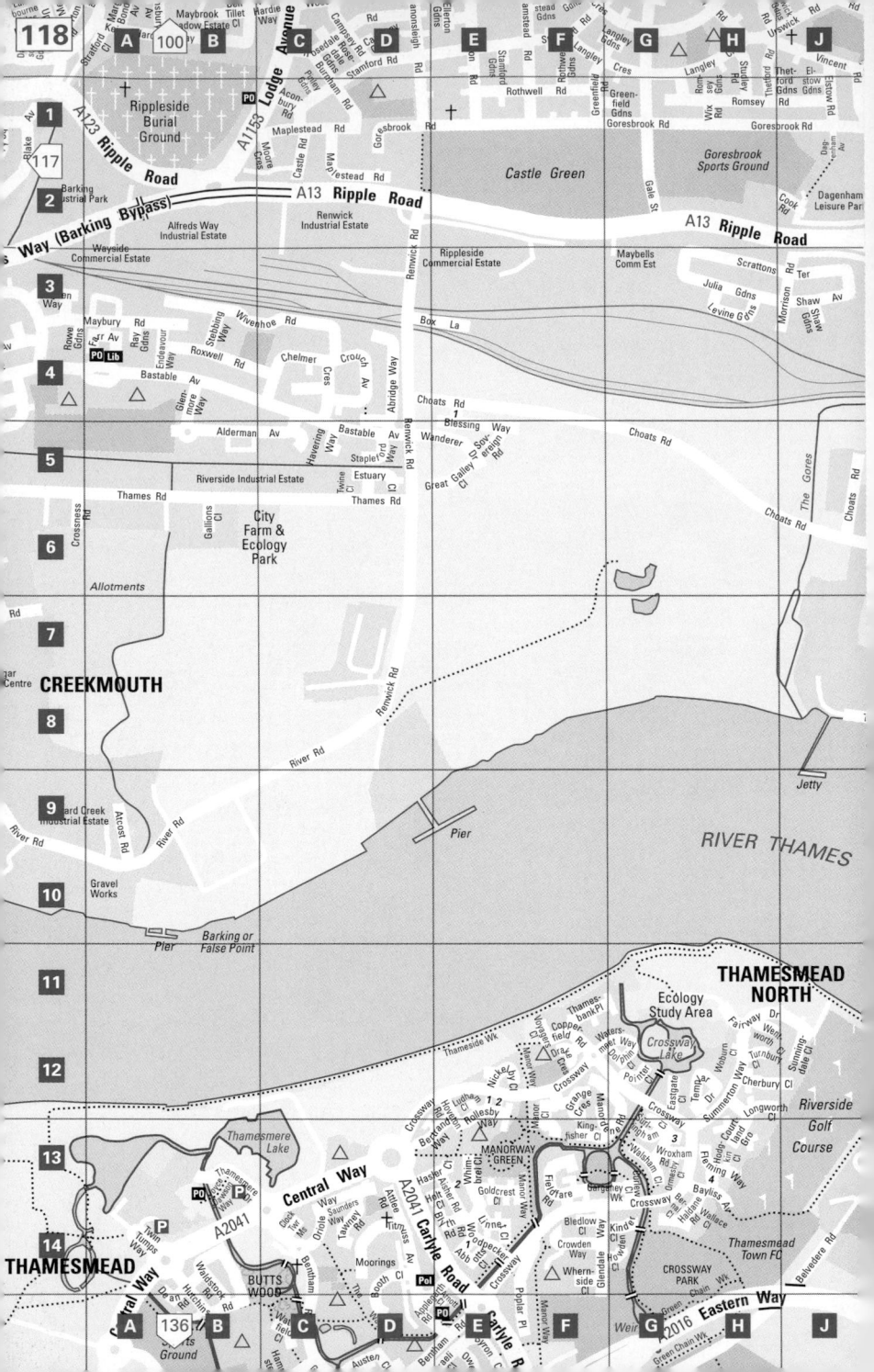

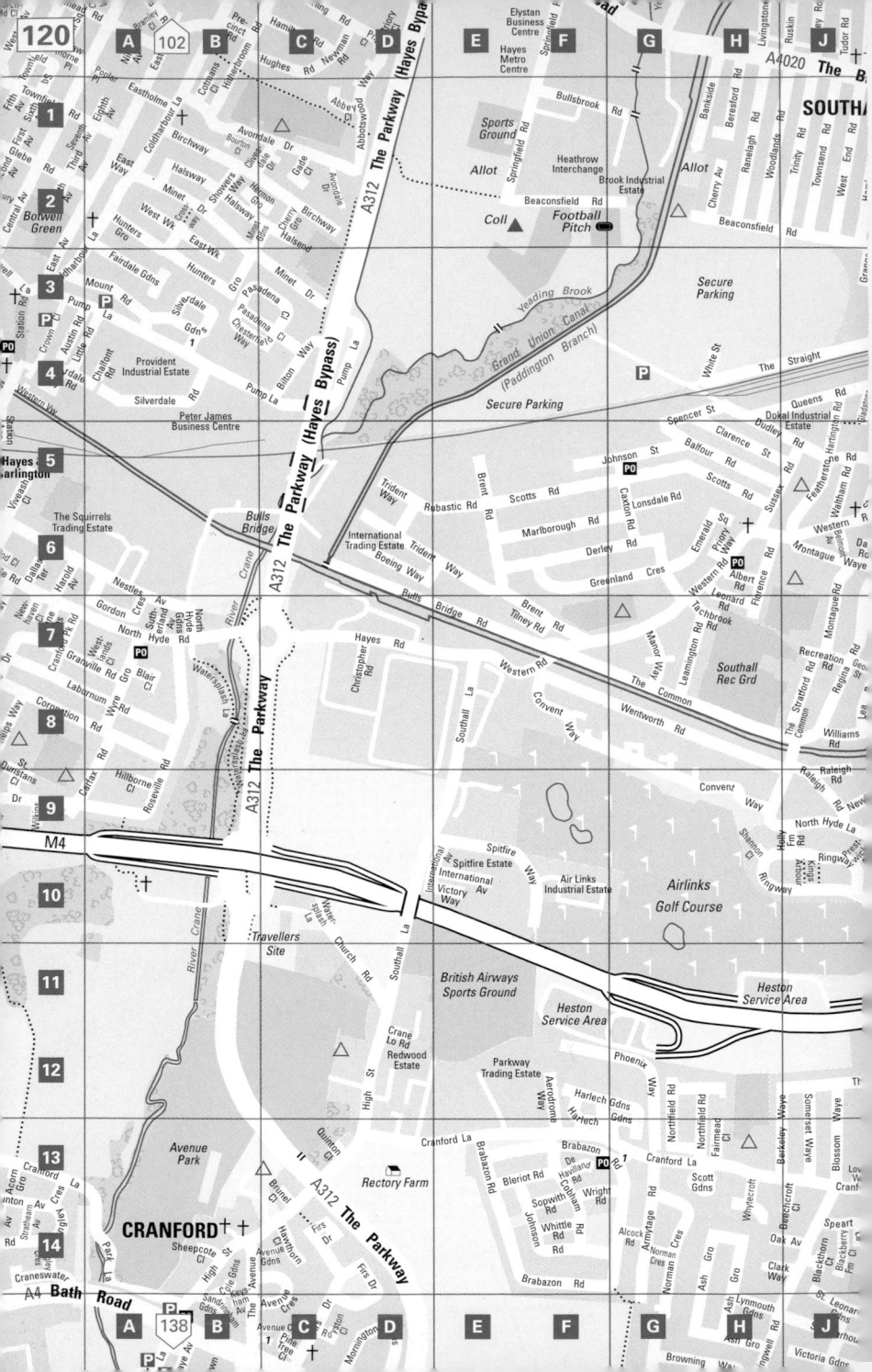

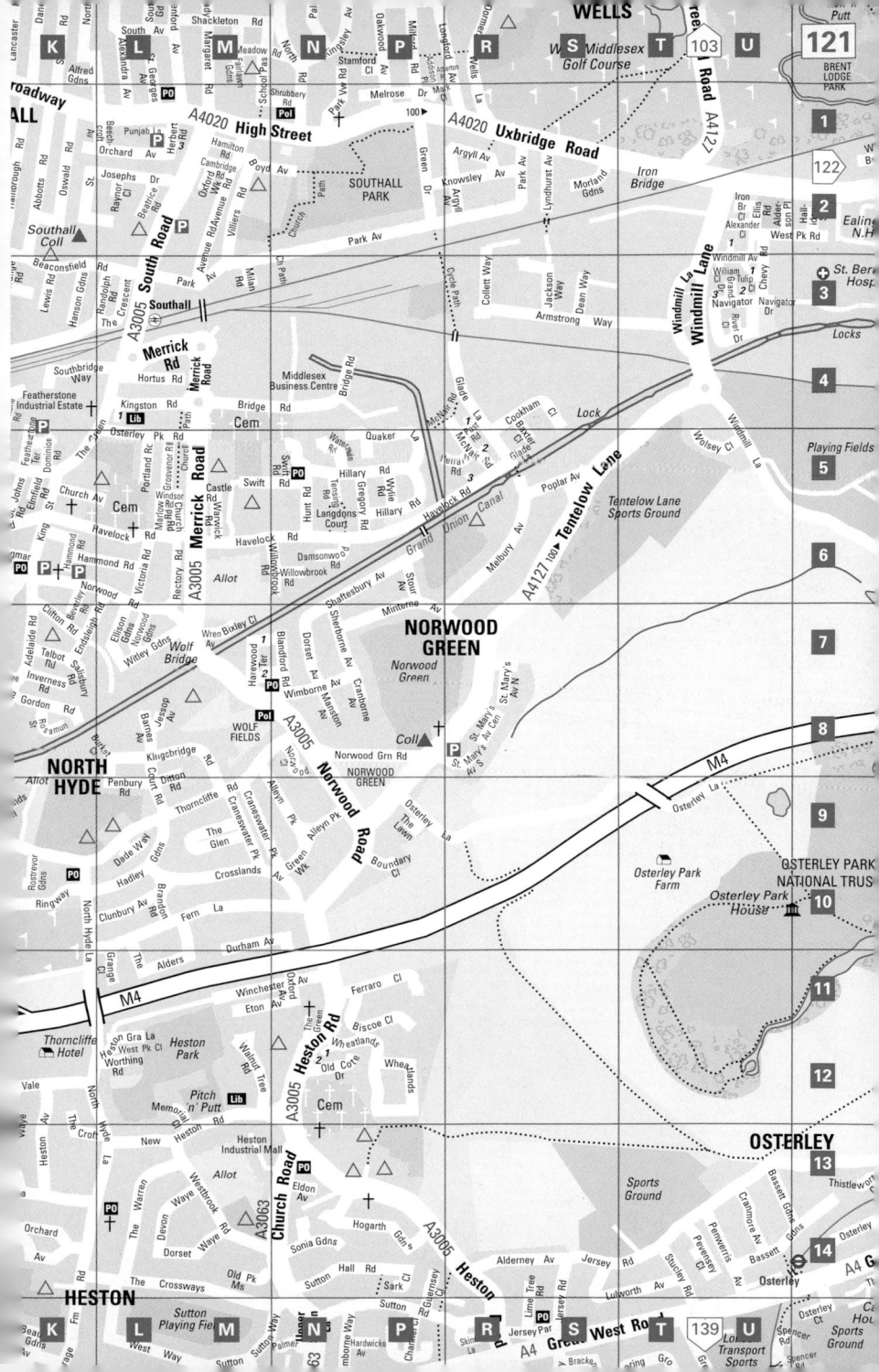

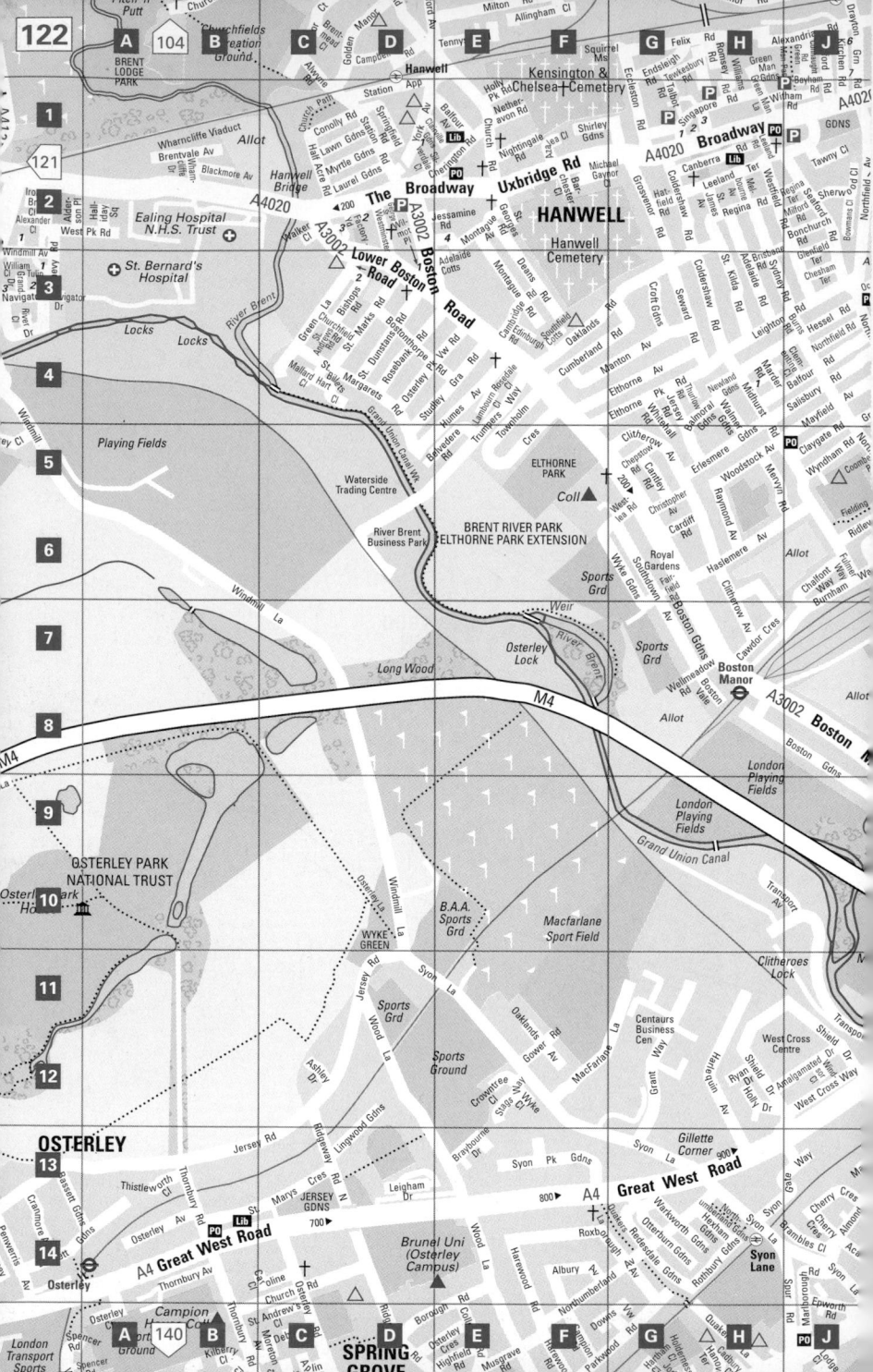

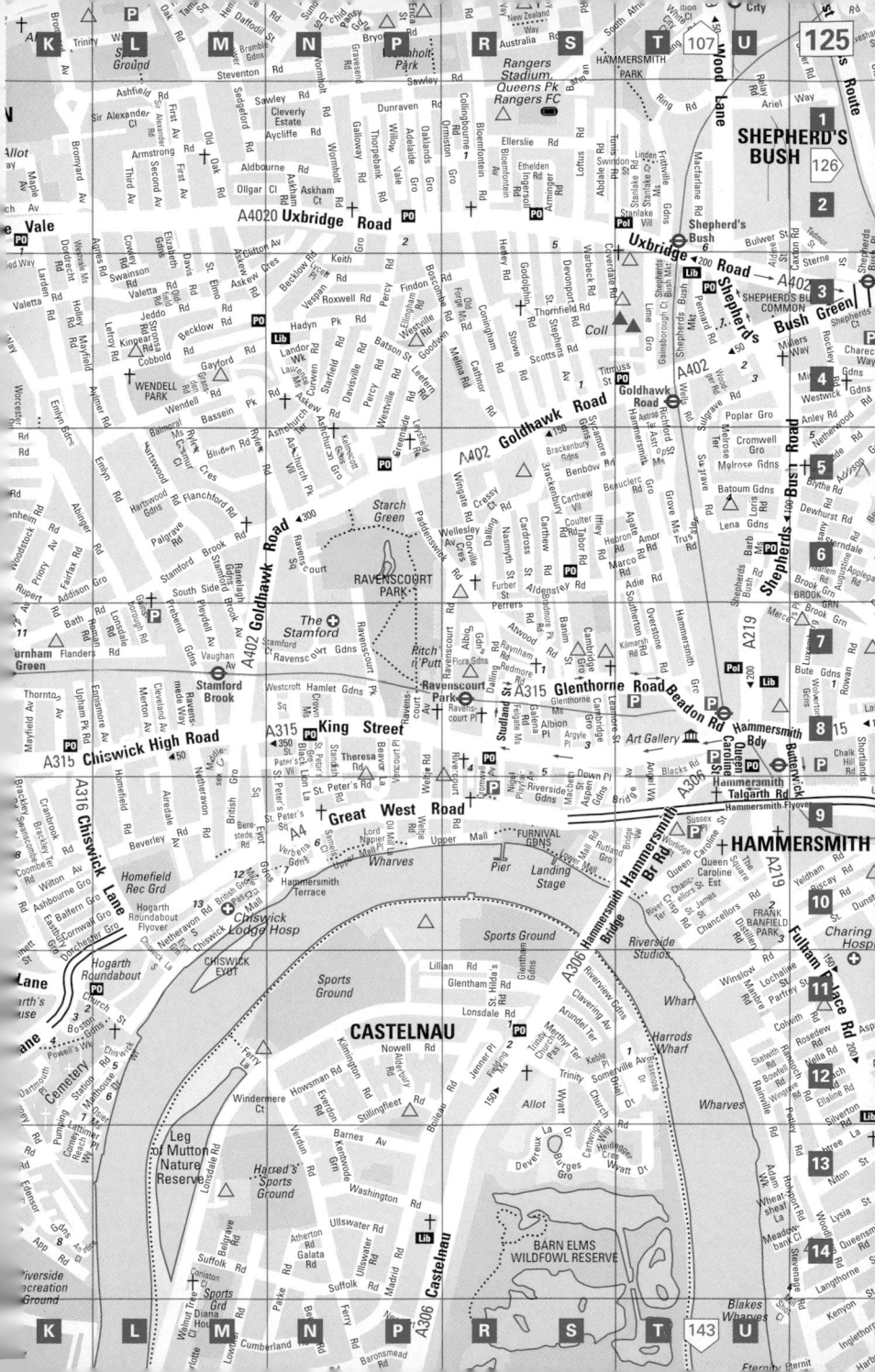

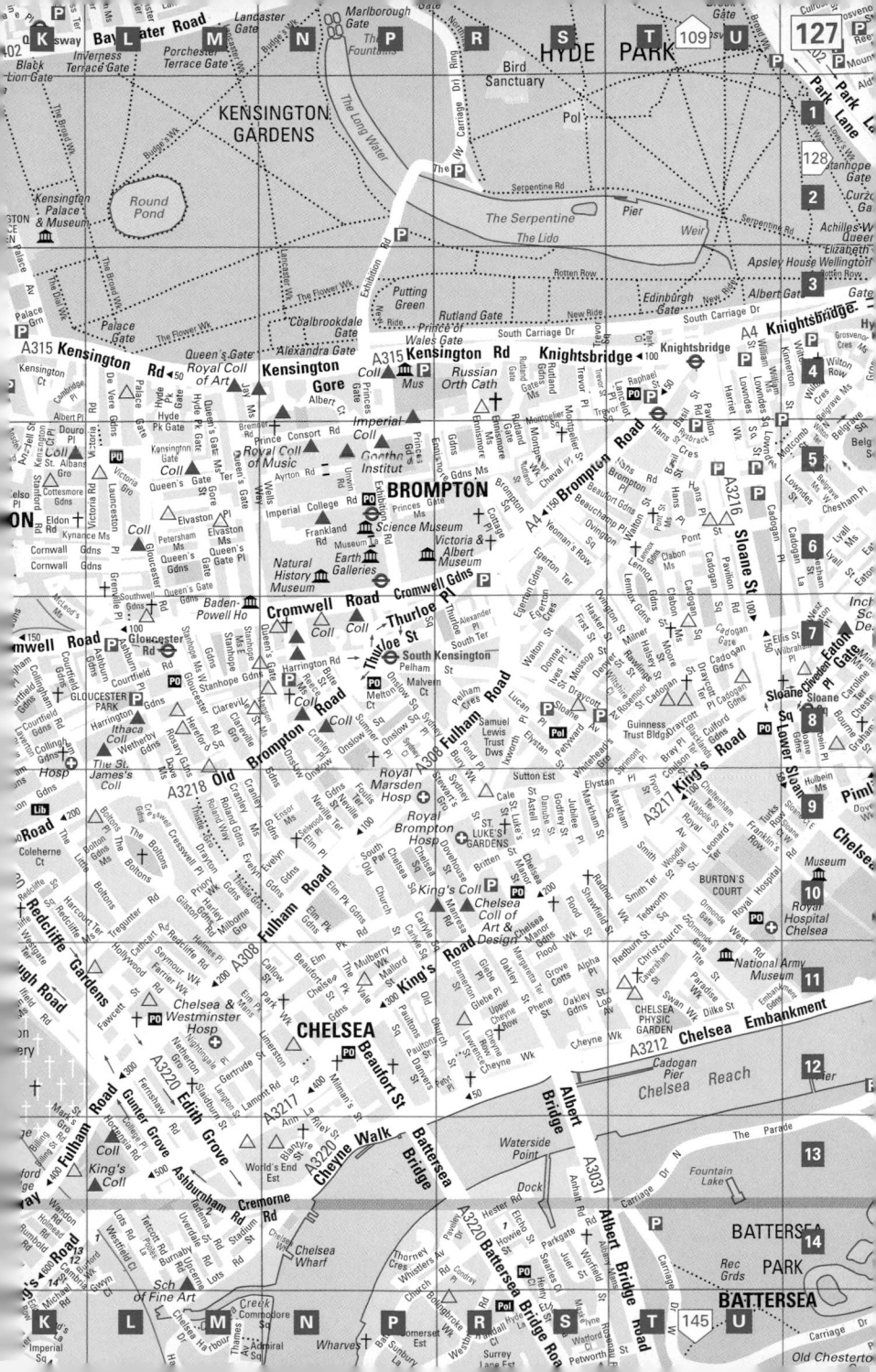

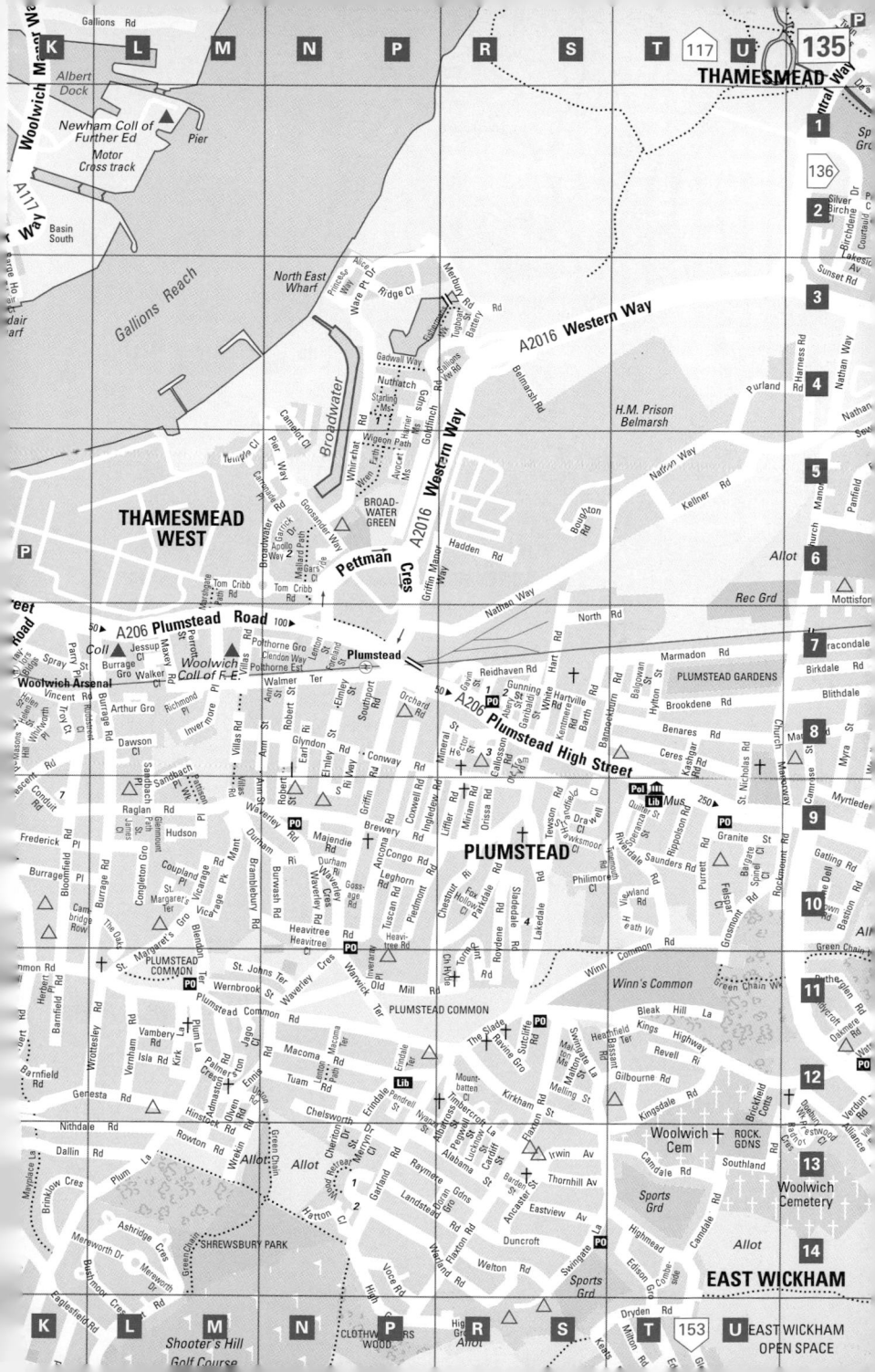

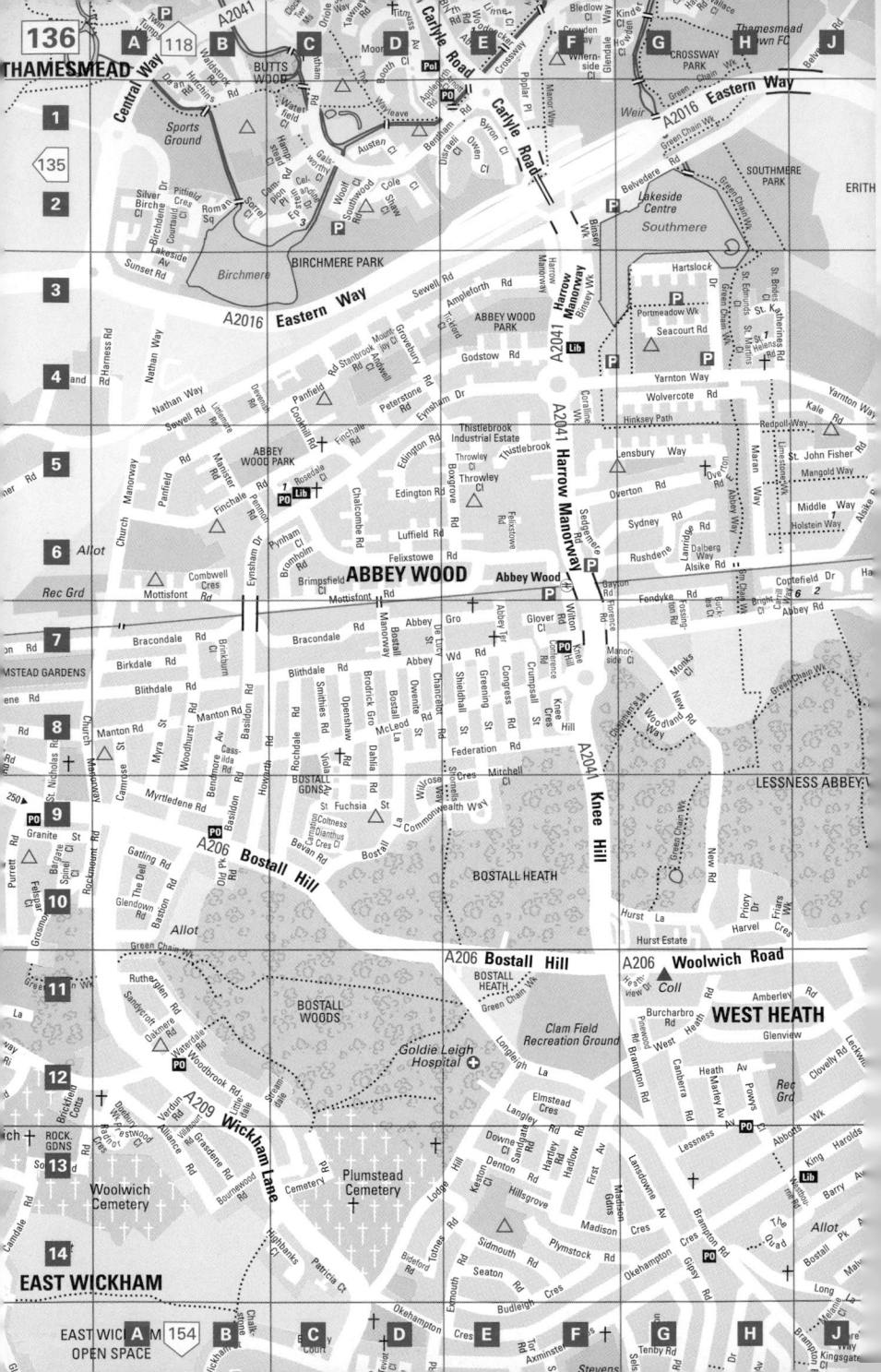

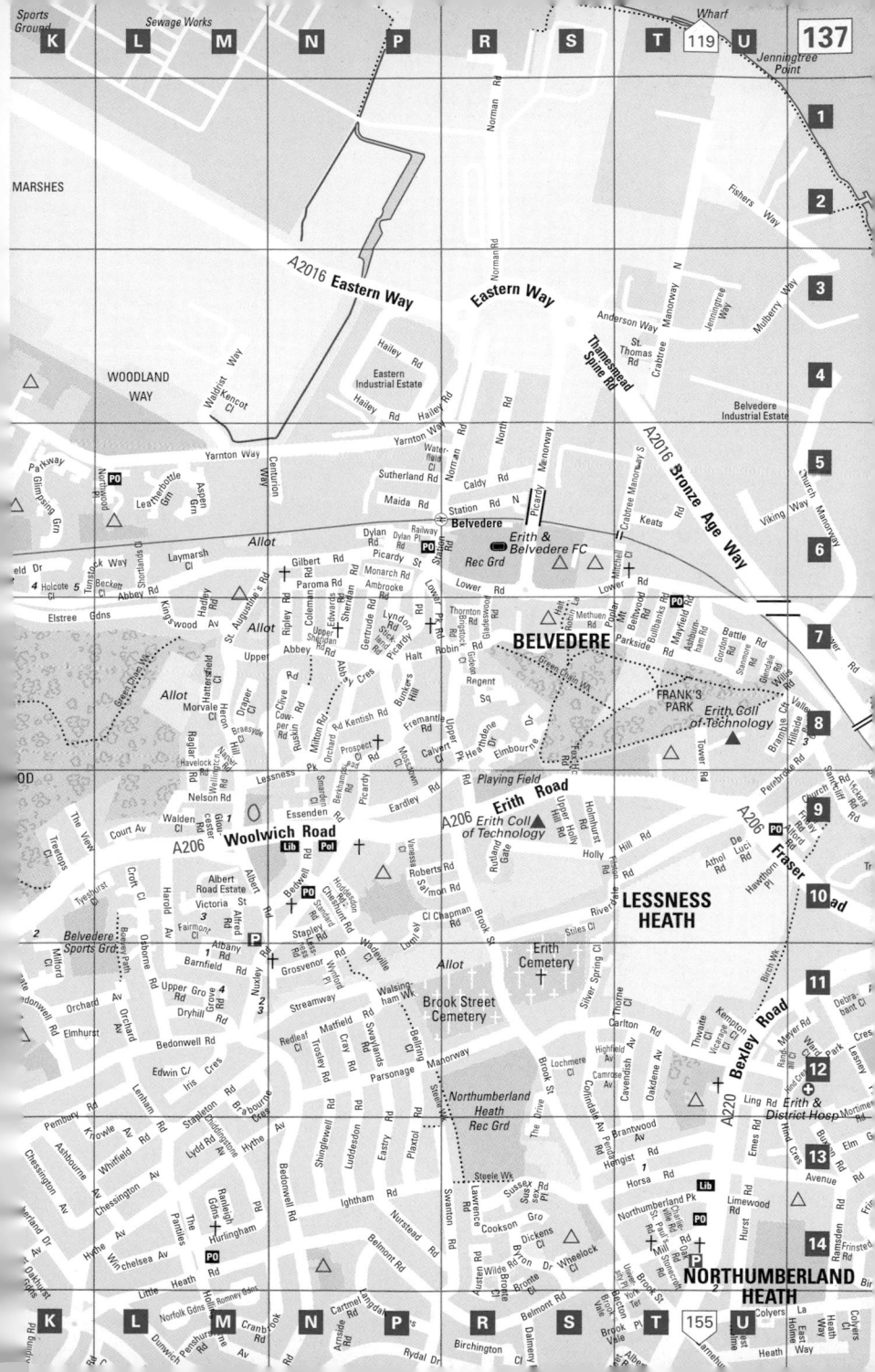

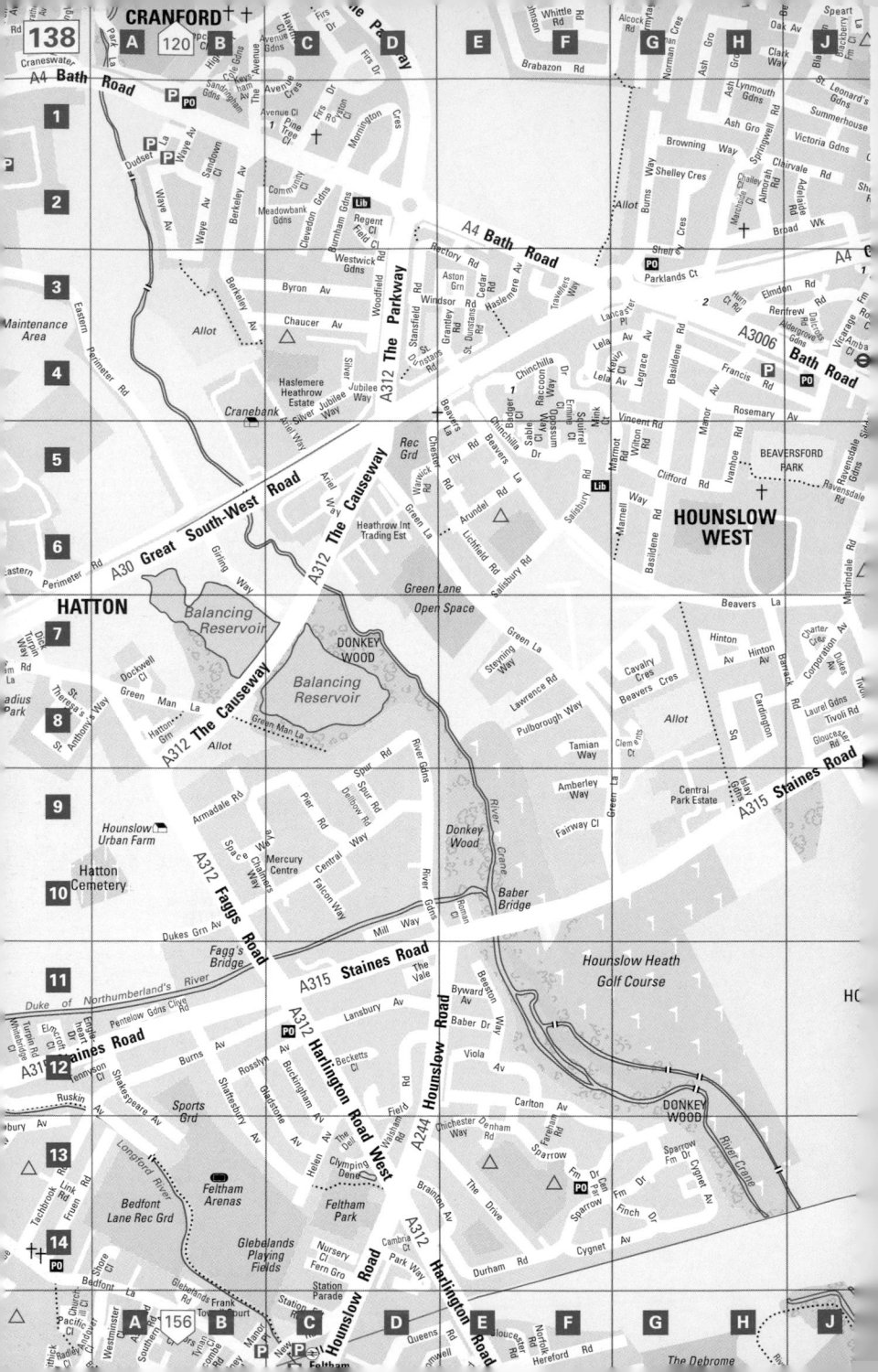

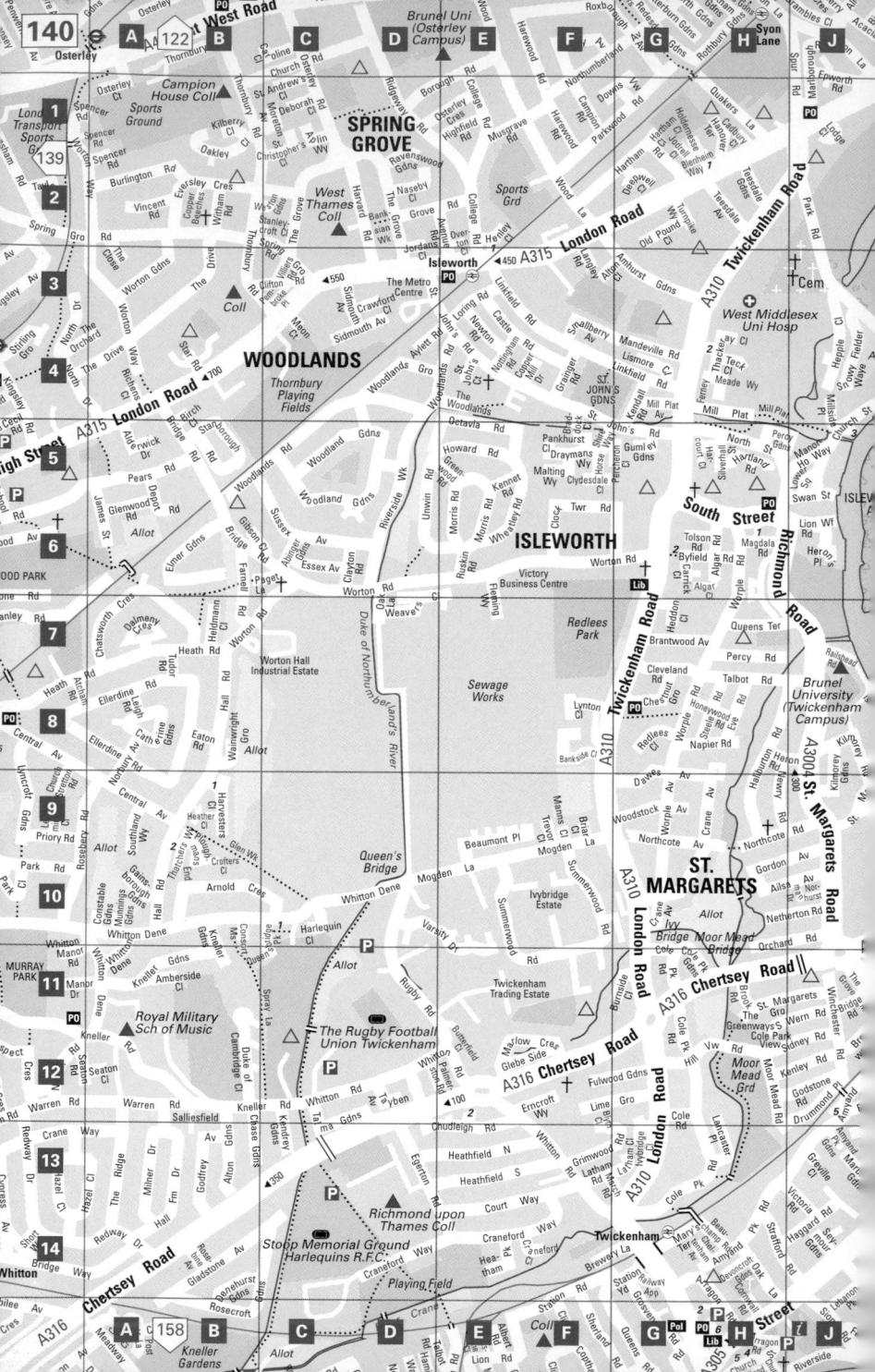

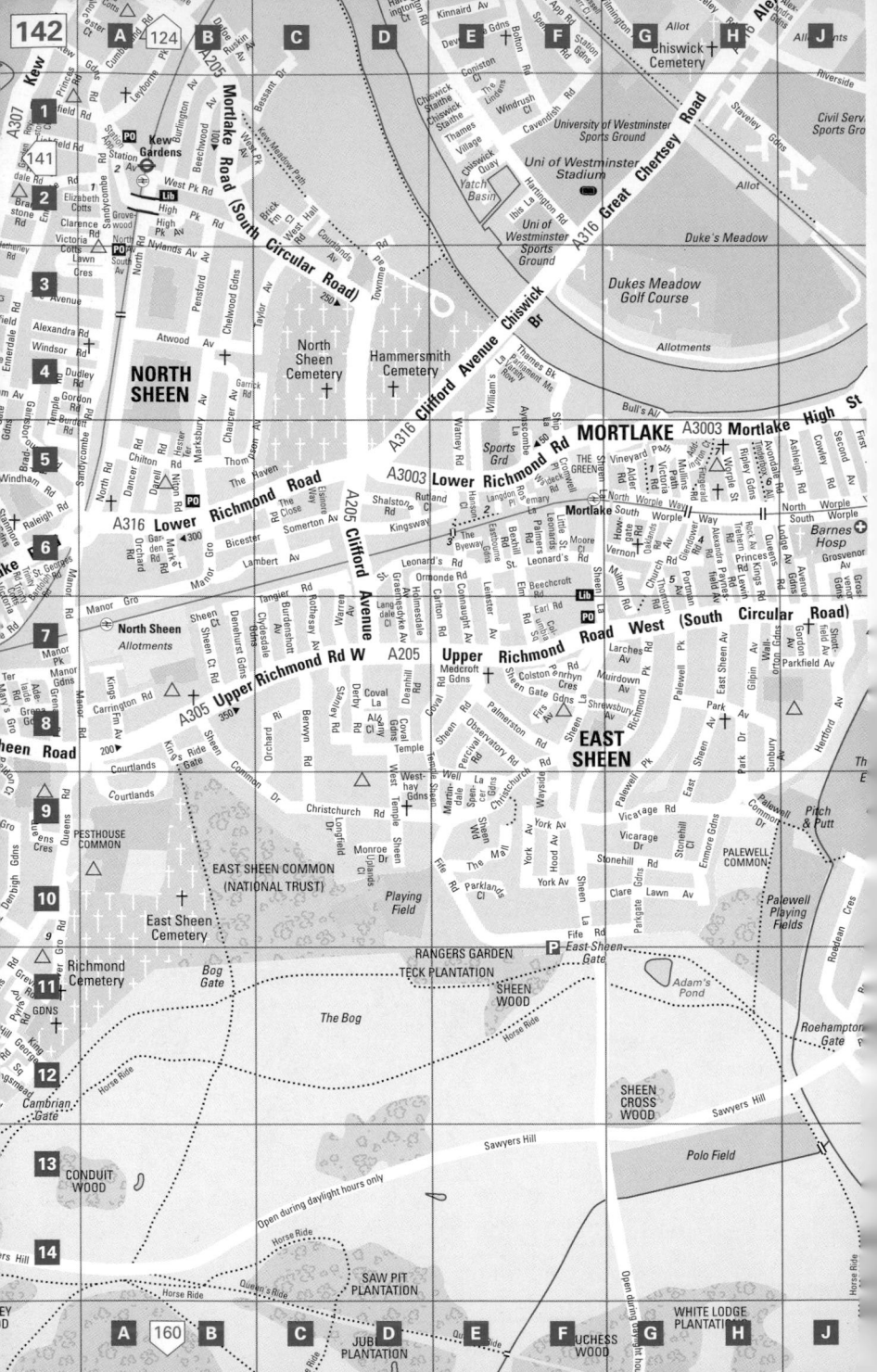

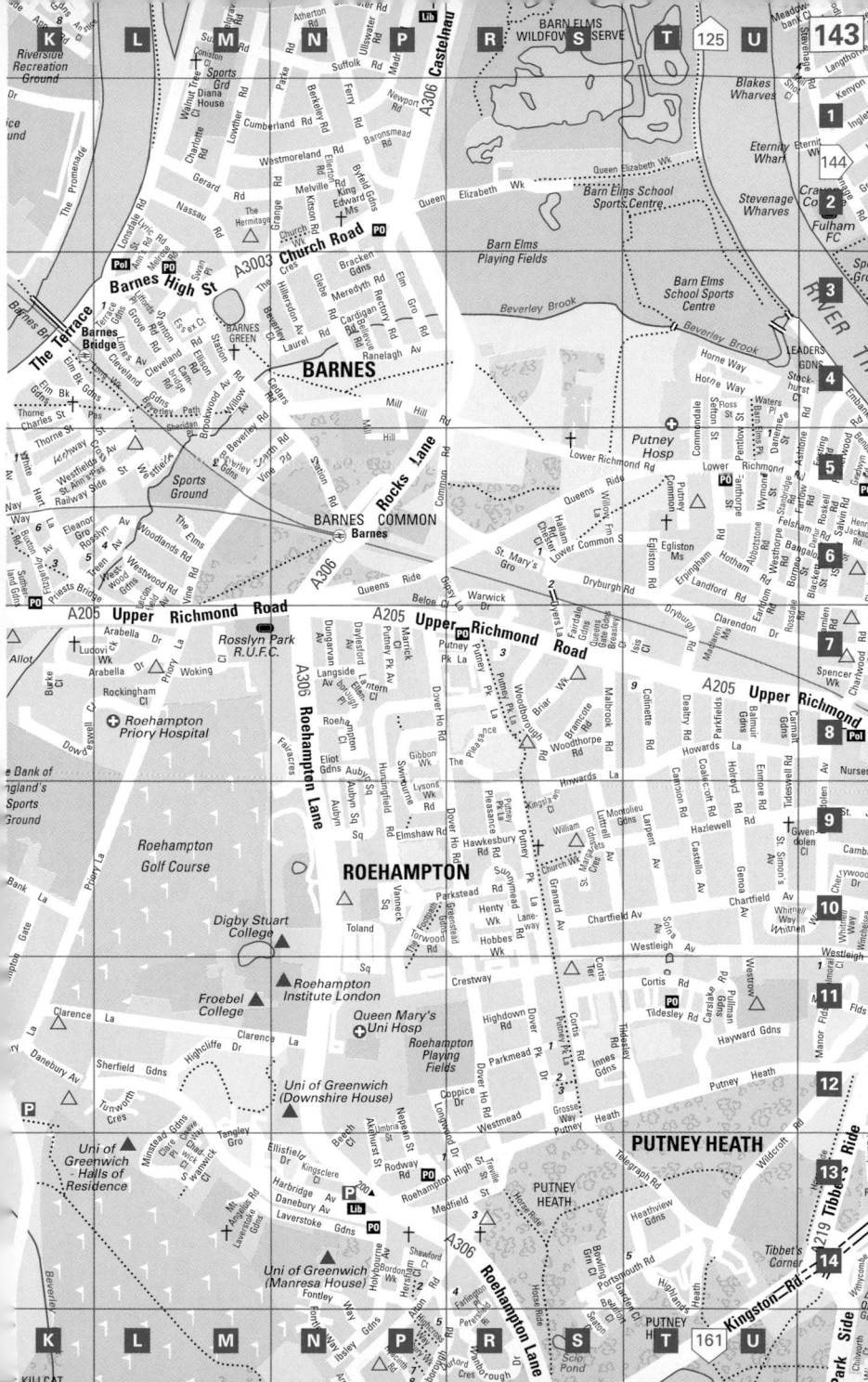

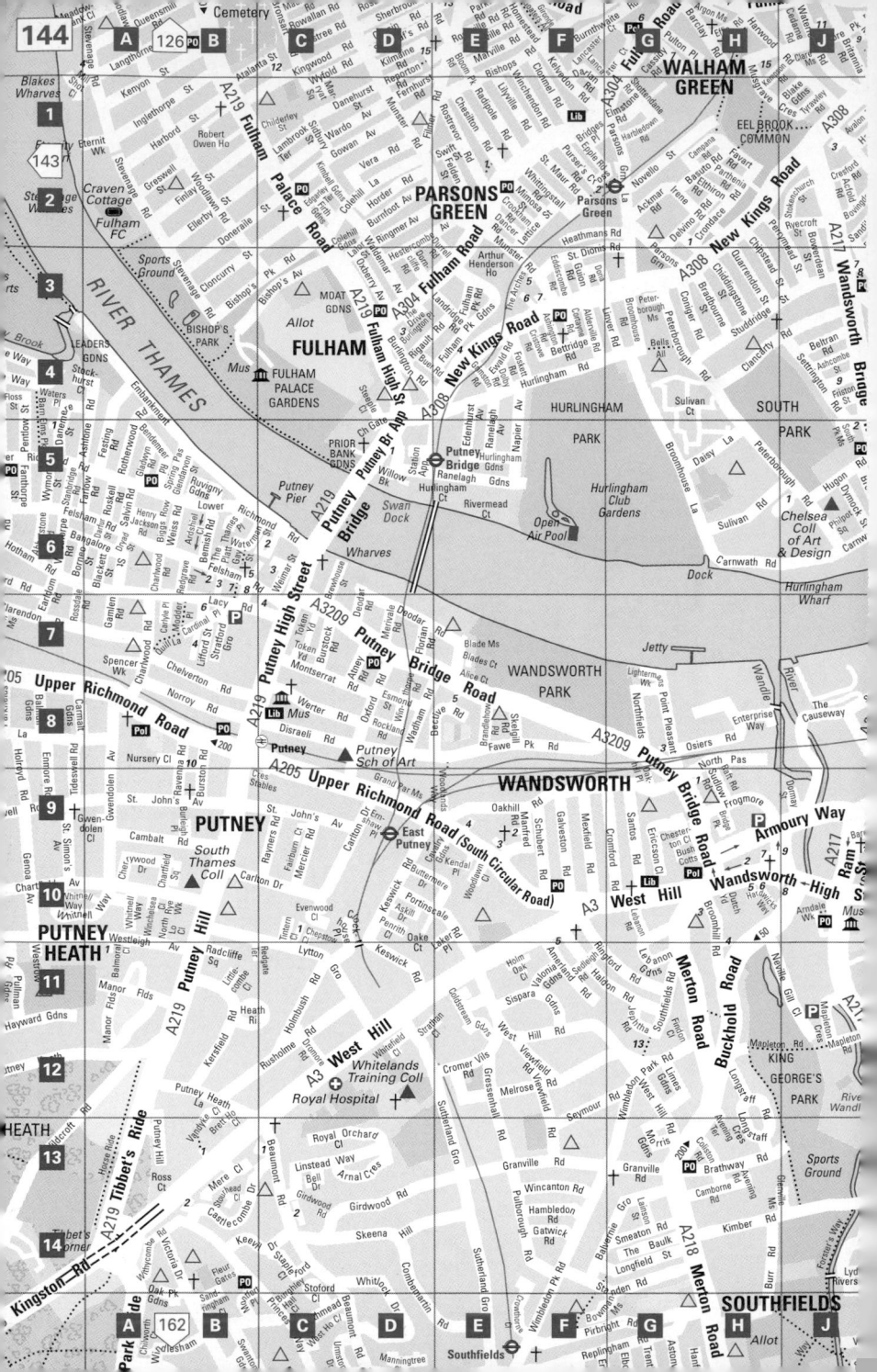

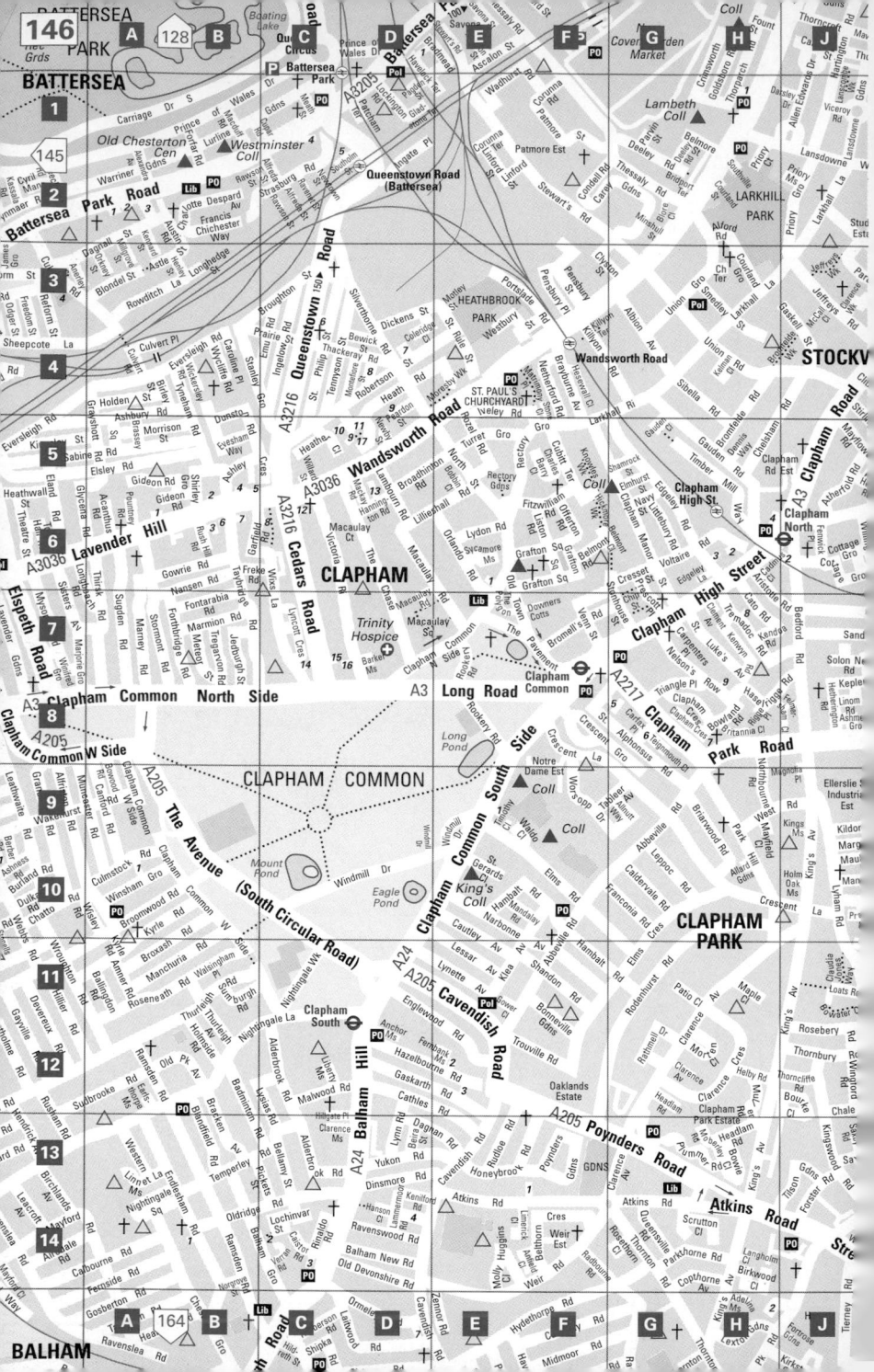

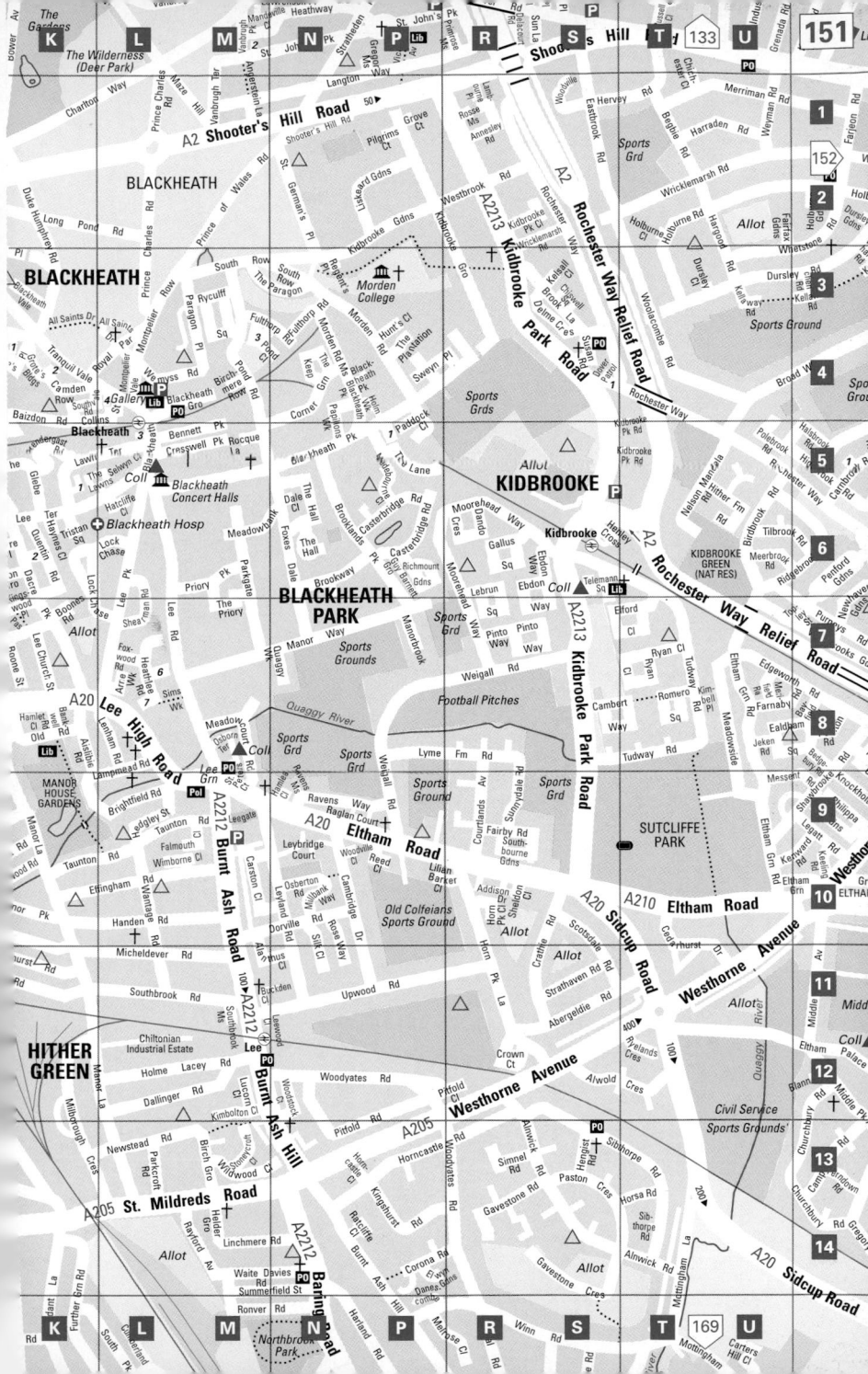

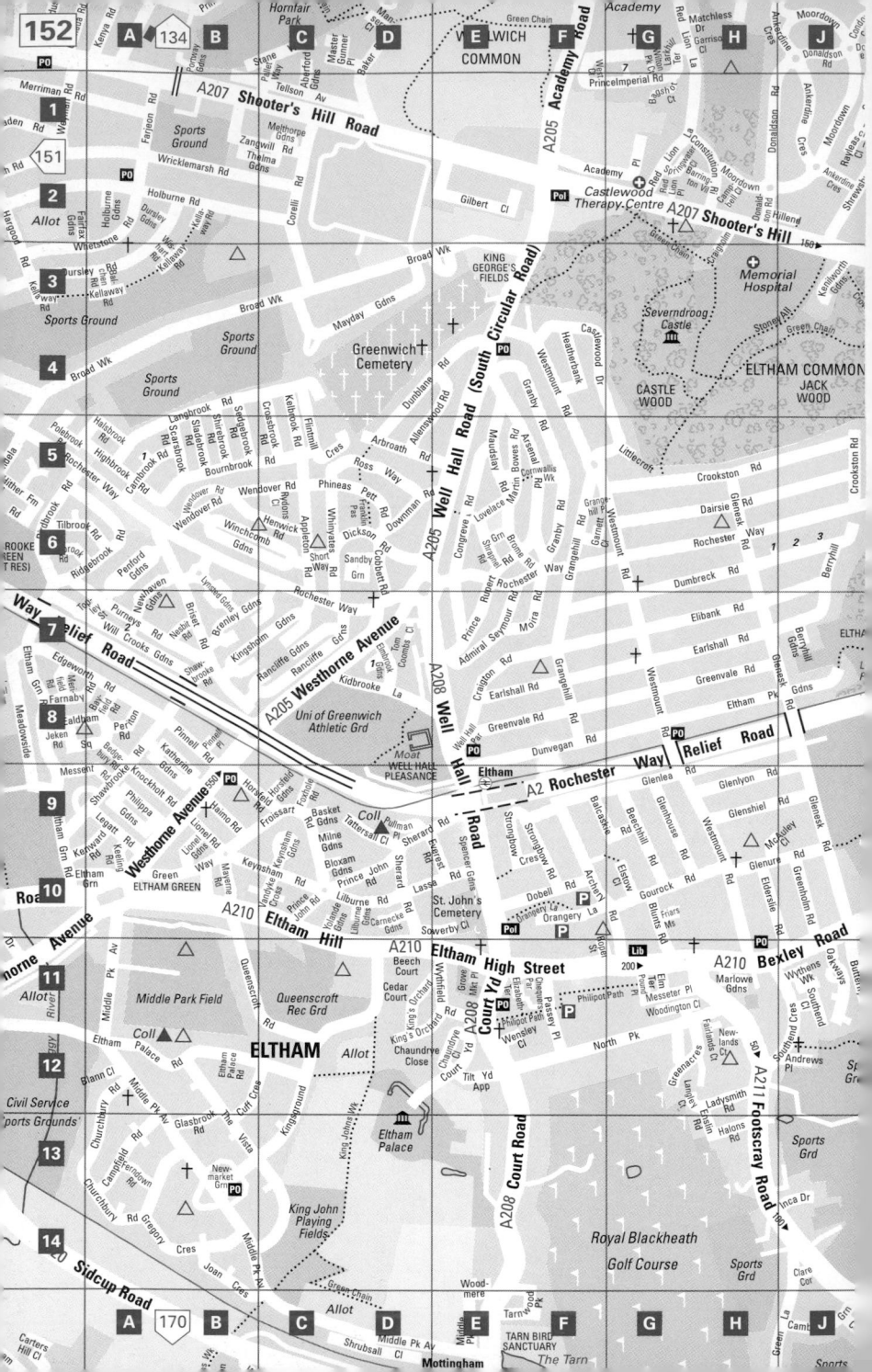

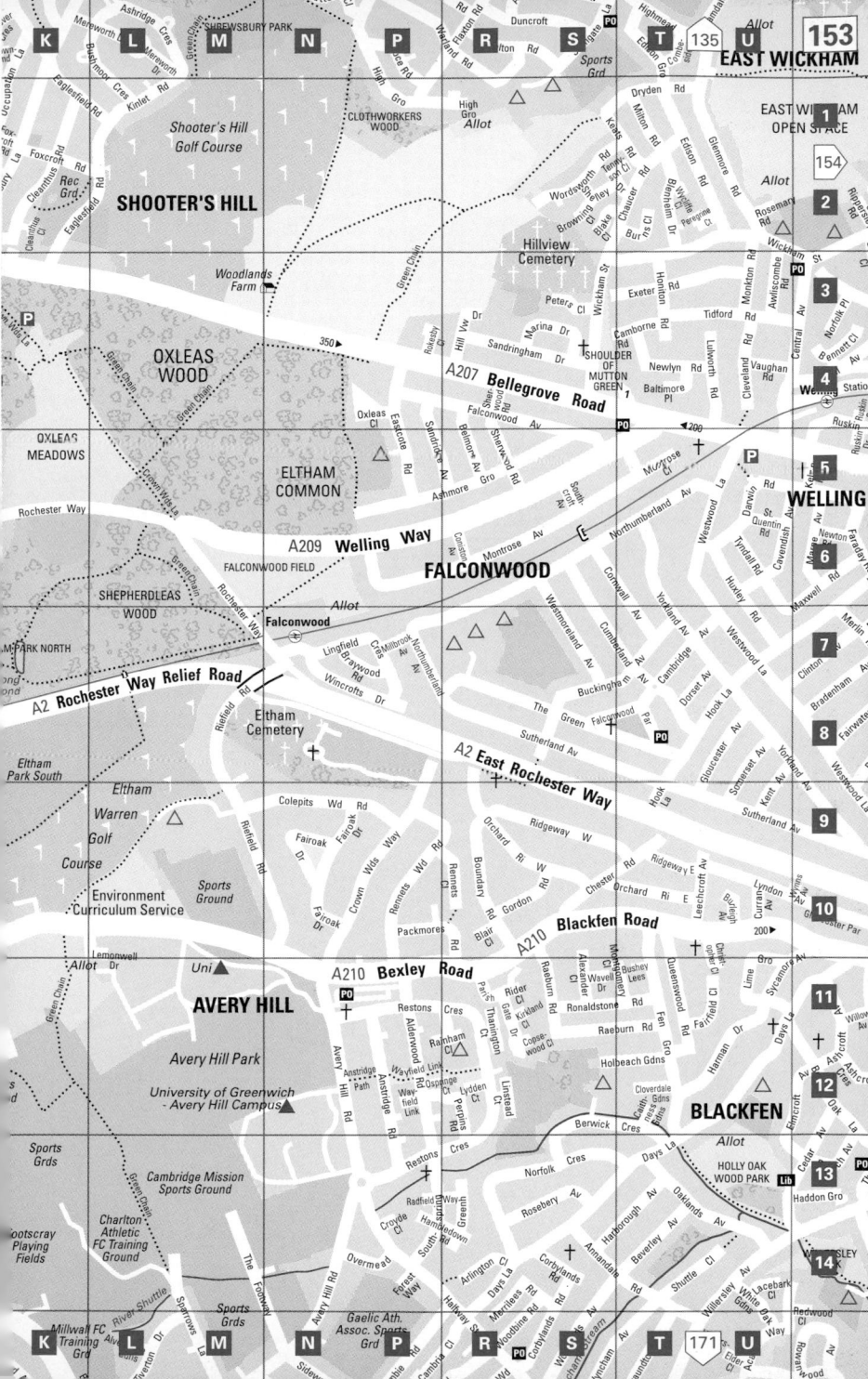

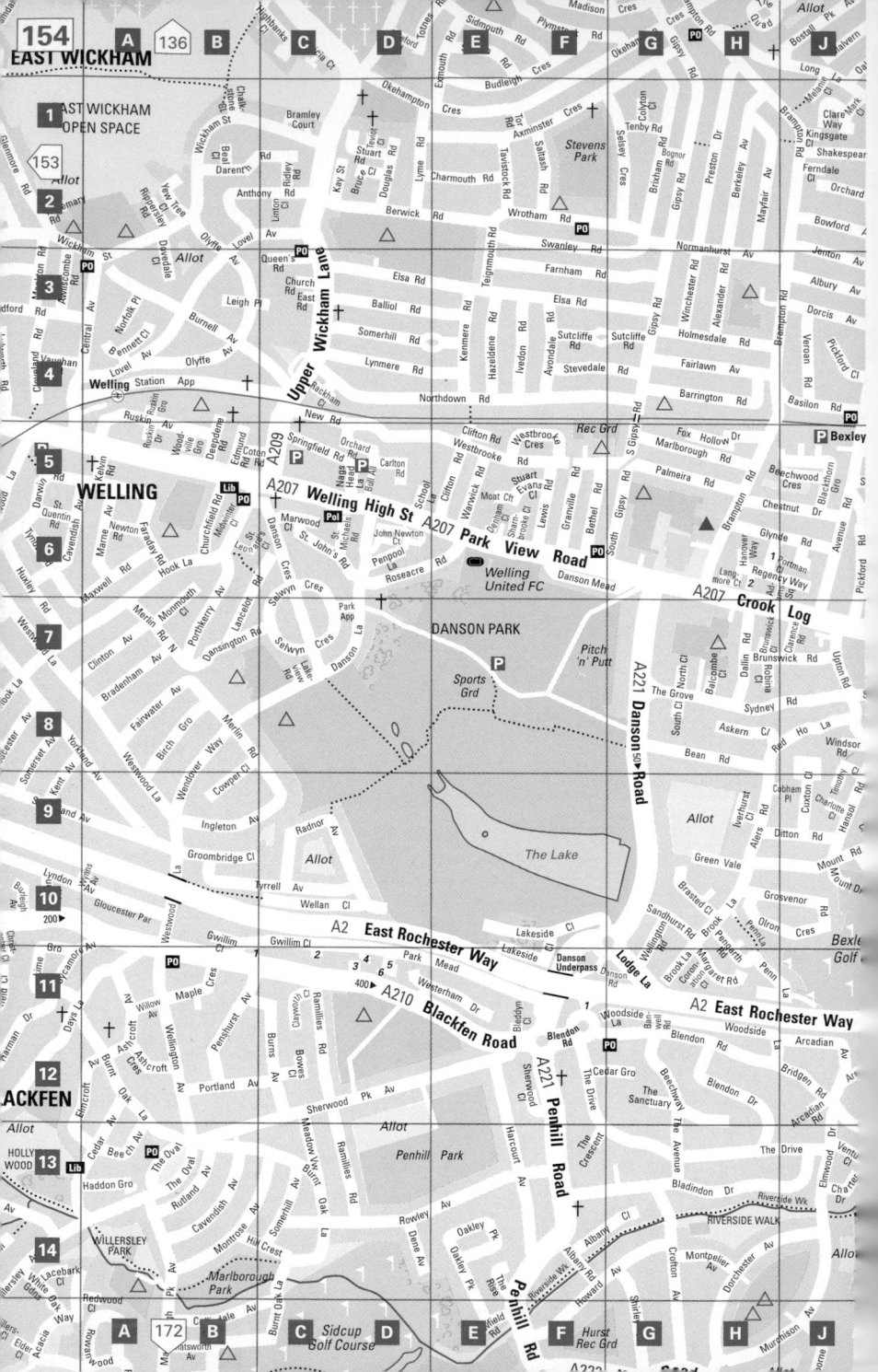

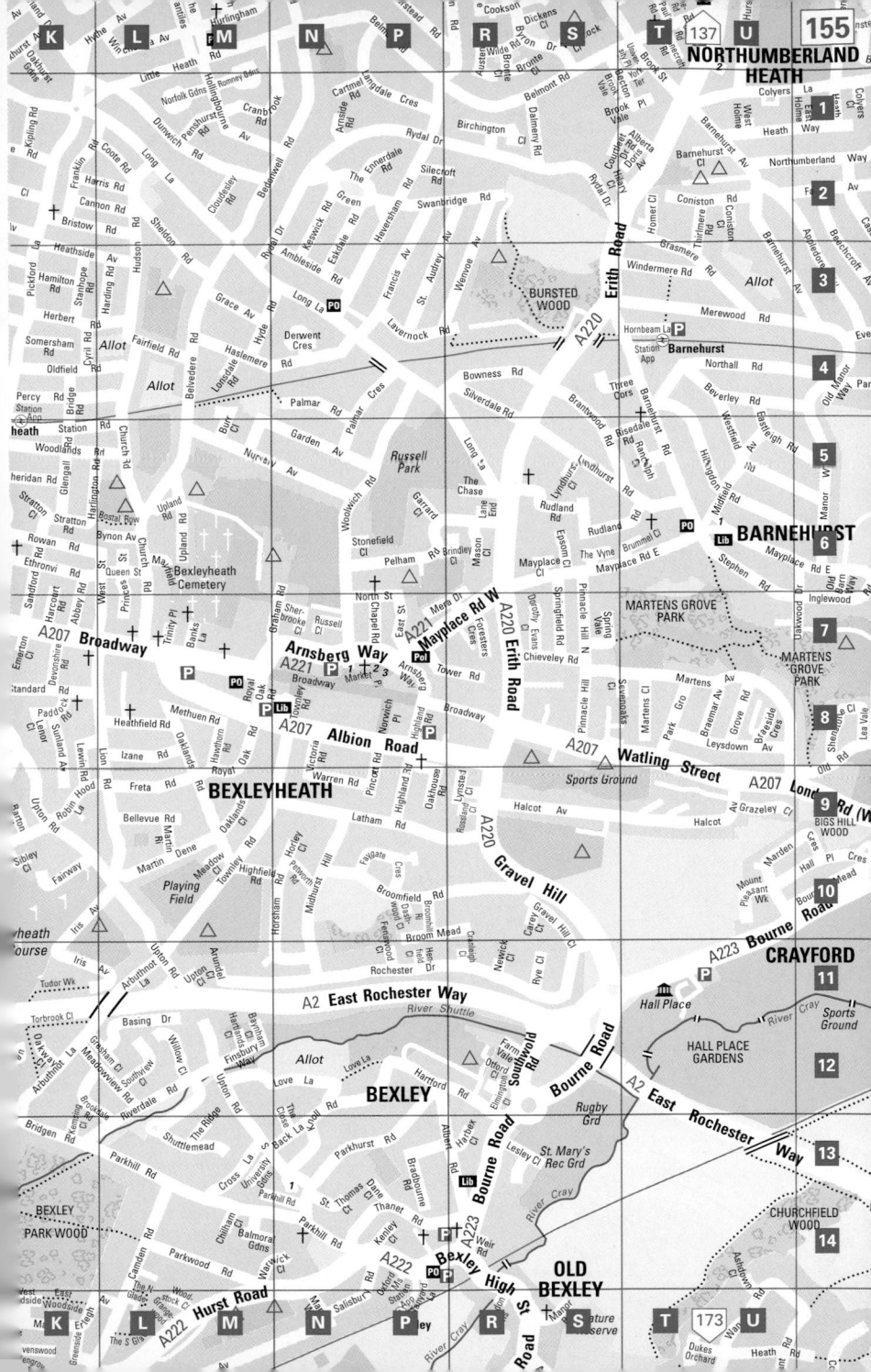

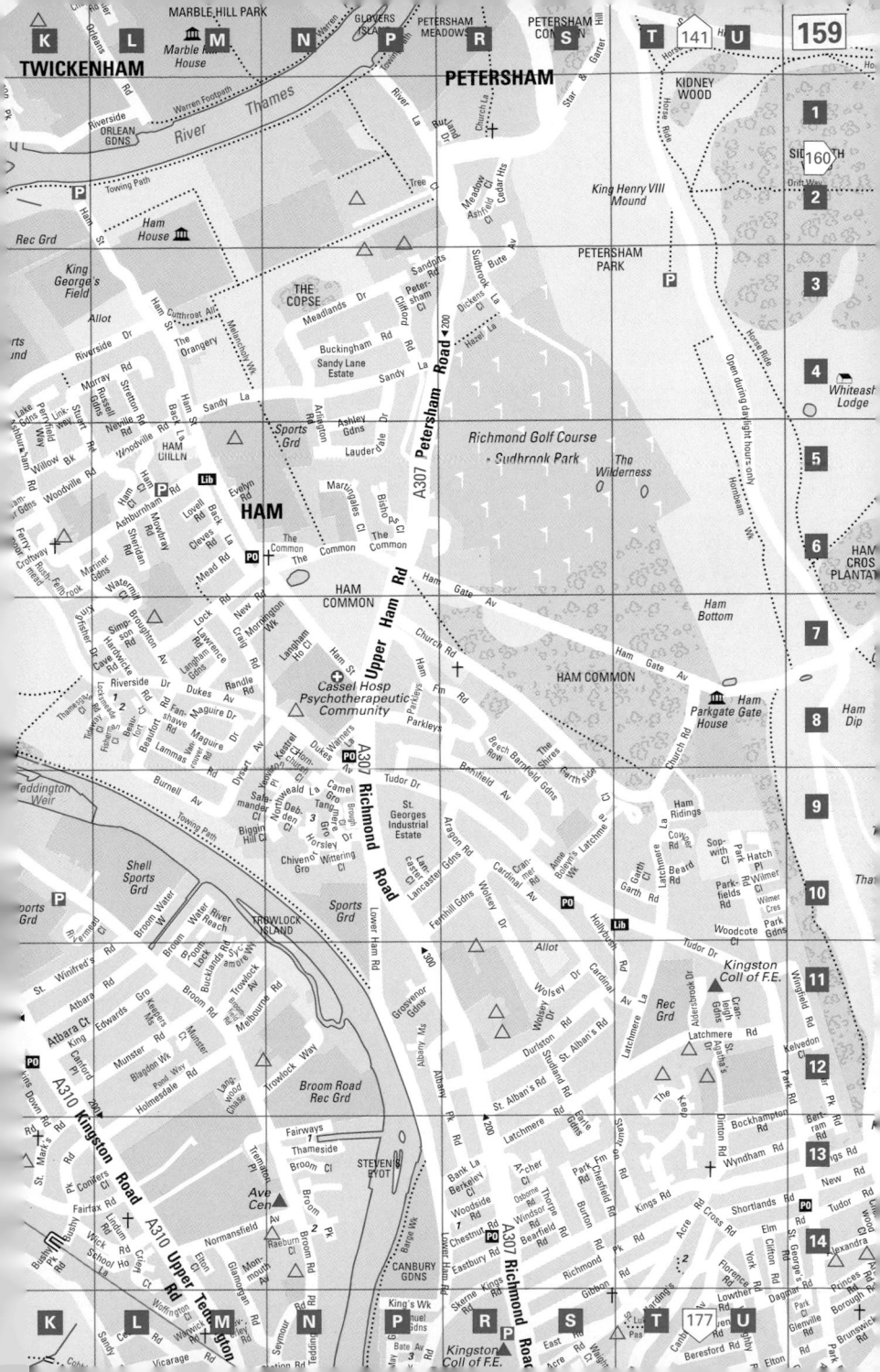

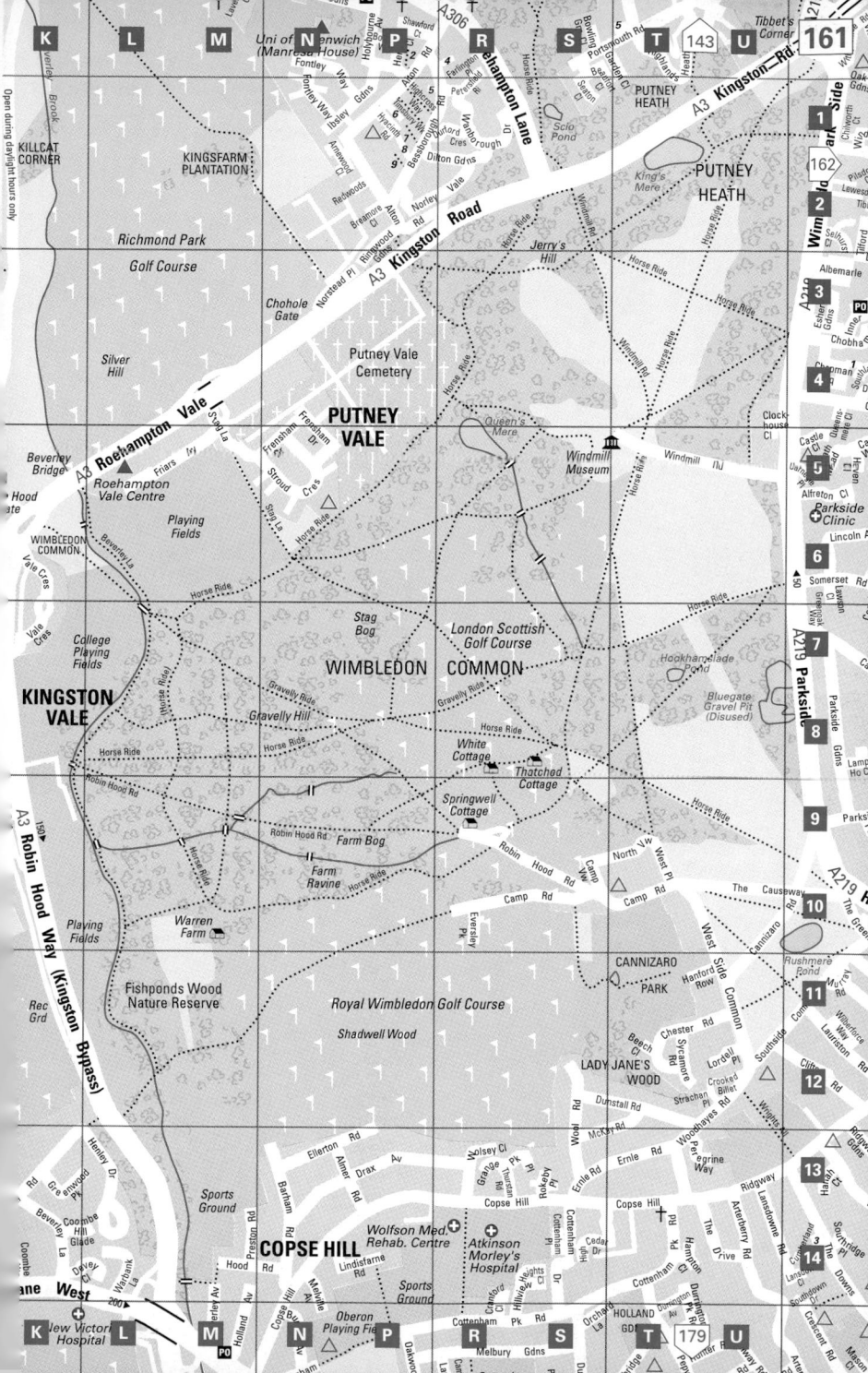

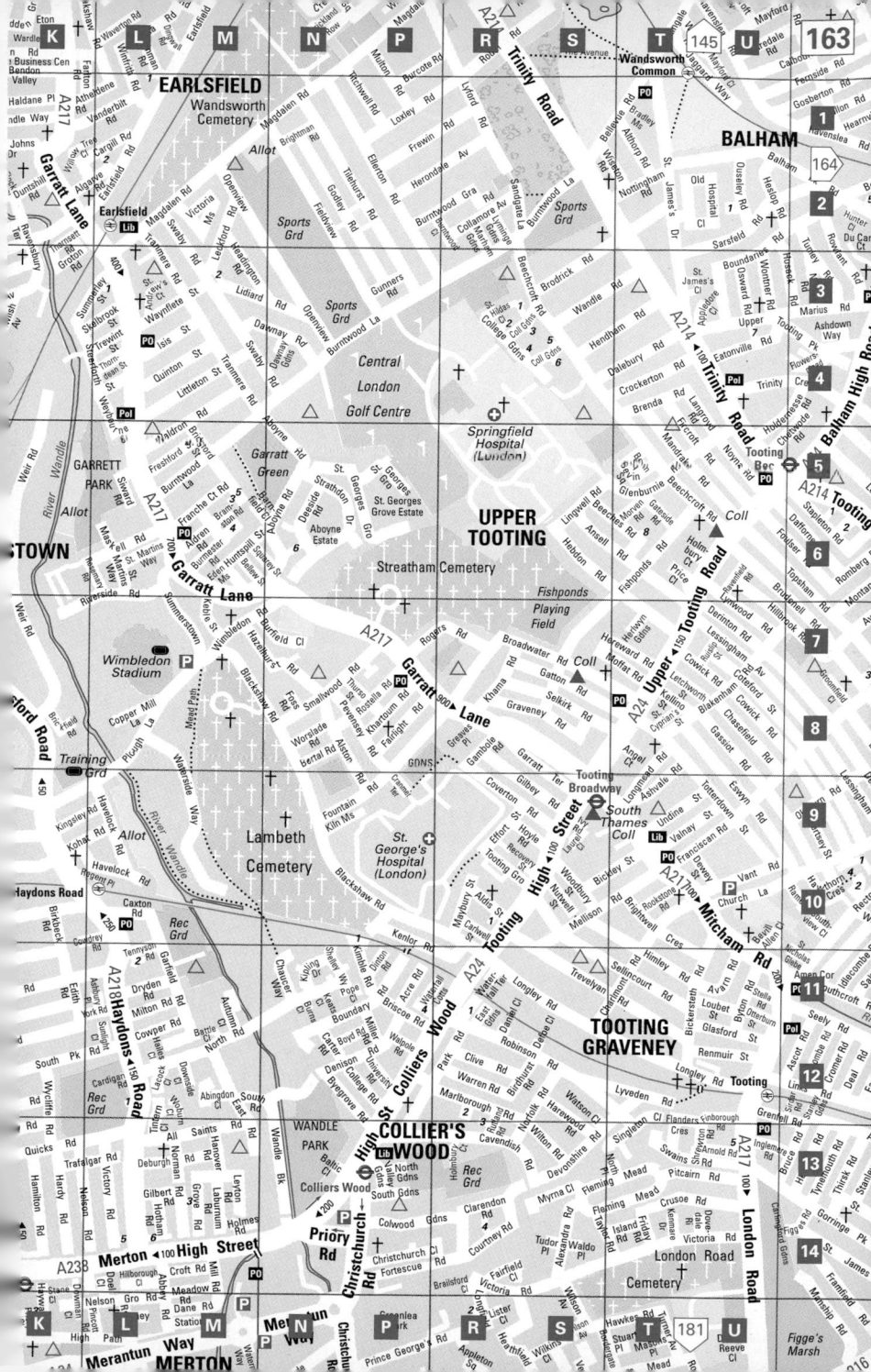

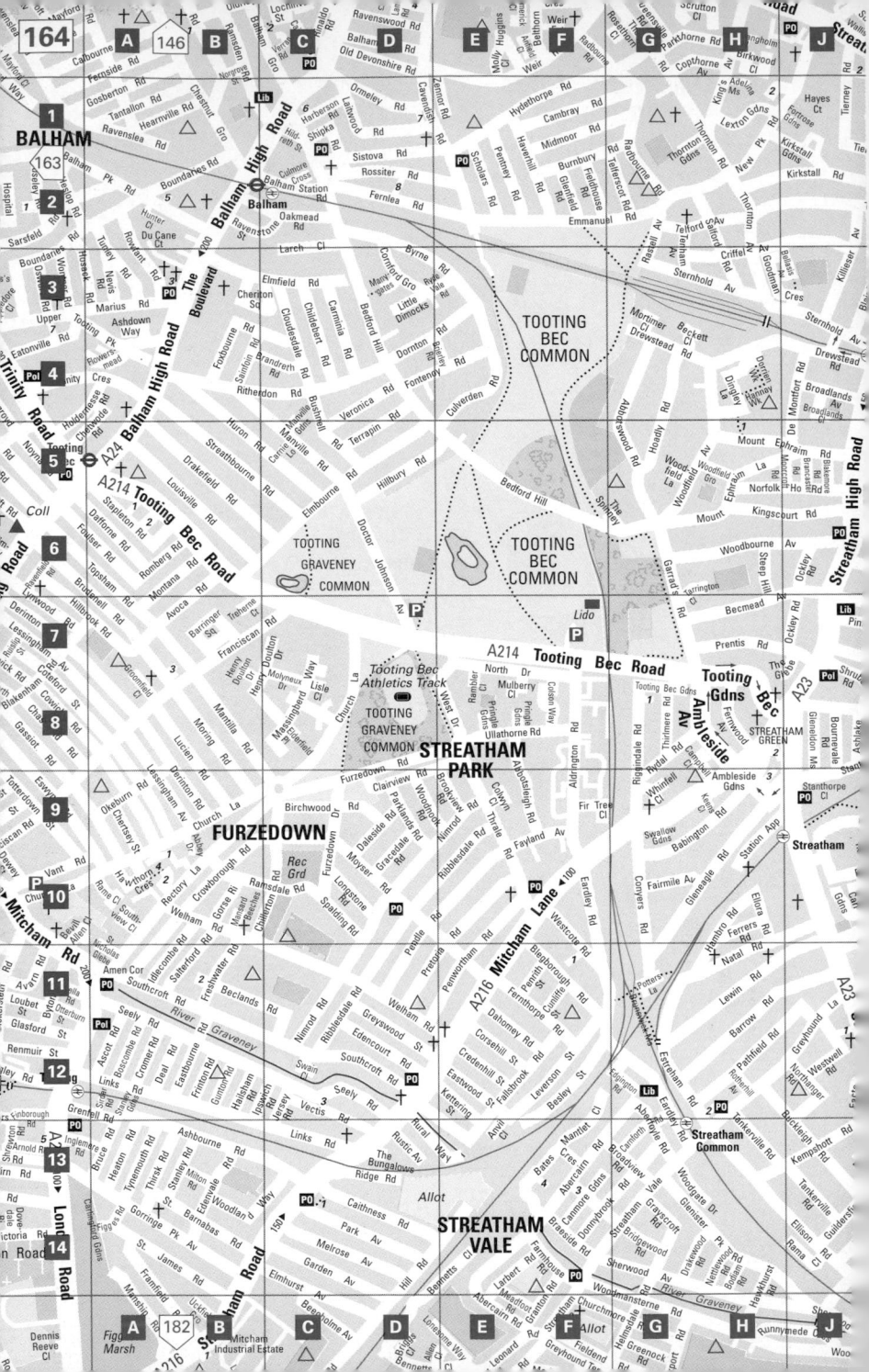

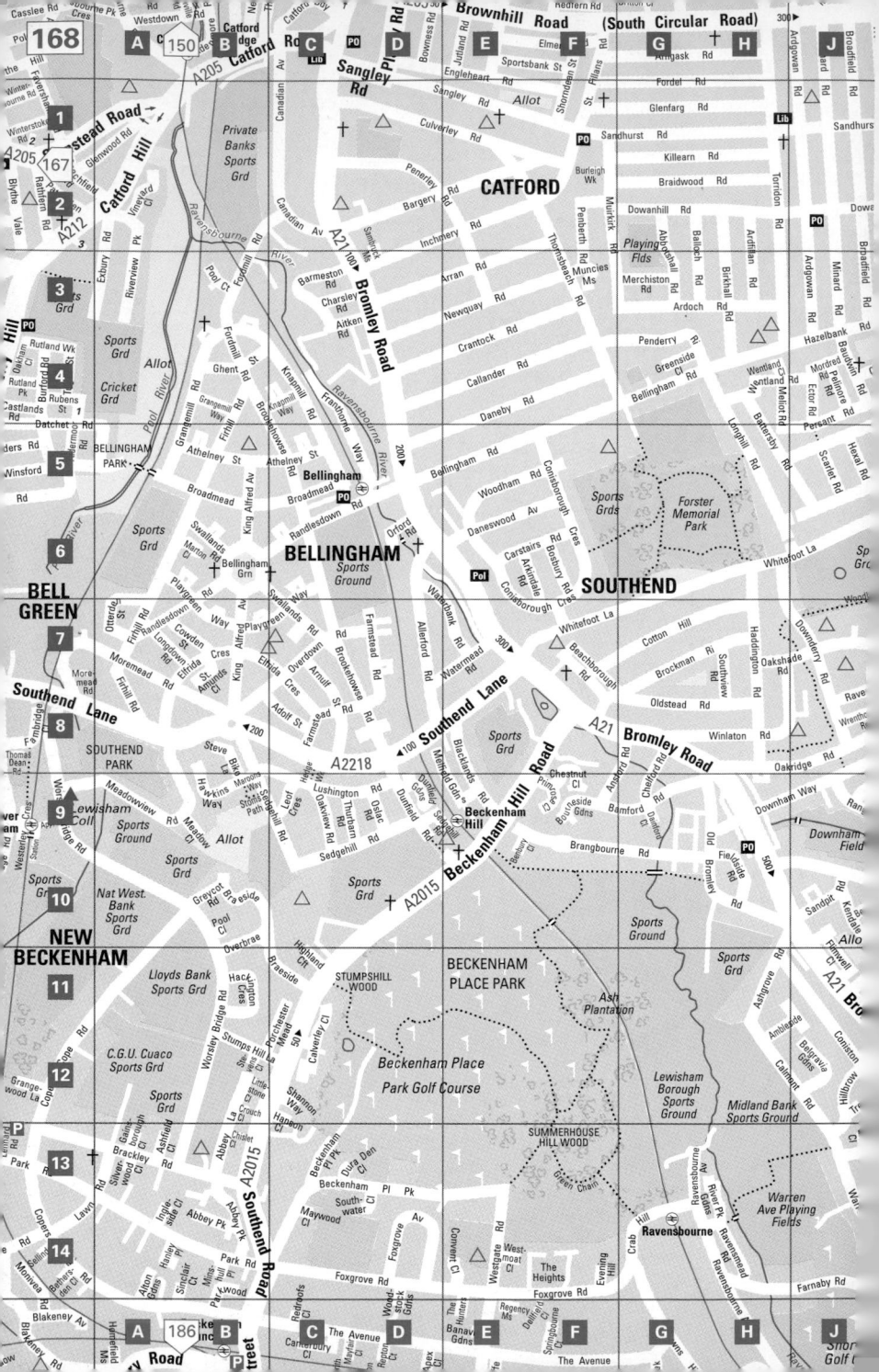

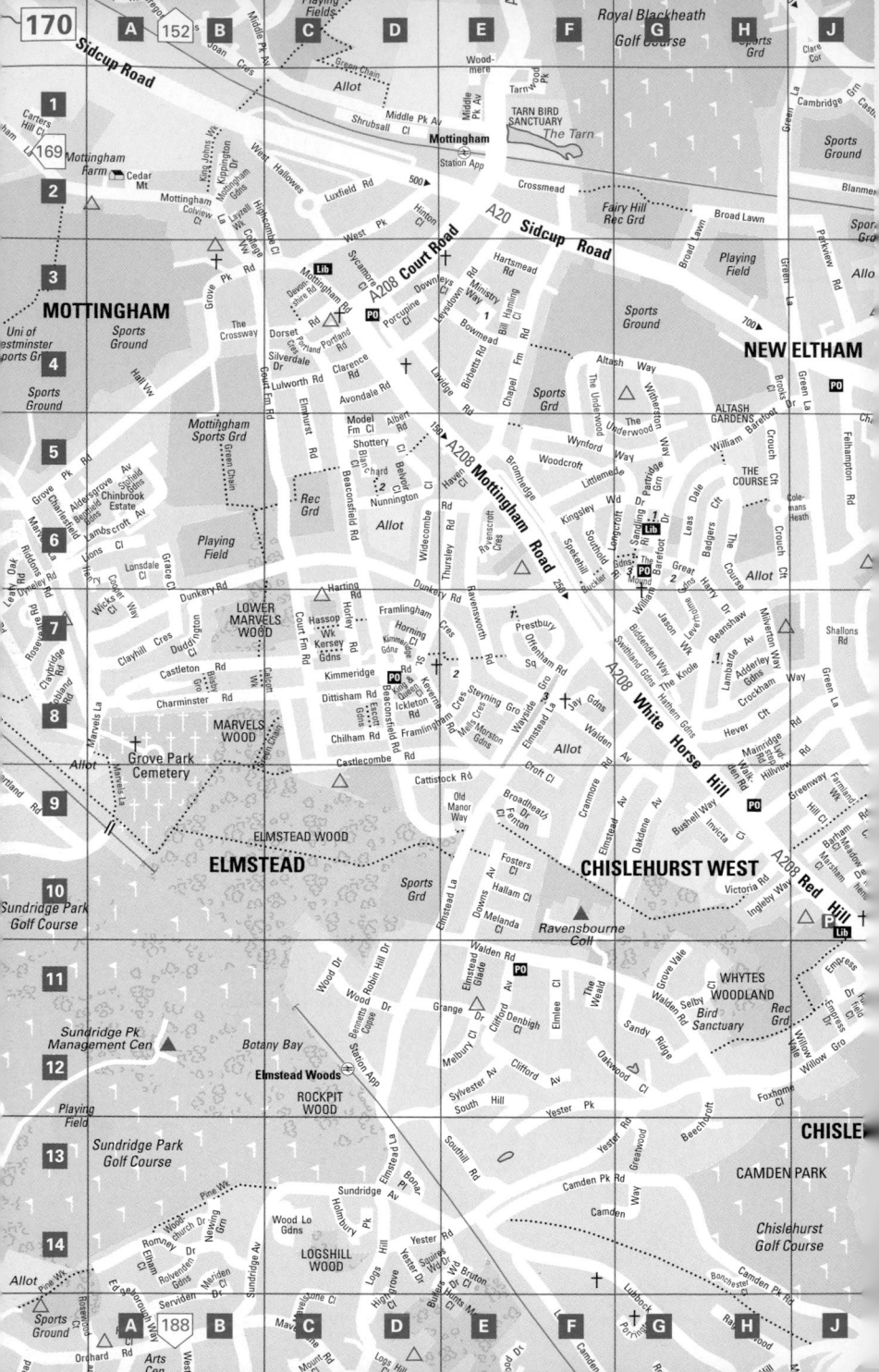

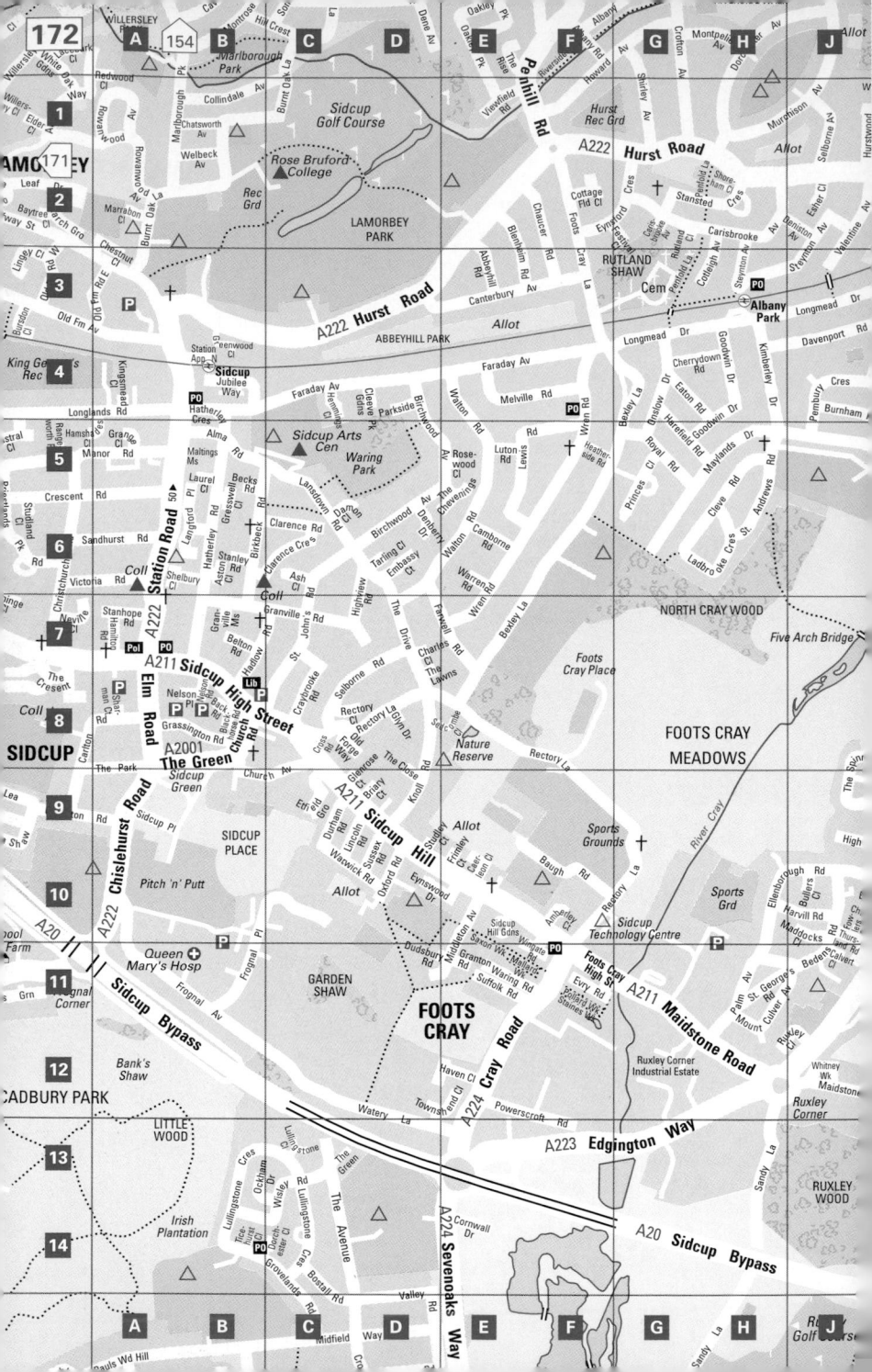

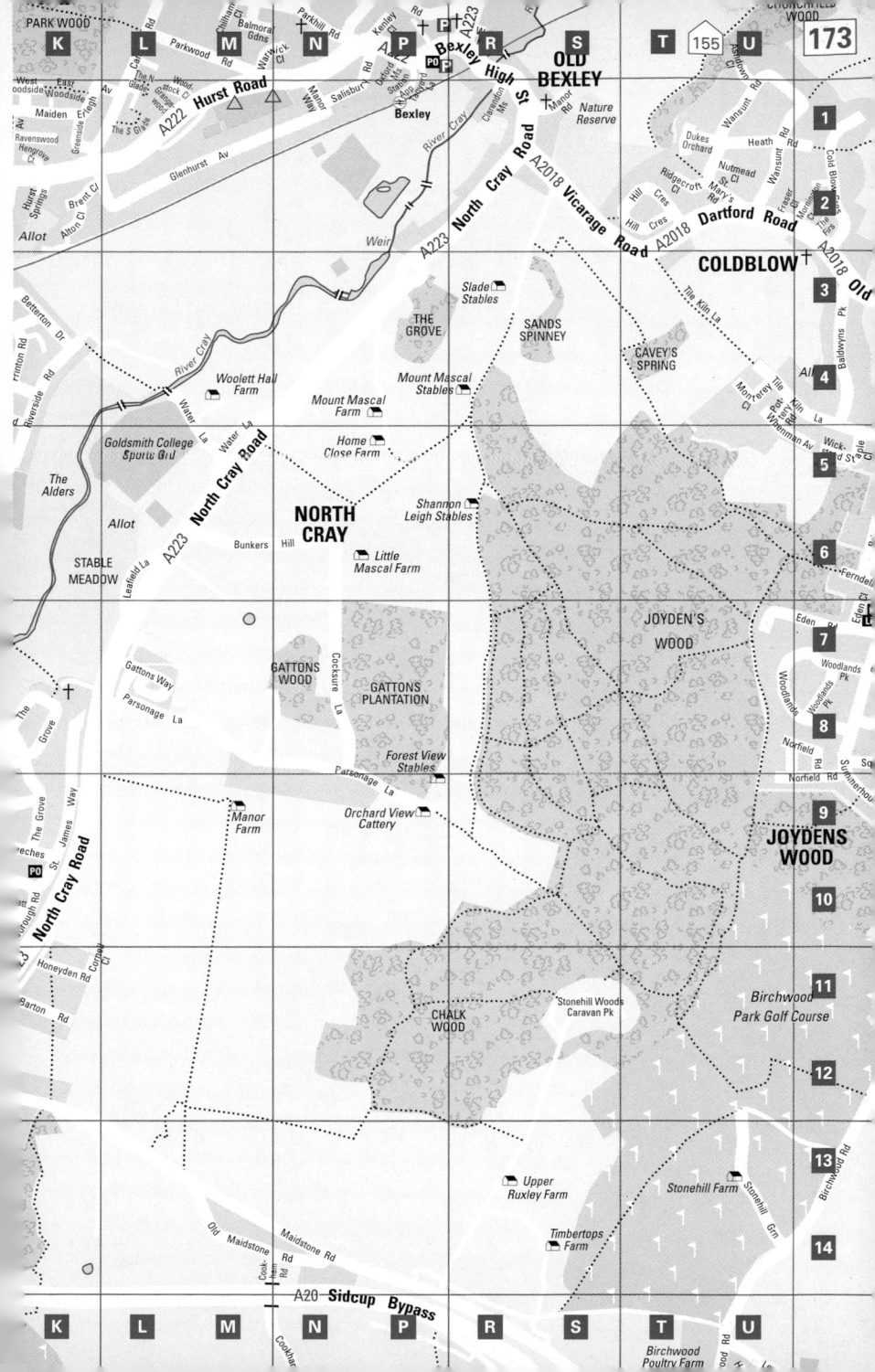

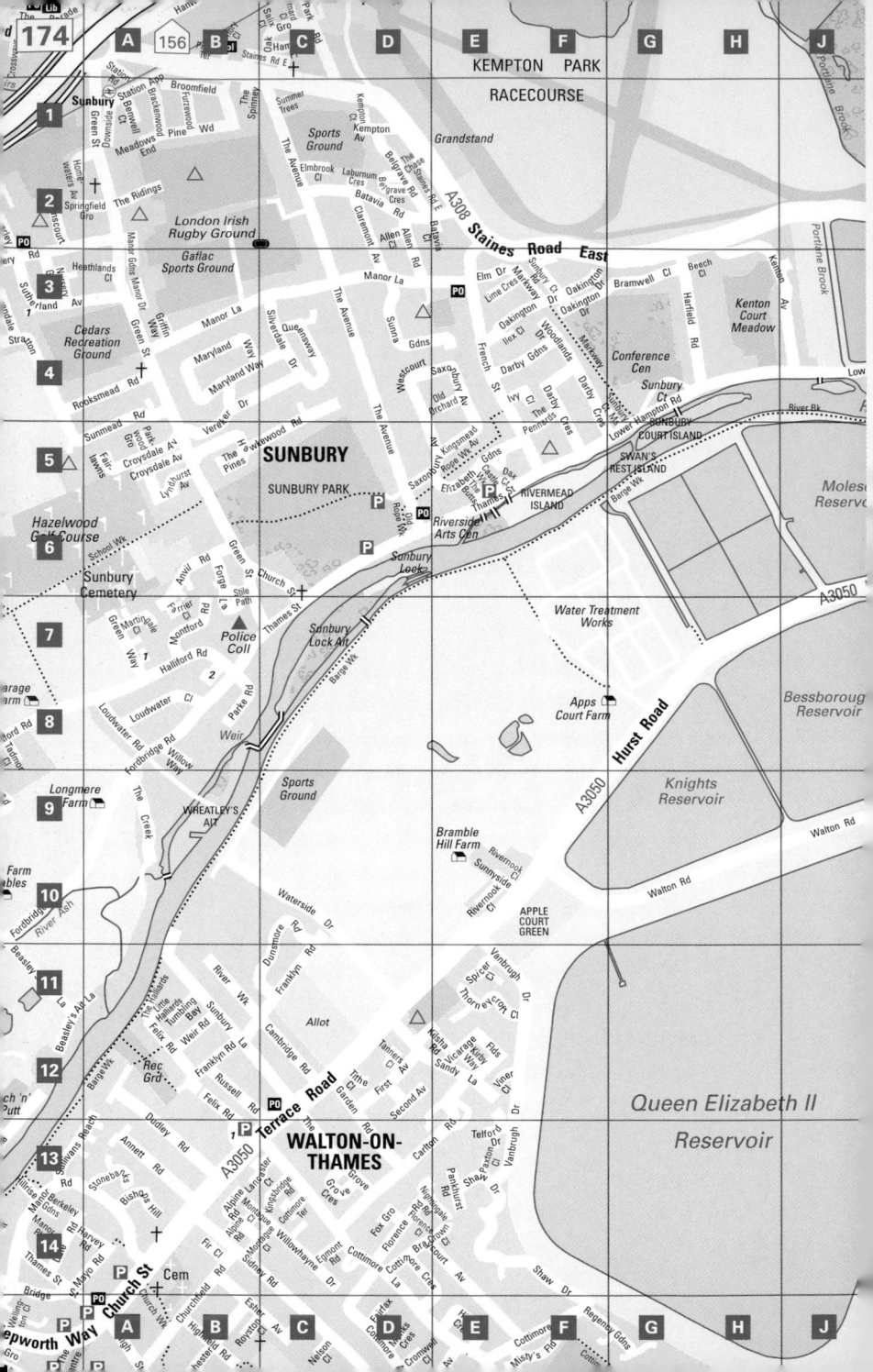

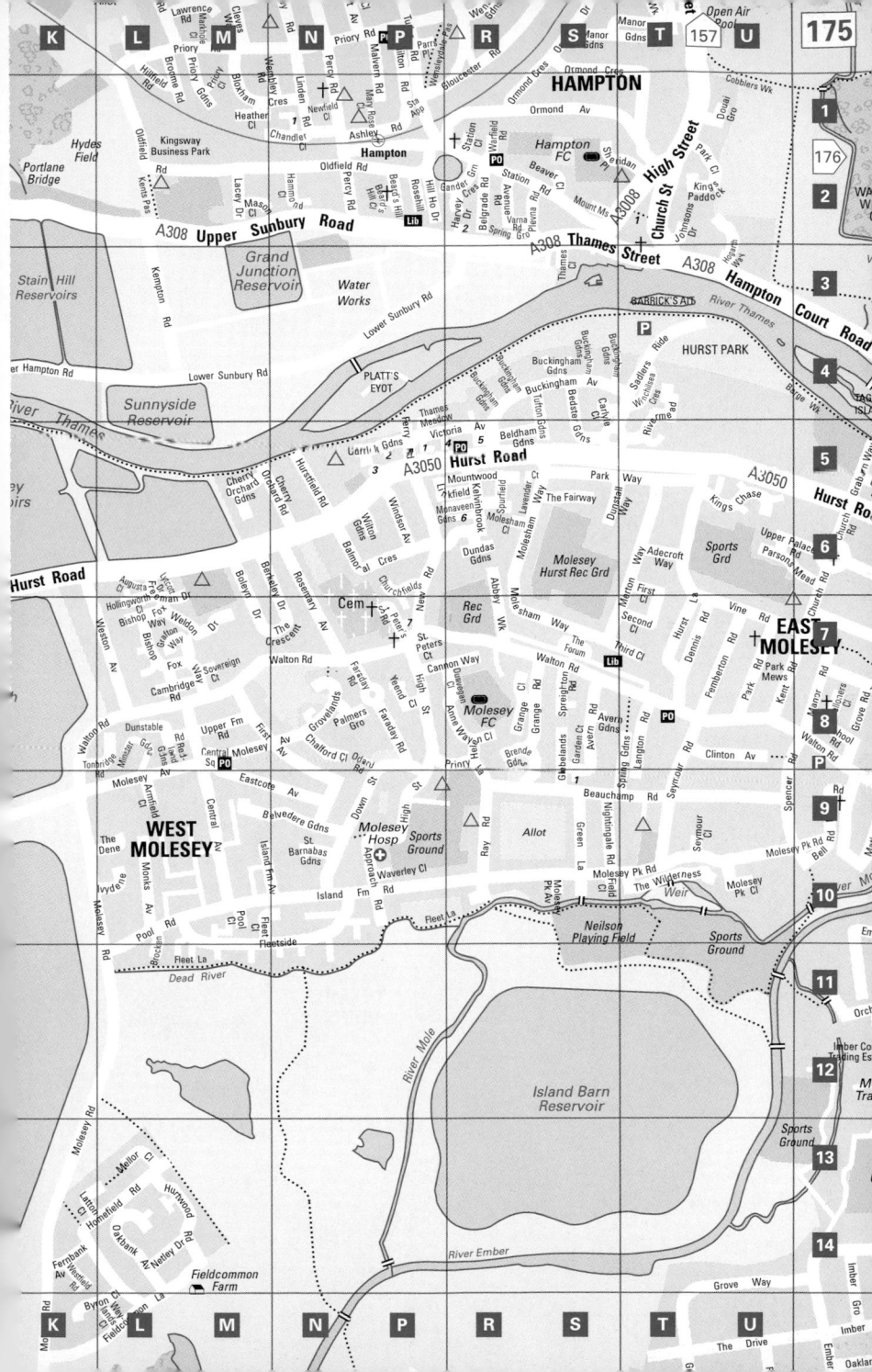

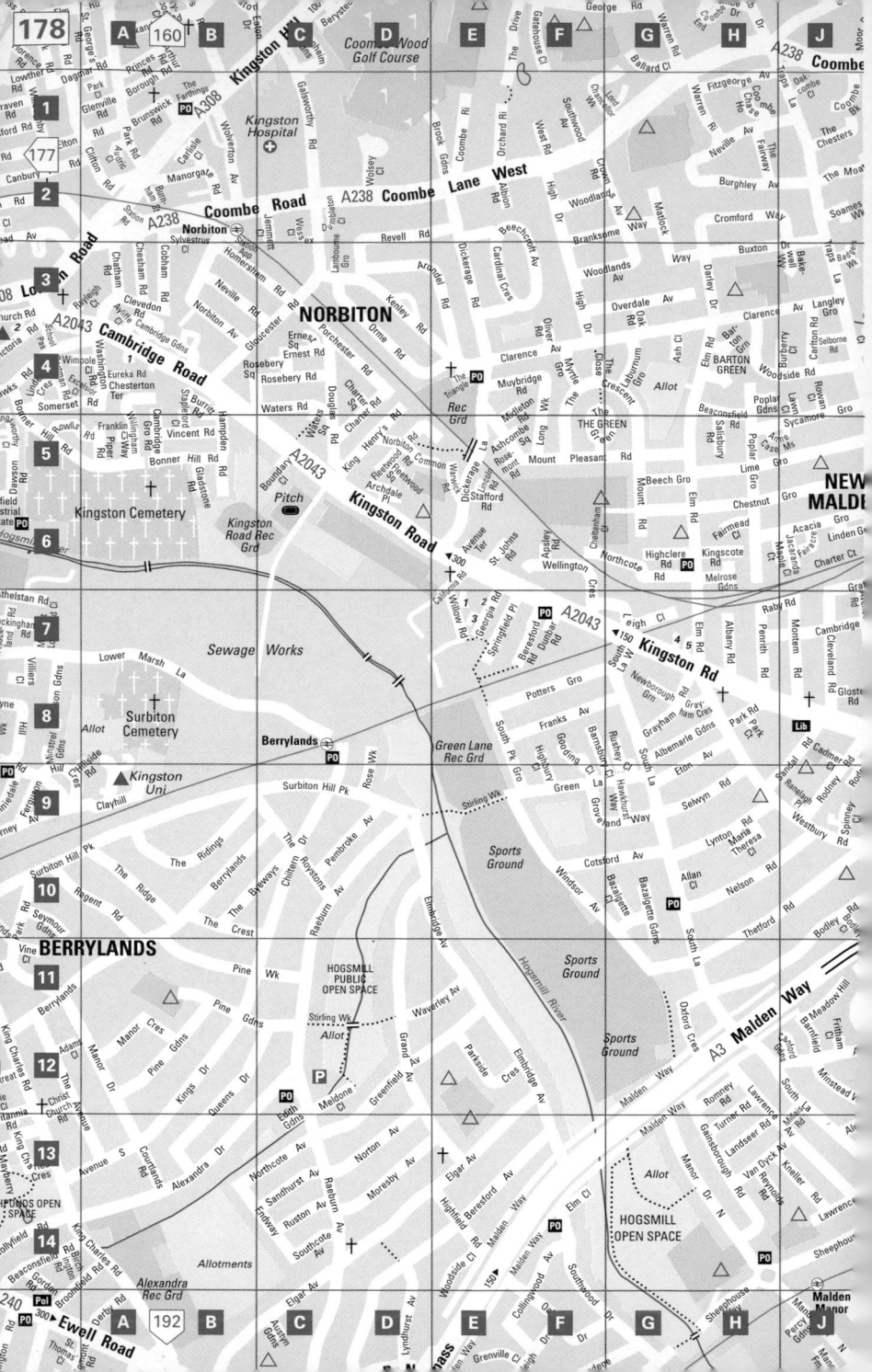

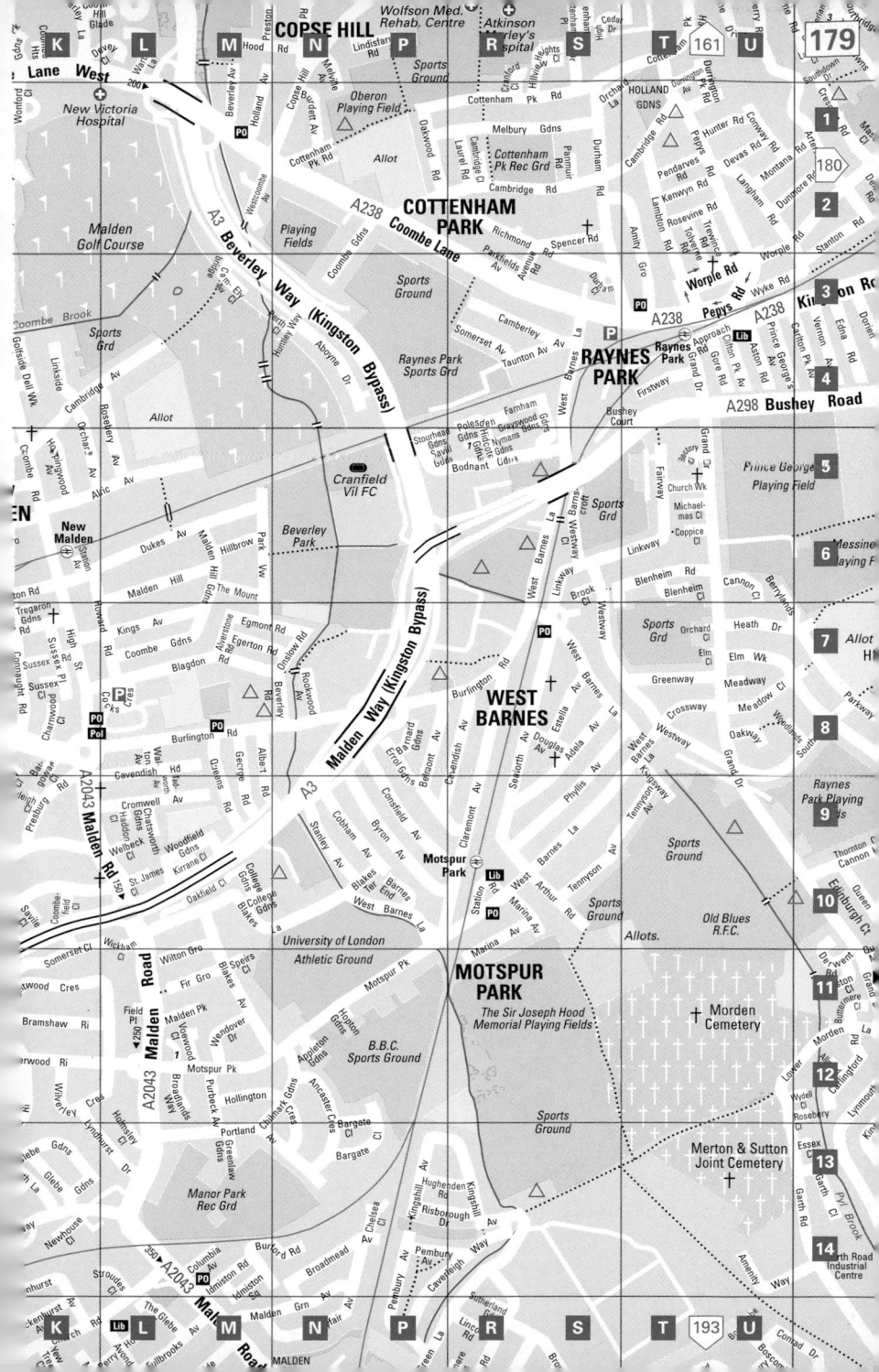

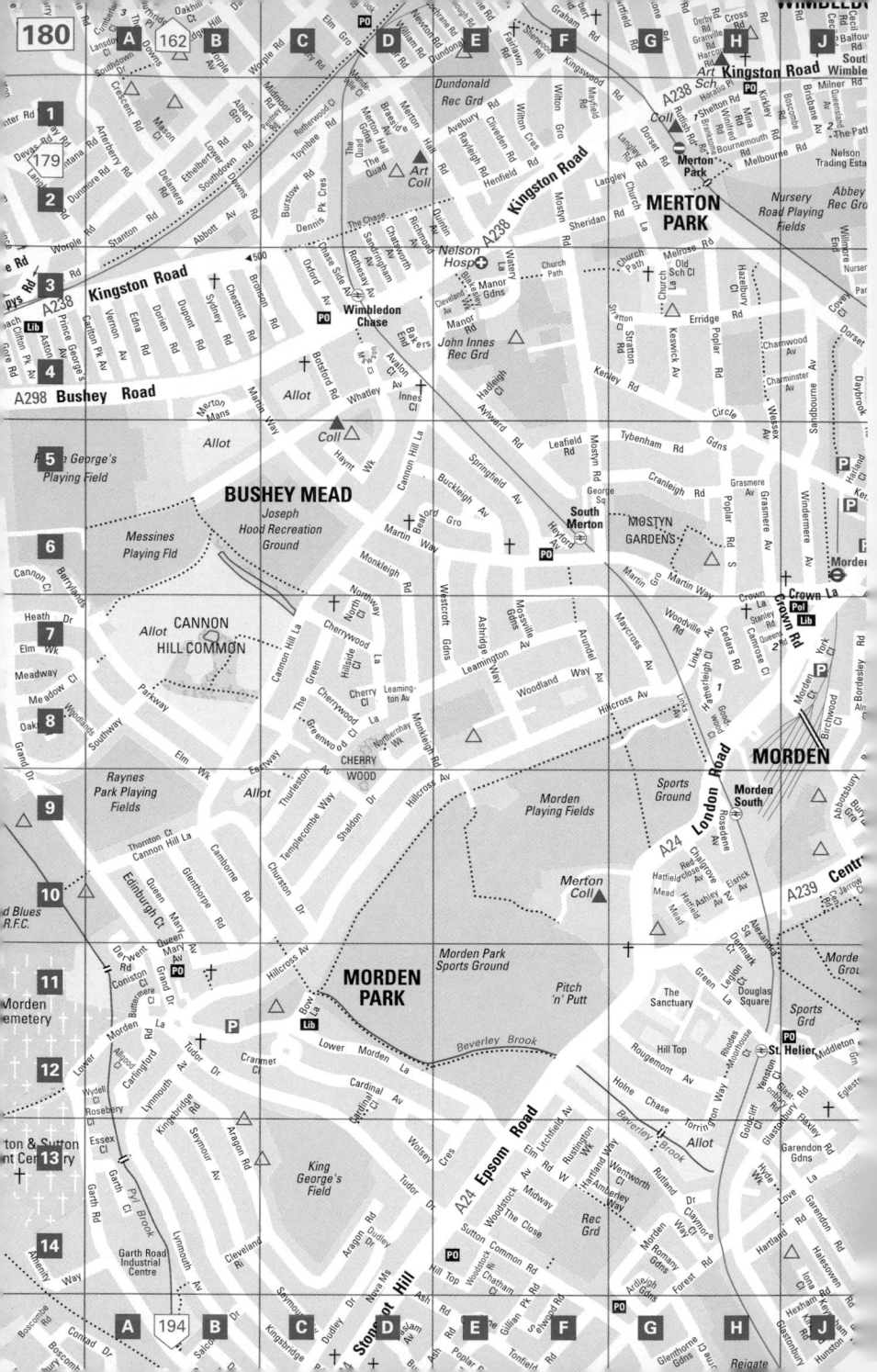

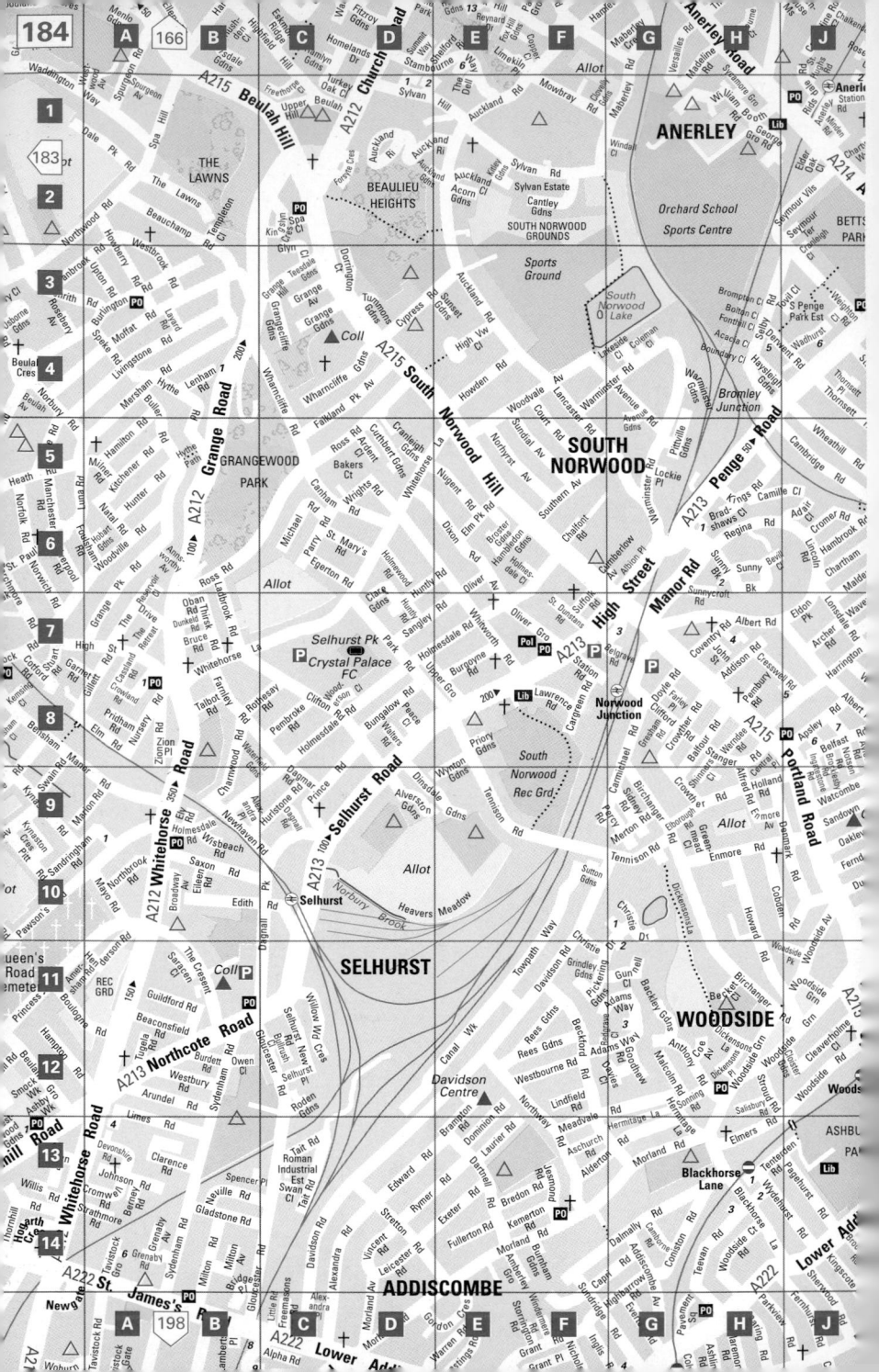

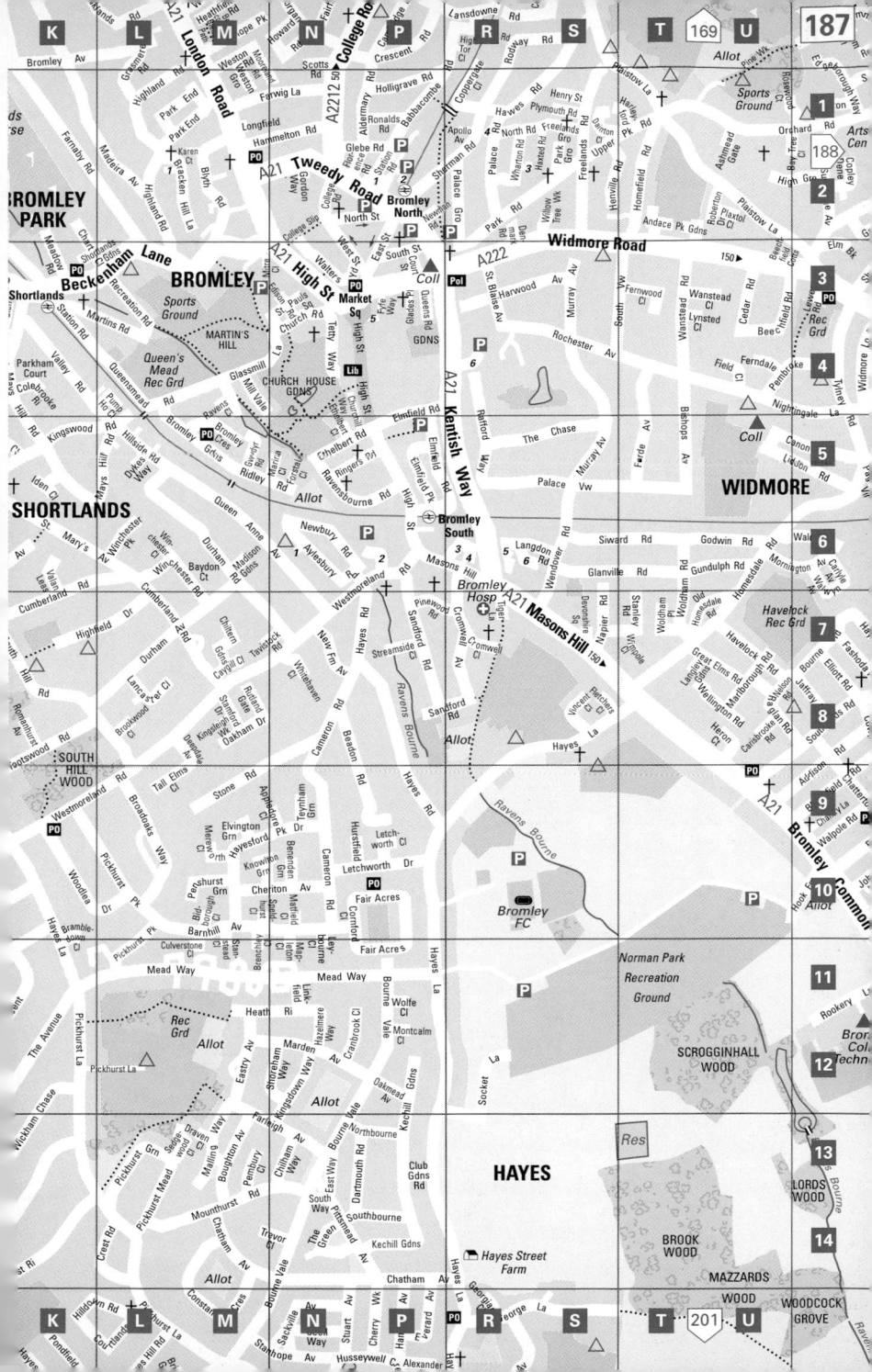

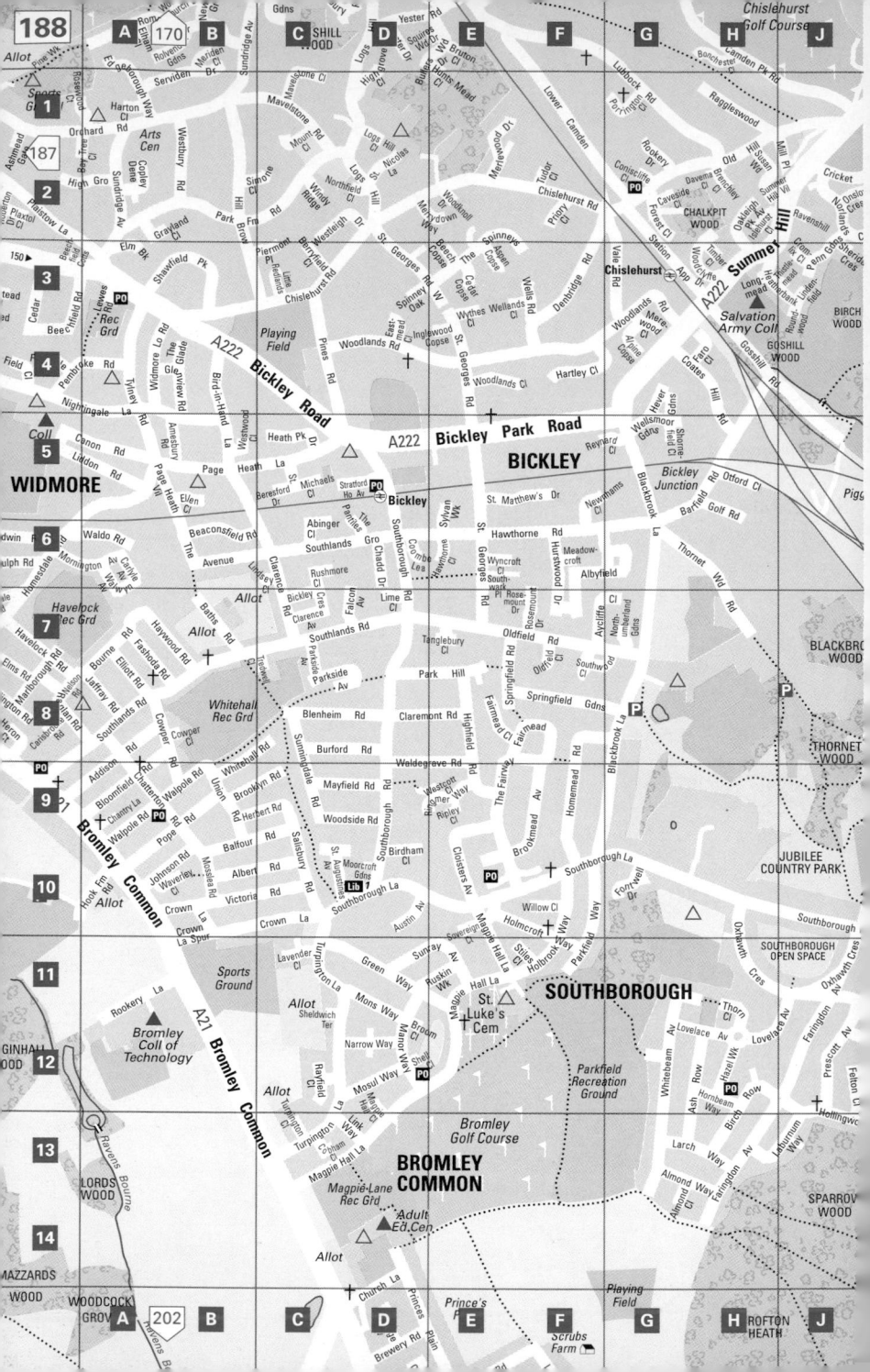

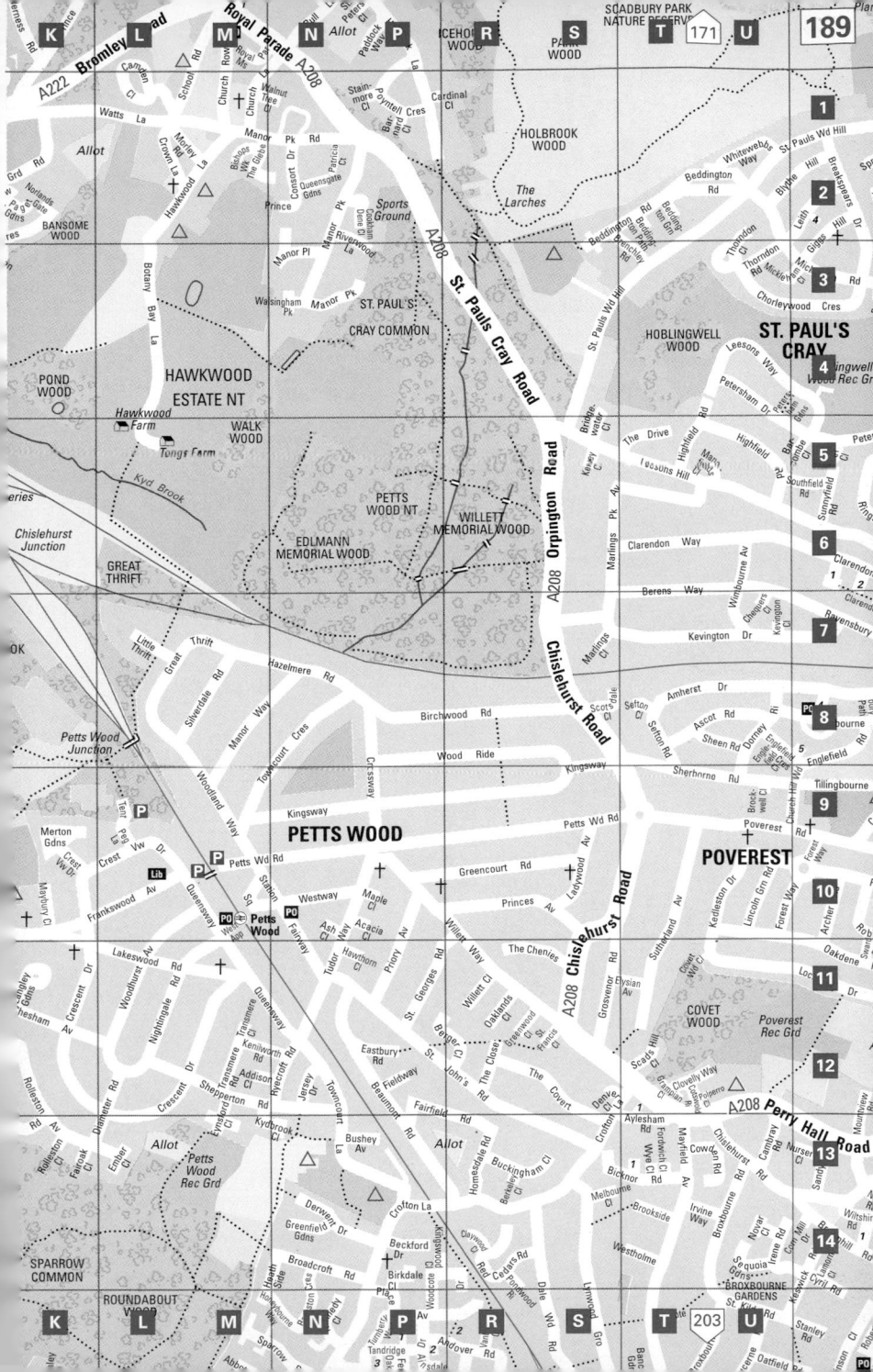

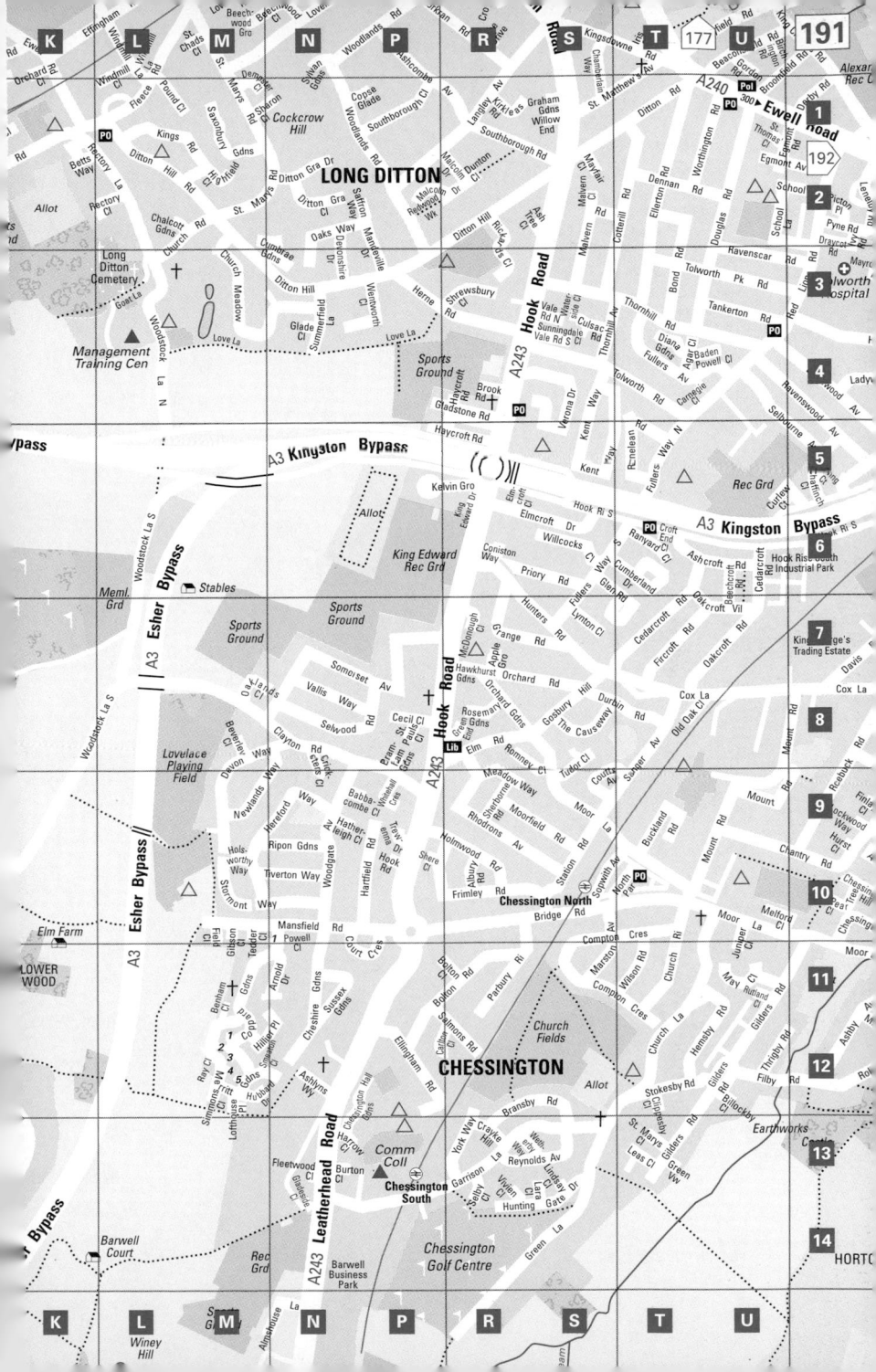

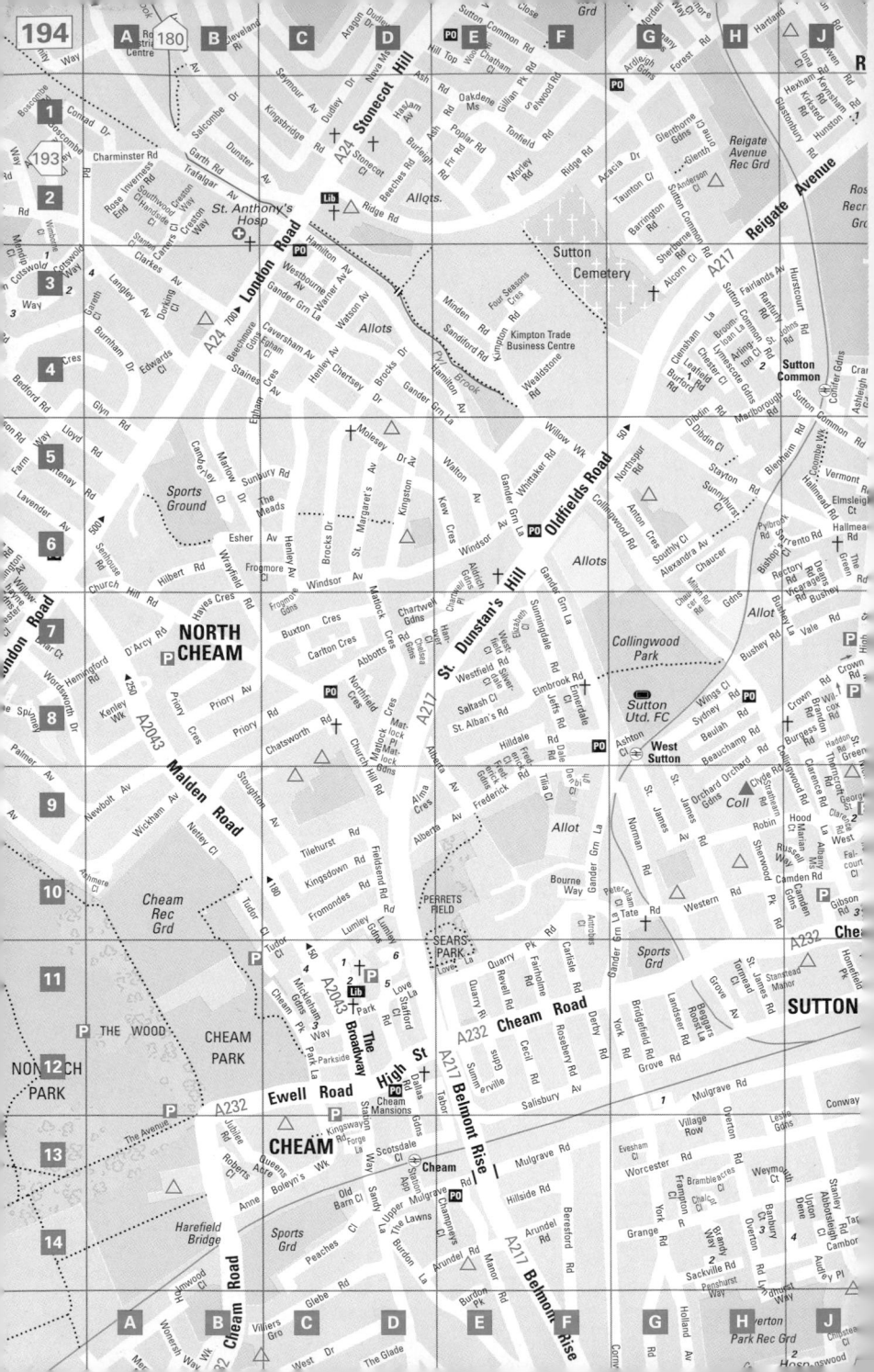

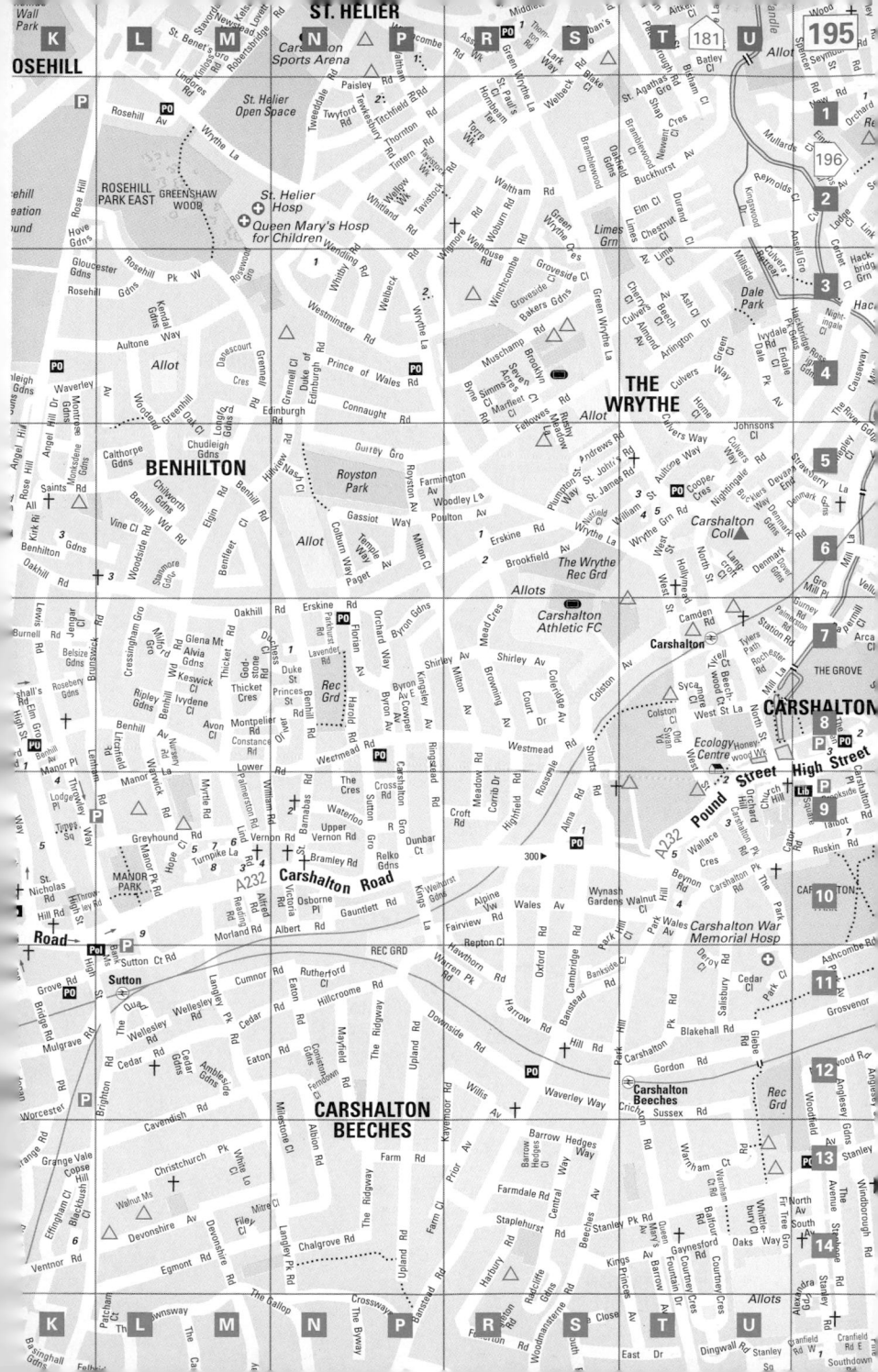

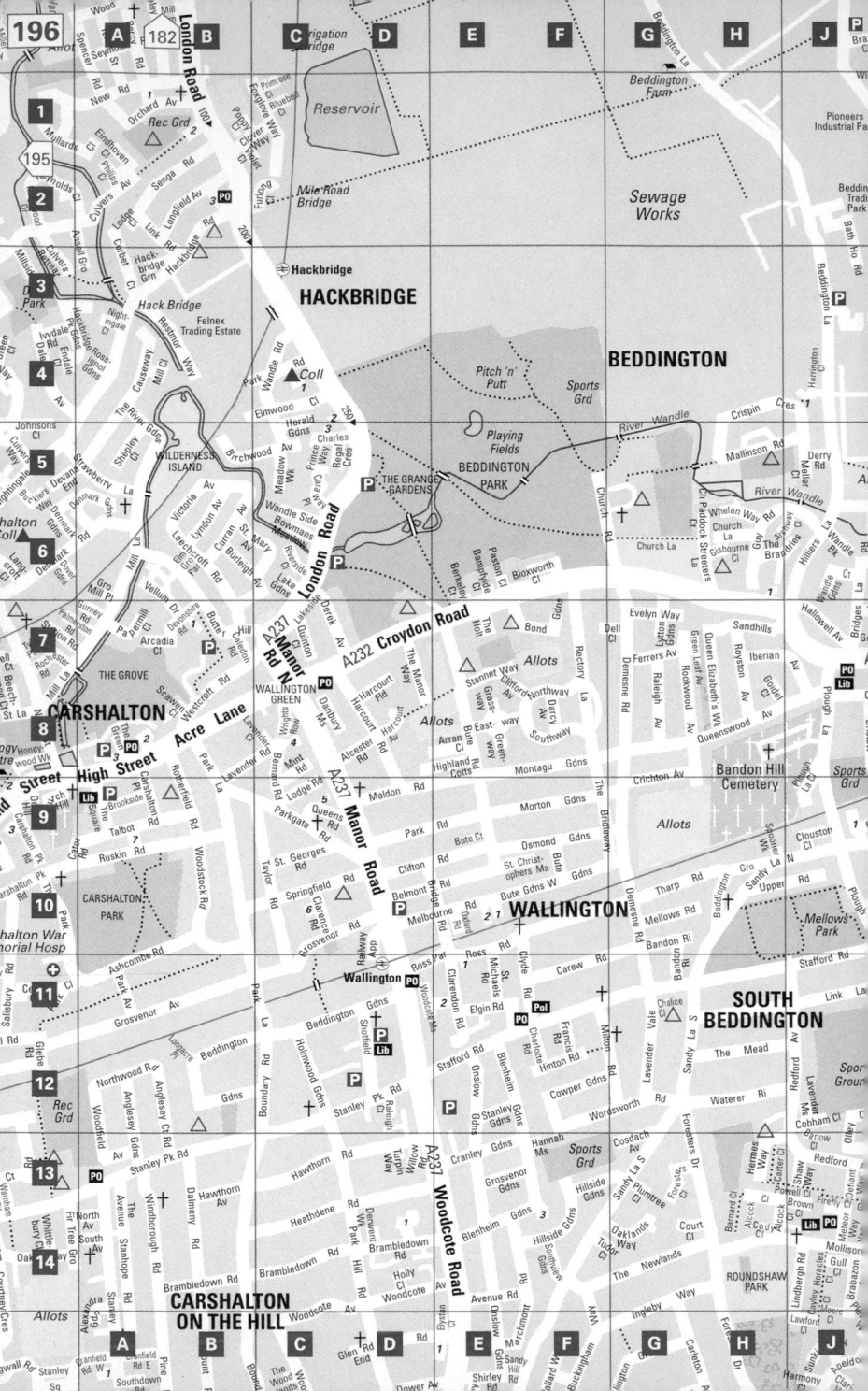

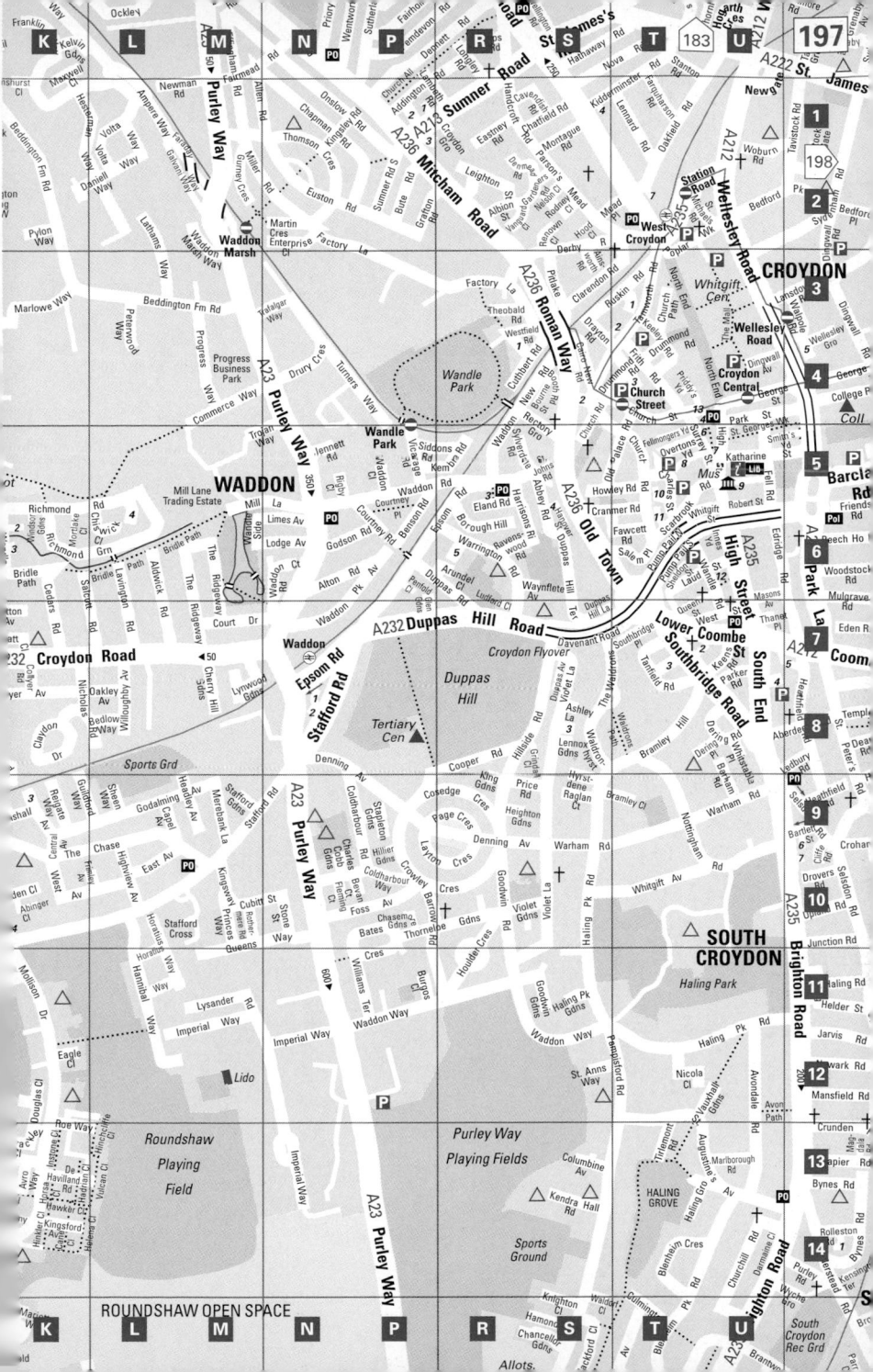

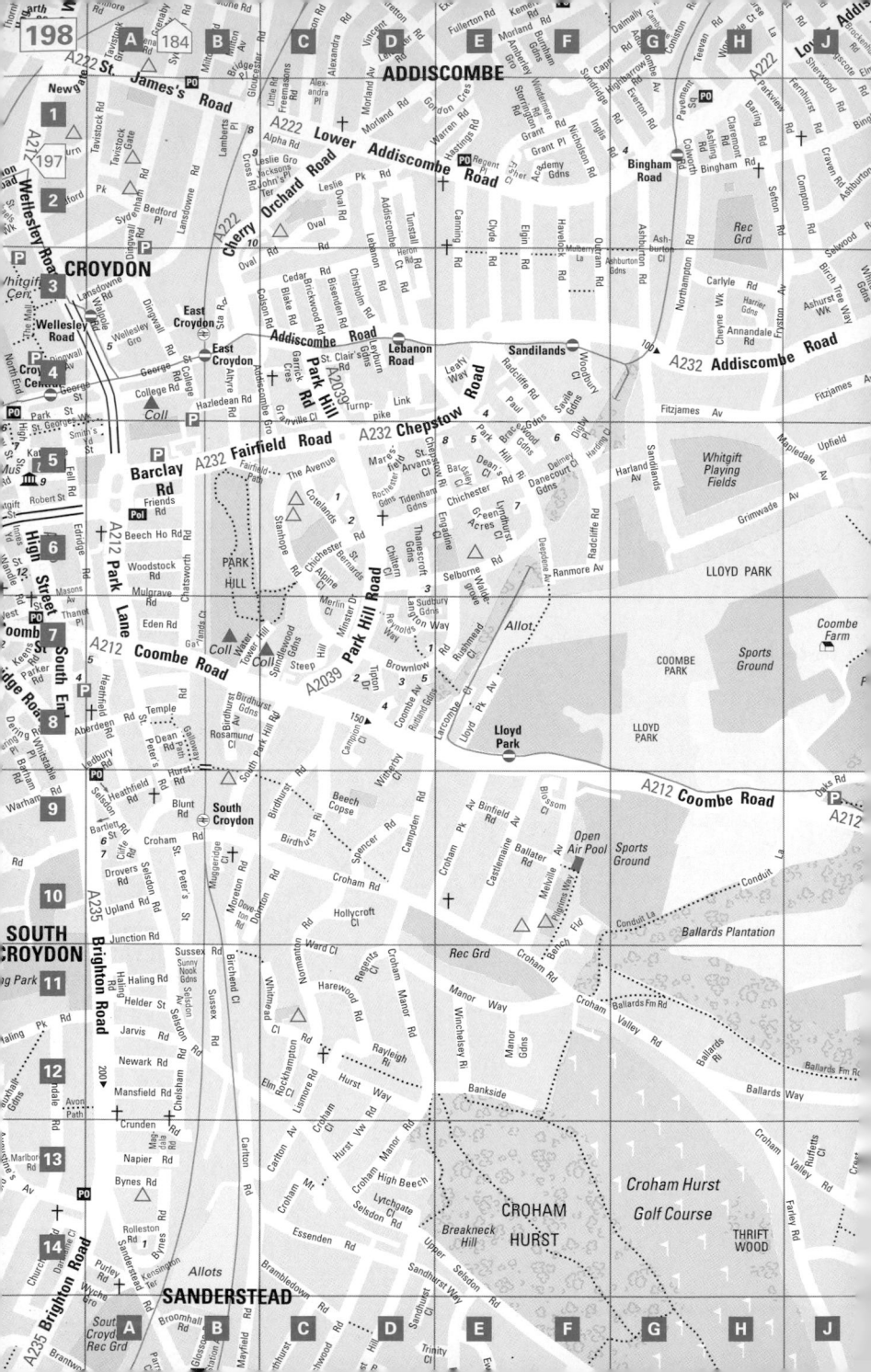

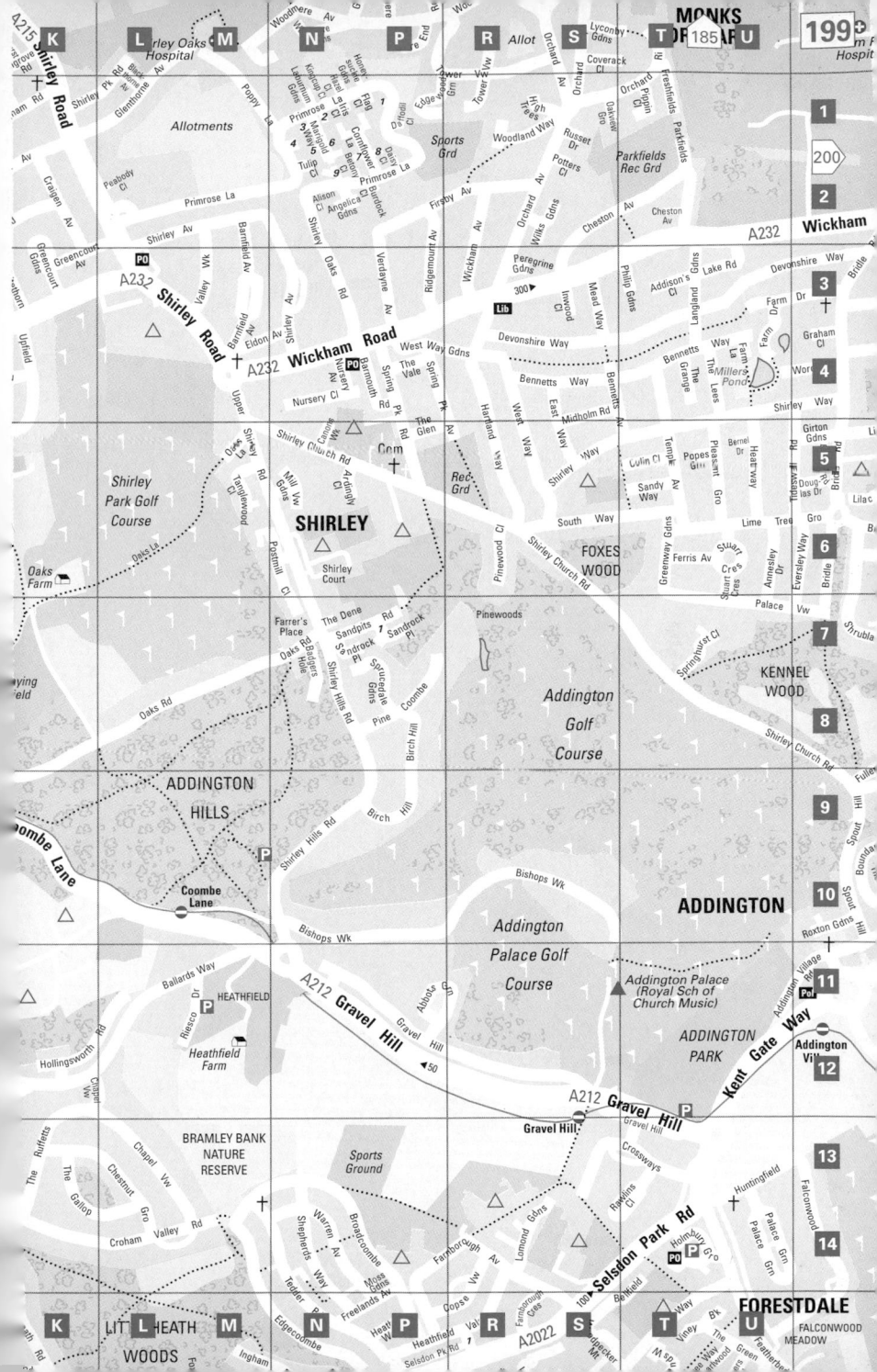

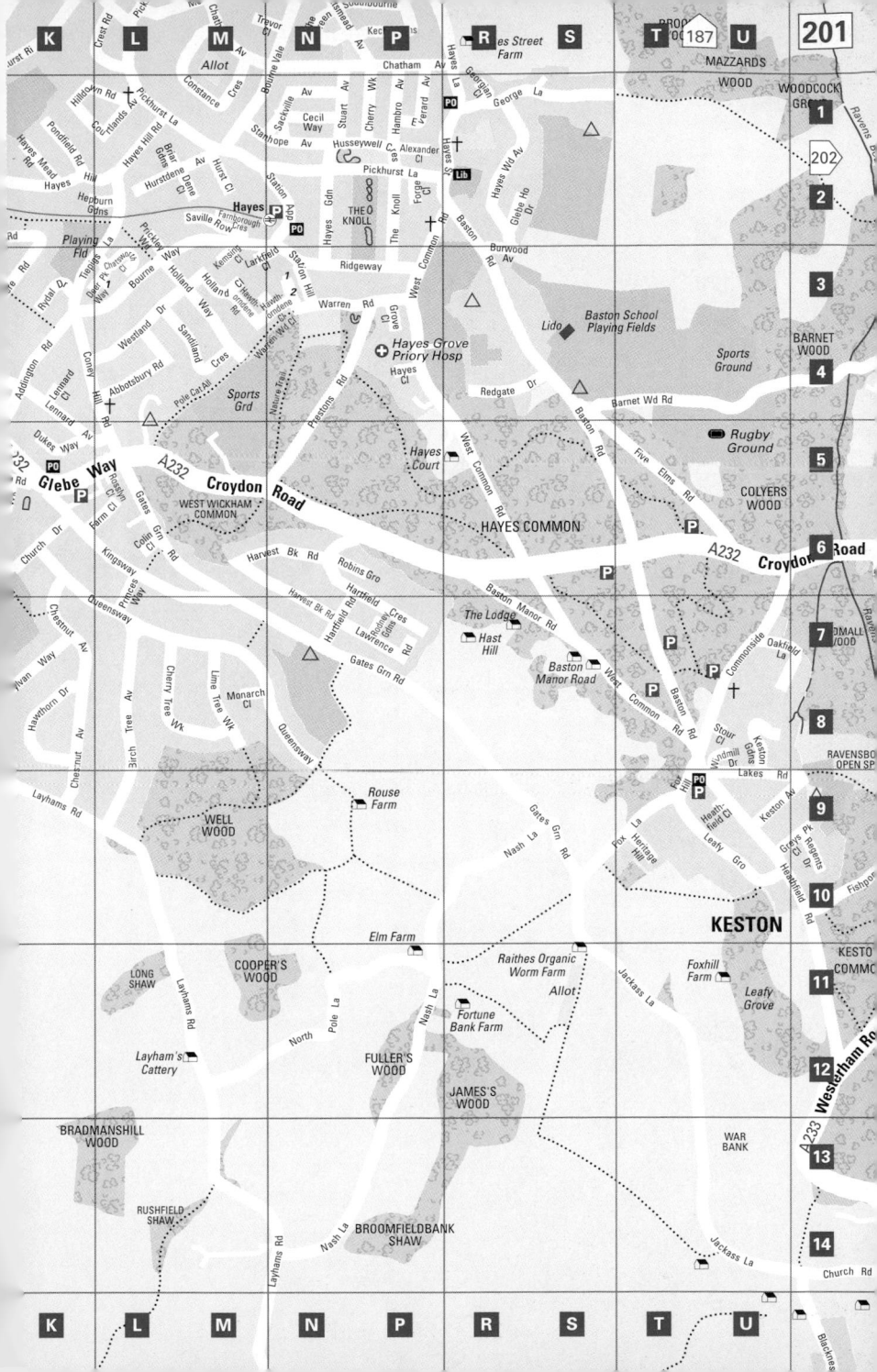

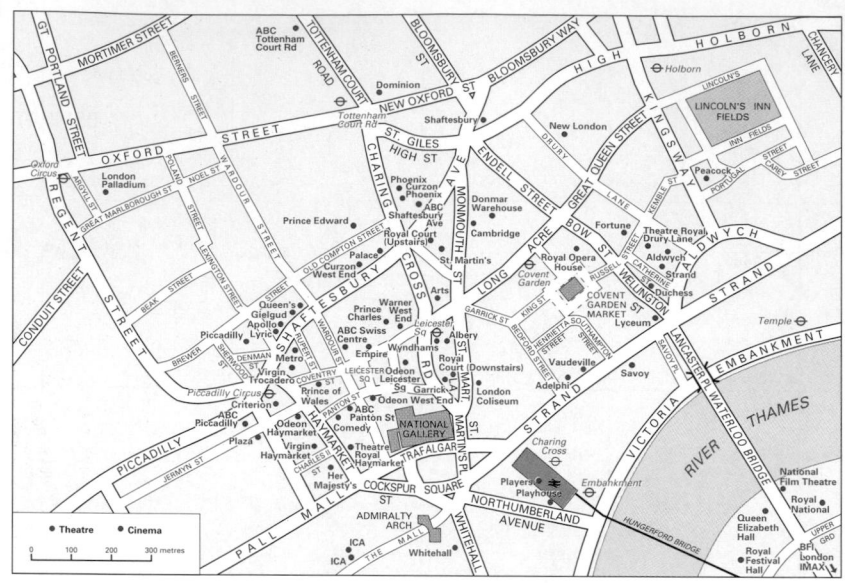

THEATRES

Adelphi *020 7344 0055*
Albery *020 7369 1730*
Aldwych *020 7416 6003*
Apollo *020 7416 6022*
Arts *020 7836 2132*
Cambridge *020 7494 5054*
Comedy *020 7369 1731*
Criterion *020 7369 1747*
Dominion *020 7656 1888*
Donmar Warehouse
  020 7369 1732
Duchess *020 7494 5075*
Fortune *020 7836 2238*
Garrick *020 7494 5085*
Gielgud *020 7494 5065*
Her Majesty's *020 7494 5400*
ICA *020 7930 3647*
London Coliseum
  020 7632 8300
London Palladium
  020 7494 5020

Lyceum *020 7420 8191*
Lyric *020 7494 5045*
New London *020 7405 0072*
Palace *020 7434 0909*
Peacock *020 7314 8800*
Phoenix *020 7369 1733*
Piccadilly *020 7369 1734*
Players *020 7369 1134*
Playhouse *020 7839 4401*
Prince Edward *020 7734 8951*
Prince of Wales
  020 7839 5987
Queen Elizabeth Hall
  020 7960 4242
Queen's *020 7494 5041*
Royal Court Theatre
Downstairs *020 7565 5000*
Royal Court Theatre Upstairs
  020 7565 5000
Royal Festival Hall
  020 7960 4242

Royal National *020 7452 3000*
Royal Opera House
  020 7304 4000
St. Martin's *020 7836 1443*
Savoy *020 7836 8888*
Shaftesbury *020 7379 5399*
Strand *020 7930 8800*
Theatre Royal, Drury Lane
  020 7494 5550
Theatre Royal, Haymarket
  020 7930 8800
Vaudeville *020 7836 9987*
Whitehall *020 7369 1735*
Wyndhams *020 7369 1736*

CINEMAS

ABC Panton St
  020 7930 0631
ABC Piccadilly
  020 7437 3561
ABC Shaftesbury Avenue
  020 7836 6279
ABC Swiss Centre
  020 7439 4470
ABC Tottenham Court Rd
  020 7636 6148
BFI London IMAX
  020 7902 1200
Curzon Phoenix *020 7369 1721*
Curzon West End
  020 7369 1722

Empire *020 7437 1234*
ICA *020 7930 3647*
Metro *020 7437 0757*
National Film Theatre
  020 7928 3232
Odeon Haymarket
  0426 915353
Odeon Leicester Sq
  020 8315 4215
Odeon Mezzanine
(Odeon Leicester Sq)
  020 8315 4215
Odeon West End
  020 8315 4221
Plaza *020 7437 1234*

Prince Charles *020 7437 8181*
Virgin Haymarket
  0870 907 0712
Virgin Trocadero
  0870 907 0716
Warner West End
  020 7437 4347

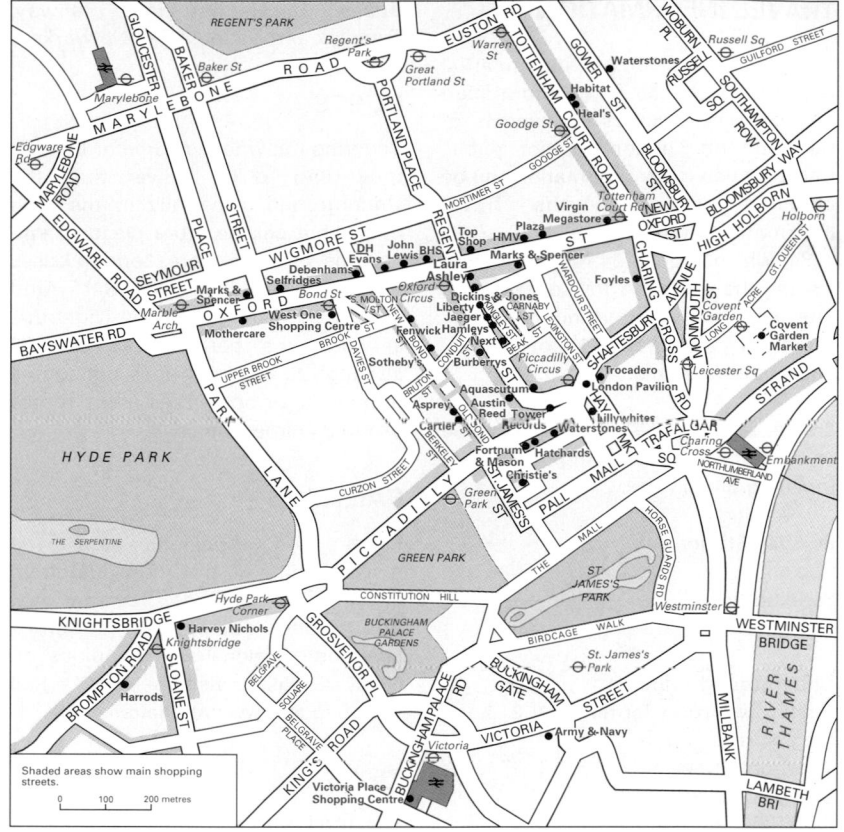

SHOPS

Aquascutum *020 7734 6090*
Army & Navy *020 7834 1234*
Asprey *020 7493 6767*
Austin Reed *020 7734 6789*
BHS (Oxford St)
  020 7629 2011
Cartier *020 7493 6962*
Christie's *020 7839 9060*
Covent Garden Market
  020 7836 9137
DH Evans *020 7629 8800*
Debenhams *020 7580 3000*
Dickins & Jones
  020 7734 7070
Fenwick *020 7629 9161*
Fortnum & Mason
  020 7734 8040
Foyles *020 7437 5660*
Habitat (Tottenham Court Rd)
  020 7631 3880
Hamleys *020 7734 3161*

Harrods *020 7730 1234*
Harvey Nichols
  020 7235 5000
Hatchards *020 7439 9921*
Heal's *020 7636 1666*
HMV *020 7631 3423*
Jaeger *020 7200 4000*
John Lewis *020 7629 7711*
Laura Ashley (Regent St)
  020 7355 1363
Liberty *020 7734 1234*
Lillywhites *020 7930 3181*
London Pavilion
  020 7437 1838
Marks & Spencer
  (Marble Arch) *020 7935 7954*
Marks & Spencer (Oxford St)
  020 7437 7722
Mothercare *020 7580 1688*
Next (Regent St)
  020 7434 2515

Plaza on Oxford St
  020 7637 8811
Selfridges *020 7629 1234*
Sotheby's *020 7493 8080*
Top Shop & Top Man
  020 7636 7700
Tower Records *020 7439 2500*
Trocadero *020 7439 1791*
Victoria Place Shopping
  Centre *020 7931 8811*
Virgin Megastore
  020 7580 5822
Waterstones (Gower St)
  020 7636 1577
Waterstones (Piccadilly)
  020 7851 2400

TRAVEL INFORMATION

Transport for London provide impartial advice through their Travel Information Service, which covers all aspects of travelling on London's major public transport networks. Information can be obtained by calling the Travel Information Call Centre (020 7222 1234) which is open 24 hours, or from visiting the Transport for London Web Site (www.transportforlondon.gov.uk), or from the network of Travel Information Centres.

Travel Information Centres can be found at the following locations (opening times vary):

Railway Stations
Euston
Paddington
Victoria

Underground Stations
Heathrow Airport Terminals 1, 2, 3
King's Cross
Liverpool Street
Oxford Circus
Piccadilly Circus
St James's Park

Bus Stations
Brent Cross Bus Station
North Greenwich Interchange
West Croydon Bus Station

THE UNDERGROUND

The Underground is the quickest way to travel around Greater London. Trains run between 05.30–24.00 Mon–Sat and 07.30–23.30 Sun (approx). It is advisable to check the details of the last train to your desired destination. Daily, weekly, monthly or annual Travelcards can provide considerable savings and can be used for travel on the Underground, London

Buses, Docklands Light Railway, Tramlink and National Rail Networks.

BUSES

Covering the whole of Greater London they tend to be slower than the Underground, especially in the rush hours, but can be more pleasant and you see so much more. London buses run 06.00–24.00 Mon–Sat and 07.30–22.00 Sun (approx). A Night Bus service runs between 23.00–05.00 although this service does not run as frequently, or operate as many routes as the daytime service.

RAILWAYS

Fares and bookings are the responsibility of the individual train operating companies. For national fares and timetable enquiries telephone National Rail enquiries on 08457 484950, or visit the National Rail Web Site at www.nationalrail.co.uk.

TAXIS

The black taxicab is one of London's best loved and instantly recognisable symbols. Most of the main tourist areas will have a taxi rank, but black cabs can also be hailed in the street when the "For Hire" sign is illuminated. Tips are discretionary but an extra 10%–15% of the fare is usually given.

RIVER SERVICES

Riverboat services operate between many of London's piers on a regular timetabled basis. For full details of services contact the London Travel Information Service for their Guide to Riverboat Services on 020 7222 1234, or visit the Transport for London Web Site (www.transportforlondon.gov.uk) and use the interactive map.

COACHES

The main provincial coach companies operate from Victoria Coach Station which is located at 164 Buckingham Palace Road, SW1. Tel 020 7730 3466 and travel all over Britain and the Continent. Booking is necessary.

LONDON AIRPORTS

London City Airport
King George V Dock, Silvertown E16
020 7474 5555

London Gatwick Airport
Perimeter Road North, Crawley, Surrey.
01293 535353

London Heathrow Airport
Bath Road, Hounslow, Hillingdon.
0870 000123

London Luton Airport
Percival Way, Luton, Beds.
01582 405100

London Southend Airport
Southend-on-Sea, Essex.
01702 608100

London Stansted Airport
Near Bishop's Stortford, Essex.
01279 680500

LOST PROPERTY

London Transport
Property lost on buses and on the Underground will be kept at the station where found for 48 hours. Any item not claimed within this time will be forwarded to the Lost Property Office, 200 Baker Street, London NW1 5RT. To claim your property you may write a letter, send a lost property enquiry form (available from any Underground Station), fax the office on 020 7918 1028, or visit the office in person between 09.30 and 14.00 Mon–Fri. The office will not take telephone enquiries.

National Rail
Enquiries should be directed to the relevant train company, or the train company at your point of departure.

Taxis
For any property lost in one of London's Licensed Taxis contact: The Public Carriage Office, 15 Penton Street, London, N1 9PU. Tel 020 7833 0996. It is advisable to leave at least 48 hours before enquiring.

Anywhere else
Apply to the nearest police station.

USEFUL WEB SITES

There are many useful web sites which cover every aspect of living in and visiting London. The sites listed here provide helpful links to many sites and provide the most up-to-date information on the city.

www.londontown.com
Official London Tourist Board Site

www.timeout.com
Entertainment Guide

www.officiallondontheatre.co.uk
Theatre Guide

www.london-uk-tours.demon.co.uk
London Tours

www.londontransport.co.uk
Transport for London

www.bbc.co.uk/weather
Weather Information

www.royalresidences.com
Offical Royal Residencies Guide

The following is a listing of named places that appear in this atlas.

Abbey Wood 136 C6
Acton 124 B1
Addington 199 T10
Addiscombe 184 D14
Aldborough Hatch 81 R6
Aldersbrook 97 S4
Alperton 105 P1
Anerley 184 G1
Arkley 39 P10
Avery Hill 153 M11

B
Balham 163 U1
Barbican 20 A3
Barking 117 K1
Barkingside 81 K6
Barnehurst 155 U6
Barnes 143 N4
Barnet 40 F6
Barnet Gate 39 M12
Barnsbury 93 L12
Battersea 145 U1
Bayswater 14 D7
Beckenham 186 E2
Beckton 116 H10
Becontree 100 J5
Becontree Heath 101 N2
Beddington 196 G4
Beddington Corner 181 U11
Bedford Park 124 H5
Belgravia 24 E12
Bell Green 167 T7
Bellingham 168 C6
Belmont 68 H4
Belsize Park 91 S13
Belvedere 137 R7
Benhilton 195 L5
Bermondsey 29 M11
Berrylands 177 U11
Bethnal Green 13 R6
Bexley 155 P12
Bexleyheath 155 M9
Bickley 188 E5
Blackfen 153 U12
Blackheath 151 K3
Blackheath Park 151 N6
Bloomsbury 18 A2
Borehamwood 38 C5
Borough, The 28 A7
Bow 113 U4
Bowes Park 59 K11
Brentford 123 K12
Brimsdown 45 T5
Brixton 147 K8
Broad Green 183 P12
Broadgate 20 F2
Brockley 149 R8
Bromley E3 114 D8
Bromley, Brom 187 L3
Bromley Common 188 D13
Bromley Park 186 J2
Brompton 23 N11
Brondesbury 90 C12
Brondesbury Park 107 U1
Brunswick Park 57 U4
Buckhurst Hill 47 S14
Burnt Oak 70 F1
Bush Hill Park 44 D10
Bushey Heath 52 C2
Bushey Mead 180 B5

C
Camberwell 35 U14
Camden Town 110 E2

Canning Town 115 N12
Canonbury 93 T12
Canons Park 53 S13
Carpenders Park 51 M4
Carshalton 195 U8
Carshalton Beeches 195 N12
Carshalton on the Hill 196 B14
Castelnau 125 N11
Catford 168 E2
Chadwell Heath 82 G11
Charlton 133 U12
Cheam 194 C13
Chelsea 31 K11
Chessington 191 R12
Chigwell 65 K6
Childs Hill 90 G3
Chingford 62 D2
Chingford Green 63 M1
Chingford Hatch 62 E7
Chipping Barnet 40 D9
Chislehurst 170 J13
Chislehurst West 170 F10
Chiswick 124 H11
Church End N3 72 D3
Church End NW10 88 J11
Clapham 146 C6
Clapham Park 146 G10
Clapton Park 95 R8
Claygate 190 D13
Clayhall 80 E4
Clerkenwell 11 P11
Cockfosters 41 U8
Coldblow 173 U3
Collier Row 83 N2
Collier's Wood 163 P13
Coombe 160 E13
Copse Hill 161 N14
Cottenham Park 179 P2
Cranbrook 98 G2
Cranford 120 A14
Crayford 155 U11
Creekmouth 117 U8
Cricklewood 90 A7
Crouch End 74 F11
Croydon 197 U3
Cubitt Town 132 F5
Custom House 116 B11

D
Dagenham 101 N11
Dalston 94 F13
Dartmouth Park 92 C6
De Beauvoir Town 112 B1
Debden 49 N5
Debden Green 49 K1
Deptford 131 T10
Dollis Hill 89 R6
Dormer's Wells 103 S13
Downham 169 L8
Ducks Island 40 A11
Dulwich 148 C13

E
Ealing 105 N13
Earls Court 126 F9
Earlsfield 163 L1
East Acton 124 J1
East Barnet 41 S12
East Dulwich 148 H12
East Finchley 73 N7
East Ham 116 B4
East Molesey 176 A7

East Sheen 142 F8
East Wickham 135 U14
Eastcote 66 F12
Eastcote Village 66 B9
Eden Park 186 A9
Edgware 54 D10
Edmonton 60 E7
Elmers End 185 R6
Elmstead 170 B10
Eltham 152 B12
Enfield 44 F5
Enfield Highway 45 M6
Enfield Town 44 A5
Enfield Wash 45 N1

F
Falconwood 153 P6
Farnborough 203 L10
Feltham 156 B4
Finchley 73 K2
Finsbury 11 L6
Finsbury Park 93 P2
Foots Cray 172 D11
Forest Gate 97 N10
Forest Hill 167 R2
Fortis Green 73 U8
Friday Hill 62 H4
Friern Barnet 57 S8
Fulham 144 C4
Fullwell Cross 81 N2
Furzedown 164 B9

G
Gants Hill 80 G10
Golders Green 72 J13
Goodmayes 100 C2
Gospel Oak 92 C9
Grange Hill 65 N11
Grange Park 43 R8
Green Street Green 203 R13
Greenford 103 S6
Greenwich 132 G14
Grove Park SE12 169 P4
Grove Park W4 124 D13
Gunnersbury 124 C7

H
Hackbridge 196 C3
Hackney 95 K13
Hackney Wick 95 U10
Hadley 40 E4
Haggerston 13 R1
Hainault 65 S13
Hale End 62 H11
Ham 159 M6
Hammersmith 125 U9
Hampstead 91 R6
Hampstead Garden Suburb 73 K10
Hampton 175 S1
Hampton Hill 157 U11
Hampton Wick 177 L2
Hanwell 122 F2
Hanworth 156 H8
Harlesden 106 J4
Harringay 75 N10
Harrow 68 A12
Harrow on the Hill 86 D2
Harrow Weald 68 C1
Hatch End 50 J12
Hayes 187 R13

Headstone 67 U9
Hendon 71 S8
Herne Hill 147 T10
Heston 121 L14
High Barnet 40 B3
High Beach 47 N2
Higham Hill 77 T4
Highams Park 62 G10
Highbury 93 T9
Highgate 73 S13
Highwood Hill 55 N4
Hinchley Wood 190 F4
Hither Green 151 K12
Holborn 18 F5
Holders Hill 72 A3
Holloway 92 J8
Homerton 95 S9
Honor Oak 149 N11
Honor Oak Park 149 T12
Hornsey 75 L5
Hounslow 139 M6
Hounslow West 138 G6
Hoxton 12 G4
Hyde, The 71 M8

I
Ilford 99 L6
Isleworth 140 E6
Islington 111 R2

J
Joydens Wood 173 U9

K
Kennington 35 K10
Kensal Green 108 A5
Kensal Rise 108 A3
Kensal Town 108 B7
Kensington 126 E3
Kentish Town 92 F10
Kenton 69 K9
Keston 201 U10
Kew 124 A12
Kidbrooke 151 R5
Kilburn 108 F2
King's Cross 10 A1
Kingsbury 70 D11
Kingsland 94 C12
Kingston upon Thames 177 S4
Kingston Vale 161 K8

L
Ladywell 150 C9
Lambeth 26 J12
Lamorbey 171 U2
Lampton 139 S2
Lea Bridge 95 N6
Lee 150 J7
Lessness Heath 137 T10
Lewisham 150 D7
Leyton 96 C3
Leytonstone 78 H14
Limehouse 113 R13
Lisson Grove 7 K11
Little Ealing 123 M7
Little Ilford 98 E9
Long Ditton 191 N2
Longlands 171 M5

Place	No.	Grid
Loughton	48	E9
Lower Clapton	95	L8
Lower Edmonton	60	G2
Lower Holloway	93	L10
Lower Sydenham	167	N7
Loxford	99	M9

M

Place	No.	Grid
Maida Hill	108	G8
Maida Vale	6	C9
Manor Park	98	C7
Mark's Gate	82	J3
Marylebone	15	T6
Mayfair	16	G12
Merry Hill	51	R2
Merton	181	M1
Merton Park	180	G2
Mile End	113	P5
Mill Hill	55	P10
Millwall	132	B6
Mitcham	181	U7
Monken Hadley	40	F2
Monks Orchard	105	T14
Morden	180	H8
Morden Park	180	D11
Mortlake	142	F5
Motspur Park	179	R11
Mottingham	169	U3
Muswell Hill	74	E5

N

Place	No.	Grid
Neasden	89	K6
New Addington	200	E14
New Barnet	40	J7
New Beckenham	167	T11
New Charlton	133	U7
New Cross	131	S14
New Cross Gate	149	N2
New Eltham	170	H4
New Malden	178	J5
New Southgate	58	G8
Newbury Park	81	R10
Newington	28	B11
Nine Elms	33	P14
Noel Park	75	P2
Norbiton	178	C3
Norbury	183	L1
North Acton	106	G9
North Beckton	116	D8
North Cheam	194	B7
North Cray	173	N5
North Finchley	57	P10
North Harrow	67	N11
North Hyde	121	K8
North Kensington	107	U11
North Sheen	142	A4
North Wembley	87	K3
North Woolwich	134	D3
Northolt	85	L13
Northumberland Heath	137	T14
Norwood	166	B10
Norwood Green	121	P7
Norwood New Town	165	U11
Notting Hill	108	D13
Nunhead	149	M6

O

Place	No.	Grid
Oakleigh Park	57	P2
Oakwood	42	G11
Old Bexley	155	S14
Old Ford	113	U1
Old Malden	192	H2
Old Oak Common	107	K9

Place	No.	Grid
Orpington	203	U2
Osidge	58	C2
Osterley	122	A13

P

Place	No.	Grid
Paddington	14	F4
Palmers Green	59	N5
Park Langley	186	G10
Park Royal	106	B5
Parsons Green	144	D2
Peckham	148	F1
Penge	167	L13
Pentonville	10	H3
Perivale	105	L2
Petersham	159	R1
Petts Wood	189	N9
Pimlico	33	L6
Pinner	67	K7
Pinner Green	66	F2
Pinnerwood Park	66	E1
Plaistow E13	115	L5
Plaistow, Brom	169	L11
Plumstead	135	R9
Ponders End	45	N9
Poplar	114	C14
Poverest	189	U10
Preston	69	R14
Primrose Hill	109	U2
Putney	144	B9
Putney Heath	143	T13
Putney Vale	161	N4

Q

Place	No.	Grid
Queensbury	69	P5

R

Place	No.	Grid
Rayners Lane	85	M1
Raynes Park	179	S4
Redbridge	80	E12
Regent's Park	8	J3
Richmond	141	S11
Roehampton	143	N10
Rosehill	181	K14
Rotherhithe	131	N5
Rowley Green	39	L8
Roxeth	86	A3
Ruislip Manor	84	A3
Rush Green	83	U14

S

Place	No.	Grid
St. Helier	181	N14
St. James's	25	R4
St. John's	150	A3
St. John's Wood	6	J6
St. Luke's	12	C9
St. Margarets	140	G10
St. Pancras	10	B8
St. Paul's Cray	189	U4
Sands End	145	L2
Selhurst	184	D11
Seven Kings	81	S14
Sewardstone	46	F2
Sewardstonebury	46	J8
Shacklewell	94	F7
Shadwell	113	M14
Shepherd's Bush	125	U1
Shirley	199	N6
Shooter's Hill	153	L2
Shoreditch	13	M11
Shortlands	187	K6
Sidcup	171	U8
Silvertown	133	U3
Snaresbrook	79	L9

Place	No.	Grid
Soho	17	R7
Somers Town	9	S4
South Acton	124	C5
South Beddington	196	H11
South Chingford	61	U9
South Croydon	197	U10
South Hackney	95	K14
South Hampstead	91	K11
South Harrow	85	R4
South Kensington	30	C1
South Lambeth	147	K1
South Norwood	184	F5
South Oxhey	50	F6
South Ruislip	84	G8
South Tottenham	76	D10
South Wimbledon	162	J13
South Woodford	79	L4
Southall	120	J1
Southborough	188	F11
Southend	168	F6
Southfields	162	H1
Southgate	58	E3
Southwark	27	R4
Spring Grove	140	C1
Stamford Hill	94	C2
Stanmore	52	H10
Stepney	113	M10
Stockwell	146	J4
Stoke Newington	94	C3
Stonebridge	106	D1
Stoneleigh	193	N10
Strand	18	B10
Stratford	96	E11
Strawberry Hill	158	C6
Streatham	165	K8
Streatham Hill	147	L14
Streatham Park	164	D8
Streatham Vale	164	E14
Stroud Green	75	L13
Sudbury	86	H9
Summerstown	162	J6
Sunbury	174	C5
Sundridge	169	S11
Surbiton	177	R11
Sutton	194	J11
Sydenham	167	L10

T

Place	No.	Grid
Teddington	158	H11
Thames Ditton	176	E11
Thamesmead	117	U14
Thamesmead North	118	H11
Thamesmead West	135	L6
Thornton Heath	183	S8
Tokyngton	88	C11
Tolworth	192	B4
Tooting Graveney	163	S11
Tottenham	60	C14
Tottenham Hale	76	J5
Totteridge	56	C2
Tufnell Park	92	H7
Tulse Hill	165	S2
Twickenham	140	J14

U

Place	No.	Grid
Underhill	40	G11
Upper Clapton	94	J2
Upper Edmonton	60	H10
Upper Elmers End	185	T11
Upper Holloway	92	F5
Upper Norwood	166	B13
Upper Sydenham	166	G7
Upper Tooting	163	R6
Upper Walthamstow	78	E6
Upton	97	S14
Upton Park	115	U2

V

Place	No.	Grid
Vauxhall	34	E7

W

Place	No.	Grid
Waddon	197	M5
Walham Green	144	G1
Wallington	196	F10
Walthamstow	78	C4
Walworth	35	U6
Wandsworth	144	E9
Wanstead	79	R13
Wapping	29	T1
Watford Heath	50	J1
Wealdstone	68	F6
Welling	154	A5
Wembley	87	S9
Wembley Park	87	U4
West Acton	106	A12
West Barnes	179	R8
West Brompton	30	A10
West Dulwich	166	A5
West Ewell	192	H13
West Green	75	U6
West Ham	97	M14
West Hampstead	91	K10
West Harrow	67	T14
West Heath	136	H11
West Hendon	71	K13
West Kilburn	108	E5
West Molesey	175	L9
West Norwood	165	S5
West Wickham	200	F3
Westbourne Green	108	G10
Westminster	25	L10
Weston Green	190	E2
Whetstone	57	K4
Whitechapel	21	R7
Whitton	139	S14
Widmore	187	U5
Willesden	89	M12
Willesden Green	89	R13
Wimbledon	162	E11
Wimbledon Park	162	E3
Winchmore Hill	43	L14
Wood Green	74	J2
Woodford	63	R12
Woodford Bridge	64	E13
Woodford Green	63	M8
Woodford Wells	63	S6
Woodlands	140	B4
Woodside	184	G11
Woolwich	134	G9
Worcester Park	193	N4
World's End	43	N6
Wrythe, The	195	T4

Y

Place	No.	Grid
Yeading	102	E6

The following is a listing of underground, light railway and main line railway stations that appear in this atlas.

Abbey Wood	136	F6
Acton Central	124	G1
Acton Main Line	106	F12
Acton Town	124	B4
Addington Village	200	A12
Albany Park	172	H3
Aldgate	21	M7
Aldgate East	21	N6
Alexandra Palace	75	K3
All Saints	114	D13
Alperton	105	R1
Anerley	184	J1
Angel	11	M3
Angel Road	61	L10
Archway	92	F3
Arena	185	L10
Arnos Grove	58	F9
Arsenal	93	P6
Avenue Road	185	P3

B

Baker Street	8	B12
Balham	164	C2
Bank	20	D8
Barbican	19	T2
Barking	99	M13
Barkingside	81	P7
Barnehurst	155	T4
Barnes	143	N6
Barnes Bridge	143	K4
Barons Court	126	C9
Battersea Park	128	C14
Bayswater	14	C10
Beckenham Hill	168	E9
Beckenham	186	B1
Junction		
Beckenham	185	R2
Road		
Beckton	116	G10
Beckton Park	116	E13
Becontree	100	G12
Beddington Lane	182	F12
Belgrave Walk	181	P7
Bellingham	168	D5
Belsize Park	91	S10
Belvedere	137	P6
Bermondsey	29	U9
Berrylands	178	C8
Bethnal Green	112	J7
Bexley	173	P1
Bexleyheath	155	K5
Bickley	188	D5
Bingham Road	198	G1
Birkbeck	185	M5
Blackfriars	19	P10
Blackheath	151	L4
Blackhorse Lane	184	H13
Blackhorse Road	77	P7
Blackwall	114	F14
Bond Street	16	G8
Borough	28	A7
Boston Manor	122	H8
Bounds Green	58	H13
Bow Church	114	B5
Bow Road	114	A6
Bowes Park	58	J13
Brent Cross	72	B13
Brentford	123	M11
Brimsdown	45	S4
Brixton	147	N7
Brockley	149	S5
Bromley North	187	P2
Bromley South	187	P6
Bromley-by-Bow	114	E6
Brondesbury	90	E13
Brondesbury Park	108	C1
Bruce Grove	76	F4
Buckhurst Hill	64	B3
Burnt Oak	70	F1

Bush Hill Park	44	E11

C

Caledonian Road	93	L11
Caledonian Road &	93	M13
Barnsbury		
Cambridge Heath	113	K3
Camden Road	92	E14
Camden Town	110	D1
Canada Water	131	M4
Canary Wharf	132	C2
Canning Town	115	K11
Cannon Street	20	C10
Canonbury	93	U10
Canons Park	53	R13
Carpenders Park	50	H5
Carshalton	195	U7
Carshalton	195	T12
Beeches		
Castle Bar Park	104	F10
Catford	150	B14
Catford Bridge	150	B14
Chadwell Heath	82	G14
Chalk Farm	92	A13
Chancery Lane	19	K3
Charing Cross	26	C1
Charlton	133	T9
Cheam	194	D13
Chessington North	191	S10
Chessington South	191	P13
Chigwell	65	K6
Chingford	46	J14
Chislehurst	188	G3
Chiswick	124	F14
Chiswick Park	124	F8
Church Street	197	T4
City Thameslink	19	P7
Clapham Common	146	F7
Clapham High	146	H6
Street		
Clapham	145	R7
Junction		
Clapham North	146	J6
Clapham South	146	D11
Clapton	95	K4
Claygate	190	C11
Clock House	185	S2
Cockfosters	42	A7
Colindale	71	K5
Colliers Wood	163	P13
Coombe Lane	199	L10
Covent Garden	18	C9
Cricklewood	90	B7
Crofton Park	149	T10
Crossharbour &	132	D5
London Arena		
Crouch Hill	75	L14
Croydon Central	197	U4
Crystal Palace	166	G12
Custom House	115	S13
Cutty Sark	132	E12
Cyprus	116	H13

D

Dagenham Dock	119	M5
Dagenham East	101	U10
Dagenham	101	M12
Heathway		
Dalston Kingsland	94	D10
Debden	49	M8
Denmark Hill	148	B4
Deptford	132	A13
Deptford Bridge	150	B1
Devons Road	114	C8
Dollis Hill	89	N10
Drayton Green	104	F12
Drayton Park	93	P9
Dundonald Road	162	E13

E

Ealing Broadway	105	P13
Ealing Common	123	U1
Earls Court	126	H9
Earlsfield	163	L2
East Acton	107	L12
East Croydon	198	B4
East Dulwich	148	D7
East Finchley	73	R8
East Ham	98	D13
East India	114	G13
East Putney	144	D9
Eastcote	66	E14
Eden Park	186	B10
Edgware	54	C11
Edgware Road	15	P3
Edmonton Green	60	H4
Elephant &	35	T1
Castle		
Elmers End	185	P7
Elmstead	170	C12
Woods		
Elstree &	38	A7
Borehamwood		
Eltham	152	E9
Elverson Road	150	D3
Embankment	26	D1
Enfield Chase	43	T6
Enfield Town	44	C6
Esher	190	A3
Essex Road	93	T14
Euston	9	P6
Euston Square	9	P9

F

Fairlop	81	P2
Falconwood	153	N7
Farringdon	19	N1
Feltham	156	C1
Fenchurch Street	21	K9
Fieldway	200	C14
Finchley Central	72	G2
Finchley Road	91	M12
Finchley Road &	91	L10
Frognal		
Finsbury Park	93	P3
Forest Gate	97	P9
Forest Hill	167	M3
Fulham Broadway	126	H13
Fulwell	158	A7

G

Gallions Reach	117	K13
Gants Hill	80	H11
Gipsy Hill	166	D9
Gloucester Road	30	F2
Golders Green	90	G1
Goldhawk	125	T4
Road		
Goodge Street	17	R2
Goodmayes	100	B1
Gordon Hill	43	S1
Gospel Oak	92	B8
Grange Hill	65	P8
Grange Park	43	S10
Gravel Hill	199	S12
Great Portland	8	J11
Street		
Green Park	25	K2
Greenford	104	B1
Greenwich	132	E13
Grove Park	169	R6
Gunnersbury	124	D9

H

Hackbridge	196	C3
Hackney Central	95	K11

Hackney Downs	94	J10
Hackney Wick	96	A12
Hainault	65	R13
Hammersmith	125	U8
Hampstead	91	M7
Hampstead Heath	91	S8
Hampton	175	P1
Hampton Court	176	D7
Hampton Wick	177	M2
Hanger Lane	105	S6
Hanwell	104	D14
Harlesden	106	H3
Harringay	75	P12
Harringay Green	75	S12
Lanes		
Harrington Road	185	K7
Harrow &	68	D7
Wealdstone		
Harrow on the Hill	68	D12
Hatch End	51	N13
Haydons Road	163	L10
Hayes	201	N2
Headstone Lane	67	S2
Hendon	71	N11
Hendon Central	71	T10
Herne Hill	147	S11
Heron Quays	132	B2
High Barnet	40	G8
High Street	22	A8
Kensington		
Highams Park	62	G11
Highbury &	93	R12
Islington		
Highgate	74	C12
Hinchley Wood	190	E5
Hither Green	150	J11
Holborn	18	E4
Holland Park	126	E1
Holloway Road	93	M9
Homerton	95	P11
Honor Oak Park	149	P12
Hornsey	75	M8
Hounslow	139	S9
Hounslow Central	139	R5
Hounslow East	139	T4
Hounslow West	138	J4
Hyde Park Corner	24	E6

I

Ilford	98	J5
Island Gardens	132	E9
Isleworth	140	E3

K

Kempton Park	156	C13
(Race days only)		
Kennington	35	P6
Kensal Green	107	U5
Kensal Rise	108	A4
Kensington	126	D5
(Olympia)		
Kent House	185	R1
Kentish Town	92	E10
Kentish Town West	92	C12
Kenton	68	J11
Kew Bridge	123	U10
Kew Gardens	142	A2
Kidbrooke	151	S6
Kilburn	90	E12
Kilburn High Road	108	J2
Kilburn Park	108	H3
King's Cross	10	C3
King's Cross	10	B5
St. Pancras		
King's Cross	10	D5
Thameslink		
Kingsbury	70	B10
Kingston	177	R2

L

Ladbroke Grove	108	C11
Ladywell	150	C9
Lambeth North	27	K9
Lancaster Gate	15	K10
Latimer Road	108	B13
Lebanon Road	198	D4
Lee	151	M12
Leicester Square	17	U10
Lewisham	150	E5
Leyton	96	F6
Leyton Midland Road	96	E1
Leytonstone	97	K1
Leytonstone High Road	97	K3
Limehouse	113	R12
Liverpool Street	20	H3
Lloyd Park	198	E8
London Bridge	28	F3
London Fields	95	K14
Loughborough Junction	147	S5
Loughton	48	D10
Lower Sydenham	167	U9

M

Maida Vale	6	D6
Malden Manor	178	J14
Manor House	75	T14
Manor Park	98	B8
Mansion House	20	A9
Marble Arch	16	A8
Maryland	96	J11
Marylebone	7	T12
Maze Hill	132	J11
Merton Park	180	G1
Mile End	113	T6
Mill Hill Broadway	55	K11
Mill Hill East	56	C13
Mitcham	181	S8
Mitcham Junction	182	B10
Monument	20	F10
Moorgate	20	D3
Morden	180	J6
Morden Road	181	K3
Morden South	180	H9
Mornington Crescent	9	M2
Mortlake	142	F5
Motspur Park	179	R10
Mottingham	170	E1
Mudchute	132	D7

N

Neasden	89	K9
New Barnet	41	N9
New Beckenham	167	T13
New Cross	131	T14
New Cross Gate	149	R1
New Eltham	171	L2
New Malden	179	K6
New Southgate	58	C10
Newbury Park	81	P11
Norbiton	178	B2
Norbury	183	L2
North Acton	106	H9
North Dulwich	148	B10
North Ealing	105	U12
North Greenwich	132	J3
North Harrow	67	R10
North Sheen	142	A7
North Wembley	87	N6
North Woolwich	134	H3
Northfields	123	L6
Northolt	85	N12
Northolt Park	85	S8
Northumberland Park	61	K14

Northwick Park	68	J13
Northwood Hills	66	B3
Norwood Junction	184	G8
Notting Hill Gate	126	G1
Nunhead	149	M4

O

Oakleigh Park	41	P13
Oakwood	42	F9
Old Street	12	E8
Orpington	203	S3
Osterley	122	A14
Oval	35	K12
Oxford Circus	17	L7

P

Paddington	14	J6
Palmers Green	59	M7
Park Royal	106	A7
Parsons Green	144	G2
Peckham Rye	148	G3
Penge East	167	M12
Penge West	167	K12
Perivale	104	H3
Petts Wood	189	M10
Phipps Bridge	181	N6
Piccadilly Circus	17	R11
Pimlico	33	S6
Pinner	67	K7
Plaistow	115	N3
Plumstead	135	P7
Ponders End	45	R10
Poplar	114	C14
Preston Road	87	R1
Prince Regent	115	T13
Pudding Mill Lane	114	D2
Putney	144	C8
Putney Bridge	144	E5

Q

Queen's Park	108	E4
Queens Road Peckham	149	L1
Queensbury	69	U5
Queenstown Road (Battersea)	146	D2
Queensway	14	C11

R

Ravensbourne	168	G14
Ravenscourt Park	125	R8
Rayners Lane	67	M14
Raynes Park	179	T3
Rectory Road	94	F6
Redbridge	80	B11
Regent's Park	8	H12
Richmond	141	R8
Roding Valley	64	A7
Rotherhithe	131	M3
Royal Albert	116	C13
Royal Oak	14	C4
Royal Victoria	115	N13
Ruislip Gardens	84	B7
Ruislip Manor	84	A2
Russell Square	10	B12

S

St. Helier	180	H12
St. James Street	77	S10
St. James's Park	25	S9
St. John's	150	B3
St. John's Wood	7	K2
St. Margarets	141	K12
St. Pancras	10	A5
St. Paul's	19	T7
Sandilands	198	F4
Selhurst	184	C10
Seven Kings	99	S2
Seven Sisters	76	D9

Shadwell	113	K13
Shepherd's Bush	126	A3
Shoreditch	13	P11
Shortlands	187	K3
Sidcup	172	B4
Silver Street	60	F9
Silvertown & London City Airport	134	C2
Sloane Square	32	C3
Snaresbrook	79	N9
South Acton	124	E6
South Bermondsey	131	L9
South Croydon	198	B9
South Ealing	123	N5
South Greenford	104	D5
South Hampstead	91	M14
South Harrow	85	U5
South Kensington	31	L2
South Kenton	87	M2
South Merton	180	F6
South Quay	132	C3
South Ruislip	84	E9
South Tottenham	76	E10
South Wimbledon	163	K14
South Woodford	79	R4
Southall	121	L3
Southbury	45	K8
Southfields	162	E1
Southgate	58	G1
Southwark	27	N4
Stamford Brook	125	M7
Stamford Hill	76	D13
Stanmore	53	N8
Stepney Green	113	N8
Stockwell	147	K3
Stoke Newington	94	E3
Stonebridge Park	88	C14
Stoneleigh	193	N10
Stratford	96	G12
Strawberry Hill	158	E5
Streatham	164	H9
Streatham Common	164	G13
Streatham Hill	164	J4
Sudbury & Harrow Road	87	K9
Sudbury Hill	86	D8
Sudbury Hill Harrow	80	D8
Sudbury Town	87	K11
Sunbury	174	A1
Sundridge Park	169	R13
Surbiton	177	R11
Surrey Quays	131	N7
Sutton	195	L11
Sutton Common	194	J4
Swiss Cottage	91	N13
Sydenham	167	M8
Sydenham Hill	166	E6
Syon Lane	122	H14

T

Teddington	158	G11
Temple	18	H10
Thames Ditton	176	E13
Therapia Lane	183	K13
Thornton Heath	183	T7
Tolworth	192	D4
Tooting	163	U12
Tooting Bec	164	A5
Tooting Broadway	163	S9
Tottenham Court Road	17	T5
Tottenham Hale	76	H7
Totteridge & Whetstone	57	L3
Tower Gateway	21	M10
Tower Hill	21	L11
Tufnell Park	92	E7
Tulse Hill	165	S3
Turnham Green	125	K7
Turnpike Lane	75	R6

Twickenham	140	G14

U

Upney	99	U13
Upper Holloway	92	G4
Upton Park	115	T1

V

Vauxhall	34	D8
Victoria	33	K1

W

Waddon	197	N7
Waddon Marsh	197	M2
Wallington	196	D11
Walthamstow Central	78	B9
Walthamstow Queens Road	78	A9
Wandle Park	197	P4
Wandsworth Common	145	T14
Wandsworth Road	146	F4
Wandsworth Town	145	K8
Wanstead	79	R12
Wanstead Park	97	R8
Wapping	131	L2
Warren Street	9	M10
Warwick Avenue	6	E12
Waterloo	26	J5
Waterloo East	27	L4
Waterloo International	26	H5
Wellesley Road	198	A3
Welling	154	A4
Wembley Central	87	R10
Wembley Park	88	B5
Wembley Stadium	87	U9
West Acton	106	B11
West Brompton	126	H10
West Croydon	197	T2
West Dulwich	166	A2
West Ealing	104	J14
West Finchley	56	J12
West Ham	114	J5
West Hampstead	90	H12
West Hampstead (Thameslink)	90	H11
West Harrow	67	T12
West India Quay	114	B14
West Kensington	126	E9
West Norwood	165	S6
West Sutton	194	G8
West Wickham	186	F14
Westbourne Park	108	F9
Westcombe Park	133	P10
Westferry	114	A13
Westminster	26	B7
White City	107	U14
White Hart Lane	60	E13
Whitechapel	112	J9
Whitton	139	T14
Willesden Green	89	U11
Willesden Junction	107	M5
Wimbledon	162	F12
Wimbledon Chase	180	D3
Wimbledon Park	162	H6
Winchmore Hill	59	R1
Wood Green	75	N3
Wood Street	78	F7
Woodford	63	S11
Woodgrange Park	98	B9
Woodside	184	J12
Woodside Park	56	J8
Woolwich Arsenal	135	K7
Woolwich Dockyard	134	E7
Worcester Park	193	N2

INDEX TO HOSPITALS

The following is a listing of hospitals that appear in this atlas.

A

Acton Hospital	124	B3
Athlone House	91	T1
Atkinson Morley's Hospital	161	R14

B

B.U.P.A. Bushey Hospital	52	E1
Barnes Hospital	142	J6
Barnet General Hospital	40	A8
Beckenham Hospital	185	U4
Bethlem Royal Hospital	186	A14
Blackheath Hospital, The	151	L6
Bolingbroke Hospital	145	S10
Bromley Hospital	187	R7

C

Carshalton War Memorial Hospital	195	U11
Cassel Hospital Psychotherapeutic Community	159	N7
Central Middlesex Hospital	106	F5
Chadwell Heath Hospital	82	D10
Charing Cross Hospital	126	A11
Charter Nightingale Hospital	15	S1
Chelsea & Westminster Hospital	30	G11
Chiswick Lodge Hospital	125	M10
Churchill Private Clinic	27	L10
Clayponds Hospital	123	R8
Clementine Churchill Hospital	86	E5
Colindale Hospital	70	J4
Collingham Gardens Hospital	30	D4
Coppetts Wood Hospital	73	U1
Cromwell Hospital, The	30	B1

D

| Devonshire Hospital | 16 | E2 |

E

Ealing Hospital N.H.S. Trust	122	B2
East Ham Memorial Hospital	98	B13
Eastman Dental Hospital	10	F9
Edgware Community Hospital	54	D14

F

| Farnborough Hospital | 202 | H6 |
| Finchley Memorial Hospital | 57 | M13 |

G

Garden Hospital, The	71	T5
Goldie Leigh Hospital	136	E12
Goodmayes Hospital	82	B9
Gordon Hospital	33	R3
Great Ormond Street Hospital for Children	10	D12
Greenwich District Hospital	133	L10
Guy's Hospital	28	E5

H

Hammersmith Hospital	107	R11
Hayes Grove Priory Hospital	201	P4
Heart Hospital, The	16	F3
Holly House Hospital	63	S4
Homerton Hospital	95	N9
Hornsey Central Hospital	74	G9
Hospital of St. John & St. Elizabeth	7	K3
Huntley Centre	9	R12

K

| King Edward VII Hospital for Officers | 16 | F2 |
| King George Hospital (Barley La) | 81 | N11 |

King George Hospital (Eastern Av)	82	C9
King's College Hospital	148	A4
King's College Hospital Dulwich	148	D8
Kingsbury Hospital	70	A7
Kingston Hospital	178	C1

L

Ladywell Mental Health Unit - University Hospital Lewisham	150	B11
Latimer Day Hospital	17	L2
Lister Hospital	32	G8
London Bridge Hospital	28	F2
London Chest Hospital	113	M3
London Clinic, The	8	F12
London Foot Hospital & School of Podiatric Medicine	9	M12
London Independent Hospital	113	N9

M

Mayday Hospital	183	R11
Maudsley Hospital, The	148	B4
Memorial Hospital	152	H3
Middlesex Hospital	17	N3
Mildmay Mission Hospital	13	L7
Molesey Hospital	175	P9
Moorfields Eye Hospital	12	C7
Morland Road Day Hospital	101	P14

N

National Hospital for Neurology & Neurosurgery, The	10	D12
Nelson Hospital	180	E3
New Victoria Hospital	179	K1
Newham General Hospital	115	U7
North London Blood Transfusion Centre	70	H4
North London Nuffield Hospital	43	P3
North Middlesex Hospital	60	E9
Northwick Park Hospital	68	J14
Northwood & Pinner Community Hospital	66	A2

O

| Orpington Hospital | 203 | U7 |

P

Parkside Clinic	162	A5
Plaistow Hospital	115	T4
Portland Hospital for Women & Children, The	8	J12
Princess Grace Hospital, The	8	D12
Princess Louise Kensington Hospital	108	A10
Putney Hospital	143	T4

Q

Queen Charlotte and Chelsea Hospital	107	P12
Queen Elizabeth Hospital	134	D13
Queen Mary's Hospital	91	M6
Queen Mary's Hospital (Sidcup)	172	B11
Queen Mary's Hospital for Children	195	M2
Queen Mary's University Hospital (Roehampton)	143	P11

R

Roding Hospital	80	A6
Roehampton Priory Hospital	143	L8
Royal Brompton Hospital	31	N6
Royal Free Hospital, The	91	S9

Royal Hospital Chelsea	32	B8
Royal Hospital Richmond	141	R6
Royal Hospital for Neuro-Disability	144	C12
Royal London Homeopathic Hospital	18	D1
Royal London Hospital (Mile End)	113	P7
Royal London Hospital (St. Clements)	113	U6
Royal London Hospital (Whitechapel)	112	J10
Royal Marsden Hospital (Fulham)	31	M5
Royal National Orthopaedic Hospital W1	9	K11
Royal National Orthopaedic Hospital, Stan	53	L3
Royal National Throat, Nose & Ear Hospital	10	E6

S

St. Andrew's Hospital	114	D7
St. Andrew's at Harrow (Bowden House Hospital)	86	D4
St. Ann's Hospital	75	U10
St. Anthony's Hospital	194	B2
St. Bartholomew's Hospital	19	S4
St. Bernard's Hospital	122	A3
St. Charles Hospital	108	B9
St. George's Hospital (London)	163	P9
St. Helier Hospital	195	M2
St. Joseph's Hospice	113	K1
St. Luke's Woodside Hospital	74	B7
St. Lukes Hospital for the Clergy	9	L11
St. Mary's Hospital	15	L5
St. Pancras Hospital & Hospital for Tropical Diseases	110	G2
St. Thomas's Hospital	26	F9
Shirley Oaks Hospital	185	M14
Sloane Hospital, The	186	H2
South Western Hospital	147	K6
Southwood Hospital	74	B13
Springfield Hospital (London)	163	R4
Stamford, The	125	N7
Stepney Day Hospital	113	M12
Surbiton General Hospital	177	S12

T

Tavistock Centre	91	N12
Teddington Memorial Hospital	158	D11
Thorpe Coombe Hospital	78	E5
Tolworth Hospital	192	A3
Trinity Hospice	146	D7

U

United Elizabeth Garrett Anderson Hospital & Soho Hospital for Women	9	T7
University Lewisham Hospital	150	D10
University of London - U.C.L. - University College Hospital	9	P11

W

Wellington Hospital North	7	L3
Wellington Hospital South	7	M4
West Middlesex University Hospital	140	H3
Whipps Cross Hospital	78	H11
Whittington Hospital	92	E3
Willesden Community Hospital	89	P14
Winifred House	39	L12
Wolfson Medical Rehabilitation Centre	161	R14

General Abbreviations

All	Alley	Ct	Court	Hts	Heights	Rds	Roads
Allot	Allotments	Cts	Courts	Ind	Industrial	Rec	Recreation
Amb	Ambulance	Ctyd	Courtyard	Int	International	Res	Reservoir
App	Approach	Dep	Depot	Junct	Junction	Ri	Rise
Arc	Arcade	Dev	Development	La	Lane	S	South
Av	Avenue	Dr	Drive	Las	Lanes	Sch	School
Bdy	Broadway	Dws	Dwellings	Lib	Library	Sec	Secondary
Bk	Bank	E	East	Lo	Lodge	Shop	Shopping
Bldgs	Buildings	Ed	Education	Lwr	Lower	Sq	Square
Boul	Boulevard	Elec	Electricity	Mag	Magistrates	St.	Saint
Bowl	Bowling	Embk	Embankment	Mans	Mansions	St	Street
Br	Bridge	Est	Estate	Mem	Memorial	Sta	Station
C of E	Church of	Ex	Exchange	Mkt	Market	Sts	Streets
	England	Exhib	Exhibition	Mkts	Markets	Sub	Subway
Cath	Cathedral	FB	Footbridge	Ms	Mews	Swim	Swimming
Cem	Cemetery	FC	Football Club	Mt	Mount	TA	Territorial Army
Cen	Central, Centre	Fld	Field	Mus	Museum	TH	Town Hall
Cft	Croft	Flds	Fields	N	North	Tenn	Tennis
Cfts	Crofts	Fm	Farm	NT	National Trust	Ter	Terrace
Ch	Church	Gall	Gallery	Nat	National	Thea	Theatre
Chyd	Churchyard	Gar	Garage	PH	Public House	Trd	Trading
Cin	Cinema	Gdn	Garden	PO	Post Office	Twr	Tower
Circ	Circus	Gdns	Gardens	Par	Parade	Twrs	Towers
Cl	Close	Govt	Government	Pas	Passage	Uni	University
Co	County	Gra	Grange	Pav	Pavilion	Vil	Villa, Villas
Coll	College	Grd	Ground	Pk	Park	Vw	View
Comm	Community	Grds	Grounds	Pl	Place	W	West
Conv	Convent	Grn	Green	Pol	Police	Wd	Wood
Cor	Corner	Grns	Greens	Prec	Precinct	Wds	Woods
Coron	Coroners	Gro	Grove	Prim	Primary	Wf	Wharf
Cors	Corners	Gros	Groves	Prom	Promenade	Wk	Walk
Cotts	Cottages	Gt	Great	Pt	Point	Wks	Works
Cov	Covered	Ho	House	Quad	Quadrant	Yd	Yard
Crem	Crematorium	Hos	Houses	RC	Roman Catholic		
Cres	Crescent	Hosp	Hospital	Rd	Road		

Abbreviations of Post Towns

Bark	Barking	Esher	Esher	S Croy	South Croydon
Barn	Barnet	Felt	Feltham	Sid	Sidcup
Beck	Beckenham	Grnf	Greenford	Stan	Stanmore
Belv	Belvedere	Har	Harrow	Sthl	Southall
Bex	Bexley	Hayes	Hayes	Sun	Sunbury-on-
Bexh	Bexleyheath	Hmptn	Hampton		Thames
Borwd	Borehamwood	Houns	Hounslow	Surb	Surbiton
Brent	Brentford	Ilf	Ilford	Sutt	Sutton
Brom	Bromley	Islw	Isleworth	Swan	Swanley
Buck H	Buckhurst Hill	Kes	Keston	T Ditt	Thames Ditton
Bushey	Bushey	Kings T	Kingston upon Thames	Tedd	Teddington
Cars	Carshalton	Loug	Loughton	Th Hth	Thornton Heath
Chess	Chessington	Mitch	Mitcham	Twick	Twickenham
Chig	Chigwell	Mord	Morden	W Mol	West Molesey
Chis	Chislehurst	N Mal	New Malden	W Wick	West Wickham
Croy	Croydon	Nthlt	Northolt	Wal Abb	Waltham Abbey
Dag	Dagenham	Nthwd	Northwood	Wall	Wallington
Dart	Dartford	Orp	Orpington	Walt	Walton-on-Thames
E Mol	East Molesey	Pnr	Pinner	Wat	Watford
Edg	Edgware	Pot B	Potters Bar	Wdf Grn	Woodford Green
Enf	Enfield	Rain	Rainham	Well	Welling
Epp	Epping	Rich	Richmond	Wem	Wembley
Epsom	Epsom	Rom	Romford	Wor Pk	Worcester Park
Erith	Erith	Ruis	Ruislip		

Notes

Each street name is followed by its Postal District (or, if outside the London Postal District, by its Post Town) and then by a page and map square where the name can be found. For example Oxford St W1 17 N6 will be found in the Postal District of W1 on page 17 in square N6.

There are entries in the index which are followed by a number in **bold italics**. These numbers can be found on the map where there is insufficient space to show the street name in full. For example the location of Abbots Wk, W8 **2** 22 B11 will be found by a number **2** in the square B11 on page 22.

Name	Page	Grid
Aaron Hill Rd E6	116	H9
Abbess Cl E6	116	D10
Abbess Cl SW2	165	R2
Abbeville Rd N8	74	H8
Abbeville Rd SW4	146	G9
Abbey Av, Wem	105	S3
Abbey Cl, Hayes	120	C1
Abbey Cl, Nthlt **1**	103	L6
Abbey Cl, Pnr	66	D5
Abbey Cres, Belv	137	N7
Abbey Dr SW17	164	B9
Abbey Gdns NW8	6	G3
Abbey Gdns W6	126	C12
Abbey Gro SE2	136	D7
Abbey Ind Est, Wem	105	T1
Abbey La E15	114	F3
Abbey La, Beck	168	B13
Abbey Orchard St SW1	25	T10
Abbey Pk, Beck	168	B14
Abbey Retail Pk, Bark	117	K1
Abbey Rd E15	114	J3
Abbey Rd NW6	6	H4
Abbey Rd NW8	109	M4
Abbey Rd NW10	106	E6
Abbey Rd SE2	136	H7
Abbey Rd SW19	163	L14
Abbey Rd, Bark	117	K1
Abbey Rd, Belv	136	H7
Abbey Rd, Bexh	155	K7
Abbey Rd, Croy	197	S5
Abbey Rd, Enf	44	D9
Abbey Rd, Ilf	81	N10
Abbey Rd Est NW8	109	K1
Abbey St E13	115	P7
Abbey St SE1	29	M9
Abbey Ter SE2	136	E7
Abbey Vw NW7	55	M5
Abbey Wk, W Mol	175	R6
Abbey Way SE2	136	H5
Abbey Wf Ind Est, Bark	117	P4
Abbey Wd Rd SE2	136	D7
Abbeydale Rd, Wem	105	U2
Abbeyfield Est SE16	131	L8
Abbeyfield Rd SE16	131	L7
Abbeyfields Cl NW10	106	B4
Abbeyhill Rd, Sid	172	E3
Abbot St E8	94	E11
Abbots Cl N1	93	T12
Abbots Cl, Orp	203	M1
Abbots Cl, Ruis	84	G6
Abbots Dr, Har	85	P4
Abbots Gdns N2	73	N7
Abbots Gdns, W8 **3**	22	B11
Abbots Grn, Croy	199	P11
Abbots La SE1	28	J4
Abbots Manor Est SW1	32	H5
Abbots Pk SW2	165	N2
Abbot's Pl NW6	108	J1
Abbot's Rd E6	116	B2
Abbots Rd, Edg	54	J13
Abbots Ter N8	74	J12
Abbots Wk, W8 **2**	22	B11
Abbots Way, Beck	185	R9
Abbotsbury Cl E15	114	F3
Abbotsbury Cl W14	126	E4
Abbotsbury Gdns, Pnr	66	E12
Abbotsbury Ms SE15	149	L6
Abbotsbury Rd W14	126	E4
Abbotsbury Rd, Brom	201	L4
Abbotsbury Rd, Mord	181	K7
Abbotsford Av N15	75	U8
Abbotsford Gdns, Wdf Grn	63	N14
Abbotsford Rd, Ilf	100	B4
Abbotshade Rd SE16	131	P1
Abbotshall Av N14	58	F6
Abbotshall Rd SE6	168	G2
Abbotsleigh Cl, Sutt	194	J13
Abbotsleigh Rd SW16	164	E8
Abbotsmede Cl, Twick	158	E4
Abbotstone Rd SW15	143	U6
Abbotswell Rd SE4	149	U10
Abbotswood Cl, Belv **2**	136	J6
Abbotswood Gdns, Ilf	80	F6
Abbotswood Rd SE22	148	D7
Abbotswood Rd SW16	164	G4
Abbotswood Way, Hayes	120	D1
Abbott Av SW20	180	B2
Abbott Cl, Hmptn	157	K11
Abbott Cl, Nthlt	85	L12
Abbott Rd E14	114	E10
Abbotts Cl SE28	118	E14
Abbotts Cl, Rom	83	R5
Abbotts Cres E4	62	H8
Abbotts Cres, Enf	43	S3
Abbotts Dr, Wem	86	J3
Abbotts Pk Rd E10	78	E13
Abbotts Rd, Barn	40	J8
Abbotts Rd, Mitch	182	G6
Abbotts Rd, Sthl	121	K2
Abbotts Rd, Sutt	194	D7
Abbotts Wk, Bexh	136	H13
Abchurch La EC4	20	E9
Abdale Rd W12	125	S2
Aberavon Rd E3	113	S6
Abercairn Rd SW16	164	F13
Aberconway Rd, Mord	181	K6
Abercorn Cl NW7	56	C14
Abercorn Cl NW8	6	F5
Abercorn Cres, Har	85	S2
Abercorn Gdns, Har	69	N13
Abercorn Gdns, Rom	82	C11
Abercorn Pl NW8	6	F4
Abercorn Rd NW7	56	D14
Abercorn Rd, Stan	53	L13
Abercorn Way SE1	37	S5
Abercrombie Dr, Enf	44	G1
Abercrombie St SW11	145	S3
Aberdare Cl, W Wick	200	F4
Aberdare Gdns NW6	91	K14
Aberdare Gdns NW7	56	A14
Aberdare Rd, Enf	45	L7
Aberdeen La N5	93	T9
Aberdeen Pk N5	93	T9
Aberdeen Pk Ms N5	93	U8
Aberdeen Pl NW8	6	J10
Aberdeen Rd N5	93	T7
Aberdeen Rd N18	60	H9
Aberdeen Rd NW10	89	M9
Aberdeen Rd, Croy	197	U8
Aberdeen Rd, Har	68	E4
Aberdeen Ter SE3	150	G3
Aberdour Rd, Ilf	100	C5
Aberdour St SE1	36	G1
Aberfeldy St E14	114	F11
Aberford Gdns SE18	152	C1
Aberford Rd, Borwd	38	A4
Aberfoyle Rd SW16	164	G12
Abergeldie Rd SE12	151	S11
Abernethy Rd SE13	150	J8
Abersham Rd E8	94	F9
Abery St SE18	135	R8
Abingdon Cl SW19	163	M12
Abingdon Rd N3	73	L3
Abingdon Rd SW16	182	J2
Abingdon Rd W8	126	H5
Abingdon St SW1	26	B9
Abingdon Vil W8	126	H6
Abinger Cl, Bark	100	A8
Abinger Cl, Brom	188	C6
Abinger Cl, Wall	197	K10
Abinger Gdns, Islw	140	C6
Abinger Gro SE8	131	T12
Abinger Ms W9	108	G7
Abinger Rd W4	125	K5
Ablett St SE16	131	L10
Abney Gdns, N16 **1**	94	E4
Aboyne Dr SW20	179	N4
Aboyne Est SW17	163	N6
Aboyne Rd NW10	88	J5
Aboyne Rd SW17	163	N4
Abridge Rd, Chig	49	R11
Abyssinia Cl SW11	145	S8
Acacia Av N17	60	B13
Acacia Av, Brent	122	J14
Acacia Av, Mitch **5**	182	C4
Acacia Av, Ruis	66	B14
Acacia Av, Wem	87	R9
Acacia Cl SE8	131	R8
Acacia Cl SE20	184	H4
Acacia Cl, Orp	189	P10
Acacia Cl, Stan	52	D11
Acacia Dr, Sutt	194	F2
Acacia Gdns NW8	7	L2
Acacia Gdns, W Wick	200	E4
Acacia Gro SE21	166	B4
Acacia Gro, N Mal	178	J6
Acacia Pl NW8	7	M1
Acacia Rd E11	97	K4
Acacia Rd E17	77	S12
Acacia Rd N22	75	P1
Acacia Rd NW8	7	M1
Acacia Rd SW16	183	K1
Acacia Rd W3	106	F13
Acacia Rd, Beck	185	T5
Acacia Rd, Enf	44	B1
Acacia Rd, Hmptn	157	P11
Acacia Rd, Mitch	182	C4
Acacia Way, Sid	171	U1
Academy Gdns, Croy	198	F2
Academy Gdns, Nthlt	102	H4
Academy Pl SE18	152	F2
Academy Rd SE18	152	F1
Acanthus Dr SE1	37	S6
Acanthus Rd SW11	146	A5
Accommodation Rd NW11	72	F14
Acer Av, Hayes	102	J9
Acfold Rd SW6	144	J2
Achilles Cl SE1	37	T6
Achilles Rd NW6	90	G9
Achilles St SE14	131	S14
Achilles Way W1	24	E4
Acklam Rd W10	108	E10
Acklington Dr NW9	70	J1
Ackmar Rd SW6	144	G2
Ackroyd Dr E3	113	U9
Ackroyd Rd SE23	149	P13
Acland Cl, SE18 **2**	135	P13
Acland Cres SE5	148	A7
Acland Rd NW2	89	S11
Acol Cres, Ruis	84	D9
Acol Rd NW6	90	J14
Aconbury Rd, Dag	118	C1
Acorn Cl E4	62	C9
Acorn Cl, Chis	171	M10
Acorn Cl, Enf	43	R2
Acorn Cl, Hmptn	157	R11
Acorn Cl, Stan	53	K14
Acorn Ct, Ilf	81	R10
Acorn Gdns SE19	184	E2
Acorn Gdns W3	106	H10
Acorn Wk SE16	131	S1
Acorn Way SE23	167	P5
Acorn Way, Orp	203	K8
Acorns, The, Chig	65	R8
Acre Dr SE22	148	G8
Acre La SW2	147	L8
Acre La, Cars	196	B8
Acre La, Wall	196	B8
Acre Rd SW19	163	P11
Acre Rd, Dag	101	S13
Acre Rd, KingsT	177	S1
Acris St SW18	145	M10
Acton Cl N9	60	H3
Acton Hill Ms W3	124	C1
Acton La NW10	106	F6
Acton La W3	124	F4
Acton La W4	124	G6
Acton Ms E8	112	E1
Acton Pk Ind Est W3	124	H3
Acton St WC1	10	F7
Acuba Rd SW18	162	J3
Acworth Cl N9	45	L14
Ada Gdns, E14 **3**	114	G11
Ada Gdns E15	115	M2
Ada Pl E2	112	H2
Ada Rd SE5	130	C14
Ada Rd, Wem	87	M5
Ada St E8	112	J2
Adair Cl SE25	184	J6
Adair Rd W10	108	D8
Adam & Eve Ms W8	126	H5
Adam Pl N16	94	E4
Adam Rd E4	61	T12
Adam St, WC2 **14**	18	D12
Adam Wk SW6	125	U13
Adams Cl, N3 **2**	56	H14
Adams Cl NW9	88	D3
Adams Cl, Surb	177	U12
Adams Ct, EC2 **9**	20	F6
Adams Pl E14	132	C1
Adams Pl N7	93	M10
Adams Rd N17	76	C3
Adams Rd, Beck	185	R9
Adams Row W1	16	E11
Adams Sq, Bexh	154	H6
Adams Wk, KingsT	177	R3
Adams Way, Croy	184	G11
Adamson Rd E16	115	P12
Adamson Rd NW3	91	P13
Adamsrill Cl, Enf	44	B11
Adamsrill Rd SE26	167	R7
Adare Wk SW16	165	L5
Adderley Gdns SE9	170	H7
Adderley Gro, SW11 **1**	146	A10
Adderley Rd, Har	68	E2
Adderley St E14	114	E12
Addington Ct SW14	142	G5
Addington Dr N12	57	M12
Addington Gro SE26	167	R8
Addington Rd E3	114	A5
Addington Rd E16	115	K8
Addington Rd N4	75	N12
Addington Rd, Croy	197	P1
Addington Rd, W Wick	201	K4
Addington Sq SE5	36	B12
Addington St SE1	26	G7
Addington Village Rd, Croy	200	B10
Addis Cl, Enf	45	N1
Addiscombe Av, Croy	184	G14
Addiscombe Cl, Har	69	L8
Addiscombe Ct Rd, Croy	198	D2
Addiscombe Gro, Croy	198	B4
Addiscombe Rd, Croy	198	C4
Addison Av N14	42	E11
Addison Av W11	126	C1
Addison Av, Houns	139	T2
Addison Br Pl W14	126	D7
Addison Cl, Nthwd	66	A1
Addison Cl, Orp	189	M12
Addison Cres W14	126	E5
Addison Dr SE12	151	R10
Addison Gdns W14	126	A5
Addison Gdns, Surb	177	U8
Addison Gro W4	125	K6
Addison Pl W11	126	C2
Addison Pl, Sthl	103	P14
Addison Rd E11	79	P11
Addison Rd E17	78	D9
Addison Rd SE25	184	H7
Addison Rd W14	126	D4
Addison Rd, Brom	188	A9
Addison Rd, Enf	45	M1
Addison Rd, Ilf	81	M2
Addison Rd, Tedd	158	J12
Addison Way NW11	72	G8
Addison Way, Hayes	102	B12
Addison's Cl, Croy	199	T3
Addle Hill EC4	19	S9
Addle St EC2	20	A4
Adecroft Way, W Mol	175	T6
Adela Av, N Mal	179	S8
Adela St W10	108	C7
Adelaide Av SE4	149	T8
Adelaide Cl, Stan	52	G7

Name	No	Grid
Adelaide Cotts W7	122	E3
Adelaide Gdns, Rom	82	J9
Adelaide Gro W12	125	P1
Adelaide Rd E10	96	E6
Adelaide Rd NW3	91	R14
Adelaide Rd, SW18 1	144	H9
Adelaide Rd W13	122	H3
Adelaide Rd, Chis	171	K10
Adelaide Rd, Houns	138	J2
Adelaide Rd, Ilf	99	K3
Adelaide Rd, Rich	141	U8
Adelaide Rd, Sthl	121	K7
Adelaide Rd, Surb	177	R10
Adelaide Rd, Tedd	158	F11
Adelaide St, WC2 13	18	B12
Adelaide Ter, Brent	123	N10
Adelaide Wk, SW9 10	147	P8
Adelina Gro E1	113	L9
Adelina Ms SW12	164	H1
Adeline Pl WC1	17	T4
Adeliza Cl, Bark	99	L13
Adelphi Ter, WC2 9	18	D12
Aden Gro N16	94	A7
Arden Rd, Enf	45	S8
Aden Rd, Ilf	81	K14
Aden Ter N16	94	A7
Adeney Cl W6	126	B12
Adenmore Rd SE6	150	B14
Adie Rd W6	125	T6
Adine Rd E13	115	R7
Adler St E1	21	S5
Adley St E5	95	S9
Adlington Cl N18	60	C9
Admaston Rd SE18	135	M12
Admiral Pl SE16	131	S1
Admiral Seymour Rd SE9	152	E7
Admiral Sq SW10	145	M1
Admiral St SE8	150	B2
Admiral Wk W9	108	H9
Admirale Cl E18	79	S7
Admirals Wk, NW3 2	91	M6
Admirals Way E14	132	B3
Admiralty Rd, Tedd	158	E12
Adolf St SE6	168	C3
Adolphus Rd N4	93	S2
Adolphus St SE8	131	U13
Adomar Rd, Dag	100	H6
Adpar St W2	7	K12
Adrian Av NW2	89	R1
Adrian Ms SW10	30	C10
Adrienne Av, Sthl	103	M6
Advance Rd SE27	165	T7
Advent Way N18	61	P9
Adys Rd SE15	148	F6
Aerodrome Rd NW4	71	N5
Aerodrome Rd NW9	71	L4
Aerodrome Way, Houns	120	F12
Aeroville NW9	71	K4
Affleck St, N1 2	10	G4
Afghan Rd SW11	145	R4
Agamemnon Rd NW6	90	F9
Agar Cl, Surb	191	T4
Agar Gro NW1	92	G13
Agar Gro Est NW1	92	G14
Agar Pl NW1	92	F14
Agar St WC2	18	C11
Agate Cl E16	116	B12
Agate Rd W6	125	T6
Agatha Cl, E1 14	131	K1
Agaton Rd SE9	171	M3
Agave Rd NW2	89	T8
Agdon St EC1	11	P9
Agincourt Rd NW3	91	T8
Agnes Av, Ilf 2	98	J7
Agnes Cl E6	116	H13
Agnes Gdns, Dag	100	H7
Agnes Rd W3	125	L2
Agnes St E14	113	U11
Agnesfield Cl N12	57	S12
Agnew Rd SE23	149	P13
Agricola Pl, Enf	44	F9
Aidan Cl, Dag	100	J7
Aileen Wk E15	97	M13
Ailsa Av, Twick	140	H10
Ailsa Rd, Twick	140	J10
Ailsa St E14	114	F9
Ainger Ms, NW3 5	91	U14
Ainger Rd NW3	91	T14
Ainsdale Cl, Orp	203	P1
Ainsdale Cres, Pnr	67	P5
Ainsdale Dr SE1	37	S8
Ainsdale Rd W5	105	P8
Ainsdale Rd, Wat	50	E5
Ainsley Av, Rom	83	S12
Ainsley Cl N9	60	C1
Ainsley St E2	113	K6
Ainslie Wk, SW12 2	146	C14
Ainslie Wd Cres E4	62	C10
Ainslie Wd Gdns E4	62	C8
Ainslie Wd Rd E4	62	C10
Ainsty Est SE16	131	N4
Ainsworth Cl NW2	89	P5
Ainsworth Cl SE15	148	D3
Ainsworth Rd E9	95	L14
Ainsworth Rd, Croy	197	S3
Ainsworth Way NW8	109	L1
Aintree Av E6	116	C2
Aintree Cres, Ilf	81	M3
Aintree Rd, Grnf	105	K3
Aintree St SW6	126	D14
Air Links Ind Est, Houns	120	F10
Air St W1	17	P12
Airdrie Cl N1	93	L14
Airdrie Cl, Hayes	102	J10
Airedale Av W4	125	L9
Airedale Av S, W4 13	125	M10
Airedale Rd SW12	145	U14
Airedale Rd W5	123	M5
Airlie Gdns W8	126	G2
Airlie Gdns, Ilf	99	K2
Airport Roundabout, E16 1	134	B1
Airthrie Rd, Ilf	100	C3
Aisgill Av W14	126	F10
Aisher Rd SE28	118	E13
Aislibie Rd SE12	151	K8
Aitken Cl E8	112	G1
Aitken Cl, Mitch	181	T14
Aitken Rd SE6	168	C3
Aitken Rd, Barn	39	T10
Ajax Av NW9	70	J6
Ajax Rd NW6	90	G9
Akabusi Cl, Croy 2	184	G11
Akehurst St SW15	143	P12
Akenside Rd NW3	91	N10
Akerman Rd SW9	147	R2
Akerman Rd, Surb	177	M11
Alabama St SE18	135	R13
Alacross Rd W5	123	M4
Alan Dr, Barn	40	C11
Alan Gdns, Rom	83	N14
Alan Hocken Way E15	115	J4
Alba Cl, Hayes	102	H8
Alba Pl W11	108	E11
Albacore Cres SE13	150	C11
Alban Cres, Borwd	38	C1
Albany, The, Wdf Grn	63	L7
Albany Cl N15	75	S8
Albany Cl SW14	142	D8
Albany Cl, Bex	154	F14
Albany Ct E4	46	C12
Albany Ctyd W1	17	N12
Albany Cres, Edg	54	B13
Albany Cres, Esher	190	C12
Albany Mans SW11	127	S14
Albany Ms, SE5 1	36	B11
Albany Ms, Brom	169	P11
Albany Ms, Kings T	159	P12
Albany Ms, Sutt	194	J10
Albany Pk Av, Enf	45	M1
Albany Pk Rd, Kings T	159	P12
Albany Pas, Rich	141	T10
Albany Pl N7	93	N8
Albany Pl, Brent 5	123	R12
Albany Rd E10	78	B13
Albany Rd E12	98	B8
Albany Rd E17	77	S11
Albany Rd N4	75	M12
Albany Rd N18	61	K10
Albany Rd SE5	36	C11
Albany Rd SW19	162	J9
Albany Rd W13	105	K13
Albany Rd, Belv	137	M11
Albany Rd, Bex	154	F14
Albany Rd, Brent	123	P12
Albany Rd, Chis	171	K10
Albany Rd, N Mal	178	H7
Albany Rd, Rom	83	L11
Albany St NW1	8	J7
Albany Vw, Buck H	63	P1
Albatross St SE18	135	R13
Albatross Way SE16	131	N4
Albemarle SW19	162	A3
Albemarle App, Ilf 1	81	K12
Albemarle Av, Twick	157	L2
Albemarle Gdns, Ilf	81	K12
Albemarle Gdns, N Mal	178	G8
Albemarle Pk, Stan 2	53	L10
Albemarle Rd, Barn	41	S14
Albemarle Rd, Beck	186	D2
Albemarle St W1	17	L12
Albemarle Way EC1	11	P11
Alberon Gdns NW11	72	E8
Albert Av E4	62	A8
Albert Av, SW8 6	129	L14
Albert Br SW3	31	R12
Albert Br SW11	127	S12
Albert Br Rd SW11	127	S14
Albert Carr Gdns SW16	164	J10
Albert Cl E9	113	K2
Albert Cl N22	74	G1
Albert Ct SW7	23	K8
Albert Dr SW19	162	C3
Albert Embk SE1	34	D5
Albert Gdns E1	113	N12
Albert Gate SW1	24	B6
Albert Gro SW20	180	B1
Albert Hall Mans SW7	23	K8
Albert Ms W8	22	F10
Albert Pl N3	72	G1
Albert Pl W8	22	D8
Albert Rd E10	96	F3
Albert Rd E16	134	C2
Albert Rd E17	78	A10
Albert Rd E18	79	S5
Albert Rd N4	93	M1
Albert Rd N15	76	C11
Albert Rd N22	74	E2
Albert Rd NW4	72	B7
Albert Rd NW6	108	F4
Albert Rd NW7	55	M9
Albert Rd SE9	170	D5
Albert Rd SE20	167	N12
Albert Rd SE25	184	H7
Albert Rd W5	105	K8
Albert Rd, Barn	41	N7
Albert Rd, Belv	137	M10
Albert Rd, Bex	155	P13
Albert Rd, Brom	188	B10
Albert Rd, Buck H	64	B3
Albert Rd, Dag	101	M2
Albert Rd, Hmptn	157	U9
Albert Rd, Har	67	U6
Albert Rd, Houns	139	P8
Albert Rd, Ilf	99	K6
Albert Rd, Kings T	177	T4
Albert Rd, Mitch	181	U5
Albert Rd, N Mal	179	M8
Albert Rd, Rich	141	S9
Albert Rd, Sthl	120	H6
Albert Rd, Sutt	195	N10
Albert Rd, Tedd	158	F12
Albert Rd, Twick	158	E1
Albert Rd Est, Belv	137	M10
Albert Sq E15	97	K10
Albert Sq SW8	129	L14
Albert St N12	57	L9
Albert St NW1	9	K1
Albert Ter NW1	110	A2
Albert Ter NW10	106	G2
Albert Ter, Buck H	64	B3
Albert Ter Ms NW1	110	A1
Albert Way SE15	130	J13
Alberta Av, Sutt	194	D9
Alberta Est SE17	35	S6
Alberta Rd, Enf	44	F11
Alberta Rd, Erith	155	T1
Alberta St SE17	35	P6
Albion Av N10	74	A1
Albion Av SW8	146	G3
Albion Cl W2	15	R9
Albion Dr E8	94	G14
Albion Est SE16	131	N4
Albion Gdns W6	125	R7
Albion Gro N16	94	C7
Albion Hill SE13	150	D3
Albion Hill, Loug	47	U10
Albion Ms N1	111	N1
Albion Ms NW6	90	E13
Albion Ms W2	15	R9
Albion Pk, Loug	48	A10
Albion Pl EC1	19	P1
Albion Pl SE25	184	G6
Albion Pl W6	125	S8
Albion Rd E17	78	F5
Albion Rd N16	94	B8
Albion Rd N17	76	F4
Albion Rd, Bexh	155	N8
Albion Rd, Houns	139	P8
Albion Rd, Kings T	178	E2
Albion Rd, Sutt	195	N13
Albion Rd, Twick	158	D2
Albion Sq E8	94	F14
Albion St SE16	131	M4
Albion St W2	15	R8
Albion St, Croy	197	R2
Albion Ter E8	94	E14
Albion Vil Rd SE26	167	L5
Albion Way, EC1 8	19	T4
Albion Way SE13	150	F7
Albion Way, Wem	88	B6
Albion Yd E1	113	K9
Albrighton Rd SE22	148	D6
Albuhera Cl, Enf	43	P1
Albury Av, Bexh	154	J3
Albury Av, Islw	122	F14
Albury Cl, Hmptn	157	P12
Albury Dr, Pnr	50	G14
Albury Ms E12	97	T3
Albury Rd, Chess	191	R10
Albury St SE8	132	A12
Albyfield, Brom	188	F6
Albyn Rd SE8	150	A2
Alcester Cres E5	95	K3
Alcester Rd, Wall	196	D8
Alcock Cl, Wall	196	H14
Alcock Rd, Houns	120	G14
Aconbury Rd E5	94	G4
Alcorn Cl, Sutt	194	G3
Alcott Cl W7	104	E10
Alcuin Cl, Stan	53	L13
Aldborough Rd, Dag	101	U12
Aldborough Rd N, Ilf	81	U6
Aldborough Rd S, Ilf	99	R2
Aldbourne Rd W12	125	M2
Aldbridge St SE17	36	J6
Aldburgh Ms W1	16	F6
Aldbury Av, Wem	88	C13
Aldbury Ms N9	44	B14
Aldebert Ter SW8	129	K14
Aldeburgh Pl, Wdf Grn	57	P7
Aldeburgh St SE10	133	P9
Alden Av E15	115	L7
Aldenham St NW1	9	P4
Aldensley Rd W6	125	S6
Alder Cl SE15	37	N12
Alder Gro NW2	89	R4
Alder Ms, N19 10	92	E4
Alder Rd SW14	142	G5
Alder Rd, Sid	171	T6

Name	Page	Grid
Alder Wk, Ilf	99	N10
Alderbrook Rd SW12	146	C13
Alderbury Rd SW13	125	P12
Aldergrove Gdns, Houns	138	H3
Alderman Av, Bark	118	B5
Aldermanbury EC2	20	B6
Aldermanbury Sq EC2	20	B4
Aldermans Hill N13	59	K7
Alderman's Wk EC2	20	H4
Aldermary Rd, Brom	187	P1
Aldermoor Rd SE6	167	U5
Alderney Av, Houns	121	R14
Alderney Gdns, Nthlt	85	L13
Alderney Rd E1	113	N7
Alderney St SW1	33	K5
Alders, The N21	43	P12
Alders, The, Felt	157	K8
Alders, The, Houns	121	L11
Alders, The, W Wick	200	C2
Alders Av, Wdf Grn	62	J12
Alders Cl E11	97	R3
Alders Cl W5	123	N5
Alders Cl, Edg	54	E9
Alders Gro, E Mol	176	B9
Alders Rd, Edg	54	E9
Aldersbrook Av, Enf	44	C3
Aldersbrook Dr, Kings T	159	T11
Aldersbrook La E12	98	F6
Aldersbrook Rd E11	97	R3
Aldersbrook Rd E12	98	C6
Aldersey Gdns, Bark	99	P12
Aldersford Cl SE4	149	P9
Aldersgate St EC1	19	T2
Aldersgrove Av SE9	169	U6
Aldershot Rd NW6	108	F1
Aldersmead Av, Croy	185	P11
Aldersmead Rd, Beck	167	R14
Alderson Pl, Sthl	121	U2
Alderson St W10	108	D7
Alderton Cl NW10	88	H5
Alderton Cl, Loug	48	G8
Alderton Cres NW4	71	R10
Alderton Hall La, Loug	48	G8
Alderton Hill, Loug	48	D9
Alderton Ms, Loug 1	48	G7
Alderton Ri, Loug	48	G8
Alderton Rd SE24	147	T6
Alderton Rd, Croy	184	F13
Alderton Way NW4	71	R10
Alderton Way, Loug	48	F10
Alderville Rd SW6	144	F3
Alderwick Dr, Houns	140	A5
Alderwood Rd SE9	153	P11
Aldford St W1	24	E1
Aldgate EC3	21	L8
Aldgate Av, E1 4	21	M6
Aldgate High St EC3	21	L7
Aldine St W12	125	U3
Aldington Cl, Dag	100	F1
Aldington Rd SE18	134	B6
Aldis Ms, SW17 1	163	R10
Aldis St SW17	163	R10
Aldred Rd NW6	90	G9
Aldren Rd SW17	163	M6
Aldrich Gdns, Sutt	194	E6
Aldrich Ter, SW18 2	163	M3
Aldriche Way E4	62	E12
Aldridge Av, Edg	54	D5
Aldridge Av, Ruis	84	G3
Aldridge Av, Stan	69	S2
Aldridge Ri, N Mal	178	J13
Aldridge Rd Vil W11	108	F10
Aldridge Wk N14	42	J14
Aldrington Rd SW16	164	F9
Aldsworth Cl W9	6	A12
Aldwick Cl SE9	171	N5
Aldwick Rd, Croy	197	L6
Aldworth Gro SE13	150	E11
Aldworth Rd E15	96	J14
Aldwych WC2	18	G8
Aldwych Av, Ilf	81	M8
Alers Rd, Bexh	154	H9
Alestan Beck Rd E16	116	B11
Alexa Ct W8	30	A1
Alexander Av NW10	89	S14
Alexander Cl, Barn	41	N8
Alexander Cl, Brom	201	P1
Alexander Cl, Sid	153	S11
Alexander Cl, Sthl	121	U2
Alexander Cl, Twick	158	E4
Alexander Ms W2	14	A6
Alexander Pl SW7	31	N1
Alexander Rd N19	92	J4
Alexander Rd, Bexh	154	H3
Alexander Rd, Chis	171	K11
Alexander Sq SW3	31	P1
Alexander St W2	108	H11
Alexandra Av N22	74	H2
Alexandra Av SW11	146	A1
Alexandra Av W4	124	H14
Alexandra Av, Har	85	P6
Alexandra Av, Sthl	103	L14
Alexandra Av, Sutt	194	G6
Alexandra Cl, Har	85	R6
Alexandra Cotts SE14	149	U2
Alexandra Ct N14	42	E10
Alexandra Ct, Wem	87	U8
Alexandra Cres, Brom	169	L11
Alexandra Dr SE19	166	C10
Alexandra Dr, Surb	178	B13
Alexandra Gdns N10	74	D7
Alexandra Gdns W4	124	J14
Alexandra Gdns, Houns	139	R8
Alexandra Gro N4	93	S2
Alexandra Gro N12	57	K11
Alexandra Ms N2	73	U6
Alexandra Palace N22	74	G4
Alexandra Palace Way N22	74	F7
Alexandra Pk Rd N10	74	C3
Alexandra Pk Rd N22	74	H3
Alexandra Pl NW8	109	M1
Alexandra Pl SE25	184	B9
Alexandra Pl, Croy	198	C1
Alexandra Rd E6	116	G5
Alexandra Rd E10	96	E6
Alexandra Rd E17	77	U12
Alexandra Rd E18	79	R6
Alexandra Rd, N9 1	44	J13
Alexandra Rd N10	58	C13
Alexandra Rd N15	76	A9
Alexandra Rd NW4	72	A7
Alexandra Rd NW8	91	M14
Alexandra Rd SE26	167	N12
Alexandra Rd SW14	142	H6
Alexandra Rd SW19	162	G10
Alexandra Rd W4	124	H4
Alexandra Rd, Brent 1	123	P12
Alexandra Rd, Croy	184	C14
Alexandra Rd, Enf	45	P7
Alexandra Rd, Houns	139	S5
Alexandra Rd, Kings T	160	A14
Alexandra Rd, Mitch	163	S14
Alexandra Rd, Rich	141	U3
Alexandra Rd (Chadwell Heath),	82	J11
Alexandra Rd, T Ditt	176	F10
Alexandra Rd, Twick	141	M12
Alexandra Sq, Mord	180	H10
Alexandra St E16	115	N9
Alexandra St SE14	151	S13
Alexandra Wk, SE19 7	166	C10
Alexandria Rd W13	104	H14
Alexis St SE16	37	T1
Alfearn Rd E5	95	L7
Alford Grn, Croy	200	G12
Alford Pl N1	12	B4
Alford Rd SW8	146	H2
Alford Rd, Erith	137	U9
Alfoxton Av N15	75	R7
Alfred Cl W4	124	G8
Alfred Gdns, Sthl	103	K14
Alfred Ms W1	17	R2
Alfred Pl WC1	17	R2
Alfred Rd E15	97	L9
Alfred Rd SE25	184	H9
Alfred Rd W2	108	H9
Alfred Rd W3	124	F2
Alfred Rd, Belv	137	M10
Alfred Rd, Buck H	64	B3
Alfred Rd, Felt	156	E3
Alfred Rd, Kings T	177	T6
Alfred Rd, Sutt	195	M10
Alfred St E3	113	U5
Alfreda St SW11	146	C2
Alfred's Gdns, Bark	117	S3
Alfreds Way, Bark	117	M5
Alfreds Way Ind Est, Bark	118	B2
Alfreton Cl SW19	162	A5
Alfriston Av, Croy	183	K13
Alfriston Av, Har	67	R13
Alfriston Cl, Surb	177	T10
Alfriston Rd SW11	145	U9
Algar Cl, Islw	140	H6
Algar Cl, Stan	52	F10
Algar Rd, Islw	140	H6
Algarve Rd SW18	163	K2
Algernon Rd NW4	71	N12
Algernon Rd NW6	108	G2
Algernon Rd SE13	150	C8
Algers Cl, Loug	48	B10
Algers Mead, Loug	48	B10
Algers Rd, Loug	48	B10
Algiers Rd SE13	150	B8
Alibon Gdns, Dag	101	P9
Alibon Rd, Dag	101	M9
Alice Ct SW15	144	F7
Alice Gilliatt Ct W14	126	E11
Alice La E3	113	T2
Alice Ms, Tedd	158	E10
Alice St SE1	28	G11
Alice Thompson Cl SE12	169	T4
Alice Walker Cl SE24	147	S8
Alice Way, Houns	139	R8
Alicia Av, Har	69	K8
Alicia Cl, Har	69	L8
Alicia Gdns, Har	69	L7
Alie St E1	21	N7
Alington Cres NW9	88	F1
Alison Cl E6	116	H12
Alison Cl, Croy	199	N2
Aliwal Rd SW11	145	S8
Alkerden Rd, W4 8	125	K9
Alkham Rd N16	94	F4
All Hallows Rd N17	76	D1
All Saints Cl N9	60	G4
All Saints Dr SE3	151	K3
All Saints Ms, Har	52	D12
All Saints Pas, SW18 7	144	H9
All Saints Rd SW19	163	M13
All Saints Rd W3	124	E5
All Saints Rd W11	108	E10
All Saints St N1	10	E1
All Souls Av NW10	107	S3
All Souls Pl W1	17	K4
Allan Barclay Cl N15	76	E12
Allan Cl, N Mal	178	G10
Allan Way W3	106	E9
Allandale Av N3	72	D5
Allard Cres, Bushey	51	T2
Allard Gdns SW4	146	H10
Allardyce St SW4	147	L7
Allbrook Cl, Tedd	158	C9
Allcroft Rd NW5	92	B10
Allen Cl, Mitch	182	D1
Allen Cl, Sun	174	D2
Allen Edwards Dr SW8	146	J1
Allen Pl, Twick 5	158	H1
Allen Rd E3	113	T3
Allen Rd N16	94	C7
Allen Rd, Beck	185	N4
Allen Rd, Croy	197	M1
Allen Rd, Sun	174	D2
Allen St W8	126	H5
Allenby Cl, Grnf	103	P6
Allenby Rd SE23	167	R5
Allenby Rd, Sthl	103	P12
Allendale Av, Sthl	103	N12
Allendale Cl, SE5 8	148	A2
Allendale Cl SE26	167	P10
Allendale Rd, Grnf	86	J11
Allens Rd, Enf	45	M10
Allensbury Pl NW1	92	H14
Allenswood Rd SE9	152	D5
Allerford Ct, Har	67	S9
Allerford Rd SE6	168	D7
Allerton Rd N16	93	U3
Allestree Rd SW6	126	C14
Alleyn Cres SE21	166	B4
Alleyn Pk SE21	166	B6
Alleyn Pk, Sthl	121	N9
Alleyn Rd SE21	166	B4
Alleyndale Rd, Dag	100	E3
Allfarthing La SW18	145	L12
Allgood Cl, Mord	180	A12
Allgood St E2	13	P4
Allhallows La EC4	20	C11
Allhallows Rd E6	116	C11
Alliance Cl, Wem	87	N8
Alliance Rd E13	115	T8
Alliance Rd SE18	136	A13
Alliance Rd W3	106	C8
Allied Way W3	124	J3
Allingham Cl W7	104	F14
Allingham Ms, N1 2	11	T1
Allingham St N1	11	T1
Allington Av N17	60	D12
Allington Cl, Grnf	85	U14
Allington Ct, SW19 2	162	B10
Allington Ct, Enf	45	P10
Allington Rd NW4	71	S11
Allington Rd W10	108	C5
Allington Rd, Har	67	T9
Allington Rd, Orp	203	R2
Allington St SW1	25	K11
Allison Cl SE10	150	F2
Allison Gro SE21	166	D1
Allison Rd N8	75	P9
Allison Rd W3	106	F12
Allitsen Rd NW8	7	N2
Allnutt Way SW4	146	G9
Alloa Rd SE8	131	R9
Alloa Rd, Ilf	100	B3
Allonby Gdns, Wem	87	M2
Alloway Rd E3	113	S5
Allsop Pl NW1	8	B12
Allum Way N20	57	L2
Allwood Cl SE26	167	P8
Alma Av E4	62	F13
Alma Cres, Sutt	194	D9
Alma Gro SE1	37	P3
Alma Pl NW10	107	S6
Alma Pl SE19	166	E13
Alma Pl, Th Hth	183	P10
Alma Rd N10	58	C14
Alma Rd SW18	145	L9
Alma Rd, Cars	195	S9
Alma Rd, Enf	45	R10
Alma Rd, Esher	190	C1
Alma Rd, Sid	172	B5
Alma Rd, Sthl	102	J13
Alma Row, Har	68	B1
Alma Sq NW8	6	G5
Alma St E15	96	H11
Alma St NW5	92	D11
Alma Ter SW18	145	P13
Alma Wk E5	95	L8
Almeida St N1	93	R14
Almer Rd SW20	161	N13
Almeric Rd SW11	145	T8
Almington St N4	93	K2
Almond Av W5	123	R5
Almond Av, Cars	195	T4
Almond Cl SE15	148	H4
Almond Cl, Brom	188	G14
Almond Cl, Brom	122	J14
Brent		
Almond Rd N17	60	H14
Almond Rd SE16	131	K7
Almond Way, Borwd	38	C7
Almond Way, Brom	188	G13
Almond Way, Har	67	S4
Almond Way, Mitch	182	H9
Almonds Av, Buck H	63	N4
Almorah Rd N1	94	A14

Name	Page	Ref
Almorah Rd, Houns	138	H2
Alnwick Gro, Mord	181	K8
Alnwick Rd E16	115	U12
Alnwick Rd SE12	151	T14
Alperton La, Grnf	105	M5
Alperton La, Wem	105	R4
Alperton St W10	108	D7
Alpha Cl, NW1 *1*	7	S8
Alpha Gro E14	132	B4
Alpha Pl NW6	108	H3
Alpha Pl SW3	31	S9
Alpha Rd E4	62	B6
Alpha Rd N18	60	G11
Alpha Rd SE14	149	U1
Alpha Rd, Croy	198	C1
Alpha Rd, Enf	45	S8
Alpha Rd, Surb	177	T12
Alpha Rd,Tedd	158	A9
Alpha St SE15	148	G4
Alphabet Gdns, Cars	181	P12
Alphabet Sq E3	114	B10
Alphea Cl, SW19 *4*	163	R14
Alpine Av, Surb	192	E3
Alpine Cl, Croy	198	C6
Alpine Copse, Brom	188	G4
Alpine Gro E9	95	M14
Alpine Rd SE16	131	M8
Alpine Rd, Walt	174	B14
Alpine Vw, Cars	195	R10
Alpine Wk, Stan	52	D3
Alpine Way E6	116	G9
Alric Av NW10	88	H14
Alric Av, N Mal	179	K5
Alroy Rd N4	75	P13
Alsace Rd SE17	36	G6
Alscot Rd SE1	29	N12
Alscot Way SE1	37	M2
Alsike Rd SE2	136	G6
Alsike Rd, Erith	136	J6
Alsom Av, Wor Pk	193	M7
Alston Cl, Surb	177	K13
Alston Rd N18	60	J10
Alston Rd SW17	163	N8
Alston Rd, Barn	40	C5
Alt Gro SW19	162	E13
Altair Cl N17	60	F12
Altash Way SE9	170	F4
Altenburg Av W13	123	K5
Altenburg Gdns SW11	145	T7
Altham Rd, Pnr	51	K14
Althea St SW6	145	K4
Althorne Gdns E18	79	L8
Althorne Way, Dag	101	N3
Althorp Cl, Barn	39	N14
Althorp Rd SW17	163	T1
Althorpe Ms, SW11 *1*	145	P1
Althorpe Rd, Har	67	U9
Altmore Av E6	98	E13
Alton Av, Stan	52	F14
Alton Cl, Bex	173	K2
Alton Cl, Islw	140	F3
Alton Gdns, Beck	168	A14
Alton Gdns, Twick	140	B13
Alton Rd N17	76	B6
Alton Rd SW15	161	P1
Alton Rd, Croy	197	N6
Alton Rd, Rich	141	S8
Alton St E14	114	C10
Altyre Cl, Beck	185	T10
Altyre Rd, Croy	198	B4
Altyre Way, Beck	185	T10
Alva Way, Wat	50	H3
Alvanley Gdns NW6	90	J9
Alverston Gdns SE25	184	D9
Alverstone Av SW19	162	G4
Alverstone Av, Barn	57	S1
Alverstone Gdns SE9	171	L1
Alverstone Rd E12	98	G8
Alverstone Rd NW2	89	T13
Alverstone Rd, N Mal	179	M7
Alverstone Rd, Wem	87	U1
Alverton St SE8	131	T10
Alveston Av, Har	69	K6
Alvey Est SE17	36	G4
Alvey St SE17	36	G6
Alvia Gdns, Sutt	195	M7
Alvington Cres E8	94	E9
Alway Av, Epsom	192	F10
Alwold Cres SE12	151	S12
Alwyn Av W4	124	G10
Alwyn Cl, Croy	200	D14
Alwyn Gdns NW4	71	P7
Alwyn Gdns W3	106	D11
Alwyne La N1	93	S13
Alwyne Pl N1	93	T12
Alwyne Rd N1	93	T13
Alwyne Rd SW19	162	E11
Alwyne Rd W7	104	C14
Alwyne Sq N1	93	T11
Alwyne Vil N1	93	S13
Alyth Gdns NW11	72	F11
Amalgamated Dr, Brent	122	H12
Amanda Cl, Chig *3*	65	P12
Amanda Ms, Rom	83	U10
Amazon St, E1 *4*	112	J12
Ambassador Cl, Houns	138	J4
Ambassador Gdns E6	116	E10
Ambassador's Ct, SW1 *2*	25	N4
Amber Av E17	77	S1
Amber Gro NW2	90	B1
Amber St E15	96	H12
Amberden Av N3	72	H5
Ambergate St SE17	35	P6
Amberley Cl, Orp	203	U9
Amberley Cl, Pnr	67	L6
Amberley Ct, Sid	172	F10
Amberley Gdns, Enf	44	D14
Amberley Gdns, Epsom	193	L8
Amberley Gro SE26	166	J9
Amberley Gro, Croy	184	E14
Amberley Rd E10	78	B13
Amberley Rd N13	59	L4
Amberley Rd SE2	136	H11
Amberley Rd W9	108	H9
Amberley Rd, Buck H	63	U2
Amberley Rd, Enf	44	E12
Amberley Way, Houns	138	F9
Amberley Way, Mord	180	F13
Amberley Way, Rom	83	S7
Amberside Cl, Islw	140	B11
Amberwood Ri, N Mal	178	J12
Amblecote Cl SE12	169	S6
Amblecote Meadows SE12	169	R6
Amblecote Rd SE12	169	R6
Ambler Rd N4	93	R5
Ambleside, Brom	168	H12
Ambleside Av SW16	164	H8
Ambleside Av, Beck	185	S10
Ambleside Cl E9	95	M9
Ambleside Cl E10	78	C14
Ambleside Cres, Enf	45	N5
Ambleside Gdns SW16	164	H9
Ambleside Gdns, Ilf	80	D8
Ambleside Gdns, Sutt	195	M12
Ambleside Gdns, Wem	87	N1
Ambleside Rd NW10	89	L14
Ambleside Rd, Bexh	155	N3
Ambrooke Rd, Belv	137	P6
Ambrosden Av SW1	25	N12
Ambrose Av NW11	72	D13
Ambrose Cl, E6 *5*	116	E10
Ambrose Cl, Orp	203	T6
Ambrose Ms SW11	145	S4
Ambrose St SE16	130	J7
Amelia St SE17	35	T5
Amen Cor EC4	19	R7
Amen Cor SW17	164	A11
Amenity Way, Mord	179	U14
America Sq EC3	21	L9
America St SE1	27	U4
Amerland Rd SW18	144	F11
Amersham Av N18	60	A11
Amersham Gro SE14	131	T13
Amersham Rd SE14	149	T1
Amersham Rd, Croy	183	U11
Amersham Vale SE14	131	T13
Amery Gdns NW10	107	S2
Amery Rd, Har	86	G4
Amesbury Av SW2	165	L4
Amesbury Cl, Wor Pk	193	U2
Amesbury Dr E4	46	D12
Amesbury Rd, Brom	188	B5
Amesbury Rd, Dag	100	G13
Amesbury Rd, Felt	156	H3
Amethyst Rd E15	96	H8
Amherst Av W13	105	L12
Amherst Rd W13	105	L12
Amhurst Gdns, Islw	140	G3
Amhurst Pk N16	76	C13
Amhurst Pas E8	94	G9
Amhurst Rd E8	94	J10
Amhurst Rd N16	94	G8
Amhurst Ter E8	94	G8
Amidas Gdns, Dag	100	D8
Amiel St, E1 *10*	113	M7
Amies St SW11	145	T5
Amis Av, Epsom	192	C10
Amity Gro SW20	179	T2
Amity Rd E15	115	L1
Amner Rd SW11	146	A11
Amor Rd W6	125	T6
Amott Rd SE15	149	S8
Amoy Pl E14	114	A12
Ampere Way, Croy	183	K13
Ampleforth Rd SE2	136	E3
Ampthill Sq Est NW1	9	P4
Ampton Pl, WC1 *3*	10	F7
Ampton St WC1	10	F8
Amroth Cl SE23	167	K1
Amsterdam Rd E14	132	F6
Amwell Cl, Enf	44	A9
Amwell Cl Est N4	93	U2
Amwell St EC1	11	K5
Amy Cl, Wall	197	K14
Amy Warne Cl, E6 *1*	116	D8
Amyand Cotts, Twick *5*	140	J12
Amyand La,Twick *7*	141	K13
Amyand Pk Gdns, Twick	140	J13
Amyand Pk Rd, Twick	140	H14
Amyruth Rd SE4	150	A9
Anatola Rd N19	92	D3
Ancaster Cres, N Mal	179	N12
Ancaster Ms, Beck	185	P6
Ancaster Rd, Beck	185	N6
Ancaster St SE18	135	R14
Anchor & Hope La SE7	133	S6
Anchor Ms SW12	146	D11
Anchor St SE16	130	J8
Anchor Yd, EC1 *5*	12	A9
Anchorage Cl, SW19 *1*	162	H10
Anchorage Pt Ind Est SE7	133	T6
Ancill Cl W6	126	C12
Ancona Rd NW10	107	N3
Ancona Rd SE18	135	P9
Andace Pk Gdns, Brom	187	T2
Andalus Rd SW9	147	K6
Ander Cl, Wem	87	N8
Anderson Cl N21	43	L9
Anderson Cl W3	106	H12
Anderson Cl, Sutt	194	G2
Anderson Pl, Houns	139	R8
Anderson Rd E9	95	N11
Anderson Rd, Wdf Grn	80	B5
Anderson St SW3	31	U5
Anderson Way, Belv	137	S3
Anderton Cl SE5	148	B6
Andmark Ct, Sthl *3*	121	L1
Andover Av, E16 *22*	116	A12
Andover Cl, Grnf	103	S7
Andover Pl NW6	6	B3
Andover Rd N7	93	L4
Andover Rd, Orp	203	P1
Andover Rd, Twick	158	B2
Andre St E8	94	H9
Andrew Borde St, WC2 *6*	17	T6
Andrew Cl, Ilf	65	P12
Andrew St E14	114	E11
Andrewes Gdns E6	116	C11
Andrews Cl, Buck H	63	U3
Andrews Cl, Har	68	B14
Andrews Cl, Wor Pk *4*	194	A3
Andrews Pl SE9	152	J12
Andrew's Rd E8	112	J2
Andwell Cl SE2	136	D4
Anerley Gro SE19	166	F13
Anerley Hill SE19	166	F12
Anerley Pk SE20	166	J13
Anerley Pk Rd SE20	166	J13
Anerley Rd SE19	166	G14
Anerley Rd SE20	184	J2
Anerley Sta Rd SE20	184	J1
Anerley St SW11	145	U3
Anerley Vale SE19	166	G13
Anfield Cl SW12	146	F14
Angel All E1	21	P5
Angel Cl N18	60	F8
Angel Cor Par, N18 *4*	60	G9
Angel Ct EC2	20	E6
Angel Ct SW17	163	T8
Angel Gate EC1	11	R5
Angel Hill, Sutt	195	K5
Angel Hill Dr, Sutt	195	K5
Angel La E15	96	H11
Angel Ms N1	11	L3
Angel Pas EC4	20	D11
Angel Pl N18	60	G9
Angel Rd N18	60	J9
Angel Rd, Har	68	D11
Angel Rd,T Ditt	190	H1
Angel St EC1	19	T5
Angel Wk W6	125	T8
Angelfield, Houns	139	R8
Angelica Dr E6	116	H6
Angelica Gdns, Croy	199	N2
Angell Pk Gdns SW9	147	P5
Angell Rd SW9	147	R5
Angerstein La SE3	133	M14
Angle Grn, Dag	100	F2
Anglers Cl, Rich *1*	159	L8
Angler's La NW5	92	D11
Angles Rd SW16	165	K7
Anglesea Av, SE18 *3*	134	J8
Anglesea Rd SE18	134	J8
Anglesea Rd, Kings T	177	P8
Anglesey Ct Rd, Cars	196	A12
Anglesey Gdns, Cars	196	A12
Anglesey Rd, Enf	45	K7
Anglesey Rd, Wat	50	E10
Anglesmede Cres, Pnr	67	N5
Anglesmede Way, Pnr	67	N6
Anglia Cl N17	60	J14
Anglia Wk, E6 *2*	116	G2
Anglian Rd E11	96	H5
Anglo Rd E3	113	U3
Angus Cl, Chess	192	A10
Angus Dr, Ruis	84	E7
Angus Gdns NW9	70	H2
Angus Rd E13	115	U6
Angus St SE14	131	S13
Anhalt Rd SW11	31	S14
Ankerdine Cres SE18	134	H14
Anlaby Rd,Tedd	158	C10
Anley Rd W14	126	A4
Annersh Gro, Stan	69	P2
Ann La SW10	31	K12
Ann Moss Way SE16	131	L5
Ann St SE18	135	N8
Anna Cl E8	112	F1

Name	Page	Grid
Anna Neagle Cl, E7 *3*	97	P7
Annabel Cl E14	114	C12
Annandale Rd SE10	133	L10
Annandale Rd W4	124	J9
Annandale Rd, Croy	198	H3
Annandale Rd, Sid	153	S14
Anne Boleyn's Wk, Kings T	159	S10
Anne Boleyn's Wk, Sutt	194	B14
Anne Case Ms, N Mal	178	H5
Anne St E13	115	N7
Anne Way, Ilf	65	M12
Anne Way, W Mol	175	R8
Annesley Av NW9	70	H6
Annesley Cl NW10	88	J5
Annesley Dr, Croy	199	U6
Annesley Rd SE3	151	R1
Annesley Wk N19	92	E3
Annett Rd, Walt	174	A13
Annette Cl, Har	68	D3
Annette Cres N1	93	U13
Annette Rd N7	93	M8
Annie Besant Cl E3	113	U2
Anning St EC2	13	K9
Annington Rd N2	73	U6
Annis Rd E9	95	R12
Ann's Cl SW1	24	B8
Ann's Pl E1	21	M4
Annsworthy Av, Th Hth	184	B6
Annsworthy Cres, SE25 *1*	184	B4
Ansdell Rd SE15	149	L3
Ansdell St W8	22	C9
Ansdell Ter W8	22	C9
Ansell Gro, Cars	196	A2
Ansell Rd SW17	163	S6
Anselm Cl, Croy *5*	198	E5
Anselm Rd SW6	126	G12
Anselm Rd, Pnr	51	M14
Ansford Rd, Brom	168	F9
Ansleigh Pl W11	108	B14
Anson Cl, Rom	83	R3
Anson Rd N7	92	G8
Anson Rd NW2	90	B9
Anson Ter, Nthlt	85	S11
Anstey Rd SE15	148	G5
Anstey Wk N15	75	S8
Anstice Cl W4	125	K14
Anstridge Path SE9	153	P12
Anstridge Rd SE9	153	P12
Antelope Rd SE18	134	E6
Anthony Cl NW7	55	K8
Anthony Cl, Wat	50	F1
Anthony Rd SE25	184	G12
Anthony Rd, Grnf	104	C4
Anthony Rd, Well	154	B2
Anthony St E1	112	J12
Antigua Cl SE19	166	B9
Antigua Wk, SE19 *7*	166	B9
Antill Rd E3	113	S5
Antill Rd N15	76	G7
Antill Ter E1	113	N11
Antlers Hill E4	46	E10
Anton Cres, Sutt	194	G6
Anton St E8	94	H9
Antoneys Cl, Pnr	66	G4
Antrim Gro NW3	91	T11
Antrim Mans NW3	91	S11
Antrim Rd NW3	91	T11
Antrobus Cl, Sutt	194	F10
Antrobus Rd W4	124	F7
Anvil Cl SW16	164	E13
Anvil Rd, Sun	174	B6
Anworth Cl, Wdf Grn	63	R11
Apex Cl, Beck	186	D1
Apex Cor NW7	54	H7
Aplin Way, Islw	140	C1
Apollo Av, Brom	187	R1
Apollo Av, Nthwd	50	A10
Apollo Pl E11	96	J5
Apollo Pl SW10	31	K13
Apollo Way SE28	135	N6
Apostle Way, Th Hth	183	S4
Apothecary St, EC4 *6*	19	P8

Name	Page	Grid
Appach Rd SW2	147	N11
Apple Garth, Brent	123	P8
Apple Gro, Chess	191	R7
Apple Gro, Enf	44	D6
Apple Rd E11	96	J6
Apple Tree Yd SW1	25	P1
Appleby Cl, E4 *1*	62	E12
Appleby Cl N15	76	A10
Appleby Cl, Twick	158	A4
Appleby Rd E8	94	H13
Appleby Rd E16	115	M12
Appleby St E2	13	M2
Appledore Av, Ruis	84	D5
Appledore Cl SW17	163	T3
Appledore Cl, Brom	187	M9
Appledore Cl, Edg	70	A2
Appledore Cres, Sid	171	T6
Appleford Rd W10	108	D8
Applegarth, Croy	200	D13
Applegarth, Esher	190	F10
Applegarth Dr, Ilf	81	U8
Applegarth Rd SE28	136	D1
Applegarth Rd W14	126	A6
Appleton Gdns, N Mal	179	N12
Appleton Rd SE9	152	C6
Appleton Rd, Loug	49	K5
Appleton Sq, Mitch	181	R1
Appletree Cl SE20	185	K1
Appletree Gdns, Barn	41	R7
Applewood Cl N20	57	R1
Applewood Cl NW2	89	R5
Appold St EC2	20	H1
Apprentice Way E5	95	K7
Approach, The, NW4 *2*	72	A9
Approach, The W3	106	H12
Approach, The, Enf	44	J3
Approach, The, Orp	203	U3
Approach Rd E2	113	L4
Approach Rd SW20	179	T14
Approach Rd, Barn	41	M8
Approach Rd, W Mol	175	P9
Aprey Gdns NW4	71	U7
April Cl W7	104	D13
April Cl, Felt	156	B6
April Cl, Orp	203	T10
April Glen SE23	167	P6
April St E8	94	F8
Apsley Cl, Har	67	T9
Apsley Rd SE25	184	J8
Apsley Rd, N Mal	178	F6
Apsley Way NW2	89	N3
Aquarius Business Pk NW2	89	N2
Aquarius Way, Nthwd	50	A9
Aquila St NW8	7	M1
Aquinas St SE1	27	L3
Arabella Dr SW15	143	L7
Arabia Cl E4	46	G14
Arabin Rd SE4	149	T7
Aragon Av, T Ditt	176	E10
Aragon Cl, Brom	202	F1
Aragon Cl, Loug	48	D11
Aragon Dr, Ilf	65	L13
Aragon Dr, Ruis	84	G2
Aragon Ms E1	29	S2
Aragon Rd, Kings T	159	R9
Aragon Rd, Mord	180	B13
Aran Dr, Stan	53	M8
Arandora Cres, Rom	82	C13
Arbery Rd E3	113	R5
Arbor Cl, Beck	186	C3
Arbor Rd E4	62	H6
Arborfield Cl SW2	165	L2
Arbour Rd, Enf	45	P7
Arbour Sq E1	113	N1
Arbroath Grn, Wat	50	B5
Arbroath Rd SE9	152	D5
Arbrook La, Esher	190	A11
Arbuthnot La, Bex	153	U14
Arbuthnot Rd SE14	149	N3
Arbutus St E8	112	E1
Arcade, The EC2	20	G4
Arcade, The, Croy *7*	197	U5
Arcadia Av N3	72	G2
Arcadia Cl, Cars	196	A7

Name	Page	Grid
Arcadia St E14	114	B11
Arcadian Av, Bex	154	J12
Arcadian Cl, Bex	154	J12
Arcadian Gdns N22	59	N13
Arcadian Rd, Bex	154	J12
Arch St SE1	27	U12
Archangel St SE16	131	P4
Archbishops Pl SW2	147	M12
Archdale Pl, N Mal	178	D5
Archdale Rd SE22	148	F9
Archel Rd W14	126	E11
Archer Cl, Kings T	159	R13
Archer Rd SE25	184	J7
Archer St W1	17	R10
Archers Dr, Enf	45	L4
Archery Cl, Har	68	F5
Archery Rd SE9	152	F10
Arches, The SW6	144	E3
Arches, The WC2	26	C1
Arches, The, Har	85	S3
Archibald Ms W1	24	F1
Archibald Rd N7	92	G7
Archibald St E3	114	A6
Archway Cl SW19	162	J6
Archway Cl W10	108	B10
Archway Cl, Wall	196	H6
Archway Mall N19	92	F3
Archway Rd N6	74	C12
Archway Rd N19	92	E2
Archway St SW13	143	K5
Arcola St E8	94	E9
Arctic St NW5	92	C10
Arcus Rd, Brom	169	K11
Ardbeg Rd SE24	148	B11
Arden Cl, Har	86	A6
Arden Ct Gdns N2	73	P12
Arden Cres E14	132	B7
Arden Cres, Dag	100	F13
Arden Est N1	12	H3
Arden Gro, Orp	203	K8
Arden Ms, E17 *5*	78	D9
Arden Mhor, Pnr	66	D7
Arden Rd N3	72	E5
Arden Rd W13	105	L14
Ardent Cl SE25	184	D5
Ardfern Av SW16	183	N5
Ardfillan Rd SE6	168	H2
Ardgowan Rd SE6	150	J14
Ardilaun Rd N5	93	T7
Ardingly Cl, Croy	199	N5
Ardleigh Gdns, Sutt	180	G14
Ardleigh Ms, Ilf *5*	98	J6
Ardleigh Rd E17	77	U2
Ardleigh Rd N1	94	C12
Ardleigh Ter E17	77	U2
Ardley Cl NW10	88	J5
Ardley Cl SE6	167	S6
Ardlui Rd SE27	165	T4
Ardmay Gdns, Surb	177	R9
Ardmere Rd SE13	150	H11
Ardmore La, Buck H	63	S1
Ardmore Pl, Buck H	47	S14
Ardoch Rd SE6	168	G3
Ardra Rd N9	61	N5
Ardrossan Gdns, Wor Pk	193	N5
Ardshiel Cl SW15	144	B6
Ardwell Av, Ilf	81	L10
Ardwell Rd SW2	165	K3
Ardwick Rd NW2	90	G7
Arewater Grn, Loug	48	G2
Argall Av E10	77	N14
Argall Way E10	95	P1
Argent St SE1	27	S5
Argenta Way NW10	88	C13
Argon Ms SW6	126	H14
Argon Rd N18	61	N10
Argus Cl, Rom	83	R2
Argus Way W3	124	D5
Argus Way, Nthlt	102	J5
Argyle Av, Houns	139	R10
Argyle Cl W13	104	G7
Argyle Pas N17	76	F1
Argyle Pl W6	125	S8
Argyle Rd E1	113	N7
Argyle Rd E15	96	J8
Argyle Rd E16	115	S12
Argyle Rd N12	56	J10
Argyle Rd N17	76	G1

Name	Page	Grid
Argyle Rd N18	60	H8
Argyle Rd W13	104	J13
Argyle Rd, Barn	39	U7
Argyle Rd, Grnf	104	H9
Argyle Rd, Har	67	R11
Argyle Rd, Houns	139	R9
Argyle Rd, Ilf	98	H3
Argyle Rd, Tedd	158	D9
Argyle Sq WC1	10	C6
Argyle St WC1	10	C6
Argyle Way SE16	37	U7
Argyll Av, Sthl	121	R1
Argyll Gdns, Edg	70	D3
Argyll Rd W8	126	G4
Argyll St W1	17	L7
Arica Rd SE4	149	R6
Ariel Rd NW6	90	G12
Ariel Way W12	125	U1
Ariel Way, Houns	138	C4
Aristotle Rd SW4	146	H6
Arkell Gro SE19	165	S14
Arkindale Rd SE6	168	E6
Arkley Cres E17	77	T10
Arkley Dr, Barn	39	P8
Arkley La, Barn	39	P6
Arkley Rd E17	77	T10
Arkley Vw, Barn	39	R8
Arklow Rd SE14	131	T12
Arkwright Rd NW3	91	L10
Arlesey Cl, SW15 *1*	144	C10
Arlesford Rd SW9	147	K5
Arlingford Rd SW2	147	N11
Arlington N12	56	G6
Arlington Av N1	111	U2
Arlington Cl, Sid	153	R14
Arlington Cl, Sutt	194	H4
Arlington Cl, Twick	141	L11
Arlington Dr, Cars	195	T4
Arlington Gdns W4	124	E9
Arlington Gdns, Ilf	98	G1
Arlington Lo SW2	147	M8
Arlington Ms, Twick	141	K11
Arlington Pl, SE10 *7*	132	E14
Arlington Rd N14	58	D3
Arlington Rd NW1	110	D2
Arlington Rd W13	105	K12
Arlington Rd, Rich	159	N4
Arlington Rd, Surb	177	P12
Arlington Rd, Tedd	158	E8
Arlington Rd, Twick	141	L11
Arlington Rd, Wdf Grn	63	P14
Arlington Sq N1	111	U2
Arlington St W1	25	L2
Arlington Way EC1	11	M6
Arliss Way, Nthlt	102	F2
Arlow Rd N21	59	P2
Armada St SE8	132	B11
Armada Way E6	117	K13
Armadale Cl N17	76	J8
Armadale Rd SW6	126	G12
Armadale Rd, Felt	138	B9
Armagh Rd E3	113	U2
Armfield Cl, W Mol	175	L9
Armfield Cres, Mitch	181	U3
Armfield Rd, Enf	44	A2
Arminger Rd W12	125	S2
Armistice Gdns, SE25 *1*	184	H6
Armitage Rd NW11	90	E1
Armitage Rd SE10	133	L9
Armour Cl N7	93	L12
Armoury Rd SE8	150	D4
Armoury Way SW18	144	H9
Armstead Wk, Dag	101	N14
Armstrong Av, Wdf Grn	62	J11
Armstrong Cl E6	116	E11
Armstrong Cl, Dag	82	F14
Armstrong Cl, Pnr	66	A11
Armstrong Cres, Barn	41	N6
Armstrong Rd SW7	22	J11
Armstrong Rd W3	125	L1
Armstrong Rd, Felt	156	J10
Armstrong Way, Sthl	121	S3
Armytage Rd, Houns	120	G14

Arnal Cres SW18	144	C13
Arncliffe Cl, N11 *3*	58	B11
Arndale Wk SW18	144	J10
Arne Gro, Orp	203	T5
Arne St WC2	18	C7
Arne Wk SE3	151	L8
Arneway St, SW1 *4*	25	T12
Arneways Av, Rom	82	H6
Arnewood Cl SW15	161	N1
Arney's La, Mitch	182	A11
Arngask Rd SE6	150	G14
Arnhem Pl E14	132	A6
Arnison Rd, E Mol	176	A8
Arnold Circ E2	13	M8
Arnold Cl, Har	69	U13
Arnold Cres, Islw	140	B10
Arnold Dr, Chess	191	N11
Arnold Est SE1	29	P8
Arnold Gdns N13	59	R9
Arnold Rd E3	114	A6
Arnold Rd N15	76	E6
Arnold Rd SW17	163	U13
Arnold Rd, Dag	101	M14
Arnold Rd, Nthlt	85	K12
Arnos Gro N14	58	G7
Arnos Rd N11	58	F9
Arnott Cl SE28	136	E1
Arnott Cl W4	124	H8
Arnould Av SE5	148	B7
Arnsberg Way, Bexh	155	N7
Arnside Gdns, Wem	87	N1
Arnside Rd, Bexh	155	N1
Arnside St SE17	36	B9
Arnulf St SE6	168	C7
Arnulls Rd SW16	165	R11
Arodene Rd SW2	147	M11
Arosa Rd, Twick	141	P12
Arragon Gdns SW16	164	J14
Arragon Gdns, W Wick	200	D5
Arragon Rd E6	116	B2
Arragon Rd SW18	162	J2
Arragon Rd, Twick	158	H1
Arran Cl, Wall	196	E8
Arran Dr E12	98	A3
Arran Ms W5	123	T2
Arran Rd SE6	168	E3
Arran Wk N1	93	T13
Arras Av, Mord	181	M9
Arrol Rd, Beck	185	M5
Arrow Rd E3	114	C5
Arrowsmith Cl, Chig	65	T9
Arrowsmith Path, Chig	65	T9
Arrowsmith Rd, Chig	65	S9
Arrowsmith Rd, Loug	48	D6
Arsenal Rd SE9	152	F5
Arterberry Rd SW20	161	U13
Artesian Cl NW10	88	H13
Artesian Gro, Barn	41	M7
Artesian Rd W2	108	G12
Artesian Wk, E11 *5*	96	J5
Arthingworth St E15	114	J1
Arthur Ct W2	14	B6
Arthur Gro SE18	135	L8
Arthur Henderson Ho SW6	144	E3
Arthur Horsley Wk E7	97	M9
Arthur Rd E6	116	F3
Arthur Rd N7	93	L7
Arthur Rd N9	60	E3
Arthur Rd SW19	162	G6
Arthur Rd, Kings T	160	B14
Arthur Rd, N Mal	179	S10
Arthur Rd, Rom	82	G12
Arthur St EC4	20	E11
Arthurdon Rd SE4	150	A9
Artichoke Hill, E1 *1*	112	J14
Artichoke Pl, SE5 *4*	148	A1
Artillery Cl, Ilf	81	M11
Artillery La E1	20	J3
Artillery La W12	107	P11
Artillery Pl SE18	134	F8
Artillery Pl SW1	25	R11
Artillery Row SW1	25	R11
Artington Cl, Orp	203	M7
Artisan Cl E6	116	J13
Artizan St E1	21	K5
Arundel Av, Mord	180	F7
Arundel Cl E15	97	K8
Arundel Cl SW11	145	R9
Arundel Cl, Bex	155	M11
Arundel Cl, Croy	197	R6
Arundel Cl, Hmptn	157	S10
Arundel Ct N12	57	R11
Arundel Ct, Har	85	P7
Arundel Dr, Borwd	38	E9
Arundel Dr, Har	85	M8
Arundel Dr, Wdf Grn	63	P14
Arundel Gdns N21	59	P2
Arundel Gdns W11	108	E13
Arundel Gdns, Edg	54	H14
Arundel Gdns, Ilf	100	A3
Arundel Great Ct WC2	18	H9
Arundel Gro N16	94	C9
Arundel Pl N1	93	N12
Arundel Rd, Barn	41	S5
Arundel Rd, Croy	184	A12
Arundel Rd, Houns	138	E6
Arundel Rd, Kings T	178	D3
Arundel Rd, Sutt	194	F14
Arundel Sq N7	93	N12
Arundel St WC2	18	H9
Arundel Ter SW13	125	S11
Arvon Rd N5	93	P9
Ascalon St SW8	128	E14
Ascham Dr, E4 *2*	62	C13
Ascham End E17	77	S1
Ascham St NW5	92	E9
Aschurch Rd, Croy	184	F13
Ascot Cl, Borwd	38	A10
Ascot Cl, Ilf	65	R12
Ascot Cl, Nthlt	85	N10
Ascot Gdns, Sthl	103	M8
Ascot Rd E6	116	E5
Ascot Rd N15	76	A10
Ascot Rd N18	60	H8
Ascot Rd SW17	164	A12
Ascot Rd, Orp	189	T8
Ascott Av W5	123	R3
Ash Cl SE20	185	L3
Ash Cl, Cars	195	T3
Ash Cl, Edg	54	F8
Ash Cl, N Mal	178	G4
Ash Cl, Orp	189	N10
Ash Cl, Sid	172	C6
Ash Cl, Stan	52	G12
Ash Ct, Epsom	192	E7
Ash Gro E8	112	J2
Ash Gro N13	59	T6
Ash Gro NW2	90	B8
Ash Gro SE20	185	L3
Ash Gro W5	123	R4
Ash Gro, Enf	44	C13
Ash Gro, Houns	138	H1
Ash Gro, Sthl	103	P9
Ash Gro, Wem	86	H8
Ash Gro, W Wick	200	F3
Ash Hill Cl, Bushey	51	S1
Ash Hill Dr, Pnr	66	F5
Ash Island, E Mol	176	B5
Ash Rd E15	97	K10
Ash Rd, Croy	200	A3
Ash Rd, Orp	203	U13
Ash Rd, Sutt	180	D14
Ash Row, Brom	188	H12
Ash Tree Cl, Croy	185	R11
Ash Tree Cl, Surb	191	S2
Ash Tree Dell NW9	70	G9
Ash Tree Way, Croy	185	R10
Ash Wk SW2	165	M2
Ash Wk, Wem	87	M7
Ashbourne Av E18	79	S7
Ashbourne Av N20	57	T3
Ashbourne Av NW11	72	E9
Ashbourne Av, Bexh	137	K13
Ashbourne Av, Har	86	A3
Ashbourne Cl N12	57	K8
Ashbourne Cl W5	106	A9
Ashbourne Gro NW7	54	H10
Ashbourne Gro SE22	148	E9
Ashbourne Gro W4	125	K10
Ashbourne Ri, Orp	203	P7
Ashbourne Rd W5	105	U8
Ashbourne Rd, Mitch	164	B13
Ashbourne Ter, SW19 *1*	162	G13
Ashbourne Way NW11	72	F9
Ashbridge Rd E11	79	L13
Ashbridge St NW8	7	P11
Ashbrook Rd N19	92	G2
Ashbrook Rd, Dag	101	S6
Ashburn Gdns SW7	30	E2
Ashburn Pl SW7	30	F3
Ashburnham Av, Har	68	F12
Ashburnham Cl, N2 *3*	73	P6
Ashburnham Cl, Wat	50	A5
Ashburnham Dr, Wat	50	A5
Ashburnham Gdns, Har	68	F12
Ashburnham Gro SE10	132	D14
Ashburnham Pl SE10	132	D14
Ashburnham Retreat, SE10 *15*	132	D14
Ashburnham Rd NW10	107	T5
Ashburnham Rd SW10	30	G14
Ashburnham Rd, Belv	137	T7
Ashburnham Rd, Rich	159	L6
Ashburton Av, Croy	198	J2
Ashburton Av, Ilf	99	R8
Ashburton Cl, Croy	198	G2
Ashburton Ct, Pnr	66	H5
Ashburton Gdns, Croy	198	F3
Ashburton Gro N7	93	N8
Ashburton Rd E16	115	P11
Ashburton Rd, Croy	198	G2
Ashburton Rd, Ruis	84	A3
Ashburton Ter, E13 *4*	115	N3
Ashbury Gdns, Rom	82	G10
Ashbury Pl SW19	163	L11
Ashbury Rd SW11	146	A5
Ashby Av, Chess	192	A12
Ashby Gro N1	93	U13
Ashby Ms SE4	149	T4
Ashby Rd N15	76	G9
Ashby Rd SE4	149	U4
Ashby St EC1	11	R7
Ashby Wk, Croy	183	U12
Ashchurch Gro W12	125	N4
Ashchurch Pk Vil W12	125	N5
Ashchurch Ter W12	125	N5
Ashcombe Av, Surb	177	P14
Ashcombe Gdns, Edg	54	A8
Ashcombe Pk NW2	89	K6
Ashcombe Rd SW19	162	H10
Ashcombe Rd, Cars	196	A11
Ashcombe Sq, N Mal	178	E5
Ashcombe St SW6	144	J4
Ashcroft, Pnr	51	P12
Ashcroft Av, Sid	154	A12
Ashcroft Cres, Sid	154	A12
Ashcroft Rd E3	113	R6
Ashcroft Rd, Chess	191	T6
Ashdale Cl, Twick	139	T13
Ashdale Gro, Stan	52	F12
Ashdale Rd SE12	169	S2
Ashdale Way, Twick	139	S13
Ashdene SE15	148	J1
Ashdene, Pnr	66	F6
Ashdon Cl, Wdf Grn	63	R11
Ashdon Rd NW10	107	L1
Ashdown Cl, Beck	186	D4
Ashdown Cl, Bex	155	U14
Ashdown Cres, NW5 *4*	92	A10
Ashdown Rd, Enf	45	L5
Ashdown Rd, Kings T	177	R4
Ashdown Wk E14	132	B7
Ashdown Wk, Rom	83	S3
Ashdown Way SW17	164	A3
Ashen E6	116	H11
Ashen Gro SW19	162	G5
Ashenden Rd E5	95	R9
Ashentree Ct, EC4 *20*	19	M8
Asher Loftus Way N11	57	U11
Asher Way E1	29	T1
Ashfield Av, Felt	156	D2
Ashfield Cl, Beck	168	A13
Ashfield Cl, Rich	159	R2
Ashfield La, Chis	171	L12
Ashfield Par N14	58	G2
Ashfield Rd N4	75	U11
Ashfield Rd N14	58	E5
Ashfield Rd W3	125	L1
Ashfield St E1	112	J10
Ashfield Yd, E1 *2*	113	L10
Ashfields, Loug	48	E3
Ashford Av N8	74	J8
Ashford Av, Hayes	102	H12
Ashford Cl, E17 *2*	77	T11
Ashford Cres, Enf	45	M3
Ashford Grn, Wat	50	G10
Ashford Rd E6	98	G12
Ashford Rd E18	79	S4
Ashford Rd NW2	90	A8
Ashford St N1	12	G6
Ashgrove Rd, Brom	168	H11
Ashgrove Rd, Ilf	100	A2
Ashingdon Cl E4	62	F6
Ashington Rd SW6	144	F3
Ashlake Rd SW16	164	J8
Ashland Pl W1	16	D2
Ashlar Pl, SE18 *4*	135	K8
Ashleigh Gdns, Sutt	194	J4
Ashleigh Rd SE20	185	K5
Ashleigh Rd SW14	142	J5
Ashley Av, Ilf	81	K4
Ashley Av, Mord	180	H10
Ashley Cl NW4	71	U3
Ashley Cl, Pnr	66	C4
Ashley Cres N22	75	P4
Ashley Cres SW11	146	B5
Ashley Dr, Borwd	38	G10
Ashley Dr, Islw	122	C12
Ashley Dr, Twick	157	R1
Ashley Gdns N13	59	U8
Ashley Gdns SW1	25	N11
Ashley Gdns, Orp	203	S9
Ashley Gdns, Rich	159	N5
Ashley Gdns, Wem	87	S4
Ashley La NW4	71	U5
Ashley La, Croy	197	S8
Ashley Pl SW1	25	M11
Ashley Rd E4	62	A11
Ashley Rd E7	97	U14
Ashley Rd N17	76	H5
Ashley Rd N19	92	J1
Ashley Rd SW19	162	J11
Ashley Rd, Enf	45	M4
Ashley Rd, Hmptn	175	N1
Ashley Rd, Rich *1*	141	R6
Ashley Rd, T Ditt	176	F12
Ashley Rd, Th Hth	183	M8
Ashley Wk NW7	56	A14
Ashlin Rd E15	96	H8
Ashling Rd, Croy	198	H1
Ashlone Rd SW15	144	A5
Ashlyns Way, Chess	191	N12
Ashmead N14	42	F10
Ashmead Gate, Brom	187	U1
Ashmead Rd SE8	150	A3
Ashmead Rd, Felt	156	A1
Ashmere Av, Beck	186	G4
Ashmere Cl, Sutt	193	U10
Ashmere Gro SW2	146	J8
Ashmill St NW1	15	P1
Ashmole Pl SW8	34	H12
Ashmole St SW8	34	H12
Ashmore Ct, Houns *1*	121	N12
Ashmore Gro, Well	153	P5
Ashmore Rd W9	108	E7

Name	Page	Grid
Ashmount Rd N15	76	E9
Ashmount Rd N19	74	F14
Ashmount Ter W5	123	N7
Ashneal Gdns, Har	86	A5
Ashness Gdns, Grnf	86	J12
Ashness Rd SW11	145	U10
Ashridge Cl, Har	69	M12
Ashridge Cres SE18	135	L14
Ashridge Dr, Wat	50	E9
Ashridge Gdns N13	58	H9
Ashridge Gdns, Pnr	66	J7
Ashridge Way, Mord	180	E7
Ashridge Way, Sun	156	B12
Ashtead Rd E5	76	H13
Ashton Cl, Sutt	194	G8
Ashton Gdns, Houns	139	L7
Ashton Gdns, Rom	83	K11
Ashton Rd E15	96	G10
Ashton St, E14 *5*	114	E13
Ashtree Av, Mitch	181	P3
Ashtree Cl, Orp *1*	203	K7
Ashurst Cl SE20	185	K1
Ashurst Dr, Ilf	81	K11
Ashurst Rd N12	57	S9
Ashurst Rd, Barn	41	U9
Ashurst Wk, Croy	198	J3
Ashvale Rd SW17	163	T9
Ashville Rd E11	96	H3
Ashwater Rd SE12	169	P2
Ashwell Cl, E6 *30*	116	D11
Ashwin St E8	94	E11
Ashwood Gdns, Croy	200	D12
Ashwood Rd E4	62	H6
Ashworth Cl SE5	148	A3
Ashworth Rd W9	6	C7
Aske St N1	12	H5
Askern Cl, Bexh	154	H8
Askew Cres W12	125	M3
Askew Rd W12	125	N4
Askham Ct W12	125	N2
Askham Rd W12	125	N2
Askill Dr SW15	144	D10
Asland Rd E15	114	H2
Aslett St SW18	145	L13
Asmara Rd NW2	90	D9
Asmuns Hill NW11	72	G10
Asmuns Pl NW11	72	F9
Asolando Dr, SE17 *1*	36	B4
Aspen Cl, N19 *13*	92	E4
Aspen Cl W5	123	T4
Aspen Copse, Brom	188	E3
Aspen Dr, Wem	86	H6
Aspen Gdns W6	125	S9
Aspen Gdns, Mitch	182	A10
Aspen Grn, Erith	137	M5
Aspen La, Nthlt	103	K6
Aspen Way E14	114	B14
Aspen Way, Felt	156	C6
Aspenlea Rd W6	126	A11
Aspern Gro NW3	91	S10
Aspinall Rd SE4	149	P5
Aspinden Rd SE16	131	K7
Aspley Rd SW18	145	L10
Asplins Rd E17	76	H11
Asquith Cl, Dag	100	F1
Ass Ho La, Har	51	R7
Assam St E1	21	R6
Assembly Pas E1	113	M9
Assembly Wk, Cars	181	R14
Assurance Cotts, Belv *1*	137	M9
Astall Cl, Har	68	C1
Astbury Rd SE15	149	L1
Aste St E14	132	E4
Astell St SW3	31	R5
Asthall Gdns, Ilf	81	M7
Astle St SW11	146	A3
Astley Av NW2	89	U9
Aston Av, Har	69	M13
Aston Cl, Sid	172	B6
Aston Grn, Houns	138	E3
Aston Ms, Rom	82	F13
Aston Rd SW20	179	U4
Aston Rd W5	105	P11
Aston Rd, Esher	190	C10
Aston St E14	113	R10
Astonville St SW18	162	G1
Astor Av, Rom	83	T11
Astor Cl, Kings T	160	D11
Astoria Wk SW9	147	N6
Astrop Ms W6	125	T5
Astrop Ter W6	125	T4
Astwood Ms SW7	30	D2
Asylum Rd SE15	131	K13
Atalanta St SW6	144	B1
Atbara Ct, Tedd	159	K12
Atbara Rd, Tedd	159	K11
Atcham Rd, Houns	139	U7
Atcost Rd, Bark	118	A9
Atheldene Rd SW18	163	K1
Athelney St SE6	168	B5
Athelstan Rd, Kings T	177	U7
Athelstane Gro E3	113	T4
Athelstone Rd, Har	68	B4
Athena Cl, Har	86	B3
Athena Cl, Kings T *1*	177	T5
Athenaeum Pl, N10	74	C6
Athenaeum Rd N20	57	N2
Athenlay Rd SE15	149	N10
Atherden Rd E5	95	L7
Atherfold Rd SW9	146	J5
Atherley Way, Houns	139	M14
Atherstone Ms SW7	30	G1
Atherton Dr SW19	162	B7
Atherton Hts, Wem	87	M12
Atherton Ms E7	97	M11
Atherton Pl, Har	68	A6
Atherton Pl, Sthl	103	P14
Atherton Rd E7	97	M11
Atherton Rd SW13	125	N14
Atherton Rd, Ilf	80	D3
Atherton St SW11	145	T3
Athlon Rd, Wem	105	N3
Athlone, Esher	190	C12
Athlone Cl E5	95	K9
Athlone Rd SW2	147	M14
Athlone St NW5	92	B11
Athol Cl, Pnr	66	D2
Athol Gdns, Pnr	66	D2
Athol Rd, Erith	137	U10
Athol Sq E14	114	F12
Athole Gdns, Enf	44	C10
Atholl Rd, Ilf	82	A14
Atkins Dr, W Wick	200	H4
Atkins Rd, E10 *2*	78	D12
Atkins Rd SW12	146	H13
Atkinson Rd E16	115	U10
Atlantic Rd SW9	147	N7
Atlas Gdns SE7	133	T7
Atlas Ms E8	94	F11
Atlas Ms N7	93	M12
Atlas Rd E13	115	P4
Atlas Rd N11	58	C12
Atlas Rd NW10	107	K6
Atlas Rd, Wem	88	E7
Atley Rd E3	114	A1
Atlip Rd, Wem	105	R1
Atney Rd SW15	144	D7
Atria Rd, Nthwd	50	A10
Attenborough Cl, Wat	50	J6
Atterbury Rd N4	75	R12
Atterbury St SW1	34	A4
Attewood Av NW10	88	J5
Attewood Rd, Nthlt	84	J12
Attfield Cl N20	57	N3
Attlee Cl, Hayes	102	C5
Attlee Cl, Th Hth	183	T11
Attlee Rd SE28	118	D13
Attlee Rd, Hayes	102	B5
Attlee Ter E17	78	D7
Attneave St WC1	10	J8
Atwater Cl SW2	165	N1
Atwell Cl E10	78	D12
Atwell Pl, T Ditt	190	F1
Atwell Rd, SE15 *5*	148	H4
Atwood Av, Rich	142	A4
Atwood Rd W6	125	R7
Aubert Pk N5	93	R7
Aubert Rd N5	93	S7
Aubrey Pl NW8	6	F3
Aubrey Rd E17	78	B6
Aubrey Rd N8	75	K10
Aubrey Rd W8	126	F2
Aubrey Wk W8	126	F2
Aubyn Hill SE27	165	U8
Aubyn Sq SW15	143	N8
Auckland Cl SE19	184	E2
Auckland Gdns SE19	184	D2
Auckland Hill SE27	165	T7
Auckland Ri SE19	184	D1
Auckland Rd E10	96	D5
Auckland Rd SE19	184	E1
Auckland Rd SW11	145	S8
Auckland Rd, Ilf	99	K1
Auckland Rd, Kings T	177	U7
Auckland St SE11	34	E8
Auden Pl NW1	110	A1
Audleigh Pl, Chig	64	G11
Audley Cl N10	58	C13
Audley Cl, SW11 *5*	146	B5
Audley Cl, Borwd	38	A5
Audley Ct E18	79	M8
Audley Ct, Pnr	66	E4
Audley Dr E16	133	R1
Audley Gdns, Ilf	99	T4
Audley Gdns, Loug	49	M3
Audley Pl, Sutt	194	J14
Audley Rd NW4	71	R11
Audley Rd W5	105	U10
Audley Rd, Enf	43	R3
Audley Rd, Rich	141	T9
Audley Sq, W1 *2*	24	F2
Audrey Cl, Beck	186	C11
Audrey Gdns, Wem	87	K3
Audrey Rd, Ilf	98	J6
Audrey St E2	12	S1
Audric Cl, Kings T	178	A1
Augurs La, E13 *2*	115	S5
Augusta Cl, W Mol	175	L6
Augusta Rd, Twick	157	T4
Augusta St E14	114	C11
Augustine Rd W14	126	A6
Augustine Rd, Har	67	S2
Augustus Cl, Brent	123	P14
Augustus Rd SW19	162	C2
Augustus St NW1	9	K5
Aulton Pl SE11	35	L8
Aultone Way, Cars	195	T5
Aultone Way, Sutt	195	L4
Aurelia Gdns, Croy	183	L10
Aurelia Rd, Croy	183	K12
Auriga Ms N16	94	B9
Auriol Cl, Wor Pk	193	K6
Auriol Dr, Grnf	86	A13
Auriol Pk Rd, Wor Pk	193	K6
Auriol Rd W14	126	C8
Austell Gdns NW7	55	K6
Austen Cl SE28	136	D1
Austen Cl, Loug	49	N6
Austen Rd, Erith	137	R14
Austen Rd, Har	85	R3
Austin Av, Brom	188	D10
Austin Cl SE23	149	T13
Austin Cl, Twick	141	L10
Austin Friars EC2	20	F6
Austin Friars Pas, EC2	20	F5
Austin Friars Sq EC2	20	G5
Austin Rd SW11	146	A2
Austin St E2	13	L7
Austral Cl, Sid	171	T5
Austral St SE11	35	N1
Australia Rd W12	107	S13
Austyn Gdns, Surb	192	C1
Autumn Cl SW19	163	M11
Autumn Cl, Enf	44	H2
Autumn St E3	114	B2
Avalon Cl SW20	180	D4
Avalon Cl W13	104	G9
Avalon Cl, Enf	43	P3
Avalon Rd SW6	144	J1
Avalon Rd W13	104	G7
Avard Gdns, Orp	203	M8
Avarn Rd SW17	163	U11
Av Maria La EC4	19	S7
Avebury Pk, Surb	177	P13
Avebury Rd, E11 *2*	96	H1
Avebury Rd SW19	180	E1
Avebury Rd, Orp	203	N6
Avebury St, N1 *7*	112	A2
Aveline St SE11	34	J7
Aveling Pk Rd E17	78	B3
Avenell Rd N5	93	R6
Avening Rd SW18	144	H13
Avening Ter SW18	144	H12
Avenons Rd E13	115	N8
Avenue, The E4	62	G11
Avenue, The (Leytonstone) E11	97	M3
Avenue, The (Wanstead) E11	97	N1
Avenue, The N3	72	G3
Avenue, The N8	75	N6
Avenue, The N10	74	F3
Avenue, The N11	58	C8
Avenue, The N17	76	D4
Avenue, The NW6	108	C1
Avenue, The SE7	133	T13
Avenue, The SE10	132	G13
Avenue, The SW4	146	B9
Avenue, The SW11	145	S14
Avenue, The SW18	145	S14
Avenue, The W4	124	J5
Avenue, The W13	104	J12
Avenue, The, Barn	40	C6
Avenue, The, Beck	186	F1
Avenue, The, Bex	154	G12
Avenue, The, Brom	188	B6
Avenue, The, Cars	196	A13
Avenue, The, Croy	198	C5
Avenue, The, Epsom	193	R13
Avenue, The, Esher	190	C11
Avenue, The, Hmptn	157	M11
Avenue, The, Har	68	E1
Avenue, The, Houns	139	R10
Avenue, The (Cranford), Houns	138	B1
Avenue, The, Kes	202	B6
Avenue, The, Loug	48	B11
Avenue, The, Orp	203	U4
Avenue, The (St. Paul's Cray), Orp	172	C13
Avenue, The, Pnr	67	L11
Avenue, The (Hatch End), Pnr	51	N13
Avenue, The, Rich	141	U3
Avenue, The, Sun	174	C1
Avenue, The, Surb	177	U12
Avenue, The (Cheam), Sutt	194	A13
Avenue, The, Twick	141	L10
Avenue, The, Wem	87	S1
Avenue, The, W Wick	186	F14
Avenue, The, Wor Pk	193	M3
Avenue Cl N14	42	F11
Avenue Cl NW8	109	S2
Avenue Cl, Houns	138	B1
Avenue Cres W3	124	C3
Avenue Cres, Houns	138	C1
Avenue Elmers, Surb	177	S9
Avenue Gdns SE25	184	G4
Avenue Gdns SW14	142	J6
Avenue Gdns W3	124	D3
Avenue Gdns, Houns	120	C14
Avenue Gdns, Tedd	158	F13
Avenue Gate, Loug	47	U12
Avenue Ind Est E4	62	A12
Avenue Pk Rd SE27	165	S3
Avenue Rd E7	97	R8
Avenue Rd N6	74	G13
Avenue Rd N12	57	L8
Avenue Rd N14	42	D13
Avenue Rd N15	76	B10
Avenue Rd NW3	91	N14
Avenue Rd NW8	109	R1
Avenue Rd NW10	107	L4
Avenue Rd SE20	185	M1
Avenue Rd SE25	184	G4
Avenue Rd SW16	182	G4
Avenue Rd SW20	179	R3
Avenue Rd W3	124	C3
Avenue Rd, Beck	185	N2
Avenue Rd, Bexh	154	J6
Avenue Rd, Brent	123	M9
Avenue Rd, Hmptn	175	R2
Avenue Rd, Islw	140	E2
Avenue Rd, Kings T	177	S5
Avenue Rd, N Mal	178	J7

Avenue Rd, Pnr	66	J5
Avenue Rd	82	D14
(Chadwell Heath),		
Rom		
Avenue Rd, Sthl	121	M2
Avenue Rd, Tedd	158	G13
Avenue Rd, Wall	196	E14
Avenue Rd, Wdf Grn	63	U11
Avenue S, Surb	178	A13
Avenue Ter, N Mal	178	E6
Averil Gro SW16	165	R12
Averill St W6	126	A12
Avern Gdns, W Mol	175	S8
Avern Rd, W Mol	175	S8
Avery Fm Row,	32	G4
SW1 *2*		
Avery Gdns, Ilf	80	F10
Avery Hill Rd SE9	153	N12
Avery Row W1	16	H9
Aviary Cl E16	115	M10
Aviemore Cl, Beck	185	T10
Aviemore Way,	185	R10
Beck		
Avignon Rd SE4	149	P5
Avington Gro SE20	167	L13
Avion Cres NW9	71	N2
Avis Sq E1	113	P11
Avoca Rd SW17	164	A7
Avocet Ms SE28	13b	P5
Avon Cl, Hayes	102	E8
Avon Cl, Sutt	195	M8
Avon Cl, Wor Pk	193	N3
Avon Ct, Grnf	103	R7
Avon Ms, Pnr	51	L14
Avon Path, S Croy	197	U12
Avon Pl SE1	28	B7
Avon Rd E17	78	G6
Avon Rd SE4	150	A5
Avon Rd, Grnf	103	R7
Avon Way E18	79	P6
Avondale Av N12	56	J10
Avondale Av NW2	89	K5
Avondale Av, Barn	57	T1
Avondale Av, Esher	190	G5
Avondale Av,	193	L1
Wor Pk		
Avondale Cl, Loug	48	E13
Avondale Ct E11	96	J1
Avondale Ct E16	115	K9
Avondale Ct E18	79	R1
Avondale Cres, Enf	45	R6
Avondale Cres, Ilf	80	B10
Avondale Dr, Hayes	120	C2
Avondale Dr, Loug	48	E13
Avondale Gdns,	139	M10
Houns		
Avondale Pk Gdns,	108	C14
W11 *1*		
Avondale Pk Rd	108	C13
W11		
Avondale Ri SE15	148	E5
Avondale Rd E16	115	K9
Avondale Rd E17	78	A13
Avondale Rd N3	73	L2
Avondale Rd N13	59	P4
Avondale Rd N15	75	S9
Avondale Rd SE9	170	C4
Avondale Rd SW14	142	H5
Avondale Rd SW19	162	J9
Avondale Rd, Brom	169	K12
Avondale Rd, Har	68	F5
Avondale Rd, S Croy	197	U12
Avondale Rd, Well	154	F4
Avondale Sq SE1	37	R8
Avonley Rd SE14	131	M13
Avonmore Pl, W14 *5*	126	D7
Avonmore Rd W14	126	E7
Avonmouth St SE1	27	U9
Avonwick Rd, Houns	139	R3
Avril Way E4	62	F9
Avro Way, Wall	197	K13
Awlfield Av N17	76	B2
Awliscombe Rd,	153	U3
Well		
Axe St, Bark	117	M1
Axholme Av, Edg	70	C1
Axminster Cres,	154	E1
Well		
Axminster Rd N7	93	K5
Aybrook St W1	16	D3

Aycliffe Cl, Brom	188	F7
Aycliffe Rd W12	125	M1
Aylands Cl, Wem	87	S3
Ayles Rd, Hayes	102	C6
Aylesbury Cl E7	97	M11
Aylesbury Est SE17	36	E8
Aylesbury Rd SE17	36	E7
Aylesbury Rd, Brom	187	N6
Aylesbury St EC1	11	N11
Aylesbury St NW10	88	H6
Aylesford Av, Beck	185	R10
Aylesford St SW1	33	S7
Aylesham Cl, NW7 *2*	55	N14
Aylesham Rd, Orp	189	T13
Aylestone Av NW6	90	A14
Aylett Rd SE25	184	J8
Aylett Rd, Islw	140	D4
Ayley Cft, Enf	44	G10
Ayliffe Cl, Kings T	178	A3
Aylmer Cl, Stan	52	H7
Aylmer Dr, Stan	52	G7
Aylmer Rd E11	79	L14
Aylmer Rd N2	73	S10
Aylmer Rd W12	125	L4
Aylmer Rd, Dag	100	J6
Ayloffe Rd, Dag	101	L11
Aylward Rd SE23	167	P4
Aylward Rd SW20	180	E4
Aylward St E1 L1	113	L11
Aylwards Ri, Stan	52	G7
Aylwyn Est SE1	29	K10
Aynhoe Rd W14	126	B7
Aynscombe La	142	F5
SW14		
Ayr Ct W3	106	A10
Ayres Cl E13	115	P6
Ayres Cres NW10	88	G14
Ayres St SE1	28	A5
Ayrsome Rd N16	94	C5
Ayrton Rd SW7	22	J10
Aysgarth Rd SE21	148	C12
Aytoun Pl SW9	147	M4
Aytoun Rd SW9	147	M4
Azalea Cl W7	122	F1
Azalea Cl, Ilf	98	J10
Azalea Wk, Pnr	66	C10
Azenby Rd SE15	148	E3
Azof St SE10	133	K8

B

Baalbec Rd N5	93	S10
Babbacombe Cl,	191	N9
Chess		
Babbacombe Gdns,	80	C7
Ilf		
Babbacombe Rd,	187	P1
Brom		
Baber Dr, Felt	138	E11
Babington Ri, Wem	88	B11
Babington Rd NW4	71	S7
Babington Rd	164	G9
SW16		
Babington Rd, Dag	100	F9
Babmaes St SW1	17	P12
Bacchus Wk, N1 *1*	12	H3
Baches St N1	12	F7
Back Ch La E1	21	S8
Back Hill EC1	11	K12
Back La N8	74	J10
Back La NW3	91	M7
Back La, Bex	155	N13
Back La, Brent	123	P12
Back La, Edg	70	E2
Back La, Rich	159	L4
Back La, Rom	82	H13
Back Rd, Sid	172	B8
Backhouse Pl SE17	36	J4
Backley Gdns SE25	184	G11
Bacon Gro SE1	29	L12
Bacon La, Edg	70	B1
Bacon La, NW9	70	B1
Bacon St E1	13	P10
Bacon St E2	13	P10
Bacons La N6	92	B1
Bacton St E2	113	M5
Baddow Cl, Dag	119	N1

Baddow Cl, Wdf Grn	64	A11
Baddow Wk N1	111	T1
Baden Pl SE1	28	D6
Baden Powell Cl,	119	K1
Dag		
Baden Powell Cl,	191	T4
Surb		
Baden Rd N8	74	H7
Baden Rd, Ilf	98	J9
Badger Cl, Felt	156	B6
Badger Cl, Houns	138	E5
Badger Cl, Har	68	A12
Badgers Cl, Enf	43	S6
Badgers Cl, Har	68	A12
Badgers Copse, Orp	203	T4
Badgers Copse,	193	M3
Wor Pk		
Badgers Cft N20	56	D1
Badgers Cft SE9	170	H6
Badgers Hole, Croy	199	N7
Badgers Wk, N Mal	178	J3
Badlis Rd E17	78	A4
Badminton Cl,	38	A4
Borwd *2*		
Badminton Cl, Har	68	C7
Badminton Cl, Nthlt	85	P12
Badminton Ms,	133	P1
E16 *10*		
Badminton Rd SW12	146	B12
Badsworth Rd SE5	147	T1
Bagley's La SW6	145	K2
Bagleys Spring, Rom	83	K7
Bagshot Ct SE18	152	G1
Bagshot Rd, Enf	44	E12
Bagshot St SE17	36	J7
Baildon St SE8	131	U14
Bailey Cl E4	62	E7
Bailey Pl SE26	167	N11
Bainbridge Rd, Dag	101	M7
Bainbridge St WC1	17	U5
Baines Cl, S Croy *7*	198	A9
Baird Av, Sthl	103	S13
Baird Cl NW9	70	F12
Baird Gdns SE19	166	D8
Baird Rd, Enf	44	J7
Baird St, EC1 *2*	12	B10
Baizdon Rd SE3	150	J4
Baker La, Mitch	182	A4
Baker Rd NW10	106	J2
Baker Rd SE18	134	D14
Baker St NW1	8	B12
Baker St W1	16	C4
Baker St, Enf	44	B4
Bakers Av E17	78	C12
Bakers Ct SE25	184	D5
Bakers End SW20	180	D3
Bakers Fld N7	92	H7
Bakers Gdns, Cars	195	R3
Bakers Hill E5	95	L2
Bakers Hill, Barn	41	K4
Bakers La N6	73	U10
Baker's Ms W1	16	D5
Bakers Ms, Orp *2*	203	T12
Baker's Rents, E2 *2*	13	L7
Bakers Row E15	114	J3
Baker's Row, EC1 *10*	11	K11
Bakery Cl SW9	147	M1
Bakery Pl, SW11 *4*	145	T7
Bakewell Way,	178	J3
N Mal		
Balaam St E13	115	P7
Balaams La N14	58	G4
Balaclava Rd SE1	37	P3
Balaclava Rd, Surb	177	M13
Balcaskie Rd SE9	152	F9
Balchen Rd SE3	152	A8
Balchier Rd SE22	148	J11
Balcombe Cl, Bexh	154	H8
Balcombe St NW1	7	T11
Balcon Way, Borwd	38	F1
Balcorne St E9	95	M14
Balder Ri SE12	169	S4
Balderton St W1	16	E8
Baldock St E3	114	C4
Baldry Gdns SW16	165	L12
Baldwin Cres SE5	147	L2
Baldwin St EC1	12	C8
Baldwin Ter N1	11	T2
Baldwin's Gdns EC1	18	J2
Baldwins Hill, Loug	48	E2

Baldwyn Gdns W3	106	F13
Balfe St N1	10	D3
Balfern Gro W4	125	K10
Balfern St SW11	145	S3
Balfour Av W7	122	E1
Balfour Gro N20	57	T6
Balfour Ms N9	60	G5
Balfour Ms W1	24	E1
Balfour Pl, SW15 *3*	143	R7
Balfour Pl W1	16	E12
Balfour Rd N5	93	T8
Balfour Rd SE25	184	G8
Balfour Rd SW19	162	J14
Balfour Rd W3	106	F10
Balfour Rd W13	122	J4
Balfour Rd, Brom	188	B9
Balfour Rd, Cars	195	U13
Balfour Rd, Har	68	B10
Balfour Rd, Houns	139	R5
Balfour Rd, Ilf	99	M1
Balfour Rd, Sthl	120	G5
Balfour St SE17	36	C2
Balgonie Rd E4	62	G2
Balgowan Cl, N Mal	179	K8
Balgowan Rd, Beck	185	T4
Balgowan St SE18	135	T8
Balham Gro SW12	146	B14
Balham High Rd	164	B2
SW12		
Balham High Rd	164	A5
SW17		
Balham Hill SW12	146	D13
Balham New Rd	146	D14
SW12		
Balham Pk Rd SW12	163	U13
Balham Rd N9	60	H3
Balham Sta Rd	164	C2
SW12		
Balladier Wk E14	114	C9
Ballamore Rd, Brom	169	N5
Ballance Rd E9	95	R11
Ballantine St,	145	L8
SW18 *14*		
Ballard Cl, Kings T	160	G14
Ballards Cl, Dag	119	R1
Ballards Fm Rd,	198	J12
Croy		
Ballards Fm Rd,	198	G11
S Croy		
Ballards La N3	72	H4
Ballards La N12	57	L12
Ballards Ms, Edg	54	A12
Ballards Ri, S Croy	198	H12
Ballards Rd NW2	89	N4
Ballards Rd, Dag	119	R3
Ballards Way, Croy	199	L11
Ballards Way,	198	H12
S Croy		
Ballast Quay SE10	132	H9
Ballater Cl, Wat	50	D7
Ballater Rd SW2	147	K7
Ballater Rd, S Croy	198	F9
Ballina St SE23	149	P13
Ballingdon Rd SW11	146	A11
Balliol Av E4	62	J8
Balliol Rd N17	76	C2
Balliol Rd W10	107	U11
Balliol Rd, Well	154	D3
Balloch Rd SE6	168	G2
Ballogie Av NW10	89	K7
Balls Pond Pl, N1 *1*	94	B11
Balls Pond Rd N1	94	C11
Balmain Cl W5	123	P1
Balmer Rd E3	113	T4
Balmes Rd N1	112	B1
Balmoral Av, Beck	185	S8
Balmoral Cl SW15	144	A11
Balmoral Cres,	175	N6
W Mol		
Balmoral Dr, Borwd	38	H6
Balmoral Dr, Sthl	103	R7
Balmoral Gdns W13	122	G4
Balmoral Gdns, Bex	155	M14
Balmoral Gdns, Ilf	99	T2
Balmoral Gro N7	93	L12
Balmoral Ms W12	125	L5
Balmoral Rd E7	97	T9
Balmoral Rd E10	96	D4
Balmoral Rd NW2	89	R11

Name	No.	Grid
Balmoral Rd, Har	85	N7
Balmoral Rd, Kings T	177	T7
Balmoral Rd, Wor Pk	193	R4
Balmore Cres, Barn	42	B9
Balmore St N19	92	D4
Balmuir Gdns SW15	143	U8
Balnacraig Av NW10	89	K7
Balniel Gate SW1	33	T7
Baltic Cl SW19	163	N13
Baltic Ct SE16	131	P3
Baltic Pl N1	112	D1
Baltic St E EC1	11	U11
Baltic St W EC1	11	T11
Baltimore Pl, Well	153	T4
Balvaird Pl SW1	33	T8
Balvernie Gro SW18	144	F14
Bamborough Gdns, W12 2	125	U4
Bamford Av, Wem	105	T2
Bamford Rd, Bark	99	L12
Bamford Rd, Brom	168	F9
Bampfylde Cl, Wall	196	E6
Bampton Dr NW7	55	P14
Bampton Rd SE23	167	N5
Banavie Gdns, Beck	186	E1
Banbury Cl, Enf	43	S2
Banbury Ct, WC2 3	18	B9
Banbury Ct, Sutt	194	H14
Banbury Rd E9	95	N14
Banbury Rd E17	61	R14
Banbury St SW11	145	S3
Banchory Rd SE3	133	R13
Bancroft Av N2	73	R9
Bancroft Av, Buck H	63	R4
Bancroft Ct, Nthlt	102	F2
Bancroft Gdns, Har	67	T2
Bancroft Gdns, Orp	203	T1
Bancroft Rd E1	113	P7
Bancroft Rd, Har 1	67	U3
Bandon Ri, Wall	196	G10
Bangalore St SW15	143	U6
Bangor Cl, Nthlt	85	R10
Banim St W6	125	S7
Banister Rd W10	108	B5
Bank, The N6	92	C1
Bank Av, Mitch	181	P4
Bank End SE1	28	B1
Bank La SW15	143	K10
Bank La, Kings T	159	R13
Bank Ms, Sutt	195	L11
Bankfoot Rd, Brom	169	K8
Bankhurst Rd SE6	149	U13
Banks La, Bexh	155	M7
Banks Rd, Borwd	38	F3
Banksia Rd N18	61	M9
Banksian Wk, Islw	140	D2
Bankside SE1	19	U12
Bankside, Enf	43	S2
Bankside, S Croy	198	E12
Bankside, Sthl	120	H1
Bankside Av, Nthlt	102	B4
Bankside Cl, Cars	195	S11
Bankside Cl, Islw	140	F8
Bankside Dr, T Ditt	190	J2
Bankside Rd, Ilf	99	N10
Bankton Rd SW2	147	P8
Bankwell Rd SE13	151	K8
Banner St EC1	12	B10
Banning St SE10	132	J9
Bannister Cl SW2	165	N1
Bannister Cl, Grnf	86	A9
Bannockburn Rd SE18	135	S8
Banstead Gdns N9	60	B5
Banstead Rd, Cars	195	S11
Banstead St SE15	149	L5
Banstead Way, Wall 3	197	K9
Banstock Rd, Edg	54	D12
Banting Dr N21	43	L10
Banton Cl, Enf	44	J3
Bantry St SE5	130	B14
Banwell Rd, Bex	154	G11
Banyard Rd SE16	131	K6
Baptist Gdns NW5	92	A11
Barandon Wk W11	108	B13
Barb Ms W6	125	U6
Barbara Brosnan Ct NW8	7	K2
Barbara Hucklesby Cl, N22 3	75	R4
Barbauld Rd N16	94	C6
Barber Cl N21	43	P14
Barber's All E13	115	R5
Barbers Rd E15	114	C3
Barbican, The EC2	20	A2
Barbican Rd, Grnf	103	S11
Barbon Cl WC1	18	E1
Barbot Cl N9	60	G6
Barchard St SW18	144	J9
Barchester Cl W7	122	F2
Barchester Rd, Har	68	B3
Barchester St E14	114	C10
Barclay Cl, SW6 7	126	G14
Barclay Oval, Wdf Grn	63	P7
Barclay Path E17	78	E10
Barclay Rd E11	97	L1
Barclay Rd E13	115	T8
Barclay Rd E17	78	E10
Barclay Rd N18	60	B12
Barclay Rd SW6	126	H14
Barclay Rd, Croy	198	A5
Barcombe Av SW2	165	L4
Barcombe Cl, Orp	189	U5
Bard Rd W10	108	A13
Barden St SE18	135	R13
Bardfield Av, Rom	82	G6
Bardney Rd, Mord	181	K7
Bardolph Rd N7	92	J7
Bardolph Rd, Rich	141	U6
Bardsey Pl, E1 14	113	L8
Bardsley Cl, Croy	198	E5
Bardsley La SE10	132	E12
Barfett St W10	108	E7
Barfield Av N20	57	T3
Barfield Rd E11	97	L1
Barfield Rd, Brom	188	G6
Barfields, Loug	48	H8
Barfields Gdns, Loug	48	G7
Barfields Path, Loug	48	H8
Barford Cl NW4	71	P2
Barford St N1	111	P2
Barforth Rd SE15	149	K6
Barfreston Way, SE20 3	185	K1
Bargate Cl SE18	135	U10
Bargate Cl, N Mal	179	N13
Barge Ho Rd E16	135	K3
Barge Ho St SE1	27	L1
Barge Wk, E Mol	176	G9
Barge Wk, Kings T	159	P14
Barge Wk, Walt	174	G5
Bargery Rd SE6	168	D2
Bargrove Cl SE20	166	G13
Barham Cl, Brom	202	D2
Barham Cl, Chis	170	J9
Barham Cl, Rom	83	R4
Barham Cl, Wem	87	K11
Barham Rd SW20	161	N13
Barham Rd, Chis	170	J9
Barham Rd, S Croy	197	U9
Baring Cl SE12	169	P3
Baring Rd SE12	151	N14
Baring Rd, Barn	41	P6
Baring Rd, Croy	198	H1
Baring St N1	112	A2
Bark Pl W2	14	B10
Barker Dr NW1	92	F14
Barker Ms SW4	146	D7
Barker St SW10	30	F10
Barker Wk, SW16 1	164	H5
Barkham Rd N17	60	B13
Barking Ind Pk, Bark	117	U2
Barking Rd E6	116	B3
Barking Rd E13	115	S6
Barking Rd E16	115	M9
Barkston Gdns SW5	30	A8
Barkwood Cl, Rom	83	U9
Barkworth Rd SE16	131	K10
Barlborough St SE14	131	N13
Barlby Gdns W10	108	A8
Barlby Rd W10	108	B8
Barley La, Ilf	100	B1
Barley La, Rom	82	D8
Barley Mow Pas W4	124	G9
Barleycorn Way E14	113	T14
Barleyfields Cl, Rom	82	D12
Barlow Cl, Wall	196	J13
Barlow Pl, W1 4	17	K11
Barlow Rd NW6	90	F11
Barlow Rd W3	124	D1
Barlow Rd, Hmptn	157	P13
Barlow St SE17	36	F3
Barmeston Rd SE6	168	C3
Barmor Cl, Har	67	S3
Barmouth Av, Grnf	104	F4
Barmouth Rd SW18	145	M12
Barmouth Rd, Croy	199	P4
Barn Cl, Nthlt	102	E3
Barn Cres, Stan	53	L12
Barn Elms Pk SW15	143	U4
Barn Hill, Wem	88	C4
Barn Ms, Har	85	N6
Barn Ri, Wem	88	B4
Barn St N16	94	C4
Barn Way, Wem	88	B2
Barnabas Ct N21	43	P9
Barnabas Rd E9	95	P10
Barnaby Cl, Har	85	T4
Barnaby Pl SW7	31	K3
Barnaby Way, Chig	64	J6
Barnard Cl, SE18 3	134	H6
Barnard Cl, Chis	189	P1
Barnard Cl, Sun	156	C14
Barnard Cl, Wall	196	H14
Barnard Gdns, Hayes	102	D8
Barnard Gdns, N Mal	179	P8
Barnard Gro E15	97	L14
Barnard Hill N10	74	C2
Barnard Ms SW11	145	S7
Barnard Rd SW11	145	S7
Barnard Rd, Enf	45	K3
Barnard Rd, Mitch	182	A5
Barnardo Dr, Ilf 1	81	M7
Barnardo St E1	113	N12
Barnardos Village, Ilf	81	M7
Barnard's Inn, EC1 2	19	L5
Barnby Sq, E15 6	114	J1
Barnby St E15	114	J1
Barnby St NW1	9	N5
Barncroft Cl, Loug	48	G10
Barncroft Grn, Loug	48	G10
Barncroft Rd, Loug	48	G10
Barnehurst Av, Bexh	155	U2
Barnehurst Av, Erith	155	U1
Barnehurst Cl, Erith	155	T1
Barnehurst Rd, Bexh	155	T4
Barnes Av SW13	125	N13
Barnes Av, Sthl	121	L8
Barnes Br SW13	143	K3
Barnes Br W4	143	K3
Barnes Cl E12	98	B8
Barnes Ct, E16 11	115	U9
Barnes Ct, Wdf Grn	64	A9
Barnes End, N Mal	179	P10
Barnes High St SW13	143	L3
Barnes Pikle W5	105	N14
Barnes Rd N18	61	L7
Barnes Rd, Ilf	99	M9
Barnes St E14	113	R12
Barnes Ter SE8	131	U10
Barnet Bypass, Barn	38	H11
Barnet Dr, Brom	202	D3
Barnet Gate La, Barn	39	M12
Barnet Gro E2	13	S6
Barnet Hill, Barn	40	G8
Barnet La N20	56	E1
Barnet La, Barn	40	F12
Barnet La, Borwd	38	G11
Barnet Rd (Arkley), Barn	39	T8
Barnet Trd Est, Barn	40	F6
Barnet Way NW7	54	H3
Barnet Wd Rd, Brom	202	B4
Barnett St, E1 8	112	J11
Barney Cl SE7	133	T9
Barnfield, N Mal	178	J11
Barnfield Av, Croy	199	M2
Barnfield Av, Kings T	159	R8
Barnfield Av, Mitch	182	D7
Barnfield Cl N4	75	K14
Barnfield Cl SW17	163	N5
Barnfield Gdns, Kings T	159	R8
Barnfield Pl E14	132	B8
Barnfield Rd SE18	135	K12
Barnfield Rd W5	105	L7
Barnfield Rd, Belv	137	M11
Barnfield Rd, Edg	70	E2
Barnfield Wd Cl, Beck	186	H11
Barnfield Wd Rd, Beck	186	H11
Barnham Rd, Grnf	103	T5
Barnham St SE1	28	J5
Barnhill, Pnr	66	F9
Barnhill Av, Brom	187	M10
Barnhill La, Hayes	102	D7
Barnhill Rd, Hayes	102	D7
Barnhill Rd, Wem	88	F5
Barnhurst Path, Wat	50	E9
Barningham Way NW9	70	G11
Barnlea Cl, Felt	157	K4
Barnmead Gdns, Dag	101	M9
Barnmead Rd, Beck	185	R1
Barnmead Rd, Dag	101	L10
Barnsbury Cl, N Mal	178	F8
Barnsbury Cres, Surb	192	E2
Barnsbury Gro, N7 7	93	M13
Barnsbury La, Surb	192	D3
Barnsbury Pk N1	93	N13
Barnsbury Rd N1	111	N2
Barnsbury Sq N1	93	N13
Barnsbury St N1	93	P14
Barnsbury Ter, N1 8	93	M14
Barnscroft SW20	179	S5
Barnsdale Av E14	132	B7
Barnsdale Rd W9	108	F7
Barnsley St E1	113	K7
Barnstaple Rd, Ruis	84	E5
Barnwell Rd SW2	147	P9
Barnwood Cl W9	6	C12
Baron Cl N11	58	B10
Baron Gdns, Ilf	81	M5
Baron Gro, Mitch	181	S7
Baron Rd, Dag	100	G1
Baron St, N1 4	11	K2
Baron Wk E16	115	L9
Baron Wk, Mitch	181	R7
Baroness Rd E2	13	N5
Baronet Gro N17	76	G1
Baronet Rd N17	76	H1
Barons, The, Twick	141	K11
Barons Ct Rd W14	126	D9
Barons Gate, Barn	41	R9
Barons Keep W14	126	C9
Barons Mead, Har	68	D7
Barons Pl SE1	27	M7
Barons Wk, Croy	185	S11
Baronsfield Rd, Twick	141	K12
Baronsmead Rd SW13	143	P1
Baronsmede W5	123	T4
Baronsmere Rd N2	73	S7
Barque Ms, SE8 4	132	A11
Barrack Rd, Houns	138	H7
Barratt Av N22	75	L3
Barratt Way, Har	68	B5
Barrenger Rd N10	73	T2
Barrett Rd E17	78	F8
Barrett St W1	16	E7
Barretts Grn Rd NW10	106	F4
Barretts Gro N16	94	D9
Barrhill Rd SW2	165	K3
Barrie Est W2	14	J10
Barriedale SE14	149	S3
Barrier App SE7	134	A6
Barringer Sq SW17	164	B7
Barrington Cl NW5	92	A9
Barrington Cl, Ilf	80	F2
Barrington Cl, Loug	49	L6
Barrington Grn, Loug	49	L7
Barrington Rd E12	98	G11

Name	Page	Grid
Barrington Rd N8	74	H9
Barrington Rd SW9	147	R6
Barrington Rd, Bexh	154	G4
Barrington Rd, Loug	49	L7
Barrington Rd, Sutt	194	G2
Barrington Vil SE18	152	H2
Barrow Av, Cars	195	T14
Barrow Cl N21	59	S4
Barrow Hedges Cl, Cars	195	R13
Barrow Hedges Way, Cars	195	S13
Barrow Hill, Wor Pk	192	J3
Barrow Hill Cl, Wor Pk	192	J3
Barrow Hill Rd, NW8 1	7	N4
Barrow Pt Av, Pnr	66	J3
Barrow Pt La, Pnr	66	J3
Barrow Rd SW16	164	H12
Barrow Rd, Croy	197	P10
Barrow Wk, Brent 1	123	M10
Barrowdene Cl, Pnr	66	J3
Barrowell Grn N21	59	T4
Barrowfield Cl N9	61	K5
Barrowgate Rd W4	124	F10
Barrs Rd NW10	88	G13
Barry Av N15	76	F12
Barry Av, Bexh	136	J13
Barry Cl, Orp	203	R5
Barry Rd E6	116	D11
Barry Rd NW10	88	F13
Barry Rd SE22	148	H9
Barset Rd SE15	149	L5
Barson Cl SE20	167	M13
Barston Rd SE27	165	U5
Barstow Cres SW2	165	L2
Barter St WC1	18	C4
Barth Rd SE18	135	S8
Bartholomew Cl EC1	19	T4
Bartholomew Cl SW18	145	M8
Bartholomew La EC2	20	E6
Bartholomew Pl, EC1 6	19	T3
Bartholomew Rd NW5	92	F11
Bartholomew Sq EC1	12	B9
Bartholomew St SE1	28	E12
Bartholomew Vil NW5	92	E12
Bartle Av E6	116	D3
Bartle Rd W11	108	B12
Bartlett Cl E14	114	B11
Bartlett Ct, EC4 6	19	L5
Bartlett St, S Croy	198	A9
Barton Av, Rom	101	S2
Barton Cl, E6 1	116	F11
Barton Cl E9	95	M9
Barton Cl NW4	71	P9
Barton Cl SE15	149	K5
Barton Cl, Bexh	155	K9
Barton Cl, Chig	65	L4
Barton Grn, N Mal	178	H4
Barton Meadows, Ilf	81	K7
Barton Rd W14	126	C10
Barton Rd, Sid	173	K11
Barton St, SW1 1	26	A10
Barton Way, Borwd	38	A4
Bartram Rd SE4	149	S10
Barwell Business Pk, Chess	191	N14
Barwick Rd E7	97	R7
Barwood Av, W Wick	200	D1
Basden Gro, Felt	157	N4
Basedale Rd, Dag	100	C13
Baseing Cl E6	116	H13
Bashley Rd NW10	106	H7
Basil Av E6	116	D5
Basil Gdns SE27	165	T9
Basil Gdns, Croy 9	199	N2
Basil St SW3	23	U8
Basildene Rd, Houns	138	G4
Basildon Av, Ilf	80	H2
Basildon Rd SE2	136	B9
Basilon Rd, Bexh	154	J4
Basin S E16	135	K2
Basing Cl, T Ditt	176	F13
Basing Ct SE15	148	F2
Basing Dr, Bex	155	L11
Basing Hill NW11	90	E2
Basing Hill, Wem	88	A2
Basing Ho Yd E2	12	J6
Basing Pl E2	13	K5
Basing St W11	108	E11
Basing Way N3	72	H5
Basing Way, T Ditt	176	F13
Basingdon Way SE5	148	A7
Basingfield Rd, T Ditt	176	E13
Basinghall Av EC2	20	C4
Basinghall St EC2	20	C5
Basire St N1	111	U1
Baskerville Rd SW18	145	R13
Basket Gdns SE9	152	C9
Baslow Cl, Har	68	B1
Baslow Wk E5	95	P7
Basnett Rd, SW11 4	146	B5
Bassano St SE22	148	E9
Bassant Rd SE18	135	T12
Bassein Pk Rd W12	125	M4
Bassett Gdns, Islw	121	U14
Bassett Rd W10	108	B11
Bassett St NW5	92	A11
Bassett Way, Grnf	103	R11
Bassetts Cl, Orp	202	J8
Bassetts Way, Orp	202	J8
Bassingham Rd SW18	145	L13
Bassingham Rd, Wem	87	N12
Basswood Cl SE15	149	K6
Bastable Av, Bark	117	S4
Bastion Rd SE2	136	A10
Baston Manor Rd, Brom	201	R6
Baston Rd, Brom	201	T8
Bastwick St EC1	11	T10
Basuto Rd SW6	144	H2
Batavia Cl, Sun	174	E2
Batavia Ms, SE14 9	131	S14
Batavia Rd SE14	131	S14
Batavia Rd, Sun	174	D2
Batchelor St N1	11	K1
Bate St E14	113	U13
Bateman Cl, Bark 4	99	M12
Bateman Rd E4	62	A11
Bateman St W1	17	S8
Bateman's Row EC2	12	J9
Bates Cres SW16	164	F13
Bates Cres, Croy	197	P10
Bateson St, SE18 2	135	R8
Bath Cl SE15	131	K14
Bath Ct, EC1 12	11	K11
Bath Ho Rd, Croy	196	J2
Bath Pl, EC2 6	12	G8
Bath Pl, Barn	40	E5
Bath Rd E7	98	B12
Bath Rd N9	61	K3
Bath Rd W4	125	K7
Bath Rd, Houns	139	M5
Bath Rd, Mitch	181	N5
Bath Rd, Rom	82	J12
Bath St EC1	12	C8
Bath Ter SE1	27	U11
Bathgate Rd SW19	162	B6
Baths Rd, Brom	188	B7
Bathurst Av, SW19 2	180	J1
Bathurst Gdns NW10	107	S4
Bathurst Ms W2	15	L9
Bathurst Rd, Ilf	99	K2
Bathurst St W2	15	L9
Bathway, SE18 1	134	H7
Batley Cl, Mitch	181	T14
Batley Pl N16	94	E6
Batley Rd N16	94	E6
Batley Rd, Enf	44	A1
Batman Cl W12	125	S1
Batoum Gdns W6	125	U5
Batson St W12	125	P4
Batsworth Rd, Mitch	181	P5
Batten Cl, E6 6	116	F12
Batten St SW11	145	S5
Battersby Rd SE6	168	H4
Battersea Br SW3	31	M13
Battersea Br SW11	127	P13
Battersea Br Rd SW11	127	R14
Battersea Ch Rd SW11	145	P1
Battersea High St SW11	145	P2
Battersea Pk SW11	32	C14
Battersea Pk Rd SW8	33	U10
Battersea Pk Rd SW11	145	U2
Battersea Ri SW11	145	S8
Battery Rd SE28	135	R3
Battishill St, N1 5	93	R14
Battle Br La SE1	28	G3
Battle Br Rd NW1	10	A3
Battle Cl SW19	163	M11
Battle Rd, Belv	137	U7
Battle Rd, Erith	137	U7
Battledean Rd N5	93	R9
Batty St E1	21	T6
Baudwin Rd SE6	168	J4
Baugh Rd, Sid	172	F10
Baulk, The SW18	144	G14
Bavant Rd SW16	183	K3
Bavaria Rd N19	92	J3
Bavdene Ms NW4	71	nn
Bavent Rd SE5	147	U4
Bawdale Rd SE22	148	F10
Bawdsey Av, Ilf	81	U8
Bawtree Rd SE14	131	R13
Bawtry Rd N20	57	T6
Baxendale N20	57	M4
Baxendale St E2	13	R5
Baxter Cl, Sthl	121	R5
Baxter Rd E16	115	U11
Baxter Rd N1	94	B12
Baxter Rd N18	60	J8
Baxter Rd NW10	106	J8
Baxter Rd, Ilf	98	J9
Bay Ct W5	123	S5
Bay Tree Cl, Brom	188	A2
Baycroft Cl, Pnr	66	E5
Baydon Ct, Brom	187	M6
Bayes Cl SE26	167	L9
Bayfield Rd SE9	152	A8
Bayford Rd NW10	108	A6
Bayford St, E8 11	95	K14
Bayham Pl NW1	110	F2
Bayham Rd W4	124	H5
Bayham Rd W13	104	J14
Bayham Rd, Mord	181	K7
Bayham St NW1	110	E2
Bayley St WC1	17	S3
Bayley Wk, SE2 2	137	K10
Baylis Rd SE1	27	K7
Bayliss Av SE28	118	H13
Bayliss Cl N21	43	K9
Bayne Cl E6	116	E12
Baynes Cl, Enf	44	H2
Baynes Ms, NW3 4	91	P11
Baynes St NW1	92	F14
Baynham Cl, Bex	155	M11
Bayonne Rd W6	126	C12
Bayshill Ri, Nthlt	85	S11
Bayston Rd N16	94	E5
Bayswater Rd W2	15	N10
Baythorne St E3	113	U9
Baytree Cl, Sid	171	U2
Baytree Rd SW2	147	L8
Bazalgette Cl, N Mal	178	G10
Bazalgette Gdns, N Mal	178	G10
Bazely St E14	114	E13
Bazile Rd N21	43	P11
Beach Gro, Felt	157	N4
Beacham Cl SE7	134	B10
Beachborough Rd, Brom	168	F7
Beachcroft Rd E11	97	K5
Beachcroft Way N19	92	H2
Beachy Rd E3	96	A14
Beacon Gate SE14	149	N4
Beacon Gro, Cars 2	196	A8
Beacon Hill N7	92	J9
Beacon Rd SE13	150	G11
Beacons Cl, E6 20	116	D10
Beaconsfield Cl N11	58	B8
Beaconsfield Cl SE3	133	N11
Beaconsfield Cl W4	124	E10
Beaconsfield Rd E10	96	F4
Beaconsfield Rd E16	115	L8
Beaconsfield Rd E17	77	U12
Beaconsfield Rd N9	60	H6
Beaconsfield Rd N11	58	A7
Beaconsfield Rd N15	76	U8
Beaconsfield Rd NW10	89	M12
Beaconsfield Rd SE3	133	N12
Beaconsfield Rd SE9	170	C5
Beaconsfield Rd SE17	36	F9
Beaconsfield Rd W4	124	G6
Beaconsfield Rd W5	123	M3
Beaconsfield Rd, Brom	188	B6
Beaconsfield Rd, Croy	184	A11
Beaconsfield Rd, Esher	190	D14
Beaconsfield Rd, Hayes	120	F2
Beaconsfield Rd, N Mal	178	H4
Beaconsfield Rd, Sthl	121	K3
Beaconsfield Rd, Surb	177	U14
Beaconsfield Rd, Twick	141	K12
Beaconsfield Ter, Rom	82	H12
Beaconsfield Ter Rd, W14 1	126	C6
Beaconsfield Wk, SW6 2	144	F2
Beacontree Av E17	78	H2
Beacontree Rd E11	97	M1
Beadlow Cl, Cars	181	P12
Beadman Pl, SE27 6	165	S7
Beadman St SE27	165	S7
Beadnell Rd SE23	167	N1
Beadon Rd W6	125	T8
Beadon Rd, Brom	187	N8
Beaford Gro SW20	180	D6
Beagle Cl, Felt	156	C7
Beak St W1	17	N9
Beal Cl, Well	154	B1
Beal Rd, Ilf	98	H4
Beale Cl N13	59	S10
Beale Pl E3	113	T3
Beale Rd E3	113	T2
Beam Av, Dag	119	R2
Beaminster Gdns, Ilf	80	J4
Beamish Dr, Bushey	51	U2
Beamish Rd N9	60	H2
Bean Rd, Bexh	154	G8
Beanacre Cl E9	95	U11
Beanshaw SE9	170	H7
Beansland Gro, Rom	83	K4
Bear All EC4	19	P5
Bear Cl, Rom	83	R11
Bear Gdns SE1	27	U1
Bear La SE1	27	R3
Bear Rd, Felt	156	H8
Bear St, WC2 6	17	U10
Beard Rd, Kings T	159	T10
Beardell St SE19	166	E11
Beardow Gro N14	42	E12
Beard's Hill, Hmptn	175	P2
Beard's Hill Cl, Hmptn	175	P2
Beardsfield E13	115	N2
Beardsley Way W3	124	G3
Bearfield Rd, Kings T	159	S14
Bearstead Ri SE4	149	T10
Beatrice Av SW16	183	L4
Beatrice Av, Wem	87	S10
Beatrice Cl E13	115	N7
Beatrice Cl, Pnr	66	B7
Beatrice Ct, Buck H	63	L8
Beatrice Pl W8	22	A12
Beatrice Rd E17	78	B2
Beatrice Rd N4	75	P14
Beatrice Rd N9	45	L13
Beatrice Rd SE1	37	U4
Beatrice Rd, Rich 2	141	T9
Beatrice Rd, Sthl	121	L2

Name	No.	Ref	Name	No.	Ref	Name	No.	Ref	Name	No.	Ref
Beatson Wk SE16	131	P1	Beaumont Wk NW3	91	U13	Bede Rd, Rom	82	F11	Beech Lawns N12	57	P9
Beattock Ri N10	74	C7	Beauvais Ter, Nthlt	102	G4	Bedens Rd, Sid	172	J11	Beech Rd N11	59	K11
Beatty Rd N16	94	D7	Beauval Rd SE22	148	E11	Bedfont Cl, Mitch	182	A4	Beech Rd SW16	183	K4
Beatty Rd, Stan	53	M11	Beaver Cl, SE20 *2*	166	H13	Bedfont Av WC1	17	T4	Beech Row, Rich	159	R8
Beatty St NW1	9	L1	Beaver Cl, Hmptn	175	S2	Bedford Av, Barn	40	E10	Beech St EC2	20	A1
Beattyville Gdns, Ilf	80	J7	Beaver Gro, Nthlt	102	J6	Bedford Av, Hayes	102	C11	Beech St, Rom	83	U8
Beauchamp Cl, W4 *3*	124	F5	Beaverbank Rd SE9	171	N2	Bedford Cl N10	58	B14	Beech Tree Cl, Stan	53	M10
Beauchamp Pl SW3	23	S10	Beavers Cres, Houns	138	G8	Bedford Cl, W4 *7*	125	K12	Beech Tree Glade E4	63	L1
Beauchamp Rd E7	97	R13	Beavers La, Houns	138	H7	Bedford Ct WC2	18	B11	Beech Tree Pl, Sutt	195	K9
Beauchamp Rd SE19	184	A2	Beaverwood Rd, Chis	171	S10	Bedford Gdns W8	126	G2	Beech Wk NW7	54	J11
Beauchamp Rd SW11	145	S7	Beavor La W6	125	P8	Bedford Hill SW12	164	D3	Beech Way NW10	88	G13
Beauchamp Rd, E Mol	175	S9	Bebbington Rd, SE18 *3*	135	R8	Bedford Hill SW16	164	E5	Beech Way, Twick	157	P5
Beauchamp Rd, Sutt	194	H8	Bebletts Cl, Orp *9*	203	U10	Bedford Ms N2	73	R5	Beechcroft, Chis	170	G13
Beauchamp Rd, Twick	140	H14	Bec Cl, Ruis	84	H5	Bedford Pk, Croy	197	U2	Beechcroft Av NW11	72	E13
Beauchamp Rd, W Mol	175	S9	Beccles Dr, Bark	99	T11	Bedford Pas, SW6 *11*	126	D13	Beechcroft Av, Har	67	N14
Beauchamp St EC1	19	K3	Beccles St E14	113	U13	Bedford Pl, W1 *2*	17	N2	Beechcroft Av, N Mal	178	E2
Beauchamp Ter, SW15 *2*	143	S6	Beck Cl SE13	150	C2	Bedford Pl WC1	18	B1	Beechcroft Av, Sthl	121	L1
Beauclerc Rd W6	125	T5	Beck Ct, Beck	185	N5	Bedford Pl, Croy	198	A2	Beechcroft Cl, Houns	120	J13
Beauclerk Cl, Felt	156	D2	Beck La, Beck	185	N5	Bedford Rd E6	116	G1	Beechcroft Cl, Orp	203	P8
Beaufort, E6 *6*	116	H11	Beck Rd E8	112	J1	Bedford Rd E17	78	B4	Beechcroft Gdns, Wem	87	T6
Beaufort Av, Har	68	H7	Beck Way, Beck	185	U6	Bedford Rd E18	79	P4	Beechcroft Rd, E18 *1*	79	S4
Beaufort Cl E4	62	D11	Beckenham Business Cen, Beck	167	S11	Bedford Rd N2	73	R5	Beechcroft Rd SW14	142	F6
Beaufort Cl SW15	143	S14	Beckenham Gdns N9	60	C6	Bedford Rd N8	74	H11	Beechcroft Rd SW17	163	R3
Beaufort Cl W5	105	U9	Beckenham Gro, Brom	186	H4	Bedford Rd N9	44	J13	Beechcroft Rd, Chess	191	U7
Beaufort Cl, Rom	83	T7	Beckenham Hill Rd SE6	168	E10	Bedford Rd N15	76	C7	Beechcroft Rd, Orp	203	P8
Beaufort Ct, Rich	159	L8	Beckenham Hill Rd, Beck	168	E10	Bedford Rd N22	74	J2	Beechdale N21	59	M3
Beaufort Dr NW11	72	G7	Beckenham La, Brom	187	K3	Bedford Rd NW7	54	J4	Beechdale Rd SW2	147	L11
Beaufort Gdns NW4	71	T12	Beckenham Pl Pk, Beck	168	C13	Bedford Rd SW4	146	J7	Beechen Cliff Way, Islw *1*	140	E3
Beaufort Gdns SW3	23	S10	Beckenham Rd, Beck	185	R2	Bedford Rd W4	124	H6	Beechen Gro, Pnr	67	L6
Beaufort Gdns SW16	165	M14	Beckenham Rd, W Wick	186	D14	Bedford Rd W13	104	J14	Beeches, The, Houns	139	R2
Beaufort Gdns, Houns SW16	139	K1	Becket Av E6	116	G5	Bedford Rd, Har	67	U11	Beeches Av, Cars	195	S14
Beaufort Gdns, Ilf	98	G1	Becket Cl SE25	184	H11	Bedford Rd, Ilf	99	K6	Beeches Cl SE20	185	L2
Beaufort Pk NW11	72	G7	Becket Fold, Har *1*	68	F10	Bedford Rd, Sid	171	R6	Beeches Rd SW17	163	S5
Beaufort Rd W5	105	U10	Becket Rd N18	61	L8	Bedford Rd, Twick	158	B5	Beeches Rd, Sutt	194	D2
Beaufort Rd, Kings T	177	S7	Becket St SE1	28	D9	Bedford Rd, Wor Pk	193	U4	Beechfield Cotts, Brom	187	U3
Beaufort Rd, Rich	159	L8	Beckett Cl NW10	88	H12	Bedford Row WC1	18	G2	Beechfield Gdns, Rom	83	U13
Beaufort Rd, Twick	141	M13	Beckett Cl SW16	164	G3	Bedford Sq WC1	17	T3	Beechfield Rd N4	75	U12
Beaufort St SW3	31	L11	Beckett Cl, Belv	137	L6	Bedford St WC2	18	C11	Beechfield Rd SE6	167	U1
Beaufort Way, Epsom	193	P14	Beckett Wk, Beck	167	R12	Bedford Way WC1	9	U11	Beechfield Rd, Brom	187	U4
Beaufoy Rd N17	60	D14	Becketts Cl, Felt	138	C12	Bedfordbury WC2	18	B10	Beechhill Rd SE9	152	G9
Beaufoy Wk SE11	34	H4	Becketts Cl, Orp	203	T5	Bedgebury Gdns SW19	162	D3	Beechmont Cl, Brom	168	J10
Beaulieu Av E16	133	R1	Becketts Pl, Kings T	177	N2	Bedgebury Rd SE9	152	A8	Beechmore Gdns, Sutt	194	B4
Beaulieu Av SE26	166	J8	Beckford Dr, Orp	189	P14	Bedivere Rd, Brom	169	P5	Beechmore Rd SW11	145	U2
Beaulieu Cl NW9	71	K7	Beckford Pl, SE17 *1*	36	B7	Bedlow Way, Croy	197	L8	Beechmount Av W7	104	B10
Beaulieu Cl SE5	148	B5	Beckford Rd, Croy	184	F11	Bedonwell Rd SE2	137	K11	Beecholme Av, Mitch	182	C1
Beaulieu Cl, Houns	139	L9	Becklow Rd W12	125	N3	Bedonwell Rd, Belv	137	L12	Beechvale Cl N12	57	S9
Beaulieu Cl, Mitch	182	A2	Becks Rd, Sid	172	B5	Bedonwell Rd, Bexh	155	M2	Beechway, Bex	154	G12
Beaulieu Cl, Twick	141	N13	Beckton Rd E16	115	M9	Bedser Cl, SE11 *2*	34	G10	Beechwood Av N3	72	G6
Beaulieu Cl, Wat	50	F2	Beckway Rd SW16	182	G4	Bedser Cl, Th Hth	183	T6	Beechwood Av, Grnf	103	R6
Beaulieu Dr, Pnr	66	H13	Beckway St SE17	36	F3	Bedser Dr, Grnf	86	A9	Beechwood Av, Har	85	S5
Beaulieu Gdns N21	43	T14	Beckwith Rd SE24	148	A10	Bedster Gdns, W Mol	175	S4	Beechwood Av, Orp	203	R10
Beaumanor Gdns, SE9 *1*	170	H7	Beclands Rd SW17	164	B11	Bedwardine Rd SE19	166	C13	Beechwood Av, Rich	142	B2
Beaumaris Dr, Wdf Grn	64	A13	Becmead Av SW16	164	H7	Bedwell Rd N17	76	C1	Beechwood Av, Sun	156	A11
Beaumont Av W14	126	E9	Becmead Av, Har	69	K9	Bedwell Rd, Belv	137	N10	Beechwood Av, Th Hth	183	R7
Beaumont Av, Har	67	S12	Becondale Rd SE19	166	D10	Beeby Rd E16	115	R10	Beechwood Cl NW7	54	H10
Beaumont Av, Rich	141	T6	Becontree Av, Dag	100	C7	Beech Av N20	57	S2	Beechwood Cl, Surb	177	M14
Beaumont Av, Wem	87	L9	Bective Pl, SW15 *5*	144	E8	Beech Av W3	124	J2	Beechwood Cl, Cars	195	U8
Beaumont Cl, Kings T	160	B13	Bective Rd E7	97	P7	Beech Av, Brent	123	K13	Beechwood Cl, Sun	156	B11
Beaumont Cres W14	126	E9	Bective Rd SW15	144	E8	Beech Av, Buck H	63	R4	Beechwood Cres, Bexh	154	H5
Beaumont Gdns NW3	90	H5	Becton Pl, Erith	155	T1	Beech Av, Ruis	84	C1	Beechwood Dr, Kes	202	B7
Beaumont Gro, E1 *21*	113	N8	Bedale St SE1	28	D3	Beech Av, Sid	154	A13	Beechwood Dr, Wdf Grn	63	M10
Beaumont Ms W1	16	E2	Beddington Fm Rd, Croy	197	N1	Beech Cl N9	44	H12	Beechwood Gdns, Har	85	S6
Beaumont Pl W1	9	N10	Beddington Gdns, Cars	196	B12	Beech Cl, SE8 *5*	131	U12	Beechwood Gro, Ilf	80	G8
Beaumont Pl, Barn	40	F1	Beddington Gdns, Wall	196	C11	Beech Cl SW15	143	N13	Beechwood Gro, Surb	177	M14
Beaumont Pl, Islw	140	E9	Beddington Grn, Orp	189	T2	Beech Cl SW19	161	T12	Beechwood Ms N9	60	G4
Beaumont Ri N19	74	H14	Beddington Gro, Wall	196	H10	Beech Cl, Cars	195	T3	Beechwood Pk E18	79	N6
Beaumont Rd E10	78	D14	Beddington La, Croy	182	E11	Beech Cl, Loug	49	K5	Beechwood Ri, Chis	171	K8
Beaumont Rd E13	115	S6	Beddington Path, Orp	189	S2	Beech Cl, Sun	174	H3	Beechwood Rd E8	94	E11
Beaumont Rd SE19	165	T12	Beddington Rd, Ilf	81	T13	Beech Copse, Brom	188	E3	Beechwood Rd N8	74	H7
Beaumont Rd SW19	144	C13	Beddington Rd, Orp	189	S2	Beech Copse, S Croy	198	C9	Beechworth Cl NW3	90	H4
Beaumont Rd W4	124	F5	Beddington Trd Pk W, Croy	196	J2	Beech Ct SE9	152	D11	Beecroft Rd SE4	149	S9
Beaumont Rd, Orp	189	P12	Bede Cl, Pnr	66	H1	Beech Ct, Ilf	98	H6	Beehive Cl E8	94	E13
Beaumont Sq E1	113	N8				Beech Ct, Surb	177	R13			
Beaumont St W1	16	E1				Beech Dell, Kes	202	E8			
						Beech Dr N2	73	T5			
						Beech Gdns W5	123	R4			
						Beech Gdns, Dag	101	T13			
						Beech Gro, Ilf	65	S11			
						Beech Gro, Mitch	182	G8			
						Beech Gro, N Mal	178	G5			
						Beech Hall Cres E4	62	G13			
						Beech Hall Rd E4	62	G13			
						Beech Hill Av, Barn	41	N2			
						Beech Ho Rd, Croy	198	A6			
						Beech La, Buck H	63	R4			

Beehive La, Ilf 80 E9
Beehive Pl, SW9 2 147 N6
Beeken Dene, Orp 2 203 L8
Beeleigh Rd, Mord 181 K7
Beeston Cl, Wat 50 G7
Beeston Pl SW1 24 J10
Beeston Rd, Barn 41 P11
Beeston Way, Felt 138 E11
Beethoven St W10 108 D5
Beeton Cl, Pnr 51 N14
Begbie Rd SE3 151 T1
Beggars Hill, Epsom 193 M14
Beggars Roost La, Sutt 194 H11
Begonia Cl, E6 11 116 D9
Begonia Pl, Hmptn 1 157 N11
Beira St SW12 146 D13
Bekesbourne St E14 113 R12
Belcroft Cl, Brom 169 M14
Beldham Gdns, W Mol 175 R5
Belfairs Dr, Rom 82 F14
Belfairs Grn, Wat 50 G10
Belfast Rd N16 94 E3
Belfast Rd SE25 184 J8
Belfont Wk N7 93 K7
Belford Gro SE18 134 G8
Belfort Rd SE15 149 M3
Belfry Cl, SE16 9 131 K9
Belgrade Rd N16 94 D8
Belgrade Rd, Hmptn 175 R2
Belgrave Cl N14 42 F9
Belgrave Cl NW7 54 G10
Belgrave Cl W3 124 D3
Belgrave Cres, Sun 174 D2
Belgrave Gdns N14 42 G9
Belgrave Gdns NW8 109 L2
Belgrave Gdns, Stan 1 53 M9
Belgrave Ms N SW1 24 C8
Belgrave Ms S SW1 24 E10
Belgrave Ms W SW1 24 C10
Belgrave Pl SW1 24 E11
Belgrave Rd E10 96 E1
Belgrave Rd E11 97 N3
Belgrave Rd E13 115 T6
Belgrave Rd E17 78 B11
Belgrave Rd SE25 184 G7
Belgrave Rd SW1 33 M4
Belgrave Rd SW13 125 M14
Belgrave Rd, Houns 139 L6
Belgrave Rd, Ilf 98 E2
Belgrave Rd, Mitch 181 M5
Belgrave Rd, Sun 174 D1
Belgrave Sq SW1 24 E8
Belgrave St E1 113 P11
Belgrave Ter, Wdf Grn 63 N6
Belgrave Wk, Mitch 181 P6
Belgrave Yd, SW1 4 24 H11
Belgravia Cl, Barn 40 E5
Belgravia Gdns, Brom 168 J12
Belgravia Ms, Kings T 177 P8
Belgrove St WC1 10 C5
Belhaven Ct, Borwd 38 A2
Belinda Rd SW9 147 S6
Belitha Vil N1 93 M13
Bell Cl, Pnr 66 F5
Bell Ct, Surb 192 D3
Bell Dr SW18 144 C13
Bell Fm Av, Dag 101 T5
Bell Gdns E17 77 T10
Bell Grn SE26 167 T6
Bell Grn La SE26 167 T9
Bell Hill, Croy 4 197 U4
Bell Ho Rd, Rom 101 T1
Bell Inn Yd EC3 20 F8
Bell La E1 21 L4
Bell La E16 133 N1
Bell La NW4 72 A8
Bell La, Twick 158 H1
Bell La, Wem 87 P4
Bell Meadow, SE19 2 166 D8
Bell Rd, E Mol 176 A9
Bell Rd, Enf 44 B2
Bell Rd, Houns 139 R7
Bell St NW1 15 N2

Bell Water Gate, SE18 1 134 H5
Bell Wf La EC4 20 B11
Bell Yd WC2 18 J7
Bellamy Cl, E14 2 132 A3
Bellamy Cl, W14 13 126 F10
Bellamy Cl, Edg 54 F5
Bellamy Dr, Stan 68 J2
Bellamy Rd E4 62 D12
Bellamy Rd, Enf 44 A3
Bellamy St SW12 146 C13
Bellasis Av SW2 164 J3
Belle Vue, Grnf 104 A1
Belle Vue La, Bushey 52 B1
Belle Vue Pk, Th Hth 183 T6
Belle Vue Rd E17 78 G3
Bellefields Rd SW9 147 M6
Bellegrove Cl, Well 1 153 T4
Bellegrove Rd, Well 153 R4
Bellenden Rd SE15 148 F6
Bellestaines Pleasaunce E4 62 B3
Belleville Rd SW11 145 S10
Bellevue Ms, N11 1 58 A9
Bellevue Pl, E1 12 113 L8
Bellevue Rd N11 58 A9
Bellevue Rd SW13 143 P3
Bellevue Rd SW17 163 S1
Bellevue Rd W13 104 J8
Bellevue Rd, Bexh 155 L9
Bellevue Rd, Kings T 177 S6
Bellew St SW17 163 M6
Bellfield Av, Har 52 A12
Bellflower Cl, E6 31 116 C9
Bellgate Ms NW5 92 C7
Bellingham Grn SE6 168 B6
Bellingham Rd SE6 168 G4
Bello Cl SE24 147 R14
Bellot Gdns SE10 133 K9
Bellot St SE10 133 K9
Bellring Cl, Belv 137 P12
Bells All SW6 144 G4
Bells Hill, Barn 40 B7
Belltrees Gro SW16 165 M9
Bellwood Rd SE15 149 P8
Belmarsh Rd SE28 135 R4
Belmont Av N9 60 H1
Belmont Av N13 59 K9
Belmont Av N17 75 T6
Belmont Av, Barn 41 T9
Belmont Av, N Mal 179 P9
Belmont Av, Sthl 120 J6
Belmont Av, Well 153 R4
Belmont Av, Wem 105 T1
Belmont Circle, Har 68 J2
Belmont Cl E4 62 H10
Belmont Cl N20 56 J2
Belmont Cl SW4 146 G6
Belmont Cl, Barn 41 U7
Belmont Cl, Wdf Grn 63 R7
Belmont Ct NW11 72 F9
Belmont Gro SE13 150 G5
Belmont Gro W4 124 H8
Belmont Hill SE13 150 G6
Belmont La, Chis 171 L9
Belmont La, Stan 53 L14
Belmont Ms, SW19 1 162 A4
Belmont Pk SE13 150 J7
Belmont Pk Cl, SE13 3 150 H7
Belmont Pk Rd E10 78 D12
Belmont Ri, Sutt 194 E12
Belmont Rd N15 75 T6
Belmont Rd N17 75 T7
Belmont Rd SE25 184 J10
Belmont Rd SW4 146 F6
Belmont Rd W4 124 G8
Belmont Rd, Beck 185 T4
Belmont Rd, Chis 171 K10
Belmont Rd, Erith 137 P14
Belmont Rd, Har 68 G5
Belmont Rd, Ilf 99 L5
Belmont Rd, Twick 158 A3
Belmont Rd, Wall 196 D10
Belmont St NW1 92 B13
Belmor, Borwd 38 A10
Belmore Av, Hayes 102 A11

Belmore La N7 92 H10
Belmore St SW8 146 G1
Beloe Cl SW15 143 P6
Belsham St E9 95 L11
Belsize Av N13 59 L11
Belsize Av NW3 91 R10
Belsize Av W13 123 K6
Belsize Ct NW3 91 P9
Belsize Cres NW3 91 P10
Belsize Gdns, Sutt 195 K7
Belsize Gro NW3 91 S11
Belsize La NW3 91 N12
Belsize Pk NW3 91 N12
Belsize Pk Gdns NW3 91 R11
Belsize Pk Ms, NW3 1 91 P11
Belsize Pl NW3 91 P10
Belsize Rd NW6 91 M14
Belsize Rd, Har 52 A13
Belsize Sq NW3 91 P12
Belsize Ter NW3 91 P11
Belson Rd SE18 134 F7
Beltane Dr SW19 162 B5
Belthorn Cres SW12 146 F14
Belton Rd E7 97 S13
Belton Rd E11 96 J7
Belton Rd N17 76 D5
Belton Rd NW2 89 P11
Belton Rd, Sid 172 B7
Belton Way E3 114 A9
Beltran Rd SW6 144 J4
Beltwood Rd, Belv 137 T7
Belvedere Av SW19 162 D9
Belvedere Av, Ilf 80 J4
Belvedere Bldgs SE1 27 S7
Belvedere Cl, Tedd 158 C10
Belvedere Ct N2 73 P9
Belvedere Dr SW19 162 D10
Belvedere Gdns, W Mol 175 M9
Belvedere Gro SW19 162 C10
Belvedere Ind Est, Belv 137 U4
Belvedere Ms SE15 149 K6
Belvedere Pl SE1 27 S8
Belvedere Rd E10 95 S1
Belvedere Rd SE1 26 G4
Belvedere Rd SE2 136 G2
Belvedere Rd SE19 166 F13
Belvedere Rd W7 122 D5
Belvedere Rd, Bexh 155 M4
Belvedere Sq SW19 162 C10
Belvedere Strand NW9 71 L4
Belvedere Way, Har 69 S12
Belvoir Cl SE9 170 D5
Belvoir Rd SE22 148 H14
Belvue Cl, Nthlt 85 N13
Belvue Rd, Nthlt 85 P13
Bembridge Cl NW6 90 B13
Bemerton Est N1 93 K14
Bemerton St N1 111 L1
Bemish Rd SW15 144 B6
Bempton Dr, Ruis 84 C5
Bemsted Rd E17 77 U5
Ben Hale Cl, Stan 52 J9
Ben Jonson Rd E1 113 R10
Ben Smith Way, SE16 4 29 U9
Ben Tillet Cl, Bark 100 B14
Ben Tillett Cl, E16 3 134 E2
Benares Rd SE18 135 T8
Benbow Rd W6 125 S5
Benbow St SE8 132 B11
Benbury Cl, Brom 168 E9
Bench Fld, S Croy 198 F11
Bencroft Rd, SW16 3 164 F13
Bencurtis Pk, W Wick 200 H5
Bendall Ms NW1 15 R1
Bendemeer Rd SW15 144 A5
Bendish Rd E6 98 C14
Bendmore Av SE2 136 B9
Bendon Valley SW18 145 K14

Benedict Cl, Belv 5 137 K6
Benedict Cl, Orp 203 S6
Benedict Rd SW9 147 M5
Benedict Rd, Mitch 181 P6
Benedict Way N2 73 L5
Benenden Grn, Brom 187 N9
Benett Gdns SW16 182 J3
Benfleet Cl, Sutt 195 M6
Bengal Rd, Ilf 98 J7
Bengarth Dr, Har 68 B3
Bengarth Rd, Nthlt 102 J1
Bengeworth Rd SE5 147 T5
Bengeworth Rd, Har 86 H4
Benham Cl SW11 145 N6
Benham Cl, Chess 191 M11
Benham Gdns, Houns 139 M8
Benham Rd W7 104 D10
Benhams Pl, NW3 2 91 L7
Benhill Av, Sutt 195 L8
Benhill Rd SE5 130 B14
Benhill Rd, Sutt 195 N8
Benhill Wd Rd, Sutt 195 L8
Benhilton Gdns, Sutt 195 K6
Benhurst Ct SW16 165 N10
Benhurst La SW16 165 N10
Benin St SE13 150 H13
Benjafield Ct N18 60 J7
Benjamin Cl E8 112 H1
Benjamin St EC1 19 N1
Benledi St E14 114 G11
Benn St E9 95 S11
Bennerley Rd SW11 145 S9
Bennet's Hill, EC4 1 19 S9
Bennett Cl, Kings T 177 M2
Bennett Cl, Well 154 A4
Bennett Gro SE13 150 D2
Bennett Pk SE3 151 L5
Bennett Rd E13 115 T8
Bennett Rd N16 94 C8
Bennett Rd, Rom 83 K13
Bennett St SW1 25 M2
Bennett St W4 125 K11
Bennetts Av, Croy 199 S4
Bennetts Av, Grnf 104 C2
Bennetts Castle La, Dag 100 F7
Bennetts Cl, Mitch 164 D14
Bennetts Copse, Chis 170 C12
Bennetts Way, Croy 199 R4
Benningholme Rd, Edg 54 J11
Bennington Rd N17 76 C3
Bennington Rd, Wdf Grn 2 62 J14
Benn's Wk, Rich 141 R7
Benrek Cl, Ilf 81 L1
Bensbury Cl, SW15 5 143 T14
Bensham Cl, Th Hth 183 T8
Bensham Gro, Th Hth 183 T4
Bensham La, Croy 183 R13
Bensham La, Th Hth 183 S9
Bensham Manor Rd, Th Hth 183 U8
Bensley Cl N11 57 T10
Benson Av E6 115 U4
Benson Cl, Houns 139 N7
Benson Quay E1 113 L14
Benson Rd SE23 167 M1
Benson Rd, Croy 197 P6
Bentfield Gdns SE9 170 A6
Benthal Rd N16 94 G5
Bentham Rd E9 95 N12
Bentham Rd SE28 118 C14
Bentham Wk NW10 88 F10
Bentinck Ms W1 16 F5
Bentinck Pl NW8 7 N3
Bentinck St W1 16 F5
Bentley Dr NW2 90 E5
Bentley Dr, Ilf 81 L11
Bentley Ms, Enf 44 B11
Bentley Rd N1 94 D12
Bentley Way, Stan 52 G10
Bentley Way, Wdf Grn 63 N5

Benton Rd, Ilf	99	N1
Benton Rd, Wat	50	H9
Bentons La SE27	165	U8
Bentons Ri SE27	166	A9
Bentry Cl, Dag	101	K4
Bentry Rd, Dag	101	K3
Bentworth Rd W12	107	R12
Benwell Ct, Sun	174	A1
Benwell Rd N7	93	N9
Benwick Cl SE16	131	K7
Benworth St E3	113	U5
Benyon Rd N1	112	B1
Berber Rd SW11	145	U9
Berberry Cl, Edg 1	54	F7
Bercta Rd SE9	171	L3
Bere St E1	113	P13
Berens Rd NW10	108	A6
Berens Way, Chis	189	T6
Beresford Av N20	57	T3
Beresford Av W7	104	B10
Beresford Av, Surb	178	E14
Beresford Av, Twick	141	M11
Beresford Av, Wem	106	B1
Beresford Dr, Brom	188	B5
Beresford Dr, Wdf Grn	63	T7
Beresford Gdns, Enf	44	C7
Beresford Gdns, Houns	139	M10
Beresford Gdns, Rom	83	K10
Beresford Rd E4	62	J1
Beresford Rd E17	78	C1
Beresford Rd N2	73	R6
Beresford Rd N5	94	A10
Beresford Rd N8	75	P9
Beresford Rd, Har	68	A9
Beresford Rd, Kings T	177	T1
Beresford Rd, N Mal	178	F7
Beresford Rd, Sthl	120	H1
Beresford Rd, Sutt	194	F14
Beresford Sq SE18	134	J7
Beresford St SE18	134	J6
Beresford Ter N5	93	U10
Berestede Rd W6	125	M9
Bergen Sq, SE16 8	131	S5
Berger Cl, Orp	189	P12
Berger Rd E9	95	N12
Berghem Ms W14	126	A6
Bergholt Av, Ilf	80	C9
Bergholt Cres N16	76	C13
Bergholt Ms NW1	92	F14
Bering Wk E16	116	A12
Berisford Ms SW18	145	L11
Berkeley Av, Bexh	154	H2
Berkeley Av, Grnf	86	D12
Berkeley Av, Houns	138	B2
Berkeley Av, Ilf	80	H3
Berkeley Cl, Borwd	38	A9
Berkeley Cl, Kings T	159	R13
Berkeley Cl, Orp	189	R14
Berkeley Cl, Ruis	84	A5
Berkeley Ct N14	42	E12
Berkeley Ct, Wall	196	E6
Berkeley Cres, Barn	41	P10
Berkeley Dr, W Mol	175	M6
Berkeley Gdns N21	44	A13
Berkeley Gdns, W8 7	126	H2
Berkeley Gdns, Esher	190	H12
Berkeley Ms W1	16	B7
Berkeley Pl SW19	162	B12
Berkeley Rd E12	98	C10
Berkeley Rd N8	74	H10
Berkeley Rd N15	76	B12
Berkeley Rd NW9	70	B8
Berkeley Rd SW13	143	N1
Berkeley Sq W1	16	J11
Berkeley St W1	25	K1
Berkeley Waye, Houns	120	H13
Berkhampstead Rd, Belv	137	N9
Berkhamsted Av, Wem	87	U11
Berkley Gro, NW1 2	92	A14
Berkley Rd NW1	91	U14
Berkshire Gdns N13	59	N12

Berkshire Gdns N18	60	J10
Berkshire Rd E9	95	U11
Berkshire Way, Mitch	182	J8
Bermans Way NW10	89	L8
Bermondsey Sq, SE1 3	28	J10
Bermondsey St SE1	28	H5
Bermondsey Wall E SE16	130	J4
Bermondsey Wall W SE16	29	R6
Bernal Cl SE28	118	G13
Bernard Ashley Dr SE7	133	R10
Bernard Av W13	123	K5
Bernard Cassidy St E16	115	M9
Bernard Gdns SW19	162	F10
Bernard Rd N15	76	F9
Bernard Rd, Rom	83	T13
Bernard Rd, Wall	196	C8
Bernard St WC1	10	C11
Bernards Cl, Ilf	65	M12
Bernays Cl, Stan	53	L11
Bernays Gro SW9	147	M7
Berne Rd, Th Hth	183	T9
Bernel Dr, Croy	199	U5
Berners Dr W13	104	G12
Berners Ms W1	17	N4
Berners Pl W1	17	P5
Berners Rd N1	111	P3
Berners Rd N22	75	N2
Berners St W1	17	N5
Berney Rd, Croy	184	A13
Bernville Way, Har	69	U9
Bernwell Rd E4	63	K6
Berridge Grn, Edg	54	C14
Berridge Rd SE19	166	B9
Berriman Rd N7	93	M5
Berriton Rd, Har	85	M2
Berry Cl N21	59	S1
Berry Cl NW10	88	J13
Berry Ct, Houns	139	L10
Berry Hill, Stan	53	P7
Berry La SE21	166	B7
Berry Pl EC1	11	R8
Berry St, EC1 2	11	R10
Berry Way W5	123	R5
Berrybank Cl E4	62	E3
Berrydale Rd, Hayes	102	J7
Berryfield Cl E17	78	D8
Berryfield Cl, Brom	188	C3
Berryfield Rd SE17	35	S6
Berryhill SE9	152	J7
Berryhill Gdns SE9	152	J7
Berrylands SW20	179	U6
Berrylands, Surb	178	B10
Berrylands Rd, Surb	177	T11
Berryman Cl, Dag 1	100	F6
Berrymans La SE26	167	P8
Berrymead Gdns W3	124	F3
Berrymede Rd W4	124	G5
Bert Rd, Th Hth	183	T10
Bertal Rd SW17	163	N8
Berthon St SE8	132	B13
Bertie Rd NW10	89	N12
Bertie Rd SE26	167	P11
Bertram Cotts SW19	162	G13
Bertram Rd NW4	71	P12
Bertram Rd, Enf	44	F7
Bertram Rd, Kings T	160	A13
Bertram St N19	92	C4
Bertram Way, Enf	44	F8
Bertrand St SE13	150	C5
Bertrand Way SE28	118	D13
Berwick Av, Hayes	102	H13
Berwick Cl, Stan	52	F12
Berwick Cres, Sid	153	S12
Berwick Rd E16	115	S12
Berwick Rd N22	75	R1
Berwick Rd, Well	154	D2
Berwick St W1	17	R8
Berwyn Av, Houns	139	R2
Berwyn Rd SE24	165	R1
Berwyn Rd, Rich	142	C8
Beryl Av E6	116	D9
Beryl Rd W6	126	A10
Berystede, Kings T	160	C14

Besant Rd NW2	90	C7
Besant Way NW10	88	F10
Besley St SW16	164	F12
Bessant Dr, Rich	142	C1
Bessborough Gdns SW1	33	U6
Bessborough Pl SW1	33	S6
Bessborough Rd SW15	161	P1
Bessborough Rd, Har	68	B14
Bessborough St SW1	33	S6
Bessemer Rd SE5	147	U4
Bessie Lansbury Cl E6	116	G12
Bessingby Rd, Ruis	84	B4
Besson St SE14	149	N1
Bessy St, E2 3	113	M5
Bestwood St SE8	131	P8
Beswick Ms, NW6 1	91	K10
Betchworth Cl, Sutt 2	195	N9
Betchworth Rd, Ilf	99	S4
Betham Rd, Grnf	104	B6
Bethecar Rd, Har	68	C9
Bethel Rd, Well	154	F6
Bethell Av E16	115	M7
Bethell Av, Ilf	80	G14
Bethersden Cl, Beck	167	U14
Bethnal Grn Rd E1	13	M10
Bethnal Grn Rd E2	13	S8
Bethune Av N11	57	U8
Bethune Rd N16	94	C1
Bethune Rd NW10	106	H8
Bethwin Rd SE5	35	T13
Betjeman Cl, Pnr	67	N8
Betony Cl, Croy	199	N2
Betoyne Av E4	62	J7
Betstyle Rd N11	58	D8
Betterton Dr, Sid	173	K3
Betterton St WC2	18	B7
Bettons Pk E15	115	K2
Bettridge Rd SW6	144	F4
Betts Cl, Beck	185	R4
Betts Rd E16	115	S13
Betts St E1	112	J13
Betts Way SE20	185	K2
Betts Way, Surb	191	K1
Beulah Av, Th Hth	183	U4
Beulah Cl, Edg	54	C6
Beulah Cres, Th Hth	183	U4
Beulah Gro, Croy	183	U12
Beulah Hill SE19	165	S12
Beulah Rd E17	78	D9
Beulah Rd SW19	162	F13
Beulah Rd, Sutt	194	H8
Beulah Rd, Th Hth	183	T5
Bev Callender Cl, SW8 9	146	D5
Bevan Av, Bark	100	B13
Bevan Ct, Croy	197	P10
Bevan Rd SE2	136	C9
Bevan Rd, Barn	41	T7
Bevan St N1	111	U2
Bevenden St N1	12	E5
Beveridge Rd, NW10 1	89	K13
Beverley Av SW20	179	M1
Beverley Av, Houns	139	M8
Beverley Av, Sid	153	T14
Beverley Cl N21	59	T2
Beverley Cl SW11	145	N7
Beverley Cl SW13	143	M3
Beverley Cl, Chess	191	M8
Beverley Cl, Enf	44	C8
Beverley Ct N14	42	E13
Beverley Ct SE4	149	U5
Beverley Cres, Wdf Grn	79	R1
Beverley Dr, Edg	70	D5
Beverley Gdns NW11	72	C13
Beverley Gdns SW13	143	M5
Beverley Gdns, Stan	68	G2
Beverley Gdns, Wem	87	U2
Beverley Gdns, Wor Pk	193	P2

Beverley La SW15	161	L6
Beverley La, Kings T	161	K14
Beverley Ms E4	62	G11
Beverley Path SW13	143	L4
Beverley Rd E4	62	G12
Beverley Rd E6	116	B5
Beverley Rd, SE20 6	184	J4
Beverley Rd SW13	143	M5
Beverley Rd W4	125	L9
Beverley Rd, Bexh	155	U4
Beverley Rd, Brom	202	D4
Beverley Rd, Dag	101	K7
Beverley Rd, Kings T	177	M1
Beverley Rd, Mitch	182	G7
Beverley Rd, N Mal	179	N7
Beverley Rd, Ruis	84	D4
Beverley Rd, Sthl	121	K7
Beverley Rd, Wor Pk	193	T4
Beverley Way SW20	179	M2
Beverley Way, N Mal	179	N8
Beversbrook Rd N19	92	G5
Beverston Ms W1	15	U3
Beverstone Rd SW2	147	M9
Beverstone Rd, Th Hth	183	R8
Bevill Allen Cl SW17	163	U10
Bevill Cl SE25	184	H6
Bevin Cl SE16	131	R1
Bevin Rd, Hayes	102	B6
Bevin Sq SW17	163	T5
Bevington Rd W10	108	D9
Bevington Rd, Beck	186	C3
Bevington St SE16	29	T8
Bevis Marks EC3	20	J6
Bewcastle Gdns, Enf	43	K8
Bewdley St N1	93	N13
Bewick St SW8	146	D4
Bewley St E1	113	K13
Bewlys Rd SE27	165	S9
Bexhill Cl, Felt	156	J3
Bexhill Rd N11	58	G10
Bexhill Rd SE4	149	U12
Bexhill Rd SW14	142	E6
Bexhill Wk E15	115	K2
Bexley Gdns N9	60	B6
Bexley Gdns, Rom	82	C10
Bexley High St, Bex	155	P14
Bexley La, Sid	172	E7
Bexley Rd SE9	152	H11
Bexley Rd, Erith	137	U12
Beynon Rd, Cars	195	T10
Bianca Rd SE15	37	R11
Bibsworth Rd N3	72	F4
Bibury Cl SE15	37	K12
Bicester Rd, Rich	142	B6
Bickenhall St W1	16	A2
Bickersteth Rd SW17	163	T11
Bickerton Rd N19	92	E4
Bickley Cres, Brom	188	C7
Bickley Pk Rd, Brom	188	E5
Bickley Rd E10	78	C13
Bickley Rd, Brom	188	C4
Bickley St SW17	163	S10
Bicknell Rd SE5	147	U6
Bicknoller Rd, Enf	44	D1
Bicknor Rd, Orp	189	S13
Bidborough Cl, Brom	187	M10
Bidborough St WC1	10	A7
Biddenden Way SE9	170	G7
Bidder St E16	114	J9
Biddestone Rd N7	93	L8
Biddulph Rd W9	6	C7
Bideford Av, Grnf	104	A4
Bideford Cl, Edg	70	A2
Bideford Cl, Felt	157	M5
Bideford Gdns, Enf	44	D13
Bideford Rd, Brom	169	L6
Bideford Rd, Ruis	84	D6
Bideford Rd, Well	136	D14
Bidwell Gdns N11	58	F14
Bidwell St SE15	149	K2
Big Hill E5	95	K1
Bigbury Rd N17	60	C13
Biggerstaff Rd E15	114	F1
Biggerstaff St N4	93	N4
Biggin Av, Mitch	181	T2
Biggin Hill SE19	165	S14

Biggin Hill Cl, KingsT	159	N9
Biggin Way SE19	165	T14
Bigginwood Rd SW16	165	R14
Biggs Row SW15	144	A6
Bigland St E1	112	J12
Bignell Rd SE18	134	J10
Bignold Rd E7	97	P8
Bigwood Rd NW11	72	J11
Bill Hamling Cl SE9	170	E4
Billet Cl, Rom	82	H5
Billet Rd E17	77	P3
Billet Rd, Rom	82	F6
Billets Hart Cl W7	122	C4
Billing Pl SW10	30	C13
Billing Rd SW10	30	D13
Billing St SW10	30	D13
Billingford Cl SE4	149	P7
Billington Rd SE14	131	P14
Billiter Sq, EC3 **6**	20	J9
Billiter St EC3	20	J8
Billockby Cl, Chess	191	U12
Billson St E14	132	F8
Bilsby Gro SE9	170	B8
Bilton Rd, Grnf	105	K2
Bilton Way, Hayes	120	C4
Bina Gdns SW5	30	F4
Bincote Rd, Enf	43	M6
Binden Rd W12	125	M5
Bindon Grn, Mord **3**	181	K7
Binfield Rd SW4	147	K2
Binfield Rd, S Croy	198	E9
Bingfield St N1	111	K1
Bingham Pl W1	16	D1
Bingham Rd, Croy	198	H2
Bingham St N1	94	A11
Bingley Rd E16	115	T11
Bingley Rd, Grnf	103	U8
Bingley Rd, Sun	156	A13
Binney St, W1 **2**	16	F9
Binns Rd W4	124	J9
Binsey Wk SE2	136	F3
Binyon Cres, Stan	52	E10
Birbetts Rd SE9	170	E4
Birch Av N13	59	T6
Birch Cl E16	115	K9
Birch Cl, N19 **14**	92	E4
Birch Cl, Brent	122	J14
Birch Cl, Buck H	64	A5
Birch Cl, Houns	140	B4
Birch Cl, Rom	83	R6
Birch Cl, Tedd	158	G9
Birch Gdns, Dag	101	U6
Birch Gro E11	96	J6
Birch Gro SE12	151	M13
Birch Gro W3	124	A1
Birch Gro, Well	154	A8
Birch Hill, Croy	199	P8
Birch Mead, Orp	202	H3
Birch Pk, Har	51	T13
Birch Rd, Felt	156	H10
Birch Rd, Rom	83	R5
Birch Row, Brom	188	H13
Birch Tree Av, W Wick	201	L8
Birch Tree Way, Croy	198	J3
Birch Wk, Borwd	38	A1
Birch Wk, Erith	137	U11
Birch Wk, Mitch	182	C2
Birchanger Rd SE25	184	G9
Birchdale Gdns, Rom	82	G13
Birchdale Rd E7	97	U10
Birchdene Dr SE28	136	A2
Birchen Cl NW9	88	H3
Birchen Gro NW9	88	G4
Birchend Cl, S Croy	198	B11
Birches, The N21	43	L11
Birches, The SE7	133	S11
Birches, The Orp	202	G8
Birches Cl, Mitch	181	T6
Birches Cl, Pnr	66	J9
Birchfield St E14	114	A13
Birchin La EC3	20	F8
Birchington Cl, Bexh	155	R1
Birchington Rd N8	74	G11
Birchington Rd NW6	108	H1
Birchington Rd, Surb	177	U14
Birchlands Av SW12	145	U13

Birchmead Av, Pnr	66	F8
Birchmere Row SE3	151	M4
Birchmore Wk N5	93	T6
Birchway, Hayes	120	C2
Birchwood Av N10	74	B6
Birchwood Av, Beck	185	T7
Birchwood Av, Sid	172	D6
Birchwood Av, Wall	196	B5
Birchwood Cl, Mord	180	J8
Birchwood Ct N13	59	R9
Birchwood Ct, Edg	70	E4
Birchwood Dr NW3	91	K6
Birchwood Gro, Hmptn	157	P11
Birchwood Rd SW17	164	C9
Birchwood Rd, Orp	189	P8
Bird in Bush Rd SE15	37	T13
Bird St W1	16	F7
Bird Wk, Twick	157	M1
Bird-in-Hand La, Brom	188	B4
Bird-in-Hand Pas SE23	167	M3
Birdbrook Cl, Dag	101	U13
Birdbrook Rd SE3	151	U6
Birdcage Wk SW1	25	N8
Birdham Cl, Brom	188	D10
Birdhurst Av, S Croy	190	D8
Birdhurst Gdns, S Croy	198	B8
Birdhurst Ri, S Croy	198	C9
Birdhurst Rd SW18	145	L9
Birdhurst Rd SW19	163	R12
Birdhurst Rd, S Croy	198	C9
Birdlip Cl SE15	36	G12
Birds Fm Av, Rom	83	S1
Birdsfield La E3	113	T1
Birdwood Cl, Tedd	158	C7
Birkbeck Av W3	106	F13
Birkbeck Av, Grnf	103	U1
Birkbeck Gdns, Wdf Grn	63	N4
Birkbeck Gro W3	124	G3
Birkbeck Hill SE21	165	S2
Birkbeck Pl SE21	165	T2
Birkbeck Rd E8	94	E10
Birkbeck Rd N8	75	K8
Birkbeck Rd N12	57	L10
Birkbeck Rd N17	76	E1
Birkbeck Rd NW7	55	M9
Birkbeck Rd SW19	163	K10
Birkbeck Rd W3	124	G2
Birkbeck Rd W5	123	M7
Birkbeck Rd, Beck	185	P2
Birkbeck Rd, Ilf	81	N10
Birkbeck Rd, Sid	172	B6
Birkbeck St E2	113	K6
Birkbeck Way, Grnf	103	U1
Birkdale Av, Pnr	67	P5
Birkdale Cl SE16 **1**	130	J10
Birkdale Cl, Orp	189	P14
Birkdale Gdns, Croy **1**	199	P7
Birkdale Gdns, Wat	50	G5
Birkdale Rd SE2	136	A7
Birkdale Rd W5	105	R8
Birkenhead Av, KingsT	177	T3
Birkenhead St WC1	10	C5
Birkhall Rd SE6	168	H3
Birkwood Cl SW12	146	H14
Birley Rd N20	57	L4
Birley St SW11	146	A4
Birnam Rd N4	93	L4
Birse Cres NW10	89	K7
Birstall Grn, Wat	50	G7
Birstall Rd N15	76	D9
Biscay Rd W6	126	A10
Biscoe Cl, Houns	121	P11
Biscoe Way SE13	150	M4
Bisenden Rd, Croy	198	C3
Bisham Cl, Cars	181	T14
Bisham Gdns N6	92	B1
Bishop Butt Cl, Orp	203	T6
Bishop Cl W4	124	E9
Bishop Fox Way, W Mol	175	L7
Bishop Ken Rd, Har	68	F3
Bishop Kings Rd W14	126	D7

Bishop Rd N14	42	C14
Bishop St N1	111	T1
Bishop Way NW10	88	J14
Bishop Wilfred Wd Cl, SE15 **6**	148	H3
Bishop's Av E13	115	R1
Bishop's Av SW6	144	C3
Bishops Av, Brom	187	T4
Bishops Av, Rom	82	F11
Bishops Ave, The N2	73	P13
Bishops Br W2	14	H4
Bishops Br Rd W2	14	E6
Bishops Cl, E17 **5**	78	D8
Bishops Cl SE9	171	L3
Bishops Cl, Barn	40	A11
Bishops Cl, Enf	44	J3
Bishops Cl, Rich	159	P5
Bishop's Cl, Sutt	181	N11
Bishop's Ct, EC4 **3**	19	P6
Bishop's Ct WC2	18	J6
Bishops Dr, Nthlt	103	K1
Bishops Gro N2	73	P11
Bishops Gro, Hmptn	157	M8
Bishop's Hall, KingsT	177	P3
Bishops Hill, Walt	174	A13
Bishops Pk, SW6	144	B3
Bishops Pk Rd SW6	144	B3
Bishops Pk Rd SW16	183	K1
Bishops Pl, Sutt **4**	195	M10
Bishops Rd N6	74	B12
Bishops Rd SW6	126	E14
Bishops Rd W7	122	C3
Bishops Rd, Croy	183	R14
Bishops Ter SE11	35	L2
Bishops Wk, Chis	189	M2
Bishops Wk, Croy	199	N10
Bishops Way E2	113	L3
Bishopsford Rd, Mord	181	N12
Bishopsgate EC2	20	J3
Bishopsgate Arc EC2	20	J3
Bishopsgate Chyd EC2	20	G4
Bishopsthorpe Rd SE26	167	N7
Bishopswood Rd N6	73	T14
Bisley Cl, Wor Pk	193	U2
Bispham Rd NW10	105	T6
Bisson Rd E15	114	F3
Bisterne Av E17	78	H5
Bittacy Hill NW7	56	A11
Bittacy Pk Av NW7	56	C13
Bittacy Ri NW7	56	A11
Bittacy Rd NW7	56	B12
Bittern Cl, Hayes	102	H10
Bittern St SE1	27	U7
Bittoms, The, KingsT	177	P5
Bixley Cl, Sthl	121	M7
Black Boy La N15	75	U9
Black Fan Cl, Enf	43	T2
Black Friars Ct, EC4 **3**	19	P9
Black Friars La EC4	19	P9
Black Horse Ct SE1	28	E10
Black Lion La W6	125	N8
Black Path E10	95	P1
Black Prince Rd SE1	34	F3
Black Prince Rd SE11	34	J5
Black Swan Yd SE1	28	H6
Blackall St EC2	12	G9
Blackberry Fm Cl, Houns	120	J14
Blackbird Hill NW9	88	F4
Blackbird Yd, E2 **3**	13	P5
Blackborne Rd, Dag	101	N12
Blackbrook La, Brom	188	G5
Blackburn Rd NW6	90	J12
Blackburne's Ms W1	16	D10
Blackbush Av, Rom	82	G10
Blackbush Cl, Sutt	195	K14
Blackdown Cl N2	73	M4
Blackett St SW15	144	A6
Blackfen Rd, Sid	153	S10
Blackford Rd, Wat	50	G10
Blackfriars Br EC4	19	P10
Blackfriars Br SE1	19	P10

Blackfriars Pas EC4	19	P10
Blackfriars Rd SE1	27	P3
Blackheath Av SE10	132	J14
Blackheath Gro SE3	151	L4
Blackheath Hill SE10	150	E2
Blackheath Pk SE3	151	N5
Blackheath Ri SE13	150	E4
Blackheath Rd SE10	150	C1
Blackheath Vale SE3	151	K3
Blackheath Village SE3	151	L5
Blackhorse La E17	77	P7
Blackhorse La, Croy	184	H13
Blackhorse Rd E17	77	P8
Blackhorse Rd SE8	131	S10
Blackhorse Rd, Sid	172	B8
Blacklands Rd SE6	168	E8
Blacklands Ter SW3	31	L4
Blackmore Av, Sthl	122	B2
Blackmore Rd, Buck H	48	C14
Blackmores Gro, Tedd	158	G11
Blackpool Rd SE15	148	J4
Blacks Rd W6	125	T8
Blackshaw Rd SW17	163	M7
Blacksmiths Cl, Rom	82	E11
Blackstock Ms, N4 **1**	93	R4
Blackstock Rd N4	93	R4
Blackstock Rd N5	93	R4
Blackstone Est E8	94	J14
Blackstone Rd NW2	89	U9
Blackthorn Ct, Houns	120	J14
Blackthorn Gro, Bexh	154	J5
Blackthorn St E3	114	B8
Blackthorne Av, Croy	185	L14
Blackthorne Dr E4	62	H7
Blacktree Ms SW9	147	P6
Blackwall La SE10	133	K9
Blackwall Pier E14	114	J14
Blackwall Tunnel E14	132	H1
Blackwall Tunnel App SE10	132	J4
Blackwall Tunnel Northern App E3	114	E7
Blackwall Tunnel Northern App E14	114	E7
Blackwall Way E14	114	G14
Blackwater Cl E7	97	M8
Blackwater Rd, Sutt **1**	195	K8
Blackwater St SE22	148	E9
Blackwell Cl E5	95	P7
Blackwell Cl, Har	52	A14
Blackwell Gdns, Edg	54	B7
Blackwood St SE17	36	C6
Blade Ms SW15	144	E7
Blades Cl SW15	144	E7
Bladindon Dr, Bex	154	G13
Bladon Gdns, Har	67	S11
Blagdens Cl N14	58	F3
Blagdens La N14	58	G3
Blagdon Rd SE13	150	D7
Blagdon Rd, N Mal	179	L7
Blagdon Wk, Tedd	159	L12
Blagrove Rd W10	108	D10
Blair Av NW9	70	J14
Blair Cl N1	93	U11
Blair Cl, Hayes	120	A7
Blair Cl, Sid	153	R10
Blair St E14	114	G12
Blairderry Rd SW2	164	J3
Blairhead Dr, Wat	50	C5
Blake Av, Bark	117	S2
Blake Cl W10	107	U9
Blake Cl, Cars	195	S1
Blake Cl, Well	153	S1
Blake Gdns SW6	144	J1
Blake Hall Cres E11	97	P2
Blake Hall Rd E11	97	P1
Blake Rd E16	115	L8
Blake Rd N11	58	F13
Blake Rd, Croy	198	C3
Blake Rd, Mitch	181	R5
Blake St SE8	132	A11
Blakeden Dr, Esher	190	F12
Blakehall Rd, Cars	195	T11

Blakemore Rd SW16	164	J5
Blakemore Rd, Th Hth	183	M9
Blakemore Way, Belv 4	137	K6
Blakeney Av, Beck	185	U1
Blakeney Cl N20	57	L2
Blakeney Cl, NW1 5	92	G14
Blakeney Rd, Beck	185	U1
Blakenham Rd SW17	163	U8
Blaker Ct SE7	133	T13
Blaker Rd E15	114	E2
Blakes Av, N Mal	179	M11
Blake's Grn, W Wick	186	E14
Blakes La, N Mal	179	M10
Blakes Rd SE15	36	J14
Blakes Ter, N Mal	179	N10
Blakesley Av W5	105	M11
Blakesley Wk SW20	180	E3
Blakesware Gdns N9	44	B14
Blakewood Cl, Felt	156	F8
Blanch Cl SE15	131	L14
Blanchard Cl SE9	170	D5
Blanchard Way E8	94	H12
Blanche St E16	115	M8
Blanchedowne SE5	148	B7
Blanchland Rd, Mord	180	J9
Bland St, SE9 2	152	A7
Blandfield Rd SW12	146	B12
Blandford Av, Beck	185	R3
Blandford Av, Twick	157	S1
Blandford Cl N2	73	M8
Blandford Cl, Croy 3	197	K6
Blandford Cl, Rom	83	R7
Blandford Cres E4	46	E14
Blandford Rd W4	124	J5
Blandford Rd W5	123	P3
Blandford Rd, Beck	185	N4
Blandford Rd, Sthl	121	S7
Blandford Rd, Tedd	158	B10
Blandford Sq NW1 7		S11
Blandford St W1	16	C4
Blandford Waye, Hayes	102	F12
Blaney Cres E6	116	J5
Blanmerle Rd SE9	170	J2
Blann Cl SE9	151	U12
Blantyre St SW10	30	J13
Blashford St SE13	150	H13
Blasker Wk E14	132	C9
Blawith Rd, Har	68	D8
Blaydon Cl N17	60	J13
Blaydon Wk N17	60	J13
Bleak Hill La SE18	135	T11
Blean Gro SE20	167	L14
Bleasdale Av, Grnf	104	G3
Blechynden St, W10 2	108	B13
Bleddyn Cl, Sid	154	E11
Bledlow Cl SE28	118	F14
Bledlow Ri, Grnf	103	T3
Bleeding Heart Yd, EC1 4	19	M3
Blegborough Rd SW16	164	F11
Blendon Dr, Bex	154	H12
Blendon Path, Brom	169	M14
Blendon Rd, Bex	154	F11
Blendon Ter SE18	135	M10
Blenheim Av, Ilf	80	G12
Blenheim Cl N21	59	T1
Blenheim Cl SW20	179	T6
Blenheim Cl, Grnf	104	B4
Blenheim Cl, Rom	83	T7
Blenheim Cl, Wall 3	196	F13
Blenheim Ct N19	92	J3
Blenheim Ct, Sid	171	P5
Blenheim Cres W11	108	D12
Blenheim Cres, S Croy	197	T14
Blenheim Dr, Well	153	T2
Blenheim Gdns NW2	89	U10
Blenheim Gdns SW2	147	L11
Blenheim Gdns, Kings T	160	C14
Blenheim Gdns, Wall	196	E12
Blenheim Gdns, Wem	87	S6
Blenheim Gro SE15	148	G4
Blenheim Ri N15	76	E8
Blenheim Rd E6	116	A5
Blenheim Rd E15	97	K7
Blenheim Rd E17	77	R6
Blenheim Rd NW8 6		G1
Blenheim Rd SE20	167	M14
Blenheim Rd SW20	179	T6
Blenheim Rd W4	124	J5
Blenheim Rd, Barn	40	B6
Blenheim Rd, Brom	188	C8
Blenheim Rd, Har	67	R11
Blenheim Rd, Nthlt	85	S11
Blenheim Rd, Sid	172	E2
Blenheim Rd, Sutt	194	H5
Blenheim St, W1 1	16	H8
Blenheim Ter NW8 6		E2
Blenheim Way, Islw	140	G2
Blenkarne Rd SW11	145	T12
Bleriot Rd, Houns	120	E13
Blessbury Rd, Edg	70	E1
Blessing Way, Bark	118	E5
Blessington Cl SE13	150	H7
Blessington Rd SE13	150	H6
Bletchingley Cl, Th Hth	183	R8
Bletchley Ct N1	12	C3
Bletchley St N1	12	B3
Bletsoe Wk N1	12	A2
Blincoe Cl SW19	162	B4
Blind La, Loug	47	K3
Blissett St SE10	150	E1
Blisworth Cl, Hayes	103	K7
Blithbury Rd, Dag	100	D12
Blithdale Rd SE2	136	A8
Blithfield St W8	22	A11
Blockley Rd, Wem	86	J4
Bloemfontein Av W12	125	R1
Bloemfontein Rd W12	125	R1
Blomfield Cres, Ilf	81	K12
Blomfield Pl W1	16	J10
Blomfield Rd N6	74	B12
Blomfield Rd SE18	135	K10
Blomfield Rd, Brom	188	A9
Blomfield Rd, Kings T	177	S7
Bloomfield Ter SW1	32	E5
Bloomhall Rd SE19	166	B10
Bloomsbury Ct W5	105	U13
Bloomsbury Ct, Pnr	67	L5
Bloomsbury Pl SW18	145	L9
Bloomsbury Pl, WC1 1	18	C2
Bloomsbury Sq WC1	18	C3
Bloomsbury St WC1	17	U3
Bloomsbury Way WC1	18	B5
Blore Cl SW8	146	G2
Blossom Cl W5	123	S4
Blossom Cl, Dag	119	L2
Blossom Cl, S Croy	198	F9
Blossom La, Enf	43	T1
Blossom Pl, E1 1	13	K12
Blossom St E1	21	K1
Blossom Waye, Houns	120	J13
Blount St E14	113	S11
Bloxam Gdns SE9	152	C10
Bloxhall Rd E10	95	T1
Bloxham Cres, Hmptn	175	M1
Bloxworth Cl, Wall	196	F6
Blucher Rd SE5	129	U14
Blue Anchor All, Rich 3	141	S7
Blue Anchor La SE16	37	U1
Blue Anchor Yd E1	21	R10
Blue Ball Yd SW1	25	M3
Bluebell Av E12	98	B9
Bluebell Cl E9	113	L1
Bluebell Cl SE26	166	F8
Bluebell Cl, Orp	203	L4
Bluebell Cl, Wall	196	C1
Bluebell Way, Ilf	98	J11
Blueberry Cl, Wdf Grn	63	P11
Bluefield Cl, Hmptn	157	N10
Bluegates, Epsom	193	P14
Bluehouse Rd E4	62	J5
Blundell Rd, Edg	70	H1
Blundell St N7	93	K12
Blunden Cl, Dag	100	F1
Blunt Rd, S Croy	198	B9
Blunts Rd SE9	152	G10
Blurton Rd E5	95	M8
Blyth Cl E14	132	G7
Blyth Cl, Twick	140	F12
Blyth Rd E17	77	T14
Blyth Rd SE28	118	E14
Blyth Rd, Brom	187	M2
Blythe Cl SE6	149	T14
Blythe Hill SE6	149	T14
Blythe Hill, Orp	189	U2
Blythe Hill La SE6	149	T14
Blythe Rd W14	126	C6
Blythe St E2	112	J5
Blythe Vale SE6	167	U2
Blythswood Rd, Ilf	100	A1
Blythwood Rd N4	75	K13
Blythwood Rd, Pnr	66	G1
Boadicea St, N1 1	111	L2
Boakes Cl NW9	70	E8
Boardman Av E4	46	D10
Boardman Cl, Barn	40	C10
Boardwalk Pl E14	132	E1
Boat Lifter Way SE16	131	S7
Boathouse Wk SE15	37	P13
Boathouse Wk, Rich	141	R2
Bob Anker Cl, E13 1	115	P5
Bob Marley Way, SE24 13	147	P8
Bobbin Cl SW4	146	E5
Bobby Moore Way N10	57	U14
Bockhampton Rd, Kings T	159	U13
Bocking St E8	112	J1
Boddicott Cl SW19	162	C4
Bodiam Cl, Enf	44	B3
Bodiam Rd SW16	164	H14
Bodley Cl, N Mal	178	J10
Bodley Rd, N Mal	178	J10
Bodmin Cl, Har	85	M6
Bodmin Gro, Mord	181	K9
Bodmin St SW18	162	H2
Bodnant Gdns SW20	179	R5
Bodney Rd E8	94	J9
Boeing Way, Sthl	120	D6
Boevey Path, Belv	137	L10
Bognor Gdns, Wat	50	E10
Bognor Rd, Well	154	G1
Bohemia Pl E8	95	K11
Bohun Gro, Barn	41	S11
Boileau Rd SW13	125	P13
Boileau Rd W5	105	U11
Bolden St SE8	150	C3
Bolderwood Way, W Wick	200	C3
Boldmere Rd, Pnr	66	F13
Boleyn Av, Enf	44	J1
Boleyn Cl E17	78	A7
Boleyn Cl, Loug 2	48	D11
Boleyn Ct, Buck H	63	P2
Boleyn Dr, Ruis	84	G3
Boleyn Dr, W Mol	175	M6
Boleyn Gdns, Dag	101	T13
Boleyn Gdns, W Wick	200	D4
Boleyn Gro, W Wick	200	E4
Boleyn Rd E6	116	A3
Boleyn Rd E7	97	R14
Boleyn Rd N16	94	D10
Boleyn Way, Barn	41	L6
Boleyn Way, Ilf	65	L12
Bolina Rd SE16	131	M9
Bolingbroke Gro SW11	145	R9
Bolingbroke Rd W14	126	B5
Bolingbroke Wk SW11	145	P1
Bolliger Ct NW10	106	F7
Bollo Br Rd W3	124	D5
Bollo La W3	124	C4
Bollo La W4	124	E8
Bolney Gate SW7	23	N8
Bolney St SW8	129	L14
Bolney Way, Felt	157	L5
Bolsover St W1	17	K1
Bolstead Rd, Mitch	182	C2
Bolt Ct, EC4 10	19	L7
Boltmore Cl NW4	72	B6
Bolton Cl SE20	184	H3
Bolton Cl, Chess	191	R11
Bolton Cres SE5	35	N12
Bolton Gdns NW10	108	A4
Bolton Gdns SW5	30	C5
Bolton Gdns, Brom	169	L12
Bolton Gdns, Tedd	158	G12
Bolton Gdns Ms SW10	30	D6
Bolton Rd E15	97	M12
Bolton Rd N18	60	F9
Bolton Rd NW8	109	K2
Bolton Rd NW10	107	K2
Bolton Rd W4	124	F14
Bolton Rd, Chess	191	P11
Bolton Rd, Har	67	U8
Bolton St W1	24	J2
Boltons, The SW10	30	E7
Boltons, The, Wem	86	F7
Boltons, The, Wdf Grn	63	P8
Boltons Pl SW5	30	E5
Bombay St SE16	130	J7
Bomore Rd W11	108	B13
Bonar Pl, Chis	170	D13
Bonar Rd SE15	130	G14
Bonchester Cl, Chis	170	H14
Bonchurch Cl, Sutt 6	195	K14
Bonchurch Rd W10	108	C9
Bonchurch Rd W13	122	J2
Bond Ct EC4	20	D8
Bond Gdns, Wall	196	F7
Bond Rd, Mitch	181	T3
Bond Rd, Surb	191	T3
Bond St E15	96	J9
Bond St W4	124	J8
Bond St W5	105	N14
Bondfield Av, Hayes	102	B5
Bondfield Rd, E6 4	116	E10
Bondway SW8	34	C10
Boneta Rd SE18	134	E6
Bonfield Rd SE13	150	F7
Bonham Gdns, Dag	100	H4
Bonham Rd SW2	147	L10
Bonham Rd, Dag	100	H7
Bonheur Rd W4	124	H4
Bonhill St EC2	12	E11
Boniface Gdns, Har	51	R14
Boniface Wk, Har	51	S14
Bonner Hill Rd, Kings T	178	A5
Bonner Rd E2	113	L3
Bonner St E2	113	M4
Bonnersfield Cl, Har	68	F11
Bonnersfield La, Har	68	H11
Bonneville Gdns SW4	146	F11
Bonnington Sq SW8	34	F10
Bonny St NW1	92	E4
Bonser Rd, Twick	158	E4
Bonsor St SE5	130	C14
Bonville Gdns, NW4 2	71	P7
Bonville Rd, Brom	169	M10
Booker Cl E14	113	U10
Booker Rd N18	60	G9
Boone Ct N9	61	L5

Name	Page	Ref
Boone St SE13	151	K7
Boones Rd SE13	151	K7
Boord St SE10	133	K5
Boot St N1	12	G7
Booth Cl, E9 **10**	113	K2
Booth Cl SE28	118	D14
Booth Rd NW9	70	J4
Booth Rd, Croy	197	S4
Boothby Rd, N19 **3**	92	G3
Booth's Pl W1	17	M4
Bordars Rd W7	104	D10
Bordars Wk W7	104	D9
Borden Av, Enf	44	B12
Border Cres SE26	166	J9
Border Gdns, Croy	200	C7
Border Rd SE26	167	K9
Bordergate, Mitch	181	S1
Borders La, Loug	48	G7
Bordesley Rd, Mord	180	J8
Bordon Wk SW15	143	P14
Boreas Wk, N1 **3**	11	R4
Boreham Av E16	115	N12
Boreham Cl E11	96	E1
Boreham Rd N22	75	T2
Borehamwood Ind Pk, Borwd	38	G3
Borgard Rd SE18	134	E7
Borkwood Pk, Orp	203	T8
Borkwood Way, Orp	203	R7
Borland Rd SE15	149	M8
Borland Rd, Tedd	158	J12
Borneo St SW15	143	U6
Borough High St SE1	27	U8
Borough Hill, Croy	197	R6
Borough Rd SE1	27	R9
Borough Rd, Islw	140	D1
Borough Rd, Kings T	178	A1
Borough Rd, Mitch	181	R3
Borrett Cl SE17	35	T7
Borrodaile Rd SE18	145	K11
Borrowdale Av, Har	68	G4
Borrowdale Cl, Ilf	80	D7
Borrowdale Ct, Enf	43	U2
Borthwick Ms, E15 **10**	96	J8
Borthwick Rd E15	96	J8
Borthwick Rd, NW9 **1**	71	M12
Borthwick St SE8	132	A10
Borwick Av E17	77	T6
Bosbury Rd SE6	168	F6
Boscastle Rd NW5	92	C6
Bosco Cl, Orp	203	T7
Boscobel Pl SW1	32	F1
Boscobel St NW8	7	L12
Boscombe Av E10	78	F13
Boscombe Cl E5	95	R9
Boscombe Gdns, SW16 **2**	165	K12
Boscombe Rd SW17	164	A12
Boscombe Rd SW19	180	J1
Boscombe Rd W12	125	P3
Boscombe Rd, Wor Pk	193	U1
Bosgrove E4	62	E2
Boss St SE1	29	L5
Bostal Row, Bexh	155	L6
Bostall Heath SE2	136	E11
Bostall Hill SE2	136	B9
Bostall La SE2	136	D9
Bostall Manorway SE2	136	D7
Bostall Pk Av, Bexh	136	J14
Bostall Rd, Orp	172	C14
Boston Gdns W4	125	K11
Boston Gdns W7	122	G7
Boston Gdns, Brent	122	J8
Boston Manor Rd, Brent	122	J8
Boston Pk Rd, Brent	123	M10
Boston Pl NW1	7	T11
Boston Rd E6	116	C5
Boston Rd E17	78	A12
Boston Rd W7	123	M11
Boston Rd, Croy	183	M12
Boston Rd, Edg	54	E14
Boston St E2	13	S2
Boston Vale W7	122	H7
Bostonthorpe Rd W7	122	D3
Bosun Cl E14	132	B3
Boswell Rd, Th Hth	183	T8
Boswell St WC1	18	D1
Bosworth Cl E17	77	T2
Bosworth Rd N11	58	H11
Bosworth Rd W10	108	D8
Bosworth Rd, Barn	40	H6
Bosworth Rd, Dag	101	P7
Botany Bay La, Chis	189	L3
Botany Cl, Barn	41	R8
Boteley Cl E4	62	H4
Botha Rd E13	115	S9
Botham Cl, Edg	54	E14
Bothwell Cl E16	115	M10
Bothwell St, W6 **2**	126	B12
Botolph La, EC3 **3**	20	G11
Botsford Rd SW20	180	C4
Botts Pas W2	108	H12
Boucher Cl, Tedd	158	E10
Boughton Av, Brom	187	M13
Boughton Rd SE28	135	S6
Boulcott St E1	113	P12
Boulevard, The SW17	164	B3
Boulogne Rd, Croy	183	U11
Boulton Rd, Dag	101	L5
Boultwood Rd E6	116	E12
Bounces La N9	60	J3
Bounces Rd N9	60	J2
Boundaries Rd SW12	164	A2
Boundaries Rd, Felt	156	F2
Boundary Av, E17 **1**	77	U13
Boundary Cl SE20	184	H4
Boundary Cl, Barn	40	E2
Boundary Cl, Ilf	99	R8
Boundary Cl, Kings T	178	C5
Boundary Cl, Sthl	121	P9
Boundary La E13	116	A6
Boundary La SE17	36	B11
Boundary Rd E13	115	U4
Boundary Rd E17	77	U13
Boundary Rd N9	45	M12
Boundary Rd N22	75	S5
Boundary Rd NW8	109	N1
Boundary Rd SW19	163	N11
Boundary Rd, Bark	117	M3
Boundary Rd, Cars	196	C12
Boundary Rd, Pnr	66	G13
Boundary Rd, Sid	153	R9
Boundary Rd, Wall	196	C12
Boundary Rd, Wem	87	R5
Boundary Row SE1	27	N6
Boundary St E2	13	L9
Boundary Way, Croy	200	A10
Boundfield Rd SE6	169	K4
Bounds Grn Rd N11	58	F11
Bounds Grn Rd N22	75	L1
Bourchier St W1	17	S9
Bourdon Pl, W1 **3**	16	J10
Bourdon Rd SE20	185	L4
Bourdon St W1	16	H11
Bourke Cl NW10	89	K12
Bourke Cl SW4	146	J12
Bourlet Cl W1	17	M4
Bourn Av N15	76	A7
Bourn Av, Barn	41	P10
Bournbrook Rd SE3	152	B5
Bourne, The N14	58	H2
Bourne Av N14	58	J3
Bourne Av, Ruis	84	E10
Bourne Ct, Ruis	84	D9
Bourne Dr, Mitch	181	N4
Bourne Est EC1	18	J1
Bourne Gdns E4	62	D8
Bourne Hill N13	59	M4
Bourne Pl W4	124	H9
Bourne Rd E7	97	M6
Bourne Rd N8	75	K11
Bourne Rd, Bex	155	R13
Bourne Rd, Brom	188	A7
Bourne Rd, Dart	155	U11
Bourne St SW1	32	D4
Bourne St, Croy	197	S4
Bourne Ter W2	14	C2
Bourne Vale, Brom	187	P11
Bourne Vw, Grnf	86	F11
Bourne Way, Brom	201	L3
Bourne Way, Epsom	192	E8
Bourne Way, Sutt	194	F10
Bournemead Av, Nthlt	102	B4
Bournemead Cl, Nthlt	102	A5
Bournemead Way, Nthlt	102	C4
Bournemouth Cl SE15	148	H4
Bournemouth Rd SE15	148	H4
Bournemouth Rd SW19	180	H1
Bourneside Cres N14	58	G2
Bourneside Gdns SE6	168	F9
Bournevale Rd SW16	164	J8
Bournewood Rd SE18	136	B13
Bournville Rd SE6	150	A14
Bournwell Cl, Barn	41	T5
Bourton Cl, Hayes	120	B1
Bousfield Rd SE14	149	N3
Boutflower Rd SW11	145	R8
Bouverie Gdns, Har	69	P12
Bouverie Ms N16	94	D4
Bouverie Pl W2	15	M5
Bouverie Rd N16	94	C3
Bouverie Rd, Har	67	U12
Bouverie St EC4	19	M7
Boveney Rd SE23	149	N13
Bovill Rd SE23	149	P14
Bovingdon Av, Wem	88	B12
Bovingdon La NW9	55	K14
Bovingdon Rd SW6	144	J2
Bow Br Est E3	114	D5
Bow Common La E3	113	T8
Bow Ind Pk E15	96	B13
Bow La EC4	20	B8
Bow La N12	57	L14
Bow La, Mord	180	C11
Bow Rd E3	114	B5
Bow St E15	96	J10
Bow St WC2	18	D8
Bowater Cl NW9	70	G10
Bowater Cl SW2	146	J11
Bowater Pl SE3	133	S13
Bowater Rd SE18	134	B6
Bowden Cl, Felt	35	L7
Bowden St SE11	131	T9
Bowdon Rd E17	78	B13
Bowen Dr SE21	166	D6
Bowen Rd, Har	67	U13
Bowen St E14	114	C11
Bower Av SE10	133	K14
Bower Cl, Nthlt	102	E3
Bower St E1	113	N12
Bowerdean St SW6	144	J3
Bowerman Av SE14	131	S12
Bowers Wk, E6 **28**	116	D11
Bowes Cl, Sid	154	C12
Bowes Rd N11	58	E9
Bowes Rd N13	58	H10
Bowes Rd W3	106	J13
Bowes Rd, Dag	100	F8
Bowfell Rd W6	125	U12
Bowford Av, Bexh	154	J2
Bowhill Cl SW9	35	L14
Bowie Cl SW4	146	H13
Bowl Ct EC2	13	K11
Bowland Rd SW4	146	H8
Bowland Rd, Wdf Grn	63	U10
Bowland Yd, SW1 **2**	24	C7
Bowles Rd SE1	37	S9
Bowley Cl SE19	166	E11
Bowley La SE19	166	E10
Bowling Grn Cl SW15	143	S14
Bowling Grn La EC1	11	L10
Bowling Grn Pl SE1	28	D6
Bowling Grn Row, SE18 **1**	134	E7
Bowling Grn St SE11	35	K10
Bowling Grn Wk N1	12	G6
Bowls, The, Chig	65	S7
Bowls Cl, Stan	52	J9
Bowman Av E16	115	M13
Bowman Ms SW18	162	F1
Bowmans Cl W13	122	J2
Bowmans Lea SE23	149	M13
Bowmans Meadow, Wall	196	C6
Bowmans Ms, E1 **3**	21	S9
Bowmans Ms N7	93	K6
Bowmans Pl, N7 **2**	93	K6
Bowmead SE9	170	E3
Bowness Cres SW15	160	J9
Bowness Dr, Houns	139	K7
Bowness Rd SE6	150	D14
Bowness Rd, Bexh	155	R4
Bowood Rd SW11	146	A9
Bowood Rd, Enf	45	N3
Bowring Grn, Wat	50	E10
Bowrons Av, Wem	87	P14
Bowsley Ct, Felt **1**	156	B3
Bowyer Cl E6	116	F9
Bowyer Pl SE5	36	B14
Bowyer St SE5	36	A14
Box La, Bark	118	D3
Boxall Rd SE21	148	C12
Boxgrove Rd SE2	136	E5
Boxley Rd, Mord	181	M8
Boxley St E16	133	R2
Boxmoor Rd, Har	68	J7
Boxoll Rd, Dag	101	L7
Boxted Cl, Buck H	64	D1
Boxtree La, Har	52	A14
Boxtree Rd, Har	52	B13
Boxworth Cl, N12 **4**	57	N10
Boxworth Gro, N1 **2**	111	M1
Boyard Rd SE18	134	J9
Boyce St SE1	26	H4
Boyce Way E13	115	P7
Boycroft Av NW9	70	F11
Boyd Av, Sthl	121	M1
Boyd Rd SW19	163	N12
Boyd St E1	21	S8
Boyfield St SE1	27	R7
Boyland Rd, Brom	169	M10
Boyle Av, Stan	52	H11
Boyle Fm Island, T Ditt	176	H11
Boyle Rd, T Ditt	176	G12
Boyle St W1	17	L10
Boyne Av NW4	72	B2
Boyne Rd SE13	150	G5
Boyne Rd, Dag	101	N6
Boyne Ter Ms W11	126	E1
Boyseland Ct, Edg	54	E3
Boyson Rd SE17	36	C10
Boyton Cl E1	113	N7
Boyton Rd N8	75	K6
Brabant Ct, EC3 **4**	20	G9
Brabant Rd N22	75	M3
Brabazon Av, Wall	196	J14
Brabazon Rd, Houns	120	F13
Brabazon Rd, Nthlt	104	N4
Brabazon St E14	114	C11
Brabourn Gro SE15	149	L4
Brabourne Cl SE19	166	C10
Brabourne Cres, Bexh	137	M12
Brabourne Hts NW7	55	K6
Brabourne Ri, Beck	186	G9
Bracewell Av, Grnf	86	F10
Bracewell Rd W10	107	T10
Bracewood Gdns, Croy	198	E5
Bracey St N4	93	K3
Bracken, The, E4 **1**	62	F3
Bracken Av SW12	146	B12
Bracken Av, Croy	200	C6
Bracken Cl E6	116	E10
Bracken Cl, Borwd	38	C5
Bracken Cl, Twick **4**	139	N13
Bracken Dr, Chig	65	K11
Bracken End, Islw **1**	140	H4
Bracken Gdns SW13	143	N3

Bracken Hill Cl, Brom 1 — 187 L2
Bracken Hill La, Brom — 187 L2
Bracken Ind Est, Ilf — 81 T1
Bracken Ms, E4 2 — 62 F2
Bracken Ms, Rom — 83 R12
Brackenbridge Dr, Ruis — 84 G6
Brackenbury Gdns W6 — 125 S5
Brackenbury Rd N2 — 73 M5
Brackenbury Rd W6 — 125 S5
Brackendale N21 — 59 M3
Brackendale Cl, Houns — 139 S1
Brackens, The, Enf — 44 C13
Brackenwood, Sun — 174 A1
Brackley Cl, Wall — 197 K13
Brackley Rd W4 — 125 K9
Brackley Rd, Beck — 168 A13
Brackley Sq, Wdf Grn — 64 A13
Brackley St EC1 — 20 A1
Brackley Ter W4 — 125 K9
Bracklyn Cl N1 — 12 C1
Bracklyn Ct N1 — 12 C1
Bracklyn St N1 — 12 C1
Bracknell Cl N22 — 75 P2
Bracknell Gdns NW3 — 90 J8
Bracknell Gate NW3 — 90 J9
Bracknell Way NW3 — 90 J8
Bracondale Rd SE2 — 136 A7
Brad St SE1 — 27 L4
Bradbourne Rd, Bex — 155 P13
Bradbourne St SW6 — 144 H3
Bradbury Cl, Borwd — 38 C2
Bradbury Cl, Sthl 2 — 121 M7
Bradbury St N16 — 94 D10
Braddock Cl, Islw — 140 F5
Braddon Rd, Rich — 141 U5
Braddyll St SE10 — 132 J10
Braden St W9 — 6 B11
Bradenham Av, Well — 154 A8
Bradenham Cl SE17 — 36 C10
Bradenham Rd, Har — 68 J7
Bradfield Dr, Bark — 100 A9
Bradfield Rd E16 — 133 P3
Bradfield Rd, Ruis — 85 K9
Bradford Cl SE26 — 166 H7
Bradford Cl, Brom — 202 E2
Bradford Dr, Epsom — 193 L12
Bradford Rd W3 — 124 J3
Bradford Rd, Ilf — 99 P1
Bradgate Rd SE6 — 150 C12
Brading Cres E11 — 97 R3
Brading Rd SW2 — 147 M13
Brading Rd, Croy — 183 L12
Bradiston Rd W9 — 108 F5
Bradley Cl N7 — 93 K12
Bradley Gdns W13 — 105 K12
Bradley Ms SW17 — 163 T1
Bradley Rd N22 — 75 L3
Bradley Rd SE19 — 165 T11
Bradley Stone Rd E6 — 116 E10
Bradley's Cl N1 — 11 L2
Bradman Row, Edg 3 — 54 E14
Bradmead SW8 — 128 D14
Bradmore Pk Rd W6 — 125 S6
Bradshaw Cl SW19 — 162 G11
Bradshaws Cl SE25 — 184 H6
Bradstock Rd E9 — 95 P12
Bradstock Rd, Epsom — 193 R10
Bradwell Av, Dag — 101 P3
Bradwell Cl E18 — 79 L7
Bradwell Ms, N18 7 — 60 H8
Bradwell Rd, Buck H — 64 D1
Bradwell St E1 — 113 P6
Brady Av, Loug — 49 L3
Brady St E1 — 112 J8
Bradymead E6 — 116 H11
Braemar Av N22 — 75 K2
Braemar Av NW10 — 88 H5
Braemar Av SW19 — 162 G4
Braemar Av, Bexh — 155 T8
Braemar Av, Th Hth — 183 P5
Braemar Av, Wem — 87 P14
Braemar Gdns NW9 — 70 H2

Braemar Gdns, Sid — 171 P5
Braemar Gdns, W Wick — 200 E2
Braemar Rd E13 — 115 M8
Braemar Rd N15 — 76 C9
Braemar Rd, Brent — 123 P11
Braemar Rd, Wor Pk — 193 R5
Braes St N1 — 93 S13
Braeside, Beck — 168 B10
Braeside Av SW19 — 180 D1
Braeside Cl, Pnr — 51 N13
Braeside Cres, Bexh — 155 U8
Braeside Rd SW16 — 164 F14
Braesyde Cl, Belv — 137 M8
Brafferton Rd, Croy 3 — 197 T7
Braganza St SE17 — 35 P7
Braham St E1 — 21 N7
Braid Av W3 — 106 J12
Braid Cl, Felt — 157 L3
Braidwood Rd SE6 — 168 G2
Braidwood St, SE1 1 — 28 H3
Brailsford Cl, Mitch — 163 R14
Brailsford Rd SW2 — 147 P11
Brainton Av, Felt — 138 D13
Braintree Av, Ilf — 80 C8
Braintree Rd, Dag — 101 N5
Braintree Rd, Ruis — 84 D7
Braintree St E2 — 113 L6
Braithwaite Av, Rom — 83 N13
Braithwaite Gdns, Stan — 69 L1
Braithwaite Rd, Enf — 45 T5
Bramah Grn SW9 — 147 P1
Bramalea Cl N6 — 74 A12
Bramall Cl E15 — 97 L9
Bramber Ct, Brent 2 — 123 R8
Bramber Rd N12 — 57 R10
Bramber Rd W14 — 126 E11
Bramble Cl, Croy — 200 B7
Bramble Cl, Stan — 53 P14
Bramble Cft, Erith — 137 U8
Bramble Gdns W12 — 107 M14
Bramble La, Hmptn — 157 M11
Brambleacres Cl, Sutt — 194 G13
Bramblebury Rd SE18 — 135 M10
Brambledown Cl, W Wick — 187 K10
Brambledown Rd, Cars — 196 B14
Brambledown Rd, S Croy — 198 C14
Brambledown Rd, Wall — 196 D14
Brambles, The, Chig 1 — 65 M11
Brambles Cl, Islw — 122 J14
Bramblewood Cl, Cars — 195 T1
Bramblings, The E4 — 62 H7
Bramcote Av, Mitch — 181 T8
Bramcote Gro SE16 — 131 L10
Bramcote Rd SW15 — 143 S8
Bramdean Cres SE12 — 169 N2
Bramdean Gdns SE12 — 169 N2
Bramerton Rd, Beck — 185 U5
Bramerton St SW3 — 31 N9
Bramfield Rd SW11 — 145 T10
Bramford Ct N14 — 58 G3
Bramford Rd SW18 — 145 L8
Bramham Gdns SW5 — 30 B5
Bramham Gdns, Chess — 191 P8
Bramhope La SE7 — 133 S11
Bramlands Cl SW11 — 145 R5
Bramley Cl E17 — 77 S4
Bramley Cl N14 — 42 C10
Bramley Cl, Hayes — 102 A14
Bramley Cl, Orp — 203 K1
Bramley Cl, S Croy — 197 T9
Bramley Cl, Twick — 139 T11
Bramley Cl, Well — 154 C1
Bramley Cres SW8 — 33 U14
Bramley Cres, Ilf — 80 H12

Bramley Gdns, Wat — 50 F11
Bramley Hill, S Croy — 197 T8
Bramley Rd N14 — 42 C10
Bramley Rd W5 — 123 L6
Bramley Rd W10 — 108 B13
Bramley Rd, Sutt — 195 N9
Bramley Way, Houns — 139 L9
Bramley Way, W Wick — 200 C4
Brampton Cl E5 — 95 K3
Brampton Gdns N15 — 75 T9
Brampton Gro NW4 — 71 S8
Brampton Gro, Har — 68 J8
Brampton Gro, Wem — 88 A2
Brampton La NW4 — 71 U8
Brampton Pk Rd N22 — 75 N5
Brampton Rd E6 — 116 B6
Brampton Rd N15 — 75 T10
Brampton Rd NW9 — 70 B8
Brampton Rd SE2 — 136 G12
Brampton Rd, Bexh — 136 G14
Brampton Rd, Croy — 184 E13
Brampton Rd, Wat — 50 B5
Bramshaw Gdns, Wat — 50 G9
Bramshaw Ri, N Mal — 179 K11
Bramshaw Rd E9 — 95 P12
Bramshill Cl, Chig — 65 S9
Bramshill Gdns NW5 — 92 D5
Bramshill Rd NW10 — 107 L3
Bramshot Av SE7 — 133 P11
Bramshot Way, Wat — 50 B4
Bramston Cl, Ilf — 65 U11
Bramston Rd NW10 — 107 N3
Bramston Rd SW17 — 163 M6
Bramwell Cl, Sun — 174 G3
Bramwell Ms N1 — 111 M1
Brancaster Dr NW7 — 55 N14
Brancaster Pl, Loug — 48 E5
Brancaster Rd E12 — 98 F8
Brancaster Rd SW16 — 164 J5
Brancaster Rd, Ilf — 81 R12
Brancepeth Gdns, Buck H 1 — 63 N4
Branch Hill NW3 — 91 L6
Branch Pl N1 — 112 B1
Branch Rd E14 — 113 R13
Branch St SE15 — 130 D14
Brancker Rd, Har — 69 N6
Brancroft Way, Enf — 45 T2
Brand St SE10 — 132 E14
Brandlehow Rd SW15 — 144 E8
Brandon Est SE17 — 35 R11
Brandon Rd, E17 3 — 78 F6
Brandon Rd N7 — 92 J13
Brandon Rd, Sthl — 121 L10
Brandon Rd, Sutt — 194 J8
Brandon St SE17 — 36 A3
Brandram Rd SE13 — 150 J6
Brandreth Rd E6 — 116 F11
Brandreth Rd SW17 — 164 C4
Brandries, The, Wall — 196 H6
Brandville Gdns, Ilf — 81 K7
Brandy Way, Sutt — 194 H14
Brangbourne Rd, Brom — 168 F9
Brangton Rd SE11 — 34 H7
Brangwyn Cres SW19 — 181 N2
Branksea St SW6 — 126 C14
Branksome Av N18 — 60 E13
Branksome Rd SW2 — 147 K9
Branksome Rd SW19 — 180 H1
Branksome Way, Har — 69 S11
Branksome Way, N Mal — 178 F2
Bransby Rd, Chess — 191 R12
Branscombe Gdns N21 — 43 N14

Branscombe St SE13 — 150 D5
Bransdale Cl NW6 — 108 H1
Bransgrove Rd, Edg — 69 T1
Branston Cres, Orp — 203 N1
Branstone Rd, Rich — 141 U2
Brants Wk W7 — 104 D8
Brantwood Av, Erith — 137 T13
Brantwood Av, Islw — 140 G7
Brantwood Cl E17 — 78 E6
Brantwood Gdns, Enf — 42 J8
Brantwood Gdns, Ilf — 80 D8
Brantwood Rd N17 — 60 H12
Brantwood Rd SE24 — 147 T9
Brantwood Rd, Bexh — 155 S4
Brasenose Dr SW13 — 125 T12
Brasher Cl, Grnf 2 — 86 A9
Brassey Rd NW6 — 90 F11
Brassey Sq SW11 — 146 A5
Brassie Av W3 — 106 J12
Brasted Cl SE26 — 167 L7
Brasted Cl, Bexh — 154 G10
Brasted Cl, Orp — 203 U3
Brathway Rd SW18 — 144 H13
Bratley St E1 — 13 S11
Braund Av, Grnf — 103 R8
Braundton Av, Sid — 171 T1
Braunston Dr, Hayes — 102 J7
Bravington Pl, W9 3 — 108 E7
Bravington Rd W9 — 108 E5
Braxfield Rd SE4 — 149 T7
Braxted Pk SW16 — 165 L11
Bray Cl, Borwd — 38 F2
Bray Cres SE16 — 131 N3
Bray Dr E16 — 115 M13
Bray Pas, E16 3 — 115 N13
Bray Pl SW3 — 31 U4
Bray Rd NW7 — 56 B12
Brayards Rd SE15 — 148 J4
Brayards Rd Est SE15 — 148 J3
Braybourne Dr, Islw — 122 E13
Braycourt Av, Walt — 174 D14
Braydon Rd N16 — 76 G14
Brayfield Ter N3 — 93 N14
Brayton Gdns, Enf — 42 H8
Braywood Rd SE9 — 153 N7
Brazil Cl, Croy — 182 J14
Breach La, Dag — 119 N5
Bread St EC4 — 20 A9
Breakspears Ms SE4 — 150 A4
Breakspears Rd SE4 — 150 A4
Bream Cl N17 — 77 K8
Bream Gdns E6 — 116 G6
Bream St E3 — 96 B14
Breamore Cl SW15 — 161 P2
Breamore Rd, Ilf — 99 T4
Bream's Bldgs EC4 — 19 K6
Breamwater Gdns, Rich — 158 J5
Brearley Cl, Edg 4 — 54 E14
Breasley Cl SW15 — 143 S7
Brechin Pl SW7 — 30 G4
Brecknock Rd N7 — 92 G9
Brecknock Rd N19 — 92 F8
Brecknock Rd Est N7 — 92 F8
Brecon Cl, Mitch — 182 J6
Brecon Cl, Wor Pk — 193 T3
Brecon Rd W6 — 126 D12
Brecon Rd, Enf — 45 L7
Brede Cl E6 — 116 G5
Bredgar Rd N19 — 92 E4
Bredhurst Cl SE20 — 167 L11
Bredon Rd SE5 — 147 U5
Bredon Rd, Croy — 184 E13
Breer St SW6 — 144 J5
Breezers Hill E1 — 21 U11
Brember Rd, Har — 85 T4
Bremer Ms E17 — 78 D8
Bremner Rd SW7 — 22 H9
Brenchley Cl, Brom — 187 M11
Brenchley Cl, Chis — 188 H2
Brenchley Gdns SE23 — 149 M11

Brenchley Rd, Orp	189	T2
Brenda Rd SW17	163	T4
Brende Gdns,	175	R8
W Mol		
Brendon Av NW10	89	K8
Brendon Gdns, Har	85	S7
Brendon Gdns, Ilf	81	S9
Brendon Gro N2	73	M4
Brendon Rd SE9	171	N4
Brendon Rd, Dag	101	M2
Brendon St W1	15	R5
Brendon Way, Enf	44	C13
Brenley Cl, Mitch	182	B6
Brenley Gdns SE9	152	B7
Brent Cl, Bex	173	K2
Brent Cres NW10	105	T4
Brent Cross Gdns,	72	A12
NW4 3		
Brent Cross Shop	71	T13
Cen NW4		
Brent Grn NW4	72	A10
Brent Grn Wk, Wem	88	F5
Brent Lea, Brent	123	M14
Brent Pk NW10	88	H9
Brent Pk Rd NW4	71	R14
Brent Pk Rd NW9	71	R14
Brent Pl, Barn	40	F10
Brent Rd E16	115	P10
Brent Rd SE18	134	J13
Brent Rd, Brent	123	M12
Brent Rd, Sthl	120	E5
Brent Side, Brent	123	M12
Brent St NW4	71	U9
Brent Ter NW2	89	U2
Brent Vw Rd NW9	71	N12
Brent Way N3	56	G12
Brent Way, Brent	123	N13
Brent Way, Wem	88	D11
Brentcot Cl W13	104	J8
Brentfield NW10	88	E14
Brentfield Cl NW10	88	G11
Brentfield Gdns	72	A13
NW2		
Brentfield Rd NW10	88	H14
Brentford Business	123	L13
Cen, Brent		
Brentford Cl, Hayes	102	H7
Brentham Way W5	105	N7
Brenthouse Rd E9	95	L12
Brenthurst Rd NW10	89	M11
Brentmead Cl W7	104	C14
Brentmead Gdns	105	U4
NW10		
Brenton St E14	113	S11
Brentside Cl W13	104	F7
Brentside	123	K12
Executive Cen,		
Brent		
Brentvale Av, Sthl	122	A1
Brentvale Av, Wem	105	T2
Brentwick Gdns,	123	R8
Brent		
Brentwood Cl SE9	171	L2
Brereton Rd N17	60	E14
Bressenden Pl SW1	25	K10
Bressey Av, Enf	44	G2
Bressey Gro E18	79	M4
Brett Cl N16	94	C4
Brett Cl, Nthlt	102	G5
Brett Cr N9	61	L4
Brett Cres NW10	106	G1
Brett Gdns, Dag	100	J13
Brett Ho Cl SW15	144	B13
Brett Rd E8	95	K10
Brett Rd, Barn	39	T10
Brettell St SE17	36	D2
Brettenham Av E17	78	B2
Brettenham Rd E17	78	B2
Brettenham Rd N18	60	H7
Brewer St W1	17	P10
Brewer's Grn,	25	P10
SW1 6		
Brewers Hall Gdns,	20	B4
EC2 4		
Brewers La, Rich 9	141	P9
Brewery Cl, Wem	86	H9
Brewery La, Twick	140	F14
Brewery Rd N7	92	J12
Brewery Rd SE18	135	P9
Brewery Rd, Brom	202	D1

Brewhouse La E1	131	K2
Brewhouse Rd SE18	134	F7
Brewhouse St SW15	144	C6
Brewhouse Wk	131	R2
SE16		
Brewood Rd, Dag	100	D11
Brewster Gdns W10	107	T9
Brewster Rd E10	96	D1
Brian Rd, Rom	82	E10
Briant St SE14	149	N1
Briants Cl, Pnr	67	L3
Briar Av SW16	165	M13
Briar Cl N2	73	K5
Briar Cl N13	59	U6
Briar Cl, Buck H	64	A4
Briar Cl, Hmptn	157	L10
Briar Cl, Islw	140	F9
Briar Ct, Sutt	193	U7
Briar Cres, Nthlt	85	R12
Briar Gdns, Brom	201	L1
Briar La, Croy	200	C7
Briar Pas SW16	183	K6
Briar Pl SW16	183	L6
Briar Rd NW2	89	U7
Briar Rd SW16	183	K6
Briar Rd, Har	69	L10
Briar Rd, Twick	158	C2
Briar Wk, SW15	143	S8
Briar Wk, Edg	54	F14
Briarbank Rd W13	104	H11
Briardale Gdns NW3	90	G6
Briarfield Av N3	72	J4
Briaris Cl N17	60	J14
Briarswood Way,	203	T10
Orp		
Briarwood Cl NW9	70	F11
Briarwood Dr,	66	B3
Nthwd		
Briarwood Rd SW4	146	H9
Briarwood Rd,	193	P11
Epsom		
Briary Cl NW3	91	R13
Briary Ct, Sid	172	D9
Briary Gdns, Brom	169	R9
Briary Gro, Edg	70	C3
Briary La N9	60	E6
Brick Ct EC4	18	J8
Brick Fm Cl, Rich	142	C2
Brick La E1	21	N1
Brick La E2	13	N8
Brick La, Enf	44	J4
Brick La, Stan	53	N14
Brick St W1	24	G4
Brickfield Cl, Brent	123	L13
Brickfield Cotts	135	U12
SE18		
Brickfield Fm Gdns,	203	L8
Orp 3		
Brickfield La, Barn	39	L11
Brickfield Rd SW19	163	K8
Brickfield Rd, Th Hth	183	S1
Brickfields, Har	86	B3
Bricklayer's Arms	36	J2
SE1		
Brickwood Cl SE26	167	K6
Brickwood Rd, Croy	198	C3
Bride La EC4	19	N8
Bride St N7	93	N11
Bridewain St SE1	29	M9
Bridewell Pl, E1 13	131	K2
Bridewell Pl EC4	19	N8
Bridford Ms W1	16	J1
Bridge, The, Har	68	D6
Bridge App NW1	92	A13
Bridge Av W6	125	T9
Bridge Av W7	104	B10
Bridge Cl W10	108	B12
Bridge Cl, Enf	45	K3
Bridge Cl, Tedd	158	E7
Bridge Dr N13	59	M8
Bridge End E17	78	E1
Bridge Gdns, E Mol	176	B8
Bridge Gate N21	43	U13
Bridge Ho Quay E14	132	F1
Bridge La NW11	72	C9
Bridge La SW11	145	S2
Bridge Meadows	131	N11
SE14		
Bridge Pk SW18	144	H9
Bridge Pl SW1	33	N2

Bridge Pl, Croy	184	B14
Bridge Rd E6	98	F13
Bridge Rd E15	96	H14
Bridge Rd E17	77	T14
Bridge Rd N9	60	G5
Bridge Rd N22	74	J2
Bridge Rd NW10	88	J11
Bridge Rd, Beck	167	T14
Bridge Rd, Bexh	155	K4
Bridge Rd, Chess	191	S10
Bridge Rd, E Mol	176	C7
Bridge Rd, Houns	140	A5
Bridge Rd, Islw	140	B6
Bridge Rd, Sthl	121	N4
Bridge Rd, Sutt	195	K11
Bridge Rd, Twick	140	J11
Bridge Rd, Wall	196	D10
Bridge Rd, Wem	88	B5
Bridge Row,	198	B1
Croy 8		
Bridge St SW1	26	B7
Bridge St W4	124	G8
Bridge St, Pnr	66	J6
Bridge St, Rich	141	P10
Bridge Ter, E15 2	96	H14
Bridge Vw W6	125	T9
Bridge Way NW11	72	F9
Bridge Way, Twick	139	U14
Bridge Wf Rd,	140	J5
Islw 3		
Bridge Yd SE1	28	F2
Bridgefield Rd, Sutt	194	G11
Bridgefoot SE1	34	C8
Bridgeland Rd E16	115	P13
Bridgeman Rd N1	93	L14
Bridgeman Rd, Tedd	158	G11
Bridgeman St NW8	7	N3
Bridgen Rd, Bex	154	J12
Bridgend Rd SW18	145	L7
Bridgenhall Rd, Enf	44	E1
Bridgeport Pl, E1 1	29	T1
Bridges Ct SW11	145	N5
Bridges La, Croy	196	J7
Bridges Ms SW19	162	J12
Bridges Pl SW6	144	F1
Bridges Rd SW19	162	J12
Bridges Rd, Stan	52	E10
Bridgetown Cl,	166	C9
SE19 6		
Bridgeview Ct, Ilf	65	P12
Bridgewater Cl, Chis	189	S5
Bridgewater Gdns,	69	T3
Edg		
Bridgewater Rd,	84	C7
Ruis		
Bridgewater Rd,	105	N1
Wem		
Bridgewater Sq,	19	U1
EC2 2		
Bridgewater St,	19	U1
EC2 9		
Bridgeway, Bark	99	U14
Bridgeway, Wem	87	S13
Bridgeway St NW1	9	R3
Bridgewood Cl,	166	J14
SE20 5		
Bridgewood Rd	164	G14
SW16		
Bridgewood Rd,	193	P7
Wor Pk		
Bridgford St SW18	163	M5
Bridgman Rd W4	124	E6
Bridgwater Rd E15	114	E2
Bridle Cl, Epsom	192	G9
Bridle Cl, Kings T	177	P7
Bridle La W1	17	P9
Bridle Path, Croy	197	L6
Bridle Path, The,	62	J13
Wdf Grn		
Bridle Rd, Croy	200	A3
Bridle Rd, Esher	190	J11
Bridle Rd, Pnr	66	D11
Bridle Way, Croy	200	B9
Bridle Way, Orp	203	L8
Bridleway, The,	196	F9
Wall		
Bridlington Rd N9	44	J14
Bridlington Rd, Wat	50	G5
Bridport Av, Rom	83	R12
Bridport Pl N1	12	E1

Bridport Rd N18	60	D10
Bridport Rd, Grnf	103	R1
Bridport Rd, Th Hth	183	P5
Bridport Ter SW8	146	G2
Bridstow Pl W2	108	H11
Brief St SE5	147	R2
Brierley Av N9	61	M2
Brierley Cl, SE25 5	184	J8
Brierley Rd E11	96	G7
Brierley Rd SW12	164	E4
Brierly Gdns E2	113	M4
Brig Ms SE8	132	A12
Brigade Cl, Har	86	A3
Brigadier Av, Enf	43	U1
Briggeford Cl, E5 1	94	H4
Briggs Cl, Mitch	182	D1
Bright Cl, Belv	136	H7
Bright St E14	114	D11
Brightfield Rd SE12	151	L9
Brightling Rd SE4	149	U12
Brightlingsea Pl,	113	T13
E14 9		
Brightman Rd SW18	163	N1
Brighton Av E17	77	T10
Brighton Dr, Nthlt	85	N12
Brighton Gro SE14	149	R1
Brighton Rd E6	116	H5
Brighton Rd N2	73	L4
Brighton Rd N16	94	D7
Brighton Rd, S Croy	198	A11
Brighton Rd, Surb	177	N11
Brighton Rd, Sutt	195	L12
Brighton Ter SW9	147	M7
Brightside, The, Enf	45	R1
Brightside Rd SE13	150	H11
Brightwell Cl,	197	P1
Croy 1		
Brightwell Cres	163	T10
SW17		
Brigstock Rd, Belv	137	R7
Brigstock Rd, Th Hth	183	P10
Brill Pl NW1	9	T4
Brim Hill N2	73	P8
Brimpsfield Cl SE2	136	C6
Brimsdown Av, Enf	45	S4
Brimsdown Ind Est,	45	U3
Enf		
Brindle Gate, Sid	171	R2
Brindley Cl, Bexh	155	P6
Brindley Cl, Wem	105	N1
Brindley St SE14	149	T2
Brindley Way, Brom	169	P10
Brindley Way, Sthl	103	R13
Brindwood Rd E4	62	A5
Brinkburn Cl SE2	136	C7
Brinkburn Cl, Edg	70	C4
Brinkburn Gdns, Edg	70	B5
Brinkley Rd, Wor Pk	193	R3
Brinklow Cres SE18	135	K13
Brinkworth Rd, Ilf	80	C5
Brinkworth Way,	95	U11
E9 5		
Brinsdale Rd NW4	72	A6
Brinsley Rd, Har	68	A3
Brinsley St E1	113	K12
Brinsworth Cl,	158	B2
Twick		
Brion Pl E14	114	E10
Brisbane Av SW19	180	J1
Brisbane Rd E10	96	D4
Brisbane Rd W13	122	H3
Brisbane Rd, Ilf	81	K14
Brisbane St SE5	130	A14
Briscoe Cl E11	97	L4
Briscoe Rd SW19	163	P11
Briset Rd SE9	152	B7
Briset St EC1	19	P1
Briset Way N7	93	M4
Bristol Gdns W9	6	D12
Bristol Ms W9	6	D12
Bristol Pk Rd,	77	S7
E17 2		
Bristol Rd E7	98	A12
Bristol Rd, Grnf	103	R2
Bristol Rd, Mord	181	L9
Briston Gro N8	75	K12
Briston Ms NW7	55	N14
Bristow Rd SE19	166	C10
Bristow Rd, Bexh	155	K2

Bristow Rd, Croy	196	J8
Bristow Rd, Houns	139	S6
Britannia Cl SW4	146	H8
Britannia Cl, Nthlt	102	H6
Britannia Gate E16	133	P1
Britannia La, Twick	139	T13
Britannia Rd,	132	B8
E14 *5*		
Britannia Rd N12	57	M6
Britannia Rd SW6	126	J14
Britannia Rd, Ilf	98	J6
Britannia Rd, Surb	177	U13
Britannia Row N1	111	S1
Britannia St WC1	10	E5
Britannia Wk N1	12	C6
Britannia Way NW10	106	D7
Britannia Way,	127	K14
SW6 *10*		
British Gro W4	125	M9
British Gro Pas W4	125	M10
British Gro S,	125	M10
W4 *12*		
British Legion Rd E4	63	L3
British St E3	113	U6
Brittain Rd, Dag	101	K5
Britten Cl NW11	90	J1
Britten Dr, Sthl	103	N12
Britten St SW3	31	N7
Brittenden Cl, Orp	203	S11
Britten's Ct E1	112	H13
Britton Cl SE6	150	G14
Britton St EC1	11	N12
Brixham Cres, Ruis	84	B2
Brixham Gdns, Ilf	99	S9
Brixham Rd, Well	154	G2
Brixham St E16	134	F2
Brixton Est, Edg	70	C4
Brixton Hill SW2	147	M9
Brixton Hill Pl,	147	K14
SW2 *1*		
Brixton Oval,	147	N8
SW2 *8*		
Brixton Rd SW9	35	K14
Brixton Sta Rd SW9	147	P7
Brixton Water La	147	M10
SW2		
Broad Grn Av, Croy	183	R13
Broad La EC2	20	G2
Broad La N15	76	F8
Broad La, Hmptn	157	S12
Broad Lawn SE9	170	G3
Broad Oak, Wdf Grn	63	S10
Broad Oak Cl E4	62	B10
Broad Sanctuary	25	U9
SW1		
Broad St, Dag	101	N13
Broad St, Tedd	158	E11
Broad St Av, EC2 *5*	20	G4
Broad St Pl EC2	20	F3
Broad Vw NW9	70	B12
Broad Wk N21	59	L3
Broad Wk NW1	8	G8
Broad Wk SE3	151	U4
Broad Wk W1	15	U10
Broad Wk, Houns	138	H2
Broad Wk, Rich	123	T13
Broad Wk, The W8	22	E5
Broad Wk, The,	176	F6
E Mol		
Broad Wk La NW11	72	F14
Broad Yd EC1	11	N12
Broadbent Cl N6	92	C1
Broadbent St W1	16	H10
Broadberry Ct,	60	J11
N18 *2*		
Broadbridge Cl SE3	133	N13
Broadcoombe,	199	N14
S Croy		
Broadcroft Av, Stan	69	P3
Broadcroft Rd, Orp	189	N14
Broadfield Cl NW2	89	T6
Broadfield Ct,	52	C3
Bushey		
Broadfield La,	92	J13
NW1 *1*		
Broadfield Rd SE6	150	J14
Broadfield Sq, Enf	45	K4
Broadfield Way,	63	U6
Buck H		
Broadfields, E Mol	176	C11

Broadfields, Har	67	S3
Broadfields Av N21	43	N13
Broadfields Av, Edg	54	C8
Broadfields Hts, Edg	54	B8
Broadfields La, Wat	50	C1
Broadfields Way	89	L9
NW10		
Broadgate Rd E16	116	A11
Broadgates Av, Barn	41	K2
Broadhead Strand	71	L2
NW9		
Broadheath Dr, Chis	170	E9
Broadhinton Rd	146	D5
SW4		
Broadhurst Av, Edg	54	C7
Broadhurst Av, Ilf	99	T8
Broadhurst Cl NW6	91	L12
Broadhurst Cl,	141	U10
Rich *9*		
Broadhurst Gdns	90	J12
NW6		
Broadhurst Gdns,	65	L8
Chig		
Broadhurst Gdns,	84	F3
Ruis		
Broadlands, Felt	157	M6
Broadlands Av	164	J4
SW16		
Broadlands Av, Enf	45	K6
Broadlands Cl N6	74	A13
Broadlands Cl SW16	164	J4
Broadlands Cl, Enf	45	K6
Broadlands Rd N6	73	U13
Broadlands Rd, Brom	169	S8
Broadlands Way,	179	L12
N Mal		
Broadlawns Ct, Har	68	F2
Broadley St NW8	15	N1
Broadley Ter NW1	7	R11
Broadmead SE6	168	B5
Broadmead Av,	179	N14
Wor Pk		
Broadmead Cl,	157	P12
Hmptn		
Broadmead Cl, Pnr	51	K13
Broadmead Est,	63	T14
Wdf Grn		
Broadmead Rd,	102	J8
Hayes		
Broadmead Rd,	103	K6
Nthlt		
Broadmead Rd,	63	N11
Wdf Grn		
Broadoaks, Surb	192	C3
Broadoaks Way,	187	L9
Brom		
Broadstone Pl W1	16	C3
Broadview Rd SW16	164	G13
Broadwalk E18	79	L5
Broadwalk, Har	67	P9
Broadwall SE1	27	L1
Broadwater Gdns,	203	K7
Orp		
Broadwater Rd N17	76	D3
Broadwater Rd SE28	135	N6
Broadwater Rd	163	R7
SW17		
Broadway E15	96	H13
Broadway SW1	25	S9
Broadway W13	122	H1
Broadway, Bark	117	L1
Broadway, Bexh	155	K7
Broadway, Surb	192	C2
Broadway, The E4	62	F12
Broadway, The E13	115	R4
Broadway, The N8	74	J11
Broadway, The N9	60	H5
Broadway, The N22	75	N3
Broadway, The NW7	55	K10
Broadway, The	162	H13
SW19		
Broadway, The W5	105	P13
Broadway, The W7	122	D2
Broadway, The,	103	T7
Grnf		
Broadway, The, Har	68	D3
Broadway, The,	49	M7
Loug		
Broadway, The, Pnr	51	L14
Broadway, The, Sthl	102	J14

Broadway, The, Stan	53	L9
Broadway, The, Sutt	194	D12
Broadway, The,	190	C1
T Ditt *3*		
Broadway, The, Wem	87	T6
Broadway, The,	63	S11
Wdf Grn		
Broadway Av, Croy	184	B10
Broadway Av, Twick	140	J12
Broadway Cl,	63	S11
Wdf Grn		
Broadway Ct SW19	162	F12
Broadway Gdns,	181	S7
Mitch		
Broadway Mkt E8	112	H2
Broadway Ms E5	76	E14
Broadway Ms,	59	M10
N13 *1*		
Broadway Par N8	74	J11
Broadwick St W1	17	N8
Brocas Cl NW3	91	S13
Brock Pl E3	114	C8
Brock Rd E13	115	S9
Brock St, SE15 *1*	149	L5
Brockdish Av, Bark	99	T10
Brockenhurst,	175	L11
W Mol		
Brockenhurst Av,	193	K1
Wor Pk		
Brockenhurst Gdns	55	K10
NW7		
Brockenhurst	99	L9
Gdns, Ilf		
Brockenhurst Ms,	60	G8
N18 *2*		
Brockenhurst Rd,	184	J14
Croy		
Brockenhurst Way	182	H3
SW16		
Brocket Cl, Chig	65	T8
Brocket Way, Chig	65	S9
Brockham Cl SW19	162	E10
Brockham Cres,	200	G13
Croy		
Brockham Dr SW2	147	L13
Brockham Dr, Ilf	81	L11
Brockham St SE1	28	A9
Brockhurst Cl, Stan	52	E11
Brockill Cres SE4	149	R7
Brocklebank Rd SE7	133	R7
Brocklebank Rd	145	L13
SW18		
Brocklehurst St	131	P13
SE14		
Brocklesby Rd SE25	184	J8
Brockley Av, Stan	53	R6
Brockley Cl, Stan	53	R6
Brockley Cross SE4	149	S5
Brockley Footpath	149	L7
SE15		
Brockley Gdns SE4	149	U3
Brockley Gro SE4	149	S10
Brockley Hall Rd	149	S10
SE4		
Brockley Hill, Stan	53	M2
Brockley Ms SE4	149	R10
Brockley Pk SE23	149	R14
Brockley Ri SE23	149	S12
Brockley Rd SE4	149	T6
Brockley Vw SE23	149	S13
Brockley Way SE4	149	P9
Brocklyside, Stan	53	P7
Brockman Ri, Brom	168	G7
Brocks Dr, Sutt	194	D4
Brockshot Cl, Brent	123	N10
Brockway Cl E11	97	K3
Brockwell Cl, Orp	189	U9
Brockwell Pk Gdns	147	R14
SE24		
Brodewater Rd,	38	C2
Borwd		
Brodia Rd N16	94	D5
Brodie Rd E4	62	F2
Brodie St SE1	37	N6
Brodlove La E1	113	N13
Brodrick Gro SE2	136	D7
Brodrick Rd SW17	163	S3
Brograve Gdns,	186	C4
Beck		
Broke Wk E8	112	F1

Broken Wf, EC4 *6*	19	U10
Brokesley St E3	113	T6
Bromar Rd SE5	148	D5
Bromborough Grn,	50	E9
Wat		
Brome Rd SE9	152	E6
Bromefield, Stan	69	M2
Bromehead Rd E1	113	L11
Bromell's Rd SW4	146	F7
Bromfelde Rd SW4	146	H5
Bromfelde Wk SW4	146	J4
Bromfield St N1	11	M1
Bromhall Rd, Dag	100	C11
Bromhedge SE9	170	E5
Bromholm Rd SE2	136	C6
Bromleigh Ct,	166	J3
SE23 *4*		
Bromley Av, Brom	169	K14
Bromley Common,	188	A9
Brom		
Bromley Cres, Brom	187	M5
Bromley Gdns, Brom	187	L5
Bromley Gro, Brom	186	H4
Bromley Hall Rd E14	114	E9
Bromley High St E3	114	C5
Bromley Hill, Brom	168	J11
Bromley La, Chis	171	N13
Bromley Pl, W1 *1*	17	M1
Bromley Rd E10	78	D12
Bromley Rd E17	78	B4
Bromley Rd N17	60	B6
Bromley Rd N18	76	F1
Bromley Rd SE6	168	G8
Bromley Rd, Beck	186	C2
Bromley Rd, Brom	186	F3
Bromley Rd	168	D3
(Downham), Brom		
Bromley Rd, Chis	171	K14
Bromley St E1	113	P11
Brompton Arc,	24	A7
SW3 *4*		
Brompton Cl SE20	184	H3
Brompton Cl, Houns	139	M9
Brompton Gro N2	73	S8
Brompton Pk Cres	30	A11
SW6		
Brompton Pl SW3	23	S10
Brompton Rd SW1	23	S10
Brompton Rd SW3	23	S10
Brompton Rd SW7	23	S10
Brompton Sq SW3	23	P10
Bromwich Av N6	92	B4
Bromyard Av W3	125	K1
Brondesbury Ct	90	A12
NW2		
Brondesbury Ms	90	G14
NW6		
Brondesbury Pk	89	U13
NW2		
Brondesbury Pk	89	U13
NW6		
Brondesbury Rd	108	E3
NW6		
Brondesbury Vil	108	G3
NW6		
Bronsart Rd SW6	126	C14
Bronson Rd SW20	180	B3
Bronte Cl E7	97	P7
Bronte Cl, Erith	137	R14
Bronte Cl, Ilf	80	H9
Bronti Cl SE17	36	B6
Bronze Age Way,	137	T5
Belv		
Bronze Age Way,	137	T5
Erith		
Bronze St SE8	133	B13
Brook Av, Dag	101	S13
Brook Av, Edg	54	C11
Brook Av, Wem	88	A5
Brook Cl SW20	179	S6
Brook Cl W3	124	A2
Brook Cl, Borwd	38	C5
Brook Cres E4	62	B7
Brook Cres N9	60	J7
Brook Dr SE11	35	N1
Brook Dr, Har	67	U7
Brook Gdns E4	62	C7
Brook Gdns,	143	M5
SW13 *2*		
Brook Gdns, Kings T	178	E1

Name	No.	Ref
Brook Gate W1	16	B11
Brook Grn W6	126	A6
Brook Ind Est, Hayes	120	G2
Brook La SE3	151	S3
Brook La, Bex	154	G11
Brook La, Brom	169	N11
Brook La N, Brent	123	N10
Brook Mead, Epsom	193	K12
Brook Meadow N12	56	J6
Brook Meadow Cl, Wdf Grn	62	J12
Brook Ms N W2	14	H9
Brook Par, Chig	64	J6
Brook Pk Cl N21	43	R10
Brook Path, Loug	48	D8
Brook Pl, Barn	40	G9
Brook Ri, Chig	64	H5
Brook Rd N8	74	J7
Brook Rd N22	75	M4
Brook Rd NW2	89	M3
Brook Rd, Borwd	38	C4
Brook Rd, Buck H	63	N3
Brook Rd, Ilf	81	R11
Brook Rd, Loug	48	D9
Brook Rd, Surb	191	R4
Brook Rd, Th Hth	183	T7
Brook Rd, Twick	140	H11
Brook Rd S, Brent	123	P11
Brook St N17	76	F4
Brook St W1	16	F9
Brook St W2	15	M9
Brook St, Belv	137	R10
Brook St, Erith	137	S12
Brook St, Kings T	177	R4
Brook Vale, Erith	155	S1
Brook Wk N2	73	P1
Brook Wk, Edg	54	G12
Brook Way, Chig	64	H5
Brookbank Av W7	104	B9
Brookbank Rd SE13	150	B6
Brookdale N11	58	E7
Brookdale Rd E17	78	A6
Brookdale Rd SE6	150	C12
Brookdale Rd, Bex	155	K12
Brookdene Av, Wat	50	E1
Brookdene Rd SE18	135	T8
Brooke Av, Har	85	U5
Brooke Rd E5	94	J5
Brooke Rd E17	78	F8
Brooke Rd N16	94	F5
Brooke St EC1	19	K3
Brookehowse Rd SE6	168	B4
Brookend Rd, Sid	171	R2
Brookes Mkt, EC1 3	19	K2
Brookfield N6	92	A5
Brookfield Av E17	78	E8
Brookfield Av NW7	55	S12
Brookfield Av W5	105	P7
Brookfield Av, Sutt	195	R6
Brookfield Cl NW7	55	S12
Brookfield Ct, Grnf	103	U5
Brookfield Ct, Har	69	P9
Brookfield Cres NW7	55	S12
Brookfield Cres, Har	69	R10
Brookfield Gdns, Esher	190	F11
Brookfield Pk NW5	92	C5
Brookfield Path, Wdf Grn	62	J12
Brookfield Rd E9	95	S12
Brookfield Rd N9	60	J6
Brookfield Rd W4	124	H4
Brookfields, Enf	45	P7
Brookfields Av, Mitch	181	R9
Brookhill Cl SE18	134	J10
Brookhill Cl, Barn	41	R10
Brookhill Rd SE18	134	J9
Brookhill Rd, Barn	41	R10
Brookhouse Gdns E4	62	J8
Brooking Rd E7	97	P9
Brookland Cl NW11	72	J8
Brookland Garth NW11	72	J7
Brookland Hill NW11	72	H8
Brookland Ri NW11	72	H8
Brooklands Av SW19	162	J3
Brooklands Av, Sid	171	P3
Brooklands Dr, Grnf	105	N2
Brooklands Pk SE3	151	N5
Brooklands Rd, T Ditt	190	F2
Brooklea Cl NW9	71	K1
Brooklyn Av SE25	185	K7
Brooklyn Av, Loug	48	D8
Brooklyn Cl, Cars	195	R4
Brooklyn Gro, SE25 8	185	K7
Brooklyn Rd SE25	185	K7
Brooklyn Rd, Brom	188	B9
Brookmead Av, Brom	188	F10
Brookmead Rd, Croy	182	F12
Brookmeads Est, Mitch	181	S8
Brookmill Rd SE8	150	B2
Brooks Av E6	116	E7
Brooks Cl SE9	170	H4
Brooks La W4	124	B11
Brook's Ms W1	16	H9
Brooks Rd E13	115	N2
Brooks Rd W4	124	B10
Brooksbank St E9	95	M12
Brooksby St N1	93	N14
Brooksby's Wk E9	95	N9
Brookscroft Rd E17	78	C2
Brookshill, Har	52	B10
Brookshill Av, Har	52	B10
Brookshill Dr, Har	52	A9
Brookside N21	43	M12
Brookside, Barn	41	S11
Brookside, Cars	196	A9
Brookside, Ilf	65	M11
Brookside, Orp	189	T14
Brookside Cl, Barn	40	C11
Brookside Cl, Felt	156	B6
Brookside Cl, Har	69	P10
Brookside Cl (Kenton), Har	85	K7
Brookside Cres, Wor Pk	193	P2
Brookside Rd N9	60	J7
Brookside Rd N19	92	F4
Brookside Rd NW11	72	D11
Brookside Rd, Hayes	102	F13
Brookside S, Barn	42	B14
Brookside Wk N3	72	C3
Brookside Wk N12	56	H10
Brookside Wk NW4	72	C8
Brookside Wk NW11	72	E7
Brookside Way, Croy	185	N11
Brooksville Av NW6	108	D2
Brookview Rd SE16	164	E9
Brookville Rd SW6	126	E14
Brookway SE3	151	N6
Brookwood Av SW13	143	M5
Brookwood Cl, Brom	187	L8
Brookwood Rd SW18	162	F2
Brookwood Rd, Houns	139	S2
Broom Cl, Brom	188	D11
Broom Cl, Tedd	159	N13
Broom Gdns, Croy	200	B6
Broom Lock, Tedd	159	M11
Broom Mead, Bexh	155	P10
Broom Pk, Tedd	159	N13
Broom Rd, Croy	200	A6
Broom Rd, Tedd	159	M11
Broom Water, Tedd	159	L11
Broom Water W, Tedd	159	L10
Broomcroft Av, Nthlt	102	F5
Broome Rd, Hmptn	157	L14
Broome Way SE5	129	U14
Broomfield, E17 3	77	U13
Broomfield, Sun	174	B1
Broomfield Av N13	59	L9
Broomfield Av, Loug	48	F12
Broomfield La N13	59	L8
Broomfield Pl W13	123	K1
Broomfield Rd N13	59	K10
Broomfield Rd W13	123	K1
Broomfield Rd, Beck	185	T6
Broomfield Rd, Bexh	155	P10
Broomfield Rd, Rich	141	U1
Broomfield Rd, Rom	82	G14
Broomfield Rd, Surb	191	U1
Broomfield Rd, Tedd	159	M11
Broomfield St E14	114	B10
Broomgrove Gdns, Edg	70	B2
Broomgrove Rd SW9	147	M4
Broomhall Ri, Bexh	155	P10
Broomhill Rd SW18	144	H10
Broomhill Rd, Ilf	100	B3
Broomhill Rd, Wdf Grn	63	N12
Broomhill Wk, Wdf Grn	63	M13
Broomhouse La SW6	144	G5
Broomhouse Rd SW6	144	G3
Broomloan La, Sutt	194	H4
Broomsleigh St NW6	90	F10
Broomwood Cl, Croy	185	P9
Broomwood Rd SW11	146	A10
Broseley Gro SE26	167	R9
Broster Gdns SE25	184	E6
Brough Cl, SW8 3	129	K14
Brough Cl, Kings T	159	N9
Brougham Rd E8	112	H1
Brougham Rd W3	106	F12
Brougham St, SW11 4	145	U3
Broughinge Rd, Borwd	38	C3
Broughton Av N3	72	C5
Broughton Av, Rich	159	L7
Broughton Dr SW9	147	P8
Broughton Gdns N6	74	F12
Broughton Rd SW6	145	K3
Broughton Rd SW13	105	K14
Broughton Rd, Orp	203	N4
Broughton Rd, Th Hth	183	N11
Broughton Rd App, SW6 7	144	J3
Broughton St SW8	146	C3
Brouncker Rd W3	124	E4
Browells La, Felt	156	E3
Brown Cl, Wall	196	J13
Brown Hart Gdns W1	16	E9
Brown St W1	15	T5
Brownfield St E14	114	D12
Brownhill Rd SE6	150	E14
Browning Av W7	104	F11
Browning Av, Sutt	195	R7
Browning Av, Wor Pk	193	S1
Browning Cl E17	78	E7
Browning Cl, W9 2	6	H11
Browning Cl, Hmptn	157	M8
Browning Cl, Well	153	S2
Browning Est SE17	36	A6
Browning Ms W1	16	E7
Browning Rd E11	79	L14
Browning Rd E12	98	E10
Browning St SE17	36	A4
Browning Way, Houns	138	G1
Brownlea Gdns, Ilf	100	A4
Brownlow Ms WC1	10	G10
Brownlow Rd, E7 2	97	P7
Brownlow Rd E8	112	G1
Brownlow Rd N3	56	J13
Brownlow Rd N11	58	J12
Brownlow Rd NW10	89	K14
Brownlow Rd, W13 3	122	H1
Brownlow Rd, Borwd	38	B7
Brownlow Rd, Croy	198	D7
Brownlow St WC1	18	G3
Brown's Bldgs EC3	20	J7
Browns La NW5	92	C10
Browns Rd E17	78	B6
Browns Rd, Surb	177	T13
Brownspring Dr SE9	171	K7
Brownswell Rd N2	73	N3
Brownswood Rd N4	93	T4
Broxash Rd SW11	146	A11
Broxbourne Av E18	79	R7
Broxbourne Rd E7	97	N6
Broxbourne Rd, Orp	189	U14
Broxholm Rd SE27	165	N6
Broxted Rd SE6	167	T3
Broxwood Way NW8	109	S2
Bruce Castle Rd N17	76	E1
Bruce Cl W10	108	B9
Bruce Cl, Well	154	D2
Bruce Gdns, N20 2	57	T6
Bruce Gro N17	76	E3
Bruce Hall Ms, SW17 3	164	A7
Bruce Rd E3	114	C6
Bruce Rd NW10	88	H14
Bruce Rd SE25	184	B7
Bruce Rd, Barn	40	D5
Bruce Rd, Har	68	C4
Bruce Rd, Mitch	164	A13
Bruckner St W10	108	D6
Brudenell Rd SW17	163	U6
Bruffs Meadow, Nthlt	85	K12
Bruges Pl, NW1 2	92	F14
Brumfield Rd, Epsom	192	E9
Brummel Cl, Bexh	155	T6
Brune St E1	21	M3
Brunel Cl SE19	166	E12
Brunel Cl, Houns	120	C13
Brunel Cl, Nthlt	103	L6
Brunel Est W2	108	G9
Brunel Pl, Sthl 1	103	R12
Brunel Rd E17	77	S12
Brunel Rd SE16	131	L4
Brunel Rd W3	106	J10
Brunel Rd, Wdf Grn	64	E10
Brunel St E16	115	L12
Brunel Wk N15	76	C8
Brunel Wk, Twick 2	139	N13
Brunner Cl NW11	73	K10
Brunner Rd E17	77	S10
Brunner Rd W5	105	N7
Bruno Pl NW9	88	E3
Brunswick Av N11	58	A6
Brunswick Cen WC1	10	B10
Brunswick Cl, Bexh	154	H7
Brunswick Cl, T Ditt	190	F2
Brunswick Cl, Twick	158	A5
Brunswick Ct SE1	29	K7
Brunswick Ct, Barn	41	P9
Brunswick Cres N11	58	A5
Brunswick Gdns W5	105	S7
Brunswick Gdns W8	126	H2
Brunswick Gdns, Ilf	65	L14
Brunswick Gro N11	58	A6
Brunswick Ind Pk N11	58	D7
Brunswick Ms SW16	164	G11
Brunswick Ms W1	16	A6
Brunswick Pk SE5	148	C1
Brunswick Pk Gdns N11	58	A4
Brunswick Pk Rd N11	58	C7
Brunswick Pl N1	12	E7
Brunswick Pl SE19	166	G13
Brunswick Quay SE16	131	P6
Brunswick Rd E10	78	E14
Brunswick Rd E14 7	114	F12
Brunswick Rd N15	76	C8
Brunswick Rd W5	105	S7
Brunswick Rd, Bexh	154	H7
Brunswick Rd, Kings T	178	A1
Brunswick Rd, Sutt	195	K7
Brunswick Sq N17	60	E12
Brunswick Sq WC1	10	C10
Brunswick St E17	78	E9

Name	Page	Grid
Brunswick Vil SE5	148	C1
Brunswick Way N11	58	C7
Brunton Pl, E14 5	113	S12
Brushfield St E1	21	L2
Brussels Rd SW11	145	P8
Bruton Cl, Chis	170	E14
Bruton La W1	17	K12
Bruton Pl W1	16	J11
Bruton Rd, Mord	181	L8
Bruton St W1	16	J11
Bruton Way W13	104	G10
Bryan Av NW10	89	S14
Bryan Cl, Sun	156	A13
Bryan Rd SE16	131	T3
Bryan's All, SW6 8	144	J3
Bryanston Av, Twick	157	S1
Bryanston Cl, Sthl 1	121	M7
Bryanston Ms E W1	15	U4
Bryanston Ms W W1	15	T4
Bryanston Pl W1	15	T4
Bryanston Sq W1	15	U4
Bryanston St W1	16	A8
Bryanstone Rd N8	74	H10
Bryant Cl, Barn	40	F10
Bryant Ct E2	13	M1
Bryant Rd, Nthlt	102	E5
Bryant St E15	96	H14
Bryantwood Rd N7	93	N9
Bryce Rd, Dag	100	E7
Brycedale Cres N14	58	G6
Bryden Cl SE26	167	R9
Brydges Rd E15	96	H9
Bryett Rd N7	93	K5
Brymay Cl E3	114	B4
Bryn-y-Mawr Rd, Enf	44	F7
Brynmaer Rd SW11	145	T2
Bryony Cl, Loug	48	J8
Bryony Rd W12	107	P14
Bryony Way, Sun	156	A11
Buchan Rd SE15	149	M5
Buchanan Cl, N21 4	43	L9
Buchanan Ct, Borwd 2	38	F3
Buchanan Gdns NW10	107	S4
Bucharest Rd SW18	145	L13
Buck La NW9	70	G10
Buck St NW1	92	D14
Buckden Cl SE12	151	M11
Buckfast Rd, Mord	181	K8
Buckfast St E2	13	T8
Buckhold Rd SW18	144	H12
Buckhurst Av, Cars	195	T2
Buckhurst St E1	113	K8
Buckhurst Way, Buck H	64	A8
Buckingham Av N20	41	M14
Buckingham Av, Felt	138	C12
Buckingham Av, Grnf	104	H2
Buckingham Av, Th Hth	183	N2
Buckingham Av, Well	153	S7
Buckingham Av, W Mol	175	R4
Buckingham Cl W5	105	L9
Buckingham Cl, Enf	44	D3
Buckingham Cl, Hmptn 3	157	L9
Buckingham Cl, Orp	189	R13
Buckingham Ct NW4	71	P5
Buckingham Dr, Chis	171	K9
Buckingham Gdns, Edg	53	S14
Buckingham Gdns, Th Hth	183	P3
Buckingham Gdns, W Mol	175	S4
Buckingham Gate SW1	25	M8
Buckingham La, SE23 1	149	S14
Buckingham Ms, N1 6	94	D12
Buckingham Ms NW10	107	M3
Buckingham Ms, SW1 1	25	L9
Buckingham Palace Rd SW1	32	H3
Buckingham Pl SW1	25	M10
Buckingham Rd E10	96	D5
Buckingham Rd E11	79	T9
Buckingham Rd E15	97	L9
Buckingham Rd E18	79	M2
Buckingham Rd N1	94	C12
Buckingham Rd N22	74	J2
Buckingham Rd NW10	107	M3
Buckingham Rd, Borwd	38	G8
Buckingham Rd, Edg	53	S14
Buckingham Rd, Hmptn	157	N11
Buckingham Rd, Har	68	B9
Buckingham Rd, Ilf	99	P3
Buckingham Rd, Kings T	177	U7
Buckingham Rd, Mitch 1	182	J9
Buckingham Rd, Rich	159	N4
Buckingham St WC2	18	C12
Buckland Cres NW3	91	N13
Buckland Ri, Pnr	66	F1
Buckland Rd E10	96	E3
Buckland Rd, Chess	191	T9
Buckland Rd, Orp	203	S7
Buckland St N1	12	F3
Buckland Wk, Mord 2	181	L8
Buckland Way, Wor Pk	193	T1
Bucklands Rd, Tedd	159	M11
Buckle St E1	21	P6
Buckleigh Av SW20	180	E5
Buckleigh Rd SW16	164	J12
Buckleigh Way, SE19 6	166	E14
Buckler Gdns SE9	170	F7
Bucklers All SW6	126	F12
Bucklers Way, Cars	195	U5
Bucklersbury, EC4 4	20	C8
Bucklersbury Pas, EC4 4	20	C8
Buckles Ct, Belv	136	H6
Buckley Rd NW6	90	F14
Buckley St, SE1 2	26	J4
Buckmaster Cl, SW9 1	147	N5
Buckmaster Rd SW11	145	S8
Bucknall St WC2	17	U6
Bucknell Cl SW2	147	L8
Buckner Rd SW2	147	M8
Buckrell Rd E4	62	H4
Buckstone Cl SE23	149	L12
Buckstone Rd N18	60	G10
Buckters Rents SE16	131	R2
Buckthorne Rd SE4	149	R10
Budd Cl N12	57	K7
Buddings Circle, Wem	88	E5
Budge La, Mitch	181	T14
Budge's Wk W2	22	G1
Budleigh Cres, Well	154	E1
Budoch Ct, Ilf	100	B4
Budoch Dr, Ilf	100	A4
Buer Rd SW6	144	D4
Bugsby's Way SE7	133	R8
Bugsby's Way SE10	133	P7
Bulganak Rd, Th Hth	183	T7
Bulinga St SW1	33	U3
Bull All, Well	154	D5
Bull La N18	60	D10
Bull La, Chis	171	N14
Bull La, Dag	101	R5
Bull Rd E15	115	L3
Bull Wf La EC4	20	A10
Bullards Pl E2	113	N5
Bullbanks Rd, Belv	137	T7
Bullen St SW11	145	R3
Buller Cl SE15	130	G14
Buller Rd N17	76	G4
Buller Rd N22	75	N3
Buller Rd NW10	108	B6
Buller Rd, Bark	99	R13
Buller Rd, Th Hth	184	A4
Bullers Cl, Sid	172	J10
Bullers Wd Dr, Chis	188	D1
Bullescroft Rd, Edg	54	B5
Bullhead Rd, Borwd	38	E4
Bullied Way SW1	32	J3
Bullivant St E14	114	E12
Bullrush Cl, Croy	184	C12
Bull's All SW14	142	G4
Bulls Br Rd, Sthl	120	D6
Bulls Gdns, SW3 3	31	S2
Bullsbrook Rd, Hayes	120	F1
Bulmer Gdns, Har	69	N13
Bulmer Ms, W11 4	108	G14
Bulmer Pl W11	126	G1
Bulstrode Av, Houns	139	N5
Bulstrode Gdns, Houns	139	M5
Bulstrode Pl W1	16	F4
Bulstrode Rd, Houns	139	N5
Bulstrode St W1	16	F4
Bulwer Ct Rd E11	96	G1
Bulwer Gdns, Barn	41	L7
Bulwer Rd E11	96	G1
Bulwer Rd N18	60	D8
Bulwer Rd, Barn	41	K8
Bulwer St W12	125	U2
Bunces La, Wdf Grn	63	M13
Bungalow Rd SE25	184	D8
Bungalows, The SW16	164	D13
Bungalows, The, Wall 6	196	C10
Bunhill Row EC1	12	C11
Bunhouse Pl SW1	32	D5
Bunkers Hill NW11	73	L13
Bunkers Hill, Belv	137	P8
Bunkers Hill, Sid	173	M6
Bunning Way N7	93	K13
Bunns La NW7	55	N13
Bunsen St, E3 5	113	R3
Bunting Cl N9	61	N2
Bunting Cl, Mitch	181	U9
Buntingbridge Rd, Ilf	81	N10
Bunton St, SE18 2	134	H6
Bunyan Rd E17	77	S6
Burbage Cl SE1	28	D11
Burbage Rd SE21	148	B13
Burbage Rd SE24	147	U12
Burberry Cl, N Mal	178	J4
Burbridge Way N17	76	F4
Burcham St E14	114	D11
Burcharbro Rd SE2	136	G11
Burchell Rd E10	96	C1
Burchell Rd SE15	149	K2
Burchett Way, Rom	83	L12
Burcote Rd SW18	163	P1
Burden Cl, Brent	123	M10
Burden Way E11	97	S3
Burdenshott Av, Rich	142	C7
Burder Cl N1	94	D11
Burder Rd, N1 5	94	D11
Burdett Cl, Sid	172	J10
Burdett Ms W2	14	B6
Burdett Rd E3	113	T9
Burdett Rd E14	113	T9
Burdett Rd, Croy	184	B12
Burdett Rd, Rich	141	U4
Burdett St SE1	27	K9
Burdetts Rd, Dag	119	L2
Burdock Cl, Croy	199	P2
Burdock Rd N17	76	H5
Burdon La, Sutt	194	D14
Burfield Cl SW17	163	N7
Burford Cl, Dag	100	F6
Burford Cl, Ilf	81	L7
Burford Gdns N13	59	M6
Burford Rd E6	116	C5
Burford Rd E15	114	G1
Burford Rd SE6	167	U4
Burford Rd, Brent	123	R10
Burford Rd, Brom	188	C8
Burford Rd, Sutt	194	G4
Burford Rd, Wor Pk	179	M14
Burford Wk SW6	127	K14
Burford Way, Croy	200	F12
Burge St SE1	28	E12
Burges Ct E6	98	H13
Burges Gro SW13	125	S13
Burges Rd E6	98	D14
Burgess Av NW9	70	G11
Burgess Cl, Felt	156	J7
Burgess Hill NW2	90	G7
Burgess Rd E15	96	J8
Burgess Rd, Sutt	194	J8
Burgess St E14	114	A10
Burgh St N1	11	S2
Burghill Rd SE26	167	P7
Burghley Av, Borwd	38	F9
Burghley Av, N Mal	178	H2
Burghley Hall Cl SW19	162	C1
Burghley Pl, Mitch 1	181	U9
Burghley Rd E11	97	K1
Burghley Rd N8	75	N5
Burghley Rd NW5	92	D8
Burghley Rd SW19	162	C8
Burgon St, EC4 10	19	R8
Burgos Cl, Croy	197	P11
Burgos Gro SE10	150	C1
Burgoyne Rd N4	75	R11
Burgoyne Rd SE25	184	E7
Burgoyne Rd SW9	147	M5
Burham Cl SE20	167	M14
Burhill Gro, Pnr	66	J3
Burke Cl SW15	143	K7
Burke Cl E16	115	M10
Burket Cl, Sthl	121	L8
Burland Rd SW11	145	U10
Burleigh Av, Sid	153	U10
Burleigh Av, Wall	196	B6
Burleigh Gdns N14	58	F1
Burleigh Pl SW15	144	B9
Burleigh Rd, Enf	44	D7
Burleigh Rd, Sutt	194	D1
Burleigh St, WC2 1	18	D10
Burleigh Way, Enf 1	44	A6
Burley Cl E4	62	A10
Burley Cl SW16	182	H3
Burley Rd E16	115	T10
Burlington Arc W1	17	L12
Burlington Av, Rich	142	B1
Burlington Av, Rom	83	S11
Burlington Cl, E6 29	116	D11
Burlington Cl W9	108	G7
Burlington Cl, Orp	202	J4
Burlington Cl, Pnr	66	D5
Burlington Gdns W1	17	L12
Burlington Gdns W3	124	F2
Burlington Gdns W4	124	F10
Burlington Gdns, Rom	83	K13
Burlington La W4	124	J12
Burlington Ms, SW15 4	144	E9
Burlington Ms, W3 3	124	F2
Burlington Pl SW6	144	D4
Burlington Pl, Wdf Grn	63	R6
Burlington Ri, Barn	41	T14
Burlington Rd N10	74	A5
Burlington Rd N17	76	G2
Burlington Rd SW6	144	D4
Burlington Rd W4	124	F10
Burlington Rd, Enf	44	A1
Burlington Rd, Islw	140	A2
Burlington Rd, N Mal	179	R8
Burlington Rd, Th Hth	184	A3
Burma Rd N16	94	A7
Burmester Rd SW17	163	M6
Burn Side N9	61	M5
Burnaby Cres W4	124	D11
Burnaby Gdns W4	124	E11
Burnaby St SW10	127	L14
Burnbrae Cl N12	57	K12
Burnbury Rd SW12	164	F2
Burncroft Av, Enf	45	M4

Burne Jones Ho W14	126	E8
Burne St NW1	15	N2
Burnell Av, Rich	159	L9
Burnell Av, Well	154	B3
Burnell Gdns, Stan	69	N3
Burnell Rd, Sutt	195	K7
Burnels Av E6	116	G6
Burnett Cl E9	95	M10
Burney Av, Surb	177	U9
Burney Dr, Loug	49	K4
Burney St SE10	132	F13
Burnfoot Av SW6	144	D2
Burnfoot Ct SE22	166	J1
Burnham Cl NW7	55	N14
Burnham Cl, Har	68	G7
Burnham Ct NW4	71	U7
Burnham Cres E11	79	T8
Burnham Dr, Wor Pk	194	A4
Burnham Gdns, Croy	184	F14
Burnham Gdns, Houns	138	C3
Burnham Rd E4	61	T9
Burnham Rd, Dag	100	C14
Burnham Rd, Mord	181	K9
Burnham Rd, Rom	83	U6
Burnham Rd, Sid	172	J4
Burnham St E2	113	L5
Burnham St, Kings T	178	A2
Burnham Way SE26	167	T9
Burnham Way W13	122	J6
Burnhill Rd, Beck	186	B3
Burnley Cl, Wat	50	F9
Burnley Rd NW10	89	N10
Burnley Rd SW9	147	L3
Burns Av, Felt	138	B12
Burns Av, Rom	82	E14
Burns Av, Sid	154	C12
Burns Av, Sthl	103	P13
Burns Cl E17	78	E8
Burns Cl SW19	163	N11
Burns Cl, Well	153	T2
Burns Rd NW10	107	L1
Burns Rd SW11	145	T3
Burns Rd W13	122	J3
Burns Rd, Wem	105	R3
Burns Way, Houns	138	G2
Burnsall St SW3	31	R6
Burnside Av E4	61	U11
Burnside Cl SE16	131	P1
Burnside Cl, Barn	40	H6
Burnside Cl, Twick	140	G11
Burnside Cres, Wem	105	N1
Burnside Rd, Dag	100	F4
Burnt Ash Hill SE12	151	M12
Burnt Ash La, Brom	169	R9
Burnt Ash Rd SE12	151	M9
Burnt Oak Bdy, Edg	70	C1
Burnt Oak Flds, Edg	70	E1
Burnt Oak La, Sid	154	A12
Burnthwaite Rd SW6	126	F14
Burntwood Cl SW18	163	P2
Burntwood Gra Rd SW18	163	P2
Burntwood La SW17	163	S2
Burntwood Vw, SE19 *8*	166	E10
Buross St E1	113	K12
Burr Cl E1	29	R2
Burr Cl, Bexh	155	M5
Burr Rd SW18	144	H14
Burrage Gro SE18	135	L7
Burrage Pl SE18	135	K10
Burrage Rd SE18	135	L10
Burrard Rd E16	115	R11
Burrard Rd NW6	90	G9
Burrell Cl, Croy	185	S11
Burrell Cl, Edg	54	D3
Burrell Row, Beck *4*	186	A3
Burrell St SE1	27	P2
Burrells Wf Sq E14	132	C9
Burritt Rd, Kings T	178	B4
Burroughs, The NW4	71	S8
Burroughs Gdns NW4	71	R8
Burrow Cl, Chig	65	U9
Burrow Grn, Chig	65	U9
Burrow Rd SE22	148	C8
Burrow Rd, Chig	65	T9
Burrow Wk SE21	147	T14
Burrows Ms SE1	27	N5
Burrows Rd NW10	107	U5
Bursdon Cl, Sid	171	U3
Bursland Rd, Enf	45	N7
Burslem St E1	21	U7
Burstock Rd SW15	144	C7
Burston Rd SW15	144	B9
Burstow Rd SW20	180	C2
Burt Rd E16	133	U2
Burtenshaw Rd, T Ditt	176	H13
Burtley Cl N4	93	T1
Burton Cl, Chess	191	N13
Burton Gdns, Houns	139	M2
Burton Gro SE17	36	D7
Burton La SW9	147	P3
Burton Ms SW1	32	F3
Burton Pl WC1	9	U9
Burton Rd, E18 *1*	79	R6
Burton Rd NW6	90	F14
Burton Rd SW9	147	R3
Burton Rd, Kings T	159	S14
Burton Rd, Loug	49	M7
Burton St WC1	9	U8
Burtonhole Cl NW7	56	B8
Burtonhole La NW7	55	U9
Burtons Rd, Hmptn	157	U9
Burtwell La SE27	166	B7
Burwash Rd SE18	135	N10
Burwell Av, Grnf	86	D12
Burwell Cl, E1 *5*	113	K12
Burwell Rd E10	95	R1
Burwell Wk E3	114	B7
Burwood Av, Brom	201	R3
Burwood Av, Pnr	66	E10
Burwood Cl, Surb	192	B2
Burwood Pl W2	15	R6
Bury Cl SE16	131	P1
Bury Ct EC3	20	J6
Bury Gro, Mord	180	J9
Bury Pl WC1	18	C4
Bury Rd E4	46	J7
Bury Rd N22	75	P5
Bury Rd, Dag	101	S9
Bury St EC3	20	J7
Bury St N9	60	J2
Bury St SW1	25	N2
Bury St W N9	44	D14
Bury Wk SW3	31	N4
Busby Ms NW5	92	G11
Busby Pl NW5	92	G11
Busby St, E2 *1*	13	P9
Bush Cl, Ilf	81	P10
Bush Cotts SW18	144	G9
Bush Ct W12	126	B3
Bush Gro NW9	70	E13
Bush Gro, Stan	69	N1
Bush Hill N21	43	U13
Bush Hill Rd N21	44	A12
Bush Hill Rd, Har	69	T11
Bush Ind Est NW10	106	G7
Bush La EC4	20	D10
Bush Rd E8	112	J2
Bush Rd E11	79	N14
Bush Rd SE8	131	P8
Bush Rd, Buck H	64	A8
Bush Rd, Rich	123	U11
Bushbaby Cl, SE1 *2*	28	H11
Bushberry Rd E9	95	S11
Bushell Cl SW2	165	M3
Bushell Grn, Bushey	52	A3
Bushell St E1	29	T3
Bushell Way, Chis	170	G9
Bushey Av E18	79	M6
Bushey Av, Orp	189	P13
Bushey Cl E4	62	F6
Bushey Ct SW20	179	T4
Bushey Hill Rd SE5	148	E2
Bushey La, Sutt	194	H7
Bushey Lees, Sid	153	T11
Bushey Rd E13	115	T4
Bushey Rd N15	76	C11
Bushey Rd SW20	179	U4
Bushey Rd, Croy	200	A4
Bushey Rd, Sutt	194	J7
Bushey Way, Beck	186	G10
Bushfield Cl, Edg	54	D3
Bushfield Cres, Edg	54	C4
Bushfields, Loug	48	H9
Bushgrove Rd, Dag	100	G7
Bushmead Cl, N15 *2*	76	F7
Bushmoor Cres SE18	135	L14
Bushnell Rd SW17	164	C4
Bushway, Dag	100	G7
Bushwood E11	97	L2
Bushwood Dr SE1	37	P4
Bushwood Rd, Rich	124	A12
Bushy Pk, Hmptn	176	D2
Bushy Pk, Tedd	176	D2
Bushy Pk Gdns, Tedd	158	B10
Bushy Pk Rd, Tedd	159	K14
Bushy Rd, Tedd	158	E12
Butcher Row E1	113	P13
Butcher Row E14	113	P13
Butchers Rd E16	115	N12
Bute Av, Rich	159	R3
Bute Ct, Wall	196	E9
Bute Gdns W6	126	A7
Bute Gdns, Wall	196	F9
Bute Gdns W, Wall	196	E10
Bute Rd, Croy	197	P2
Bute Rd, Ilf	81	K9
Bute Rd, Wall	196	E8
Bute St SW7	31	K2
Butler Av, Har	68	B13
Butler Pl, SW1 *2*	25	R10
Butler Rd NW10	89	L13
Butler Rd, Dag	100	C7
Butler Rd, Har	67	T13
Butler St E2	113	M5
Butter Hill, Cars	196	B7
Butter Hill, Wall	196	B7
Butterfield Cl N17	59	U12
Butterfield Cl, SE16 *1*	130	J4
Butterfield Cl, Twick	140	E11
Butterfield Sq, E6 *7*	116	E12
Butterfields E17	78	F10
Butterfly La SE9	152	J11
Butterfly Wk, SE5 *5*	148	A2
Butteridges Cl, Dag	119	M2
Buttermere Cl, E15 *10*	96	H8
Buttermere Cl, SE1 *1*	37	M2
Buttermere Cl, Mord	180	A11
Buttermere Dr SW15	144	D10
Buttermere Wk E8	94	F12
Butterwick W6	126	A8
Butterworth Gdns, Wdf Grn	63	P10
Buttesland St N1	12	F6
Buttfield Cl, Dag	101	S12
Buttmarsh Cl, SE18 *7*	135	K9
Butts, The, Brent	123	M12
Butts, The, Sun	174	E5
Butts Cotts, Felt	157	L5
Butts Cres, Felt	157	N5
Butts Piece, Nthlt	102	C4
Butts Rd, Brom	169	K9
Buttsbury Rd, Ilf	99	M10
Buxted Rd E8	94	E13
Buxted Rd N12	57	R9
Buxted Rd SE22	148	D8
Buxton Cl, Wdf Grn	64	A12
Buxton Ct, N1 *1*	12	A5
Buxton Cres, Sutt	194	C7
Buxton Dr E11	79	K8
Buxton Dr, N Mal	178	H3
Buxton Gdns W3	106	C14
Buxton Path, Wat	50	E5
Buxton Rd E4	46	H14
Buxton Rd E6	116	C5
Buxton Rd E15	96	J9
Buxton Rd E17	77	S8
Buxton Rd N19	92	H2
Buxton Rd NW2	89	S11
Buxton Rd SW14	143	K6
Buxton Rd, Ilf	81	R12
Buxton Rd, Th Hth	183	R10
Buxton St E1	13	R12
Buzzard Creek Ind Est, Bark	117	U9
By the Wd, Wat	51	L3
Byam St SW6	145	L4
Byards Cft SW16	182	G2
Bycroft Rd, Sthl	103	P8
Bycroft St, SE20 *4*	167	N13
Bycullah Av, Enf	43	S5
Bycullah Rd, Enf	43	S5
Bye, The W3	107	K11
Bye Way, The, Har	68	E2
Byegrove Rd SW19	163	N12
Byeway, The SW14	142	E6
Byeways, Twick	157	R5
Byeways, The, Surb	178	B10
Byfeld Gdns SW13	143	N2
Byfield Cl SE16	131	S3
Byfield Pas, Islw *2*	140	G6
Byfield Rd, Islw	140	G6
Byford Cl E15	97	K14
Bygrove, Croy	200	C12
Bygrove St, E14 *3*	114	C12
Byland Cl N21	43	L13
Bylands Cl, SE2 *1*	136	C5
Bylands Cl, SE16 *7*	131	P1
Byne Rd SE26	167	M11
Byne Rd, Cars	195	R4
Bynes Rd, S Croy	198	A13
Byng Pl WC1	9	S11
Byng Rd, Barn	40	A5
Byng St E14	132	B3
Bynon Av, Bexh	155	L6
Byre, The N14	42	B12
Byre Rd N14	42	B12
Byrne Rd SW12	164	D3
Byron Av E12	98	C12
Byron Av E18	79	L4
Byron Av NW9	70	D7
Byron Av, Borwd	38	B9
Byron Av, Houns	138	C3
Byron Av, N Mal	179	P9
Byron Av, Sutt	195	P8
Byron Av E, Sutt	195	P7
Byron Cl E8	112	G1
Byron Cl SE28	136	E1
Byron Cl, Hmptn	157	M8
Byron Ct W9	108	H7
Byron Ct, Enf	43	S3
Byron Ct, Har	68	D11
Byron Dr N2	73	P12
Byron Dr, Erith	137	R14
Byron Gdns, Sutt	195	P7
Byron Hill Rd, Har	86	B2
Byron Ms NW3	91	S8
Byron Rd E10	96	C1
Byron Rd E17	78	B6
Byron Rd NW2	89	R4
Byron Rd NW7	55	N9
Byron Rd W5	123	U1
Byron Rd, Har	68	D11
Byron Rd (Wealdstone), Har	68	F6
Byron Rd, Wem	87	M5
Byron St E14	114	E11
Byron Ter N9	45	L13
Byron Way, Nthlt	102	J6
Bysouth Cl, N15 *1*	76	B7
Bysouth Cl, Ilf	80	J2
Bythorn St SW9	147	L6
Byton Rd SW17	163	U11
Byward Av, Felt	138	E11
Byward St EC3	20	J11
Bywater Pl SE16	131	S1
Bywater St SW3	31	T5
Byway, The, Epsom	193	M8
Bywell Pl W1	17	M4
Bywood Av, Croy	185	M11

C

Cabbell St NW1	15	P4
Cabinet Way E4	61	T11
Cable Pl SE10	150	F11
Cable St E1	21	S10
Cable Trade Pk SE7	133	T8
Cabot Sq E14	132	B1
Cabot Way, E6 *2*	116	B2
Cabul Rd SW11	145	R4

Name	Page	Grid
Cactus Cl SE15	148	D3
Cadbury Cl, Islw	140	H1
Caddington Cl, Barn	41	R9
Caddington Rd NW2	90	C6
Caddis Cl, Stan	52	F13
Cade Rd SE10	150	G1
Cadell Cl E2	13	P4
Cader Rd SW18	145	L12
Cadet Dr SE1	37	P5
Cadet Pl SE10	132	J9
Cadiz Rd, Dag	101	U13
Cadiz St SE17	36	B7
Cadley Ter SE23	167	L3
Cadmer Cl, N Mal	178	J8
Cadmus Cl SW4	146	H6
Cadogan Cl, Beck	186	H2
Cadogan Cl, Har	85	S8
Cadogan Cl, Tedd	158	D10
Cadogan Ct, Sutt	195	K12
Cadogan Gdns E18	79	S6
Cadogan Gdns N3	72	J2
Cadogan Gdns N21	43	N10
Cadogan Gdns SW3	32	A2
Cadogan Gate SW1	32	A1
Cadogan La SW1	24	C11
Cadogan Pl SW1	24	B11
Cadogan Rd, Surb	177	N9
Cadogan Sq SW1	24	A12
Cadogan St SW3	31	U3
Cadogan Ter E9	95	U13
Cadoxton Av N15	76	F11
Cadwallon Rd SE9	171	K3
Caedmon Rd N7	93	M7
Caerleon Cl, Sid	172	E10
Caernarvon Cl, Mitch	182	J6
Caernarvon Dr, Ilf	80	H1
Caesars Wk, Mitch	181	U9
Cahill St, EC1 *3*	12	B11
Cahir St E14	132	C8
Caird St W10	108	D6
Cairn Av W5	123	N2
Cairn Way, Stan	52	F11
Cairndale Cl, Brom	169	M13
Cairnfield Av NW2	89	K7
Cairngorm Cl, Tedd	158	F10
Cairns Av, Wdf Grn	64	D12
Cairns Rd SW11	145	S9
Cairo New Rd, Croy	197	S4
Cairo Rd E17	78	B7
Caishowe Rd, Borwd	38	C2
Caistor Ms, SW12 *3*	146	C14
Caistor Pk Rd E15	115	M2
Caistor Rd SW12	146	C14
Caithness Gdns, Sid	153	T12
Caithness Rd W14	126	B6
Caithness Rd, Mitch	164	C13
Calabria Rd N5	93	R11
Calais Gate SE5	147	R1
Calais St SE5	147	S1
Calbourne Rd SW12	145	U14
Calcott Wk SE9	170	C8
Caldbeck Av, Wor Pk	193	R2
Caldecot Rd SE5	147	U3
Caldecott Way E5	95	N5
Calder Av, Grnf	104	E4
Calder Cl, Enf	44	C6
Calder Gdns, Edg	70	A5
Calder Rd, Mord	181	L9
Calderon Pl, W10 *1*	107	T10
Calderon Rd E11	96	F7
Caldervale Rd SW4	146	G10
Calderwood St SE18	134	H7
Caldicot Grn NW9	70	J11
Caldwell Rd, Wat	50	H7
Caldwell St SW9	129	M14
Caldy Rd, Belv	137	R5
Cale St SW3	31	P5
Caleb St, SE1 *3*	27	U6
Caledon Rd E6	116	D1
Caledon Rd, Wall	196	B7
Caledonia St N1	10	D2
Caledonian Cl, Ilf *2*	100	C2
Caledonian Rd N1	10	E2
Caledonian Rd N7	93	L12
Caledonian Wf E14	132	G8
Caletock Way SE10	133	L9
Calico Row, SW11 *6*	145	M5
Calidore Cl SW2	147	L12
California La, Bushey	52	B2
California Rd, N Mal	178	E7
Callaghan Cl SE13	150	J7
Callander Rd SE6	168	E4
Callard Av N13	59	R8
Callcott Rd NW6	90	E14
Callcott St, W8 *10*	126	G1
Callendar Rd SW7	22	J9
Callingham Cl, E14 *3*	113	U10
Callis Rd E17	77	T11
Callow St SW3	30	J9
Calmont Rd, Brom	168	H12
Calne Av, Ilf	80	J2
Calonne Rd SW19	162	A7
Calshot St N1	10	F3
Calshot Way, Enf	43	S6
Calthorpe Gdns, Edg	53	S9
Calthorpe Gdns, Sutt	195	L5
Calthorpe St WC1	10	G10
Calton Av SE21	148	D10
Calton Rd, Barn	41	M11
Calverley Cl, Beck	168	C12
Calverley Cres, Dag	101	N4
Calverley Gdns, Har	69	P13
Calverley Gro N19	92	H2
Calverley Rd, Epsom	193	N11
Calvert Av E2	13	L8
Calvert Cl, Belv	137	P8
Calvert Cl, Sid	172	J11
Calvert Rd SE10	133	L10
Calvert Rd, Barn	40	B4
Calvert St, NW1 *5*	110	A1
Calverton SE5	36	G9
Calverton Rd E6	116	G1
Calvin St E1	13	M12
Calydon Rd SE7	133	S10
Calypso Way SE16	131	T6
Cam Rd E15	114	G1
Camac Rd, Twick	158	B2
Cambalt Rd SW15	144	A9
Camberley Av SW20	179	R3
Camberley Av, Enf	44	C8
Camberley Cl, Sutt	194	B5
Cambert Way SE3	151	S8
Camberwell Ch St SE5	148	A1
Camberwell Glebe SE5	148	C1
Camberwell Grn SE5	148	A1
Camberwell Gro SE5	148	B2
Camberwell New Rd SE5	35	M13
Camberwell Pas, SE5 *2*	147	U1
Camberwell Rd SE5	36	B13
Camberwell Sta Rd SE5	147	T2
Cambeys Rd, Dag	101	S10
Camborne Av W13	123	K4
Camborne Ms W11	108	C12
Camborne Rd SW18	144	H13
Camborne Rd, Croy	184	G14
Camborne Rd, Mord	180	B9
Camborne Rd, Sid	172	E6
Camborne Rd, Sutt	194	J14
Camborne Rd, Well	153	T3
Camborne Way, Houns	139	N1
Cambourne Av N9	45	N14
Cambray Rd SW12	164	F1
Cambray Rd, Orp	189	U13
Cambria Cl, Houns	139	P8
Cambria Cl, Sid	171	P1
Cambria Cl, Felt	138	D14
Cambria Rd SE5	147	T5
Cambria St SW6	127	K14
Cambrian Av, Ilf	81	S9
Cambrian Cl SE27	165	R5
Cambrian Rd E10	78	A14
Cambrian Rd, Rich	141	T12
Cambridge Av NW6	108	H3
Cambridge Av, Grnf	86	E10
Cambridge Av, N Mal	179	M3
Cambridge Av, Well	153	T7
Cambridge Barracks Rd SE18	134	F8
Cambridge Circ WC2	17	U8
Cambridge Cl, E17 *3*	77	U12
Cambridge Cl, N22 *1*	75	N2
Cambridge Cl NW10	88	F6
Cambridge Cl SW20	179	R1
Cambridge Cl, Houns	139	K7
Cambridge Cotts, Rich	124	A12
Cambridge Cres E2	112	J4
Cambridge Cres, Tedd	158	G9
Cambridge Dr SE12	151	N10
Cambridge Dr, Ruis	84	G3
Cambridge Gdns N10	74	B1
Cambridge Gdns N13	59	N10
Cambridge Gdns N17	60	A13
Cambridge Gdns N21	44	A13
Cambridge Gdns NW6	108	H3
Cambridge Gdns W10	108	C11
Cambridge Gdns, Enf	44	H3
Cambridge Gdns, Kings T	178	A3
Cambridge Gate NW1	8	J8
Cambridge Gate Ms NW1	8	J8
Cambridge Grn SE9	170	J1
Cambridge Gro, SE20 *2*	184	J1
Cambridge Gro W6	125	S7
Cambridge Gro Rd, Kings T	178	A4
Cambridge Heath Rd E1	113	K6
Cambridge Heath Rd E2	113	K6
Cambridge Pk E11	79	N13
Cambridge Pk, Twick	141	N13
Cambridge Pk Rd E11	79	M13
Cambridge Pl W8	22	D8
Cambridge Rd E4	62	G2
Cambridge Rd E11	79	M12
Cambridge Rd NW6	108	G5
Cambridge Rd SE20	184	J5
Cambridge Rd SW11	145	T2
Cambridge Rd SW13	143	M4
Cambridge Rd SW20	179	T1
Cambridge Rd W7	122	E3
Cambridge Rd, Bark	99	L13
Cambridge Rd, Brom	169	P13
Cambridge Rd, Cars	195	S11
Cambridge Rd, Hmptn	157	M13
Cambridge Rd, Har	67	N9
Cambridge Rd, Houns	139	K7
Cambridge Rd, Ilf	99	T2
Cambridge Rd, Kings T	178	A4
Cambridge Rd, Mitch	182	E6
Cambridge Rd, N Mal	178	J7
Cambridge Rd, Rich	124	A13
Cambridge Rd, Sid	171	S7
Cambridge Rd, Sthl	121	M1
Cambridge Rd, Tedd	158	F8
Cambridge Rd, Twick	141	N11
Cambridge Rd, Walt	174	C11
Cambridge Rd, W Mol	175	L8
Cambridge Rd N W4	124	C9
Cambridge Row SE18	135	K10
Cambridge Sq W2	15	P6
Cambridge St SW1	33	K5
Cambridge Ter N13	59	N10
Cambridge Ter, NW1 *5*	8	H8
Cambridge Ter Ms, NW1 *4*	8	J8
Cambstone Cl N11	58	B4
Cambus Cl, Hayes	103	K10
Cambus Rd E16	115	P9
Camdale Rd SE18	135	T13
Camden Av, Felt	156	E3
Camden Av, Hayes	102	G13
Camden Cl, Chis	171	L14
Camden Est SE15	148	E1
Camden Gdns, NW1 *5*	92	D14
Camden Gdns, Sutt	194	J10
Camden Gdns, Th Hth	183	S5
Camden Gro, Chis	171	K12
Camden High St NW1	110	D2
Camden Hill Rd SE19	166	D11
Camden La N7	92	H10
Camden Lock Pl NW1	92	C14
Camden Ms NW1	92	G12
Camden Pk Rd NW1	92	H11
Camden Pk Rd, Chis	170	F13
Camden Pas, N1 *2*	11	N1
Camden Rd E11	79	S11
Camden Rd E17	77	T11
Camden Rd N7	92	H10
Camden Rd NW1	92	F13
Camden Rd, Bex	155	L14
Camden Rd, Cars	195	T7
Camden Rd, Sutt	194	H10
Camden Row SE3	151	K4
Camden Sq NW1	92	G12
Camden St NW1	110	E1
Camden Ter NW1	92	G12
Camden Wk N1	111	R2
Camden Way, Chis	170	F14
Camden Way, Th Hth	183	S5
Camdenhurst St E14	113	S11
Camel Gro, Kings T	159	N9
Camel Rd E16	134	B1
Camelford Wk, W11 *14*	108	C12
Camellia Pl, Twick	139	R13
Camellia St SW8	128	J14
Camelot Cl SE28	135	N4
Camelot Cl SW19	162	G7
Camera Pl SW10	30	J10
Cameron Cl N18	61	K8
Cameron Cl N20	57	P3
Cameron Rd, SE6 *1*	167	U4
Cameron Rd, Brom	187	N8
Cameron Rd, Croy	183	S12
Cameron Rd, Ilf	99	R2
Cameron Sq, Mitch	181	R1
Camerton Cl E8	94	F12
Camilla Rd SE16	130	J8
Camille Cl SE25	184	H5
Camlan Rd, Brom	169	M7
Camlet St E2	13	L9
Camlet Way, Barn	40	G3
Camley St NW1	9	U1
Camm Gdns, Kings T *2*	177	U4
Camm Gdns, T Ditt	176	E14
Camms Ter, Dag	101	T10
Camomile Av, Mitch *3*	181	T2
Camomile St EC3	20	H5
Camp Rd SW19	161	T10
Camp Vw SW19	161	S10
Campana Rd SW6	144	G1
Campbell Av, Ilf	81	L8
Campbell Cl SE18	152	H2

Campbell Cl SW16 164 G8
Campbell Cl, Ruis 66 B12
Campbell Cl, Twick 158 A3
Campbell Cft, Edg 54 A9
Campbell Gordon Way NW2 89 R7
Campbell Rd E3 114 B5
Campbell Rd E6 116 D2
Campbell Rd E15 97 L8
Campbell Rd E17 77 U7
Campbell Rd N17 76 F1
Campbell Rd W7 104 D14
Campbell Rd, Croy 183 R13
Campbell Rd, E Mol 176 D5
Campbell Rd, Twick 158 A3
Campdale Rd N7 92 G6
Campden Cres, Dag 100 D7
Campden Cres, Wem 87 K5
Campden Gro W8 126 H3
Campden Hill W8 126 G3
Campden Hill Gdns W8 126 G1
Campden Hill Pl, W11 *15* 126 F1
Campden Hill Rd W8 126 H3
Campden Hill Sq W8 126 F1
Campden Ho Cl, W8 *1* 126 H3
Campden Rd, S Croy 198 D9
Campden St W8 126 G2
Campen Cl SW19 162 C4
Camperdown St E1 21 P7
Campfield Rd SE9 152 A13
Campion Cl E6 116 F13
Campion Cl, Croy 198 C8
Campion Cl, Har 69 U12
Campion Gdns, Wdf Grn 63 P9
Campion Pl SE28 136 C2
Campion Rd SW15 143 T8
Campion Rd, Islw 140 F1
Campion Ter NW2 90 A6
Campion Way, Edg 54 F8
Camplin Rd, Har 69 R9
Camplin St SE14 131 P13
Campsbourne, The, N8 *2* 75 K7
Campsbourne Rd N8 75 K6
Campsey Gdns, Dag 100 D14
Campsey Rd, Dag 100 C14
Campsfield Rd N8 75 K6
Campshill Pl SE13 150 F9
Campshill Rd SE13 150 F10
Campus Rd E17 77 U11
Camrose Av, Edg 54 B14
Camrose Av, Erith 137 S12
Camrose Av, Felt 156 D7
Camrose Cl, Croy 185 R13
Camrose Cl, Mord 180 H7
Camrose St SE2 136 A9
Canada Av N18 59 U11
Canada Cres W3 106 E9
Canada Est SE16 131 M5
Canada Gdns SE13 150 F9
Canada Rd W3 106 E9
Canada Sq E14 132 C1
Canada St SE16 131 N4
Canada Way W12 107 S13
Canadian Av SE6 168 C1
Canal App SE8 131 S10
Canal Cl E1 113 R7
Canal Cl W10 108 B7
Canal Gro SE15 37 U9
Canal Head SE15 148 G1
Canal Path E2 112 E2
Canal Rd E3 113 S8
Canal St SE5 36 D11
Canal Wk N1 112 B1
Canal Wk SE26 167 M9
Canal Wk, Croy 184 E12
Canal Way NW8 7 N9
Canal Way NW10 107 K5
Canal Way W10 108 A8
Canal Way Wk W10 107 T7
Canberra Cl, NW4 *1* 71 P5
Canberra Dr, Hayes 102 F6
Canberra Dr, Nthlt 102 F6
Canberra Rd, E6 *1* 116 F2
Canberra Rd SE7 134 A12
Canberra Rd W13 122 G2
Canberra Rd, Bexh 136 G12
Canbury Av, Kings T 177 T1
Canbury Ms, SE26 *2* 166 G6
Canbury Pk Rd, Kings T 177 U2
Canbury Pas, Kings T 177 P2
Cancell Rd SW9 147 P1
Candahar Rd SW11 145 R4
Candler St N15 76 B11
Candover St W1 17 M3
Candy St E3 113 U1
Cane Cl, Wall 197 K14
Caney Ms NW2 90 A4
Canfield Dr, Ruis 84 D9
Canfield Gdns NW6 91 K13
Canfield Pl NW6 91 L12
Canfield Rd, Wdf Grn 64 C14
Canford Av, Nthlt 103 K2
Canford Cl, Enf 43 P4
Canford Gdns, N Mal 178 J12
Canford Pl, Tedd 159 K12
Canford Rd SW11 146 A9
Canham Rd SE25 184 C5
Canham Rd W3 124 J4
Canmore Gdns SW16 164 F14
Cann Hall Rd E11 97 M6
Canning Cres N22 75 M1
Canning Cross SE5 148 C4
Canning Pas W8 22 E8
Canning Pl W8 22 E9
Canning Pl Ms W8 22 E9
Canning Rd E15 114 J4
Canning Rd E17 77 S7
Canning Rd N5 93 S5
Canning Rd, Croy 198 E2
Canning Rd, Har 68 E5
Cannington Rd, Dag 100 E11
Cannizaro Rd SW19 161 U10
Cannon Cl SW20 179 U6
Cannon Cl, Hmptn 157 S11
Cannon Dr E14 114 A14
Cannon Hill N14 58 J5
Cannon Hill NW6 90 H9
Cannon Hill La SW20 180 C7
Cannon La NW3 91 N6
Cannon La, Pnr 84 J1
Cannon Pl NW3 91 N6
Cannon Pl SE7 134 D9
Cannon Rd N14 58 J6
Cannon Rd, Bexh 155 K2
Cannon St EC4 20 A8
Cannon St Rd E1 112 J12
Cannon Trd Est, Wem 88 C7
Cannon Way, W Mol 175 P7
Cannon Wf Business Cen SE8 131 R8
Cannonbury Av, Pnr 66 G12
Canon Av, Rom 82 F10
Canon Beck Rd SE16 131 M3
Canon Mohan Cl, N14 *1* 42 B12
Canon Rd, Brom 187 U5
Canon Row SW1 26 B6
Canon St N1 111 T2
Canonbie Rd SE23 149 L13
Canonbury Cres N1 93 T13
Canonbury Gro N1 93 T13
Canonbury La N1 93 R13
Canonbury Pk N N1 93 T12
Canonbury Pk S N1 93 T12
Canonbury Pl N1 93 S12
Canonbury Rd N1 93 S13
Canonbury Rd, Enf 44 C1
Canonbury Sq N1 93 R13
Canonbury St N1 93 T13
Canonbury Vil N1 93 S14
Canonbury Yd N1 111 U1
Canons Cl N2 73 P13
Canons Cl, Edg 53 U11
Canons Cor, Edg 53 S7
Canons Dr, Edg 53 S11
Canons Pk Cl, Edg 53 R13
Canons Wk, Croy 199 N5
Canonsleigh Rd, Dag 100 D14
Canopus Way, Nthwd 50 A8
Canrobert St E2 112 J5
Cantelowes Rd NW1 92 H12
Canterbury Av, Ilf 80 D13
Canterbury Av, Sid 172 E3
Canterbury Cl, E6 *16* 116 E12
Canterbury Cl, Beck 186 C1
Canterbury Cl, Chig 65 T6
Canterbury Cl, Grnf 103 R11
Canterbury Cres SW9 147 N6
Canterbury Gro SE27 165 R6
Canterbury Pl SE17 35 R4
Canterbury Rd E10 78 F13
Canterbury Rd NW6 108 G4
Canterbury Rd, Borwd 38 B3
Canterbury Rd, Croy 183 N13
Canterbury Rd, Felt 157 K1
Canterbury Rd, Har 67 S9
Canterbury Rd, Mord 181 L10
Canterbury Ter NW6 108 F3
Cantley Gdns SE19 184 F2
Cantley Gdns, Ilf 81 L11
Cantley Rd W7 122 G5
Canton St E14 114 A12
Cantrell Rd E3 113 U8
Cantwell Rd SE18 134 J13
Canute Gdns, SE16 *7* 131 N7
Canvey St SE1 27 S2
Cape Rd, N17 *2* 76 G6
Capel Av, Wall 197 L9
Capel Cl N20 57 M5
Capel Cl, Brom 202 D1
Capel Ct EC2 20 E7
Capel Ct SE20 185 L1
Capel Gdns, Ilf 99 U7
Capel Gdns, Pnr 67 M7
Capel Rd E7 97 R7
Capel Rd E12 98 B7
Capel Rd, Barn 41 R12
Capener's Cl, SW1 *5* 24 C8
Capern Rd, SW18 *2* 163 L2
Capital Business Cen, Wem 105 N2
Capital Interchange Way, Brent 124 A9
Capitol Ind Pk NW9 70 F6
Capitol Way NW9 70 F6
Capland St NW8 7 M11
Caple Rd NW10 107 L4
Capper St WC1 9 P12
Caprea Cl, Hayes 102 H9
Capri Rd, Croy 184 F14
Capstan Cl, Rom 82 D11
Capstan Ride, Enf 43 N3
Capstan Rd SE8 131 T7
Capstan Sq E14 132 F4
Capstan Way SE16 131 S2
Capstone Rd, Brom 169 L7
Capthorne Av, Har 85 K2
Capuchin Cl, Stan 52 J12
Capulet Ms, E16 *5* 133 P1
Capworth St E10 96 A1
Caradoc Cl W2 108 G11
Caradoc St SE10 132 J9
Caradon Way N15 76 A8
Caravel Ms, SE8 *5* 132 A11
Caraway Cl E13 115 R9
Caraway Pl, Wall 196 C5
Carberry Rd SE19 166 D12
Carbery Av W3 123 U3
Carbis Cl E4 62 G1
Carbis Rd E14 113 T11
Carbuncle Pas Way N17 76 H3
Carburton St W1 17 K1
Cardale St, E14 *3* 132 E5
Carden Rd SE15 148 J6
Cardiff Rd W7 122 G6
Cardiff Rd, Enf 45 K7
Cardiff St SE18 135 R13
Cardigan Gdns, Ilf 100 B3
Cardigan Rd E3 113 U3
Cardigan Rd SW13 143 N3
Cardigan Rd SW19 163 L12
Cardigan Rd, Rich 141 R11
Cardigan St SE11 34 J6
Cardinal Av, Borwd 38 C6
Cardinal Av, Kings T 159 R10
Cardinal Av, Mord 180 D12
Cardinal Bourne St SE1 28 E11
Cardinal Cl, Chis 189 P1
Cardinal Cl, Edg 54 F13
Cardinal Cl, Mord 180 D13
Cardinal Cl, Wor Pk 193 N7
Cardinal Cres, N Mal 178 E3
Cardinal Dr, Ilf 65 L12
Cardinal Pl SW15 144 B7
Cardinal Rd, Felt 156 D2
Cardinal Rd, Ruis 84 G1
Cardinal Way, Har 68 D5
Cardinals Wk, Hmptn 157 T13
Cardinals Way N19 92 G1
Cardine Ms SE15 130 J13
Cardington Sq, Houns 138 H8
Cardington St NW1 9 P7
Cardozo Rd N7 93 K9
Cardrew Av N12 57 P9
Cardrew Cl, N12 *3* 57 R9
Cardross St W6 125 R6
Cardwell Rd N7 92 J7
Cardwell Rd SE18 134 F8
Carew Cl N7 93 M4
Carew Rd N17 76 G4
Carew Rd W13 123 L3
Carew Rd, Mitch 182 A3
Carew Rd, Th Hth 183 S7
Carew Rd, Wall 196 F11
Carew St SE5 147 T3
Carew Way, Wat 51 L5
Carey Ct, Bexh 155 R10
Carey Gdns SW8 146 F2
Carey La EC2 19 U6
Carey Pl, SW1 *2* 33 S4
Carey Rd, Dag 101 K8
Carey St WC2 18 H7
Carey Way, Wem 88 E8
Carfax Pl SW4 146 G8
Carfree Cl N1 93 P13
Cargill Rd SW18 163 L1
Cargreen Rd SE25 184 F8
Carholme Rd SE23 167 T2
Carisbrooke Av, Bex 172 G2
Carisbrooke Cl, Enf 44 E2
Carisbrooke Cl, Stan 69 P3
Carisbrooke Gdns SE15 37 P14
Carisbrooke Rd E17 77 S8
Carisbrooke Rd, Brom 187 U8
Carisbrooke Rd, Mitch 182 H8
Carker's La NW5 92 C9
Carleton Cl, Esher 190 A2
Carleton Rd N7 92 G9
Carlile Cl E3 113 U4
Carlina Gdns, Wdf Grn 63 R10
Carlingford Gdns, Mitch 163 U13
Carlingford Rd N15 75 R6
Carlingford Rd NW3 91 P7
Carlingford Rd, Mord 180 A12
Carlisle Av EC3 21 K8
Carlisle Av W3 106 J12
Carlisle Cl, Kings T 178 B2
Carlisle Cl, Pnr 66 J14
Carlisle Gdns, Har 69 P13
Carlisle Gdns, Ilf 80 C12
Carlisle La SE1 26 H10
Carlisle Ms NW8 15 M1

Carlisle Pl N11 58 C8
Carlisle Pl SW1 25 M12
Carlisle Rd E10 96 B3
Carlisle Rd N4 75 P14
Carlisle Rd NW6 108 D2
Carlisle Rd NW9 70 E5
Carlisle Rd, Hmptn 157 S13
Carlisle Rd, Sutt 194 F11
Carlisle St W1 17 R7
Carlisle Way, SW17 **2** 164 A10
Carlos Pl W1 16 F11
Carlow St NW1 9 L1
Carlton Av N14 42 G9
Carlton Av, Felt 138 E12
Carlton Av, Har 68 J10
Carlton Av, S Croy 198 C13
Carlton Av E, Wem 87 N3
Carlton Av W, Wem 87 L4
Carlton Cl NW3 90 H3
Carlton Cl, Borwd 38 H8
Carlton Cl, Chess 191 P12
Carlton Cl, Edg 54 A10
Carlton Ct SW9 147 R1
Carlton Ct, Ilf 81 N6
Carlton Cres, Sutt 194 C7
Carlton Dr SW15 148 B10
Carlton Dr, Ilf 81 N6
Carlton Gdns SW1 25 S3
Carlton Gdns W5 105 M12
Carlton Gro SE15 148 J1
Carlton Hill NW8 6 C3
Carlton Ho Ter SW1 25 S3
Carlton Pk Av SW20 179 U3
Carlton Rd E11 97 L1
Carlton Rd E12 98 B8
Carlton Rd E17 77 S2
Carlton Rd N4 75 N14
Carlton Rd N11 58 A9
Carlton Rd SW14 142 E6
Carlton Rd W4 124 G4
Carlton Rd W5 105 L12
Carlton Rd, Erith 137 T11
Carlton Rd, N Mal 178 J4
Carlton Rd, Sid 171 U8
Carlton Rd, S Croy 198 B13
Carlton Rd, Walt 174 D13
Carlton Rd, Well 154 D5
Carlton Sq, E1 **17** 113 N7
Carlton St, SW1 **9** 17 S12
Carlton Ter E11 79 R9
Carlton Ter N18 60 B6
Carlton Ter SE26 167 L6
Carlton Twr Pl SW1 24 B9
Carlton Vale NW6 6 A4
Carlwell St SW17 163 R10
Carlyle Av, Brom 188 A6
Carlyle Av, Sthl 103 L13
Carlyle Cl N2 73 M11
Carlyle Cl NW10 106 H2
Carlyle Cl, W Mol 175 S4
Carlyle Gdns, Sthl 103 L13
Carlyle Pl SW15 144 A7
Carlyle Rd E12 98 C8
Carlyle Rd SE28 118 D14
Carlyle Rd NW6 123 M9
Carlyle Rd, Croy 198 H3
Carlyle Sq SW3 31 M8
Carlyon Av, Har 85 M7
Carlyon Cl, Wem 105 R2
Carlyon Rd, Hayes 102 F12
Carlyon Rd, Wem 105 T2
Carmalt Gdns SW15 143 U8
Carmel Ct W8 22 A6
Carmel Ct, Wem 88 C3
Carmelite Cl, Har 67 U2
Carmelite Rd, Har 67 A4
Carmelite St EC4 19 M10
Carmelite Wk, Har 67 T2
Carmelite Way, Har 67 U3
Carmen St E14 114 C11
Carmichael Cl, SW11 **10** 145 P6
Carmichael Cl, Ruis 84 B7
Carmichael Ms SW18 145 P13
Carmichael Rd SE25 184 G9
Carminia Rd SW17 164 C3
Carnaby St W1 17 M8
Carnac St SE27 166 A7

Carnanton Rd E17 78 G2
Carnarvon Av, Enf 44 E4
Carnarvon Rd E10 78 F11
Carnarvon Rd E15 97 L11
Carnarvon Rd E18 79 L2
Carnarvon Rd, Barn 40 C5
Carnation St SE2 136 C9
Carnbrook Rd SE3 152 A5
Carnecke Gdns SE9 152 D10
Carnegie Cl, Surb 191 T4
Carnegie Pl SW19 162 A5
Carnegie St N1 111 L2
Carnforth Cl, Epsom 192 C11
Carnforth Rd SW16 164 G13
Carnie Lo SW17 164 C5
Carnoustie Dr N1 93 L14
Carnwath Rd SW6 144 J6
Carol St NW1 110 E1
Carolina Cl E15 96 J10
Carolina Rd, Th Hth 183 S3
Caroline Cl N10 74 C4
Caroline Cl SW16 165 M7
Caroline Cl W2 14 C12
Caroline Cl, Croy **3** 198 D7
Caroline Cl, Islw 122 C14
Caroline Gdns SE15 130 J13
Caroline Pl SW11 146 B4
Caroline Pl W2 14 C10
Caroline Pl Ms, W2 **3** 14 C11
Caroline Rd SW19 162 E13
Caroline St E1 113 P12
Caroline Ter SW1 32 D3
Caroline Wk W6 126 C12
Carpenders Av, Wat 51 K4
Carpenders Pk, Wat 51 K4
Carpenter Gdns N21 59 S3
Carpenter St W1 16 G11
Carpenters Ct, Twick 158 C4
Carpenters Pl SW4 146 G7
Carpenters Rd E15 96 E13
Carr Gro SE18 134 D7
Carr Rd E17 78 A3
Carr Rd, Nthlt 85 E13
Carr St E14 113 S11
Carriage Dr E SW11 32 E14
Carriage Dr N SW11 32 E12
Carriage Dr S SW11 146 A1
Carriage Dr W SW11 127 T14
Carriage Ms, Ilf 99 M3
Carriage Pl N16 94 B6
Carrick Cl, Islw 140 G6
Carrick Dr, Ilf 81 L2
Carrick Gdns N17 60 C14
Carrick Ms, SE8 **3** 132 A11
Carrill Way, Belv 136 H7
Carrington Av, Borwd 38 D10
Carrington Av, Houns 139 R10
Carrington Cl, Barn 39 P9
Carrington Cl, Borwd 38 E10
Carrington Cl, Croy **1** 185 S13
Carrington Cl, Kings T 160 F9
Carrington Gdns, E7 **4** 97 P7
Carrington Rd, Rich 142 A8
Carrington Sq, Har 51 U13
Carrington St W1 24 H3
Carrol Cl NW5 92 C8
Carroll Cl E15 97 L10
Carroll Hill, Loug 48 F5
Carron Cl E14 114 D11
Carronade Pl SE28 135 M5
Carroun Rd SW8 34 F14
Carrow Rd, Dag 100 D13
Carroway La, Grnf **1** 104 B5
Carrs La N21 43 U9
Carshalton Gro, Sutt 195 P8
Carshalton Pk Rd, Cars 195 U9
Carshalton Pl, Cars 196 A8
Carshalton Rd, Cars 195 N10
Carshalton Rd, Mitch 182 A9

Carshalton Rd, Sutt 195 N10
Carslake Rd SW15 143 T11
Carson Rd E16 115 P8
Carson Rd SE21 166 A3
Carson Rd, Barn 41 T8
Carstairs Rd SE6 168 E6
Carston Cl SE12 151 M10
Carswell Cl, Ilf 80 B7
Carswell Rd SE6 150 E13
Cart La E4 46 H14
Carter Cl, Wall 196 H13
Carter La EC4 19 S8
Carter Pl SE17 36 A7
Carter Rd E13 115 R2
Carter Rd SW19 163 N12
Carter St SE17 35 T8
Carteret St SW1 25 S8
Carteret Way SE8 131 S8
Carterhatch La, Enf 44 J3
Carterhatch Rd, Enf 44 G3
Carters Cl, Wor Pk 194 A3
Carters Hill Cl SE9 169 U1
Carters Yd, SW18 **2** 144 H10
Carthew Rd W6 125 S6
Carthew Vil W6 125 S5
Carthusian St EC1 19 T1
Cartier Circle E14 132 D2
Carting La WC2 18 D11
Cartmel Cl N17 61 K13
Cartmel Gdns, Mord 181 L10
Cartmel Rd, Bexh 155 N1
Carton St W1 16 B5
Cartwright Gdns WC1 10 A8
Cartwright Rd, Dag 101 L13
Cartwright St E1 21 P10
Cartwright Way SW13 125 S13
Carver Cl W4 124 F5
Carver Rd SE24 147 T11
Carville Cres, Brent 123 R9
Cary Rd E11 97 K7
Carysfort Rd N8 74 G9
Carysfort Rd N16 94 A6
Cascade Av N10 74 H7
Cascade Cl, Buck H 64 B5
Cascade Rd, Buck H 64 B4
Casella Rd SE14 131 N14
Casewick Rd SE27 165 R7
Casimir Rd E5 95 L5
Casino Av SE24 148 A9
Caspian St SE5 36 C14
Caspian Wk E16 116 A12
Cassandra Cl, Nthlt 86 A8
Casselden Rd NW10 88 H14
Cassidy Rd SW6 126 A13
Cassilda Rd SE2 136 B8
Cassilis Rd, Twick 141 K11
Cassiobury Rd E17 77 L3
Cassis Ct, Loug **2** 49 L7
Cassland Rd E9 95 N3
Cassland Rd, Th Hth 184 A7
Casslee Rd SE6 149 U14
Casson St E1 21 R3
Castell Rd, Loug 49 L2
Castellain Rd W9 6 C7
Castellane Cl, Stan **1** 52 F13
Castello Av SW15 143 T9
Castelnau SW13 125 P14
Castelnau Pl, SW13 **2** 125 R12
Castelnau Row, SW13 **1** 125 R11
Casterbridge Rd SE3 151 P6
Castillon Rd SE6 168 J4
Castlands Rd SE6 167 T4
Castle Av E4 62 H10
Castle Baynard St EC4 19 R9
Castle Cl SW19 162 A5
Castle Cl W3 124 D4
Castle Cl, Brom 186 J6
Castle Ct SE26 167 S7
Castle Dr, Ilf 80 C12
Castle La SW1 25 N9
Castle Ms N12 57 M10
Castle Ms NW1 92 C12
Castle Par, Epsom 193 N14

Castle Pl NW1 92 D12
Castle Rd N12 57 M10
Castle Rd NW1 92 C12
Castle Rd, Dag 118 C2
Castle Rd, Enf 45 R1
Castle Rd, Islw 140 E3
Castle Rd, Nthlt 85 R12
Castle Rd, Sthl 121 M5
Castle St E6 115 U3
Castle St, Kings T 177 R3
Castle Wk, Sun 174 E5
Castle Way SW19 162 A5
Castle Way, Felt 156 F7
Castle Yd N6 74 B14
Castle Yd SE1 27 R1
Castle Yd, Rich **7** 141 P10
Castlebar Hill W5 105 K10
Castlebar Ms W5 105 L9
Castlebar Pk W5 105 K8
Castlebar Rd W5 105 N12
Castlebrook Cl SE11 35 N2
Castlecombe Dr SW19 144 B14
Castlecombe Rd SE9 170 C8
Castledine Rd SE20 166 J14
Castleford Av SE9 170 J1
Castleford Cl N17 60 E12
Castlegate, Rich 141 T6
Castlehaven Rd NW1 92 D13
Castleleigh Ct, Enf 44 B9
Castlemaine Av, S Croy 198 E10
Castlereagh St W1 15 T5
Castleton Av, Wem 87 R7
Castleton Cl, Croy 185 S12
Castleton Gdns, Wem 87 R6
Castleton Rd E17 78 H3
Castleton Rd SE9 170 A7
Castleton Rd, Ilf 100 C2
Castleton Rd, Mitch 182 G8
Castleton Rd, Ruis 84 G2
Castletown Rd W14 126 D10
Castleview Cl N4 93 T3
Castleview Gdns, Ilf 80 C14
Castlewood Dr SE9 152 F3
Castlewood Rd N15 76 G11
Castlewood Rd N16 76 G13
Castlewood Rd, Barn 41 P6
Castor La E14 114 C14
Cat Hill, Barn 41 S11
Caterham Av, Ilf 80 G3
Caterham Rd SE13 150 F6
Catesby St SE17 36 E3
Catford Bdy SE6 150 C14
Catford Hill SE6 168 A2
Catford Rd SE6 150 B14
Cathall Rd E11 96 H5
Cathay St SE16 131 K4
Cathcart Dr, Orp 203 R3
Cathcart Hill N19 92 E6
Cathcart Rd SW10 30 F9
Cathcart St NW5 92 C11
Cathedral St SE1 28 D2
Catherall Rd N5 93 U6
Catherine Cl, Loug 48 E11
Catherine Ct, N14 **2** 42 F10
Catherine Dr, Rich 141 S7
Catherine Gdns, Houns 140 A8
Catherine Griffiths Ct EC1 11 L10
Catherine Gro SE10 150 C1
Catherine Rd, Surb 177 P9
Catherine St WC2 18 E9
Catherine Wheel All E1 21 K4
Catherine Wheel Rd, Brent 123 N13
Catherine Wheel Yd SW1 25 L4
Cathles Rd SW12 146 D12
Cathnor Rd W12 125 R4
Catlin St SE16 37 U6
Catling Cl SE23 167 M6

Catlins La, Pnr	66	D6
Cato Rd SW4	146	H7
Cato St W1	15	S5
Cator La, Beck	185	U3
Cator Rd SE26	167	P11
Cator Rd, Cars	195	U9
Cator St SE15	37	M12
Catterick Cl N11	58	B11
Cattistock Rd SE9	170	D9
Cattley Cl, Barn	40	C7
Catton St WC1	18	E4
Caulfield Rd E6	116	D1
Caulfield Rd SE15	149	K3
Causeway The N2	73	R7
Causeway, The SW18	144	J8
Causeway, The SW19	161	U10
Causeway, The, Cars	196	A4
Causeway, The, Chess	191	S8
Causeway, The, Esher	190	F13
Causeway, The, Felt	138	C6
Causeway, The, Tedd	158	F11
Causeyware Rd N9	45	K13
Causton Rd N6	74	D14
Causton St SW1	33	T4
Cautley Av SW4	148	E10
Cavalier Cl, Rom	82	G7
Cavalry Cres, Houns	138	G7
Cavalry Rd SW15	144	E9
Cavaye Pl SW10	30	H8
Cave Rd E13	115	S4
Cave Rd, Rich	159	L7
Cave St N1	111	M2
Cavell Dr, Enf	43	P3
Cavell Rd N17	60	A14
Cavell St E1	113	K11
Cavendish Av N3	72	G4
Cavendish Av NW8	7	L4
Cavendish Av W13	104	G11
Cavendish Av, Erith	137	T12
Cavendish Av, Har	86	C8
Cavendish Av, N Mal	179	R9
Cavendish Av, Ruis	84	C9
Cavendish Av, Sid	154	B14
Cavendish Av, Well	153	U6
Cavendish Av, Wdf Grn	79	R1
Cavendish Cl N18	61	K9
Cavendish Cl NW6	90	E12
Cavendish Cl, NW8 2	7	L5
Cavendish Cres, Borwd	38	A8
Cavendish Dr E11	96	G1
Cavendish Dr, Edg	53	U11
Cavendish Dr, Esher	190	C9
Cavendish Gdns, Bark	99	S10
Cavendish Gdns, Ilf	98	G1
Cavendish Gdns, Rom	83	K10
Cavendish Ms N, W1 4	16	J2
Cavendish Ms S, W1 2	16	J3
Cavendish Pl W1	16	J5
Cavendish Rd E4	62	E12
Cavendish Rd N4	75	R11
Cavendish Rd N18	60	J9
Cavendish Rd NW6	90	D13
Cavendish Rd SW12	146	E11
Cavendish Rd SW19	163	R13
Cavendish Rd W4	142	F1
Cavendish Rd, Barn	39	U6
Cavendish Rd, Croy	197	R1
Cavendish Rd, N Mal	179	L8
Cavendish Rd, Sutt	195	L13
Cavendish Sq W1	16	H5
Cavendish St N1	12	C3
Cavendish Ter, Felt	156	B4
Cavendish Way, W Wick	200	C2
Cavenham Gdns, Ilf	99	N6
Caverleigh Way, Wor Pk	179	P14
Caversham Av N13	59	N5
Caversham Av, Sutt	194	C3
Caversham Flats, SW3 2	31	U9
Caversham Rd N15	75	U7
Caversham Rd NW5	75	U7
Caversham Rd, Kings T	177	T3
Caversham St SW3	31	T9
Caverswall St, W12 2	107	T11
Cawdor Cres W7	122	H7
Cawnpore St SE19	166	D10
Caxton Gro E3	114	A5
Caxton Ms, Brent	123	N12
Caxton Rd N22	75	M4
Caxton Rd SW19	163	L10
Caxton Rd W12	126	A3
Caxton Rd, Sthl	120	G5
Caxton St SW1	25	R9
Caxton St N, E16 5	115	M13
Caygill Cl, Brom	187	M7
Cayley Rd, Sthl 2	121	R5
Cayton Pl, FC1 1	12	C7
Cayton Rd, Grnf	104	D4
Cayton St EC1	12	C7
Cazenove Rd E17	78	B2
Cazenove Rd N16	94	F3
Cecil Av, Bark	99	N13
Cecil Av, Enf	44	E7
Cecil Av, Wem	87	T10
Cecil Cl W5	105	P9
Cecil Cl, Chess	191	P8
Cecil Cl, Barn	40	B5
Cecil Pk, Pnr	67	K7
Cecil Pl, Mitch	181	U9
Cecil Rd E11	97	K5
Cecil Rd E13	115	P1
Cecil Rd E17	78	B1
Cecil Rd N10	74	D3
Cecil Rd N14	58	E1
Cecil Rd NW9	70	J6
Cecil Rd NW10	106	J2
Cecil Rd SW19	162	J14
Cecil Rd W3	106	F10
Cecil Rd, Croy	183	L12
Cecil Rd, Enf	44	A7
Cecil Rd, Har	68	C5
Cecil Rd, Houns	139	U5
Cecil Rd, Ilf	98	J7
Cecil Rd, Rom	82	H13
Cecil Rd, Sutt	194	F12
Cecil Way, Brom	201	N1
Cecile Pk N8	75	K12
Cecilia Cl N2	73	L5
Cecilia Rd E8	94	F9
Cedar Av, Barn	41	R13
Cedar Av, Enf	45	M3
Cedar Av, Hayes	102	A12
Cedar Av, Rom	82	J9
Cedar Av, Ruis	84	F10
Cedar Av, Sid	154	A13
Cedar Av, Twick	139	S11
Cedar Cl SE21	165	U2
Cedar Cl SW15	160	G8
Cedar Cl, Borwd	38	C8
Cedar Cl, Brom	202	C5
Cedar Cl, Buck H	64	B4
Cedar Cl, Cars	195	U11
Cedar Cl, E Mol 2	176	C8
Cedar Cl, Rom	83	U7
Cedar Copse, Brom	188	E3
Cedar Ct, N1 3	93	U13
Cedar Ct SE9	152	D11
Cedar Ct SW19	162	B6
Cedar Cres, Brom	202	C6
Cedar Dr N2	73	R8
Cedar Dr, Loug	49	K4
Cedar Dr, Pnr	51	P12
Cedar Gdns, Sutt	195	M12
Cedar Gro W5	123	R4
Cedar Gro, Bex	154	F12
Cedar Gro, Sthl	103	P9
Cedar Hts, Rich	159	R2
Cedar Lawn Av, Barn	40	D9
Cedar Mt SE9	170	A2
Cedar Pk Gdns, Rom	82	G13
Cedar Pl SE7	133	T9
Cedar Ri N14	42	B13
Cedar Rd N17	76	F1
Cedar Rd NW2	89	U7
Cedar Rd, Brom	187	U3
Cedar Rd, Croy	198	C3
Cedar Rd, E Mol	176	C8
Cedar Rd, Houns	138	E3
Cedar Rd, Rom	83	U7
Cedar Rd, Sutt	195	L12
Cedar Rd, Tedd	158	G10
Cedar Ter, Rich	141	T7
Cedar Tree Gro SE27	165	R9
Cedar Wk, Esher	190	E11
Cedar Way NW1	92	G14
Cedarcroft Rd, Chess	191	U6
Cedarhurst Dr SE9	151	T10
Cedarne Rd SW6	126	J14
Cedars, The, Buck H	63	P2
Cedars, The, Tedd	158	F11
Cedars Av E17	78	A9
Cedars Av, Mitch	182	C5
Cedars Cl NW4	72	A6
Cedars Cl N9	60	D3
Cedars Ms, SW4 15	146	C7
Cedars Rd E15	97	K11
Cedars Rd N9	60	G4
Cedars Rd N21	59	S3
Cedars Rd SW4	146	C6
Cedars Rd SW13	143	N4
Cedars Rd W4	124	E10
Cedars Rd, Beck	185	T3
Cedars Rd, Croy	197	K6
Cedars Rd, Kings T	177	L1
Cedars Rd, Mord	180	H7
Cedarville Gdns SW16	165	M12
Cedric Rd SE9	171	L5
Celadon Cl, Enf	45	R5
Celandine Cl E14	114	A10
Celandine Dr SE28	136	C2
Celandine Way E15	115	K5
Celbridge Ms W2	14	C5
Celestial Gdns SE13	150	H7
Celia Rd N19	92	F8
Celtic Av, Brom	186	J6
Celtic St E14	114	D9
Cemetery La SE7	134	D11
Cemetery Rd E7	97	M8
Cemetery Rd N17	60	D14
Cemetery Rd SE2	136	C13
Cenacle Cl NW3	90	H5
Centaur St SE1	26	J10
Centaurs Business Cen, Islw	122	G11
Centenary Est, Enf	45	T7
Centenary Rd, Enf	45	T8
Centenary Wk, Loug	47	S5
Central Av E11	96	G4
Central Av N2	73	N4
Central Av N9	60	D5
Central Av, Enf	44	J3
Central Av, Houns	140	A9
Central Av, Pnr	67	L12
Central Av, Wall	197	K9
Central Av, Well	154	A4
Central Av, W Mol	175	M9
Central Hill SE19	166	B11
Central Mkts EC1	19	R2
Central Par, Felt	138	F13
Central Par, Grnf	104	B5
Central Pk Av, Dag	101	S6
Central Pk Est, Houns	138	G9
Central Pk Rd E6	115	U4
Central Pl SE25	184	H9
Central Rd, Mord	180	J10
Central Rd, Wem	86	J10
Central Rd, Wor Pk	193	R3
Central Sch Footpath, SW14 2	142	J7
Central Sq NW11	72	J11
Central Sq, Wem 2	87	R10
Central Sq, W Mol	175	M8
Central St EC1	11	T7
Central Way NW10	106	F4
Central Way SE28	118	C13
Central Way, Cars	195	S14
Central Way, Felt	138	C10
Centre, The, Felt	156	C2
Centre Av W3	124	H2
Centre Common Rd, Chis	171	L12
Centre Rd E7	97	P5
Centre Rd E11	97	P5
Centre Rd, Dag	119	S3
Centre St E2	112	J4
Centre Way E17	62	E14
Centre Way N9	61	M3
Centreway, Ilf	99	L4
Centric Cl NW1	110	B1
Centurion Cl N7	93	M13
Centurion La, E3 13	113	U13
Centurion Way, Erith	137	N5
Century Cl NW4	72	A9
Century Ms E5	95	L8
Century Rd E17	77	R6
Cephas Av E1	113	M7
Cephas St E1	113	L8
Ceres Rd SE18	135	T8
Cerise Rd SE15	148	H2
Cerne Cl, Hayes	102	F13
Cerne Rd, Mord	181	L11
Cerney Ms W2	14	J9
Corvantes Ct W2	14	C8
Cester St, E2 6	112	G2
Ceylon Rd W14	126	B6
Chadacre Av, Ilf	80	E5
Chadacre Rd, Epsom	193	R10
Chadbourn St E14	114	D10
Chadd Dr, Brom	188	D6
Chadd Grn E13	115	N2
Chadview Ct, Rom	82	H12
Chadville Gdns, Rom	82	G10
Chadway, Dag	100	F2
Chadwell Av, Rom	82	D14
Chadwell Heath La, Rom	82	D8
Chadwell St EC1	11	L5
Chadwick Av, E4 2	62	H7
Chadwick Av N21	43	L8
Chadwick Av SW19	162	G10
Chadwick Cl SW15	143	M13
Chadwick Cl W7	104	E10
Chadwick Cl, Tedd	158	H11
Chadwick Pl, Surb	177	L13
Chadwick Rd E11	79	K12
Chadwick Rd NW10	107	L1
Chadwick Rd SE15	148	F4
Chadwick Rd, Ilf	99	K5
Chadwick St SW1	25	S12
Chadwick Way, SE28 4	118	H13
Chadwin Rd E13	115	R9
Chadworth Way, Esher	190	B10
Chaffinch Av, Croy	185	N11
Chaffinch Cl N9	61	N2
Chaffinch Cl, Croy	185	N10
Chaffinch Cl, Surb	192	A5
Chaffinch Rd, Beck	185	S2
Chafford Way, Rom	82	E8
Chagford St NW1	7	U11
Chailey Av, Enf	44	E3
Chailey Cl, Houns	138	H2
Chailey St E5	95	M6
Chalbury Wk N1	10	H2
Chalcombe Rd SE2	136	D5
Chalcot Cl, Sutt	194	G13
Chalcot Cres NW1	109	U1
Chalcot Gdns NW3	91	T12
Chalcot Ms SW16	165	K5
Chalcot Rd NW1	92	A14
Chalcot Sq NW1	92	A14
Chalcott Gdns, Surb	191	L2
Chalcroft Rd SE13	150	J10
Chaldon Path, Th Hth	183	R7
Chaldon Rd SW6	126	C13
Chale Rd SW2	146	J12
Chalet Est NW7	55	N8
Chalfont Av, Wem	88	D11
Chalfont Ct NW9	71	L6
Chalfont Grn N9	60	D5

Chalfont Rd N9	60	D5
Chalfont Rd SE25	184	F6
Chalfont Rd, Hayes	120	A4
Chalfont Way W13	122	J6
Chalford Cl, W Mol	175	N8
Chalford Rd SE21	166	B7
Chalford Wk, Wdf Grn	80	A1
Chalgrove Av, Mord	180	H9
Chalgrove Cres, Ilf	80	C3
Chalgrove Gdns N3	72	D6
Chalgrove Rd N17	76	J1
Chalgrove Rd, Sutt	195	N14
Chalice Cl, Wall	196	G11
Chalk Fm Rd NW1	92	B13
Chalk Hill Rd W6	126	A8
Chalk La, Barn	41	U7
Chalk Pit Way, Sutt 9	195	L10
Chalk Rd E13	115	T9
Chalkenden Cl SE20	166	J14
Chalkhill Rd, Wem	88	E5
Chalklands, Wem	88	E5
Chalkley Cl, Mitch	181	U4
Chalkmill Rd, Enf	44	J5
Chalkstone Cl, Well	154	B1
Chalkwell Pk Av, Enf	44	C8
Challice Way SW2	165	M1
Challin St SE20	185	L1
Challis Rd, Brent	123	N9
Challoner Cl N2	73	N4
Challoner Cres, W14 9	126	E10
Challoner St W14	126	E9
Challoners Cl, E Mol	176	A8
Chalmers Way, Felt	138	B10
Chaloner Ct, SE1 2	28	C6
Chalsey Rd SE4	149	U7
Chalton Dr N2	73	M11
Chalton St NW1	9	T5
Chamber St E1	21	P9
Chamberlain Cl, SE28 2	135	N6
Chamberlain Cres, W Wick	200	C1
Chamberlain La, Pnr	66	B7
Chamberlain Pl, E17 1	77	S5
Chamberlain Rd N2	73	L4
Chamberlain Rd N9	60	G5
Chamberlain Rd, W13 1	122	H4
Chamberlain St, NW1 3	91	U14
Chamberlain Way, Pnr	66	D6
Chamberlain Way, Surb	177	S14
Chamberlayne Rd NW10	108	A5
Chambers Gdns, N2 1	73	N2
Chambers La NW10	89	S13
Chambers Pl, S Croy 1	198	A14
Chambers Rd N7	92	J7
Chambers St SE16	29	S7
Chambord St E2	13	N7
Champion Cres SE26	167	R7
Champion Gro SE5	148	B5
Champion Hill SE5	148	B6
Champion Hill Est SE5	148	C6
Champion Pk SE5	148	B4
Champion Rd SE26	167	S7
Champness Cl, SE27 5	166	A7
Champneys Cl, Sutt	194	E13
Chance St E1	13	M10
Chance St E2	13	M10
Chancel St SE1	27	P3
Chancellor Gro SE21	165	U5
Chancellor Pas, E14 8	132	B2
Chancellor Pl NW9	71	L4
Chancellors Rd W6	125	U10
Chancellors St W6	125	T10

Chancelot Rd SE2	136	D7
Chancery La WC2	18	J6
Chancery La, Beck	186	D3
Chanctonbury Cl SE9	171	K5
Chanctonbury Gdns, Sutt 4	194	J14
Chanctonbury Way N12	56	H9
Chandler Av E16	115	N9
Chandler Cl, Hmptn	175	N1
Chandler Rd, Loug	49	K2
Chandler St E1	131	K1
Chandler Way SE15	130	E14
Chandlers Ms E14	132	A3
Chandlers Way SW2	147	P14
Chandos Av E17	78	B4
Chandos Av N14	58	F5
Chandos Av N20	57	M1
Chandos Av W5	123	M7
Chandos Cl, Buck H	63	R4
Chandos Cres, Edg	53	U14
Chandos Pl WC2	18	B11
Chandos Rd E15	96	G9
Chandos Rd N2	73	P4
Chandos Rd N17	76	D3
Chandos Rd NW2	89	T10
Chandos Rd NW10	106	J7
Chandos Rd, Har	67	U10
Chandos Rd, Pnr	66	F13
Chandos St W1	16	J4
Chandos Way NW11	90	J1
Channel Cl, Houns	139	P1
Channel Gate Rd NW10	107	L6
Channelsea Rd E15	114	G1
Chant Sq E15	96	H14
Chant St E15	96	H14
Chantress Cl, Dag	119	U1
Chantrey Rd SW9	147	M6
Chantry Cl NW7	39	M12
Chantry Cl, Har	69	U10
Chantry Cl, Sid	172	J10
Chantry La, Brom	188	A9
Chantry Pl, Har 1	67	R1
Chantry Rd, Chess	191	U9
Chantry Rd, Har	67	R1
Chantry St N1	111	S2
Chantry Way, Mitch	181	P6
Chapel Ct N2	73	R6
Chapel Cl SE1	28	C5
Chapel Fm Rd SE9	170	E4
Chapel Ho St E14	132	D9
Chapel La, Chig	65	U6
Chapel La, Pnr	66	H6
Chapel La, Rom	82	H13
Chapel Mkt N1	11	K2
Chapel Path E11	79	P11
Chapel Pl EC2	12	H8
Chapel Pl N1	11	L1
Chapel Pl N17	60	F13
Chapel Pl W1	16	H6
Chapel Rd SE27	165	S8
Chapel Rd W13	123	K1
Chapel Rd, Bexh	155	P7
Chapel Rd, Houns	139	S6
Chapel Rd, Ilf	98	H5
Chapel Rd, Twick	141	L14
Chapel Side W2	14	A10
Chapel Stones N17	76	F1
Chapel St NW1	15	P3
Chapel St SW1	24	F8
Chapel St, Enf	44	A5
Chapel Ter, Loug	48	C7
Chapel Vw, S Croy	199	K12
Chapel Wk NW4	71	S8
Chapel Way, N7 3	93	L5
Chapel Yd, SW18 8	144	J10
Chapelmount Rd, Wdf Grn	64	F11
Chaplin Cl SE1	27	M6
Chaplin Rd E15	115	K3
Chaplin Rd N17	76	E5
Chaplin Rd NW2	89	P11
Chaplin Rd, Dag	101	K13
Chaplin Rd, Wem	87	L11
Chaplin Sq N12	57	N14
Chapman Cres, Har	69	S10
Chapman Pk Ind Est NW10	89	M11

Chapman Rd E9	95	T12
Chapman Rd, Belv	137	P10
Chapman Rd, Croy	197	N1
Chapman Sq SW19	162	A4
Chapman St E1	112	J13
Chapman's La SE2	136	F8
Chapone Pl W1	17	S7
Chapter Cl, W4 4	124	F5
Chapter Rd NW2	89	R11
Chapter Rd SE17	35	S9
Chapter St SW1	33	S4
Chapter Way, Hmptn	157	N8
Chara Pl W4	124	G11
Charcroft Gdns, Enf	45	P7
Chardin Rd, W4 3	124	J8
Chardmore Rd N16	94	G2
Chardwell Cl E6	116	E11
Charecroft Way W12	126	A4
Charford Rd E16	115	P10
Chargeable La E13	115	M7
Chargeable St E16	115	M7
Chargrove Cl, SE16 17	131	P3
Charing Cl, Orp	203	T7
Charing Cross SW1	26	A2
Charing Cross Rd WC2	17	T6
Charlbert St NW8	7	P2
Charlbury Av, Stan	53	N10
Charlbury Gdns, Ilf	99	U3
Charlbury Gro W5	105	M11
Charldane Rd SE9	170	J5
Charlecote Gro SE26	167	K5
Charlecote Rd, Dag	100	J6
Charlemont Rd E6	116	F6
Charles Barry Cl SW4	146	F5
Charles Cl, Sid	172	D7
Charles Cobb Gdns, Croy	197	N9
Charles Coveney Rd, SE15 1	148	E1
Charles Cres, Har	68	B14
Charles Flemwell Ms, E16 9	133	P2
Charles Grinling Wk SE18	134	G7
Charles La NW8	7	N2
Charles Pl, NW1 3	9	N8
Charles Rd E7	97	T14
Charles Rd, SW19 1	180	C3
Charles Rd, Rom	82	G12
Charles II St SW1	25	S1
Charles Sevright Dr NW7	56	B10
Charles Sq N1	12	F7
Charles St E16	134	A2
Charles St SW13	143	K4
Charles St W1	24	H1
Charles St, Croy	197	T5
Charles St, Enf	44	E9
Charles St, Houns	139	L3
Charles Whincup Rd, E16 15	133	R1
Charlesfield SE9	169	U6
Charleston Cl, Felt 3	156	B5
Charleston St SE17	36	A4
Charleville Circ SE26	166	H9
Charleville Rd W14	126	D10
Charlieville Rd, Erith	137	T14
Charlmont Rd SW17	163	S11
Charlotte Cl, Bexh	154	J9
Charlotte Despard Av SW11	146	B2
Charlotte Ms W1	17	P2
Charlotte Ms W10	108	A12
Charlotte Ms, W14 1	126	C7
Charlotte Pl, NW9 2	70	F10
Charlotte Pl, SW1 3	33	M3
Charlotte Rd EC2	12	H9
Charlotte Rd SW13	143	M1
Charlotte Rd, Dag	101	R12
Charlotte Rd, Wall	196	F11
Charlotte St W1	17	P3

Charlotte Ter N1	111	M2
Charlow Cl, SW6 2	145	L4
Charlton Ch La SE7	133	T10
Charlton Cres, Bark	117	T3
Charlton Dene SE7	133	U14
Charlton Kings Rd NW5	92	G9
Charlton La SE7	134	A9
Charlton Pk La SE7	134	A13
Charlton Pk Rd SE7	134	B11
Charlton Pl N1	11	N1
Charlton Rd N9	61	N1
Charlton Rd NW10	107	K1
Charlton Rd SE3	133	P13
Charlton Rd SE7	133	R12
Charlton Rd, Har	69	P8
Charlton Rd, Wem	87	U2
Charlton Way SE3	151	K1
Charlwood Cl, Har	52	D12
Charlwood Pl SW1	33	N4
Charlwood Rd SW15	144	A6
Charlwood Sq, Mitch	181	N5
Charlwood St SW1	33	P4
Charlwood Ter, SW15 4	144	B7
Charmian Av, Stan	69	N5
Charminster Av SW19	180	J4
Charminster Ct, Surb	177	N13
Charminster Rd SE9	170	A8
Charminster Rd, Wor Pk	194	A1
Charmouth Rd, Well	154	E2
Charnock Rd E5	94	J6
Charnwood Av SW19	180	H4
Charnwood Cl, N Mal	179	K8
Charnwood Dr E18	79	R6
Charnwood Gdns E14	132	B7
Charnwood Pl N20	57	L5
Charnwood Rd SE25	184	B9
Charnwood St E5	94	H4
Charrington Rd, Croy 2	197	T3
Charrington St NW1	9	R2
Charsley Rd SE6	168	C3
Chart Cl, Brom	187	K2
Chart Cl, Croy 3	185	L11
Chart St N1	12	E6
Charter Av, Ilf	81	P14
Charter Ct, N Mal	178	J6
Charter Cres, Houns	138	J7
Charter Dr, Bex	154	J13
Charter Rd, Kings T	178	D5
Charter Rd, The, Wdf Grn	62	J11
Charter Sq, Kings T	178	D4
Charter Way N3	72	E7
Charter Way N14	42	F12
Charterhouse Av, Wem	87	L9
Charterhouse Bldgs, EC1 4	11	S11
Charterhouse Ms EC1	19	R1
Charterhouse Sq EC1	19	S1
Charterhouse St EC1	19	N3
Charteris Rd N4	93	N2
Charteris Rd NW6	108	F2
Charteris Rd, Wdf Grn	63	S12
Charters Cl SE19	166	C13
Chartfield Av SW15	143	U10
Chartfield Sq SW15	144	A10
Chartham Gro, SE27 2	165	R6
Chartham Rd SE25	184	J6
Chartley Av NW2	89	K6
Chartley Av, Stan	52	F11
Charton Cl, Belv 2	137	M11
Chartridge Cl, Barn	39	P9
Chartwell Cl SE9	171	N4
Chartwell Cl, Grnf	103	S1
Chartwell Dr, Orp	203	N9

Chartwell Gdns, Sutt 194 D7
Chartwell Pl, Har 86 B3
Chartwell Pl, Sutt 194 E7
Chartwell Way SE20 184 J1
Charwood SW16 165 N8
Chase, The E12 98 A7
Chase, The SW4 146 D6
Chase, The SW16 165 M13
Chase, The SW20 180 D2
Chase, The, Bexh 155 R5
Chase, The, Brom 187 R5
Chase, The, Chig 65 L7
Chase, The, Edg 70 C1
Chase, The, Loug 47 U13
Chase, The, Pnr 67 L8
Chase, The (Eastcote), Pnr 66 E11
Chase, The (Chadwell Heath), Rom 82 J11
Chase, The, Stan 52 G11
Chase, The, Sun 174 D1
Chase, The, Wall 197 K9
Chase Ct Gdns, Enf 43 T5
Chase Gdns E4 62 A8
Chase Gdns, Twick 140 B12
Chase Grn, Enf 43 U5
Chase Grn Av, Enf 43 S4
Chase Hill, Enf 43 T5
Chase La, Ilf 81 N9
Chase Ridings, Enf 43 N4
Chase Rd N14 58 G1
Chase Rd NW10 106 H7
Chase Rd W3 106 H7
Chase Side N14 58 F1
Chase Side, Enf 43 U5
Chase Side Av SW20 180 C2
Chase Side Av, Enf 43 U3
Chase Side Cres, Enf 43 U2
Chase Way N14 58 D3
Chasefield Rd SW17 163 U8
Chaseley Dr W4 124 C9
Chaseley St E14 113 R11
Chasemore Cl, Mitch 4 181 U13
Chasemore Gdns, Croy 197 P10
Chaseville Pk Rd N21 43 K10
Chasewood Av, Enf 43 R3
Chasewood Pk, Har 86 D5
Chatfield Rd SW11 145 M6
Chatfield Rd, Croy 197 S1
Chatham Av, Brom 187 M14
Chatham Cl NW11 72 H10
Chatham Cl, Sutt 180 E14
Chatham Pl E9 95 L11
Chatham Rd E17 77 S6
Chatham Rd, E18 1 79 L3
Chatham Rd SW11 145 T11
Chatham Rd, Kings T 178 A3
Chatham Rd, Orp 203 M9
Chatham St SE17 36 E2
Chatsfield Pl W5 105 S11
Chatsworth Av NW4 71 T4
Chatsworth Av SW20 180 D2
Chatsworth Av, Brom 169 R9
Chatsworth Av, Sid 172 B1
Chatsworth Av, Wem 87 U10
Chatsworth Cl NW4 71 T3
Chatsworth Cl, Borwd 38 A5
Chatsworth Cl, W Wick 201 L3
Chatsworth Ct, W8 1 126 H7
Chatsworth Ct, Stan 53 M10
Chatsworth Cres, Houns 140 A7
Chatsworth Dr, Enf 44 G13
Chatsworth Gdns W3 124 C1

Chatsworth Gdns, Har 85 R2
Chatsworth Gdns, N Mal 179 L9
Chatsworth Pl, Mitch 181 T6
Chatsworth Pl, Tedd 158 G7
Chatsworth Ri W5 105 U8
Chatsworth Rd E5 95 N8
Chatsworth Rd E15 97 L9
Chatsworth Rd NW2 90 D12
Chatsworth Rd W4 124 F12
Chatsworth Rd W5 105 T8
Chatsworth Rd, Croy 198 B7
Chatsworth Rd, Hayes 102 D7
Chatsworth Rd, Sutt 194 C8
Chatsworth Way SE27 165 S5
Chatterton Rd N4 93 R5
Chatterton Rd, Brom 188 A9
Chatto Rd SW11 145 U10
Chaucer Av, Hayes 102 B10
Chaucer Av, Houns 138 C3
Chaucer Av, Rich 142 B5
Chaucer Cl N11 58 F9
Chaucer Dr SE1 37 N4
Chaucer Gdns, Sutt 194 H6
Chaucer Grn, Croy 185 L13
Chaucer Rd E7 97 P12
Chaucer Rd E11 79 N12
Chaucer Rd E17 78 F2
Chaucer Rd SE24 147 P10
Chaucer Rd W3 124 F1
Chaucer Rd, Sid 172 F2
Chaucer Rd, Sutt 194 G7
Chaucer Rd, Well 153 T2
Chaucer Way SW19 163 N11
Chauncey Cl N9 60 G5
Chaundrye Cl SE9 152 D12
Chauntler Cl, E16 1 115 S13
Cheam Common Rd, Wor Pk 193 S5
Cheam Mans, Sutt 194 D12
Cheam Pk Way, Sutt 194 C11
Cheam Rd, Sutt 194 J10
Cheam St, SE15 6 149 K5
Cheapside, EC2 3 19 U6
Cheapside, N13 1 59 U8
Cheddar Waye, Hayes 102 C11
Cheddington Rd N18 60 C6
Chedworth Cl, E16 5 115 L11
Cheeseman Cl, Hmptn 157 K12
Cheesemans Ter, W14 12 126 E10
Chelford Rd, Brom 168 G9
Chelmer Cres, Bark 118 C4
Chelmer Rd E9 95 P9
Chelmsford Cl E6 116 E12
Chelmsford Cl, W6 5 126 B11
Chelmsford Gdns, Ilf 80 D14
Chelmsford Rd E11 96 H1
Chelmsford Rd E17 78 A11
Chelmsford Rd E18 79 L1
Chelmsford Rd N14 42 F14
Chelmsford Sq NW10 107 T2

Chelsea Br SW1 32 G9
Chelsea Br SW8 32 G9
Chelsea Br Rd SW1 32 D6
Chelsea Cl NW10 106 H2
Chelsea Cl, Edg 70 A4
Chelsea Cl, Hmptn 157 U10
Chelsea Cl, Wor Pk 179 P14
Chelsea Embk SW3 32 C10
Chelsea Gdns, Sutt 194 D7
Chelsea Harbour SW10 145 N2
Chelsea Harbour Dr SW10 145 M1
Chelsea Manor Gdns SW3 31 P9

Chelsea Manor St SW3 31 P6
Chelsea Pk Gdns SW3 31 K10
Chelsea Sq SW3 31 M6
Chelsea Wf SW10 127 N14
Chelsfield Av N9 45 N13
Chelsfield Gdns SE26 167 M6
Chelsfield Grn N9 45 N12
Chelsham Rd SW4 146 H5
Chelsham Rd, S Croy 198 B12
Chelston App, Ruis 84 B3
Chelston Rd, Ruis 84 B2
Chelsworth Dr SE18 135 N12
Cheltenham Av, Twick 140 H14
Cheltenham Cl, N Mal 178 F6
Cheltenham Cl, Nthlt 85 R11
Cheltenham Gdns E6 116 C4
Cheltenham Gdns, Loug 48 D12
Cheltenham Pl W3 124 D2
Cheltenham Pl, Har 69 R7
Cheltenham Rd E10 78 E12
Cheltenham Rd SE15 149 M8
Cheltenham Ter SW3 32 A5
Chelverton Rd SW15 144 B7
Chelwood Cl, E4 1 46 C12
Chelwood Gdns, Rich 142 B3
Chelwood Wk SE4 149 R8
Chenappa Cl E13 115 N6
Chenduit Way, Stan 52 F10
Cheney Rd NW1 10 A3
Cheney Row E17 77 T1
Cheney St, Pnr 66 E10
Cheneys Rd E11 97 K6
Chenies, The, Orp 189 R11
Chenies Ms WC1 9 U12
Chenies Pl NW1 9 T2
Chenies St WC1 17 R2
Cheniston Gdns, W8 1 22 A10
Chepstow Cl SW15 144 C10
Chepstow Cres W11 108 G13
Chepstow Cres, Ilf 81 S12
Chepstow Gdns, Sthl 103 M12
Chepstow Pl W2 108 H13
Chepstow Ri, Croy 198 D5
Chepstow Rd W2 108 H11
Chepstow Rd W7 122 G5
Chepstow Rd, Croy 198 D5
Chepstow Vil W11 108 F13
Chepstow Way SE15 148 F1
Chequer St, EC1 4 12 B11
Chequers Cl NW9 70 J6
Chequers Cl, Orp 189 U7
Chequers Gdns N13 59 R9
Chequers Par SE9 152 F11
Chequers Rd, Loug 48 H9
Chequers Way N13 59 T9
Cherbury Cl SE28 118 H12
Cherbury St N1 12 E3
Cherchefelle Ms, S Croy 52 J9
Cherimoya Gdns, W Mol 6 175 R6
Cherington Rd W7 122 D2
Cheriton Av, Brom 187 M10
Cheriton Av, Ilf 80 G3
Cheriton Cl W5 105 M9
Cheriton Cl, Barn 41 T6
Cheriton Dr SE18 135 N13
Cheriton Sq SW17 164 B3
Cherry Av, Sthl 120 H2
Cherry Blossom Cl N13 59 S9

Cherry Cl SW2 147 N13
Cherry Cl W5 123 N6
Cherry Cl, Cars 195 T3

Cherry Cl, Mord 180 D8
Cherry Cres, Brent 122 J14
Cherry Gdn St SE16 130 J4
Cherry Gdns, Dag 101 L9
Cherry Gdns, Nthlt 85 S13
Cherry Garth, Brent 123 P9
Cherry Gro, Hayes 120 C2
Cherry Hill, Barn 41 K12
Cherry Hill, Har 52 D13
Cherry Hill Gdns, Croy 197 M7
Cherry Hills, Wat 50 J9
Cherry Orchard Gdns, Croy 198 B2
Cherry Orchard Gdns, W Mol 175 M5
Cherry Orchard Rd, Brom 202 D3
Cherry Orchard Rd, Croy 198 B2
Cherry Orchard Rd, W Mol 175 N5
Cherry Tree Cl, E9 2 113 M1
Cherry Tree Cl, Wem 86 G7
Cherry Tree Ct NW9 70 E9
Cherry Tree Dr SW16 165 K5
Cherry Tree Ho, Buck H 63 U7
Cherry Tree Rd, E15 3 96 J9
Cherry Tree Rd N2 73 T8
Cherry Tree Wk, EC1 12 12 B12
Cherry Tree Wk, Beck 185 U7
Cherry Tree Wk, W Wick 201 L7
Cherry Tree Way, Stan 53 K11
Cherry Wk, Brom 201 P1
Cherry Way, Epsom 192 G11
Cherry Way W5 106 A10
Cherrycot Hill, Orp 203 N8
Cherrycot Ri, Orp 203 M8
Cherrycroft Gdns, Pnr 51 N13
Cherrydown Av E4 62 A6
Cherrydown Cl E4 61 U6
Cherrydown Rd, Sid 172 G4
Cherrydown Wk, Rom 83 S3
Cherrywood Cl E3 113 S5
Cherrywood Cl, Kings T 160 B14
Cherrywood Dr SW15 144 A10
Cherrywood La, Mord 180 C7
Cherston Gdns, Loug 48 H7
Cherston Rd, Loug 48 H8
Chertsey Dr, Sutt 194 C4
Chertsey Rd E11 96 H2
Chertsey Rd, Ilf 99 N8
Chertsey Rd, Twick 140 H11
Chertsey St SW17 164 A9
Chervil Cl, Felt 156 B5
Chervil Ms, SE28 2 136 C2
Cherwell Ct, Epsom 192 E8
Cheryls Cl SW6 145 K1
Cheseman St SE26 167 K5
Chesfield Rd, Kings T 159 S13
Chesham Av, Orp 189 K11
Chesham Cl, SW1 1 24 D11
Chesham Cres SE20 185 M2
Chesham Ms SW1 24 C10
Chesham Pl SW1 24 D11
Chesham Rd SE20 185 M3
Chesham Rd, Kings T 163 P10
Chesham St NW10 88 G6
Chesham St SW1 24 C12
Chesham Ter W13 122 J3

Name	Page	Ref
Cheshire Cl E17	78	D1
Cheshire Cl SE4	149	T3
Cheshire Cl, Mitch	182	J6
Cheshire Ct, EC4 *14*	19	M7
Cheshire Gdns, Chess	191	N12
Cheshire Rd N22	59	L13
Cheshire St E2	13	S10
Chesholm Rd N16	94	D5
Cheshunt Rd E7	97	S12
Cheshunt Rd, Belv	137	N10
Chesil Ct E2	113	K4
Chesilton Rd SW6	144	E1
Chesley Gdns E6	116	B4
Chesney Cres, Croy	200	E13
Chesney St, SW11 *1*	146	A2
Chesnut Est N17	76	F6
Chesnut Gro N17	76	F5
Chesnut Rd N17	76	F5
Chessington Av N3	72	D6
Chessington Av, Bexh	137	K13
Chessington Cl, Epsom	192	E12
Chessington Ct, Pnr	67	L8
Chessington Hall Gdns, Chess	191	N13
Chessington Hill Pk, Chess	192	A10
Chessington Rd, Epsom	192	E12
Chessington Way, W Wick	200	C3
Chesson Rd W14	126	E11
Chesswood Way, Pnr	66	G3
Chester Av, Rich	141	T11
Chester Av, Twick	157	L1
Chester Cl SW1	24	F8
Chester Cl SW13	143	S6
Chester Cl, Loug	49	L1
Chester Cl, Sutt	194	H4
Chester Cl N SW1	8	H5
Chester Cl S SW1	8	J7
Chester Cotts SW1	32	D3
Chester Ct NW1	8	J6
Chester Ct SE5	129	U14
Chester Cres E8	94	F10
Chester Dr, Har	67	P11
Chester Gdns W13	104	J12
Chester Gdns, Enf	45	K11
Chester Gdns, Mord	181	L11
Chester Gate NW1	8	H8
Chester Grn, Loug	49	L2
Chester Ms SW1	24	G9
Chester Path, Loug	49	L1
Chester Pl NW1	8	J6
Chester Rd E7	98	A13
Chester Rd E11	79	S12
Chester Rd E16	115	K8
Chester Rd E17	77	P10
Chester Rd N9	61	K2
Chester Rd N17	76	B5
Chester Rd N19	92	D4
Chester Rd NW1	8	G7
Chester Rd SW19	161	T11
Chester Rd, Borwd	38	G5
Chester Rd, Chig	64	H5
Chester Rd, Houns	138	D5
Chester Rd, Ilf	99	U1
Chester Rd, Loug	49	K2
Chester Rd, Sid	153	S10
Chester Row SW1	32	E3
Chester Sq SW1	24	G12
Chester Sq Ms, SW1 *5*	24	H12
Chester St E2	13	U9
Chester St SW1	24	F9
Chester Ter NW1	8	H6
Chester Way SE11	35	L4
Chesterfield Dr, Esher	190	G4
Chesterfield Gdns N4	75	S10
Chesterfield Gdns SE10	132	G14
Chesterfield Gdns, W1 *3*	24	G2
Chesterfield Gro SE22	148	E9
Chesterfield Hill W1	24	G1
Chesterfield Ms, N4 *1*	75	S10
Chesterfield Rd E10	78	F12
Chesterfield Rd N3	56	H11
Chesterfield Rd W4	124	F11
Chesterfield Rd, Barn	40	A10
Chesterfield Rd, Epsom	192	G14
Chesterfield St W1	24	G2
Chesterfield Wk SE10	150	H1
Chesterfield Way, SE15 *2*	131	L14
Chesterfield Way, Hayes	120	B3
Chesterford Gdns NW3	91	K8
Chesterford Rd E12	98	F10
Chesters, The, N Mal	178	J1
Chesterton Cl SW18	144	G9
Chesterton Cl, Grnf	103	R3
Chesterton Rd E13	115	N5
Chesterton Rd W10	108	B10
Chesterton Ter E13	115	N5
Chesterton Ter, Kings T	178	A4
Chesthunte Rd N17	75	U2
Chestnut All, SW6 *7*	126	F12
Chestnut Av E7	97	R8
Chestnut Av N8	74	J9
Chestnut Av, SW14 *5*	142	G6
Chestnut Av, Brent	123	P8
Chestnut Av, Buck H	64	B6
Chestnut Av, E Mol	176	F3
Chestnut Av, Edg	53	S12
Chestnut Av, Epsom	192	J7
Chestnut Av, Esher	176	B14
Chestnut Av, Hmptn	157	N13
Chestnut Av, Tedd	176	F3
Chestnut Av, Wem	86	J9
Chestnut Av, W Wick	201	K7
Chestnut Av N E17	78	G8
Chestnut Av S E17	78	F8
Chestnut Cl N14	42	F10
Chestnut Cl N16	94	B4
Chestnut Cl SE6	168	F8
Chestnut Cl SW16	165	N8
Chestnut Cl, Buck H	64	B4
Chestnut Cl, Cars	195	T2
Chestnut Cl, Sid	172	A2
Chestnut Ct, SW6 *6*	126	F11
Chestnut Ct, Surb *2*	177	S13
Chestnut Dr E11	79	N12
Chestnut Dr, Bexh	154	H5
Chestnut Dr, Har	52	E14
Chestnut Dr, Pnr	66	H12
Chestnut Gro SE20	167	K14
Chestnut Gro SW12	164	B13
Chestnut Gro W5	123	P5
Chestnut Gro, Barn	41	T10
Chestnut Gro, Ilf	65	S11
Chestnut Gro, Islw	140	G8
Chestnut Gro, Mitch	182	H8
Chestnut Gro, N Mal	178	H6
Chestnut Gro, S Croy	199	L13
Chestnut Gro, Wem	86	J9
Chestnut La N20	56	C1
Chestnut Ri SE18	135	R10
Chestnut Rd SE27	165	T5
Chestnut Rd SW20	180	B3
Chestnut Rd, Kings T	159	R14
Chestnut Rd, Twick	158	C3
Chestnut Wk, Wdf Grn	63	N9
Chestnut Way, Felt	156	D6
Chestnuts, The SE14	149	T2
Cheston Av, Croy	199	S2
Chettle Ct N8	75	N11
Chetwode Rd SW17	163	U5
Chetwood Wk E6	116	D11
Chetwynd Av, Barn	57	T1
Chetwynd Rd NW5	92	D6
Cheval Pl SW7	23	R10
Cheval St E14	132	A5
Chevalier Cl, Stan	53	R7
Chevening Rd NW6	108	C2
Chevening Rd SE10	133	M10
Chevening Rd SE19	166	A12
Chevenings, The, Sid	172	E5
Cheverton Rd N19	92	G1
Chevet St, E9 *6*	95	R10
Cheviot Cl, Enf	44	B3
Cheviot Gdns NW2	90	C4
Cheviot Gdns SE27	165	S8
Cheviot Gate NW2	90	D3
Cheviot Rd SE27	165	P9
Cheviot Way, Ilf	81	R8
Chevron Cl E16	115	P11
Chevy Rd, Sthl	121	U3
Chewton Rd E17	77	R8
Cheyne Av E18	79	L5
Cheyne Av, Twick	157	M2
Cheyne Cl, NW4 *4*	71	S10
Cheyne Cl, Brom	202	C6
Cheyne Ct SW3	31	T10
Cheyne Gdns SW3	31	S10
Cheyne Hill, Surb	177	T8
Cheyne Ms SW3	31	S11
Cheyne Pl SW3	31	U10
Cheyne Row SW3	31	P11
Cheyne Wk N21	43	R9
Cheyne Wk NW4	71	T11
Cheyne Wk SW3	31	S11
Cheyne Wk SW10	31	P12
Cheyne Wk, Croy	198	H4
Cheyneys Av, Edg	53	P12
Chichele Gdns, Croy *1*	198	D7
Chichele Rd NW2	90	A9
Chicheley Gdns, Har	51	T14
Chicheley Rd, Har	51	T13
Chicheley St SE1	26	G5
Chichester Cl E6	116	D12
Chichester Cl SE3	133	T14
Chichester Cl, Hmptn *3*	157	L11
Chichester Ct, Stan	69	S5
Chichester Gdns, Ilf	80	D14
Chichester Ms SE27	165	P7
Chichester Rd E11	97	K6
Chichester Rd N9	60	G3
Chichester Rd NW6	108	G3
Chichester Rd W2	14	D2
Chichester Rd, Croy	198	E5
Chichester St SW1	33	P8
Chichester Way, E14 *1*	132	G7
Chichester Way, Felt	138	E13
Chicksand St E1	21	P3
Chiddingfold N12	56	H6
Chiddingstone Av, Bexh	137	M13
Chiddingstone St SW6	144	H3
Chieveley Rd, Bexh	155	R7
Chignell Pl, W13 *2*	122	G1
Chigwell Hill E1	112	J14
Chigwell Hurst Ct, Pnr	66	G4
Chigwell La, Loug	49	L9
Chigwell Pk, Chig	64	J7
Chigwell Pk Dr, Chig	64	G6
Chigwell Ri, Chig	64	J5
Chigwell Rd E18	79	S5
Chigwell Rd, Wdf Grn	79	U3
Chilcot Cl, E14 *2*	114	C12
Childebert Rd SW17	164	C3
Childeric Rd SE14	131	S14
Childerley St SW6	144	C1
Childers, The, Wdf Grn	64	E10
Childers St SE8	131	T11
Childs Hill Wk, NW2 *2*	90	F5
Childs La SE19	166	D12
Child's Pl, SW5 *3*	126	H8
Child's St SW5	126	H8
Childs Way NW11	72	F9
Chilham Cl, Bex	155	M14
Chilham Cl, Grnf	104	H3
Chilham Rd SE9	170	C8
Chilham Way, Brom	187	N13
Chillerton Rd SW17	164	B10
Chillingworth Gdns, Twick *1*	158	F5
Chillingworth Rd N7	93	N10
Chilmark Gdns, N Mal	179	M13
Chilmark Rd SW16	182	G3
Chiltern Av, Twick	157	N2
Chiltern Cl, Croy	198	D6
Chiltern Cl, Wor Pk *1*	193	U3
Chiltern Dene, Enf	43	M7
Chiltern Dr, Surb	178	C10
Chiltern Gdns NW2	90	B5
Chiltern Gdns, Brom	187	M7
Chiltern Rd E3	114	B8
Chiltern Rd, Ilf	81	S8
Chiltern Rd, Pnr	66	F9
Chiltern St W1	16	C2
Chiltern Way, Wdf Grn	63	N6
Chilthorne Cl SE6	149	U13
Chilton Av W5	123	P7
Chilton Gro SE8	131	R7
Chilton Rd, Edg	54	A12
Chilton Rd, Rich	142	A5
Chilton St E2	13	P9
Chiltonian Ind Est SE12	151	L12
Chiltons, The, E18 *3*	79	N4
Chilver St SE10	133	M9
Chilwell Gdns, Wat	50	F7
Chilworth Cl SW19	162	A11
Chilworth Gdns, Sutt	195	L5
Chilworth Ms W2	14	H7
Chilworth St W2	14	G7
Chimes Av N13	59	P9
Chinbrook Cres, SE12 *2*	169	R6
Chinbrook Est SE9	170	A5
Chinbrook Rd SE12	169	S6
Chinchilla Dr, Houns	138	E4
Chine, The N10	74	E8
Chine, The N21	43	S11
Chine, The, Wem	87	K9
Ching Ct, WC2 *1*	18	A7
Ching Way E4	61	T12
Chingdale Rd E4	63	K6
Chingford Av E4	62	B5
Chingford Hall Est E4	61	T11
Chingford Ind Cen E4	61	S9
Chingford La, Wdf Grn	63	L8
Chingford Mt Rd E4	62	B8
Chingford Rd E4	62	B12
Chingford Rd E17	78	B5
Chingley Cl, Brom	169	K11
Chinnery Cl, Enf	44	F1
Chinnor Cres, Grnf	103	T4
Chip St SW4	146	G7
Chipka St E14	132	E4
Chipley St SE14	131	R12
Chipmunk Gro, Nthlt	102	J5
Chippendale St E5	95	N6
Chippenham Av, Wem	88	D10
Chippenham Gdns NW6	108	G6
Chippenham Ms W9	108	G8
Chippenham Rd W9	108	G7
Chipping Cl, Barn	40	D5
Chipstead Av, Th Hth	183	S8
Chipstead Cl SE19	166	F13

Name	No.	Ref.
Chipstead Gdns NW2	89	S4
Chipstead St SW6	144	H2
Chirk Cl, Hayes 2	103	K7
Chisenhale Rd E3	113	R3
Chisholm Rd, Croy	198	D3
Chisholm Rd, Rich	141	T12
Chislehurst Av N12	57	L14
Chislehurst Rd, Brom	188	C3
Chislehurst Rd, Chis	188	F2
Chislehurst Rd, Orp	189	S7
Chislehurst Rd, Rich	141	S10
Chislehurst Rd, Sid	172	A10
Chislet Cl, Beck	168	B13
Chisley Rd N15	76	C11
Chiswell Sq SE3	151	S3
Chiswell St EC1	20	C1
Chiswick Br SW14	142	F3
Chiswick Br W4	142	F3
Chiswick Cl, Croy	197	L6
Chiswick Common Rd W4	124	H8
Chiswick Ct, Pnr	67	L5
Chiswick High Rd W4	125	K8
Chiswick High Rd, Brent	123	U10
Chiswick Ho Grds W4	124	H12
Chiswick La W4	125	K9
Chiswick La S W4	125	L10
Chiswick Mall W4	125	M10
Chiswick Mall W6	125	M10
Chiswick Quay W4	142	E2
Chiswick Rd N9	60	H3
Chiswick Rd W4	124	E8
Chiswick Sq, W4 3	125	K11
Chiswick Staithe W4	142	D1
Chiswick Village W4	124	B11
Chiswick Wf W4	125	L12
Chitty St W1	17	N2
Chitty's La, Dag	100	G3
Chivalry Rd SW11	145	R9
Chivenor Gro, Kings T	159	N10
Chivers Rd E4	62	D6
Choats Rd, Bark	118	D4
Choats Rd, Dag	118	J6
Chobham Gdns SW19	162	A3
Chobham Rd E15	96	G9
Cholmeley Cres N6	74	C14
Cholmeley Pk N6	74	D14
Cholmley Rd, T Ditt	176	J12
Cholmondeley Av NW10	107	N3
Cholmondeley Wk, Rich	141	M9
Choppins Ct E1	131	K1
Chopwell Cl, E15 4	96	J14
Chorleywood Cres, Orp	189	U3
Choumert Gro SE15	148	G4
Choumert Rd SE15	148	F4
Choumert Sq SE15	148	G4
Chrisp St E14	114	C10
Christ Ch Rd, Beck 1	186	B3
Christ Ch Rd, Surb	177	U12
Christchurch Av N12	57	L12
Christchurch Av NW6	90	D13
Christchurch Av, Har	68	G7
Christchurch Av, Tedd	158	G10
Christchurch Av, Wem	87	S12
Christchurch Cl SW19	163	P14
Christchurch Cl, Enf	43	T4
Christchurch Gdns, Har	68	G7
Christchurch Grn, Wem	87	S12
Christchurch Hill NW3	91	N6
Christchurch La, Barn	40	D4
Christchurch Pk, Sutt	195	L13
Christchurch Pas, NW3 5	91	M6
Christchurch Pas, Barn	40	D5
Christchurch Rd N8	74	J12
Christchurch Rd SW2	165	L1
Christchurch Rd SW14	142	E9
Christchurch Rd SW19	163	P14
Christchurch Rd, Ilf	99	K1
Christchurch Rd, Sid	171	U7
Christchurch Sq E9	113	L2
Christchurch St SW3	31	U9
Christchurch Ter, SW3 1	31	U9
Christchurch Way SE10	133	K9
Christian Ct SE16	131	T2
Christian Flds SW16	165	P14
Christian St E1	21	U7
Christie Dr, Croy	184	G10
Christie Gdns, Rom	82	D11
Christie Rd E9	95	R12
Christina Sq N4	93	S2
Christina St EC2	12	H10
Christine Worsley Cl, N21 1	59	S2
Christopher Av W7	122	G5
Christopher Cl, SE16 12	131	N3
Christopher Gdns, Dag	100	G9
Christopher Pl, NW1 1	9	T7
Christopher Rd, Sthl	120	D7
Christopher St EC2	12	E12
Christopher's Ms, W11 13	126	D1
Chryssell Rd SW9	129	P14
Chubworthy St SE14	131	R12
Chudleigh Cres, Ilf	99	S8
Chudleigh Gdns, Sutt	195	M5
Chudleigh Rd NW6	90	A14
Chudleigh Rd SE4	149	U10
Chudleigh Rd, Twick	140	E13
Chudleigh St E1	113	N11
Chudleigh Way, Ruis	84	B2
Chulsa Rd SE26	166	J9
Chumleigh St SE5	36	H10
Chumleigh Wk, Surb	177	T8
Church All, Croy	197	P1
Church App SE21	166	B6
Church Av E4	62	G11
Church Av NW1	92	D12
Church Av SW14	142	G6
Church Av, Beck	186	B2
Church Av, Nthlt	85	L14
Church Av, Pnr	67	K12
Church Av, Sid	172	B9
Church Av, Sthl	121	K5
Church Cl N20	57	S6
Church Cl, Edg	54	F10
Church Cl, Loug	48	F4
Church Cres E9	95	N13
Church Cres N3	72	F2
Church Cres N10	74	C8
Church Cres N20	57	R5
Church Dr NW9	88	G2
Church Dr, Har	67	P11
Church Dr, W Wick	201	K6
Church Elm La, Dag	101	P12
Church End E17	78	D8
Church End NW4	71	S6
Church Fm La, Sutt 5	194	D11
Church Gdns SW5	123	N4
Church Gdns, Wem	86	H8
Church Gate SW6	144	D5
Church Gro SE13	150	D8
Church Gro, Kings T	177	M2
Church Hill E17	78	B8
Church Hill N21	43	M13
Church Hill SE18	134	F6
Church Hill SW19	162	E10
Church Hill, Cars	195	U9
Church Hill, Har	86	D1
Church Hill, Loug	48	E5
Church Hill Rd E17	78	D7
Church Hill Rd, Barn	58	A1
Church Hill Rd, Surb	177	R10
Church Hill Rd, Sutt	194	A6
Church Hill Wd, Orp	189	U9
Church Hyde SE18	135	R11
Church La E11	97	K2
Church La E17	78	D8
Church La N2	73	N5
Church La N8	75	L8
Church La N9	60	G3
Church La N17	76	D1
Church La NW9	70	G14
Church La SW17	164	C8
Church La SW19	180	G2
Church La W5	123	M3
Church La, Brom	202	D1
Church La, Chess	191	T12
Church La, Chis	189	M1
Church La, Dag	101	S13
Church La, Enf	44	B6
Church La, Har	68	E2
Church La, Loug	48	F6
Church La, Pnr	67	K6
Church La, Rich	159	R1
Church La, Tedd	158	F10
Church La, T Ditt	176	F12
Church La, Twick	158	H1
Church La, Wall	196	H6
Church Manorway SE2	136	A6
Church Meadow, Surb	191	M3
Church Mt N2	73	N10
Church Paddock Ct, Wall	196	H5
Church Pas, Surb	177	R10
Church Path E11	79	P10
Church Path N12	57	L9
Church Path N20	57	LG
Church Path NW10	89	K13
Church Path, SW14 7	142	H5
Church Path SW19	180	G3
Church Path W4	124	F5
Church Path W7	121	N2
Church Path, Croy	197	T3
Church Path, Mitch	181	R6
Church Path, Sthl	121	M5
Church Pl W5	123	N4
Church Pl, Mitch	181	S6
Church Ri SE23	167	N3
Church Ri, Chess	191	T11
Church Rd E10	96	C3
Church Rd E12	98	C9
Church Rd E17	77	R4
Church Rd N6	74	A12
Church Rd N17	76	D1
Church Rd NW4	71	T7
Church Rd NW10	89	K12
Church Rd SE19	184	D1
Church Rd SW13	143	N3
Church Rd (Wimbledon) SW19	162	D8
Church Rd W3	124	E3
Church Rd W7	122	E1
Church Rd, Bark	99	L12
Church Rd, Bexh	155	L5
Church Rd, Brom	187	N3
Church Rd (Shortlands), Brom	186	J5
Church Rd, Buck H	63	R2
Church Rd, Croy	197	S5
Church Rd, E Mol	176	A6
Church Rd, Enf	45	M11
Church Rd (West Ewell), Epsom	192	H13
Church Rd, Esher	190	F12
Church Rd, Felt	156	G9
Church Rd (Cranford), Houns	120	C10
Church Rd (Heston), Houns	121	N14
Church Rd, Ilf	81	R12
Church Rd, Islw	122	C14
Church Rd, Kes	202	A14
Church Rd, Kings T	177	U3
Church Rd, Loug	47	N6
Church Rd, Mitch	181	N3
Church Rd, Nthlt	85	M14
Church Rd (Farnborough), Orp	203	N10
Church Rd, Rich	141	S9
Church Rd (Ham), Rich	159	T8
Church Rd, Sid	172	B8
Church Rd, Sthl	121	L5
Church Rd, Stan	53	K10
Church Rd, Surb	191	L3
Church Rd, Sutt 2	194	C11
Church Rd, Tedd	158	D8
Church Rd, Wall	196	F5
Church Rd, Well	154	C3
Church Rd, Wor Pk	193	K1
Church Rd Merton SW19	181	P2
Church Row NW3	91	L8
Church Row, Chis	189	M1
Church St E15	115	K1
Church St E16	134	J2
Church St N9	60	G4
Church St NW8	7	N11
Church St W2	15	L2
Church St W4	125	K11
Church St, Croy	197	T4
Church St, Dag	101	S12
Church St, Enf	43	U6
Church St, Hmptn	175	T2
Church St, Islw	140	J5
Church St, Kings T	177	P3
Church St, Sun	174	C6
Church St, Sutt 5	195	K9
Church St, Twick	158	H1
Church St Est NW8	7	M12
Church St N E15	115	K1
Church St Pas E15	115	K1
Church Stretton Rd, Houns	139	U9
Church Ter NW4	71	S6
Church Ter SE13	150	J6
Church Ter SW8	146	H3
Church Ter, Rich	141	P9
Church Vale N2	73	T5
Church Vale SE23	167	N3
Church Wk N16	94	B8
Church Wk NW2	90	F5
Church Wk NW4	71	T6
Church Wk SW13	143	N2
Church Wk SW15	143	S10
Church Wk SW16	182	F4
Church Wk SW20	179	T5
Church Wk, Brent	123	M11
Church Wk, Enf	44	B6
Church Wk, T Ditt	176	F12
Church Way N20	57	R5
Church Way, Barn	41	U7
Church Way, Edg	54	B12
Churchbury Cl, Enf	44	C4
Churchbury La, Enf	44	B5
Churchbury Rd SE9	152	A13
Churchbury Rd, Enf	44	C3
Churchcroft Cl, SW12 8	146	B14
Churchdown, Brom	169	K7
Churchfield Rd N12	57	N11
Churchfield Cl, Har	67	T8
Churchfield Rd W3	124	E2
Churchfield Rd W7	122	C3
Churchfield Rd W13	123	K1
Churchfield Rd, Well	154	B6
Churchfields E18	79	P1
Churchfields, SE10 4	132	E12
Churchfields, Loug	48	D8
Churchfields, W Mol	175	P6
Churchfields Av, Felt	157	M5

Churchfields Rd, Beck	185	R3	Clandon Cl W3	124	D3	Claremont Way NW2	89	T2	Clarendon Way, Chis	189	T6

Churchfields Rd, Beck 185 R3
Churchill Av, Har 68 J12
Churchill Ct W5 105 T7
Churchill Gdns SW1 33 M8
Churchill Gdns W3 106 B12
Churchill Gdns Rd SW1 33 L9
Churchill Ms, Wdf Grn 63 M12
Churchill Pl E14 132 C1
Churchill Rd E16 115 T12
Churchill Rd NW2 89 R11
Churchill Rd NW5 92 D7
Churchill Rd, Edg 53 U12
Churchill Rd, S Croy 197 U14
Churchill Ter, E4 1 62 B6
Churchill Wk E9 95 M9
Churchill Way, Brom 187 N4
Churchill Way, Sun 156 A10
Churchley Rd SE26 167 K7
Churchmead Cl, Barn 41 R12
Churchmead Rd NW10 89 N12
Churchmore Rd SW16 182 F1
Churchview Rd, Twick 158 A2
Churchway NW1 9 T7
Churchwell Path E9 95 L10
Churchwood Gdns, Wdf Grn 63 P8
Churchyard Row SE11 35 R2
Churston Av E13 115 S1
Churston Cl SW2 165 P2
Churston Dr, Mord 180 C10
Churston Gdns N11 58 F12
Churton Pl, SW1 7 33 N3
Churton St SW1 33 N4
Chusan Pl E14 113 U12
Chyngton Cl, Sid 171 T5
Cibber Rd SE23 167 P3
Cicada Rd SW18 145 M10
Cicely Rd SE15 148 H2
Cinderford Way, Brom 169 K8
Cinema Par W5 105 T7
Cinnamon Cl, Croy 182 J13
Cinnamon Row, SW11 3 145 M5
Cinnamon St E1 131 K2
Cintra Pk SE19 166 E13
Circle, The NW2 89 K5
Circle, The NW7 54 H11
Circle Gdns SW19 180 H4
Circuits, The, Pnr 66 E7
Circular Rd N17 76 F5
Circular Way SE18 134 F11
Circus Ms, W1 1 15 T2
Circus Pl EC2 20 E4
Circus Rd NW8 7 K5
Circus St SE10 132 E14
Cirencester St W2 14 A2
Cissbury Ring N N12 56 F9
Cissbury Ring S N12 56 F10
Cissbury Rd N15 76 B10
Citadel Pl SE11 34 E5
Citizen Rd N7 93 N7
City Gdn Row N1 11 S3
City Rd EC1 12 E11
Civic Way, Ilf 81 M7
Civic Way, Ruis 84 G9
Clabon Ms SW1 23 U12
Clack St SE16 131 M4
Clacton Rd E6 116 A5
Clacton Rd E17 77 R11
Clacton Rd, N17 4 76 E4
Claigmar Gdns N3 72 J2
Claire Ct N12 57 L6
Claire Ct, Bushey 52 B2
Claire Ct, Pnr 51 M13
Claire Gdns, Stan 53 L9
Claire Pl E14 132 B5
Clairvale Rd, Houns 138 H1
Clairview Rd SW16 164 D9
Clairville Gdns W7 122 D1
Clamp Hill, Stan 52 B8
Clancarty Rd SW6 144 H4

Clandon Cl W3 124 D3
Clandon Cl, Epsom 193 M11
Clandon Gdns N3 72 H6
Clandon Rd, Ilf 99 S3
Clandon St SE8 150 B3
Clanricarde Gdns W2 108 H14
Clap La, Dag 101 S4
Clapham Common N Side SW4 146 D7
Clapham Common S Side SW4 146 D10
Clapham Common W Side SW4 145 U8
Clapham Cres SW4 146 G8
Clapham High St SW4 146 G7
Clapham Junct Est SW11 145 R7
Clapham Manor St SW4 146 G5
Clapham Pk Est SW4 146 H12
Clapham Pk Rd SW4 146 G8
Clapham Rd SW9 34 J14
Clapham Rd Est SW4 146 H5
Claps Gate La E6 116 J7
Clapton Common E5 76 G14
Clapton Pas E5 95 L9
Clapton Sq E5 95 L9
Clapton Ter N16 94 H1
Clapton Way E5 94 H7
Clara Pl SE18 134 H7
Clare Cl N2 73 L5
Clare Cor SE9 152 J14
Clare Gdns E7 97 N8
Clare Gdns W11 108 D12
Clare Gdns, Bark 99 U12
Clare La N1 93 U14
Clare Lawn Av SW14 142 G10
Clare Mkt WC2 18 G7
Clare Ms SW6 126 J14
Clare Pl SW15 143 L13
Clare Rd E11 78 H12
Clare Rd NW10 89 P13
Clare Rd SE14 149 T2
Clare Rd, Grnf 86 B11
Clare Rd, Houns 139 L6
Clare St E2 113 K4
Clare Way, Bexh 154 J1
Claredale St E2 13 U4
Claremont Av, Har 69 S10
Claremont Av, N Mal 179 R9
Claremont Av, Sun 174 D2
Claremont Cl E16 134 H2
Claremont Cl N1 11 L4
Claremont Cl SW2 165 L1
Claremont Cl, Orp 202 H8
Claremont Ct, Surb 1 177 R11
Claremont Gdns, Ilf 99 S3
Claremont Gdns, Surb 177 R9
Claremont Gro, W4 8 125 K14
Claremont Gro, Wdf Grn 63 T11
Claremont Pk N3 72 D2
Claremont Rd E7 97 R10
Claremont Rd E17 77 S4
Claremont Rd N6 74 E13
Claremont Rd NW2 90 B5
Claremont Rd W9 108 E4
Claremont Rd W13 104 G9
Claremont Rd, Brom 188 D8
Claremont Rd, Croy 198 H1
Claremont Rd, Esher 190 C14
Claremont Rd, Har 68 D4
Claremont Rd, Surb 177 R10
Claremont Rd, Tedd 158 F9
Claremont Rd, Twick 141 K12
Claremont Sq N1 10 J4
Claremont St E16 134 H2
Claremont St N18 60 G11
Claremont St SE10 132 D12

Claremont Way SW4 89 T2
Clarence Av SW4 146 G12
Clarence Av, Brom 188 C7
Clarence Av, Ilf 80 G11
Clarence Av, N Mal 178 E4
Clarence Cres SW4 146 H12
Clarence Cres, Sid 172 C6
Clarence Gdns NW1 9 K7
Clarence La SW15 143 K11
Clarence Ms E5 95 K9
Clarence Ms SE16 131 N2
Clarence Ms SW12 146 C13
Clarence Pas NW1 10 A3
Clarence Pl E5 95 K9
Clarence Rd E5 95 K9
Clarence Rd E12 98 A9
Clarence Rd E16 115 K8
Clarence Rd E17 77 P3
Clarence Rd N15 75 U9
Clarence Rd N22 59 K14
Clarence Rd NW6 90 E14
Clarence Rd SE9 170 C4
Clarence Rd SW19 162 J12
Clarence Rd, W4 1 124 B10
Clarence Rd, Bexh 154 J7
Clarence Rd, Brom 188 C6
Clarence Rd, Croy 184 A13
Clarence Rd, Enf 45 L10
Clarence Rd, Rich 141 U2
Clarence Rd, Sid 172 C6
Clarence Rd, Sutt 194 J8
Clarence Rd, Tedd 158 G12
Clarence Rd, Wall 196 C10
Clarence St, Kings T 177 S2
Clarence St, Rich 4 141 R7
Clarence St, Sthl 120 H5
Clarence Ter NW1 8 A10
Clarence Ter, Houns 139 R7
Clarence Wk SW4 146 J3
Clarence Way NW1 92 C13
Clarence Way Est NW1 92 D13
Clarendon Cl, E9 3 95 M14
Clarendon Cl W2 15 P9
Clarendon Cres, Twick 158 A6
Clarendon Cross W11 108 D14
Clarendon Dr SW15 143 U7
Clarendon Gdns NW4 71 R5
Clarendon Gdns W9 6 G11
Clarendon Gdns, Ilf 98 F1
Clarendon Gdns, Wem 87 S7
Clarendon Gro NW1 9 S5
Clarendon Gro, Mitch 181 U5
Clarendon Ms, W2 1 15 P9
Clarendon Ms, Bex 173 R1
Clarendon Ms, Borwd 38 B5
Clarendon Pl W2 15 P9
Clarendon Ri SE13 150 F7
Clarendon Rd E11 96 H1
Clarendon Rd E17 78 C11
Clarendon Rd E18 79 P5
Clarendon Rd N8 75 M6
Clarendon Rd N15 75 S8
Clarendon Rd N18 60 G11
Clarendon Rd N22 75 L4
Clarendon Rd SW19 163 R13
Clarendon Rd W5 105 R7
Clarendon Rd W11 126 D1
Clarendon Rd, Borwd 38 B5
Clarendon Rd, Croy 197 S3
Clarendon Rd, Har 68 D12
Clarendon Rd, Wall 196 E11
Clarendon St SW1 32 J6
Clarendon Ter, W9 3 6 H10
Clarendon Wk W11 108 C12
Clarendon Way N21 43 U12

Clarendon Way, Chis 189 T6
Clarens St SE6 167 T4
Claret Gdns SE25 184 D7
Clareville Gro SW7 30 H3
Clareville Rd, Orp 203 L3
Clareville St SW7 30 H3
Clarewood Wk SW9 147 P7
Clarges Ms W1 24 H1
Clarges St W1 24 J2
Claribel Rd SW9 147 R3
Claridge Rd, Dag 100 H2
Clarissa Rd, Rom 2 82 G13
Clarissa St E8 112 E1
Clark St E1 113 L10
Clark Way, Houns 120 H14
Clarkes Av, Wor Pk 194 A3
Clarke's Ms, W1 5 16 F2
Clarks Pl EC2 20 H6
Clarks Rd, Ilf 99 P3
Clarkson Rd E16 115 L11
Clarkson Row NW1 9 K2
Clarkson St E2 112 J5
Clarksons, The, Bark 117 M3
Claude Rd E10 96 F2
Claude Rd E13 115 R1
Claude Rd SE15 148 J4
Claude St, E14 2 132 A7
Claudia Jones Way SW2 146 J11
Claudia Pl SW19 162 C2
Claughton Rd E13 115 U14
Clauson Av, Nthlt 85 T9
Clave St, E1 5 131 L2
Clavell St, SE10 2 132 E11
Claverdale Rd SW2 147 M14
Clavering Av SW13 125 S11
Clavering Cl, Twick 2 158 G7
Clavering Rd E12 98 A2
Claverings Ind Est N9 61 N3
Claverley Gro N3 72 J1
Claverley Vil N3 72 H1
Claverton St SW1 33 P8
Claxton Gro W6 126 B10
Clay Av, Mitch 182 D3
Clay Rd, The, Loug 48 D3
Clay St W1 16 B3
Claybank Gro SE13 150 C5
Claybourne Ms, SE19 11 166 D13
Claybridge Rd SE12 169 U8
Claybrook Cl N2 73 N5
Claybrook Rd W6 126 B11
Claybury Bdy, Ilf 80 C5
Claybury Rd, Wdf Grn 64 D13
Claydon Dr, Croy 197 K8
Claydown Ms, SE18 9 134 H9
Clayfarm Rd SE9 171 M4
Claygate Cres, Croy 200 F12
Claygate La, Esher 190 G3
Claygate La, T Ditt 190 G2
Claygate Lo Cl, Esher 190 C14
Claygate Rd W13 122 J5
Clayhall Av, Ilf 80 C5
Clayhill, Surb 178 A9
Clayhill Cres SE9 170 A7
Claylands Pl SW8 34 J13
Claylands Rd SW8 34 G11
Claymore Cl, Mord 180 G14
Claypole Dr, Houns 139 K2
Claypole Rd E15 114 F3
Clayponds Av, Brent 123 R8
Clayponds Gdns W5 123 P8
Clayponds La, Brent 123 R9
Clays La E15 96 D9
Clay's La, Loug 48 G1
Clays La Cl E15 96 D10
Clayside, Chig 65 M11
Clayton Av, Wem 87 S13
Clayton Cl E6 116 F11
Clayton Cres, Brent 123 N9
Clayton Fld NW9 55 K14
Clayton Ms SE10 150 G1

Clayton Rd SE15	148	H2	Cleveland Rd E18	79	P6	Clifton Rd, Ilf	81	N12	Close, The N14	58	G3
Clayton Rd, Chess	191	N8	Cleveland Rd N1	94	B14	Clifton Rd, Islw	140	C3	Close, The N20	56	F3
Clayton Rd, Islw	140	C6	Cleveland Rd,	45	K14	Clifton Rd, Kings T	159	U14	Close, The, Barn	41	U10
Clayton Rd, Rom	101	T1	N9 2			Clifton Rd, Loug	48	C7	Close, The, Beck	185	R7
Clayton St SE11	34	J10	Cleveland Rd SW13	143	L4	Clifton Rd, Sid	171	S7	Close, The, Bex	155	N12
Clayton Ter, Hayes	102	H9	Cleveland Rd,	124	F6	Clifton Rd, Sthl	121	K7	Close, The, Har	67	U4
Claywood Cl, Orp	189	R14	W4 6			Clifton Rd, Tedd	158	D8	Close, The, Islw	140	A3
Clayworth Cl, Sid	154	C11	Cleveland Rd W13	104	J10	Clifton Rd, Wall	196	D10	Close, The, Mitch	181	T8
Cleanthus Cl SE18	153	K2	Cleveland Rd, Ilf	99	K6	Clifton Rd, Well	154	E5	Close, The, N Mal	178	G4
Cleanthus Rd SE18	153	K2	Cleveland Rd, Islw	140	G7	Clifton St EC2	12	G11	Close, The, Orp	189	R12
Clearbrook Way E1	113	M11	Cleveland Rd,	178	J7	Clifton Ter N4	93	N3	Close, The	66	E13
Clearwell Dr W9	6	C12	N Mal			Clifton Vil W9	14	D1	(Eastcote), Pnr		
Cleave Av, Orp	203	S11	Cleveland Rd, Well	153	U4	Clifton Wk, E6 25	116	C11	Close, The, Rich	142	C5
Cleaveland Rd, Surb	177	N10	Cleveland Rd,	193	K3	Clifton Way SE15	131	L14	Close, The, Rom	82	J11
Cleaver Sq SE11	35	M7	Wor Pk			Clifton Way, Borwd	38	A1	Close, The, Sid	172	D8
Cleaver St SE11	35	L6	Cleveland Row SW1	25	M4	Clifton Way, Wem	105	S1	Close, The, Sutt	180	E14
Cleaverholme Cl	184	J12	Cleveland Sq W2	14	F8	Clinch Ct, E16 2	115	P10	Close, The (Barnhill	88	F5
SE25			Cleveland St W1	9	L12	Cline Rd N11	58	F12	Rd), Wem		
Cleeve Hill SE23	167	K1	Cleveland Ter W2	14	F7	Clinger Ct, N1 1	112	C2	Close, The (Lyon	87	R12
Cleeve Pk Gdns, Sid	172	D4	Cleveland Way E1	113	L8	Clink St SE1	28	B1	Pk Ave), Wem		
Cleeve Way SW15	143	M13	Cleveley Cl SE7	134	B7	Clinton Av, E Mol	175	T8	Cloth Cl, EC1 4	19	S3
Clegg St E1	131	K1	Cleveley Cres W5	105	S4	Clinton Av, Well	154	A7	Cloth Fair EC1	19	S3
Clegg St E13	115	P3	Cleveleys Rd E5	95	K5	Clinton Cres, Ilf	65	R11	Cloth St, EC1 5	19	T2
Cleland Path, Loug	49	K2	Cleverly Est W12	125	N1	Clinton Rd E3	113	R6	Clothier St, E1 3	21	K5
Clem Attlee Ct SW6	126	F12	Cleves Cl, Loug	48	D11	Clinton Rd E7	97	P8	Clothworkers Rd,	135	P13
Clematis Gdns,	63	P10	Cleves Rd E6	116	A2	Clinton Rd N15	76	A8	SE18 1		
Wdf Grn			Cleves Rd, Rich	159	M6	Clipper Cl,	131	N3	Cloudberry Rd,	164	C3
Clematis St W12	107	N13	Cleves Wk, Ilf	65	M14	SE16 10			SW17		
Clemence Rd, Dag	119	U1	Cleves Way, Hmptn	157	M14	Clipper Way SE13	160	EU	Cloudesdale Rd	164	C3
Clemence St E14	113	T10	Cleves Way, Ruis	84	H2	Clippesby Cl, Chess	191	T12	SW17		
Clement Av SW4	146	H7	Clewer Cres, Har	68	A2	Clipstone Ms W1	17	L1	Cloudesley Pl N1	111	N2
Clement Cl NW6	89	U14	Clichy Est E1	113	L10	Clipstone Rd, Houns	139	N5	Cloudesley Rd N1	111	N1
Clement Cl W4	124	G7	Clifden Rd E5	95	N9	Clipstone St W1	17	L2	Cloudesley Rd, Bexh	155	M2
Clement Rd SW19	162	C10	Clifden Rd, Brent	123	N11	Clissold Cl N2	73	U6	Cloudesley Sq N1	111	N1
Clement Rd, Beck	185	P4	Clifden Rd, Twick	158	F1	Clissold Ct, N4	93	U4	Cloudesley St N1	111	P2
Clementhorpe Rd,	100	E12	Cliff Rd NW1	92	H11	Clissold Cres N16	94	A7	Clouston Cl, Wall	196	J9
Dag			Cliff Ter SE8	150	B3	Clissold Rd N16	94	B6	Clova Rd E7	97	N10
Clementina Rd E10	95	T2	Cliff Vil NW1	92	H11	Clitheroe Av, Har	85	N2	Clove Cres E14	114	G13
Clementine Cl W13	122	J4	Cliff Wk E16	115	M9	Clitheroe Gdns, Wat	50	G6	Clove Hitch Quay	145	M6
Clements Av E16	115	N13	Cliffe Rd, S Croy	198	A9	Clitheroe Rd SW9	146	J4	SW11		
Clements Ct, Houns	138	G8	Clifford Av SW14	142	D4	Clitherow Av W7	122	G5	Clove St, E13 6	115	N8
Clement's Inn WC2	18	G8	Clifford Av, Chis	170	E11	Clitherow Pas,	123	K10	Clovelly Av NW9	71	L7
Clements La EC4	20	E9	Clifford Av, Ilf	80	J2	Brent			Clovelly Cl, Pnr	66	D5
Clements La, Ilf	98	J5	Clifford Av, Wall	196	E7	Clitherow Rd, Brent	123	K9	Clovelly Gdns SE19	184	F1
Clements Pl, Brent	123	N9	Clifford Cl, Nthlt	103	K2	Clitterhouse Cres	89	U2	Clovelly Gdns, Enf	44	C14
Clements Rd E6	98	D14	Clifford Dr SW9	147	R7	NW2			Clovelly Gdns, Rom	83	S2
Clements Rd SE16	130	H6	Clifford Gdns NW10	107	U4	Clitterhouse Rd	89	U2	Clovelly Rd N8	74	H7
Clements Rd, Ilf	98	J5	Clifford Rd E16	115	L8	NW2			Clovelly Rd W4	124	G4
Clendon Way SE18	135	N7	Clifford Rd E17	78	E4	Clive Av N18	60	G11	Clovelly Rd W5	123	M4
Clennam St,	28	A5	Clifford Rd N9	45	M12	Clive Ct W9	6	G9	Clovelly Rd, Bexh	136	J12
SE1 4			Clifford Rd SE25	184	G8	Clive Pas, SE21 1	166	B6	Clovelly Rd, Houns	139	P3
Clensham La, Sutt	194	G4	Clifford Rd, Barn	41	K5	Clive Rd SE21	166	B6	Clovelly Way, Har	85	L5
Clenston Ms W1	15	U6	Clifford Rd, Houns	138	G5	Clive Rd SW19	163	R12	Clovelly Way, Orp	189	T12
Clephane Rd N1	93	U12	Clifford Rd, Rich	159	P3	Clive Rd, Belv	137	N8	Clover Cl, E11 2	96	H4
Clere St EC2	12	F10	Clifford Rd, Wem	105	N1	Clive Rd, Enf	44	G7	Clover Ms SW3	32	A10
Clerkenwell Cl EC1	11	M10	Clifford St W1	17	L11	Clive Rd, Felt	138	B11	Clover Way, Wall	196	B1
Clerkenwell Grn EC1	11	M11	Clifford Way NW10	89	L7	Clive Rd, Twick	158	G7	Cloverdale Gdns,	153	T12
Clerkenwell Rd EC1	11	P12	Cliffview Rd SE13	150	B6	Clive Way, Enf	44	G8	Sid		
Clerks Piece, Loug	48	F6	Clifton Av E17	77	P6	Cliveden Cl N12	57	L8	Cloverleys, Loug	48	B9
Clermont Rd E9	113	L1	Clifton Av N3	72	F2	Cliveden Pl SW1	32	C3	Clowders Rd SE6	167	T5
Cleve Rd NW6	90	H13	Clifton Av W12	125	M2	Cliveden Rd SW19	180	E1	Clowser Cl, Sutt 8	195	M10
Cleve Rd, Sid	172	H6	Clifton Av, Felt	156	E6	Clivedon Ct W13	104	J9	Cloyster Wd, Edg	53	P13
Clevedon Gdns,	138	C2	Clifton Av, Stan	69	K3	Clivedon Rd E4	62	J10	Cloysters Grn E1	29	S1
Houns			Clifton Av, Wem	87	U11	Clivesdale Dr, Hayes	120	B1	Club Gdns Rd,	187	P13
Clevedon Rd SE20	185	N2	Clifton Cl, Orp	203	L9	Cloak La EC4	20	B9	Brom		
Clevedon Rd,	178	A3	Clifton Ct N8	6	J10	Clock Ho Rd, Beck	185	S4	Club Row E1	13	M9
Kings T			Clifton Cres SE15	131	K14	Clock Twr Ms N1	111	U2	Club Row E2	13	M9
Clevedon Rd, Twick	141	N11	Clifton Gdns N15	76	F12	Clock Twr Ms SE28	118	C14	Clunbury Av, Sthl	121	L10
Cleveland Av SW20	180	E3	Clifton Gdns NW11	72	F11	Clock Twr Pl N7	92	J11	Clunbury St, N1 1	12	F3
Cleveland Av W4	125	L7	Clifton Gdns,	124	H8	Clock Twr Rd, Islw	140	F6	Cluny Est SE1	28	H9
Cleveland Av,	157	L13	W4 1			Clockhouse Av, Bark	117	L1	Cluny Ms SW5	126	F9
Hmptn			Clifton Gdns W9	6	F11	Clockhouse Cl SW19	161	U4	Cluny Pl SE1	28	H10
Cleveland Cres,	38	E9	Clifton Gdns, Enf	42	J8	Clockhouse La SW15	144	D10	Cluse Ct N1	11	U1
Borwd			Clifton Gro E8	94	G11	Cloister Cl, Tedd	158	J10	Clutton St E14	114	D10
Cleveland Gdns N4	75	T10	Clifton Hill NW8	6	D1	Cloister Gdns SE25	184	J12	Clydach Rd, Enf	44	F7
Cleveland Gdns	90	B3	Clifton Pk Av SW20	179	U3	Cloister Gdns, Edg	54	F9	Clyde Pl E10	78	C14
NW2			Clifton Pl SE16	131	M3	Cloister Rd NW2	90	E5	Clyde Rd N15	76	D7
Cleveland Gdns	143	L4	Clifton Pl W2	15	L9	Cloister Rd W3	106	F10	Clyde Rd N22	74	G1
SW13			Clifton Ri SE14	131	S14	Cloisters Av, Brom	188	E10	Clyde Rd, Croy	198	E2
Cleveland Gdns W2	14	F7	Clifton Rd E7	98	B12	Clonard Way, Pnr	51	P12	Clyde Rd, Sutt	194	H9
Cleveland Gdns,	193	K3	Clifton Rd E16	115	K9	Clonbrock Rd N16	94	C7	Clyde Rd, Wall	196	F11
Wor Pk			Clifton Rd N3	73	M1	Cloncurry St SW6	144	B3	Clyde St SE8	131	U12
Cleveland Gro,	113	L8	Clifton Rd N8	74	G11	Clonmel Cl, Har	86	B3	Clyde Ter SE23	167	M4
E1 13			Clifton Rd N22	74	F2	Clonmel Rd SW6	126	F14	Clyde Vale SE23	167	M4
Cleveland Ms W1	17	M1	Clifton Rd NW10	107	N4	Clonmel Rd, Tedd	158	B7	Clydesdale, Enf	45	N8
Cleveland Pk Av E17	78	A7	Clifton Rd SE25	184	C8	Clonmore St SW18	162	F2	Clydesdale Av, Stan	69	N5
Cleveland Pk Cres	78	A7	Clifton Rd SW19	162	A12	Cloonmore Av, Orp	203	U8	Clydesdale Cl,	38	G10
E17			Clifton Rd W9	6	G10	Clorane Gdns NW3	90	G6	Borwd		
Cleveland Pl SW1	25	P2	Clifton Rd, Grnf	103	U7	Close, The E4	62	F14	Clydesdale Cl, Islw	140	F5
Cleveland Ri, Mord	180	B14	Clifton Rd, Har	69	T9						

Name	Page	Grid
Clydesdale Gdns, Rich	142	C7
Clydesdale Rd W11	108	F11
Clymping Dene, Felt	138	C13
Clyston St SW8	146	F3
Coach & Horses Yd, W1 2	17	L10
Coach Ho La N5	93	R8
Coach Ho La SW19	162	A7
Coach Ho Ms, SE23 1	149	M12
Coach Ho Rd, SW18 6	145	K8
Coach Yd Ms N19	93	K1
Coachhouse Ms SE20	166	J13
Coalecroft Rd SW15	143	T8
Coate St E2	13	U3
Coates Av SW18	145	R11
Coates Hill Rd, Brom	188	G4
Coates Wk, Brent	123	R10
Cobb Cl, Borwd	38	F10
Cobb St E1	21	L4
Cobbett Rd SE9	152	D6
Cobbett Rd, Twick	157	P1
Cobbett St SW8	129	M14
Cobbetts Av, Ilf	80	B10
Cobblers Wk, Hmptn	175	U1
Cobblers Wk, Kings T	177	K1
Cobblers Wk, Tedd	176	H1
Cobblestone Pl, Croy 7	197	T2
Cobbold Est NW10	89	M12
Cobbold Rd E11	97	M5
Cobbold Rd NW10	89	L12
Cobbold Rd W12	125	L4
Cobb's Rd, Houns	139	L8
Cobden Rd E11	97	K4
Cobden Rd SE25	184	H10
Cobden Rd, Orp	203	N8
Cobham Av, N Mal	179	N9
Cobham Cl SW11	145	S11
Cobham Cl, Brom	188	C13
Cobham Cl, Edg	70	C4
Cobham Cl, Sid 4	154	D11
Cobham Cl, Wall	196	J12
Cobham Ms NW1	92	G13
Cobham Pl, Bexh	154	H9
Cobham Rd E17	78	F2
Cobham Rd N22	75	R5
Cobham Rd, Houns	120	F13
Cobham Rd, Ilf	99	S4
Cobham Rd, Kings T	178	A3
Cobland Rd SE12	169	U8
Coborn Rd E3	113	T5
Coborn St E3	113	U5
Cobourg Rd SE5	37	M9
Cobourg St NW1	9	N7
Coburg Cl SW1	33	N1
Coburg Cres SW2	165	N2
Coburg Gdns, Ilf	80	B4
Coburg Rd N22	75	L5
Cochrane Ms NW8	7	M3
Cochrane Rd SW19	162	D14
Cochrane St NW8	7	M3
Cock La EC1	19	P4
Cockayne Way SE8	131	S9
Cockerell Rd E17	77	S12
Cockfosters Rd, Barn	42	A7
Cockpit Steps, SW1 2	25	T7
Cockpit Yd WC1	18	G1
Cocks Cres, N Mal	179	L8
Cocksett Av, Orp	203	R11
Cockspur Ct SW1	25	T2
Cockspur St SW1	25	T1
Cocksure La, Sid	173	N7
Code St E1	13	P11
Codling Cl, E1 3	29	U2
Codling Way, Wem	88	E14
Codrington Hill SE23	149	S13
Codrington Ms W11	108	D12
Cody Cl, Har	69	P6
Cody Cl, Wall	196	H14
Cody Rd E16	114	H8
Cody Rd Business Cen E16	114	H8
Coe Av SE25	184	H12
Coe's All, Barn	40	C7
Coffers Circle, Wem	88	C5
Cogan Av E17	77	R1
Coin St SE1	27	K2
Coity Rd NW5	92	B11
Coke St E1	21	S6
Cokers La SE21	165	U2
Colas Ms NW6	108	H1
Colbeck Ms SW7	30	D3
Colbeck Rd, Har	67	U14
Colberg Pl N16	76	D14
Colborne Way, Wor Pk	193	T5
Colburn Av, Pnr	51	K12
Colburn Way, Sutt	195	N6
Colby Ms SE19	166	D9
Colby Rd SE19	166	D9
Colchester Av E12	98	F6
Colchester Dr, Pnr	66	G10
Colchester Rd E10	78	F13
Colchester Rd E17	78	A12
Colchester Rd, Edg	54	F13
Colchester Rd, Nthwd	66	A4
Colchester St, E1 7	21	P6
Cold Blow La SE14	131	P12
Cold Blows, Mitch	181	T6
Cold Harbour E14	132	F2
Coldbath Sq, EC1 4	11	K10
Coldbath St SE13	150	D2
Coldershaw Rd W13	122	H3
Coldfall Av N10	73	U3
Coldharbour La SE5	147	U4
Coldharbour La SW9	147	R7
Coldharbour La, Hayes	102	B13
Coldharbour Pl, SE5 12	148	A3
Coldharbour Rd, Croy	197	P9
Coldharbour Way, Croy	197	P10
Coldstream Gdns SW18	144	E11
Cole Cl SE28	136	D2
Cole Gdns, Houns	120	B14
Cole Pk Gdns, Twick	140	G11
Cole Pk Rd, Twick	140	G11
Cole Pk Vw, Twick	140	H12
Cole Rd, Twick	140	G12
Cole St SE1	28	B8
Colebeck Ms N1	93	S12
Colebert Av E1	113	L7
Colebrook Cl, SW15 1	144	B13
Colebrook Gdns, Loug	49	K4
Colebrook La, Loug	49	L2
Colebrook Path, Loug 2	49	K3
Colebrook Rd SW16	183	K2
Colebrook Way N11	58	D10
Colebrooke Av W13	104	J11
Colebrooke Dr E11	79	S13
Colebrooke Pl N1	111	S2
Colebrooke Ri, Brom	187	K4
Colebrooke Row N1	11	P2
Coledale Dr, Stan	69	L1
Coleford Rd SW18	145	L9
Colegrave Rd E15	96	G9
Colegrove Rd SE15	37	P12
Coleherne Ct SW5	30	C7
Coleherne Ms SW10	30	B7
Coleherne Rd SW10	30	B7
Colehill Gdns SW6	144	C2
Colehill La SW6	144	D2
Coleman Cl SE25	184	G4
Coleman Flds N1	111	U1
Coleman Rd SE5	36	G13
Coleman Rd, Belv	137	N7
Coleman Rd, Dag	101	K12
Coleman St EC2	20	C6
Colemans Heath SE9	170	H5
Colenso Rd E5	95	M7
Colenso Rd, Ilf	99	R1
Colepits Wd Rd SE9	153	N9
Coleraine Rd N8	75	P5
Coleraine Rd SE3	133	M12
Coleridge Av E12	98	D11
Coleridge Av, Sutt	195	S7
Coleridge Cl SW8	146	D4
Coleridge Gdns NW6	91	L14
Coleridge La N8	74	J11
Coleridge Rd E17	77	T7
Coleridge Rd N4	93	N4
Coleridge Rd N8	74	H12
Coleridge Rd N12	57	L10
Coleridge Rd, Croy	185	L13
Coleridge Sq W13	104	F12
Coleridge Way NW11	72	G8
Coleridge Way, Hayes	102	A11
Coles Cres, Har	85	R4
Coles Grn, Bushey	51	U1
Coles Grn, Loug	48	H2
Coles Grn Ct NW2	89	P3
Coles Grn Rd NW2	89	P2
Colesburg Rd, Beck	185	T5
Coleshill Rd, Tedd	158	D11
Colestown St, SW11 3	145	S3
Colet Cl N13	59	S11
Colet Gdns W14	126	B8
Coley St WC1	10	H11
Colfe Rd SE23	167	R2
Colin Cl NW9	71	K8
Colin Cl, Croy	199	T5
Colin Cl, W Wick	201	L6
Colin Cres NW9	71	M7
Colin Dr NW9	71	M9
Colin Gdns NW9	71	M8
Colin Pk Rd NW9	70	J7
Colin Rd NW10	89	N11
Colina Ms N15	75	S8
Colina Rd N15	75	S9
Colindale Av NW9	70	H6
Colindale Business Pk NW9	70	F5
Colindeep Gdns NW4	71	P9
Colindeep La NW4	71	K6
Colindeep La NW9	71	K6
Colinette Rd SW15	143	T7
Colinton Rd, Ilf	100	D3
Coliston Rd SW18	144	H13
Collamore Av SW18	163	R2
Collapit Cl, Har	67	S11
Collard Av, Loug	49	M3
Collard Grn, Loug	49	M3
College App SE10	132	F11
College Av, Har	68	C1
College Cl E9	95	M9
College Cl N18	60	F9
College Cl, Har	52	D14
College Cl, Twick	158	A1
College Cres NW3	91	N12
College Cross N1	93	P13
College Dr, Ruis	66	A14
College Gdns E4	46	C14
College Gdns N18	60	F9
College Gdns SE21	166	C1
College Gdns SW17	163	R3
College Gdns, Enf	44	A2
College Gdns, Ilf	80	C9
College Gdns, N Mal	179	M10
College Grn SE19	166	C13
College Gro NW1	110	F2
College Hill EC4	20	B10
College Hill Rd, Har	68	E2
College La NW5	92	C8
College Ms SW1	26	B10
College Ms, SW18 12	145	K10
College Pk Cl SE13	150	G8
College Pl E17	78	J7
College Pl NW1	110	F2
College Pl SW10	30	E13
College Rd E17	78	E11
College Rd N17	60	E12
College Rd N21	59	P4
College Rd NW10	107	T5
College Rd SE19	166	F9
College Rd SE21	166	C1
College Rd SW19	163	P12
College Rd W13	104	J12
College Rd, Brom	169	N14
College Rd, Croy	198	B4
College Rd, Enf	44	B3
College Rd (Harrow on the Hill), Har	68	C12
College Rd (Harrow Weald), Har	68	C1
College Rd, Islw	140	E2
College Rd, Wem	87	P2
College Row E9	95	N10
College Slip, Brom	187	N2
College St EC4	20	C10
College Ter E3	113	T5
College Ter, N3 2	72	F3
College Vw SE9	170	B2
College Yd, NW5 2	92	D8
Collent St E9	95	M12
Colless Rd N15	76	E9
Collett Rd SE16	29	U11
Collett Way, Sthl	121	R3
Collier Cl E6	116	J13
Collier Cl, Epsom	192	B12
Collier Dr, Edg	70	A3
Collier Row Rd, Rom	83	L3
Collier St N1	10	E3
Colliers Shaw, Kes	202	B9
Colliers Water La, Th Hth	183	P9
Collindale Av, Erith	137	S12
Collindale Av, Sid	172	B1
Collingbourne Rd W12	125	R1
Collingham Gdns SW5	30	D4
Collingham Pl SW5	30	B3
Collingham Rd SW5	30	D3
Collings Cl N22	59	L11
Collingtree Rd SE26	167	L7
Collingwood Av N10	74	A6
Collingwood Av, Surb	192	E1
Collingwood Cl, SE20 1	185	K1
Collingwood Cl, Twick	139	P13
Collingwood Rd, E17 1	78	A12
Collingwood Rd N15	76	C7
Collingwood Rd, Mitch	181	R4
Collingwood Rd, Sutt	194	F5
Collingwood St E1	113	K8
Collins Av, Stan	69	R3
Collins Dr, Ruis	84	F3
Collins Rd N5	93	U7
Collins Sq, SE3 4	151	L4
Collins St SE3	151	K4
Collin's Yd N1	111	R2
Collinson St SE1	27	T7
Collinwood Av, Enf	45	M6
Collinwood Gdns, Ilf	80	G9
Collis All, Twick 2	158	D2
Colls Rd SE15	149	L1
Collyer Av, Croy	196	J8
Collyer Pl SE15	148	F2
Collyer Rd, Croy	197	K7
Colman Rd E16	115	T10
Colmar Cl, E1 16	113	N7
Colmer Pl, Har	52	A14
Colmer Rd SW16	183	K1
Colmore Ms SE15	148	J2
Colmore Rd, Enf	45	M7
Colnbrook St SE1	27	P11
Colne Ct, Epsom	192	E7
Colne Rd E5	95	R8
Colne Rd N21	44	A14
Colne Rd, Twick	158	D2
Colne St E13	115	N6
Colney Hatch La N10	74	C4
Colney Hatch La N11	57	U11
Cologne Rd SW11	145	N8
Colomb St SE10	133	K10
Colombo Rd, Ilf	81	L14
Colombo St SE1	27	N3

Street	Page	Grid
Colonels Wk, Enf	43	R4
Colonial Av, Twick	139	T10
Colonnade WC1	10	C12
Colonnade Wk SW1	32	H3
Colonnades, The, W2 *2*	14	D6
Colson Gdns, Loug	48	H8
Colson Path, Loug	48	H7
Colson Rd, Croy	198	C3
Colson Rd, Loug	48	H7
Colson Way SW16	164	F7
Colsterworth Rd N15	76	E7
Colston Av, Cars	195	S8
Colston Cl, Cars	195	T8
Colston Rd E7	98	A12
Colston Rd SW14	142	F7
Colthurst Cres N4	93	S3
Coltness Cres SE2	136	C9
Colton Gdns N17	75	U5
Colton Rd, Har	68	D9
Columbia Av, Edg	70	C1
Columbia Av, Ruis	84	D1
Columbia Av, Wor Pk	179	M14
Columbia Ctyd E14	132	A1
Columbia Rd E2	13	M6
Columbia Rd E13	115	M8
Columbia Sq SW14	142	F7
Columbine Av E6	116	C10
Columbine Av, S Croy	197	S13
Columbine Way SE13	150	E4
Columbus Gdns, Nthwd	66	A1
Colvestone Cres E8	94	E10
Colview Ct SE9	170	B2
Colville Est N1	112	C2
Colville Gdns W11	108	F12
Colville Hos W11	108	E12
Colville Ms W11	108	F12
Colville Rd E11	96	F5
Colville Rd E17	77	S4
Colville Rd N9	60	J1
Colville Rd W3	124	D6
Colville Rd W11	108	F12
Colville Sq W11	108	E12
Colville Ter W11	108	F12
Colvin Cl SE26	167	L9
Colvin Gdns E4	62	F5
Colvin Gdns E11	79	S7
Colvin Gdns, Ilf	65	L14
Colvin Rd E6	98	C14
Colvin Rd, Th Hth	183	N10
Colwall Gdns, Wdf Grn	63	P10
Colwell Rd SE22	148	E10
Colwick Cl N6	74	G13
Colwith Rd W6	125	U11
Colwood Gdns SW19	163	P14
Colworth Gro SE17	36	A4
Colworth Rd E11	78	J12
Colworth Rd, Croy	198	G1
Colwyn Av, Grnf	104	F4
Colwyn Cl SW16	164	E9
Colwyn Cres, Houns	139	T2
Colwyn Grn, NW9 *4*	70	J11
Colwyn Rd NW2	89	S6
Colyer Cl N1	10	H1
Colyer Cl SE9	171	K4
Colyers La, Erith	155	U1
Colyton Cl, Well	154	G1
Colyton Cl, Wem	87	L11
Colyton Rd SE22	149	K10
Colyton Way N18	60	G10
Combe Av SE3	133	M13
Combe Lo SE7	133	U11
Combe Ms SE3	133	M13
Combedale Rd, SE10 *1*	133	N10
Combemartin Rd SW18	144	D14
Comber Cl NW2	89	R5
Comber Gro SE5	129	U14
Combermere Rd SW9	147	L5
Combermere Rd, Mord	181	K11
Comberton Rd E5	95	K3
Combeside SE18	135	T14
Combwell Cres SE2	136	B6
Comely Bank Rd E17	78	E9
Comer Cres, Sthl *1*	121	U3
Comeragh Ms, W14 *7*	126	D10
Comeragh Rd W14	126	C10
Comerford Rd SE4	149	S8
Comet Cl E12	98	B7
Comet Pl SE8	132	A14
Comet St SE8	132	A14
Commerce Rd N22	75	L1
Commerce Rd, Brent	123	L13
Commerce Way, Croy	197	M4
Commercial Rd E1	21	R6
Commercial Rd E14	113	S12
Commercial Rd N17	60	D12
Commercial Rd N18	60	D10
Commercial St E1	13	L12
Commercial Way NW10	106	D4
Commercial Way SE15	130	E14
Commerell St SE10	133	K9
Commodity Quay E1	21	P12
Commodore Sq SW10	145	N1
Commodore St E1	113	R8
Common, The W5	123	S1
Common, The, Rich	159	P6
Common, The, Sthl	120	J8
Common, The, Stan	53	L9
Common La, Esher	190	G14
Common Rd SW13	143	P5
Common Rd, Esher	190	G13
Common Rd, Stan	52	B6
Commondale SW15	143	T5
Commonside, Kes	201	U7
Commonside E, Mitch	182	A5
Commonside W, Mitch	182	A6
Commonwealth Av W12	107	R14
Commonwealth Rd N17	60	H13
Commonwealth Way SE2	136	D9
Community Cl, Houns	138	C2
Community La N7	92	H9
Community Rd E15	96	H10
Community Rd, Grnf	103	U2
Como Rd SE23	167	R3
Compass Hill, Rich	141	P11
Compayne Gdns NW6	90	J13
Compton Av E6	116	A3
Compton Av N1	93	R12
Compton Av N6	73	R14
Compton Cl E3	114	B9
Compton Cl NW11	90	B5
Compton Cl W13	104	G11
Compton Cl, Edg *2*	54	E14
Compton Ct SE19	166	C10
Compton Cres N17	59	U13
Compton Cres W4	124	E11
Compton Cres, Chess	191	S10
Compton Cres, Nthlt	102	H1
Compton Pl WC1	10	B9
Compton Pl, Wat	50	J7
Compton Ri, Pnr	67	K10
Compton Rd N1	93	S12
Compton Rd N21	59	R1
Compton Rd NW10	108	A6
Compton Rd SW19	162	E11
Compton Rd, Croy	198	J2
Compton St EC1	11	P10
Compton Ter N1	93	R12
Comreddy Cl, Enf	43	R1
Comus Pl SE17	36	G3
Comyn Rd SW11	145	S8
Comyns, The, Bushey	51	U1
Comyns Cl E16	115	L9
Comyns Rd, Dag	101	N13
Conant Ms E1	21	S9
Concanon Rd SW2	147	L7
Concert Hall App SE1	26	G3
Concord Cl, Nthlt	102	J5
Concord Rd W3	106	C8
Concord Rd, Enf	45	K10
Concorde Cl, Houns	139	R4
Concorde Dr E6	116	E10
Concourse, The NW9	71	L3
Condell Rd SW8	146	F2
Conder St E14	113	R11
Conderton Rd SE5	147	T5
Condover Cres SE18	134	J14
Condray Pl SW11	127	R14
Conduit Ct, WC2 *5*	18	B9
Conduit La N18	61	L9
Conduit La, Croy	198	H10
Conduit La, S Croy	198	G10
Conduit Ms W2	14	J8
Conduit Pas W2	15	K8
Conduit Pl W2	15	K7
Conduit Rd SE18	135	K9
Conduit St W1	17	K10
Conduit Way NW10	88	E13
Conewood St N5	93	R6
Coney Acre SE21	165	U2
Coney Burrows E4	62	J3
Coney Hill Rd, W Wick	201	K4
Coney Way SW8	34	G12
Conference Cl E4	62	E3
Conference Rd SE2	136	F7
Congleton Gro SE18	135	L10
Congo Rd SE18	135	P9
Congress Rd SE2	136	E7
Congreve Rd SE9	152	E6
Congreve St SE17	36	H3
Congreve Wk, E16 *7*	116	A10
Conical Cor, Enf	43	T4
Conifer Cl, Orp	203	P8
Conifer Gdns SW16	165	L6
Conifer Gdns, Enf	44	C12
Conifer Gdns, Sutt	194	J4
Conifer Way, Hayes	102	A14
Conifer Way, Wem	87	M6
Conifers Cl, Tedd	159	K13
Coniger Rd SW6	144	G3
Coningham Ms, W12 *2*	125	P2
Coningham Rd W12	125	R3
Coningsby Cotts, W5 *1*	123	N4
Coningsby Gdns E4	62	C11
Coningsby Rd N4	75	R13
Coningsby Rd W5	123	N4
Conington Rd SE13	150	E4
Conisbee Ct N14	42	F10
Conisborough Cres SE6	168	F5
Coniscliffe Cl, Chis	188	G2
Coniscliffe Rd N13	59	U6
Coniston Av, Bark	99	R14
Coniston Av, Grnf	105	K5
Coniston Av, Well	153	R6
Coniston Cl N20	57	M6
Coniston Cl SW13	125	M14
Coniston Cl SW20	180	A11
Coniston Cl W4	142	E1
Coniston Cl, Bark *1*	99	R14
Coniston Cl, Bexh	155	U2
Coniston Gdns N9	61	M2
Coniston Gdns NW9	70	G10
Coniston Gdns, Ilf	80	D8
Coniston Gdns, Pnr	66	A8
Coniston Gdns, Sutt	195	N12
Coniston Gdns, Wem	87	M1
Coniston Rd N10	74	C4
Coniston Rd N17	60	G12
Coniston Rd, Bexh	155	T2
Coniston Rd, Brom	168	J12
Coniston Rd, Croy	184	G14
Coniston Rd, Twick	139	S12
Coniston Way, Chess	191	R6
Conistone Way N7	93	K13
Conlan St W10	108	C7
Conley Rd NW10	89	K12
Conley St, SE10 *2*	133	K9
Connaught Av E4	46	H13
Connaught Av SW14	142	E6
Connaught Av, Barn	57	U1
Connaught Av, Enf	44	D4
Connaught Av, Houns	139	K9
Connaught Av, Loug	48	B8
Connaught Br E16	134	A1
Connaught Cl E10	95	R3
Connaught Cl W2	15	P8
Connaught Cl, Enf	44	D4
Connaught Dr NW11	72	H7
Connaught Gdns N10	74	D9
Connaught Gdns N13	59	S8
Connaught Gdns, Mord	181	M8
Connaught Hill, Loug	48	B7
Connaught La, Ilf	99	M4
Connaught Ms SE18	134	H9
Connaught Ms W2	15	T8
Connaught Ms, Ilf *4*	99	N4
Connaught Pl W2	15	T9
Connaught Rd, E4 *1*	62	J1
Connaught Rd E11	96	H2
Connaught Rd E16	134	B1
Connaught Rd E17	78	A10
Connaught Rd N4	75	N14
Connaught Rd NW10	107	K2
Connaught Rd SE18	134	H9
Connaught Rd W13	104	J14
Connaught Rd, Barn	40	B11
Connaught Rd, Har	68	F2
Connaught Rd, Ilf	99	N4
Connaught Rd, N Mal	179	K7
Connaught Rd, Rich *5*	141	T9
Connaught Rd, Sutt	195	N4
Connaught Rd, Tedd	158	A9
Connaught Roundabout E16	116	A13
Connaught Sq W2	15	S8
Connaught St W2	15	R8
Connaught Way N13	59	S8
Connell Cres W5	105	U7
Connemara Cl, Borwd	38	F11
Connington Cres E4	62	G5
Connor Rd, Dag	101	L7
Connor St E9	113	N1
Conolly Rd W7	122	C1
Conrad Dr, Wor Pk	193	U1
Cons St SE1	27	M5
Consfield Av, N Mal	179	P9
Consort Ms, Islw	140	B10
Consort Rd SE15	148	J2
Constable Av E16	133	R1
Constable Cl NW11	73	K12
Constable Cres N15	76	G9
Constable Gdns, Edg	70	A2
Constable Gdns, Islw	140	A10
Constable Ms, Dag	100	D8
Constable Wk SE21	166	D5
Constance Cres, Brom	201	M1
Constance Rd, Croy	183	S13
Constance Rd, Enf	44	C12
Constance Rd, Sutt	195	M8
Constance Rd, Twick	139	S14
Constance St, E16 *1*	134	C2
Constantine Rd NW3	91	S8

Name	No	Grid
Constitution Hill SW1	24	J6
Constitution Ri SE18	152	H1
Consul Av, Dag	119	U7
Content St SE17	36	B3
Contessa Cl, Orp 6	203	R10
Convent Cl, Beck	168	E14
Convent Gdns W5	123	L8
Convent Gdns W11	108	D12
Convent Hill SE19	165	T12
Convent Way, Sthl	120	H9
Conway Cl, Stan	52	G11
Conway Cres, Grnf	104	D2
Conway Cres, Rom	82	E13
Conway Dr, Sutt	194	J12
Conway Gdns, Mitch	182	J7
Conway Gdns, Wem	69	L14
Conway Gro W3	106	H10
Conway Ms W1	9	M12
Conway Rd N14	59	K5
Conway Rd N15	75	S9
Conway Rd NW2	89	T4
Conway Rd SE18	135	P8
Conway Rd SW20	179	U1
Conway Rd, Felt	156	H9
Conway Rd, Houns	139	N13
Conway St E13	115	N8
Conway St W1	9	M12
Conybeare NW3	91	S13
Conyer St E3	113	R4
Conyers Cl, Wdf Grn 1	62	J12
Conyers Rd SW16	164	G10
Conyers Way, Loug	49	K5
Cooden Cl, Brom	169	S14
Cooderidge Cl, N17 2	60	F12
Cook Rd, Dag	118	J2
Cookes Cl E11	97	L4
Cookes La, Sutt 1	194	C11
Cookham Cl, Sthl	121	R4
Cookham Cres, SE16 16	131	N3
Cookham Dene Cl, Chis	189	P2
Cookham Rd, Swan	173	M14
Cookhill Rd SE2	136	C4
Cooks Cl, Rom	83	U1
Cook's Rd E15	114	D3
Cooks Rd SE17	35	P10
Cookson Gro, Erith	137	R14
Cool Oak La NW9	71	K14
Coolfin Rd E16	115	P12
Coolgardie Av E4	62	G10
Coolgardie Av, Chig	64	H6
Coolhurst Rd N8	74	G11
Coomassie Rd W9	108	E7
Coombe Av, Croy	198	D8
Coombe Bank, Kings T	178	J1
Coombe Cl, Edg	69	T4
Coombe Cl, Houns	139	P8
Coombe Cor N21	59	R2
Coombe Cres, Hmptn	157	K13
Coombe Dr, Kings T	160	H14
Coombe Dr, Ruis	84	D2
Coombe End, Kings T	160	H14
Coombe Gdns SW20	179	N3
Coombe Gdns, N Mal	179	L7
Coombe Hts, Kings T	161	K14
Coombe Hill Glade, Kings T	161	K14
Coombe Hill Rd, Kings T	160	J14
Coombe Ho Chase, N Mal	178	H1
Coombe La SW20	179	P2
Coombe La, Croy	199	K9
Coombe La W, Kings T	160	J14
Coombe Lea, Brom	188	D6
Coombe Neville, Kings T	160	G14
Coombe Pk, Kings T	160	G10
Coombe Ridings, Kings T	160	E10
Coombe Ri, Kings T	178	E2
Coombe Rd N22	75	P3
Coombe Rd NW10	88	G5
Coombe Rd SE26	166	J7
Coombe Rd W4	125	K10
Coombe Rd W13	122	J5
Coombe Rd, Croy	198	G9
Coombe Rd, Hmptn	157	L12
Coombe Rd, Kings T	178	B2
Coombe Rd, N Mal	179	K5
Coombe Wk, Sutt	194	J5
Coombe Wd Rd, Kings T	160	F10
Coombefield Cl, N Mal	179	K10
Coombehurst Cl, Barn	41	T3
Coomber Way, Croy	182	G13
Coombes Rd, Dag	119	M1
Coombewood Dr, Rom	83	M12
Coombs St N1	11	S4
Coomer Ms, SW6 8	126	F12
Coomer Pl, SW6 9	126	F12
Coomer Rd SW6	126	F12
Cooper Av E17	77	R1
Cooper Cl SE1	27	M8
Cooper Cres, Cars	195	T5
Cooper Rd NW4	72	A12
Cooper Rd NW10	89	N10
Cooper Rd, Croy	197	R8
Cooper St E16	115	M10
Coopers Cl E1	113	M8
Coopers Cl, Dag	101	R11
Coopers Cres, Borwd	38	F2
Coopers La E10	96	D1
Coopers La NW1	9	T2
Cooper's La SE12	169	R4
Coopers Rd SE1	37	P6
Cooper's Row EC3	21	U3
Coopers Wk, E15 5	96	J10
Cooper's Yd SE19	166	D11
Coopersale Cl, Wdf Grn	63	U14
Coopersale Rd E9	95	P9
Coote Gdns, Dag	101	L5
Coote Rd, Bexh	155	L1
Coote Rd, Dag	101	M5
Cope Pl W8	126	G6
Cope St SE16	131	N7
Copeland Dr E14	132	B7
Copeland Rd E17	78	B15
Copeland Rd SE15	148	J4
Copeman Cl SE26	167	L10
Copenhagen Gdns W4	124	F4
Copenhagen Pl E14	113	T12
Copenhagen St N1	111	K2
Copers Cope Rd, Beck	167	U12
Copford Cl, Wdf Grn	64	C12
Copgate Path SW16	165	P12
Copland Av, Wem	87	N10
Copland Cl, Wem	87	M9
Copland Ms, Wem 2	87	R11
Copland Rd, Wem	87	R11
Copleston Ms SE15	148	E4
Copleston Pas SE15	148	E5
Copleston Rd SE15	148	E5
Copley Cl, SE17 3	35	T11
Copley Cl W7	104	E8
Copley Dene, Brom	188	A2
Copley Pk SW16	165	L12
Copley Rd, Stan	53	M9
Coppard Gdns, Chess	191	M12
Copped Hall SE21	166	B3
Coppelia Rd, SE3 6	151	L7
Coppen Rd, Dag	83	L14
Copper Beech Cl, NW3 6	91	N11
Copper Beech Cl, Ilf	80	G1
Copper Beech Ct, Loug 1	48	G2
Copper Beeches, Islw	140	B2
Copper Cl SE19	166	F14
Copper Mead Cl NW2	89	T5
Copper Mill Dr, Islw	140	E4
Copper Mill La SW17	163	L8
Copper Row SE1	29	M4
Copperas St SE8	132	C12
Copperbeech Cl, NW3 13	91	N10
Copperdale Rd, Hayes 1	120	B4
Copperfield, Chig	65	M10
Copperfield App, Chig	65	N12
Copperfield Ct, Pnr	67	M7
Copperfield Dr N15	76	F7
Copperfield Ms N18	60	D8
Copperfield Rd E3	113	S8
Copperfield Rd SE28	118	F11
Copperfield St SE1	27	S5
Copperfield Way, Chis	171	M11
Copperfield Way, Pnr	67	M7
Coppergate Cl, Brom	187	R1
Coppermill La E17	77	M11
Coppetts Cl N12	57	S13
Coppetts Rd N10	73	U1
Coppice, The, Enf	43	R7
Coppice Cl SW20	179	T6
Coppice Cl, Stan	52	E12
Coppice Dr SW15	143	R12
Coppice Wk N20	56	G5
Coppice Way E18	79	M6
Coppies Gro N11	58	B8
Copping Cl, Croy 2	198	D7
Coppins, The, Croy	200	D12
Coppins, The, Har	52	D12
Coppock Cl SW11	145	R4
Coppsfield, W Mol 3	175	P5
Copse, The E4	63	L2
Copse Av, W Wick	200	C6
Copse Cl SE7	133	S12
Copse Glade, Surb	191	P1
Copse Hill SW20	161	T13
Copse Hill, Sutt	195	K13
Copsewood Cl, Sid	153	R11
Coptefield Dr, Belv	136	H6
Copthall Av EC2	20	E6
Copthall Dr NW7	55	N13
Copthall Gdns NW7	55	P13
Copthall Gdns, Twick	158	F1
Copthorne Av SW12	146	G14
Copthorne Av, Brom	202	E3
Copthorne Av, Ilf	65	K12
Coptic St WC1	18	A4
Copwood Cl N12	57	P8
Coral Cl, Rom	82	F7
Coral Row, SW11 2	145	M6
Coral St SE1	27	L7
Coraline Cl, Sthl	103	M6
Coralline Wk SE2	136	F4
Coram St WC1	10	A11
Coran Cl N9	45	N13
Corban Rd, Houns	139	P6
Corbar Cl, Barn	41	P1
Corbet Cl, Wall	196	A2
Corbet Ct, EC3 15	20	F8
Corbet Pl E1	21	M1
Corbett Gro N22	58	J14
Corbett Rd E11	79	T11
Corbett Rd E17	78	F5
Corbetts La SE16	131	L8
Corbetts Pas SE16	131	L8
Corbicum E11	79	K13
Corbiere Ct, SW19 1	162	B12
Corbins La, Har	85	S6
Corbridge Cres E2	112	J3
Corby Cres, Enf	43	K7
Corby Rd NW10	106	G4
Corby Way E3	114	A8
Corbylands Rd, Sid	153	S14
Corbyn St N4	93	K2
Cordelia Cl SE24	147	S7
Cordelia St E14	114	C11
Cording St E14	114	D10
Cordova Rd E3	113	R5
Cordwainers Wk E13	115	N4
Cordwell Rd SE13	150	J9
Corelli Rd SE3	152	C2
Corfe Av, Har	85	N7
Corfe Cl, Hayes	102	E11
Corfield Rd N21	43	L9
Corfield St E2	113	K6
Corfton Rd W5	105	R11
Coriander Av E14	114	G12
Cories Cl, Dag	100	H3
Corinium Cl, Wem 4	87	T8
Corinne Rd N19	92	F7
Cork Sq E1	130	J1
Cork St W1	17	L11
Cork St Ms W1	17	L11
Cork Tree Way E4	61	S9
Corker Wk N7	93	M4
Corkran Rd, Surb	177	P14
Corkscrew Hill, W Wick	200	H5
Corlett St NW1	15	N2
Cormont Rd SE5	147	R2
Cormorant Cl E17	61	P14
Cormorant Rd E7	97	M9
Corn Mill Dr, Orp	189	U14
Corn Way E11	96	H6
Cornbury Rd, Edg	53	P13
Cornelia St N7	93	M12
Cornell Cl, Sid	173	K11
Corner Grn SE3	151	N4
Corner Ho St, WC2 2	26	B1
Corner Mead NW9	71	M1
Corney Reach Way W4	125	K13
Corney Rd W4	125	K12
Cornflower La, Croy	199	P1
Cornflower Ter SE22	148	J11
Cornford Cl, Brom	187	N10
Cornford Gro SW12	164	D3
Cornhill EC3	20	F8
Cornish Ct N9	44	J14
Cornish Gro SE20	185	K1
Cornmill La SE13	150	D6
Cornmow Dr NW10	89	M9
Cornshaw Rd, Dag	100	H1
Cornthwaite Rd E5	95	L6
Cornwall Av E2	113	L6
Cornwall Av N3	56	H14
Cornwall Av N22	75	K2
Cornwall Av, Sthl	103	M10
Cornwall Av, Well	153	S6
Cornwall Cl, Bark	99	U12
Cornwall Cres W11	108	C12
Cornwall Dr, Orp	172	E14
Cornwall Gdns NW10	89	S12
Cornwall Gdns SW7	22	E11
Cornwall Gdns Wk SW7	22	C11
Cornwall Gro W4	125	K10
Cornwall Ms S SW7	22	E12
Cornwall Ms W, SW7 7	22	C11
Cornwall Rd N4	75	N14
Cornwall Rd N15	76	A10
Cornwall Rd, N18 6	60	H9
Cornwall Rd SE1	27	L5
Cornwall Rd, Croy 1	197	R4
Cornwall Rd, Esher	190	G13
Cornwall Rd, Har	67	T11
Cornwall Rd, Pnr	51	M14
Cornwall Rd, Twick	140	H14
Cornwall St, E1 7	113	K13
Cornwall Ter, NW1 1	8	B11
Cornwall Ter Ms NW1	8	B11
Cornwallis Av N9	61	K3

Name	Page	Grid
Cornwallis Av SE9	171	N4
Cornwallis Gro N9	61	K3
Cornwallis Rd E17	77	P8
Cornwallis Rd N9	61	K3
Cornwallis Rd N19	92	J3
Cornwallis Rd, Dag	100	J8
Cornwallis Sq N19	92	J3
Cornwallis Wk SE9	152	F5
Cornwood Cl N2	73	N9
Cornwood Dr E1	113	L11
Cornworthy Rd, Dag	100	E10
Corona Rd SE12	151	P14
Coronation Av, N16 *2*	94	E7
Coronation Cl, Bex	154	G11
Coronation Cl, Ilf	81	M8
Coronation Rd E13	115	U6
Coronation Rd NW10	106	B7
Coronation Wk, Twick	157	N1
Coronet St N1	12	G7
Corporation Av, Houns	138	J7
Corporation Row EC1	11	M9
Corporation St E15	115	L4
Corporation St N7	92	J10
Corrance Rd SW2	147	K7
Corri Av N14	58	H7
Corrib Dr, Sutt	195	R9
Corringham Ct NW11	72	H14
Corringham Rd NW11	72	G13
Corringham Rd, Wem	88	A3
Corringway NW11	72	J14
Corringway W5	106	A8
Corscombe Cl, Kings T	160	E10
Corsehill St SW16	164	E11
Corsham St N1	12	E7
Corsica St N5	93	R11
Cortayne Rd SW6	144	F3
Cortis Rd SW15	143	T11
Cortis Ter SW15	143	S11
Corunna Rd SW8	146	F1
Corunna Ter SW8	146	E1
Corvette Sq, SE10 *5*	132	H11
Cosbycote Av SE24	147	T9
Cosdach Av, Wall	196	G13
Cosedge Cres, Croy	197	P9
Cosgrove Cl N21	59	T4
Cosgrove Cl, Hayes *2*	102	H7
Cosmo Pl, WC1 *7*	18	C1
Cosmur Cl W12	125	M5
Cossall Wk SE15	149	K2
Cosser St SE1	26	J10
Costa St SE15	148	G4
Costons Av, Grnf	104	A6
Costons La, Grnf	104	A7
Cosway St NW1	15	R1
Cotall St E14	114	B11
Coteford Cl, Loug	48	J3
Coteford Cl, Pnr	66	A10
Coteford St SW17	163	U7
Cotelands, Croy	198	C5
Cotesbach Rd E5	95	L6
Cotesmore Gdns, Dag	100	E8
Cotford Rd, Th Hth	183	U7
Cotham St SE17	36	B4
Cotherstone Rd SW2	165	L1
Cotleigh Av, Bex	172	H3
Cotleigh Rd NW6	90	G13
Cotman Cl NW11	73	L11
Cotman Cl, SW15 *1*	144	A11
Cotman Gdns, Edg	70	A3
Cotmans Cl, Hayes	120	B1
Coton Rd, Well	154	C5
Cotsford Av, N Mal	178	F10
Cotswold Av, Esher	190	E5
Cotswold Cl, Kings T	160	E12
Cotswold Ct N11	58	A8
Cotswold Gdns E6	116	B5
Cotswold Gdns NW2	90	B3
Cotswold Gdns, Ilf	81	P13
Cotswold Gate NW2	90	C2
Cotswold Ms SW11	145	P2
Cotswold Ri, Orp	189	T12
Cotswold Rd, Hmptn	157	N11
Cotswold St, SE27 *7*	165	S7
Cotswold Way, Enf	43	L6
Cotswold Way, Wor Pk	193	U3
Cottage Av, Brom	202	D1
Cottage Fld Cl, Sid	172	F2
Cottage Grn SE5	36	G14
Cottage Gro SW9	146	J6
Cottage Gro, Surb	177	N12
Cottage Homes NW7	55	P8
Cottage Pl SW3	23	P10
Cottage Rd, Epsom	192	H13
Cottage St E14	114	D13
Cottenham Dr NW9	71	L5
Cottenham Dr SW20	161	S13
Cottenham Pk Rd SW20	161	T14
Cottenham Pl SW20	161	S13
Cottenham Rd E17	77	U7
Cotterill Rd, Surb	191	T2
Cottesbrook St, SE14 *6*	131	R13
Cottesloe Ms, SE1 *1*	27	L9
Cottesmore Av, Ilf	80	G4
Cottesmore Gdns W8	22	D10
Cottimore Cres, Walt	174	D14
Cottimore Ter, Walt	174	C14
Cottingham Chase, Ruis	84	B6
Cottingham Rd SE20	167	N14
Cottingham Rd SW8	34	G13
Cottington Rd, Felt	156	H7
Cottington St, SE11 *1*	35	N5
Cotton Av W3	106	H11
Cotton Hill, Brom	168	G7
Cotton Row SW11	145	N5
Cotton St E14	114	E13
Cottongrass Cl, Croy *7*	199	N1
Cottons Gdns E2	13	K6
Cottons La SE1	28	F2
Cotts Cl W7	104	F11
Couchmore Av, Esher	190	C4
Couchmore Av, Ilf	80	E4
Coulgate St SE4	149	S6
Coulson Cl, Dag	82	F14
Coulson St SW3	31	U5
Coulter Cl, Hayes	102	J7
Coulter Rd W6	125	S6
Councillor St SE5	129	T14
Counter Ct, SE1 *3*	28	C4
Counter St SE1	28	G3
Countess Rd NW5	92	E9
Countisbury Av, Enf	44	E13
Country Way, Felt	156	G8
Country Way, Sun	156	C13
County Gate SE9	171	M5
County Gate, Barn	41	K12
County Gro SE5	147	T1
County Rd E6	116	J10
County Rd, Th Hth	183	R4
County St SE1	28	B12
Coupland Pl SE18	135	L10
Courcy Rd N8	75	N5
Courier Rd, Dag	119	T7
Courland Gro SW8	146	H3
Courland St SW8	146	H2
Course, The SE9	170	H6
Court, The, Ruis	84	J8
Court Av, Belv	137	L9
Court Cl, Har	69	R6
Court Cl, Twick	157	R5
Court Cl, Wall	196	G14
Court Cres, Chess	191	N10
Court Downs Rd, Beck	186	C3
Court Dr, Croy	197	M7
Court Dr, Stan	53	R8
Court Dr, Sutt	195	R8
Court Fm Av, Epsom	192	H10
Court Fm Rd SE9	170	B4
Court Fm Rd, Nthlt	85	N14
Court Gdns N7	93	P12
Court Ho Gdns N3	56	H12
Court La SE21	148	C12
Court La Gdns SE21	148	D13
Court Mead, Nthlt	103	M5
Court Par, Wem	86	J6
Court Rd SE9	170	D3
Court Rd SE25	184	F4
Court Rd, Sthl	121	L8
Court St E1	112	J9
Court St, Brom	187	P3
Court Way NW9	71	K7
Court Way W3	106	E9
Court Way, Ilf	81	M6
Court Way, Twick	140	E13
Court Yd SE9	152	E12
Courtauld Cl SE28	136	A2
Courtauld Rd N19	92	H2
Courtenay Av N6	73	R13
Courtenay Av, Har	67	U3
Courtenay Dr, Beck	186	G4
Courtenay Gdns, Har	67	U3
Courtenay Ms, E17 *1*	77	S9
Courtenay Pl E17	77	S9
Courtenay Rd E11	97	L5
Courtenay Rd E17	77	P8
Courtenay Rd SE20	167	P12
Courtenay Rd, Wem	87	P5
Courtenay Rd, Wor Pk	193	U5
Courtenay Sq, SE11 *2*	34	J7
Courtenay St SE11	34	J6
Courtens Ms, Stan	53	L13
Courtfield W5	105	L10
Courtfield Av, Har	68	F10
Courtfield Cres, Har	68	F10
Courtfield Gdns SW5	30	C2
Courtfield Gdns W13	104	H12
Courtfield Ms, SW5 *3*	30	E3
Courtfield Ri, W Wick	200	H5
Courtfield Rd SW7	30	E2
Courthill Rd SE13	150	D8
Courthope Rd NW3	91	U8
Courthope Rd SW19	162	C10
Courthope Vil SW19	162	D13
Courthouse Rd N12	56	J11
Courtland Av E4	63	J3
Courtland Av NW7	54	H5
Courtland Av SW16	165	M14
Courtland Av, Ilf	98	F3
Courtland Dr, Chig	65	L5
Courtland Gro SE28	118	H13
Courtland Rd E6	116	C1
Courtlands, Rich	142	A8
Courtlands Av SE12	151	R9
Courtlands Av, Brom	201	L1
Courtlands Av, Hmptn	157	L12
Courtlands Av, Rich	142	C2
Courtlands Dr, Epsom	193	K12
Courtlands Rd, Surb	178	A13
Courtleet Dr, Erith	155	S2
Courtleigh Gdns NW11	72	C8
Courtman Rd N17	59	U14
Courtmead Cl SE24	147	U11
Courtnell St W2	108	G12
Courtney Cl SE19	166	C12
Courtney Cres, Cars	195	T14
Courtney Pl, Croy	197	P5
Courtney Rd N7	93	N9
Courtney Rd SW19	163	R14
Courtney Rd, Croy	197	P5
Courtrai Rd SE23	149	R11
Courtside N8	74	G12
Courtway, Wdf Grn	63	T9
Courtway, The, Wat	51	K3
Courtyard, The N1	93	M13
Cousin La EC4	20	C11
Couthurst Rd SE3	133	S13
Coutts Av, Chess	191	S9
Coutts Cres NW5	92	B5
Coval Gdns SW14	142	D8
Coval La SW14	142	D8
Coval Rd SW14	142	E8
Covelees Wall E6	116	H11
Covent Gdn WC2	18	D9
Coventry Cl E6	116	E12
Coventry Cl NW6	108	H3
Coventry Rd E2	113	K7
Coventry Rd SE25	184	H7
Coventry Rd, Ilf	98	H3
Coventry St W1	17	S11
Coverack Cl N14	42	E12
Coverack Cl, Croy	185	S14
Coverdale Cl, Stan	53	K9
Coverdale Gdns, Croy *7*	198	E5
Coverdale Rd N11	58	A11
Coverdale Rd NW2	90	B13
Coverdale Rd W12	125	S2
Coverdales, The, Bark	117	N3
Coverley Cl E1	21	T1
Covert, The, Orp	189	S12
Covert Rd, Ilt	65	T11
Covert Way, Barn	41	M3
Coverton Rd SW17	163	R9
Coverts Rd, Esher	190	F14
Covet Wd Cl, Orp	189	T11
Covey Cl SW19	180	J3
Covington Gdns SW16	165	S14
Covington Way SW16	165	P13
Cow La, Grnf	104	A4
Cow Leaze E6	116	H11
Cowan Cl E6	116	D10
Cowbridge La, Bark	98	J13
Cowbridge Rd, Har	69	U8
Cowcross St EC1	19	N2
Cowden Rd, Orp	189	T13
Cowden St SE6	168	A7
Cowdenbeath Path N1	11	L1
Cowdrey Cl, Enf	44	C3
Cowen Av, Har	86	A4
Cowgate Rd, Grnf	104	B6
Cowick Rd SW17	163	T7
Cowings Mead, Nthlt	85	K12
Cowland Av, Enf	45	M7
Cowleaze Rd, Kings T	177	S2
Cowley Hill, Borwd	38	D1
Cowley La, E11 *6*	96	J5
Cowley Pl NW4	71	U9
Cowley Rd E11	79	R9
Cowley Rd SW9	147	P1
Cowley Rd SW14	142	J5
Cowley Rd W3	125	L2
Cowley Rd, Ilf	80	F14
Cowley St SW1	26	A10
Cowling Cl W11	108	C14
Cowper Av E6	98	C13
Cowper Av, Sutt	195	P8
Cowper Cl, Brom	188	B8
Cowper Cl, Well	154	B9
Cowper Gdns N14	42	E12
Cowper Gdns, Wall	196	F12
Cowper Rd N14	58	D2
Cowper Rd N16	94	C9
Cowper Rd N18	60	G10
Cowper Rd SW19	163	K1
Cowper Rd W3	124	G1
Cowper Rd W7	104	E13
Cowper Rd, Belv	137	N8
Cowper Rd, Brom	188	A8
Cowper Rd, Kings T	159	T9
Cowper St EC2	12	E9
Cowper Ter W10	108	A10
Cowslip Rd E18	79	R5
Cowthorpe Rd, SW8 *1*	146	H1
Cox La, Chess	192	A8

Cox La, Epsom 192 E9
Coxe Pl, Har 68 G7
Coxmount Rd SE7 134 A9
Cox's Wk SE21 166 H3
Coxson Pl, SE1 *4* 29 M7
Coxwell Rd SE18 135 P9
Coxwell Rd SE19 166 D13
Crab Hill, Beck 168 G14
Crabbs Cft Cl, Orp *4* 203 L9
Crabtree Av, Rom 82 H7
Crabtree Av, Wem 105 S3
Crabtree Cl E2 13 M3
Crabtree La SW6 126 A13
Crabtree Manorway N, Belv 137 T4
Crabtree Manorway S, Belv 137 T6
Craddock Rd, Enf 44 E6
Craddock St NW5 92 A12
Cradley Rd SE9 171 N1
Craig Gdns E18 79 M3
Craig Pk Rd N18 60 J9
Craig Rd, Rich 159 M7
Craigen Av, Croy 199 K2
Craigerne Rd SE3 133 R12
Craigholm SE18 152 H3
Craigmuir Pk, Wem 105 U1
Craignair Rd SW2 147 N13
Craignish Av SW16 183 M3
Craigs Ct SW1 26 A2
Craigton Rd SE9 152 E8
Craigweil Cl, Stan 53 N10
Craigweil Dr, Stan 53 N9
Craigwell Av, Felt 156 A6
Crail Row SE17 36 E3
Cramer St W1 16 E3
Cramond Cl, W6 *3* 126 C11
Crampton Rd SE20 167 L12
Crampton St SE17 35 T4
Cranberry Cl, Nthlt *2* 102 H3
Cranberry La E16 114 J7
Cranborne Av, Sthl 121 P8
Cranborne Av, Surb 192 B5
Cranborne Rd, Bark 117 N1
Cranborne Waye, Hayes 102 E13
Cranbourn All, WC2 *7* 17 U10
Cranbourn Pas, SE16 *2* 130 J4
Cranbourn St WC2 17 U10
Cranbourne Av E11 79 R7
Cranbourne Cl SW16 183 K6
Cranbourne Dr, Pnr 66 G9
Cranbourne Gdns NW11 72 D9
Cranbourne Gdns, Ilf 81 M5
Cranbourne Rd, E12 *1* 98 C9
Cranbourne Rd E15 96 F8
Cranbourne Rd N10 74 D4
Cranbrook Cl, Brom 187 N12
Cranbrook Dr, Twick 139 R14
Cranbrook Ms E17 77 T9
Cranbrook Pk N22 75 N2
Cranbrook Ri, Ilf 80 F12
Cranbrook Rd SE8 150 B2
Cranbrook Rd SW19 162 D13
Cranbrook Rd W4 125 K9
Cranbrook Rd, Barn 41 P11
Cranbrook Rd, Bexh 155 M1
Cranbrook Rd, Houns 139 L7
Cranbrook Rd, Ilf 98 H2
Cranbrook Rd, Th Hth 183 U3
Cranbrook St E2 113 P4
Cranbury Rd SW6 145 K4
Crane Av W3 106 F13
Crane Av, Islw 140 H9
Crane Cl, Dag 101 P12
Crane Cl, Har 85 T5
Crane Ct, Epsom 192 E8
Crane Gro N7 93 P12

Crane Lo Rd, Houns 120 D12
Crane Mead SE16 131 N8
Crane Pk Rd, Twick 157 R3
Crane Rd, Twick 158 D1
Crane St SE10 132 G10
Crane St SE15 148 E1
Crane Way, Twick 139 U13
Cranebrook, Twick 157 U3
Craneford Cl, Twick 140 F14
Craneford Way, Twick 140 D14
Cranes Dr, Surb 177 S8
Cranes Pk, Surb 177 S8
Cranes Pk Av, Surb 177 S8
Cranes Pk Cres, Surb 177 T8
Cranes Way, Borwd 38 F9
Craneswater Pk, Sthl 121 M9
Cranfield Dr NW9 54 J14
Cranfield Rd SE4 149 T5
Cranfield Row, SE1 *3* 27 M9
Cranford Av N13 59 K9
Cranford Cl SW20 179 R1
Cranford La (Heston), Houns 120 J13
Cranford St E1 113 P13
Cranford Way N8 75 M9
Cranhurst Rd NW2 89 U10
Cranleigh Cl SE20 184 J3
Cranleigh Cl, Bex 155 R10
Cranleigh Gdns N21 43 P10
Cranleigh Gdns SE25 184 D5
Cranleigh Gdns, Bark 99 N13
Cranleigh Gdns, Har 69 R10
Cranleigh Gdns, Kings T 159 U11
Cranleigh Gdns, Loug 48 F12
Cranleigh Gdns, Sthl 103 L11
Cranleigh Gdns, Sutt 194 J4
Cranleigh Gdns Ind Est, Sthl 103 L10
Cranleigh Ms SW11 145 S4
Cranleigh Rd N15 75 T9
Cranleigh Rd SW19 180 G5
Cranleigh St NW1 9 P3
Cranley Dene Ct N10 74 C8
Cranley Dr, Ilf 81 L13
Cranley Gdns N10 74 C8
Cranley Gdns N13 59 M5
Cranley Gdns SW7 30 J6
Cranley Ms SW7 30 H5
Cranley Pl SW7 31 K4
Cranley Rd E13 115 R9
Cranley Rd, Ilf 81 L12
Cranmer Av W13 123 K6
Cranmer Cl, Mord 180 B12
Cranmer Cl, Ruis 84 G2
Cranmer Cl, Stan 53 M13
Cranmer Ct SW3 31 S4
Cranmer Ct, SW4 *4* 146 H6
Cranmer Ct, Hmptn 157 R9
Cranmer Fm Cl, Mitch 181 U8
Cranmer Gdns, Dag 101 T8
Cranmer Rd E7 97 S7
Cranmer Rd SW9 35 L14
Cranmer Rd, Croy 197 S5
Cranmer Rd, Edg 54 D6
Cranmer Rd, Hmptn 157 S9
Cranmer Rd, Kings T 159 R10
Cranmer Rd, Mitch 181 U8
Cranmer Ter SW17 163 P9
Cranmore Av, Islw 121 U13
Cranmore Rd, Brom 169 K6
Cranmore Rd, Chis 170 F9
Cranmore Way N10 74 E8
Cranston Cl, Houns 139 K4
Cranston Est N1 12 E3
Cranston Gdns E4 62 C10
Cranston Rd SE23 167 R3

Cranswick Rd, SE16 *14* 131 K10
Crantock Rd SE6 168 E4
Cranwell Cl E3 114 C8
Cranwich Av N21 44 A13
Cranwich Rd N16 76 C13
Cranwood St EC1 12 E8
Cranworth Cres E4 62 G2
Cranworth Gdns SW9 147 N1
Craster Rd SW2 147 M13
Crathie Rd SE12 151 S11
Cravan Av, Felt 156 A4
Craven Av W5 105 L14
Craven Av, Sthl 103 L10
Craven Cl, Hayes 102 B12
Craven Gdns SW19 162 H10
Craven Gdns, Bark 117 R4
Craven Gdns, Ilf 81 N4
Craven Hill W2 14 G9
Craven Hill Gdns W2 14 F10
Craven Hill Ms W2 14 G9
Craven Pk NW10 88 J14
Craven Pk Ms NW10 88 J14
Craven Pk Rd N15 76 F12
Craven Pk Rd NW10 107 K1
Craven Pas, WC2 *1* 26 B2
Craven Rd NW10 106 H1
Craven Rd W2 14 J8
Craven Rd W5 105 M14
Craven Rd, Croy 198 J1
Craven Rd, Kings T 177 U1
Craven St WC2 26 B1
Craven Ter W2 14 H9
Craven Wk N16 76 G13
Crawford Av, Wem 87 N10
Crawford Cl, Islw 140 D3
Crawford Est SE5 147 U3
Crawford Gdns N13 59 R5
Crawford Gdns, Nthlt 103 M5
Crawford Ms W1 15 U3
Crawford Pas EC1 11 K11
Crawford Pl W1 15 R5
Crawford Rd SE5 147 U2
Crawford St W1 16 B3
Crawley Rd E10 96 D2
Crawley Rd N22 75 T4
Crawley Rd, Enf 44 D14
Crawthew Gro SE22 148 F8
Cray Rd, Belv 137 N12
Cray Rd, Sid 172 E12
Craybrooke Rd, Sid 172 C8
Craybury End SE9 171 L4
Crayford Cl E6 116 C10
Crayford Rd N7 92 H7
Crayke Hill, Chess 191 R13
Crealock Gro, Wdf Grn 63 L10
Crealock St SW18 145 K12
Creasy Est SE1 28 H12
Crebor St SE22 148 H11
Credenhall Dr, Brom 202 E2
Credenhill St SW16 164 E12
Crediton Hill NW6 90 J10
Crediton Rd E16 115 N11
Crediton Rd NW10 108 A2
Crediton Way, Esher 190 G10
Credon Rd E13 115 T3
Credon Rd SE16 131 K9
Creechurch La EC3 20 J7
Creechurch Pl, EC3 *4* 21 K7
Creed La EC4 19 R8
Creek, The, Sun 174 A9
Creek Rd SE8 131 U11
Creek Rd SE10 132 D12
Creek Rd, Bark 117 T6
Creek Rd, E Mol 176 C7
Creekside SE8 132 C13
Creeland Gro, SE6 *3* 167 U2
Crefeld Cl W6 126 B12
Creffield Rd W3 106 A14
Creffield Rd W5 106 A14
Creighton Av E6 116 A3
Creighton Av N2 73 R5

Creighton Av N10 74 B4
Creighton Rd N17 60 D13
Creighton Rd NW6 108 B3
Creighton Rd W5 123 N5
Cremer St E2 13 L4
Cremorne Est SW10 31 K13
Cremorne Rd SW10 127 M14
Crescent EC3 21 L10
Crescent, The E17 77 S10
Crescent, The N11 58 A8
Crescent, The NW2 89 S5
Crescent, The SW13 143 M3
Crescent, The SW19 162 H6
Crescent, The W3 106 J12
Crescent, The, Barn 40 J4
Crescent, The, Beck 186 B2
Crescent, The, Bex 154 F13
Crescent, The, Croy 184 B11
Crescent, The, Har 85 U2
Crescent, The, Ilf 80 G12
Crescent, The, Loug 48 B11
Crescent, The, N Mal 178 F4
Crescent, The, Sid 171 U7
Crescent, The, Sthl 121 L3
Crescent, The, Surb 177 R10
Crescent, The, Sutt 195 N9
Crescent, The, Wem 86 J4
Crescent, The, W Mol 175 N7
Crescent, The, W Wick 186 J12
Crescent Ct, Surb 177 P10
Crescent Dr, Orp 189 K11
Crescent Gdns SW19 162 H6
Crescent Gdns, Ruis 66 D13
Crescent Gro SW4 146 G8
Crescent Gro, Mitch 181 R8
Crescent La SW4 146 H10
Crescent Ms N22 74 J2
Crescent Pl SW3 31 R1
Crescent Ri N22 74 G1
Crescent Ri, Barn 41 R9
Crescent Rd E4 47 K14
Crescent Rd E6 115 U1
Crescent Rd E10 96 C3
Crescent Rd E13 115 P1
Crescent Rd E18 79 T2
Crescent Rd N3 72 F1
Crescent Rd N8 74 H13
Crescent Rd N9 60 H1
Crescent Rd N11 57 U8
Crescent Rd N15 75 R6
Crescent Rd N22 74 H1
Crescent Rd SE18 135 K9
Crescent Rd SW20 180 A1
Crescent Rd, Barn 41 R10
Crescent Rd, Beck 186 D4
Crescent Rd, Brom 169 P14
Crescent Rd, Dag 101 R7
Crescent Rd, Enf 43 S7
Crescent Rd, Kings T 160 B13
Crescent Rd, Sid 171 U5
Crescent Row EC1 11 T11
Crescent Stables SW15 144 B9
Crescent St N1 93 M13
Crescent Vw, Loug 48 B10
Crescent Way SE4 150 A6
Crescent Way N12 57 R12
Crescent Way SW16 165 M12
Crescent Way, Orp *5* 203 S9
Crescent Wd Rd SE26 166 G6
Cresford Rd SW6 144 J2
Crespigny Rd NW4 71 S11
Cressage Cl, Sthl 103 N7
Cresset Rd E9 95 M12
Cresset St SW4 146 G6
Cressfield Cl NW5 92 B9
Cressida Rd N19 92 F1
Cressingham Gro, Sutt 195 L7
Cressingham Rd SE13 150 F5
Cressingham Rd, Edg 54 G12

Name	No.	Grid
Cressington Cl N16	94	D9
Cresswell Gdns SW5	30	F5
Cresswell Pk SE3	151	L5
Cresswell Pl SW10	30	G6
Cresswell Rd SE25	184	H7
Cresswell Rd, Felt	156	J7
Cresswell Rd, Twick	141	N11
Cresswell Way N21	43	P13
Cressy Cl, E1 3	113	M9
Cressy Ct W6	125	R5
Cressy Pl E1	113	M9
Cressy Rd NW3	91	T8
Crest, The N13	59	N7
Crest, The NW4	71	U9
Crest, The, Surb	178	B10
Crest Gdns, Ruis	84	F5
Crest Rd NW2	89	N4
Crest Rd, Brom	187	L14
Crest Rd, S Croy	198	J13
Crest Vw, Pnr	66	G8
Crest Vw Dr, Orp	189	K10
Crestbrook Av N13	59	R5
Crestbrook Pl N13	59	R5
Crestfield St WC1	10	C5
Creston Way, Wor Pk	194	B2
Crestway SW15	143	R11
Crestwood Way, Houns	139	L9
Creswick Rd W3	106	C13
Creswick Wk NW11	72	F8
Creton St SE18	134	H6
Crewdson Rd SW9	129	N14
Crewe Pl NW10	107	L5
Crews St E14	132	A7
Crewys Rd NW2	90	F4
Crewys Rd SE15	149	K4
Crichton Av, Wall	196	G9
Crichton Rd, Cars	195	T12
Cricket Grn, Mitch	181	T7
Cricket Grd Rd, Chis	188	J2
Cricket La, Beck	167	S11
Cricketers Arms Rd, Enf	43	U4
Cricketers Cl N14	42	E13
Cricketers Cl, Chess	191	N8
Cricketers Ct, SE11 3	35	P4
Cricketfield Rd E5	95	K8
Cricklade Av SW2	165	L3
Cricklewood Bdy NW2	90	B8
Cricklewood La NW2	90	B7
Cridland St E15	115	L1
Crieff Ct, Tedd	159	L14
Crieff Rd SW18	145	M11
Criffel Av SW2	164	H3
Crimscott St SE1	29	K12
Crimsworth Rd SW8	146	H1
Crinan St N1	10	D1
Cringle St SW8	33	M13
Cripplegate St, EC2 3	19	U1
Crisp Rd W6	125	T10
Crispen Rd, Felt	156	J7
Crispian Cl NW10	89	K8
Crispin Cl, Croy 1	196	J4
Crispin Cres, Croy	196	H4
Crispin Rd, Edg	54	F12
Crispin St E1	21	L3
Cristowe Rd SW6	144	F4
Criterion Ms N19	92	G3
Crockerton Rd SW17	163	T4
Crockham Way SE9	170	H8
Crocus Cl, Croy 8	199	P1
Crocus Fld, Barn	40	F11
Croft, The E4	62	J3
Croft, The NW10	107	L3
Croft, The W5	105	R10
Croft, The, Barn	40	C7
Croft, The, Houns	121	K12
Croft, The, Loug	48	H3
Croft, The, Ruis	84	E7
Croft, The, Wem	87	L9
Croft Av, W Wick	200	F2
Croft Cl NW7	54	J6
Croft Cl, Belv	137	L10
Croft Cl, Chis	170	E8
Croft End Cl, Chess	191	T6
Croft Gdns W7	122	G3
Croft Lo Cl, Wdf Grn	63	S11
Croft Ms N12	57	L6
Croft Rd SW16	183	P1
Croft Rd SW19	163	L14
Croft Rd, Brom	169	P12
Croft Rd, Enf	45	R2
Croft Rd, Sutt	195	R9
Croft St SE8	131	R8
Croft Way, Sid	171	R5
Croftdown Rd NW5	92	C6
Crofters Cl, Islw	140	B10
Crofters Way NW1	110	G1
Crofton Av W4	124	G13
Crofton Av, Bex	154	G14
Crofton Av, Orp	203	M4
Crofton Gro E4	62	G8
Crofton La, Orp	203	N2
Crofton Pk Rd SE4	149	T12
Crofton Rd E13	115	R7
Crofton Rd SE5	148	D2
Crofton Rd, Orp	203	R3
Crofton Ter, Rich	141	T7
Crofton Way, Barn	40	J11
Crofton Way, Enf	43	N3
Croftongate Way SE4	149	S9
Crofts Rd, Har	68	G10
Crofts St E1	21	R11
Croftside, SE25 2	184	H6
Croftway NW3	90	H7
Croftway, Rich	159	R6
Crogsland Rd NW1	92	A13
Croham Cl, S Croy	198	C13
Croham Manor Rd, S Croy	198	D13
Croham Mt, S Croy	198	C13
Croham Pk Av, S Croy	198	E10
Croham Rd, S Croy	198	A9
Croham Valley Rd, S Croy	198	F11
Croindene Rd SW16	183	K2
Cromartie Rd N19	74	H14
Cromarty Rd, Edg	54	D4
Crombie Cl, Ilf	80	E10
Crombie Rd, Sid	171	P1
Cromer Pl, Orp 2	203	P1
Cromer Rd E10	78	G12
Cromer Rd N17	76	G3
Cromer Rd SE25	184	D6
Cromer Rd SW17	164	A12
Cromer Rd, Barn	41	L7
Cromer Rd, Rom	83	U11
Cromer Rd (Chadwell Heath), Rom	83	K11
Cromer Rd, Wdf Grn	63	P8
Cromer St WC1	10	D7
Cromer Vil Rd SW18	144	E12
Cromford Cl, Orp	203	S6
Cromford Rd SW18	144	G9
Cromford Way, N Mal	178	H2
Cromlix Cl, Chis	188	J2
Crompton St W2	6	J12
Cromwell Av N6	92	D1
Cromwell Av W6	125	R9
Cromwell Av, Brom	187	R7
Cromwell Av, N Mal	179	L9
Cromwell Cl N2	73	N7
Cromwell Cl W3	124	F2
Cromwell Cl, Brom	187	R7
Cromwell Cres SW5	126	G7
Cromwell Gdns SW7	23	M12
Cromwell Gro W6	125	U5
Cromwell Ind Est E10	95	R1
Cromwell Ms SW7	31	L1
Cromwell Pl N6	92	D1
Cromwell Pl SW7	31	L1
Cromwell Pl SW14	142	F5
Cromwell Pl, W3 1	124	F1
Cromwell Rd E7	97	T13
Cromwell Rd E17	78	E10
Cromwell Rd N3	73	L2
Cromwell Rd N10	58	B13
Cromwell Rd SW5	30	B2
Cromwell Rd SW7	30	J1
Cromwell Rd SW9	147	R1
Cromwell Rd SW19	162	J10
Cromwell Rd, Beck	185	S4
Cromwell Rd, Croy	184	A13
Cromwell Rd, Felt	156	D1
Cromwell Rd, Houns	139	N8
Cromwell Rd, Kings T	177	S2
Cromwell Rd, Tedd	158	G12
Cromwell Rd, Wem	105	R3
Cromwell Rd, Wor Pk	192	H5
Cromwell St, Houns	139	P7
Crondace Rd SW6	144	H2
Crondall St N1	12	F4
Cronin St SE15	130	E14
Crook Log, Bexh	154	H7
Crooke Rd SE8	131	R9
Crooked Billet SW19	161	U12
Crooked Billet Roundabout E17	78	C1
Crooked Usage N3	72	C6
Crookham Rd SW6	144	E2
Crookston Rd SE9	152	H5
Croombe Rd F16	115	T10
Crooms Hill SE10	132	G13
Crooms Hill Gro SE10	132	F14
Cropley St N1	12	C1
Croppath Rd, Dag	101	P8
Cropthorne Ct W9	6	G8
Crosby Cl, Felt	156	J7
Crosby Ct SE1	28	D6
Crosby Rd E7	97	N11
Crosby Rd, Dag	119	R2
Crosby Row SE1	28	D7
Crosby Wk E8	94	E12
Crosby Wk SW2	147	P13
Crosland Pl, SW11 7	146	B6
Cross Av SE10	132	H12
Cross Cl SE15	148	J3
Cross Deep, Twick	158	G3
Cross Deep Gdns, Twick	158	F3
Cross Keys Cl, N9 1	60	H4
Cross Keys Cl W1	16	F4
Cross Keys Sq EC1	19	T4
Cross Lances Rd, Houns	139	R8
Cross La, EC3 2	20	H11
Cross La N8	75	L7
Cross La, Bex	155	M13
Cross Rd E4	62	J1
Cross Rd N11	58	D9
Cross Rd N22	59	P13
Cross Rd SE5	148	D3
Cross Rd SW19	162	H14
Cross Rd, Brom	202	C3
Cross Rd, Croy	198	B1
Cross Rd, Enf	44	D8
Cross Rd, Felt	156	J7
Cross Rd, Har	68	A8
Cross Rd (South Harrow), Har	85	R5
Cross Rd (Wealdstone), Har	68	H4
Cross Rd, Kings T	159	U14
Cross Rd, Rom	83	P7
Cross Rd (Chadwell Heath), Rom	82	E14
Cross Rd, Sid	172	C8
Cross Rd, Sutt	195	P9
Cross Rd, Wdf Grn	64	E11
Cross Rds, Loug	47	S3
Cross St N1	111	S1
Cross St SW13	143	L5
Cross St, Hmptn	157	U10
Cross Way, The, Har	68	D3
Crossbow Rd, Chig	65	U9
Crossbrook Rd SE3	152	C4
Crossfield Rd N17	75	T6
Crossfield Rd NW3	91	P12
Crossfield St SE8	132	A13
Crossfields, Loug	48	J9
Crossford St SW9	147	L4
Crossgate, Edg	54	A6
Crossgate, Grnf	87	K11
Crossland Rd, Th Hth	183	R12
Crosslands Av W5	123	T2
Crosslands Av, Sthl	121	M10
Crosslands Rd, Epsom	192	G12
Crosslet St SE17	36	F2
Crosslet Vale SE10	150	C1
Crossley St N7	93	N11
Crossmead SE9	170	E2
Crossmead Av, Grnf	103	P5
Crossness Rd, Bark	117	U6
Crossthwaite Av SE5	148	B8
Crosswall EC3	21	L9
Crossway N12	57	P12
Crossway N16	94	D10
Crossway NW9	71	M8
Crossway SE28	118	D13
Crossway SW20	179	T8
Crossway W13	104	G8
Crossway, Dag	100	E6
Crossway, Enf	44	C13
Crossway, Hayes	120	B2
Crossway, Orp	189	P8
Crossway, Pnr	66	D3
Crossway, Ruis	84	F7
Crossway, Wdf Grn	63	U8
Crossway, The N22	59	S14
Crossway, The SE9	170	B3
Crossways N21	43	T12
Crossways, S Croy	199	T13
Crossways, The, Houns	121	L14
Crossways, The, Wem	88	B3
Crossways Rd, Beck	186	A8
Crossways Rd, Mitch	182	D5
Croston St E8	112	H1
Crothall Cl N13	59	M5
Crouch Av, Bark	118	D4
Crouch Cl, Beck	168	B12
Crouch Cft SE9	170	H5
Crouch End Hill N8	74	H13
Crouch Hall Rd N8	74	H11
Crouch Hill N4	75	K14
Crouch Hill N8	75	K14
Crouch Rd NW10	88	G13
Crouchman's Cl SE26	166	F6
Crow La, Rom	83	M13
Crowborough Path, Wat	50	H6
Crowborough Rd SW17	164	B10
Crowden Way SE28	118	F14
Crowder St E1	112	J13
Crowfoot Cl, E9 4	95	U10
Crowhurst Cl SW9	147	P3
Crowland Gdns N14	42	J14
Crowland Rd N15	76	F10
Crowland Rd, Th Hth	184	A8
Crowland Ter N1	94	A13
Crowland Wk, Mord	181	K11
Crowlands Av, Rom	83	S11
Crowley Cres, Croy	197	P10
Crowmarsh Gdns SE23	149	M14
Crown Cl E3	114	A1
Crown Cl NW6	90	J11
Crown Cl NW7	55	M3
Crown Cl, Walt	174	E14
Crown Ct SE12	151	R12
Crown Dale SE19	165	T10
Crown Hill, Croy 13	197	T4
Crown La N14	58	F1
Crown La SW16	165	P10
Crown La, Brom	188	B10
Crown La, Chis	189	L1
Crown La, Mord	180	J6
Crown La Gdns SW16	165	P10
Crown La Spur, Brom	188	B10

Crown Ms E13 115 T2
Crown Ms W6 125 N8
Crown Office Row 19 K9
  EC4
Crown Pas SW1 25 N3
Crown Pl EC2 20 G2
Crown Pl NW5 92 D11
Crown Rd N10 58 B14
Crown Rd, Borwd 38 B1
Crown Rd, Enf 44 J7
Crown Rd, Ilf 81 N7
Crown Rd, Mord 180 J7
Crown Rd, N Mal 178 G2
Crown Rd, Ruis 84 H9
Crown Rd, Sutt 194 J7
Crown Rd, Twick 141 K12
Crown St SE5 36 A14
Crown St W3 124 D2
Crown St, Dag 101 T12
Crown St, Har 86 B2
Crown Ter, Rich 141 U7
Crown Wk, Wem 87 U5
Crown Wds La SE9 153 L5
Crown Wds La SE18 152 J3
Crown Wds Way 153 P10
  SE9
Crown Wks, E2 **13** 112 J4
Crown Yd, Houns 139 T5
Crowndale Rd NW1 9 P1
Crownfield Av, Ilf 81 R10
Crownfield Rd E15 96 H8
Crownhill Rd NW10 107 L2
Crownhill Rd, 64 D14
  Wdf Grn
Crownmead Way, 83 R7
  Rom
Crownstone Rd SW2 147 N10
Crowntree Cl, Islw 122 E12
Crows Rd E15 114 H5
Crowshott Av, Stan 69 P2
Crowther Av, Brent 123 R8
Crowther Rd SE25 184 G8
Crowthorne Cl 162 E1
  SW18
Crowthorne Rd W10 108 A12
Croxden Cl, Edg 70 A5
Croxden Wk, Mord 181 L11
Croxford Gdns N22 59 T14
Croxley Rd W9 108 F6
Croxted Cl SE21 147 U13
Croxted Rd SE21 147 T13
Croxted Rd SE24 147 T13
Croyde Av, Grnf 103 U6
Croyde Cl, Sid 153 P13
Croydon Flyover, 197 S7
  Croy
Croydon Gro, Croy 197 R1
Croydon Rd E13 115 M8
Croydon Rd SE20 185 L3
Croydon Rd, Beck 185 U4
Croydon Rd, Brom 201 M5
Croydon Rd, Croy 197 K7
Croydon Rd, Kes 201 U6
Croydon Rd, Mitch 182 B8
Croydon Rd, Wall 196 D7
Croydon Rd, W Wick 200 J5
Croyland Rd N9 60 H3
Croylands Dr, Surb 177 R14
Croysdale Av, Sun 174 A5
Crozier Ter E9 95 P10
Crucible Cl, Rom 82 D11
Crucifix La SE1 28 H5
Cruden St N1 111 S2
Cruikshank Rd E15 97 K8
Cruikshank St WC1 10 J5
Crummock Gdns 70 J10
  NW9
Crumpsall St SE2 136 F7
Crundale Av NW9 70 B10
Crunden Rd, S Croy 198 A13
Crusader Gdns, 198 D6
  Croy **2**
Crusoe Ms N16 94 B3
Crusoe Rd, Mitch 163 T13
Crutched Friars EC3 21 K9
Crutchley Rd SE6 169 K4
Crystal Palace Par 166 F11
  SE19
Crystal Palace Pk 166 J9
  Rd SE26

Crystal Palace Rd 148 G7
  SE22
Crystal Palace Sta 166 G12
  Rd, SE19 **1**
Crystal Ter SE19 166 A11
Crystal Way, Dag 100 F1
Crystal Way, Har 68 F9
Cuba Dr, Enf 45 L4
Cuba St E14 132 A3
Cubitt Sq, Sthl 121 U2
Cubitt Steps, 132 B1
  E14 **6**
Cubitt St WC1 10 G8
Cubitt St, Croy 197 M10
Cubitt Ter SW4 146 F5
Cubitts Yd WC2 18 C9
Cuckoo Av W7 104 D8
Cuckoo Dene W7 104 B9
Cuckoo Hall La N9 45 N13
Cuckoo Hill, Pnr 66 E7
Cuckoo Hill Dr, Pnr 66 F6
Cuckoo Hill Rd, Pnr 66 F8
Cuckoo La W7 104 D13
Cudas Cl, Epsom 193 L7
Cuddington Av, 193 L6
  Wor Pk
Cudham La N, Orp 203 R14
Cudham St SE6 150 E13
Cudworth St E1 113 K7
Cuff Cres SE9 152 B12
Culford Gdns SW3 32 A4
Culford Gro N1 94 C12
Culford Ms N1 94 C11
Culford Rd N1 94 C13
Culgaith Gdns, Enf 42 J8
Cullen Way NW10 106 F8
Culling Rd SE16 131 L5
Cullington Cl, Har 68 G8
Cullingworth Rd 89 P10
  NW10
Culloden Cl SE16 37 U8
Culloden Rd, Enf 43 R4
Culloden St E14 114 F11
Cullum St EC3 20 H9
Culmington Rd W13 123 M3
Culmore Cross 164 C2
  SW12
Culmore Rd SE15 131 K14
Culmstock Rd SW11 146 A10
Culpeper Cl, Ilf 65 K12
Culross Cl N15 75 T8
Culross St W1 16 C11
Culsac Rd, Surb 191 S3
Culver Gro, Stan 69 N5
Culverden Rd SW12 164 E4
Culverden Rd, Wat 50 C5
Culverhouse Gdns 165 L6
  SW16
Culverlands Cl, Stan 52 H8
Culverley Rd SE6 168 D1
Culvers Av, Cars 196 A2
Culvers Retreat, 195 U3
  Cars
Culvers Way, Cars 195 T4
Culverstone Cl, 187 L11
  Brom
Culvert Pl SW11 146 A4
Culvert Rd N15 76 C10
Culvert Rd SW11 145 U3
Culworth St NW8 7 P3
Cumberland Av 106 C6
  NW10
Cumberland Av, 153 S7
  Well
Cumberland Cl E8 94 F12
Cumberland Cl 162 A14
  SW20
Cumberland Cl, Ilf 81 L2
Cumberland Cl, 140 J11
  Twick **1**
Cumberland Cres, 126 D7
  W14 **4**
Cumberland Dr, 137 K13
  Bexh
Cumberland Dr, 191 T6
  Chess
Cumberland Dr, 190 G4
  Esher
Cumberland Gdns 72 B3
  NW4

Cumberland Gdns 10 J6
  WC1
Cumberland Gate 15 U9
  W1
Cumberland Mkt 9 K6
  NW1
Cumberland Mkt 9 K5
  Est NW1
Cumberland Mills 132 G9
  Sq, E14 **9**
Cumberland Pk W3 107 P5
Cumberland Pl NW1 8 H5
Cumberland Pl SE6 169 L1
Cumberland Pl, 174 B7
  Sun **2**
Cumberland Rd E12 98 A8
Cumberland Rd E13 115 R8
Cumberland Rd E17 77 R3
Cumberland Rd N9 61 L2
Cumberland Rd N22 75 L3
Cumberland Rd 185 K11
  SE25
Cumberland Rd 143 M1
  SW13
Cumberland Rd W3 106 F13
Cumberland Rd W7 122 F4
Cumberland Rd, 187 K7
  Brom
Cumberland Rd, Har 67 R9
Cumberland Rd, 124 A14
  Rich
Cumberland Rd, 69 U6
  Stan
Cumberland St SW1 32 J5
Cumberland Ter 8 H5
  NW1
Cumberland Ter 8 H3
  Ms NW1
Cumberlow Av SE25 184 F6
Cumberton Rd N17 76 B2
Cumbrae Gdns, 191 M2
  Surb
Cumbrian Gdns 90 B4
  NW2
Cumming St N1 10 G3
Cumnor Gdns, 193 P12
  Epsom
Cumnor Rd, Sutt 195 M11
Cunard Cres N21 44 A12
Cunard Pl EC3 20 J7
Cunard Rd NW10 106 H6
Cunard Wk SE16 131 R7
Cundy Rd E16 115 T12
Cundy St SW1 32 F4
Cundy St Est SW1 32 F4
Cunliffe Rd, Epsom 193 M7
Cunliffe St SW16 164 F11
Cunningham Cl, Rom 82 E10
Cunningham Cl, 200 C4
  W Wick
Cunningham Pk, 67 U9
  Har
Cunningham Pl NW8 7 K9
Cunningham Rd N15 76 G7
Cunnington St W4 124 F7
Cupar Rd SW11 146 C1
Cupola Cl, Brom 169 R9
Cureton St SW1 33 U4
Curlew Cl SE28 118 G13
Curlew Ct, Surb 191 U5
Curlew St SE1 29 M5
Curlew Way, Hayes 102 G10
Curnick's La, 165 T8
  SE27 **3**
Curran Av, Sid 153 U10
Curran Av, Wall 196 B6
Currey Rd, Grnf 85 U11
Curricle St, W3 **2** 124 J2
Currie Hill Cl SW19 162 F8
Curry Ri NW7 56 B11
Cursitor St EC4 18 J5
Curtain Rd EC2 12 H11
Curthwaite Gdns, 42 H8
  Enf
Curtis Dr W3 106 H11
Curtis Fld Rd SW16 165 M7
Curtis La, Wem 87 R10
Curtis Rd, Epsom 192 F7
Curtis Rd, Houns 139 L14
Curtis St SE1 37 L1

Curtis Way SE1 37 L1
Curve, The W12 107 N13
Curwen Av, E7 **1** 97 R7
Curwen Rd W12 125 N4
Curzon Av, Enf 45 P9
Curzon Av, Stan 68 G2
Curzon Cl, Orp 203 P7
Curzon Cres NW10 89 L14
Curzon Cres, Bark 117 T5
Curzon Gate W1 24 E3
Curzon Pl W1 24 F3
Curzon Pl, Pnr 66 E9
Curzon Rd N10 74 D3
Curzon Rd W5 105 K7
Curzon Rd, Th Hth 183 N11
Curzon St W1 24 G2
Cusack Cl, 158 E7
  Twick **1**
Custom Ho Reach 131 T4
  SE16
Custom Ho Wk EC3 20 G12
Cut, The SE1 27 M5
Cutcombe Rd SE5 147 U4
Cuthberga Cl, 99 L13
  Bark **2**
Cuthbert Gdns SE25 184 D5
Cuthbert Rd, 78 F6
  E17 **1**
Cuthbert Rd, 60 G9
  N18 **5**
Cuthbert Rd, Croy 197 R4
Cuthbert St W2 7 K12
Cuthill Wk SE5 148 A2
Cutler St E1 21 K5
Cutlers Sq, E14 **7** 132 B8
Cutthroat All, Rich 159 L3
Cuxton Cl, Bexh 154 J9
Cyclamen Cl, 157 N11
  Hmptn **4**
Cyclamen Way, 192 E9
  Epsom
Cyclops Ms E14 132 A8
Cygnet Av, Felt 138 F14
Cygnet Cl NW10 88 H10
Cygnet Cl, Borwd 38 F2
Cygnet St E1 13 N10
Cygnet Way, Hayes 102 H11
Cygnets, The, Felt 156 J7
Cygnus Business 89 L11
  Cen NW10
Cymbeline Ct, Har 68 E12
Cynthia St N1 10 H3
Cyntra Pl, E8 **10** 95 K13
Cypress Av, Twick 139 U13
Cypress Gro, Ilf 65 S11
Cypress Pl W1 9 N12
Cypress Rd SE25 184 D3
Cypress Rd, Har 68 A3
Cyprus Av N3 72 D3
Cyprus Gdns N3 72 D3
Cyprus Pl E2 113 M4
Cyprus Pl E6 116 H13
Cyprus Rd N3 72 E4
Cyprus Rd N9 60 F3
Cyprus St E2 113 M4
Cyrena Rd SE22 148 F10
Cyril Mans SW11 145 U2
Cyril Rd, Bexh 155 K4
Cyrus St EC1 11 R9
Czar St SE8 132 A11

D

Dabbs Hill La, Nthlt 85 R9
Dabin Cres SE10 150 E13
Dacca St SE8 131 U11
Dace Rd E3 114 A1
Dacre Av, Ilf 80 H3
Dacre Cl, Chig 65 M8
Dacre Cl, Grnf 103 S3
Dacre Gdns SE13 150 J7
Dacre Gdns, Borwd 38 G10
Dacre Gdns, Chig 65 M8
Dacre Pk SE13 151 K6
Dacre Pl SE13 150 J6
Dacre Rd, E11 **1** 97 L1
Dacre Rd E13 115 R1

Name	Page	Ref
Dacre Rd, Croy	183	K13
Dacre St SW1	25	S9
Dacres Rd SE23	167	M5
Dade Way, Sthl	121	L9
Daerwood Cl, Brom	202	E2
Daffodil Cl, Croy	199	P1
Daffodil Gdns, Ilf	98	J9
Daffodil Pl, Hmptn *6*	157	N11
Daffodil St W12	107	M14
Dafforne Rd SW17	164	A6
Dagenham Av, Dag	118	J1
Dagenham Rd E10	95	U1
Dagenham Rd, Dag	101	S7
Dagmar Av, Wem	87	T8
Dagmar Gdns NW10	108	A4
Dagmar Rd N4	75	P13
Dagmar Rd, N15 *2*	76	A8
Dagmar Rd N22	74	H1
Dagmar Rd SE5	148	C2
Dagmar Rd SE25	184	C9
Dagmar Rd, Dag	101	U13
Dagmar Rd, Kings T	177	U1
Dagmar Rd, Sthl	120	J6
Dagmar Ter N1	111	S1
Daynall Pk SE26	184	C11
Dagnall Rd SE25	184	C9
Dagnall St SW11	146	A3
Dagnan Rd SW12	146	D13
Dagonet Gdns, Brom	169	N6
Dagonet Rd, Brom *3*	169	N6
Dahlia Gdns, Ilf	99	K11
Dahlia Gdns, Mitch	182	G7
Dahlia Rd SE2	136	D8
Dahomey Rd SW16	164	E11
Daimler Way, Wall	196	J13
Daines Cl E12	98	F6
Dainford Cl, Brom	168	G9
Dainton Cl, Brom	187	S1
Daintry Cl, Har	68	H8
Daintry Way, E9 *2*	95	T11
Dairsle Rd SE9	152	H6
Dairy Cl NW10	107	P2
Dairy Cl, Th Hth	183	T3
Dairy La SE18	134	E8
Dairy Ms SW9	147	K6
Dairy Wk SW19	162	C7
Dairyman Cl NW2	90	B6
Daisy Cl, Croy	199	P1
Daisy La SW6	144	H5
Daisy Rd, E16 *1*	114	J7
Daisy Rd E18	79	R4
Dakota Gdns E6	116	D8
Dalberg Rd SW2	147	N9
Dalberg Way SE2	136	G6
Dalby Rd SW18	145	L8
Dalby St NW5	92	C12
Dalcross Rd, Houns	138	J3
Dale, The, Kes	202	B7
Dale Av, Edg	69	U3
Dale Av, Houns	139	K5
Dale Cl SE3	151	N5
Dale Cl, Barn	41	K11
Dale Cl, Pnr	66	C2
Dale Gdns, Wdf Grn	63	R7
Dale Grn Rd N11	58	D6
Dale Gro N12	57	L10
Dale Pk Av, Cars	195	U4
Dale Pk Rd SE19	184	A1
Dale Rd NW5	92	B9
Dale Rd SE17	35	S12
Dale Rd, Grnf	103	R10
Dale Rd, Sutt	194	F8
Dale Row, W11 *11*	108	D12
Dale St W4	124	J9
Dale Vw Av E4	62	F4
Dale Vw Cres E4	62	F5
Dale Vw Gdns E4	62	G5
Dale Wd Rd, Orp	189	S14
Dalebury Rd SW17	163	S4
Daleham Gdns NW3	91	N10
Daleham Ms NW3	91	N11
Dalemain Ms E16	133	P1
Dales Rd, Borwd	38	G10
Daleside Gdns, Chig	65	M5
Daleside Rd SW16	164	D9
Daleside Rd, Epsom	192	G12
Daleview Rd N15	76	D12
Dalewood Gdns, Wor Pk	193	S3
Daley St E9	95	P11
Daley Thompson Way, SW8 *11*	146	D5
Dalgarno Gdns W10	107	T9
Dalgarno Way W10	107	T8
Dalgleish St E14	113	S12
Daling Way E3	113	S2
Dalkeith Gro, Stan	53	P10
Dalkeith Rd SE21	165	U1
Dalkeith Rd, Ilf	99	M5
Dallas Rd NW4	71	P13
Dallas Rd SE26	166	J6
Dallas Rd W5	105	T9
Dallas Rd, Sutt	194	D12
Dallin Rd SE18	135	K13
Dallin Rd, Bexh	154	H7
Dalling Rd W6	125	R6
Dallinger Rd SE12	151	L12
Dallington St EC1	11	R10
Dalmain Rd SE23	167	N1
Dalmally Rd, Croy	184	G14
Dalmeny Av N7	92	H9
Dalmeny Av SW16	183	N4
Dalmeny Cl, Wem	87	M11
Dalmeny Cres, Houns	140	A7
Dalmeny Rd N7	92	H8
Dalmeny Rd, Barn	41	M12
Dalmeny Rd, Cars	196	B13
Dalmeny Rd, Erith	155	S1
Dalmeny Rd, Wor Pk	193	S5
Dalmeyer Rd NW10	89	L11
Dalmore Av, Esher	190	E12
Dalmore Rd SE21	165	U3
Dalrymple Cl N14	42	H13
Dalrymple Rd SE4	149	S8
Dalston Gdns, Stan	69	R2
Dalston La E8	94	F11
Dalton Av, Mitch	181	R3
Dalton Cl, Orp	203	S5
Dalton Rd, Har	68	B4
Dalton St SE27	165	S4
Dalwood St SE5	148	D1
Dalyell Rd SW9	147	L5
Damask Cres E16	115	K7
Dame St N1	11	U1
Damer Ter, SW10 *2*	127	M14
Dames Rd E7	97	N6
Damien St E1	113	K11
Damon Cl, Sid	172	C6
Damsonwood Rd, Sthl	121	N6
Dan Leno Wk, SW6 *9*	126	J14
Danbrook Rd SW16	183	K1
Danbury Cl, Rom	82	G6
Danbury Ms, Wall	196	C8
Danbury Rd, Loug	48	D13
Danbury St N1	11	S2
Danbury Way, Wdf Grn	63	T12
Danby St SE15	148	E5
Dancer Rd SW6	144	E2
Dancer Rd, Rich	144	A5
Dando Cres SE3	151	R6
Dandridge Cl SE10	133	M8
Dane Cl, Bex	155	P13
Dane Cl, Orp	203	N9
Dane Pl E3	113	T3
Dane Rd N18	61	L7
Dane Rd SW19	181	M1
Dane Rd W13	123	L1
Dane Rd, Ilf	99	L10
Dane Rd, Sthl	103	K14
Dane St WC1	18	F3
Danebury, Croy	200	D12
Danebury Av SW15	143	N13
Daneby Rd SE6	166	E4
Danecourt Gdns, Croy	198	F5
Danecroft Rd SE24	147	U9
Danehurst Gdns, Ilf	80	D10
Danehurst St SW6	144	D1
Daneland, Barn	41	U12
Danemead Gro, Nthlt	85	R9
Danemere St SW15	143	U5
Danes Ct, Wem	88	C6
Danes Gate, Har	68	C6
Danes Rd, Rom	83	T13
Danesbury Rd, Felt	156	D2
Danescombe SE12	151	P14
Danescourt Cres, Sutt	195	M4
Danescroft NW4	72	B10
Danescroft Av NW4	72	B10
Danescroft Gdns NW4	72	B10
Danesdale Rd E9	95	R12
Danesfield SE5	36	G9
Daneswood Av SE6	168	E6
Danethorpe Rd, Wem	87	N12
Danette Gdns, Dag	101	N4
Daneville Rd SE5	148	A2
Dangan Rd E11	79	N12
Daniel Bolt Cl E14	114	D9
Daniel Cl N18	61	L8
Daniel Cl SW17	163	R11
Daniel Gdns SE15	37	M13
Daniel Rd W5	105	U14
Daniell Way, Croy	197	K7
Daniels Ms SE4	149	U7
Daniels Rd SE15	146	U6
Dansey Pl W1	17	S10
Dansington Rd, Well	154	B7
Danson Cres, Well	154	C6
Danson La, Well	154	C7
Danson Mead, Well	154	F6
Danson Pk, Bexh	154	E7
Danson Rd, Bex	154	F11
Danson Rd, Bexh	154	G8
Danson Underpass, Sid	154	F11
Dante Pl SE11	35	R3
Dante Rd SE11	35	P2
Danube St SW3	31	R5
Danvers Rd N8	74	G7
Danvers St SW3	31	M11
Danziger Way, Borwd	38	E2
Daphne Gdns E4	62	F5
Daphne St SW18	145	L12
D'Arblay St W1	17	P7
Darby Cres, Sun	174	F4
Darby Gdns, Sun	174	E4
Darcy Av, Wall	196	F8
Darcy Cl N20	57	N4
D'Arcy Dr, Har	69	P8
Darcy Gdns, Dag	119	M1
D'Arcy Gdns, Har	69	R8
Darcy Rd SW16	182	J3
Darcy Rd, Islw *1*	140	H2
D'Arcy Rd, Sutt	194	A7
Darell Rd, Rich	142	A5
Darenth Rd N16	94	F1
Darenth Rd, Well	154	B2
Darfield Rd SE4	149	T9
Darfield Way W10	108	A12
Darfur St SW15	144	A6
Dargate Cl, SE19 *10*	166	F13
Darien Rd SW11	144	P6
Darlan Rd SW6	126	F14
Darlaston Rd SW19	162	B14
Darley Cl, Croy	185	R12
Darley Dr, N Mal	178	H3
Darley Gdns, Mord	181	L12
Darley Rd N9	60	F1
Darley Rd SW11	145	T11
Darling Rd SE4	150	A5
Darling Row E1	113	K8
Darlington Rd SE27	165	S9
Darmaine Cl, S Croy	197	U14
Darndale Cl E17	77	T4
Darnley Rd E9	95	L12
Darnley Rd, Wdf Grn	79	P1
Darnley Ter W11	126	B1
Darrell Rd SE22	148	G10
Darren Cl N4	75	M13
Darrick Wd Rd, Orp	203	N3
Darris Cl, Hayes	103	K8
Darsley Dr SW8	146	H1
Dart St W10	108	D5
Dartford Av N9	45	M12
Dartford Gdns, Rom	82	D10
Dartford Rd, Bex	173	U2
Dartford St SE17	36	A10
Dartmouth Cl W11	108	F11
Dartmouth Gro SE10	150	F2
Dartmouth Hill SE10	150	F2
Dartmouth Pk Av NW5	92	D5
Dartmouth Pk Hill N19	92	D3
Dartmouth Pk Hill NW5	92	E6
Dartmouth Pk Rd NW5	92	C6
Dartmouth Pl, SE23 *3*	167	M4
Dartmouth Pl W4	125	K12
Dartmouth Rd E16	115	N11
Dartmouth Rd NW2	90	C11
Dartmouth Rd NW4	71	P12
Dartmouth Rd SE23	167	L5
Dartmouth Rd SE26	167	L5
Dartmouth Rd, Brom	187	N14
Dartmouth Rd, Ruis	84	B6
Dartmouth Row SE10	150	F3
Dartmouth St SW1	25	S8
Dartmouth Ter SE10	150	G2
Darville Rd N16	94	F5
Darwell Cl E6	116	G4
Darwin Cl N11	58	C6
Darwin Cl, Orp	203	N9
Darwin Dr, Sthl	103	S12
Darwin Gdns, Wat	50	F9
Darwin Rd N22	75	R3
Darwin Rd W5	123	M9
Darwin Rd, Well	153	U5
Darwin St SE17	36	E3
Daryngton Dr, Grnf	104	C3
Dashwood Cl, Bexh	155	P10
Dashwood Rd N8	75	L12
Dassett Rd SE27	165	S9
Datchelor Pl SE5	148	B1
Datchet Rd SE6	167	U5
Date St SE17	36	B7
Daubeney Gdns N17	59	U13
Daubeney Rd E5	95	R9
Daubeney Rd N17	59	U13
Dault Rd SW18	145	L11
Davema Cl, Chis	188	G2
Davenant Rd N19	92	H4
Davenant Rd, Croy	197	S7
Davenant St E1	21	T3
Davenport Cl, Tedd	158	G12
Davenport Rd SE6	150	E12
Davenport Rd, Sid	172	J4
Daventer Dr, Stan	52	F13
Daventry Av E17	78	B10
Daventry St NW1	15	P1
Davern Cl SE10	133	L8
Davey Rd E9	93	M12
Davey St SE15	37	N12
David Av, Grnf	104	C5
David Ms W1	16	B1
David Rd, Dag	100	J3
David St E15	96	H11
Davidge St SE1	27	P7
Davids Rd SE23	167	M2
David's Way, Ilf	65	R13
Davidson Gdns SW8	128	J13
Davidson La, Har	86	E1
Davidson Rd, Croy	184	C14
Davies Cl, Croy	184	G12
Davies La E11	97	L3
Davies Ms W1	16	G9
Davies St E13	16	H10
Davington Gdns, Dag	100	D10
Davington Rd, Dag	100	D10
Davinia Cl, Wdf Grn	64	E12
Davis Rd W3	125	M3
Davis Rd, Chess	192	B7
Davis St E13	115	S4
Davisville Rd W12	125	N4

Dawes Av, Islw	140	G9
Dawes Ho SE17	36	D4
Dawes Rd SW6	126	E13
Dawes St SE17	36	E6
Dawlish Av N13	58	J8
Dawlish Av SW18	162	J3
Dawlish Av, Grnf	104	H4
Dawlish Dr, Ilf	99	S7
Dawlish Dr, Pnr	67	K10
Dawlish Dr, Ruis	84	B3
Dawlish Rd E10	96	E3
Dawlish Rd N17	76	F5
Dawlish Rd NW2	90	B11
Dawn Cl, Houns	139	K5
Dawn Cres E15	114	H1
Dawnay Gdns SW18	163	N4
Dawnay Rd SW18	163	M3
Dawpool Rd NW2	89	L4
Daws Hill E4	46	E4
Daws La NW7	55	M10
Dawson Av, Bark	99	T14
Dawson Cl SE18	135	L8
Dawson Gdns, Bark	99	U14
Dawson Hts Est SE22	148	H13
Dawson Pl W2	108	H13
Dawson Rd NW2	89	U9
Dawson Rd, Kings T	177	U5
Dawson St E2	13	N3
Dax Ct, Sun	174	E5
Daybrook Rd SW19	180	J4
Daylesford Av SW15	143	P7
Daymer Gdns, Pnr	66	D7
Days La, Sid	153	R14
Daysbrook Rd SW2	165	L2
Dayton Gro SE15	149	L1
De Barowe Ms, N5 *3*	93	S8
De Beauvoir Cres N1	112	C1
De Beauvoir Est N1	112	B1
De Beauvoir Rd N1	94	C14
De Beauvoir Sq N1	94	D14
De Bohun Av N14	42	C11
De Brome Rd, Felt	156	F2
De Crespigny Pk SE5	148	A3
De Frene Rd SE26	167	R7
De Havilland Rd, Edg	70	B4
De Havilland Rd, Houns	120	F13
De Havilland Rd, Wall	197	K13
De Laune St SE17	35	N8
De Luci Rd, Erith	137	U9
De Lucy St SE2	136	D7
De Montfort Rd SW16	164	J5
De Morgan Rd SW6	145	K5
De Quincey Ms, E16 *7*	133	P1
De Quincey Rd N17	76	A1
De Vere Gdns W8	22	E8
De Vere Gdns, Ilf	98	F3
De Vere Ms, W8 *1*	22	E9
De Walden St, W1 *2*	16	F3
Deacon Ms N1	94	B14
Deacon Rd NW2	89	P10
Deacon Rd, Kings T	177	T2
Deacon Way SE17	35	U1
Deacon Way, Wdf Grn	64	E12
Deacons Cl, Borwd	38	A8
Deacons Cl, Pnr	66	D3
Deacon's Hill Rd, Borwd	38	A10
Deacons Leas, Orp	203	P7
Deacons Ri N2	73	N9
Deal Ms W5	123	N8
Deal Porters Way SE16	131	N5
Deal Rd SW17	164	A12
Deal St E1	21	S1
Deal Wk, SW9 *1*	129	P13
Deal's Gateway SE10	150	B1
Dealtry Rd SW15	143	T8
Dean Bradley St SW1	26	B12
Dean Cl E9	95	M9
Dean Cl SE16	131	P2
Dean Ct, Wem	87	K5
Dean Dr, Stan	69	S4
Dean Farrar St SW1	25	S9
Dean Gdns E17	78	G7
Dean Gdns W13	122	J1
Dean Rd NW2	89	T12
Dean Rd SE28	118	A14
Dean Rd, Croy	198	A8
Dean Rd, Hmptn	157	N9
Dean Rd, Houns	139	S10
Dean Ryle St SW1	34	A1
Dean Stanley St, SW1 *4*	26	B12
Dean St E7	97	N9
Dean St W1	17	S7
Dean Trench St, SW1 *3*	26	A12
Dean Way, Sthl	121	S3
Deancross St E1	113	L12
Deane Av, Ruis	84	E10
Deane Cft Rd, Pnr	66	E12
Deane Way, Ruis	66	C12
Deanery Cl N2	73	R7
Deanery Ms, W1 *1*	24	F2
Deanery Rd E15	97	K12
Deanery St W1	24	E2
Deanhill Rd SW14	142	D8
Deans Bldgs SE17	36	D4
Deans Cl W4	124	D11
Dean's Cl, Croy	198	E5
Deans Cl, Edg	54	E12
Deans Ct, EC4 *8*	19	S8
Deans Dr N13	59	R11
Deans Dr, Edg	54	G10
Dean's Gate Cl SE23	167	N6
Deans La, W4 *5*	124	D12
Deans La, Edg	54	E11
Deans Ms W1	16	J5
Dean's Pl SW1	33	S5
Deans Rd W7	122	F3
Deans Rd, Sutt	194	A6
Deans Way, Edg	54	E10
Dean's Yd SW1	25	U9
Deansbrook Cl, Edg	54	E13
Deansbrook Rd, Edg	54	F13
Deanscroft Av NW9	88	E2
Deansway N2	73	P8
Deansway N9	60	C5
De'Arn Gdns, Mitch	181	S5
Dearne Cl, Stan	52	H9
Dearsley Rd, Enf	44	H6
Deason St E15	114	F2
Debden Cl, Kings T	159	N9
Debden Cl, Wdf Grn	64	A13
Debnams Rd, SE16 *3*	131	L8
Deborah Cl, Islw	140	C1
Deburgh Rd SW19	163	L13
Decima St SE1	28	G10
Deck Cl SE16	131	P3
Decoy Av NW11	72	D8
Dee Rd, Rich	141	U7
Dee St E14	114	F11
Deeley Rd SW8	146	G1
Deena Cl W3	105	U11
Deepdale SW19	162	B8
Deepdale Av, Brom	187	M8
Deepdale Cl, N11 *1*	58	B11
Deepdene W5	105	T7
Deepdene Av, Croy	198	F6
Deepdene Cl E11	79	N7
Deepdene Ct N21	43	S12
Deepdene Gdns SW2	147	L13
Deepdene Path, Loug	48	H8
Deepdene Rd SE5	148	A7
Deepdene Rd, Loug	48	H8
Deepdene Rd, Well	154	B5
Deepwell Cl, Islw	140	G2
Deepwood La, Grnf	104	B5
Deer Pk Cl, Kings T	160	C13
Deer Pk Gdns, Mitch	181	N7
Deer Pk Rd SW19	181	L3
Deer Pk Way, W Wick	201	K3
Deerbrook Rd SE24	165	R1
Deerdale Rd SE24	147	T7
Deerhurst Cl, Felt	156	B7
Deerhurst Cres, Hmptn	157	U10
Deerhurst Rd NW2	90	B12
Deerhurst Rd SW16	165	L10
Deerings Dr, Pnr	66	B9
Deerleap Gro E4	46	D10
Deeside Rd SW17	163	N6
Defiance Wk SE18	134	E5
Defiant Way, Wall	196	J13
Defoe Av, Rich	124	B14
Defoe Cl SE16	131	T4
Defoe Cl SW17	163	S12
Defoe Rd N16	94	C5
Degema Rd, Chis	170	J10
Dehar Cres NW9	71	M14
Dehavilland Cl, Nthlt	102	G6
Dekker Rd SE21	148	C12
Delacourt Rd SE3	133	R14
Delafield Rd SE7	133	S9
Delaford Rd SE16	131	K9
Delaford St SW6	126	D13
Delamare Cres, Croy	185	L12
Delamere Gdns NW7	54	G10
Delamere Rd SW20	180	A2
Delamere Rd W5	123	S2
Delamere Rd, Borwd	38	D2
Delamere Rd, Hayes	102	G13
Delamere Ter W2	14	D1
Delancey Pas NW1	110	D2
Delancey St NW1	110	C2
Delaware Rd W9	6	A9
Delawyk Cres SE24	147	U11
Delcombe Av, Wor Pk	193	T2
Delft Way, SE22 *4*	148	D9
Delhi Rd, Enf	44	E14
Delhi St N1	111	K1
Delia St SW18	145	K13
Delius Gro E15	114	G3
Dell, The SE2	136	A10
Dell, The SE19	184	E1
Dell, The, Brent	123	M11
Dell, The, Felt	138	C13
Dell, The, Pnr	66	H4
Dell, The, Wem	87	K9
Dell, The, Wdf Grn	63	R6
Dell Cl E15	114	H1
Dell Cl, Wall	196	G7
Dell Cl, Wdf Grn	63	R6
Dell La, Epsom	193	N10
Dell Rd, Epsom	193	P11
Dell Wk, N Mal	179	K4
Dell Way W13	105	L11
Dellbow Rd, Felt	138	C9
Dellfield Cl, Beck	186	E1
Dellors Cl, Barn	40	A9
Dellow Cl, Ilf	81	N13
Dellow St E1	113	K13
Dells Cl E4	46	C13
Dell's Ms, SW1 *6*	33	N4
Dellwood Gdns, Ilf	80	H6
Delmare Cl SW9	147	M7
Delme Cres SE3	151	S3
Delmey Cl, Croy	198	F5
Deloraine St SE8	150	A2
Delorme St W6	126	B12
Delta Cl, Wor Pk	193	L5
Delta Ct NW2	89	P3
Delta Gain, Wat	50	H5
Delta Gro, Nthlt	102	H5
Delta Rd, Wor Pk	193	K5
Delta St E2	13	R6
Delvan Cl, SE18 *6*	134	G13
Delvers Mead, Dag	101	T7
Delverton Rd SE17	35	R7
Delvino Rd SW6	144	G2
Demesne Rd, Wall	196	G7
Demeta Cl, Wem	88	F5
Dempster Cl, Surb	177	M14
Dempster Rd SW18	145	L9
Den Cl, Beck	186	H6
Den Rd, Brom	186	H6
Denberry Dr, Sid	172	D6
Denbigh Cl NW10	88	J14
Denbigh Cl, W11 *8*	108	F13
Denbigh Cl, Chis	170	E11
Denbigh Cl, Sthl	103	M11
Denbigh Cl, Sutt	194	F9
Denbigh Gdns, Rich	141	U10
Denbigh Ms, SW1 *5*	33	M4
Denbigh Pl SW1	33	M6
Denbigh Rd E6	116	A6
Denbigh Rd W11	108	F13
Denbigh Rd W13	105	K12
Denbigh Rd, Houns	139	S3
Denbigh Rd, Sthl	103	M11
Denbigh St SW1	33	M3
Denbigh Ter W11	108	F13
Denbridge Rd, Brom	188	F3
Dene, The W13	104	J10
Dene, The, Croy	199	N7
Dene, The, Wem	87	R7
Dene, The, W Mol	175	L9
Dene Av, Houns	139	M5
Dene Av, Sid	154	D14
Dene Cl SE4	149	R6
Dene Cl, Brom	201	M2
Dene Cl, Wor Pk	193	L3
Dene Ct, Stan	53	M9
Dene Gdns, Stan	53	M9
Dene Gdns, T Ditt	190	G3
Dene Rd N11	57	U2
Dene Rd, Buck H	64	B2
Denehurst Gdns NW4	71	T12
Denehurst Gdns W3	124	C2
Denehurst Gdns, Rich	142	B7
Denehurst Gdns, Twick	140	B14
Denehurst Gdns, Wdf Grn	63	R7
Denewood, Barn	41	M10
Denewood Rd N6	73	T12
Denham Cl, Well	154	E6
Denham Dr, Ilf	81	L11
Denham Rd N20	57	T5
Denham Rd, Felt	138	E13
Denham St SE10	133	N9
Denham Way, Bark	117	S1
Denham Way, Borwd	38	F1
Denholme Rd W9	108	F5
Denison Cl N2	73	L6
Denison Rd SW19	163	N12
Denison Rd W5	105	M7
Deniston Av, Bex	172	H2
Denleigh Gdns N21	43	N14
Denleigh Gdns, T Ditt	176	D11
Denman Dr NW11	72	H9
Denman Dr, Esher	190	G10
Denman Dr N NW11	72	H9
Denman Dr S NW11	72	H9
Denman Rd SE15	148	E2
Denman St W1	17	R11
Denmark Av SW19	162	C13
Denmark Ct, Mord	180	H10
Denmark Gdns, Cars	195	U5
Denmark Gro N1	10	J1
Denmark Hill, SE5 *2*	148	B5
Denmark Hill Dr NW9	71	M7
Denmark Hill Est SE5	148	B7
Denmark Rd N8	75	M7
Denmark Rd NW6	108	F4
Denmark Rd SE5	147	T2
Denmark Rd SE25	184	J9
Denmark Rd SW19	162	B12
Denmark Rd W13	105	K14
Denmark Rd, Brom	187	R2
Denmark Rd, Cars	195	U6
Denmark Rd, Kings T	177	R6
Denmark Rd, Twick	158	B5
Denmark St, E11 *8*	96	J6

Name	No	Ref
Denmark St E13	115	R9
Denmark St N17	76	J1
Denmark St WC2	17	T7
Denmark Wk SE27	165	T8
Denmead Rd, Croy	197	R1
Dennan Rd, Surb	191	T2
Denne Ter E8	112	F2
Denner Rd E4	62	B4
Dennett Rd, Croy	183	P14
Dennetts Gro SE14	149	N3
Dennetts Rd SE14	149	M2
Denning Av, Croy	197	N8
Denning Cl NW8	6	H6
Denning Cl, Hmptn	157	L11
Denning Rd NW3	91	P7
Dennington Pk Rd NW6	90	H11
Denningtons, The, Wor Pk	193	K3
Dennis Av, Wem	87	T9
Dennis Gdns, Stan	53	L9
Dennis La, Stan	52	J6
Dennis Pk Cres SW20	180	C2
Dennis Reeve Cl, Mitch	181	U1
Dennis Rd, E Mol	175	T7
Dennis Way SW4	146	H5
Denny Cl E6	116	C10
Denny Cres, SE11 *1*	35	L5
Denny Gdns, Dag	100	D13
Denny Rd N9	60	J1
Denny St SE11	35	L5
Densham Rd E15	115	K1
Densole Cl, Beck	185	R1
Densworth Gro N9	61	L4
Denton Cl, Barn	39	T9
Denton Rd N8	75	M10
Denton Rd N18	60	D7
Denton Rd, Twick	141	N12
Denton Rd, Well	136	E13
Denton St SW18	145	K11
Denton Way E5	95	P5
Dents Rd SW11	145	T12
Denver Cl, Orp	189	S12
Denver Rd N16	76	C13
Denyer St SW3	31	S3
Denzil Rd NW10	89	L10
Deodar Rd SW15	144	D7
Deodara Cl, N20 *1*	57	S5
Depot Rd, Houns	140	A5
Deptford Br SE8	150	B1
Deptford Bdy SE8	150	B1
Deptford Ch St SE8	132	B12
Deptford Ferry Rd, E14 *4*	132	B8
Deptford Grn SE8	132	B11
Deptford High St SE8	132	A13
Deptford Strand SE8	131	U8
Deptford Wf SE8	131	T7
Derby Av N12	57	L10
Derby Av, Har	68	A2
Derby Av, Rom	83	T12
Derby Est, Houns	139	P7
Derby Gate SW1	26	B6
Derby Hill SE23	167	L4
Derby Hill Cres SE23	167	L4
Derby Rd E7	98	A13
Derby Rd E9	113	N1
Derby Rd E18	79	L1
Derby Rd N18	61	L9
Derby Rd SW14	142	D8
Derby Rd SW19	162	G14
Derby Rd, Croy	197	S2
Derby Rd, Enf	45	K9
Derby Rd, Grnf	103	R1
Derby Rd, Houns	139	R7
Derby Rd, Surb	192	A1
Derby Rd, Sutt	194	F11
Derby St W1	24	F3
Derbyshire St E2	13	U8
Dereham Pl EC2	12	J8
Dereham Rd, Bark	99	U11
Derek Av, Epsom	192	B10
Derek Av, Wall	196	C7
Derek Av, Wem	88	C13
Derek Cl, Epsom	192	C10
Derek Walcott Cl, SE24 *21*	147	S8
Dericote St, E8 *7*	112	H1
Derifall Cl, E6 *3*	116	F9
Dering Pl, Croy	197	T8
Dering Rd, Croy	197	U8
Dering St W1	16	H7
Derinton Rd SW17	163	U7
Derley Rd, Sthl	120	F6
Dermody Gdns SE13	150	G9
Dermody Rd SE13	150	G9
Deronda Rd SE24	165	R1
Deroy Cl, Cars	195	T11
Derrick Gdns SE7	133	T6
Derrick Rd, Beck	185	T6
Derry Rd, Croy	196	J5
Derry St W8	22	B8
Dersingham Av E12	98	F7
Dersingham Rd NW2	90	D5
Derwent Av N18	60	A9
Derwent Av NW7	54	H11
Derwent Av SW15	160	J7
Derwent Av, Barn	57	T2
Derwent Av, Pnr	51	K12
Derwent Cl, Esher	190	D12
Derwent Cres N20	57	M6
Derwent Cres, Bexh	155	N4
Derwent Cres, Stan	69	M3
Derwent Dr NW9	70	J9
Derwent Dr, Orp	189	N14
Derwent Gdns, Ilf	80	D8
Derwent Gdns, Wem	69	M14
Derwent Gro SE22	148	E7
Derwent Ri NW9	70	J11
Derwent Rd N13	59	L6
Derwent Rd SE20	184	H4
Derwent Rd SW20	180	A11
Derwent Rd W5	123	L5
Derwent Rd, Sthl	103	M11
Derwent Rd, Twick	139	S12
Derwent St SE10	132	J9
Derwent Wk, Wall	196	D13
Derwentwater Rd W3	124	E1
Desborough St, W2 *1*	14	A2
Desenfans Rd SE21	148	D12
Desford Rd E16	115	K8
Desmond St SE14	131	S12
Despard Rd N19	92	E2
Detling Rd, Brom	169	N9
Detmold Rd E5	95	L3
Devalls Cl E6	116	H13
Devana End, Cars	195	U5
Devas Rd SW20	179	U1
Devas St E3	114	D7
Devenay Rd E15	97	L14
Devenish Rd SE2	136	B4
Deventer Cres, SE22 *6*	148	C9
Deverell St SE1	28	D11
Devereux La SW13	125	R13
Devereux Rd SW11	145	U11
Devey Cl, KingsT	161	K14
Devizes St, N1 *8*	112	B2
Devon Av, Twick	157	U1
Devon Cl N17	76	F5
Devon Cl, Buck H	63	R3
Devon Cl, Grnf	105	M2
Devon Gdns N4	75	S11
Devon Ri N2	73	P8
Devon Rd, Bark	117	R1
Devon St SE15	131	K12
Devon Way, Chess	191	M9
Devon Way, Epsom	192	C10
Devon Waye, Houns	121	L14
Devoncroft Gdns, Twick	140	H14
Devonia Gdns N18	59	T11
Devonia Rd N1	11	R1
Devonport Gdns, Ilf	80	E11
Devonport Rd, W12 *5*	125	S2
Devonport St E1	113	M12
Devonport Rd W12	125	S3
Devons Est E3	114	D6
Devons Rd E3	114	B9
Devonshire Av, Sutt	195	L14
Devonshire Cl E15	97	K8
Devonshire Cl N13	59	N7
Devonshire Cl W1	16	G1
Devonshire Cres NW7	56	A14
Devonshire Dr SE10	132	D14
Devonshire Dr, Surb	191	N2
Devonshire Gdns N17	59	U12
Devonshire Gdns N21	43	U13
Devonshire Gdns W4	124	E14
Devonshire Gro SE15	131	K12
Devonshire Hill La N17	59	S12
Devonshire Ms, W4 *5*	124	J9
Devonshire Ms N W1 *1*	16	G1
Devonshire Ms S W1	16	G1
Devonshire Ms W W1	8	F12
Devonshire Pas, W4 *10*	124	J10
Devonshire Pl NW2	90	G5
Devonshire Pl W1	8	F12
Devonshire Pl, W4 *9*	124	J10
Devonshire Pl, W8 *4*	22	B12
Devonshire Pl Ms W1	8	F12
Devonshire Rd E16	115	S11
Devonshire Rd E17	78	B11
Devonshire Rd N9	61	M2
Devonshire Rd N13	59	N7
Devonshire Rd N17	59	U12
Devonshire Rd NW7	56	A13
Devonshire Rd SE9	170	C3
Devonshire Rd SE23	149	N13
Devonshire Rd SW19	163	S13
Devonshire Rd W4	124	J9
Devonshire Rd W5	123	L5
Devonshire Rd, Bexh	155	K8
Devonshire Rd, Cars	196	B7
Devonshire Rd, Croy	184	A13
Devonshire Rd, Felt	156	J6
Devonshire Rd, Har	68	A11
Devonshire Rd, Ilf	81	R13
Devonshire Rd (Eastcote), Pnr	66	E12
Devonshire Rd (Hatch End), Pnr	67	L1
Devonshire Rd, Sthl	103	N9
Devonshire Rd, Sutt	195	M14
Devonshire Row EC2	20	J4
Devonshire Row Ms W1	8	J12
Devonshire Sq EC2	21	K5
Devonshire Sq, Brom	187	S7
Devonshire St W1	16	G1
Devonshire St W4	124	J10
Devonshire Ter W2	14	G8
Devonshire Way, Croy	199	U3
Devonshire Way, Hayes	102	D12
Dewar St SE15	148	H6
Dewberry Gdns E6	116	C10
Dewberry St E14	114	E10
Dewey Rd N1	10	J1
Dewey Rd, Dag	101	T11
Dewey St SW17	163	U10
Dewhurst Rd W14	126	A5
Dewsbury Cl, Pnr	67	K11
Dewsbury Ct, W4 *3*	124	F8
Dewsbury Gdns, Wor Pk	193	N5
Dewsbury Rd NW10	89	N9
Dexter Rd, Barn	40	A11
Deyncourt Rd N17	75	U1
Deynecourt Gdns E11	79	T8
D'Eynsford Rd SE5	148	A1
Dial Wk, The W8	22	D5
Diameter Rd, Orp	189	K13
Diamond Cl, Dag	100	F2
Diamond Rd, Ruis	84	H8
Diamond St SE15	130	D14
Diamond Ter SE10	150	F1
Diamond Way, SE8 *9*	132	A13
Diana Cl E18	79	S2
Diana Gdns, Surb	191	T4
Diana Ho SW13	143	M1
Diana Pl NW1	9	L10
Diana Rd E17	77	U5
Dianne Way, Barn	41	R9
Dianthus Cl SE2	136	C9
Dibden St N1	111	T1
Dibdin Cl, Sutt	194	H5
Dibdin Rd, Sutt	194	G5
Dicey Av NW2	89	T8
Dickens Av N3	73	M2
Dickens Cl, Erith	137	S14
Dickens Cl, Rich	159	R3
Dickens Dr, Chis	171	M11
Dickens Est SE1	29	R7
Dickens Est SE16	29	S9
Dickens La N18	60	D9
Dickens Ri, Chig	64	J6
Dickens Rd E6	116	B3
Dickens Sq SE1	28	B10
Dickens St SW8	146	D3
Dickenson Cl N9	60	H2
Dickenson Rd N8	75	K13
Dickenson Rd, Felt	156	F10
Dickensons La SE25	184	G10
Dickensons Pl SE25	184	H12
Dickenswood Cl SE19	165	S13
Dickerage La, N Mal	178	E5
Dickerage Rd, KingsT	178	E3
Dickerage Rd, N Mal	178	E3
Dickson Fold, Pnr	66	H7
Dickson Rd SE9	152	D6
Didsbury Cl E6	116	F2
Digby Cres N4	93	T4
Digby Gdns, Dag	119	N1
Digby Pl, Croy	198	F5
Digby Rd E9	95	N11
Digby Rd, Bark	99	T14
Digby St E2	113	M6
Dighton Ct SE5	35	T11
Dighton Rd SW18	145	L9
Digswell St, N7 *1*	93	P11
Dilhorne Cl SE12	169	R5
Dilke St SW3	32	A10
Dillwyn Cl SE26	167	S7
Dilston Cl, Nthlt *4*	102	F5
Dilton Gdns SW15	161	P1
Dimes Pl, W6 *3*	125	S8
Dimmock Dr, Grnf	86	B10
Dimond Cl E7	97	P8
Dimsdale Dr NW9	88	F2
Dimsdale Dr, Enf	44	G12
Dimson Cres E3	114	A7
Dingle Cl, Barn	39	M11
Dingle Gdns E14	114	B14
Dingley La SW16	164	H4
Dingley Pl EC1	12	A7
Dingley Rd EC1	11	U7
Dingwall Av, Croy	197	U4
Dingwall Gdns NW11	72	F12
Dingwall Rd SW18	145	L14
Dingwall Rd, Croy	198	A3
Dinmont St, E2 *11*	112	H4
Dinsdale Gdns SE25	184	D9
Dinsdale Gdns, Barn	41	K10
Dinsdale Rd SE3	133	L11
Dinsmore Rd SW12	146	D13
Dinton Rd SW19	163	P11
Dinton Rd, KingsT	159	U13
Diploma Av N2	73	R7
Dirleton Rd E15	115	L1
Disbrowe Rd W6	126	D12
Discovery Wk E1	112	J14
Dishforth La NW9	70	J1
Disney Ms, N4 *2*	75	S11

Disney Pl SE1 28 A6
Disney St SE1 28 A6
Dison Cl, Enf 45 N2
Disraeli Cl SE28 136 E1
Disraeli Rd E7 97 P11
Disraeli Rd NW10 106 G4
Disraeli Rd SW15 144 C8
Disraeli Rd W5 123 N2
Diss St E2 13 M5
Distaff La EC4 19 T9
Distillery La, W6 2 125 U10
Distillery Rd W6 125 U10
Distin St SE11 34 J3
District Rd, Wem 86 J10
Ditch All SE10 150 C2
Ditchburn St E14 114 F14
Ditchfield Rd, Hayes 102 J8
Dittisham Rd SE9 170 C8
Ditton Cl, T Ditt 1 176 G14
Ditton Gra Cl, Surb 191 N2
Ditton Gra Dr, Surb 191 N2
Ditton Hill, Surb 191 R2
Ditton Hill Rd, Surb 191 L1
Ditton Lawn, T Ditt 2 190 G1
Ditton Pl, SE20 4 185 K1
Ditton Reach, T Ditt 176 J12
Ditton Rd, Bexh 154 J9
Ditton Rd, Sthl 121 L8
Ditton Rd, Surb 191 T1
Dittoncroft Cl, Croy 4 198 D8
Divis Way, SW15 3 143 S12
Dixon Cl E6 116 F11
Dixon Pl, W Wick 200 C2
Dixon Rd SE14 149 S1
Dixon Rd SE25 184 E6
Dixon's All, SE16 5 130 J4
Dobbin Cl, Har 68 H3
Dobell Rd SE9 152 F10
Dobree Av NW10 89 S14
Dobson Cl NW6 91 N13
Dock Hill Av SE16 131 P3
Dock Rd E16 115 M14
Dock Rd, Brent 123 P13
Dock St E1 21 S10
Dockers Tanner Rd, E14 1 132 B7
Dockhead SE1 29 P7
Dockland St E16 134 G2
Dockley Rd SE16 29 S11
Dockwell Cl, Felt 138 A7
Doctor Johnson Av SW17 164 D6
Doctors Cl SE26 167 L9
Docwra's Bldgs N1 94 C11
Dod St E14 114 A11
Dodbrooke Rd SE27 165 P6
Doddington Gro SE17 35 P9
Doddington Pl SE17 35 N9
Dodsley Pl N9 61 L6
Dodson St SE1 27 M8
Doebury Wk SE18 136 A12
Doel Cl SW19 163 L14
Dog Kennel Hill SE22 148 C6
Dog Kennel Hill Est SE22 148 D5
Dog La NW10 89 K8
Doggets Ct, Barn 41 R10
Doggett Rd SE6 150 B12
Doherty Rd E13 115 P7
Dokal Ind Est, Sthl 120 J4
Dolben St SE1 27 P3
Dolby Rd SW6 144 E4
Dolland St SE11 34 H7
Dollis Av N3 72 E3
Dollis Brook Wk, Barn 40 C12
Dollis Cres, Ruis 84 E1
Dollis Hill Av NW2 89 T5
Dollis Hill Est NW2 89 N6
Dollis Hill La NW2 89 T5
Dollis Pk N3 72 F1
Dollis Rd N3 56 F14
Dollis Rd NW7 56 D14

Dollis Valley Grn Wk N20 41 K14
Dollis Valley Grn Wk, Barn 40 C12
Dollis Valley Way, Barn 40 E11
Dolman Rd W4 124 G8
Dolman St SW4 147 L7
Dolphin Cl, SE16 11 131 N3
Dolphin Cl SE28 118 G12
Dolphin Cl, Surb 177 P10
Dolphin Ct NW11 72 C11
Dolphin La, E14 11 114 C13
Dolphin Rd, Nthlt 103 M3
Dolphin Sq SW1 33 P8
Dolphin Sq W4 125 K13
Dolphin St, Kings T 177 R2
Dombey St WC1 18 E1
Dome Hill Pk SE26 166 F7
Domett Cl, SE5 4 148 B7
Domfe Pl E5 95 L7
Domingo St, EC1 9 11 U11
Dominica Cl, E13 4 116 A4
Dominion Rd, Croy 184 E13
Dominion Rd, Sthl 121 K5
Dominion St EC2 20 E2
Domonic Dr SE9 170 J6
Domville Cl N20 57 N4
Don Phelan Cl SE5 148 B1
Donald Dr, Rom 82 E9
Donald Rd E13 115 R1
Donald Rd, Croy 183 M12
Donald Wds Gdns, Surb 192 D4
Donaldson Rd NW6 108 F2
Donaldson Rd SE18 152 H1
Doncaster Dr, Nthlt 85 L10
Doncaster Gdns, N4 1 75 T11
Doncaster Gdns, Nthlt 85 L9
Doncaster Grn, Wat 50 E9
Doncaster Rd N9 44 J14
Doncel Ct E4 46 H13
Donegal St N1 10 H3
Doneraile St SW6 144 B2
Dongola Rd E13 115 R6
Dongola Rd N17 76 C5
Dongola Rd W E13 115 R6
Donington Av, Ilf 81 M10
Donkey La, Enf 44 G3
Donne Ct SE24 147 U12
Donne Pl SW3 31 R2
Donne Rd, Mitch 182 D7
Donne Rd, Dag 100 E3
Donnefield Av, Edg 53 R13
Donnington Rd NW10 107 S1
Donnington Rd, Har 69 N11
Donnington Rd, Wor Pk 193 P4
Donnybrook Rd SW16 164 F14
Donovan Av N10 74 D4
Doon St SE1 26 J2
Doone Cl, Tedd 158 G11
Dora Rd SW19 162 G8
Dora St E14 113 T11
Doral Way, Cars 3 195 U9
Doran Gro SE18 135 R13
Doran Mans N2 73 T10
Doran Wk E15 96 F14
Dorchester Av N13 59 T7
Dorchester Av, Bex 154 H14
Dorchester Av, Har 67 S12
Dorchester Cl, Nthlt 85 S9
Dorchester Cl, Orp 172 C14
Dorchester Ct N14 42 D13
Dorchester Ct SE24 147 U9
Dorchester Dr SE24 147 T9
Dorchester Gdns, E4 1 62 A8
Dorchester Gdns NW11 72 H7
Dorchester Gro W4 125 K11

Dorchester Ms, N Mal 5 178 G7
Dorchester Ms, Twick 141 L13
Dorchester Rd, Mord 181 K13
Dorchester Rd, Nthlt 85 S9
Dorchester Rd, Wor Pk 193 T2
Dorchester Way, Har 69 U11
Dorchester Waye, Hayes 102 E12
Dorcis Av, Bexh 154 J3
Dordrecht Rd W3 125 K2
Dore Av E12 98 G10
Dore Gdns, Mord 181 K13
Doreen Av NW9 88 H1
Dorell Cl, Sthl 103 M10
Doria Rd SW6 144 F3
Doric Way NW1 9 S6
Dorien Rd SW20 180 A3
Doris Av, Erith 155 T2
Doris Rd E7 97 P13
Dorking Cl SE8 131 T11
Dorking Cl, Wor Pk 194 A3
Dorlcote Rd SW18 145 R13
Dorma Trd Pk E10 95 P1
Dorman Pl N9 60 H4
Dorman Way NW8 109 N1
Dormay St SW18 144 J9
Dormer Cl E15 97 L11
Dormer Cl, Barn 40 A10
Dormers Av, Sthl 103 N12
Dormers Ri, Sthl 103 S12
Dormers Wells La, Sthl 103 P12
Dornberg Cl SE3 133 P13
Dorncliffe Rd SW6 144 D3
Dorney Ri, Orp 189 U8
Dorney Way, Houns 139 K10
Dornfell St NW6 90 F10
Dornton Rd SW12 164 D4
Dornton Rd, S Croy 198 B10
Dorothy Av, Wem 87 S14
Dorothy Evans Cl, Bexh 155 R7
Dorothy Gdns, Dag 100 D8
Dorothy Rd SW11 145 T6
Dorrell Pl, SW9 7 147 N7
Dorrien Wk SW16 164 H4
Dorrington Ct SE25 184 C3
Dorrington St EC1 19 K2
Dorrit Ms N18 60 D8
Dorrit Way, Chis 171 M11
Dors Cl NW9 88 G1
Dorset Av, Sthl 121 N7
Dorset Av, Well 153 T8
Dorset Bldgs EC4 19 N8
Dorset Cl NW1 15 U1
Dorset Dr, Edg 53 U12
Dorset Est E2 13 N5
Dorset Gdns, Mitch 183 L7
Dorset Ms N3 72 H1
Dorset Ms SW1 24 G10
Dorset Pl E15 96 G11
Dorset Pl SW1, 1 33 S5
Dorset Ri EC4 19 N8
Dorset Rd E7 97 U14
Dorset Rd N15 76 B7
Dorset Rd N22 75 K2
Dorset Rd SE9 170 C4
Dorset Rd SW8 34 E14
Dorset Rd SW19 180 G1
Dorset Rd W5 123 M5
Dorset Rd, Beck 185 N6
Dorset Rd, Har 67 U11
Dorset Rd, Mitch 181 S3
Dorset Sq NW1 7 U12
Dorset St W1 16 B3
Dorset Way, Twick 158 A1
Dorset Way, Houns 121 L14
Dorville Cres W6 125 R6
Dorville Rd SE12 151 N10
Douai Gro, Hmptn 175 U1
Doubleday Rd, Loug 49 S6
Doughty Ms WC1 10 F11
Doughty St WC1 10 F10
Douglas Av E17 78 A1
Douglas Av, N Mal 179 S8
Douglas Av, Wem 87 S13

Douglas Cl, Stan 52 H10
Douglas Cl, Wall 197 K13
Douglas Cres, Hayes 102 F8
Douglas Dr, Croy 200 A5
Douglas Est N1 93 U12
Douglas Ms, NW2 3 90 D6
Douglas Rd E4 47 K14
Douglas Rd E16 115 P9
Douglas Rd N1 93 T13
Douglas Rd N22 75 P1
Douglas Rd NW6 108 F1
Douglas Rd, Houns 139 S6
Douglas Rd, Ilf 82 B12
Douglas Rd, Kings T 178 C4
Douglas Rd, Surb 191 U2
Douglas Rd, Well 154 D2
Douglas Sq, Mord 180 H11
Douglas St SW1 33 S4
Douglas Way SE8 131 U14
Doulton Ms, NW6 1 91 K11
Dounesforth Gdns SW18 162 J2
Douro Pl W8 22 D9
Douro St E3 114 A3
Douthwaite Sq, E1 4 29 U2
Dove App E6 116 C10
Dove Cl, Nthlt 102 H7
Dove Ct, EC2 2 20 C7
Dove Ho Gdns E4 62 A4
Dove Ms SW5 30 F4
Dove Pk, Pnr 51 N14
Dove Rd N1 94 B11
Dove Row E2 112 G2
Dove Wk SW1 32 D6
Dovecot Cl, Pnr 66 D9
Dovecote Av, N22 1 75 P5
Dovecote Gdns, SW14 6 142 H5
Dovedale Av, Har 69 M11
Dovedale Av, Ilf 80 G3
Dovedale Cl, Well 154 A3
Dovedale Ri, Mitch 163 U13
Dovedale Rd SE22 149 K10
Dovedon Cl N14 58 J4
Dovehouse Mead, Bark 117 N3
Dovehouse St SW3 31 N7
Dover Cl NW2 90 A4
Dover Cl, Rom 83 T4
Dover Gdns, Cars 195 U6
Dover Ho Rd SW15 143 P7
Dover Pk Dr SW15 143 R11
Dover Patrol SE3 151 S4
Dover Rd E12 97 U3
Dover Rd N9 61 L3
Dover Rd SE19 166 B11
Dover Rd, Rom 83 K12
Dover St W1 25 L1
Dover Yd W1 25 L1
Dovercourt Av, Th Hth 183 P8
Dovercourt Est N1 94 B12
Dovercourt Gdns, Stan 53 R9
Dovercourt La, Sutt 3 195 U5
Dovercourt Rd SE22 148 D12
Doverfield Rd SW2 147 K13
Doveridge Gdns N13 59 R8
Doves Cl, Brom 202 C3
Dove's Yd N1 111 N2
Doveton Rd, S Croy 198 B10
Doveton St E1 113 L7
Dowanhill Rd SE6 168 G2
Dowdeswell Cl SW15 142 K8
Dowding Pl, Stan 52 H11
Dowgate Hill EC4 20 C10
Dowland St W10 108 D5
Dowlas St SE5 36 G14
Dowlas St SE5 36 G14
Dowlerville Rd, Orp 203 U13
Dowman Cl SW19 181 K1
Down Cl, Nthlt 102 D4
Down Hall Rd, Kings T 177 P2

Name	Page	Grid
Down Pl W6	125	S8
Down Rd, Tedd	159	K12
Down St W1	24	G4
Down St, W Mol	175	N9
Down St Ms W1	24	G5
Down Way, Nthlt	102	D5
Downage NW4	71	T5
Downalong, Bushey	52	A2
Downbarns Rd, Ruis	84	G6
Downderry Rd, Brom	168	J7
Downe Cl, Well	136	E13
Downe Rd, Mitch	181	U3
Downend SE18	134	J14
Downers Cotts SW4	146	F7
Downes Cl, Twick 4	141	K11
Downes Ct N21	59	N1
Downfield, Wor Pk	193	M2
Downfield Cl W9	6	A12
Downham Rd N1	94	A14
Downham Way, Brom	168	H9
Downhills Av N17	76	A6
Downhills Pk Rd N17	76	A6
Downhills Way N17	75	T5
Downhurst Av NW7	54	G10
Downing Cl, Har	67	U6
Downing Dr, Grnf	104	B2
Downing Rd, Dag	119	M1
Downing St SW1	26	A5
Downings E6	116	H11
Downland Cl N20	57	L1
Downleys Cl SE9	170	D3
Downman Rd SE9	152	D6
Downs, The SW20	162	A14
Downs Av, Chis	170	E10
Downs Av, Pnr	67	K12
Downs Br Rd, Beck	186	G2
Downs Hill, Beck	186	G1
Downs Pk Rd E5	94	J9
Downs Pk Rd E8	94	F9
Downs Rd E5	94	H7
Downs Rd, Beck	186	D3
Downs Rd, Enf	44	D8
Downs Rd, Th Hth	183	T1
Downs Vw, Islw	140	F1
Downsbury Ms, SW18 3	144	H10
Downsell Rd E15	96	G8
Downsfield Rd E17	77	S12
Downshall Av, Ilf	81	S12
Downshire Hill NW3	91	P8
Downside, Sun	174	A1
Downside, Twick	158	E5
Downside Cl SW19	163	M12
Downside Cres NW3	91	S10
Downside Cres W13	104	G8
Downside Rd, Sutt	195	P11
Downside Wk, Nthlt	103	L6
Downsview Gdns, SE19	165	T14
Downsview Rd SE19	165	T14
Downsway, Orp 4	203	R9
Downton Av SW2	165	L3
Downtown Rd SE16	131	S3
Downway N12	57	R13
Dowrey St, N1 1	111	N1
Dowsett Rd N17	76	G4
Dowson Cl, SE5 5	148	B7
Doyce St SE1	27	U5
Doyle Gdns NW10	107	P1
Doyle Rd SE25	184	G8
D'Oyley St SW1	32	C1
Doynton St N19	92	D4
Draco St SE17	35	T9
Dragmire La, Mitch	181	P7
Dragon Rd SE15	36	H12
Dragonfly Cl E13	115	S5
Dragoon Rd SE8	131	T10
Dragor Rd NW10	106	F7
Drake Ct, Har	85	M2
Drake Cres SE28	118	F12
Drake Rd SE4	150	A5
Drake Rd, Chess	192	B9
Drake Rd, Croy	183	M14
Drake Rd, Har	85	M3
Drake Rd, Mitch	182	A11
Drake St WC1	18	E3
Drake St, Enf	44	A1
Drakefell Rd SE4	149	R5
Drakefell Rd SE14	149	N4
Drakefield Rd SW17	164	B5
Drakeley Ct N5	93	R7
Drakes Ctyd, NW6 2	90	F13
Drakes Wk E6	116	G2
Drakewood Rd SW16	164	G14
Draper Cl, Belv	137	M8
Drapers Rd E15	96	G8
Drapers Rd N17	76	E6
Drapers Rd, Enf	43	R3
Drappers Way, SE16 4	37	U2
Draven Cl, Brom	187	M13
Drawdock Rd SE10	132	H3
Drawell Cl SE18	135	S9
Drax Av SW20	161	P13
Draxmont SW19	162	D11
Dray Gdns SW2	147	M10
Draycot Rd E11	79	R13
Draycot Rd, Surb	192	A2
Draycott Av SW3	31	T3
Draycott Av, Har	69	K11
Draycott Cl, Har	69	K11
Draycott Ms, SW6 6	144	F3
Draycott Pl SW3	31	U4
Draycott Ter SW3	32	A3
Drayford Cl W9	108	F7
Draymans Way, Islw	140	F5
Drayside Ms, Sthl 1	121	L4
Drayson Ms W8	126	H4
Drayton Av W13	104	H13
Drayton Av, Loug	48	F12
Drayton Av, Orp	203	K2
Drayton Br Rd W7	104	E13
Drayton Br Rd W13	104	F12
Drayton Cl, Houns	139	L9
Drayton Cl, Ilf	99	N2
Drayton Gdns N21	43	S14
Drayton Gdns SW10	30	G7
Drayton Gdns W13	104	H13
Drayton Grn W13	104	H13
Drayton Grn Rd W13	104	J14
Drayton Gro W13	104	H13
Drayton Pk N5	93	P9
Drayton Pk Ms N5	93	N9
Drayton Rd E11	96	H1
Drayton Rd N17	76	D3
Drayton Rd NW10	107	L1
Drayton Rd W13	104	H13
Drayton Rd, Borwd	38	B7
Drayton Rd, Croy	197	S3
Drayton Waye, Har	69	K11
Dreadnought St SE10	133	K6
Dresden Cl NW6	91	K11
Dresden Rd N19	92	F1
Dressington Av SE4	150	B11
Drew Av NW7	56	C11
Drew Gdns, Grnf	86	F11
Drew Rd E16	134	C2
Drewstead Rd SW16	164	G3
Driffield Rd E3	113	R3
Drift, The, Brom	202	B6
Drift Way, Rich	160	A2
Driftway, The, Mitch 1	182	B1
Drinkwater Rd, Har	85	R3
Drive, The E4	46	H14
Drive, The E17	78	D6
Drive, The E18	79	N5
Drive, The N3	56	G13
Drive, The N6	73	T9
Drive, The N11	58	G12
Drive, The NW10	89	M14
Drive, The NW11	72	C13
Drive, The SW6	144	D3
Drive, The SW16	183	L5
Drive, The SW20	161	U14
Drive, The W3	106	F12
Drive, The, Barn	99	U13
Drive, The, Barn	40	C6
Drive, The (New Barnet), Barn	41	L11
Drive, The, Beck	186	A2
Drive, The, Bex	154	F12
Drive, The, Buck H	47	U14
Drive, The, Chis	189	T5
Drive, The, Edg	54	B9
Drive, The, Enf	44	B2
Drive, The, Epsom	193	L12
Drive, The, Erith	137	S13
Drive, The, Felt	138	E13
Drive, The, Har	67	P14
Drive, The, Houns	139	U4
Drive, The, Ilf	80	D11
Drive, The, Islw	140	B3
Drive, The, Kings T	160	E14
Drive, The, Loug	48	C6
Drive, The, Mord	181	N10
Drive, The, Orp	203	U4
Drive, The, Sid	172	D7
Drive, The, Surb	177	R14
Drive, The, Th Hth	184	A7
Drive, The, Wem	88	E4
Drive, The, W Wick	186	G14
Driveway, The E17	78	B11
Droitwich Cl SE26	166	G6
Dromey Gdns, Har	52	E13
Dromore Rd SW15	144	C12
Dronfield Gdns, Dag	100	F9
Droop St W10	108	D7
Drover La SE15	131	K13
Drovers Pl SE15	131	K13
Droveway, Loug	49	K3
Druce Rd SE21	148	D12
Druid St SE1	28	J5
Druids Way, Brom	186	H7
Drum St, E1 8	21	P6
Drumaline Ridge, Wor Pk	192	J4
Drummond Cres NW1	9	R6
Drummond Dr, Stan	52	F13
Drummond Gate SW1	33	T6
Drummond Pl, Rich	141	R8
Drummond Pl, Twick	140	J12
Drummond Rd E11	79	S11
Drummond Rd SE16	130	J5
Drummond Rd, Croy	197	T4
Drummond St NW1	9	L9
Drummonds, The, Buck H	63	R4
Drury Cres, Croy	197	N4
Drury La WC2	18	E8
Drury Rd, Har	67	U13
Drury Way NW10	88	H9
Drury Way Ind Est NW10	88	F9
Dryad St SW15	144	A6
Dryburgh Gdns NW9	70	B5
Dryburgh Rd SW15	143	T7
Dryden Av W7	104	E12
Dryden Cl, Ilf	65	U11
Dryden Ct SE11	35	M3
Dryden Rd SW19	163	L11
Dryden Rd, Enf	44	D11
Dryden Rd, Har	68	F2
Dryden Rd, Well	153	T1
Dryden Rd WC2	18	C7
Dryfield Cl NW10	88	F12
Dryfield Rd, Edg	54	F12
Dryfield Wk, SE8 1	132	A11
Dryhill Rd, Belv	137	M11
Dryland Av, Orp	203	T7
Drylands Rd N8	75	K11
Drysdale Av E4	46	D12
Drysdale Pl N1	12	J6
Drysdale St N1	12	J6
Du Burstow Ter, W7 2	122	D3
Du Cane Cl W12	107	T2
Du Cane Ct SW17	164	A2
Du Cane Rd W12	107	P12
Du Cros Dr, Stan	53	N11
Dublin Av E8	112	H1
Ducal St E2	13	N8
Duchess Cl N11	58	C10
Duchess Cl, Sutt	195	M7
Duchess Gro, Buck H	63	S3
Duchess Ms W1	17	J3
Duchess of Bedford's Wk W8	126	G4
Duchess St W1	17	K3
Duchy St SE1	27	L1
Ducie St SW4	147	L7
Duck La W1	17	R8
Duck Lees La, Enf	45	S8
Duckett Ms N4	75	R11
Duckett Rd N4	75	R11
Duckett St E1	113	P9
Ducks Wk, Twick	141	M10
Dudden Hill La NW10	89	M10
Duddington Cl SE9	170	B7
Dudley Av, Har	69	L6
Dudley Ct NW11	72	F8
Dudley Dr, Mord	180	D14
Dudley Dr, Ruis	84	D10
Dudley Gdns W13	123	K3
Dudley Gdns, Har	86	A2
Dudley Rd E17	78	B4
Dudley Rd N3	72	J4
Dudley Rd NW6	108	D3
Dudley Rd SW19	162	G12
Dudley Rd, Har	85	T3
Dudley Rd, Ilf	99	K7
Dudley Rd, Kings T	177	T5
Dudley Rd, Rich	142	A4
Dudley Rd, Sthl	120	H5
Dudley Rd, Walt	174	A12
Dudley St W2	14	J4
Dudlington Rd E5	95	M3
Dudmaston Ms SW3	31	L6
Dudsbury Rd, Sid	172	D11
Dudset La, Houns	138	A1
Duff St E14	114	C12
Dufferin Av EC1	12	C11
Dufferin St EC1	12	B11
Duffield Cl, Har	68	F10
Duffield Dr N15	76	F7
Dufour's Pl W1	17	N8
Dugard Way SE11	35	P3
Duke Humphrey Rd SE3	151	K2
Duke of Cambridge Cl, Twick	140	B12
Duke of Edinburgh Rd, Sutt	195	N4
Duke of Wellington Pl SW1	24	F6
Duke of York St SW1	25	P1
Duke Rd W4	124	H9
Duke Rd, Ilf	81	N8
Duke Shore Pl E14	113	T14
Duke St SW1	25	N1
Duke St W1	16	E7
Duke St, Rich	141	P9
Duke St, Sutt	195	N7
Duke St Hill SE1	28	E2
Dukes Av N3	72	J1
Dukes Av N10	74	D5
Dukes Av W4	124	H9
Dukes Av, Edg	53	T11
Dukes Av, Har	67	M12
Dukes Av (Wealdstone), Har	68	C7
Dukes Av, Houns	138	J7
Dukes Av, Kings T	159	N8
Dukes Av, N Mal	179	L6
Dukes Av, Nthlt	85	K14
Dukes Av, Rich	159	M8
Dukes Cl, Hmptn	157	L9
Dukes Ct E6	116	H1
Dukes Grn Av, Felt	138	A10
Dukes La W8	126	H3
Dukes Ms N10	74	D5
Duke's Ms W1	16	E6
Dukes Orchard, Bex	173	T1
Duke's Pas E17	78	E6
Dukes Pl EC3	21	K7
Dukes Rd E6	116	G2
Dukes Rd W3	106	A8
Duke's Rd WC1	9	T8
Dukes Way, W Wick	201	K5
Duke's Yd W1	16	F9
Dukesthorpe Rd SE26	167	P8
Dulas St N4	93	M2
Dulford St W11	108	C13

Name	Page	Grid
Dulka Rd SW11	145	U10
Dulverton Rd SE9	171	N3
Dulverton Rd, Ruis	84	B3
Dulwich Common SE21	166	D2
Dulwich Common SE22	166	D2
Dulwich Lawn Cl, SE22 *7*	148	E10
Dulwich Oaks, The SE21	166	E5
Dulwich Rd SE24	147	R10
Dulwich Village SE21	148	C11
Dulwich Wd Av SE19	166	D8
Dulwich Wd Pk SE19	166	D8
Dumbarton Rd SW2	147	K12
Dumbleton Cl, Kings T	178	C2
Dumbreck Rd SE9	152	G6
Dumont Rd N16	94	D5
Dumpton Pl NW1	92	A14
Dunbar Av SW16	183	N4
Dunbar Av, Beck	185	S7
Dunbar Av, Dag	101	N6
Dunbar Cl, Hayes	102	B10
Dunbar Ct, Sutt	195	P9
Dunbar Gdns, Dag	101	P10
Dunbar Rd E7	97	P12
Dunbar Rd N22	75	P1
Dunbar Rd, N Mal	178	F7
Dunbar St SE27	165	T6
Dunblane Cl, Edg *1*	54	C4
Dunblane Rd SE9	152	D4
Dunboyne Rd NW3	91	T9
Dunbridge St E2	112	H7
Duncan Cl, Barn	41	L8
Duncan Gro W3	106	J11
Duncan Rd E8	112	J1
Duncan Rd, Rich	141	S7
Duncan St N1	11	N2
Duncan Ter N1	11	N2
Duncannon St WC2	18	A12
Dunch St, E1 *12*	113	K12
Duncombe Hill SE23	149	R13
Duncombe Rd N19	92	G2
Duncrievie Rd SE13	150	H12
Duncroft SE18	135	R14
Dundalk Rd SE4	149	R6
Dundas Gdns, W Mol	175	R6
Dundas Rd SE15	149	L3
Dundee Rd E13	115	R4
Dundee Rd SE25	184	J10
Dundee St E1	130	J2
Dundee Way, Enf	45	S5
Dundela Gdns, Wor Pk	193	S8
Dundonald Rd SW19	162	E14
Dunedin Rd E10	96	D6
Dunedin Rd, Ilf	99	M1
Dunedin Way, Hayes	102	F7
Dunelm Gro SE27	165	T6
Dunelm St E1	113	N11
Dunfield Gdns SE6	168	D9
Dunfield Rd SE6	168	D9
Dunford Rd N7	93	M8
Dungarvan Av SW15	143	N7
Dunheved Cl, Th Hth	183	N11
Dunheved Rd N, Th Hth	183	P11
Dunheved Rd S, Th Hth	183	P11
Dunheved Rd W, Th Hth	183	N11
Dunholme Grn N9	60	E5
Dunholme La, N9 *1*	60	E6
Dunholme Rd N9	60	F5
Dunkeld Rd SE25	184	B7
Dunkeld Rd, Dag	100	D4
Dunkery Rd SE9	170	B7
Dunkirk St SE27	165	T7
Dunlace Rd E5	95	N8
Dunleary Cl, Houns	139	M14
Dunley Dr, Croy	200	E12
Dunloe Av N17	76	B6
Dunloe St E2	13	L3
Dunlop Pl SE16	29	P11
Dunmore Rd NW6	108	C2
Dunmore Rd SW20	179	U2
Dunmow Cl, Felt *1*	156	J7
Dunmow Cl, Loug	48	C12
Dunmow Cl, Rom	82	E9
Dunmow Rd E15	96	H8
Dunn Mead NW9	55	L14
Dunn St E8	94	E9
Dunnage Cres SE16	131	S7
Dunnock Cl N9	61	N2
Dunnock Cl, Borwd	38	A8
Dunnock Rd E6	116	D11
Dunollie Pl, NW5 *3*	92	F9
Dunollie Rd NW5	92	F9
Dunoon Rd SE23	149	M13
Dunraven Dr, Enf	43	P3
Dunraven Rd W12	125	P1
Dunraven St W1	16	B9
Dunsany Rd W14	126	A6
Dunsfold Way, Croy	200	E13
Dunsford Way, SW15 *2*	143	S12
Dunsmore Cl, Hayes *1*	102	H7
Dunsmore Rd, Walt	174	C11
Dunsmure Rd N16	94	D1
Dunspring La, Ilf	80	J4
Dunstable Ms, W1 *6*	16	F2
Dunstable Rd, Rich	141	S8
Dunstable Rd, W Mol	175	L8
Dunstall Rd SW20	161	T12
Dunstall Way, W Mol	175	S6
Dunstan Cl, N2 *1*	73	L5
Dunstan Rd NW11	92	F7
Dunstans Gro SE22	148	J11
Dunstans Rd SE22	148	J11
Dunster Av, Mord	194	B1
Dunster Cl, Barn	40	B8
Dunster Cl, Rom	83	T4
Dunster Ct EC3	20	J9
Dunster Dr NW9	88	E2
Dunster Gdns NW6	90	F13
Dunster Way, Har	85	K5
Dunsterville Way SE1	28	F7
Dunston Rd E8	112	E2
Dunston Rd SW11	146	B5
Dunston St E8	112	E1
Dunton Cl, Surb	191	R2
Dunton Rd E10	78	C13
Dunton Rd SE1	37	L5
Duntshill Rd SW18	163	K2
Dunvegan Cl, W Mol	175	R7
Dunvegan Rd SE9	152	F8
Dunwich Rd, Bexh	155	L1
Dunworth Ms, W11 *15*	108	E11
Duplex Ride SW1	24	B7
Dupont Rd SW20	180	B3
Dupont St E14	113	S10
Duppas Av, Croy	197	S8
Duppas Hill La, Croy	197	S7
Duppas Hill Rd, Croy	197	P7
Duppas Hill Ter, Croy	197	S6
Duppas Rd, Croy	197	P6
Dupree Rd SE7	133	R9
Dura Den Cl, Beck	168	C13
Durand Cl, Cars	195	T2
Durand Gdns SW9	147	M1
Durand Way NW10	88	E14
Durands Wk, SE16 *4*	131	S3
Durant St E2	13	S5
Durants Pk Av, Enf	45	N7
Durants Rd, Enf	45	M7
Durban Gdns, Dag	101	U13
Durban Rd E15	114	J5
Durban Rd E17	77	T1
Durban Rd N17	60	D12
Durban Rd SE27	165	U7
Durban Rd, Beck	185	T4
Durban Rd, Ilf	99	R1
Durbin Rd, Chess	191	S8
Durdans Rd, Sthl	103	M12
Durell Gdns, Dag	100	G8
Durell Rd, Dag	100	G9
Durford Cres SW15	161	P1
Durham Av, Brom	187	L7
Durham Av, Houns	121	M10
Durham Av, Wdf Grn	64	A9
Durham Cl SW20	179	S3
Durham Hill, Brom	169	M7
Durham Ho St WC2	18	C12
Durham Pl SW3	31	U8
Durham Pl, Ilf *2*	99	M8
Durham Ri SE18	135	M9
Durham Rd E12	98	A8
Durham Rd E16	115	K8
Durham Rd N2	73	T5
Durham Rd N7	93	M3
Durham Rd N9	60	G3
Durham Rd SW20	179	S1
Durham Rd W5	123	P6
Durham Rd, Borwd	38	F5
Durham Rd, Brom	187	M6
Durham Rd, Dag	101	T9
Durham Rd, Felt	138	E14
Durham Rd, Har	67	S10
Durham Rd, Sid	172	C9
Durham Row E1	113	P10
Durham St SE11	34	F8
Durham Ter W2	14	A5
Durham Wf, Brent *2*	123	M13
Durham Yd, E2 *1*	112	J5
Durley Av, Pnr	67	K12
Durley Rd N16	76	C14
Durlston Rd E5	94	G3
Durlston Rd, Kings T	159	S12
Durnell Way, Loug	48	H6
Durnford St N15	76	D10
Durnford St, SE10 *3*	132	F12
Durning Rd SE19	166	B10
Durnsford Av SW19	162	H4
Durnsford Rd N11	58	G14
Durnsford Rd SW19	162	H4
Durrant Way, Orp	203	P9
Durrell Rd SW6	144	E3
Durrington Av SW20	179	T1
Durrington Pk Rd SW20	161	U14
Durrington Rd E5	95	R8
Dursley Cl SE3	151	T3
Dursley Gdns SE3	152	A2
Dursley Rd SE3	151	U3
Durward St E1	112	H9
Durweston Ms, W1 *3*	16	B2
Durweston St W1	16	A3
Dury Rd, Barn	40	E2
Dutch Gdns, Kings T	160	C12
Dutch Yd SW18	144	H10
Duthie St, E14 *8*	114	F14
Dutton St SE10	150	E1
Duxberry Cl, Brom *1*	188	D10
Dwight Ct, SW6 *3*	144	B2
Dye Ho La E3	114	B2
Dyers Hall Rd E11	96	J2
Dyers La SW15	143	S6
Dykes Way, Brom	187	L5
Dylan Rd SE24	147	S8
Dylan Rd, Belv	137	P6
Dylways SE5	148	B7
Dymchurch Cl, Ilf	80	G4
Dymchurch Cl, Orp *1*	203	S7
Dymes Path, SW19 *2*	162	B4
Dymock St SW6	144	J5
Dyne Rd NW6	90	E13
Dyneley Rd SE12	169	U7
Dynevor Rd N16	94	D6
Dynevor Rd, Rich	141	S9
Dynham Rd NW6	90	G13
Dyott St WC1	18	A6
Dysart Av, Kings T	159	M9
Dysart St EC2	12	F12
Dyson Rd E11	79	K12
Dyson Rd E15	97	M12
Dysons Rd N18	61	K11

E

Name	Page	Grid
Eade Rd N4	75	U13
Eagans Cl N2	73	P6
Eagle Av, Rom	82	J12
Eagle Cl, Enf	45	M8
Eagle Cl, Wall	197	K12
Eagle Ct EC1	19	P1
Eagle Dr NW9	71	K3
Eagle Hill, SE19 *1*	166	B12
Eagle La E11	79	N8
Eagle Ms N1	94	C12
Eagle Pl SW7	30	G5
Eagle Rd, Wem	87	P13
Eagle St WC1	18	F3
Eagle Ter, Wdf Grn	63	R13
Eagle Wf Rd N1	12	A2
Eaglesfield Rd SE18	153	K2
Ealdham Sq SE9	151	U8
Ealing Cl, Borwd	38	G2
Ealing Grn W5	123	N1
Ealing Pk Gdns W5	123	L8
Ealing Rd, Brent	123	R11
Ealing Rd, Nthlt	85	N14
Ealing Rd, Wem	87	R12
Ealing Village W5	105	S12
Eamont St NW8	7	P2
Eardley Cres SW5	126	H9
Eardley Rd SW16	164	F10
Eardley Rd, Belv	137	P9
Earl Cl N11	58	C10
Earl Ri SE18	135	N8
Earl Rd SW14	142	F7
Earl St EC2	20	F1
Earldom Rd SW15	143	U7
Earle Gdns, Kings T	159	S13
Earlham Gro E7	97	M10
Earlham Gro N22	59	M14
Earlham St WC2	18	A8
Earls Ct Gdns SW5	30	A4
Earls Ct Rd SW5	126	H7
Earls Ct Rd W8	126	G6
Earls Ct Sq SW5	30	A5
Earls Cres, Har	68	C7
Earl's Path, Loug	47	U5
Earls Ter W8	126	F6
Earls Wk W8	126	G6
Earls Wk, Dag	100	C7
Earlsferry Way N1	93	L14
Earlsfield Rd SW18	145	M14
Earlshall Rd SE9	152	E8
Earlsmead, Har	85	M8
Earlsmead Rd N15	76	E9
Earlsmead Rd NW10	107	T5
Earlsthorpe Ms SW12	146	A12
Earlsthorpe Rd SE26	167	N8
Earlstoke St EC1	11	P6
Earlston Gro, E9 *9*	113	K2
Earlswood Av, Th Hth	183	P10
Earlswood Cl, SE10 *5*	133	K10
Earlswood Gdns, Ilf	80	G6
Earlswood St SE10	133	K10
Early Ms NW1	110	D1
Earnshaw St WC2	17	U6
Earsby St W14	126	D7
Easby Cres, Mord	181	K12
Easebourne Rd, Dag	100	E10
Easley's Ms W1	16	F6
East Acton La W3	107	K13
East Arbour St E1	113	N11
East Av E12	98	D13
East Av E17	78	C8
East Av, Hayes	102	A14
East Av, Sthl	103	L13
East Av, Wall	197	L10
East Bank N16	94	D1
East Barnet Rd, Barn	41	R11

Name	Page	Grid
East Churchfield Rd W3	124	G1
East Cl W5	106	A8
East Cl, Barn	42	B8
East Cl, Grnf	103	U4
East Ct, Wem	87	M4
East Cres, Enf	44	D9
East Cres N11	57	U7
East Cross Route E3	114	A2
East Duck Lees La, Enf	45	S8
East Dulwich Gro SE22	148	D9
East Dulwich Rd SE15	148	G7
East Dulwich Rd SE22	148	F7
East End Rd N2	73	L5
East End Rd N3	72	G4
East End Way, Pnr	67	K5
East Entrance, Dag 1	119	S4
East Ferry Rd E14	132	D8
East Gdns SW17	163	R11
East Ham Ind Est E6	116	C8
East Ham Manor Way E6	116	G12
East Harding St EC4	19	M6
East Heath Rd NW3	91	N5
East Hill SW18	145	M9
East Hill, Wem	88	A3
East India Dock Rd E14	114	A12
East La SE16	29	S8
East La, Kings T	177	P5
East La, Wem	87	L5
East Mascalls, SE7 1	133	T12
East Mead, Ruis	84	G6
East Mt St E1	113	K10
East Parkside SE10	133	L4
East Pas EC1	19	S2
East Pier E1	130	J2
East Pl, SE27 2	165	T7
East Poultry Av EC1	19	P3
East Rd E15	115	N2
East Rd N1	12	D6
East Rd SW19	163	M12
East Rd, Barn	58	A1
East Rd, Edg	70	D1
East Rd, Kings T	177	S1
East Rd (Chadwell Heath), Rom	82	J9
East Rd, Well	154	C3
East Rochester Way SE9	153	R8
East Rochester Way, Bex	154	H11
East Rochester Way, Sid	153	R8
East Row E11	79	M11
East Row W10	108	D8
East Sheen Av SW14	142	H8
East Smithfield E1	21	P12
East St SE17	36	B6
East St, Bark	99	M14
East St, Bexh	155	P7
East St, Brent	123	L13
East St, Brom	187	P3
East Surrey Gro SE15	130	E14
East Tenter St E1	21	P8
East Twrs, Pnr	66	G11
East Vw E4	62	F9
East Vw, Barn	40	E5
East Wk, Barn	58	B1
East Wk, Hayes	120	B2
East Way E11	79	S9
East Way, Brom	187	N13
East Way, Croy	199	S4
East Way, Hayes	120	A1
East Way, Ruis	84	A1
East Woodside, Bex	173	K1
Eastbank Rd, Hmptn	157	T10
Eastbourne Av W3	106	G12
Eastbourne Gdns SW14	142	E6
Eastbourne Ms W2	14	G6
Eastbourne Rd E6	116	H5
Eastbourne Rd E15	115	K2
Eastbourne Rd N15	76	D12
Eastbourne Rd SW17	164	B12
Eastbourne Rd W4	124	F11
Eastbourne Rd, Brent	123	M10
Eastbourne Rd, Felt	156	H3
Eastbourne Ter W2	14	H5
Eastbournia Av N9	61	K5
Eastbrook Av N9	45	M14
Eastbrook Av, Dag	101	T7
Eastbrook Rd SE3	151	S1
Eastbury Av, Bark	117	R1
Eastbury Av, Enf	44	D1
Eastbury Ct, Bark	117	S1
Eastbury Gro W4	125	K10
Eastbury Ho, Bark	117	T1
Eastbury Rd E6	116	H8
Eastbury Rd, Kings T	159	R14
Eastbury Rd, Orp	189	P12
Eastbury Sq, Bark	117	T1
Eastbury Ter E1	113	N8
Eastcastle St W1	17	M6
Eastcheap EC3	20	G10
Eastcombe Av SE7	133	R11
Eastcote, Orp	203	T1
Eastcote Av, Grnf	86	H10
Eastcote Av, Har	85	S4
Eastcote Av, W Mol	175	M9
Eastcote La, Har	85	T5
Eastcote La, Nthlt	85	M13
Eastcote La N, Nthlt	85	N12
Eastcote Pl, Pnr	66	C11
Eastcote Rd, Har	85	T6
Eastcote Rd, Pnr	66	H9
Eastcote Rd (Eastcote Village), Pnr	66	C10
Eastcote Rd, Well	153	P4
Eastcote St SW9	147	L4
Eastcote Vw, Pnr	66	F8
Eastcroft Rd, Epsom	193	K14
Eastdown Pk SE13	150	G8
Eastern Av E11	79	U11
Eastern Av, Ilf	80	D11
Eastern Av, Pnr	66	F13
Eastern Av, Rom	81	K11
Eastern Av W, Rom	82	J8
Eastern Ind Est, Erith	137	P4
Eastern Rd E13	115	S3
Eastern Rd E17	78	F9
Eastern Rd N2	73	U6
Eastern Rd N22	74	J1
Eastern Rd SE4	150	B8
Eastern Way SE2	136	H1
Eastern Way SE28	136	C3
Eastern Way, Belv	137	N3
Eastern Way, Erith	137	R3
Easternville Gdns, Ilf	81	M12
Eastfield Gdns, Dag	101	N8
Eastfield Rd E17	78	B7
Eastfield Rd N8	74	J6
Eastfield Rd, Dag	101	N8
Eastfields, Pnr	66	F10
Eastfields Rd W3	106	E10
Eastfields Rd, Mitch	182	B3
Eastgate Cl SE28	118	G12
Eastglade, Pnr	67	L5
Eastham Cl, Barn	40	D10
Eastholm N11	73	K8
Eastholme, Hayes	120	A1
Eastlake Rd SE5	147	T4
Eastlands Cres SE21	148	E12
Eastlea Ms E16	115	K8
Eastleigh Av, Har	85	R4
Eastleigh Cl NW2	89	K6
Eastleigh Cl, Sutt 5	195	K14
Eastleigh Rd E17	77	T4
Eastleigh Rd, Bexh	155	U5
Eastleigh Wk SW15 2	143	P14
Eastleigh Way, Felt	156	A2
Eastman Rd W3	124	H3
Eastmead Av, Grnf	103	R6
Eastmead Cl, Brom	188	D4
Eastmearn Rd SE21	165	U4
Eastmont Rd, Esher	190	D4
Eastmoor Pl, SE7 3	134	A6
Eastmoor St SE7	134	A6
Eastney Rd, Croy	197	R1
Eastney St SE10	132	H10
Eastnor Rd SE9	171	M2
Easton Gdns, Borwd	38	H8
Easton St WC1	11	K9
Eastry Av, Brom	187	M12
Eastry Rd, Erith	137	P13
Eastside Rd NW11	72	E8
Eastview Av SE18	135	S13
Eastville Av NW11	72	E10
Eastway E9	95	T11
Eastway E10	96	H4
Eastway E15	96	B9
Eastway, Mord	180	B9
Eastway, Wall	96	B9
Eastway Commercial Cen E9	96	A9
Eastwell Cl, Beck	185	R1
Eastwood Cl E18	79	P4
Eastwood Cl N17	60	J14
Eastwood Rd E18	79	P3
Eastwood Rd N10	74	A4
Eastwood Rd, Ilf	82	B14
Eastwood St SW16	164	E12
Eatington Rd E10	78	G10
Eaton Cl SW1	32	D3
Eaton Cl, Stan	53	K8
Eaton Dr SW9	147	R8
Eaton Dr, Kings T	160	B14
Eaton Gdns, Dag	100	J13
Eaton Gate SW1	32	E1
Eaton La SW1	24	J11
Eaton Ms N SW1	24	E12
Eaton Ms S SW1	24	G12
Eaton Ms W SW1	32	E2
Eaton Pk Rd N13	59	P4
Eaton Pl SW1	24	D12
Eaton Ri E11	79	T9
Eaton Ri W5	105	N11
Eaton Rd NW4	71	U9
Eaton Rd, Enf	44	D7
Eaton Rd, Houns	140	B8
Eaton Rd, Sid	172	G4
Eaton Rd, Sutt	195	N11
Eaton Row SW1	24	H11
Eaton Sq SW1	24	F11
Eaton Ter SW1	32	E3
Eaton Ter Ms, SW1 3	32	D1
Eatons Mead E4	62	J8
Eatonville Rd SW17	163	U4
Eatonville Vil, SW17 7	163	U3
Ebbisham Dr SW8	34	F11
Ebbisham Rd, Wor Pk	193	T3
Ebbsfleet Rd NW2	90	C8
Ebdon Way SE3	151	R6
Ebenezer St, N1 2	12	C6
Ebenezer Wk SW16	182	E2
Ebley Cl SE15	37	M12
Ebner St SW18	145	K9
Ebor St E1	13	L10
Ebrington Rd, Har	69	N12
Ebsworth St SE23	149	P14
Eburne Rd N7	93	K6
Ebury Br SW1	32	G5
Ebury Br Est SW1	32	G6
Ebury Br Rd SW1	32	F7
Ebury Cl, Kes	202	D6
Ebury Ms SE27	165	S5
Ebury Ms SW1	32	G2
Ebury Ms E SW1	32	G1
Ebury Sq SW1	32	F4
Ebury St SW1	24	H12
Eccles Rd SW11	145	T7
Ecclesbourne Cl N13	59	N10
Ecclesbourne Gdns N13	59	N9
Ecclesbourne Rd N1	93	U14
Ecclesbourne Rd, Th Hth	183	T9
Eccleston Br SW1	32	J2
Eccleston Cl, Barn	41	S8
Eccleston Cl, Orp	203	P3
Eccleston Cres, Rom	82	C13
Eccleston Ms SW1	24	F11
Eccleston Pl SW1	32	H1
Eccleston Rd W13	104	G14
Eccleston Sq SW1	33	K4
Eccleston Sq Ms, SW1 4	33	L3
Eccleston St SW1	24	G12
Ecclestone Pl, Wem	87	U9
Echo Hts E4	62	C2
Eckford St N1	10	J2
Eckstein Rd SW11	145	S7
Eclipse Rd E13	115	R9
Ector Rd SE6	168	J4
Edbrooke Rd W9	108	G8
Eddiscombe Rd SW6	144	F3
Eddy Cl, Rom	83	R12
Eddystone Rd SE4	149	S10
Ede Cl, Houns	139	M6
Eden Cl NW3	90	H4
Eden Cl W8	126	H5
Eden Cl, Wem	105	N2
Eden Gro E17	78	D9
Eden Gro N7	93	M10
Eden Ms SW17	163	M6
Eden Pk Av, Beck	185	S7
Eden Rd E17	78	D10
Eden Rd SE27	165	S9
Eden Rd, Beck	185	R7
Eden Rd, Croy	190	A7
Eden St, Kings T	177	P4
Eden Way, Beck	185	U10
Edenbridge Cl, SE16 4	130	J10
Edenbridge Rd E9	95	P14
Edenbridge Rd, Enf	44	D12
Edencourt Rd SW16	164	D11
Edenfield Gdns, Wor Pk	193	L5
Edenham Way W10	108	E9
Edenhurst Av SW6	144	E5
Edensor Gdns W4	125	K13
Edensor Rd W4	124	J13
Edenvale Rd, Mitch	164	B14
Edenvale St SW6	145	K4
Ederline Av SW16	183	N5
Edgar Kail Way SE22	148	D6
Edgar Rd E3	114	D5
Edgar Rd, Houns	139	M13
Edgar Rd, Rom	82	G13
Edgarley Ter SW6	144	C2
Edgbaston Rd, Wat 1	50	C5
Edge Hill SE18	134	J11
Edge Hill SW19	162	B13
Edge Hill Av N3	72	G7
Edge Hill Ct SW19	162	B14
Edge St W8	126	H1
Edgeborough Way, Brom	170	A14
Edgebury, Chis	171	K8
Edgebury Wk, Chis	171	L7
Edgecoombe Cl, Kings T	160	G13
Edgecot Gro N15	76	C9
Edgecote Cl W3	124	E3
Edgefield Av, Bark	99	U13
Edgefield Gdns, Dag	101	N7
Edgehill Rd W13	105	L10
Edgehill Rd, Chis	171	L6
Edgel St, SW18 4	145	K8
Edgeley La SW4	146	G6
Edgeley Rd SW4	146	G5
Edgepoint Cl SE27	165	R10
Edgewood Grn, Croy	199	P1
Edgeworth Av NW4	71	P9
Edgeworth Cl NW4	71	N9
Edgeworth Cres NW4	71	P9
Edgeworth Rd SE9	151	U12
Edgeworth Rd, Barn	41	R7
Edgington Rd SW16	164	F12
Edgington Way, Sid	172	F13
Edgware Rd NW2	89	R2
Edgware Rd NW9	70	G5
Edgware Rd W2	15	R6
Edgware Way, Edg	54	E7

Edgwarebury Gdns, Edg	54	B9
Edgwarebury La, Edg	54	B8
Edinburgh Cl E2	113	L4
Edinburgh Cl, Pnr	66	H14
Edinburgh Ct SW20	180	A10
Edinburgh Dr, Rom	83	T7
Edinburgh Gate SW1	23	U6
Edinburgh Rd E13	115	R3
Edinburgh Rd E17	78	A9
Edinburgh Rd N18	60	H9
Edinburgh Rd W7	122	E3
Edinburgh Rd, Sutt	195	M4
Edington Rd SE2	136	D5
Edington Rd, Enf	45	M4
Edis St NW1	110	A1
Edison Cl E17	78	A9
Edison Dr, Sthl	103	S12
Edison Gro SE18	135	T14
Edison Rd N8	74	H12
Edison Rd, Brom	187	N3
Edison Rd, Enf	45	U3
Edison Rd, Well	153	T1
Edith Gdns, Surb	178	C13
Edith Gro SW10	30	G13
Edith Rd E6	98	B13
Edith Rd E15	96	H9
Edith Rd N11	58	H14
Edith Rd SE25	184	B10
Edith Rd SW19	163	K11
Edith Rd W14	126	C8
Edith Rd, Rom 3	82	G13
Edith Row SW6	145	K1
Edith St E2	13	R2
Edith Ter SW10	30	F13
Edith Vil W14	126	E8
Edith Yd SW10	30	H13
Edithna St SW9	147	K5
Edmansons Cl N17	76	E2
Edmeston Cl E9	95	S11
Edmond Halley Way SE10	132	J4
Edmonds Ct, W Mol 1	175	S9
Edmund Gro, Felt	157	L4
Edmund Rd, Mitch	181	S5
Edmund Rd, Well	154	B5
Edmund St SE5	36	E14
Edmunds Cl, Hayes	102	E10
Edmunds Wk N2	73	R8
Edna Rd SW20	180	A3
Edna St SW11	145	R2
Edric Rd SE14	131	N13
Edrick Rd, Edg	54	E12
Edrick Wk, Edg	54	E12
Edridge Rd, Croy	197	U6
Edulf Rd, Borwd	38	D2
Edward Av E4	62	C11
Edward Av, Mord	181	N10
Edward Cl N9	44	F14
Edward Cl, Hmptn	157	U10
Edward Cl, Nthlt	102	F4
Edward Ct E16	115	N9
Edward Gro, Barn	41	N9
Edward Ms, NW1 1	8	J5
Edward Pl SE8	131	U12
Edward Rd E17	77	P9
Edward Rd SE20	167	N13
Edward Rd, Barn	41	N9
Edward Rd, Brom	169	S13
Edward Rd, Chis	171	K10
Edward Rd, Croy	184	E12
Edward Rd, Hmptn	157	U10
Edward Rd, Har	67	U6
Edward Rd, Nthlt	102	E4
Edward Rd, Rom	82	H12
Edward St E16	115	N8
Edward St SE8	131	T13
Edward St SE14	131	S13
Edward Temme Av E15	97	L14
Edward Tyler Rd SE12	169	S4
Edwardes Sq W8	126	G6
Edward's Av, Ruis	84	D11
Edwards Cl, Wor Pk	194	A4
Edwards Cotts, N1 3	93	R12
Edwards Dr N11	58	H13
Edwards La N16	94	C5
Edwards Ms N1	93	P13
Edwards Ms W1	16	D7
Edwards Rd, Belv	137	N6
Edwin Av E6	116	G4
Edwin Cl, Bexh	137	L12
Edwin Pl, Croy 9	198	B1
Edwin Rd, Edg	54	G12
Edwin Rd, Twick	158	E2
Edwin St E1	113	M7
Edwin St E16	115	N10
Edwina Gdns, Ilf	80	C10
Edwin's Mead, E9 5	95	S7
Edwyn Cl, Barn	39	U11
Eel Brook Studios, SW6 15	126	H14
Eel Pie Island, Twick	158	H2
Effie Pl, SW6 8	126	H14
Effie Rd SW6	126	H14
Effingham Cl, Sutt	195	K14
Effingham Rd N8	75	P9
Effingham Rd SE12	151	K10
Effingham Rd, Croy	183	M14
Effingham Rd, Surb	177	K14
Effort St SW17	163	R9
Effra Par SW2	147	P10
Effra Rd SW2	147	N8
Effra Rd SW19	162	J11
Egbert St NW1	110	A1
Egerton Cl, Pnr	66	A8
Egerton Cres SW3	31	R1
Egerton Dr SE10	150	D1
Egerton Gdns NW4	71	S8
Egerton Gdns NW10	107	T2
Egerton Gdns SW3	31	R1
Egerton Gdns W13	104	J11
Egerton Gdns, Ilf	99	T5
Egerton Gdns Ms SW3	23	R11
Egerton Pl SW3	23	R11
Egerton Rd N16	76	F13
Egerton Rd SE25	184	C6
Egerton Rd, N Mal	179	M7
Egerton Rd, Twick	140	D13
Egerton Rd, Wem	87	T14
Egerton Ter SW3	23	R12
Egham Cl SW19	162	C4
Egham Cl, Sutt	194	C4
Egham Cres, Sutt	194	B5
Egham Rd E13	115	S9
Eglantine Rd SW18	145	L10
Egleston Rd, Mord	180	J12
Eglington Ct SE17	35	T9
Eglington Rd E4	46	G14
Eglinton Hill SE18	135	K13
Eglinton Rd SE18	134	J11
Egliston Ms SW15	143	T6
Egliston Rd SW15	143	T6
Eglon Ms, NW1 7	91	U14
Egmont Av, Surb	191	U1
Egmont Rd, N Mal	179	M7
Egmont Rd, Surb	191	U1
Egmont Rd, Sutt	195	L14
Egmont Rd, Walt	174	C14
Egmont St SE14	131	P14
Egremont Rd SE27	165	P6
Egret Way, Hayes 7	102	H10
Eider Cl E7	97	M9
Eider Cl, Hayes 1	102	G10
Eighteenth Rd, Mitch 2	182	J8
Eighth Av E12	98	E7
Eighth Av, Hayes	120	A1
Eileen Rd SE25	184	B10
Eindhoven Cl, Cars	196	A1
Eisenhower Dr E6	116	D9
Elaine Gro NW5	92	A9
Elam Cl SE5	147	S4
Elam St SE5	147	S3
Eland Pl, Croy 3	197	R5
Eland Rd SW11	145	U5
Eland Rd, Croy	197	R5
Elba Pl SE17	36	B2
Elberon Av, Croy	182	F12
Elborough Rd SE25	184	G9
Elborough St SW18	162	G1
Elbury Dr E16	115	P12
Elcho St SW11	127	R14
Elcot Av SE15	130	J13
Elder Av N8	75	K10
Elder Cl, Sid	171	U1
Elder Ct, Bushey	52	C3
Elder Oak Cl SE20	184	J2
Elder Rd SE27	165	U9
Elder St E1	13	L12
Elder Wk, N1 6	111	S1
Elderberry Gro, SE27 4	165	T8
Elderberry Rd W5	123	R4
Elderfield Pl SW17	164	C8
Elderfield Rd E5	95	M7
Elderfield Wk E11	79	R9
Elderflower Way E15	96	J13
Elderslie Cl, Beck	186	C10
Elderslie Rd SE9	152	H10
Elderton Rd SE26	167	R8
Eldertree Pl, Mitch	182	E2
Eldertree Way, Mitch	182	E2
Eldon Av, Borwd	38	B4
Eldon Av, Croy	199	M4
Eldon Av, Houns	121	N13
Eldon Gro NW3	91	P9
Eldon Pk SE25	184	J7
Eldon Rd E17	77	U8
Eldon Rd N9	61	L2
Eldon Rd N22	75	S2
Eldon Rd W8	22	D11
Eldon St EC2	20	F3
Eldon Way NW10	106	C4
Eldred Rd, Bark	117	R1
Eldridge Cl, Felt	156	A2
Eleanor Cl N15	76	E6
Eleanor Cl SE16	131	N3
Eleanor Cres NW7	56	A8
Eleanor Gdns, Barn	40	A10
Eleanor Gdns, Dag	101	L5
Eleanor Gro SW13	143	K6
Eleanor Rd E8	94	J12
Eleanor Rd E15	97	M12
Eleanor Rd N11	58	J12
Eleanor St E3	114	A6
Electric Av SW9	147	N7
Electric La SW9	147	N7
Electric Par, Surb	177	N12
Elephant & Castle SE1	27	S12
Elephant La SE16	131	L3
Elephant Rd SE17	35	T1
Elers Rd W13	123	L4
Eleven Acre Ri, Loug	48	E6
Eley Est N18	61	M9
Eley Rd N18	61	N9
Elf Row E1	113	M13
Elfin Gro, Tedd	158	E10
Elfindale Rd SE24	147	U9
Elford Cl SE3	151	S7
Elfort Rd N5	93	P7
Elfrida Cres SE6	168	B7
Elfwine Rd W7	104	D9
Elgal Cl, Orp	203	K9
Elgar Av NW10	88	H11
Elgar Av SW16	182	J5
Elgar Av W5	123	S3
Elgar Av, Surb	178	E13
Elgar Cl E13	115	T3
Elgar Cl SE8	132	A14
Elgar Cl, Buck H	64	A4
Elgar St SE16	131	S5
Elgin Av W9	6	B8
Elgin Av, Har	68	J4
Elgin Cres W11	108	D12
Elgin Est W9	108	G8
Elgin Ms W11	108	D12
Elgin Ms N W9	6	D6
Elgin Ms S W9	6	D6
Elgin Rd N22	74	F3
Elgin Rd, Croy	198	F2
Elgin Rd, Ilf	99	S2
Elgin Rd, Sutt	195	M6
Elgin Rd, Wall	196	E11
Elgood Av, Nthwd	50	A12
Elham Cl, Brom	170	A14
Elia Ms N1	11	P3
Elia St N1	11	P3
Elias Pl SW8	34	J12
Elibank Rd SE9	152	G7
Elim Est SE1	28	G9
Elim Way E13	115	M6
Eliot Bank SE23	167	K3
Eliot Cotts, SE3 1	151	K4
Eliot Dr, Har	85	R3
Eliot Gdns SW15	143	N8
Eliot Hill SE13	150	F4
Eliot Ms NW8	6	G3
Eliot Pk SE13	150	F4
Eliot Pl SE3	150	J4
Eliot Rd, Dag	100	H8
Eliot Vale SE3	150	H4
Elizabeth Av N1	94	A14
Elizabeth Av, Enf	43	S5
Elizabeth Av, Ilf 5	99	P3
Elizabeth Br SW1	32	H3
Elizabeth Cl E14	114	C12
Elizabeth Cl W9	6	H10
Elizabeth Cl, Barn	40	A6
Elizabeth Cl, Rom	83	R2
Elizabeth Cl, Sutt	194	E7
Elizabeth Clyde Cl N15	76	C6
Elizabeth Cotts, Rich	142	A2
Elizabeth Ct SW1	25	T11
Elizabeth Est SE17	36	C9
Elizabeth Fry Rd E8	95	K14
Elizabeth Gdns W3	125	L2
Elizabeth Gdns, Stan	53	M10
Elizabeth Gdns, Sun	174	E5
Elizabeth Ms NW3	91	S12
Elizabeth Pl N15	76	B7
Elizabeth Ride N9	45	K14
Elizabeth Rd E6	116	A1
Elizabeth Rd N15	76	D9
Elizabeth Sq, SE16 5	113	R14
Elizabeth St SW1	32	F2
Elizabeth Ter SE9	152	E11
Elizabeth Way SE19	166	A14
Elizabeth Way, Felt	156	E7
Elkanette Ms N20	57	L4
Elkington Rd E13	115	R8
Elkstone Rd W10	108	E9
Ella Rd N8	75	K13
Ellaline Rd W6	126	A12
Ellanby Cres N18	60	J8
Elland Rd SE15	149	M8
Ellen Cl, Brom	188	B5
Ellen Ct N9	61	L4
Ellen St E1	21	T8
Ellen Webb Dr, Har	68	D6
Ellenborough Pl SW15	143	N7
Ellenborough Rd N22	75	T2
Ellenborough Rd, Sid	172	H10
Elleray Rd, Tedd	158	E11
Ellerby St SW6	144	B2
Ellerdale Cl NW3	91	L8
Ellerdale Rd NW3	91	M9
Ellerdale St SE13	150	C7
Ellerdine Rd, Houns	140	A8
Ellerker Gdns, Rich	141	R11
Ellerman Av, Twick	157	M2
Ellerslie Gdns NW10	107	P1
Ellerslie Rd W12	125	R1
Ellerslie Sq Ind Est SW2	146	J9
Ellerton Gdns, Dag	100	E14
Ellerton Rd SW13	143	N2
Ellerton Rd SW18	163	P1
Ellerton Rd SW20	161	N13
Ellerton Rd, Dag	100	E14
Ellerton Rd, Surb	191	T2
Ellery Rd SE19	166	A14
Ellery St SE15	148	J4
Ellesborough Cl, Wat	52	F9
Ellesmere Av NW7	54	G6
Ellesmere Av, Beck	186	D4
Ellesmere Cl E11	79	M10
Ellesmere Gdns, Ilf	80	D10
Ellesmere Gro, Barn	40	E9

Ellesmere Rd E3	113	R3
Ellesmere Rd NW10	89	N9
Ellesmere Rd W4	124	G11
Ellesmere Rd, Grnf	103	T8
Ellesmere Rd, Twick	141	L11
Ellesmere St E14	114	C11
Ellingfort Rd E8	95	K13
Ellingham Rd E15	96	G8
Ellingham Rd W12	125	P3
Ellingham Rd, Chess	191	P12
Ellington Rd N10	74	C8
Ellington Rd, Houns	139	S4
Ellington St N7	93	N12
Elliot Cl E15	96	J13
Elliot Rd NW4	71	R12
Elliot Rd, Stan	52	H11
Elliott Av, Ruis	84	C3
Elliott Cl, Wem	88	A5
Elliott Rd SW9	129	R14
Elliott Rd W4	124	J8
Elliott Rd, Brom	188	A7
Elliott Rd, Th Hth	183	S8
Elliott Sq NW3	91	S13
Elliott's Pl N1	111	S2
Elliotts Row SE11	35	P1
Ellis Cl, NW10 1	89	T12
Ellis Cl SE9	171	L3
Ellis Ct W7	104	E10
Ellis Ms SE7	133	T11
Ellis Rd, Mitch	181	U12
Ellis Rd, Sthl	121	U2
Ellis St SW1	32	B2
Elliscombe Rd SE7	133	T11
Ellisfield Dr SW15	143	N13
Ellison Gdns, Sthl	121	L7
Ellison Rd SW13	143	M4
Ellison Rd SW16	164	J14
Ellison Rd, Sid	171	P2
Ellora Rd SW16	164	H10
Ellsworth St E2	112	J5
Elm Av W5	123	T2
Elm Av, Ruis	84	B1
Elm Bank, Brom	188	A3
Elm Bank Gdns SW13	143	K4
Elm Cl E11	79	S11
Elm Cl N19	92	E4
Elm Cl NW4	72	A10
Elm Cl SW20	179	U7
Elm Cl, Buck H	64	B4
Elm Cl, Cars	195	T2
Elm Cl, Har	67	R12
Elm Cl, Hayes	102	A12
Elm Cl, Rom	83	S2
Elm Cl, S Croy	198	C12
Elm Cl, Surb	178	F14
Elm Cl, Twick	157	R4
Elm Ct EC4	19	K9
Elm Cres W5	123	S2
Elm Cres, Kings T	177	S2
Elm Dr, Har	67	R11
Elm Dr, Sun	174	E3
Elm Friars Wk NW1	92	H13
Elm Gdns N2	73	M6
Elm Gdns, Esher	190	F12
Elm Gdns, Mitch	182	H7
Elm Grn W3	106	J12
Elm Gro N8	75	K12
Elm Gro NW2	90	B7
Elm Gro SE15	148	G3
Elm Gro SW19	162	C14
Elm Gro, Har	67	N14
Elm Gro, Kings T	177	S2
Elm Gro, Orp	203	T3
Elm Gro, Sutt	195	K8
Elm Gro, Wdf Grn	63	M10
Elm Gro Par, Wall	196	B6
Elm Gro Rd SW13	143	P3
Elm Gro Rd W5	123	R3
Elm Hall Gdns E11	79	S11
Elm Ms, Rich	141	T12
Elm Pk SW2	147	M13
Elm Pk, Stan	53	K10
Elm Pk Av N15	76	F10
Elm Pk Ct, Pnr	66	F5
Elm Pk Gdns NW4	72	A10
Elm Pk Gdns SW10	31	K7
Elm Pk La SW3	30	J8
Elm Pk Mans SW10	30	H10
Elm Pk Rd E10	95	S2
Elm Pk Rd N3	56	F14
Elm Pk Rd N21	43	T14
Elm Pk Rd SE25	184	E6
Elm Pk Rd SW3	31	K9
Elm Pk Rd, Pnr	66	H5
Elm Pl SW7	31	K6
Elm Quay Ct SW8	33	S11
Elm Rd E7	97	M11
Elm Rd E11	96	G4
Elm Rd E17	78	F10
Elm Rd N22	75	R2
Elm Rd SW14	142	F6
Elm Rd, Barn	40	E7
Elm Rd, Beck	185	T3
Elm Rd, Chess	191	R8
Elm Rd, Epsom	193	M12
Elm Rd, Esher	190	E11
Elm Rd, Kings T	177	T2
Elm Rd, N Mal	178	H4
Elm Rd, Rom	83	S3
Elm Rd, Sid	172	A7
Elm Rd, Th Hth	184	A8
Elm Rd, Wall 3	196	B2
Elm Rd, Wem	87	R9
Elm Rd W, Sutt	180	F13
Elm Row, NW3 4	91	M6
Elm St WC1	10	H11
Elm Ter SE9	152	G11
Elm Ter, Har	52	B14
Elm Tree Av, Esher	176	B14
Elm Tree Cl NW8	7	K5
Elm Tree Cl, Nthlt	103	N4
Elm Tree Rd NW8	7	K6
Elm Wk NW3	90	H4
Elm Wk SW20	179	U7
Elm Wk, Orp	202	F5
Elm Way N11	58	B12
Elm Way NW10	88	J7
Elm Way, Epsom	192	H10
Elm Way, Wor Pk	193	T5
Elmar Rd N15	76	B8
Elmbank N14	43	K13
Elmbank Av, Barn	39	T8
Elmbank Way W7	104	B9
Elmbourne Dr, Belv	137	R8
Elmbourne Rd SW17	164	C6
Elmbridge Av, Surb	178	D10
Elmbridge Cl, Ruis	66	A11
Elmbridge Wk E8	94	H13
Elmbrook Cl, Sun	174	C2
Elmbrook Gdns SE9	152	D7
Elmbrook Rd, Sutt	194	F8
Elmcourt Rd SE27	165	S3
Elmcroft N8	75	L9
Elmcroft Av E11	79	S8
Elmcroft Av N9	45	K11
Elmcroft Av NW11	72	F13
Elmcroft Av, Sid	153	U12
Elmcroft Cl E11	79	S8
Elmcroft Cl W5	105	N11
Elmcroft Cl, Chess	191	R5
Elmcroft Cres NW11	72	C13
Elmcroft Cres, Har	67	P6
Elmcroft Dr, Chess	191	R6
Elmcroft Gdns NW9	70	A9
Elmcroft St E5	95	L7
Elmdale Rd N13	59	M10
Elmdene, Surb	192	F1
Elmdene Cl, Beck	185	T10
Elmdene Rd SE18	134	J10
Elmdon Rd, Houns	138	H3
Elmer Cl, Enf	43	L5
Elmer Gdns, Edg	54	C13
Elmer Gdns, Islw	140	A6
Elmer Rd SE6	150	F14
Elmers End Rd SE20	185	L3
Elmers End Rd, Beck	185	N6
Elmers Rd SE25	184	H13
Elmerside Rd, Beck	185	R7
Elmfield Av N8	74	J9
Elmfield Av, Mitch	182	A2
Elmfield Av, Tedd	158	F9
Elmfield Cl, Har	86	C4
Elmfield Pk, Brom	187	P5
Elmfield Rd E4	62	F3
Elmfield Rd E17	77	P11
Elmfield Rd N2	73	N5
Elmfield Rd SW17	164	C3
Elmfield Rd, Brom	187	P5
Elmfield Rd, Sthl	121	K5
Elmfield Way W9	108	G9
Elmgate Av, Felt	156	E6
Elmgate Gdns, Edg	54	F9
Elmgreen Cl E15	115	K1
Elmgrove Cres, Har	68	F9
Elmgrove Gdns, Har	68	G9
Elmgrove Rd, Croy	184	J14
Elmgrove Rd, Har	68	F9
Elmhurst, Belv	137	K12
Elmhurst Av N2	73	N6
Elmhurst Av, Mitch	164	C14
Elmhurst Dr E18	79	P3
Elmhurst Gdns E18	79	R2
Elmhurst Rd E7	97	R13
Elmhurst Rd N17	76	E3
Elmhurst Rd SE9	170	C4
Elmhurst St SW4	146	G5
Elmhurst Way, Loug	48	E13
Elmington Cl, Bex	155	R12
Elmington Est SE5	36	E14
Elmington Rd SE5	130	B14
Elmira St SE13	150	D6
Elmlee Cl, Chis	170	F12
Elmley Cl, E6 21	116	D10
Elmley St SE18	135	N8
Elmore Cl, Wem	105	R3
Elmore Rd E11	96	F6
Elmore Rd, Enf	45	N1
Elmore St N1	94	A13
Elmores, Loug	48	G6
Elms, The SW13	143	L6
Elms Av N10	74	D5
Elms Av NW4	72	A10
Elms Ct, Wem	86	F8
Elms Cres SW4	146	G11
Elms Gdns, Dag	101	L7
Elms Gdns, Wem	86	G8
Elms La, Wem	86	H8
Elms Ms W2	14	J10
Elms Pk Av, Wem	86	G8
Elms Rd SW4	146	F10
Elms Rd, Har	52	C14
Elmscott Gdns N21	43	U12
Elmscott Rd, Brom	169	L9
Elmsdale Rd E17	77	T7
Elmshaw Rd SW15	143	P9
Elmshurst Cres N2	73	M7
Elmside, Croy	200	C11
Elmside Rd, Wem	88	A6
Elmsleigh Av, Har	69	K7
Elmsleigh Ct, Sutt	194	J6
Elmsleigh Rd, Twick	158	B3
Elmslie Cl, Wdf Grn	64	E12
Elmstead Av, Chis	170	F9
Elmstead Av, Wem	87	T3
Elmstead Cl N20	56	G4
Elmstead Cl, Epsom	193	K10
Elmstead Cres, Well	136	F12
Elmstead Gdns, Wor Pk	193	N5
Elmstead Glade, Chis	170	E11
Elmstead La, Chis	170	F8
Elmstead Rd, Ilf	99	S3
Elmstone Rd SW6	144	G1
Elmsworth Av, Houns	139	R3
Elmton Way E5	94	H6
Elmtree Rd, Tedd	158	D8
Elmwood Av N13	59	K9
Elmwood Av, Borwd	38	D8
Elmwood Av, Felt	156	E5
Elmwood Av, Har	68	H10
Elmwood Cl, Epsom	193	P13
Elmwood Cl, Wall	196	C4
Elmwood Cl, Wem	86	H6
Elmwood Cres NW9	70	F8
Elmwood Dr, Bex	154	J13
Elmwood Dr, Epsom	193	P13
Elmwood Gdns W7	104	D12
Elmwood Rd SE24	148	B3
Elmwood Rd W4	124	E11
Elmwood Rd, Croy	183	S13
Elmwood Rd, Mitch	181	U5
Elmworth Gro SE21	166	A4
Elnathan Ms W9	6	C11
Elphinstone Rd E17	77	U3
Elphinstone St N5	93	R7
Elrington Rd E8	94	G12
Elrington Rd, Wdf Grn	63	P10
Elsa Rd, Well	154	D3
Elsa St E1	113	R10
Elsdale St E9	95	M12
Elsden Ms E2	113	M4
Elsden Rd N17	76	E2
Elsenham Rd E12	98	F10
Elsenham St SW18	162	F22
Elsham Rd E11	97	K6
Elsham Rd W14	126	C4
Elsham Ter W14	126	C4
Elsie Rd SE22	148	E7
Elsiedene Rd N21	43	U14
Elsiemaud Rd SE4	149	U9
Elsinore Gdns NW2	90	C5
Elsinore Rd SE23	167	S2
Elsinore Way, Rich	142	C5
Elsley Rd SW11	146	A5
Elspeth Rd SW11	145	U7
Elspeth Rd, Wem	87	R10
Elsrick Av, Mord	180	H10
Elstan Way, Croy	185	R13
Elsted St SE17	36	F4
Elstow Cl SE9	152	G10
Elstow Cl, Ruis	66	G14
Elstow Gdns, Dag	100	J14
Elstow Rd, Dag	118	J1
Elstree Gdns N9	61	K2
Elstree Gdns, Belv	137	K7
Elstree Gdns, Ilf	99	L10
Elstree Hill, Brom	168	J13
Elstree Pk, Borwd	38	G12
Elstree Way, Borwd	38	H5
Elswick Rd SE13	150	C4
Elswick St SW6	145	L3
Elsworthy, T Ditt	176	D12
Elsworthy Ri NW3	91	S13
Elsworthy Rd NW3	109	R1
Elsworthy Ter NW3	91	S14
Elsynge Rd SW18	145	N9
Eltham Grn SE9	151	U10
Eltham Grn Rd SE9	151	U9
Eltham High St SE9	152	D11
Eltham Hill SE9	152	C10
Eltham Palace Rd SE9	152	A12
Eltham Pk Gdns SE9	152	H8
Eltham Rd SE9	151	T10
Eltham Rd SE12	151	N9
Elthiron Rd SW6	144	H2
Elthorne Av W7	122	G4
Elthorne Ct, Felt	156	F2
Elthorne Pk Rd W7	122	G4
Elthorne Rd N19	92	G3
Elthorne Rd NW9	70	G13
Elthorne Way NW9	70	H12
Elthruda Rd SE13	150	H12
Eltisley Rd, Ilf	98	J7
Elton Av, Barn	40	F9
Elton Av, Grnf	86	E12
Elton Av, Wem	87	K9
Elton Cl, Kings T	159	M14
Elton Pl N16	94	C9
Elton Rd, Kings T	177	U1
Eltringham St SW18	145	M7
Elvaston Ms SW7	22	H10
Elvaston Pl SW7	22	F11
Elveden Pl NW10	106	A3
Elveden Rd NW10	106	B3
Elvendon Rd N13	58	J11
Elver Gdns E2	13	U5
Elverson Rd SE8	150	C3
Elverton St SW1	33	S1
Elvington Grn, Brom	187	M9
Elvington La NW9	70	J1
Elvino Rd SE26	167	R10
Elvis Rd NW2	89	T11
Elwill Way, Beck	186	E7
Elwin St E2	13	R5
Elwood St N5	93	R6
Elwyn Gdns SE12	151	P14
Ely Cl, N Mal	179	M3
Ely Gdns, Borwd	38	H9
Ely Gdns, Dag	101	U5
Ely Pl EC1	19	M3
Ely Pl, Wdf Grn	64	G10
Ely Rd E10	78	E13

Ely Rd, Croy	184	B9
Ely Rd (Hounslow W), Houns	138	E5
Elyne Rd N4	75	N12
Elysian Av, Orp	189	S11
Elysium St, SW6 4	144	E4
Elystan Business Cen, Hayes	102	F14
Elystan Pl SW3	31	S5
Elystan St SW3	31	R4
Elystan Wk N1	111	N2
Emanuel Av W3	106	F12
Emanuel Dr, Hmptn	157	M9
Emba St SE16	29	U7
Embankment SW15	144	A4
Embankment, The, Twick	158	H2
Embankment Gdns SW3	32	B10
Embankment Pl WC2	26	C2
Embassy Ct, Sid	172	D6
Ember Cl, Orp	189	L13
Ember Fm Av, E Mol	176	B11
Ember Fm Way, E Mol	176	A10
Ember Gdns, T Ditt	176	C13
Ember La, E Mol	190	A1
Ember La, Esher	190	A1
Embercourt Rd, T Ditt	176	D12
Emberton SE5	36	G9
Embleton Rd SE13	150	C7
Embleton Rd, Wat	50	B5
Embry Cl, Stan	52	H8
Embry Dr, Stan	52	H11
Embry Way, Stan	52	H9
Emden St, SW6 4	145	K1
Emerald Cl E16	116	C12
Emerald Gdns, Dag	101	N2
Emerald Sq, Sthl	120	G6
Emerald St WC1	18	F1
Emerson Gdns, Har	69	T12
Emerson Rd, Ilf	80	G13
Emerson St SE1	27	U1
Emerton Cl, Bexh	155	K7
Emery Hill St SW1	25	P12
Emery St SE1	27	L9
Emes Rd, Erith	137	U13
Emilia Cl, Enf	45	K9
Emily Pl N7	93	P7
Emlyn Gdns W12	125	K4
Emlyn Rd W12	125	L5
Emma Rd E13	115	M4
Emma St E2	112	J3
Emmanuel Rd SW12	164	F2
Emmaus Way, Chig	64	G9
Emmott Av, Ilf	81	L9
Emmott Cl E1	113	S8
Emmott Cl NW11	73	L12
Emms Pas, Kings T	177	N4
Emperor's Gate SW7	22	D12
Empire Av N18	59	U11
Empire Ct, Wem	88	G7
Empire Rd, Grnf	105	M2
Empire Way, Wem	87	U7
Empire Wf Rd E14	132	G8
Empire Yd N7	93	K5
Empress Av E4	62	C14
Empress Av E12	97	U4
Empress Av, Ilf	98	G3
Empress Av, Wdf Grn	63	L14
Empress Dr, Chis	170	J11
Empress Pl SW6	126	G10
Empress St SE17	36	A9
Empson St E3	114	D8
Emsworth Cl N9	61	L1
Emsworth Rd, Ilf	81	K3
Emsworth St SW2	165	L4
Emu Rd SW8	146	C4
Ena Rd SW16	183	K5
Enbrook St W10	108	D6
Endale Cl, Cars	195	U4
Endeavour Way SW19	162	J7

Endeavour Way, Bark	118	A4
Endeavour Way, Croy	182	J13
Endell St WC2	18	B7
Enderby St SE10	132	H10
Enderley Cl, Har	68	C2
Enderley Rd, Har	68	C2
Endersby Rd, Barn	39	T9
Endersleigh Gdns NW4	71	N8
Endlebury Rd E4	62	D3
Endlesham Rd SW12	146	A13
Endsleigh Gdns WC1	9	S9
Endsleigh Gdns, Ilf	98	F2
Endsleigh Gdns, Surb	177	M12
Endsleigh Pl WC1	9	T10
Endsleigh Rd W13	104	G14
Endsleigh Rd, Sthl	121	K7
Endsleigh St WC1	9	S9
Endway, Surb	178	C14
Endwell Rd SE4	149	S4
Endymion Rd N4	75	R13
Endymion Rd SW2	147	L12
Energen Cl NW10	88	J12
Enfield Retail Pk, Enf	44	J5
Enfield Rd N1	94	D14
Enfield Rd W3	124	C4
Enfield Rd, Brent	123	N9
Enfield Rd, Enf	42	J7
Enfield Wk, Brent	123	N9
Enford St W1	15	T2
Engadine Cl, Croy	198	E6
Engadine St SW18	162	F1
Engate St SE13	150	E8
Engel Pk NW7	55	U12
Engineer Cl SE18	134	H11
Engineers Way, Wem	88	A7
Englands La NW3	91	T12
Englands La, Loug	48	G3
Englefield Cl, Croy 2	183	T12
Englefield Cl, Enf	43	N4
Englefield Cl, Orp	189	U8
Englefield Cres, Orp	189	U8
Englefield Rd N1	94	A12
Engleheart Rd SE6	150	E14
Englewood Rd SW12	146	D11
English Grds SE1	28	H3
English St E3	113	T7
Enid St SE16	29	P10
Enmore Av SE25	184	H9
Enmore Gdns SW14	142	H10
Enmore Rd SE25	184	H10
Enmore Rd SW15	143	U8
Enmore Rd, Sthl	103	P7
Ennerdale Av, Stan	69	L5
Ennerdale Cl (Cheam), Sutt	194	F8
Ennerdale Dr NW9	70	J10
Ennerdale Gdns, Wem	87	M2
Ennerdale Rd, Bexh	155	P2
Ennerdale Rd, Rich	141	U2
Ennersdale Rd SE13	150	G10
Ennis Rd N4	93	N2
Ennis Rd SE18	135	M12
Ennismore Av W4	125	L7
Ennismore Av, Grnf	86	D11
Ennismore Gdns SW7	23	N7
Ennismore Gdns, T Ditt	176	D12
Ennismore Gdns Ms SW7	23	N9
Ennismore Ms SW7	23	P8
Ennismore St SW7	23	P10
Ensign Dr N13	59	T5
Ensign St E1	21	S10
Enslin Rd SE9	152	H13
Ensor Ms SW7	30	J6
Enstone Rd, Enf	45	R5
Enterprise Cl, Croy	197	N2
Enterprise Way NW10	107	N6

Enterprise Way SW18	144	H8
Enterprise Way, Tedd	158	F10
Enterprize Way SE8	131	T7
Epirus Ms, SW6 3	126	G13
Epirus Rd SW6	126	F13
Epping Cl E14	132	B7
Epping Cl, Rom	83	S6
Epping Glade E4	46	E12
Epping New Rd, Buck H	63	R4
Epping New Rd, Loug	47	S12
Epping Pl N1	93	N12
Epping Way E4	46	D12
Epple Rd SW6	144	F1
Epsom Cl, Bexh	155	S6
Epsom Cl, Nthlt	85	M10
Epsom Rd E10	78	F12
Epsom Rd, Croy	197	P6
Epsom Rd, Ilf	81	T12
Epsom Rd, Mord	180	E13
Epsom Rd, Sutt	180	E13
Epstein Rd SE28	136	C2
Epworth Rd, Islw	122	J14
Epworth St EC2	12	E11
Erasmus St SW1	33	U3
Erconwald St W12	107	L12
Eresby Dr, Beck	200	B1
Eresby Pl, NW6 4	90	G14
Eric Clarke La, Bark	117	L6
Eric Cl, E7 6	97	N8
Eric Rd E7	97	N8
Eric Rd NW10	89	L12
Eric Rd, Rom	82	H13
Eric St E3	113	T7
Erica Gdns, Croy	200	C7
Erica St W12	107	P14
Ericcson Cl SW18	144	G9
Eridge Rd W4	124	H5
Erin Cl, Brom	168	J13
Erin Cl, Ilf	82	B12
Erindale SE18	135	P12
Erindale Ter SE18	135	P12
Erith Cres, Rom	83	T1
Erith Rd, Belv	137	R9
Erith Rd, Bexh	155	R7
Erith Rd, Erith	155	S3
Erlanger Rd SE14	149	P3
Erlesmere Gdns W13	122	H5
Ermine Cl, Houns	138	F4
Ermine Rd N15	76	E11
Ermine Rd SE13	150	C6
Ermine Side, Enf	44	G9
Ermington Rd SE9	171	M4
Ernald Av E6	116	D3
Erncroft Way, Twick	140	F12
Ernest Av SE27	165	S7
Ernest Cl, Beck	186	A9
Ernest Gdns W4	124	D12
Ernest Gro, Beck	185	U9
Ernest Rd, Kings T	178	C4
Ernest Sq, Kings T	178	C4
Ernest St E1	113	P8
Ernle Rd SW20	161	T13
Ernshaw Pl SW15	144	D9
Erpingham Rd SW15	143	T6
Erridge Rd SW19	180	H3
Errington Rd W9	108	F7
Errol Gdns, Hayes	102	D7
Errol Gdns, N Mal	179	P8
Errol St EC1	12	B12
Erskine Cl, Sutt	195	R6
Erskine Cres N17	76	J7
Erskine Hill NW11	72	H10
Erskine Ms, NW3 6	91	U14
Erskine Rd E17	77	U7
Erskine Rd NW3	91	U14
Erskine Rd, Sutt	195	R6
Erskine Rd, Wat	50	F6
Erwood Rd SE7	134	D9
Esam Way SW16	165	P10
Escot Way, Barn	39	T9
Escott Gdns SE9	170	D8
Escreet Gro SE18	134	G7
Esher Av, Rom	83	T11
Esher Av, Sutt	194	B6

Esher Bypass, Chess	191	L7
Esher Bypass, Esher	191	L10
Esher Cl, Bex	172	J2
Esher Gdns SW19	162	A3
Esher Ms, Mitch	181	U5
Esher Rd, E Mol	176	B10
Esher Rd, Ilf	99	S5
Esk Rd E13	115	P7
Eskdale Av, Nthlt	103	M1
Eskdale Cl, Wem	87	N3
Eskdale Rd, Bexh	155	N3
Eskmont Ridge SE19	166	C14
Esmar Cres NW9	71	N13
Esmeralda Rd SE1	37	T4
Esmond Rd NW6	108	F2
Esmond Rd W4	124	H6
Esmond St SW15	144	D8
Esparto St SW18	145	K13
Essenden Rd, Belv	137	N9
Essenden Rd, S Croy	198	C14
Essendine Rd W9	108	H6
Essex Av, Islw	140	C6
Essex Cl E17	77	R7
Essex Cl, Mord	180	A13
Essex Cl, Rom	83	R7
Essex Cl, Ruis	84	H1
Essex Ct, EC4 19	18	J8
Essex Ct SW13	143	L3
Essex Gdns N4	75	S11
Essex Gro SE19	166	B12
Essex Pk N3	56	J12
Essex Pk Ms, W3 1	125	K2
Essex Pl W4	124	F8
Essex Rd E4	62	J1
Essex Rd E10	78	E11
Essex Rd E12	98	D10
Essex Rd E17	77	R11
Essex Rd E18	79	S4
Essex Rd N1	111	S1
Essex Rd NW10	89	K13
Essex Rd W3	106	E13
Essex Rd W4	124	G8
Essex Rd, Bark	99	P14
Essex Rd, Borwd	38	B5
Essex Rd, Dag	101	T9
Essex Rd, Enf	44	A8
Essex Rd, Rom	83	R7
Essex Rd (Chadwell Heath), Rom	82	E14
Essex Rd S E11	78	G13
Essex St E7	97	N9
Essex St WC2	18	J8
Essex Vil W8	126	G4
Essex Wf E5	95	N4
Essian St E1	113	R9
Essoldo Way, Edg	69	U5
Estate Way E10	95	U1
Estcourt Rd SE25	185	K11
Estcourt Rd SW6	126	E13
Este Rd SW11	145	S5
Estella Av, N Mal	179	S8
Estelle Rd NW3	91	U8
Esterbrooke St, SW1 1	33	S3
Esther Cl N21	43	P13
Esther Rd E11	78	J13
Estoria Cl SW2	147	N14
Estreham Rd SW16	164	G12
Estridge Cl, Houns	139	N7
Estuary Cl, Bark	118	D5
Eswyn Rd SW17	163	U9
Etchingham Pk Rd N3	57	K13
Etchingham Rd E15	96	F7
Eternit Wk SW6	143	U1
Etfield Gro, Sid	172	C9
Ethel Rd E16	115	R12
Ethel St SE17	36	A4
Ethelbert Cl, Brom	187	N4
Ethelbert Gdns, Ilf	80	F10
Ethelbert Rd SW20	180	B2
Ethelbert Rd, Brom	187	N5
Ethelbert Rd, Erith 1	137	T13
Ethelbert St, SW12 8	164	D2

Place	Page	Grid
Ethelburga St SW11	145	S1
Ethelden Rd W12	125	R1
Etheldene Av N10	74	E8
Etheridge Rd NW2	71	T14
Etheridge Rd, Loug	49	L5
Etherley Rd N15	75	U9
Etherow St SE22	148	G12
Etherstone Grn SW16	165	M8
Etherstone Rd SW16	165	N8
Ethnard Rd SE15	130	J12
Ethronvi Rd, Bexh	155	K6
Etloe Rd E10	96	A3
Eton Av N12	57	M13
Eton Av NW3	91	S12
Eton Av, Barn	41	S11
Eton Av, Houns	121	M11
Eton Av, N Mal	178	G9
Eton Av, Wem	87	K8
Eton Cl SW18	145	K14
Eton College Rd NW3	91	U12
Eton Ct, Wem	87	M8
Eton Garages NW3	91	S12
Eton Gro NW9	70	B7
Eton Gro SE13	150	J6
Eton Pl NW3	92	A13
Eton Rd NW3	91	T13
Eton Rd, Ilf	99	L9
Eton St, Rich	141	R9
Eton Vil NW3	91	U12
Etta St SE8	131	S11
Ettrick St E14	114	G11
Etwell Pl, Surb	177	T11
Eugenia Rd SE16	131	M8
Eureka Rd, Kings T	178	A4
Europa Pl EC1	11	U8
Europe Rd SE18	134	F6
Eustace Rd E6	116	D5
Eustace Rd SW6	126	G13
Eustace Rd, Rom	82	H13
Euston Gro NW1	9	S8
Euston Rd N1	10	B6
Euston Rd NW1	9	M10
Euston Rd, Croy	197	N2
Euston Sq NW1	9	S8
Euston St NW1	9	P8
Eva Rd, Rom	82	F13
Evandale Rd SW9	147	P3
Evangelist Rd NW5	92	D8
Evans Gro, Felt	157	N4
Evans Rd SE6	169	K4
Evanston Av E4	62	F14
Evanston Gdns, Ilf	80	C11
Eve Rd E11	96	J8
Eve Rd E15	115	K3
Eve Rd N17	76	D5
Eve Rd, Islw	140	H8
Evelina Rd SE15	149	L5
Evelina Rd SE20	167	M14
Eveline Lowe Est SE16	29	S12
Eveline Rd, Mitch	181	T2
Evelyn Av NW9	70	G7
Evelyn Av, Ruis	66	A12
Evelyn Cl, Twick	139	R13
Evelyn Ct, Twick	12	D3
Evelyn Denington Rd E6	116	D8
Evelyn Dr, Pnr	50	H14
Evelyn Fox Ct W10	107	U10
Evelyn Gdns SW7	30	J7
Evelyn Gdns, Rich	141	S6
Evelyn Gro W5	123	U2
Evelyn Gro, Sthl	103	L12
Evelyn Rd E16	133	R1
Evelyn Rd E17	78	F8
Evelyn Rd SW19	162	J10
Evelyn Rd W4	124	G6
Evelyn Rd, Barn	41	T8
Evelyn Rd, Rich	141	R6
Evelyn Rd (Ham), Rich	159	M5
Evelyn St SE8	131	S9
Evelyn Ter, Rich	141	R6
Evelyn Wk N1	12	D3
Evelyn Way, Wall	196	G7
Evelyn Yd W1	17	S5
Evening Hill, Beck	168	F14
Evenwood Cl SW15	144	C10
Everard Av, Brom	201	P1
Everard Way, Wem	87	R6
Everatt Cl, SW18 5	144	F10
Everdon Rd SW13	125	N12
Everest Pl E14	114	E9
Everest Rd SE9	152	E10
Everett Cl, Bushey	52	C1
Everglade Strand NW9	71	M2
Everilda St N1	111	M2
Evering Rd E5	94	J4
Evering Rd N16	94	E6
Everington Rd N10	73	U3
Everington St W6	126	B12
Everitt Rd NW10	106	H6
Everleigh St N4	93	M2
Eversfield Gdns NW7	54	J12
Eversfield Rd, Rich	141	T3
Evershed Wk W4	124	F6
Eversholt St NW1	9	P4
Evershot Rd N4	93	L1
Eversleigh Rd E6	116	B1
Eversleigh Rd N3	56	F14
Eversleigh Rd SW11	146	B4
Eversleigh Rd, Barn	41	L10
Eversley Av, Wem	88	B3
Eversley Cres N21	43	M11
Eversley Cres, Islw	140	B2
Eversley Mt N21	43	M11
Eversley Pk SW19	161	R10
Eversley Pk Rd N21	43	M12
Eversley Rd SE7	133	R11
Eversley Rd SE19	166	A13
Eversley Rd, Surb	177	T8
Eversley Way, Croy	200	A6
Everthorpe Rd SE15	148	E6
Everton Bldgs NW1	9	L7
Everton Dr, Stan	69	T5
Everton Rd, Croy	198	G1
Evesham Av E17	78	B3
Evesham Cl, Grnf	103	R3
Evesham Cl, Sutt	194	G13
Evesham Grn, Mord	100	J12
Evesham Rd E15	97	L14
Evesham Rd N11	58	F10
Evesham Rd, Mord	181	K12
Evesham St W11	108	A14
Evesham Wk, SE5 5	148	A3
Evesham Wk SW9	147	N3
Evesham Way SW11	146	B5
Evesham Way, Ilf	80	H6
Evry Rd, Sid	172	F11
Ewald Rd SW6	144	E4
Ewanrigg Ter, Wdf Grn	63	T10
Ewart Gro N22	75	N2
Ewart Pl E3	113	T3
Ewart Rd SE23	149	P14
Ewe Cl N7	93	K11
Ewell Bypass, Epsom	193	N13
Ewell Cl, Epsom	193	K10
Ewell Pk Gdns, Epsom	193	N13
Ewell Pk Way, Epsom	193	N12
Ewell Rd, Surb	192	C2
Ewell Rd (Long Ditton), Surb	177	K14
Ewell Rd, Sutt	194	C12
Ewellhurst Rd, Ilf	80	D4
Ewelme Rd SE23	167	M1
Ewen Cres SW2	147	N14
Ewer St SE1	27	T3
Ewhurst Rd SE4	149	U11
Exbury Rd SE6	168	A3
Excelsior Cl, Kings T	177	U4
Excelsior Gdns, SE13 3	150	F4
Exchange Sq EC2	20	H2
Exeter Cl E6	116	E11
Exeter Gdns, Ilf	98	E1
Exeter Ms NW6	90	J12
Exeter Rd E16	115	P10
Exeter Rd E17	78	A9
Exeter Rd N9	61	L4
Exeter Rd N14	42	C14
Exeter Rd NW2	90	C11
Exeter Rd, Croy	184	E14
Exeter Rd, Dag	101	S12
Exeter Rd, Enf	45	N6
Exeter Rd, Felt	157	M5
Exeter Rd, Har	85	K5
Exeter Rd, Well	153	T3
Exeter St WC2	18	E10
Exeter Way SE14	131	T14
Exford Gdns SE12	169	R2
Exford Rd SE12	169	R2
Exhibition Cl W12	107	T14
Exhibition Rd SW7	23	L6
Exmoor Cl, Ilf	81	L2
Exmoor St W10	108	B9
Exmouth Mkt EC1	11	K9
Exmouth Ms, NW1 2	9	N8
Exmouth Pl E8	94	J14
Exmouth Rd E17	77	U10
Exmouth Rd, Brom 4	187	R6
Exmouth Rd, Ruis	84	E5
Exmouth Rd, Well	154	E1
Exmouth St E1	113	M11
Exning Rd E16	115	L8
Exon St SE17	30	H4
Express Dr, Ilf	100	C1
Exton Cres NW10	88	F14
Exton Gdns, Dag	100	F9
Exton St SE1	27	K4
Eyhurst Cl NW2	89	P3
Eylewood Rd SE27	165	U9
Eynella Rd SE22	148	E13
Eynham Rd W12	107	T11
Eynsford Cl, Orp	189	M13
Eynsford Cres, Bex	172	F2
Eynsford Rd, Ilf	99	S3
Eynsham Dr SE2	136	B6
Eynswood Dr, Sid	172	D10
Eyot Gdns W6	125	M9
Eyot Grn W4	125	M10
Eyre Ct NW8	7	K2
Eyre St Hill EC1	11	K11
Eythorne Rd SW9	147	P1
Ezra St E2	13	P5

F

Place	Page	Grid
Faber Gdns NW4	71	P10
Fabian Rd SW6	126	F13
Fabian St E6	116	D7
Factory La N17	76	F4
Factory Rd E16	134	C2
Factory Sq SW16	164	J12
Factory Yd W7	122	D2
Faggs Rd, Felt	138	B10
Fair Acres, Brom	187	P10
Fair St SE1	29	K5
Fair St, Houns 2	139	T6
Fairacre, N Mal	178	J6
Fairacres SW15	143	N8
Fairbairn Grn SW9	147	R1
Fairbank Av, Orp	202	J3
Fairbanks Rd N17	76	F6
Fairbourne Rd N17	76	C5
Fairbridge Rd N19	92	H3
Fairbrook Cl N13	59	P10
Fairbrook Rd N13	59	P10
Fairburn Cl, Borwd	38	A2
Fairburn Ct SW15	144	C10
Fairby Rd SE12	151	R9
Faircharm Trd Est SE8	132	C13
Fairchild Cl SW11	145	P4
Fairchild Pl, EC2 2	13	K11
Fairchild St, EC2 3	13	K11
Fairclough St E1	21	T7
Faircross Av, Bark	99	M11
Fairdale Gdns SW15	143	S7
Fairdale Gdns, Hayes	120	A3
Fairfax Gdns SE3	151	U2
Fairfax Ms E16	133	R1
Fairfax Pl NW6	91	M14
Fairfax Rd N8	75	P8
Fairfax Rd NW6	91	M13
Fairfax Rd W4	125	K6
Fairfax Rd, Tedd	158	H12
Fairfax Way N10	58	B13
Fairfield Av NW4	71	S12
Fairfield Av, Edg	54	C12
Fairfield Av, Twick	157	S1
Fairfield Av, Wat	50	G5
Fairfield Cl N12	57	M8
Fairfield Cl, Enf 1	45	R8
Fairfield Cl, Epsom	192	J10
Fairfield Cl, Mitch	163	R14
Fairfield Cl, Sid	153	T11
Fairfield Ct NW10	107	N2
Fairfield Cres, Edg	54	C12
Fairfield Dr SW18	145	K9
Fairfield Dr, Grnf	105	M2
Fairfield Dr, Har	67	U6
Fairfield E, Kings T	177	S3
Fairfield Gdns N8	75	K10
Fairfield Gro SE7	134	A10
Fairfield Ind Est, Kings T	177	U6
Fairfield Path, Croy	198	B5
Fairfield Pl, Kings T	177	S5
Fairfield Rd E3	114	B4
Fairfield Rd E17	77	S4
Fairfield Rd N8	75	K10
Fairfield Rd N18	60	G9
Fairfield Rd W7	122	G6
Fairfield Rd, Beck	186	B3
Fairfield Rd, Bexh	155	L4
Fairfield Rd, Brom	169	N14
Fairfield Rd, Croy	198	B5
Fairfield Rd, Ilf	99	K11
Fairfield Rd, Kings T	177	S4
Fairfield Rd, Orp	189	P12
Fairfield Rd, Sthl	103	L11
Fairfield Rd, Wdf Grn	63	N12
Fairfield S, Kings T	177	S5
Fairfield St SW18	145	K9
Fairfield Way, Barn	40	H9
Fairfield Way, Epsom	192	J10
Fairfield W, Kings T	177	S4
Fairfields Cl NW9	70	F9
Fairfields Cres NW9	70	F8
Fairfields Rd, Houns 3	139	T6
Fairfoot Rd E3	114	A8
Fairford Av, Croy	185	P10
Fairford Cl, Croy	185	P10
Fairford Gdns, Wor Pk	193	M5
Fairgreen, Barn	41	T5
Fairgreen E, Barn	41	T5
Fairgreen Rd, Th Hth	183	S10
Fairhaven Av, Croy	185	N12
Fairhaven Cres, Wat	50	B5
Fairhazel Gdns NW6	91	L13
Fairholme Gdns N3	72	D7
Fairholme Rd W14	126	D10
Fairholme Rd, Croy	183	P14
Fairholme Rd, Har	68	E10
Fairholme Rd, Ilf	80	F13
Fairholme Rd, Sutt	194	F11
Fairholt Cl N16	94	C1
Fairholt Rd N16	94	B1
Fairholt St SW7	23	R10
Fairland Rd E15	97	L12
Fairlands Av, Buck H	63	P3
Fairlands Av, Sutt	194	H3
Fairlands Av, Th Hth	183	M8
Fairlands Ct SE9	153	N11
Fairlawn SE7	133	T12
Fairlawn Av N2	73	S7
Fairlawn Av W4	124	F7
Fairlawn Av, Bexh	154	G4
Fairlawn Cl N14	42	F12
Fairlawn Cl, Esher	190	F12
Fairlawn Cl, Felt	157	S7
Fairlawn Cl, Kings T	160	E11
Fairlawn Dr, Wdf Grn	63	P14
Fairlawn Gdns, Sthl	103	M14
Fairlawn Gro W4	124	F7
Fairlawn Pk SE26	167	S9
Fairlawn Rd SW19	162	E14

Entry	No.	Grid
Fairlawns, Pnr	66	F4
Fairlawns, Sun	174	A5
Fairlawns, Twick	141	M12
Fairlea Pl W5	105	M8
Fairlie Gdns SE23	149	M14
Fairlight Av E4	62	G4
Fairlight Av NW10	107	K3
Fairlight Av, Wdf Grn	63	P12
Fairlight Cl E4	62	G4
Fairlight Cl, Wor Pk	193	T7
Fairlight Rd SW17	163	P8
Fairlop Gdns, Ilf	65	M14
Fairlop Rd E11	78	H14
Fairlop Rd, Ilf	81	L4
Fairmead, Brom	188	F8
Fairmead, Surb	192	D2
Fairmead Cl, Brom	188	E8
Fairmead Cl, Houns	120	H13
Fairmead Cl, N Mal	178	H6
Fairmead Cres, Edg	54	E5
Fairmead Gdns, Ilf	80	B10
Fairmead Rd N19	92	H6
Fairmead Rd, Croy	183	M14
Fairmead Rd, Loug	47	S9
Fairmead Side, Loug	47	U10
Fairmeads, Loug	48	J4
Fairmile Av SW16	164	G10
Fairmont Cl, Belv	137	M10
Fairmount Rd SW2	147	L11
Fairoak Cl, Orp	189	K13
Fairoak Dr SE9	153	N10
Fairseat Cl, Bushey	52	C4
Fairthorn Rd SE7	133	P9
Fairview Av, Wem	87	N11
Fairview Cl E17	77	S2
Fairview Cl, Chig	65	S8
Fairview Cres, Har	85	N1
Fairview Dr, Chig	65	S9
Fairview Dr, Orp	203	P8
Fairview Gdns, Wdf Grn	79	S1
Fairview Pl SW2	147	L13
Fairview Rd N15	76	F11
Fairview Rd SW16	183	L2
Fairview Rd, Chig	65	S8
Fairview Rd, Enf	43	N2
Fairview Rd, Sutt	195	R10
Fairview Way, Edg	54	A8
Fairwater Av, Well	154	A8
Fairway SW20	179	T5
Fairway, Bexh	155	K10
Fairway, Orp	189	N10
Fairway, Wdf Grn	63	U9
Fairway, The N13	60	A5
Fairway, The N14	42	C11
Fairway, The NW7	54	J4
Fairway, The W3	106	J11
Fairway, The, Barn	41	K11
Fairway, The, Brom	188	E9
Fairway, The, N Mal	178	H1
Fairway, The, Nthlt	85	T12
Fairway, The, Ruis	84	F8
Fairway, The, Wem	87	K5
Fairway, The, W Mol	175	S5
Fairway Av NW9	70	D6
Fairway Av, Borwd	38	C4
Fairway Cl NW11	73	L13
Fairway Cl, Croy	185	R10
Fairway Cl, Epsom	192	F7
Fairway Cl, Houns	188	T9
Fairway Ct NW7	54	G5
Fairway Dr SE28	118	H11
Fairway Dr, Grnf	85	S14
Fairway Gdns, Beck	186	H11
Fairway Gdns, Ilf	99	L9
Fairways, Stan	69	R3
Fairways, Tedd	159	N13
Fairweather Cl N15	76	C7
Fairweather Rd N16	76	G12
Fairwyn Rd SE26	167	N14
Fakenham Cl, NW7 *1*	55	N14
Fakenham Cl, Nthlt	85	M11
Fakruddin St E1	13	T11
Falcon Av, Brom	188	D7
Falcon Cl SE1	27	S2
Falcon Cl W4	124	D11
Falcon Ct, EC4 *16*	19	K8
Falcon Cres, Enf	45	P10
Falcon Gro SW11	145	R5
Falcon La SW11	145	S6
Falcon Pk Ind Est NW10	89	L9
Falcon Rd SW11	145	R5
Falcon Rd, Enf	45	N10
Falcon Rd, Hmptn	157	M13
Falcon St E13	115	N7
Falcon Ter SW11	145	S6
Falcon Way E11	79	P7
Falcon Way E14	132	D7
Falcon Way NW9	71	K4
Falcon Way, Felt	138	C10
Falcon Way, Har	69	R10
Falconberg Ct, W1 *7*	17	T6
Falconberg Ms, W1 *4*	17	S6
Falconwood Av, Well	153	R4
Falconwood Par, Well	153	S8
Falconwood Rd, Croy	200	A13
Falcourt Cl, Sutt	194	J10
Falkirk Gdns, Wat	50	G10
Falkirk St N1	12	J4
Falkland Av N3	56	H14
Falkland Av N11	58	C7
Falkland Pk Av SE25	184	C5
Falkland Rd N8	75	P8
Falkland Rd NW5	92	E9
Falkland Rd, Barn	40	C4
Fallaize Av, Ilf	98	H7
Falloden Way NW11	72	G7
Fallow Cl, Chig	65	U10
Fallow Ct SE16 *2*	37	U8
Fallow Ct Av N12	57	L12
Fallow Flds, Loug	47	U13
Fallowfield, Stan	52	G6
Fallowfield Ct, Stan	52	G6
Fallowfields Dr N12	57	S12
Fallows Cl N2	73	M3
Fallsbrook Rd SW16	164	E12
Falman Cl N9	60	G1
Falmer Rd E17	78	C6
Falmer Rd N15	75	U9
Falmer Rd, Enf	44	D7
Falmouth Av E4	62	H10
Falmouth Cl N22	59	L14
Falmouth Cl SE12	151	L9
Falmouth Gdns, Ilf	80	B7
Falmouth Rd SE1	28	A12
Falmouth St, E15 *7*	96	H10
Fambridge Cl SE26	167	U8
Fambridge Rd, Dag	83	N14
Fane St W14	126	F10
Fann St EC1	11	U12
Fann St EC2	11	U12
Fanshaw St N1	12	G5
Fanshawe Av, Bark	99	M12
Fanshawe Cres, Dag	101	L9
Fanshawe Rd, Rich	159	M8
Fanthorpe St SW15	143	U5
Faraday Av, Sid	172	C4
Faraday Rd E15	97	L12
Faraday Rd SW19	162	J11
Faraday Rd W3	106	F13
Faraday Rd W10	108	C9
Faraday Rd, Sthl	103	R13
Faraday Rd, Well	154	A6
Faraday Rd, W Mol	175	N7
Faraday Way SE18	134	B6
Faraday Way, Croy	197	M1
Fareham Rd, Felt	138	F13
Fareham St, W1 *9*	17	R6
Farewell Pl, Mitch *1*	181	R2
Faringdon Av, Brom	188	J12
Faringford Rd E15	96	J14
Farjeon Rd SE3	152	A1
Farleigh Av, Brom	187	M13
Farleigh Pl N16	94	E7
Farleigh Rd N16	94	E7
Farley Dr, Ilf	99	S2
Farley Pl SE25	184	G8
Farley Rd SE6	150	E13
Farley Rd, S Croy	198	J13
Farlington Pl SW15	143	R14
Farlow Rd SW15	144	A5
Farlton Rd SW18	163	K1
Farm Av NW2	90	D6
Farm Av SW16	165	K7
Farm Av, Har	87	N13
Farm Av, Wem	87	M12
Farm Cl, Barn	39	T10
Farm Cl, Buck H	63	T6
Farm Cl, Dag	101	T14
Farm Cl, Sthl	103	R13
Farm Cl, Sutt	195	P14
Farm Cl, W Wick	201	K6
Farm Ct NW4	71	P5
Farm Dr, Croy	199	U3
Farm End E4	46	J9
Farm La N14	42	B12
Farm La SW6	126	H12
Farm La, Croy	199	U4
Farm Pl W8	126	G1
Farm Rd N21	59	T2
Farm Rd, Edg	54	D11
Farm Rd, Houns	157	K1
Farm Rd, Mord	185	K10
Farm Rd, Sutt	195	P13
Farm St W1	16	G12
Farm Vale, Bex	155	R12
Farm Way, Buck H	63	T7
Farm Way, Wor Pk	193	U5
Farmborough Cl, Har	86	B1
Farmcote Rd SE12	169	P2
Farmdale Rd SE10	133	P9
Farmdale Rd, Cars	195	R13
Farmer Rd E10	96	D1
Farmer St, W8 *12*	126	G1
Farmers Rd SE5	129	S14
Farmfield Rd, Brom	168	J10
Farmhouse Rd SW16	164	F14
Farmilo Rd E17	78	A13
Farmington Av, Sutt	195	P5
Farmland Wk, Chis	170	J9
Farmlands, Enf	43	N2
Farmlands, Pnr	66	B7
Farmlands, The, Nthlt	85	N12
Farmleigh N14	42	E13
Farmstead Rd SE6	168	C8
Farmstead Rd, Har	68	B2
Farmway, Dag	100	F5
Farnaby Rd SE9	151	U8
Farnaby Rd, Brom	168	J14
Farnan Av E17	78	C4
Farnan Rd SW16	165	K10
Farnborough Av E17	77	R6
Farnborough Av, S Croy	199	P14
Farnborough Cl, Wem *1*	88	D4
Farnborough Common, Orp	202	E5
Farnborough Cres, Brom	201	M2
Farnborough Hill, Orp	203	P9
Farnborough Way, Orp	203	S11
Farncombe St SE16	29	U7
Farndale Av N13	59	S5
Farndale Cres, Grnf	103	U5
Farnell Ms, SW5 *1*	30	A6
Farnell Rd, Islw	140	B6
Farnham Cl N20	41	L13
Farnham Gdns SW20	179	R4
Farnham Pl SE1	27	S3
Farnham Rd, Ilf	81	U13
Farnham Rd, Well	154	F3
Farnham Royal SE11	34	G8
Farningham Rd N17	60	H13
Farnley Rd E4	46	J14
Farnley Rd SE25	184	B8
Faro Cl, Brom	188	H4
Faroe Rd W14	126	B6
Farorna Wk, Enf	43	N1
Farquhar Rd SE19	166	E9
Farquhar Rd SW19	162	H5
Farquharson Rd, Croy	197	T1
Farr Av, Bark	118	A4
Farr Rd, Enf	44	B2
Farrance Rd, Rom	83	K13
Farrance St E14	113	U12
Farrans Ct, Har	69	K13
Farrant Av N22	75	P4
Farren Rd SE23	167	R3
Farrer Ms N8	74	F8
Farrer Rd N8	74	F8
Farrer Rd, Har	69	R9
Farrer's Pl, Croy	199	N7
Farrier Cl, Sun	174	A7
Farrier Rd, Nthlt	103	P3
Farrier St NW1	92	E13
Farrier Wk SW10	30	F9
Farriers Way, Borwd	38	F11
Farringdon La EC1	11	L11
Farringdon Rd EC1	19	M1
Farringdon St EC4	19	N5
Farrington Pl, Chis	171	N13
Farrins Rents SE16	131	R2
Farrow La SE14	131	M13
Farrow Pl SE16	131	R5
Farthing All, SE1 *2*	29	R7
Farthing Flds, E1 *11*	131	K1
Farthing St, Orp	202	E14
Farthingale Wk E15	96	G14
Farthings, The, Kings T	178	B1
Farthings Cl E4	63	K5
Farthings Cl, Pnr	66	C11
Farwell Rd, Sid	172	D7
Farwig La, Brom	187	M1
Fashion St E1	21	N3
Fashoda Rd, Brom	188	A7
Fassett Rd E8	94	G11
Fassett Rd, Kings T	177	R7
Fassett Sq E8	94	G11
Fauconberg Rd W4	124	E11
Faulkner Cl, Dag	82	G14
Faulkner St, SE14	149	M1
Fauna Cl, Rom	82	E12
Faunce St SE17	35	P8
Favart Rd SW6	144	H1
Faversham Av E4	63	K2
Faversham Av, Enf	44	B12
Faversham Rd SE6	149	U14
Faversham Rd, Beck	185	U3
Faversham Rd, Mord	181	K11
Fawcett Cl SW11	145	P4
Fawcett Cl SW16	165	N8
Fawcett Est E5	94	H1
Fawcett Rd NW10	89	L14
Fawcett Rd, Croy	197	T6
Fawcett St SW10	30	E11
Fawcus Cl, Esher	190	D12
Fawe Pk Rd SW15	144	E8
Fawe St E14	114	D10
Fawley Rd NW6	90	J10
Fawn Rd E13	115	T3
Fawn Rd, Chig	65	U10
Fawnbrake Av SE24	147	T8
Fawood Av NW10	88	G14
Faygate Cres, Bexh	155	P10
Faygate Rd SW2	165	L4
Fayland Av SW16	164	E9
Fearnley Cres, Hmptn	157	L11
Fearon St SE10	133	N9
Feathers Pl SE10	132	H11
Featherstone Av, SE23 *7*	167	L4
Featherstone Gdns, Borwd	38	F8
Featherstone Ind Est, Sthl	121	K4
Featherstone Rd NW7	55	R12
Featherstone Rd, Sthl	120	J5
Featherstone St EC1	12	C10
Featherstone Ter, Sthl	121	K5

Featley Rd SW9	147	R5
Federal Rd, Grnf	105	M3
Federation Rd SE2	136	E8
Fee Fm Rd, Esher	190	F13
Felbridge Av, Stan	68	H2
Felbridge Cl SW16	165	N7
Felbrigge Rd, Ilf	99	T3
Felday Rd SE13	150	C11
Felden Cl, Pnr	51	K14
Felden St SW6	144	E2
Feldman Cl N16	94	G1
Felgate Ms W6	125	R8
Felhampton Rd SE9	170	J5
Felhurst Cres, Dag	101	S7
Felix Av N8	74	J11
Felix Rd W13	104	G14
Felix Rd, Walt	174	A11
Felix St E2	113	K3
Felixstowe Rd N9	60	H7
Felixstowe Rd N17	76	E5
Felixstowe Rd NW10	107	S5
Felixstowe Rd SE2	136	D6
Fell Rd, Croy	197	U5
Fellbrigg Rd SE22	148	F10
Fellbrigg St E1	113	K8
Fellbrook, Rich	159	K6
Fellmongers Yd, Croy	197	T5
Fellowes Cl, Hayes	102	H7
Fellowes Rd, Cars	195	R5
Fellows Ct E2	13	M4
Fellows Rd NW3	91	T13
Felltram Way SE7	133	P9
Felmersham Cl SW4	146	J8
Felmingham Rd SE20	185	L4
Felnex Trd Est, Wall	196	B3
Fels Cl, Dag	101	S5
Fels Fm Av, Dag	101	U6
Felsberg Rd SW2	147	K12
Felsham Rd SW15	144	B6
Felspar Cl SE18	135	U10
Felstead Av, Ilf	80	G2
Felstead Gdns, E14	132	E10
Felstead Rd E11	79	P13
Felstead Rd, Loug	48	C13
Felstead St E9	95	U12
Felsted Rd E16	116	A12
Feltham Av, K Mol	176	C7
Feltham Business Complex, Felt	156	D3
Feltham Hill Rd, Felt	156	D9
Feltham Rd, Mitch	182	A3
Felthambrook Way, Felt	156	D6
Felton Cl, Orp	188	J12
Felton Gdns, Bark 3	117	S3
Felton Lea, Sid	171	T9
Felton Rd W13	123	L3
Felton Rd, Bark	117	S3
Felton St N1	112	B2
Fen Ct EC3	20	H9
Fen Gro, Sid	153	T11
Fen St E16	115	M13
Fencepiece Rd, Chig	65	M12
Fencepiece Rd, Ilf	65	M12
Fenchurch Av EC3	20	H8
Fenchurch Bldgs EC3	20	J8
Fenchurch Pl EC3	20	J9
Fenchurch St EC3	20	H9
Fendall Rd, Epsom	192	F9
Fendall St SE1	29	K11
Fendt Cl E16	115	M12
Fendyke Rd, Belv	136	G6
Fenelon Pl W14	126	F8
Fenham Rd SE15	130	N14
Fenman Ct N17	77	K1
Fenman Gdns, Ilf	100	C1
Fenn Cl, Brom	169	N12
Fenn St E9	95	M10
Fennel Cl, E16 4	115	K7
Fennel Cl, Croy 1	199	P1
Fennel St SE18	134	H12
Fenner Cl SE16	131	K7
Fenner Sq, SW11 9	145	P6
Fenning St, SE1 2	28	G5
Fenstanton Av N12	57	N10
Fenswood Cl, Bex	155	P10
Fentiman Rd SW8	34	G13
Fenton Cl E8	94	F11
Fenton Cl, SW9 5	147	L4
Fenton Cl, Chis	170	E9
Fenton Rd N17	59	U13
Fentons Av E13	115	R4
Fenwick Cl SE18	134	G12
Fenwick Gro SE15	148	G6
Fenwick Pl SW9	146	J6
Fenwick Rd SE15	148	G6
Ferdinand Pl NW1	92	C13
Ferdinand St NW1	92	B12
Fergus Rd N5	93	S10
Ferguson Av, Surb	177	U9
Ferguson Cl E14	132	B8
Ferguson Cl, Brom	186	F5
Ferguson Dr W3	106	H11
Ferme Pk Rd N4	75	M13
Ferme Pk Rd N8	75	L11
Fermor Rd SE23	167	S2
Fermoy Rd W9	108	E8
Fermoy Rd, Grnf	103	R8
Fern Av, Mitch	182	H7
Fern Dene, W13 2	105	K10
Fern Gro, Felt	138	C14
Fern La, Houns	121	M10
Fern St E3	114	B8
Fern Wk SE16	37	U7
Fernbank, Buck H	63	R2
Fernbank Av, Walt	175	K14
Fernbank Av, Wem	86	E8
Fernbank Ms SW12	146	E12
Fernbrook Cres SE13	150	J11
Fernbrook Dr, Har	67	R13
Fernbrook Rd SE13	150	J11
Ferncliff Rd E8	94	G9
Ferncroft Av N12	57	T11
Ferncroft Av NW3	90	H6
Ferncroft Av, Ruis	84	F3
Ferndale, Brom	187	U4
Ferndale Av E17	78	G9
Ferndale Av, Houns	139	K5
Ferndale Cl, Bexh	154	J2
Ferndale Ct SE3	133	M13
Ferndale Rd E7	97	S3
Ferndale Rd E11	97	L3
Ferndale Rd N15	76	F10
Ferndale Rd SE25	184	J10
Ferndale Rd, SW4 4	147	K7
Ferndale Rd SW9	146	J7
Ferndale Rd, Rom	83	U3
Ferndale St E6	116	J13
Ferndale Ter, Har	68	E8
Ferndale Way, Orp	203	P9
Ferndene Rd SE24	147	U7
Ferndown, Nthwd	66	B3
Ferndown Av, Orp	203	P1
Ferndown Cl, Pnr	50	J13
Ferndown Cl, Sutt	195	N12
Ferndown Rd SE9	152	A13
Ferndown Rd, Wat	50	E6
Ferney Meade Way, Islw	140	G4
Ferney Rd, Barn	42	B14
Fernhall Dr, Ilf	80	B10
Fernham Rd, Th Hth	183	T6
Fernhead Rd W9	108	F8
Fernhill Ct E17	78	H4
Fernhill Gdns, Kings T	159	P10
Fernhill St E16	134	F2
Fernholme Rd SE15	149	N9
Fernhurst Gdns, Edg	54	A11
Fernhurst Rd SW6	144	D1
Fernhurst Rd, Croy	198	J1
Fernlea Rd SW12	164	D2
Fernlea Rd, Mitch	182	A3
Fernleigh Cl, Croy 1	197	N8
Fernleigh Ct, Har	67	S3
Fernleigh Ct, Wem	87	R3
Fernleigh Rd N21	59	P3
Ferns Rd E15	97	L12
Fernsbury St WC1	11	K7
Fernshaw Rd SW10	30	F12
Fernside NW11	90	G3
Fernside, Buck H	63	R1
Fernside Av NW7	54	H6
Fernside Av, Felt	156	D7
Fernside Rd SW12	164	A1
Fernthorpe Rd SW16	164	E11
Ferntower Rd N5	94	A9
Fernways, Ilf	98	J7
Fernwood Av SW16	164	H8
Fernwood Av, Wem	87	L11
Fernwood Cl, Brom	187	T3
Fernwood Cres N20	57	T5
Ferranti Cl SE18	134	B6
Ferraro Cl, Houns	121	N11
Ferrers Av, Wall	196	G7
Ferrers Rd SW16	164	H10
Ferrestone Rd, N8 1	75	L8
Ferriby Cl N1	93	N13
Ferrier St SW18	145	K8
Ferring Cl, Har	85	U1
Ferrings SE21	166	D5
Ferris Av, Croy	199	T6
Ferris Rd SE22	148	G8
Ferron Rd E5	94	J6
Ferrour Ct, N2 4	73	N5
Ferry La N17	76	J7
Ferry La SW13	125	M12
Ferry La, Brent	123	R12
Ferry La, Rich	123	U12
Ferry Pl SE18	134	H6
Ferry Rd SW13	143	N1
Ferry Rd, Tedd	158	J9
Ferry Rd, T Ditt	176	J12
Ferry Rd, Twick	158	J1
Ferry Rd, W Mol	175	P5
Ferry Sq, Brent 7	123	R12
Ferry St E14	132	E9
Ferryhills Cl, Wat	50	F5
Ferrymead Av, Grnf	103	S4
Ferrymead Dr, Grnf	103	P4
Ferrymead Gdns, Grnf	103	T4
Ferrymoor, Rich	159	K6
Festing Rd SW15	144	A5
Festival Cl, Bex	172	G2
Festival Wk, Cars 2	195	U9
Fetter La EC4	19	L7
Ffinch St SE8	132	A13
Field Cl E4	62	C11
Field Cl, Brom	187	U4
Field Cl, Buck H	63	U6
Field Cl, Chess	191	M10
Field Cl, Houns	138	D2
Field Cl, W Mol	175	S10
Field Ct WC1	18	H3
Field End, Barn	39	S8
Field End, Nthlt	84	H12
Field End, Ruis	84	F11
Field End, Twick	158	E7
Field End Rd, Pnr	66	D11
Field End Rd, Ruis	85	K9
Field La, Brent	123	L13
Field La, Tedd	158	G10
Field Mead NW7	55	K14
Field Mead NW9	55	K14
Field Pl, N Mal	179	L11
Field Rd E7	97	N8
Field Rd N17	76	B5
Field Rd W6	126	C10
Field Rd, Felt	138	D12
Field St WC1	10	E5
Field Way NW10	88	F14
Field Way, Croy	200	D11
Field Way, Grnf	103	R2
Fieldend SW16	182	F1
Fielders Cl, Enf 1	48	C1
Fielders Cl, Har	85	U2
Fieldfare Rd SE28	118	F13
Fieldgate La, Mitch	181	S4
Fieldgate St E1	21	U4
Fieldhouse Cl E18	79	P2
Fieldhouse Rd SW12	164	F2
Fielding Av, Twick	157	U5
Fielding Ms SW13	125	R12
Fielding Rd W4	124	J5
Fielding Rd W14	126	B5
Fielding St SE17	36	A9
Fielding Wk W13	122	J6
Fieldings, The SE23	167	L1
Fields Est E8	94	H14
Fields Pk Cres, Rom	82	G9
Fieldsend Rd, Sutt	194	D9
Fieldside Cl, Orp	203	L8
Fieldside Rd, Brom	168	H9
Fieldview SW18	163	N2
Fieldway, Dag	100	E7
Fieldway, Orp	189	P12
Fieldway Cres N5	93	P10
Fiennes Cl, Dag	100	E1
Fiesta Dr, Dag	119	T8
Fife Rd E16	115	N10
Fife Rd N22	59	S14
Fife Rd SW14	142	E10
Fife Rd, Kings T	177	R3
Fife Ter N1	10	G1
Fifield Path SE23	167	N5
Fifth Av E12	98	E7
Fifth Av W10	108	C6
Fifth Cross Rd, Twick	158	A4
Fifth Way, Wem	88	C7
Fig Tree Cl, NW10 1	106	J1
Figges Rd, Mitch	164	A14
Filby Rd, Chess	191	U12
Filey Av N16	94	G2
Filey Cl, Sutt	195	M14
Filey Waye, Ruis	84	B4
Fillebrook Av, Enf	44	D3
Fillebrook Rd E11	96	H1
Filmer Rd SW6	144	D1
Filston Rd, Erith	137	S10
Finborough Rd SW10	30	C9
Finborough Rd SW17	163	U12
Finch Av SE27	166	A8
Finch Cl, NW10 1	88	G10
Finch Cl, Barn	40	G10
Finch Dr, Felt	138	G14
Finch La EC3	20	F7
Finch Ms SE15	148	E1
Finchale Rd SE2	136	B5
Finchingfield Av, Wdf Grn	63	U13
Finchley Ct N3	56	J12
Finchley La NW4	72	A7
Finchley Pk N12	57	M7
Finchley Pl NW8	6	J1
Finchley Rd NW2	90	G4
Finchley Rd NW3	91	M12
Finchley Rd NW8	109	N2
Finchley Rd NW11	90	G4
Finchley Way N3	56	G13
Finck St SE1	26	G8
Finden Rd E7	97	T10
Findhorn Av, Hayes	102	C9
Findhorn St E14	114	F11
Findon Cl SW18	144	G11
Findon Cl, Har	85	S6
Findon Rd N9	60	J2
Findon Rd W12	125	P3
Fingal St SE10	133	M9
Finland Quay SE16	131	R6
Finland Rd SE4	149	R6
Finland St SE16	131	R6
Finlay St SW6	144	B2
Finlays Cl, Chess	192	A9
Finnis St E2	113	K6
Finnymore Rd, Dag	101	K13
Finsbury Av, EC2 1	20	F3
Finsbury Circ EC2	20	E4
Finsbury Cotts N22	59	K14
Finsbury Est EC1	11	N8
Finsbury Mkt EC2	12	G12
Finsbury Pk Av N4	75	T12
Finsbury Pk Rd N4	93	S5
Finsbury Pavement EC2	20	E2
Finsbury Rd N22	75	L1
Finsbury Sq EC2	20	E1
Finsbury St EC2	20	D2
Finsbury Way, Bex	155	M12
Finsen Rd SE5	147	U6
Finstock Rd W10	108	A11
Finucane Ri, Bushey	51	U3

Name	Page	Grid
Fir Cl, Walt	174	B14
Fir Dene, Orp	202	F6
Fir Gro, N Mal	179	L11
Fir Rd, Felt	156	H10
Fir Rd, Sutt	194	E2
Fir Tree Av, Mitch	182	A3
Fir Tree Cl SW16	164	F9
Fir Tree Cl W5	105	S11
Fir Tree Cl, Epsom	193	M8
Fir Tree Cl, Orp	203	U10
Fir Tree Gdns, Croy	200	B7
Fir Tree Gro, Cars	195	U13
Fir Tree Rd, Houns	139	K8
Fir Tree Wk, Dag	101	T6
Fir Tree Wk, Enf	44	B5
Fir Trees Cl SE16	131	S2
Firbank Cl E16	116	A9
Firbank Cl, Enf	43	T7
Firbank Rd SE15	149	K3
Fircroft Gdns, Har	86	C5
Fircroft Rd SW17	163	T4
Fircroft Rd, Chess	191	T7
Firdene, Surb	192	E2
Fire Bell All, Surb	177	S12
Fire Sta All, Barn	40	D5
Firecrest Dr NW3	91	K6
Firefly Cl, Wall	196	J13
Firefly Gdns E6	116	C8
Firethorn Cl, Edg	54	E7
Firhill Rd SE6	168	B5
Firs, The N20	57	P2
Firs, The W5	105	N10
Firs Av N10	74	B6
Firs Av N11	58	A12
Firs Av SW14	142	F8
Firs Cl N10	74	B6
Firs Cl SE23	149	R14
Firs Cl, Esher	190	D12
Firs Cl, Mitch	182	C3
Firs Dr, Houns	120	D14
Firs Dr, Loug	48	G2
Firs La N13	59	T7
Firs La N21	59	U4
Firs Pk Av N21	60	A2
Firs Pk Gdns N21	59	U2
Firs Wk, Wdf Grn	63	N9
Firsby Av, Croy	199	P2
Firsby Rd N16	94	G1
Firscroft N13	59	U5
Firside Gro, Sid	171	T2
First Av E12	98	D9
First Av E13	115	P5
First Av E17	78	B9
First Av N18	61	L8
First Av NW4	71	U7
First Av SW14	142	J5
First Av W3	125	L1
First Av W10	108	E7
First Av, Bexh	136	F13
First Av, Dag	119	S3
First Av, Enf	44	E11
First Av, Rom	82	F9
First Av, Walt	174	D12
First Av, Wem	87	P3
First Av, W Mol	175	M8
First Cl, W Mol	175	T6
First Cross Rd, Twick	158	C3
First Dr NW10	88	E14
First St SW3	31	S1
First Way, Wem	88	C8
Firstway SW20	179	T4
Firswood Av, Epsom	193	L9
Firth Gdns SW6	144	C2
Fish St Hill EC3	20	F11
Fisher Cl, Croy	198	E2
Fisher Cl, Grnf	103	N5
Fisher Rd, Har	68	F3
Fisher St E16	115	N9
Fisher St WC1	18	E4
Fisherman Cl, Rich	159	L8
Fishermans Dr SE16	131	P3
Fisherman's Wk E14	132	A1
Fishermans Wk SE28	135	P3
Fishers Ct, SE14 [4]	149	N1
Fishers La W4	124	H8
Fishers Way, Belv	137	U2
Fishersdene, Esher	190	G13
Fisherton St NW8	7	K10
Fishponds Rd SW17	163	T6
Fishponds Rd, Kes	202	A10
Fisons Rd E16	133	N2
Fitzalan Rd N3	72	E5
Fitzalan Rd, Esher	190	D14
Fitzalan St SE11	34	J2
Fitzgeorge Av W14	126	C8
Fitzgeorge Av, N Mal	178	H1
Fitzgerald Av SW14	143	K6
Fitzgerald Cl, E11 [1]	79	N10
Fitzgerald Rd E11	79	N10
Fitzgerald Rd SW14	142	H5
Fitzgerald Rd, T Ditt	176	G12
Fitzhardinge St W1	16	D6
Fitzhugh Gro SW18	145	P12
Fitzhugh Gro Est SW18	145	P11
Fitzjames Av W14	126	D8
Fitzjames Av, Croy	198	G4
Fitzjohn Av, Barn	40	D10
Fitzjohn's Av NW3	91	M8
Fitzmaurice Pl W1	24	J1
Fitzneal St W12	107	L11
Fitzroy Cl N6	91	U2
Fitzroy Cres W4	124	G13
Fitzroy Gdns SE19	166	D14
Fitzroy Ms W1	9	L12
Fitzroy Pk N6	92	A1
Fitzroy Rd NW1	110	A1
Fitzroy Sq W1	9	L12
Fitzroy St W1	9	M12
Fitzroy Yd, NW1 [3]	110	A1
Fitzstephen Rd, Dag	100	C9
Fitzwarren Gdns N19	92	E1
Fitzwilliam Av, Rich	141	T4
Fitzwilliam Ms, E16 [4]	133	N1
Fitzwilliam Rd SW4	146	F5
Fitzwygram Cl, Hmptn	157	T10
Five Acre NW9	71	L2
Five Bell All, E14 [12]	113	U13
Five Elms Rd, Brom	201	T5
Five Elms Rd, Dag	101	L6
Five Flds Cl, Wat	51	L4
Fiveacre Cl, Th Hth	183	P12
Fives Ct SE11	35	P1
Fiveways Rd SW9	147	P3
Fladbury Rd N15	76	B11
Fladgate Rd E11	79	K11
Flag Cl, Croy	199	P1
Flag Wk, Pnr	66	B11
Flambard Rd, Har	68	H12
Flamborough Rd, Ruis	84	B5
Flamborough St E14	113	R12
Flamstead Gdns, Dag	100	F14
Flamstead Rd, Dag	100	F14
Flamsted Av, Wem	88	B12
Flamsteed Rd SE7	134	C10
Flanchford Rd W12	125	M5
Flanders Cres SW17	163	T12
Flanders Rd E6	116	F4
Flanders Rd W4	125	K7
Flanders Way E9	95	N11
Flank St E1 [2]	21	R10
Flask Wk NW3	91	M7
Flavell Ms SE10	133	K9
Flaxen Cl E4	62	D6
Flaxen Rd E4	62	D6
Flaxley Rd, Mord	180	J12
Flaxman Rd SE5	147	S4
Flaxman Ter WC1	9	U8
Flaxton Rd SE18	135	R14
Flecker Cl, Stan	52	F9
Fleece Dr, N9 [3]	60	G7
Fleece Rd, Surb	191	L1
Fleece Wk, N7 [9]	93	K11
Fleeming Cl, E17 [4]	77	U3
Fleeming Rd E17	77	U3
Fleet Cl, W Mol	175	M10
Fleet La, W Mol	175	P10
Fleet Rd NW3	91	T9
Fleet Sq, WC1 [7]	10	G8
Fleet St EC4	19	K7
Fleet St Hill E1	13	R11
Fleetside, W Mol	175	M10
Fleetway Business Pk, Grnf	105	K3
Fleetwood Cl E16	116	A9
Fleetwood Cl, N Mal	191	N13
Fleetwood Cl, Chess	198	E5
Fleetwood Cl, Croy [8]		
Fleetwood Gro W3	106	J14
Fleetwood Rd NW10	89	N9
Fleetwood Rd, Kings T	178	D5
Fleetwood Sq, Kings T	178	D5
Fleetwood St N16	94	D4
Fleetwood Way, Wat	50	E8
Fleming Ct, W2 [2]	14	J2
Fleming Ct, Croy	197	N10
Fleming Dr, N21 [1]	43	L9
Fleming Mead, Mitch	163	S13
Fleming Rd SE17	35	R10
Fleming Rd, Sthl	103	S12
Fleming Way SE28	118	H13
Fleming Way, Islw	140	E7
Flemming Av, Ruis	84	C2
Flempton Rd E10	95	S1
Fletcher Cl, E6 [2]	116	J12
Fletcher La E10	78	E14
Fletcher Rd W4	124	F5
Fletcher Rd, Chig	65	U9
Fletcher St E1	21	T10
Fletchers Cl, Brom	187	S8
Fletching Rd E5	95	L6
Fletching Rd SE7	134	A11
Fletton Rd N11	58	J13
Fleur de Lis St E1	13	K12
Fleur Gates SW19	144	B14
Flexmere Rd N17	76	B1
Flight App NW9	71	L4
Flimwell Cl, Brom	168	J11
Flint St SE17	36	E4
Flintmill Cres SE3	152	C5
Flinton St SE17	36	J5
Flitcroft St WC2	17	U6
Flock Mill Pl SW18	162	J2
Flockton St, SE16 [1]	29	S8
Flodden Rd SE5	147	T1
Flood La, Twick	158	H1
Flood St SW3	31	S8
Flood Wk SW3	31	R9
Flora Cl E14	114	C12
Flora Gdns W6	125	R7
Flora Gdns, Rom	82	E12
Flora St, Belv [3]	137	M10
Floral St WC2	18	B9
Florence Av, Enf	43	T5
Florence Av, Mord	181	M10
Florence Cl, Walt	174	D14
Florence Dr, Enf	43	T5
Florence Gdns W4	124	E12
Florence Rd E6	115	U1
Florence Rd E13	115	M4
Florence Rd N4	93	N1
Florence Rd SE2	136	F7
Florence Rd SE14	149	U2
Florence Rd SW19	162	J12
Florence Rd W4	124	G5
Florence Rd W5	105	R14
Florence Rd, Beck	185	P4
Florence Rd, Brom	187	N2
Florence Rd, Felt	156	D2
Florence Rd, Kings T	159	U14
Florence Rd, Sthl	120	H7
Florence Rd, Walt	174	D14
Florence St E16	115	M7
Florence St N1	93	R14
Florence St NW4	71	T7
Florence Ter SE14	149	U1
Florence Way, SW12 [1]	163	U2
Florfield Pas, E8 [7]	95	K12
Florfield Rd E8	94	J12
Florian Av, Sutt	195	N7
Florian Rd SW15	144	D7
Florida Cl, Bushey	52	A3
Florida Rd, Th Hth	183	S2
Florida St E2	13	T7
Floriston Cl, Stan	69	K1
Floriston Gdns, Stan	69	K1
Floss St SW15	143	U4
Flower & Dean Wk E1	21	N4
Flower La NW7	55	L10
Flower Pot Cl N15	76	E12
Flower Wk, The SW7	22	G6
Flowersmead SW17	164	A4
Floyd Rd SE7	133	T9
Fludyer St SE13	150	J7
Foley Ms, Esher	190	D13
Foley Rd, Esher	190	D13
Foley St W1	17	M3
Folgate St E1	21	K1
Foliot St W12	107	L12
Folkestone Rd E6	116	H4
Folkestone Rd E17	78	C7
Folkestone Rd N18	60	G8
Folkingham La, NW9 [1]	70	J2
Folkington Cor N12	56	E10
Follett St E14	114	E12
Folly La E4	61	S14
Folly La E17	77	S1
Folly Wall E14	132	F4
Font Hills N2	73	L3
Fontaine Rd SW16	165	L13
Fontarabia Rd SW11	146	B7
Fontayne Av, Chig	65	M8
Fontenoy Rd SW12	164	D4
Fonteyne Gdns, Wdf Grn	80	A3
Fonthill Cl SE20	184	H3
Fonthill Ms N4	93	N3
Fonthill Rd N4	93	N3
Fontley Way SW15	143	N14
Fontwell Cl, Har	52	C13
Fontwell Cl, Nthlt	85	P11
Fontwell Dr, Brom	188	G10
Football La, Har	86	E1
Footpath, The SW15	143	P10
Foots Cray High St, Sid	172	F11
Foots Cray La, Sid	172	F2
Footscray Rd SE9	171	M3
Footway, The SE9	153	M14
Forbes Cl NW2	89	P5
Forbes St E1	21	T8
Forbes Way, Ruis	84	C3
Forburg Rd N16	94	G2
Ford Cl E3	113	S3
Ford Cl, Har	68	B13
Ford Cl, Th Hth	183	S11
Ford End, Wdf Grn	63	R12
Ford Rd E3	113	T3
Ford Rd, Dag	101	M13
Ford Sq E1	113	K10
Ford St E3	113	S2
Ford St E16	115	L11
Fordbridge Rd, Sun	174	A8
Forde Av, Brom	187	T5
Fordel Rd SE6	168	G1
Fordham Cl, Barn	41	R6
Fordham Rd, Barn	41	R6
Fordham St E1	21	U5
Fordhook Av W5	105	U14
Fordingley Rd W9	108	F6
Fordington Rd N6	73	T9
Fordmill Rd SE6	168	B3
Fords Gro N21	59	T2
Fords Pk Rd E16	115	N11
Fordwich Cl, Orp	189	T13
Fordwych Rd NW2	90	C9
Fordyce Rd SE13	150	F11
Fordyke Rd, Dag	101	L3
Fore St EC2	20	B3
Fore St N9	60	G7
Fore St N18	60	G11
Fore St, Pnr	66	A10
Fore St EC2	20	C4
Foreland Ct NW4	72	C2
Foreland St SE18	135	N7
Foremark Cl, Ilf	65	T11
Foreshore SE8	131	T8
Forest, The E11	79	K7
Forest App E4	46	J13

Name	Pg	Grid
Forest App, Wdf Grn	63	M13
Forest Av E4	47	K14
Forest Av, Chig	64	G9
Forest Business Pk E17	77	P14
Forest Cl E11	79	M10
Forest Cl, Chis	188	G2
Forest Cl, Wdf Grn	63	R7
Forest Ct E4	63	M2
Forest Ct E11	79	K8
Forest Cft SE23	167	K3
Forest Dr E12	98	B6
Forest Dr, Kes	202	C8
Forest Dr, Wdf Grn	62	J14
Forest Dr E E11	78	H13
Forest Dr W E11	78	F14
Forest Edge, Buck H	63	U7
Forest Gdns N17	76	E3
Forest Gate NW9	70	J9
Forest Glade E4	62	J8
Forest Glade E11	78	J12
Forest Gro E8	94	E12
Forest Hts, Buck H	63	P3
Forest Hill Business Cen SE23	167	M4
Forest Hill Rd SE22	148	J10
Forest Hill Rd SE23	149	L12
Forest Ind Pk, Ilf	81	S1
Forest La E7	97	P9
Forest La E15	97	K11
Forest La, Chig	64	H9
Forest Mt Rd, Wdf Grn	62	H14
Forest Ridge, Beck	186	A5
Forest Ridge, Kes	202	D8
Forest Ri E17	78	G9
Forest Rd E7	97	P7
Forest Rd E8	94	E12
Forest Rd E11	78	G14
Forest Rd E17	77	M7
Forest Rd N9	61	K1
Forest Rd N17	77	M7
Forest Rd, Felt	156	D4
Forest Rd, Ilf	81	N3
Forest Rd, Loug	48	C7
Forest Rd, Rich	124	B13
Forest Rd, Rom	83	R6
Forest Rd, Sutt	180	G14
Forest Rd, Wdf Grn	63	N6
Forest Side E4	63	L12
Forest Side, E7 *7*	97	R7
Forest Side, Buck H	63	T1
Forest Side, Wor Pk	193	L2
Forest St E7	97	N9
Forest Vw E4	46	H13
Forest Vw E11	79	M14
Forest Vw Av E10	78	H9
Forest Vw Rd E12	98	C7
Forest Vw Rd E17	78	F1
Forest Vw Rd, Loug	48	B8
Forest Way, N19 *11*	92	E4
Forest Way, Loug	48	D5
Forest Way, Sid	153	P14
Forest Way, Wdf Grn	63	R7
Forestdale N14	58	H7
Forester Rd SE15	149	K6
Foresters Cl, Wall	196	G13
Foresters Cres, Bexh	155	R7
Foresters Dr E17	78	H8
Foresters Dr, Wall	196	G12
Forestholme Cl SE23	167	L3
Forfar Rd N22	75	R1
Forfar Rd SW11	146	B3
Forge Cl, Brom	201	P2
Forge Dr, Esher	190	G13
Forge La, Felt	156	J9
Forge La, Sun	174	B6
Forge La, Sutt	194	D13
Forge Pl NW1	92	B12
Forman Pl, N16 *7*	94	F7
Formby Av, Stan	69	L5
Formosa St W9 *6*	6	D12
Formunt Cl E16	115	M10
Forres Gdns NW11	72	G12
Forrest Gdns SW16	183	L6
Forrester Path SE26	167	M8
Forset St W1	15	S6
Forstal Cl, Brom	187	N5
Forster Rd E17	77	R11
Forster Rd N17	76	E5
Forster Rd SW2	146	J14
Forster Rd, Beck	185	R6
Forster Rd, Croy *1*	183	U13
Forsters Cl, Rom	83	L12
Forster's Way SW18	144	J14
Forsters Way, Hayes	102	C12
Forston St N1	12	B2
Forsyte Cres SE19	184	C2
Forsyth Gdns SE17	35	R10
Forsyth Pl, Enf	44	C10
Forsythia Cl, Ilf	98	J10
Fort Rd SE1	37	P3
Fort Rd, Nthlt	85	P14
Fort St E1	21	K3
Fort St E16	133	S2
Forterie Gdns, Ilf	100	A7
Fortescue Av, Twick	157	U5
Fortescue Av, E8 *9*	95	K14
Fortescue Rd SW19	163	P14
Fortescue Rd, Edg	70	G1
Fortess Gro NW5	92	E9
Fortess Rd NW5	92	E8
Fortess Wk, NW5 *5*	92	D9
Forthbridge Rd SW11	146	A7
Fortis Cl E16	115	T12
Fortis Grn N2	73	S7
Fortis Grn N10	73	S7
Fortis Grn Av N2	73	U6
Fortis Grn Rd N10	74	B6
Fortismere Av N10	74	B6
Fortnam Rd N19	92	H4
Fortnums Acre, Stan	52	F11
Fortrose Gdns SW2	164	J1
Fortuna Cl N7	93	L11
Fortune Gate Rd NW10	107	K1
Fortune Grn Rd NW6	90	G9
Fortune St EC1	12	A12
Fortune Way NW10	107	N6
Fortunes Mead, Nthlt	85	K12
Forty Acre La E16	115	N10
Forty Av, Wem	87	U4
Forty Cl, Wem	87	U5
Forty Footpath, SW14 *3*	142	E6
Forty La, Wem	88	D4
Forum, The, W Mol	175	S7
Forum Way, Edg	54	B12
Forumside, Edg	54	B12
Forval Cl, Mitch	181	T9
Forward Dr, Har	68	F8
Fosbury Ms, W2 *4*	14	D11
Foscote Ms, W9 *1*	108	H8
Foscote Rd NW4	71	R11
Foskett Rd SW6	144	E4
Foss Av, Croy	197	P10
Foss Rd SW17	163	N8
Fossdene Rd SE7	133	S10
Fossdyke Cl, Hayes	103	K9
Fosse Way W13	104	G9
Fossil Rd SE13	150	B6
Fossington Rd, Belv	136	G7
Fossway, Dag	100	F3
Foster La EC2	19	U6
Foster Rd E13	115	N7
Foster Rd W3	106	J13
Foster Rd W4	124	H9
Foster St NW4	71	T8
Foster Wk, NW4 *2*	71	U8
Fosters Cl E18	79	S2
Fosters Cl, Chis	170	E10
Fothergill Cl E13	115	N3
Fothergill Dr N21	43	L10
Fotheringham Rd, Enf	44	E8
Foubert's Pl W1	17	M8
Foulden Rd N16	94	E7
Foulden Ter N16	94	E7
Foulis Ter SW7	31	L5
Foulser Rd SW17	163	U6
Foulsham Rd, Th Hth	183	U6
Founder Cl, E6 *3*	116	J12
Founders Gdns SE19	165	U13
Foundry Cl SE16	131	R1
Foundry Ms, NW1 *1*	9	N9
Fount St SW8	128	H14
Fountain Ct, EC4 *1*	19	K9
Fountain Dr SE19	166	F8
Fountain Dr, Cars	195	T14
Fountain Pl SW9	147	P2
Fountain Rd SW17	163	N9
Fountain Rd, Th Hth	183	T4
Fountain Sq, SW1 *1*	32	J2
Fountains Av, Felt	157	M5
Fountains Cl, Felt	157	M4
Fountains Cres N14	42	J13
Fountayne Rd N15	76	H8
Fountayne Rd N16	94	G4
Four Seasons Cl E3	114	A3
Four Seasons Cres, Sutt	194	E3
Four Wents, The, E4 *2*	62	H3
Fouracres, Enf	45	R2
Fourland Wk, Edg	54	F12
Fournier St E1	21	N2
Fourth Av E12	98	F8
Fourth Av W10	108	C6
Fourth Cross Rd, Twick	158	A4
Fourth Way, Wem	88	E8
Fowey Av, Ilf	80	B9
Fowey Cl E1	130	J1
Fowler Cl SW11	145	N6
Fowler Rd E7	97	N7
Fowler Rd N1	93	S14
Fowler Rd, Mitch	182	B3
Fowlers Cl, Sid	172	J10
Fowlers Wk W5	105	N7
Fownes St SW11	145	S5
Fox & Knot St, EC1 *2*	19	R1
Fox Cl E1	113	M7
Fox Cl E16	115	N10
Fox Gro, Walt	174	D14
Fox Hill SE19	166	E14
Fox Hill, Kes	201	T9
Fox Hill Gdns SE19	166	E14
Fox Hollow Cl SE18	135	R10
Fox Hollow Dr, Bexh	154	G5
Fox Ho Rd, Belv	137	N4
Fox La N13	59	L5
Fox La W5	105	S9
Fox La, Kes	201	T9
Fox Rd E16	115	L10
Foxberry Rd SE4	149	S7
Foxborough Gdns SE4	150	A11
Foxbourne Rd SW17	164	B4
Foxbury Av, Chis	171	P11
Foxbury Cl, Brom	169	R12
Foxbury Rd, Brom	169	P12
Foxcombe, Croy	200	D11
Foxcombe Cl, E6 *5*	116	A3
Foxcombe Rd, SW15 *6*	161	P1
Foxcote SE5	36	J8
Foxcroft Rd SE18	153	K1
Foxes Dale SE3	151	N6
Foxes Dale, Brom	186	H5
Foxfield Rd, Orp	203	N4
Foxglove Cl, Sthl	103	K13
Foxglove Gdns E11	79	T7
Foxglove La, Chess	192	B8
Foxglove St W12	107	L13
Foxglove Way, Wall	196	C1
Foxgrove, N14 *1*	58	J6
Foxgrove Av, Beck	168	D14
Foxgrove Path, Wat	50	D10
Foxgrove Rd, Beck	168	C14
Foxham Rd N19	92	G6
Foxhole Rd SE9	152	C9
Foxholt Gdns NW10	88	E14
Foxhome Cl, Chis	170	H12
Foxlands Cres, Dag	101	T9
Foxlands La, Dag	101	U9
Foxlands Rd, Dag	101	T10
Foxlees, Wem	86	H7
Foxley Cl E8	94	G9
Foxley Cl, Loug	49	K4
Foxley Rd SW9	129	P13
Foxley Rd, Th Hth	183	R7
Foxley Sq SW9	147	R1
Foxleys, Wat	50	J5
Foxmead Cl, Enf	43	L6
Foxmore St SW11	145	T2
Fox's Path, Mitch	181	R4
Foxton Gro, Mitch	181	N4
Foxwell, Ms, SE4 *1*	149	S6
Foxwell St SE4	149	R5
Foxwood Cl NW7	54	J8
Foxwood Cl, Felt	156	C6
Foxwood Grn Cl, Enf	44	D11
Foxwood Rd SE3	151	L7
Foyle Rd N17	76	H1
Foyle Rd SE3	133	L12
Framfield Cl N12	56	G6
Framfield Ct, Enf	44	C11
Framfield Rd N5	93	R9
Framfield Rd W7	104	E12
Framfield Rd, Mitch	164	A14
Framlingham Cres SE9	170	D7
Frampton Cl, Sutt	194	G13
Frampton Pk Rd E9	95	L12
Frampton Rd, Houns	139	K9
Frampton St NW8	7	L11
Francemary Rd SE4	150	B9
Frances Rd E4	62	B11
Frances St SE18	134	E7
Franche Ct Rd SW17	163	M6
Francis Av, Bexh	155	P3
Francis Av, Felt	156	A5
Francis Av, Ilf	99	N3
Francis Barber Cl, SW16 *1*	165	M8
Francis Chichester Way SW11	146	B2
Francis Cl, E14 *3*	132	G7
Francis Cl, Epsom	192	G7
Francis Gro SW19	162	E12
Francis Rd E10	96	E2
Francis Rd N2	73	U7
Francis Rd, Croy	183	S13
Francis Rd, Grnf	105	K3
Francis Rd, Har	68	G9
Francis Rd, Houns	138	H4
Francis Rd, Ilf *2*	99	N3
Francis Rd, Pnr	66	F10
Francis Rd, Wall	196	F11
Francis St E15	96	J10
Francis St SW1	33	N1
Francis St, Ilf *3*	99	N3
Franciscan Rd SW17	164	B7
Francklyn Gdns, Edg	54	B5
Franconia Rd SW4	146	F10
Frank Burton Cl SE7	133	S10
Frank Dixon Cl SE21	166	D1
Frank Dixon Way SE21	166	C1
Frank St E13	115	P8
Frank Towell Ct, Felt	156	B1
Frankfurt Rd SE24	147	U9
Frankham St SE8	132	B14
Frankland Cl, SE16 *5*	131	L7
Frankland Cl, Wdf Grn	63	T10
Frankland Rd E4	62	A9
Frankland Rd SW7	22	J11
Franklin Cl N20	41	L13
Franklin Cl SE13	150	C2
Franklin Cl SE27	165	R6
Franklin Cl, Kings T	178	A5
Franklin Cres, Mitch	182	F7
Franklin Pas SE9	152	D5
Franklin Rd SE20	167	M14
Franklin Rd, Bexh	155	K2
Franklin Sq W14	126	F10
Franklin St E3	114	D5
Franklin St N15	76	C12
Franklin Way, Croy	183	K14
Franklins Ms, Har	85	T3

Franklin's Row SW3	32	B6
Franklyn Gdns, Ilf	65	P12
Franklyn Rd NW10	89	L13
Franklyn Rd, Walt	174	C11
Franks Av, N Mal	178	F8
Frankswood Av, Orp	189	K10
Franlaw Cres N13	59	U8
Fransfield Gro SE26	167	K6
Frant Cl SE20	167	M14
Frant Rd, Th Hth	183	R9
Franthorne Way SE6	168	C4
Fraser Cl E6	116	C11
Fraser Cl, Bex	173	U2
Fraser Rd E17	78	D10
Fraser Rd N9	60	J6
Fraser Rd, Erith	137	U9
Fraser Rd, Grnf	105	L2
Fraser St W4	124	J10
Frating Cres, Wdf Grn	63	P12
Frazer Av, Ruis	84	E10
Frazier St SE1	26	J7
Frean St SE16	29	R10
Freda Corbett Cl SE15	37	R14
Frederic Ms, SW1 4	24	C7
Frederic St E17	77	S10
Frederica Rd E4	46	H14
Frederica St, N7 2	93	L13
Frederick Cl W2	15	S9
Frederick Cl, Sutt	194	F8
Frederick Ct NW2	90	D6
Frederick Cres SW9	129	R14
Frederick Cres, Enf	45	M3
Frederick Gdns, Sutt	194	E8
Frederick Pl SE18	135	K9
Frederick Rd SE17	35	R9
Frederick Rd, Sutt	194	E9
Frederick Sq, SE16 1	113	R14
Frederick St WC1	10	F7
Frederick Ter E8	94	E14
Frederick's Pl, EC2 1	20	C7
Fredericks Pl N12	57	L7
Frederick's Row, EC1 1	11	P5
Freedom Cl E17	77	P7
Freedom Rd N17	76	B4
Freedom St SW11	145	U3
Freegrove Rd N7	93	K9
Freeland Pk NW4	72	C3
Freeland Rd W5	105	T13
Freelands Gro, Brom	187	S1
Freelands Rd, Brom	187	S2
Freeling St, N1 5	93	L14
Freeman Cl, Nthlt	85	K13
Freeman Dr, W Mol	175	L6
Freeman Rd, Mord	181	N9
Freemantle Av, Enf	45	P9
Freemantle St SE17	36	H5
Freemasons Rd E16	115	R11
Freemasons Rd, Croy	198	C1
Freesia Cl, Orp	203	T10
Freethorpe Cl SE19	184	C1
Freke Rd SW11	146	B6
Fremantle Rd, Belv	137	P8
Fremantle Rd, Ilf	81	L4
Fremont St E9	113	K1
French Pl, E1 4	13	K8
French St, Sun	174	E4
Frendsbury Rd SE4	149	R7
Frensham Cl, Sthl	103	M7
Frensham Dr SW15	161	N4
Frensham Dr, Croy	200	E14
Frensham Rd SE9	171	N4
Frensham St SE15	37	T11
Frere St SW11	145	S3
Fresh Wf Rd, Bark	117	K2
Freshfield Av E8	94	E14
Freshfield Cl, SE13 2	150	G7
Freshfield Dr N14	42	D13
Freshfields, Croy	185	T14
Freshford St SW18	163	L5
Freshwater Cl, SW17 2	164	B11
Freshwater Rd SW17	164	B11
Freshwater Rd, Dag	100	H1
Freshwell Av, Rom	82	E8
Freshwood Cl, Beck	186	C2
Freston Gdns, Barn	42	A9
Freston Pk N3	72	E3
Freston Rd W10	108	B14
Freston Rd W11	108	B14
Freta Rd, Bexh	155	L9
Frewin Rd SW18	163	P1
Friar Ms SE27	165	R6
Friar Rd, Hayes	102	G8
Friar St, EC4 9	19	R8
Friars, The, Chig	65	R8
Friars Av N20	57	S6
Friars Av SW15	161	L5
Friars Cl E4	62	F6
Friars Cl N2	73	P7
Friars Cl, Nthlt 3	102	G5
Friars Gdns W3	106	G12
Friars Gate Cl, Wdf Grn	63	P8
Friars La, Rich	141	N9
Friars Mead E14	132	E6
Friars Ms SE9	152	G10
Friars Pl La W3	106	H13
Friars Rd E6	116	B2
Friars Stile Rd, Rich	141	S12
Friars Wk N14	58	C1
Friars Wk SE2	136	H10
Friars Way W3	106	G12
Friary Cl N12	57	S9
Friary Ct SW1	25	N4
Friary Est SE15	37	U12
Friary La, Wdf Grn	63	N8
Friary Rd N12	57	N8
Friary Rd SE15	37	U14
Friary Rd W3	106	G12
Friary Way N12	57	R8
Friday Hill E4	62	J5
Friday Hill E E4	62	J5
Friday Hill W E4	62	J3
Friday Rd, Mitch	163	T14
Friday St EC4	19	U8
Frideswide Pl, NW5 4	92	E10
Friend St EC1	11	N5
Friendly Pl, SE13 5	150	D2
Friendly St SE8	150	A3
Friends Rd, Croy	198	A5
Friern Barnet La N11	57	T9
Friern Barnet La N20	57	M4
Friern Barnet Rd N11	57	U10
Friern Br Retail Pk	58	C11
Friern Ct N20	57	N5
Friern Mt Dr N20	41	M13
Friern Pk N12	57	M9
Friern Rd SE22	148	H9
Friern Watch Av N12	57	M8
Frigate Ms, SE8 2	132	A11
Frimley Av, Wall	197	K9
Frimley Cl SW19	162	D4
Frimley Cl, Croy	200	F13
Frimley Ct, Sid	172	E10
Frimley Cres, Croy	200	F14
Frimley Gdns, Mitch	181	R5
Frimley Rd, Chess	191	R10
Frimley Rd, Ilf	99	S6
Frimley Way E1	113	N7
Frinton Cl, Wat	50	C4
Frinton Dr, Wdf Grn	62	H14
Frinton Ms, Ilf	80	H11
Frinton Rd E6	116	A6
Frinton Rd N15	76	D12
Frinton Rd SW17	164	B12
Frinton Rd, Sid	172	J4
Friston Path, Chig	65	S10
Friston St SW6	144	J4
Friswell Pl, Bexh 1	155	N7
Frith Ct NW7	56	D14
Frith La NW7	56	C14
Frith Rd E11	96	G7
Frith Rd, Croy	197	T4
Frith St W1	17	S7
Fritham Cl, N Mal	178	J12
Frithville Gdns W12	125	T1
Frizlands La, Dag	101	R7
Frobisher Cl, Pnr	66	G13
Frobisher Pas, E14 10	132	B1
Frobisher Rd E6	116	F11
Frobisher Rd N8	75	P8
Frobisher St SE10	133	K10
Frogley Rd SE22	148	F8
Frogmore SW18	144	H9
Frogmore Cl, Sutt	194	C6
Frogmore Est, Ruis	84	G9
Frogmore Gdns, Sutt	194	C7
Frogmore Ind Est NW10	106	F6
Frognal NW3	91	M10
Frognal Av, Har	68	E8
Frognal Av, Sid	172	B11
Frognal Ct NW3	91	L9
Frognal Ct NW3	91	M11
Frognal Gdns NW3	91	L7
Frognal La NW3	91	K9
Frognal Par, NW3 1	91	L11
Frognal Pl, Sid	172	B11
Frognal Ri NW3	91	L6
Frognal Way NW3	91	L8
Froissart Rd SE9	152	C9
Frome Rd N22	75	R5
Frome St N1	11	T1
Fromondes Rd, Sutt	194	C10
Frostic Wk E1	21	P3
Froude St, SW8 7	146	D4
Fry Rd E6	98	A14
Fry Rd NW10	107	M1
Fryatt Rd N17	60	B14
Fryatt St E14	114	J12
Fryent Cl NW9	70	A10
Fryent Cres NW9	70	J12
Fryent Flds NW9	71	K11
Fryent Gro NW9	70	J12
Fryent Way NW9	70	C14
Frye's Bldgs, N1 1	11	M2
Frying Pan All E1	21	K3
Fryston Av, Croy	198	H3
Fuchsia St SE2	136	C9
Fulbeck Dr NW9	70	J1
Fulbeck Way, Har	67	T4
Fulbourne Rd E17	78	E1
Fulbourne St, E1 1	112	J9
Fulbrook Ms, N19 2	92	E7
Fulford Gro, Wat	50	D4
Fulford Rd, Epsom	192	G14
Fulford St SE16	131	K4
Fulham Bdy SW6	126	H14
Fulham High St SW6	144	D3
Fulham Palace Rd SW6	144	B1
Fulham Palace Rd W6	126	A10
Fulham Pk Gdns SW6	144	E4
Fulham Pk Rd SW6	144	E3
Fulham Rd SW3	31	P3
Fulham Rd SW6	30	D14
Fulham Rd SW10	30	F11
Fullbrooks Av, Wor Pk	193	L1
Fuller Cl E2	13	R10
Fuller Cl, Orp	203	U10
Fuller Rd, Dag	100	E7
Fuller St NW4	71	T7
Fullers Av, Surb	191	T4
Fullers Av, Wdf Grn	63	M14
Fullers Rd E18	79	M1
Fullers Way N, Surb	191	T5
Fullers Way S, Chess	191	S7
Fullers Wd, Croy	200	A9
Fullerton Rd SW18	145	L9
Fullerton Rd, Croy	184	E14
Fullwell Av, Ilf	80	F2
Fullwell Cross Roundabout, Ilf	81	M3
Fullwoods Ms, N1 4	12	E5
Fulmar Ct, Surb	177	T11
Fulmead St SW6	145	K2
Fulmer Cl, Hmptn	157	K10
Fulmer Rd E16	116	A10
Fulmer Way W13	122	J6
Fulready Rd E10	78	G10
Fulstone Cl, Houns	139	L7
Fulthorp Rd SE3	151	M3
Fulton Ms, W2 4	14	E10
Fulton Rd, Wem	88	B6
Fulwell Pk Av, Twick	157	T4
Fulwell Rd, Tedd	158	B8
Fulwood Av, Wem	105	T3
Fulwood Gdns, Twick	140	F12
Fulwood Pl WC1	18	H3
Fulwood Wk SW19	162	C1
Furber St W6	125	R6
Furham Feild, Pnr	51	P13
Furley Rd SE15	130	H14
Furlong Cl, Wall	196	C2
Furlong Rd N7	93	P11
Furmage St SW18	145	K13
Furneaux Av SE27	165	S10
Furness Rd NW10	107	P4
Furness Rd SW6	145	K3
Furness Rd, Har	85	S1
Furness Rd, Mord	181	K12
Furnival St EC4	19	K5
Furrow La E9	95	M10
Fursby Av N3	56	G11
Further Acre NW9	71	L3
Further Grn Rd SE6	169	K1
Furtherfield Cl, Croy	183	N12
Furze Cl, Wat	50	F9
Furze Fm Cl, Rom	83	K4
Furze Rd, Th Hth	183	U5
Furze St E3	114	B9
Furzedown Dr SW17	164	C10
Furzedown Rd SW17	164	C9
Furzefield Cl, Chis	170	J11
Furzefield Rd SE3	133	R12
Furzehill Rd, Borwd	38	F10
Furzewood, Sun	174	B1
Fyfe Way, Brom	187	P3
Fyfield Cl, Brom	186	H7
Fyfield Ct E7	97	N11
Fyfield Rd E17	78	G6
Fyfield Rd SW9	147	P5
Fyfield Rd, Enf	44	C6
Fyfield Rd, Wdf Grn	63	T13
Fynes St SW1	33	S2

G

GEC Est, Wem	87	P5
Gable Cl, Pnr	51	N14
Gable Ct SE26	167	K8
Gables, The, Wem	87	U7
Gables Cl SE5	148	C1
Gables Cl SE12	169	N2
Gabriel Cl, Felt	156	H7
Gabriel St SE23	149	P13
Gabrielle Ct, Wem	87	T5
Gabrielle Ct NW3	91	P12
Gad Cl E13	115	R5
Gaddesden Av, Wem	87	U11
Gade Cl, Hayes	120	C2
Gadesden Rd, Epsom	192	F11
Gadsbury Cl NW9	71	L11
Gadwall Cl E16	115	R11
Gadwall Way SE28	135	P4
Gage Rd, E16 1	115	K9
Gage St, WC1 6	18	D2
Gainford St N1	111	N1
Gainsboro Gdns, Grnf	86	D9
Gainsborough Av E12	98	G9
Gainsborough Cl, Beck	168	A13
Gainsborough Cl, Esher 2	190	C1
Gainsborough Ct N12	57	K10
Gainsborough Ct W12	125	T4
Gainsborough Gdns NW3	91	P6

Street	Page	Grid
Gainsborough Gdns NW11	72	D14
Gainsborough Gdns, Edg	69	U4
Gainsborough Gdns, Islw	140	A10
Gainsborough Ms, SE26 *3*	166	J6
Gainsborough Pl, Chig	65	U6
Gainsborough Rd E11	79	K14
Gainsborough Rd E15	115	K6
Gainsborough Rd N12	57	K10
Gainsborough Rd W4	125	L6
Gainsborough Rd, Dag	100	C7
Gainsborough Rd, N Mal	178	H13
Gainsborough Rd, Rich	141	U4
Gainsborough Rd, Wdf Grn *2*	64	D12
Gainsborough Sq, Dexh *2*	154	H6
Gainsford Rd E17	77	T7
Gainsford St SE1	29	M5
Gairloch Rd SE5	148	D3
Gaisford St NW5	92	E11
Gaitskell Rd SE9	171	L2
Galahad Rd, Brom	169	P7
Galata Rd SW13	125	N14
Galatea Sq SE15	148	J5
Galbraith St E14	132	E5
Galdana Av, Barn	41	L6
Gale Cl, Hmptn	157	K11
Gale Cl, Mitch	181	P6
Gale St E3	114	B9
Gale St, Dag	118	G2
Galeborough Av, Wdf Grn	62	H13
Galen Pl WC1	18	B4
Galena Rd W6	125	S8
Gales Gdns E2	113	K6
Gales Way, Wdf Grn	64	D13
Galesbury Rd SW18	145	L12
Galgate Cl SW19	162	C2
Gallants Fm Rd, Barn	57	T2
Galleon Cl, SE16 *8*	131	M3
Gallery Gdns, Nthlt	102	H4
Gallery Rd SE21	166	B8
Galley La, Barn	39	T7
Galleywall Rd SE16	131	K8
Gallia Rd N5	93	S10
Galliard Cl N9	45	L11
Galliard Rd N9	60	G1
Gallions Cl, Bark	118	B6
Gallions Rd E16	117	K14
Gallions Rd SE7	133	S8
Gallions Roundabout E16	116	J13
Gallions Vw Rd SE28	135	R4
Gallon Cl SE7	133	U8
Gallop, The, S Croy	199	K13
Gallosson Rd SE18	135	R8
Galloway Path, Croy	198	B8
Galloway Rd W12	125	P1
Gallus Cl N21	43	M11
Gallus Sq SE3	151	R6
Galpins Rd, Th Hth	183	L7
Galsworthy Av, Rom	82	C13
Galsworthy Cl SE28	136	C1
Galsworthy Rd NW2	90	D7
Galsworthy Rd, Kings T	178	C1
Galsworthy Ter N16	94	C5
Galton St W10	108	C7
Galva Cl, Barn	42	A8
Galvani Way, Croy	197	L1
Galveston Rd SW15	144	F9
Galway Cl, SE16 *6*	131	K10
Galway St EC1	12	A8
Gambetta St, SW8 *8*	146	D4
Gambia St SE1	27	R4
Gambole Rd SW17	163	R8
Games Rd, Barn	41	T6
Gamlen Rd SW15	144	A7
Gamuel Cl E17	78	A12
Gander Grn Cres, Hmptn	175	R2
Gander Grn La, Sutt	194	C3
Gandhi Cl E17	78	B11
Gandolfi St, SE15 *2*	36	J12
Ganton St W1	17	M9
Ganton Wk, Wat	50	H7
Gap Rd SW19	162	J9
Garage Rd W3	106	A12
Garbutt Pl W1	16	E2
Gard St EC1	11	S6
Garden Av, Bexh	155	N5
Garden Av, Mitch	164	C14
Garden City, Edg *1*	54	B11
Garden Cl E4	62	A10
Garden Cl SE12	169	R5
Garden Cl SW15	143	S14
Garden Cl, Barn	39	T8
Garden Cl, Hmptn	157	M10
Garden Cl, Nthlt	103	K1
Garden Cl, Wall	197	K10
Garden Ct EC4	18	J9
Garden Ct, Rich	141	U2
Garden Ct, Stan	53	M9
Garden Ct, W Mol	175	S8
Garden La, SW2 *3*	165	L1
Garden La, Brom	169	S12
Garden Ms W2	108	H14
Garden Rd NW8	6	H5
Garden Rd SE20	185	M2
Garden Rd, Brom	169	S13
Garden Rd, Rich	142	A6
Garden Rd, Walt	174	D12
Garden Row SE1	27	P11
Garden St E1	113	P10
Garden Ter SW1	33	R5
Garden Wk EC2	12	H8
Garden Wk, Beck	185	T2
Garden Way NW10	88	F11
Gardeners Cl N11	58	B3
Gardeners Rd, Croy	197	S2
Gardenia Rd, Enf	44	C7
Gardenia Way, Wdf Grn	63	P10
Gardens, The SE22	148	H8
Gardens, The, Beck	186	F2
Gardens, The, Har	67	T12
Gardens, The, Pnr	67	M11
Gardiner Av NW2	89	T9
Gardiner Cl, Dag *1*	100	G8
Gardiner Cl, Enf	45	N11
Gardiner Cl E11	79	R11
Gardner Gro, Felt	157	M4
Gardner Rd E13	115	R8
Gardners La, EC4 *5*	19	U10
Gardnor Rd NW3	91	N7
Garendon Gdns, Mord	180	J13
Garendon Rd, Mord	180	J13
Gareth Cl, Wor Pk	194	A3
Gareth Gro, Brom	169	N7
Garfield Ms, SW11 *8*	146	C6
Garfield Rd E4	62	H1
Garfield Rd E13	115	M8
Garfield Rd SW11	146	B6
Garfield Rd SW19	163	S11
Garfield Rd, Enf	45	M8
Garfield Rd, Twick *6*	158	H1
Garford St E14	114	A14
Garganey Wk SE28	118	F13
Garibaldi St SE18	135	R8
Garland Rd SE18	135	P13
Garland Rd, Stan	69	R1
Garlands Ct, Croy	198	B7
Garlick Hill EC4	20	A9
Garlies Rd SE23	167	R5
Garlinge Rd NW2	90	E12
Garman Cl N18	60	B10
Garman Rd N17	61	L14
Garnault Ms EC1	11	L7
Garnault Pl EC1	11	L8
Garner Rd E17	78	E1
Garner St E2	13	U3
Garnet Rd NW10	89	K12
Garnet Rd, Th Hth	183	U7
Garnet St E1	131	L1
Garnet Wk E6	116	D9
Garnett Cl SE9	152	F6
Garnett Rd NW3	91	T9
Garnett Way, E17 *3*	77	R1
Garnham St N16	94	E4
Garnies Cl SE15	37	M13
Garrad's Rd SW16	164	G6
Garrard Cl, Bexh	155	P5
Garrard Cl, Chis	171	K9
Garratt Cl, Croy	196	J7
Garratt La SW17	163	M6
Garratt La SW18	145	K12
Garratt Rd, Edg	54	B13
Garratt Ter SW17	163	S8
Garrett Cl W3	106	H10
Garrett St EC1	12	A10
Garrick Av NW11	72	D12
Garrick Cl SW18	145	M8
Garrick Cl W5	105	S7
Garrick Cl, Rich *1*	141	N0
Garrick Cres, Croy	198	C4
Garrick Dr NW4	71	U4
Garrick Dr SE28	135	N6
Garrick Gdns, W Mol	175	N5
Garrick Pk NW4	72	A4
Garrick Rd NW9	71	M11
Garrick Rd, Grnf	103	S8
Garrick Rd, Rich	142	B4
Garrick St WC2	18	A10
Garrick Way NW4	72	A7
Garrison Cl SE18	134	H14
Garrison Cl, Houns	139	L9
Garrison La, Chess	191	R13
Garsdale Cl N11	58	A11
Garside Cl SE28	135	N6
Garside Cl, Hmptn	157	R12
Garsington Ms SE4	149	U6
Garter Way SE16	131	N4
Garth, The, Hmptn	157	S11
Garth, The, Har	69	U11
Garth Cl W4	124	G10
Garth Cl, Kings T	159	T10
Garth Cl, Mord	180	A13
Garth Cl, Ruis	84	G2
Garth Ct W4	124	F10
Garth Rd NW2	90	E4
Garth Rd SW20	124	G11
Garth Rd, Kings T	159	T10
Garth Rd, Mord	180	A13
Garth Rd Ind Cen, Mord	180	A13
Garthland Dr, Barn	39	T9
Garthorne Rd SE23	149	P14
Garthside, Rich	159	S9
Garthway N12	57	R12
Gartmoor Gdns SW19	162	E2
Gartmore Rd, Ilf	99	U2
Garton Pl SW18	145	L12
Gartons Cl, Enf	45	M8
Gartons Way SW11	145	M6
Garvary Rd E16	115	S12
Garway Rd W2	14	A8
Gascoigne Gdns, Wdf Grn	63	K14
Gascoigne Pl E2	13	M7
Gascoigne Rd, Bark	117	M2
Gascony Av NW6	90	G14
Gascoyne Rd E9	95	P13
Gaselee St E14	114	F14
Gasholder Pl SE11	34	A8
Gaskarth Rd SW12	146	D12
Gaskarth Rd, Edg	70	E2
Gaskell Rd N6	73	U11
Gaskell St SW4	146	J3
Gaskin St N1	111	R1
Gaspar Cl SW5 *1*	30	D2
Gaspar Ms SW5	30	D2
Gassiot Rd SW17	163	U8
Gassiot Way, Sutt	195	N6
Gastein Rd W6	126	B11
Gaston Bell Cl, Rich	141	T5
Gaston Rd, Mitch	182	A5
Gataker St SE16	131	K5
Gatcombe Rd E16	133	P1
Gatcombe Rd N19	92	G6
Gatcombe Way, Barn	41	T6
Gate Cl, Borwd	38	E2
Gate End, Nthwd	50	A13
Gate Ms SW7	23	R8
Gate St WC2	18	E5
Gateforth St NW8	7	N11
Gatehouse Cl, Kings T	160	F14
Gateley Rd SW9	147	M6
Gater Dr, Enf	44	A2
Gates Grn Rd, Kes	201	S9
Gates Grn Rd, W Wick	201	L5
Gatesborough St, EC2 *4*	12	H10
Gateside Rd SW17	163	T5
Gatestone Rd SE19	166	D12
Gateway SE17	36	B10
Gateway Ind Est NW10	107	M6
Gateway Ms, E8 *5*	94	E9
Gateway Rd F10	96	C6
Gateways, The, SW3 *3*	31	S4
Gatfield Gro, Felt	157	N4
Gathorne Rd N22	75	N3
Gathorne St, E2 *6*	113	P4
Gatley Av, Epsom	192	C9
Gatliff Rd SW1	32	G7
Gatling Rd SE2	136	A9
Gatting Cl, Edg	54	E14
Gatton Rd SW17	163	S7
Gattons Way, Sid	173	L7
Gatward Cl N21	43	R12
Gatward Grn N9	60	D3
Gatwick Rd SW18	144	F14
Gauden Cl SW4	146	G4
Gauden Rd SW4	146	H5
Gaunt St SE1	27	T10
Gauntlet Cl, Nthlt	84	J13
Gauntlett Ct, Wem	86	H9
Gauntlett Rd, Sutt	195	N10
Gautrey Rd SE15	149	M3
Gautrey Sq, E6 *9*	116	F12
Gavel St SE17	36	F2
Gaverick St E14	132	A7
Gavestone Cres SE12	151	S14
Gavestone Rd SE12	151	S14
Gaviller Pl, E5 *1*	95	K7
Gavin St SE18	135	R7
Gavina Cl, Mord	181	R10
Gawber St E2	113	L5
Gawsworth Cl E15	97	K9
Gawthorne Av, NW7 *1*	56	D10
Gay Cl NW2	89	S9
Gay Gdns, Dag	101	T8
Gay Rd E15	114	G3
Gay St SW15	144	B6
Gaydon La NW9	70	J2
Gayfere Rd, Epsom	193	P10
Gayfere Rd, Ilf	80	E5
Gayfere St SW1	26	A11
Gayford Rd W12	125	M4
Gayhurst SE17	36	E9
Gayhurst Rd E8	94	G13
Gaylor Rd, Nthlt	85	L10
Gaynes Hill Rd, Wdf Grn	64	C12
Gaynesford Rd SE23	167	N4
Gaynesford Rd, Cars	195	T14
Gaysham Av, Ilf	80	H10
Gaysham Hall, Ilf	80	J6
Gayton Ct, Har	68	E12
Gayton Cres NW3	91	N7
Gayton Rd NW3	91	N7
Gayton Rd SE2	136	F6
Gayton Rd, Har	68	G12
Gayville Rd SW11	145	U11
Gaywood Cl SW2	165	N1
Gaywood Est SE1	27	R11
Gaywood Rd E17	78	B5

Name	Page	Grid
Gaywood St SE1	27	R11
Gaza St SE17	35	P7
Geariesville Gdns, Ilf	81	K7
Geary Rd NW10	89	N9
Geary St N7	93	M10
Geddes Pl, Bexh 2	155	P7
Gedeney Rd N17	75	U1
Gedling Pl SE1	29	N9
Gee St EC1	11	T10
Geere Rd E15	115	M2
Geffrye St E2	13	L2
Geldart Rd SE15	130	J14
Geldeston Rd E5	94	H4
Gellatly Rd SE14	149	M3
Gemini Gro, Nthlt	102	J6
General Gordon Pl, SE18 2	134	J7
General Wolfe Rd SE10	150	H1
Genesta Rd SE18	135	K12
Geneva Dr SW9	147	P7
Geneva Gdns, Rom	82	J9
Geneva Rd, Kings T	177	S7
Geneva Rd, Th Hth	183	T9
Genever Cl E4	62	B9
Genista Rd N18	61	K10
Genoa Av SW15	143	U10
Genoa Rd SE20	185	L2
Genotin Rd, Enf	44	B6
Genotin Ter, Enf 3	44	B6
Gentian Row SE13	150	E2
Gentlemans Row, Enf	43	U6
Gentry Gdns E13	115	P6
Geoffrey Cl SE5	147	T4
Geoffrey Gdns E6	116	C4
Geoffrey Rd SE4	149	T5
George Beard Rd, SE8 5	131	T8
George Cres N10	58	A14
George V Av, Pnr	67	N5
George V Cl, Pnr	67	N6
George V Way, Grnf	105	K1
George Gange Way, Har	68	E6
George Gro Rd SE20	184	H1
George Inn Yd, SE1 4	28	D4
George La E18	79	P4
George La SE13	150	G12
George La, Brom	201	R1
George Lowe Ct, W2 2	14	A2
George Mathers Rd SE11	35	P3
George Ms NW1	9	N8
George Rd E4	62	A11
George Rd, Kings T	160	D13
George Rd, N Mal	179	M8
George Row SE16	29	S8
George Sq SW19	180	F5
George St, E16 6	115	L12
George St W1	16	D5
George St W7	122	D2
George St, Bark	99	L14
George St, Croy	198	A4
George St, Houns	139	L3
George St, Rich	141	P9
George St, Sthl	120	J7
George St, Sutt	194	J9
George Wyver Cl, SW19 2	144	C14
George Yd EC3	20	F8
George Yd W1	16	F9
George's Rd N7	93	M10
Georgetown Cl, SE19 5	166	C9
Georgette Pl SE10	132	F14
Georgeville Gdns, Ilf	81	K7
Georgia Rd, N Mal	178	E7
Georgia Rd, Th Hth	183	S2
Georgian Cl, Brom	187	R14
Georgian Cl, Stan	52	G13
Georgian Ct, Wem	88	B11
Georgian Way, Har	86	B4
Georgiana St NW1	110	E1
Georgina Gdns E2	13	N6
Geraint Rd, Brom	169	P7
Gerald Ms, SW1 5	32	F2
Gerald Rd E16	115	L7
Gerald Rd SW1	32	F2
Gerald Rd, Dag	101	L3
Geraldine Rd SW18	145	L10
Geraldine Rd W4	124	B11
Geraldine St SE11	27	N12
Gerard Av, Houns	139	N14
Gerard Rd SW13	143	M2
Gerard Rd, Har	68	H11
Gerards Cl SE16	131	L10
Gerda Rd SE9	171	L4
Germander Way E15	115	K5
Gernon Rd E3	113	R4
Geron Way NW2	89	T3
Gerrard Gdns, Pnr	66	B9
Gerrard Pl, W1 2	17	T9
Gerrard Rd N1	11	R1
Gerrard St W1	17	T10
Gerrards Cl N14	42	F9
Gerridge St SE1	27	L8
Gerry Raffles Sq E15	96	H12
Gertrude Rd, Belv	117	P7
Gertrude St SW10	30	H12
Gervase Cl, Wem	88	F5
Gervase St SE15	131	K13
Ghent St SE6	168	B4
Ghent Way, E8 2	94	F11
Giant Arches Rd SE24	147	U13
Giant Tree Hill, Bushey	52	A2
Gibbard Ms SW19	162	B10
Gibbfield Cl, Rom	82	J5
Gibbins Rd E15	96	F14
Gibbon Rd SE15	149	M4
Gibbon Rd W3	106	J13
Gibbon Rd, Kings T	177	S1
Gibbon Wk SW15	143	P8
Gibbons Rd NW10	88	J12
Gibbs Av SE19	166	B10
Gibbs Cl SE19	166	B10
Gibbs Couch, Wat	50	H5
Gibbs Grn W14	126	F9
Gibbs Grn, Edg	54	F8
Gibbs Rd N18	61	L8
Gibbs Sq SE19	166	A10
Gibraltar Wk E2	13	P8
Gibson Cl, E1 9	113	M7
Gibson Cl N21	43	N11
Gibson Cl, Chess	191	M10
Gibson Gdns N16	94	L4
Gibson Rd SE11	34	G3
Gibson Rd, Dag	100	F1
Gibson Rd, Sutt	194	J10
Gibson Sq N1	111	P1
Gibson St SE10	132	J10
Gibson's Hill SW16	165	R12
Gideon Cl, Belv	137	R7
Gideon Ms W5	123	N3
Gideon Rd SW11	146	A5
Giesbach Rd N19	92	F3
Giffard St N1 8	60	D10
Giffin St SE8	132	B13
Gifford Gdns W7	104	B10
Gifford St N1	93	K14
Gift La E15	115	L1
Giggs Hill Gdns, T Ditt	190	H1
Giggs Hill Rd, T Ditt	176	G14
Gilbert Cl SE18	152	E2
Gilbert Gro, Edg	70	G1
Gilbert Pl WC1	18	B4
Gilbert Rd SE11	35	M3
Gilbert Rd SW19	163	L13
Gilbert Rd, Belv	137	N6
Gilbert Rd, Brom	169	N13
Gilbert Rd, Pnr	66	G7
Gilbert St E15	96	J8
Gilbert St W1	16	F8
Gilbert St, Houns 1	139	T5
Gilbey Rd SW17	163	R9
Gilbourne Rd SE18	135	T12
Gilda Av, Enf	45	R9
Gilda Cres N16	94	H2
Gildea Cl, Pnr	51	N14
Gildea St W1	17	K3
Gilden Cres NW5	92	A10
Gilders Rd, Chess	191	U11
Gildersome St SE18	134	H11
Giles Coppice SE19	166	E8
Gilkes Cres SE21	148	C11
Gilkes Pl SE21	148	C12
Gill Av E16	115	P12
Gill St E14	113	U13
Gillan Grn, Bushey	51	U3
Gillards Ms, E17 2	78	A8
Gillards Way E17	78	A8
Gillender St E3	114	E8
Gillender St E14	114	E8
Gillespie Rd N5	93	R6
Gillett Av E6	116	C3
Gillett Rd, Th Hth	184	A8
Gillett St N16	94	D10
Gillette Cor, Islw	122	G13
Gillham Ter N17	60	G12
Gillian Pk Rd, Sutt	194	E1
Gillian St SE13	150	C9
Gillies St NW5	92	B10
Gilling Ct NW3	91	S11
Gillingham Ms, SW1 2	33	L2
Gillingham Rd NW2	90	C6
Gillingham Row SW1	33	L2
Gillingham St SW1	33	L2
Gillison Wk SE16	29	U10
Gillman Dr E15	115	L2
Gillum Cl, Barn	57	T1
Gilmore Rd SE13	150	G7
Gilpin Av SW14	142	H8
Gilpin Cl, Mitch	181	R3
Gilpin Cres N18	60	F10
Gilpin Cres, Twick	139	R13
Gilpin Rd E5	95	R7
Gilsland Rd, Th Hth 1	184	A8
Gilstead Rd SW6	145	K3
Gilston Rd SW10	30	G8
Gilton Rd SE6	169	K5
Giltspur St EC1	19	R5
Gilwell Cl E4	46	D8
Gilwell La E4	46	E8
Gilwell Pk E4	46	G6
Gippeswyck Cl, Pnr 1	66	H2
Gipsy Hill SE19	166	D9
Gipsy La SW15	143	R6
Gipsy Rd SE27	165	U8
Gipsy Rd, Well	136	G14
Gipsy Rd Gdns SE27	165	U8
Giralda Cl E16	116	A10
Giraud St E14	114	C11
Girdlers Rd W14	126	B7
Girdlestone Wk N19	92	E3
Girdwood Rd SW18	144	D14
Girling Way, Felt	138	B6
Gironde Rd SW6	126	F14
Girton Av NW9	70	B6
Girton Cl, Nthlt	85	T12
Girton Gdns, Croy	200	A5
Girton Rd SE26	167	N9
Girton Rd, Nthlt	85	T12
Girton Vil W10	108	B11
Gisbourne Cl, Wall	196	H6
Gisburn Rd N8	75	M7
Gittens Cl, Brom	169	L7
Given Wilson Wk E13	115	L4
Glacier Way, Wem	105	P3
Gladbeck Way, Enf	43	S8
Gladding Rd E12	98	B7
Glade, The N21	43	L12
Glade, The SE7	133	T13
Glade, The, Brom	188	B4
Glade, The, Croy	185	N9
Glade, The, Enf	43	N5
Glade, The, Epsom	193	P11
Glade, The, Ilf	80	E1
Glade, The, W Wick	200	D6
Glade Cl, Surb	191	N3
Glade Gdns, Croy	185	S13
Glade La, Sthl	121	R5
Glades Pl, Brom	187	P3
Gladeside N21	43	L12
Gladeside, Croy	185	N11
Gladeside Cl, Chess	191	N13
Gladesmore Rd N15	76	E11
Gladeswood Rd, Belv	137	R7
Gladiator St SE23	149	S12
Glading Ter N16	94	E6
Gladioli Cl, Hmptn 5	157	N11
Gladsdale Dr, Pnr	66	B8
Gladsmuir Rd N19	92	F2
Gladsmuir Rd, Barn	40	D4
Gladstone Av E12	98	D13
Gladstone Av N22	75	N3
Gladstone Av, Felt	138	B12
Gladstone Av, Twick	140	B14
Gladstone Ms, NW6 1	90	E13
Gladstone Ms SE20	167	L14
Gladstone Pk Gdns NW2	89	T5
Gladstone Pl E3	113	U3
Gladstone Pl, Barn	40	B7
Gladstone Rd SW19	162	G13
Gladstone Rd W4	124	G6
Gladstone Rd, Buck H	63	T1
Gladstone Rd, Croy	184	B14
Gladstone Rd, Kings T	178	B5
Gladstone Rd, Orp	203	M9
Gladstone Rd, Sthl	120	J4
Gladstone Rd, Surb	191	P4
Gladstone St SE1	27	N10
Gladstone Ter SE27	165	U8
Gladstone Ter SW8	146	D1
Gladstone Way, Har	68	D6
Gladwell Rd N8	75	L11
Gladwell Rd, Brom	169	P11
Gladwyn Rd SW15	144	A5
Glamis Pl E1	113	M13
Glamis Rd E1	113	M14
Glamis Way, Nthlt	85	T12
Glamorgan Cl, Mitch	182	J6
Glamorgan Rd, Kings T	159	M14
Glanfield Rd, Beck	185	U7
Glanleam Rd, Stan	53	N7
Glanville Rd SW2	147	K10
Glanville Rd, Brom	187	S6
Glasbrook Av, Twick	157	L2
Glasbrook Rd SE9	152	B13
Glaserton Rd N16	76	D14
Glasford St SW17	163	U11
Glasgow Rd E13	115	R4
Glasgow Rd N18	60	J9
Glasgow Ter SW1	33	L7
Glass St, E2 6	113	K7
Glass Yd SE18	134	H5
Glasse Cl W13	104	G13
Glasshill St SE1	27	R6
Glasshouse Flds E1	113	N13
Glasshouse St W1	17	N11
Glasshouse Wk SE11	34	D6
Glasslyn Rd N8	74	G10
Glassmill La, Brom	187	M4
Glastonbury Av, Wdf Grn	64	A13
Glastonbury Rd N9	60	F2
Glastonbury Rd, Mord	180	H12
Glastonbury St NW6	90	F10
Glaucus St E3	114	C9
Glazbury Rd W14	126	D8
Glazebrook Cl SE21	166	A3
Glazebrook Rd, Tedd	158	E13
Glebe, The SE3	151	K5
Glebe, The SW16	164	H7
Glebe, The, Chis	189	M2
Glebe, The, Wor Pk	193	L1
Glebe Av, Enf	43	R5
Glebe Av, Har	69	R6
Glebe Av, Mitch	181	R4
Glebe Av, Ruis	84	D12
Glebe Av, Wdf Grn	63	N12
Glebe Cl, W4 6	124	J9
Glebe Ct W7	104	B13
Glebe Ct, Mitch	181	T5

Name	Page	Grid
Glebe Ct, Stan	53	L10
Glebe Cres NW4	71	U7
Glebe Cres, Har	69	S6
Glebe Gdns, N Mal	179	K13
Glebe Ho Dr, Brom	201	R2
Glebe Hyrst, SE19 3	166	D8
Glebe La, Barn	39	N10
Glebe La, Har	69	R8
Glebe Path, Mitch	181	T6
Glebe Pl SW3	31	N9
Glebe Rd E8	94	E13
Glebe Rd N3	73	M2
Glebe Rd N8	75	L8
Glebe Rd NW10	89	M12
Glebe Rd SW13	143	N3
Glebe Rd, Brom	187	N1
Glebe Rd, Cars	195	U12
Glebe Rd, Dag	101	S12
Glebe Rd, Stan	53	L9
Glebe Side, Twick	140	E12
Glebe St W4	124	H9
Glebe Way, Felt	157	P5
Glebe Way, W Wick	200	G3
Glebelands, W Mol	175	S9
Glebelands Av E18	79	N4
Glebelands Av, Ilf	81	P13
Glebelands Rd, Felt	138	R14
Glebeway, Wdf Grn	63	U9
Gledhow Gdns SW5	30	E4
Gledstanes Rd W14	126	D10
Gleed Av, Bushey	52	A3
Gleeson Dr, Orp	203	T9
Glegg Pl, SW15 6	144	B7
Glen, The, Brom	186	J4
Glen, The, Croy	199	P4
Glen, The, Enf	43	S7
Glen, The, Orp	202	G5
Glen, The, Pnr	67	K13
Glen, The (Eastcote), Pnr	66	D9
Glen, The, Sthl	121	M9
Glen, The, Wem	87	R7
Glen Albyn Rd SW19	162	B3
Glen Cres, Wdf Grn	63	R12
Glen Gdns, Croy	197	P7
Glen Ri, Wdf Grn	63	R12
Glen Rd E13	115	T7
Glen Rd E17	77	U9
Glen Rd, Chess	191	S6
Glen Ter E14	132	E3
Glen Wk, Islw	140	B9
Glena Mt, Sutt	195	M7
Glenaffric Av, E14 6	132	G8
Glenalmond Rd, Har	69	R7
Glenalvon Way SE18	134	C7
Glenarm Rd E5	95	L8
Glenavon Cl, Esher	190	G13
Glenavon Rd E15	97	K13
Glenbow Rd, Brom	169	K9
Glenbrook N, Enf	43	L7
Glenbrook Rd NW6	90	G10
Glenbrook S, Enf	43	L7
Glenbuck Rd, Surb	177	P12
Glenburnie Rd SW17	163	T5
Glencairn Dr W5	105	L8
Glencairn Rd SW16	164	J14
Glencairne Cl, E16 2	116	A9
Glencoe Av, Ilf	81	R14
Glencoe Dr, Dag	101	P7
Glencoe Rd, Hayes	103	K10
Glencorse Grn, Wat	50	H8
Glendale Av N22	59	N13
Glendale Av, Edg	53	U7
Glendale Av, Rom	82	E13
Glendale Cl, SE9 1	152	H6
Glendale Dr SW19	162	F10
Glendale Gdns, Wem	87	P2
Glendale Ms, Beck	186	D2
Glendale Rd, Erith	138	U7
Glendall St SW9	147	L6
Glendarvon St SW15	144	B5
Glendevon Cl, Edg 2	54	C5
Glendish Rd N17	76	J2
Glendor Gdns NW7	54	H8
Glendower Gdns, SW14 4	142	H6
Glendower Pl SW7	31	K2
Glendower Rd, E4 4	62	G1
Glendower Rd SW14	142	G6
Glendown Rd SE2	136	A10
Glendun Rd W3	107	K13
Gleneagle Ms, SW16 3	164	H9
Gleneagle Rd SW16	164	G10
Gleneagles, Stan	52	J12
Gleneagles Cl, SE16 2	130	J10
Gleneagles Cl, Orp	203	P2
Gleneagles Cl, Wat	50	G8
Gleneagles Grn, Orp 3	203	P1
Gleneldon Ms SW16	164	J8
Gleneldon Rd SW16	165	K8
Glenelg Rd SW2	147	K9
Glenesk Rd SE9	152	H5
Glenfarg Rd SE6	168	G1
Glenfield Rd SW12	104	I2
Glenfield Rd W13	123	K3
Glenfield Ter W13	122	J3
Glenfinlas Way SE5	35	S14
Glenforth St SE10	133	M9
Glengall Causeway E14	132	A5
Glengall Gro E14	132	E5
Glengall Rd NW6	108	F1
Glengall Rd SE15	37	R12
Glengall Rd, Bexh	155	K5
Glengall Rd, Edg	54	D5
Glengall Rd, Wdf Grn	63	P12
Glengall Ter SE15	37	P9
Glengarnock Av E14	132	F8
Glengarry Rd SE22	148	D7
Glenham Dr, Ilf	81	K10
Glenhaven Av, Borwd	38	A6
Glenhead Cl, SE9 3	152	J6
Glenhill Cl N3	72	G3
Glenhouse Rd SE9	152	G9
Glenhurst Av NW5	92	B7
Glenhurst Av, Bex	173	L2
Glenhurst Ri SE19	165	U14
Glenhurst Rd N12	57	P9
Glenhurst Rd, Brent	123	M11
Glenilla Rd NW3	91	R11
Glenister Pk Rd SW16	164	G13
Glenister Rd SE10	133	L9
Glenister St E16	134	H3
Glenlea Rd SE9	152	G9
Glenloch Rd NW3	91	R11
Glenloch Rd, Enf	45	M3
Glenluce Rd SE3	133	P12
Glenlyon Rd SE9	152	H9
Glenmere Av NW7	55	N13
Glenmill, Hmptn	157	M9
Glenmore Rd NW3	91	R11
Glenmore Rd, Well	153	U1
Glenmore Way, Bark	184	B4
Glenmount Path SE18	135	L9
Glennie Rd SE27	165	N6
Glenny Rd, Bark	99	M12
Glenorchy Cl, Hayes	103	K9
Glenparke Rd E7	97	R11
Glenrosa St SW6	145	L3
Glenrose Ct, Sid	172	C9
Glenroy St W12	107	T11
Glensdale Rd SE4	149	U6
Glenshiel Rd SE9	152	H9
Glenside, Chig	65	K11
Glentanner Way, SW17 6	163	N6
Glentham Gdns SW13	125	R11
Glentham Rd SW13	125	R11
Glenthorne Av, Croy	199	L1
Glenthorne Cl, Sutt	194	G1
Glenthorne Gdns, Ilf	80	H6
Glenthorne Gdns, Sutt	194	G1
Glenthorne Ms W6	125	S8
Glenthorne Rd E17	77	R9
Glenthorne Rd N11	57	U9
Glenthorne Rd W6	125	S8
Glenthorne Rd, Kings T	177	T7
Glenthorpe Rd, Mord	180	B10
Glenton Rd SE13	150	J7
Glentrammon Av, Orp	203	U12
Glentrammon Cl, Orp	203	U11
Glentrammon Gdns, Orp	203	T11
Glentrammon Rd, Orp	203	U11
Glentworth St NW1	8	A11
Glenure Rd SE9	152	H10
Glenview SE2	136	H11
Glenview Rd, Brom	188	B4
Glenville Gro SE8	131	U14
Glenville Ms SW18	144	J13
Glenville Rd, Kings T	178	A1
Glenwood Av NW9	88	J1
Glenwood Cl, Har	68	F10
Glenwood Gdns, Ilf	80	G9
Glenwood Gro NW9	88	E2
Glenwood Rd N15	75	S9
Glenwood Rd NW7	55	K5
Glenwood Rd SE6	167	U1
Glenwood Rd, Epsom	193	N11
Glenwood Rd, Houns	140	A5
Glenwood Way, Croy	185	P12
Glenworth Av, E14 5	132	G8
Gliddon Rd W14	126	C8
Glimpsing Grn, Erith	137	R1
Global App E3	114	D4
Globe Pond Rd SE16	131	R2
Globe Rd E1	113	N7
Globe Rd E2	113	M6
Globe Rd E15	97	L10
Globe Rd, Wdf Grn	63	U11
Globe Rope Wk E14	132	E8
Globe St SE1	28	B9
Globe Ter, E2 1	113	L5
Globe Yd W1	16	H8
Gloster Rd, N Mal	178	J8
Gloucester Arc, SW7 2	30	F2
Gloucester Av NW1	110	B2
Gloucester Av, Sid	171	S4
Gloucester Av, Well	153	U8
Gloucester Circ SE10	132	F13
Gloucester Cl NW10	88	G13
Gloucester Cl, T Ditt	190	G1
Gloucester Ct EC3	20	J11
Gloucester Ct, Rich	124	A14
Gloucester Cres NW1	110	C1
Gloucester Dr N4	93	S3
Gloucester Dr NW11	72	H7
Gloucester Gdns NW11	72	E13
Gloucester Gdns W2	14	D6
Gloucester Gdns, Barn	42	B8
Gloucester Gdns, Ilf	80	D13
Gloucester Gdns, Sutt	195	K3
Gloucester Gate NW1	8	G1
Gloucester Gate Ms, NW1 1	8	G1
Gloucester Gro, Edg	70	G1
Gloucester Gro Est SE15	37	K12
Gloucester Ms E10	78	A14
Gloucester Ms W2	14	H7
Gloucester Ms W W2	14	F7
Gloucester Par, Sid	154	A10
Gloucester Pl NW1	16	A3
Gloucester Pl W1	7	U11
Gloucester Pl Ms W1	16	A4
Gloucester Rd E10	78	A14
Gloucester Rd E11	79	S10
Gloucester Rd E12	98	E7
Gloucester Rd E17	77	P3
Gloucester Rd N17	76	B5
Gloucester Rd N18	60	E9
Gloucester Rd SW7	30	G3
Gloucester Rd W3	124	F3
Gloucester Rd W5	123	M4
Gloucester Rd, Barn	41	M10
Gloucester Rd, Belv	137	M9
Gloucester Rd, Croy	198	B1
Gloucester Rd, Felt	156	E1
Gloucester Rd, Hmptn	175	R1
Gloucester Rd, Har	67	R9
Gloucester Rd, Houns	138	J8
Gloucester Rd, Kings T	178	B4
Gloucester Rd, Rich	124	A13
Gloucester Rd, Tedd	158	C10
Gloucester Rd, Twick	157	U2
Gloucester Sq E2	112	F2
Gloucester Sq W2	15	N8
Gloucester St SW1	33	M5
Gloucester Ter W2	14	J9
Gloucester Wk W8	126	H3
Gloucester Way EC1	11	M8
Glover Cl SE2	136	F7
Glover Dr N18	61	L11
Glover Rd, Pnr	66	H11
Gloxinia Wk, Hmptn	157	N11
Glycena Rd SW11	145	U5
Glyn Av, Barn	41	N7
Glyn Cl SE25	184	C3
Glyn Ct SW16	165	M6
Glyn Dr, Sid	172	D8
Glyn Rd E5	95	P9
Glyn Rd, Enf	45	L7
Glyn Rd, Wor Pk	194	A4
Glyn St SE11	34	E8
Glynde Ms SW3	23	S12
Glynde Rd, Bexh	154	H6
Glynde St SE4	149	U11
Glyndebourne Pk, Orp	203	K4
Glyndon Rd SE18	135	N8
Glynfield Rd NW10	89	K14
Glynne Rd N22	75	P4
Glynwood Ct, SE23 4	167	M4
Goat La, Surb	191	L3
Goat Rd, Mitch	182	A12
Goat St, SE1 1	29	L6
Goat Wf, Brent	123	R12
Godalming Av, Wall	197	L9
Godalming Rd E14	114	C10
Godbold Rd E15	114	J6
Goddard Rd, Beck	185	P8
Goddards Way, Ilf	99	N2
Godfrey Av, Nthlt	102	J1
Godfrey Av, Twick	140	B13
Godfrey Hill SE18	134	D8
Godfrey Rd SE18	134	E8
Godfrey St E15	114	F3
Godfrey St SW3	31	N5
Godfrey Way, Houns	139	L13
Goding St SE11	34	D7
Godley Rd SW18	163	N2
Godliman St EC4	19	T8
Godman Rd, SE15 11	148	J4
Godolphin Cl N13	59	R12
Godolphin Pl W3	125	H14
Godolphin Rd W12	125	R13
Godson Rd, Croy	197	N6
Godson St N1	11	K2
Godstone Rd, Sutt	195	M7
Godstone Rd, Twick	140	J12
Godstow Rd SE2	136	E4

Name	Page	Grid
Godwin Cl N1	12	B2
Godwin Cl, Epsom	192	E11
Godwin Ct NW1	9	P1
Godwin Rd E7	97	S8
Godwin Rd, Brom	187	T6
Goffers Rd SE3	150	J3
Goidel Cl, Wall	196	H7
Golborne Gdns, W10 1	108	D8
Golborne Ms, W10 5	108	C9
Golborne Rd W10	108	D9
Gold Hill, Edg	54	H12
Gold La, Edg	54	G12
Golda Cl, Barn	40	B11
Goldbeaters Gro, Edg	54	J13
Goldcliff Cl, Mord	180	H13
Goldcrest Cl E16	116	A9
Goldcrest Cl SE28	118	E13
Goldcrest Ms, W5 1	105	N9
Goldcrest Way, Bushey	51	T1
Golden Cross Ms, W11 17	108	E11
Golden La EC1	12	A12
Golden La Est EC1	11	U12
Golden Manor W7	104	C14
Golden Plover Cl, E16 5	115	R11
Golden Sq W1	17	N10
Golders Cl, Edg	54	D9
Golders Gdns NW11	72	D14
Golders Grn Cres NW11	72	F14
Golders Grn Rd NW11	72	D12
Golders Manor Dr NW11	72	B12
Golders Pk Cl NW11	90	H2
Golders Ri NW4	72	A9
Golders Way NW11	72	F14
Goldfinch Rd SE28	135	P5
Goldfinch Way, Borwd	38	B7
Goldhawk Ms, W12 1	125	S4
Goldhawk Rd W6	125	M7
Goldhawk Rd W12	125	R5
Goldhaze Cl, Wdf Grn	63	U13
Goldhurst Ter NW6	91	L14
Golding Cl, Chess 1	191	M12
Golding St E1	21	U8
Goldingham Av, Loug	49	L4
Goldings Hill, Loug	48	F1
Goldings Ri, Loug	48	G1
Goldings Rd, Loug	48	G2
Goldington Cres NW1	9	R1
Goldington St NW1	9	S1
Goldman Cl E2	13	R9
Goldney Rd W9	108	G8
Goldrill Dr N11	58	B4
Goldsboro Rd SW8	146	H1
Goldsborough Cres E4	62	D4
Goldsdown Cl, Enf	45	R4
Goldsdown Rd, Enf	45	P4
Goldsmid St, SE18 4	135	S10
Goldsmith Av E12	98	D11
Goldsmith Av NW9	71	K11
Goldsmith Av W3	106	G13
Goldsmith Av, Rom	83	P14
Goldsmith Cl W3	124	H1
Goldsmith Cl, Har	85	R2
Goldsmith La NW9	70	D8
Goldsmith Rd E10	96	C2
Goldsmith Rd E17	77	P4
Goldsmith Rd N11	57	T10
Goldsmith Rd SE15	148	H1
Goldsmith Rd W3	124	G1
Goldsmith St, EC2 2	20	A6
Goldsmith's Row E2	13	T2
Goldsmith's Sq E2	13	T1
Goldsworthy Gdns SE16	131	M8
Goldwell Rd, Th Hth	183	M7
Goldwin Cl SE14	149	L1
Goldwing Cl E16	115	P12
Golf Cl, Stan	53	L13
Golf Cl, Th Hth	183	P2
Golf Club Dr, Kings T	160	H13
Golf Rd W5	105	U11
Golf Rd, Brom	188	H6
Golf Side, Twick	158	B6
Golfe Rd, Ilf	99	N6
Golfside Cl N20	57	R6
Golfside Cl, N Mal	179	K4
Goliath Cl, Wall	196	J13
Gollogly Ter SE7	133	T10
Gomer Gdns, Tedd	158	G11
Gomer Pl, Tedd	158	G11
Gomm Rd SE16	131	L6
Gomshall Av, Wall	196	J9
Gondar Gdns NW6	90	E9
Gonson Pl SE8	132	B12
Gonson St SE8	132	C12
Gonston Cl SW19	162	C4
Gonville Cres, Nthlt	85	S12
Gonville Rd, Th Hth	183	M9
Gonville St, SW6 1	144	D5
Goodall Rd E11	96	F7
Gooden Ct, Har 1	86	C5
Goodenough Rd SW19	162	E13
Goodge Pl W1	17	N3
Goodge St W1	17	P3
Goodhall St NW10	107	L5
Goodhart Pl E14	113	S13
Goodhart Way, W Wick	186	J11
Goodhew Rd, Croy	184	G12
Gooding Cl, N Mal	178	F8
Goodinge Cl N7	92	J11
Goodman Cres SW2	164	H3
Goodman Rd E10	78	F14
Goodmans Ct, Wem	87	P8
Goodman's Stile E1	21	R7
Goodmans Yd E1	21	M10
Goodmayes Av, Ilf	100	A1
Goodmayes La, Ilf	100	A7
Goodmayes Rd, Ilf	100	B2
Goodrich Rd SE22	148	G11
Goods Way NW1	10	A2
Goodson Rd NW10	89	K13
Goodway Gdns, E14 2	114	G11
Goodwin Cl SE16	29	F12
Goodwin Cl, Mitch	181	P5
Goodwin Dr, Sid	172	H4
Goodwin Gdns, Croy	197	S11
Goodwin Rd N9	61	M2
Goodwin Rd W12	125	P4
Goodwin Rd, Croy	197	R10
Goodwin St N4	93	N4
Goodwood Cl, Mord	180	H8
Goodwood Cl, Stan	53	M10
Goodwood Dr, Nthlt	85	N11
Goodwood Rd SE14	131	R14
Goodwyn Av NW7	55	K10
Goodwyns Vale N10	74	C2
Goodyers Gdns NW4	72	A10
Goosander Way SE28	135	N5
Gooseacre La, Har	69	P9
Gooseley La E6	116	H5
Goossens Cl, Sutt 5	195	M9
Gophir La EC4	20	D10
Gopsall St N1	112	B2
Gordon Av E4	62	J11
Gordon Av SW14	142	J7
Gordon Av, Stan	52	H12
Gordon Av, Twick	158	H6
Gordon Cl E17	78	A11
Gordon Cl N19	92	E3
Gordon Cres, Croy	198	D1
Gordon Cres, Hayes	120	A7
Gordon Gdns, Edg	70	D3
Gordon Gro SE5	147	S4
Gordon Hill, Enf	43	T1
Gordon Ho Rd NW5	92	B8
Gordon Pl W8	126	H3
Gordon Rd E4	47	K14
Gordon Rd E11	79	N12
Gordon Rd E15	96	F8
Gordon Rd E18	79	S2
Gordon Rd N3	56	F14
Gordon Rd N9	61	K3
Gordon Rd N11	58	H13
Gordon Rd SE15	148	J3
Gordon Rd W4	124	D11
Gordon Rd W5	105	M13
Gordon Rd W13	105	K13
Gordon Rd, Bark	117	R2
Gordon Rd, Beck	185	T6
Gordon Rd, Belv	137	U7
Gordon Rd, Cars	195	T12
Gordon Rd, Enf	44	A3
Gordon Rd, Esher	190	C13
Gordon Rd, Har	68	C6
Gordon Rd, Houns	139	T7
Gordon Rd, Ilf	99	N5
Gordon Rd, Kings T	177	T2
Gordon Rd, Rich	141	U4
Gordon Rd, Rom	83	L11
Gordon Rd, Sid	153	R10
Gordon Rd, Sthl	121	K8
Gordon Rd, Surb	177	U14
Gordon Sq WC1	9	S10
Gordon St E13	115	P6
Gordon St WC1	9	R9
Gordon Way, Barn	40	F7
Gordon Way, Brom	187	N2
Gordonbrock Rd SE4	150	A9
Gordondale Rd SW19	162	H4
Gore Ct NW9	70	B10
Gore Rd E9	113	M2
Gore Rd SW20	179	U4
Gore St SW7	22	G10
Gorefield Pl NW6	108	G3
Goresbrook Rd, Dag	118	D1
Gorham Pl W11	108	C14
Goring Cl, Rom	83	T1
Goring Gdns, Dag	100	E8
Goring Rd N11	58	J12
Goring St, EC3 2	21	K6
Goring Way, Grnf	103	U4
Gorleston Rd N15	76	A9
Gorleston St W14	126	D7
Gorman Rd SE18	134	F8
Gorringe Pk Av, Mitch	164	A14
Gorse Cl E16	115	N12
Gorse Ri SW17	164	B10
Gorse Rd, Croy	200	B6
Gorst Rd NW10	106	G7
Gorst Rd SW11	145	T12
Gorsuch Pl E2	13	L5
Gorsuch St E2	13	L5
Gosberton Rd SW12	164	A1
Gosbury Hill, Chess	191	S8
Gosfield Rd, Dag	101	P3
Gosfield St W1	17	L2
Gosford Gdns, Ilf	80	E9
Gosforth La, Wat	50	F5
Gosforth Path, Wat 3	50	B5
Goslett Yd, WC2 5	17	T7
Gosling Cl, Grnf	103	N5
Gosling Way SW9	147	P1
Gospatrick Rd N17	75	U1
Gospel Oak Est NW5	91	U9
Gosport Rd E17	77	U10
Gossage Rd SE18	135	P10
Gosset St E2	13	P7
Gosshill Rd, Chis	188	H4
Gossington Cl, Chis	171	K8
Gosterwood St SE8	131	S11
Gostling Rd, Twick	157	P1
Goston Gdns, Th Hth	183	N6
Goswell Rd EC1	11	T11
Gothic Rd, Twick	158	B3
Gottfried Ms, NW5 1	92	E7
Goudhurst Rd, Brom	169	K9
Gough Rd E15	97	L8
Gough Rd, Enf	44	J3
Gough Sq, EC4 12	19	L6
Gough St WC1	10	G10
Gould Rd, Twick	158	C2
Gould Ter E8	95	K10
Goulding Gdns, Th Hth	183	T3
Goulston St E1	21	M5
Goulton Rd E5	95	K8
Gourley Pl N15	76	C10
Gourley St N15	76	D10
Gourock Rd SE9	152	G10
Govan St E2	112	H2
Govier Cl E15	97	K14
Gowan Av SW6	144	C1
Gowan Rd NW10	89	R12
Gower Cl SW4	146	E11
Gower Ct WC1	9	R10
Gower Ms WC1	17	T3
Gower Pl WC1	9	P10
Gower Rd E7	97	P12
Gower Rd, Islw	122	F12
Gower St WC1	9	S12
Gower's Wk E1	21	S7
Gowland Pl, Beck	185	T4
Gowlett Rd SE15	148	G6
Gowrie Rd SW11	146	A6
Graburn Way, E Mol	176	A5
Grace Av, Bexh	155	M3
Grace Cl SE9	170	A6
Grace Cl, Borwd	38	G2
Grace Cl, Edg	54	E14
Grace Cl, Ilf	65	U12
Grace Jones Cl, E8 2	94	G12
Grace Pl E3	114	D6
Grace Rd, Croy	183	T12
Grace St E3	114	D6
Gracechurch St EC3	20	F9
Gracedale Rd SW16	164	D9
Gracefield Gdns SW16	165	K6
Grace's All E1	21	S10
Graces Ms SE5	148	B3
Graces Rd SE5	148	C3
Gradient, The SE26	166	G8
Graeme Rd, Enf	44	C3
Graemesdyke Av SW14	142	D6
Grafton Cl W13	104	G12
Grafton Cl, Houns	157	K1
Grafton Cl, Wor Pk	193	K5
Grafton Cres NW1	92	C12
Grafton Gdns N4	75	T11
Grafton Gdns, Dag	101	K3
Grafton Ms W1	9	M11
Grafton Pk Rd, Wor Pk	192	J4
Grafton Pl NW1	9	S7
Grafton Rd NW5	92	B10
Grafton Rd W3	106	F13
Grafton Rd, Croy	197	P2
Grafton Rd, Dag	101	K6
Grafton Rd, Enf	43	L5
Grafton Rd, Har	67	U10
Grafton Rd, N Mal	178	J6
Grafton Rd, Wor Pk	192	H6
Grafton Sq SW4	146	F6
Grafton St W1	17	K12
Grafton Ter NW5	91	U10
Grafton Way W1	9	L12
Grafton Way WC1	9	N11
Grafton Way, W Mol	175	L7
Graham Yd NW5	92	D11
Graham Av W13	122	J4
Graham Av, Mitch	182	A2
Graham Cl, Croy	200	A4
Graham Gdns, Surb	191	S1
Graham Rd E8	94	H11
Graham Rd E13	115	N6
Graham Rd N15	75	R6
Graham Rd NW4	71	R11
Graham Rd SW19	162	F14
Graham Rd W4	124	G5
Graham Rd, Bexh	155	N7
Graham Rd, Hmptn	157	N7
Graham Rd, Har	68	C5
Graham Rd, Mitch	182	A2
Graham St N1	11	S3
Graham Ter SW1	32	D4

Name	No	Ref
Grahame Pk Way NW7	71	L4
Grahame Pk Way NW9	71	L4
Grainger Cl, Nthlt	85	T10
Grainger Rd N22	75	T2
Grainger Rd, Islw	140	F4
Gramer Cl, E11 3	96	H4
Grampian Cl, Orp	189	T12
Grampian Gdns NW2	90	C2
Granard Av SW15	143	S10
Granard Rd SW12	145	T13
Granary Cl N9	45	L14
Granary Rd E1	112	J8
Granary St NW1	110	G2
Granby Bldgs SE11	34	E3
Granby Rd SE9	152	F4
Granby St E2	13	P10
Granby Ter NW1	9	L4
Grand Av EC1	19	R3
Grand Av N10	74	A7
Grand Av, Surb	178	D12
Grand Av, Wem	88	A10
Grand Av E, Wem	88	C10
Grand Depot Rd SE18	134	H10
Grand Dr SW20	179	T4
Grand Dr, Sthl	121	U3
Grand Junct Wf N1	11	T3
Grand Par Ms SW15	144	D9
Grand Union Canal Wk W7	122	D4
Grand Union Cres E8	94	H14
Grand Union Ind Est NW10	106	C3
Grand Union Wk NW1	92	D14
Granden Rd SW16	183	K4
Grandison Rd SW11	145	U9
Grandison Rd, Wor Pk	193	T4
Granfield St SW11	145	P2
Grange, The N20	57	M1
Grange, The SE1	29	L10
Grange, The SW19	162	B11
Grange, The, Croy	199	T4
Grange, The, Wem	88	A14
Grange, The, Wor Pk	192	H6
Grange Av N12	67	L9
Grange Av N20	40	C14
Grange Av SE25	184	C3
Grange Av, Barn	57	S1
Grange Av, Stan	69	K3
Grange Av, Twick	158	D3
Grange Av, Wdf Grn	63	N12
Grange Cl, Edg	54	F10
Grange Cl, Houns	121	L11
Grange Cl, Sid	172	A5
Grange Cl, W Mol	175	R8
Grange Cl, Wdf Grn	63	N13
Grange Ct, Loug	48	B10
Grange Ct, Nthlt	102	F3
Grange Cres SE28	118	F12
Grange Cres, Chig	65	P9
Grange Dr, Chis	170	D11
Grange Fm Cl, Har	85	U3
Grange Gdns N14	58	H2
Grange Gdns NW3	91	K6
Grange Gdns SE25	184	C3
Grange Gdns, Pnr	67	L7
Grange Gro N1	93	T11
Grange Hill SE25	184	C3
Grange Hill, Edg	54	F10
Grange La SE21	166	E4
Grange Mans, Epsom	193	M14
Grange Ms SE10	132	G14
Grange Pk W5	123	R1
Grange Pk Av N21	43	T12
Grange Pk Pl SW20	161	R13
Grange Pk Rd E10	96	C2
Grange Pk Rd, Th Hth	184	A7
Grange Pl NW6	90	G14
Grange Rd E10	96	B2
Grange Rd E13	115	L6
Grange Rd E17	77	R10
Grange Rd N6	74	A12
Grange Rd N17	60	G12
Grange Rd N18	60	G12
Grange Rd NW10	89	S12
Grange Rd SE1	29	L11
Grange Rd SE19	184	B5
Grange Rd SE25	184	B5
Grange Rd SW13	143	N2
Grange Rd W4	124	D9
Grange Rd W5	123	R1
Grange Rd, Chess	191	R7
Grange Rd, Edg	54	H12
Grange Rd, Har	68	G10
Grange Rd (South Harrow), Har	86	A4
Grange Rd, Ilf	99	K7
Grange Rd, Kings T	177	R5
Grange Rd, Orp	203	M4
Grange Rd, Sthl	120	J3
Grange Rd, Sutt	195	K13
Grange Rd, Th Hth	184	B5
Grange Rd, W Mol	175	S8
Grange Vale, Sutt	195	K13
Grange Vw Rd N20	57	M1
Grange Wk SE1	29	M10
Grange Yd SE1	29	L11
Grangecliffe Gdns SE25	184	C3
Grangecourt Rd N16	94	C1
Grangehill Pl SE9	152	F5
Grangehill Rd SE9	152	F6
Grangemill Rd SE6	168	A5
Grangemill Way SE6	168	B4
Grangeway N12	57	K7
Grangeway NW6	90	G13
Grangeway, Wdf Grn	63	U8
Grangeway, The N21	43	S11
Grangeway Gdns, Ilf	80	D9
Grangewood, Bex	173	L1
Grangewood Cl, Pnr	66	A9
Grangewood La, Beck	167	U12
Grangewood St E6	116	A1
Granham Gdns N9	60	F4
Granite St SE18	135	U9
Granleigh Rd E11	96	J4
Gransden Av E8	95	K14
Gransden Rd W12	125	M4
Grant Cl N14	42	E14
Grant Pl, Croy	198	F1
Grant Rd SW11	145	P6
Grant Rd, Croy	198	F1
Grant Rd, Har	68	E5
Grant St E13	115	N6
Grant St N1	11	K2
Grant Way, Islw	122	C12
Grantbridge St N1	11	R2
Grantchester Cl, Har	86	F5
Grantham Cl, Edg	53	R5
Grantham Gdns, Rom	83	L12
Grantham Grn, Borwd	38	G9
Grantham Pl W1	24	G4
Grantham Rd E12	98	G7
Grantham Rd SW9	147	K4
Grantham Rd W4	124	J13
Grantley Rd, Houns	138	E3
Grantley St E1	113	N6
Grantock Rd E17	78	H2
Granton Rd SW16	182	F1
Granton Rd, Ilf	100	A2
Granton Rd, Sid	172	E11
Grants Cl NW7	55	U13
Grantully Rd W9	6	A7
Granville Av N9	61	L5
Granville Av, Felt	156	A4
Granville Av, Houns	139	N10
Granville Cl, Croy	198	C4
Granville Gdns SW16	183	L1
Granville Gdns W5	123	U1
Granville Gro SE13	150	F6
Granville Ms, Sid	172	B7
Granville Pk SE13	150	F5
Granville Pl (North Finchley) N12	57	M13
Granville Pl W1	16	C8
Granville Rd E17	78	C11
Granville Rd E18	79	S4
Granville Rd N4	75	M12
Granville Rd N12	57	L13
Granville Rd N13	59	L11
Granville Rd N22	75	S2
Granville Rd NW2	90	E3
Granville Rd NW6	108	H4
Granville Rd SW18	144	G13
Granville Rd SW19	162	H14
Granville Rd, Barn	39	U7
Granville Rd, Ilf	98	J3
Granville Rd, Sid	172	C7
Granville Rd, Well	154	F6
Granville Sq SE15	37	K14
Granville Sq WC1	10	H7
Granville St WC1	10	H7
Grape St WC2	18	B5
Graphite Sq, SE11 1	34	E5
Grasdene Rd SE18	136	B13
Grasmere Av SW15	160	H8
Grasmere Av SW19	180	H5
Grasmere Av W3	106	F13
Grasmere Av, Houns	139	R12
Grasmere Av, Orp	202	J5
Grasmere Av, Wem	69	M14
Grasmere Cl, Loug	48	F4
Grasmere Ct N22	59	L12
Grasmere Gdns, Har	68	H4
Grasmere Gdns, Ilf	80	D9
Grasmere Gdns, Orp	202	J5
Grasmere Rd, E13 6	115	N3
Grasmere Rd N10	74	D2
Grasmere Rd N17	60	G12
Grasmere Rd SE25	185	K10
Grasmere Rd SW16	165	L9
Grasmere Rd, Bexh	155	T3
Grasmere Rd, Brom	187	L1
Grasmere Rd, Orp	202	J5
Grass Pk N3	72	E2
Grassington Cl N11	58	B8
Grassington Rd, Sid	172	A8
Grassmount, SE23 1	167	K3
Grassway, Wall	196	E7
Grasvenor Av, Barn	40	H10
Gratton Rd W14	126	C0
Gratton Ter NW2	90	A6
Gravel Hill N3	72	F3
Gravel Hill, Bexh	155	R10
Gravel Hill, Croy	199	P11
Gravel Hill Cl, Bexh	155	S10
Gravel La E1	21	L6
Gravel La, Chig	49	U9
Gravel Rd, Brom	202	C4
Gravel Rd, Twick	158	C2
Graveley Av, Borwd	38	E9
Gravelly Ride SW19	161	N7
Gravelwood Cl, Chis	171	L6
Graveney Gro SE20	167	L14
Graveney Rd SW17	163	R8
Gravesend Rd W12	107	P14
Gray Av, Dag	101	M1
Gray St SE1	27	M7
Grayham Cres, N Mal	178	G8
Grayham Rd, N Mal	178	G8
Grayling Cl, E16 3	115	K7
Grayling Rd N16	94	B4
Grayling Sq, E2 2	13	U5
Gray's Inn WC1	18	J3
Gray's Inn Rd WC1	18	H3
Gray's Inn Rd WC1	10	H7
Gray's Inn Sq WC1	18	H2
Gray's Yd, W1 1	16	H1
Grayscroft Rd SW16	164	G13
Grayshott Rd SW11	144	K4
Grayswood Gdns SW20	179	S4
Graywood Ct N12	57	L13
Grazebrook Rd N16	94	B4
Grazeley Cl, Bexh	155	U9
Grazeley Ct, SE19 4	166	C9
Great Brownings SE21	166	F7
Great Bushey Dr N20	57	K1
Great Cambridge Rd N9	60	B5
Great Cambridge Rd N17	60	A10
Great Cambridge Rd N18	60	A10
Great Cambridge Rd, Enf	44	H9
Great Castle St W1	17	K6
Great Cen Av, Ruis	84	F9
Great Cen St NW1	15	T1
Great Cen Way NW10	88	J10
Great Cen Way, Wem	88	E8
Great Chapel St W1	17	R6
Great Chertsey Rd W4	142	G2
Great Chertsey Rd, Felt	157	P5
Great Ch La W6	126	B9
Great College St SW1	26	A10
Great Cross Av SE10	132	J14
Great Cumberland Ms, W1 1	15	U7
Great Cumberland Pl W1	15	U6
Great Dover St SE1	28	D10
Great Eastern Rd E15	96	G13
Great Eastern St EC2	12	H9
Great Elms Rd, Brom	187	T7
Great Fld NW9	71	K1
Great Fleete Way, Bark 1	118	E4
Great Galley Cl, Bark	118	D5
Great George St SW1	25	U7
Great Guildford St SE1	27	T2
Great Harry Dr SE9	170	G6
Great James St WC1	10	F12
Great Marlborough St W1	17	M8
Great Maze Pond SE1	28	E5
Great New St EC4	19	L6
Great Newport St, WC2 7	18	A10
Great N Rd N2	73	S9
Great N Rd N6	73	S9
Great N Rd (New Barnet), Barn	40	J10
Great N Way NW4	72	C7
Great Oaks, Chig	65	M8
Great Ormond St WC1	18	D1
Great Owl Rd, Chig	64	G6
Great Percy St WC1	10	H6
Great Peter St SW1	25	T11
Great Portland St W1	8	J12
Great Pulteney St W1	17	P9
Great Queen St WC2	18	D6
Great Russell St WC1	17	T5
Great St. Helens, EC3 1	20	H6
Great St. Thomas Apostle, EC4 3	20	B9
Great Scotland Yd SW1	26	B2
Great Smith St SW1	25	U10
Great South-West Rd, Houns	138	A6
Great Spilmans SE22	148	C10
Great Strand NW9	71	M3
Great Suffolk St SE1	27	S6
Great Sutton St EC1	11	R11
Great Swan All EC2	20	D5

Great Thrift, Orp 189 L7
Great Titchfield St 17 L4
W1
Great Twr St EC3 20 H10
Great Trinity La EC4 20 A9
Great W Rd W4 124 C10
Great W Rd W6 125 N9
Great W Rd, Brent 123 K12
Great W Rd, Houns 139 S1
Great W Rd, Islw 122 G13
Great Western Rd 108 F9
W2
Great Western Rd 108 F9
W9
Great Western Rd 108 F9
W11
Great Winchester 20 F5
St EC2
Great Windmill St 17 R11
W1
Greatdown Rd W7 104 E8
Greatfield Av E6 116 E7
Greatfield Cl N19 92 E7
Greatfield Cl SE4 150 B8
Greatfields Rd, Bark 117 P2
Greatham Wk, 161 P2
SW15 9
Greatorex St E1 21 S2
Greatwood, Chis 170 G13
Greaves Cl, Bark 99 P14
Greaves Pl SW17 163 R8
Grebe Av, 102 H11
Hayes 4
Grebe Cl E7 97 M9
Grebe Cl E17 61 R14
Grecian Cres SE19 165 S11
Greek St W1 17 T8
Greek Yd WC2 18 A10
Green, The E4 62 F1
Green, The E11 79 R12
Green, The E15 97 K12
Green, The N9 60 H4
Green, The N14 58 G5
Green, The N21 43 P14
Green, The SW14 142 F5
Green, The SW19 162 A10
Green, The W3 107 K11
Green, The, Bexh 155 N2
Green, The, Brom 187 N14
Green, The, Cars 196 A8
Green, The, Esher 190 E12
Green, The, Felt 156 C3
Green, The, Houns 121 N11
Green, The, Mord 180 C8
Green, The, N Mal 178 F5
Green, The (St. 172 C13
Paul's Cray), Orp
Green, The, Rich 141 N9
Green, The, Sid 172 A8
Green, The, Sthl 121 K5
Green, The, Sutt 194 J6
Green, The, Twick 158 D3
Green, The, Well 153 S8
Green, The, Wem 86 H3
Green, The, Wdf Grn 63 P9
Green Acres, Croy 198 E6
Green Arbour Ct 19 P5
EC1
Green Av NW7 54 J7
Green Av W13 123 K5
Green Bank E1 131 K2
Green Bank N12 57 K7
Green Cl NW9 70 F11
Green Cl N11 73 L13
Green Cl, Brom 186 J5
Green Cl, Cars 195 U4
Green Cl, Felt 156 J9
Green Dale SE5 148 B8
Green Dale SE22 148 C9
Green Dale Cl SE22 148 C10
Green Dragon Ct, 28 D2
SE1 2
Green Dragon La 43 S12
N21
Green Dragon La, 123 S10
Brent
Green Dragon Yd E1 21 R4
Green Dr, Sthl 121 P1
Green End N21 59 S4
Green End, Chess 191 R8

Green Gdns, Orp 203 L9
Green Hill, Buck H 63 T1
Green Hundred Rd 37 U12
SE15
Green La E4 46 H5
Green La NW4 72 B9
Green La SE9 170 H1
Green La SE20 167 N14
Green La SW16 165 L14
Green La W7 122 C3
Green La, Chess 191 R14
Green La, Chis 171 K9
Green La, Dag 100 F3
Green La, Edg 53 T7
Green La, Felt 156 J9
Green La, Har 86 D6
Green La, Houns 138 F9
Green La, Ilf 99 N4
Green La, Mord 180 H11
Green La, N Mal 178 F9
Green La, Stan 52 J8
Green La, Th Hth 183 S3
Green La, Wat 50 F2
Green La, W Mol 175 S9
Green La, Wor Pk 193 P1
Green La Gdns, 183 S3
Th Hth
Green Las N4 93 U5
Green Las N8 75 R7
Green Las N13 59 M12
Green Las N15 75 R7
Green Las N16 94 A8
Green Las N21 59 S1
Green Lawns, Ruis 84 E1
Green Leaf Av, Wall 196 G7
Green Man Gdns 104 H14
W13
Green Man La W13 104 H14
Green Man La, Felt 138 B8
Green Man Pas W13 104 J14
Green Man 79 M13
Roundabout E11
Green Moor Link 43 S14
N21
Green Pk Way, Grnf 86 C14
Green Pond Cl E17 77 S5
Green Pond Rd E17 77 S5
Green Ride, Loug 47 N10
Green Rd N14 42 C11
Green Rd N20 57 M5
Green St E7 97 T13
Green St E13 115 U3
Green St W1 16 C9
Green St, Enf 45 R5
Green St, Sun 174 A1
Green Vale W5 105 T11
Green Vale, Bexh 154 H9
Green Verges, Stan 53 N13
Green Vw, Chess 191 T13
Green Wk NW4 72 B9
Green Wk SE1 28 G11
Green Wk, Buck H 48 C14
Green Wk, Sthl 121 N10
Green Wk, Wdf Grn 64 D12
Green Wk, The E4 62 F1
Green Way SE9 152 A10
Green Way, Brom 188 D11
Green Way, Sun 174 A7
Green Wrythe 195 S2
Cres, Cars
Green Wrythe La, 181 P12
Cars
Greenacre Cl, Nthlt 85 L9
Greenacre Gdns E17 78 F7
Greenacre Pl, 196 C4
Wall 1
Greenacre Sq, 131 P3
SE16 14
Greenacre Wk N14 58 H5
Greenacres SE9 152 G12
Greenacres, Bushey 52 B3
Greenacres Cl, 203 L8
Orp 1
Greenacres Dr, Stan 52 J13
Greenaway Gdns 90 J8
NW3
Greenbank Av, Wem 86 H9
Greenbank Cl E4 62 E3
Greenbank Cres 72 C7
NW4

Greenbay Rd SE7 134 B13
Greenberry St NW8 7 P4
Greenbrook Av, 41 M2
Barn
Greencoat Pl SW1 33 P1
Greencoat Row SW1 25 P12
Greencourt Av, Croy 199 K3
Greencourt Av, Edg 70 C2
Greencourt Gdns, 199 K3
Croy
Greencourt Rd, Orp 189 R10
Greencrest Pl NW2 89 P6
Greencroft Av, Ruis 84 E4
Greencroft Cl E6 116 C10
Greencroft Gdns 91 L13
NW6
Greencroft Gdns, 44 C5
Enf
Greencroft Rd, 139 L2
Houns
Greenend Rd W4 124 J4
Greenfarm Cl, Orp 203 T10
Greenfield Av, Surb 178 D12
Greenfield Av, Wat 50 H3
Greenfield Gdns 90 D4
NW2
Greenfield Gdns, 118 G1
Dag
Greenfield Gdns, 189 N14
Orp
Greenfield Rd E1 21 T4
Greenfield Rd N15 76 D9
Greenfield Rd, Dag 118 F1
Greenfield Way, Har 67 R5
Greenfields, Loug 48 G8
Greenfields Cl, 48 G8
Loug 2
Greenford Av W7 104 D13
Greenford Av, Sthl 103 L13
Greenford Gdns, 103 T5
Grnf
Greenford Rd, Grnf 104 B2
Greenford Rd, Har 86 E7
Greenford Rd, Sthl 103 T13
Greenford Rd, Sutt 194 J8
Greengate St E13 115 R4
Greengate, Grnf 86 J11
Greenhalgh Wk N2 73 L8
Greenham Cl SE1 27 K8
Greenham Cres, 61 U12
E4 4
Greenham Rd N10 74 A3
Greenheys Dr E18 79 M5
Greenhill NW3 91 N8
Greenhill SE18 134 F9
Greenhill, Sutt 195 L4
Greenhill, Wem 88 D3
Greenhill Gdns, 103 L4
Nthlt
Greenhill Gro E12 98 C9
Greenhill Pk NW10 106 J2
Greenhill Pk, Barn 41 K10
Greenhill Rd NW10 106 J2
Greenhill Rd, Har 68 D11
Greenhill Ter SE18 134 F9
Greenhill Ter, Nthlt 103 L4
Greenhill Way, Har 68 C12
Greenhill Way, Wem 88 D3
Greenhill's Rents, 19 P2
EC1 1
Greenhithe Cl, Sid 153 R13
Greenholm Rd SE9 152 J3
Greenhurst Rd SE27 165 P9
Greening St SE2 136 E7
Greenland Cres, 120 F6
Sthl
Greenland Pl, 110 D1
NW1 7
Greenland Quay 131 P7
SE16
Greenland Rd NW1 110 E1
Greenland Rd, Barn 39 U11
Greenland St, 110 D1
NW1 8
Greenlaw Gdns, 179 M13
N Mal
Greenlaw St SE18 134 G6
Greenlea Pk SW19 181 P1
Greenleaf Cl SW2 147 N13
Greenleaf Rd E6 115 U2

Greenleaf Rd E17 77 U6
Greenleafe Dr, Ilf 81 K7
Greenman St N1 93 T14
Greenmead Cl SE25 184 H9
Greenmoor Rd, Enf 45 L3
Greenoak Way 162 A6
SW19
Greenock Rd SW16 182 G1
Greenock Rd W3 124 D6
Greenpark Ct, Wem 87 M13
Greens Clo, The, 48 G4
Loug
Green's End SE18 134 J7
Greenshank Cl, 61 R14
E17 1
Greenside, Bex 173 K1
Greenside, Dag 100 E2
Greenside Cl N20 57 N4
Greenside Cl SE6 168 G4
Greenside Rd W12 125 P5
Greenside Rd, Croy 183 P14
Greenslade Rd, Bark 99 P14
Greenstead Av, 63 U12
Wdf Grn
Greenstead Cl, 63 U12
Wdf Grn
Greenstead Gdns, 143 R10
SW15
Greenstead Gdns, 63 T12
Wdf Grn
Greensted Rd, Loug 48 D14
Greenstone Ms E11 79 N11
Greenvale Rd SE9 152 E8
Greenview Av, Beck 185 S11
Greenview Av, Croy 185 R11
Greenway N14 58 J4
Greenway N20 56 J3
Greenway SW20 179 T7
Greenway, Chis 170 J9
Greenway, Dag 100 F3
Greenway, Har 69 R10
Greenway, Hayes 102 B5
Greenway, Pnr 66 D3
Greenway, Wall 196 E8
Greenway, Wdf Grn 63 T9
Greenway, The, Har 68 D2
Greenway, The, 139 L7
Houns
Greenway, The, Pnr 67 M12
Greenway Av E17 78 G7
Greenway Cl N4 93 U4
Greenway Cl N11 58 B12
Greenway Cl, 76 F7
N15 1
Greenway Cl N20 56 H4
Greenway Cl NW9 70 G4
Greenway Gdns 70 G4
NW9
Greenway Gdns, 199 T6
Croy
Greenway Gdns, 103 P6
Grnf
Greenway Gdns, 68 D3
Har
Greenways, Beck 186 B4
Greenways, Esher 190 D7
Greenways, The, 140 H11
Twick
Greenwell St W1 9 K12
Greenwich Ch St 132 F12
SE10
Greenwich Cres, 116 C10
E6 15
Greenwich Foot 132 E11
Tunnel E14
Greenwich Foot 132 E11
Tunnel SE10
Greenwich High Rd 132 C14
SE10
Greenwich Ind Est 133 R8
SE7
Greenwich Pk SE10 132 J13
Greenwich Pk St 132 H10
SE10
Greenwich S St 150 E1
SE10
Greenwich Vw Pl 132 C6
E14
Greenwood Av, Dag 101 S7

Name	Page	Grid
Greenwood Av, Enf	45	P2
Greenwood Cl, Mord	180	C8
Greenwood Cl, Orp	189	R12
Greenwood Cl, Sid	172	B4
Greenwood Cl, T Ditt	190	H2
Greenwood Ct SW1	33	M6
Greenwood Dr E4	62	G9
Greenwood Gdns N13	59	R4
Greenwood Gdns, Ilf	65	M14
Greenwood La, Hmptn	157	S10
Greenwood Pk, Kings T	161	K13
Greenwood Pl NW5	92	D9
Greenwood Rd E8	94	H12
Greenwood Rd, E13 2	115	M3
Greenwood Rd, Croy	183	S13
Greenwood Rd, Islw	140	E5
Greenwood Rd, Mitch	182	G6
Greenwood Rd, T Ditt	190	H3
Greenwood Ter NW10	106	H2
Greer Rd, Har	67	U1
Greet St SE1	27	M4
Greg Cl E10	78	E11
Gregor Ms SE3	133	P14
Gregory Cres SE9	152	A14
Gregory Pl W8	22	A6
Gregory Rd, Rom	82	G7
Gregory Rd, Sthl	121	P5
Gregson Cl, Borwd	38	F2
Greig Cl N8	74	J9
Greig Ter SE17	35	S10
Grena Gdns, Rich	141	U8
Grena Rd, Rich	141	U8
Grenaby Av, Croy	184	A14
Grenaby Rd, Croy	184	A14
Grenada Rd SE7	133	U14
Grenade St E14	113	U13
Grenadier St E16	134	F2
Grendon Gdns, Wem	88	B4
Grendon St NW8	7	N10
Grenfell Cl, Borwd	38	F1
Grenfell Gdns, Har	69	R13
Grenfell Rd W11	108	B13
Grenfell Rd, Mitch	163	U12
Grenfell Wk W11	108	B13
Grennell Cl, Sutt	195	N4
Grennell Rd, Sutt	195	M4
Grenoble Gdns N13	59	N11
Grenville Cl N3	72	D2
Grenville Cl, Surb	192	E1
Grenville Gdns, Wdf Grn	79	T1
Grenville Ms, SW7 4	30	G3
Grenville Ms, Hmptn	157	R9
Grenville Pl NW7	54	G10
Grenville Pl SW7	22	E12
Grenville Rd N19	92	J2
Grenville St WC1	10	C11
Gresham Av N20	57	T7
Gresham Cl, Bex	155	K12
Gresham Cl, Enf	43	T6
Gresham Dr, Rom	82	D11
Gresham Gdns NW11	90	D1
Gresham Rd E6	116	F4
Gresham Rd E16	115	S12
Gresham Rd NW10	88	H10
Gresham Rd SE25	184	G8
Gresham Rd SW9	147	P6
Gresham Rd, Beck	185	R4
Gresham Rd, Edg	53	U12
Gresham Rd, Hmptn	157	N11
Gresham Rd, Houns	139	T1
Gresham St EC2	20	A6
Gresham Way SW19	162	J5
Gresley Cl E17	77	R12
Gresley Cl N15	76	A8
Gresley Rd N19	92	F1
Gresse St W1	17	R4
Gressenhall Rd SW18	144	E12
Gresswell Cl, Sid	172	B5
Greswell St SW6	144	A2
Gretton Rd N17	60	D14
Greville Cl, Twick	140	J13
Greville Pl NW6	6	C1
Greville Rd E17	78	F8
Greville Rd NW6	6	D1
Greville Rd, Rich	141	U11
Greville St EC1	19	L2
Grey Cl NW11	73	L11
Grey Eagle St E1	21	M1
Greycoat Pl SW1	25	R11
Greycoat St SW1	25	R12
Greycot Rd, Beck	168	B10
Greyfell Cl, Stan 1	53	K9
Greyhound Hill NW4	71	R6
Greyhound La SW16	164	J12
Greyhound Rd N17	76	D6
Greyhound Rd NW10	107	S5
Greyhound Rd W6	126	C11
Greyhound Rd W14	126	C11
Greyhound Rd, Sutt	195	L9
Greyhound Ter SW16	182	F1
Greys Pk Cl, Kes	201	U9
Greystead Rd SE23	149	L13
Greystoke Av, Pnr	67	P5
Greystoke Gdns W5	105	S8
Greystoke Gdns, Enf	42	H8
Greystoke Pk Ter W5	105	P6
Greystone Gdns, Har	69	L11
Greystone Gdns, Ilf	81	M3
Greystone Path, E11 3	79	L14
Greyswood St SW16	164	D11
Grierson Rd SE23	149	R12
Griffin Cl NW10	89	S10
Griffin Manor Way SE28	135	P6
Griffin Rd N17	76	C4
Griffin Rd SE18	135	P9
Griffin Way, Sun	174	A3
Griffith Cl, Dag 1	100	F1
Griffiths Cl, Wor Pk	193	S4
Griffiths Rd SW19	162	H13
Griggs App, Ilf	99	L3
Griggs Pl SE1	28	J11
Griggs Rd E10	78	F12
Grilse Cl N9	61	K7
Grimsby St E2	13	P11
Grimsdyke Cres, Barn	39	T6
Grimsdyke Rd, Pnr	51	K13
Grimshaw Cl N6	74	A14
Grimston Rd SW6	144	E4
Grimwade Av, Croy	198	H6
Grimwade Cl SE15	149	L4
Grimwood Rd, Twick	140	F13
Grindal St SE1	26	J7
Grindall Cl, Croy	197	S8
Grindleford Av N11	58	R4
Grindley Gdns, Croy	184	F11
Grinling Pl, SE8 7	132	A12
Grinstead Rd SE8	131	R10
Grittleton Av, Wem	88	C12
Grittleton Rd W9	108	G7
Grizedale Ter SE23	167	K3
Grocer's Hall Ct EC2	20	C7
Grogan Cl, Hmptn	157	L11
Groom Cres SW18	145	N13
Groom Pl SW1	24	F9
Groombridge Cl, Well	154	B9
Groombridge Rd E9	95	N14
Groomfield Cl SW17	164	A7
Grooms Dr, Pnr	66	A10
Grosmont Rd SE18	135	U10
Grosse Way SW15	143	S12
Grosvenor Av N5	93	U10
Grosvenor Av SW14	142	J6
Grosvenor Av, Cars	196	A11
Grosvenor Av, Har	67	S12
Grosvenor Av, Rich	141	R10
Grosvenor Cl, Loug	49	K2
Grosvenor Cotts SW1	32	C2
Grosvenor Ct N14	42	E12
Grosvenor Ct NW6	108	B1
Grosvenor Cres NW9	70	B8
Grosvenor Cres SW1	24	E7
Grosvenor Cres Ms SW1	24	D7
Grosvenor Dr, Loug	49	K2
Grosvenor Est SW1	33	T2
Grosvenor Gdns E6	116	A5
Grosvenor Gdns N10	74	E6
Grosvenor Gdns N14	42	G8
Grosvenor Gdns NW2	89	U10
Grosvenor Gdns NW11	72	E11
Grosvenor Gdns SW1	24	H10
Grosvenor Gdns SW14	142	J6
Grosvenor Gdns, Kings T	159	P11
Grosvenor Gdns, Wall	196	E13
Grosvenor Gdns, Wdf Grn	63	P12
Grosvenor Gdns Ms E, SW1 2	24	J10
Grosvenor Gdns Ms N SW1	24	H11
Grosvenor Gdns Ms S, SW1 3	24	J11
Grosvenor Gate W1	16	B12
Grosvenor Hill SW19	162	C11
Grosvenor Hill W1	16	H10
Grosvenor Pk SE5	35	U12
Grosvenor Pk Rd E17	78	C10
Grosvenor Path, Loug 3	49	K2
Grosvenor Pl SW1	24	F7
Grosvenor Ri E E17	78	D10
Grosvenor Rd E6	116	B1
Grosvenor Rd E7	97	R12
Grosvenor Rd E10	78	F10
Grosvenor Rd E11	79	R10
Grosvenor Rd N3	56	F13
Grosvenor Rd N9	61	K1
Grosvenor Rd N10	74	D2
Grosvenor Rd, SE25 3	184	G7
Grosvenor Rd SW1	33	S9
Grosvenor Rd W4	124	D10
Grosvenor Rd W7	122	G2
Grosvenor Rd, Belv	137	N11
Grosvenor Rd, Bexh	154	H10
Grosvenor Rd, Borwd	38	B5
Grosvenor Rd, Brent	123	P12
Grosvenor Rd, Dag	101	M1
Grosvenor Rd, Houns	139	L6
Grosvenor Rd, Ilf	99	L5
Grosvenor Rd, Orp	189	S11
Grosvenor Rd, Rich	141	R9
Grosvenor Rd, Sthl	121	L5
Grosvenor Rd, Twick	140	G14
Grosvenor Rd, Wall	196	C14
Grosvenor Rd, W Wick	200	D2
Grosvenor Sq W1	16	E11
Grosvenor St W1	16	G10
Grosvenor Ter SE5	35	U12
Grosvenor Way E5	95	L3
Grosvenor Wf Rd E14	132	G8
Grote's Bldgs SE3	151	K4
Grote's Pl SE3	151	J3
Groton Rd SW18	163	K3
Grotto Pas, W1 8	16	E2
Grotto Rd, Twick	158	F3
Grove, The E15	96	J11
Grove, The N3	56	G14
Grove, The N4	75	L14
Grove, The N6	92	A1
Grove, The N8	74	H9
Grove, The N13	59	N9
Grove, The N14	42	F9
Grove, The NW9	70	G10
Grove, The NW11	72	D13
Grove, The W5	123	P1
Grove, The, Bexh	154	G8
Grove, The, Edg	54	D8
Grove, The, Enf	43	N4
Grove, The, Grnf	103	T11
Grove, The, Islw	140	C2
Grove, The, Sid	173	K8
Grove, The, Stan	52	H3
Grove, The, Tedd	158	G8
Grove, The, Twick	140	J11
Grove, The, Walt	174	C13
Grove, The, W Wick	200	E4
Grove Av N3	56	H14
Grove Av N10	74	E3
Grove Av N7	104	D12
Grove Av, Pnr	67	K8
Grove Av, Sutt	194	H11
Grove Av, Twick	158	E1
Grove Bank, Wat	50	G2
Grove Cl SE23	167	P1
Grove Cl, Brom	201	P3
Grove Cl, Felt	156	J8
Grove Cl, Kings T	177	T7
Grove Cotts SW3	31	R9
Grove Ct SE3	151	P1
Grove Ct, E Mol	176	B9
Grove Cres E18	79	M3
Grove Cres NW9	70	F7
Grove Cres SE5	148	C4
Grove Cres, Felt	156	J8
Grove Cres, Kings T	177	R6
Grove Cres, Walt	174	C13
Grove Cres Rd E15	96	J12
Grove End E18	79	L3
Grove End La, Esher	190	B1
Grove End Rd NW8	6	J7
Grove Fm Ct, Mitch	181	T8
Grove Footpath, Surb 3	177	S8
Grove Gdns E15	96	J12
Grove Gdns NW4	71	N9
Grove Gdns NW8	7	R7
Grove Gdns, Dag	101	U6
Grove Gdns, Tedd	158	G8
Grove Grn Rd E11	96	H4
Grove Hall Ct NW8	6	H6
Grove Hill E18	79	M3
Grove Hill, Har	86	D1
Grove Hill Rd SE5	148	C5
Grove Hill Rd, Har	68	D13
Grove Ho N8	74	J8
Grove La SE5	148	A2
Grove La, Chig	65	U5
Grove La, SE5	177	S7
Grove Mkt Pl SE9	152	E11
Grove Ms W6	125	T5
Grove Mill Pl, Cars	196	A6
Grove Pk E11	79	R10
Grove Pk NW9	70	F7
Grove Pk SE5	148	C4
Grove Pk Av E4	62	C14
Grove Pk Gdns W4	124	D13
Grove Pk Ms W4	124	D13
Grove Pk Rd N15	76	D7
Grove Pk Rd SE9	169	U5
Grove Pk Rd W4	124	E14
Grove Pk Rd W4	124	D13
Grove Pas E2	112	J3
Grove Pas, Tedd	158	H8
Grove Pl NW3	91	N6
Grove Pl, Bark	99	L14
Grove Rd E3	113	P2
Grove Rd E4	62	E6
Grove Rd E17	79	L14
Grove Rd E18	78	D10
Grove Rd E18	79	M3
Grove Rd N11	58	D9
Grove Rd N12	57	N10
Grove Rd N15	76	C10

Name	Page	Grid
Grove Rd NW2	89	T11
Grove Rd SW13	143	L3
Grove Rd SW19	163	M13
Grove Rd W3	124	F2
Grove Rd W5	105	P14
Grove Rd, Barn	41	R6
Grove Rd, Belv	137	M11
Grove Rd, Bexh	155	U8
Grove Rd, Borwd	38	A2
Grove Rd, Brent	123	M9
Grove Rd, E Mol	176	A8
Grove Rd, Edg	54	A11
Grove Rd, Houns	139	R7
Grove Rd, Islw	140	D2
Grove Rd, Mitch	182	E2
Grove Rd, Pnr	67	L9
Grove Rd, Rich	141	T12
Grove Rd, Rom	82	D13
Grove Rd, Surb	177	P9
Grove Rd, Sutt	195	K11
Grove Rd, Th Hth	183	N8
Grove Rd, Twick	158	B6
Grove St N18	60	F10
Grove St SE8	131	T7
Grove Ter NW5	92	B7
Grove Ter, Tedd	158	G8
Grove Ter Ms NW5	92	C6
Grove Vale SE22	148	E7
Grove Vale, Chis	170	G11
Grove Vil, E14 *14*	114	D13
Grove Way, Esher	175	U14
Grove Way, Wem	88	D9
Grovebury Rd SE2	136	D3
Grovedale Rd N19	92	G3
Groveland Av SW16	165	M13
Groveland Rd, Beck	185	T6
Groveland Way, N Mal	178	F9
Grovelands, W Mol	175	N8
Grovelands Cl SE5	148	C4
Grovelands Cl, Har	85	R6
Grovelands Ct N14	42	G14
Grovelands Rd N13	59	M7
Grovelands Rd N15	76	G11
Grovelands Rd, Orp	172	C14
Groveside Cl W3	106	B11
Groveside Cl, Cars	195	S3
Groveside Rd E4	63	K5
Groveway SW9	147	N2
Groveway, Dag	100	G7
Grovewood, Rich	142	A2
Grovewood Pl, Wdf Grn	64	F11
Grummant Rd SE15	148	E2
Grundy St E14	114	C12
Gruneisen Rd N3	56	J13
Gubyon Av SE24	147	S9
Guernsey Cl, Houns	139	P1
Guernsey Gro SE24	147	T13
Guernsey Rd E11	96	G2
Guibal Rd SE12	169	R1
Guild Rd SE7	134	B10
Guildersfield Rd SW16	164	J14
Guildford Gro SE10	150	D1
Guildford Rd E6	116	D12
Guildford Rd E17	78	F1
Guildford Rd SW8	147	K1
Guildford Rd, Croy	184	A11
Guildford Rd, Ilf	99	S4
Guildford Way, Wall	197	K9
Guildhall Yd EC2	20	B6
Guildhouse St SW1	33	L2
Guildown Av N12	56	J7
Guildsway E17	77	T1
Guilford Av, Surb	177	T9
Guilford Pl WC1	10	E11
Guilford St WC1	10	B12
Guilsborough Cl NW10	88	J14
Guinness Bldgs SE1	28	H12
Guinness Cl E9	95	R14
Guinness Sq SE1	36	H1
Guinness Trust Bldgs SE11	35	R5
Guinness Trust Bldgs SW3	31	U3
Guinness Trust Bldgs SW9	147	R8
Guion Rd SW6	144	F3
Gull Cl, Wall	196	J14
Gulliver Cl, Nthlt	103	L1
Gulliver Rd, Sid	171	R4
Gulliver St SE16	131	S5
Gulston Wk W11	108	E11
Gumleigh Rd W5	123	L7
Gumley Gdns, Islw	140	G5
Gumping Rd, Orp	203	M3
Gun St E1	21	L3
Gundulph Rd, Brom	187	T6
Gunmakers La E3	113	S2
Gunnell Cl SE26	166	G8
Gunnell Cl, Croy	184	G11
Gunner La SE18	134	H10
Gunners Gro E4	62	E5
Gunners Rd SW18	163	P3
Gunnersbury Av W3	123	U4
Gunnersbury Av W4	123	U4
Gunnersbury Av W5	123	U4
Gunnersbury Ct W3	124	C4
Gunnersbury Cres W3	124	B4
Gunnersbury Dr W5	123	U4
Gunnersbury Gdns W3	124	A4
Gunnersbury La W3	124	B4
Gunnersbury Ms, W4 *5*	124	D9
Gunnersbury Pk W3	123	T6
Gunnersbury Pk W5	123	T6
Gunning St SE18	135	R7
Gunpowder Sq, EC4 *13*	19	M6
Gunstor Rd N16	94	D7
Gunter Gro SW10	30	E12
Gunter Gro, Edg	70	G1
Gunterstone Rd W14	126	C8
Gunthorpe St E1	21	P4
Gunton Rd E5	95	K4
Gunton Rd SW17	164	B12
Gunwhale Cl, SE16 *6*	131	P2
Gurdon Rd SE7	133	P10
Gurnell Gro W13	104	F7
Gurney Cl E15	97	K9
Gurney Cl E17	77	P1
Gurney Cl, Bark	98	J12
Gurney Cres, Croy	197	M1
Gurney Dr N2	73	N8
Gurney Rd E15	96	J9
Gurney Rd, Cars	196	A7
Gurney Rd, Nthlt	102	E5
Guthrie St SW3	31	N5
Gutter La EC2	20	A6
Guy Barnett Gro SE3	151	P6
Guy Rd, Wall	196	H6
Guy St SE1	28	F6
Guyatt Gdns, Mitch	182	B3
Guyscliff Rd SE13	150	E10
Gwalior Rd, SW15 *3*	144	B6
Gwendolen Av SW15	144	A9
Gwendolen Cl SW15	144	A9
Gwendoline Av E13	115	R1
Gwendwr Rd W14	126	D9
Gwillim Cl, Sid	154	B10
Gwydor Rd, Beck	185	P6
Gwydyr Rd, Brom	187	M5
Gwyn Cl SW6	127	L14
Gwynne Av, Croy	185	N13
Gwynne Cl, W4 *5*	125	L12
Gwynne Pk Av, Wdf Grn	64	E12
Gwynne Pl, WC1 *6*	10	H7
Gylcote Cl SE5	148	B8
Gyles Pk, Stan	69	M1
Gyllyngdune Gdns, Ilf	99	U5

H

Name	Page	Grid
Ha-Ha Rd SE18	134	F11
Haarlem Rd W14	126	A6
Haberdasher Pl, N1 *5*	12	F5
Haberdasher St N1	12	E6
Habgood Rd, Loug	48	C6
Haccombe Rd, SW19 *1*	163	L12
Hackbridge Grn, Wall	196	A3
Hackbridge Pk Gdns, Cars	196	A3
Hackbridge Rd, Wall	196	B3
Hackford Rd SW9	147	M1
Hackforth Cl, Barn	39	S10
Hackington Cres, Beck	168	B11
Hackney Cl, Borwd	38	H10
Hackney Gro E8	95	K12
Hackney Rd E2	13	L6
Hadden Rd SE28	135	R6
Hadden Way, Grnf	86	B11
Haddington Rd, Brom	168	H7
Haddo St SE10	132	D12
Haddon Cl, Borwd	38	A4
Haddon Cl, Enf	44	G12
Haddon Cl, N Mal	179	L9
Haddon Gro, Sid	154	A13
Haddon Rd, Sutt	194	J8
Haddonfield SE8	131	P8
Hadfield Cl, Sthl	103	M6
Hadleigh Cl, E1 *7*	113	L7
Hadleigh Cl SW20	180	E4
Hadleigh Rd N9	44	J13
Hadleigh St E2	113	L6
Hadleigh Wk E6	116	D11
Hadley Cl N21	43	P11
Hadley Common, Barn	40	H4
Hadley Gdns W4	124	G10
Hadley Gdns, Sthl	121	L10
Hadley Grn, Barn	40	E4
Hadley Grn Rd, Barn	40	E4
Hadley Grn W, Barn	40	E4
Hadley Gro, Barn	40	D4
Hadley Highstone, Barn	40	E5
Hadley Ridge, Barn	40	E5
Hadley Rd (New Barnet), Barn	41	K7
Hadley Rd, Belv	137	M7
Hadley Rd, Enf	43	L1
Hadley Rd, Mitch	182	G7
Hadley St NW1	92	C12
Hadley Way N21	43	P12
Hadlow Pl SE19	166	G13
Hadlow Rd, Sid	172	B7
Hadlow Rd, Well	136	F13
Hadrian Cl, Wall	197	K13
Hadrian Est E2	13	T4
Hadrian St SE10	132	J9
Hadrians Ride, Enf	44	F14
Hadyn Pk Rd W12	125	N3
Hafer Rd SW11	145	T8
Hafton Rd SE6	169	K2
Haggard Rd, Twick	140	J14
Haggerston Rd E8	112	F1
Hague St E2	13	U8
Haig Rd, Stan	53	L10
Haig Rd E E13	115	U5
Haig Rd W E13	115	T5
Haigville Gdns, Ilf	81	K7
Hailes Cl SW19	163	L12
Hailey Rd, Erith	137	P4
Haileybury Av, Enf	44	F12
Hailsham Av SW2	165	L4
Hailsham Cl, Surb	177	P3
Hailsham Dr, Har	68	B6
Hailsham Rd SW17	164	B12
Hailsham Ter N18	59	U9
Haimo Rd SE9	152	B9
Hainault Ct E17	78	H8
Hainault Gore, Rom	83	K10
Hainault Gro, Chig	65	L3
Hainault Rd E11	96	E1
Hainault Rd, Chig	65	L8
Hainault Rd, Rom	83	U5
Hainault Rd (Chadwell Heath), Rom	83	M11
Hainault Rd (Hainault), Rom	82	C2
Hainault St SE9	171	K2
Hainault St, Ilf	99	K4
Hainford Cl SE4	149	P7
Haining Cl, W4 *3*	124	B10
Hainthorpe Rd SE27	165	R6
Hainton Cl E1	113	K12
Halberd Ms E5	94	J3
Halbutt Gdns, Dag	101	L6
Halbutt St, Dag	101	L7
Halcomb St N1	112	C2
Halcot Av, Bexh	155	R9
Halcrow St, E1 *3*	113	K10
Haldan Rd E4	62	F12
Haldane Cl N10	58	B13
Haldane Pl SW18	162	J1
Haldane Rd E6	116	C5
Haldane Rd SE28	118	G14
Haldane Rd SW6	126	F13
Haldane Rd, Sthl	103	T13
Haldon Cl, Chig	65	S9
Haldon Rd SW18	144	F11
Hale, The E4	62	G14
Hale, The N17	76	G6
Hale Cl E4	62	E5
Hale Cl, Edg	54	F10
Hale Cl, Orp	203	M7
Hale Dr NW7	54	H11
Hale End Cl, Ruis	66	A12
Hale End Rd E4	62	G12
Hale End Rd E17	78	G3
Hale End Rd, Wdf Grn	78	G1
Hale Gdns, N17 *1*	76	G6
Hale Gdns W3	124	B1
Hale Gro Gdns NW7	54	J9
Hale La NW7	54	G10
Hale La, Edg	54	C10
Hale Path SE27	165	R8
Hale Rd E6	116	D8
Hale Rd N17	76	H6
Hale St E14	114	C13
Hale Wk W7	104	D10
Halefield Rd N17	76	J2
Hales St, SE8 *11*	132	A14
Halesowen Rd, Mord	180	J14
Halesworth Rd SE13	150	C5
Haley Rd NW4	71	U12
Half Acre, Brent	123	N12
Half Acre Rd W7	122	C1
Half Moon Ct EC1	19	T3
Half Moon Cres N1	10	H1
Half Moon La SE24	147	U11
Half Moon St W1	24	J2
Halford Cl, Edg	70	C4
Halford Rd E10	78	G10
Halford Rd SW6	126	H12
Halford Rd, Rich	141	R10
Halfway St, Sid	153	R14
Haliburton Rd, Twick	140	H9
Haliday Wk N1	94	B11
Halidon Cl E9	95	L9
Halifax Rd, Enf	43	U3
Halifax Rd, Grnf	103	S2
Halifax St SE26	167	K7
Halifield Dr, Belv	136	J6
Haling Gro, S Croy	197	T14
Haling Pk, S Croy	197	U11
Haling Pk Gdns, S Croy	197	S11
Haling Pk Rd, S Croy	197	S10
Haling Rd, S Croy	198	A11
Halkin Arc, SW1 *2*	24	C9
Halkin Ms SW1	24	C9
Halkin Pl SW1	24	C10
Halkin St SW1	24	E8
Hall, The SE3	151	N5
Hall Av N18	60	B11
Hall Cl W5	105	R10
Hall Ct, Tedd	156	B9
Hall Dr SE26	167	L9
Hall Dr W7	104	D11
Hall Fm Cl, Stan	53	J7
Hall Fm Dr, Twick	140	A14
Hall Gdns E4	61	U8
Hall Gate NW8	6	H6
Hall La E4	61	S9
Hall La NW4	71	P2

Name	Page	Grid
Hall Pl W2	15	K1
Hall Rd E6	116	F1
Hall Rd E15	96	H7
Hall Rd NW8	6	G7
Hall Rd, Islw	140	A10
Hall Rd, Rom	82	G12
Hall St EC1	11	R5
Hall St N12	57	L9
Hall Vw SE9	170	A4
Hallam Cl, Chis	170	E10
Hallam Gdns, Pnr	51	K14
Hallam Ms W1	16	J2
Hallam Rd N15	75	S8
Hallam Rd SW13	143	S6
Hallam St W1	17	K2
Halley Gdns SE13	150	H7
Halley Rd E7	97	T12
Halley Rd E12	98	B10
Halley St E14	113	R10
Hallfield Est W2	14	F7
Halliards, The, Walt	174	A11
Halliday Sq, Sthl	122	A2
Halliford Rd, Sun	174	A7
Halliford St N1	93	U14
Hallingbury Ct E17	78	D5
Halliwell Rd SW2	147	L11
Halliwick Rd N10	74	A2
Hallmead Rd, Sutt	194	J6
Hallowell Av, Croy	196	J7
Hallowell Cl, Mitch	182	A5
Hallowes Cres, Wat	50	A5
Hallowfield Way, Mitch	181	P6
Hallsville Rd E16	115	L12
Hallswelle Rd NW11	72	E9
Hallywell Cres E6	116	F10
Halons Rd SE9	152	H13
Halpin Pl SE17	36	F4
Halsbrook Rd SE3	152	A5
Halsbury Cl, Stan	52	J9
Halsbury Rd, W12 1	125	R1
Halsbury Rd E, Nthlt	85	U8
Halsbury Rd W, Nthlt	85	S9
Halsend, Hayes	120	C2
Halsey Ms SW3	31	T2
Halsey St SW3	31	T2
Halsham Cres, Bark	99	T11
Halsmere Rd SE5	147	S1
Halstead Cl, Croy 10	197	T5
Halstead Ct N1	12	E4
Halstead Gdns N21	60	A1
Halstead Rd E11	79	R9
Halstead Rd N21	60	A1
Halstead Rd, Enf	44	D7
Halston Cl SW11	145	T11
Halstow Rd NW10	108	A5
Halstow Rd SE10	133	N10
Halsway, Hayes	120	B2
Halt Robin La, Belv	137	S7
Halt Robin Rd, Belv	137	P7
Halter Cl, Borwd	38	G10
Halton Cross St, N1 6	93	S14
Halton Pl, N1 1	111	T1
Halton Rd N1	93	S14
Ham, The, Brent	123	M14
Ham Cl, Rich	159	L5
Ham Common, Rich	159	S8
Ham Fm Rd, Rich	159	P7
Ham Gate Av, Rich	159	P9
Ham Pk Rd E7	97	M13
Ham Pk Rd E15	97	M13
Ham Ridings, Rich	159	T9
Ham St, Rich	159	L3
Ham Vw, Croy	185	S12
Hambalt Rd SW4	146	E10
Hamble Ct, KingsT 2	159	N14
Hamble St SW6	145	K5
Hambledon Gdns SE25	184	F6
Hambledon Pl SE21	166	D2
Hambledon Rd SW18	144	F14
Hambledown Rd, Sid	153	P13
Hambleton Cl, Wor Pk 2	193	U3
Hambridge Way SW2	147	P14
Hambro Av, Brom	201	P1
Hambro Rd SW16	164	H11
Hambrook Rd SE25	184	J6
Hambrough Rd, Sthl	120	J2
Hamden Cres, Dag	101	R5
Hamel Cl, Har	69	N7
Hameway E6	116	G6
Hamfrith Rd E15	97	L11
Hamilton Av N9	44	G13
Hamilton Av, Ilf	81	K8
Hamilton Av, Surb	192	C3
Hamilton Av, Sutt	194	C2
Hamilton Cl N17	76	F6
Hamilton Cl NW8	6	J8
Hamilton Cl, SE16 1	131	S4
Hamilton Cl, Barn	41	S7
Hamilton Cl, Stan	52	E4
Hamilton Ct W5	105	T13
Hamilton Ct, W9 1	6	E6
Hamilton Cres N13	59	P8
Hamilton Cres, Har	85	M5
Hamilton Cres, Houns	130	R10
Hamilton Gdns NW8	6	G5
Hamilton La N5	93	S8
Hamilton Ms, W1 1	24	G5
Hamilton Pk N5	93	S8
Hamilton Pk W N5	93	R8
Hamilton Pl W1	24	F4
Hamilton Pl, Sun	156	C14
Hamilton Rd E15	115	K6
Hamilton Rd E17	77	S4
Hamilton Rd N2	73	L5
Hamilton Rd N9	44	G14
Hamilton Rd NW10	89	N10
Hamilton Rd NW11	72	B14
Hamilton Rd SE27	166	A7
Hamilton Rd SW19	163	K13
Hamilton Rd W4	124	J4
Hamilton Rd W5	105	S13
Hamilton Rd, Barn	41	S7
Hamilton Rd, Bexh	155	K3
Hamilton Rd, Brent	123	N11
Hamilton Rd, Har	68	D7
Hamilton Rd, Hayes	102	C14
Hamilton Rd, Ilf	98	J7
Hamilton Rd, Sid	172	A7
Hamilton Rd, Sthl	121	M1
Hamilton Rd, Th Hth	184	A5
Hamilton Rd, Twick	158	D1
Hamilton Rd, Wat	50	D5
Hamilton Sq SE1	28	E6
Hamilton St SE8	132	A12
Hamilton Ter NW8	6	H8
Hamilton Way N3	56	G12
Hamilton Way N13	59	R8
Hamlea Cl SE12	151	N9
Hamlet, The, SE5	148	B6
Hamlet Cl SE13	151	K8
Hamlet Gdns W6	125	N7
Hamlet Rd SE19	166	F14
Hamlet Sq NW2	90	C5
Hamlet Way, SE1 1	28	E6
Hamlets Way E3	113	T7
Hamlin Cres, Pnr	66	F10
Hamlyn Cl, Edg	53	R5
Hamlyn Gdns SE19	166	C14
Hammelton Rd, Brom	187	M1
Hammers La NW7	55	P8
Hammersmith Br SW13	125	S10
Hammersmith Br W6	125	S10
Hammersmith Br Rd W6	125	T10
Hammersmith Bdy W6	125	U8
Hammersmith Flyover W6	125	U9
Hammersmith Gro W6	125	T7
Hammersmith Rd W6	126	B8
Hammersmith Rd W14	126	B8
Hammersmith Ter W6	125	N10
Hammet Cl, Hayes	102	G9
Hammond Av, Mitch	182	C4
Hammond Cl, Barn	40	D10
Hammond Cl, Grnf 5	86	B9
Hammond Cl, Hmptn	175	N2
Hammond Rd, Enf	45	K4
Hammond Rd, Sthl	121	K6
Hammond St NW5	92	E11
Hammonds Cl, Dag	100	E6
Hamonde Cl, Edg	54	C4
Hampden Av, Beck	185	S4
Hampden Cl, NW1 2	9	T3
Hampden Gurney St, W1 2	15	U7
Hampden La N17	76	F2
Hampden Rd N8	75	N7
Hampden Rd N10	58	B14
Hampden Rd N17	76	G1
Hampden Rd N19	92	H4
Hampden Rd, Beck	185	S4
Hampden Rd, Har	67	U2
Hampden Rd, KingsT	178	B5
Hampden Way N14	58	C2
Hampermill La, Wat	50	B2
Hampshire Cl N18	60	J10
Hampshire Hog La, W6 4	125	R8
Hampshire Rd N22	59	L13
Hampshire St NW5	92	G10
Hampson Way SW8	147	L1
Hampstead Cl SE28	136	C1
Hampstead Gdns NW11	72	G12
Hampstead Gdns, Rom	82	C10
Hampstead Grn NW3	91	R9
Hampstead Gro NW3	91	M6
Hampstead Hts N2	73	M7
Hampstead High St NW3	91	M7
Hampstead Hill Gdns NW3	91	P8
Hampstead La N6	92	A1
Hampstead La NW3	91	N1
Hampstead Rd NW1	9	M5
Hampstead Sq NW3	91	M6
Hampstead Way NW11	72	H11
Hampton Cl N11	58	C10
Hampton Cl NW6	108	G5
Hampton Cl SW20	161	T14
Hampton Ct, N1 2	93	R12
Hampton Ct Av, E Mol	176	B10
Hampton Ct Cres, E Mol	176	B5
Hampton Ct Palace, E Mol	176	E7
Hampton Ct Par, E Mol 1	176	D7
Hampton Ct Rd, E Mol	177	L4
Hampton Ct Rd, Hmptn	175	U3
Hampton Ct Rd, KingsT	177	L4
Hampton Ct Way, E Mol	176	D8
Hampton Ct Way, T Ditt	190	C1
Hampton Fm Ind Est, Felt	157	K5
Hampton La, Felt	157	K8
Hampton Mead, Loug 3	48	J5
Hampton Ms NW10	106	G6
Hampton Ri, Har	69	R12
Hampton Rd E4	61	T9
Hampton Rd E7	97	R9
Hampton Rd E11	96	H2
Hampton Rd, Croy	183	U12
Hampton Rd, Hmptn	158	B10
Hampton Rd, Ilf	99	K8
Hampton Rd, Tedd	158	B10
Hampton Rd, Twick	158	B5
Hampton Rd, Wor Pk	193	P4
Hampton Rd E, Felt	157	M6
Hampton Rd W, Felt	157	K5
Hampton St SE1	35	S3
Hampton St SE17	35	S3
Hamshades Cl, Sid	171	U5
Hanah Ct SW19	162	A13
Hanameel St E16	133	R2
Hanbury Dr N21	43	M9
Hanbury Ms, N1 4	111	U2
Hanbury Rd N17	76	J3
Hanbury Rd W3	124	C4
Hanbury St E1	21	N1
Hancock Ct, Borwd 1	38	F3
Hancock Rd E3	114	E5
Hancock Rd SE19	166	A12
Hand Ct, WC1 4	18	G3
Handcroft Rd, Croy	197	R1
Handel Cl, Edg	53	T11
Handel Pl NW10	88	H11
Handel St WC1	10	B10
Handel Way, Edg	54	A13
Handen Rd SE12	151	L10
Handforth Rd SW9	34	J14
Handforth Rd, Ilf 4	99	K5
Handley Rd E9	95	M14
Handowe Cl NW4	71	P7
Hands Wk E16	115	P11
Handside Cl, Wor Pk 1	194	A2
Handsworth Av E4	62	G11
Handsworth Rd N17	76	B6
Handsworth Way, Wat	50	A5
Handtrough Way, Bark	117	K3
Hanford Cl SW18	162	G1
Hanford Row SW19	161	J11
Hangar Ruding, Wat	51	L6
Hanger Grn W5	106	A7
Hanger La W5	105	T7
Hanger Vale La W5	105	U10
Hanger Vw Way W3	106	A11
Hankey Pl SE1	28	E8
Hankins La NW7	54	J5
Hanley Pl, Beck	168	A14
Hanley Rd N4	93	K2
Hannah Cl NW10	88	F8
Hannah Cl, Beck	186	E5
Hannah Ms, Wall	196	F13
Hannay La N8	74	H13
Hannay Wk SW16	164	H4
Hannell Rd SW6	126	C13
Hannen Rd, SE27 4	165	S6
Hannibal Rd E1	113	M9
Hannibal Way, Croy	197	L11
Hannington Rd SW4	146	D6
Hanover Av E16	133	N1
Hanover Av, Felt	156	A2
Hanover Cl, Rich	124	A13
Hanover Cl, Sutt	194	E7
Hanover Dr, Chis	171	L8
Hanover Gdns SE11	34	J12
Hanover Gdns, Ilf	65	L14
Hanover Pk SE15	148	G2
Hanover Pl E3	113	T6
Hanover Rd N15	76	F8
Hanover Rd NW10	107	U1
Hanover Rd SW19	163	M13
Hanover Sq W1	17	K8
Hanover St W1	17	K8
Hanover St, Croy	197	S6
Hanover Ter NW1	7	T8
Hanover Ter, Islw	140	H1
Hanover Ter Ms NW1	7	S7
Hanover Way, Bexh	154	H6
Hanover W Ind Est NW10	106	G5
Hans Cres SW1	23	U9

Name	Page	Ref
Hans Pl SW1	23	U10
Hans Rd SW3	23	T10
Hans St SW1	24	A11
Hansard Ms W14	126	B3
Hansart Way, Enf	43	P2
Hanselin Cl, Stan	52	F10
Hansen Dr N21	43	L9
Hansha Dr, Edg	70	G1
Hansler Gro, E Mol	176	A8
Hansler Rd SE22	148	F9
Hansol Rd, Bexh	154	J9
Hanson Cl SW12	146	D14
Hanson Cl SW14	142	E5
Hanson Cl, Beck	168	C12
Hanson Cl, Loug	49	L4
Hanson Dr, Loug	49	L4
Hanson Gdns, Sthl	121	K3
Hanson Grn, Loug	49	L3
Hanson St W1	17	L2
Hanway Pl W1	17	S5
Hanway Rd W7	104	B11
Hanway St W1	17	S5
Hanworth Rd, Felt	156	C1
Hanworth Rd, Hmptn	157	R11
Hanworth Rd, Houns	139	S6
Hanworth Rd, Sun	156	B14
Hanworth Ter, Houns	139	R7
Hanworth Trd Est, Felt	157	K5
Hapgood Cl, Grnf	86	A10
Harben Rd NW6	91	M13
Harberson Rd E15	115	L1
Harberson Rd SW12	164	C1
Harberton Rd N19	92	F2
Harbet Rd E4	61	S11
Harbet Rd N18	61	P10
Harbet Rd W2	15	M3
Harbex Cl, Bex	155	R13
Harbinger Rd E14	132	C8
Harbledown Rd SW6	144	G1
Harbord Cl, SE5 11	148	A3
Harbord St SW6	144	A1
Harborne Cl, Wat	50	E10
Harborough Av, Sid	153	S14
Harborough Rd SW16	165	L8
Harbour Av SW10	145	M2
Harbour Ex Sq E14	132	D4
Harbour Rd SE5	147	T5
Harbridge Av SW15	143	N13
Harbury Rd, Cars	195	R14
Harbut Rd SW11	145	N7
Harcombe Rd N16	94	C6
Harcourt Av E12	98	E8
Harcourt Av, Edg	54	E6
Harcourt Av, Sid	154	E13
Harcourt Av, Wall	196	D8
Harcourt Cl, Islw	140	H5
Harcourt Fld, Wall	196	D7
Harcourt Rd E15	115	L3
Harcourt Rd N22	74	G1
Harcourt Rd SE4	149	S7
Harcourt Rd SW19	162	H14
Harcourt Rd, Bexh	155	K7
Harcourt Rd, Th Hth	183	N11
Harcourt Rd, Wall	196	D8
Harcourt St W1	15	S3
Harcourt Ter SW10	30	D8
Hardcastle Cl, Croy 3	184	G11
Hardcourts Cl, W Wick	200	D6
Hardel Ri SW2	165	R3
Hardens Manorway SE7	134	A6
Harders Rd SE15	148	J3
Hardess St SE24	147	T6
Hardie Cl NW10	88	G9
Hardie Rd, Dag	101	T6
Harding Cl, SE17 2	35	T11
Harding Cl, Croy	198	F5
Harding Cl, Bexh	155	L3
Hardinge La, E1 10	113	M12
Hardinge Rd N18	60	C10
Hardinge Rd NW10	107	T2
Hardinge St E1	113	M12
Harding's Cl, Kings T	177	T1
Hardings La SE20	167	N12
Hardman Rd, SE7 3	133	R9
Hardman Rd, Kings T	177	S3
Hardwick Cl, Stan	53	L9
Hardwick Grn W13	105	K9
Hardwick St EC1	11	L7
Hardwicke Av, Houns	139	N1
Hardwicke Rd N13	58	J11
Hardwicke Rd W4	124	G7
Hardwicke Rd, Rich	159	L7
Hardwicke St, Bark	117	L2
Hardwicks Way SW18	144	H10
Hardwidge St SE1	28	H6
Hardy Av E16	133	P1
Hardy Av, Ruis	84	D10
Hardy Cl SE16	131	P4
Hardy Cl, Barn	40	D11
Hardy Cl, Pnr	66	H13
Hardy Rd, E4 3	61	U11
Hardy Rd SE3	133	M12
Hardy Rd SW19	163	K13
Hardy Way, Enf	43	P2
Hare & Billet Rd SE3	150	H3
Hare Ct EC4	19	K8
Hare La, Esher	190	B11
Hare Marsh, E2 1	13	S10
Hare Row, E2 15	113	K3
Hare St SE18	134	H6
Hare Wk N1	12	J3
Harebell Dr E6	116	H10
Harecastle Cl, Hayes	102	J7
Harecourt Rd N1	93	T11
Haredale Rd SE24	147	U8
Haredon Cl SE23	149	M13
Harefield, Esher	190	D7
Harefield Cl, Enf	43	P1
Harefield Ms SE4	149	T5
Harefield Rd N8	74	G9
Harefield Rd SE4	149	T6
Harefield Rd SW16	165	M14
Harefield Rd, Sid	172	G4
Haresfield Rd, Dag	101	P12
Harewood Av NW1	7	S12
Harewood Av, Nthlt	85	L14
Harewood Cl, Nthlt	85	L14
Harewood Dr, Ilf	80	E3
Harewood Pl W1	16	J7
Harewood Rd SW19	163	S12
Harewood Rd, Islw	140	F1
Harewood Rd, S Croy	198	C11
Harewood Rd, Wat	50	D5
Harewood Row NW1	15	S1
Harewood Ter, Sthl	121	M7
Harfield Gdns SE5	148	C5
Harfield Rd, Sun	174	G3
Harford Cl E4	46	D13
Harford Rd E4	46	D13
Harford St E1	113	R8
Harford Wk N2	73	P8
Hargood Cl, Har	69	S11
Hargood Rd SE3	151	U2
Hargrave Pk N19	92	E4
Hargrave Pl N7	92	G10
Hargrave Rd N19	92	F4
Hargwyne St SW9	147	L5
Haringey Pk N8	74	J11
Haringey Pas N4	75	R9
Haringey Pas N8	75	R9
Haringey Rd N8	74	J8
Harington Ter N9	60	A6
Harington Ter N18	60	A6
Harkett Cl, Har	68	E4
Harkett Ct, Har	68	E3
Harland Av, Croy	198	G5
Harland Av, Sid	171	R4
Harland Cl SW19	180	J5
Harland Rd SE12	169	N1
Harlands Gro, Orp	203	K8
Harlech Gdns, Houns	120	F12
Harlech Gdns, Pnr	66	H14
Harlech Rd N14	59	K6
Harlequin Av, Brent	122	H12
Harlequin Cl, Hayes 2	102	G10
Harlequin Cl, Islw	140	C10
Harlequin Rd, Tedd	158	J13
Harlescott Rd SE15	149	N8
Harlesden Gdns NW10	107	L1
Harlesden La NW10	107	N2
Harlesden Rd NW10	107	P1
Harley Cl, Wem	87	N11
Harley Cres, Har	68	B8
Harley Gdns SW10	30	G8
Harley Gdns, Orp	203	R8
Harley Gro E3	113	U5
Harley Pl W1	16	G4
Harley Rd NW3	91	P14
Harley Rd NW10	107	K4
Harley Rd, Har	68	B7
Harley St W1	16	H3
Harleyford, Brom	187	T1
Harleyford Rd SE11	34	F9
Harleyford St SE11	34	J11
Harlinger St SE18	134	C5
Harlington Rd, Bexh	155	K6
Harlington Rd E, Felt	138	D14
Harlington Rd W, Felt	138	C12
Harlow Rd N13	60	A5
Harlyn Dr, Pnr	66	C5
Harman Av, Wdf Grn	63	L13
Harman Cl E4	62	H8
Harman Cl NW2	90	D6
Harman Dr NW2	90	D6
Harman Dr, Sid	153	U12
Harman Rd, Enf	44	E9
Harmony Cl NW11	72	C10
Harmony Way NW4	71	U8
Harmood Gro NW1	92	C13
Harmood Pl NW1	92	C13
Harmood St NW1	92	C12
Harmsworth Ms, SE11 1	27	N12
Harmsworth St SE17	35	N8
Harmsworth Way N20	56	F2
Harness Rd SE28	136	A4
Harold Av, Belv	137	L10
Harold Est SE1	28	J12
Harold Pl SE11	34	J8
Harold Rd E4	62	E6
Harold Rd E11	96	J2
Harold Rd E13	115	S2
Harold Rd N8	75	L9
Harold Rd N15	76	F9
Harold Rd NW10	106	G5
Harold Rd SE19	166	B14
Harold Rd, Sutt	195	N8
Harold Rd, Wdf Grn	79	P1
Haroldstone Rd E17	77	P9
Harp Island Cl NW10	88	H4
Harp La EC3	20	H11
Harp Rd W7	104	E9
Harpenden Rd E12	97	T3
Harpenden Rd SE27	165	R4
Harper Cl, N14 1	42	F9
Harper Rd E6	116	E12
Harper Rd SE1	27	U9
Harpers Yd, N17 1	76	F1
Harpley Sq E1	113	N6
Harpour Rd, Bark	99	L12
Harpsden St, SW11 3	146	A2
Harpur Ms WC1	18	E1
Harpur St WC1	18	E2
Harraden Rd SE3	151	T1
Harrap St E14	114	F14
Harrier Av E11	79	S11
Harrier Ms SE28	135	P4
Harrier Rd NW9	71	K3
Harrier Way E6	116	F10
Harriers Cl W5	105	R14
Harries Rd, Hayes	102	F8
Harriet Cl, E8 1	112	G1
Harriet Gdns, Croy	198	H3
Harriet St SW1	24	A8
Harriet Tubman Cl, SW2 1	147	N14
Harriet Wk SW1	24	A8
Harringay Gdns N8	75	R8
Harringay Rd N15	75	S9
Harrington Cl NW10	88	G6
Harrington Cl, Croy	196	J4
Harrington Gdns SW7	30	E3
Harrington Hill E5	95	K2
Harrington Rd E11	97	K1
Harrington Rd SE25	184	J7
Harrington Rd SW7	31	K2
Harrington Sq NW1	9	M3
Harrington St NW1	9	L5
Harrington Way SE18	134	B5
Harriott Cl SE10	133	L8
Harris Cl, Enf	43	R2
Harris Cl, Houns	139	N2
Harris Rd, Bexh	155	K2
Harris Rd, Dag	101	L10
Harris St E17	77	T14
Harris St SE5	130	B14
Harrison Cl N20	57	S2
Harrison Rd, Dag	101	R12
Harrison St WC1	10	D7
Harrisons Ri, Croy	197	R5
Harrogate Rd, Wat	50	E5
Harrold Rd, Dag	100	D9
Harrow Av, Enf	44	F12
Harrow Cl, Chess	191	N13
Harrow Dr N9	60	E1
Harrow Flds Gdns, Har	86	D5
Harrow La E14	114	E14
Harrow Manorway SE2	136	F3
Harrow Pk, Har	86	D3
Harrow Pl E1	21	K5
Harrow Rd E6	116	C1
Harrow Rd E11	97	K5
Harrow Rd NW10	107	U6
Harrow Rd W2	15	L3
Harrow Rd W9	14	A2
Harrow Rd W10	108	E7
Harrow Rd, Bark	117	S1
Harrow Rd, Cars	195	R11
Harrow Rd, Ilf	99	M8
Harrow Rd, Wem	86	F7
Harrow Rd (Tokyngton), Wem	88	C12
Harrow Vw, Har	68	B10
Harrow Vw, Hayes	102	B12
Harrow Vw Rd W5	105	K7
Harrow Way, Wat	50	J5
Harrow Weald Pk, Har	52	B11
Harroway Rd SW11	145	N4
Harrowby St W1	15	S5
Harrowdene Cl, Wem	87	N8
Harrowdene Gdns, Tedd	158	H13
Harrowdene Rd, Wem	87	N6
Harrowes Meade, Edg	54	B5
Harrowgate Rd E9	95	R12
Hart Cres, Chig	65	U10
Hart Gro W5	124	A2
Hart Gro, Sthl	103	P9
Hart St EC3	20	J10
Harte Rd, Houns	139	M3
Hartfield Av, Borwd	38	A9
Hartfield Av, Nthlt	102	D4
Hartfield Cl, Borwd	38	A10
Hartfield Cres SW19	162	F13
Hartfield Cres, W Wick	201	N6
Hartfield Gro SE20	185	L1
Hartfield Rd SW19	162	G14
Hartfield Rd, Chess	191	P10
Hartfield Rd, W Wick	201	N7
Hartfield Ter E3	114	B4
Hartford Av, Har	68	H6
Hartford Rd, Bex	155	P12
Hartford Rd, Epsom	193	R8
Hartforde Rd, Borwd	38	B3
Hartham Cl N7	93	K10
Hartham Cl, Islw	140	G1

Name	Page	Grid
Hartham Rd N7	92	J10
Hartham Rd, N17 2	76	E3
Hartham Rd, Islw	140	G2
Harting Rd SE9	170	C6
Hartington Cl, Har	86	C8
Hartington Ct W4	124	D14
Hartington Rd E16	115	R12
Hartington Rd E17	77	R11
Hartington Rd SW8	128	J14
Hartington Rd W4	124	D13
Hartington Rd W13	105	K14
Hartington Rd, Sthl	120	J5
Hartington Rd, Twick	140	J13
Hartismere Rd SW6	126	F13
Hartlake Rd E9	95	P12
Hartland Cl N21	43	U12
Hartland Cl, Edg	54	B4
Hartland Dr, Edg	54	C4
Hartland Dr, Ruis	84	D6
Hartland Rd E15	97	L14
Hartland Rd N11	57	U10
Hartland Rd NW1	92	C13
Hartland Rd NW6	108	E3
Hartland Rd, Hmptn	157	S8
Hartland Rd, Islw	140	H5
Hartland Rd, Mord	180	H14
Hartland Way, Croy	199	R4
Hartland Way, Mord	180	F13
Hartlands Cl, Bex	155	M11
Hartley Av E6	116	C2
Hartley Av NW7	55	L10
Hartley Cl NW7	55	L10
Hartley Cl, Brom	188	F4
Hartley Rd E11	97	M1
Hartley Rd, Croy	183	T13
Hartley Rd, Well	166	H3
Hartley St, E2 2	113	M5
Hartmann Rd E16	134	A1
Hartnoll St N7	93	M9
Harton Cl, Brom	188	A1
Harton Rd N9	61	K4
Harton St SE8	150	A1
Harts La SE14	149	R1
Harts La, Bark	99	K12
Hartsbourne Av, Bushey	51	U4
Hartsbourne Cl, Bushey	52	A4
Hartsbourne Rd, Bushey	52	A4
Hartshorn Gdns E6	116	G7
Hartslock Dr SE2	136	G3
Hartsmead Rd SE9	170	E3
Hartsway, Enf	45	K8
Hartswood Gdns W12	125	L5
Hartswood Grn, Bushey	52	A3
Hartswood Rd W12	125	L5
Hartsworth Cl E13	115	M4
Hartville Rd SE18	135	S8
Hartwell Dr E4	62	E12
Hartwell St E8	94	E11
Harvard Hill, W4 4	124	D11
Harvard La W4	124	E10
Harvard Rd SE13	150	F10
Harvard Rd W4	124	D10
Harvard Rd, Islw	140	D2
Harvel Cres SE2	136	H10
Harvest Bank Rd, W Wick	201	M6
Harvest La, T Ditt	176	G12
Harvest Rd, Felt	156	A6
Harvesters Cl, Islw	140	B9
Harvey Dr, Hmptn	175	R2
Harvey Gdns E11	97	L1
Harvey Gdns SE7	133	U9
Harvey Gdns, Loug	49	K5
Harvey Rd E11	97	L1
Harvey Rd N8	75	L9
Harvey Rd, SE5 3	148	A1
Harvey Rd, Houns	139	M13
Harvey Rd, Ilf	99	K10
Harvey Rd, Nthlt	84	F14
Harvey Rd, Walt	174	A14
Harvey St N1	112	B1
Harvill Rd, Sid	172	J10
Harvington Wk E8	94	H13
Harvist Est N7	93	N7
Harvist Rd NW6	108	C4
Harwater Dr, Loug	48	F3
Harwell Pas, N2 1	73	T7
Harwich La EC2	20	J1
Harwood Av, Brom	187	R3
Harwood Av, Mitch	181	S6
Harwood Cl, N12 2	57	S12
Harwood Cl, Wem	87	N7
Harwood Rd SW6	126	H14
Harwood Ter SW6	144	J1
Harwoods Yd N21	43	P13
Hascombe Ter SE5	148	A3
Haselbury Rd N9	60	D6
Haselbury Rd N18	60	D8
Haseley End SE23	149	M14
Haselrigge Rd SW4	146	H8
Haseltine Rd SE26	167	T8
Haselwood Dr, Enf	43	S7
Haskard Rd, Dag	100	G8
Hasker St SW3	31	S1
Haslam Av, Sutt	194	D1
Haslam Cl N1	93	P13
Haslam St SE15	130	F14
Haslemere Av NW4	72	A11
Haslemere Av SW18	162	J3
Haslemere Av W7	122	H6
Haslemere Av W13	122	H6
Haslemere Av, Barn	57	T2
Haslemere Av, Houns	138	E3
Haslemere Av, Mitch	181	N4
Haslemere Cl, Hmptn	157	M10
Haslemere Cl, Wall 4	197	K10
Haslemere Gdns N3	72	E6
Haslemere Heathrow Est, Houns	138	C4
Haslemere Rd N8	74	H13
Haslemere Rd N21	59	R3
Haslemere Rd, Bexh	155	M4
Haslemere Rd, Ilf	99	T3
Haslemere Rd, Th Hth	183	R9
Hasler Cl SE28	118	D13
Hasluck Gdns, Barn	41	K11
Hassard St, E2 1	13	N4
Hassendean Rd SE3	133	R12
Hassett Rd E9	95	P11
Hassock Wd, Kes	202	B8
Hassocks Cl SE26	167	K5
Hassocks Rd SW16	182	G2
Hassop Rd NW2	90	A7
Hassop Wk SE9	170	C7
Hasted Rd SE7	134	A9
Hastings Av, Ilf	81	L8
Hastings Cl SE15	130	G14
Hastings Cl, Barn	41	L7
Hastings Dr, Surb	177	M12
Hastings Rd N11	58	F10
Hastings Rd N17	76	A5
Hastings Rd W13	105	K14
Hastings Rd, Brom	202	D2
Hastings Rd, Croy	188	E1
Hastings St WC1	10	A7
Hastingwood Trd Est N18	61	P11
Hastoe Cl, Hayes	102	J7
Hatch, The, Enf	45	N2
Hatch Gro, Rom	83	K8
Hatch La E4	62	G7
Hatch Pl, Kings T	159	U10
Hatch Rd SW16	183	K3
Hatch Side, Chig	64	H9
Hatcham Pk Ms SE14	149	P1
Hatcham Pk Rd SE14	149	P1
Hatcham Rd SE15	131	L12
Hatchard Rd N19	92	H3
Hatchcroft NW4	71	N6
Hatchwood Cl, Wdf Grn	63	M7
Hatcliffe Cl SE3	151	L5
Hatcliffe St SE10	133	L9
Hatfield Cl SE14	131	N14
Hatfield Cl, Ilf	81	K5
Hatfield Cl, Mitch	181	N8
Hatfield Mead, Mord	180	G10
Hatfield Rd E15	97	K9
Hatfield Rd W4	124	H3
Hatfield Rd W13	122	G2
Hatfield Rd, Dag	101	K13
Hatfields SE1	27	M2
Hatfields, Loug	48	J6
Hathaway Cl, Brom	202	E2
Hathaway Cl, Stan	52	G10
Hathaway Cres E12	98	F11
Hathaway Gdns W13	104	F10
Hathaway Gdns, Rom	82	G9
Hathaway Rd, Croy	183	S14
Hatherleigh Cl, Chess	191	N9
Hatherleigh Cl, Mord	180	H8
Hatherleigh Rd, Ruis	84	A4
Hatherley Cres, Sid	172	B4
Hatherley Gdns E6	116	B4
Hatherley Gdns N8	74	J11
Hatherley Gro W2	14	B6
Hatherley Ms E17	78	A7
Hatherley Rd E17	78	A7
Hatherley Rd, Rich	141	U3
Hatherley Rd, Sid	172	B6
Hatherley St SW1	33	P3
Hathern Gdns SE9	170	G8
Hatherop Rd, Hmptn	157	L13
Hathorne Cl SE15	149	K3
Hathway St, SE15 8	149	N4
Hatley Av, Ilf	81	L8
Hatley Cl N11	57	T9
Hatley Rd N4	93	M3
Hatteraick St, SE16 4	131	L3
Hattersfield Cl, Belv	137	M7
Hatton Cl SE18	135	N14
Hatton Gdn EC1	19	L2
Hatton Gdns, Mitch	181	U9
Hatton Grn, Felt	138	A8
Hatton Pl EC1	19	L1
Hatton Rd, Croy 2	197	P1
Hatton Row, NW8 2	7	L12
Hatton St NW8	7	L12
Hatton Wall EC1	19	K1
Haunch of Venison Yd, W1 1	16	H9
Havana Rd SW19	162	H4
Havannah St, E14 4	132	B4
Havant Rd E17	78	E6
Havelock Pl, Har	68	D12
Havelock Rd N17	76	H4
Havelock Rd SW19	163	L9
Havelock Rd, Belv	137	L8
Havelock Rd, Brom	187	U7
Havelock Rd, Croy	198	F2
Havelock Rd, Har	68	C5
Havelock Rd, Sthl	121	P5
Havelock St N1	111	K1
Havelock St, Ilf	99	K4
Havelock Ter SW8	128	D14
Havelock Wk SE23	167	M2
Haven, The, SE26 2	167	K10
Haven, The, Rich	142	B5
Haven Cl SE9	170	E5
Haven Cl SW19	162	A5
Haven Cl, Sid	172	D12
Haven Grn W5	105	P13
Haven Grn Ct W5	105	R12
Haven La W5	105	R12
Haven Pl W5	105	P13
Haven St NW1	92	C14
Havenhurst Ri, Enf	43	N4
Havenwood, Wem	88	D5
Haverfield Gdns, Rich	113	A13
Haverfield Rd E3	113	R5
Haverford Way, Edg	69	U2
Haverhill Rd, E4 1	62	E1
Haverhill Rd SW12	164	F1
Havering Gdns, Rom	82	G9
Havering St E1	113	N12
Havering Way, Bark	118	C5
Haversfield Est, Brent	123	S11
Haversham Cl, Twick	141	P12
Haversham Pl N6	91	U3
Haverstock Hill NW3	91	U12
Haverstock Rd NW5	92	A10
Haverstock St N1	11	S4
Haverthwaite Rd, Orp	203	P5
Havil St SE5	130	C14
Havisham Pl SE19	165	S12
Hawarden Gro SE24	147	T13
Hawarden Hill NW2	89	P6
Hawarden Rd E17	77	P8
Hawbridge Rd E11	96	G1
Hawes La, W Wick	200	F1
Hawes Rd N18	60	J11
Hawes Rd, Brom	187	R1
Hawes St N1	93	S14
Hawgood St E3	114	B10
Hawkdene E4	46	D11
Hawke Pk Rd N22	75	S5
Hawke Rd SE19	166	C11
Hawker Cl, Wall	197	K13
Hawkes Rd, Mitch	181	T1
Hawkesbury Rd SW15	143	R9
Hawkesfield Rd SE23	167	S4
Hawkesley Cl, Twick	158	F7
Hawkewood Rd, Sun	174	B5
Hawkhurst Gdns, Chess	191	R7
Hawkhurst Rd SW16	182	H1
Hawkhurst Way, N Mal	178	G9
Hawkhurst Way, W Wick	200	C3
Hawkins Cl NW7	54	G9
Hawkins Cl, Borwd	38	F3
Hawkins Cl, Har	68	A13
Hawkins Rd, Tedd	159	K12
Hawkins Way SE6	168	B9
Hawkley Gdns SE27	165	S4
Hawkridge Cl, Rom	82	F12
Hawks Ms, SE10 8	132	F14
Hawks Rd, Kings T	177	U4
Hawksbrook La, Beck	186	C11
Hawkshaw Cl, SW2 2	146	J14
Hawkshead Cl, Brom	169	K13
Hawkshead Rd NW10	89	L13
Hawkshead Rd W4 1	124	J4
Hawksdale Rd SE15	149	N9
Hawksley Rd N16	94	C5
Hawksmoor Cl E6	116	C11
Hawksmoor Cl SE18	135	S9
Hawksmoor Ms E1	112	J13
Hawksmoor St, W6 3	126	B12
Hawksmouth E4	46	D14
Hawkstone Rd SE16	131	M7
Hawkwood Cres E4	46	D11
Hawkwood La, Chis	189	L2
Hawkwood Mt E5	95	K1
Hawlands Dr, Pnr	66	J13
Hawley Cl, Hmptn	157	L12
Hawley Cres NW1	92	D14
Hawley Ms, NW1 3	92	C13
Hawley Rd N18	61	P10
Hawley Rd NW1	92	D13
Hawley St NW1	92	C13
Hawstead Rd SE6	150	C12
Hawsted, Buck H	47	S14
Hawthorn Av N13	59	K9
Hawthorn Av, Cars	196	B13
Hawthorn Av, Th Hth	183	R2
Hawthorn Cen, Har	68	F8
Hawthorn Cl, Hmptn	157	N10
Hawthorn Cl, Houns	120	C14
Hawthorn Cl, Orp	189	N11
Hawthorn Cres SW17	164	A10

Hawthorn Dr, Har	67	M12
Hawthorn Dr, W Wick	201	K8
Hawthorn Gdns W5	123	P6
Hawthorn Gro SE20	167	K14
Hawthorn Gro, Barn	39	M12
Hawthorn Hatch, Brent	123	K14
Hawthorn Ms NW7	72	C2
Hawthorn Pl, Erith	137	U10
Hawthorn Rd N8	74	H6
Hawthorn Rd N18	60	E11
Hawthorn Rd NW10	89	P13
Hawthorn Rd, Bexh	155	M8
Hawthorn Rd, Brent	123	K14
Hawthorn Rd, Buck H	64	A8
Hawthorn Rd, Sutt	195	R11
Hawthorn Rd, Wall	196	C13
Hawthornden Cl, N12 **3**	57	S12
Hawthorndene Cl, Brom	201	M3
Hawthorndene Rd, Brom	201	M3
Hawthorne Av, Har	68	H11
Hawthorne Av, Mitch	181	P3
Hawthorne Av, Ruis	66	C13
Hawthorne Cl N1	94	C11
Hawthorne Cl, Brom	188	E6
Hawthorne Fm Av, Nthlt	103	K2
Hawthorne Gro NW9	70	F13
Hawthorne Ms, Grnf	103	U12
Hawthorne Rd E17	78	B5
Hawthorne Rd, Brom	188	E6
Hawthorne Way N9	60	E4
Hawthorns, Wdf Grn	63	N5
Hawthorns, The, Epsom	193	M13
Hawthorns, The, Loug	48	G7
Hawtrey Av, Nthlt	102	G3
Hawtrey Dr, Ruis	66	A14
Hawtrey Rd NW3	91	R14
Haxted Rd, Brom	187	S2
Hay Cl E15	97	K13
Hay Cl, Borwd	38	F3
Hay Currie St E14	114	D11
Hay Hill W1	17	K12
Hay La NW9	70	F8
Hay St E2	112	H2
Haycroft Gdns NW10	107	P2
Haycroft Rd SW2	147	K10
Haycroft, Surb	191	R4
Hayday Rd E16	115	N9
Hayden Way, Rom	83	U3
Haydens Pl W11	108	E11
Haydns Ms, W3 **1**	106	F12
Haydock Av, Nthlt	85	N11
Haydock Grn, Nthlt	85	N11
Haydon Cl NW9	70	F8
Haydon Cl, Enf	44	C11
Haydon Dr, Pnr	66	C7
Haydon Pk Rd SW19	162	J9
Haydon Rd, Dag	100	F4
Haydon St EC3	21	M9
Haydons Rd SW19	163	L11
Hayes Bypass, Hayes	102	G5
Hayes Chase, W Wick	186	J11
Hayes Cl, Brom	201	P4
Hayes Ct SW2	164	J1
Hayes Cres NW11	72	E9
Hayes Cres, Sutt	194	B7
Hayes Gdn, Brom	201	N2
Hayes Hill, Brom	201	K2
Hayes Hill Rd, Brom	201	L2
Hayes La, Beck	186	E6
Hayes La, Brom	187	S8
Hayes Mead Rd, Brom	201	K1
Hayes Metro Cen, Hayes	102	E14
Hayes Pl NW1	7	S12
Hayes Rd, Brom	187	P7
Hayes Rd, Sthl	120	D7

Hayes St, Brom	201	R1
Hayes Way, Beck	186	E6
Hayes Wd Av, Brom	201	R2
Hayesford Pk Dr, Brom	187	M9
Hayfield Pas E1	113	M8
Hayfield Yd E1	113	M8
Haygarth Pl, SW19 **1**	162	B10
Haygreen Cl, Kings T	160	C12
Hayland Cl NW9	70	G8
Hayles St SE11	35	P1
Haylett Gdns, Kings T	177	P8
Hayling Av, Felt	156	A6
Hayling Rd, Wat	50	G4
Haymarket SW1	17	S12
Haymer Gdns, Wor Pk	193	P5
Haymerle Rd SE15	37	S12
Haymill Cl, Grnf	104	E5
Hayne Rd, Beck	185	U2
Hayne St EC1	19	S2
Haynes Cl N11	58	A5
Haynes Cl N17	60	J13
Haynes Cl SE3	151	K6
Haynes La SE19	166	D12
Haynes Rd, Wem	87	R13
Haynt Wk SW20	180	C5
Hay's La SE1	28	G2
Hay's Ms W1	16	H12
Haysleigh Gdns SE20	184	J4
Hayter Rd SW2	147	L9
Hayward Cl SW19	163	K14
Hayward Gdns SW15	143	U11
Hayward Rd N20	57	L4
Hayward Rd, T Ditt	190	G1
Haywards Cl, Rom	82	D10
Hayward's Pl EC1	11	N11
Haywood Cl, Pnr	66	G4
Haywood Ri, Orp	203	S8
Haywood Rd, Brom	188	A7
Hayworth Cl, Enf	45	S4
Hazel Cl N13	60	A6
Hazel Cl N19	92	E4
Hazel Cl SE15	148	H4
Hazel Cl, Brent	123	K13
Hazel Cl, Croy	199	N1
Hazel Cl, Mitch	182	H8
Hazel Cl, Twick	140	A13
Hazel Gdns, Edg	54	C7
Hazel Gro SE26	167	P8
Hazel Gro, Enf	44	G12
Hazel Gro, Orp	202	J3
Hazel Gro, Rom	82	J5
Hazel Gro, Wem	105	S2
Hazel Gro Est SE26	167	P8
Hazel La, Rich	159	R4
Hazel Mead, Barn	39	R9
Hazel Rd E15	96	J9
Hazel Rd NW10	107	T5
Hazel Wk, Brom	188	H12
Hazel Way E4	61	T11
Hazelbank, Surb	192	E2
Hazelbank Rd SE6	168	J4
Hazelbourne Rd SW12	146	D12
Hazelbrouck Gdns, Ilf	65	P13
Hazelbury Cl SW19	180	H3
Hazelbury Grn N9	60	D6
Hazelbury La N9	60	D6
Hazelcroft, Pnr	51	R12
Hazeldean Rd NW10	88	H14
Hazeldene Dr, Pnr	66	F5
Hazeldene Rd, Ilf	100	D3
Hazeldene Rd, Well	154	E4
Hazeldon Rd SE4	149	S10
Hazeleigh Gdns, Wdf Grn	64	D10
Hazelgreen Cl N21	59	S1
Hazelhurst, Beck	186	G2
Hazelhurst Rd SW17	163	M7
Hazell Cres, Rom	83	R1
Hazellville Rd N19	92	H1
Hazelmere Cl, Nthlt	103	M3
Hazelmere Dr, Nthlt	103	M3

Hazelmere Rd NW6	108	F2
Hazelmere Rd, Nthlt	103	M3
Hazelmere Rd, Orp	189	N7
Hazelmere Wk, Nthlt	103	M3
Hazelmere Way, Brom	187	N12
Hazeltree La, Nthlt	103	K6
Hazelwood, Loug	48	A9
Hazelwood Av, Mord	181	K7
Hazelwood Cl W5	123	S3
Hazelwood Cl, Har	67	R8
Hazelwood Cl, NW10 **1**	88	J6
Hazelwood Cres N13	59	P7
Hazelwood Cft, Surb	177	S11
Hazelwood Dr, Pnr	66	C4
Hazelwood La N13	59	P7
Hazelwood Pk Cl, Chig	65	S10
Hazelwood Rd E17	77	R9
Hazelwood Rd, Enf	44	F11
Hazlebury Rd SW6	145	K3
Hazledean Rd, Croy	198	B4
Hazledene Rd W4	124	E11
Hazlemere Gdns, Wor Pk	193	P2
Hazlewell Rd SW15	143	T9
Hazlewood Cl E5	95	R6
Hazlewood Cres W10	108	D8
Hazlitt Rd W14	126	C6
Head St E1	113	N12
Headcorn Pl, Th Hth	183	M7
Headcorn Rd N17	60	E14
Headcorn Rd, Brom	169	M9
Headcorn Rd, Th Hth	183	M7
Headfort Pl SW1	24	F7
Headingley Cl, Ilf	65	U12
Headington Rd SW18	163	M3
Headlam Rd SW4	146	G12
Headlam St E1	113	K8
Headley App, Ilf	80	H10
Headley Av, Wall	197	M9
Headley Cl, Epsom	192	B11
Headley Ct SE26	167	L9
Headley Dr, Croy	200	F13
Headley Dr, Ilf	81	K11
Head's Ms, W11 **5**	108	G12
Headstone Dr, Har	68	D6
Headstone Gdns, Har	67	U7
Headstone La, Har	67	S4
Headstone Rd, Har	68	C10
Headway Cl, Rich **2**	159	L8
Heald St SE14	150	A1
Healey Dr, Orp	203	U7
Healey St NW1	92	C12
Hearn Ri, Nthlt	102	H1
Hearn St EC2	12	J12
Hearne Rd W4	124	A11
Hearn's Bldgs SE17	36	F4
Hearnville Rd SW12	164	A1
Heath, The, W7 **3**	122	C2
Heath Av, Bexh	136	G12
Heath Brow NW3	91	L5
Heath Cl NW11	72	J14
Heath Cl W5	105	U8
Heath Ct, Houns	139	M8
Heath Dr NW3	90	J8
Heath Dr SW20	179	U7
Heath Gdns, Twick	158	E2
Heath Gro SE20	167	L14
Heath Hurst Rd NW3	91	R8
Heath La SE3	150	H4
Heath Mead SW19	162	A5
Heath Pk Dr, Brom	188	C5
Heath Pas NW3	91	K3
Heath Ri SW15	144	B11
Heath Ri, Brom	187	M11
Heath Rd SW8	146	D4
Heath Rd, Bex	173	U1
Heath Rd, Har	67	U13
Heath Rd, Houns	139	S8
Heath Rd, Rom	82	J14
Heath Rd, Th Hth	183	U5
Heath Rd, Twick	158	F2
Heath Side NW3	91	P7

Heath Side, Orp	189	M14
Heath St NW3	91	M8
Heath Vw N2	73	M7
Heath Vw Cl N2	73	L7
Heath Vil SE18	135	T10
Heath Way, Erith	155	U1
Heatham Pk, Twick	140	E14
Heathbourne Rd, Bushey	52	D3
Heathbourne Rd, Stan	52	D3
Heathcote Av, Ilf	80	F3
Heathcote Gro E4	62	E5
Heathcote Rd, Twick	141	K11
Heathcote St WC1	10	E9
Heathcroft NW11	91	K1
Heathcroft W5	105	U8
Heathdale Av, Houns	139	K6
Heathdene Dr, Belv	137	R8
Heathdene Rd SW16	165	L14
Heathdene Rd, Wall	196	C13
Heathedge SE26	167	K4
Heather Cl E6	116	H12
Heather Cl SE13	150	H13
Heather Cl SW8	146	C5
Heather Cl, Hmptn	175	M1
Heather Cl, Islw	140	B9
Heather Dr, Enf	43	R3
Heather Gdns NW11	72	C11
Heather Gdns, Sutt **1**	194	G12
Heather Pk Dr, Wem	88	A14
Heather Rd E4	61	U11
Heather Rd NW2	89	M4
Heather Rd SE12	169	P3
Heather Wk, Edg	54	D9
Heather Way, Stan	52	F12
Heatherbank SE9	152	F4
Heatherbank, Chis	188	H3
Heatherdale Cl, Kings T	160	B12
Heatherdene Cl N12	57	M14
Heatherdene Cl, Mitch	181	P8
Heatherlands, Sun	156	A12
Heatherley Dr, Ilf	80	D5
Heatherset Gdns SW16	165	L14
Heatherside Rd, Epsom	192	G14
Heatherside Rd, Sid	172	T5
Heatherwood Cl E12	97	T4
Heathfield E4	62	E5
Heathfield, Chis	171	M12
Heathfield Av SW18	145	P13
Heathfield Cl E16	116	A9
Heathfield Cl, Kes	201	T9
Heathfield Dr, Mitch	181	R1
Heathfield Gdns NW11	72	B12
Heathfield Gdns, SW18 **5**	145	N11
Heathfield Gdns W4	124	F10
Heathfield Gdns, Croy **5**	198	A7
Heathfield La, Chis	171	K11
Heathfield N, Twick	140	E13
Heathfield Pk NW2	89	T12
Heathfield Pk Dr, Rom	82	C10
Heathfield Rd SW18	145	N11
Heathfield Rd W3	124	C3
Heathfield Rd, Bexh	155	L8
Heathfield Rd, Brom	169	M14
Heathfield Rd, Croy	198	A7
Heathfield Rd, Kes	201	U10
Heathfield S, Twick	140	E13
Heathfield Sq SW18	145	N13
Heathfield Ter SE18	135	S11
Heathfield Ter W4	124	F9
Heathfields Ct, Houns **1**	139	K9
Heathgate NW11	72	J11
Heathland Rd N16	94	C1
Heathlands Cl, Twick	158	E3
Heathlands Way, Houns	139	K9
Heathlee Rd SE3	151	L7

Heathley End, Chis	171	L11
Heathmans Rd SW6	144	F2
Heathrow	120	F2
Interchange,		
Hayes		
Heathrow Int Trd	138	D6
Est, Houns		
Heaths Cl, Enf	44	C4
Heathside, Esher	190	D5
Heathside, Houns	139	M14
Heathside Av, Bexh	155	K3
Heathside Cl, Esher	190	C5
Heathstan Rd W12	107	P12
Heathview Cl,	162	A3
SW19 1		
Heathview Dr SE2	136	G11
Heathview Gdns	143	T13
SW15		
Heathview Rd, Th	183	N7
Hth		
Heathville Rd N19	75	K14
Heathwall St SW11	145	U5
Heathway SE3	133	N14
Heathway, Croy	199	U5
Heathway, Dag	101	N14
Heathway, Wdf Grn	63	U8
Heathwood Gdns	134	C9
SE7		
Heaton Cl E4	62	F0
Heaton Rd SE15	148	J5
Heaton Rd, Mitch	164	A13
Heaver Rd,	145	P5
SW11 16		
Heavitree Cl SE18	135	N10
Heavitree Rd SE18	135	N10
Hebdon Rd SW17	163	S6
Heber Rd NW2	90	A9
Heber Rd SE22	148	F11
Hebron Rd W6	125	S6
Hecham Cl E17	77	R3
Heckfield Pl,	126	G14
SW6 6		
Heckford St E1	113	P13
Hector St SE18	135	R8
Heddington Gro N7	93	L9
Heddon Cl, Islw	140	G7
Heddon Ct Av, Barn	41	U9
Heddon Rd, Barn	41	U9
Heddon St W1	17	M10
Hedge Hill, Enf	43	R2
Hedge La N13	59	R5
Hodgo Wk SE6	168	C8
Hedgeley, Ilf	80	E8
Hedgemans Rd, Dag	100	G13
Hedgemans Way,	100	J12
Dag		
Hedger St SE11	35	P1
Hedgerley Gdns,	103	T4
Grnf		
Hedgers Gro E9	95	R12
Hedgewood Gdns,	80	G8
Ilf		
Hedgley St SE12	151	L9
Hedingham Cl,	93	T14
N1 5		
Hedingham Rd, Dag	100	C10
Hedley Rd, Twick	139	N13
Hedley Row N5	94	A9
Heenan Cl, Bark 3	99	M12
Heene Rd, Enf	44	A2
Heidegger Cres	125	S13
SW13		
Heigham Rd E6	98	C14
Heighton Gdns, Croy	197	R9
Heights, The SE7	133	U10
Heights, The, Beck	168	F14
Heights, The, Loug	48	E4
Heights, The, Nthlt	85	M9
Heights Cl SW20	161	S14
Heiron St SE17	35	S11
Helby Rd SW4	146	H12
Helder Gro SE12	151	M14
Helder St, S Croy	198	A11
Heldmann Cl, Houns	140	B7
Helen Av, Felt	138	C13
Helen Cl N2	73	L5
Helen Cl, W Mol	175	R8
Helen St SE18	135	K8
Helena Cl, Wall	197	L14
Helena Rd E13	115	N4

Helena Rd E17	78	A10
Helena Rd NW10	89	R9
Helena Rd W5	105	P9
Helena Sq, SE16 4	113	R14
Helen's Pl E2	113	L5
Helenslea Av NW11	90	F2
Helix Gdns SW2	147	M11
Helix Rd SW2	147	M11
Hellings St E1	29	T3
Helme Cl SW19	162	F10
Helmet Row EC1	12	A9
Helmsdale Rd SW16	182	G1
Helmsley Pl E8	94	J14
Helsinki Sq,	131	S5
SE16 9		
Helston Cl, Pnr	51	M14
Helvetia St SE6	167	T4
Hemans St SW8	33	U14
Hemberton Rd SW9	146	J5
Hemery Rd,	86	A9
Grnf 3		
Heming Rd, Edg	54	C13
Hemingford Cl,	57	N10
N12 3		
Hemingford Rd N1	93	M14
Hemingford Rd,	193	U8
Sutt		
Hemington Av N11	57	T9
Hemlock Rd W12	107	M14
Hemming Cl,	175	N1
Hmptn 1		
Hemming St E1	13	U11
Hemmings Cl, Sid	172	C4
Hemp Wk SE17	36	E2
Hempstead Cl,	63	N4
Buck H		
Hempstead Rd E17	78	G4
Hemsby Rd, Chess	191	T12
Hemstal Rd NW6	90	G13
Hemswell Dr NW9	70	J1
Hemsworth Ct,	12	G1
N1 4		
Hemsworth St N1	12	G1
Hemus Pl SW3	31	R7
Henbury Way, Wat	50	G5
Henchman St W12	107	L11
Hendale Av NW4	71	R6
Henderson Cl NW10	88	F11
Henderson Dr NW8	7	K9
Henderson Rd E7	97	T11
Henderson Rd N9	60	J1
Henderson Rd SW18	145	R13
Henderson Rd, Croy	184	A11
Henderson Rd,	102	B6
Hayes		
Hendham Rd SW17	163	S4
Hendon Av N3	72	D2
Hendon La N3	72	C6
Hendon Pk Row	72	F11
NW11		
Hendon Rd N9	60	H3
Hendon Way NW2	90	D3
Hendon Way NW4	71	T11
Hendon Wd La NW7	39	L12
Hendre Rd SE1	36	J3
Hendren Cl, Grnf	86	B10
Hendrick Av SW12	145	U13
Heneage St E1	21	P2
Henfield Cl N19	72	F2
Henfield Cl, Bex	155	P11
Henfield Rd SW19	180	E2
Hengelo Gdns,	181	N8
Mitch		
Hengist Rd SE12	151	S13
Hengist Rd, Erith	137	S13
Hengist Way, Brom	186	J7
Hengrave Rd SE23	149	M13
Hengrove Ct, Bex	173	K1
Henley Av, Sutt	194	C4
Henley Cl, Grnf	103	U4
Henley Cl, Islw	142	E2
Henley Ct N14	42	E14
Henley Cross SE3	151	S6
Henley Dr SE1	37	N1
Henley Dr, Kings T	161	L13
Henley Gdns, Pnr	66	C6
Henley Gdns, Rom	82	J9
Henley Rd E16	134	F3
Henley Rd N18	60	C7
Henley Rd NW10	107	U1

Henley Rd, Ilf	99	K8
Henley St SW11	146	B3
Henley Way, Felt	156	H9
Hennel Cl SE23	167	M5
Henniker Gdns E6	116	B5
Henniker Ms SW3	30	J9
Henniker Rd E15	96	H10
Henning St SW11	145	R2
Henningham Rd N17	76	A1
Henrietta Cl SE8	132	B11
Henrietta Ms,	10	C9
WC1 2		
Henrietta Pl W1	16	G7
Henrietta St E15	96	F9
Henrietta St WC2	18	C10
Henriques St E1	21	T6
Henry Cooper Way	170	A6
SE9		
Henry Darlot Dr	56	B10
NW7		
Henry Dickens Ct	108	B14
W11		
Henry Doulton Dr	164	B7
SW17		
Henry Jackson Rd	144	A6
SW15		
Henry Macaulay	177	P2
Av, Kings T		
Henry Rd E6	116	D3
Henry Rd N4	93	S2
Henry Rd, Barn	41	N9
Henry St, Brom	187	S1
Henry's Av, Wdf Grn	63	L10
Henry's Wk, Ilf	65	N13
Henryson Rd SE4	150	A9
Hensford Gdns,	167	K7
SE26 1		
Henshall St, N1 2	94	B11
Henshaw St SE17	36	D2
Henshawe Rd, Dag	100	H6
Henslowe Rd SE22	148	H10
Henson Av NW2	89	T9
Henson Cl, Orp	203	K4
Henson Path, Har	69	N7
Henson Pl, Nthlt	7	N1
Henty Cl SW11	127	S14
Henty Wk SW15	143	R10
Henville Rd, Brom	187	S2
Henwick Rd SE9	152	C6
Henwood Side,	64	F11
Wdf Grn		
Hepburn Gdns, Brom	201	K2
Hepburn Ms,	145	U10
SW11 1		
Hepple Cl, Islw	140	J4
Hepplestone Cl,	143	S12
SW15 1		
Hepscott Rd E9	96	A13
Hepworth Gdns,	100	B9
Bark		
Hepworth Rd SW16	165	K14
Hepworth Wk NW3	91	S10
Heracles Cl, Wall	196	J14
Herald Gdns, Wall	196	C4
Herald St, E2 7	113	K7
Herald's Ct,	35	N3
SE11 1		
Herald's Pl SE11	35	M2
Herbal Hill EC1	11	L11
Herbert Cres SW1	24	A10
Herbert Gdns NW10	107	S3
Herbert Gdns W4	124	C12
Herbert Gdns, Rom	82	H13
Herbert Pl SE18	135	K11
Herbert Rd E12	98	C8
Herbert Rd E17	77	T13
Herbert Rd N11	58	J13
Herbert Rd N15	76	F9
Herbert Rd NW9	71	N12
Herbert Rd SE18	134	H14
Herbert Rd SW19	162	F13
Herbert Rd, Bexh	155	R3
Herbert Rd, Brom	188	B9
Herbert Rd, Ilf	99	R3
Herbert Rd, Kings T	177	T6
Herbert Rd, Sthl	121	L1
Herbert St E13	115	P4
Herbert St NW5	92	A11
Herbert Ter SE18	134	J13

Herbrand St WC1	10	A10
Hercules Pl, N7 1	93	K6
Hercules Rd SE1	26	J10
Hercules St N7	93	K6
Hereford Av, Barn	57	T2
Hereford Gdns, Ilf	80	D13
Hereford Gdns, Pnr	66	J9
Hereford Gdns,	157	U2
Twick		
Hereford Ms W2	108	H12
Hereford Pl SE14	131	T13
Hereford Retreat	37	S13
SE15		
Hereford Rd E11	79	S9
Hereford Rd W2	108	H13
Hereford Rd W3	106	D13
Hereford Rd W5	123	M6
Hereford Rd, Felt	156	F1
Hereford Sq SW7	30	G3
Hereford St E2	13	S9
Hereford Way,	191	N9
Chess		
Herent Dr, Ilf	80	D7
Hereward Gdns N13	59	P10
Hereward Grn, Loug	49	L2
Hereward Rd SW17	163	S7
Herga Ct, Har	86	D5
Herga Rd, Har	68	E7
Heriot Av E4	62	A4
Heriot Rd NW4	71	U9
Heriots Cl, Stan	52	H7
Heritage Cl SW9	147	S6
Heritage Hill, Kes	201	T9
Heritage Vw, Har	86	F5
Herlwyn Gdns SW17	163	T7
Hermes St, N1 7	10	J4
Hermes Way, Wall	196	H13
Hermiston Av N8	75	K9
Hermit Pl NW6	108	H2
Hermit Rd E16	115	L9
Hermit St EC1	11	N6
Hermitage, The	167	L1
SE23		
Hermitage, The	143	M2
SW13		
Hermitage, The,	141	R10
Rich		
Hermitage Cl E18	79	M8
Hermitage Cl, Enf	43	S4
Hermitage Cl, Esher	190	G11
Hermitage Ct E18	79	N8
Hermitage Ct NW2	90	G5
Hermitage Gdns	90	G5
NW2		
Hermitage Gdns	165	U12
SE19		
Hermitage La N18	60	B9
Hermitage La NW2	90	G5
Hermitage La SE25	184	G12
Hermitage La SW16	165	L14
Hermitage La, Croy	184	G13
Hermitage Path,	183	K1
SW16 1		
Hermitage Rd N4	75	S13
Hermitage Rd N15	76	A11
Hermitage Rd SE19	166	A11
Hermitage Row,	94	H10
E8 2		
Hermitage St,	15	K3
W2 1		
Hermitage Wk E18	79	M7
Hermitage Wall E1	29	T3
Hermitage Way,	68	H2
Stan		
Hermon Gro, Hayes	120	B2
Hermon Hill E11	79	P7
Hermon Hill E18	79	P7
Herndon Rd SW18	145	L10
Herne Cl NW10	88	H10
Herne Hill SE24	147	T10
Herne Hill Rd SE24	147	T6
Herne Ms, N18 8	60	H8
Herne Pl SE24	147	S10
Herne Rd, Surb	191	P3
Heron Cl E17	77	T3
Heron Cl NW10	89	K12
Heron Ct, Buck H	63	P7
Heron Ct, Brom	187	U8
Heron Cres, Sid	171	R7
Heron Dr N4	93	T4

Heron Hill, Belv	137	M8
Heron Ms, Ilf	98	J4
Heron Pl SE16	131	S1
Heron Quay E14	132	A2
Heron Rd SE24	147	T7
Heron Rd, Croy	198	D3
Heron Rd, Twick	140	H8
Herondale Av SW18	163	P2
Herongate Rd E12	97	U3
Herons, The E11	79	M12
Heron's Pl, Islw	140	J6
Herons Ri, Barn	41	S8
Heronsforde W13	105	L11
Heronsgate, Edg	54	B10
Heronslea Dr, Stan	53	R9
Heronway, Wdf Grn	63	U8
Herrick Rd N5	93	T5
Herrick St SW1	33	U4
Herries St W10	108	D4
Herringham Rd SE7	133	U6
Herrongate Cl, Enf	44	E4
Hersant Cl NW10	107	P1
Herschell Rd SE23	149	P14
Hersham Cl SW15	143	P14
Hertford Av SW14	142	J8
Hertford Cl, Barn	41	N5
Hertford Pl W1	9	M12
Hertford Rd N1	112	D1
Hertford Rd N2	73	R5
Hertford Rd N9	60	J3
Hertford Rd, Bark	98	J13
Hertford Rd, Barn	41	M6
Hertford Rd, Enf	45	L11
Hertford Rd, Ilf	81	R11
Hertford St W1	24	G4
Hertford Way, Mitch	182	J8
Hertslet Rd N7	93	L6
Hertsmere Rd E14	114	A14
Hervey Cl N3	72	H2
Hervey Pk Rd E17	77	S7
Hervey Rd SE3	151	S1
Hesa Rd, Hayes	102	A12
Hesewall Cl SW4	146	F4
Hesketh Pl, W11 *3*	108	C14
Hesketh Rd E7	97	N6
Heslop Rd SW12	163	U2
Hesper Ms SW5	30	B4
Hesperus Cres E14	132	C8
Hessel Rd W13	122	J3
Hessel St E1	112	J12
Hester Rd N18	60	G10
Hester Rd SW11	127	R14
Hester Ter, Rich	142	B5
Hestercombe Av SW6	144	D3
Hesterman Way, Croy	197	K1
Heston Av, Houns	121	K13
Heston Gra La, Houns	121	L12
Heston Ind Mall, Houns	121	M13
Heston Rd, Houns	121	N12
Heston St SE14	150	A1
Heswall Grn, Wat *2*	50	B5
Hetherington Rd SW4	146	J8
Hetley Gdns SE19	166	E14
Hetley Rd W12	125	R2
Heton Gdns NW4	71	P7
Hevelius Cl SE10	133	L9
Hever Cft SE9	170	H8
Hever Gdns, Brom	188	G4
Heverham Rd, SE18 *1*	135	R7
Heversham Rd, Bexh	155	P2
Hewer St W10	108	B9
Hewett Cl, Stan	53	K8
Hewett Rd, Dag	100	G8
Hewett St EC2	12	J11
Hewish Rd N18	60	C8
Hewison St E3	113	U3
Hewitt Av N22	75	R4
Hewitt Cl, Croy	200	B5
Hewitt Rd N8	75	P9
Hewlett Rd E3	113	S3
Hexagon, The N6	91	U2
Hexal Rd SE6	168	J5

Hexham Gdns, Islw	122	H14
Hexham Rd SE27	165	T4
Hexham Rd, Barn	41	K7
Hexham Rd, Mord	194	J1
Heybourne Rd N17	61	K13
Heybridge Av SW16	165	L12
Heybridge Dr, Ilf	81	N5
Heybridge Way E10	77	S14
Heyford Av SW8	34	D13
Heyford Av SW20	180	F6
Heyford Rd, Mitch	181	S3
Heygate St SE17	36	A2
Heynes Rd, Dag	100	F7
Heysham Dr, Wat	50	G10
Heysham La NW3	91	K6
Heysham Rd N15	76	B12
Heythrop St SW18	162	F2
Heywood Av NW9	70	J2
Heyworth Rd E5	94	J7
Heyworth Rd E15	97	L3
Hibbert Rd E17	77	T14
Hibbert Rd, Har	68	F3
Hibbert St SW11	145	N6
Hibernia Gdns, Houns	139	P8
Hibernia Rd, Houns	139	P7
Hibiscus Cl, Edg	54	H8
Hichisson Rd SE15	149	M9
Hickin Cl SE7	134	A8
Hickin St, E14 *2*	132	E5
Hickling Rd, Ilf	99	K9
Hickman Av E4	62	F11
Hickman Cl, E16 *3*	116	A10
Hickman Rd, Rom	82	F13
Hickmore Wk SW4	146	F5
Hickory Cl N9	44	G14
Hicks Av, Grnf	104	B4
Hicks Cl SW11	145	R5
Hicks St SE8	131	R9
Hidcote Gdns SW20	179	R5
Hide, E6 *12*	116	H11
Hide Pl SW1	33	S3
Hide Rd, Har	68	A8
High Beech, S Croy	198	D13
High Beech Rd, Loug	48	C7
High Beeches, Sid	172	J9
High Br SE10	132	H10
High Br Wf SE10	132	G10
High Broom Cres, W Wick	186	D14
High Cedar Dr SW20	161	S14
High Coombe Pl, Kings T	160	G13
High Cross Cen N15	76	H8
High Cross Rd N17	76	G6
High Dr, N Mal	178	F2
High Elms, Chig	65	S7
High Elms, Wdf Grn	63	N10
High Elms Rd, Orp	203	M13
High Foleys, Esher	190	J14
High Gables, Loug	48	B9
High Gro SE18	135	P14
High Gro, Brom	187	U2
High Hill Ferry E5	95	K1
High Holborn WC1	18	E4
High La W7	104	B11
High Lawns, Har	86	C5
High Level Dr SE26	166	G8
High Mead, Chig	65	L4
High Mead, Har	68	D9
High Mead, W Wick	200	H3
High Meadow Cl, Pnr	66	E7
High Meadow Cres NW9	70	G10
High Meadows, Chig	65	N10
High Meads Rd E16	116	A11
High Mt NW4	71	P11
High Pk Av, Rich	142	A2
High Pk Rd, Rich	142	A2
High Path SW19	181	K1
High Pt SE9	171	K6
High Rd N2	73	P4
High Rd N11	58	D9
High Rd N12	73	M1
High Rd N15	76	F6
High Rd N17	76	E10
High Rd N20	57	M4

High Rd N22	75	P5
High Rd	89	S12
(Willesden) NW10		
High Rd, Buck H	63	R4
High Rd, Bushey	52	B2
High Rd, Chig	64	G9
High Rd (Harrow Weald), Har	52	C14
High Rd, Ilf	98	J5
High Rd (Seven Kings), Ilf	99	N4
High Rd, Loug	47	U12
High Rd, Pnr	66	E8
High Rd (Chadwell Heath), Rom	82	E14
High Rd, Wem	87	R10
High Rd Leyton E10	96	D3
High Rd Leyton E15	96	F7
High Rd Leytonstone E11	97	K3
High Rd Leytonstone E15	97	K3
High Rd Woodford Grn E18	63	M14
High Rd Woodford Grn, Wdf Grn	63	N10
High Silver, Loug	48	A8
High St E11	79	N9
High St E13	115	N3
High St E15	114	F2
High St E17	77	T9
High St N8	74	J7
High St N14	58	G3
High St NW7	55	R8
High St (Harlesden) NW10	107	M3
High St SE20	167	M13
High St (South Norwood) SE25	184	F7
High St W3	124	E2
High St W5	124	E2
High St, Barn	40	F7
High St, Beck	186	B2
High St, Brent	123	R12
High St, Brom	187	N3
High St, Cars	196	A8
High St, Chis	171	K11
High St, Croy	197	U5
High St, Edg	54	B13
High St (Ponders End), Enf	45	L9
High St (Claygate), Esher	190	E12
High St, Felt	156	B4
High St, Hmptn	157	U10
High St, Har	86	C2
High St (Wealdstone), Har	68	C3
High St, Houns	139	T5
High St (Cranford), Houns	120	D12
High St, Ilf	81	M4
High St, Kings T	177	P4
High St (Hampton Wick), Kings T	177	M2
High St, N Mal	179	K7
High St (Farnborough), Orp	203	M9
High St (Green St Grn), Orp	217	T13
High St, Pnr	66	J6
High St, Sthl	121	M1
High St, Sutt	194	J7
High St (Cheam), Sutt	194	D12
High St, Tedd	158	G10
High St, T Ditt	176	G12
High St, Th Hth	183	U7
High St (Whitton), Twick	139	T13
High St, Wem	87	U8
High St, W Mol	175	P7
High St, W Wick	200	D2
High St Colliers Wd SW19	163	P13
High St Ms SW19	162	C10
High St N E6	98	C11
High St N E12	98	C11
High St S E6	116	E4

High St Wimbledon SW19	162	B10
High Timber St EC4	19	U10
High Tor Cl, Brom	169	R14
High Trees SW2	165	P1
High Trees, Barn	41	S9
High Trees, Croy	199	S1
High Vw, Pnr	66	F7
High Vw Cl SE19	184	E4
High Vw Cl, Loug	47	U9
High Vw Rd E18	79	L4
High Worple, Har	67	K14
Higham Hill Rd E17	77	R2
Higham Pl E17	77	S5
Higham Rd N17	76	A5
Higham Rd, Wdf Grn	63	N12
Higham Sta Av E4	62	C11
Higham St E17	77	R5
Highams Lo Business Cen E17	77	P5
Highams Pk Ind Est E4	62	F11
Highbank Way N8	75	N11
Highbanks Cl, Well	136	B14
Highbanks Rd, Pnr	51	R10
Highbarrow Rd, Croy	198	G1
Highbridge Rd, Bark	116	J1
Highbrook Rd SE3	152	A5
Highbury Av, Th Hth	183	R3
Highbury Cl, N Mal	178	F8
Highbury Cl, W Wick	200	D4
Highbury Cor N5	93	P11
Highbury Cres N5	93	P11
Highbury Est N5	93	U10
Highbury Gdns, Ilf	99	R3
Highbury Gra N5	93	T8
Highbury Gro N5	93	S10
Highbury Hill N5	93	P6
Highbury Ms N7	93	P11
Highbury New Pk N5	93	T10
Highbury Pk N5	93	S7
Highbury Pl N5	93	R11
Highbury Quad N5	93	T6
Highbury Rd SW19	162	D10
Highbury Sta Rd N1	93	P12
Highbury Ter N5	93	R9
Highbury Ter Ms N5	93	R10
Highclere Rd, N Mal	178	G6
Highclere St SE26	167	R8
Highcliffe Dr SW15	143	M12
Highcliffe Gdns, Ilf	80	C9
Highcombe SE7	133	S11
Highcombe Cl SE9	170	B2
Highcroft NW9	70	H9
Highcroft Av, Wem	88	A14
Highcroft Gdns NW11	72	E12
Highcroft Rd N19	74	J14
Highcross Way SW15	161	P1
Highdaun Dr SW16	183	L7
Highdown, Wor Pk	193	L3
Highdown Rd SW15	143	R11
Highfield, Felt	156	A2
Highfield, Wat	51	L5
Highfield Av NW9	70	F9
Highfield Av NW11	72	B13
Highfield Av, Erith	137	S12
Highfield Av, Grnf	86	E9
Highfield Av, Orp	203	U11
Highfield Av, Pnr	67	L10
Highfield Av, Wem	87	S5
Highfield Cl N22	75	N1
Highfield Cl NW9	70	F9
Highfield Cl SE13	150	G13
Highfield Cl, Surb	191	M2
Highfield Ct N14	42	F11
Highfield Dr, Brom	187	K7
Highfield Dr, Epsom	193	L13
Highfield Dr, W Wick	200	D5
Highfield Gdns NW11	72	C12
Highfield Hill SE19	166	B14
Highfield Rd N21	59	S3
Highfield Rd NW11	72	D12
Highfield Rd W3	106	D9
Highfield Rd, Bexh	155	M10
Highfield Rd, Brom	188	E8
Highfield Rd, Chis	189	T5

Name	Page	Grid
Highfield Rd, Felt	156	B2
Highfield Rd, Islw	140	E1
Highfield Rd, Surb	178	E14
Highfield Rd, Sutt	195	R9
Highfield Rd, Wdf Grn	64	C14
Highfields Gro N6	91	U2
Highgate Av N6	74	C13
Highgate CI N6	74	A14
Highgate High St N6	92	C1
Highgate Hill N6	92	E2
Highgate Hill N19	92	E2
Highgate Rd NW5	92	C8
Highgate Wk SE23	167	L3
Highgate W Hill N6	92	A2
Highgrove CI N11	58	B10
Highgrove CI, Chis	188	D1
Highgrove Ms, Cars 3	195	T5
Highgrove Rd, Dag	100	E9
Highgrove Way, Ruis	66	A12
Highland Av W7	104	C11
Highland Av, Dag	101	T5
Highland Av, Loug	48	D12
Highland Cotts, Wall	196	E8
Highland Ct E10	70	S1
Highland Cft, Beck	168	C11
Highland Rd SE19	166	C11
Highland Rd, Bexh	155	P8
Highland Rd, Brom	187	L2
Highlands, Wat	50	E2
Highlands, The, Edg	70	D3
Highlands, The, Pot B	40	H9
Highlands Av N21	43	M9
Highlands Av W3	106	E14
Highlands CI, N4 2	75	K13
Highlands CI, Houns	139	S2
Highlands Gdns, Ilf	98	E1
Highlands Heath SW15	143	T14
Highlands Rd, Barn	40	H9
Highlea CI NW9	71	K1
Highlever Rd W10	107	U10
Highmead SE18	135	T14
Highmead Cres, Wem	87	U13
Highmore Rd SE3	133	K13
Highshore Rd SE15	148	F3
Highstone Av E11	79	N12
Highview Av, Edg	54	E8
Highview Av, Wall	197	L9
Highview Gdns N3	72	C7
Highview Gdns N11	58	E10
Highview Gdns, Edg	54	E8
Highview Rd SE19	166	B12
Highview Rd W13	104	H11
Highview Rd, Sid	172	D7
Highway, The E1	21	U11
Highway, The E14	112	J14
Highway, The, Stan	52	G14
Highwood, Brom	186	J5
Highwood Av N12	57	L7
Highwood CI, Orp	203	L4
Highwood Dr, Orp	203	L4
Highwood Gdns, Ilf	80	F8
Highwood Gro NW7	54	H9
Highwood Hill NW7	55	M5
Highwood La, Loug	48	H10
Highwood Rd N19	92	J6
Highworth Rd N11	58	H11
Hilary Av, Mitch	182	A5
Hilary CI SW6	30	B14
Hilary CI, Erith	155	T2
Hilary Rd W12	107	M13
Hilbert Rd, Sutt	194	A6
Hilborough Way, Orp	203	P9
Hilda Rd E6	98	A14
Hilda Rd E16	115	K8
Hilda Ter SW9	147	P3
Hilda Vale CI, Orp	202	J8
Hilda Vale Rd, Orp	202	J8
Hildenborough Gdns, Brom	169	K11
Hildenlea PI, Brom	186	J3
Hildreth St SW12	164	C1
Hildyard Rd SW6	126	H11
Hiley Rd NW10	107	T5
Hilgrove Rd NW6	91	M14
Hiliary Gdns, Stan	69	M4
Hill Brow, Brom	188	B2
Hill CI NW2	89	R6
Hill CI NW11	72	H11
Hill CI, Barn	39	T10
Hill CI, Chis	170	J9
Hill CI, Har	86	C6
Hill Cres N20	56	J3
Hill Cres, Bex	173	T2
Hill Cres, Har	68	G10
Hill Cres, Surb	177	U9
Hill Cres, Wor Pk	193	U4
Hill Crest, Sid	154	B14
Hill Dr NW9	88	E2
Hill Dr SW16	183	L5
Hill End, Orp	203	U3
Hill Fm Rd W10	107	U9
Hill Gro, Felt	157	M4
Hill Ho Av, Stan	52	F13
Hill Ho CI N21	43	N13
Hill Ho Dr, Hmptn	175	P2
Hill Ho Rd SW16	165	L10
Hill Path SW16	165	L10
Hill Ri N9	45	K12
Hill Ri NW11	73	K8
Hill Ri SE23	167	K2
Hill Ri, Esher	190	J4
Hill Ri, Grnf	85	T14
Hill Ri, Rich	141	P10
Hill Rd N10	73	U2
Hill Rd NW8	6	H4
Hill Rd, Cars	195	S12
Hill Rd, Har	68	G10
Hill Rd, Mitch	164	D14
Hill Rd, Pnr	66	J10
Hill Rd, Sutt	195	K10
Hill Rd, Wem	86	J5
Hill St W1	16	G12
Hill St, Rich	141	P10
Hill Top NW11	73	K7
Hill Top, Loug	48	G5
Hill Top, Mord	180	G12
Hill Top, Sutt	180	E14
Hill Top CI, Loug	48	G5
Hill Top PI, Loug	48	G5
Hill Top Vw, Wdf Grn	64	F11
Hill Vw Cres, Orp 3	203	T2
Hill Vw Dr, Well	153	R4
Hill Vw Gdns NW9	70	H9
Hill Vw Rd, Esher	190	H13
Hill Vw Rd, Orp	203	T2
Hill Vw Rd, Twick	140	G12
Hillary Ri, Barn	40	H7
Hillary Rd, Sthl	121	P5
Hillbeck CI, SE15 1	131	L13
Hillbeck Way, Grnf	104	A1
Hillborne CI, Hayes	120	A9
Hillborough CI SW19	163	L14
Hillbrook Rd SW17	163	U7
Hillbrow, N Mal	179	M6
Hillbrow Rd, Brom	168	J12
Hillbury Av, Har	69	K10
Hillbury Rd SW17	164	D5
Hillcote Av SW16	165	N13
Hillcourt Av N12	56	J11
Hillcourt Est N16	94	B2
Hillcourt Rd SE22	148	H12
Hillcrest N6	74	B13
Hillcrest N21	43	R13
Hillcrest Av NW11	72	D9
Hillcrest Av, Edg	54	C8
Hillcrest Av, Pnr	66	H8
Hillcrest CI SE26	166	G8
Hillcrest CI, Beck	185	T10
Hillcrest Gdns N3	72	C7
Hillcrest Gdns NW2	89	N6
Hillcrest Gdns, Esher	190	F6
Hillcrest Rd E17	78	H3
Hillcrest Rd E18	79	N3
Hillcrest Rd W3	124	B2
Hillcrest Rd W5	105	S9
Hillcrest Rd, Brom	169	N8
Hillcrest Rd, Loug	48	B12
Hillcrest Vw, Beck	185	T11
Hillcroft, Loug	48	H3
Hillcroft Av, Pnr	67	L12
Hillcroft Cres W5	105	P11
Hillcroft Cres, Ruis	84	G5
Hillcroft Cres, Wat	50	D3
Hillcroft Cres, Wem	87	U7
Hillcroft Rd E6	116	J9
Hillcroome Rd, Sutt	195	N11
Hillcross Av, Mord	180	F8
Hilldale Rd, Sutt	194	E8
Hilldown Rd SW16	165	K13
Hilldown Rd, Brom	201	K1
Hilldrop Cres N7	92	H9
Hilldrop Est N7	92	G9
Hilldrop La N7	92	H10
Hilldrop Rd N7	92	H9
Hilldrop Rd, Brom	169	P11
Hillend SE18	152	H2
Hillersdon Av SW13	143	N3
Hillersdon Av, Edg	53	T9
Hillery CI SE17	36	E3
Hillfield Av N8	75	K8
Hillfield Av NW9	71	K9
Hillfield Av, Wem	87	S13
Hillfield CI, Har	67	U8
Hillfield Ct NW3	91	R10
Hillfield Par, Mord	181	P11
Hillfield Pk N10	74	D7
Hillfield Pk N21	59	N3
Hillfield Pk Ms N10	74	C7
Hillfield Rd NW6	90	F10
Hillfield Rd, Hmptn	157	L14
Hillfoot Av, Rom	83	T1
Hillfoot Rd, Rom	83	U2
Hillgate PI SW12	146	C13
Hillgate PI W8	126	G1
Hillgate St, W8 11	126	G1
Hilliards Ct, E1 4	131	L1
Hillier CI, Barn	40	J11
Hillier Gdns, Croy	197	P9
Hillier PI, Chess	191	M12
Hillier Rd SW11	145	U11
Hilliers La, Croy	196	J6
Hillingdon Rd, Bexh	155	T5
Hillingdon St, SE5 1	35	P12
Hillingdon St SE17	35	S12
Hillington Gdns, Wdf Grn	80	B4
Hillman Dr W10	107	U8
Hillman St E8	95	K11
Hillmarton Rd N7	93	K9
Hillmead Dr SW9	147	R7
Hillmont Rd, Esher	190	D5
Hillmore Gro SE26	167	P9
Hillreach SE18	134	E9
Hillrise Rd N19	74	J14
Hills Ms W5	105	S14
Hills PI W1	17	M7
Hills Rd, Buck H	63	R2
Hillsborough Grn, Wat	50	B5
Hillsborough Rd SE22	148	D10
Hillsgrove, Well	136	E13
Hillside NW9	70	G8
Hillside SW19	106	G1
Hillside SW19	162	B12
Hillside, Barn	41	M10
Hillside Av N11	57	T11
Hillside Av, Borwd	38	C8
Hillside Av, Wem	87	T8
Hillside Av, Wdf Grn	63	U8
Hillside CI NW8	6	C2
Hillside CI, Mord	180	C7
Hillside CI, Wdf Grn	63	T10
Hillside Cres, Har	85	T2
Hillside Cres, Nthwd	66	B1
Hillside Gdns, Nthwd	50	B14
Hillside Gdns, Wall	196	F13
Hillside Gro N14	42	G14
Hillside Gro NW7	55	N13
Hillside La, Brom 2	201	N3
Hillside Pas, SW2 1	165	M4
Hillside Ri, Nthwd	50	B14
Hillside Rd N15	76	D13
Hillside Rd SW2	165	N4
Hillside Rd W5	105	S10
Hillside Rd, Brom	187	L5
Hillside Rd, Croy	197	R8
Hillside Rd, Nthwd	50	B14
Hillside Rd, Pnr	50	D14
Hillside Rd, Sthl	103	N7
Hillside Rd, Surb	177	U9
Hillside Rd, Sutt	194	E13
Hillsleigh Rd W8	126	F1
Hillstowe St E5	95	M4
Hilltop Gdns NW4	71	S3
Hilltop Gdns, Orp	203	R4
Hilltop Rd NW6	90	H13
Hilltop Way, Stan	52	H6
Hillview SW20	179	R1
Hillview, Mitch	182	J7
Hillview Av, Har	69	R9
Hillview CI, Pnr	51	M12
Hillview Cres, Ilf	80	E12
Hillview Gdns NW4	72	B7
Hillview Gdns, Har	67	P6
Hillview Rd NW7	56	A8
Hillview Rd, Chis	170	H9
Hillview Rd, Pnr	51	L13
Hillview Rd, Sutt	195	M5
Hillway N6	92	B3
Hillway NW9	88	J1
Hillworth Rd SW2	147	N14
Hilly Flds Cres SE4	150	A6
Hillyard Rd W7	104	D9
Hillyard St SW9	147	N2
Hillyfield E17	77	R4
Hillyfields, Loug	48	H3
Hilsea St E5	95	L7
Hilton Av N12	57	P10
Hilversum Cres, SE22 5	148	D9
Himley Rd SW17	163	T11
Hinchcliffe CI, Wall	197	L13
Hinchley CI, Esher	190	F7
Hinchley Dr, Esher	190	F6
Hinchley Way, Esher	190	G5
Hinckley Rd SE15	148	G7
Hind CI, Chig	65	T10
Hind Ct, EC4 15	19	M7
Hind Cres, Erith	137	U12
Hind Gro E14	114	A12
Hinde St W1	16	E5
Hindes Rd, Har	68	B10
Hindhead CI N16	94	D1
Hindhead Gdns, Nthlt	102	J1
Hindhead Grn, Wat	50	E9
Hindhead Way, Wall 1	196	J9
Hindmans Rd SE22	148	G10
Hindmans Way, Dag	119	L8
Hindmarsh CI E1	21	U10
Hindrey Rd E5	95	K9
Hindsley's PI SE23	167	M3
Hinkler CI, Wall	197	K14
Hinkler Rd, Har	69	N6
Hinksey Path SE2	136	G4
Hinstock Rd SE18	135	M12
Hinton Av, Houns	138	H7
Hinton CI SE9	170	D2
Hinton Rd N18	60	C8
Hinton Rd SE24	147	S6
Hinton Rd, Wall	196	F12
Hippodrome PI, W11 5	108	D14
Hitcham Rd E17	77	T14
Hitchin Sq E3	113	S3
Hither Fm Rd SE3	151	L15
Hither Grn La SE13	150	F9
Hitherbroom Rd, Hayes	120	B1

Hitherfield Rd SW16	165	M4
Hitherfield Rd, Dag	100	J4
Hitherwell Dr, Har	68	A1
Hitherwood Dr SE19	166	E8
Hive Cl, Bushey	52	B3
Hive Rd, Bushey	52	B3
Hoadly Rd SW16	164	G5
Hobart Cl N20	57	R3
Hobart Cl, Hayes	102	G7
Hobart Dr, Hayes	102	G7
Hobart Gdns, Th Hth	184	A6
Hobart La, Hayes	102	G7
Hobart Pl SW1	24	G10
Hobart Pl, Rich	141	T13
Hobart Rd, Dag	100	H7
Hobart Rd, Hayes	102	G7
Hobart Rd, Ilf	81	M4
Hobart Rd, Wor Pk	193	R5
Hobbayne Rd W7	104	B11
Hobbes Wk SW15	143	R10
Hobbs Grn N2	73	M5
Hobbs Ms, Ilf	99	T4
Hobbs Rd SE27	165	U8
Hobday St, E14 *5*	114	C11
Hobill Wk, Surb	177	T12
Hoblands End, Chis	171	S12
Hobsons Pl E1	21	R1
Hobury St SW10	30	H11
Hocker St E2	13	M7
Hockett Cl SE8	131	S7
Hockley Av E6	116	C3
Hockley Ms, Bark	117	S4
Hocroft Av NW2	90	E6
Hocroft Rd NW2	90	E7
Hocroft Wk NW2	90	F6
Hodder Dr, Grnf	104	F4
Hoddesdon Rd, Belv	137	N10
Hodford Rd NW11	90	F3
Hodgkin Cl SE28	118	H13
Hodnet Gro SE16	131	N7
Hodson Cl, Har	85	M5
Hoe, The, Wat	50	H3
Hoe St E17	78	B10
Hofland Rd W14	126	C5
Hogan Ms W2	14	J2
Hogan Way E5	94	H3
Hogarth Cl, E16 *1*	116	A9
Hogarth Cl W5	105	S9
Hogarth Ct SE19	166	F8
Hogarth Cres SW19	181	N2
Hogarth Cres, Croy	183	U14
Hogarth Gdns, Houns	121	P14
Hogarth La W4	124	J11
Hogarth Pl, SW5 *2*	30	A3
Hogarth Reach, Loug	48	E9
Hogarth Rd SW5	30	A3
Hogarth Rd, Dag	100	D9
Hogarth Rd, Edg	70	A3
Hogarth Roundabout W4	125	L11
Hogarth Roundabout Flyover W4	125	L10
Hogarth Way, Hmptn	175	U3
Hogsmill Way, Epsom	192	E8
Holbeach Gdns, Sid	153	S12
Holbeach Ms, SW12 *6*	164	C1
Holbeach Rd SE6	158	B13
Holbeck Row SE15	130	H14
Holbein Ms SW1	32	C5
Holbein Pl SW1	32	D4
Holberton Gdns NW10	107	R5
Holborn EC1	19	L4
Holborn Circ EC1	19	M4
Holborn Pl WC1	18	F4
Holborn Rd E13	115	S9
Holborn Viaduct EC1	19	N4
Holborn Way, Mitch	181	T4
Holbrook Cl N19	92	D2
Holbrook Cl, Enf	44	F1
Holbrook La, Chis	171	P14
Holbrook Rd E15	115	L3
Holbrook Way, Brom	188	F11

Holbrooke Ct N7	93	K7
Holbrooke Pl, Rich	141	P10
Holburne Cl SE3	151	T2
Holburne Gdns SE3	152	A2
Holburne Rd SE3	151	T2
Holcombe Rd N17	76	F5
Holcombe Rd, Ilf	80	G14
Holcombe St, W6 *5*	125	S8
Holcote Cl, Belv	137	K6
Holcroft Rd E9	95	M14
Holden Av N12	57	K9
Holden Av NW9	88	F2
Holden Cl, Dag	100	D5
Holden Rd N12	56	J9
Holden St SW11	146	A4
Holdenby Rd SE4	149	S10
Holdenhurst Av N12	57	L14
Holder Cl N3	57	K13
Holderness Way SE27	165	S10
Holdernesse Cl, Islw	140	G1
Holdernesse Rd SW17	163	U5
Holders Hill Av NW4	72	A4
Holders Hill Circ NW7	56	C14
Holders Hill Cres NW4	72	B5
Holders Hill Dr NW4	72	B5
Holders Hill Gdns NW4	72	C3
Holders Hill Rd NW4	72	C2
Holders Hill Rd NW7	72	C2
Holdgate St, SE7 *1*	134	A6
Holford Pl WC1	10	H5
Holford Rd NW3	91	M6
Holford St WC1	10	J5
Holgate Av SW11	145	N6
Holgate Gdns, Dag	101	N11
Holgate Rd, Dag	101	N10
Holland Av SW20	179	M1
Holland Cl, Barn	41	N13
Holland Cl, Brom	201	M3
Holland Cl, Rom	83	U9
Holland Cl, Stan	52	J9
Holland Dr SE23	167	R6
Holland Gdns W14	126	D5
Holland Gro SW9	129	P14
Holland Pk W8	126	F4
Holland Pk W11	126	E2
Holland Pk Av W11	126	C3
Holland Pk Av, Ilf	81	S11
Holland Pk Gdns W14	126	C3
Holland Pk Ms W11	126	E2
Holland Pk Rd W14	126	E6
Holland Pl, W8 *1*	22	A6
Holland Rd E6	116	F1
Holland Rd E15	115	K5
Holland Rd NW10	107	R3
Holland Rd SE25	184	H9
Holland Rd W14	126	C4
Holland Rd, Wem	87	N12
Holland St SE1	27	R1
Holland St W8	126	H3
Holland Vil Rd W14	126	C3
Holland Wk W8	126	F3
Holland Wk, Stan	52	H9
Holland Way, Brom	201	L3
Hollands, The, Felt	156	H7
Hollands, The, Wor Pk	193	M2
Hollar Rd N16	94	E6
Hollen St W1	17	R6
Holles Cl, Hmptn	157	P11
Holles St W1	16	J6
Holley Rd W3	125	K3
Hollickwood Av N12	57	T11
Holliday Sq, SW11 *8*	145	N6
Hollidge Way, Dag	101	R13
Hollies, The, Har	68	G7
Hollies Av, Sid	171	T3
Hollies Cl SW16	165	P12
Hollies Cl, Twick	158	E3
Hollies End NW7	55	S9
Hollies Rd W5	123	L7
Holligrave Rd, Brom	187	P1

Hollingbourne Av, Bexh	155	M1
Hollingbourne Gdns W13	104	J10
Hollingbourne Rd SE24	147	U10
Hollingsworth Rd, Croy	199	K12
Hollington Cres, N Mal	179	M12
Hollington Rd E6	116	E6
Hollington Rd N17	76	H3
Hollingworth Cl, W Mol	175	L7
Hollingworth Rd, Orp	188	J12
Hollman Gdns SW16	165	R12
Hollow, The, Wdf Grn	63	M7
Holloway Rd E6	116	F6
Holloway Rd E11	96	H6
Holloway Rd N7	93	L7
Holloway Rd N19	92	G4
Holloway St, Houns	139	S5
Hollowfield Wk, Nthlt	84	J12
Hollows, The, Brent	123	U11
Holly Av, Stan	69	S4
Holly Bush Hill NW3	91	L7
Holly Bush La, Hmptn	157	M13
Holly Bush Vale, NW3 *4*	91	M7
Holly Cl NW10	88	J13
Holly Cl, Buck H	64	A6
Holly Cl, Felt	156	J9
Holly Cl, Wall	196	D14
Holly Cres, Beck	185	U10
Holly Cres, Wdf Grn	62	H13
Holly Dr E4	46	D14
Holly Dr, Brent	122	H12
Holly Fm Rd, Sthl	120	H9
Holly Gro NW9	70	F13
Holly Gro SE15	148	F3
Holly Gro, Pnr	67	K2
Holly Hedge Ter SE13	150	G9
Holly Hill N21	43	L11
Holly Hill NW3	91	M7
Holly Lo Gdns N6	92	A3
Holly Ms SW10	30	H7
Holly Mt NW3	91	M7
Holly Pk N3	72	F6
Holly Pk N4	75	L14
Holly Pk Gdns N3	72	G5
Holly Pk Rd N11	58	A9
Holly Pk Rd W7	122	E1
Holly Rd E11	79	M13
Holly Rd, W4 *2*	124	H8
Holly Rd, Hmptn	157	T11
Holly Rd, Houns	139	S7
Holly Rd, Twick	158	G1
Holly St E8	94	F13
Holly St Est E8	94	E13
Holly Ter, N20 *1*	57	M4
Holly Vw Cl NW4	71	P11
Holly Wk NW3	91	L7
Holly Wk, Enf	44	A5
Holly Wk, Rich	141	S3
Holly Way, Mitch	182	H7
Hollybank Cl, Hmptn	157	N10
Hollyberry La, NW3 *1*	91	L7
Hollybrake Cl, Chis	171	N14
Hollybush Cl E11	79	N9
Hollybush Cl, Har	68	D1
Hollybush Gdns E2	113	K5
Hollybush Hill E11	79	M10
Hollybush Pl E2	113	K5
Hollybush Rd, Kings T	159	S10
Hollybush St E13	115	S5
Hollybush Wk SW9	147	R8
Hollycroft Av NW3	90	H6
Hollycroft Av, Wem	87	T4
Hollycroft Cl, S Croy	198	C10
Hollydale Cl, Nthlt	85	R8
Hollydale Dr, Brom	202	E5
Hollydale Rd SE15	149	L2
Hollydene SE15	148	J1

Hollydown Way E11	96	H5
Hollyfield Av N11	57	T10
Hollyfield Rd, Surb	177	U14
Hollymead, Cars	195	T6
Hollymount Cl SE10	150	E1
Hollytree Cl SW19	162	B2
Hollywood Ct, Borwd	38	A7
Hollywood Gdns, Hayes	102	C11
Hollywood Ms, SW10 *2*	30	F9
Hollywood Rd E4	61	S9
Hollywood Rd SW10	30	F9
Hollywood Way, Wdf Grn	62	H13
Holm Oak Cl SW15	144	E11
Holm Oak Ms SW4	146	J10
Holm Wk SE3	151	P4
Holman Rd SW11	145	N4
Holman Rd, Epsom	192	E9
Holmbridge Gdns, Enf	45	N7
Holmbrook Dr NW4	72	B9
Holmbury Ct SW17	163	T6
Holmbury Ct SW19	163	R13
Holmbury Gro, Croy	199	T14
Holmbury Pk, Brom	170	C13
Holmbury Vw E5	95	K1
Holmbush Rd SW15	144	C11
Holmcote Gdns N5	93	T9
Holmcroft Way, Brom	188	E10
Holmdale Gdns NW4	72	B9
Holmdale Rd NW6	90	G10
Holmdale Rd, Chis	171	L10
Holmdale Ter N15	76	D13
Holmdene Av NW7	55	N12
Holmdene Av SE24	147	U10
Holmdene Av, Har	67	R6
Holmdene Cl, Beck	186	E4
Holme Lacey Rd SE12	151	L12
Holme Rd E6	116	D1
Holme Way, Stan	52	F12
Holmead Rd SW6	127	K14
Holmebury Cl, Bushey	52	C3
Holmefield Ct NW3	91	S11
Holmes Av E17	77	T5
Holmes Av NW7	56	D10
Holmes Pl SW10	30	H9
Holmes Rd NW5	92	C11
Holmes Rd SW19	163	M14
Holmes Rd, Twick	158	F4
Holmes Ter SE1	27	K5
Holmesdale Av SW14	142	D6
Holmesdale Cl SE25	184	E6
Holmesdale Rd N6	74	D13
Holmesdale Rd SE25	184	D7
Holmesdale Rd, Bexh	154	G3
Holmesdale Rd, Croy	184	B9
Holmesdale Rd, Rich	141	U2
Holmesdale Rd, Tedd	159	L12
Holmesley Rd SE23	149	R11
Holmewood Gdns SW2	147	L14
Holmewood Rd SE25	184	D6
Holmewood Rd SW2	147	K14
Holmfield Av NW4	72	B9
Holmhurst Rd, Belv	137	S9
Holmleigh Rd N16	94	D1
Holms St E2	13	S2
Holmshaw Cl SE26	167	S7
Holmside Ri, Wat	50	C5
Holmside Rd SW12	146	B12
Holmsley Cl, N Mal	179	L12
Holmstall Av, Edg	70	E5
Holmwood Cl, Har	67	T5
Holmwood Cl, Nthlt	85	S11
Holmwood Gdns N3	72	H4
Holmwood Gdns, Wall	196	C12

Name	No.	Ref
Holmwood Gro NW7	54	H10
Holmwood Rd, Chess	191	R9
Holmwood Rd, Ilf	99	S4
Holmwood Vil SE7	133	P9
Holne Chase N2	73	M11
Holne Chase, Mord	180	G12
Holness Rd E15	97	L12
Holroyd Rd SW15	143	U8
Holstein Way, Erith	136	J6
Holstock Rd, Ilf	99	L4
Holsworth Cl, Har	67	T9
Holsworthy Sq, WC1 1	10	H12
Holsworthy Way, Chess	191	M9
Holt, The, Ilf	65	M12
Holt, The, Wall	196	E7
Holt Cl N10	74	A8
Holt Cl SE28	118	D13
Holt Cl, Chig	65	T9
Holt Ct E15	96	E9
Holt Rd E16	134	D2
Holt Rd, Wem	87	K5
Holt Way, Chig	65	T9
Holton St E1	113	N7
Holtwhite Av, Enf	43	U3
Holtwhites Hill, Enf	43	T3
Holwell Pl, Pnr	66	J8
Holwood Pk Av, Orp	202	F8
Holwood Pl, SW4 6	146	G8
Holybourne Av SW15	143	P14
Holyhead Cl E3	114	B6
Holyhead Cl, E6 2	116	E9
Holyoak Rd SE11	35	P2
Holyoake Ct, SE16 6	131	T3
Holyoake Wk N2	73	L6
Holyoake Wk W5	105	L7
Holyport Rd SW6	125	U13
Holyrood Av, Har	85	K8
Holyrood Gdns, Edg	70	C4
Holyrood Ms, E16 8	133	P1
Holyrood Rd, Barn	41	M12
Holyrood St SE1	28	H4
Holywell Cl, SE3 1	133	P11
Holywell Cl, SE16 13	131	K9
Holywell La EC2	12	J10
Holywell Row EC2	12	G11
Home Cl, Cars	195	T4
Home Cl, Nthlt	103	L5
Home Ct, Felt	156	B2
Home Fm Cl, T Ditt	176	E13
Home Gdns, Dag	101	T6
Home Lea, Orp	203	T10
Home Mead, Stan	69	M1
Home Pk Rd SW19	162	H6
Home Pk Wk, Kings T	177	P8
Home Rd SW11	145	R3
Homecroft Gdns, Loug	48	J7
Homecroft Rd N22	75	T1
Homecroft Rd SE26	167	M10
Homefarm Rd W7	104	E12
Homefield Av, Ilf	81	R10
Homefield Cl NW10	88	F12
Homefield Cl, Hayes	102	F8
Homefield Gdns N2	73	N6
Homefield Gdns, Mitch	181	M3
Homefield Ms, Beck	186	A1
Homefield Pk, Sutt	194	J11
Homefield Rd SW19	162	C10
Homefield Rd W4	125	L8
Homefield Rd, Brom	187	T2
Homefield Rd, Edg	54	G12
Homefield Rd, Walt	175	K14
Homefield Rd, Wem	86	H8
Homefield St, N1 2	12	H3
Homelands Dr SE19	166	C14
Homeleigh Rd SE15	149	N9
Homemead Rd, Brom	188	F9
Homemead Rd, Croy	182	G12
Homer Cl, Bexh	155	T2
Homer Dr E14	132	A7
Homer Rd E9	95	S12
Homer Rd, Croy	185	N12
Homer Row W1	15	S3
Homer St W1	15	S3
Homersham Rd, Kings T	178	B3
Homerton Gro E9	95	N10
Homerton High St E9	95	N10
Homerton Rd E9	96	A8
Homerton Row E9	95	M10
Homerton Ter E9	95	M11
Homesdale Cl E11	79	N10
Homesdale Rd, Brom	187	U7
Homesdale Rd, Orp	189	R13
Homesfield NW11	72	G9
Homestall Rd SE22	149	L9
Homestead, The N11	58	D8
Homestead Gdns, Esher	190	C10
Homestead Paddock N14	42	D10
Homestead Pk NW2	89	M6
Homestead Rd SW6	128	E14
Homestead Rd, Dag	101	L4
Homewillow Cl N21	43	S11
Homewood Cl, Hmptn 2	157	L11
Homewood Cres, Chis	171	R12
Honduras St, EC1 7	11	U10
Honey Cl, Dag	101	S11
Honeybourne Rd NW6	90	J10
Honeybourne Way, Orp	203	M1
Honeybrook Rd SW12	146	E13
Honeycroft, Loug	48	H8
Honeyden Rd, Sid	173	K11
Honeyman Cl NW6	90	A13
Honeypot Cl NW9	69	U7
Honeypot La NW9	69	T6
Honeypot La, Stan	69	T6
Honeysett Rd, N17 5	76	F4
Honeysuckle Cl, Sthl	102	J13
Honeysuckle Gdns, Croy	185	P14
Honeywell Rd SW11	145	T11
Honeywood Rd NW10	107	L4
Honeywood Rd, Islw	140	G8
Honeywood Wk, Cars	195	U8
Honister Cl, Stan	69	K1
Honister Gdns, Stan	53	K14
Honister Pl, Stan	69	K1
Honiton Rd NW6	108	E3
Honiton Rd, Well	153	T3
Honley Rd SE6	150	D13
Honor Oak Pk SE23	149	M12
Honor Oak Ri SE23	149	M12
Honor Oak Rd SE23	149	M13
Hood Av N14	42	D12
Hood Av SW14	142	F10
Hood Cl, Croy	197	S2
Hood Rd SW20	161	M14
Hood Wk, Rom	83	R2
Hoodcote Gdns N21	43	R13
Hook, The, Barn	41	N12
Hook Fm Rd, Brom	188	A10
Hook La, Well	153	T9
Hook Ri N, Surb	192	B5
Hook Ri S, Surb	192	A6
Hook Ri S Ind Pk, Surb	192	A6
Hook Rd, Chess	191	P10
Hook Rd, Epsom	192	E14
Hook Rd, Surb	191	R3
Hook Wk, Edg	54	F13
Hookers Rd E17	77	P6
Hooking Grn, Har	67	R9
Hooks Hall Dr, Dag	101	U6
Hookstone Way, Wdf Grn	64	A14
Hoop La NW11	72	F14
Hooper Rd E16	115	P12
Hooper St E1	21	S8
Hooper's Ct, SW3 3	23	U8
Hope Cl N1	93	U11
Hope Cl SE12	169	R5
Hope Cl, Sutt	195	L10
Hope Cl, Wdf Grn 2	63	U11
Hope Pk, Brom	169	M14
Hope St SW11	145	N6
Hopedale Rd SE7	133	R12
Hopefield Av NW6	108	D3
Hopes Cl, Houns 2	121	N12
Hopetown St E1	21	P3
Hopewell St SE5	130	B14
Hopewell Yd, SE5 2	130	B14
Hopgood St, W12 6	125	U2
Hopkins Cl N10	58	B13
Hopkins Ms E15	115	M2
Hopkins St W1	17	P8
Hopkinsons Pl, NW1 2	110	A1
Hoppers Rd N13	59	P4
Hoppers Rd N21	59	P4
Hoppett Rd E4	62	J4
Hopping La N1	93	S12
Hoppingwood Av, N Mal	179	K5
Hopton Gdns SE1	27	R2
Hopton Gdns, N Mal	179	N11
Hopton Rd SW16	164	J9
Hopton St SE1	27	R1
Hopwood Cl, SW17 4	163	M6
Hopwood Rd SE17	36	E9
Hopwood Wk E8	94	H13
Horace Av, Rom	101	U2
Horace Rd E7	97	R8
Horace Rd, Ilf	81	L5
Horace Rd, Kings T	177	T6
Horatio Pl E14	132	F2
Horatio Pl SW19	180	H1
Horatio St E2	13	R4
Horatius Way, Croy	197	L11
Horbury Cres W11	108	G14
Horbury Ms W11	108	F14
Horder Rd SW6	144	D2
Horizon Way SE7	133	S8
Horley Cl, Bexh	155	N9
Horley Rd SE9	170	C7
Hormead Rd W9	108	E8
Horn La E13	133	N9
Horn La W3	106	F11
Horn La, Wdf Grn	63	P12
Horn Link Way SE10	133	P7
Horn Pk Cl SE12	151	R10
Horn Pk La SE12	151	R10
Hornbeam Cl, SE11 1	34	J1
Hornbeam Cl, Borwd	38	A1
Hornbeam Cl, Buck H	64	B6
Hornbeam Cl, Ilf	99	N10
Hornbeam Cl, Nthlt	85	M10
Hornbeam Cres, Brent	123	K13
Hornbeam Gro E4	63	L5
Hornbeam La E4	47	K9
Hornbeam La, Bexh	155	T3
Hornbeam Rd, Buck H	64	B6
Hornbeam Rd, Hayes	102	F9
Hornbeam Ter, Cars	195	R1
Hornbeam Wk, Rich	159	U5
Hornbeam Way, Brom	188	H12
Hornbeams Ri, N11 7	58	B12
Hornblower Cl, SE16 2	131	R7
Hornbuckle Cl, Har	86	A4
Hornby Cl NW3	91	P13
Horncastle Cl SE12	151	P13
Horncastle Rd SE12	151	P13
Hornchurch Cl, Kings T	159	N8
Horndean Cl, SW15 5	161	P1
Horndon Cl, Rom	83	U1
Horndon Grn, Rom	83	U2
Horndon Rd, Rom	83	U2
Horne Way SW15	143	T4
Horner La, Mitch 6	181	P4
Hornfair Rd SE7	134	A12
Horniman Dr SE23	149	L14
Horning Cl SE9	170	D7
Horns End Pl, Pnr	66	E8
Horns Rd, Ilf	81	M11
Hornsey La N6	92	D1
Hornsey La N19	74	F14
Hornsey La Gdns N6	74	E14
Hornsey Pk Rd N8	75	M5
Hornsey Ri N19	74	J14
Hornsey Ri Gdns N19	74	H13
Hornsey Rd N7	93	L4
Hornsey Rd N19	93	L4
Hornsey St N7	93	M9
Hornshay St SE15	131	M12
Hornton Pl, W8 3	126	H4
Hornton St W8	126	H3
Horsa Cl, Wall	197	K13
Horsa Rd SE12	151	T13
Horsa Rd, Erith	137	T13
Horse & Dolphin Yd, W1 1	17	T9
Horse Fair, Kings T	177	P3
Horse Guards Av SW1	26	B4
Horse Guards Rd SW1	25	U4
Horse Leaze E6	116	H11
Horse Ride SW1	25	P4
Horse Shoe Cres, Nthlt	103	N3
Horse Yd N1	11	S1
Horsebridge Cl, Dag	119	K2
Horsecroft Rd, Edg	54	H13
Horseferry Pl SE10	132	E12
Horseferry Rd E14	113	R13
Horseferry Rd SW1	33	U1
Hursell Rd N5	93	N10
Horselydown La SE1	29	M4
Horsenden Av, Grnf	86	D9
Horsenden Cres, Grnf	86	E9
Horsenden La N, Grnf	86	G14
Horsenden La S, Grnf	104	H3
Horseshoe Cl E14	132	E9
Horseshoe Cl NW2	89	R3
Horseshoe La N20	56	A1
Horsfeld Gdns SE9	152	C9
Horsfeld Rd SE9	152	B9
Horsford Rd SW2	147	L10
Horsham Av N12	57	S9
Horsham Rd, Bexh	155	N10
Horsley Dr, Croy	200	E14
Horsley Dr, Kings T	159	N9
Horsley Rd E4	62	F3
Horsley Rd, Brom 4	187	R1
Horsley St SE17	36	C9
Horsmonden Cl, Orp 1	189	T13
Horsmonden Rd SE4	149	T10
Hortensia Rd SW10	30	E13
Horticultural Pl W4	124	G9
Horton Av NW2	90	D8
Horton Rd E8	94	J11
Horton St SE13	150	D5
Horton Way, Croy	185	P9
Hortus Rd E4	62	F3
Hortus Rd, Sthl	121	L4
Hosack Rd SW17	163	U3
Hoser Av SE12	169	N3
Hosier La EC1	19	P4
Hoskins Cl E16	115	U11

Hoskins St SE10	132	H10
Hospital Br Rd,	139	R13
Twick		
Hospital Rd E9	95	N9
Hospital Rd, Houns	139	N6
Hotham Cl,	175	P5
W Mol 2		
Hotham Rd SW15	143	U6
Hotham Rd SW19	163	L14
Hotham Rd Ms,	163	L14
SW19 6		
Hotham St E15	114	J1
Hothfield Pl SE16	131	M6
Hotspur Rd, Nthlt	103	N3
Hotspur St SE11	34	J5
Houblon Rd, Rich	141	S9
Houghton Cl E8	94	F12
Houghton Cl, Hmptn	157	K11
Houghton Rd,	76	E8
N15 3		
Houghton St,	18	G8
WC2 2		
Houlder Cres, Croy	197	R11
Houndsden Rd N21	43	N12
Houndsditch EC3	20	J5
Houndsfield Rd N9	44	J14
Hounslow Av,	139	S9
Houns		
Hounslow Gdns,	139	S9
Houns		
Hounslow Rd	156	C1
(Feltham), Felt		
Hounslow Rd	156	H6
(Hanworth), Felt		
Hounslow Rd, Twick	139	T12
Houseman Way,	130	B14
SE5 3		
Houston Pl,	190	C1
Esher 1		
Houston Rd SE23	167	S5
Houston Rd, Surb	177	K12
Hove Av E17	77	T10
Hove Gdns, Sutt	195	K2
Hoveden Rd NW2	90	C9
Hoveton Rd SE28	118	E12
Howard Av, Bex	172	F1
Howard Cl N11	58	A4
Howard Cl NW2	90	C7
Howard Cl W3	106	C11
Howard Cl, Hmptn	157	T13
Howard Cl, Loug	48	D11
Howard Dr, Borwd	38	H8
Howard Ms N5	93	S8
Howard Rd E6	116	F3
Howard Rd E11	97	K5
Howard Rd E17	78	C6
Howard Rd N15	76	D11
Howard Rd N16	94	B8
Howard Rd NW2	90	A8
Howard Rd SE20	185	L1
Howard Rd SE25	184	H10
Howard Rd, Bark	117	P2
Howard Rd, Brom	169	M14
Howard Rd, Ilf	98	J8
Howard Rd, Islw	140	E5
Howard Rd, N Mal	179	K7
Howard Rd, Sthl	103	S12
Howard Rd, Surb	177	T12
Howard St, T Ditt	177	K13
Howard Wk N2	73	M7
Howard Way, Barn	40	B10
Howards Cl, Pnr	66	D3
Howards Crest Cl,	186	F4
Beck		
Howards La SW15	143	T8
Howards Rd E13	115	N5
Howarth Ct, E15 3	96	E9
Howarth Rd SE2	136	B9
Howberry Cl, Edg	53	P12
Howberry Rd, Edg	53	P13
Howberry Rd, Stan	53	P11
Howberry Rd, Th Hth	184	A2
Howbury Rd SE15	149	L13
Howcroft Cres N3	56	H13
Howcroft La, Grnf	104	B5
Howden Cl SE28	118	G14
Howden Rd SE25	184	E4
Howden St SE15	148	G5
Howe Cl, Rom	83	P2
Howell Cl, Rom	82	G10
Howell Wk SE1	35	S3
Howes Cl N3	72	G5
Howfield Pl N17	76	E5
Howgate Rd SW14	142	G6
Howick Pl SW1	25	N11
Howie St SW11	127	R14
Howitt Rd NW3	91	R11
Howland Est SE16	131	M5
Howland Ms E W1	17	P1
Howland St W1	17	M1
Howland Way SE16	131	S4
Howletts Rd,	147	U11
SE24 1		
Howley Pl W2	14	G2
Howley Rd, Croy	197	S5
Hows St E2	13	M1
Howsman Rd SW13	125	N12
Howson Rd SE4	149	S8
Howson Ter, Rich	141	R11
Howton Pl, Bushey	52	A2
Hoxton Mkt, N1 1	12	G7
Hoxton Sq N1	12	H7
Hoxton St N1	12	J6
Hoy St E16	115	M12
Hoylake Gdns, Mitch	182	E5
Hoylake Gdns, Ruis	84	D1
Hoylake Gdns, Wat	50	G8
Hoylake Rd W3	107	K12
Hoyland Cl,	130	J13
SE15 5		
Hoyle Rd SW17	163	S9
Hubbard Dr, Chess	191	M12
Hubbard Rd SE27	165	U7
Hubbard St E15	114	J2
Hubbinet Ind Est,	83	U6
Rom		
Hubert Gro SW9	147	K6
Hubert Rd E6	116	A5
Huddart St E3	113	U9
Huddleston Cl E2	113	L3
Huddleston Rd N7	92	F6
Huddlestone Rd E7	97	M7
Huddlestone Rd	89	S11
NW2		
Hudson Gdns,	203	T12
Orp 1		
Hudson Pl SE18	135	L9
Hudson Rd, Bexh	155	L3
Hudson's Pl SW1	33	K1
Huggin Ct EC4	20	A9
Huggins Pl SW2	165	M1
Hugh Dalton Av,	126	E12
SW6 4		
Hugh Gaitskell Cl	126	E12
SW6		
Hugh Ms SW1	32	J3
Hugh Pl SW1	33	S2
Hugh St SW1	32	J3
Hughan Rd E15	96	H9
Hughenden Av, Har	69	K9
Hughenden Gdns,	102	F5
Nthlt		
Hughenden Rd,	179	P13
Wor Pk		
Hughendon Ter,	96	F7
E15 9		
Hughes Rd, Hayes	102	C14
Hughes Wk,	183	T13
Croy 3		
Hugo Rd N19	92	F7
Hugon Rd SW6	144	J5
Huguenot Pl E1	21	P2
Huguenot Pl SW18	145	L9
Huguenot Sq,	148	J5
SE15 4		
Hull Cl SE16	131	P2
Hull St EC1	11	U7
Hullbridge Ms N1	112	A1
Hulse Av, Bark	99	P11
Hulse Av, Rom	83	S1
Humber Dr W10	108	A8
Humber Rd NW2	89	S4
Humber Rd SE3	133	M11
Humberstone Rd	115	T6
E13		
Humberton Cl,	95	R10
E9 2		
Humbolt Rd W6	126	C12
Hume Ter E16	115	S10
Hume Way, Ruis	66	A12
Humes Av W7	122	E5
Humphrey Cl, Ilf	80	E2
Humphrey St SE1	37	M6
Humphries Cl, Dag	101	L7
Hundred Acre NW9	71	L3
Hungerdown E4	62	E1
Hungerford Br SE1	26	D2
Hungerford Br WC2	26	D2
Hungerford La WC2	26	B1
Hungerford Rd N7	92	J10
Hungerford St,	113	K11
E1 9		
Hunsdon Cl, Dag	101	K12
Hunsdon Rd SE14	131	N12
Hunslett St E2	113	M4
Hunston Rd, Mord	194	J1
Hunt Rd, Sthl	121	N6
Hunt St W11	126	B1
Hunter Cl SE1	28	F11
Hunter Cl SW12	164	A2
Hunter Cl, Borwd	38	F10
Hunter Rd SW20	179	U1
Hunter Rd, Ilf	99	K10
Hunter Rd, Th Hth	184	A6
Hunter St WC1	10	C9
Hunter Wk E13	115	N3
Huntercrombe	50	E9
Gdns, Wat		
Hunters, The, Beck	186	E1
Hunters Ct, Rich	141	N9
Hunters Gro, Har	69	M7
Hunters Gro, Hayes	120	B3
Hunters Gro, Orp	203	K8
Hunters Hall Rd, Dag	101	P8
Hunters Hill, Ruis	84	F5
Hunters Meadow,	166	D8
SE19 1		
Hunters Rd, Chess	191	R7
Hunters Sq, Dag	101	P8
Hunters Way,	198	D7
Croy 5		
Hunters Way, Enf	43	P1
Hunting Gate Cl, Enf	43	N5
Hunting Gate Dr,	191	R14
Chess		
Hunting Gate Ms,	195	K6
Sutt 3		
Hunting Gate Ms,	158	C2
Twick 1		
Huntingdon Cl,	182	J6
Mitch		
Huntingdon Gdns	124	F13
W4		
Huntingdon Gdns,	193	T6
Wor Pk		
Huntingdon Rd N2	73	R6
Huntingdon Rd N9	61	M2
Huntingdon St E16	115	M12
Huntingdon St N1	93	L14
Huntingfield, Croy	199	U13
Huntingfield Rd	143	P8
SW15		
Huntings Rd, Dag	101	P12
Huntley Dr N3	56	H12
Huntley St WC1	9	R12
Huntley Way SW20	179	N4
Huntly Rd SE25	184	D7
Hunton St E1	13	R12
Hunt's Cl SE3	151	P4
Hunts La E15	114	E4
Hunts Mead, Enf	45	P5
Hunts Mead Cl, Chis	170	E14
Hunts Slip Rd SE21	166	C5
Huntsman St SE17	36	F4
Huntsmans Cl, Felt	156	C7
Huntsmoor Rd,	192	G9
Epsom		
Huntspill St SW17	163	M6
Huntsworth Ms NW1	7	U11
Hurley Cres,	131	P3
SE16 15		
Hurley Rd SE11	35	M4
Hurley Rd, Grnf	103	R10
Hurlingham Ct SW6	144	E5
Hurlingham Gdns	144	E5
SW6		
Hurlingham Rd SW6	144	F4
Hurlingham Rd,	137	M14
Bexh		
Hurlingham Sq,	144	J5
SW6 1		
Hurlock St N5	93	S6
Hurlstone Rd SE25	184	C9
Hurn Ct Rd, Houns	138	H3
Huron Cl, Orp 5	203	T12
Huron Rd SW17	164	B4
Hurren Cl SE3	150	J5
Hurry Cl E15	97	K14
Hursley Rd, Chig	65	U10
Hurst Av E4	62	A6
Hurst Av N6	74	F12
Hurst Cl E4	62	A6
Hurst Cl NW11	72	J11
Hurst Cl, Brom	201	M1
Hurst Cl, Chess	192	A9
Hurst Cl, Nthlt	85	M10
Hurst Est SE2	136	G10
Hurst La SE2	136	G10
Hurst La, E Mol	175	T7
Hurst Ri, Barn	40	H6
Hurst Rd E17	78	C6
Hurst Rd N21	59	P2
Hurst Rd, Bex	172	G1
Hurst Rd, Buck H	64	B2
Hurst Rd, Croy	198	B9
Hurst Rd, E Mol	176	A5
Hurst Rd, Erith	137	U14
Hurst Rd, Sid	172	D3
Hurst Rd, Walt	175	K6
Hurst Rd, W Mol	175	R5
Hurst Springs, Bex	173	K2
Hurst St SE24	147	S11
Hurst Vw Rd, S Croy	198	C13
Hurst Way, S Croy	198	C12
Hurstbourne, Esher	190	F12
Hurstbourne Gdns,	99	R11
Bark		
Hurstbourne Rd	167	S2
SE23		
Hurstcourt Rd, Sutt	194	J3
Hurstdene Av, Brom	201	L2
Hurstdene Gdns N15	76	D13
Hurstfield, Brom	187	N9
Hurstfield Rd,	175	N5
W Mol		
Hurstleigh Gdns, Ilf	80	F2
Hurstmead Ct, Edg	54	D7
Hurstway Wk W11	108	B13
Hurstwood Av E18	79	S7
Hurstwood Av, Bex	172	J1
Hurstwood Dr, Brom	188	F6
Hurstwood Rd	72	E8
NW11		
Hurtwood Rd, Walt	175	L13
Huson Cl NW3	91	R13
Hussars Cl, Houns	139	K6
Husseywell Cres,	201	N1
Brom		
Hutchings St,	132	A4
E14 3		
Hutchings Wk NW11	73	K8
Hutchins Cl, E15 1	96	F14
Hutchins Rd SE28	118	B14
Hutchinson Ter,	87	P6
Wem		
Hutton Cl, Grnf 1	86	A9
Hutton Cl, Wdf Grn	63	R11
Hutton Gdns, Har	51	U13
Hutton Gro N12	57	L11
Hutton La, Har	52	A14
Hutton Row, Edg	54	E13
Hutton St EC4	19	M8
Hutton Wk, Har	51	U13
Huxbear St SE4	149	U10
Huxley Cl, Nthlt	103	K3
Huxley Dr, Rom	82	C14
Huxley Gdns NW10	105	U5
Huxley Par N18	59	U9
Huxley Pl N13	59	S7
Huxley Rd E10	96	E4
Huxley Rd N18	60	C7
Huxley Rd, Well	153	U6
Huxley Sayze N18	60	A9
Huxley St W10	108	C6
Hyacinth Cl,	157	N11
Hmptn 2		
Hyacinth Cl, Ilf	98	J11
Hyacinth Ct, Pnr 1	66	E5
Hyacinth Rd SW15	161	P1

Hycliffe Gdns, Chig	65	L7
Hyde, The NW9	71	L10
Hyde Cl E13	115	P3
Hyde Cl, Barn	40	E6
Hyde Ct N20	57	P5
Hyde Cres NW9	71	K10
Hyde Est Rd NW9	71	L10
Hyde La SW11	145	R1
Hyde Pk SW7	23	U2
Hyde Pk W1	23	U2
Hyde Pk W2	23	U2
Hyde Pk Av N21	60	A2
Hyde Pk Cor W1	24	E6
Hyde Pk Cres W2	15	P7
Hyde Pk Gdns N21	59	U2
Hyde Pk Gdns W2	15	M9
Hyde Pk Gdns Ms W2	15	M9
Hyde Pk Gate SW7	22	G8
Hyde Pk Gate Ms, SW7 *1*	22	G8
Hyde Pk Pl W2	15	S9
Hyde Pk Sq W2	15	N8
Hyde Pk Sq Ms W2	15	P8
Hyde Pk St W2	15	P8
Hyde Rd N1	112	C2
Hyde Rd, Bexh	155	M4
Hyde Rd, Rich *1*	141	T9
Hyde St SE8	132	A12
Hyde Vale SE10	132	G14
Hyde Wk, Mord	180	H13
Hyde Way N9	60	E4
Hydefield Cl N21	60	A2
Hydefield Ct N9	60	D3
Hyderabad Way, E15 *6*	96	J13
Hydes Pl, N1 *4*	93	R13
Hydeside Gdns N9	60	E4
Hydethorpe Av N9	60	E4
Hydethorpe Rd SW12	164	E1
Hylands Rd E17	78	H4
Hylton St SE18	135	T8
Hyndewood SE23	167	N5
Hyndman St, SE15 *1*	130	J11
Hynton Rd, Dag	100	F4
Hyrstdene, S Croy	197	S8
Hyson Rd SE16	131	K9
Hythe Av, Bexh	137	M13
Hythe Cl N18	60	H8
Hythe Path, Th Hth	184	D5
Hythe Rd NW10	107	N7
Hythe Rd, Th Hth	184	A4
Hyver Hill NW7	38	H13

I

Ibbetson Path, Loug	49	K6
Ibbotson Av E16	115	M11
Ibbott St E1	113	M7
Iberian Av, Wall	196	H7
Ibis La W4	142	E2
Ibis Way, Hayes *5*	102	H11
Ibscott Cl, Dag	101	T12
Ibsley Gdns SW15	161	N1
Ibsley Way, Barn	41	S8
Iceland Rd E3	114	B2
Ickburgh Rd E5	94	J5
Ickleton Rd SE9	170	D8
Icknield Dr, Ilf	81	K9
Ickworth Pk Rd E17	77	S7
Ida Rd N15	76	B9
Ida St E14	114	E12
Iden Cl, Brom	187	K5
Idlecombe Rd SW17	164	A11
Idmiston Rd E15	97	L9
Idmiston Rd SE27	165	U4
Idmiston Rd, Wor Pk	179	M14
Idmiston Sq, Wor Pk	179	M14
Idol La EC3	20	H11
Idonia St SE8	131	U13
Iffley Rd W6	125	S6
Ifield Rd SW10	30	C10
Ifor Evans Pl, E1 *18*	113	P8
Ightham Rd, Erith	137	N13
Ilbert St W10	108	D6
Ilchester Gdns W2	14	A9
Ilchester Pl W14	126	E5
Ilchester Rd, Dag	100	C9
Ildersly Gro SE21	166	B4
Ilderton Rd SE15	131	L11
Ilderton Rd SE16	131	L9
Ilex Cl, Sun	174	E4
Ilex Rd NW10	89	L12
Ilex Way SW16	165	N10
Ilford Hill, Ilf	98	H5
Ilford La, Ilf	99	K7
Ilfracombe Gdns, Rom	82	C14
Ilfracombe Rd, Brom	169	L6
Iliffe St SE17	35	S5
Iliffe Yd SE17	35	S5
Ilkley Cl SE19	166	B12
Ilkley Rd E16	115	T10
Ilkley Rd, Wat	50	H9
Illingworth Cl, Mitch	181	N6
Illingworth Way, Enf	44	D8
Ilmington Rd, Har	69	N11
Ilminster Gdns SW11	145	S7
Imber Cl N14	42	F13
Imber Cl, Esher	190	A2
Imber Ct Trd Est, E Mol	176	A12
Imber Gro, Esher	176	A14
Imber Pk Rd, Esher	190	A1
Imber St N1	112	A2
Imer Pl, T Ditt	176	E13
Imperial Av, N16 *1*	94	D7
Imperial Cl, Har	67	N12
Imperial College Rd SW7	22	J11
Imperial Dr, Har	67	N13
Imperial Gdns, Mitch	182	C6
Imperial Ms E6	116	A4
Imperial Rd N22	74	J1
Imperial Rd SW6	145	K2
Imperial Rd SW6	145	K1
Imperial St E3	114	E6
Imperial Way, Chis	171	M8
Imperial Way, Croy	197	N12
Imperial Way, Har	69	S11
Inca Dr SE9	152	J14
Inchmery Rd SE6	168	D2
Inchwood, Croy	200	C7
Indopendent Pl E8	94	F9
Independents Rd, SE3 *3*	151	L5
Inderwick Rd N8	75	M11
Indescon Ct E14	132	C4
India St, EC3 *2*	21	L8
India Way W12	107	R13
Indigo Ms, E14 *14*	114	E13
Indigo Ms N16	94	A6
Indus Rd SE7	133	U14
Industry Ter, SW9 *3*	147	N6
Ingal Rd E13	115	N8
Ingate Pl SW8	146	D2
Ingatestone Rd E12	97	T2
Ingatestone Rd SE25	184	J8
Ingatestone Rd, Wdf Grn	63	P13
Ingelow Rd SW8	146	C4
Ingersoll Rd W12	125	R2
Ingestre Pl W1	17	P8
Ingestre Rd E7	97	P7
Ingestre Rd NW5	92	D7
Ingham Rd NW6	90	G8
Ingle Cl, Pnr	67	K6
Inglebert St EC1	11	K5
Ingleborough St, SW9 *4*	147	N3
Ingleby Dr, Har	86	A5
Ingleby Rd, Dag	101	R12
Ingleby Rd, Ilf	98	J2
Ingleby Way, Chis	170	H10
Ingledew Rd SE18	135	P9
Inglehurst Gdns, Ilf	80	E10
Inglemere Rd SE23	167	N5
Inglemere Rd, Mitch	163	U13
Inglesham Wk, E9 *3*	95	U11
Ingleside Cl, Beck	168	A14
Ingleside Gro SE3	133	M12
Inglethorpe St SW6	144	A1
Ingleton Av, Well	154	B9
Ingleton Rd N18	60	G11
Ingleton St, SW9 *3*	147	N3
Ingleway N12	57	R11
Inglewood Cl, E14 *12*	132	B7
Inglewood Cl, Ilf	65	T11
Inglewood Copse, Brom	188	D4
Inglewood Rd NW6	90	H10
Inglis Barracks NW7	56	C10
Inglis Rd W5	105	U14
Inglis Rd, Croy	198	F1
Inglis St SE5	147	S2
Ingram Av NW11	73	L14
Ingram Cl SE11	34	G1
Ingram Cl, Stan	53	L10
Ingram Rd N2	73	S7
Ingram Rd, Th Hth	183	T1
Ingram Way, Grnf	104	A2
Ingrave St SW11	145	P5
Ingress St, W4 *7*	124	J9
Inigo Jones Rd SE7	134	C13
Inkerman Rd NW5	92	C11
Inks Grn E4	62	E10
Inman Rd NW10	106	J1
Inman Rd SW18	145	L14
Inmans Row, Wdf Grn	63	P8
Inner Circle NW1	8	C9
Inner Pk Rd SW19	162	A3
Inner Temple La EC4	19	K8
Innes Cl SW20	180	D4
Innes Gdns SW15	143	S12
Innes Yd, Croy	197	U6
Inniskilling Rd E13	115	U4
Innovation Cl, Wem	105	R1
Inskip Cl E10	96	C4
Inskip Rd, Dag	100	H2
Institute Pl E8	94	J10
Instone Cl, Wall	197	K13
Integer Gdns E11	78	G14
International Av, Houns	120	D10
International Trd Est, Sthl	120	D6
Inver Ct W2	14	C7
Inveraray Pl SE18	135	P11
Inverclyde Gdns, Rom	82	G8
Inveresk Gdns, Wor Pk	193	M6
Inverforth Cl NW3	91	L4
Inverforth Rd N11	58	D10
Inverine Rd SE7	133	S10
Invermore Pl SE18	135	M8
Inverness Av, Enf	44	D2
Inverness Dr, Ilf	65	S12
Inverness Gdns W8	22	A4
Inverness Ms W2	14	D10
Inverness Pl W2	14	C10
Inverness Rd N18	60	J9
Inverness Rd, Houns	139	M7
Inverness Rd, Sthl	121	K7
Inverness Rd, Wor Pk	194	A2
Inverness St NW1	110	C1
Inverness Ter W2	14	D9
Inverton Rd SE15	149	N8
Invicta Cl, Chis	170	H9
Invicta Gro, Nthlt	103	L6
Invicta Plaza SE1	27	P1
Invicta Rd SE3	133	P13
Inville Rd SE17	36	F7
Inwen Ct SE8	131	S10
Inwood Av, Houns	139	T6
Inwood Cl, Croy	199	S3
Inwood Rd, Houns	139	S7
Inworth St SW11	145	S3
Ion Sq E2	13	S4
Iona Cl SE6	150	A13
Iona Cl, Mord	180	J14
Ipswich Rd SW17	164	B12
Ireland Cl E6	116	E10
Ireland Pl N22	59	K13
Ireland Yd EC4	19	R8
Irene Rd SW6	144	G2
Irene Rd, Orp	189	U14
Ireton Cl N10	58	B13
Ireton St E3	114	A7
Iris Av, Bex	155	K10
Iris Cl E6	116	D9
Iris Cl, Croy	199	N1
Iris Cl, Surb	177	T14
Iris Ct, Pnr	66	E6
Iris Cres, Bexh	137	M12
Iris Rd, Epsom	192	D9
Iris Way E4	61	U11
Irkdale Av, Enf	44	F1
Iron Br Cl NW10	88	J10
Iron Br Cl, Sthl	121	U2
Iron Mill Pl SW18	145	K12
Iron Mill Rd SW18	145	K11
Ironmonger La EC2	20	C7
Ironmonger Row EC1	12	A7
Ironmongers Pl, E14 *4*	132	B8
Ironside Cl SE16	131	N3
Irvine Av, Har	68	H5
Irvine Cl N20	57	R4
Irvine Way, Orp	189	T14
Irving Av, Nthlt	102	H2
Irving Gro SW9	147	L4
Irving Rd W14	126	B5
Irving St WC2	17	U11
Irving Way NW9	71	M10
Irwin Av SE18	135	S13
Irwin Gdns NW10	107	S2
Isabel Hill Cl, Hmptn *2*	175	R2
Isabel St SW9	147	M1
Isabella Cl N14	42	F13
Isabella Dr, Orp	203	L8
Isabella Rd, E9 *3*	95	M10
Isabella St SE1	27	N4
Isambard Ms E14	132	F6
Isambard Pl, SE16 *8*	131	M2
Isham Rd SW16	182	J3
Isis Cl SW15	143	T7
Isis St SW18	163	L4
Isla Rd SE18	135	L12
Island Fm Av, W Mol	175	M9
Island Fm Rd, W Mol	175	N10
Island Rd, Mitch	163	T14
Island Row E14	113	T12
Islay Gdns, Houns	138	H9
Isledon Rd N7	93	N5
Islehurst Cl, Chis	188	H2
Isleworth Prom, Twick	140	J8
Islington Grn N1	111	R2
Islington High St N1	11	N2
Islington Pk Ms N1	93	R13
Islington Pk St N1	93	P13
Islip Gdns, Edg	54	G13
Islip Gdns, Nthlt	85	K14
Islip Manor Rd, Nthlt	85	K13
Islip St NW5	92	E10
Ismailia Rd E7	97	R13
Isom Cl E13	115	T6
Ivanhoe Dr, Har	68	J4
Ivanhoe Rd SE5	148	E6
Ivanhoe Rd, Houns	138	H5
Ivatt Pl W14	126	F10
Ivatt Way N17	75	S6
Ive Fm Cl E10	96	B3
Ive Fm La E10	96	A3
Iveagh Av NW10	106	A4
Iveagh Cl E9	113	P1
Iveagh Cl, NW10 *1*	106	B4
Ivedon Rd, Well	154	F4
Iveley Rd SW4	146	E4
Ivere Dr, Barn	40	J11
Iverhurst Cl, Bexh	154	H9
Iverna Ct W8	126	H5
Iverna Gdns W8	126	H5
Ivers Way, Croy	200	D13
Iverson Rd NW6	90	G12
Ives Rd E16	114	J10
Ives St SW3	31	R2

Name	Page	Grid
Ivestor Ter SE23	149	M13
Ivimey St E2	13	T6
Ivinghoe Cl, Enf	44	C3
Ivinghoe Rd, Dag	100	C10
Ivor Gro SE9	171	K2
Ivor Pl NW1	7	T11
Ivor St NW1	92	E13
Ivory Sq, SW11 1	145	M6
Ivorydown, Brom	169	N7
Ivy Cl, Har	85	L7
Ivy Cl, Pnr	66	F13
Ivy Cl, Sun	174	E4
Ivy Cotts E14	114	D13
Ivy Ct SE16	37	U7
Ivy Cres W4	124	E7
Ivy Gdns N8	74	J12
Ivy Gdns, Mitch	182	G6
Ivy La, Houns	139	L7
Ivy Rd E16	115	N11
Ivy Rd E17	78	B12
Ivy Rd N14	42	G14
Ivy Rd NW2	89	U7
Ivy Rd SE4	149	T8
Ivy Rd SW17	163	S9
Ivy Rd, Houns	139	S8
Ivy Rd, Surb	192	A3
Ivy St N1	12	G2
Ivy Wk, Dag	100	J12
Ivybridge Cl, Twick	140	G13
Ivybridge Est, Islw	140	F10
Ivybridge La WC2	18	D11
Ivychurch Cl SE20	167	L14
Ivychurch La, SE17 1	37	L6
Ivydale Rd SE15	149	N6
Ivydale Rd, Cars	195	U4
Ivyday Gro SW16	165	L6
Ivydene, W Mol	175	L10
Ivydene Cl, Sutt	195	M8
Ivyhouse Rd, Dag	100	G12
Ivymount Rd SE27	165	P6
Ixworth Pl SW3	31	P5
Izane Rd, Bexh	155	L8

J

Name	Page	Grid
Jacaranda Cl, N Mal	178	J6
Jack Barnett Way N22	75	M4
Jack Clow Rd E15	115	K4
Jack Cornwell St E12	98	G8
Jack Dash Way E6	116	C8
Jack Walker Ct N5	93	S7
Jackass La, Kes	201	T11
Jacklin Grn, Wdf Grn	63	N8
Jackman Ms NW10	88	J6
Jackman St E8	112	J2
Jackson Cl E9	95	M14
Jackson Rd N7	93	M8
Jackson Rd, Bark	117	P2
Jackson Rd, Barn	41	R12
Jackson Rd, Brom	202	E3
Jackson St SE18	134	H11
Jackson Way, Sthl	121	S3
Jacksons La N6	74	B13
Jacksons Pl, Croy	198	B2
Jacksons Way, Croy	200	B5
Jacob St SE1	29	R6
Jacobs Cl, Dag	101	S6
Jacob's Well Ms W1	16	E5
Jacqueline Cl, Nthlt	103	L1
Jade Cl E16	116	B12
Jade Cl NW2	72	B14
Jade Cl, Dag	100	F1
Jaffe Rd, Ilf	99	N2
Jaffray Pl, SE27 4	145	T14
Jaffray Rd, Brom	188	A8
Jaggard Way SW12	145	T14
Jago Cl SE18	135	M12
Jago Wk SE5	130	A14
Jamaica Rd SE1	29	P8
Jamaica Rd SE16	130	J4
Jamaica Rd,Th Hth	183	R11
Jamaica St E1	113	M10
James Av NW2	89	U9
James Av, Dag	101	M2
James Bedford Cl, Pnr	66	E3
James Boswell Cl, SW16 1	165	N7
James Cl E13	115	P3
James Cl NW11	72	C11
James Collins Cl W9	108	E7
James Ct N1	93	U14
James Dudson Ct NW10	88	E13
James Gdns N22	59	T14
James Joyce Wk, SE24 18	147	S8
James La E10	78	G13
James La E11	78	J11
James Newman Ct, SE9 2	170	G6
James Pl N17	60	E14
James St W1	16	F7
James St WC2	18	C8
James St, Bark	99	L14
James St, Enf	44	F9
James St, Houns	140	A5
James Yd E4	62	G11
Jameson Cl, W3 1	124	F3
Jameson St, W8 13	126	H1
James's Cotts, Rich	124	A13
Jamestown Rd NW1	110	C1
Jamestown Way E14	114	H14
Jane St, E1 10	112	J11
Janet St E14	132	B5
Janeway Pl, SE16 4	130	J4
Janeway St SE16	29	U8
Jansen Wk SW11	145	N7
Janson Cl E15	96	J9
Janson Cl NW10	88	J5
Janson Rd E15	97	K9
Jansons Rd N15	76	D6
Japan Cres N4	75	L14
Japan Rd, Rom	82	H12
Jardine Rd E1	113	P13
Jarrett Cl SW2	165	R2
Jarrow Cl, Mord	180	J10
Jarrow Rd N17	76	J8
Jarrow Rd SE16	131	L8
Jarrow Rd, Rom	82	F11
Jarrow Way E9	95	S8
Jarvis Cl, Bark	117	N1
Jarvis Cl, Barn	40	B10
Jarvis Rd SE22	148	D8
Jarvis Rd, S Croy	198	A11
Jasmin Rd, Epsom	192	D10
Jasmine Cl, Ilf	99	K10
Jasmine Cl, Orp	202	J3
Jasmine Cl, Sthl 2	103	K13
Jasmine Gdns, Croy	200	C6
Jasmine Gdns, Har	85	P4
Jasmine Gro SE20	185	K1
Jason Wk SE9	170	G7
Jasper Pas SE19	166	E11
Jasper Rd E16	116	B12
Jasper Rd SE19	166	E11
Jasper Wk N1	12	C5
Javelin Way, Nthlt	102	H6
Jay Gdns, Chis	170	F8
Jay Ms SW7	22	J8
Jaycroft, Enf	43	P2
Jebb Av SW2	147	K12
Jebb St E3	114	B4
Jedburgh Rd E13	115	T5
Jedburgh St SW11	146	B7
Jeddo Rd W12	125	L3
Jefferson Cl W13	123	K6
Jefferson Cl, Ilf	81	K9
Jefferson Wk, SE18 4	134	H12
Jeffreys Pl, NW1 1	92	E13
Jeffreys Rd SW4	146	J3
Jeffreys Rd, Enf	45	T7
Jeffreys St NW1	92	D13
Jeffreys Wk SW4	146	J3
Jeffs Cl, Hmptn	157	S11
Jeffs Rd, Sutt	194	F8
Jeger Av E2	112	E2
Jeken Rd SE9	151	U8
Jelf Rd SW2	147	P9
Jellicoe Gdns, Stan	52	F11
Jellicoe Rd E13	115	P8
Jellicoe Rd N17	60	A14
Jemmett Cl, Kings T	178	C2
Jengar Cl, Sutt	195	K7
Jenkins La E6	116	H4
Jenkins La, Bark	117	L4
Jenkins Rd E13	115	S8
Jenner Av W3	106	H10
Jenner Pl SW13	125	R12
Jenner Rd N16	94	F5
Jennett Rd, Croy	197	N5
Jennifer Rd, Brom	169	M5
Jennings Cl, Surb	177	L13
Jennings Rd SE22	148	F11
Jennings Way, Barn	39	U6
Jenningtree Way, Belv	137	U3
Jenny Hammond Cl, E11 2	97	L5
Jenson Way, SE19 13	166	E14
Jenton Av, Bexh	154	J2
Jephson Rd E7	97	T13
Jephson St, SE5 6	148	A2
Jephtha Rd SW18	144	G11
Jeppos La, Mitch	181	T8
Jerdan Pl SW6	126	G13
Jeremiah St, E14 4	114	C12
Jeremys Grn N18	61	K7
Jermyn St SW1	25	N1
Jerningham Av, Ilf	80	J3
Jerningham Rd SE14	149	P4
Jerome Cres NW8	7	N9
Jerome St E1	13	M12
Jerrard St, N1 3	12	J4
Jerrard St SE13	150	D5
Jersey Av, Stan	69	L4
Jersey Dr, Orp	189	N12
Jersey Par, Houns	139	R1
Jersey Rd E11	96	G2
Jersey Rd E16	115	S10
Jersey Rd SW17	164	C12
Jersey Rd W7	122	G4
Jersey Rd, Houns	139	S1
Jersey Rd, Ilf	99	K8
Jersey Rd, Islw	122	B13
Jersey St E2	112	J5
Jervis Ct W1	17	K8
Jerviston Gdns SW16	165	P10
Jesmond Av, Wem	87	U11
Jesmond Cl, Mitch	182	B6
Jesmond Rd, Croy	184	F13
Jesmond Way, Stan	53	S9
Jessam Av E5	94	J2
Jessamine Rd W7	122	D2
Jesse Rd E10	96	E2
Jessel Dr, Loug	49	M3
Jessica Rd SW18	145	M11
Jessie Blythe La, N19 1	74	J14
Jessop Av, Sthl	121	L8
Jessop Rd, SE24 3	147	T8
Jessop Sq, E14 9	132	A2
Jessops Way, Croy	182	F12
Jessup Cl SE18	135	L7
Jetstar Way, Nthlt	102	H6
Jevington Way SE12	169	S2
Jewel Rd E17	78	A5
Jewry St, EC3 1	21	L8
Jew's Row SW18	145	K7
Jews Wk SE26	167	K7
Jeymer Av NW2	89	S10
Jeymer Dr, Grnf	103	T2
Jeypore Rd SW18	145	M13
Jillian Cl, Hmptn	157	P13
Jim Bradley Cl SE18	134	H7
Joan Cres SE9	152	B14
Joan Gdns, Dag	100	J3
Joan Rd, Dag	100	J3
Joan St SE1	27	N4
Jocelyn Rd, Rich	141	R6
Jocelyn St SE15	148	G1
Jockey's Flds WC1	18	G1
Jodane St SE8	131	T8
Jodrell Cl, Islw	140	G1
Jodrell Rd E3	113	U1
Joel St, Nthwd	66	A5
Joel St, Pnr	66	C9
Johanna St, SE1 1	27	K7
John Adam St WC2	26	C1
John Aird Ct W2	14	G2
John Archer Way SW18	145	P11
John Ashby Cl SW2	147	K11
John Austin Cl, Kings T	177	T2
John Barnes Wk E15	97	L11
John Bradshaw Rd N14	58	G2
John Burns Dr, Bark	99	S14
John Campbell Rd N16	94	D10
John Carpenter St EC4	19	M9
John Felton Rd SE16	29	S7
John Fisher St E1	21	R10
John Gooch Dr, Enf	43	R2
John Harrison Way SE10	133	L6
John Islip St SW1	34	A3
John Maurice Cl SE17	36	D2
John McKenna Wk, SE16 3	29	U10
John Newton Ct, Well	154	D6
John Parker Cl, Dag	101	R13
John Parker Sq, SW11 12	145	P6
John Penn St SE13	150	D2
John Perrin Pl, Har	69	S13
John Princes St W1	17	K6
John Roll Way SE16	29	T10
John Ruskin St SE5	35	R13
John Silkin La SE8	131	P9
John Smith Av SW6	126	E13
John Spencer Sq N1	93	S11
John St E15	115	L2
John St SE25	184	H7
John St WC1	10	G12
John St, Enf	44	E9
John St, Houns	139	K3
John Williams Cl SE14	131	N12
John Williams Cl, Kings T 3	177	P1
John Wilson St SE18	134	H7
John Woolley Cl, SE13 4	150	J7
Johns Av NW4	71	T7
Johns La, Mord	181	M10
John's Ms WC1	10	F11
John's Pl E1	113	K11
John's Ter, Croy	198	B2
Johnson Cl E8	112	H1
Johnson Rd, Brom	188	A10
Johnson Rd, Croy	184	A13
Johnson Rd, Houns	120	F14
Johnson St E1	113	M12
Johnson St, Sthl	120	F5
Johnsons Cl, Cars	195	U5
Johnsons Dr, Hmptn	175	T2
Johnson's Pl SW1	33	M7
Johnsons Way NW10	106	C7
Johnston Cl, SW9 3	147	M2
Johnston Rd, Wdf Grn	63	N10
Johnstone Rd E6	116	F6
Joiner St SE1	28	F3
Joiner's Arms Yd, SE5 7	148	A2
Jollys La, Har	86	A2
Jollys La, Hayes	102	H9
Jonathan St SE11	34	F5
Jones Rd E13	115	S8
Jonquil Gdns, Hmptn	157	N11
Jonson Cl, Hayes	102	B9
Jonson Cl, Mitch	182	D6
Jordan Cl, Dag	101	R7
Jordan Cl, Har 1	85	M6
Jordan Rd, Grnf	105	L1

Jordans Cl, Islw	140	D2
Joseph Av W3	106	G12
Joseph Powell Cl, SW12 2	146	E12
Joseph Ray Rd E11	96	J3
Joseph St E3	113	U8
Josephine Av SW2	147	M10
Joshua St E14	114	E11
Joubert St SW11	145	U4
Jowett St SE15	130	F14
Joyce Av N18	60	F10
Joyce Dawson Way SE28	118	B13
Joyce Page Cl, SE7 3	134	A11
Joyce Wk SW2	147	N11
Joydon Dr, Rom	82	D11
Joyners Cl, Dag	101	L7
Jubilee Av E4	62	F11
Jubilee Av, Rom	83	T10
Jubilee Av, Twick	157	T1
Jubilee Cl NW9	70	G11
Jubilee Cl, Pnr	66	E3
Jubilee Cl, Rom	83	S10
Jubilee Cres E14	132	F6
Jubilee Cres N9	60	G1
Jubilee Dr, Ruis	84	H7
Jubilee Gdns, Sthl	103	P10
Jubilee Pl SW3	31	S5
Jubilee Rd, Grnf	104	J1
Jubilee Rd, Sutt	194	B13
Jubilee St E1	113	L10
Jubilee Wk, Wat	50	D7
Jubilee Way SW19	181	K2
Jubilee Way, Chess	192	B7
Jubilee Way, Sid	172	B4
Judd St WC1	10	B8
Jude St E16	115	L12
Judge Wk, Esher	190	C11
Juer St SW11	127	S14
Julia Gdns, Bark	118	H3
Julia Garfield Ms E16	133	S1
Julia St NW5	92	A8
Julian Av W3	106	D13
Julian Cl, Barn	40	J6
Julian Hill, Har	86	D4
Julian Pl E14	132	D9
Juliana Cl N2	73	K5
Julien Rd W5	123	L7
Juliette Rd E13	115	M4
Junction App SE13	150	E5
Junction App SW1	145	S7
Junction Ms W2	15	P5
Junction Pl, W2 1	15	M5
Junction Rd E13	115	S3
Junction Rd N9	60	G2
Junction Rd N17	76	G5
Junction Rd N19	92	E6
Junction Rd W5	123	N8
Junction Rd, Brent	123	N8
Junction Rd, Har	68	C12
Junction Rd, S Croy	198	A10
Junction Rd E, Rom 1	82	J13
Junction Rd W, Rom	82	J13
Juniper Cl, Barn	40	B10
Juniper Cl, Chess	191	U11
Juniper Cl, Wem	87	U9
Juniper Cres NW1	92	B14
Juniper Gdns SW16	182	E2
Juniper La E6	116	D10
Juniper Rd, Ilf	98	H6
Juniper St E1	113	L13
Juno Way SE14	131	P11
Jupiter Way N7	93	M11
Jupp Rd E15	96	G14
Jupp Rd W E15	114	G1
Justice Wk SW3	31	N11
Justin Cl, Brent	123	P14
Justin Rd E4	61	U12
Jute La, Enf	45	S4
Jutland Cl N19	92	J2
Jutland Rd E13	115	P8
Jutland Rd SE6	150	E14
Jutsums Av, Rom	83	S12
Jutsums La, Rom	83	S11
Juxon Cl, Har	67	S2
Juxon St SE11	34	G1

K

Kaduna Cl, Pnr	66	B10
Kale Rd, Erith	136	J4
Kambala Rd SW11	145	P4
Kangley Br Rd SE26	167	T10
Kaplan Dr N21	43	K10
Kara Way NW2	90	A7
Karen Ct, Brom	187	L1
Karina Cl, Chig	65	S10
Karoline Gdns, Grnf	104	A3
Kashgar Rd SE18	135	T8
Kashmir Rd SE7	134	A13
Kassala Rd SW11	145	U2
Katella Trd Est, Bark	117	S5
Kates Cl, Barn	39	N10
Katharine St, Croy	197	U5
Katherine Cl SE16	131	N2
Katherine Gdns SE9	152	A8
Katherine Gdns, Ilf	65	M13
Katherine Rd E6	116	C2
Katherine Rd E7	97	U13
Katherine Rd, Twick 2	158	G1
Katherine Sq, W11 12	126	C1
Kathleen Av W3	106	F9
Kathleen Av, Wem	87	S14
Kathleen Rd SW11	145	T6
Kay Rd SW9	147	K4
Kay St E2	13	T2
Kay St E15	96	H14
Kay St, Well	154	C2
Kayemoor Rd, Sutt	195	R13
Kean St WC2	18	E7
Keatley Grn E4	61	T12
Keats Av E16	133	R1
Keats Cl E11	79	R9
Keats Cl NW3 1	91	R8
Keats Cl SE1	37	M4
Keats Cl SW19	163	N11
Keats Cl, Chig	65	M11
Keats Cl, Enf	45	N9
Keats Cl, Hayes	102	B9
Keats Gro NW3	91	R8
Keats Pl EC2	20	D4
Keats Rd, Belv	137	T6
Keats Rd, Well	153	S1
Keats Way, Croy	185	M12
Keats Way, Grnf	103	R10
Keble Cl, Nthlt	85	U10
Keble Cl, Wor Pk	193	M2
Keble Pl SW13	125	S12
Keble St SW17	163	M7
Kechill Gdns, Brom	187	P13
Kedleston Dr, Orp	189	U10
Keedonwood Rd, Brom	169	K9
Keel Cl SE16	131	P2
Keeley Rd, Croy	197	T3
Keeley St WC2	18	E7
Keeling Rd SE9	152	A10
Keely Cl, Barn	41	S9
Keemor Cl SE18	134	G13
Keens Cl SW16	164	H9
Keens Rd, Croy	197	U7
Keens Yd N1	93	S12
Keep, The SE3	151	N4
Keep, The, Kings T	159	T12
Keep La, N11 1	58	B3
Keepers Ms, Tedd	159	L11
Keesey St SE17	36	D10
Keetons Rd SE16	130	J5
Keevil Dr SW19	144	B14
Keighley Cl N7	93	K8
Keightley Dr SE9	171	M2
Keildon Rd SW11	145	T8
Keir Hardie Way, Bark	100	A14
Keir Hardie Way, Hayes	102	B6
Keith Connor Cl, SW8 10	146	C5
Keith Gro W12	125	N3
Keith Rd E17	77	U2
Keith Rd, Bark	117	P3
Kelbrook Rd SE3	152	C4
Kelby Path SE9	171	K6
Kelceda Cl NW2	89	P3
Kelfield Gdns W10	107	U11
Kelfield Ms W10	108	A11
Kell St SE1	27	R9
Kelland Cl N8	74	H9
Kelland Rd E13	115	P7
Kellaway Rd SE3	151	U3
Keller Cres E12	98	B7
Kellerton Rd SE13	150	J9
Kellett Rd SW2	147	N8
Kelling Gdns, Croy	183	R13
Kellino St SW17	163	T8
Kellner Rd SE28	135	T5
Kelly Av SE15	130	F14
Kelly Cl NW10	88	H5
Kelly Ct, Borwd	38	G3
Kelly Rd NW7	56	C11
Kelly St NW1	92	D12
Kelly Way, Rom	82	J10
Kelman Cl SW4	146	H4
Kelmore Gro SE22	148	G7
Kelmscott Cl E17	77	T2
Kelmscott Gdns W12	125	N5
Kelmscott Rd SW11	145	S10
Kelross Rd N5	93	T7
Kelsall Cl SE3	151	S3
Kelsey La, Beck	186	A4
Kelsey Pk Av, Beck	186	C4
Kelsey Pk Rd, Beck	186	B3
Kelsey Sq, Beck	186	A3
Kelsey St E2	13	U9
Kelsey Way, Beck	186	A5
Kelsie Way, Ilf	65	R13
Kelso Pl W8	22	C11
Kelso Rd, Cars	181	M14
Kelston Rd, Ilf	81	K3
Kelvedon Cl, Kings T	159	U12
Kelvedon Rd SW6	126	F14
Kelvedon Way, Wdf Grn	64	E11
Kelvin Av N13	59	L11
Kelvin Av, Tedd	158	D12
Kelvin Cl, Epsom	192	B12
Kelvin Cres, Har	52	D13
Kelvin Dr, Twick	141	K11
Kelvin Gdns, Croy	183	K14
Kelvin Gdns, Sthl	103	N11
Kelvin Gro SE26	166	J6
Kelvin Gro, Chess	191	P5
Kelvin Ind Est, Grnf	85	S14
Kelvin Par, Orp	203	R2
Kelvin Rd N5	93	T8
Kelvin Rd, Well	154	A5
Kelvinbrook, W Mol	175	R5
Kelvington Cl, Croy	185	S13
Kelvington Rd SE15	149	N10
Kember St, N1 3	93	L14
Kemble Dr, Brom	202	D5
Kemble Rd N17	76	G2
Kemble Rd SE23	167	P2
Kemble Rd, Croy	197	R5
Kemble St WC2	18	E8
Kemerton Rd SE5	147	T6
Kemerton Rd, Beck	186	D4
Kemerton Rd, Croy	184	F14
Kemeys St, E9 1	95	R10
Kemnal Rd, Chis	171	M11
Kemp Gdns, Croy	183	T12
Kempe Rd NW6	108	B4
Kemplay Rd NW3	91	N8
Kemps Dr E14	113	M13
Kemps Gdns, SE13 2	150	F10
Kempsford Gdns SW5	126	H10
Kempsford Rd SE11	35	M3
Kempshott Rd SW16	164	J13
Kempson Rd SW6	144	H1
Kempt St SE18	134	G12
Kempthorne Rd SE8	131	S7
Kempton Av, Nthlt	85	P10
Kempton Av, Sun	174	D1
Kempton Cl, Erith	137	U11
Kempton Ct, Sun	174	D1
Kempton Rd E6	116	E1
Kempton Rd, Hmptn	175	L12
Kempton Wk, Croy	185	R12
Kemsing Cl, Bex	155	K13
Kemsing Cl, Brom	201	M3
Kemsing Cl, Th Hth	183	U8
Kemsing Rd SE10	133	N9
Ken Way, Wem	88	F4
Kenbury St SE5	147	T3
Kenchester Cl SW8	129	K14
Kencot Cl, Erith	137	M4
Kendal Av N18	60	A8
Kendal Av W3	106	B8
Kendal Av, Bark	99	R14
Kendal Cl SW9	35	N14
Kendal Cl, Wdf Grn	63	N4
Kendal Gdns N18	60	B8
Kendal Gdns, Sutt	195	L3
Kendal Par N18	60	A8
Kendal Pl SW15	144	E10
Kendal Rd NW10	89	P8
Kendal St W2	15	R8
Kendale Rd, Brom	168	J10
Kendall Av, Beck	185	R3
Kendall Pl W1	16	C4
Kendall Rd, Beck	185	R3
Kendall Rd, Islw	140	G4
Kendalmere Cl N10	74	D2
Kender St SE14	131	M14
Kendoa Rd SW4	146	H7
Kendon Cl E11	79	S10
Kendra Hall Rd, S Croy	197	S13
Kendrey Gdns, Twick	140	C13
Kendrick Ms, SW7 2	31	K2
Kendrick Pl SW7	31	K3
Kenelm Cl, Har	86	G5
Kenerne Dr, Barn	40	C10
Kenilford Rd SW12	146	D13
Kenilworth Av E17	78	B4
Kenilworth Av SW19	162	G8
Kenilworth Av, Har	85	L7
Kenilworth Cl, Borwd	38	F6
Kenilworth Ct, SW15 2	144	C6
Kenilworth Cres, Enf	44	D1
Kenilworth Dr, Borwd	38	F6
Kenilworth Gdns SE18	152	J3
Kenilworth Gdns, Ilf	99	U3
Kenilworth Gdns, Loug	48	E11
Kenilworth Gdns, Sthl	103	M6
Kenilworth Gdns, Wat	50	E9
Kenilworth Rd E3	113	R3
Kenilworth Rd NW6	108	F1
Kenilworth Rd SE20	185	N1
Kenilworth Rd W5	123	R2
Kenilworth Rd, Edg	54	E6
Kenilworth Rd, Epsom	193	N10
Kenilworth Rd, Orp	189	M12
Kenley Av NW9	70	J3
Kenley Cl, Barn	41	R7
Kenley Cl, Bex	155	P14
Kenley Cl, Chis	189	S5
Kenley Gdns, Th Hth	183	R8
Kenley Rd SW19	180	F4
Kenley Rd, Kings T	178	D3
Kenley Rd, Twick	140	H12
Kenley Wk W11	108	C14
Kenley Wk, Sutt	194	A8
Kenlor Rd SW17	163	P10
Kenmare Dr, Mitch	163	T13
Kenmare Gdns N13	59	S8
Kenmare Rd, Th Hth	183	N11
Kenmere Gdns, Wem	106	A1
Kenmere Rd, Well	154	E4
Kenmont Gdns NW10	107	R5
Kenmore Av, Har	124	A13
Kenmore Cl, Rich	124	A13
Kenmore Gdns, Edg	70	D3

Kenmore Rd, Har	69	P6
Kenmure Rd E8	95	K10
Kenmure Yd E8	95	K10
Kennacraig Cl, E16 *11*	133	P2
Kennard Rd E15	96	G14
Kennard Rd N11	57	T10
Kennard St E16	134	E2
Kennard St SW11	146	A2
Kennedy Av, Enf	45	M11
Kennedy Cl E13	115	P4
Kennedy Cl, Mitch *3*	182	A3
Kennedy Cl, Orp	203	N1
Kennedy Cl, Pnr	51	M12
Kennedy Rd W7	104	D8
Kennedy Rd, Bark	117	R2
Kennet Cl SW11	145	N7
Kennet Rd W9	108	F7
Kennet Rd, Islw	140	E5
Kennet Sq, Mitch	181	R2
Kennet St E1	29	T1
Kennet Wf La EC4	20	A10
Kenneth Av, Ilf	98	J7
Kenneth Cres NW2	89	T10
Kenneth Gdns, Stan	52	G12
Kenneth More Rd, Ilf *3*	99	K5
Kenneth Rd, Rom	82	J13
Kennett Dr, Hayes	102	J9
Kenning St, SE16 *5*	131	M3
Kenning Ter N1	112	B2
Kenninghall Rd E5	94	H6
Kenninghall Rd N18	61	L9
Kennings Way SE11	35	M6
Kennington Grn, SE11 *5*	35	K8
Kennington Gro, SE11 *1*	34	G9
Kennington La SE11	34	G8
Kennington Oval SE11	34	H9
Kennington Pk Est SE11	35	K11
Kennington Pk Gdns SE11	35	N10
Kennington Pk Pl SE11	35	M8
Kennington Pk Rd SE11	35	L9
Kennington Rd SE1	27	K10
Kennington Rd SE11	35	K2
Kenny Rd NW7	56	C10
Kenrick Pl W1	16	C2
Kensal Rd W10	108	C7
Kensington Av E12	98	D12
Kensington Av, Th Hth	183	P2
Kensington Ch Ct W8	22	A7
Kensington Ch St W8	126	H1
Kensington Ch Wk W8	22	A6
Kensington Cl N11	58	B11
Kensington Ct W8	22	D8
Kensington Ct Ms, W8 *2*	22	D8
Kensington Ct Pl W8	22	C9
Kensington Dr, Wdf Grn	80	B3
Kensington Gdns W2	22	G2
Kensington Gdns, Ilf	98	F2
Kensington Gdns, Kings T	177	P6
Kensington Gdns Sq W2	14	B8
Kensington Gate W8	22	F9
Kensington Gore SW7	22	J8
Kensington Hall Gdns, W14 *8*	126	E9
Kensington High St W8	126	F5
Kensington High St W14	126	F5
Kensington Mall, W8 *6*	126	H1
Kensington Palace Gdns W8	22	A1
Kensington Pk Gdns W11	108	E14
Kensington Pk Ms, W11 *16*	108	E12
Kensington Pk Rd W11	108	F13
Kensington Pl W8	126	G2
Kensington Rd SW7	23	M7
Kensington Rd W8	22	D7
Kensington Rd, Nthlt	103	N5
Kensington Rd, Rom	83	U11
Kensington Sq W8	22	B8
Kensington Ter, S Croy	198	A14
Kent Av W13	104	J9
Kent Av, Dag	119	P8
Kent Av, Well	153	U9
Kent Cl, Mitch	183	K7
Kent Cl, Orp	203	S11
Kent Dr, Barn	42	B9
Kent Dr, Tedd	158	C10
Kent Gdns W13	105	K9
Kent Gdns, Ruis	66	B12
Kent Gate Way, Croy	199	U12
Kent Ho La, Beck	167	S10
Kent Ho Rd SE26	167	R9
Kent Ho Rd, Beck	167	R12
Kent Pas NW1	7	T9
Kent Rd N21	44	A14
Kent Rd W4	124	F6
Kent Rd, Dag	101	S9
Kent Rd, E Mol	175	U8
Kent Rd, Kings T *1*	177	P5
Kent Rd, Rich	124	A13
Kent Rd, W Wick	200	D2
Kent St E2	13	N1
Kent St E13	115	T6
Kent Ter NW1	7	S8
Kent Vw Gdns, Ilf	99	S4
Kent Way, SE15 *3*	148	F1
Kent Way, Surb	191	S5
Kent Yd SW7	23	R8
Kentford Way, Nthlt	102	J2
Kentish Bldgs, SE1 *6*	28	C4
Kentish Rd, Belv	137	N8
Kentish Town Rd NW1	92	D14
Kentish Town Rd NW5	92	D14
Kentish Way, Brom	187	R4
Kentmere Rd SE18	135	S8
Kenton Av, Har	68	E13
Kenton Av, Sthl	103	P14
Kenton Av, Sun	174	H3
Kenton Gdns, Har	69	L9
Kenton La, Har	68	J3
Kenton Pk Av, Har	69	N8
Kenton Pk Cl, Har	69	M8
Kenton Pk Cres, Har	69	N8
Kenton Pk Rd, Har	69	M8
Kenton Rd E9	95	N12
Kenton Rd, Har	69	U9
Kenton St WC1	10	B9
Kents Pas, Hmptn	175	L2
Kentwode Grn SW13	125	N13
Kenver Av N12	57	N12
Kenward Rd SE9	151	U10
Kenway, Rom	83	T3
Kenway Rd SW5	30	A3
Kenwood Av N14	42	H10
Kenwood Av, SE14 *3*	149	N1
Kenwood Cl NW3	91	N1
Kenwood Dr, Beck	186	E5
Kenwood Gdns E18	79	R5
Kenwood Gdns, Ilf	80	G8
Kenwood Rd N6	73	U11
Kenwood Rd N9	60	H2
Kenworthy Rd E9	95	R10
Kenwyn Dr NW2	89	L5
Kenwyn Rd SW4	146	H7
Kenwyn Rd SW20	179	T2
Kenya Rd SE7	134	A14
Kenyngton Dr, Sun	156	A10
Kenyngton Pl, Har	69	L10
Kenyon St SW6	144	A1
Keogh Rd E15	97	K11
Kepler Rd SW4	146	J8
Keppel Rd E6	98	E14
Keppel Rd, Dag	100	J7
Keppel Row SE1	27	U3
Keppel St WC1	17	T2
Kerbela St E2	13	R10
Kerbey St E14	114	D12
Kerfield Cres SE5	148	A2
Kerfield Pl SE5	148	B2
Kerri Cl, Barn	39	T7
Kerridge Ct, N1 *3*	94	D11
Kerrison Pl W5	123	P2
Kerrison Rd E15	114	G1
Kerrison Rd SW11	145	R5
Kerrison Rd W5	123	P2
Kerry Av, Stan	53	N7
Kerry Cl E16	115	R12
Kerry Cl N13	59	M4
Kerry Ct, Stan	53	N8
Kerry Path SE14	131	T12
Kerry Rd SE14	131	T12
Kersey Gdns SE9	170	C7
Kersfield Rd SW15	144	B12
Kershaw Cl SW18	145	N12
Kershaw Rd, Dag	101	P5
Kersley Ms, SW11 *2*	145	T2
Kersley Rd N16	94	D5
Kersley St SW11	145	T3
Kerswell Cl N15	76	C10
Kerwick Cl N7	93	K13
Keslake Rd NW6	108	B4
Kessock Cl N17	76	J9
Kesteven Cl, Ilf	65	U11
Kestlake Rd, Bex *1*	154	F11
Keston Av, Kes	201	U9
Keston Cl N18	60	B6
Keston Cl, Well	136	E13
Keston Gdns, Kes	201	U8
Keston Pk Cl, Kes	202	E6
Keston Rd N17	76	A6
Keston Rd SE15	148	G6
Keston Rd, Th Hth	183	N11
Kestrel Av E6	116	C10
Kestrel Av SE24	147	S9
Kestrel Cl NW9	70	J3
Kestrel Cl NW10	88	G10
Kestrel Cl, Kings T	159	N8
Keswick Av SW15	160	J10
Keswick Av SW19	180	G3
Keswick Cl, Sutt	195	M7
Keswick Gdns, Ilf	80	D9
Keswick Gdns, Wem	87	R8
Keswick Ms W5	123	R2
Keswick Rd SW15	144	D11
Keswick Rd, Bexh	155	N3
Keswick Rd, Twick	139	T12
Keswick Rd, W Wick	200	J3
Kett Gdns SW2	147	M9
Kettering St SW16	164	E12
Kettlebaston Rd E10	95	T2
Kettlewell Cl N11	58	B11
Kevelioc Rd N17	75	U2
Kevin Cl, Houns	138	G4
Kevington Cl, Orp	189	U7
Kevington Dr, Chis	189	T7
Kew Br, Brent	123	U11
Kew Br, Rich	123	U11
Kew Br Ct W4	124	A10
Kew Br Rd, Brent	123	T11
Kew Cres, Sutt	194	E5
Kew Foot Rd, Rich	141	R7
Kew Gdns Rd, Rich	123	U14
Kew Grn, Rich	124	A12
Kew Meadow Path, Rich	142	C1
Kew Palace, Rich	123	S13
Kew Rd, Rich	141	U1
Key Cl E1	113	K8
Keyes Rd NW2	90	B9
Keymer Rd SW2	165	M4
Keynes Cl N2	73	U6
Keynsham Av, Wdf Grn	63	K8
Keynsham Gdns SE9	152	C10
Keynsham Rd SE9	152	B10
Keynsham Rd, Mord	194	J1
Keynsham Wk, Mord *1*	194	J1
Keyse Rd, SE1 *1*	29	M12
Keysham Av, Houns	138	B1
Keystone Cres N1	10	D4
Keywood Dr, Sun	156	B11
Keyworth Cl E5	95	R7
Keyworth St SE1	27	R10
Kezia St SE8	131	R10
Khama Rd SW17	163	R8
Khartoum Rd E13	115	R6
Khartoum Rd SW17	163	P8
Khartoum Rd, Ilf	99	K10
Khyber Rd SW11	145	R4
Kibworth St SW8	129	L14
Kidbrooke Gdns SE3	151	N3
Kidbrooke Gro SE3	151	P2
Kidbrooke La SE9	152	D8
Kidbrooke Pk Cl SE3	151	R2
Kidbrooke Pk Rd SE3	151	R3
Kidbrooke Way, SE3 *1*	151	S4
Kidd Pl SE7	134	D9
Kidderminster Pl, Croy *4*	197	S1
Kidderminster Rd, Croy	197	S1
Kidderpore Av NW3	90	H7
Kidderpore Gdns NW3	90	H7
Kidlington Way NW9	70	J3
Kielder Cl, Ilf	65	U11
Kiffen St EC2	12	F10
Kilberry Cl, Islw	140	B1
Kilburn High Rd NW6	90	F13
Kilburn La W9	108	B6
Kilburn La W10	108	D4
Kilburn Pk Rd NW6	6	A3
Kilburn Pl NW6	108	H2
Kilburn Priory NW6	108	J2
Kilburn Vale, NW6 *1*	108	J2
Kildare Cl, Ruis	84	E1
Kildare Gdns W2	108	H11
Kildare Rd E16	115	N9
Kildare Ter W2	108	H11
Kildoran Rd SW2	146	J9
Kildowan Rd, Ilf	100	B2
Kilgour Rd SE23	149	R11
Kilkie St SW6	145	L4
Killarney Rd SW18	145	M12
Killburns Mill Cl, Wall *2*	196	C4
Killearn Rd SE6	168	G1
Killester Gdns, Wor Pk	193	S8
Killick St N1	10	E3
Killieser Av SW2	164	J3
Killip Cl E16	115	M11
Killowen Av, Nthlt	85	U9
Killowen Rd, E9 *2*	95	N12
Killyon Rd SW8	146	F4
Killyon Ter SW8	146	F3
Kilmaine Rd SW6	126	D14
Kilmarnock Gdns, Dag	100	F6
Kilmarnock Rd, Wat	50	H7
Kilmarsh Rd W6	125	T7
Kilmartin Av SW16	183	N5
Kilmartin Rd, Ilf	100	B4
Kilmington Rd SW13	125	N12
Kilmorey Gdns, Twick	140	J8
Kilmorey Rd, Twick	140	J8
Kilmorie Rd SE23	167	R2
Kiln Ms SW17	163	N9
Kiln Pl NW5	92	B8
Kilner St E14	114	A10
Kilnside, Esher	190	G13
Kilpatrick Way, Hayes	103	K10
Kilravock St W10	108	C6

Kilsby Wk, Dag	100	C12
Kilsha Rd, Walt	174	D11
Kimbell Gdns SW6	144	C2
Kimbell Pl SE3	151	U8
Kimber Rd SW18	144	H14
Kimberley Av E6	116	C3
Kimberley Av SE15	149	L5
Kimberley Av, Ilf	81	R14
Kimberley Av, Rom	83	T12
Kimberley Dr, Sid	172	H4
Kimberley Gdns N4	75	S10
Kimberley Gdns, Enf	44	E6
Kimberley Rd E4	63	K2
Kimberley Rd E11	96	H3
Kimberley Rd E16	115	L7
Kimberley Rd E17	77	T1
Kimberley Rd N17	76	G4
Kimberley Rd N18	61	K11
Kimberley Rd NW6	108	D1
Kimberley Rd SW9	147	K4
Kimberley Rd, Beck	185	P3
Kimberley Rd, Croy	183	S11
Kimberley Way E4	63	K1
Kimble Rd SW19	163	P11
Kimbolton Cl SE12	151	M12
Kimbolton Grn, Borwd	38	E8
Kimmeridge Gdns SE9	170	D7
Kimmeridge Rd SE9	170	C7
Kimpton Rd SE5	148	A1
Kimpton Rd, Sutt	194	E4
Kimpton Trade Business Cen, Sutt	194	F4
Kinburn St SE16	131	N3
Kincaid Rd SE15	130	J14
Kinch Gro, Wem	69	T13
Kinder Cl SE28	118	G14
Kinder St E1	112	J12
Kinfauns Rd SW2	165	P4
Kinfauns Rd, Ilf	100	C2
King Alfred Av SE6	168	B6
King & Queen Cl SE9	170	D8
King & Queen St SE17	36	B5
King Arthur Cl SE15	131	L14
King Charles Cres, Surb	177	U13
King Charles Rd, Surb	177	U12
King Charles St SW1	25	U6
King Charles Ter, E1 *3*	113	K14
King Charles Wk, SW19 *3*	162	C2
King David La E1	113	L13
King Edward Dr, Chess	191	R6
King Edward Ms SW13	143	N2
King Edward Rd E10	96	E1
King Edward Rd E17	77	R6
King Edward Rd, Barn	40	H7
King Edward St EC1	19	T5
King Edward III Ms SE16	131	K4
King Edward Wk SE1	27	L10
King Edward's Gdns W3	124	B2
King Edwards Gro, Tedd	159	K12
King Edward's Pl, W3 *2*	124	B2
King Edwards Rd E9	113	K1
King Edwards Rd N9	44	J13
King Edwards Rd, Bark	117	N2
King Edward's Rd, Enf	45	P8
King Gdns, Croy	197	R9
King George Av E16	116	A11
King George Av, Ilf	81	P10
King George Cl, Rom	83	U6
King George VI Av, Mitch	181	U8
King George Sq, Rich	141	U12
King George St SE10	132	F14
King Georges Dr, Sthl	103	M9
King George's Trd Est, Chess	192	A7
King Harolds Way, Bexh	136	J13
King Henry Ms, Orp *7*	203	U10
King Henry St N16	94	C9
King Henry Ter, E1 *5*	113	K14
King Henry's Rd NW3	91	R14
King Henry's Rd, Kings T	178	D5
King Henry's Wk N1	94	C11
King James St SE1	27	R8
King John Ct EC2	12	J10
King John St E1	113	P10
King Johns Wk SE9	170	B2
King Sq EC1	11	T7
King Stairs Cl SE16	131	K3
King St E13	115	N8
King St EC2	20	B7
King St N2	73	N1
King St N17	76	E1
King St SW1	25	N2
King St W3	124	D2
King St W6	125	N8
King St WC2	18	B10
King St, Rich	141	N9
King St, Sthl	121	K6
King St, Twick	158	G2
King William IV Gdns, SE20 *1*	167	M12
King William La, SE10 *4*	132	J10
King William St EC4	20	E11
King William Wk SE10	132	F11
Kingcup Cl, Croy	185	N14
Kingdon Rd NW6	90	H11
Kingfield Rd W5	105	P7
Kingfield St E14	132	F7
Kingfisher Av E11	79	S11
Kingfisher Cl SE28	118	F13
Kingfisher Cl, Har	52	E14
Kingfisher Dr, Rich	159	K7
Kingfisher Sq SE8	131	T11
Kingfisher St E6	116	D10
Kingfisher Wk NW9	71	K4
Kingfisher Way NW10	88	H10
Kingfisher Way, Beck	185	N9
Kingham Cl SW18	145	L13
Kingham Cl W11	126	C3
Kinghorn St, EC1 *7*	19	T3
Kinglake Est SE17	37	K5
Kinglake St SE17	36	J6
Kingly St W1	17	M9
Kings Arbour, Sthl	120	J10
Kings Arms Yd EC2	20	D6
Kings Av N10	74	B5
Kings Av N21	59	R1
Kings Av SW4	146	J10
Kings Av SW12	164	H1
Kings Av W5	105	P11
Kings Av, Brom	169	L12
Kings Av, Buck H	64	A3
Kings Av, Cars	195	S14
Kings Av, Grnf	103	R11
Kings Av, Houns	139	S2
Kings Av, N Mal	179	L7
Kings Av, Rom	83	M11
Kings Av, Wdf Grn	63	U8
Kings Bench St SE1	27	R6
Kings Bench Wk EC4	19	L9
Kings Chase, E Mol	175	U5
Kings Cl E10	78	C14
Kings Cl NW4	72	B8
Kings Cl, T Ditt	176	H12
Kings College Rd NW3	91	R13
Kings Ct E13	115	S2
Kings Ct, Wem	88	C4
Kings Cres N4	93	T5
Kings Cres Est N4	93	T4
King's Cross Br, N1 *2*	10	D5
King's Cross Rd WC1	10	G7
Kings Dr, Edg	53	T8
Kings Dr, Surb	178	B12
Kings Dr, Tedd	158	B10
Kings Dr, T Ditt	176	J12
Kings Dr, Wem	88	C3
Kings Fm Av, Rich	142	A7
Kings Gdns NW6	90	H14
Kings Gdns, Ilf	99	N1
King's Garth Ms, SE23 *1*	167	L3
Kings Grn, Loug	48	D6
Kings Gro SE15	131	K14
Kings Hall Rd, Beck	167	T13
Kings Head Hill E4	46	D14
Kings Head Yd SE1	28	D3
Kings Highway SE18	135	T11
Kings Hill, Loug	48	D4
Kings Keep, Kings T	177	R8
Kings La, Sutt	195	P10
Kings Mead Pk, SE9	190	D13
Kings Ms SW4	146	J9
King's Ms WC1	10	H12
Kings Ms, Chig	65	L4
Kings Oak, Rom	83	P6
Kings Orchard SE9	152	D11
Kings Paddock, Hmptn	175	T2
King's Pas E11	78	J14
Kings Pas, Kings T	177	N4
Kings Pl, SE1 *10*	27	U8
Kings Pl W4	124	F9
Kings Pl, Buck H	63	U4
Kings Ride Gate, Rich	142	B8
Kings Rd E4	62	G2
Kings Rd E6	115	U1
Kings Rd E11	78	J14
King's Rd N17	76	E1
Kings Rd N18	60	H9
Kings Rd N22	75	M1
Kings Rd NW10	89	R13
Kings Rd SE25	184	H5
King's Rd SW1	32	A5
King's Rd SW3	32	A5
Kings Rd SW6	145	K1
Kings Rd SW10	145	K1
Kings Rd SW14	142	H6
Kings Rd SW19	162	G12
Kings Rd W5	105	P10
Kings Rd, Bark *1*	99	L13
Kings Rd, Barn	39	U6
Kings Rd, Felt	156	E2
Kings Rd, Har	85	M6
Kings Rd, Kings T	160	A13
Kings Rd, Mitch	182	B5
Kings Rd, Orp	203	T7
Kings Rd, Rich	141	T9
Kings Rd, Surb	191	L1
Kings Rd, Tedd	158	B9
Kings Rd, Twick	141	K12
Kings Rd Bungalows, Har	85	M6
King's Scholars Pas SW1	25	L12
King's Ter NW1	110	E2
King's Wk, Kings T	177	P1
Kings Way, Har	68	C7
Kingsand Rd SE12	169	P3
Kingsash Dr, Hayes	102	J7
Kingsbridge Av W3	123	U3
Kingsbridge Cres, Sthl	103	L10
Kingsbridge Rd W10	107	U11
Kingsbridge Rd, Bark	117	P4
Kingsbridge Rd, Sthl	121	L8
Kingsbridge Rd, Walt	174	C14
Kingsbury Circle NW9	70	A9
Kingsbury Rd N1	94	D11
Kingsbury Rd NW9	70	J10
Kingsbury Ter, N1 *2*	94	D11
Kingsbury Trd Est NW9	70	G11
Kingsclere Cl SW15	143	N13
Kingsclere Pl, Enf	43	U4
Kingscliffe Gdns SW19	162	E2
Kingscote Rd W4	124	G6
Kingscote Rd, Croy	184	J14
Kingscote Rd, N Mal	178	H6
Kingscote St EC4	19	N9
Kingscourt Rd SW16	164	H6
Kingscroft Rd NW2	90	D11
Kingsdale Gdns W11	126	B2
Kingsdale Rd SE18	135	T12
Kingsdale Rd SE20	167	N14
Kingsdown Av W3	107	K13
Kingsdown Av W13	123	K4
Kingsdown Cl, SE16 *12*	131	K10
Kingsdown Cl W10	108	B12
Kingsdown Rd E11	97	K6
Kingsdown Rd N19	92	J5
Kingsdown Rd, Sutt	194	C10
Kingsdown Way, Brom	187	N12
Kingsdowne Rd, Surb	177	S14
Kingsfield Av, Har	67	S8
Kingsfield Rd, Har	68	B14
Kingsford Av, Wall	197	K14
Kingsford St NW5	91	U9
Kingsford Way E6	116	F10
Kingsgate, Wem	88	E5
Kingsgate Av N3	72	G6
Kingsgate Cl, Bexh	154	J1
Kingsgate Pl NW6	90	G14
Kingsgate Rd NW6	90	G14
Kingsgate Rd, Kings T	177	R2
Kingsground SE9	252	C13
Kingshall Ms SE13	150	F5
Kingshill Av, Har	69	K7
Kingshill Av, Hayes	102	B5
Kingshill Av, Nthlt	102	B5
Kingshill Av, Wor Pk	179	R13
Kinghill Dr, Har	68	J6
Kingshold Rd E9	95	M14
Kingsholm Gdns SE9	152	B7
Kingshurst Rd SE12	151	P13
Kingsland Grn E8	94	D11
Kingsland High St E8	94	E10
Kingsland Pas, E8 *8*	94	D11
Kingsland Rd E2	13	K4
Kingsland Rd E8	94	E13
Kingsland Rd E13	115	U6
Kingslawn Cl SW15	143	R9
Kingsleigh Pl, Mitch *3*	181	T6
Kingsleigh Wk, Brom	187	M8
Kingsley Av W13	104	G11
Kingsley Av, Houns	139	T3
Kingsley Av, Sthl	103	N14
Kingsley Av, Sutt	195	P7
Kingsley Cl N2	73	L9
Kingsley Cl, Dag	101	R7
Kingsley Cl, Edg	54	D4
Kingsley Dr, Wor Pk *1*	193	M3
Kingsley Gdns E4	62	B9
Kingsley Ms E1 *16*	113	K14
Kingsley Ms W8	22	C11
Kingsley Ms, Chis	171	K12
Kingsley Pl N6	74	B14
Kingsley Rd E7	97	P13
Kingsley Rd E17	78	E4
Kingsley Rd N13	59	P7
Kingsley Rd NW6	108	F1
Kingsley Rd SW19	163	K9
Kingsley Rd, Croy	197	N1

Name	Page	Grid
Kingsley Rd, Har	85	T6
Kingsley Rd, Houns	139	S2
Kingsley Rd, Ilf	81	M1
Kingsley Rd, Loug	49	N6
Kingsley Rd, Orp	203	T12
Kingsley Rd, Pnr	67	M8
Kingsley St SW11	145	U5
Kingsley Way N2	73	L11
Kingsley Wd Dr SE9	170	F6
Kingslyn Cres SE19	184	C2
Kingsman Par, SE18 1	134	F6
Kingsman St SE18	134	G7
Kingsmead, Barn	40	G7
Kingsmead, Rich	141	U12
Kingsmead Av N9	60	J2
Kingsmead Av NW9	70	G14
Kingsmead Av, Mitch	182	F5
Kingsmead Av, Sun	174	E5
Kingsmead Av, Surb	192	B3
Kingsmead Av, Wor Pk	193	S5
Kingsmead Cl, Epsom	192	H14
Kingsmead Cl, Sid	172	A4
Kingsmead Cl, Tedd	158	J12
Kingsmead Dr, Nthlt	85	M13
Kingsmead Rd SW2	165	N4
Kingsmead Way E9	95	S8
Kingsmere Cl, SW15 5	144	B6
Kingsmere Pk NW9	88	D2
Kingsmere Rd SW19	162	B3
Kingsmill Gdns, Dag	101	M10
Kingsmill Rd, Dag	101	M10
Kingsmill Ter NW8	7	L2
Kingsnympton Pk, Kings T	160	C12
Kingspark Ct E18	79	N5
Kingsridge, SW19 1	162	D3
Kingsthorpe Rd SE26	167	N8
Kingston Av, Sutt	194	D6
Kingston Br, Kings T	177	N3
Kingston Bypass SW15	161	K11
Kingston Bypass SW20	161	K11
Kingston Bypass, Esher	190	J5
Kingston Bypass, N Mal	179	P7
Kingston Bypass, Surb	192	D2
Kingston Cl, Nthlt	85	M14
Kingston Cl, Rom	82	J5
Kingston Cl, Tedd	158	J12
Kingston Cres, Beck	185	U2
Kingston Gdns, Croy 2	197	K6
Kingston Hall Rd, Kings T	177	P5
Kingston Hill, Kings T	160	E10
Kingston Hill Av, Rom	83	K5
Kingston Hill Pl, Kings T	160	F8
Kingston La, Tedd	158	H10
Kingston Pk Est, Kings T	160	D12
Kingston Pl, Har	52	E13
Kingston Rd N9	60	H3
Kingston Rd SW15	161	U1
Kingston Rd SW19	162	H14
Kingston Rd SW20	180	A3
Kingston Rd, Barn	41	P10
Kingston Rd, Epsom	192	G7
Kingston Rd, Ilf	99	K8
Kingston Rd, Kings T	178	G7
Kingston Rd, N Mal	178	G7
Kingston Rd, Sthl	121	L4
Kingston Rd, Surb	192	J9
Kingston Rd, Tedd	158	J10
Kingston Wor Pk	192	E5
Kingston Sq SE19	166	B9
Kingston Vale SW15	160	H7
Kingstown St NW1	110	A1
Kingsway N12	57	M11
Kingsway SW14	142	D6
Kingsway WC2	18	E6
Kingsway, Croy	197	M10
Kingsway, Enf	45	K9
Kingsway, N Mal	179	T8
Kingsway, Orp	189	N9
Kingsway, Wem	87	S7
Kingsway, W Wick	201	L6
Kingsway, Wdf Grn	63	T9
Kingsway Business Pk, Hmptn	175	L1
Kingsway Cres, Har	67	T8
Kingsway Rd, Sutt	194	C13
Kingswear Rd NW5	92	C5
Kingswear Rd, Ruis	84	A4
Kingswood Av NW6	108	D2
Kingswood Av, Belv	137	L7
Kingswood Av, Brom	186	J7
Kingswood Av, Hmptn	157	R12
Kingswood Av, Houns	139	L2
Kingswood Av, Th Hth	183	P10
Kingswood Cl N20	41	L13
Kingswood Cl, SW8 4	129	K14
Kingswood Cl, Enf	44	E8
Kingswood Cl, N Mal 1	179	L12
Kingswood Cl, Orp	189	P14
Kingswood Cl, Surb	177	S13
Kingswood Dr SE19	166	E8
Kingswood Dr, Cars	195	U2
Kingswood Pk N3	72	E3
Kingswood Pl SE13	151	K6
Kingswood Rd E11	79	K14
Kingswood Rd SE20	167	L12
Kingswood Rd SW2	146	J13
Kingswood Rd SW19	162	F14
Kingswood Rd W4	124	E6
Kingswood Rd, Brom	186	H7
Kingswood Rd, Ilf	100	A1
Kingswood Rd, Wem	88	A6
Kingswood Ter W4	124	E6
Kingswood Way, Wall 2	197	K9
Kingsworth Cl, Beck	185	R9
Kingsworthy Cl, Kings T	177	U5
Kingthorpe Rd NW10	88	G13
Kingthorpe Ter NW10	88	H12
Kingwood Rd SW6	126	C14
Kinlet Rd SE18	153	L1
Kinloch Dr NW9	70	J14
Kinloch St N7	93	M6
Kinloss Ct N3	72	E7
Kinloss Gdns N3	72	E7
Kinloss Rd, Cars	181	M14
Kinnaird Av W4	124	E14
Kinnaird Av, Brom	169	M12
Kinnaird Cl, Brom	169	M12
Kinnaird Way, Wdf Grn	64	E12
Kinnear Rd W12	125	L3
Kinnerton Pl N, SW1 1	24	C7
Kinnerton Pl S, SW1 3	24	C7
Kinnerton St SW1	24	C8
Kinnerton Yd, SW1 6	24	C8
Kinnoul Rd W6	126	C11
Kinross Av, Wor Pk	193	N4
Kinross Cl, Edg	54	C4
Kinross Cl, Har	69	S10
Kinsale Rd SE15	148	H6
Kintyre Cl SW16	183	M4
Kinveachy Gdns SE7	134	C9
Kinver Rd SE26	167	M7
Kipling Dr SW19	163	N11
Kipling Pl, Stan	52	E11
Kipling Rd, Bexh	155	K1
Kipling St SE1	28	E7
Kipling Ter N9	60	B5
Kippington Dr SE9	170	B2
Kirby Cl, Epsom	193	L10
Kirby Cl, Ilf	65	R12
Kirby Cl, Loug	48	C13
Kirby Est SE16	130	J5
Kirby Gro SE1	28	G6
Kirby St EC1	19	M2
Kirby Way, Walt	174	E12
Kirchen Rd W13	104	J14
Kirk La SE18	135	M12
Kirk Ri, Sutt	195	K6
Kirk Rd E17	77	U11
Kirkby Cl, N11 2	58	A11
Kirkcaldy Grn, Wat	50	E5
Kirkdale SE26	166	J4
Kirkdale Rd E11	79	K14
Kirkfield Cl W13	123	K1
Kirkham Rd E6	116	D11
Kirkham St SE18	135	R12
Kirkland Av, Ilf	80	H4
Kirkland Cl, Sid	153	R11
Kirkland Wk, E8 11	94	E12
Kirkleas Rd, Surb	191	R1
Kirklees Rd, Dag	100	E10
Kirklees Rd, Th Hth	183	N9
Kirkley Rd SW19	180	H1
Kirkmichael Rd E14	114	F11
Kirks Pl E14	113	T10
Kirkside Rd SE3	133	N11
Kirkstall Av N17	76	A7
Kirkstall Gdns SW2	164	J1
Kirkstall Rd SW2	164	J2
Kirksted Rd, Mord	194	J1
Kirkstone Way, Brom	169	K12
Kirkton Rd N15	76	C9
Kirkwall Pl E2	113	M5
Kirkwood Rd SE15	149	K3
Kirn Rd, W13 7	104	J14
Kirrane Cl, N Mal	179	L10
Kirtley Rd SE26	167	S7
Kirtling St SW8	33	M13
Kirton Cl W4	124	H8
Kirton Rd E13	115	T3
Kirton Wk, Edg	54	F14
Kirwyn Way SE5	35	S13
Kitcat Ter E3	114	B5
Kitchener Rd E7	97	R12
Kitchener Rd E17	78	D2
Kitchener Rd N2	73	R6
Kitchener Rd N17	76	C6
Kitchener Rd, Dag	101	T11
Kitchener Rd, Th Hth	184	A5
Kite Pl, E2 3	13	T5
Kitley Gdns SE19	184	E2
Kitson Rd SE5	36	C13
Kitson Rd SW13	143	N2
Kittiwake Rd, Nthlt	102	H5
Kittiwake Way, Hayes	102	G10
Kitto Rd SE14	149	P4
Kiver Rd N19	92	H4
Kiwi Cl, Twick	141	K12
Klea Av SW4	146	E11
Knapdale Cl SE23	167	K3
Knapmill Rd SE6	168	C4
Knapmill Way SE6	168	C4
Knapp Cl NW10	89	K11
Knapp Rd E3	114	A8
Knaresborough Dr SW18	162	J2
Knaresborough Pl SW5	30	B2
Knatchbull Rd SE5	147	T2
Knatchbull Rd NW10	106	H1
Knebworth Av E17	78	B1
Knebworth Path, Borwd	38	H8
Knebworth Rd N16	94	C6
Knee Hill SE2	136	F7
Knee Hill Cres SE2	136	F8
Kneller Gdns, Islw	140	B10
Kneller Rd SE4	149	S7
Kneller Rd, N Mal	178	J13
Kneller Rd, Twick	140	B12
Knighten St E1	29	U3
Knightland Rd E5	94	J3
Knighton Cl, Wdf Grn	63	S8
Knighton Dr, Wdf Grn	63	P7
Knighton La, Buck H	63	S4
Knighton Pk Rd SE26	167	P9
Knighton Rd E7	97	P6
Knighton Rd, Rom	83	U11
Knightrider Ct, EC4 1	19	T9
Knights Arc, SW1 2	23	U7
Knights Av W5	123	S4
Knights Ct, Kings T	177	R5
Knights Hill SE27	165	S9
Knights Hill Sq, SE27 5	165	S7
Knights La N9	60	H5
Knights Pk, Kings T	177	S5
Knights Rd E16	133	P3
Knights Rd, Stan	53	M8
Knights Wk, SE11 2	35	N3
Knights Way, Ilf	65	L12
Knightsbridge SW1	24	B7
Knightsbridge SW7	23	R7
Knightsbridge Grn, SW1 1	23	U8
Knightswood Cl, Edg	54	E4
Knightwood Cres, N Mal	178	J11
Knivet Rd SW6	126	G12
Knobs Hill Rd E15	114	C1
Knockholt Rd SE9	152	A9
Knole, The SE9	170	G8
Knole Cl, Croy 2	185	L11
Knole Gate, Sid	171	S5
Knoll, The W13	105	L10
Knoll, The, Beck	186	C2
Knoll, The, Beck	201	P2
Knoll Dr N14	42	B14
Knoll Ri, Orp	203	U2
Knoll Rd SW18	145	L10
Knoll Rd, Bex	155	N13
Knoll Rd, Sid	172	D9
Knollmead, Surb	192	F2
Knolls Cl, Wor Pk	193	R5
Knollys Cl SW16	165	P5
Knollys Rd SW16	165	N5
Knottisford St E2	113	M5
Knotts Grn Ms E10	78	D11
Knotts Grn Rd E10	78	D12
Knowle Av, Bexh	137	K13
Knowle Cl SW9	147	N5
Knowle Rd, Brom	202	E3
Knowle Rd, Twick	158	D2
Knowles Hill Cres SE13	150	G10
Knowles Wk SW4	146	F5
Knowlton Grn, Brom	187	M10
Knowsley Av, Sthl	121	R2
Knowsley Rd SW11	145	T4
Knox Rd E7	97	N12
Knox St W1	15	U2
Knoyle St, SE14 1	131	R12
Kohat Rd SW19	163	K9
Kossuth St SE10	132	J9
Kotree Way SE1	37	U4
Kramer Ms SW5	126	H10
Kreedman Wk E8	94	G10
Kreisel Wk, Rich	123	U12
Kuala Gdns SW16	183	L1
Kuhn Way E7	97	P9
Kydbrook Cl, Orp	189	M13
Kylemore Cl, E6 6	116	B3
Kylemore Rd NW6	90	G13
Kymberley Rd, Har	68	C12
Kynance Gdns, Stan	69	L2
Kynance Ms SW7	22	E11
Kynance Pl SW7	22	E11
Kynaston Av, Th Hth	183	T10
Kynaston Cres, Th Hth	52	B14
Kynaston Rd N16	94	D5
Kynaston Rd, Brom	169	P10
Kynaston Rd, Enf	44	B2
Kynaston Rd, Th Hth	183	U9
Kynaston Wd, Har	52	B13

Kynersley Cl, Cars	195	T6
4		
Kynock Rd N18	61	M8
Kyrle Rd SW11	146	A10
Kyverdale Rd N16	94	F4

L

La Tourne Gdns, Orp	203	M5
Laburnum Av N9	60	D4
Laburnum Av N17	60	A13
Laburnum Av, Sutt **2**	195	R6
Laburnum Cl E4	61	U11
Laburnum Cl N11	58	B12
Laburnum Cl SE15	149	L1
Laburnum Ct, Stan	53	L8
Laburnum Cres, Sun	174	C2
Laburnum Gdns N21	59	T3
Laburnum Gdns, Croy	185	N14
Laburnum Gro N21	59	T3
Laburnum Gro NW9	70	F13
Laburnum Gro, Houns	139	M7
Laburnum Gro, N Mal	178	G4
Laburnum Gro, Sthl	103	M8
Laburnum Rd SW19	163	M14
Laburnum Rd, Mitch	182	B4
Laburnum St E2	112	E2
Laburnum Way, Brom	188	H13
Lacebark Cl, Sid	153	U14
Lacey Cl N9	60	H4
Lacey Dr, Dag	100	D7
Lacey Dr, Edg	53	T8
Lacey Dr, Hmptn	175	M2
Lacey Wk E3	114	A3
Lackington St EC2	20	E2
Lacock Cl SW19	163	L12
Lacon Rd SE22	148	G8
Lacy Rd SW15	144	B7
Ladas Rd SE27	165	T8
Ladbroke Cres W11	108	D12
Ladbroke Gdns W11	108	E13
Ladbroke Gro W10	108	C10
Ladbroke Gro W11	108	E14
Ladbroke Rd W11	126	E1
Ladbroke Rd, Enf	44	F11
Ladbroke Sq W11	108	F14
Ladbroke Ter W11	108	F14
Ladbroke Wk W11	126	F1
Ladbrook Cl, Pnr	67	L10
Ladbrook Rd SE25	184	B6
Ladbrooke Cres, Sid	172	G6
Ladderstile Ride, Kings T	160	D10
Ladderswood Way N11	58	E10
Lady Booth Rd, Kings T	177	R4
Lady Hay, Wor Pk	193	L3
Lady Margaret Rd N19	92	F8
Lady Margaret Rd NW5	92	E10
Lady Margaret Rd, Sthl	103	M6
Lady Somerset Rd NW5	92	D8
Ladycroft Gdns, Orp **5**	203	M9
Ladycroft Rd SE13	150	C6
Ladycroft Wk, Stan	69	P2
Ladycroft Way, Orp	203	L9
Ladyfield Cl, Loug	49	K8
Ladyfields, Loug	49	K8
Ladysmith Av E6	116	C3
Ladysmith Av, Ilf	81	R14
Ladysmith Rd E16	115	L6
Ladysmith Rd N17	76	G4
Ladysmith Rd N18	61	K10
Ladysmith Rd SE9	152	H12
Ladysmith Rd, Enf	44	D6
Ladysmith Rd, Har	68	C4
Ladywell Cl SE4	150	A8
Ladywell Hts SE4	149	T11

Ladywell Rd SE13	150	A9
Ladywell St, E15 **1**	115	L2
Ladywood Av, Orp	189	S10
Ladywood Rd, Surb	192	A4
Lafone Av, Felt	156	E2
Lafone St SE1	29	M5
Lagado Ms SE16	131	P2
Lagonda Av, Ilf	65	T12
Laidlaw Dr, N21 **2**	43	L9
Laing Cl, Ilf	65	P12
Laing Dean, Nthlt	102	F2
Laings Av, Mitch	181	T3
Lainlock Pl, Houns	139	S2
Lainson St SW18	144	G13
Lairdale Cl SE21	147	T14
Lairs Cl N7	93	K10
Laitwood Rd SW12	164	D1
Lake, The, Bushey	51	U1
Lake Av, Brom	169	P12
Lake Dr, Bushey	51	U3
Lake Gdns, Dag	101	N9
Lake Gdns, Rich	159	K4
Lake Gdns, Wall	196	C6
Lake Ho Rd E11	97	N4
Lake Rd SW19	162	E10
Lake Rd, Croy	199	U3
Lake Rd, Rom	82	H8
Lake Vw, Edg	52	T10
Lakedale Rd SE18	135	S10
Lakefield Rd, N22 **4**	75	S4
Lakehall Gdns, Th Hth	183	S10
Lakehall Rd, Th Hth	183	S10
Lakehurst Rd, Epsom	192	J10
Lakeland Cl, Har	52	A11
Lakenheath N14	42	G10
Laker Pl SW15	144	E10
Lakes Rd, Kes	201	U9
Lakeside N3	73	K3
Lakeside W13	105	L11
Lakeside, Beck	186	D5
Lakeside, Enf	42	H8
Lakeside, Wall	196	C7
Lakeside Av SE28	136	A2
Lakeside Av, Ilf	80	A8
Lakeside Cl SE25	184	F4
Lakeside Cl, Chig	65	T7
Lakeside Cl, Sid	154	E11
Lakeside Ct N4	93	S3
Lakeside Cres, Barn	41	U10
Lakeside Dr, Brom	202	D5
Lakeside Rd N13	59	L6
Lakeside Rd W14	126	A5
Lakeside Way, Wem	88	A8
Lakeswood Rd, Orp	189	L11
Lakeview Ct SW19	162	D4
Lakeview Rd SE27	165	P10
Lakeview Rd, Well	154	C7
Lakis Cl NW3	91	M7
Laleham Av NW7	54	G5
Laleham Rd SE6	150	E13
Lalor St SW6	144	D3
Lamb La E8	94	J14
Lamb St E1	21	L1
Lamb Wk SE1	28	H8
Lambarde Av SE9	170	H8
Lamberhurst Rd SE27	165	P8
Lamberhurst Rd, Dag	101	L2
Lambert Av, Rich	142	B6
Lambert Rd E16	115	R11
Lambert Rd N12	57	M10
Lambert Rd SW2	147	K10
Lambert St N1	93	N14
Lambert Wk, Wem	87	P6
Lambert Way N12	57	M10
Lamberts Pl, Croy	198	B1
Lamberts Rd, Surb	177	S10
Lambeth Br SE1	34	C1
Lambeth Br SW1	34	C1
Lambeth High St SE1	34	E3
Lambeth Hill EC4	19	U9
Lambeth Palace Rd SE1	26	F10
Lambeth Rd SE1	27	L11
Lambeth Rd SE11	26	F12

Lambeth Rd, Croy	183	P14
Lambeth Wk SE11	34	H1
Lamble St NW5	92	A9
Lambley Rd, Dag	100	D12
Lambolle Pl NW3	91	S12
Lambolle Rd NW3	91	R12
Lambourn Cl W7	122	E4
Lambourn Rd SW4	146	D5
Lambourne Av SW19	162	F7
Lambourne Gdns E4	62	B3
Lambourne Gdns, Bark	99	U14
Lambourne Gdns, Enf	44	E4
Lambourne Gro, Kings T	178	C3
Lambourne Pl SE3	151	R1
Lambourne Rd E11	78	G14
Lambourne Rd, Bark	99	T14
Lambourne Rd, Chig	65	S7
Lambourne Rd, Ilf	99	S3
Lambrook Ter SW6	144	C1
Lamb's Bldgs EC1	12	C11
Lamb's Conduit St WC1	10	E12
Lambs Meadow, Wdf Grn	80	A4
Lamb's Pas EC1	20	C1
Lambs Ter N9	60	B4
Lambs Wk, Enf	43	U4
Lambscroft Av SE9	170	A6
Lambton Pl, W11 **9**	108	F13
Lambton Rd N19	92	J1
Lambton Rd SW20	179	T2
Lamerock Rd, Brom	169	M7
Lamerton Rd, Ilf	81	K3
Lamerton St SE8	132	A12
Lamford Cl N17	60	B13
Lamington St, W6 **1**	125	S7
Lamlash St SE11	35	P1
Lammas Av, Mitch	182	A4
Lammas Grn SE26	166	J5
Lammas Pk W5	123	L4
Lammas Pk Gdns W5	123	M3
Lammas Pk Rd W5	123	M2
Lammas Rd E9	95	P14
Lammas Rd E10	95	R3
Lammas Rd, Rich	159	L8
Lammermoor Rd SW12	146	D14
Lamont Rd SW10	30	J12
Lamorbey Cl, Sid	171	T2
Lamorna Cl E17	78	F3
Lamorna Gro, Stan	69	N2
Lamp Office Ct WC1	10	D12
Lampard Gro N16	94	F2
Lampern Sq E2	13	T5
Lampeter Sq, W6 **2**	126	C12
Lamplighter Cl, E1 **11**	113	L8
Lampmead Rd SE12	151	K9
Lamport Cl SE18	134	F7
Lampton Av, Houns	139	R2
Lampton Ho Cl SW19	162	A8
Lampton Pk Rd, Houns	139	R5
Lampton Rd, Houns	139	R4
Lanacre Av NW9	71	L3
Lanark Cl W5	105	M9
Lanark Pl W9	6	H10
Lanark Rd W9	6	C4
Lanark Sq E14	132	D5
Lanbury Rd SE15	149	N8
Lancaster Av E18	79	R7
Lancaster Av SE27	165	T4
Lancaster Av SW19	162	B9
Lancaster Av, Bark	99	S14
Lancaster Av, Mitch	182	J9
Lancaster Cl N1	94	D14
Lancaster Cl N17	60	G14
Lancaster Cl NW9	55	L14
Lancaster Cl, Brom	187	L8

Lancaster Cl, Kings T	159	P10
Lancaster Cotts, Rich **8**	141	R11
Lancaster Ct SE27	165	S4
Lancaster Ct SW6	126	F14
Lancaster Ct W2	14	H11
Lancaster Ct, Walt	174	B13
Lancaster Dr, E14 **12**	132	F2
Lancaster Dr NW3	91	R12
Lancaster Dr, Loug	48	D11
Lancaster Gdns SW19	162	C9
Lancaster Gdns W13	123	K3
Lancaster Gdns, Kings T	159	P10
Lancaster Gate W2	14	H11
Lancaster Gro NW3	91	P12
Lancaster Ms, SW18 **11**	145	K10
Lancaster Ms W2	14	H10
Lancaster Ms, Rich **6**	141	R11
Lancaster Pk, Rich	141	R10
Lancaster Pl SW19	162	B10
Lancaster Pl WC2	18	E10
Lancaster Pl, Houns	138	F3
Lancaster Pl, Ilf **3**	99	M8
Lancaster Pl, Twick	140	H12
Lancaster Rd E7	97	P13
Lancaster Rd E11	97	K4
Lancaster Rd E17	77	P4
Lancaster Rd N4	75	N14
Lancaster Rd N11	58	H11
Lancaster Rd N18	60	F10
Lancaster Rd NW10	89	N9
Lancaster Rd SE25	184	F4
Lancaster Rd SW19	162	B10
Lancaster Rd W11	108	E11
Lancaster Rd, Barn	41	N9
Lancaster Rd, Enf	44	A1
Lancaster Rd, Har	67	P10
Lancaster Rd, Nthlt	85	T12
Lancaster Rd, Sthl	103	K14
Lancaster St SE1	27	R7
Lancaster Ter W2	15	K10
Lancaster Wk W2	22	J5
Lance Rd, Har	67	U14
Lancefield St W10	108	E6
Lancell St N16	94	D5
Lancelot Av, Wem	87	P7
Lancelot Cres, Wem	87	P8
Lancelot Gdns, Barn	42	A14
Lancelot Pl SW7	23	T8
Lancelot Rd, Ilf	65	R13
Lancelot Rd, Well	154	B7
Lancelot Rd, Wem	87	P9
Lancey Cl SE7	134	C7
Lanchester Rd N6	73	U9
Lancing Gdns N9	60	F2
Lancing Rd, W13 **6**	104	J14
Lancing Rd, Croy	183	M12
Lancing Rd, Ilf	81	N12
Lancing St NW1	9	S7
Landcroft Rd SE22	148	E11
Landells Rd SE22	148	G11
Landford Rd SW15	143	T6
Landgrove Rd SW19	162	G9
Landmann Way SE14	131	P10
Landon Pl SW1	23	U10
Landon Wk E14	114	D13
Landons Cl E14	132	F1
Landor Rd SW9	147	K5
Landor Wk W12	125	N4
Landra Gdns N21	43	R11
Landridge Rd SW6	144	E3
Landrock Rd N8	75	K11
Landscape Rd, Wdf Grn	63	S14
Landseer Av E12	98	G9
Landseer Cl, SW19 **19**	181	M2
Landseer Cl, Edg	70	B3
Landseer Rd N19	92	J5
Landseer Rd, Enf	44	G10
Landseer Rd, N Mal	178	H13
Landseer Rd, Sutt	194	G11

Landstead Rd SE18	135	P13
Lane, The NW8	6	E2
Lane, The SE3	151	P5
Lane App NW7	56	D10
Lane Cl NW2	89	R5
Lane End, Bexh	155	R6
Lane Ms E12	98	E6
Lanercost Cl SW2	165	P3
Lanercost Gdns N14	42	J13
Lanercost Rd SW2	165	P3
Lanesborough Pl, SW1 7	24	E6
Laneside, Chis	171	K9
Laneside, Edg	54	F10
Laneside Av, Dag	83	M14
Laneway SW15	143	R10
Lanfranc Rd E3	113	S4
Lanfrey Pl, W14 10	126	E10
Lang St E1	113	L7
Langbourne Av N6	92	A4
Langbourne Way, Esher	190	G11
Langbrook Rd SE3	152	B5
Langcroft Cl, Cars	195	U6
Langdale Av, Mitch	181	U5
Langdale Cl SE17	35	U10
Langdale Cl SW14	142	D7
Langdale Cl, Dag	100	E2
Langdale Cl, Orp	202	J5
Langdale Cres, Bexh	155	P1
Langdale Rd SE10	132	E14
Langdale Rd, Th Hth	183	P7
Langdale St, E1 11	112	J12
Langdon Ct NW10	106	J1
Langdon Cres E6	116	H3
Langdon Dr NW9	88	E1
Langdon Pk Rd N6	74	D13
Langdon Pl SW14	142	E5
Langdon Rd E6	116	G2
Langdon Rd, Brom	187	R6
Langdon Rd, Mord	181	M10
Langdon Shaw, Sid	171	T9
Langdon Wk, Mord	181	L10
Langdons Ct, Sthl	121	N5
Langford Cl E8	94	G9
Langford Cl N15	76	C11
Langford Cl NW8	6	H2
Langford Cl NW8	6	H3
Langford Cres, Barn	41	T7·
Langford Grn SE5	148	C6
Langford Pl NW8	6	H2
Langford Pl, Sid	172	B6
Langford Rd, SW6 6	145	K3
Langford Rd, Barn	41	T7
Langford Rd, Wdf Grn	63	U12
Langfords, Buck H	64	A3
Langham Dr, Rom	82	C11
Langham Gdns N21	43	P9
Langham Gdns W13	105	K13
Langham Gdns, Edg	54	F13
Langham Gdns, Rich	159	M7
Langham Gdns, Wem	87	L4
Langham Ho Cl, Rich	159	N7
Langham Pl N15	75	S6
Langham Pl W1	16	J4
Langham Pl, W4 4	125	K12
Langham Rd N15	75	T7
Langham Rd SW20	179	U2
Langham Rd, Edg	54	F12
Langham Rd, Tedd	158	J10
Langham St W1	17	K4
Langhedge Cl N18	60	F11
Langhedge La N18	60	F11
Langhedge La Ind Est N18	60	F12
Langholm Cl SW12	146	H14
Langholme, Bushey 4	51	T1
Langhorne, Dag	101	N13
Langland Cres, Stan	69	P4
Langland Dr, Pnr	50	J14
Langland Gdns NW3	91	K9
Langland Gdns, Croy	199	T3
Langler Rd NW10	107	U4
Langley Av, Ruis	84	D3
Langley Av, Surb	191	R1
Langley Av, Wor Pk	194	A3
Langley Ct SE9	152	G12
Langley Ct, WC2 2	18	B9
Langley Ct, Beck	186	D9
Langley Cres E11	79	T13
Langley Cres, Dag	100	F14
Langley Cres, Edg	54	F6
Langley Dr E11	79	S13
Langley Dr W3	124	D3
Langley Gdns, Brom	187	T7
Langley Gdns, Dag	100	G14
Langley Gdns, Orp	189	K11
Langley Gro, N Mal	178	J3
Langley La SW8	34	D10
Langley Meadow, Loug	49	N3
Langley Pk NW7	54	J11
Langley Pk Rd, Sutt	195	M11
Langley Rd SW19	180	G1
Langley Rd, Beck	185	R7
Langley Rd, Islw	140	F3
Langley Rd, Surb	177	S13
Langley Rd, Well	136	E12
Langley Row, Barn	40	E1
Langley St WC2	18	B8
Langley Way, W Wick	186	J14
Langmead Dr, Bushey	52	B1
Langmead St, SE27 1	165	T7
Langmore Ct, Bexh	154	H6
Langridge Ms, Hmptn 4	157	L12
Langroyd Rd SW17	163	T4
Langside Av SW15	143	N7
Langside Cres N14	58	H6
Langston Hughes Cl, SE24 16	147	S7
Langston Rd, Loug	49	M9
Langthorn Ct, EC2 7	20	E5
Langthorne Rd E11	96	F5
Langthorne St SW6	126	A14
Langton Av E6	116	G5
Langton Av N20	41	M14
Langton Cl WC1	10	G9
Langton Ri SE23	148	J13
Langton Rd NW2	89	U6
Langton Rd SW9	129	S14
Langton Rd, Har	51	T14
Langton Rd, W Mol	175	T8
Langton St SW10	30	H12
Langton Way SE3	151	N1
Langton Way, Croy	198	D7
Langtry Rd NW8	108	J2
Langtry Rd, Nthlt	102	H3
Langwood Chase, Tedd	159	M12
Langworth Dr, Hayes	102	C12
Lanhill Rd W9	108	G7
Lanier Rd SE13	150	G11
Lanigan Dr, Houns	139	R10
Lankaster Gdns N2	73	N2
Lankers Dr, Har	67	M11
Lankton Cl, Beck	186	E2
Lannoy Rd SE9	171	L2
Lanrick Rd E14	114	H11
Lanridge Rd SE2	136	G6
Lansbury Av N18	60	B10
Lansbury Av, Bark	100	A13
Lansbury Av, Felt	138	C11
Lansbury Av, Rom	83	K10
Lansbury Cl NW10	88	F10
Lansbury Est E14	114	C11
Lansbury Gdns, E14 5	114	G11
Lansbury Rd, Enf	45	N2
Lansbury Way N18	60	C10
Lanscombe Wk SW8	146	J1
Lansdell Rd, Mitch	182	A4
Lansdown Rd E7	97	U13
Lansdown Rd, Sid	172	C5
Lansdowne Av, Bexh	136	G13
Lansdowne Av, Orp	203	K2
Lansdowne Cl SW20	162	A14
Lansdowne Cl, Surb	192	C4
Lansdowne Cl, Twick	158	E1
Lansdowne Cres W11	108	E14
Lansdowne Dr E8	94	H14
Lansdowne Gdns SW8	146	J1
Lansdowne Gro NW10	89	K8
Lansdowne Hill SE27	165	R5
Lansdowne La SE7	134	A10
Lansdowne Ms SE7	134	A10
Lansdowne Pl, SE1 2	28	E10
Lansdowne Pl SE19	166	E13
Lansdowne Ri W11	108	D14
Lansdowne Rd E4	62	A4
Lansdowne Rd E11	97	L4
Lansdowne Rd E17	78	A10
Lansdowne Rd E18	79	P5
Lansdowne Rd N3	56	F13
Lansdowne Rd N10	74	E4
Lansdowne Rd N17	76	G2
Lansdowne Rd SW20	161	U13
Lansdowne Rd W11	108	D14
Lansdowne Rd, Brom	169	R14
Lansdowne Rd, Croy	198	B2
Lansdowne Rd, Epsom	192	G13
Lansdowne Rd, Har 2	68	C13
Lansdowne Rd, Houns	139	R5
Lansdowne Rd, Ilf	99	T1
Lansdowne Rd, Stan	53	L12
Lansdowne Ter WC1	10	D11
Lansdowne Wk W11	126	D1
Lansdowne Way SW8	146	J1
Lansdowne Wd Cl, SE27 3	165	R5
Lansfield Av, N18 1	60	H8
Lant St SE1	27	U6
Lantern Cl SW15	143	P7
Lantern Cl, Wem	87	P10
Lanterns Ct E14	132	C4
Lanvanor Rd SE15	149	L4
Lapford Cl W9	108	F7
Lapponum Wk, Hayes 4	102	J9
Lapse Wd Wk SE23	166	J2
Lapstone Gdns, Har	69	M11
Lapwing Ct, Surb	192	A5
Lapwing Way, Hayes 6	102	H11
Lara Cl SE13	150	F12
Lara Cl, Chess	191	S13
Larbert Rd SW16	164	E14
Larch Av W3	124	J2
Larch Cl E13	115	T7
Larch Cl N11	58	A13
Larch Cl, N19 9	92	E4
Larch Cl, SE8 3	131	U12
Larch Cl SW12	164	C3
Larch Cres, Epsom	192	D11
Larch Cres, Hayes	102	F8
Larch Gro, Sid	171	U2
Larch Rd E10	96	B4
Larch Rd NW2	89	U7
Larch Tree Way, Croy	200	B6
Larch Way, Brom	188	G13
Larchdene, Orp	202	H4
Larches, The N13	59	T6
Larches Av SW14	142	G7
Larchwood Rd SE9	171	K3
Larcom St SE17	36	A4
Larcombe Cl, Croy	198	E8
Larden Rd W3	125	K3
Largewood Av, Surb	192	A4
Larissa St, SE17 2	36	F5
Lark Row E2	113	L2
Lark Way, Cars	181	S14
Larkbere Rd SE26	167	S8
Larken Dr, Bushey	51	U1
Larkfield Av, Har	69	K5
Larkfield Cl, Brom	201	M3
Larkfield Rd, Rich	141	S8
Larkfield Rd, Sid	171	T6
Larkhall La SW4	146	H3
Larkhall Ri SW4	146	F5
Larkhill Ter SE18	134	G14
Larks Gro, Bark	99	S14
Larksfield Gro, Enf	45	K2
Larkshall Ct, Rom	83	T4
Larkshall Cres E4	62	F8
Larkshall Rd E4	62	G7
Larkspur Cl E6	116	C9
Larkspur Cl N17	60	A14
Larkspur Cl NW9	70	D10
Larkspur Gro, Edg	54	F7
Larkspur Way, Epsom	192	D10
Larkswood Ct E4	62	H9
Larkswood Ri, Pnr	66	E8
Larkswood Rd E4	62	C8
Larkway Cl NW9	70	H8
Larnach Rd W6	126	A12
Larpent Av SW15	143	T9
Larwood Cl, Grnf	86	A10
Lascelles Av, Har	68	A14
Lascelles Cl, E11 4	96	H4
Lascotts Rd N22	59	L12
Lassa Rd SE9	152	D10
Lassell St SE10	132	H10
Latchett Rd E18	79	S2
Latchingdon Ct E17	77	P7
Latchingdon Gdns, Wdf Grn	64	D11
Latchmere Cl, Rich	159	S9
Latchmere La, KingsT	159	T10
Latchmere Rd SW11	145	T4
Latchmere Rd, KingsT	159	R13
Latchmere St SW11	145	T3
Lateward Rd, Brent	123	P12
Latham Cl E6	116	D11
Latham Cl, Twick	140	G13
Latham Rd, Bexh	155	N9
Latham Rd, Twick	140	F13
Lathams Way, Croy	197	L2
Lathkill Cl, Enf	44	F13
Lathom Rd E6	98	D14
Latimer SE17	36	G8
Latimer Av E6	116	F1
Latimer Cl, Pnr	66	E2
Latimer Cl, Wor Pk	193	S7
Latimer Gdns, Pnr	66	E2
Latimer Pl W10	107	U11
Latimer Rd E7	97	S7
Latimer Rd N15	76	C11
Latimer Rd SW19	162	J12
Latimer Rd W10	107	U11
Latimer Rd, Barn	40	J5
Latimer Rd, Croy 4	197	S5
Latimer Rd, Tedd	158	E9
Latona Rd SE15	37	R11
Latymer Pl W14	125	K12
Latton Cl, Walt	175	K13
Latymer Ct W6	126	A8
Latymer Rd N9	60	F3
Latymer Way N9	60	C4
Laud St SE11	34	E6
Laud St, Croy	197	T6
Lauder Cl, Nthlt	102	G3
Lauderdale Dr, Rich	159	P5
Lauderdale Rd W9	6	C8
Laughton Ct, Borwd	38	F3
Laughton Rd, Nthlt	102	H2
Laughton Rd, Brom	169	P8
Launcelot St, SE1 2	26	J7
Launceston Gdns, Grnf	105	L1
Launceston Pl W8	22	E11
Launceston Rd, Grnf	105	L2
Launch St E14	132	E5
Laundry La N16	94	H5
Laundry Rd W6	126	C12
Laura Cl E11	79	T9
Laura Cl, Enf	44	C10

Lau-Lee 295

Laura PI E5	95	L8
Lauradale Rd N2	73	U7
Laurel Av, Twick	158	E1
Laurel Bank Gdns, SW6 7	144	F3
Laurel Bank Rd, Enf	43	U2
Laurel CI N19	92	E4
Laurel CI SW17	163	S9
Laurel CI, Ilf	65	M12
Laurel CI, Sid	172	B5
Laurel Cres, Croy	200	B6
Laurel Dr N21	43	N13
Laurel Gdns E4	46	C13
Laurel Gdns NW7	54	G6
Laurel Gdns W7	122	C2
Laurel Gdns, Houns	138	J8
Laurel Gro SE20	167	K13
Laurel Gro SE24	167	P8
Laurel Pk, Har	52	E14
Laurel Rd SW13	143	N4
Laurel Rd SW20	179	R1
Laurel Rd, Hmptn	158	A10
Laurel St E8	94	F12
Laurel Vw N12	56	J6
Laurel Way E18	79	M7
Laurel Way N20	56	H5
Laurence Ms W12	125	N4
Laurence Pountney Hill, EC4 5	20	D10
Laurence Pountney La EC4	20	D11
Laurie Gro SE14	149	S1
Laurie Rd W7	104	C9
Laurier Rd NW5	92	C6
Laurier Rd, Croy	184	E13
Laurimel CI, Stan	53	K12
Laurino PI, Bushey	51	U4
Lauriston Rd E9	113	N1
Lauriston Rd SW19	162	A11
Lausanne Rd N8	75	P7
Lausanne Rd SE15	149	M2
Lavell St N16	94	B8
Lavender Av NW9	88	E1
Lavender Av, Mitch	181	T2
Lavender Av, Wor Pk	193	U5
Lavender CI, SW3 1	31	M11
Lavender CI, Brom	188	C11
Lavender CI, Cars	196	C8
Lavender CI, W Mol	175	R6
Lavender Gdns SW11	145	U7
Lavender Gdns, Enf	43	S1
Lavender Gdns, Har	52	D12
Lavender Gro E8	94	G14
Lavender Gro, Mitch	181	S2
Lavender Hill SW11	145	U6
Lavender Hill, Enf	43	P1
Lavender Ms, Wall	196	J12
Lavender PI, Ilf	98	J9
Lavender Rd SE16	131	R1
Lavender Rd SW11	145	P5
Lavender Rd, Cars	196	B9
Lavender Rd, Croy	183	L12
Lavender Rd, Enf	44	B1
Lavender Rd, Epsom	192	D10
Lavender Rd, Sutt	195	N7
Lavender Sq E11	96	H5
Lavender St, E15 2	96	J12
Lavender Sweep SW11	145	T7
Lavender Ter, SW11 2	145	S5
Lavender Vale, Wall	196	G12
Lavender Wk SW11	145	T7
Lavender Wk, Mitch 1	182	A5
Lavender Way, Croy	185	P12
Lavengro Rd SE27	165	T3
Lavenham Rd SW18	162	F13
Lavernock Rd, Bexh	155	P3
Lavers Rd N16	94	D5
Laverstoke Gdns SW15	143	N13
Laverton Ms SW5	30	C4
Laverton PI SW5	30	C4
Lavidge Rd SE9	170	D4
Lavina Gro N1	10	E1

Lavington Rd W13	123	K2
Lavington Rd, Croy	197	L6
Lavington St SE1	27	S3
Law St SE1	28	F10
Lawdons Gdns, Croy 3	197	S8
Lawford Rd N1	94	C14
Lawford Rd NW5	92	E12
Lawford Rd W4	124	F13
Lawless St E14	114	D13
Lawley Rd N14	42	C14
Lawley St E5	95	M7
Lawn, The, Sthl	121	P9
Lawn CI N9	44	F14
Lawn CI, Brom	169	S12
Lawn CI, N Mal	178	J4
Lawn Cres, Rich	142	A3
Lawn Fm Gro, Rom	82	J7
Lawn Gdns W7	122	C1
Lawn Ho CI E14	132	E3
Lawn La SW8	34	E11
Lawn Rd NW3	91	T10
Lawn Rd, Beck	167	U14
Lawn Ter SE3	151	K5
Lawn Vale, Pnr	66	H3
Lawns, The E4	62	B10
Lawns, The SE3	151	K5
Lawns, The SE19	184	A2
Lawns, The, Pnr	81	R13
Lawns, The, Sid	172	D7
Lawns, The, Sutt	194	D14
Lawnside, SE3 7	151	L8
Lawrence Av E12	98	G8
Lawrence Av E17	77	P2
Lawrence Av N13	59	R8
Lawrence Av NW7	55	K7
Lawrence Av, N Mal	178	H12
Lawrence Bldgs N16	94	E5
Lawrence Campe CI N20	57	P5
Lawrence CI E3	114	A4
Lawrence CI N15	76	C6
Lawrence Ct NW7	55	K9
Lawrence Rd E13	115	R1
Lawrence Rd N15	76	C7
Lawrence Rd N18	60	J8
Lawrence Rd SE25	184	F8
Lawrence Rd W5	123	N7
Lawrence Rd, Erith	137	R14
Lawrence Rd, Hmptn	157	L14
Lawrence Rd, Houns	138	E8
Lawrence Rd, Pnr	66	H10
Lawrence Rd, Rich	159	M7
Lawrence Rd, W Wick	201	P7
Lawrence St E16	115	M10
Lawrence St NW7	55	N6
Lawrence St SW3	31	N11
Lawrence Way NW10	88	F7
Lawrie Pk Av SE26	167	K9
Lawrie Pk Cres SE26	167	K10
Lawrie Pk Gdns SE26	167	K9
Lawrie Pk Rd SE26	167	L9
Lawson CI E16	115	U10
Lawson CI SW19	162	A6
Lawson Est SE1	28	C11
Lawson Gdns, Pnr	66	D6
Lawson Rd, Enf	45	L2
Lawson Rd, Sthl	103	M8
Lawton Rd E3	113	S6
Lawton Rd E10	96	E2
Lawton Rd, Barn	41	N6
Lawton Rd, Loug	48	J5
Laxcon CI NW10	88	F9
Laxey Rd, Orp	203	T11
Laxley CI SE5	35	S14
Laxton PI, NW1 4	9	K9
Layard Rd SE16	131	K7
Layard Rd, Enf	44	F1

Layard Rd, Th Hth	184	B3
Layard Sq SE16	131	K7
Laycock St N1	93	P12
Layer Gdns W3	106	A14
Layfield CI NW4	71	S13
Layfield Cres NW4	71	R14
Layfield Rd NW4	71	R14
Layhams Rd, Kes	201	L11
Layhams Rd, W Wick	200	H6
Laymarsh CI, Belv	137	L6
Laymead CI, Nthlt	84	J12
Laystall St EC1	10	J12
Layton Cres, Croy	197	P9
Layton Rd N1	11	M1
Layton Rd, Brent	123	N10
Layton Rd, Houns	139	S8
Laytons Bldgs, SE1 3	28	C6
Layzell Wk SE9	170	B2
Le May Av SE12	169	R5
Lea Br Rd E5	95	L5
Lea Br Rd E10	95	T1
Lea Br Rd E17	78	D12
Lea Gdns, Wem	87	T8
Lea Hall Rd E10	96	B1
Lea Rd, Beck 2	186	B3
Lea Rd, Enf	44	A1
Lea Rd, Sthl	120	J8
Lea Valley Rd E4	45	U11
Lea Valley Rd, Enf	45	U11
Lea Valley Trd Est N18	61	P11
Lea Valley Viaduct E4	61	P9
Lea Valley Viaduct N18	61	P9
Leabank CI, Har	86	D5
Leabank Sq E9	96	A11
Leabank Vw N15	76	G11
Leabourne Rd N16	76	G13
Leacroft Av SW12	145	U13
Leadale Av E4	62	A4
Leadale Rd N15	76	G12
Leadale Rd N16	76	G12
Leadbeaters CI, N11 1	57	T10
Leadenhall PI EC3	20	G8
Leadenhall St EC3	20	H7
Leader Av E12	98	H10
Leadings, The, Wem	88	E5
Leaf CI, T Ditt	176	D10
Leaf Gro SE27	165	P9
Leafield CI SW16	165	R12
Leafield La, Sid	173	L6
Leafield Rd SW20	180	F5
Leafield Rd, Sutt	194	G4
Leafy Gro, Kes	201	U9
Leafy Oak Rd SE12	169	U7
Leafy Way, Croy	198	E4
Leagrave St E5	95	M5
Leahurst Rd SE13	150	J11
Leake CI SE1	26	G6
Leake St SE1	26	H6
Lealand Rd N15	76	E11
Leamington Av E17	78	B10
Leamington Av, Orp	203	R7
Leamington Av, Mord	180	E7
Leamington CI E12	98	E10
Leamington CI, Brom	169	T9
Leamington CI, Houns	139	U9
Leamington Cres, Har	85	K6
Leamington Gdns, Ilf	99	U3
Leamington Pk W3	106	G10
Leamington Rd, Sthl	120	G8
Leamington Rd Vil W11	108	F10
Leamore St W6	125	S8
Leamouth Rd, E6 18	116	C10
Leamouth Rd E14	114	H12
Leander Ct SE8	150	A2

Leander Rd SW2	147	N12
Leander Rd, Nthlt	103	N4
Leander Rd, Th Hth	183	M8
Learner Dr, Har	85	P4
Learoyd Gdns E6	116	G13
Leas CI, Chess	191	T13
Leas Dale SE9	170	G6
Leas Grn, Chis	171	T11
Leaside Av N10	74	A6
Leaside Rd E5	95	L2
Leasowes Rd E10	96	B1
Leather CI, Mitch	182	A4
Leather Gdns E15	115	K2
Leather La EC1	19	L4
Leatherbottle Grn, Erith	137	L5
Leatherdale St, E1 4	113	N6
Leatherhead CI N16	94	E1
Leatherhead Rd, Chess	191	N14
Leathermarket Ct SE1	28	G8
Leathermarket St SE1	28	G7
Leathersellers CI, Barn 1	40	C7
Leathsail Rd, Har	85	S6
Leathwaite Rd SW11	145	U9
Leathwell Rd SE8	150	U4
Leaveland CI, Beck	186	B8
Leaver Gdns, Grnf	104	C4
Leavesden Rd, Stan	52	H12
Leaway E10	95	P2
Lebanon Av, Felt	156	G9
Lebanon Gdns SW18	144	G11
Lebanon Pk, Twick	158	J1
Lebanon Rd SW18	144	G10
Lebanon Rd, Croy	198	D2
Lebrun Sq SE3	151	R7
Lechmere App, Wdf Grn 2	79	U4
Lechmere Av, Chig	65	L8
Lechmere Av, Wdf Grn	80	A3
Lechmere Rd NW2	89	S12
Leckford Rd SW18	163	M3
Leckwith Av, Bexh	136	J12
Lecky St SW7	31	K6
Leconfield Av SW13	143	L6
Leconfield Rd N5	94	A8
Leda Rd SE18	134	F6
Ledbury Est SE15	130	J13
Ledbury Ms N W11	108	G13
Ledbury Ms W, W11 1	108	F11
Ledbury Rd W11	108	F11
Ledbury Rd, Croy	198	A8
Ledbury St SE15	37	U13
Ledrington Rd SE19	166	G12
Ledway Dr, Wem	69	T14
Lee Av, Rom	82	J12
Lee Br SE13	150	F6
Lee Ch St SE13	151	K7
Lee CI E17	77	N2
Lee CI, Barn	41	M7
Lee Conservancy Rd E9	95	T9
Lee Grn SE12	151	M9
Lee Gro, Chig	64	J4
Lee High Rd SE12	151	L8
Lee High Rd SE13	150	G6
Lee Pk SE3	151	L7
Lee Pk Way N9	61	R5
Lee Pk Way N18	61	P8
Lee Rd NW7	56	B14
Lee Rd SE3	151	L7
Lee Rd SW19	181	K2
Lee Rd, Enf	44	G11
Lee Rd, Grnf	105	L1
Lee St E8	112	E1
Lee Ter SE3	151	K6
Lee Ter SE13	151	K6
Lee Valley Technopark N17	76	H6
Lee Vw, Enf	43	R1
Leechcroft Av, Sid	153	T10
Leechcroft Rd, Wall	196	B6
Leecroft Rd, Barn	40	C8

Leeds Pl N4 93 L2
Leeds Rd, Ilf 99 P1
Leeds St N18 60 G9
Leefern Rd W12 125 P4
Leegate SE12 151 M9
Leeke St WC1 10 E5
Leeland Rd W13 122 H1
Leeland Ter W13 122 H2
Leeland Way NW10 89 L7
Leerdam Dr E14 132 F6
Lees, The, Croy 199 U4
Lees Pl W1 16 D10
Leeside, Barn 40 D11
Leeside Cres NW11 72 E11
Leeside Rd N17 61 L12
Leeson Rd, SE24 *12* 147 P8
Leesons Way, Orp 189 U4
Leeward Gdns SW19 162 D10
Leeway SE8 131 T9
Leeway Cl, Pnr 51 L14
Leewood Cl SE12 151 N11
Lefevre Wk E3 114 A2
Lefroy Rd W12 125 L3
Legard Rd N5 93 S6
Legatt Rd SE9 152 A9
Leggatt Rd E15 114 F4
Legge St SE13 150 E9
Leghorn Rd NW10 107 N3
Leghorn Rd E11 135 P10
Legion Cl N1 93 P13
Legion Ct, Mord 180 H11
Legion Rd, Grnf 103 U2
Legion Way N12 57 R13
Legon Av, Rom 101 U2
Legrace Av, Houns 138 G4
Leicester Av, Mitch *1* 183 K8
Leicester Cl, Wor Pk 193 T7
Leicester Gdns, Ilf 81 S13
Leicester Pl WC2 17 T10
Leicester Rd E11 79 S9
Leicester Rd N2 73 S6
Leicester Rd NW10 88 H13
Leicester Rd, Barn 40 J9
Leicester Rd, Croy 184 D14
Leicester Sq WC2 17 T11
Leicester St, WC2 *5* 17 T10
Leigh Av, Ilf 80 A8
Leigh Cl, N Mal 178 G7
Leigh Ct, Borwd 38 G3
Leigh Ct, Har 86 C2
Leigh Cres, Croy 200 D13
Leigh Gdns NW10 107 U3
Leigh Hunt Dr N14 58 G2
Leigh Hunt St SE1 27 U6
Leigh Orchard Cl SW16 165 L6
Leigh Pl, EC1 *2* 19 K2
Leigh Pl, Well 154 B3
Leigh Rd E6 98 G12
Leigh Rd E10 78 F14
Leigh Rd N5 93 R8
Leigh Rd, Houns 140 A8
Leigh Rodd, Wat 51 L5
Leigh St WC1 10 B8
Leigham Av SW16 165 K5
Leigham Ct Rd SW16 165 K4
Leigham Dr, Islw 122 D13
Leigham Vale SW2 165 P4
Leigham Vale SW16 165 M6
Leighton Av E12 98 H10
Leighton Av, Pnr 66 J5
Leighton Cl, Edg 70 B3
Leighton Cres, NW5 *5* 92 F9
Leighton Gdns NW10 107 T3
Leighton Gro NW5 92 F9
Leighton Pl NW5 92 F10
Leighton Rd NW5 92 H10
Leighton Rd W13 122 H3
Leighton Rd, Enf 44 G10
Leighton Rd, Har 68 A4
Leighton St, Croy 197 R2
Leila Parnell Pl, SE7 *2* 133 T12

Leinster Av SW14 142 E6
Leinster Gdns W2 14 E8
Leinster Ms W2 14 F11
Leinster Pl W2 14 E8
Leinster Rd N10 74 D7
Leinster Sq W2 108 H12
Leinster Ter W2 14 F10
Leisure Way N12 57 N14
Leith Cl NW9 88 G2
Leith Rd N22 75 R1
Leithcote Gdns SW16 165 L7
Leithcote Path SW16 165 M6
Lela Av, Houns 138 F4
Lelitia Cl E8 112 G1
Leman St E1 21 P7
Lemark Cl, Stan 53 L11
Lemmon Rd SE10 132 J11
Lemna Rd E11 79 K14
Lemonwell Dr SE9 153 L10
Lemsford Cl N15 76 H10
Lemsford Ct, Borwd 38 E8
Lemuel St, SW18 *16* 145 K12
Len Freeman Pl, SW6 *10* 126 E12
Lena Gdns W6 125 U6
Lena Kennedy Cl E4 62 E11
Lendal Ter, SW4 *2* 146 J6
Lenelby Rd, Surb 192 A2
Lenham Rd SE12 151 L8
Lenham Rd, Bexh 137 L12
Lenham Rd, Sutt 195 K8
Lenham Rd, Th Hth 184 B4
Lennard Av, W Wick 201 K4
Lennard Cl, W Wick 201 K4
Lennard Rd SE20 167 M12
Lennard Rd, Beck 167 T13
Lennard Rd, Brom 202 F1
Lennard Rd, Croy 197 T1
Lennon Rd NW2 89 T10
Lennox Gdns NW10 89 M8
Lennox Gdns SW1 23 T12
Lennox Gdns, Croy 197 S8
Lennox Gdns, Ilf 98 E1
Lennox Gdns Ms SW1 23 T12
Lennox Rd E17 77 U11
Lennox Rd N4 93 M3
Lenor Cl, Bexh 155 K8
Lens Rd E7 97 T14
Lensbury Way SE2 136 G5
Lenthall Rd E8 94 F13
Lenthall Rd, Loug 49 N8
Lenthorp Rd SE10 133 L8
Lentmead Rd, Brom 169 M6
Lenton Path SE18 135 N12
Lenton St SE18 135 N7
Leo St SE15 131 K13
Leof Cres SE6 168 C9
Leominster Rd, Mord 181 M11
Leominster Wk, Mord 181 L11
Leonard Av, Mord 181 M10
Leonard Rd E4 62 A11
Leonard Rd E7 97 N8
Leonard Rd N9 60 F6
Leonard Rd SW16 182 E1
Leonard Rd, Sthl 120 H6
Leonard St E16 134 D2
Leonard St EC2 12 E10
Leontine Cl SE15 130 H14
Leopards Ct EC1 19 K1
Leopold Av SW19 162 F9
Leopold Ms, E9 *1* 113 L1
Leopold Rd E17 78 A10
Leopold Rd N2 73 P5
Leopold Rd N18 61 K10
Leopold Rd NW10 89 K14
Leopold Rd SW19 162 F8
Leopold Rd W5 123 T1
Leopold St E3 113 U9
Leppoc Rd SW4 146 G9
Leroy St SE1 36 G1
Lescombe Cl SE23 167 S6
Lescombe Rd SE23 167 S5
Lesley Cl, Bex 155 R13
Leslie Gdns, Sutt 194 H13
Leslie Gro, Croy 198 B1

Leslie Pk Rd, Croy 198 C2
Leslie Rd E11 96 G7
Leslie Rd E16 115 R12
Leslie Rd N2 73 P5
Leslie Smith Sq, SE18 *1* 134 H12
Lessar Av SW4 146 E11
Lessing St SE23 149 R13
Lessingham Av SW17 163 U7
Lessingham Av, Ilf 80 G5
Lessington Av, Rom 83 T12
Lessness Av, Bexh 136 G13
Lessness Pk, Belv 137 M9
Lessness Rd, Belv 137 N11
Lessness Rd, Mord 181 M11
Lester Av E15 115 K7
Leswin Pl, N16 *3* 94 E6
Leswin Rd N16 94 E5
Letchford Gdns NW10 107 P5
Letchford Ms NW10 107 P5
Letchford Ter, Har 67 R1
Letchworth Cl, Brom 187 P9
Letchworth Cl, Wat 50 G10
Letchworth Dr, Brom 187 N10
Letchworth St SW17 163 T7
Lethbridge Cl SE13 150 E2
Lett Rd E15 96 G14
Letterstone Rd, SW6 *13* 126 E14
Lettice St SW6 144 F2
Lettsom St SE5 148 C3
Lettsom Wk E13 115 N3
Leucha Rd E17 77 R10
Levana Cl SW19 162 C2
Levehurst Way SW4 147 K3
Leven Cl, Wat 50 H9
Leven Rd E14 114 F10
Levendale Rd SE23 167 S4
Lever St EC1 11 U7
Leverett St, SW3 *2* 31 S2
Leverholme Gdns SE9 170 G7
Leverson St SW16 164 F12
Leverton Pl NW5 92 D9
Leverton St NW5 92 E9
Levett Gdns, Ilf 99 T7
Levett Rd, Bark 99 R12
Levine Gdns, Bark 118 H3
Levison Way N19 92 G2
Lewes Cl, Nthlt 85 P12
Lewes Rd N12 57 R10
Lewes Rd, Brom 188 A3
Lewesdon Cl SW19 162 A2
Leweston Pl N16 76 F14
Lewgars Av NW9 70 F11
Lewin Rd SW14 142 H6
Lewin Rd SW16 164 H11
Lewin Rd, Bexh 155 K8
Lewis Av E17 78 B2
Lewis Cl N14 42 E14
Lewis Cres NW10 88 G10
Lewis Gdns N2 73 N3
Lewis Rd, Mitch 181 R4
Lewis Rd, Sid *6* 141 P10
Lewis Rd, Sthl 121 K3
Lewis Rd, Sutt 195 K7
Lewis Rd, Well 154 F6
Lewis St NW1 92 D12
Lewis Way, Dag 101 S11
Lewisham High St SE13 150 F5
Lewisham Hill SE13 150 F4
Lewisham Pk SE13 150 E11
Lewisham Rd SE13 150 E3
Lewisham St SW1 25 T7
Lewisham Way SE4 149 T1
Lewisham Way SE14 149 T1
Lexden Dr, Rom 82 C11
Lexden Rd W3 124 D1
Lexden Rd, Mitch 182 G7
Lexham Ct, Grnf 104 A1
Lexham Gdns W8 30 C1
Lexham Gdns Ms W8 22 C12

Lexham Ms W8 126 H7
Lexham Wk, W8 *6* 22 C12
Lexington St W1 17 P9
Lexington Way, Barn 40 B8
Lexton Gdns SW12 164 H1
Ley St, Ilf 99 K4
Leyborne Av W13 123 L4
Leyborne Pk, Rich 142 A1
Leybourne Cl, Brom 187 N10
Leybourne Rd E11 97 M2
Leybourne Rd NW1 92 D14
Leybourne Rd NW9 70 A9
Leybourne St, NW1 *4* 92 C14
Leybridge Ct SE12 151 N9
Leyburn Cl, E17 *4* 78 D8
Leyburn Gdns, Croy 198 D4
Leyburn Gro N18 60 H11
Leyburn Rd N18 60 H11
Leycroft Cl, Loug 48 G10
Leyden St, E1 *2* 21 L4
Leydon Cl SE16 131 P2
Leyfield, Wor Pk 193 L2
Leyland Av, Enf 45 R3
Leyland Gdns, Wdf Grn 63 T9
Leyland Rd SE12 151 N10
Leylang Rd SE14 131 P13
Leys, The N2 73 M7
Leys, The, Har 69 T11
Leys Av, Dag 101 U14
Leys Cl, Dag 101 U13
Leys Cl, Har 68 B9
Leys Gdns, Barn 42 A9
Leys Rd E, Enf 45 R1
Leys Rd W, Enf 45 R1
Leysdown Av, Bexh 155 U8
Leysdown Rd SE9 170 E3
Leysfield Rd W12 125 P4
Leyspring Rd E11 97 M1
Leyswood Dr, Ilf 81 R9
Leythe Rd W3 124 F4
Leyton Business Cen E10 96 A3
Leyton Gra E10 96 C2
Leyton Gra Est E10 96 B3
Leyton Grn Rd E10 78 E12
Leyton Ind Village E10 77 N14
Leyton Pk Rd E10 96 F5
Leyton Rd E15 96 G10
Leyton Rd SW19 163 M13
Leyton Way E11 79 K13
Leytonstone Rd E15 96 J9
Leywick St E15 114 J3
Lezayre Rd, Orp 203 T12
Liardet St SE14 131 S12
Liberia Rd N5 93 S11
Liberty Av SW19 181 N2
Liberty Ms SW12 146 C12
Liberty St SW9 147 M1
Libra Rd E3 113 U3
Libra Rd E13 115 N3
Library Pl E1 113 K13
Library St SE1 27 P8
Library Way, Twick 139 T13
Lichfield Cl, Barn 41 T6
Lichfield Gdns, Rich 141 R8
Lichfield Gro N3 72 H3
Lichfield Rd E3 113 S5
Lichfield Rd E6 116 A6
Lichfield Rd N9 60 G3
Lichfield Rd NW2 90 C7
Lichfield Rd, Dag 100 D7
Lichfield Rd, Houns 138 E6
Lichfield Rd, Nthwd 66 A5
Lichfield Rd, Rich 141 U1
Lichfield Rd, Wdf Grn 63 K8
Lichfield Sq, Rich 141 R8
Lichlade Cl, Orp 203 T8
Lidbury Rd NW7 56 C11
Lidcote Gdns SW9 147 N3
Liddell Cl, Har 69 P6
Liddell Gdns NW10 107 T3
Liddell Rd NW6 90 G11
Lidding Rd, Har 69 P10
Liddington Rd E15 115 L1
Liddon Rd E13 115 R6

Liddon Rd, Brom	187	U5
Liden Cl E17	77	T14
Lidfield Rd N16	94	A8
Lidgate Rd, SE15 **2**	130	E14
Lidiard Rd SW18	163	M3
Lidlington Pl NW1	9	N3
Lido Sq N17	76	B2
Lidyard Rd N19	92	E2
Liffler Rd SE18	135	R9
Lifford St SW15	144	B7
Liffords Pl SW13	143	L3
Lightcliffe Rd N13	59	P7
Lighter Cl SE16	131	S7
Lighterman Ms E1	113	P12
Lightermans Rd E14	132	B4
Lightermans Wk SW18	144	G7
Lightfoot Rd N8	75	K9
Lightley Cl, Wem	105	S1
Ligonier St E2	13	L9
Lilac Cl E4	61	T11
Lilac Gdns W5	123	P5
Lilac Gdns, Croy	200	A5
Lilac Pl SE11	34	F4
Lilac St W12	107	N13
Lilburne Gdns SE9	152	D10
Lilburne Rd SE9	152	C10
Lilburne Wk NW10	88	E11
Lile Cres W7	104	D10
Lilestone Est NW8	7	L10
Lilestone St NW8	7	P10
Lilford Rd SE5	147	S3
Lilian Barker Cl SE12	151	P10
Lilian Board Way, Grnf	86	A9
Lilian Cl N16	94	C6
Lilian Gdns, Wdf Grn	79	S1
Lilian Rd SW16	182	E2
Lillechurch Rd, Dag	100	D11
Lilleshall Rd, Mord	181	N11
Lilley Cl E1	29	U3
Lilley La NW7	54	H9
Lillian Av W3	124	A4
Lillian Rd SW13	125	P11
Lillie Rd SW6	126	G11
Lillie Yd SW6	126	H11
Lilleshall Rd SW4	146	D6
Lillington Gdns Est SW1	33	P4
Lilliput Av, Nthlt	103	K2
Lily Cl W14	126	C8
Lily Gdns, Wem	105	M4
Lily Pl EC1	19	M1
Lily Rd E17	78	C12
Lilyville Rd SW6	144	E1
Limbourne Av, Dag	83	M14
Limburg Rd SW11	145	T8
Lime Cl E1	29	T2
Lime Cl, Brom	188	D7
Lime Cl, Buck H	64	A5
Lime Cl, Cars	195	T3
Lime Cl, Har	68	F3
Lime Cl, Rom	83	T8
Lime Cres, Sun	174	E3
Lime Gro N20	56	E1
Lime Gro W12	125	T3
Lime Gro, Ilf	65	T11
Lime Gro, N Mal	178	H5
Lime Gro, Orp	203	K3
Lime Gro, Ruis	66	C14
Lime Gro, Sid	153	U11
Lime Gro, Twick	140	F12
Lime Rd, Rich	141	T8
Lime St E17	77	R7
Lime St EC3	20	G9
Lime St Pas EC3	20	G9
Lime Tree Av, Esher	190	B1
Lime Tree Av, T Ditt	190	C1
Lime Tree Gro, Croy	199	U6
Lime Tree Pl, Mitch	182	D2
Lime Tree Rd, Houns	139	R1
Lime Tree Wk, Bushey	52	D3
Lime Tree Wk, W Wick	201	M7
Limeburner La EC4	19	P7
Limecroft Cl, Epsom	192	H14
Limedene Cl, Pnr	66	H2
Limeharbour E14	132	D5
Limehouse Causeway E14	113	U13
Limehouse Flds Est E14	113	S10
Limehouse Link E14	113	T13
Limekiln Dr SE7	133	S12
Limekiln Pl SE19	166	E14
Limerick Cl SW12	146	F14
Limerston St SW10	30	J11
Limes, The, W2 **16**	108	H14
Limes, The, Brom	202	C4
Limes, The, Har	68	F3
Limes Av E11	79	S8
Limes Av N12	57	L7
Limes Av NW7	54	J11
Limes Av NW11	72	D13
Limes Av SE20	167	K14
Limes Av SW13	143	L4
Limes Av, Cars	195	T2
Limes Av, Chig	65	M10
Limes Av, Croy	197	N6
Limes Ave, The N11	58	D9
Limes Fld Rd, SW14 **1**	143	K5
Limes Gdns SW18	144	G12
Limes Gro SE13	150	F8
Limes Pl, Croy **4**	184	A13
Limes Rd, Beck	186	D3
Limes Rd, Croy	184	A12
Limes Row, Orp	203	K9
Limes Wk SE15	149	K7
Limes Wk W5	123	P4
Limesdale Gdns, Edg	70	E3
Limesford Rd SE15	149	N8
Limestone Wk, Erith	136	H5
Limetree Cl SW2	165	M2
Limetree Wk, SW17 **4**	164	A10
Limewood Cl E17	77	T7
Limewood Cl W13	105	K11
Limewood Cl, Ilf	80	F10
Limewood Rd, Erith	137	U13
Limpsfield Av SW19	162	A3
Limpsfield Av, Th Hth	183	M10
Linacre Rd NW2	89	S11
Linberry Wk SE8	131	S8
Linchmere Rd SE12	151	M14
Lincoln Av N14	58	E4
Lincoln Av SW19	162	A6
Lincoln Av, Twick	157	S3
Lincoln Cl, Grnf	103	T1
Lincoln Cl, Har	67	M10
Lincoln Ct, Borwd	38	H9
Lincoln Cres, Enf	44	D9
Lincoln Dr, Wat	50	E5
Lincoln Gdns, Ilf	80	D13
Lincoln Grn Rd, Orp	189	U10
Lincoln Ms NW6	108	D1
Lincoln Ms, SE21 **1**	166	A2
Lincoln Rd E7	98	B12
Lincoln Rd E13	115	R8
Lincoln Rd E18	79	N2
Lincoln Rd N2	73	S6
Lincoln Rd SE25	184	J6
Lincoln Rd, Enf	44	C8
Lincoln Rd, Felt	157	L5
Lincoln Rd, Har	67	M10
Lincoln Rd, Mitch **2**	182	J9
Lincoln Rd, N Mal	178	E5
Lincoln Rd, Sid	172	D9
Lincoln Rd, Wem	87	P12
Lincoln Rd, Wor Pk	193	R1
Lincoln St E11	96	J4
Lincoln St SW3	31	U4
Lincoln Way, Enf	44	J9
Lincolns, The NW7	55	M5
Lincoln's Inn WC2	18	J6
Lincoln's Inn Flds WC2	18	G6
Lincombe Rd, Brom	169	L5
Lind Rd, Sutt	195	M9
Lind St SE8	150	B3
Lindal Cres, Enf	43	K9
Lindal Rd SE4	149	T10
Lindbergh Rd, Wall	196	J14
Linden Av NW10	108	A4
Linden Av, Enf	44	H1
Linden Av, Houns	139	R9
Linden Av, Ruis	84	A2
Linden Av, Th Hth	183	R7
Linden Av, Wem	87	T9
Linden Cl N14	42	E11
Linden Cl, Ruis	84	A2
Linden Cl, Stan	52	J9
Linden Cl, T Ditt	176	F13
Linden Ct W12	125	T1
Linden Cres, Grnf	86	E11
Linden Cres, Kings T	63	R11
Linden Cres, Wdf Grn		
Linden Gdns W2	108	H14
Linden Gdns W4	124	H9
Linden Gdns, Enf	44	H2
Linden Gro SE15	149	L6
Linden Gro SE26	167	M12
Linden Gro, N Mal	178	J6
Linden Gro, Tedd	158	E9
Linden Lawns, Wem	87	T8
Linden Lea N2	73	M10
Linden Leas, W Wick	200	G3
Linden Ms, W2 **3**	108	H14
Linden Pl, Mitch	181	S8
Linden Rd N10	74	D8
Linden Rd N11	57	U3
Linden Rd N15	75	T7
Linden Rd, Hmptn	175	N1
Linden Way N14	42	F12
Lindenfield, Chis	188	J3
Lindens, The N12	57	N9
Lindens, The W4	142	E1
Lindens, The, Croy	200	E11
Lindens, The, Loug	48	F9
Lindeth Cl, Stan	53	K12
Lindfield Gdns NW3	91	L9
Lindfield Rd W5	105	L7
Lindfield Rd, Croy	184	F12
Lindfield St E14	114	A11
Lindhill Cl, Enf	45	P2
Lindisfarne Rd SW20	161	N14
Lindisfarne Rd, Dag	100	F5
Lindisfarne Way E9	95	S8
Lindley Est SE15	37	S13
Lindley Rd E10	96	F3
Lindley St E1	113	L9
Lindo St SE15	149	M4
Lindore Rd SW11	145	T8
Lindores Rd, Cars	181	L14
Lindrop St SW6	145	L3
Lindsay Cl, Chess	191	S13
Lindsay Dr, Har	69	T10
Lindsay Rd, Hmptn	157	S8
Lindsay Rd, Wor Pk	193	S3
Lindsay Sq SW1	33	T7
Lindsell St SE10	150	E1
Lindsey Cl, Brom	188	B6
Lindsey Cl, Mitch	183	K7
Lindsey Ms N1	93	U13
Lindsey Rd, Dag	100	D7
Lindsey St EC1	19	S2
Lindum Rd, Tedd	159	L14
Lindway SE27	165	R10
Lindwood Cl E6	116	D10
Linfield Cl NW4	71	U6
Linford Rd, E17 **2**	78	F6
Linford St SW8	146	E2
Ling Rd E16	115	P9
Ling Rd, Erith	137	U12
Lingards Rd SE13	150	F8
Lingey Cl, Sid	171	U3
Lingfield Av, Kings T	177	S8
Lingfield Cl, Enf	44	C11
Lingfield Cres SE9	153	N7
Lingfield Gdns N9	45	K13
Lingfield Rd SW19	162	B1
Lingfield Rd, Wor Pk	193	U6
Lingham St SW9	147	K4
Lingholm Way, Barn	40	B9
Lingmere Cl, Chig	65	M4
Lingrove Gdns, Buck H	63	R5
Lingwell Rd SW17	163	S6
Lingwood Gdns, Islw	122	C13
Lingwood Rd E5	76	H13
Linhope St NW1	7	T10
Link, The, SE9 **1**	170	G6
Link, The W3	106	C11
Link, The, Enf	45	R1
Link, The, Nthlt	85	L10
Link, The, Pnr	66	F13
Link, The, Wem	87	M2
Link La, Wall	196	J11
Link Rd N11	58	A7
Link Rd, Dag	119	R3
Link Rd, Wall	196	A2
Link St E9	95	M11
Link Way, Brom	188	D13
Link Way, Pnr	66	H1
Linkfield, Brom	187	N11
Linkfield, W Mol	175	P5
Linkfield Rd, Islw	140	E3
Linklea Cl NW9	55	K14
Links, The E17	77	R7
Links Av, Mord	180	G7
Links Dr N20	56	H2
Links Gdns SW16	165	N14
Links Rd NW2	89	L4
Links Rd SW17	164	A12
Links Rd W3	106	A11
Links Rd, W Wick	200	F2
Links Rd, Wdf Grn	63	N10
Links Side, Enf	43	N5
Links Vw N3	56	E14
Links Vw Cl, Stan	52	H12
Links Vw Rd, Croy	200	A5
Links Vw Rd, Hmptn	157	U9
Links Way, Beck	186	B11
Links Yd E1	21	P2
Linkside N12	56	F11
Linkside, Chig	65	L9
Linkside, N Mal	179	K4
Linkside Cl, Enf	43	M6
Linkside Gdns, Enf	43	M6
Linksway NW4	72	B4
Linkway, N4 **1**	75	U13
Linkway SW20	179	T6
Linkway, Dag	100	F7
Linkway, Rich	159	K4
Linkway, The, Barn	40	J12
Linley Cres, Rom	83	T5
Linley Rd N17	76	D3
Linnell Cl NW11	72	J12
Linnell Dr NW11	72	J12
Linnell Rd N18	60	H9
Linnell Rd SE5	148	D3
Linnet Cl N9	61	N2
Linnet Cl SE28	118	E14
Linnet Ms SW12	146	A13
Linnett Cl E4	62	F8
Linom Rd SW4	146	J8
Linscott Rd E5	95	L8
Linsdell Rd, Bark	117	L2
Linsey St SE16	37	S1
Linslade Cl, Houns	139	K7
Linslade Cl, Pnr	66	C6
Linstead St SE9	153	R12
Linstead St NW6	90	G13
Linstead Way SW18	144	C13
Linster Gro, Borwd	38	E10
Linthorpe Av, Wem	87	M11
Linthorpe Rd N16	76	D14
Linthorpe Rd, Barn	41	R6
Linton Cl, Mitch	181	T14
Linton Cl, Well	154	C2
Linton Gdns E6	116	C11
Linton Rd, Bark	99	L13
Linton St N1	111	U2
Lintons, The, Bark	99	L13
Linver Rd SW6	144	G3
Linwood Cl SE5	148	E4
Linwood Cres, Enf	44	G2
Linzee Rd N8	74	J7
Lion Av, Twick	158	E2
Lion Cl SE4	150	B11
Lion Ct, Borwd	38	F2
Lion Gate Gdns, Rich	141	U5
Lion Pk Av, Chess	192	B8
Lion Rd E6	116	F10
Lion Rd N9	60	G4

Name	Pg	Ref
Lion Rd, Bexh	155	L8
Lion Rd, Croy	183	T10
Lion Rd, Twick	158	E1
Lion Way, Brent	123	N13
Lion Wf Rd, Islw	140	J6
Lion Yd, SW4 8	146	H7
Lionel Gdns SE9	152	B9
Lionel Ms W10	108	C9
Lionel Rd SE9	152	B9
Lionel Rd, Brent	123	U10
Lions Cl SE9	169	U6
Liphook Cres SE23	167	L1
Liphook Rd, Wat	50	G8
Lippitts Hill, Loug	47	M5
Lipton Cl, SE28 2	118	E13
Lipton Rd, E1 7	113	N12
Lisbon Av, Twick	157	T4
Lisburne Rd NW3	91	T8
Lisford St SE15	148	F1
Lisgar Ter W14	126	E7
Liskeard Cl, Chis	171	M12
Liskeard Gdns SE3	151	P2
Lisle Cl SW17	164	C8
Lisle St WC2	17	T10
Lismore Circ NW5	91	U9
Lismore Cl, Islw	140	G4
Lismore Rd N17	76	B6
Lismore Rd, S Croy	198	C12
Lissenden Gdns NW5	92	B7
Lisson Grn Est NW8	7	P8
Lisson Gro NW1	7	R12
Lisson Gro NW8	7	N10
Lisson St NW1	15	P1
Lister Cl W3	106	H10
Lister Cl, Mitch	181	R1
Lister Gdns N18	59	U9
Lister Rd E11	97	K2
Liston Rd N17	76	G2
Liston Rd SW4	146	F6
Liston Way, Wdf Grn	63	T14
Listowel Cl SW9	35	L14
Listowel Rd, Dag	101	P5
Listria Pk N16	94	D3
Litchfield Av E15	96	J12
Litchfield Av, Mord	180	F13
Litchfield Gdns NW10	89	P12
Litchfield Rd, Sutt	195	L8
Litchfield St WC2	17	U9
Litchfield Way NW11	73	L9
Lithos Rd NW3	91	L11
Little Acre, Beck	186	B6
Little Albany St NW1	8	J9
Little Argyll St W1	17	L7
Little Birches, Sid	171	S4
Little Boltons, The SW5	30	D7
Little Boltons, The SW10	30	D7
Little Bornes SE21	166	D7
Little Britain EC1	19	T4
Little Brownings SE23	166	J3
Little Bury St N9	60	B1
Little Cedars N12	57	L7
Little Chester St SW1	24	G9
Little College St, SW1 2	26	A10
Little Ct, W Wick	200	J4
Little Dean's Yd SW1	26	A9
Little Dimocks SW12	164	D3
Little Dorrit Ct SE1	28	A5
Little Dragons, Loug	48	A5
Little Ealing La W5	123	M7
Little Edward St, NW1 2	8	J5
Little Essex St WC2	18	D7
Little Ferry Rd, Twick 8	158	J1
Little Friday Rd E4	62	J4
Little Gearies, Ilf	81	K8
Little George St SW1	26	A7
Little Gra, Grnf	104	G5
Little Grn, Rich	141	P8
Little Grn St NW5	92	C7
Little Halliards, Walt	174	A11
Little Heath SE7	134	D10
Little Heath, Rom	82	C9
Little Heath Rd, Bexh	155	L1
Little Ilford La E12	98	F8
Little Marlborough St, W1 3	17	M8
Little Moss La, Pnr	67	K3
Little New St EC4	19	M6
Little Newport St WC2	17	U10
Little Orchard Cl, Pnr	67	K3
Little Oxhey La, Wat	50	G9
Little Pk Dr, Felt	156	H3
Little Pk Gdns, Enf	43	U6
Little Plucketts Way, Buck H	64	A1
Little Portland St W1	17	K5
Little Queens Rd, Tedd	158	E11
Little Redlands, Brom	188	C3
Little Rd, Croy	198	C1
Little Russell St WC1	18	A5
Little St. James's St SW1	25	M3
Little St. Leonards SW14	142	F6
Little Sanctuary SW1	25	U7
Little Smith St SW1	25	U10
Little Somerset St E1	21	M7
Little Strand NW9	71	M3
Little Thrift, Orp	189	L7
Little Titchfield St, W1 3	17	L4
Little Trinity La EC4	20	A9
Littlebrook Cl, Croy 4	185	P12
Littlebury Rd SW4	146	G6
Littlecombe SE7	133	S11
Littlecombe Cl SW15	144	B11
Littlecote Cl, SW19 1	144	C13
Littlecote Pl, Pnr	67	L1
Littlecroft SE9	152	G5
Littledale SE2	136	B12
Littlefield Cl N19	92	E7
Littlefield Cl, KingsT 1	177	S4
Littlefield Rd, Edg	54	E14
Littlegrove, Barn	41	S12
Littlejohn Rd W7	104	E11
Littlemead, Esher	190	A8
Littlemede SE9	170	F5
Littlemoor Rd, Ilf	99	P6
Littlemore Rd SE2	136	B4
Littlers Cl, SW19 1	181	N2
Littlestone Cl, Beck	168	B12
Littleton Av, E4 2	63	L2
Littleton Cres, Har	86	F4
Littleton Rd, Har	86	F4
Littleton St SW18	163	L4
Littlewood SE13	150	F11
Littlewood Cl W13	123	K6
Littleworth Av, Esher	190	A10
Littleworth Common Rd, Esher	190	A5
Littleworth La, Esher	190	A7
Littleworth Pl, Esher	190	A7
Littleworth Rd, Esher	190	C5
Livermere Rd E8	112	E1
Liverpool Gro SE17	36	C8
Liverpool Rd E10	78	F11
Liverpool Rd E16	115	K9
Liverpool Rd N1	111	P1
Liverpool Rd N7	93	N10
Liverpool Rd W5	123	P3
Liverpool Rd, KingsT	160	B13
Liverpool Rd, Th Hth	183	U6
Liverpool St EC2	20	G4
Livesey Cl, KingsT	177	T5
Livesey Pl SE15	37	T10
Livingstone Pl, E14 8	132	E9
Livingstone Rd E15	114	F2
Livingstone Rd E17	78	C11
Livingstone Rd N13	59	K11
Livingstone Rd, SW11 11	145	P6
Livingstone Rd, Houns	139	T7
Livingstone Rd, Sthl	102	H14
Livingstone Rd, Th Hth	184	A4
Livingstone Wk SW11	145	N6
Livonia St W1	17	P8
Lizard St EC1	12	B8
Lizban St SE3	133	S13
Llanelly Rd NW2	90	F4
Llanover Rd SE18	134	H13
Llanover Rd, Wem	87	P6
Llanthony Rd, Mord	181	N11
Llanvanor Rd NW2	90	F3
Llewellyn St SE16	29	T7
Lloyd Av SW16	183	K2
Lloyd Baker St WC1	10	J7
Lloyd Ct, Pnr	66	H9
Lloyd Pk Av, Croy	198	E8
Lloyd Rd E6	116	E2
Lloyd Rd E17	77	P8
Lloyd Rd, Dag	101	M12
Lloyd Rd, Wor Pk	193	U5
Lloyd Sq WC1	10	J6
Lloyd St WC1	10	J6
Lloyd's Av EC3	21	K9
Lloyds Pl, SE3 2	151	K4
Lloyd's Row EC1	11	M7
Lloyds Way, Beck	185	T9
Loampit Hill SE13	150	B4
Loampit Vale SE13	150	D5
Loanda Cl E8	112	E1
Loats Rd SW2	146	J11
Lobelia Cl E6	116	C9
Locarno Rd, Grnf	104	A7
Lochaber Rd SE13	150	J8
Lochaline St W6	125	U11
Lochan Cl, Hayes	102	J8
Lochinvar St SW12	146	C14
Lochmere Cl, Erith	137	S12
Lochnagar St E14	114	F10
Lock Chase SE3	151	L6
Lock Rd, Rich	159	M7
Lockesfield Pl E14	132	D9
Lockesley Sq, Surb	177	P12
Locket Rd, Har	68	D5
Lockfield Av, Enf	45	S3
Lockgate Cl, E9 3	95	T9
Lockhart Cl N7	93	L12
Lockhart Cl, Enf	45	K9
Lockhart St E3	113	U8
Lockhurst St E5	95	N7
Lockie Pl SE25	184	G5
Lockier Wk, Wem 1	87	P6
Lockington Rd SW8	146	D1
Lockmead Rd N15	76	H11
Lockmead Rd SE13	150	F5
Locks La, Mitch	182	A3
Locksley Est E14	113	T11
Locksley St E14	113	T10
Locksmeade Rd, Rich	159	L8
Lockwood Cl, Barn	41	T7
Lockwood Cl SE26	167	P8
Lockwood Ind Pk N17	76	J5
Lockwood Sq SE16	130	J5
Lockwood Way E17	77	N3
Lockwood Way, Chess	192	A9
Lockyer Est SE1	28	E6
Lockyer St SE1	28	E7
Loddiges Rd E9	95	L13
Loder St SE15	131	L14
Lodge Av SW14	142	J6
Lodge Av, Croy	197	N6
Lodge Av, Dag	118	C1
Lodge Av, Har	69	R7
Lodge Cl N18	59	U10
Lodge Cl, Edg	53	U11
Lodge Cl, Islw	140	J1
Lodge Cl, Wall	196	A2
Lodge Ct, Wem 1	87	R10
Lodge Dr N13	59	N8
Lodge Gdns, Beck	185	U10
Lodge Hill SE2	136	D13
Lodge Hill, Ilf	80	D7
Lodge Hill, Well	136	D13
Lodge La N12	57	L9
Lodge La, Bex	154	G11
Lodge La, Croy	200	B12
Lodge Pl, Sutt	195	K9
Lodge Rd NW4	71	T8
Lodge Rd NW8	7	M8
Lodge Rd, Brom	169	T13
Lodge Rd, Croy	183	S12
Lodge Rd, Wall	196	C9
Lodge Vil, Wdf Grn	63	L13
Lodgehill Pk Cl, Har	85	S3
Lodore Gdns NW9	70	J9
Lodore St E14	114	E12
Lofthouse Pl, Chess	191	M13
Loftie St SE16	29	U7
Lofting Rd N1	93	N14
Loftus Rd W12	125	S2
Logan Cl, Enf	45	N2
Logan Cl, Houns	139	L6
Logan Ms W8	126	G8
Logan Pl W8	126	G7
Logan Rd N9	61	K4
Logan Rd, Wem	87	R3
Loggetts, The SE21	166	C4
Logs Hill, Brom	170	D14
Logs Hill, Chis	170	D14
Logs Hill Cl, Chis	188	D1
Lolesworth Cl, E1 1	21	N3
Lollard St SE11	34	H2
Loman St SE1	27	S5
Lomas Cl, Croy	200	F14
Lomas St E1	21	U1
Lombard Av, Enf	45	M2
Lombard Av, Ilf	99	R2
Lombard Business Pk SW19	181	L3
Lombard Ct, EC3 2	20	F9
Lombard La EC4	19	L8
Lombard Rd N11	58	E9
Lombard Rd SW11	145	N4
Lombard Rd SW19	181	K3
Lombard St EC3	20	E8
Lombard Wall SE7	133	R7
Lombardy Pl, W2 5	14	C11
Lomond Cl N15	76	C8
Lomond Cl, Wem	87	U13
Lomond Gdns, S Croy	199	R14
Lomond Gro SE5	130	A13
Loncroft Rd SE5	37	K9
Londesborough Rd N16	94	C7
London Br EC4	28	E1
London Br SE1	28	E1
London Br SE1	28	D3
London Br Wk SE1	28	F2
London City Airport E16	116	E14
London Flds E8	94	J13
London Flds E Side E8	94	J14
London Flds W Side E8	94	H13
London La E8	95	K13
London La, Brom	169	L13
London Ms W2	15	L7
London Rd E13	115	N4
London Rd SE1	27	R10
London Rd SE23	166	J2
London Rd SW16	183	L1
London Rd SW17	163	U14
London Rd, Bark	98	F14
London Rd, Brent	123	M13
London Rd, Brom	169	M14
London Rd, Croy	183	R13
London Rd, Enf	44	B7
London Rd, Epsom	193	N14

London Rd, Har	86	C3
London Rd, Houns	140	A4
London Rd, Islw	140	F2
London Rd, Kings T	177	U3
London Rd, Mitch	181	U4
London Rd (Beddington Cor), Mitch	182	B14
London Rd, Mord	180	H9
London Rd, Rom	83	P11
London Rd, Stan	53	R7
London Rd, Sutt	194	B3
London Rd, Th Hth	183	N8
London Rd, Twick	140	G10
London Rd, Wall	196	C6
London Rd, Wem	87	S11
London Stile, W4 2	124	B10
London St EC3	20	J9
London St W2	14	J5
London Wall EC2	20	B4
London Wall Bldgs EC2	20	F4
Lonesome Way SW16	182	D1
Long Acre WC2	18	B9
Long Deacon Rd E4	62	J2
Long Dr W3	106	J11
Long Dr, Grnf	103	S2
Long Dr, Ruis	84	J6
Long Elmes, Har	68	B1
Long Fld NW9	55	K14
Long Grn, Chig	65	R8
Long Hedges, Houns	139	P3
Long La EC1	19	S3
Long La N2	73	M4
Long La N3	73	L3
Long La SE1	28	D7
Long La, Bexh	136	J14
Long La, Croy	185	N10
Long Leys E4	62	D12
Long Mark Rd, E16 8	116	A10
Long Mead NW9	71	L1
Long Meadow NW5	92	G10
Long Meadow Cl, W Wick	186	E14
Long Pond Rd SE3	151	K2
Long Reach Ct, Bark	117	P4
Long Rd SW4	146	E8
Long St E2	13	L6
Long Wk SE1	29	K10
Long Wk SE18	134	J11
Long Wk SW13	143	L4
Long Wk, N Mal	178	F5
Long Yd WC1	10	E11
Longacre Pl, Cars	196	B12
Longacre Rd E17	78	G1
Longbeach Rd SW11	145	U6
Longberrys NW2	90	E5
Longboat Row, Sthl	103	L11
Longbridge Rd, Bark	99	M13
Longbridge Rd, Dag	99	U9
Longbridge Way SE13	150	E9
Longcliffe Path, Wat	50	B5
Longcroft SE9	170	F6
Longcroft Ri, Loug	48	H10
Longcrofte Rd, Edg	53	P13
Longdon Wd, Kes	202	C7
Longdown Rd SE6	168	A7
Longfellow Rd E17	77	U12
Longfellow Rd, Wor Pk	193	R2
Longfellow Way SE1	37	N4
Longfield, Brom	187	M1
Longfield, Loug	48	A9
Longfield Av E17	77	R8
Longfield Av NW7	55	N14
Longfield Av W5	105	M13
Longfield Av, Wall	196	B2
Longfield Av, Wem	87	R2
Longfield Cres SE26	167	L5
Longfield Dr SW14	142	C9
Longfield Dr, Mitch	163	R14
Longfield Est SE1	37	N3
Longfield Rd W5	105	M13
Longfield St SW18	144	G14
Longfield Wk W5	105	M12
Longford Av, Sthl	103	P14
Longford Cl, Hmptn	157	N8
Longford Cl, Hayes	102	G13
Longford Ct, Epsom	192	F8
Longford Gdns, Hayes	102	G13
Longford Gdns, Sutt	195	M5
Longford Rd, Twick	157	P2
Longford St NW1	9	K9
Longford Wk, SW2 2	147	N13
Longhayes Av, Rom	82	H7
Longheath Gdns, Croy	185	M10
Longhedge St SW11	146	B3
Longhill Rd SE6	168	H4
Longhook Gdns, Nthlt	102	B5
Longhope Cl SE15	37	K12
Longhurst Rd SE13	150	J10
Longhurst Rd, Croy	185	K12
Longland Ct SE1	37	R6
Longland Dr N20	56	J6
Longlands Ct, W11 7	108	F13
Longlands Ct, Mitch	182	B1
Longlands Pk Cres, Sid	171	R5
Longlands Rd, Sid	171	R6
Longleat Rd, Enf	44	D10
Longleigh La SE2	136	E12
Longleigh La, Bexh	136	E12
Longley Av, Wem	105	U2
Longley Rd SW17	163	R11
Longley Rd, Croy	183	R14
Longley Rd, Har	68	A9
Longley St SE1	37	S2
Longley Way NW2	89	U6
Longmead, Chis	188	H3
Longmead Dr, Sid	172	G4
Longmead Rd SW17	163	T9
Longmead Rd, T Ditt	176	D14
Longmeadow Rd, Sid	171	R2
Longmoore St SW1	33	M3
Longmore Av, Barn	41	N11
Longnor Rd E1	113	P6
Longreach Rd, Bark	117	T7
Longridge La, Sthl	103	S13
Longridge Rd SW5	126	G8
Long's Ct WC2	17	S10
Longshaw Rd E4	62	H6
Longshore SE8	131	T8
Longstaff Cres SW18	144	H12
Longstaff Rd SW18	144	H12
Longstone Av NW10	107	M1
Longstone Rd SW17	164	D10
Longthornton Rd SW16	182	F3
Longton Av SE26	166	G7
Longton Gro SE26	166	J8
Longville Rd SE11	35	P2
Longwood Dr SW15	143	P12
Longwood Gdns, Ilf	80	E8
Longworth Cl SE28	118	H12
Loning, The NW9	71	K7
Lonsdale Av E6	116	A6
Lonsdale Av, Rom	83	T11
Lonsdale Av, Wem	87	S10
Lonsdale Cl E6	116	C7
Lonsdale Cl SE9	170	A6
Lonsdale Cl, Pnr 1	51	K14
Lonsdale Cres, Ilf	80	J11
Lonsdale Dr, Enf	43	K8
Lonsdale Gdns, Th Hth	183	L7
Lonsdale Ms, Rich 1	142	A2
Lonsdale Pl N1	93	P14
Lonsdale Rd E11	79	M13
Lonsdale Rd NW6	108	E2
Lonsdale Rd SE25	184	J7
Lonsdale Rd SW13	143	L2
Lonsdale Rd W4	125	L7
Lonsdale Rd W11	108	F12
Lonsdale Rd, Bexh	155	M4
Lonsdale Rd, Sthl	120	G5
Lonsdale Sq N1	93	N14
Loobert Rd N15	76	D6
Looe Gdns, Ilf	81	K5
Loom Ct E1	13	K12
Loop Rd, Chis	171	L12
Lopen Rd N18	60	C8
Loraine Cl, Enf	45	L9
Loraine Rd N7	93	M7
Loraine Rd W4	124	C12
Lord Amory Way E14	132	E3
Lord Av, Ilf	80	E7
Lord Chancellor Wk, Kings T	178	G1
Lord Gdns, Ilf	80	E7
Lord Hills Br W2	14	C4
Lord Hills Rd W2	14	C2
Lord Napier Pl W6	125	P9
Lord N St SW1	26	A11
Lord Roberts Ms, SW6 11	126	J14
Lord Roberts Ter SE18	134	H11
Lord St E16	134	D2
Lord Warwick St SE18	134	E6
Lordell Pl SW19	161	U12
Lorden Wk E2	13	R7
Lord's Cl SE21	165	U3
Lord's Cl, Felt	157	R4
Lord's Vw NW8	7	M7
Lordship Gro N16	94	B4
Lordship La N17	75	U2
Lordship La N22	75	R2
Lordship La SE22	148	F9
Lordship La Est SE22	166	G1
Lordship Pk N16	94	A3
Lordship Pk Ms N16	93	U3
Lordship Pl, SW3 1	31	P11
Lordship Rd N16	94	B3
Lordship Rd, Nthlt	84	J13
Lordship Ter N16	94	B4
Lordsmead Rd N17	76	D2
Lorenzo St WC1	10	F5
Loretto Gdns, Har	69	R8
Lorian Cl N12	56	J8
Loring Rd N20	57	R4
Loring Rd, Islw	140	E3
Loris Rd W6	125	U5
Lorn Ct SW9	147	N3
Lorn Rd SW9	147	M3
Lorne Av, Croy	185	P13
Lorne Cl NW8	7	R8
Lorne Gdns E11	79	T8
Lorne Gdns W11	126	B3
Lorne Gdns, Croy	185	P13
Lorne Rd E7	97	S7
Lorne Rd E17	78	A10
Lorne Rd N4	93	M1
Lorne Rd, Har	68	E4
Lorne Rd, Rich 3	141	T9
Lorraine Pk, Har	52	C14
Lorrimore Rd SE17	35	S10
Lorrimore Sq SE17	35	S9
Loseberry Rd, Esher	190	B10
Lothair Rd W5	123	N4
Lothair Rd N N4	75	R12
Lothair Rd S N4	75	P13
Lothbury EC2	20	D6
Lothian, Av, Hayes	102	D9
Lothian Cl, Wem	86	G7
Lothian Rd SW9	147	S1
Lothrop St W10	105	C5
Lots Rd SW10	127	M14
Lotus Cl SE21	165	U5
Loubet St SW17	163	U11
Loudoun Av, Ilf	81	K9
Loudoun Rd NW8	6	J2
Loudwater Cl, Sun	174	A8
Loudwater Rd, Sun	174	A8
Lough Rd N7	93	M11
Loughborough Pk SW9	147	N3
Loughborough Rd SW9	147	N3
Loughborough St SE11	34	H6
Loughton Way, Buck H	64	B2
Louis Ms N10	74	C1
Louisa Gdns, E1 19	113	N8
Louisa St E1	113	N8
Louise Bennett Cl, SE24 20	147	S8
Louise Rd E15	97	K11
Louisville Rd SW17	164	A5
Louvaine Rd SW11	145	N8
Lovage App E6	116	D10
Lovat Cl NW2	89	L6
Lovat Wk, Houns	120	J13
Lovatt Cl, Edg	54	C11
Love La EC2	20	A5
Love La N17	60	E13
Love La SE18	134	J8
Love La SE25	185	K6
Love La, Bex	155	N12
Love La, Mitch	181	T5
Love La, Mord	180	J13
Love La, Pnr	66	J6
Love La, Surb	191	M4
Love La, Sutt	194	E11
Love La, Wdf Grn	64	F11
Love Wk SE5	148	A3
Loveday Rd W13	123	K2
Lovegrove St SE1	37	T8
Lovegrove Wk E14	132	E2
Lovekyn Cl, Kings T	157	S3
Lovel Av, Well	154	B2
Lovelace Av, Brom	188	G12
Lovelace Gdns, Bark	100	A8
Lovelace Gdns, Surb	177	N13
Lovelace Grn SE9	152	E6
Lovelace Rd SE21	165	T2
Lovelace Rd, Barn	41	R13
Lovelace Rd, Surb	177	N14
Lovelinch Cl SE15	131	M12
Lovell Pl SE16	131	S5
Lovell Rd, Rich	159	M5
Lovell Rd, Sthl	103	R11
Loveridge Rd NW6	90	F12
Lovers Wk N3	56	G14
Lovers Wk NW7	56	E11
Lovers Wk SE10	132	J12
Lover's Wk W1	24	D2
Lovett Dr, Cars	181	M14
Lovett Way NW10	88	F9
Lovett's Pl, SW18 5	145	K8
Lovibonds Av, Orp	203	K5
Low Cross Wd La SE21	166	E6
Low Hall Cl E4	46	C14
Low Hall La E17	77	S11
Lowbrook Rd, Ilf	99	K9
Lowden Rd N9	61	K1
Lowden Rd SE24	147	T8
Lowden Rd, Sthl	102	J13
Lowe Av E16	115	P10
Lowell St E14	113	S11
Lower Aberdeen Wf E14	131	U2
Lower Addiscombe Rd, Croy	198	C1
Lower Addison Gdns W14	126	C4
Lower Alderton Hall La, Loug	48	H10
Lower Belgrave St SW1	24	G11
Lower Boston Rd W7	122	D3
Lower Broad St, Dag	119	N1
Lower Camden, Chis	188	F1
Lower Clapton Rd E5	95	K10
Lower Common S SW15	143	S6
Lower Coombe St, Croy	197	T7
Lower Downs Rd SW20	180	B1
Lower George St, Rich	141	P9
Lower Gravel Rd, Brom	202	E2
Lower Grn W, Mitch	181	S6

Lower Grosvenor Pl SW1	24	H10
Lower Gro Rd, Rich	141	U11
Lower Hall La E4	61	S8
Lower Ham Rd, Kings T	159	P10
Lower Hampton Rd, Sun	174	J4
Lower James St W1	17	P10
Lower John St W1	17	P10
Lower Kenwood Av, Enf	42	H9
Lower Lea Crossing E14	115	K13
Lower Lea Crossing E16	115	K13
Lower Maidstone Rd N11	58	F11
Lower Mall W6	125	S9
Lower Mardyke Av, Rain	119	U4
Lower Marsh SE1	24	J7
Lower Marsh La, Kings T	178	A7
Lower Merton Ri NW3	91	R13
Lower Morden La, Mord	179	U12
Lower Mortlake Rd, Rich	141	T7
Lower Pk Rd N11	58	E10
Lower Pk Rd, Belv	137	P6
Lower Pk Rd, Loug	48	B10
Lower Queens Rd, Buck H	64	B3
Lower Richmond Rd SW14	142	E5
Lower Richmond Rd SW15	144	B5
Lower Richmond Rd, Rich	142	A6
Lower Rd SE8	131	P7
Lower Rd SE16	131	L5
Lower Rd, Belv	137	S6
Lower Rd, Har	86	A2
Lower Rd, Loug	48	G3
Lower Rd, Sutt	195	M8
Lower Robert St, WC2 **15**	18	D12
Lower Sand Hills, T Ditt	177	M13
Lower Sloane St SW1	32	C4
Lower Sq, Islw	140	J5
Lower Strand NW9	71	M3
Lower Sunbury Rd, Hmptn	175	P4
Lower Sydenham Ind Est SE26	167	T10
Lower Tail, Wat	51	K6
Lower Teddington Rd, Kings T	177	N2
Lower Ter NW3	91	L6
Lower Thames St EC3	20	J12
Lower Wd Rd, Esher	190	J12
Loweswater Cl, Wem	87	N3
Lowfield Rd NW6	90	G13
Lowfield Rd W3	106	E11
Lowick Rd, Har	68	C9
Lowlands Gdns, Rom	83	S11
Lowlands Rd, Har	66	C12
Lowlands Rd, Pnr	66	F12
Lowman Rd N7	93	M8
Lowndes Cl SW1	24	E11
Lowndes Ct, W1 **4**	17	M8
Lowndes Pl SW1	24	D11
Lowndes Sq SW1	24	B7
Lowndes St SW1	24	C10
Lowood St, E1 **6**	113	K13
Lowry Cres, Mitch	181	R3
Lowry Rd, Dag	100	D9
Lowshoe La, Rom	83	R1
Lowth Rd SE5	147	T2
Lowther Dr, Enf	42	J7
Lowther Gdns SW7	23	L8
Lowther Hill SE23	149	R14
Lowther Rd E17	77	R4
Lowther Rd N7	93	N10
Lowther Rd SW13	143	M1
Lowther Rd, Kings T	177	U1
Lowther Rd, Stan	69	T5
Loxford Av E6	116	B3
Loxford La, Ilf	99	L10
Loxford Rd, Bark	99	K11
Loxham Rd E4	62	C13
Loxham St WC1	10	D7
Loxley Cl SE26	167	P9
Loxley Rd SW18	163	P1
Loxley Rd, Hmptn	157	L8
Loxton Rd SE23	167	P2
Loxwood Rd N17	76	C6
Lubbock Rd, Chis	170	G14
Lubbock St, SE14 **3**	131	M14
Lucan Pl SW3	31	R3
Lucan Rd, Barn	40	C5
Lucas Av E13	115	S1
Lucas Av, Har	85	N3
Lucas Cl NW10	89	P13
Lucas Ct, Har	85	N2
Lucas Rd SE20	167	M12
Lucas Sq NW11	72	G11
Lucas St SE8	150	A2
Lucerne Cl N13	58	J6
Lucerne Ct, Erith **1**	136	J6
Lucerne Gro E17	78	G8
Lucerne Ms, W8 **8**	126	H1
Lucerne Rd N5	93	S7
Lucerne Rd, Orp	203	U1
Lucerne Rd, Th Hth	183	T8
Lucey Rd SE16	29	R12
Lucien Rd SW17	164	B8
Lucien Rd SW19	162	J4
Lucknow St SE18	135	R13
Lucorn Cl SE12	151	M12
Lucton Ms, Loug	48	J8
Luctons av, Buck H	63	T1
Lucy Cres W3	106	E9
Luddesdon Rd, Erith	137	N13
Ludford Cl NW9	70	J3
Ludford Cl, Croy	197	R6
Ludgate Bdy EC4	19	P8
Ludgate Circ EC4	19	N7
Ludgate Hill EC4	19	R7
Ludgate Sq, EC4 **7**	19	R8
Ludham CI SE28	118	E12
Ludlow Cl, Brom **1**	187	N6
Ludlow Cl, Har	85	M7
Ludlow Mead, Wat	50	D5
Ludlow Rd W5	85	M7
Ludlow St EC1	11	T10
Ludlow Way N2	73	L7
Ludovick Wk SW15	143	K7
Ludwick Ms SE14	131	S13
Luffield Rd SE2	136	D6
Luffman Rd SE12	169	S5
Lugard Rd SE15	149	K2
Lugg App E12	98	G6
Luke St EC2	12	G10
Lukin Cres E4	62	G6
Lukin St E1	113	M12
Lukintone Cl, Loug **1**	48	D11
Lullingstone Cl, Orp	172	C13
Lullingstone Cres, Orp	172	C13
Lullingstone La SE13	150	G12
Lullingstone Rd, Belv **1**	137	M11
Lullington Garth N12	56	G9
Lullington Garth, Borwd	38	D10
Lullington Garth, Brom	169	K13
Lullington Rd SE20	166	H13
Lullington Rd, Dag	100	J13
Lulot Gdns N19	92	D3
Lulworth Av, Houns	121	S14
Lulworth Av, Wem	69	L13
Lulworth Cl, Har	85	L5
Lulworth Cres, Mitch	181	R4
Lulworth Dr, Pnr	66	H13
Lulworth Gdns, Har	85	K4
Lulworth Rd SE9	170	C4
Lulworth Rd SE15	149	K3
Lulworth Rd, Well	153	U4
Lulworth Waye, Hayes	102	E11
Lumen Rd, Wem	87	P3
Lumley Cl, Belv	137	P11
Lumley Gdns, Sutt	194	D10
Lumley Rd, Sutt	194	C10
Lumley St W1	16	E8
Luna Rd, Th Hth	183	U5
Lundin Wk, Wat	50	H8
Lunham Rd SE19	166	C11
Lupin Cl SW2	165	R3
Lupin Cl, Croy **2**	199	N1
Lupin Cres, Ilf	99	K11
Lupton Cl SE12	169	R6
Lupton St NW5	92	E8
Lupus St SW1	32	J8
Luralda Gdns E14	132	F9
Lurgan Av W6	126	B11
Lurline Gdns SW11	146	B1
Luscombe Ct, Brom	186	J4
Luscombe Way SW8	34	B14
Lushes Rd, Loug	49	K9
Lushington Rd NW10	107	R4
Lushington Rd SE6	168	C9
Lushington Ter E8	94	H10
Luther Cl, Edg	54	E4
Luther King Cl E17	77	S12
Luther Rd, Tedd	158	E10
Luton Pl SE10	132	F14
Luton Rd E17	77	T5
Luton Rd, Sid	172	E5
Luton St NW8	7	L11
Lutton Ter, NW3 **8**	91	M7
Luttrell Av SW15	143	S9
Lutwyche Rd SE6	167	T3
Luxborough La, Chig	64	G8
Luxborough St W1	16	D1
Luxemburg Gdns W6	126	A7
Luxfield Rd SE9	170	C2
Luxford St, SE16 **6**	131	N8
Luxmore St SE4	149	U2
Luxor St SE5	147	S4
Lyal Rd E3	113	S4
Lyall Av SE21	166	E7
Lyall Ms SW1	24	D11
Lyall Ms W SW1	24	D12
Lyall St SW1	24	D12
Lycett Pl W12	125	N3
Lyconby Gdns, Croy	185	S14
Lydd Cl, Sid	171	S6
Lydd Rd, Bexh	137	M13
Lydden Ct SE9	153	R12
Lydden Gro SW18	144	J14
Lydden Rd SW18	144	J14
Lydeard Rd E6	98	E13
Lydford Rd N15	76	B10
Lydford Rd NW2	89	U12
Lydford Rd W9	108	F7
Lydhurst Av SW2	165	M4
Lydney Cl SE15	37	K13
Lydney Cl SW19	162	D3
Lydon Rd SW4	146	E6
Lydstep Rd, Chis	170	H8
Lyford Rd SW18	163	R1
Lygon Pl SW1	24	H11
Lyham Cl SW2	147	K12
Lyham Rd SW2	146	J10
Lyle Cl, Mitch	182	A13
Lyme Fm Rd SE12	151	P8
Lyme Rd, Well	154	D2
Lyme St NW1	92	E14
Lymer Av SE19	166	F9
Lymescote Gdns, Sutt	194	H4
Lyminge Cl, Sid	171	U7
Lyminge Gdns SW18	163	R2
Lymington Av N22	75	N4
Lymington Cl E6	116	E9
Lymington Cl SW16	182	G3
Lymington Gdns, Epsom	193	L9
Lymington Rd NW6	90	J11
Lymington Rd, Dag	100	H1
Lympstone Gdns SE15	37	T14
Lyn Ms E3	113	T6
Lynbridge Gdns N13	59	R8
Lynbrook Cl SE15	36	J13
Lynchen Cl, Houns **1**	138	C1
Lyncott Cres SW4	146	C7
Lyncroft Av, Pnr	66	J9
Lyncroft Gdns NW6	90	H9
Lyncroft Gdns W13	123	L3
Lyncroft Gdns, Houns	139	U8
Lyndale NW2	90	F7
Lyndale Av NW2	90	F6
Lyndale Cl SE3	133	L12
Lyndhurst Av N12	57	T11
Lyndhurst Av NW7	54	J12
Lyndhurst Av SW16	182	H4
Lyndhurst Av, Pnr	66	D2
Lyndhurst Av, Sthl	121	S2
Lyndhurst Av, Sun	174	A5
Lyndhurst Av, Surb	192	D1
Lyndhurst Av, Twick	157	M1
Lyndhurst Cl NW10	88	H5
Lyndhurst Cl, Bexh	155	S5
Lyndhurst Cl, Croy	198	E5
Lyndhurst Cl, Orp	203	K7
Lyndhurst Dr E10	78	F14
Lyndhurst Dr, N Mal	179	K13
Lyndhurst Gdns N3	72	D2
Lyndhurst Gdns NW3	91	P9
Lyndhurst Gdns, Bark	99	R11
Lyndhurst Gdns, Enf	44	C8
Lyndhurst Gdns, Ilf	81	P12
Lyndhurst Gdns, Pnr	66	D2
Lyndhurst Gro SE15	148	E3
Lyndhurst Ri, Chig	64	H7
Lyndhurst Rd E4	62	F14
Lyndhurst Rd N18	60	H8
Lyndhurst Rd N22	59	N12
Lyndhurst Rd NW3	91	N9
Lyndhurst Rd, Bexh	155	S5
Lyndhurst Rd, Grnf	103	R7
Lyndhurst Rd, Th Hth	183	P8
Lyndhurst Sq SE15	148	F2
Lyndhurst Ter NW3	91	N9
Lyndhurst Way SE15	148	F3
Lyndhurst Way, Sutt	194	H14
Lyndon Av, Pnr	51	K12
Lyndon Av, Sid	153	U10
Lyndon Av, Wall	196	B6
Lyndon Rd, Belv	137	P7
Lyne Cres E17	77	T2
Lyneham Wk E5	95	R9
Lynett Rd, Dag	100	H3
Lynette Av SW4	146	E11
Lynford Cl, Barn	39	M10
Lynford Cl, Edg	70	E1
Lynford Gdns, Edg	54	C6
Lynford Gdns, Ilf	99	U3
Lynmere Rd, Well	154	D4
Lynmouth Av, Enf	44	F12
Lynmouth Av, Mord	180	A12
Lynmouth Dr, Ruis	84	C4
Lynmouth Gdns, Grnf	105	K1
Lynmouth Gdns, Houns	138	H1
Lynmouth Rd E17	77	R11
Lynmouth Rd N2	73	U7
Lynmouth Rd N16	94	F2
Lynmouth Rd, Grnf	105	K2
Lynn Cl, Har	68	A4
Lynn Ms E11	97	K4
Lynn Rd E11	96	J4
Lynn Rd SW12	146	D13
Lynn Rd, Ilf	81	N13
Lynn St, Enf	44	A1
Lynne Cl, Orp	203	T12
Lynne Way NW10	88	J13
Lynne Way, Nthlt	102	G3
Lynsted Cl, Bexh	155	R9
Lynsted Cl, Brom	187	T3
Lynsted Ct, Beck	185	R3
Lynsted Gdns SE9	152	B6
Lynton Av N12	57	N7

Name	Page	Grid
Lynton Av NW9	71	L8
Lynton Av W13	104	G11
Lynton Av, Rom	83	P2
Lynton Cl NW10	88	J11
Lynton Cl, Chess	191	S7
Lynton Cl, Islw	140	F8
Lynton Cres, Ilf	80	J12
Lynton Est SE1	37	R4
Lynton Gdns N11	58	F12
Lynton Gdns, Enf	44	D14
Lynton Mead N20	56	H5
Lynton Rd E4	62	D9
Lynton Rd N8	74	H10
Lynton Rd NW6	108	F2
Lynton Rd SE1	37	P4
Lynton Rd W3	106	B13
Lynton Rd, Croy	183	N12
Lynton Rd, Har	85	K5
Lynton Rd, N Mal	178	H9
Lynwood Cl E18	79	T2
Lynwood Cl, Har	85	K5
Lynwood Dr, Wor Pk	193	P4
Lynwood Gdns, Croy	197	M7
Lynwood Gdns, Sthl	103	M10
Lynwood Gro N21	59	P1
Lynwood Gro, Orp	189	S14
Lynwood Rd SW17	163	U6
Lynwood Rd W5	105	R7
Lynwood Rd, T Ditt	190	F3
Lyon Business Pk, Bark	117	S4
Lyon Mead, Stan	69	M2
Lyon Pk Av, Wem	87	U14
Lyon Rd SW19	181	M2
Lyon Rd, Har	68	E12
Lyon St N1	93	L14
Lyon Way, Grnf	104	D2
Lyons Pl NW8	7	K11
Lyons Wk W14	126	C7
Lyonsdown Av, Barn	41	L12
Lyonsdown Rd, Barn	41	L11
Lyoth Rd, Orp	203	M3
Lyric Dr, Grnf	103	S8
Lyric Rd SW13	143	L2
Lysander Gdns, Surb	177	T12
Lysander Gro N19	92	F2
Lysander Rd, Croy	197	M11
Lysander Way, Orp 2	203	M5
Lysia St SW6	126	A14
Lysias Rd SW12	146	C12
Lysons Wk SW15	143	P9
Lytchet Rd, Brom	169	R13
Lytchet Way, Enf	45	L2
Lytchgate Cl, S Croy	198	D13
Lytcott Dr, W Mol	175	L6
Lytcott Gro SE22	148	E9
Lyte St E2	113	L3
Lytham Av, Wat	50	H9
Lytham Gro W5	105	S5
Lytham St SE17	36	C8
Lyttelton Cl NW3	91	R13
Lyttelton Rd E10	96	D5
Lyttelton Rd N2	73	M9
Lyttleton Rd N8	75	P6
Lytton Av N13	59	P4
Lytton Cl N2	73	N11
Lytton Cl, Loug	49	N6
Lytton Cl, Nthlt	85	M14
Lytton Gdns, Wall	196	G7
Lytton Gro SW15	144	C11
Lytton Rd E11	78	J13
Lytton Rd, Barn	41	M7
Lytton Rd, Pnr	50	J14
Lyveden Rd SE3	133	R13
Lyveden Rd SW17	163	T12

M

Name	Page	Grid
Maberley Cres SE19	166	G14
Maberley Rd SE19	184	G1
Maberley Rd, Beck	185	P6
Mabledon Pl WC1	9	U7
Mablethorpe Rd SW6	126	C14
Mabley St E9	95	R11
Macaret Cl N20	41	K13
MacArthur Cl E7	97	P12
MacArthur Ter SE7	134	B11
Macaulay Av, Esher	190	E3
Macaulay Ct SW4	146	D6
Macaulay Rd E6	116	B3
Macaulay Rd SW4	146	D6
Macaulay Sq SW4	146	D7
Macauley Ms SE13	150	F2
Macbean St SE18	134	J6
Macbeth St W6	125	S9
Macclesfield Br NW1	7	S2
Macclesfield Rd EC1	11	T6
Macclesfield Rd SE25	185	K10
Macclesfield St, W1 3	17	T10
Macdonald Av, Dag	101	S6
Macdonald Rd E7	97	N8
Macdonald Rd E17	78	F3
Macdonald Rd N11	57	U9
Macdonald Rd N19	92	E3
Macduff Rd SW11	146	B1
Mace Cl E1	130	J1
Mace St E2	113	N4
MacFarlane La, Islw	122	F12
Macfarlane Rd W12	125	T1
Mactarren Pl, NW1 2	8	E11
Macgregor Rd E16	115	U9
Machell Rd SE15	149	L5
Mackay Rd SW4	146	D5
Mackennal St NW8	7	R2
Mackenzie Rd N7	93	M11
Mackenzie Rd, Beck	185	P3
Mackenzie Wk E14	132	A2
Mackeson Rd NW3	91	T8
Mackie Rd SW2	147	N14
Mackintosh La E9	95	P10
Macklin St WC2	18	C6
Mackrow Wk, E14 7	114	F13
Macks Rd SE16	37	T2
Mackworth St NW1	9	L5
Maclaren Ms SW15	143	T7
Maclean Rd SE23	149	R11
Macleod Rd N21	43	K9
Macleod St SE17	36	A8
Maclise Rd W14	126	C6
Macoma Rd SE18	135	N12
Macoma Ter SE18	135	N12
Maconochies Rd, E14 11	132	C9
Macquarie Way E14	132	D8
Macroom Rd W9	108	F5
Mada Rd, Orp	203	K5
Maddams St E3	114	C8
Maddison Cl, Tedd	158	F12
Maddock Way SE17	35	R11
Maddox St W1	17	K9
Madeira Av, Brom	187	L1
Madeira Gro, Wdf Grn	63	T11
Madeira Rd E11	96	H2
Madeira Rd N13	59	R7
Madeira Rd SW16	165	K9
Madeira Rd, Mitch	181	U7
Madeley Rd W5	105	R12
Madeline Gro, Ilf	99	N9
Madeline Rd SE20	166	H14
Madge Gill Way, E6 2	116	D1
Madinah Rd E8	94	G11
Madison Cres, Bexh	136	F14
Madison Gdns, Bexh	136	F13
Madison Gdns, Brom	187	M6
Madras Pl N7	93	N11
Madras Rd, Ilf	98	J8
Madrid Rd SW13	125	P14
Madrigal La SE5	129	S14
Madron St SE17	37	K5
Mafeking Av E6	116	C3
Mafeking Av, Brent	123	P11
Mafeking Av, Ilf	81	P14
Mafeking Rd E16	115	L7
Mafeking Rd N17	76	G4
Mafeking Rd, Enf	44	E6
Magdala Av N19	92	D3
Magdala Rd, Islw	140	H6
Magdala Rd, S Croy	198	A13
Magdalen Rd SW18	145	P14
Magdalen St SE1	28	H4
Magdalene Cl, SE15 10	148	J4
Magdalene Gdns E6	116	G7
Magee St, SE11 2	35	K10
Magnet Rd, Wem	87	P4
Magnin Cl, E8 3	112	H1
Magnolia Cl, E10 2	96	B3
Magnolia Cl, Kings T	160	D12
Magnolia Ct, Har	69	T13
Magnolia Pl SW4	146	H9
Magnolia Pl W5	105	P9
Magnolia Rd W4	124	C12
Magnolia Way, Epsom	192	E9
Magpie Cl E7	97	M9
Magpie Cl, NW9 5	71	K3
Magpie Cl, Enf	44	G1
Magpie Hall Cl, Brom	188	D12
Magpie Hall La, Brom	188	E10
Magpie Hall Rd, Bushey	52	D3
Maguire Dr, Rich	159	M8
Maguire St SE1	29	N5
Mahlon Av, Ruis	84	D11
Mahogany Cl, SE16 14	131	R2
Mahon Cl, Enf	44	F1
Maida Av E4	46	C14
Maida Av W2	6	H12
Maida Rd, Belv	137	P5
Maida Vale W9	6	G8
Maida Way E4	46	C14
Maiden Erlegh Av, Bex	173	K1
Maiden La NW1	91	H13
Maiden La SE1	28	B2
Maiden La WC2	18	C11
Maiden Rd E15	97	K13
Maidenstone Hill SE10	150	E1
Maidstone Av, Rom	83	T3
Maidstone Bldgs SE1	28	B4
Maidstone Rd N11	58	G11
Maidstone Rd, Sid	172	G11
Maidstone St, E2 4	13	T1
Main Av, Enf	44	E9
Main Dr, Wem	87	P5
Main Rd, Sid	171	S6
Main St, Felt	156	H10
Mainridge Rd, Chis	170	H8
Maisemore St, SE15 1	37	T13
Maitland Cl SE10	132	D14
Maitland Cl, Houns	155	L9
Maitland Pk Est NW3	91	U11
Maitland Pk Rd NW3	91	U11
Maitland Pk Vil NW3	91	U11
Maitland Rd, E15 8	97	L12
Maitland Rd SE26	167	N12
Maize Row E14	113	T13
Majendie Rd SE18	135	N9
Majestic Way, Mitch	181	U4
Major Rd E15	96	G9
Major Rd, SE16 6	29	U9
Makepeace Av N6	92	A4
Makepeace Rd E11	79	P8
Makepeace Rd, Nthlt	102	J3
Makins St SW3	31	R3
Malabar St E14	132	A4
Malam Gdns E14	114	C13
Malbrook Rd SW15	143	S8
Malcolm Ct, Stan	53	L10
Malcolm Cres NW4	71	N11
Malcolm Dr, Surb	191	R1
Malcolm Pl E2	113	L7
Malcolm Rd E1	113	L7
Malcolm Rd SE20	167	L13
Malcolm Rd SE25	184	G12
Malcolm Rd SW19	162	D12
Malcolm Way E11	79	N8
Malcolms Way N14	42	E9
Malden Av SE25	184	J6
Malden Av, Grnf	86	C10
Malden Cres NW1	92	B12
Malden Grn Av, Wor Pk	193	M1
Malden Hill, N Mal	179	L6
Malden Hill Gdns, N Mal	179	M6
Malden Pk, N Mal	179	L11
Malden Pl, NW5 6	92	A10
Malden Rd NW5	91	U10
Malden Rd, Borwd	38	B5
Malden Rd, N Mal	179	K9
Malden Rd, Sutt	194	B9
Malden Rd, Wor Pk	193	M1
Malden Way, N Mal	178	H12
Maldon Cl N1	111	T1
Maldon Cl SE5	148	C5
Maldon Rd N9	60	F5
Maldon Rd W3	106	F14
Maldon Rd, Rom	83	T13
Maldon Rd, Wall	196	D9
Maldon Wk, Wdf Grn	63	T12
Malet Pl WC1	9	S11
Malet St WC1	17	T1
Maley Av SE27	165	S3
Malford Ct E18	79	N4
Malford Gro E18	79	N5
Malfort Rd SE5	148	D5
Malham Cl, N11 5	58	B11
Malham Rd SE23	167	P1
Malins Cl, Barn	39	S9
Mall, The E15	96	H13
Mall, The N14	58	J5
Mall, The SW1	25	N6
Mall, The SW14	142	E10
Mall, The W5	105	R13
Mall, The, Croy	197	U4
Mall, The, Har	70	A10
Mall, The, Surb	177	N10
Mall Rd W6	125	S9
Mallams Ms SW9	147	P5
Mallard Cl E9	95	U11
Mallard Cl NW6	108	G2
Mallard Cl W7	122	C4
Mallard Cl, Barn	41	P12
Mallard Cl, Twick 1	139	N13
Mallard Path SE28	135	N6
Mallard Pl, Twick	158	G0
Mallard Wk, Beck	185	P9
Mallard Wk, Sid	172	E11
Mallard Way NW9	70	F14
Mallards Rd, Wdf Grn	63	S13
Mallet Dr, Nthlt	85	M9
Mallet Rd SE13	150	H11
Malling Cl, Croy	185	L11
Malling Gdns, Mord	181	L11
Malling Way, Brom	187	M13
Mallinson Rd SW11	145	S9
Mallinson Rd, Croy	196	H5
Mallord St SW3	31	L9
Mallory Cl SE4	149	R6
Mallory Gdns, Barn	42	A14
Mallory St NW8	7	R11
Mallow Cl, Croy 3	199	N1
Mallow Mead NW7	56	D14
Mallow St EC1	12	D9
Malmains Cl, Beck	186	G8
Malmains Way, Beck	186	E8
Malmesbury Rd E3	113	U4
Malmesbury Rd E16	115	K9
Malmesbury Rd E18	79	M2
Malmesbury Rd, Mord	181	L12
Malmesbury Ter E16	115	L9
Malpas Dr, Pnr	66	H9
Malpas Rd E8	94	J11
Malpas Rd SE4	149	T4
Malpas Rd, Dag	100	G12
Malt St SE1	37	S9
Malta Rd E10	78	A14
Malta St EC1	11	R9
Maltby Rd, Chess	192	A11

Maltby St SE1 29 M8
Malthouse Dr W4 125 K12
Malthouse Dr, Felt 156 G9
Malting Way, Islw 140 F5
Maltings, The, Orp 203 T2
Maltings, Sid 172 B5
Maltings Pl SW6 145 K2
Malton Ms SE18 135 S12
Malton Ms, W10 18 108 C11
Malton Rd W10 108 C11
Malton St SE18 135 S12
Maltravers St, WC2 2 18 H9
Malva Cl SW18 145 K10
Malvern Av E4 62 G13
Malvern Av, Bexh 136 J14
Malvern Av, Har 85 K6
Malvern Cl, SE20 5 184 H4
Malvern Cl W10 108 E10
Malvern Cl, Mitch 182 E6
Malvern Cl, Surb 191 S2
Malvern Ct SW7 31 M3
Malvern Dr, Felt 1 156 H9
Malvern Dr, Ilf 99 T8
Malvern Dr, Wdf Grn 63 T9
Malvern Gdns NW2 90 D3
Malvern Gdns, NW6 1 108 F4
Malvern Gdns, Har 69 S8
Malvern Gdns, Loug 48 E12
Malvern Ms NW6 108 G5
Malvern Pl NW6 108 F5
Malvern Rd E6 116 C1
Malvern Rd E8 94 G14
Malvern Rd E11 97 K3
Malvern Rd N8 75 M5
Malvern Rd N17 76 G5
Malvern Rd NW6 108 G5
Malvern Rd, Hmptn 157 P14
Malvern Rd, Surb 191 S2
Malvern Rd, Th Hth 183 P8
Malvern Ter N1 111 N1
Malvern Ter N9 60 F2
Malvern Way W13 105 K9
Malwood Rd SW12 146 C12
Malyons Rd SE13 150 C10
Malyons Ter, SE13 1 150 C9
Managers St, E14 13 132 F2
Manatee Pl, Wall 1 196 H6
Manaton Cl SE15 148 J5
Manaton Cres, Sthl 103 N11
Manbey Gro E15 96 J11
Manbey Pk Rd E15 96 J11
Manbey Rd E15 96 J11
Manbey St E15 96 J12
Manbre Rd W6 125 U11
Manbrough Av E6 116 G6
Manchester Dr W10 108 C8
Manchester Gro E14 132 E9
Manchester Ms, W1 1 16 D4
Manchester Rd E14 132 F5
Manchester Rd N15 76 B12
Manchester Rd, Th Hth 183 U5
Manchester Sq W1 16 D5
Manchester St W1 16 D3
Manchester Way, Dag 101 R8
Manchuria Rd SW11 146 A11
Manciple St SE1 28 E8
Mandalay Rd SW4 146 E10
Mandarin St, E14 3 114 A13
Mandarin Way, Hayes 102 H10
Mandela Cl NW10 88 F13
Mandela Rd E16 115 P12
Mandela St NW1 110 F1
Mandela St SW9 129 N14
Mandela Way SE1 36 J2
Mandeville Cl SE3 133 M14
Mandeville Cl SW20 162 D14
Mandeville Ct E4 61 S8
Mandeville Dr, Surb 191 P2

Mandeville Pl W1 16 F5
Mandeville Rd N14 58 D4
Mandeville Rd, Islw 140 G4
Mandeville Rd, Nthlt 85 P12
Mandeville St E5 95 R7
Mandrake Rd SW17 163 T5
Mandrake Way, E15 5 96 J13
Mandrell Rd SW2 146 J10
Manette St W1 17 T7
Manford Way, Chig 65 R8
Manfred Rd SW15 144 F9
Manger Rd N7 93 K11
Mangold Way, Erith 136 J5
Manhattan Wf E16 133 N3
Manilla St E14 132 A3
Manister Rd SE2 136 B5
Manitoba Gdns, Orp 4 203 T12
Manley Ct N16 94 E5
Manley St NW1 110 A1
Mann Cl, Croy 11 197 T6
Mannin Rd, Rom 82 C13
Manning Gdns, Har 69 P13
Manning Pl, 141 U12
Rich 7
Manning Rd, E17 6 77 R8
Manning Rd, Dag 101 N12
Manningford Cl, EC1 2 11 P6
Manningtree Cl SW19 162 D1
Manningtree Rd, Ruis 84 C7
Manningtree St, E1 3 21 R6
Mannock Dr, Loug 49 L4
Mannock Rd N22 75 S5
Manns Cl, Islw 140 F9
Manns Rd, Edg 54 B11
Manoel Rd, Twick 157 T4
Manor Av SE4 149 U4
Manor Av, Houns 138 H5
Manor Av, Nthlt 85 L14
Manor Cl NW9 70 C9
Manor Cl SE28 118 F13
Manor Cl, Barn 40 D7
Manor Cl, Wor Pk 193 K2
Manor Cotts App N2 73 L4
Manor Ct N2 73 T10
Manor Ct SW6 145 K2
Manor Ct, Twick 157 U3
Manor Ct Rd W7 104 C14
Manor Cres, Surb 178 A12
Manor Dr N14 42 D14
Manor Dr N20 57 S7
Manor Dr NW7 54 H9
Manor Dr, Epsom 193 K11
Manor Dr, Esher 190 F4
Manor Dr, Felt 2 156 H9
Manor Dr, Sun 174 A3
Manor Dr, Surb 178 A12
Manor Dr, Wem 87 U7
Manor Dr, The, Wor Pk 193 L2
Manor Dr N, N Mal 178 G13
Manor Dr N, Wor Pk 192 J1
Manor Est SE16 130 J8
Manor Fm Cl, Wor Pk 192 J1
Manor Fm Dr E4 62 J5
Manor Fm Rd, Th Hth 183 N3
Manor Fm Rd, Wem 105 N4
Manor Flds SW15 144 A11
Manor Gdns N7 93 K5
Manor Gdns SW20 180 E3
Manor Gdns W3 124 B8
Manor Gdns, Hmptn 157 T14
Manor Gdns, Rich 141 U7
Manor Gdns, Ruis 84 E10
Manor Gdns, S Croy 198 E12
Manor Gdns, Sun 174 A2
Manor Gate, Nthlt 84 J13
Manor Gro SE15 131 L12
Manor Gro, Beck 186 C3
Manor Gro, Rich 142 B6
Manor Hall Av NW4 71 U3

Manor Hall Dr NW4 72 A4
Manor Ho Dr NW6 90 B14
Manor Ho Way, Islw 140 J5
Manor La SE12 151 K12
Manor La SE13 151 K9
Manor La, Felt 156 B4
Manor La, Sun 174 B3
Manor La, Sutt 195 L9
Manor La Ter SE13 150 J8
Manor Ms NW6 2 108 H3
Manor Ms SE4 149 U3
Manor Mt SE23 167 L2
Manor Pk SE13 150 H8
Manor Pk, Chis 189 N2
Manor Pk, Rich 141 U7
Manor Pk Cl, W Wick 200 D2
Manor Pk Cres, Edg 54 A11
Manor Pk Dr, Har 67 R5
Manor Pk Gdns, Edg 54 B10
Manor Pk Rd E12 98 B8
Manor Pk Rd N2 73 M5
Manor Pk Rd NW10 107 L2
Manor Pk Rd, Chis 189 M1
Manor Pk Rd, Sutt 195 L9
Manor Pk Rd, W Wick 200 C2
Manor Pl SE17 35 T6
Manor Pl, Chis 189 N3
Manor Pl, Felt 156 B1
Manor Pl, Mitch 182 F6
Manor Pl, Sutt 195 K8
Manor Rd E10 78 B14
Manor Rd E15 114 J6
Manor Rd E16 114 J9
Manor Rd E17 77 R3
Manor Rd N16 94 C2
Manor Rd N17 76 J1
Manor Rd N22 59 K12
Manor Rd SE25 184 G7
Manor Rd SW20 180 E3
Manor Rd W13 104 H14
Manor Rd, Bark 99 U12
Manor Rd, Barn 40 D9
Manor Rd, Beck 186 C3
Manor Rd, Bex 173 S1
Manor Rd, Chig 64 J10
Manor Rd, Dag 101 U12
Manor Rd, E Mol 176 A8
Manor Rd, Enf 43 U3
Manor Rd, Har 68 H10
Manor Rd, Hayes 102 A12
Manor Rd, Loug 47 S12
Manor Rd (High Beach), Loug 47 R1
Manor Rd, Mitch 182 G5
Manor Rd, Rich 141 U6
Manor Rd (Chadwell Heath), Rom 82 G12
Manor Rd, Sid 171 U5
Manor Rd, Sutt 194 E14
Manor Rd, Tedd 158 J9
Manor Rd, Twick 157 U3
Manor Rd, Wall 196 D9
Manor Rd, W Wick 200 C3
Manor Rd, Wdf Grn 64 E11
Manor Rd N, Esher 190 F5
Manor Rd N, T Ditt 190 G3
Manor Rd N, Wall 196 C7
Manor Rd S, Esher 190 D8
Manor Sq, Dag 100 G3
Manor Vale, Brent 123 L10
Manor Vw N3 72 A4
Manor Way E4 62 G7
Manor Way NW9 70 J6
Manor Way SE3 151 N7
Manor Way SE28 118 E13
Manor Way, Beck 186 B4
Manor Way, Bex 173 N1
Manor Way, Borwd 38 F8
Manor Way, Brom 188 D12
Manor Way, Har 67 R7
Manor Way, Mitch 182 F5
Manor Way, Orp 189 M8
Manor Way, S Croy 198 E11
Manor Way, Sthl 120 D2
Manor Way, Wor Pk 193 K1
Manor Way, The, Wall 196 D7

Manorbrook SE3 151 P7
Manordene Cl, T Ditt 190 G2
Manordene Rd SE28 118 F12
Manorfields Cl, Chis 189 U5
Manorgate Rd, Kings T 178 B2
Manorhall Gdns, E10 4 96 B1
Manorside, Barn 40 C8
Manorside Cl SE2 136 F7
Manorway, Enf 44 C13
Manorway, Wdf Grn 63 U9
Manpreet Ct E12 98 E10
Manresa Rd SW3 31 N7
Mansard Beeches SW17 164 B10
Mansard Ct, Pnr 66 H6
Manse Rd N16 94 F6
Mansel Gro E17 78 A2
Mansel Rd SW19 162 D12
Mansell Rd W3 124 G3
Mansell Rd, Grnf 103 R9
Mansell St E1 21 N8
Mansergh Cl SE18 134 D14
Mansfield Av N15 76 A7
Mansfield Av, Barn 42 A11
Mansfield Av, Ruis 84 C2
Mansfield Cl N9 44 H12
Mansfield Hill E4 62 C2
Mansfield Ms W1 16 H3
Mansfield Rd E11 79 S12
Mansfield Rd E17 77 T8
Mansfield Rd NW3 91 U9
Mansfield Rd W3 106 D8
Mansfield Rd, Chess 191 N10
Mansfield Rd, Ilf 98 H3
Mansfield Rd, S Croy 198 A12
Mansfield St W1 16 H3
Mansford St E2 13 U4
Manship Rd, Mitch 164 A14
Mansion Cl, SW9 2 147 P1
Mansion Gdns NW3 91 K5
Mansion Ho EC4 20 C8
Mansion Ho Pl EC4 20 D8
Mansion Ho St EC4 20 C7
Manson Ms SW7 30 H3
Manson Pl SW7 31 K3
Mansted Gdns, Rom 82 F14
Manston Av, Sthl 121 N8
Manston Cl SE20 185 L2
Manston Gro, Kings T 3 159 N9
Manstone Rd NW2 90 C9
Manthorp Rd SE18 135 M9
Mantilla Rd SW17 164 S6
Mantle Way E15 96 J13
Mantlet Cl SW16 164 F13
Manton Av W7 122 F4
Manton Rd SE2 136 A8
Mantua St, SW11 7 145 P5
Mantus Cl E1 8 113 M7
Mantus Rd E1 113 L7
Manus Way, N20 1 57 L2
Manville Gdns SW17 164 C5
Manville Rd SW17 164 C4
Manwood Rd SE4 149 U11
Manwood St E16 134 F2
Manygates SW12 164 D3
Mape St E2 112 J7
Mapesbury Rd NW2 90 C12
Mapeshill Pl NW2 89 U12
Maple Av E4 61 T10
Maple Av W3 125 K2
Maple Av, Har 85 S4
Maple Cl N3 56 G12
Maple Cl N16 76 H12
Maple Cl SW4 146 H11
Maple Cl, Buck H 64 A5
Maple Cl, Hmptn 157 L11
Maple Cl, Hayes 102 G6
Maple Cl, Ilf 65 R10
Maple Cl, Mitch 182 D2
Maple Cl, Orp 189 P10

Maple Cl, Ruis	66	D12
Maple Ct, N Mal	178	J6
Maple Cres, Sid	154	B11
Maple Gdns, Edg	55	K13
Maple Gate, Loug	48	G4
Maple Gro NW9	70	F14
Maple Gro W5	123	P5
Maple Gro, Brent	122	J13
Maple Gro, Sthl	103	M9
Maple Leaf Dr, Sid	171	T2
Maple Leaf Sq, SE16 *13*	131	P3
Maple Ms, NW6 *1*	6	A2
Maple Ms SW16	165	M10
Maple Pl W1	9	N12
Maple Rd E11	79	K12
Maple Rd SE20	185	L1
Maple Rd, Hayes	102	F6
Maple Rd, Surb	177	R9
Maple St W1	17	M1
Maple St, Rom	83	U8
Maple Way, Felt	156	B5
Maplecroft Cl E6	116	B11
Mapledale Av, Croy	198	J5
Mapledene, Chis	171	M11
Mapledene Rd E8	94	G13
Maplehurst Cl, Kings T	177	R8
Mapleleafe Gdns, Ilf	80	J6
Maples Pl, E1 *2*	113	K9
Maplestead Rd SW2	147	L14
Maplestead Rd, Dag	118	C1
Maplethorpe Rd, Th Hth	183	R8
Mapleton Cl, Brom	187	N11
Mapleton Cres SW18	144	J11
Mapleton Rd E4	62	F6
Mapleton Rd SW18	144	J12
Mapleton Rd, Enf	45	K4
Maplin Cl N21	43	M11
Maplin Rd E16	115	P11
Maplin St E3	113	T6
Mapperley Dr, Wdf Grn	62	J13
Maran Way, Erith	136	H5
Marban Rd W9	108	E5
Marble Arch W1	16	A9
Marble Cl W3	124	C2
Marble Dr NW2	72	B14
Marble Hill Cl, Twick	141	K13
Marble Hill Gdns, Twick	140	J13
Marble Quay E1	29	R2
Marbrook Ct SE12	169	T5
Marcellina Way, Orp	203	S6
March Rd, Twick	140	F13
Marchant Rd E11	96	H4
Marchbank Rd W14	126	F11
Marchmont Rd, Rich	141	T10
Marchmont St WC1	10	B10
Marchside Cl, Houns	138	H2
Marchwood Cl, SE5 *1*	130	D14
Marchwood Cres W5	105	M11
Marcia Rd SE1	37	K4
Marcilly Rd SW18	145	N9
Marco Rd W6	125	T6
Marcon Pl E8	94	J10
Marconi Rd E10	96	A2
Marconi Way, Sthl	103	S12
Marcourt Lawns W5	105	S8
Marcus Ct E15	115	K1
Marcus Garvey Ms SE22	148	J11
Marcus Garvey Way SE24	147	P8
Marcus St E15	115	K1
Marcus St, SW18 *14*	145	K11
Marcus Ter SW18	145	K11
Mardale Dr NW9	70	H10
Mardell Rd, Croy	185	N10
Marden Av, Brom	187	N12
Marden Cres, Bex	155	U10
Marden Cres, Croy	183	M11
Marden Rd N17	76	C5
Marden Rd, Croy	183	M12
Marden Sq SE16	130	J6
Marder Rd W13	122	H4
Mare St E8	95	K14
Marechal Niel Av, Sid	171	P5
Maresfield, Croy	198	D5
Maresfield Gdns NW3	91	M10
Marfleet Cl, Cars	195	R4
Margaret Av E4	46	D12
Margaret Bondfield Av, Bark	100	A14
Margaret Bldgs N16	94	F2
Margaret Gardner Dr, SE9 *1*	170	E3
Margaret Ingram Cl, SW6 *5*	126	E12
Margaret Lockwood Cl, Kings T	177	U7
Margaret Rd N16	94	F2
Margaret Rd, Barn	41	N8
Margaret Rd, Bex	154	H11
Margaret St W1	17	L5
Margaret Way, Ilf	80	C11
Margaretta Ter SW3	31	P9
Margaretting Rd E12	97	U3
Margate Rd SW2	146	J9
Margeholes, Wat	50	J3
Margery Pk Rd E7	97	N11
Margery Rd, Dag	100	H5
Margery St WC1	10	J8
Margin Dr SW19	162	B9
Margravine Gdns W6	126	B9
Margravine Rd W6	126	B11
Marham Gdns SW18	163	R2
Marham Gdns, Mord	181	L11
Maria Cl, SE1 *2*	37	U2
Maria Ter, E1 *20*	113	N8
Maria Theresa Cl, N Mal	178	H9
Marian Cl, Hayes	102	G8
Marian Ct, Sutt	194	J9
Marian Pl E2	112	J3
Marian Rd SW16	182	F1
Marian Sq E2	13	U1
Marian St, E2 *12*	112	J3
Marian Way NW10	89	L14
Maricas Av, Har	68	A1
Marie Lloyd Wk, E8 *1*	94	G12
Marigold All, SE1 *4*	19	N12
Marigold Cl, Sthl *1*	103	K13
Marigold Rd N17	61	L14
Marigold St SE16	130	J4
Marigold Way, E4 *2*	61	U11
Marigold Way, Croy	199	N1
Marina App, Hayes	103	K10
Marina Av, N Mal	179	R10
Marina Cl, Brom	187	N5
Marina Dr, Well	153	S3
Marina Gdns, Rom	83	T11
Marina Way, Tedd *1*	159	N13
Marine Dr SE18	134	F8
Marine St SE16	29	R10
Marinefield Rd SW6	145	K3
Mariner Gdns, Rich	159	K6
Mariner Rd, E12 *1*	98	G7
Mariners Ms, E14 *2*	132	G7
Marion Cl, Ilf	65	N13
Marion Gro, Wdf Grn	63	K9
Marion Rd NW7	55	N10
Marion Rd, Th Hth	183	U9
Marischal Rd SE13	150	H3
Maritime Quay E14	132	B9
Maritime St E3	113	U8
Marius Pas, SW17 *3*	164	A3
Marius Rd SW17	164	A3
Marjorams Av, Loug	48	G4
Marjorie Gro SW11	145	U7
Marjorie Ms, E1 *6*	113	N12
Mark Av E4	46	D12
Mark Cl, Bexh	154	J1
Mark Cl, Sthl	121	P1
Mark La EC3	20	J11
Mark Rd N22	75	S3
Mark Sq EC2	12	G10
Mark St E15	96	J14
Mark St EC2	12	G10
Marke Cl, Kes	202	C7
Markeston Grn, Wat	50	H8
Market Est N7	92	J11
Market Hill SE18	134	H6
Market La, Edg	70	F2
Market Ms W1	24	G3
Market Pl N2	73	R6
Market Pl NW11	73	K8
Market Pl SE16	37	U2
Market Pl W1	17	L6
Market Pl, W3 *2*	124	E2
Market Pl, Bexh	155	N7
Market Pl, Brent	123	M13
Market Pl, Enf	44	A6
Market Pl, Kings T	177	P4
Market Rd N7	92	J12
Market Rd, Rich	142	B6
Market Sq E2	13	M6
Market Sq, Brom	187	N3
Market St E6	116	F3
Market St SE18	134	H7
Market Way, Wem	87	R10
Markfield Gdns E4	46	C13
Markfield Rd N15	76	G9
Markham Pl SW3	31	T5
Markham Sq SW3	31	T5
Markham St SW3	31	S5
Markhole Cl, Hmptn	157	M14
Markhouse Av E17	77	S11
Markhouse Rd E17	77	T12
Markmanor Av E17	77	S13
Marks Rd, Rom	83	U10
Marksbury Av, Rich	142	B5
Markway, Sun	174	F4
Markwell Cl SE26	166	J8
Markyate Rd, Dag	100	D10
Marl Rd SW18	145	L7
Marlands Rd, Ilf	80	D6
Marlborough Av E8	112	G1
Marlborough Av N14	58	E5
Marlborough Av, Edg	54	D5
Marlborough Bldgs SW3	31	R1
Marlborough Cl N20	57	U6
Marlborough Cl SE17	35	S3
Marlborough Cl, SW19 *2*	163	R12
Marlborough Cl, Orp *1*	189	T12
Marlborough Ct, W1 *5*	17	M8
Marlborough Ct W8	126	G7
Marlborough Cres W4	124	H6
Marlborough Dr, Ilf	80	D5
Marlborough Gdns N20	57	U6
Marlborough Gate Ho, W2 *2*	14	J10
Marlborough Gro SE1	37	S8
Marlborough Hill NW8	109	M2
Marlborough Hill, Har	68	E7
Marlborough La SE7	133	U13
Marlborough Pk Av, Sid	172	A1
Marlborough Pl NW8	6	H1
Marlborough Rd E4	62	C12
Marlborough Rd E7	97	T13
Marlborough Rd E15	97	K8
Marlborough Rd E18	79	P4
Marlborough Rd N9	60	F2
Marlborough Rd N19	92	H4
Marlborough Rd N22	59	K13
Marlborough Rd SW1	25	P4
Marlborough Rd SW19	163	R12
Marlborough Rd W4	124	E9
Marlborough Rd W5	123	P3
Marlborough Rd, Bexh	154	G5
Marlborough Rd, Brom	187	U8
Marlborough Rd, Dag	100	C8
Marlborough Rd, Felt	156	G3
Marlborough Rd, Hmptn	157	N12
Marlborough Rd, Islw	140	J1
Marlborough Rd, Rich	141	T11
Marlborough Rd, Rom	83	R7
Marlborough Rd, S Croy	197	U13
Marlborough Rd, Sthl	120	F6
Marlborough Rd, Sutt	194	H5
Marlborough St SW3	31	P4
Marlborough Yd N19	92	H4
Marler Rd SE23	167	T2
Marlescroft Way, Loug	48	J10
Marley Av, Bexh	136	H12
Marley Cl N15	75	S7
Marley Cl, Grnf	103	N5
Marlingdene Cl, Hmptn	157	N12
Marlings Cl, Chis	189	S7
Marlings Pk Av, Chis	189	S6
Marlins Cl, Sutt *7*	195	M9
Marloes Cl, Wem	87	N8
Marloes Rd W8	22	A11
Marlow Cl SE20	185	K5
Marlow Ct NW6	90	B13
Marlow Ct NW9	71	L6
Marlow Cres, Twick	140	E12
Marlow Dr, Sutt	194	B5
Marlow Rd E6	116	E6
Marlow Rd SE20	185	K5
Marlow Rd, Sthl	121	L6
Marlow Way SE16	131	P3
Marlowe Cl, Chis	171	N12
Marlowe Cl, Ilf	81	M2
Marlowe Gdns SE9	152	H11
Marlowe Rd E17	78	E7
Marlowe Sq, Mitch	182	E7
Marlowe Way, Croy	197	K3
Marlowes, The NW8	109	N2
Marlton St, SE10 *7*	133	M9
Marlwood Cl, Sid	171	R4
Marmadon Rd SE18	135	T7
Marmion App, E4 *2*	62	A7
Marmion Av E4	61	U7
Marmion Cl E4	61	U7
Marmion Ms, SW11 *6*	146	B6
Marmion Rd SW11	146	B7
Marmont Rd SE15	148	H1
Marmora Rd SE22	149	L11
Marmot Rd, Houns	138	G5
Marne Av N11	58	C7
Marne Av, Well	154	A6
Marne St W10	108	C5
Marnell Way, Houns	138	G6
Marney Rd SW11	146	A7
Marnfield Cres SW2	165	M1
Marnham Av NW2	90	C7
Marnham Cres, Grnf	103	S5
Marnock Rd SE4	149	T10
Maroon St E14	113	S10
Maroons Way SE6	168	B9
Marquess Rd N1	94	A11
Marquis Cl, Wem	87	U14

Name	Page	Grid
Marquis Rd N4	93	M1
Marquis Rd N22	59	M12
Marquis Rd NW1	92	H12
Marrabon Cl, Sid	172	A2
Marrick Cl SW15	143	P7
Marriots Cl NW9	71	M12
Marriott Rd E15	114	J1
Marriott Rd N4	93	L2
Marriott Rd N10	73	U2
Marriott Rd, Barn	40	B6
Marryat Pl SW19	162	C8
Marryat Rd SW19	162	C8
Marryat Sq SW6	144	C1
Marsala Rd SE13	150	D8
Marsden Rd N9	60	J4
Marsden Rd SE15	148	F6
Marsden St NW5	92	A11
Marsden Way, Orp	203	T7
Marsh Av, Mitch	181	U3
Marsh Cl NW7	55	L6
Marsh Dr NW9	71	M12
Marsh Fm Rd, Twick	158	E2
Marsh Grn Rd, Dag	119	N2
Marsh Hill E9	95	R10
Marsh La E10	96	A3
Marsh La N17	61	K14
Marsh La NW7	55	L5
Marsh La, Stan	53	N13
Marsh Rd, Pnr	67	L8
Marsh Rd, Wem	105	P4
Marsh St, E14 9	132	C8
Marsh Wall E14	132	A2
Marshall Cl, SW18 4	145	L11
Marshall Cl, Har	68	A13
Marshall Cl, Houns	139	M9
Marshall Rd E10	96	C6
Marshall Rd N17	76	B1
Marshall St W1	17	N8
Marshalls Cl N11	58	C7
Marshall's Gro SE18	134	D7
Marshalls Pl SE16	29	N11
Marshall's Rd, Sutt	194	J8
Marshalsea Rd SE1	28	A5
Marsham Cl, Chis	170	J10
Marsham St SW1	25	U11
Marshbrook Cl, SE3 1	152	A5
Marshfield St E14	132	E5
Marshgate La E15	114	D2
Marshgate Path SE28	135	M7
Marshside Cl N9	61	L2
Marsland Cl SE17	35	S7
Marston Av, Chess	191	S11
Marston Av, Dag	101	N4
Marston Cl NW6	91	M13
Marston Cl, Dag	101	N5
Marston Rd, Ilf	80	D3
Marston Rd, Tedd	158	J10
Marston Way SE19	165	S13
Marsworth Av, Pnr	66	H1
Marsworth Cl, Hayes	103	K9
Martaban Rd N16	94	D3
Martel Pl E8	94	F11
Martell Rd SE21	166	A5
Martello St E8	94	J13
Martello Ter E8	94	J14
Marten Rd E17	78	B3
Martens Av, Bexh	155	T7
Martens Cl, Bexh	155	T8
Martha Ct E2	113	K3
Martha Rd, E4 5	61	T12
Martha Rd E15	97	K11
Martha St E1	113	K12
Martham Cl, SE28 3	118	G13
Marthorne Cres, Har	68	B4
Martin Bowes Rd SE9	152	E5
Martin Cl N9	61	N2
Martin Cres, Croy	197	N2
Martin Dene, Bexh	155	L10
Martin Dr, Nthlt	66	A11
Martin Gdns, Dag	100	F8
Martin Gro, Mord	180	G6
Martin La EC4	20	E10
Martin Ri, Bexh	155	L9
Martin Rd, Dag	100	G8
Martin Way SW20	180	G6
Martin Way, Mord	180	D6
Martinbridge Ind Est, Enf	44	H10
Martindale SW14	142	E9
Martindale Av E16	115	P13
Martindale Rd, SW12 4	146	D14
Martindale Rd, Houns	138	J7
Martineau Rd N5	93	R8
Martineau St E1	113	L12
Martingale Cl, Sun	174	A7
Martingales Cl, Rich	159	N5
Martins Cl, W Wick	200	H3
Martins Mt, Barn	40	H7
Martins Rd, Brom	187	K3
Martins Wk N10	74	A1
Martinsfield Cl, Chig	65	S8
Martlet Gro, Nthlt	102	H6
Martley Dr, Ilf	80	J10
Martock Cl, Har	68	H8
Marton Cl SE6	168	B6
Marton Rd N16	94	C4
Martys Yd NW3	91	N8
Marvell Av, Hayes	102	B9
Marvels Cl SE12	169	S4
Marvels La SE12	169	S4
Marville Rd SW6	126	E14
Marvin St, E8 6	95	K11
Marwell Cl, W Wick	201	L3
Marwood Cl, Well	154	C6
Mary Adelaide Cl SW15	160	J7
Mary Ann Gdns SE8	132	A12
Mary Cl, Stan	69	U7
Mary Datchelor Cl SE5	148	B1
Mary Lawrenson Pl SE3	133	N14
Mary Peters Dr, Grnf	86	A9
Mary Pl W11	108	C14
Mary Rose Cl, Hmptn	175	P1
Mary Rose Mall E6	116	F10
Mary Seacole Cl E8	112	E1
Mary St, E16 2	115	L10
Mary St N1	111	U2
Mary Ter, NW1 10	110	D2
Maryatt Av, Har	85	R3
Marybank SE18	134	E7
Maryland Pk E15	97	K10
Maryland Pt, E15 8	96	J11
Maryland Rd E15	96	H10
Maryland Rd N22	59	N12
Maryland Rd, Th Hth	183	S2
Maryland Sq E15	97	K10
Maryland St E15	96	H10
Maryland Way, Sun	174	B4
Marylands Rd W9	108	H8
Marylebone Flyover NW1	15	L3
Marylebone Flyover W2	15	L3
Marylebone High St W1	16	E2
Marylebone La W1	16	F6
Marylebone Ms, W1 5	16	G4
Marylebone Pas, W1 1	17	N5
Marylebone Rd NW1	15	U1
Marylebone St W1	16	F3
Marylee Way SE11	34	H4
Maryon Gro SE7	134	D8
Maryon Ms NW3	91	R8
Maryon Rd SE7	134	C8
Maryon Rd SE18	134	C7
Maryrose Way N20	57	P1
Mary's Cl N17	76	F2
Mary's Ter, Twick	140	G14
Masbro Rd W14	126	B5
Mascalls Ct SE7	133	T12
Mascalls Rd SE7	133	T12
Mascotte Rd, SW15 8	144	B6
Mascotts Cl NW2	89	S6
Masefield Av, Borwd	38	D10
Masefield Av, Sthl	103	P13
Masefield Av, Stan	52	F10
Masefield Cres N14	42	E11
Masefield Gdns E6	116	G7
Masefield La, Hayes	102	D7
Masefield Rd, Hmptn	157	L7
Masefield Vw, Orp	203	L5
Mashie Rd W3	106	J11
Maskall Cl SW2	165	P2
Maskell Rd SW17	163	L6
Maskelyne Cl SW11	145	S1
Mason Cl E16	115	N12
Mason Cl SE16	37	U5
Mason Cl SW20	180	A1
Mason Cl, Bexh	155	R6
Mason Cl, Borwd	38	G3
Mason Cl, Hmptn	175	M2
Mason Rd, Sutt 4	195	K9
Mason Rd, Wdf Grn	63	K8
Mason St SE17	36	F2
Masons Arms Ms W1	17	K8
Masons Av, Croy	197	U6
Masons Av, Har	68	E7
Masons Grn La W3	106	A8
Masons Hill SE18	135	K8
Masons Hill, Brom	187	P6
Mason's Pl EC1	11	S6
Masons Pl, Mitch	181	T1
Mason's Yd SW1	25	N2
Mason's Yd SW19	162	B10
Massey Cl, N11 2	58	D9
Massie Rd, E8 4	94	G12
Massingberd Way SW17	164	C8
Massinger St SE17	36	H3
Massingham St E1	113	N7
Masson Av, Ruis	84	E12
Mast Ho Ter E14	132	B8
Mast Leisure Pk SE16	131	P5
Master Gunner Pl SE18	134	C14
Masterman Rd E6	116	C6
Masters Dr SE16	130	J10
Masters St, E1 12	113	P9
Mastmaker Rd E14	132	B4
Maswell Pk Cres, Houns	139	T9
Maswell Pk Rd, Houns	139	S9
Matcham Rd E11	97	K5
Matchless Dr SE18	134	G14
Matfield Cl, Brom	187	N10
Matfield Rd, Belv	137	N11
Matham Gro SE22	148	E8
Matham Rd, E Mol	176	A9
Matheson Rd W14	126	E8
Mathews Av E6	116	H4
Mathews Pk Av E15	97	M12
Matilda Cl SE19	166	A13
Matilda St N1	111	M1
Matlock Cl SE24	147	U8
Matlock Cl, Barn	40	B11
Matlock Cr SE5	148	A8
Matlock Cres, Sutt	194	D7
Matlock Gdns, Sutt	194	D8
Matlock Pl, Sutt	194	D8
Matlock Rd E10	78	E11
Matlock St E14	113	R11
Matlock Way, N Mal	178	G2
Matrimony Pl SW8	146	F4
Matthew Cl W10	108	A8
Matthew Ct, Mitch	182	H9
Matthew Parker St SW1	25	U8
Matthews Rd, Grnf	86	B9
Matthews St SW11	145	T3
Matthias Rd N16	94	C9
Mattison Rd N4	75	P11
Mattock La W5	123	M1
Mattock La W13	123	K1
Maud Cashmore Way SE18	134	F6
Maud Gdns E13	115	M2
Maud Gdns, Bark	117	T3
Maud Rd E10	96	F6
Maud Rd E13	115	M3
Maud St E16	115	L10
Maude Rd E17	77	S9
Maude Rd SE5	148	C2
Maude Ter E17	77	R8
Maudesville Cotts, W7 2	122	D2
Maudlin's Grn E1	29	P2
Maudslay Rd SE9	152	E5
Mauleverer Rd SW2	146	J10
Maunder Rd, W7 4	122	E2
Maunsel St SW1	33	S1
Maurice Av N22	75	S4
Maurice Brown Cl NW7	56	B10
Maurice St W12	107	R12
Maurice Wk NW11	73	L8
Maurier Cl, Nthlt	102	F1
Mauritius Rd SE10	133	K8
Maury Rd N16	94	G5
Mavelstone Cl, Brom	188	C1
Mavelstone Rd, Brom	188	C1
Maverton Rd E3	114	A2
Mavis Av, Epsom	193	K9
Mavis Cl, Epsom	193	K9
Mavis Wk E6	116	C10
Mawbey Est SE1	37	R7
Mawbey Pl SE1	37	P7
Mawbey Rd, SE1 2	37	P7
Mawbey St SW8	128	J14
Mawney Cl, Rom	83	R4
Mawney Rd, Rom	83	S3
Mawson Cl SW20	180	D4
Maxey Gdns, Dag	101	K7
Maxey Rd SE18	135	L7
Maxey Rd, Dag	100	J8
Maxfield Cl N20	41	L13
Maxim Rd N21	43	N11
Maxted Pk, Har	68	C14
Maxted Rd SE15	148	F5
Maxwell Cl, Croy	197	K1
Maxwell Gdns, Orp	203	T5
Maxwell Rd SW6	126	J14
Maxwell Rd, Borwd	38	D5
Maxwell Rd, Well	154	A6
Maxwelton Av NW7	54	H9
Maxwelton Cl NW7	54	H9
May Bate Av, Kings T	177	P1
May Cl, Chess	191	U11
May Gdns, Wem	105	M4
May Rd E4	62	A11
May Rd E13	115	P3
May Rd, Twick	158	C2
May St, W14 11	126	E10
May Tree La, Stan	52	G13
May Wk E13	115	R3
Maya Rd N2	73	L7
Mayall Rd SE24	147	R9
Maybank Av E18	79	S3
Maybank Av, Wem	86	H9
Maybank Gdns, Pnr	66	A9
Maybank Rd E18	79	T2
Maybells Commercial Est, Bark	118	G5
Mayberry Pl, Surb	177	U13
Maybourne Cl SE26	167	K10
Maybrook Meadow Est, Bark	100	B14
Maybury Cl, Loug	48	J7
Maybury Cl, Orp	189	K10
Maybury Gdns NW10	74	F13
Maybury Ms N6	74	F13
Maybury Rd E13	115	T8
Maybury Rd, Bark	118	A3
Maybury St SW17	163	R10
Maychurch Cl, Stan	53	N14
Maycroft, Pnr	66	C4
Maycross Av, Mord	180	G7
Mayday Gdns SE3	152	C3

Mayday Rd, Th Hth	183	R12
Mayerne Rd SE9	152	B10
Mayes Rd N22	75	N4
Mayesbrook Rd, Bark	117	T2
Mayesbrook Rd, Dag	100	C5
Mayesbrook Rd, Ilf	100	B5
Mayesford Rd, Rom	82	F13
Mayeswood Rd SE12	169	T6
Mayfair Av, Bexh	154	H2
Mayfair Av, Ilf	98	F3
Mayfair Av, Rom	82	H12
Mayfair Av, Twick	139	T14
Mayfair Av, Wor Pk	193	N1
Mayfair Cl, Beck	186	C1
Mayfair Cl, Surb	191	S1
Mayfair Gdns N17	60	A12
Mayfair Gdns, Wdf Grn	63	P13
Mayfair Ms, NW1 4	91	U14
Mayfair Pl W1	25	K2
Mayfair Ter N14	42	G14
Mayfield, Bexh	155	L6
Mayfield Av N12	57	N7
Mayfield Av N14	58	G4
Mayfield Av W4	125	K8
Mayfield Av W13	122	J4
Mayfield Av, Har	68	J10
Mayfield Av, Orp	189	T13
Mayfield Av, Wdf Grn	63	N13
Mayfield Cl E8	94	E12
Mayfield Cl SW4	146	H9
Mayfield Cl, T Ditt	190	J2
Mayfield Cres N9	44	J11
Mayfield Cres, Th Hth	183	L8
Mayfield Dr, Pnr	67	M7
Mayfield Gdns NW4	72	A11
Mayfield Gdns W7	104	B11
Mayfield Rd E4	62	F3
Mayfield Rd E8	94	E14
Mayfield Rd E13	115	M8
Mayfield Rd E17	77	R3
Mayfield Rd N8	75	M11
Mayfield Rd SW19	180	F1
Mayfield Rd W3	106	C13
Mayfield Rd W12	125	K3
Mayfield Rd, Belv	137	T7
Mayfield Rd, Brom	188	C9
Mayfield Rd, Dag	100	E2
Mayfield Rd, Enf	45	N4
Mayfield Rd, Sutt	195	N12
Mayfield Rd, Th Hth	183	L8
Mayfields, Wem	88	A3
Mayfields Cl, Wem	88	A3
Mayflower Cl, SE16 8	131	P7
Mayflower Rd SW9	146	J5
Mayflower St, SE16 1	131	L4
Mayfly Cl, Pnr	66	E13
Mayford Cl SW12	145	U14
Mayford Cl, Beck	185	P6
Mayford Rd SW12	145	U14
Maygood St N1	10	H1
Maygrove Rd NW6	90	F12
Mayhew Cl E4	62	A5
Mayhill Rd SE7	133	R12
Mayhill Rd, Barn	40	C11
Maylands Dr, Sid	172	H5
Maylands Rd, Wat	50	E7
Maynard Cl, SW6 12	127	K14
Maynard Rd E17	78	E9
Maynards Quay E1	113	L14
Maynooth Gdns, Cars 2	181	U13
Mayo Rd NW10	88	J12
Mayo Rd, Croy	184	A10
Mayola Rd E5	95	M7
Mayow Rd SE23	167	P5
Mayow Rd SE26	167	N8
Mayplace Cl, Bexh	155	R6
Mayplace La SE18	135	K13
Mayplace Rd E, Bexh	155	S6
Mayplace Rd W, Bexh	155	P7
Maypole Cres, Ilf	65	N13
Mayroyd Av, Surb	192	B3
Mays Hill Rd, Brom	187	K4
Mays La E4	62	G3
Mays La, Barn	39	T12
Mays Rd, Tedd	158	A9
Maysoule Rd SW11	145	N7
Mayston Ms, SE10 2	133	P10
Mayswood Gdns, Dag	101	U11
Mayton St N7	93	L6
Maytree Cl, Edg	54	E5
Maytree Gdns W5	123	N4
Maytree Wk SW2	165	N4
Mayville Rd E11	96	J4
Mayville Rd, Ilf	98	J9
Maywood Cl, Beck	168	C14
Maze Hill SE3	133	L14
Maze Hill SE10	132	J11
Maze Rd, Rich	124	B13
Mazenod Av NW6	90	H14
McAdam Dr, Enf	43	R3
McAuley Cl SE1	26	J10
McAuley Cl SE9	152	H9
McCall Cl SW4	146	J3
McCall Cres SE7	134	C10
McCarthy Rd, Felt	156	H10
McCrone Ms, NW3 5	91	P11
McCullum Rd E3	113	T2
McDermott Cl SW11	145	R5
McDermott Rd SE15	148	G5
McDonough Cl, Chess	191	R7
McDowall Cl E16	115	N10
McDowall Rd SE5	147	T2
McEntee Av E17	77	R1
McEwen Way, E15 3	114	H1
McGrath Rd E15	97	L10
McGregor Rd W11	108	E10
McIntosh Cl, Wall	196	J13
McKay Rd SW20	161	S13
McKellar Cl, Bushey	51	U3
McKerrell Rd SE15	148	H2
McLeod Rd SE2	136	D8
McLeod's Ms SW7	30	D1
McMillan St SE8	132	B12
McNair Rd, Sthl	121	R5
McNeil Rd SE5	148	C4
McNicol Dr NW10	106	E4
McRae La, Mitch	181	T14
Mead, The N2	73	M3
Mead, The W13	104	J9
Mead, The, Beck	186	E3
Mead, The, Wall	196	H12
Mead, The, Wat	50	J5
Mead, The, W Wick	200	G2
Mead Cl, Har	68	B2
Mead Cl, Loug	48	J4
Mead Ct NW9	70	F10
Mead Cres E4	62	F7
Mead Cres, Sutt	195	R7
Mead Fld, Har	85	M6
Mead Gro, Rom	82	J5
Mead Path SW17	163	M8
Mead Pl E9	95	M12
Mead Pl, Croy	197	S2
Mead Plat NW10	88	F11
Mead Rd, Chis	171	L11
Mead Rd, Edg	54	A12
Mead Rd, Rich	159	M6
Mead Row SE1	27	K10
Mead Way, Brom	187	L11
Mead Way, Croy	199	S3
Meadcroft Rd SE11	35	N11
Meade Cl W4	124	B11
Meadfield, Edg	54	D3
Meadfield Grn, Edg	54	C3
Meadfoot Rd SW16	182	E1
Meadgate Av, Wdf Grn	64	D10
Meadlands Dr, Rich	159	N3
Meadow, The, Chis	171	L11
Meadow Av, Croy	185	P11
Meadow Bank N21	43	L12
Meadow Cl E4	62	C2
Meadow Cl E9	95	U10
Meadow Cl SE6	168	B9
Meadow Cl SW20	179	U8
Meadow Cl, Barn	40	F11
Meadow Cl, Bexh	155	M10
Meadow Cl, Chis	170	J9
Meadow Cl, Esher	190	F5
Meadow Cl, Houns	139	N12
Meadow Cl, Nthlt	103	P3
Meadow Cl, Rich	159	R2
Meadow Dr N10	74	C5
Meadow Dr NW4	71	T4
Meadow Gdns, Edg	54	D11
Meadow Garth NW10	88	F12
Meadow Hill, N Mal	178	J11
Meadow Ms SW8	34	F12
Meadow Pl SW8	34	D14
Meadow Pl W4	124	J13
Meadow Rd SW8	34	F13
Meadow Rd SW19	163	M14
Meadow Rd, Bark	99	U14
Meadow Rd, Borwd	38	D3
Meadow Rd, Brom	187	K3
Meadow Rd, Dag	101	L11
Meadow Rd, Esher	190	D11
Meadow Rd, Felt	156	J3
Meadow Rd, Loug	48	C9
Meadow Rd, Pnr	66	H8
Meadow Rd, Rom	101	T1
Meadow Rd, Sthl	103	M14
Meadow Rd, Sutt	195	R9
Meadow Row SE1	27	U12
Meadow Stile, Croy 12	197	U6
Meadow Vw, Har	86	C1
Meadow Vw, Sid	154	C13
Meadow Vw Rd, Th Hth	183	R10
Meadow Wk E18	79	N7
Meadow Wk, Dag	101	L11
Meadow Wk, Epsom	193	K11
Meadow Wk, Wall	196	C5
Meadow Way NW9	70	H9
Meadow Way, Chess	191	R9
Meadow Way, Chig	65	L5
Meadow Way, Orp	202	G6
Meadow Way, Ruis	66	C12
Meadow Way, Wem	87	P7
Meadow Way, The, Har	68	D2
Meadow Waye, Houns	121	K13
Meadowbank NW3	91	T14
Meadowbank SE3	151	M6
Meadowbank, Surb	177	T11
Meadowbank Cl SW6	125	U14
Meadowbank Cl, Barn	39	M10
Meadowbank Gdns, Houns	138	C2
Meadowbank Rd NW9	70	G13
Meadowcourt Rd SE3	151	M8
Meadowcroft, Brom	188	F6
Meadowcroft Rd N13	59	P4
Meadows Cl, E10 1	96	A3
Meadows End, Sun	174	A1
Meadowside SE9	151	U8
Meadowsweet Cl, E16 5	116	A10
Meadowview Rd SE6	168	A9
Meadowview Rd, Bex	155	K12
Meads, The, Edg	54	H12
Meads, The, Sutt	194	C5
Meads La, Ilf	81	S13
Meads Rd N22	75	R4
Meads Rd, Enf	45	R2
Meadvale Rd W5	105	K7
Meadvale Rd, Croy	184	F13
Meadway N14	58	H4
Meadway NW11	73	K11
Meadway SW20	179	U7
Meadway, Barn	40	F7
Meadway, Beck	186	F2
Meadway, Ilf	99	S6
Meadway, Surb	192	E2
Meadway, Twick	158	B2
Meadway, Wdf Grn	63	T8
Meadway, The, SE3 4	150	H4
Meadway, The, Buck H	64	A2
Meadway, The, Loug	48	E12
Meadway Cl NW11	73	K11
Meadway Cl, Barn	40	G6
Meadway Cl, Pnr	51	P11
Meadway Ct NW11	73	K11
Meadway Gate NW11	72	H12
Meaford Way SE20	167	K13
Meakin Est SE1	28	H10
Meanley Rd E12	98	D8
Meard St W1	17	R8
Meath Rd E15	115	L3
Meath Rd, Ilf	99	M5
Meath St SW11	146	C1
Mechanics Path SE8	132	A13
Mecklenburgh Pl WC1	10	F10
Mecklenburgh Sq WC1	10	E9
Mecklenburgh St WC1	10	E9
Medburn St NW1	9	R2
Medcroft Gdns SW14	142	E7
Medebourne Cl SE3	151	P5
Medesenge Way N13	59	R11
Medfield St SW15	143	P13
Medhurst Rd, E3 6	113	S4
Median Rd E5	95	L9
Medina Av, Esher	190	D5
Medina Gro N7	93	N5
Medina Rd N7	93	N5
Medland Cl, Wall 2	196	B1
Medlar Cl, Nthlt 1	102	H3
Medlar St SE5	147	U1
Medley Rd NW6	90	G12
Medora Rd SW2	147	M13
Medusa Rd SE6	150	C12
Medway Bldgs, E3 10	113	S4
Medway Cl, Croy	185	L11
Medway Cl, Ilf	99	M10
Medway Dr, Grnf	104	E4
Medway Gdns, Wem	86	G13
Medway Ms, E3 7	113	S4
Medway Par, Grnf 1	104	E4
Medway Rd E3	113	S4
Medway St SW1	25	S12
Medwin St SW4	147	L7
Meerbrook Rd SE3	151	U6
Meeson Rd E15	97	L14
Meeson St E5	95	R8
Meeting Ho La SE15	130	J14
Meetinghouse All, E1 9	131	K1
Mehetabel Rd E9	95	L11
Meister Cl, Ilf	99	N2
Melancholy Wk, Rich	159	M3
Melanda Cl, Chis	170	E10
Melanie Cl, Bexh	154	J1
Melba Way SE13	150	D2
Melbourne Av N13	59	L11
Melbourne Av W13	122	H2
Melbourne Av, Pnr	67	R5
Melbourne Cl, Orp	189	S13
Melbourne Cl, Wall 2	196	E10
Melbourne Ct SE20	166	H14
Melbourne Gdns, Rom	82	J9
Melbourne Gro SE22	148	D8
Melbourne Ms SE6	150	E13
Melbourne Ms SW9	147	N2
Melbourne Pl WC2	18	G9

Name	Page	Grid
Melbourne Rd E6	116	F2
Melbourne Rd E10	78	C13
Melbourne Rd E17	77	S7
Melbourne Rd SW19	180	H1
Melbourne Rd, Ilf	99	K2
Melbourne Rd, Tedd	159	M11
Melbourne Rd, Wall	196	D10
Melbourne Sq, SW9 1	147	N2
Melbourne Way, Enf	44	F12
Melbury Av, Sthl	121	R6
Melbury Cl, Chis	170	E12
Melbury Cl, Esher	190	J12
Melbury Ct W8	126	F5
Melbury Dr SE5	130	C14
Melbury Gdns SW20	179	R1
Melbury Rd W14	126	F5
Melbury Rd, Har	69	U10
Melbury Ter NW1	7	S12
Melcombe Gdns, Har	69	U10
Melcombe Pl NW1	15	T1
Melcombe St NW1	8	A12
Meldex Cl NW7	55	T11
Meldon Cl, SW6 5	145	K2
Meldone Cl, Surb	178	C12
Meldrum Rd, Ilf	100	B4
Melfield Gdns SE6	168	D8
Melford Av, Bark	99	T11
Melford Cl, Chess	191	U10
Melford Rd E6	116	E7
Melford Rd E11	96	J4
Melford Rd E17	77	S8
Melford Rd SE22	148	H14
Melford Rd, Ilf	99	N4
Melfort Av, Th Hth	183	S6
Melfort Rd, Th Hth	183	R5
Melgund Rd N5	93	P10
Melina Pl NW8	6	J7
Melina Rd W12	125	R4
Melior Pl, SE1 3	28	G5
Melior St SE1	28	G5
Meliot Rd SE6	168	H4
Meller Cl, Croy	196	J5
Melling Dr, Enf	44	G2
Melling St SE18	135	S12
Mellish Cl, Bark	117	T2
Mellish Gdns, Wdf Grn	63	P10
Mellish St E14	132	B5
Mellison Rd SW17	163	S10
Mellitus St W12	107	L10
Mellor Cl, Walt	175	L13
Mellows Rd, Ilf	80	F5
Mellows Rd, Wall	196	G10
Mells Cres SE9	170	E8
Melody La N5	93	S9
Melody Rd SW18	145	M10
Melon Pl, W8 3	22	A5
Melon Rd E11	96	J6
Melon Rd SE15	148	G1
Melrose Av N22	75	S1
Melrose Av NW2	89	U9
Melrose Av SW16	183	N5
Melrose Av SW19	162	G5
Melrose Av, Borwd	38	C9
Melrose Av, Grnf	103	S3
Melrose Av, Mitch	164	C14
Melrose Av, Twick	139	S14
Melrose Cl SE12	169	P1
Melrose Cl, Grnf	103	R4
Melrose Cl, Hayes	102	A9
Melrose Cres, Orp	203	P8
Melrose Dr, Sthl	121	P1
Melrose Gdns W6	125	U5
Melrose Gdns, Edg	70	D4
Melrose Gdns, N Mal	178	H6
Melrose Rd SW13	143	L2
Melrose Rd SW18	144	E12
Melrose Rd SW19	180	G3
Melrose Rd, W3 5	124	E5
Melrose Rd, Pnr	67	M8
Melrose Ter W6	125	U5
Melsa Rd, Mord	181	L11
Melthorne Dr, Ruis	84	E6
Melthorpe Gdns SE3	152	C1
Melton Cl, Ruis	84	E2
Melton Ct SW7	31	L3
Melton St NW1	9	P8
Melville Av SW20	161	N14
Melville Av, Grnf	86	E10
Melville Av, S Croy	198	F10
Melville Gdns N13	59	P10
Melville Pl N1	93	T14
Melville Rd E17	77	U6
Melville Rd NW10	88	G14
Melville Rd SW13	143	N2
Melville Rd, Sid	172	E4
Melville Vil Rd, W3 4	124	G2
Melvin Rd SE20	185	L1
Melyn Cl N7	92	F8
Memel Ct, EC1 10	11	T11
Memel St EC1	11	T11
Memess Path SE18	134	H11
Memorial Av E15	115	K5
Memorial Cl, Houns	121	L12
Mendip Cl, SE26 1	167	L8
Mendip Cl, Wor Pk	193	U3
Mendip Dr NW2	90	B4
Mendip Rd SW11	145	M6
Mendip Rd, Ilf	81	R10
Mendora Rd SW6	126	D13
Menelik Rd NW2	90	D8
Menlo Gdns SE19	166	A14
Menotti St E2	13	U9
Mentmore Cl, Har	69	M11
Mentmore Ter E8	95	K14
Meon Ct, Islw	140	C3
Meon Rd W3	124	F4
Meopham Rd, Mitch	182	E2
Mepham Cres, Har	51	U13
Mepham Gdns, Har	51	U14
Mepham St SE1	26	J4
Mera Dr, Bexh	155	P7
Merantun Way SW19	181	N1
Merbury Cl SE13	150	F10
Merbury Rd SE28	135	R3
Mercator Pl E14	132	B8
Mercator Rd SE13	150	G7
Mercer Cl, T Ditt	176	F14
Mercer St WC2	18	A8
Merceron St E1	113	K8
Mercers Cl, SE10 1	133	L8
Mercers Pl W6	125	U7
Mercers Rd N19	92	H6
Merchant St E3	113	U6
Merchiston Rd SE6	168	G3
Merchland Rd SE9	171	M2
Mercia Gro SE13	150	F6
Mercier Rd SW15	144	C10
Mercury Cen, Felt	138	C10
Mercury Way SE14	131	N11
Mercy Ter SE13	150	C8
Mere Cl SW15	144	B13
Mere Cl, Orp	202	J4
Mere End, Croy	185	P14
Mere Side, Orp	202	H4
Merebank La, Croy	197	M9
Meredith Av NW2	89	U9
Meredith Cl, Pnr	50	H13
Meredith St E13	115	P6
Meredith St EC1	11	N8
Meredyth Rd SW13	143	N3
Meretone Cl SE4	149	R7
Merevale Cres, Mord	181	M11
Mereway Rd, Twick	158	C2
Merewood Cl, Brom	188	G3
Merewood Rd, Bexh	155	U13
Mereworth Cl, Brom	187	M9
Mereworth Dr SE18	135	K14
Meriden Cl, Brom	160	B14
Meriden Cl, Ilf	81	L1
Meridian Gate E14	132	E3
Meridian Pl E14	132	D3
Meridian Trd Est SE7	134	B13
Meridian Way N9	61	M8
Meridian Way N18	61	L11
Meridian Way, Enf	45	R10
Merifield Rd SE9	151	U8
Merino Cl E11	79	T8
Merino Pl, Sid 1	154	B11
Merivale Rd SW15	143	D7
Merivale Rd, Har	67	U14
Merlewood Dr, Chis	188	E2
Merley Ct NW9	88	F1
Merlin Cl, Croy	198	C7
Merlin Cl, Mitch	181	S5
Merlin Cl, Nthlt	102	F5
Merlin Cres, Edg	69	T1
Merlin Gdns, Brom	169	N6
Merlin Gro, Beck	186	A8
Merlin Gro, Ilf	65	K13
Merlin Rd E12	98	A4
Merlin Rd, Well	154	B8
Merlin Rd N, Well	154	A7
Merlin St WC1	11	K7
Merling Cl, Chess 1	191	N10
Merlins Av, Har	85	M5
Mermaid Ct SE1	28	C5
Mermaid Ct SE16	131	T2
Merredene St SW2	147	L12
Merriam Cl E4	62	F10
Merrick Rd, Sthl	121	M4
Merrick Sq SE1	28	C9
Merridene N21	43	R11
Merrielands Cres, Dag	119	M3
Merrilands Rd, Wor Pk	193	T2
Merrilees Rd, Sid	171	R1
Merrilyn Cl, Esher	190	G11
Merriman Rd SE3	151	U1
Merrington Rd SW6	126	H11
Merrion Av, Stan	53	N8
Merritt Gdns, Chess	191	M12
Merritt Rd SE4	149	T9
Merrivale N14	42	F11
Merrivale Av, Ilf	80	B8
Merrow St SE17	36	B9
Merrow Wk SE17	36	F6
Merrow Way, Croy	200	F12
Merry Hill Mt, Bushey	51	S1
Merryborn Way, Chis	188	D2
Merryfield, SE3 3	151	M4
Merryfield Gdns, Stan	53	M10
Merryfields Way SE6	150	D13
Merryhill Cl E4	46	C14
Merryhills Ct N14	42	E9
Merryhills Dr, Enf	42	J8
Mersey Rd E17	77	U5
Mersham Dr NW9	70	B10
Mersham Pl SE20	185	K1
Mersham Rd, Th Hth	184	A4
Merten Rd, Rom	83	K13
Merthyr Ter SW13	125	S11
Merton Av W4	125	L7
Merton Av, Nthlt	85	U10
Merton Gdns, Orp	189	K9
Merton Hall Gdns SW20	180	D1
Merton Hall Rd SW19	180	D1
Merton High St SW19	163	L14
Merton Ind Pk SW19	181	L2
Merton La N6	91	U3
Merton Mans SW20	180	B4
Merton Ri NW3	91	R13
Merton Rd E17	78	E10
Merton Rd SE25	184	G9
Merton Rd SW18	144	G11
Merton Rd SW19	162	J13
Merton Rd, Bark	99	U14
Merton Rd, Har	85	U2
Merton Rd, Ilf	81	T13
Merton Way, W Mol	175	T7
Merttins Rd SE15	149	P9
Meru Cl NW5	91	U2
Mervan Rd SW2	147	N8
Mervyn Av SE9	171	M5
Mervyn Rd W13	122	H5
Messaline Av W3	106	H12
Messent Rd SE9	151	U9
Messeter Pl SE9	153	M7
Messina Av NW6	90	G14
Meteor St SW11	146	B7
Meteor Way, Wall	196	J14
Metheringham Way NW9	70	J2
Methley St SE11	35	L7
Methuen Cl, Edg	54	A13
Methuen Pk N10	74	D4
Methuen Rd, Belv	137	S7
Methuen Rd, Bexh	155	L8
Methuen Rd, Edg	54	A14
Methwold Rd W10	108	A9
Metro Cen, The, Islw	140	D3
Metropolitan Cen, The, Grnf	103	R2
Metropolitan Cl, E14 12	114	B10
Mews, The N1	111	U1
Mews, The, Ilf	80	B10
Mews, The, Twick	140	J11
Mews Deck, E1 15	113	K14
Mews Pl, Wdf Grn	63	P7
Mews St E1	29	R1
Mexfield Rd SW15	144	F9
Meyer Rd, Erith	137	U12
Meymott St SE1	27	N3
Meynell Cres E9	95	N13
Meynell Gdns E9	95	N13
Meynell Rd E9	95	N13
Meyrick Rd NW10	89	N11
Meyrick Rd SW11	145	P6
Miall Wk SE26	167	S7
Micawber St N1	12	A5
Michael Faraday Ho SE17	36	G7
Michael Gaynor Cl W7	122	F2
Michael Rd E11	97	K2
Michael Rd SE25	184	C6
Michael Rd SW6	145	K1
Michaelmas Cl SW20	179	T5
Michaels Cl SE13	150	J7
Micheldever Rd SE12	151	L11
Michelham Gdns, Twick	158	F5
Michels Row, Rich	141	R7
Michigan Av E12	98	D7
Michleham Down N12	56	F7
Mickleham Cl, Orp	189	U3
Mickleham Gdns, Sutt	194	C11
Mickleham Way, Croy	200	G14
Micklethwaite Rd SW6	126	H12
Middle Dene NW7	54	H6
Middle Fld NW8	109	N1
Middle Grn Cl, Surb	177	T12
Middle La N8	74	J9
Middle La, Tedd	158	E11
Middle La Ms, N8 1	74	J10
Middle Pk Av SE9	152	A11
Middle Path, Har	86	B2
Middle Rd E13	115	N4
Middle Rd SW16	182	G3
Middle Rd, Barn	41	R11
Middle Rd, Har	86	B3
Middle Row W10	108	C8
Middle St EC1	19	T2
Middle St, Croy 6	197	U5
Middle Temple EC4	18	J9
Middle Temple La EC4	19	K8
Middle Way SW16	182	G4
Middle Way, Erith	136	J5
Middle Way, Hayes	102	F7
Middle Way, The, Har	68	E3
Middle Yd SE1	28	G2
Middlefield Gdns, Ilf	81	K12
Middlefielde W13	104	J3
Middleham Gdns N18	60	G11
Middleham Rd N18	60	H11
Middlesborough Rd N18	60	H11
Middlesex Business Cen, Sthl	121	N4
Middlesex Ct W4	125	M8

Middlesex Rd, Mitch	182	J9
Middlesex St E1	21	L4
Middlesex Wf E5	95	M4
Middleton Av E4	61	U6
Middleton Av, Grnf	104	C2
Middleton Av, Sid	172	E11
Middleton Cl E4	61	U6
Middleton Dr SE16	131	P4
Middleton Dr, Pnr	66	B6
Middleton Gdns, Ilf	81	K12
Middleton Gro N7	92	J9
Middleton Ms N7	92	J9
Middleton Rd E8	94	E14
Middleton Rd NW11	72	G13
Middleton Rd, Cars	181	U13
Middleton Rd, Mord	181	M12
Middleton St E2	112	J5
Middleton Way SE13	150	H7
Middleway NW11	73	K10
Midfield Av, Bexh	155	U6
Midfield Par, Bexh	155	U6
Midford Pl, W1 *2*	9	N12
Midholm NW11	72	J8
Midholm, Wem	88	B2
Midholm Cl NW11	72	J7
Midholm Rd, Croy	199	S5
Midhope St WC1	10	C7
Midhurst Av N10	74	A6
Midhurst Av, Croy	183	P13
Midhurst Hill, Bexh	155	N10
Midhurst Rd W13	122	H4
Midland Pl E14	132	E9
Midland Rd E10	78	E14
Midland Rd NW1	10	A5
Midland Ter NW2	90	A6
Midland Ter NW10	107	K7
Midleton Rd, N Mal	178	F4
Midlothian Rd E3	113	T9
Midmoor Rd SW12	164	F1
Midmoor Rd SW19	180	C1
Midship Cl SE16	131	P2
Midstrath Rd NW10	89	K7
Midsummer Av, Houns	139	L8
Midway, Sutt	180	F13
Midwinter Cl, Well	154	B6
Midwood Cl NW2	89	R5
Miers Cl E6	116	H1
Mighell Av, Ilf	80	B9
Milan Rd, Sthl	121	M3
Milborne Gro SW10	30	H8
Milborne St E9	95	M12
Milborough Cres SE12	151	K12
Milcote St SE1	27	P8
Mildenhall Rd E5	95	L7
Mildmay Av N1	94	B11
Mildmay Gro N N1	94	B10
Mildmay Gro S N1	94	B10
Mildmay Pk N1	94	B10
Mildmay Pl N16	94	D10
Mildmay Rd N1	94	C10
Mildmay Rd, Ilf	99	L5
Mildmay Rd, Rom	83	T9
Mildmay St N1	94	B11
Mildred Av, Borwd	38	B7
Mildred Av, Nthlt	85	S10
Mile End, The E1	77	P2
Mile End Pl E1	113	P7
Mile End Rd E1	113	K9
Mile End Rd E3	113	K9
Miles Pl NW1	15	N2
Miles Pl, Surb	177	T8
Miles Rd N8	75	K6
Miles Rd, Mitch	181	R5
Miles St SW8	34	B11
Miles Way N20	57	S4
Milespit Hill NW7	55	T12
Milestone Cl N9	60	G3
Milestone Cl, Sutt	195	N12
Milestone Rd SE19	166	E12
Milfoil St W12	107	N13
Milford Cl SE2	137	K11
Milford Gdns, Croy *1*	185	N9
Milford Gdns, Edg	54	A14
Milford Gdns, Wem	87	P9
Milford Gro, Sutt	195	L7
Milford La WC2	18	H9
Milford Ms SW16	165	M6
Milford Rd W13	122	J2
Milford Rd, Sthl	103	P14
Milk St E16	134	J2
Milk St EC2	20	A7
Milk St, Brom	169	R11
Milk Yd E1	113	L14
Milkwell Gdns, Wdf Grn	63	S13
Milkwell Yd SE5	147	U2
Milkwood Rd SE24	147	S8
Mill Cl, Cars	196	A4
Mill Cor, Barn	40	E2
Mill Ct E10	96	E6
Mill Fm Cl, Pnr	66	E4
Mill Fm Cres, Houns	157	K1
Mill Gdns SE26	167	K6
Mill Grn, Mitch	182	A13
Mill Grn Rd, Mitch	182	A13
Mill Hill SW13	143	P4
Mill Hill Circ NW7	55	L9
Mill Hill Gro, W3 *3*	124	D2
Mill Hill Rd SW13	143	P4
Mill Hill Rd W3	124	C3
Mill La NW6	90	E10
Mill La SE18	134	H10
Mill La, Cars	196	A6
Mill La, Croy	197	M5
Mill La (Chadwell Heath), Rom	82	J12
Mill La, Wdf Grn	63	M10
Mill La Trd Est, Croy	197	M5
Mill Mead Rd N17	76	J6
Mill Pl E14	113	S12
Mill Pl, Chis	188	J1
Mill Pl, Kings T	177	T5
Mill Plat, Islw	140	H4
Mill Plat Av, Islw	140	G4
Mill Ridge, Edg	53	U10
Mill Rd E16	133	S1
Mill Rd SW19	163	M14
Mill Rd, Erith	137	T14
Mill Rd, Ilf	98	H5
Mill Rd, Twick	157	U3
Mill Row N1	112	D2
Mill Shot Cl SW6	144	A1
Mill St SE1	29	P6
Mill St W1	17	L9
Mill St, Kings T	177	S5
Mill Vale, Brom	187	M4
Mill Vw Cl, Epsom	193	M14
Mill Vw Gdns, Croy	199	N5
Mill Way, Felt	138	D10
Mill Yd E1	21	S9
Millais Av E12	98	H10
Millais Gdns, Edg	70	A4
Millais Rd E11	96	G7
Millais Rd, Enf	44	F10
Millais Rd, N Mal	178	J13
Millais Way, Epsom	192	E8
Milland Ct, Borwd	38	G1
Millard Cl N16	94	D9
Millbank SW1	26	B11
Millbank Way SE12	151	N10
Millbourne Rd, Felt	157	K7
Millbrook Av, Well	153	P7
Millbrook Gdns (Chadwell Heath), Rom	83	L11
Millbrook Rd N9	60	J2
Millbrook Rd SW9	147	R6
Millender Wk SE16	131	M8
Millennium Dr E14	132	G7
Millennium Mile SE1	26	E4
Millennium Pl, E2 *17*	113	K4
Millennium Sq SE1	29	N6
Millennium Way SE10	132	J3
Miller Cl, Mitch	181	U14
Miller Cl, Pnr	66	E3
Miller Rd SW19	163	P11
Miller Rd, Croy	197	M1
Miller St NW1	9	L1
Miller Wk SE1	27	L3
Miller's Av E8	94	E9
Millers Cl NW7	55	P7
Millers Ct W4	125	M10
Millers Grn Cl, Enf	43	R6
Miller's Ter E8	94	E9
Millers Way W6	125	U4
Millet Rd, Grnf	103	S5
Millfield Av E17	77	S2
Millfield La N6	91	U4
Millfield Pl N6	92	A4
Millfield Rd, Edg	70	F3
Millfield Rd, Houns	157	K1
Millfields Rd E5	95	L7
Millgrove St SW11	146	A2
Millharbour E14	132	C5
Millhaven Cl, Rom	82	D11
Millhouse Pl, SE27 *3*	165	S8
Millicent Rd E10	95	U1
Milligan St E14	113	U14
Milliners Ct, Loug	48	G3
Milling Rd, Edg	54	H13
Millman Ms WC1	10	E11
Millman St WC1	10	F11
Millmark Gro SE14	149	S4
Millmarsh La, Enf	45	U4
Mills Ct EC2	12	H9
Mills Gro E14	114	E10
Mills Gro NW4	72	A6
Mills Row W4	124	G8
Millside, Cars	195	U3
Millside Pl, Islw	140	J4
Millsmead Way, Loug	48	F3
Millson Cl N20	57	N3
Millstream Cl N13	59	P10
Millstream Rd SE1	29	M8
Millwall Dock Rd E14	132	A5
Millway NW7	55	K10
Millway Gdns, Nthlt	85	L12
Millwell Cres, Chig	65	N9
Millwood Rd, Houns	139	T10
Millwood St, W10 *1*	108	C10
Milman Cl, Pnr	66	G5
Milman Rd NW6	108	C3
Milman's St SW10	31	K12
Milmead Ind Cen N17	76	J4
Milne Feild, Pnr	51	P13
Milne Gdns SE9	152	C9
Milner Dr, Twick	140	A13
Milner Pl N1	111	P1
Milner Rd, Cars *3*	196	A8
Milner Rd E15	114	J6
Milner Rd SW19	180	J1
Milner Rd, Dag	100	E4
Milner Rd, Kings T	177	P6
Milner Rd, Mord	181	N10
Milner Rd, Th Hth	184	A5
Milner Sq N1	93	P14
Milner St SW3	31	T1
Milner Wk SE9	171	P3
Milnthorpe Rd W4	124	G11
Milo Rd SE22	148	E12
Milson Rd W14	126	C5
Milton Av E6	98	C14
Milton Av N6	74	E13
Milton Av NW9	70	E6
Milton Av NW10	106	G2
Milton Av, Barn	40	E9
Milton Av, Croy	184	B14
Milton Av, Sutt	195	R7
Milton Cl N2	73	M11
Milton Cl SE1	37	M4
Milton Cl, Hayes	102	B11
Milton Cl, Sutt	195	P6
Milton Ct EC2	20	C2
Milton Ct Rd SE14	131	S12
Milton Cres, Ilf	81	L12
Milton Dr, Borwd	38	C9
Milton Gro N11	58	F9
Milton Gro N16	94	B8
Milton Pk N6	74	E13
Milton Pl N7	93	M9
Milton Rd E17	78	B7
Milton Rd N6	74	E14
Milton Rd N15	75	R7
Milton Rd NW7	55	N9
Milton Rd NW9 *1*	71	N13
Milton Rd SE24	147	R10
Milton Rd SW14	142	G6
Milton Rd SW19	163	L11
Milton Rd W3	124	G1
Milton Rd W7	104	E14
Milton Rd, Belv	137	N8
Milton Rd, Croy	184	B14
Milton Rd, Hmptn	157	P14
Milton Rd, Har	68	D8
Milton Rd, Mitch	164	B13
Milton Rd, Sutt	194	G6
Milton Rd, Wall	196	F11
Milton Rd, Well	153	T1
Milton St EC2	20	C2
Milverton Gdns, Ilf	99	T3
Milverton Rd NW6	89	U14
Milverton St SE11	35	L8
Milverton Way SE9	170	H7
Milward St E1	113	K10
Mimosa Rd, Hayes	102	F9
Mimosa St SW6	144	F2
Mina Rd SE17	37	K7
Mina Rd SW19	180	H1
Minard Rd SE6	150	J14
Minchenden Cres N14	58	F6
Mincing La EC3	20	H10
Minden Rd SE20	184	J1
Minden Rd, Sutt	194	E3
Minehead Rd SW16	165	L10
Minehead Rd, Har	85	N5
Minera Ms SW1	32	E2
Mineral St SE18	135	R8
Minerva Cl SW9	35	L14
Minerva Cl, Sid	171	R6
Minerva Rd, E4 *3*	62	C13
Minerva Rd NW10	106	F6
Minerva Rd, Kings T	177	T3
Minerva St E2	112	J4
Minet Av NW10	106	J3
Minet Dr, Hayes	120	C3
Minet Gdns NW10	106	J3
Minet Gdns, Hayes	120	B2
Minet Rd SW9	147	S4
Minford Gdns W14	126	A4
Ming St E14	114	B13
Ministry Way SE9	170	E3
Mink Ct, Houns	138	F5
Minniedale, Surb	177	U9
Minories EC3	21	M10
Minshull Pl, Beck	168	B14
Minshull St SW8	146	G2
Minson Rd E9	113	P1
Minstead Gdns SW15	143	L13
Minstead Way, N Mal	178	J12
Minster Av, Sutt *1*	194	G4
Minster Dr, Croy	198	C7
Minster Gdns, W Mol	175	L8
Minster Rd NW2	90	D10
Minster Rd, Brom	169	R13
Minster Wk N8	75	K8
Minstrel Gdns, Surb	177	U8
Mint Rd, Wall	196	C8
Mint St SE1	27	U6
Mint Wk, Croy *9*	197	U5
Mintern Cl N13	59	S6
Mintern St N1	12	E2
Minterne Av, Sthl	121	P7
Minterne Rd, Har	69	U10
Minterne Waye, Hayes	102	F12
Minton Ms, NW6 *2*	91	K11
Mirabel Rd SW6	126	F13
Miranda Cl, E1 *1*	113	L10
Miranda Ct W3	105	U12
Miranda Rd N19	92	F2
Mirfield St, SE7 *2*	134	A6
Miriam Rd SE18	135	R9
Mirravale Trd Est, Dag	83	L14
Mirren Cl, Har	85	L6
Missenden Gdns, Mord	181	M11
Mission Gro E17	77	S9
Mission Pl, SE15 *1*	148	H1
Mission Sq, Brent *3*	123	R11

Mistletoe Cl, Croy 5	199	N1
Mitali Pas E1	21	S7
Mitcham Gdn Village, Mitch	182	A9
Mitcham Ind Est, Mitch	182	B1
Mitcham La SW16	164	E11
Mitcham Pk, Mitch	181	T8
Mitcham Rd E6	116	D5
Mitcham Rd SW17	163	U10
Mitcham Rd, Croy	182	J12
Mitcham Rd, Ilf	81	U13
Mitchell Cl SE2	136	E8
Mitchell Cl, Belv	137	T6
Mitchell Rd N13	59	S9
Mitchell Rd, Orp	203	T7
Mitchell St EC1	11	U9
Mitchell Wk E6	116	E10
Mitchell Way NW10	88	F12
Mitchell Way, Brom 1	187	P2
Mitchellbrook Way NW10	88	G11
Mitchell's Pl, SE21 1	148	C13
Mitchison Rd N1	94	A12
Mitchley Rd N17	76	G5
Mitford Cl, Chess 4	191	M12
Mitford Rd N19	93	K3
Mitre, The E14	113	T13
Mitre Cl, Brom	187	M3
Mitre Cl, Sutt	195	M14
Mitre Ct EC4	19	L8
Mitre Rd E15	115	K3
Mitre Rd SE1	27	M6
Mitre Sq EC3	21	K7
Mitre St EC3	21	K7
Mitre Way W10	107	S9
Moat, The, N Mal	178	J2
Moat Cl, Orp	203	U12
Moat Cres N3	72	J5
Moat Cft, Well	154	E5
Moat Dr E13	115	U4
Moat Dr, Har	67	U8
Moat Fm Rd, Nthlt	85	M12
Moat Pl SW9	147	M5
Moat Pl W3	106	D11
Moatside, Enf	45	N7
Moatside, Felt	156	E8
Moberley Rd SW4	146	H13
Modbury Gdns NW5	91	U12
Modder Pl SW15	144	B7
Model Fm Cl SE9	170	C5
Moelwyn Hughes Ct N7	92	H9
Moelyn Ms, Har	68	G9
Moffat Rd N13	59	K11
Moffat Rd SW17	163	T7
Moffat Rd, Th Hth	184	A4
Mogden La, Islw	140	D10
Mohmmad Khan Rd, E11 2	97	L1
Moira Cl N17	76	C3
Moira Rd SE9	152	F7
Moland Mead SE16	131	N9
Molasses Row, SW11 5	145	M5
Mole Ct, Epsom	192	F8
Molember Ct, E Mol	176	D9
Molember Rd, E Mol	176	C9
Molescroft SE9	171	L5
Molesey Av, W Mol	175	M8
Molesey Dr, Sutt	194	D5
Molesey Pk Av, W Mol	175	S10
Molesey Pk Cl, E Mol	175	U10
Molesey Pk Rd, E Mol	175	U9
Molesey Pk Rd, W Mol	175	S10
Molesey Rd, Walt	175	K13
Molesey Rd, W Mol	175	L10
Molesford Rd, SW6 1	144	G2
Molesham Cl, W Mol	175	R6
Molesham Way, W Mol	175	R6
Molesworth St SE13	150	E7
Molineaux Pl, Tedd	158	H9
Mollison Av, Enf	45	S8
Mollison Dr, Wall	197	K11
Mollison Way, Edg	70	C3
Molly Huggins Cl SW12	146	E14
Molyneux Dr SW17	164	C7
Molyneux St W1	15	S4
Mona Rd SE15	149	M3
Mona St E16	115	M10
Monarch Cl, W Wick	201	M8
Monarch Dr E16	116	A10
Monarch Ms E17	78	C10
Monarch Ms SW16	165	P10
Monarch Pl, Buck H	63	U4
Monarch Rd, Belv	137	P6
Monastery Gdns, Enf	44	A4
Monaveen Gdns, W Mol	175	P6
Monck St SW1	25	T12
Monclar Rd SE5	148	B7
Moncorvo Cl, SW7 2	23	N8
Moncrieff Cl, E6 26	116	C11
Moncrieff Pl, SE15 3	148	G3
Moncrieff St SE15	148	H3
Monega Rd E7	97	T12
Monega Rd E12	98	B11
Monier Rd E3	96	A14
Monivea Rd, Beck	167	U14
Monk Dr E16	115	N12
Monk Pas, E16 2	115	N13
Monk St SE18	134	H7
Monkchester Cl, Loug	48	F2
Monkfrith Av N14	42	C12
Monkfrith Cl N14	42	C13
Monkfrith Way N14	42	B14
Monkhams Av, Wdf Grn	63	P9
Monkhams Dr, Wdf Grn	63	R8
Monkhams La, Wdf Grn	63	S7
Monkleigh Rd, Mord	180	D6
Monks Av, Barn	41	M12
Monks Av, W Mol	175	L10
Monks Cl SE2	136	G7
Monks Cl, Enf	43	T4
Monks Cl, Har	85	R4
Monks Cl, Ruis	84	G7
Monks Dr W3	106	A11
Monks Orchard Rd, Beck	186	B13
Monks Pk, Wem	88	D12
Monks Pk Gdns, Wem	88	D13
Monks Rd, Enf	43	T3
Monks Way NW11	72	E8
Monks Way, Beck	186	B11
Monks Way, Orp	203	M2
Monksdene Gdns, Sutt	195	K5
Monksgrove, Loug	48	H10
Monksmead, Borwd	38	E8
Monkswell Ct, N10 1	74	B1
Monkswood Gdns, Borwd	38	G8
Monkswood Gdns, Ilf	80	G6
Monkton Rd, Well	153	U3
Monkton St SE11	35	M2
Monkville Av NW11	72	E8
Monkwell Sq EC2	20	A3
Monmouth Av E18	79	S7
Monmouth Av, Kings T	159	M14
Monmouth Cl, W4 7	124	G6
Monmouth Cl, Mitch 3	183	K7
Monmouth Cl, Well	154	B7
Monmouth Gro, Brent 1	123	R8
Monmouth Pl W2	14	A7
Monmouth Rd E6	116	E6
Monmouth Rd N9	60	J3
Monmouth Rd W2	108	H12
Monmouth Rd, Dag	101	L10
Monmouth St WC2	18	A8
Monnery Rd N19	92	F5
Monnow Rd SE1	37	S5
Mono La, Felt	156	C3
Monoux Gro E17	78	A1
Monro Gdns, Har	52	C13
Monroe Cres, Enf	44	J2
Monroe Dr SW14	142	D9
Mons Way, Brom	188	D11
Monsell Rd N4	93	R5
Monson Rd NW10	107	P4
Monson Rd SE14	131	N14
Montacute Rd SE6	149	T14
Montacute Rd, Mord	181	N12
Montagu Cres N18	61	K8
Montagu Gdns N18	61	K7
Montagu Gdns, Wall	196	E8
Montagu Mans, W1 2	16	B2
Montagu Ms N W1	16	A3
Montagu Ms S W1	16	A6
Montagu Ms W W1	16	A5
Montagu Pl W1	15	U4
Montagu Rd N9	61	M3
Montagu Rd N18	61	K9
Montagu Rd NW4	71	F11
Montagu Rd Ind Est N18	61	L7
Montagu Row W1	16	B3
Montagu Sq W1	16	A4
Montagu St W1	16	A6
Montague Av SE4	149	U8
Montague Av W7	122	E2
Montague Cl SE1	28	D2
Montague Cl, Walt	174	B14
Montague Gdns W3	106	A13
Montague Pl WC1	17	U2
Montague Rd E8	94	G10
Montague Rd E11	97	L4
Montague Rd N8	75	L9
Montague Rd N15	76	G7
Montague Rd SW19	162	J13
Montague Rd W7	122	E3
Montague Rd W13	105	K11
Montague Rd, Croy	197	S1
Montague Rd, Houns	139	R5
Montague Rd, Rich	141	R11
Montague Rd, Sthl	120	J7
Montague Sq SE15	131	M14
Montague St EC1	19	T4
Montague St WC1	18	B2
Montague Waye, Sthl	120	J6
Montalt Rd, Wdf Grn	63	L9
Montana Gdns, Sutt 3	195	M10
Montana Rd SW17	164	A7
Montana Rd SW20	179	U2
Montbelle Rd SE9	171	K6
Montcalm Cl, Brom	187	P12
Montcalm Cl, Hayes	102	C6
Montcalm Rd SE7	134	A13
Montclare St, E2 4	13	M9
Monteagle Av, Bark	99	M12
Monteagle Way, SE15 5	149	K5
Montefiore St SW8	146	D4
Montego Cl, SE24 11	147	P8
Monteith Rd E3	113	T2
Montem Rd SE23	167	T1
Montem Rd, N Mal	178	J7
Montem St N4	93	L2
Montenotte Rd N8	74	F10
Monterey Cl, Bex	173	U4
Montesole Ct, Pnr	66	F4
Montford Rd SE11	34	J8
Montford Rd, Sun	174	B7
Montfort Gdns, Ilf	65	L12
Montfort Pl SW19	162	B1
Montgomery Av, Esher	190	D4
Montgomery Cl, Mitch	183	K8
Montgomery Cl, Sid	153	S10
Montgomery Rd W4	124	E7
Montgomery Rd, Edg	53	U12
Montholme Rd SW11	145	T11
Monthope Rd, E1 2	21	R3
Montolieu Gdns SW15	143	T9
Montpelier Av W5	105	M10
Montpelier Av, Bex	154	H14
Montpelier Gdns E6	116	B5
Montpelier Gdns, Rom	82	F14
Montpelier Gro NW5	92	F9
Montpelier Ms, SW7 3	23	S9
Montpelier Pl E1	113	L12
Montpelier Pl SW7	23	R9
Montpelier Ri NW11	72	C14
Montpelier Ri, Wem	87	N2
Montpelier Rd N3	73	L2
Montpelier Rd SE15	149	K1
Montpelier Rd W5	105	N9
Montpelier Rd, Sutt	195	M8
Montpelier Row SE3	151	L4
Montpelier Row, Twick	141	L13
Montpelier Sq, SW7 1	23	R8
Montpelier St SW7	23	S8
Montpelier Ter SW7	23	R8
Montpelier Vale SE3	151	L4
Montpelier Wk SW7	23	R8
Montpelier Way NW11	72	C14
Montrave Rd SE20	167	M12
Montreal Pl, WC2 1	18	F9
Montreal Rd, Ilf	81	L14
Montrell Rd SW2	165	K1
Montrose Av NW6	108	D3
Montrose Av, Edg	70	F4
Montrose Av, Sid	154	B14
Montrose Av, Twick	139	S14
Montrose Av, Well	153	R6
Montrose Cl, Well	153	T5
Montrose Cl, Wdf Grn	63	N7
Montrose Ct SW7	23	L8
Montrose Cres N12	57	L12
Montrose Cres, Wem	87	R11
Montrose Gdns, Mitch	181	U5
Montrose Gdns, Sutt	195	K4
Montrose Pl SW1	24	E8
Montrose Rd, Har	68	D4
Montrose Way SE23	167	N2
Montserrat Av, Wdf Grn	62	H14
Montserrat Cl SE19	166	B9
Montserrat Rd SW15	144	C7
Monument Gdns SE13	150	F9
Monument St EC3	20	F11
Monument Way N17	76	F6
Monza St E1	113	L14
Moodkee St SE16	131	M5
Moody Rd SE15	130	E14
Moody St E1	113	P6
Moon La, Barn	40	E6
Moon St N1	111	R1
Moor La EC2	20	C3
Moor La, Chess	192	A11
Moor Mead Rd, Twick	140	H12
Moor Pk Gdns, Kings T	160	J14
Moor Pl, EC2 2	20	D3
Moor St W1	17	T8
Moorcroft Gdns, Brom	188	D10
Moorcroft Rd SW16	164	J5

Moorcroft Way, Pnr	66	J10
Moordown SE18	152	H2
Moore Cl SW14	142	F6
Moore Cl, Mitch	182	C4
Moore Cl, Wall	196	J14
Moore Cres, Dag	118	C1
Moore Pk Rd SW6	126	J14
Moore Rd SE19	165	T11
Moore St SW3	31	U1
Moore Wk E7	97	P8
Moorefield Rd N17	76	E5
Moorehead Way	151	R5
SE3		
Mooreland Rd, Brom	169	M14
Moorey Cl, E15 *7*	115	L2
Moorfield Av W5	105	P7
Moorfield Rd, Chess	191	R9
Moorfield Rd, Enf	45	L2
Moorfields EC2	20	D3
Moorgate EC2	20	D5
Moorgate Pl,	20	D5
EC2 *5*		
Moorhouse Rd W2	108	G11
Moorhouse Rd, Har	69	P5
Moorings SE28	118	D14
Moorland Cl,	139	N13
Twick *3*		
Moorland Rd SW9	147	R7
Moorlands Av NW7	55	S12
Moorlands Est SW9	147	P7
Moormead Dr,	193	K9
Epsom		
Moorside Rd, Brom	169	L7
Moortown Rd, Wat	50	E7
Moot Ct NW9	70	A10
Mora Rd NW2	89	U7
Mora St EC1	12	A7
Morant Pl N22	75	L1
Morant St E14	114	B13
Morat St SW9	147	M1
Moravian Pl SW10	31	L12
Moravian St E2	113	M4
Moray Cl, Edg	54	D4
Moray Ms N7	93	M3
Moray Rd N4	93	L3
Mordaunt Gdns, Dag	100	J13
Mordaunt Rd NW10	106	H2
Mordaunt St SW9	147	L5
Morden Cl SE13	150	E3
Morden Ct, Mord	180	J8
Morden Gdns, Grnf	86	F9
Morden Gdns, Mitch	181	P8
Morden Hall Rd,	181	K6
Mord		
Morden Hill SE13	150	E3
Morden La SE13	150	F2
Morden Rd SE3	151	P3
Morden Rd SW19	181	K1
Morden Rd, Mitch	181	N7
Morden Rd, Rom	83	K13
Morden Rd Ms SE3	151	N3
Morden St SE13	150	D2
Morden Way, Sutt	180	G14
Morden Wf Rd SE10	132	J6
Mordon Rd, Ilf	81	T13
Mordred Rd SE6	168	J4
More Cl E16	115	L11
More Cl W14	126	B8
Morecambe Cl,	113	N9
E1 *4*		
Morecambe Gdns,	53	P8
Stan		
Morecambe St SE17	36	B4
Morecambe Ter N18	60	A7
Morecoombe Cl,	160	D13
KingsT		
Moree Way N18	60	G8
Moreland St EC1	11	R6
Moreland Way E4	62	D5
Morell Cl, Barn	41	L6
Morella Rd SW12	145	T13
Moremead Rd SE6	167	U7
Morena St SE6	150	C13
Moresby Av, Surb	178	D13
Moresby Rd E5	94	J2
Moresby Wk SW8	146	D4
Moreton Av, Islw	140	C1
Moreton Cl E5	95	K3
Moreton Cl N15	76	B11
Moreton Cl NW7	55	T12
Moreton Gdns,	64	D10
Wdf Grn		
Moreton Pl SW1	33	N5
Moreton Rd N15	76	B11
Moreton Rd, S Croy	198	B10
Moreton Rd, Wor Pk	193	P4
Moreton St SW1	33	R5
Moreton Ter SW1	33	P6
Moreton Ter Ms N,	33	N6
SW1 *1*		
Moreton Ter Ms S,	33	N6
SW1 *2*		
Morford Cl, Ruis	66	D13
Morford Way, Ruis	66	D14
Morgan Av E17	78	H8
Morgan Cl, Dag	101	N14
Morgan Rd N7	93	N10
Morgan Rd,	108	E9
W10 *9*		
Morgan Rd, Brom	169	N14
Morgan St E3	113	S6
Morgan St E16	115	M9
Morgan Way,	64	D12
Wdf Grn		
Morgans La SE1	28	H3
Moriatry Cl N7	92	J7
Morie St SW18	145	K9
Morieux Rd E10	95	T1
Moring Rd SW17	164	B8
Morkyns Wk SE21	166	C5
Morland Av, Croy	198	D1
Morland Cl NW11	91	K1
Morland Cl, Hmptn	157	L10
Morland Cl, Mitch	181	S6
Morland Gdns	88	G14
NW10		
Morland Gdns, Sthl	121	S2
Morland Ms N1	93	N14
Morland Rd E17	77	P10
Morland Rd SE20	167	P12
Morland Rd, Croy	184	G13
Morland Rd, Dag	101	P14
Morland Rd, Har	69	R9
Morland Rd, Ilf	98	J3
Morland Rd, Sutt	195	M10
Morley Av E4	62	G14
Morley Av N18	60	H8
Morley Av N22	75	N3
Morley Cl, Orp	203	K3
Morley Cres, Edg	54	E4
Morley Cres, Ruis	84	F3
Morley Cres E, Stan	69	M4
Morley Cres W, Stan	69	M5
Morley Rd E10	96	F2
Morley Rd E15	115	L3
Morley Rd SE13	150	F8
Morley Rd, Bark	117	N2
Morley Rd, Chis	189	L1
Morley Rd, Rom	82	J10
Morley Rd, Sutt	194	E2
Morley Rd, Twick	141	N12
Morley St SE1	27	L8
Morna Rd SE5	147	U3
Morning La E9	95	L11
Morningside Rd,	193	S4
Wor Pk		
Mornington Av W14	126	E8
Mornington Av,	187	U6
Brom		
Mornington Av, Ilf	80	G13
Mornington Cl,	63	N8
Wdf Grn		
Mornington Cres	9	L3
NW1		
Mornington Cres,	138	D1
Houns		
Mornington Gro E3	114	A6
Mornington Ms,	147	T1
SE5 *1*		
Mornington Pl NW1	9	K2
Mornington Rd E4	46	G14
Mornington Rd E11	97	L1
Mornington Rd SE8	131	U14
Mornington Rd,	103	R8
Grnf		
Mornington Rd,	49	L6
Loug		
Mornington Rd,	63	M7
Wdf Grn		
Mornington St NW1	9	K1
Mornington Ter	8	J1
NW1		
Mornington Wk,	159	N7
Rich		
Morocco St SE1	28	H8
Morpeth Gro E9	113	N1
Morpeth Rd E9	113	M2
Morpeth St E2	113	N5
Morpeth Ter SW1	25	M12
Morrab Gdns, Ilf	99	T5
Morris Av E12	98	E10
Morris Cl, Croy	185	R11
Morris Cl, Orp	203	R5
Morris Gdns SW18	144	G13
Morris Pl N4	93	N3
Morris Rd E14	114	C9
Morris Rd E15	96	J8
Morris Rd, Dag	101	M4
Morris Rd, Islw	140	E6
Morris St E1	113	K12
Morrish Rd SW2	147	K14
Morrison Av N17	76	C6
Morrison Rd, Bark	118	J3
Morrison Rd, Hayes	102	C6
Morrison St SW11	146	A5
Morriston Cl,	50	E10
Wat *2*		
Morse Cl E13	115	N6
Morshead Rd W9	108	H6
Morson Rd, Enf	45	R12
Morston Gdns SE9	170	E8
Morten Cl SW4	146	H1
Morteyne Rd N17	76	B1
Mortham St E15	114	J2
Mortimer Cl NW2	90	F4
Mortimer Cl SW16	164	G3
Mortimer Cres NW6	108	J2
Mortimer Cres,	192	G6
Wor Pk		
Mortimer Dr, Enf	44	C10
Mortimer Est NW6	108	J2
Mortimer Mkt WC1	9	P12
Mortimer Pl NW6	108	J2
Mortimer Rd E6	116	E6
Mortimer Rd N1	94	C14
Mortimer Rd NW10	107	U5
Mortimer Rd W13	105	L11
Mortimer Rd, Mitch	181	T2
Mortimer Sq,	108	B14
W11 *3*		
Mortimer Ter,	92	C7
NW5 *1*		
Mortlake Cl, Croy	197	K6
Mortlake Dr, Mitch	181	R2
Mortlake High St	142	H5
SW14		
Mortlake Rd E16	115	S11
Mortlake Rd, Ilf	99	L8
Mortlake Rd, Rich	142	B1
Morton Cres N14	58	G7
Morton Gdns, Wall	196	E9
Morton Ms SW5	30	B3
Morton Pl SE1	26	J11
Morton Rd E15	97	L14
Morton Rd N1	93	U14.
Morton Rd, Mord	181	P10
Morton Way N14	58	E6
Morval Rd SW2	147	N10
Morvale Cl, Belv	137	M8
Morven Rd SW17	163	T6
Morville St E3	114	A3
Morwell St WC1	17	S3
Moscow Pl W2	14	B10
Moscow Rd W2	14	A10
Moselle Av N22	75	N3
Moselle Cl N8	75	L6
Moselle Pl, N17 *3*	60	F13
Moselle St N17	60	F13
Moss Cl E1	21	T2
Moss Cl, Pnr	67	L4
Moss Gdns, Felt *2*	156	A4
Moss Gdns, S Croy	199	P14
Moss Hall Cres N12	56	K12
Moss Hall Gro N12	56	J11
Moss La, Pnr	67	L6
Moss Rd, Dag	101	P13
Mossborough Cl	57	K11
N12		
Mossbury Rd SW11	145	S6
Mossdown Cl, Belv	137	P8
Mossford Ct, Ilf	81	K5
Mossford Grn, Ilf	81	L5
Mossford La, Ilf	81	K3
Mossford St E3	113	T7
Mosslea Rd SE20	167	L12
Mosslea Rd, Brom	188	B10
Mosslea Rd, Orp	203	L5
Mossop St SW3	31	S2
Mossville Gdns,	180	E7
Mord		
Mostyn Av, Wem	87	T9
Mostyn Gdns NW10	108	A5
Mostyn Gro E3	114	A4
Mostyn Rd SW9	147	P2
Mostyn Rd SW19	180	F2
Mostyn Rd, Edg	54	J14
Mosul Way, Brom	188	D12
Motcomb St SW1	24	C9
Mothers' Sq E5	95	K8
Motley St SW8	146	E3
Motspur Pk, N Mal	179	P11
Mott St, Loug	47	K2
Mottingham Gdns	170	B2
SE9		
Mottingham La SE9	169	T1
Mottingham La	169	T1
SE12		
Mottingham Rd N9	45	N12
Mottingham Rd SE9	170	C3
Mottisfont Rd SE2	136	A6
Moulins Rd E9	113	L1
Moulton Av, Houns	139	K3
Mound, The SE9	170	G6
Moundfield Rd N16	76	G12
Mount, The N20	57	M4
Mount, The NW3	91	M7
Mount, The N Mal	179	M6
Mount, The, Wem	88	D4
Mount, The, Wor Pk	193	S8
Mount Adon Pk	148	G14
SE22		
Mount Angelus Rd	143	M13
SW15		
Mount Ararat Rd,	141	S10
Rich		
Mount Ash Rd SE26	166	J5
Mount Av E4	62	B6
Mount Av W5	105	P9
Mount Av, Sthl	103	N12
Mount Cl W5	105	M10
Mount Cl, Barn	42	A8
Mount Cl, Brom	188	C1
Mount Cor, Felt	156	H4
Mount Ct, SW15 *3*	144	C6
Mount Ct, W Wick	200	J3
Mount Culver Av,	172	H11
Sid		
Mount Dr, Bexh	154	J10
Mount Dr, Har	67	M9
Mount Dr, Wem	88	E3
Mount Echo Av E4	62	D2
Mount Echo Dr E4	62	C2
Mount Ephraim La	164	H6
SW16		
Mount Ephraim Rd	164	H5
SW16		
Mount Gdns SE26	166	J5
Mount Gro, Edg	54	F6
Mount Ms, Hmptn	175	S2
Mount Mills EC1	11	S8
Mount Nod Rd	165	L5
SW16		
Mount Pk Av, Har	86	B4
Mount Pk Cres W5	105	N12
Mount Pk Rd W5	105	N10
Mount Pk Rd, Har	86	A5
Mount Pk Rd, Pnr	66	B10
Mount Pl, W3 *1*	124	D2
Mount Pleasant	165	U7
SE27		
Mount Pleasant	10	H12
WC1		
Mount Pleasant,	41	U8
Barn		
Mount Pleasant,	84	G5
Ruis		
Mount Pleasant,	105	R1
Wem		

Name	Page	Grid
Mount Pleasant Cres N4	75	L14
Mount Pleasant Hill E5	95	L3
Mount Pleasant La E5	95	K3
Mount Pleasant Rd E17	77	S3
Mount Pleasant Rd N17	76	C2
Mount Pleasant Rd NW10	89	U14
Mount Pleasant Rd SE13	150	E11
Mount Pleasant Rd W5	105	M8
Mount Pleasant Rd, Chig	65	N8
Mount Pleasant Rd, N Mal	178	F5
Mount Pleasant Vil N4	75	L13
Mount Pleasant Wk, Bex	155	U10
Mount Rd, NW2 *1*	89	T5
Mount Rd NW4	71	P12
Mount Rd, SE19 *4*	166	B12
Mount Rd SW19	162	H3
Mount Rd, Barn	41	R9
Mount Rd, Bexh	154	J10
Mount Rd, Chess	191	U8
Mount Rd, Dag	101	M1
Mount Rd, Felt	156	J5
Mount Rd, Hayes	120	A3
Mount Rd, Ilf	98	J10
Mount Rd, Mitch	181	R3
Mount Rd, N Mal	178	G5
Mount Row W1	16	G11
Mount Sq, The, NW3 *3*	91	M6
Mount Stewart Av, Har	69	N13
Mount St W1	16	F12
Mount Ter E1	112	J10
Mount Vernon NW3	91	L7
Mount Vw NW7	54	H6
Mount Vw W5	105	P8
Mount Vw Rd E4	46	F14
Mount Vw Rd N4	75	K13
Mount Vw Rd NW9	70	H9
Mount Vil SE27	165	R6
Mountacre Cl SE26	166	G7
Mountague Pl, E14 *4*	18	E13
Mountbatten Cl SE18	135	R12
Mountbatten Cl SE19	166	C10
Mountbatten Ct, Buck H	64	B4
Mountbatten Gdns, Beck	185	S8
Mountbatten Ms, SW18 *1*	163	L1
Mountbel Rd, Stan	68	G2
Mountcombe Cl, Surb	177	R13
Mountearl Gdns SW16	165	L5
Mountfield Cl SE6	150	G13
Mountfield Rd E6	116	G4
Mountfield Rd N3	72	F5
Mountfield Rd W5	105	P12
Mountford St E1	21	R5
Mountfort Cres N1	93	N13
Mountfort Ter N1	93	N14
Mountgrove Rd N5	93	S5
Mounthurst Rd, Brom	187	M14
Mountington Pk Cl, Har	69	N11
Mountjoy Cl SE2	136	D3
Mounts Pond Rd SE3	150	G3
Mountsfield Ct SE13	150	G11
Mountside, Stan	68	G1
Mountview Ct, N8 *3*	75	R8
Mountview Rd, Esher	190	J12
Mountwood, W Mol	175	R5
Movers La, Bark	117	P1
Mowatt Cl N19	92	H2
Mowbray Rd NW6	90	D13
Mowbray Rd SE19	184	F1
Mowbray Rd, Barn	41	L8
Mowbray Rd, Edg	54	B8
Mowbray Rd, Rich	159	L6
Mowbrays Cl, Rom	83	U2
Mowbrays Rd, Rom	83	U3
Mowbrey Gdns, Loug	49	M2
Mowlem St E2	113	K3
Mowlem Trd Est N17	61	M13
Mowll St SW9	129	N14
Moxon Cl E13	115	M4
Moxon St W1	16	D3
Moxon St, Barn	40	E6
Moye Cl E2	13	T1
Moyers Rd E10	96	F1
Moylan Rd W6	126	D12
Moyne Pl NW10	106	B4
Moynihan Dr N21	43	K10
Moys Cl, Croy	182	J11
Moyser Rd SW16	164	D10
Mozart St W10	108	E6
Mozart Ter SW1	32	E4
Muchelney Rd, Mord	181	M12
Mud La W5	105	P9
Muggeridge Cl, S Croy	198	B10
Muggeridge Rd, Dag	101	R7
Muir Dr SW18	145	R11
Muir Rd E5	94	H7
Muir St E16	134	E2
Muirdown Av SW14	142	G7
Muirfield W3	107	K12
Muirfield Cl, SE16 *5*	131	K10
Muirfield Cl, Wat	50	G8
Muirfield Cres E14	132	C5
Muirfield Grn, Wat	50	E8
Muirfield Rd, Wat	50	F8
Muirkirk Rd SE6	168	F2
Mulberry Cl E4	62	B3
Mulberry Cl N8	74	J9
Mulberry Cl, NW3 *11*	91	N8
Mulberry Cl NW4	71	T6
Mulberry Cl SE7	134	A11
Mulberry Cl SE22	148	G10
Mulberry Cl SW16	164	E8
Mulberry Cl, Barn	41	P8
Mulberry Cl, Nthlt *1*	102	J3
Mulberry Ct, Bark	99	U12
Mulberry Cres, Brent	123	L13
Mulberry La, Croy	198	F3
Mulberry Ms, Wall *1*	196	E11
Mulberry Pl, W6 *7*	125	N10
Mulberry Rd E8	94	E13
Mulberry St E1	21	S5
Mulberry Way E18	79	R4
Mulberry Way, Belv	137	U3
Mulberry Way, Ilf	81	L7
Mulgrave Rd NW10	89	M8
Mulgrave Rd SW6	126	E11
Mulgrave Rd W5	105	P7
Mulgrave Rd, Croy	198	A6
Mulgrave Rd, Har	86	G4
Mulgrave Rd, Sutt	195	K12
Mulholland Cl, Mitch	182	D3
Mulkern Rd N19	92	H1
Mullards Cl, Mitch	195	U1
Muller Rd SW4	146	H12
Mullet Gdns, E2 *4*	13	T5
Mullins Path SW14	142	G5
Mullion Cl, Har	67	R1
Mullion Wk, Wat	50	H8
Mulready St NW8	7	N12
Multon Rd SW18	145	P14
Mulvaney Way SE1	28	F7
Mumford Ct EC2	20	B6
Mumford Rd SE24	147	R10
Muncaster Rd SW11	145	U9
Muncies Ms SE6	168	F3
Mund St W14	126	F10
Mundania Rd SE22	149	L10
Munday Rd E16	115	N13
Munden St W14	126	C7
Mundesley Cl, Wat	50	E7
Mundford Rd E5	95	L3
Mundon Gdns, Ilf	99	N1
Mundy St N1	12	H6
Mungo Pk Cl, Bushey	51	U3
Munnery Way, Orp	202	H4
Munnings Gdns, Islw	140	A10
Munro Dr N11	58	F12
Munro Ms W10	108	D9
Munro Ter SW10	31	K12
Munslow Gdns, Sutt *1*	195	N7
Munster Av, Houns	139	K9
Munster Ct, Tedd	159	M12
Munster Gdns N13	59	T7
Munster Rd SW6	144	E2
Munster Rd, Tedd	159	L12
Munster Sq NW1	9	K8
Munton Rd SE17	36	B1
Murchison Av, Bex	172	H1
Murchison Rd E10	96	E4
Murdock Cl E16	115	M11
Murdock St, SE15 *2*	130	J12
Murfett Cl SW19	162	C4
Muriel St N1	10	G1
Murillo Rd SE13	150	H8
Murphy St SE1	27	K8
Murray Av, Brom	187	S3
Murray Av, Houns	139	S10
Murray Cres, Pnr	66	H1
Murray Gro N1	12	C4
Murray Ms NW1	92	G13
Murray Rd SW19	162	B11
Murray Rd W5	123	M8
Murray Rd, Rich	159	K4
Murray Sq E16	115	P12
Murray St NW1	92	G13
Murray Ter, NW3 *7*	91	M7
Mursell Est SW8	147	L1
Murtwell Dr, Chig	65	L11
Musard Rd W6	126	D11
Musard Rd W14	126	D11
Musbury St E1	113	L11
Muscatel Pl SE5	130	D14
Muschamp Rd SE15	148	F6
Muschamp Rd, Cars	195	R4
Muscovy St EC3	21	K11
Museum La SW7	23	L11
Museum Pas E2	113	K5
Museum St WC1	18	B5
Musgrave Cl, Barn	41	M1
Musgrave Cres SW6	126	H14
Musgrave Rd, Islw	140	E1
Musgrove Rd SE14	149	P2
Musjid Rd, SW11 *3*	145	P4
Musquash Way, Houns *1*	138	E4
Muston Rd E5	94	J3
Mustow Pl, SW6 *5*	144	F3
Muswell Av N10	74	C3
Muswell Hill N10	74	D6
Muswell Hill Bdy N10	74	C7
Muswell Hill Pl N10	74	D7
Muswell Hill Rd N6	74	B11
Muswell Hill Rd N10	74	B8
Muswell Ms N10	74	C5
Muswell Rd N10	74	D4
Mutrix Rd NW6	108	H1
Mutton Pl NW1	92	B12
Muybridge Rd, N Mal	178	E4
Myatt Rd SW9	147	R1
Myatt's Flds S SW9	147	P1
Mycenae Rd SE3	133	N13
Myddelton Cl, Enf	43	S13
Myddelton Gdns N21	43	S13
Myddelton Pk N20	57	P4
Myddelton Pas EC1	11	L6
Myddelton Rd N8	75	K6
Myddelton Sq EC1	11	K5
Myddelton St EC1	11	L8
Myddleton Av N4	93	T3
Myddleton Ms N22	59	K13
Myddleton Rd N22	59	L13
Myers La SE14	131	N11
Mylis Cl SE26	167	K7
Mylius Cl, SE14 *1*	149	M1
Mylne St EC1	11	K4
Myra St SE2	136	A8
Myrdle St E1	21	U4
Myrna Cl SW19	163	S13
Myron Pl SE13	150	F6
Myrtle Av, Ruis	66	B14
Myrtle Cl, Barn	57	U2
Myrtle Gdns W7	122	C2
Myrtle Gro, N Mal	178	F4
Myrtle Rd, E6 *8*	116	D2
Myrtle Rd E17	77	S12
Myrtle Rd N13	59	U6
Myrtle Rd W3	124	F1
Myrtle Rd, Croy	200	B5
Myrtle Rd, Hmptn	157	T12
Myrtle Rd, Houns	139	T4
Myrtle Rd, Ilf	99	K4
Myrtle Rd, Sutt	195	M9
Myrtle Wk N1	12	H4
Myrtledene Rd SE2	136	A9
Mysore Rd SW11	145	U7
Myton Rd SE21	166	A5

N

Name	Page	Grid
Nadine St SE7	133	T10
Nafferton Rd, Loug	48	A10
Nagle Cl E17	78	G4
Nag's Head Ct EC1	11	U11
Nags Head La, Well	154	C5
Nags Head Rd, Enf	45	M8
Nairn Grn, Wat	50	A5
Nairn Rd, Ruis	84	E11
Nairn St E14	114	F10
Nairne Gro SE24	148	B9
Naish Ct N1	111	K1
Nallhead Rd, Felt	156	F9
Namba Roy Cl SW16	165	M8
Namton Dr, Th Hth	183	L7
Nan Clark's La NW7	55	L3
Nankin St E14	114	B12
Nansen Rd SW11	146	A7
Nant Rd NW2	90	F3
Nant St, E2 *3*	113	K5
Nantes Cl SW18	145	M8
Nantes Pas E1	21	L1
Naoroji St WC1	11	K7
Napier Av E14	132	B9
Napier Av SW6	144	E5
Napier Cl SE8	131	U13
Napier Cl W14	126	D5
Napier Gro N1	12	B3
Napier Pl W14	126	E6
Napier Rd E6	116	G2
Napier Rd E11	96	J6
Napier Rd E15	115	K3
Napier Rd N17	76	D5
Napier Rd NW10	107	R5
Napier Rd, SE25 *6*	184	J8
Napier Rd W14	126	D6
Napier Rd, Belv	137	M8
Napier Rd, Brom	187	S7
Napier Rd, Enf	45	P10
Napier Rd, Islw	140	G8
Napier Rd, S Croy	198	A13
Napier Rd, Wem	87	P10
Napier Ter N1	93	R14
Napoleon Rd E5	94	J6
Napoleon Rd, Twick	141	K13
Napton Cl, Hayes	102	J7
Narbonne Av SW4	146	E10
Narborough St, SW6 *9*	144	J4
Narcissus Rd NW6	90	G10
Naresby Fold, Stan	53	L11
Narford Rd E5	94	H4
Narrow St E14	113	R13
Narrow Way, Brom	188	D12
Nascot St W12	107	T11

Naseby Cl NW6	91	M13
Naseby Cl, Islw	140	D2
Naseby Rd SE19	166	B11
Naseby Rd, Dag	101	P6
Naseby Rd, Ilf	80	E2
Nash Cl, Sutt	195	N5
Nash Grn, Brom	169	P12
Nash La, Kes	201	R9
Nash Pl E14	132	C2
Nash Rd N9	61	L3
Nash Rd SE4	149	R9
Nash Rd, Rom	82	G7
Nash St NW1	8	J7
Nash Way, Har	69	K11
Nasmyth St W6	125	R6
Nassau Rd SW13	143	M2
Nassau St N1	17	M3
Nassington Rd NW3	91	S7
Natal Rd N11	58	J11
Natal Rd SW16	164	H11
Natal Rd, Ilf	98	J8
Natal Rd, Th Hth	184	A6
Natalie Ms, Twick	158	A6
Nathan Way SE28	135	R7
Nathaniel Cl E1	21	N4
Nathans Rd, Wem	87	M3
Nation Way E4	62	F1
Naval Row E14	114	F13
Navarino Gro E8	94	H11
Navarino Rd E8	94	H12
Navarre Rd E6	116	D3
Navarre St E2	13	L9
Navestock Cl E4	62	F6
Navestock Cres, Wdf Grn	79	T1
Navigator Dr, Sthl	121	U3
Navy St SW4	146	G5
Naylor Gro, Enf *1*	45	N10
Naylor Rd N20	57	L4
Naylor Rd SE15	130	J13
Nazareth Gdns SE15	148	J3
Nazrul St E2	13	L5
Neagle Cl, Borwd	38	E2
Neal Av, Sthl	103	M7
Neal Cl, Nthwd	66	A1
Neal St WC2	18	B8
Nealden St SW9	147	L5
Neale Cl N2	73	L6
Neal's Yd WC2	18	A7
Near Acre NW9	71	L2
Neasden Cl NW10	89	K9
Neasden La NW10	89	K9
Neasden La N NW10	88	H6
Neasham Rd, Dag	100	C10
Neate St SE5	37	M10
Neath Gdns, Mord	181	L12
Neathouse Pl, SW1 *1*	33	L1
Neatscourt Rd E6	116	B10
Nebraska St SE1	28	B8
Neckinger SE16	29	N10
Neckinger Est SE16	29	P10
Neckinger St, SE1 *3*	29	P8
Nectarine Way SE13	150	D3
Needham Rd, W11 *8*	108	G12
Needham Ter NW2	90	A6
Needleman St SE16	131	N4
Neeld Cres NW4	71	R10
Neeld Cres, Wem	88	A10
Neil Wates Cres SW2	165	P2
Nelgarde Rd SE6	150	B14
Nella Rd W6	126	A12
Nelldale Rd, SE16 *2*	131	L7
Nello James Gdns SE27	166	B7
Nelson Cl, Croy	197	S2
Nelson Cl, Rom	83	R2
Nelson Gdns E2	13	U5
Nelson Gdns, Houns	139	N11
Nelson Gro Rd SW19	181	L1
Nelson Mandela Cl N10	74	A3
Nelson Mandela Rd SE3	151	T6
Nelson Pas, EC1 *2*	12	A6

Nelson Pl N1	11	R4
Nelson Pl, Sid	172	A8
Nelson Rd E4	62	C12
Nelson Rd E11	79	P8
Nelson Rd N8	75	L11
Nelson Rd N9	61	K4
Nelson Rd N15	76	D7
Nelson Rd SE10	132	F12
Nelson Rd SW19	163	K13
Nelson Rd, Belv	137	M9
Nelson Rd, Brom	187	U8
Nelson Rd, Enf	45	N11
Nelson Rd, Har	86	B1
Nelson Rd, Houns	139	T13
Nelson Rd, N Mal	178	H10
Nelson Rd, Sid	172	B8
Nelson Rd, Stan	53	L11
Nelson Rd, Twick	139	U12
Nelson Sq SE1	27	P5
Nelson St E1	112	J11
Nelson St E6	116	F3
Nelson St E16	115	M13
Nelson Ter N1	11	R4
Nelson Trd Est SW19	180	J1
Nelson's Row SW4	146	G7
Nelsons Yd, NW1 *2*	9	L2
Nemoure Rd W3	100	E14
Nene Gdns, Felt	157	L5
Nepaul Rd, SW11 *1*	145	R5
Nepean St SW15	143	P12
Neptune Rd, Har	68	A12
Neptune St SE16	131	L5
Nesbit Rd SE9	152	B7
Nesbitt Cl SE3	150	J4
Nesbitt Sq, SE19 *8*	166	D13
Nesbitts All, Barn	40	E5
Nesham St E1	29	S1
Ness St SE16	29	S10
Nesta Rd, Wdf Grn	63	L11
Nestor Av N21	43	S11
Nether Cl N3	56	G13
Nether St N3	72	G1
Nether St N12	56	G14
Netheravon Rd W4	125	M8
Netheravon Rd W7	122	F1
Netheravon Rd S W4	125	L10
Netherbury Rd W5	123	N6
Netherby Gdns, Enf	42	J8
Netherby Rd SE23	149	L13
Nethercourt Av N3	56	H11
Netherfield Gdns, Bark	99	P12
Netherfield Rd N12	57	K10
Netherfield Rd, SW17 *2*	164	A6
Netherford Rd SW4	146	F4
Netherhall Gdns NW3	91	M11
Netherhall Way, NW3 *14*	91	M10
Netherlands Rd, Barn	41	N12
Netherleigh Cl N6	92	D2
Netherton Gro SW10	30	G11
Netherton Rd, N15 *4*	76	B12
Netherton Rd, Twick	140	H10
Netherwood, N2 *4*	73	P4
Netherwood Pl, W14 *5*	126	A5
Netherwood Rd W14	126	A5
Netherwood St NW6	90	F12
Netley Cl, Croy	200	F13
Netley Cl, Sutt	194	B9
Netley Dr, Walt	175	L14
Netley Gdns, Mord	181	L13
Netley Rd E17	77	U9
Netley Rd, Brent	123	R11
Netley Rd, Ilf	81	N9
Netley Rd, Mord	181	M13
Netley St NW1	9	L8
Nettleden Av, Wem	88	A11
Nettlefold Pl SE27	165	S6
Nettlestead Cl, Beck *1*	167	U14

Nettleton Rd SE14	149	P1
Nettlewood Rd SW16	164	H14
Neuchatel Rd SE6	167	T4
Nevada Cl, N Mal *2*	178	E7
Nevada St SE10	132	F13
Nevern Pl SW5	126	H8
Nevern Rd SW5	126	G8
Nevern Sq SW5	126	H8
Nevill Rd N16	94	D5
Nevill Way, Loug	48	D12
Neville Av, N Mal	178	H1
Neville Cl E11	97	M5
Neville Cl NW1	9	U3
Neville Cl NW6	108	F4
Neville Cl SE15	130	G14
Neville Cl W3	124	F3
Neville Cl, Houns	139	R3
Neville Cl, Sid	171	U7
Neville Dr N2	73	M12
Neville Gdns, Dag	100	G5
Neville Gill Cl SW18	144	H11
Neville Pl N22	75	L1
Neville Rd E7	97	R14
Neville Rd NW6	108	F4
Neville Rd W5	105	N7
Neville Rd, Croy	184	B13
Neville Rd, Dag	100	G4
Neville Rd, Ilf	81	M1
Neville Rd, Kings T	178	B3
Neville Rd, Rich	159	L5
Neville St SW7	31	K5
Neville Ter SW7	31	K5
Neville Wk, Cars *1*	181	R14
Nevilles Ct NW2	89	P6
Nevin Dr E4	62	D2
Nevinson Cl SW18	145	P11
Nevis Rd SW17	164	A3
New Ash Cl N2	73	P6
New Barn St E13	115	R8
New Barns Av, Mitch	182	G8
New Barns Way, Chig	64	J6
New Bond St W1	17	L11
New Brent St NW4	71	T9
New Br St EC4	19	N10
New Broad St EC2	20	G4
New Bdy W5	105	N14
New Burlington Ms, W1 *3*	17	M10
New Burlington Pl W1	17	L9
New Burlington St W1	17	L10
New Butt La, SE8 *13*	132	B14
New Butt La N, SE8 *12*	132	A14
New Cavendish St W1	16	J3
New Change EC4	19	U7
New Chapel Sq, Felt	156	C2
New Charles St EC1	11	R5
New Ch Rd SE5	36	B14
New City Rd E13	115	U5
New Cl SW19	181	M5
New Cl, Felt	156	J9
New College Ms N1	93	P13
New Compton St WC2	17	U7
New Ct, EC4 *2*	18	J9
New Coventry St W1	17	T11
New Crane Pl E1	131	L1
New Cross Rd SE14	131	M14
New End NW3	91	M6
New End Sq NW3	91	N7
New Fm Av, Brom	187	N7
New Ferry App SE18	134	G5
New Fetter La EC4	19	L6
New Forest La, Chig	64	H11
New Globe Wk SE1	27	U1
New Goulston St, E1 *3*	21	M5
New Grn Pl, SE19 *1*	166	C11

New Heston Rd, Houns	121	L13
New Inn Bdy, EC2 *7*	12	J9
New Inn Pas, WC2 *3*	18	G8
New Inn St, EC2 *6*	12	J9
New Inn Yd EC2	12	J10
New Kent Rd SE1	36	C1
New King St SE8	132	A11
New Kings Rd SW6	144	H2
New London St, EC3 *5*	20	J9
New Lydenburg St SE7	133	U6
New Mt St, E15 *3*	96	H14
New N Pl EC2	12	H11
New N Rd N1	12	E4
New N Rd, Ilf	65	R12
New N St WC1	18	E1
New Oak Rd N2	73	M4
New Orleans Wk N19	74	H14
New Oxford St WC1	17	T5
New Pk Av N13	60	A6
New Pk Cl, Nthlt	84	J12
New Pk Ct SW2	147	K14
New Pk Rd SW2	147	K14
New Pl Sq SE16	130	J5
New Plaistow Rd E15	115	K1
New Quebec St W1	16	B7
New Ride SW7	24	A6
New River Cres N13	59	R6
New River Wk N1	93	U12
New River Way N4	76	B13
New Rd E1	112	J10
New Rd E4	62	C7
New Rd N8	74	J10
New Rd N9	60	H4
New Rd N17	76	E1
New Rd N22	75	T1
New Rd NW7	56	C14
New Rd (Barnet Gate) NW7	39	M13
New Rd SE2	136	G8
New Rd, Brent	123	P11
New Rd, Dag	119	P3
New Rd (East Bedfont), Felt	156	C1
New Rd (Hanworth), Felt	156	J9
New Rd, Har	86	E7
New Rd, Houns	139	R8
New Rd, Ilf	99	S3
New Rd, Kings T	160	A13
New Rd, Mitch	196	A1
New Rd, Rich	159	M7
New Rd, W Mol	175	P7
New Row WC2	18	A10
New Spring Gdns Wk, SE11 *1*	34	D7
New Sq WC2	18	H6
New St EC2	20	J4
New St Hill, Brom	169	S10
New St Sq EC4	19	M6
New Trinity Rd N2	73	N4
New Union Cl E14	132	F5
New Union St EC2	20	C3
New Wanstead E11	79	N11
New Way Rd NW9	71	K8
New Wf Rd N1	10	D1
New Zealand Way W12	107	R14
Newark Cres NW10	106	G6
Newark Grn, Borwd	38	H6
Newark Knok E6	116	H10
Newark Rd, S Croy	198	A12
Newark St E1	112	J10
Newark Way NW4	71	P7
Newbiggin Path, Wat *1*	50	E7
Newbolt Av, Sutt	194	A9
Newbolt Rd, Stan	52	F11
Newborough Grn, N Mal	178	G7
Newburgh Rd W3	124	E1
Newburgh St W1	17	N8
Newburn St SE11	34	H6

Name	Pg	Ref
Newbury Cl, Nthlt	85	L11
Newbury Gdns, Epsom	193	M8
Newbury Ms NW5	92	B12
Newbury Rd E4	62	F12
Newbury Rd, Brom	187	N6
Newbury Rd, Ilf	81	R12
Newbury St EC1	19	T3
Newbury Way, Nthlt	85	K11
Newby Cl, Enf	44	D4
Newby Pl E14	114	E13
Newby St SW8	146	D5
Newcastle Cl EC4	19	N5
Newcastle Pl W2	15	L2
Newcastle Row, EC1 7	11	M10
Newcombe Gdns SW16	165	K7
Newcombe Pk NW7	55	K9
Newcombe Pk, Wem	105	U1
Newcombe St, W8 14	126	H1
Newcomen Rd E11	97	L5
Newcomen Rd SW11	145	P6
Newcomen St SE1	28	C5
Newcourt St NW8	7	P3
Newdales Cl, N9 2	60	H4
Newdene Av, Nthlt	102	G3
Newell St E14	113	T12
Newent Cl SE15	36	H13
Newent Cl, Cars	195	T1
Newfield Cl, Hmptn	175	N1
Newfield Ri NW2	89	R5
Newgale Gdns, Edg	53	T14
Newgate, Croy	197	U1
Newgate Cl, Felt	157	K4
Newgate St EC1	19	S6
Newham Way E6	116	H7
Newham Way E16	115	M10
Newhams Row SE1	28	J8
Newhaven Gdns SE9	152	A7
Newhaven La E16	115	M8
Newhaven Rd SE25	184	B9
Newhouse Av, Rom	82	H6
Newhouse Cl, N Mal	179	K14
Newhouse Wk, Mord	181	L13
Newick Cl, Bex	155	R11
Newick Rd E5	95	K6
Newing Grn, Brom	170	B14
Newington Barrow Way N7	93	L5
Newington Butts SE1	35	R3
Newington Butts SE11	35	R3
Newington Causeway SE1	27	T11
Newington Grn N1	94	B9
Newington Grn N16	94	B9
Newington Grn Rd N1	94	A11
Newland Cl, Pnr	51	K11
Newland Ct, Wem	88	A4
Newland Dr, Enf	44	J2
Newland Gdns W13	122	H4
Newland Rd N8	75	K6
Newland St E16	134	E2
Newlands, The, Wall	196	G14
Newlands Av, T Ditt	190	D1
Newlands Cl, Edg	53	R5
Newlands Cl, Sthl	120	J9
Newlands Cl, Wem	87	M11
Newlands Ct SE9	152	H12
Newlands Pk SE26	167	N11
Newlands Pl, Barn	40	A9
Newlands Quay E1	113	L14
Newlands Rd SW16	183	K4
Newlands Rd, Wdf Grn	63	M4
Newlands Way, Chess	191	M9
Newling Cl E6	116	F11
Newlyn Gdns, Har	67	L14
Newlyn Rd N17	76	E2
Newlyn Rd, Barn	40	E8
Newlyn Rd, Well	153	T4
Newman Pas W1	17	P4
Newman Rd E13	115	R6
Newman Rd, E17 1	77	P9
Newman Rd, Brom	187	P2
Newman Rd, Croy	197	M1
Newman Rd, Hayes	102	C14
Newman St W1	17	P4
Newman Yd W1	17	R5
Newmans Cl, Loug	48	J5
Newman's Ct, EC3 13	20	F7
Newmans La, Loug	48	H6
Newmans La, Surb 2	177	P11
Newman's Row WC2	18	G5
Newmans Way, Barn	41	M2
Newmarket Av, Nthlt	85	P10
Newmarket Grn SE9	152	B13
Newminster Rd, Mord	181	M12
Newnham Av, Ruis	84	F1
Newnham Cl, Loug	48	A11
Newnham Cl, Nthlt	85	T10
Newnham Cl, Th Hth	183	T4
Newnham Gdns, Nthlt	85	T10
Newnham Ms, N22 1	75	M1
Newnham Rd N22	75	M1
Newnham Ter SE1	26	J9
Newnham Way, Har	69	S9
Newnhams Cl, Brom	188	F6
Newnton Cl N4	76	A14
Newpiece, Loug	48	J5
Newport Av E13	115	S8
Newport Av E14	114	H14
Newport Mead, Wat	50	H7
Newport Pl WC2	17	U9
Newport Rd E10	96	G3
Newport Rd E17	77	S8
Newport Rd SW13	143	P1
Newport St SE11	34	F3
Newquay Cres, Har	85	K3
Newquay Gdns, Wat	50	D4
Newquay Rd SE6	168	E3
Newry Rd, Twick	140	H9
Newsam Av N15	76	A9
Newsholme Dr N21	43	L10
Newstead Av, Orp	203	P5
Newstead Rd SE12	151	L13
Newstead Wk, Cars	181	M14
Newstead Way SW19	162	B7
Newton Av N10	74	B1
Newton Av W3	124	E4
Newton Cl E17	77	S12
Newton Cl, Har	85	N4
Newton Cres, Borwd	38	D8
Newton Gro W4	124	J6
Newton Rd, E15 5	96	H9
Newton Rd N15	76	F9
Newton Rd NW2	89	T6
Newton Rd SW19	162	D14
Newton Rd W2	14	A7
Newton Rd, Har	68	C3
Newton Rd, Islw	140	E3
Newton Rd, Well	154	A6
Newton Rd, Wem	87	T13
Newton St WC2	18	D5
Newton Way N18	59	U10
Newtons Yd, SW18 6	144	H10
Newtown St, SW11 4	146	C1
Niagara Av W5	123	L7
Nibthwaite Rd, Har	68	C9
Nichol Cl N14	58	G1
Nichol La, Brom	169	P13
Nicholas Cl, Grnf	103	S3
Nicholas Ct E13	115	S5
Nicholas Gdns W5	123	N3
Nicholas La EC4	20	E9
Nicholas Rd E1	113	M7
Nicholas Rd, Croy	197	K7
Nicholas Rd, Dag	101	L5
Nicholay Rd N19	92	H2
Nicholes Rd, Houns	139	N8
Nicholl St E2	112	G2
Nichols Cl, N4 1	93	N1
Nichols Cl, Chess 2	191	M12
Nichols Grn W5	105	R9
Nicholson Rd, Croy	198	F1
Nicholson St SE1	27	P3
Nickelby Cl SE28	118	E12
Nicol Cl, Twick	141	K11
Nicola Cl, Har	68	B3
Nicola Cl, S Croy	197	T12
Nicola Ms, Ilf	65	K13
Nicoll Pl NW4	71	S12
Nicoll Rd NW10	107	K2
Nicoll Way, Borwd	38	H9
Nicolson Dr, Bushey	51	U3
Nicosia Rd SW18	145	R13
Niederwald Rd SE26	167	R7
Nigel Cl, Nthlt	102	J2
Nigel Ms, Ilf	98	J7
Nigel Playfair Av W6	125	R9
Nigel Rd E7	97	U10
Nigel Rd SE15	148	H5
Nigeria Rd SE7	133	U13
Nightingale Av E4	62	J9
Nightingale Cl E4	62	H7
Nightingale Cl W4	124	E12
Nightingale Cl, Cars	196	A3
Nightingale Cl, Pnr	66	E10
Nightingale Dr, Epsom	192	D12
Nightingale Est E5	94	J6
Nightingale Gro SE13	150	H10
Nightingale La E11	79	R10
Nightingale La N8	74	J7
Nightingale La SW4	146	B12
Nightingale La SW12	146	B12
Nightingale La, Brom	187	U4
Nightingale La, Rich	141	R13
Nightingale Ms, E3 12	113	R3
Nightingale Pl SE18	134	H11
Nightingale Pl SW10	30	G10
Nightingale Rd E5	94	J5
Nightingale Rd N9	45	M12
Nightingale Rd N22	59	L14
Nightingale Rd NW10	107	M4
Nightingale Rd W7	122	E1
Nightingale Rd, Cars	195	U5
Nightingale Rd, Hmptn	157	P11
Nightingale Rd, Orp	189	L12
Nightingale Rd, Walt	174	D13
Nightingale Rd, W Mol	175	S9
Nightingale Sq SW12	146	A14
Nightingale Vale SE18	134	H11
Nightingale Wk SW4	146	C11
Nightingale Way E6	116	D9
Nile Rd E13	115	T4
Nile St N1	12	C5
Nile Ter SE15	37	M8
Nimegen Way, SE22 1	148	C9
Nimrod Cl, Nthlt	102	H6
Nimrod Pas, N1 7	94	D12
Nimrod Rd SW16	164	E9
Nina Mackay Cl, E15 4	114	J1
Nine Acres Cl E12	98	D9
Nine Elms La SW8	128	G12
Nineteenth Rd, Mitch	182	J7
Ninhams Wd, Orp	202	G8
Ninth Av, Hayes	102	A14
Nithdale Rd SE18	135	K13
Niton Cl, Barn	40	A11
Niton Rd, Rich	142	B5
Niton St SW6	143	S4
Niven Cl, Borwd	38	F2
Nobel Rd N18	61	M9
Noble St EC2	19	U5
Noel Pk Rd N22	75	N4
Noel Rd E6	116	C8
Noel Rd N1	11	P2
Noel Rd W3	106	F11
Noel Sq, Dag	100	E7
Noel St W1	17	P7
Nolan Way E5	94	H7
Nolton Pl, Edg	69	U2
Nonsuch Cl, Ilf	65	K12
Nora Gdns NW4	72	B7
Norbiton Av, Kings T	178	B3
Norbiton Common Rd, Kings T	178	D5
Norbiton Rd E14	113	T11
Norbreck Par NW10	105	S5
Norbroke St W12	107	L13
Norburn St, W10 2	108	C10
Norbury Av SW16	183	L1
Norbury Av, Houns	140	A9
Norbury Av, Th Hth	183	R4
Norbury Cl SW16	183	P1
Norbury Ct Rd SW16	183	K4
Norbury Cres SW16	183	M2
Norbury Cross SW16	182	J5
Norbury Gdns, Rom	82	G10
Norbury Gro NW7	54	J5
Norbury Hill SW16	165	P14
Norbury Ri SW16	182	J5
Norbury Rd E4	62	A9
Norbury Rd, Th Hth	183	U4
Norcombe Gdns, Har	69	M11
Norcott Cl, Hayes	102	F8
Norcott Rd N16	94	G5
Norcroft Gdns SE22	148	G13
Norcutt Rd, Twick	158	D1
Norfield Rd, Dart	173	U8
Norfolk Av N13	59	R12
Norfolk Av N15	76	E12
Norfolk Cl N2	73	R5
Norfolk Cl N13	59	S12
Norfolk Cl, Barn	42	B8
Norfolk Cl, Twick	141	K11
Norfolk Cres W2	15	R6
Norfolk Cres, Sid	153	S13
Norfolk Gdns, Bexh	155	L1
Norfolk Gdns, Borwd	38	G8
Norfolk Ho Rd SW16	164	H5
Norfolk Ms, W10 8	108	D10
Norfolk Pl W2	15	M6
Norfolk Pl, Well	154	A3
Norfolk Rd E6	116	F1
Norfolk Rd E17	77	P3
Norfolk Rd NW8	109	P2
Norfolk Rd NW10	89	K13
Norfolk Rd SW19	163	S13
Norfolk Rd, Bark	99	R14
Norfolk Rd, Barn	40	H6
Norfolk Rd, Dag	101	S10
Norfolk Rd, Enf	45	K11
Norfolk Rd, Esher	190	C10
Norfolk Rd, Felt	156	F1
Norfolk Rd, Har	67	S10
Norfolk Rd, Ilf	99	S2
Norfolk Rd, Rom	83	U11
Norfolk Rd, Th Hth	183	U5
Norfolk Row, SE1 1	34	F1
Norfolk Sq W2	15	L7
Norfolk Sq Ms W2	15	L7
Norfolk St E7	97	N9
Norfolk Ter W6	126	C10
Norgrove St SW12	126	B14
Norhyrst Av SE25	184	E5
Norland Pl W11	126	D2
Norland Sq W11	126	D2
Norlands Cres, Chis	188	J2
Norlands Gate, Chis	188	K2
Norley Vale SW15	161	P2
Norlington Rd E10	96	F1
Norlington Rd E11	96	G2
Norman Av N22	75	T1

Norman Av, Felt	157	K4
Norman Av, Sthl	103	K13
Norman Av, Twick	141	K13
Norman Cl, Orp	203	M5
Norman Cl, Rom	83	S3
Norman Ct, Ilf	81	N13
Norman Cres, Houns	120	G14
Norman Cres, Pnr	66	F2
Norman Gro E3	113	S4
Norman Rd E6	116	F7
Norman Rd E11	96	H4
Norman Rd N15	76	F9
Norman Rd SE10	132	D13
Norman Rd SW19	163	M13
Norman Rd, Belv	137	R5
Norman Rd, Ilf	99	K10
Norman Rd, Sutt	194	G9
Norman Rd, Th Hth	183	S9
Norman St EC1	11	U8
Norman Way N14	58	J4
Norman Way W3	106	D10
Normanby Cl, SW15 3	144	E9
Normanby Rd NW10	89	M9
Normand Gdns, W14 1	126	D11
Normand Ms W14	126	D11
Normand Rd W14	126	E11
Normandy Av, Barn	40	E10
Normandy Rd SW9	147	N2
Normandy Ter E16	115	R12
Normanhurst Av, Bexh	154	G2
Normanhurst Dr, Twick	140	J10
Normanhurst Rd SW2	165	M3
Normans Cl NW10	88	G12
Normans Mead NW10	88	G11
Normansfield Av, Tedd	159	M14
Normanshire Av, E4 1	62	E7
Normanshire Dr E4	62	C8
Normanton Av SW19	162	G4
Normanton Pk E4	63	K3
Normanton Rd, S Croy	198	C11
Normanton St SE23	167	P4
Normington Cl SW16	165	N9
Norrice Lea N2	73	N10
Norris St SW1	17	S12
Norroy Rd SW15	144	B8
Norrys Cl, Barn	41	T8
Norrys Rd, Barn	41	T8
Norseman Cl, Ilf	100	D1
Norseman Way, Grnf 1	103	S2
Norstead Pl SW15	161	N3
North Access Rd E17	77	P11
North Acre NW9	71	K2
North Acton Rd NW10	106	G4
North Audley St W1	16	D8
North Av N18	60	H7
North Av W13	104	J10
North Av, Cars	196	A13
North Av, Har	67	S11
North Av, Hayes	102	A13
North Av, Rich	142	A2
North Av, Sthl	103	M13
North Bank NW8	7	N7
North Birkbeck Rd E11	96	H6
North Carriage Dr W2	109	R13
North Circular Rd E4	61	U13
North Circular Rd E18	79	U6
North Circular Rd N3	72	H7
North Circular Rd N12	73	P1
North Circular Rd N13	59	R9
North Circular Rd NW2	89	K4
North Circular Rd NW10	106	C1
North Circular Rd NW11	72	B11
North Cl, Barn	39	T9
North Cl, Bexh	154	G8
North Cl, Dag	119	P2
North Cl, Mord	180	D7
North Colonnade E14	132	B1
North Common Rd W5	105	S13
North Countess Rd E17	77	U2
North Ct W1	17	N1
North Cray Rd, Bex	173	R2
North Cray Rd, Sid	173	K10
North Cres E16	114	H7
North Cres N3	72	E4
North Cres WC1	17	R1
North Cross Rd SE22	148	F9
North Cross Rd, Ilf	81	L8
North Dene NW7	54	H5
North Dene, Houns	139	R2
North Dr SW16	164	E7
North Dr, Houns	139	U4
North Dr, Orp	203	S8
North End NW3	91	L3
North End, Buck H	47	T14
North End, Croy	197	T3
North End Av NW3	91	L3
North End Cres, W14 6	126	E8
North End Ho W14	126	D8
North End La, Orp	203	K14
North End Rd NW11	90	H1
North End Rd SW6	126	G13
North End Rd W14	126	E10
North End Rd, Wem	88	B6
North End Way NW3	91	L4
North Flockton St, SE16 3	29	S6
North Gdns SW19	163	P13
North Glade, The, Bex	155	L14
North Gower St NW1	9	N8
North Gro N6	74	A14
North Gro N15	76	A9
North Hill N6	74	A12
North Hill Av N6	73	U11
North Hyde Gdns, Hayes	120	B7
North Hyde La, Houns	121	K12
North Hyde La, Sthl	121	K10
North Hyde Rd, Hayes	120	A7
North La, Tedd	158	E11
North Lo Cl SW15	144	A10
North Ms WC1	10	G12
North Par, Chess	191	T10
North Pk SE9	152	F12
North Pas SW18	144	H8
North Peckham Est SE15	37	L14
North Pl, Mitch	163	T13
North Pl, Tedd	158	E11
North Pole La, Kes	201	N12
North Pole Rd W10	107	T10
North Ride W2	15	T10
North Rd N6	74	B13
North Rd N7	93	K10
North Rd N9	60	J1
North Rd SE18	135	S7
North Rd SW19	163	M12
North Rd W5	123	P6
North Rd, Belv	137	R5
North Rd, Brent	123	S11
North Rd, Brom	187	R1
North Rd, Edg	70	D1
North Rd, Ilf	99	R3
North Rd, Rich	142	A3
North Rd, Rom	82	J10
North Rd, Sthl	103	N13
North Rd, Surb	177	P11
North Rd, W Wick	200	D3
North Row W1	16	C9
North Side Wandsworth Common SW18	145	N9
North Sq NW11	72	H10
North St E13	115	R3
North St NW4	71	U9
North St SW4	146	E5
North St, Bark	99	K12
North St, Bexh	155	P7
North St, Brom	187	N2
North St, Cars	195	T6
North St, Islw	140	H5
North St Pas E13	115	S3
North Ter SW3	23	N12
North Vw SW19	161	T9
North Vw W5	105	L7
North Vw, Pnr	66	E14
North Vw Dr, Wdf Grn	80	A4
North Vw Rd N8	74	H6
North Vil NW1	92	H11
North Wk, Croy	200	D10
North Way N9	61	M3
North Way N11	58	E11
North Way NW9	70	C6
North Way, Pnr	66	F6
North Way, Pnr	15	K4
North Woolwich Rd E16	133	N1
North Woolwich Roundabout, E16 2	134	A2
North Worple Way SW14	142	J5
Northall Rd, Bexh	155	T4
Northampton Gro N1	93	U10
Northampton Pk N1	93	U11
Northampton Rd EC1	11	L10
Northampton Rd, Croy	198	G3
Northampton Rd, Enf	45	S8
Northampton Sq EC1	11	P7
Northampton St N1	93	T13
Northanger Rd SW16	164	J12
Northbank Rd E17	78	E3
Northborough Rd SW16	183	L4
Northbourne, Brom	187	N13
Northbourne Rd SW4	146	H8
Northbrook Rd N22	59	K13
Northbrook Rd SE13	150	H9
Northbrook Rd, Barn	40	C11
Northbrook Rd, Croy	184	A10
Northbrook Rd, Ilf	98	G3
Northburgh St EC1	11	R10
Northchurch SE17	36	E5
Northchurch Rd N1	94	A13
Northchurch Rd, Wem	87	U11
Northchurch Ter N1	94	C14
Northcliffe Cl, Wor Pk	193	K6
Northcliffe Dr N20	56	F2
Northcote, Pnr	66	E4
Northcote Av W5	105	R14
Northcote Av, Islw	140	G9
Northcote Av, Sthl	103	K14
Northcote Av, Surb	178	B13
Northcote Rd E17	77	R8
Northcote Rd NW10	89	K14
Northcote Rd SW11	158	B8
Northcote Rd, Croy	184	A12
Northcote Rd, N Mal	178	G6
Northcote Rd, Sid	171	S7
Northcote Rd, Twick	140	H9
Northcott Av N22	75	K1
Northcroft Rd W13	122	J5
Northcroft Rd, Epsom	192	J13
Northdene, Chig	65	N9
Northdene Gdns N15	76	D12
Northdown Gdns, Ilf	81	R9
Northdown Rd, Well	154	D4
Northdown St N1	10	E3
Northern Av N9	60	E4
Northern Relief Rd, Bark	99	K13
Northern Rd E13	115	S3
Northern Service Rd, Barn	40	D5
Northernhay Wk, Mord	180	D8
Northey St E14	113	S13
Northfield, Loug	48	A8
Northfield Av W5	123	L6
Northfield Av W13	122	J3
Northfield Av, Pnr	66	G7
Northfield Cl, Brom	188	C2
Northfield Cres, Sutt	194	D8
Northfield Path, Dag	101	M6
Northfield Rd E6	98	F12
Northfield Rd N16	76	D14
Northfield Rd W13	122	J4
Northfield Rd, Barn	41	R5
Northfield Rd, Borwd	38	D2
Northfield Rd, Dag	101	M7
Northfield Rd, Enf	45	K10
Northfield Rd, Houns	120	H13
Northfields SW18	144	G8
Northfields Ind Est, Wem	106	A1
Northfields Rd W3	106	D10
Northgate Dr NW9	70	J11
Northiam N12	56	H6
Northiam St E9	113	K2
Northington St WC1	10	G12
Northlands Av, Orp	203	R8
Northlands St SE5	147	T4
Northolm, Edg	54	G7
Northolme Gdns, Edg	70	B1
Northolme Ri, Orp	203	R4
Northolme Rd N5	93	T7
Northolt Av, Ruis	84	D10
Northolt Gdns, Grnf	86	F9
Northolt Rd, Har	85	S8
Northover, Brom	169	M6
Northport St, N1 9	112	B2
Northside Rd, Brom 2	187	T2
Northspur Rd, Sutt	194	G5
Northstead Rd SW2	165	P4
Northumberland All EC3	21	L8
Northumberland Av E12	97	U2
Northumberland Av WC2	26	B2
Northumberland Av, Islw	140	F1
Northumberland Av, Well	153	P7
Northumberland Cl, Erith 2	137	U14
Northumberland Gdns N9	60	F5
Northumberland Gdns, Brom	188	G7
Northumberland Gdns, Islw	122	H13
Northumberland Gdns, Mitch	182	H9
Northumberland Gro N17	60	J14
Northumberland Pk N17	60	J13
Northumberland Pk, Erith	137	T14
Northumberland Pl W2	108	G11
Northumberland Pl, Rich	141	P10
Northumberland Rd E6	116	D11
Northumberland Rd E17	78	A13
Northumberland Rd, Barn	41	M13

Name	Page	Grid
Northumberland Rd, Har	67	M9
Northumberland Row, Twick *3*	158	D2
Northumberland St WC2	26	B1
Northumberland Way, Erith	155	U2
Northumbria St E14	114	B11
Northview Cres NW10	89	L8
Northway NW11	72	J10
Northway, Mord	180	D6
Northway, Wall	196	F8
Northway Circ NW7	54	H7
Northway Cres NW7	54	H8
Northway Rd SE5	147	T6
Northway Rd, Croy	184	F12
Northweald La, Kings T	159	N9
Northwest Pl, N1 *5*	11	L2
Northwick Av, Har	68	J12
Northwick Circle, Har	69	L11
Northwick Cl, NW8 *1*	7	K10
Northwick Pk Rd, Har	68	F11
Northwick Rd, Wat	50	F7
Northwick Rd, Wem	105	P2
Northwick Ter NW8	6	J10
Northwick Wk, Har	68	E14
Northwold Est E5	94	H3
Northwold Rd E5	94	H4
Northwold Rd N16	94	E4
Northwood Gdns N12	57	N9
Northwood Gdns, Grnf	86	F10
Northwood Gdns, Ilf	80	H7
Northwood Pl, Erith	137	L5
Northwood Rd N6	74	D13
Northwood Rd SE23	167	T1
Northwood Rd, Cars	196	A12
Northwood Rd, Th Hth	183	U2
Northwood Way, SE19 *3*	166	B11
Northwood Way, Nthwd	66	A2
Norton Av, Surb	178	D13
Norton Cl E4	62	A9
Norton Cl, Borwd	38	A2
Norton Cl, Enf	44	J3
Norton Folgate E1	21	K1
Norton Rd E10	95	U1
Norton Rd, Wem	87	P12
Norval Rd, Wem	86	J3
Norway Gate SE16	131	S5
Norway Pl E14	113	T12
Norway St SE10	132	D11
Norwich Ms, Ilf	100	B2
Norwich Pl, Bexh	155	P8
Norwich Rd E7	97	N10
Norwich Rd, Dag	119	P4
Norwich Rd, Grnf	103	S2
Norwich Rd, Th Hth	183	U6
Norwich St EC4	19	K5
Norwich Wk, Edg	54	F14
Norwood Cl, Wem	105	T2
Norwood Cl, Sthl	121	N8
Norwood Cl, Twick	158	A4
Norwood Dr, Har	67	N11
Norwood Gdns, Hayes	102	F8
Norwood Gdns, Sthl	121	L7
Norwood Grn Rd, Sthl	121	N8
Norwood High St SE27	165	S6
Norwood Pk Rd SE27	165	U9
Norwood Rd SE24	147	S14
Norwood Rd SE27	165	S4
Norwood Rd, Sthl	121	N8
Notley St SE5	36	D14
Notre Dame Est SW4	146	F8
Notson Rd SE25	184	J8
Notting Barn Rd W10	108	A8
Notting Hill Gate W11	126	G1
Nottingdale Sq W11	108	C14
Nottingham Av E16	115	T10
Nottingham Ct, WC2 *2*	18	B7
Nottingham Pl W1	16	D1
Nottingham Rd E10	78	F12
Nottingham Rd SW17	163	T2
Nottingham Rd, Islw	140	E4
Nottingham Rd, S Croy	197	T9
Nottingham St W1	16	D1
Nottingham Ter, NW1 *1*	8	D12
Nova Ms, Sutt	194	D1
Nova Rd, Croy	183	S14
Novar Cl, Orp	189	U14
Novar Rd SE9	171	L2
Novello St SW6	144	G2
Novello Way, Borwd	38	G1
Nowell Rd SW13	125	P12
Nower Hill, Pnr	67	L7
Noyna Rd SW17	163	U5
Nuding Cl SE13	150	B6
Nugent Rd N19	92	J1
Nugent Rd SE25	184	E5
Nugent Ter NW8	6	G4
Nugents Ct, Pnr	67	K1
Nugents Pk, Pnr	67	K1
Nuneaton Rd, Dag	100	J13
Nunhead Cres SE15	148	J6
Nunhead Est SE15	148	J7
Nunhead Grn SE15	149	K5
Nunhead Gro SE15	149	L6
Nunhead La SE15	148	J6
Nunhead Pas, SE15 *3*	148	J6
Nunnington Cl SE9	170	D6
Nunns Rd, Enf	43	U3
Nupton Dr, Barn	39	U11
Nursery Av N3	73	K3
Nursery Av, Bexh	155	M5
Nursery Av, Croy	199	N4
Nursery Cl SE4	149	T4
Nursery Cl SW15	144	A8
Nursery Cl, Croy	199	N4
Nursery Cl, Enf	45	N1
Nursery Cl, Felt	138	C14
Nursery Cl, Rom	82	G12
Nursery Ct, N17 *4*	60	E14
Nursery Gdns, Chis	171	K12
Nursery Gdns, Enf	45	P2
Nursery Gdns, Houns	139	L10
Nursery La E2	112	E2
Nursery La E7	97	P11
Nursery La W10	107	T10
Nursery Rd E9	95	L11
Nursery Rd N2	73	P2
Nursery Rd N14	42	E13
Nursery Rd SW9	147	M7
Nursery Rd, Loug	48	B7
Nursery Rd (High Beach), Loug	47	S1
Nursery Rd, Pnr	66	E5
Nursery Rd, Sutt	195	L8
Nursery Rd, Th Hth	184	A8
Nursery Rd Merton SW19	180	J3
Nursery Rd Mitcham, Mitch	181	S7
Nursery Rd Wimbledon SW19	162	C14
Nursery Row SE17	36	D4
Nursery Row, Barn	40	D5
Nursery St N17	60	E14
Nursery Wk NW4	71	T5
Nurserymans Rd N11	58	A3
Nurstead Rd, Erith	137	P14
Nutbourne St W10	108	C5
Nutbrook St SE15	148	G6
Nutbrowne Rd, Dag	119	M1
Nutcroft Rd SE15	130	J14
Nutfield Cl N18	60	G11
Nutfield Cl, Cars	195	S6
Nutfield Gdns, Ilf	99	U3
Nutfield Gdns, Nthlt	102	F4
Nutfield Rd E15	96	F7
Nutfield Rd NW2	89	N5
Nutfield Rd SE22	148	F8
Nutfield Rd, Th Hth	183	R7
Nutfield Way, Orp	202	H4
Nutford Pl W1	15	T6
Nuthatch Gdns SE28	135	P4
Nuthurst Av SW2	165	M3
Nutley Ter NW3	91	N11
Nutmead Cl, Bex	173	U2
Nutmeg Cl, E16 *2*	115	K7
Nutmeg La E14	114	G12
Nutt Gro, Edg	53	N3
Nutt St SE15	37	N14
Nuttall St N1	12	J1
Nutter La E11	79	T10
Nutwell St SW17	163	S10
Nuxley Rd, Belv	137	M11
Nyanza St SE18	135	P12
Nye Bevan Est E5	95	P6
Nylands Av, Rich	142	A2
Nymans Gdns SW20	179	R5
Nynehead St SE14	131	R13
Nyon Gro SE6	167	T4
Nyssa Cl, Wdf Grn	64	E12
Nyton Cl N19	92	J2

O

Name	Page	Grid
Oak Apple Ct SE12	169	N3
Oak Av N8	74	J8
Oak Av N10	58	C14
Oak Av N17	60	C13
Oak Av, Croy	200	B3
Oak Av, Hmptn	157	L12
Oak Av, Houns	120	H14
Oak Bank, Croy	200	F12
Oak Cl N14	42	C14
Oak Cl, Sutt	195	M4
Oak Cottage Cl SE6	169	K2
Oak Cres E16	115	K10
Oak Dene, W13 *1*	104	J10
Oak Fm, Borwd	38	E9
Oak Gdns, Croy	200	B3
Oak Gdns, Edg	70	E3
Oak Gro NW2	90	C8
Oak Gro, Ruis	84	D1
Oak Gro, Sun	156	C14
Oak Gro, W Wick	200	F3
Oak Gro Rd SE20	185	L2
Oak Hall Rd E11	79	S12
Oak Hill, Surb	177	S13
Oak Hill, Wdf Grn	62	H13
Oak Hill Cl, Wdf Grn	62	H14
Oak Hill Cres, Surb	177	S13
Oak Hill Cres, Wdf Grn	62	H13
Oak Hill Gdns, Wdf Grn	79	K1
Oak Hill Gro, Surb	177	R12
Oak Hill Pk NW3	91	K7
Oak Hill Pk Ms NW3	91	L7
Oak Hill Rd, Surb	177	S12
Oak Hill Way NW3	91	L7
Oak La E14	113	T13
Oak La N2	73	N4
Oak La N11	58	H12
Oak La, Islw	140	D7
Oak La, Twick	140	H14
Oak La, Wdf Grn	63	M7
Oak Lo Av, Chig	65	P9
Oak Lo Cl, Stan	53	L9
Oak Lo Dr, W Wick	186	D14
Oak Manor Dr, Wem *3*	87	U10
Oak Pk Gdns SW19	144	A14
Oak Pl SW18	145	K10
Oak Ri, Buck H	64	B5
Oak Rd W5	105	P13
Oak Rd (Northumberland Heath), Erith	137	T14
Oak Rd, N Mal	178	G3
Oak Row SW16	182	E3
Oak St, Rom	83	T9
Oak Tree Cl W5	105	M12
Oak Tree Cl, Loug	49	M2
Oak Tree Cl, Stan	53	L14
Oak Tree Dell NW9	70	G10
Oak Tree Dr N20	57	K2
Oak Tree Gdns, Brom	169	S9
Oak Tree Rd NW8	7	N7
Oak Village NW5	92	B8
Oak Way N14	42	C13
Oak Way W3	124	J2
Oak Way, Croy	185	P11
Oakbank Av, Walt	175	L14
Oakbank Gro SE24	147	T7
Oakbrook Cl, Brom	169	S7
Oakbury Rd SW6	145	K4
Oakcombe Cl, N Mal	178	J1
Oakcroft Cl, Pnr	66	D4
Oakcroft Rd SE13	150	G4
Oakcroft Rd, Chess	191	U7
Oakcroft Vil, Chess	191	T7
Oakdale N14	58	D1
Oakdale Av, Har	69	R9
Oakdale Av, Nthwd	66	B3
Oakdale Cl, Wat	50	F7
Oakdale Gdns E4	62	F9
Oakdale Rd E7	97	S13
Oakdale Rd E11	96	G4
Oakdale Rd E18	79	S4
Oakdale Rd N4	75	U11
Oakdale Rd SE15	149	M5
Oakdale Rd SW16	165	K9
Oakdale Rd, Wat	50	F6
Oakdale Way, Mitch	182	A13
Oakden St SE11	35	L2
Oakdene Av, Chis	170	G9
Oakdene Av, Erith	137	T12
Oakdene Av, T Ditt	190	G1
Oakdene Cl, Pnr	51	M13
Oakdene Dr, Surb	192	F1
Oakdene Ms, Sutt	194	E1
Oakdene Pk N3	56	F13
Oake Ct SW15	144	D10
Oaken Dr, Esher	190	E11
Oaken La, Esher	190	C8
Oakenshaw Cl, Surb	177	S13
Oakes Cl E6	116	F11
Oakeshott Av N6	92	A3
Oakey La SE1	27	K10
Oakfield E4	62	C9
Oakfield Av, Har	69	K6
Oakfield Cl, N Mal	179	M10
Oakfield Ct N8	74	J13
Oakfield Ct NW2	72	A13
Oakfield Ct, Borwd	38	D6
Oakfield Gdns N18	60	C8
Oakfield Gdns SE19	166	E9
Oakfield Gdns, Beck	186	B10
Oakfield Gdns, Cars	195	S1
Oakfield Gdns, Grnf	104	A7
Oakfield La, Kes	201	U7
Oakfield Rd E6	116	C2
Oakfield Rd E17	77	S3
Oakfield Rd N3	72	J2
Oakfield Rd N4	75	N13
Oakfield Rd N14	59	K4
Oakfield Rd SE20	185	K1
Oakfield Rd SW19	162	B5
Oakfield Rd, Croy	197	T1
Oakfield Rd, Ilf	99	K5
Oakfield St SW10	30	E9
Oakfields Rd NW11	72	D11
Oakford Rd NW5	92	D8
Oakhall Ct E11	79	S11
Oakham Cl SE6	167	U4
Oakham Cl, Barn *1*	41	T6
Oakham Dr, Brom	187	M8
Oakhampton Rd NW7	56	A14
Oakhill, Esher	190	H12
Oakhill Av NW3	90	J8
Oakhill Av, Pnr	66	J3
Oakhill Ct SW19	162	B14
Oakhill Dr, Surb	177	S13
Oakhill Path, Surb	177	R12
Oakhill Pl SW15	144	G8

Name	Grid	Ref	Name	Grid	Ref	Name	Grid	Ref	Name	Grid	Ref
Oakhill Rd SW15	144	E9	Oakley Rd SE25	184	J9	Oberstein Rd SW11	145	P8	Old Clem Sq,	134	G12
Oakhill Rd SW16	183	K2	Oakley Rd, Brom	202	C4	Oborne Cl SE24	147	S10	SE18 3		
Oakhill Rd, Beck	186	E4	Oakley Rd, Har	68	C11	Observatory Gdns	126	G3	Old Compton St W1	17	S9
Oakhill Rd, Orp	203	T2	Oakley Sq NW1	9	N2	W8			Old Cote Dr, Houns	121	N12
Oakhill Rd, Sutt	195	M7	Oakley St SW3	31	P9	Observatory Ms,	132	G7	Old Ct Pl W8	22	B6
Oakhouse Rd, Bexh	155	P9	Oakley Wk W6	126	B11	E14 4			Old Deer Pk Gdns,	141	S6
Oakhurst Av, Barn	41	R13	Oakley Yd, E2 2	13	P10	Observatory Rd	142	E8	Rich		
Oakhurst Av, Barn	136	J14	Oaklodge Way NW7	55	L11	SW14			Old Devonshire Rd	146	C14
Oakhurst Cl E17	78	J7	Oakmead Av, Brom	187	P12	Occupation La SE18	153	K1	SW12		
Oakhurst Cl, Ilf	81	K2	Oakmead Gdns, Edg	54	G8	Occupation La W5	123	P7	Old Dock Cl,	124	A12
Oakhurst Cl, Tedd	158	D10	Oakmead Pl, Mitch	181	R2	Occupation Rd SE17	35	U6	Rich 1		
Oakhurst Gdns E4	63	L1	Oakmead Rd SW12	164	C2	Occupation Rd W13	122	J3	Old Dover Rd SE3	133	R14
Oakhurst Gdns E17	78	J7	Oakmead Rd, Croy	182	G11	Ocean Est E1	113	P8	Old Fm Av N14	42	F13
Oakhurst Gdns,	137	K14	Oakmeade, Pnr	51	P12	Ocean St E1	113	P9	Old Fm Av, Sid	171	P2
Bexh			Oakmere Rd SE2	136	A11	Ocean Wf E14	131	U4	Old Fm Cl, Houns	139	M7
Oakhurst Gro SE22	148	G7	Oakmoor Way, Chig	65	S10	Ockendon Rd N1	94	A12	Old Fm Pas,	175	T2
Oakhurst Rd, Epsom	192	F12	Oakmount Pl, Orp	203	P1	Ockham Dr, Orp	172	B13	Hmptn 2		
Oakington Av, Har	67	N14	Oakridge Dr N2	73	P6	Ockley Rd SW16	164	J6	Old Fm Rd N2	73	N1
Oakington Av, Wem	87	U5	Oakridge Rd, Brom	168	H8	Ockley Rd, Croy	183	L14	Old Fm Rd, Hmptn	157	M12
Oakington Dr, Sun	174	F3	Oaks, The N12	57	K7	Octavia Cl, Mitch	181	R9	Old Fm Rd E, Sid	172	A3
Oakington Manor	87	U10	Oaks, The SE18	135	L10	Octavia Rd, Islw	140	E4	Old Fm Rd W, Sid	171	U3
Dr, Wem			Oaks, The, Wat	50	F1	Octavia St SW11	145	R2	Old Fleet La EC4	19	P6
Oakington Rd W9	108	H7	Oaks, The, Wdf Grn	63	K12	Octavius St SE8	132	A13	Old Fold Cl, Barn	40	E2
Oakington Way N8	75	K12	Oaks Av SE19	166	C9	Odard Rd, W Mol	175	P8	Old Fold La, Barn	40	E2
Oakland Pl, Buck H	63	P3	Oaks Av, Felt	156	J4	Oddesey Rd, Borwd	38	D1	Old Fold Vw, Barn	39	T6
Oakland Rd E15	96	H8	Oaks Av, Rom	83	U4	Odessa Rd E7	97	M7	Old Ford Rd E2	113	L4
Oakland Way, Epsom	192	H11	Oaks Av, Wor Pk	193	S6	Odessa Rd NW10	107	P4	Old Ford Rd E3	113	T2
Oaklands N21	59	L3	Oaks Gro E4	62	J4	Odessa St SE16	131	T5	Old Forge Cl, Stan	52	H7
Oaklands, Twick	139	T13	Oaks La, Croy	199	M8	Odger St SW11	145	U3	Old Forge Ms W12	125	H3
Oaklands Av N9	45	K12	Oaks La, Ilf	81	R10	Odyssey Business	84	D9	Old Forge Way, Sid	172	D8
Oaklands Av, Esher	190	A1	Oaks Rd, Croy	199	N7	Pk, Ruis			Old Gloucester St	18	D1
Oaklands Av, Islw	122	E11	Oaks Way, Cars	195	U14	Offa's Mead E9	95	S8	WC1		
Oaklands Av, Sid	153	T13	Oaks Way, Surb	191	N2	Offenham Rd SE9	170	F7	Old Hall Cl, Pnr	67	K2
Oaklands Av, Th Hth	183	N7	Oaksford Av SE26	166	J6	Offerton Rd SW4	146	F6	Old Hall Dr, Pnr	66	J2
Oaklands Av, Wat	50	E2	Oakshade Rd, Brom	168	H7	Offham Slope N12	56	F9	Old Hill, Chis	188	H2
Oaklands Av,	200	D5	Oakshaw Rd SW18	145	K14	Offley Rd SW9	35	K13	Old Hill, Orp	203	P11
W Wick			Oakthorpe Rd N13	59	N9	Offord Cl N17	60	G12	Old Homesdale Rd,	187	T7
Oaklands Cl, Bexh	155	M9	Oaktree Av N13	59	P5	Offord Rd N1	93	L13	Brom		
Oaklands Cl, Chess	191	M8	Oaktree Gro, Ilf	99	N9	Offord St N1	93	M13	Old Hospital Cl	163	T2
Oaklands Cl, Orp	189	R11	Oakview Gdns N2	73	P7	Ogilby St SE18	134	E8	SW12		
Oaklands Ct, Wem	87	N10	Oakview Gro, Croy	199	S1	Oglander Rd SE15	148	F6	Old Ho Cl SW19	162	C10
Oaklands Est SW4	146	F12	Oakview Rd SE6	168	C9	Ogle St W1	17	M2	Old Ho Gdns, Twick	141	M11
Oaklands Gro W12	125	P1	Oakway SW20	179	U8	Oglethorpe Rd, Dag	101	M5	Old Jamaica Rd	29	R9
Oaklands La, Barn	39	R8	Oakway, Brom	186	G4	Ohio Rd E13	115	L8	SE16		
Oaklands Pk Av, Ilf	99	M4	Oakway Cl, Bex	155	K12	Oil Mill La W6	125	P9	Old James St SE15	148	J6
Oaklands Pl,	146	G8	Oakways SE9	152	J11	Okeburn Rd SW17	164	A9	Old Jewry EC2	20	C7
SW4 5			Oakwood Av N14	42	H13	Okehampton Cl N12	57	N9	Old Kent Rd SE1	28	F12
Oaklands Rd N20	40	E14	Oakwood Av, Beck	186	F4	Okehampton Cres,	154	D1	Old Kent Rd SE15	130	J12
Oaklands Rd NW2	90	A8	Oakwood Av, Borwd	38	D8	Well			Old Kenton La NW9	70	D10
Oaklands Rd SW14	142	G6	Oakwood Av,	187	R6	Okehampton Rd	107	U2	Old Kingston Rd,	192	E5
Oaklands Rd W7	122	F4	Brom 6			NW10			Wor Pk		
Oaklands Rd, Bexh	155	L8	Oakwood Av, Mitch	181	P4	Olaf St W11	108	B14	Old Lo Pl, Twick	141	K11
Oaklands Rd, Brom	169	K14	Oakwood Av, Sthl	103	P14	Old Bailey EC4	19	R7	Old Lo Way, Stan	52	H9
Oaklands Way, Wall	196	G14	Oakwood Cl N14	42	F12	Old Barn Cl, Sutt	194	C13	Old Maidstone Rd,	173	M14
Oaklea Pas, Kings T	177	P5	Oakwood Cl, Chis	170	F12	Old Barrack Yd SW1	24	C6	Sid		
Oakleafe Gdns, Ilf	80	J6	Oakwood Cl,	64	C12	Old Barrowfield,	115	K2	Old Malden La,	192	J4
Oakleigh Av N20	57	P2	Wdf Grn			E15 5			Wor Pk		
Oakleigh Av, Edg	70	C3	Oakwood Ct W14	126	E5	Old Bellgate Wf E14	132	A6	Old Manor Dr, Islw	139	U11
Oakleigh Av, Surb	192	B2	Oakwood Cres N21	43	L11	Old Bethnal Grn Rd	13	T6	Old Manor Way,	170	E9
Oakleigh Cl N20	57	U5	Oakwood Cres, Grnf	86	H11	E2			Chis		
Oakleigh Ct, Barn	41	R12	Oakwood Dr SE19	166	B11	Old Bond St W1	17	L12	Old Manor Yd SW5	30	A4
Oakleigh Ct, Edg	70	E4	Oakwood Dr, Edg	54	E11	Old Brewers Yd,	18	B8	Old Marylebone Rd	15	R4
Oakleigh Cres N20	57	S4	Oakwood Gdns, Ilf	99	T3	WC2 3			NW1		
Oakleigh Gdns N20	57	M2	Oakwood Gdns, Orp	203	M3	Old Brewery Ms,	91	N8	Old Ms, Har	68	C10
Oakleigh Gdns, Edg	53	U9	Oakwood Gdns,	194	H4	NW3 2			Old Mill Ct E18	79	T5
Oakleigh Gdns, Orp	203	S8	Sutt 2			Old Br Cl, Nthlt	103	P3	Old Mill Rd SE18	135	P11
Oakleigh Ms N20	57	M2	Oakwood Hill, Loug	48	F11	Old Br St, Kings T	177	N3	Old Montague St E1	21	R3
Oakleigh Pk Av, Chis	188	H2	Oakwood Hill Ind	49	K9	Old Broad St EC2	20	F7	Old Nichol St E2	13	L9
Oakleigh Pk N N20	57	N2	Est, Loug			Old Bromley Rd,	168	H9	Old N St, WC1 2	18	E3
Oakleigh Pk S N20	57	R3	Oakwood La W14	126	E5	Brom			Old Oak Cl, Chess	191	T8
Oakleigh Rd, Pnr	51	M11	Oakwood Pk Rd N14	42	J12	Old Brompton Rd	30	A7	Old Oak Common	107	K8
Oakleigh Rd N N20	57	U5	Oakwood Pl, Croy	183	N12	SW5			La NW10		
Oakleigh Rd S N11	58	B7	Oakwood Rd NW11	72	J9	Old Brompton Rd	30	J4	Old Oak Common	107	L11
Oakleigh Way, Mitch	182	D2	Oakwood Rd SW20	179	P1	SW7			La W3		
Oakleigh Way, Surb	192	B2	Oakwood Rd, Croy	183	N12	Old Bldgs WC2	18	H5	Old Oak La NW10	107	L6
Oakley Av W5	106	A13	Oakwood Rd, Orp	203	L3	Old Burlington St	17	L10	Old Oak Rd W3	125	M1
Oakley Av, Bark	99	U13	Oakwood Rd, Pnr	66	C3	W1			Old Orchard, Sun	174	E4
Oakley Av, Croy	197	L8	Oakwood Vw N14	42	H12	Old Castle St E1	21	M5	Old Orchard, The	91	S7
Oakley Cl E4	62	F6	Oakworth Rd W10	107	U9	Old Cavendish St	16	J6	NW3		
Oakley Cl E6	116	D11	Oarsman Pl, E Mol	176	C8	W1			Old Palace La, Rich	141	M9
Oakley Cl W7	104	C13	Oat La EC2	20	A5	Old Chelsea Ms	31	N11	Old Palace Rd, Croy	197	S5
Oakley Cl, Islw	140	B1	Oates Cl, Brom	186	G5	SW3			Old Palace Ter,	141	N9
Oakley Cres EC1	11	R4	Oatfield Rd, Orp	203	U1	Old Ch La NW9	88	F4	Rich 2		
Oakley Dr SE9	171	N2	Oatland Ri E17	77	R4	Old Ch La, Grnf	104	H5	Old Palace Yd SW1	26	B9
Oakley Dr, Brom	202	C5	Oatlands Rd, Enf	45	M2	Old Ch La, Stan	53	M13	Old Palace Yd, Rich	141	N9
Oakley Gdns N8	75	L9	Oban Cl E13	115	T8	Old Ch Rd E1	113	N12	Old Paradise St	34	T1
Oakley Gdns SW3	31	R10	Oban Rd E13	115	U6	Old Ch Rd E4	62	B6	SE11		
Oakley Pk, Bex	154	E14	Oban Rd SE25	184	B7	Old Ch St SW3	31	L7	Old Pk Av SW12	146	A12
Oakley Pl SE1	37	M7	Oban St E14	114	H11	Old Claygate La,	190	G11	Old Pk Av, Enf	43	T8
Oakley Rd N1	94	A13	Oberon Cl, Borwd	38	F1	Esher			Old Pk Gro, Enf	43	T8

Old Pk La W1	24	G4
Old Pk Ms, Houns	121	M14
Old Pk Ridings N21	43	S12
Old Pk Rd N13	59	M7
Old Pk Rd SE2	136	B10
Old Pk Rd, Enf	43	R6
Old Pk Rd S, Enf	43	R7
Old Pk Vw, Enf	43	P6
Old Perry St, Chis	171	R13
Old Pound Cl, Islw	140	G2
Old Pye St SW1	25	S10
Old Quebec St W1	16	P8
Old Queen St SW1	25	T7
Old Rectory Gdns, Edg	54	B11
Old Redding, Har	51	P10
Old Rd SE13	151	K8
Old Rd, Enf	45	L1
Old Rope Wk, Sun	174	D6
Old Royal Free Pl, N1 2	111	P2
Old Royal Free Sq N1	111	P2
Old Ruislip Rd, Nthlt	102	G3
Old Sch Cl SW19	180	G3
Old Sch Cl, Beck	185	R3
Old Sch Cres E7	97	N12
Old Sch Sq, T Ditt	176	F12
Old Seacoal La, EC4 5	19	T7
Old S Cl, Pnr	66	H2
Old S Lambeth Rd SW8	34	D13
Old Spitalfields Mkt E1	21	L2
Old Sq WC2	18	J5
Old Sta Rd, Loug	48	C9
Old St E13	115	S4
Old St EC1	12	B9
Old Swan Yd, Cars	195	T8
Old Town SW4	146	E6
Old Town, Croy	197	S6
Old Tram Yd SE18	135	M9
Old Woolwich Rd SE10	132	H10
Old York Rd SW18	145	K9
Oldberry Rd, Edg	54	H12
Oldborough Rd, Wem	87	L4
Oldbury Pl W1	16	E1
Oldbury Rd, Enf	44	H3
Oldfield Cl, Brom	188	F7
Oldfield Cl, Grnf	86	C10
Oldfield Cl, Stan	52	H9
Oldfield Fm Gdns, Grnf	104	A2
Oldfield Gdns SE16	131	N8
Oldfield La N, Grnf	86	C11
Oldfield La S, Grnf	104	A4
Oldfield Ms N6	74	E14
Oldfield Rd N16	94	C5
Oldfield Rd NW10	89	L13
Oldfield Rd SW19	162	C11
Oldfield Rd W3	125	L3
Oldfield Rd, Bexh	155	K4
Oldfield Rd, Brom	188	E7
Oldfield Rd, Hmptn	175	N2
Oldfields Circ, Nthlt	85	U11
Oldfields Rd, Sutt	194	F6
Oldham Ter W3	124	E3
Oldhill St N16	94	G1
Oldridge Rd SW12	146	B14
Oldstead Rd, Brom	168	G8
Oleander Cl, Orp	203	N9
O'Leary Sq E1	113	L9
Olinda Rd N16	76	F12
Oliphant St W10	108	B5
Olive Rd E13	115	U6
Olive Rd NW2	89	U8
Olive Rd, SW19 7	163	M13
Olive Rd W5	123	P5
Oliver Av SE25	184	E6
Oliver Cl E10	96	C4
Oliver Cl W4	124	C11
Oliver Gdns E6	116	D11
Oliver Gro SE25	184	E7
Oliver Rd E10	96	C4
Oliver Rd E17	78	F9
Oliver Rd, N Mal	178	F4
Oliver Rd, Sutt	195	N8
Oliver-Goldsmith Est SE15	148	H1
Olivers Yd EC1	12	E10
Olivette St, SW15 7	144	B6
Ollards Gro, Loug	48	B8
Ollerton Grn E3	113	U1
Ollerton Rd N11	58	G10
Olley Cl, Wall	196	J13
Ollgar Cl W12	125	M2
Olliffe St E14	132	F6
Olmar St SE1	37	R10
Olney Rd SE17	35	T10
Olron Cres, Bexh	154	H10
Olven Rd SE18	135	M12
Olveston Wk, Cars	181	P11
Olwen Ms, Pnr	66	H4
Olyffe Av, Well	154	B2
Olyffe Dr, Beck	186	E1
Olympia Ms, W2 1	14	D11
Olympia Way W14	126	D6
Olympic Retail Pk, Wem	88	C7
Olympic Way, Grnf	103	S2
Olympic Way, Wem	88	B8
Olympus Sq, E5 2	94	H6
Oman Av NW2	89	T8
O'Meara St SE1	28	A3
Omega Cl E14	132	C5
Omega Pl N1	10	D4
Omega St SE14	149	U1
Ommaney Rd SE14	149	P2
Omnibus Way E17	78	B4
On The Hill, Wat	50	J3
Ondine Rd SE15	148	F7
One Tree Cl SE23	149	M12
Onega Gate SE16	131	R5
O'Neill Path, SE18 2	134	H12
Ongar Cl, Rom	82	E9
Ongar Rd SW6	126	G11
Onra Rd E17	78	A13
Onslow Av, Rich	141	R10
Onslow Cl E4	62	F4
Onslow Cl, T Ditt	190	D1
Onslow Cres, Chis	188	J2
Onslow Dr, Sid	172	G4
Onslow Gdns E18	79	T5
Onslow Gdns N10	74	C9
Onslow Gdns N21	43	P10
Onslow Gdns SW7	31	K5
Onslow Gdns, T Ditt	190	D2
Onslow Gdns, Wall	196	E12
Onslow Ms E SW7	31	K4
Onslow Ms W SW7	30	J4
Onslow Rd, Croy	197	N1
Onslow Rd, N Mal	179	N7
Onslow Rd, Rich	141	R10
Onslow Sq SW7	31	M2
Onslow St EC1	11	M12
Onslow Way, T Ditt	190	D1
Ontario St SE1	27	S11
Ontario Way E14	114	A14
Opal Cl E16	116	B12
Opal Ms NW6	108	F1
Opal Ms, Ilf	99	K4
Opal St SE11	35	N5
Openshaw Rd SE2	136	C8
Openview SW18	163	N3
Ophelia Gdns NW2	90	C5
Ophir Ter SE15	148	G2
Opossum Way,	138	F4
Oppenheim Rd SE13	150	E3
Oppidans Ms, NW3 1	91	T14
Oppidans Rd NW3	91	T14
Orange Ct, E1 2	29	T3
Orange Gro E11	96	J5
Orange Hill Rd, Edg	54	F14
Orange Pl SE16	131	M6
Orange St WC2	17	T12
Orange Yd, W1 3	17	T7
Orangery, The, Rich	159	L4
Orangery La SE9	152	F10
Oratory La SW3	31	M5
Orb St SE17	36	D4
Orbain Rd SW6	126	D14
Orbel St SW11	145	R2
Orchard, The N14	42	D9
Orchard, The N21	44	A12
Orchard, The NW11	72	G10
Orchard, The SE3	150	H3
Orchard, The W4	124	H7
Orchard, The W5	105	P9
Orchard, The, Epsom	193	L13
Orchard, The, Houns	139	U3
Orchard Av N3	72	G6
Orchard Av N14	42	F12
Orchard Av N20	57	P4
Orchard Av, Belv	137	K11
Orchard Av, Croy	185	S14
Orchard Av, Houns	121	K14
Orchard Av, Mitch	196	A1
Orchard Av, N Mal	179	K4
Orchard Av, Sthl	121	L1
Orchard Av, T Ditt	190	H2
Orchard Cl, E4 3	62	B8
Orchard Cl E11	79	R8
Orchard Cl NW2	89	N6
Orchard Cl SE23	149	L12
Orchard Cl SW20	179	T7
Orchard Cl W10	108	D9
Orchard Cl, Bexh	154	J2
Orchard Cl, Bushey	52	B1
Orchard Cl, Edg	53	S11
Orchard Cl, Epsom	192	C11
Orchard Cl, Surb	191	K1
Orchard Cl, Wem	105	S1
Orchard Ct, Twick	158	A3
Orchard Cres, Edg	54	E10
Orchard Cres, Enf	44	E1
Orchard Dr SE3	150	J3
Orchard Dr, Edg	53	T9
Orchard Gdns, Chess		
Orchard Gdns, Sutt	194	H9
Orchard Gate NW9	70	J7
Orchard Gate, Esher	190	A2
Orchard Gate, Grnf	87	K11
Orchard Grn, Orp	203	S4
Orchard Gro SE20	166	G13
Orchard Gro, Croy	185	S13
Orchard Gro, Edg	70	B2
Orchard Gro, Har	69	U9
Orchard Gro, Orp	203	U3
Orchard Hill, SE13 3	150	D3
Orchard Hill, Cars	195	U9
Orchard La SW20	179	S1
Orchard La, E Mol	176	A11
Orchard La, Wdf Grn	63	T7
Orchard Ms N1	94	B14
Orchard Pl E14	115	K13
Orchard Pl N17	60	E14
Orchard Ri, Croy	199	T1
Orchard Ri, Kings T	178	E2
Orchard Ri, Rich	142	C8
Orchard Ri E, Sid	153	T10
Orchard Ri W, Sid	153	R9
Orchard Rd N6	74	D13
Orchard Rd SE18	135	P8
Orchard Rd, Belv	137	N8
Orchard Rd, Barn	40	E7
Orchard Rd, Brent	123	M11
Orchard Rd, Brom	187	U1
Orchard Rd, Chess	191	R7
Orchard Rd, Dag	119	P1
Orchard Rd, Enf	45	M10
Orchard Rd, Hmptn	157	M13
Orchard Rd, Hayes	102	A13
Orchard Rd, Houns	139	M9
Orchard Rd, Kings T	177	R4
Orchard Rd, Mitch 1		
Orchard Rd (Farnborough), Orp	203	K9
Orchard Rd, Rich	142	A6
Orchard Rd, Rom	83	R3
Orchard Rd, Sid	171	S7
Orchard Rd, Sun	156	B14
Orchard Rd, Sutt	194	H9
Orchard Rd, Twick	140	H10
Orchard Rd, Well	154	D5
Orchard St E17	77	R7
Orchard St W1	16	D7
Orchard Way, Beck	185	S10
Orchard Way, Croy	199	S1
Orchard Way, Enf	44	C5
Orchard Way, Sutt	195	P7
Orchardleigh Av, Enf	45	L3
Orchardmede N21	44	A11
Orchardson St NW8	7	K11
Orchid Cl E6	116	C9
Orchid Cl, Sthl	103	K12
Orchid Rd N14	42	E14
Orchid St W12	107	N14
Orde Hall St WC1	10	E12
Ordell Rd E3	113	U4
Ordnance Cl, Felt	156	B5
Ordnance Cres SE10	132	J3
Ordnance Hill NW8	109	P2
Ordnance Ms NW8	7	M2
Ordnance Rd E16	115	L9
Ordnance Rd SE18	134	G12
Oregano Dr E14	114	H12
Oregon Av E12	98	E7
Oregon Cl, N Mal 3	178	E7
Oregon Sq, Orp	203	P2
Orestes Ms NW6	90	G9
Orford Ct SE27	165	S4
Orford Gdns, Twick	158	E4
Orford Rd E17	78	B10
Orford Rd E18	79	R5
Orford Rd SE6	168	D6
Organ La E4	62	F3
Oriel Cl, Mitch	182	H7
Oriel Ct NW3	91	M8
Oriel Dr SW13	125	T12
Oriel Gdns, Ilf	80	E6
Oriel Pl, NW3 5	91	M8
Oriel Rd E9	95	P11
Orient Ind Pk E10	96	A3
Orient St SE11	35	N1
Orient Way E5	95	N6
Orient Way E10	95	S2
Oriental Rd E16	134	A1
Oriental St, E14 4	114	B13
Oriole Way SE28	118	C14
Orion Rd N11	58	C12
Orissa Rd SE18	135	R9
Orkney St SW11	146	A3
Orlando Rd SW4	146	E6
Orleans Cl, Esher	190	A3
Orleans Rd SE19	166	B12
Orleans Rd, Twick	141	L14
Orleston Ms N7	93	P11
Orleston Rd N7	93	P11
Orley Fm Rd, Har	86	C6
Orlop St SE10	132	J10
Ormanton Rd SE26	166	H8
Orme Ct W2	14	C11
Orme Ct Ms, W2 2	14	C11
Orme La W2	14	B11
Orme Rd, Kings T	178	D3
Orme Sq W2	14	B11
Ormeley Rd SW12	164	D1
Ormerod Gdns, Mitch	182	B3
Ormesby Cl SE28	118	G13
Ormesby Way, Har	69	T11
Ormiston Gro W12	125	R1
Ormiston Rd SE10	133	N10
Ormond Av, Hmptn	175	S1
Ormond Cl WC1	18	D1
Ormond Cres, Hmptn	157	S14
Ormond Dr, Hmptn	157	S13
Ormond Ms, WC1 1	10	D11
Ormond Rd N19	93	K1
Ormond Rd, Rich	141	P10
Ormond Yd SW1	25	N1
Ormonde Av, Orp	203	L3
Ormonde Gate SW3	32	A8
Ormonde Pl, SW1 6	32	D4
Ormonde Ri, Buck H	63	T1
Ormonde Rd SW14	142	D6
Ormonde Ter NW8	109	T2
Ormsby Gdns, Grnf	103	U4
Ormsby Pl N16	94	E6
Ormsby St E2	13	L1

Name	Page	Grid
Ormside St SE15	131	L11
Ormskirk Rd, Wat	50	H8
Ornan Rd NW3	91	R10
Orpen Wk N16	94	D6
Orpheus St SE5	148	A2
Orpington Gdns N18	60	C6
Orpington Rd N21	59	R2
Orpington Rd, Chis	189	S6
Orpwood Cl, Hmptn	157	L10
Orsett St SE11	34	G5
Orsett Ter W2	14	E5
Orsett Ter, Wdf Grn	79	T1
Orsman Rd N1	112	C2
Orton St E1	29	S3
Orville Rd SW11	145	P3
Orwell Ct N5	93	U8
Orwell Rd E13	115	T3
Osbaldeston Rd N16	94	F4
Osbert St SW1	33	R4
Osberton Rd SE12	151	N10
Osborn Cl, E8 *2*	112	G1
Osborn Gdns NW7	56	A14
Osborn La SE23	149	S14
Osborn St E1	21	P4
Osborn Ter SE3	151	M8
Osborne Cl, Beck	185	S7
Osborne Cl, Felt	156	G10
Osborne Gdns, Th Hth	183	U3
Osborne Gro, E17 *3*	77	T8
Osborne Rd N4	93	N1
Osborne Ms, E17 *4*	77	T8
Osborne Pl, Sutt	195	N10
Osborne Rd E7	97	R9
Osborne Rd E9	95	U11
Osborne Rd E10	96	D4
Osborne Rd N4	93	N1
Osborne Rd N13	59	P6
Osborne Rd NW2	89	R11
Osborne Rd W3	124	C4
Osborne Rd, Belv	137	L10
Osborne Rd, Buck H	63	R2
Osborne Rd, Dag	101	M9
Osborne Rd, Enf	45	R4
Osborne Rd, Houns	139	M6
Osborne Rd, Kings T	159	R13
Osborne Rd, Sthl	103	T12
Osborne Rd, Th Hth	183	T3
Osborne Sq, Dag	101	M8
Oscar St SE8	150	A3
Oseney Cres NW5	92	F11
Osgood Av, Orp	203	T10
Osgood Gdns, Orp	203	T9
O'Shea Gro E3	113	T1
Osidge La N14	58	A2
Osier Ms W4	125	L12
Osier St E1	113	M7
Osier Way E10	96	C5
Osier Way, Mitch	181	T10
Osiers Rd SW18	144	G8
Oslac Rd SE6	168	D9
Oslo Ct NW8	7	P4
Oslo Sq SE16	131	S5
Osman Cl, N15 *2*	76	B11
Osman Rd N9	60	H6
Osman Rd, W6 *4*	125	U5
Osmond Cl, Har	85	U3
Osmond Gdns, Wall	196	F9
Osmund St W12	107	M10
Osnaburgh St NW1	9	K10
Osnaburgh Ter NW1	8	J10
Osney Wk, Cars	181	P11
Osprey Cl E6	116	C10
Osprey Cl E11	79	P7
Osprey Cl E17	61	S14
Osprey Ms, Enf	45	K10
Ospringe Cl SE20	167	N14
Ospringe Ct SE9	153	P12
Ospringe Rd NW5	92	E8
Osram Rd, Wem	87	P5
Osric Path N1	12	G3
Ossian Ms N4	75	M13
Ossian Rd N4	75	L13
Ossington Bldgs W1	16	D2
Ossington Cl, W2 *15*	108	H14
Ossington St W2	14	A11
Ossory Rd SE1	37	R9
Ossulston St NW1	9	T5
Ossulton Pl, N2 *2*	73	L6
Ossulton Way N2	73	L7
Ostade Rd SW2	147	M13
Osten Ms SW7	22	D12
Osterley Av, Islw	122	A14
Osterley Ct, Islw	140	A1
Osterley Cres, Islw	140	E1
Osterley Gdns, Th Hth	183	T3
Osterley La, Islw	122	D10
Osterley La, Sthl	121	P9
Osterley Pk, Islw	122	A10
Osterley Pk Rd, Sthl	121	L5
Osterley Pk Vw Rd W7	122	D4
Osterley Rd N16	94	C7
Osterley Rd, Islw	122	C14
Ostliffe Rd N13	59	T9
Oswald Rd, Sthl	121	K2
Oswald St E5	95	P6
Oswald's Mead E9	95	S7
Osward Pl N9	60	J3
Osward Rd SW17	163	U3
Oswin St SE11	35	R1
Oswyth Rd SE5	148	D3
Otford Cl SE20	185	M1
Otford Cl, Bex	155	R12
Otford Cl, Brom	188	H5
Otford Cres SE4	149	T11
Othello Cl SE11	35	N5
Otis St E3	114	E5
Otley App, Ilf	81	K11
Otley Dr, Ilf	81	K11
Otley Rd E16	115	T11
Otley Ter E5	95	M4
Ottenden Cl, Orp	203	S6
Otter Rd, Grnf	103	U8
Otterbourne Rd E4	62	H6
Otterbourne Rd, Croy *1*	197	T3
Otterburn Gdns, Islw	122	G14
Otterburn St SW17	163	U11
Otterden St SE6	168	A7
Otto Cl SE26	166	J5
Otto St SE17	35	P11
Oulton Cl, SE28 *1*	118	E12
Oulton Cres, Bark	99	T11
Oulton Rd N15	76	B9
Oulton Way, Wat	51	L7
Ouseley Rd SW12	163	U2
Outer Circle NW1	7	S4
Outgate Rd NW10	89	L13
Outram Pl N1	111	K1
Outram Rd E6	116	C1
Outram Rd N22	74	G1
Outram Rd, Croy	198	F2
Outwich St, EC3 *7*	20	J5
Oval, The E2	112	J3
Oval, The, Sid	154	A13
Oval Pl SW8	34	F14
Oval Rd NW1	92	C14
Oval Rd, Croy	198	C2
Oval Rd N, Dag	119	P2
Oval Rd S, Dag	119	S4
Oval Way SE11	34	G8
Overbrae, Beck	168	B11
Overbrook Wk, Edg	54	A13
Overbury Av, Beck	186	E5
Overbury Rd N15	76	A12
Overbury St E5	95	P7
Overcliff Rd SE13	150	B6
Overcourt Cl, Sid *3*	154	D11
Overdale Av, N Mal	178	G3
Overdale Rd W5	123	L5
Overdown Rd SE6	168	C7
Overhill Rd SE22	148	H14
Overhill Way, Beck	186	G10
Overlea Rd E5	76	G14
Overmead, Sid	153	P14
Overstand Cl, Beck	186	B9
Overstone Gdns, Croy	185	S13
Overstone Rd W6	125	T7
Overton Cl NW10	88	E12
Overton Cl, Islw	140	E2
Overton Ct E11	79	P14
Overton Dr E11	79	P14
Overton Dr, Rom	82	F14
Overton Rd E10	95	R1
Overton Rd N14	42	J10
Overton Rd SE2	136	F5
Overton Rd SW9	147	P4
Overton Rd, Sutt	194	H12
Overton Rd E SE2	136	H5
Overtons Yd, Croy	197	T5
Ovesdon Av, Har	85	L2
Ovett Cl SE19	166	D12
Ovex Cl E14	132	F4
Ovington Gdns SW3	23	R11
Ovington Ms SW3	23	S10
Ovington Sq SW3	23	S11
Ovington St SW3	31	S1
Owen Cl SE28	136	E1
Owen Cl, Croy	184	B12
Owen Cl, Hayes	102	C5
Owen Gdns, Wdf Grn	64	D12
Owen Rd N13	59	T9
Owen Rd, Hayes	102	D6
Owen St, EC1 *5*	11	N4
Owen Way NW10	88	E11
Owenite St SE2	136	D7
Owen's Ct EC1	11	N5
Owen's Row, EC1 *3*	11	N5
Owens Way SE23	149	S14
Owgan Cl SE5	130	B14
Owl Pk, Loug	47	M4
Oxberry Av SW6	144	D3
Oxendon St SW1	17	S11
Oxenford St SE15	148	E6
Oxenpark Av, Wem	69	S14
Oxestalls Rd SE8	131	S9
Oxford Av SW20	180	C3
Oxford Av, Houns	121	N11
Oxford Cl N9	60	J3
Oxford Cl, Mitch	182	E6
Oxford Ct EC4	20	D9
Oxford Ct W3	106	A11
Oxford Ct, Felt	156	G8
Oxford Cres, N Mal	178	G11
Oxford Dr, Ruis	84	F4
Oxford Gdns N20	57	N2
Oxford Gdns N21	43	U13
Oxford Gdns W4	124	B10
Oxford Gdns W10	108	A11
Oxford Gate W6	127	B7
Oxford Ms, Bex	173	P1
Oxford Rd E15	96	H12
Oxford Rd N4	93	N1
Oxford Rd N9	61	K3
Oxford Rd NW6	108	H3
Oxford Rd SE19	166	B11
Oxford Rd SW15	144	D8
Oxford Rd W5	105	P14
Oxford Rd, Cars	195	S11
Oxford Rd, Enf	45	K10
Oxford Rd, Har	67	U11
Oxford Rd (Wealdstone), Har	68	E6
Oxford Rd, Ilf	99	M9
Oxford Rd, Sid	172	D10
Oxford Rd, Tedd	158	B10
Oxford Rd, Wall	196	E10
Oxford Rd N W4	124	C9
Oxford Rd S W4	124	C10
Oxford Sq W2	15	P7
Oxford St W1	17	N6
Oxford Wk, Sthl	121	M2
Oxford Way, Felt	156	H8
Oxgate Gdns NW2	89	S5
Oxgate La NW2	89	R3
Oxhawth Cres, Brom	188	H10
Oxhey Dr, Nthwd	50	C11
Oxhey Dr, Wat	50	G6
Oxhey La, Har	51	S12
Oxhey La, Pnr	51	S12
Oxhey La, Wat	51	M6
Oxhey Ridge Cl, Nthwd	50	B9
Oxleas E6	116	J11
Oxleas Cl, Well	153	P4
Oxleay Ct, Har	85	N2
Oxleay Rd, Har	85	N2
Oxleigh Cl, N Mal	178	J9
Oxley Cl SE1	37	P5
Oxleys Rd NW2	89	S6
Oxlip Cl, Croy *6*	199	N1
Oxlow La, Dag	101	L8
Oxonian St, SE22 *1*	148	E8
Oxted Cl, Mitch	181	N5
Oxtoby Way SW16	182	G2
Oyster Catchers Cl E16	115	R11
Oyster Row E1	113	L12
Ozolins Way E16	115	N11

P

Name	Page	Grid
Pablo Neruda Cl, SE24 *15*	147	S7
Pace Pl E1	113	K12
Pacific Rd E16	115	N11
Packington Rd, W3 *2*	124	E5
Packington Sq N1	111	T2
Packington St N1	111	S2
Packmores Rd SE9	153	P10
Padbury SE17	36	H8
Padbury Ct E2	13	N8
Paddenswick Rd W6	125	P6
Paddington Cl, Hayes	102	H7
Paddington Grn W2	15	L2
Paddington St W1	16	D2
Paddock Cl SE3	151	P5
Paddock Cl SE26	167	N7
Paddock Cl, Nthlt	103	N3
Paddock Cl, Orp *2*	203	K8
Paddock Cl, Wor Pk	192	G3
Paddock Gdns, SE19 *3*	166	D12
Paddock Rd NW2	89	P4
Paddock Rd, Bexh	155	K8
Paddock Rd, Ruis	84	H6
Paddock Way, Chis	171	P14
Paddocks, The, Barn	41	U6
Paddocks, The, Wem	88	D3
Paddocks Cl, Har	85	R7
Padfield Rd SE5	147	T5
Padnall Rd, Rom	82	G6
Padstow Rd, Enf	43	P2
Padua Rd SE20	185	L1
Pagden St SW8	146	D1
Page Cl, Dag	101	K9
Page Cl, Hmptn	157	K11
Page Cl, Har	69	T12
Page Cres, Croy	197	R9
Page Grn Rd N15	76	G9
Page Grn Ter N15	76	E9
Page Heath La, Brom	188	B5
Page Heath Vil, Brom	188	A5
Page Meadow NW7	55	P13
Page St NW7	71	P1
Page St SW1	33	U1
Pageant Av NW9	70	H1
Pageant Cres SE16	131	S1
Pageant Wk, Croy	198	C5
Pageantmaster Ct, EC4	19	P7
Pagehurst Rd, Croy	184	J13
Pages Hill N10	74	B3
Pages La N10	74	B4
Pages Wk SE1	36	H2
Pages Yd, W4 *2*	125	K11
Paget Av, Sutt	195	N6
Paget Cl, Hmptn	158	A8
Paget Gdns, Chis	189	K2
Paget La, Islw	140	B6
Paget Pl, Kings T	160	E11
Paget Pl, T Ditt	190	G2
Paget Ri SE18	134	H13
Paget Rd N16	94	B2
Paget Rd, Ilf	98	J2
Paget St EC1	11	P5
Paget Ter SE18	134	H12
Pagitts Gro, Barn	40	J2
Pagnell St SE14	131	T13
Pagoda Av, Rich	141	T6
Pagoda Gdns SE3	150	H4
Pagoda Vista, Rich	141	T3

Name	Page	Grid
Paignton Rd N15	76	C12
Paignton Rd, Ruis	84	B5
Paines Cl, Pnr	67	K5
Paines La, Pnr	66	J2
Pains Cl, Mitch	182	D4
Painters Rd, Ilf	82	A5
Paisley Rd N22	75	S1
Paisley Rd, Cars	195	N1
Pakeman St N7	93	L6
Pakenham Cl, SW12 *5*	164	A2
Pakenham St WC1	10	G8
Palace Av W8	22	C5
Palace Ct NW3	91	K9
Palace Ct W2	14	A11
Palace Ct, Har	69	R11
Palace Ct Gdns N10	74	E5
Palace Gdns, Buck H	64	A2
Palace Gdns, Enf	44	A7
Palace Gdns Ms W8	22	A1
Palace Gdns Ter W8	126	H1
Palace Gate W8	22	F8
Palace Gates Rd N22	74	H2
Palace Grn W8	22	B4
Palace Grn, Croy	199	U14
Palace Gro SE19	166	F14
Palace Gro, Brom	187	R2
Palace Ms E17	77	U8
Palace Ms SW1	32	E3
Palace Ms SW6	126	F13
Palace Pl SW1	25	L9
Palace Rd N8	74	H9
Palace Rd N11	58	H14
Palace Rd SE19	166	F13
Palace Rd SW2	165	L1
Palace Rd, Brom	187	R2
Palace Rd, E Mol	176	B7
Palace Rd, Kings T	177	P8
Palace Rd, Ruis	84	J7
Palace Rd Est SW2	165	N2
Palace Sq SE19	166	F13
Palace St SW1	25	M10
Palace Vw SE12	169	P3
Palace Vw, Brom	187	S5
Palace Vw, Croy	199	U7
Palace Vw Rd E4	62	D9
Palamos Rd E10	96	A1
Palatine Av N16	94	D8
Palatine Rd N16	94	D8
Palermo Rd NW10	107	P4
Palestine Gro SW19	181	N2
Palewell Common Dr SW14	142	H9
Palewell Pk SW14	142	G9
Paley Gdns, Loug	49	K6
Palfrey Pl SW8	34	H14
Palgrave Av, Sthl	103	N14
Palgrave Rd W12	125	L6
Palissy St E2	13	M8
Pall Mall SW1	25	P3
Pall Mall E SW1	25	T1
Pall Mall Pl SW1	25	N3
Pallant Way, Orp	202	G6
Pallet Way SE18	134	C14
Palliser Rd W14	126	C9
Palm Av, Sid	172	H11
Palm Cl E10	96	C5
Palm Gro W5	123	R5
Palm Rd, Rom	83	U9
Palmar Cres, Bexh	155	N5
Palmar Rd, Bexh	155	N4
Palmeira Rd, Bexh	154	G5
Palmer Av, Sutt	193	U8
Palmer Cl, Houns	139	N1
Palmer Cl, W Wick	200	H5
Palmer Cres, Kings T	177	R5
Palmer Gdns, Barn	40	A10
Palmer Pl N7	93	N10
Palmer Rd E13	115	S8
Palmer Rd, Dag	100	G1
Palmer St SW1	25	R9
Palmers Gro, W Mol	175	N8
Palmers La, Enf	45	K1
Palmers Rd E2	113	P4
Palmers Rd N11	58	E10
Palmers Rd SW14	142	F6
Palmers Rd SW16	183	L3
Palmers Rd, Borwd	38	D2
Palmerston Cres N13	59	L10
Palmerston Cres SE18	135	M12
Palmerston Gro, SW19 *2*	162	H14
Palmerston Rd E7	97	R11
Palmerston Rd E17	77	T7
Palmerston Rd N22	59	L13
Palmerston Rd NW6	90	F13
Palmerston Rd SW14	142	E8
Palmerston Rd SW19	162	H13
Palmerston Rd W3	124	E5
Palmerston Rd, Buck H	63	S3
Palmerston Rd, Cars	195	U7
Palmerston Rd, Croy *1*	184	A9
Palmerston Rd, Har	68	E6
Palmerston Rd, Orp	203	M8
Palmerston Rd, Sutt	195	M9
Palmerston Rd, Twick	140	E12
Palmerston Way, SW8 *1*	128	D14
Pamela Gdns, Pnr	66	D10
Pamela Wk E8	112	G1
Pampisford Rd, S Croy	197	S12
Pams Way, Epsom	192	H10
Pancras La, EC4 *1*	20	B8
Pancras Rd NW1	9	S1
Pandora Rd NW6	90	G11
Panfield Ms, Ilf	80	G11
Panfield Rd SE2	136	A5
Pangbourne Av W10	107	U9
Pangbourne Dr, Stan	53	S9
Panhard Pl, Sthl	103	S13
Pank Av, Barn	41	M10
Pankhurst Cl, SE14 *4*	131	N14
Pankhurst Cl, Islw	140	F5
Pankhurst Rd, Walt	174	E13
Panmuir Rd SW20	179	S1
Panmure Cl N5	93	R8
Panmure Rd SE26	166	J5
Pansy Gdns W12	107	N14
Panther Dr NW10	88	G9
Pantiles, The NW11	72	F8
Pantiles, The, Bexh	137	M14
Pantiles, The, Brom	188	D6
Pantiles Cl N13	59	R10
Panton St SW1	17	S12
Papermill Cl, Cars	196	A7
Papillons Wk SE3	151	N4
Papworth Gdns N7	93	M10
Papworth Way SW2	147	P13
Parade, The SW11	32	B13
Parade, The, Esher	190	C11
Parade, The (Carpenders Pk), Wat	50	J5
Parade Ms SE27	165	R3
Paradise Pas N7	93	N10
Paradise Rd SW4	146	J3
Paradise Rd, Rich	141	P9
Paradise Row E2	113	K5
Paradise St SE16	130	J4
Paradise Wk SW3	32	A10
Paragon, The SE3	151	M3
Paragon Cl E16	115	N11
Paragon Gro, Surb *2*	177	T11
Paragon Ms, SE1 *1*	36	F1
Paragon Pl SE3	151	M3
Paragon Rd E9	95	L12
Parbury Ri, Chess	191	R11
Parbury Rd SE23	149	R12
Parchmore Rd, Th Hth	183	S4
Parchmore Way, Th Hth	183	S4
Pardon St, EC1 *1*	11	S10
Pardoner St SE1	28	E10
Parfett St E1	21	U4
Parfitt Cl, NW3 *6*	91	L3
Parfrey St W6	125	U11
Parham Dr, Ilf	80	J11
Paris Gdn SE1	27	N2
Parish Gate Dr, Sid	153	R11
Parish La SE20	167	N12
Parish Ms SE20	167	N13
Park, The N6	74	B12
Park, The NW11	90	J2
Park, The SE19	166	D14
Park, The SE23	167	L2
Park, The W5	123	P2
Park, The, Cars	195	U10
Park, The, Sid	172	A9
Park App, Well	154	D7
Park Av E6	116	G2
Park Av E15	96	J12
Park Av N3	73	K1
Park Av N13	59	P7
Park Av N18	60	G8
Park Av N22	75	L3
Park Av NW2	89	T11
Park Av NW10	105	T5
Park Av NW11	90	J2
Park Av SW14	142	H8
Park Av, Bark	99	M11
Park Av, Brom	169	N12
Park Av, Cars	196	A11
Park Av, Enf	44	D12
Park Av, Houns	139	R11
Park Av, Ilf	98	H2
Park Av, Mitch	164	C14
Park Av (Farnborough), Orp	202	F5
Park Av, Sthl	121	R2
Park Av, W Wick	200	E3
Park Av, Wdf Grn	63	R9
Park Av E, Epsom	193	P12
Park Av N N8	74	H7
Park Av N NW10	89	S9
Park Av Rd N17	61	K14
Park Av S N8	74	G8
Park Av W, Epsom	193	N12
Park Chase, Wem	87	T7
Park Cl E9	113	M1
Park Cl NW2	89	R6
Park Cl NW10	105	U5
Park Cl SW1	23	T6
Park Cl W4	124	H10
Park Cl W14	126	F5
Park Cl, Cars	195	U11
Park Cl, Hmptn	175	T1
Park Cl, Har	68	D1
Park Cl, Houns	139	U10
Park Cl, Kings T	178	A1
Park Ct SE26	167	K11
Park Ct, Kings T	177	M2
Park Ct, N Mal	178	H8
Park Ct, Wem	87	S9
Park Cres N3	57	L14
Park Cres W1	8	G12
Park Cres, Enf	44	B8
Park Cres, Har	68	C2
Park Cres, Twick	158	A1
Park Cres Ms E, W1 *2*	8	J12
Park Cres Ms W W1	16	G1
Park Cft, Edg	70	F1
Park Dale N11	58	H12
Park Dr N21	43	T12
Park Dr NW11	90	J2
Park Dr SE7	134	D11
Park Dr SW14	142	H8
Park Dr W3	124	B5
Park Dr, Dag	101	U5
Park Dr (Harrow Weald), Har	67	N13
Park Dr Cl SE7	134	D10
Park End NW3	91	S7
Park End, Brom	187	L1
Park Fm Cl N2	73	M6
Park Fm Cl, Pnr	66	D10
Park Fm Rd, Brom	188	B2
Park Fm Rd, Kings T	159	S13
Park Gdns NW9	70	D6
Park Gdns, Kings T	159	U10
Park Gate N2	73	P5
Park Gate N21	43	L13
Park Gate W5	105	N9
Park Gates, Har	85	P7
Park Gro E15	115	N1
Park Gro N11	58	H14
Park Gro, Bexh	155	T8
Park Gro, Brom	187	S2
Park Gro, Edg	53	U9
Park Gro Rd E11	96	J4
Park Hall Rd N2	73	S7
Park Hall Rd SE21	166	A5
Park Hill SE23	167	K2
Park Hill SW4	146	H9
Park Hill W5	105	P10
Park Hill, Brom	188	D7
Park Hill, Cars	195	T10
Park Hill, Loug	48	B9
Park Hill, Rich	141	T11
Park Hill Cl, Cars	195	S10
Park Hill Ct, SW17 *8*	163	T6
Park Hill Ri, Croy	198	E5
Park Hill Rd, Brom	186	J4
Park Hill Rd, Croy	198	C4
Park Hill Rd, Wall	196	D14
Park Ho N21	43	L13
Park Ho Gdns, Twick	141	L11
Park La, E15 *2*	114	G1
Park La N9	60	D6
Park La N17	60	G14
Park La W1	24	F3
Park La, Cars	196	B8
Park La, Croy	198	A6
Park La, Har	85	R5
Park La, Houns	120	A14
Park La, Rich	141	P8
Park La (Chadwell Heath), Rom	82	G12
Park La, Stan	52	G6
Park La, Sutt	194	C12
Park La, Tedd	158	E11
Park La, Wall	196	B8
Park La, Wem	87	S8
Park La Cl N17	60	H14
Park Lawns, Wem	87	T8
Park Mead, Har	85	R6
Park Mead, Sid	154	D11
Park Ms SE24	147	T12
Park Ms, Chis	171	K11
Park Ms, E Mol	175	U7
Park Par NW10	107	M3
Park Pl E14	132	A1
Park Pl SW1	25	M3
Park Pl W3	124	B7
Park Pl W5	123	P2
Park Pl, Hmptn	157	T12
Park Pl, Wem	87	U8
Park Pl Vil W2	14	H1
Park Ridings N8	75	N5
Park Ri SE23	167	S1
Park Ri, Har	68	C2
Park Ri Rd SE23	167	S1
Park Rd E6	115	U1
Park Rd E10	96	B2
Park Rd E15	115	N1
Park Rd E17	77	U9
Park Rd N2	73	P5
Park Rd N8	74	G9
Park Rd N11	58	H14
Park Rd N14	42	H14
Park Rd N15	75	S8
Park Rd N18	60	G7
Park Rd NW1	7	N4
Park Rd NW4	71	S12
Park Rd NW8	7	N4
Park Rd NW9	70	G14
Park Rd NW10	106	J2
Park Rd SE25	184	D7
Park Rd SW19	163	R12
Park Rd W4	124	G11
Park Rd W7	104	F13
Park Rd, Barn	40	F7
Park Rd (New Barnet), Barn	41	P7
Park Rd, Beck	167	U13
Park Rd, Brom	187	R2
Park Rd, Chis	171	K11
Park Rd, E Mol	175	U8
Park Rd, Felt	156	G7
Park Rd, Hmptn	157	S9
Park Rd, Houns	139	T8
Park Rd, Ilf	99	N5

Name	Pg	Grid
Park Rd, Islw	140	J2
Park Rd, Kings T	159	U9
Park Rd (Hampton Wick), Kings T	158	F12
Park Rd, N Mal	178	H8
Park Rd, Rich	141	T11
Park Rd, Sun	156	C13
Park Rd, Surb	177	U10
Park Rd, Sutt	194	D11
Park Rd, Tedd	177	M2
Park Rd, Twick	141	M11
Park Rd, Wall	196	D9
Park Rd (Hackbridge), Wall	196	B4
Park Rd, Wem	87	R11
Park Rd E W3	124	D3
Park Rd N W3	124	D3
Park Rd N W4	124	H11
Park Row SE10	132	G11
Park Royal Rd NW10	106	F7
Park Royal Rd W3	106	F7
Park Sq E NW1	8	H10
Park Sq Ms NW1	8	G11
Park Sq W NW1	8	G10
Park St SE1	27	U1
Park St W1	16	D12
Park St, Croy	197	U4
Park St, Tedd	158	D11
Park Ter, Wor Pk	193	N2
Park Vw N21	43	L13
Park Vw W3	106	F10
Park Vw, N Mal	179	M6
Park Vw, Pnr	67	M1
Park Vw, Wem	88	D9
Park Vw Ct, Ilf	81	R12
Park Vw Cres N11	58	C7
Park Vw Est E2	113	N3
Park Vw Gdns NW4	71	U10
Park Vw Gdns, Ilf	80	E7
Park Vw Rd N3	73	K1
Park Vw Rd N17	76	H4
Park Vw Rd NW10	89	M7
Park Vw Rd W5	105	S10
Park Vw Rd, Pnr	50	C13
Park Vw Rd, Sthl	121	N1
Park Vw Rd, Well	154	E6
Park Village E NW1	8	J2
Park Village W NW1	8	H2
Park Vil, Rom	82	H12
Park Vista SE10	132	H12
Park Wk SE10	132	G14
Park Wk SW10	30	J10
Park Way N20	57	T7
Park Way NW11	72	D10
Park Way, Edg	70	D2
Park Way, Enf	43	N4
Park Way, Felt	138	D14
Park Way, Ruis	84	A1
Park Way, W Mol	175	S5
Park W W2	15	S7
Park W PI W2	15	R6
Parkcroft Rd SE12	151	L13
Parkdale Cres, Wor Pk	192	H5
Parkdale Rd SE18	135	R10
Parke Rd SW13	143	N1
Parke Rd, Sun	174	B8
Parker CI, E16 2	134	C2
Parker Ms WC2	18	C6
Parker Rd, Croy	197	U7
Parker St E16	134	C2
Parker St WC2	18	D6
Parkers Row SE1	29	P8
Parkes Rd, Chig	65	S10
Parkfield Av SW14	142	J7
Parkfield Av, Felt 5	156	B5
Parkfield Av, Har	67	T3
Parkfield Av, Nthlt	102	H3
Parkfield CI, Edg	54	C12
Parkfield CI, Nthlt	102	J3
Parkfield Cres, Felt	156	A5
Parkfield Cres, Har	67	T4
Parkfield Cres, Ruis	84	A4
Parkfield Dr, Nthlt	102	H3
Parkfield Gdns, Har	67	S5
Parkfield Rd NW10	89	R13
Parkfield Rd SE14	149	T1
Parkfield Rd, Felt	156	A5
Parkfield Rd, Har	85	U5
Parkfield Rd, Nthlt	102	J3
Parkfield St N1	11	M2
Parkfield Way, Brom	188	F11
Parkfields SW15	143	U8
Parkfields, Croy	199	T1
Parkfields Av NW9	88	H1
Parkfields Av SW20	179	R3
Parkfields CI, Cars 1	196	B7
Parkfields Rd, Kings T	159	U10
Parkgate SE3	151	M6
Parkgate Av, Barn	41	L1
Parkgate CI, Kings T 2	160	D11
Parkgate Cres, Barn	41	L2
Parkgate Gdns SW14	142	G10
Parkgate Rd SW11	127	S14
Parkgate Rd, Wall	196	C9
Parkham Ct, Brom	187	K4
Parkham St SW11	145	R2
Parkhill Rd E4	46	F14
Parkhill Rd NW3	91	T9
Parkhill Rd, Bex	155	M13
Parkhill Rd, Sid	171	R5
Parkhill Wk NW3	91	U10
Parkholme Rd E8	94	G12
Parkhouse St SE5	36	E13
Parkhurst Av, E16 16	133	S1
Parkhurst Gdns, Bex 1	155	N13
Parkhurst Rd E12	98	G8
Parkhurst Rd E17	77	S8
Parkhurst Rd N7	93	K7
Parkhurst Rd N11	58	B8
Parkhurst Rd N17	76	G3
Parkhurst Rd N22	59	M13
Parkhurst Rd, Bex	155	N13
Parkhurst Rd, Sutt	195	N7
Parkland CI, Chig	65	M5
Parkland Gdns SW19 3	162	B1
Parkland Rd N22	75	M3
Parkland Rd, Wdf Grn	63	P14
Parkland Wk N4	75	N14
Parkland Wk N6	74	E13
Parkland Wk N10	74	B8
Parklands N6	74	C14
Parklands, Chig	65	L4
Parklands, Surb	177	T10
Parklands CI SW14	142	E10
Parklands Ct, Houns	138	G3
Parklands Dr N3	72	C6
Parklands Rd SW16	164	D9
Parklands Way, Wor Pk	193	K4
Parklea CI NW9	71	K1
Parkleigh Rd SW19	181	K3
Parkleys, Rich	159	P8
Parkmead SW15	143	R12
Parkmead, Loug	48	H9
Parkmead Gdns NW7	55	L11
Parkmore CI, Wdf Grn	63	N8
Parkshot, Rich	141	P8
Parkside N3	72	J1
Parkside NW2	89	R6
Parkside NW7	55	N12
Parkside SE3	133	L14
Parkside SW19	162	A7
Parkside, Buck H	63	R3
Parkside, Hmptn	158	A10
Parkside, Sid	172	D4
Parkside, Sutt	194	C12
Parkside Av SW19	162	A9
Parkside Av, Brom	188	C8
Parkside CI SE20	167	M13
Parkside Cres N7	93	N6
Parkside Cres, Surb	178	E12
Parkside Dr, Edg	54	A6
Parkside Gdns SW19	162	A8
Parkside Gdns, Barn	42	A14
Parkside Rd, SW11 2	146	A2
Parkside Rd, Belv	137	T7
Parkside Rd, Houns	139	R9
Parkside Wk SE10	132	J5
Parkside Way, Har	67	S8
Parkstead Rd SW15	143	P10
Parkstone Av N18	60	E10
Parkstone Rd E17	78	E5
Parkstone Rd, SE15 4	148	H4
Parkthorne CI, Har	67	R12
Parkthorne Dr, Har	67	R11
Parkthorne Rd SW12	146	G14
Parkview Ct, SW18 4	144	H10
Parkview Dr, Mitch	181	N4
Parkview Rd SE9	170	J2
Parkview Rd, Croy	198	H1
Parkville Rd SW6	126	E14
Parkway N14	58	J3
Parkway NW1	110	C2
Parkway SW20	180	A8
Parkway, Erith	137	K5
Parkway, Ilf	99	T6
Parkway, Wdf Grn	63	U9
Parkway, The, Hayes	102	E12
Parkway, The (Cranford), Houns	120	D14
Parkway, The, Nthlt	102	G5
Parkway, The, Sthl	120	B8
Parkway Ms, Mitch 4	164	C13
Parkway Trd Est, Houns	120	E12
Parkwood N20	57	U6
Parkwood, Beck	186	B1
Parkwood Gro, Sun	174	A5
Parkwood Ms N6	74	C11
Parkwood Rd SW19	162	F10
Parkwood Rd, Bex	155	L14
Parkwood Rd, Islw	140	F1
Parliament Ct, E1 6	21	K3
Parliament Hill NW3	91	S7
Parliament Ms SW14	142	E4
Parliament Sq SW1	26	A7
Parliament St SW1	26	B4
Parma Cres SW11	145	T7
Parmiter St E2	113	K3
Parnell CI, Edg	54	D7
Parnell Rd E3	113	U2
Parnham St, E14 4	113	S11
Parolles Rd N19	92	F2
Paroma Rd, Belv	137	N6
Parr CI N9	60	J7
Parr CI N18	60	J7
Parr Ct, Felt	156	E7
Parr Rd E6	116	B2
Parr Rd, Stan	69	R1
Parr St N1	12	C1
Parrs PI, Hmptn	157	P14
Parry Av E6	116	E12
Parry CI, Epsom	193	P13
Parry PI SE18	135	K7
Parry Rd SE25	184	C6
Parry Rd W10	108	D5
Parry St SW8	34	C10
Parsifal Rd NW6	90	H8
Parsloes Av, Dag	101	M11
Parson St NW4	71	U6
Parsonage Gdns, Enf	43	U4
Parsonage La, Enf	44	B4
Parsonage La, Sid	173	L8
Parsonage Manorway, Belv	137	P12
Parsonage St E14	132	F8
Parsons Cres, Edg	54	A5
Parsons Grn SW6	144	G3
Parsons Grn La SW6	144	G1
Parsons Gro, Edg	54	B5
Parson's Mead, Croy	197	S1
Parsons Mead, E Mol	175	U6
Parsons Rd E13	115	T4
Parthenia Rd SW6	144	H2
Partingdale La NW7	56	D10
Partington CI N19	92	H1
Partridge CI, E16 6	116	A10
Partridge CI, Barn	39	U12
Partridge CI, Bushey	51	T1
Partridge CI, Stan	53	R7
Partridge Dr, Orp	203	L5
Partridge Grn SE9	170	G5
Partridge Rd, Hmptn	157	M11
Partridge Rd, Sid	171	R6
Partridge Sq, E6 2	116	D9
Partridge Way N22	75	K1
Parvin St SW8	146	G1
Pasadena CI, Hayes	120	B3
Pascal St SW8	33	U14
Pascoe Rd SE13	150	G9
Pasley CI SE17	35	T7
Pasquier Rd E17	77	S5
Passey PI SE9	152	F11
Passfield Dr E14	114	D9
Passmore Gdns N11	58	G12
Passmore St SW1	32	D4
Pasteur CI NW9	71	K4
Pasteur Gdns N18	59	T10
Paston CI, E5 2	95	N6
Paston CI, Wall	196	E6
Paston Cres SE12	151	S13
Pastor St SE11	35	R1
Pasture CI, Wem	86	J6
Pasture Rd SE6	169	K2
Pasture Rd, Dag	101	L9
Pasture Rd, Wem	86	J4
Pastures, The N20	56	F1
Patcham Ter SW8	146	D1
Pater St W8	126	G5
Paternoster Row EC4	19	T7
Path, The SW19	180	J1
Pathfield Rd SW16	164	H12
Pathway, The, Wat	50	G1
Patience Rd SW11	145	R4
Patio CI SW4	146	G11
Patmore Est SW8	146	F1
Patmore St SW8	146	F1
Patmos Rd SW9	129	R14
Paton CI E3	114	B5
Patricia Ct, Chis	189	N2
Patricia Ct, Well	136	C14
Patrick Connolly Gdns, E3 2	114	D6
Patrick Pas SW11	145	U3
Patrick Rd E13	115	U6
Patriot Sq E2	113	K4
Patrol PI SE6	150	D12
Patshull PI NW5	92	E12
Patshull Rd NW5	92	E11
Patten Rd SW18	145	R14
Pattenden Rd SE6	167	U2
Patterdale CI, Brom	169	K12
Patterdale Rd SE15	131	L13
Patterson Ct SE19	166	E13
Patterson Rd SE19	166	E12
Pattina Wk SE16	131	S2
Pattison Rd NW2	90	G6
Pattison Wk SE18	135	M8
Paul Gdns, Croy	198	E4
Paul Julius CI E14	114	G14
Paul Robeson CI E6	116	H5
Paul St E15	114	H1
Paul St EC2	12	F11
Paulet Rd SE5	147	S3
Paulhan Rd, Har	69	N7
Paulin Dr N21	43	P13
Pauline Cres, Twick	157	T1
Paul's Wk EC4	19	S10
Paultons Sq SW3	31	M10
Paultons St SW3	31	M11
Paved Ct, Rich 3	141	N9
Paveley Dr SW11	127	R14
Paveley St NW8	7	S9
Pavement, The SW4	146	E7
Pavement Ms, Rom	82	G13
Pavement Sq, Croy	198	G1
Pavet CI, Dag	101	R11
Pavilion Ms N3	72	H4
Pavilion Rd SW1	24	A8
Pavilion Rd, Ilf	80	F13
Pavilion St SW1	24	A11

Name	No.	Ref
Pavilion Ter, E Mol	176	G9
Pavilion Way, Edg	54	E14
Pavilion Way, Ruis	84	E4
Pawleyne Cl SE20	167	M14
Pawsey Cl E13	115	R1
Pawson's Rd, Croy	183	U10
Paxford Rd, Wem	86	J4
Paxton Cl, Rich	141	T3
Paxton Cl, Walt	174	E13
Paxton Pl SE27	166	C8
Paxton Rd N17	60	F14
Paxton Rd SE23	167	R5
Paxton Rd W4	124	J11
Paxton Rd, Brom	169	P13
Paxton Ter SW1	33	K9
Payne Rd E3	114	C4
Payne St SE8	131	U12
Paynell Ct, SE3 *1*	151	K5
Paynes Wk W6	126	C12
Paynesfield Av SW14	142	H7
Peabody Av SW1	32	J7
Peabody Cl SE10	150	D1
Peabody Cl, Croy	199	L2
Peabody Dws WC1	10	A10
Peabody Est EC1	12	A11
Peabody Est N17	76	C2
Peabody Est SE1	27	M3
Peabody Est SE24	147	T14
Peabody Est SW3	31	R9
Peabody Est W10	107	U9
Peabody Hill SE21	165	T2
Peabody Hill Est SE21	165	S1
Peabody Sq SE1	27	N8
Peabody Trust SE1	27	U3
Peace Cl N14	42	D10
Peace Cl SE25	184	D8
Peace Gro, Wem	88	D4
Peace St, SE18 *8*	134	H11
Peach Rd W10	108	B5
Peaches Cl, Sutt	194	C14
Peachum Rd SE3	133	M11
Peacock St SE17	35	S4
Peacock Wk, E16 *3*	115	S11
Peacock Yd SE17	35	S4
Peak, The SE26	167	M6
Peak Hill SE26	167	L7
Peak Hill Av SE26	167	L8
Peak Hill Gdns SE26	167	M8
Peaketon Av, Ilf	80	A9
Peal Gdns W13	104	G7
Peall Rd, Croy	183	L11
Pear Cl NW9	70	H8
Pear Cl SE14	131	S14
Pear Pl SE1	27	K6
Pear Rd E11	96	J5
Pear Tree Cl E2	112	E2
Pear Tree Cl, Chess	192	A10
Pear Tree Cl, Mitch *2*	181	T5
Pear Tree Ct EC1	11	L10
Pear Tree St EC1	11	T9
Pearce Cl, Mitch	182	A3
Pearce Rd, W Mol *5*	175	R5
Pearcefield Av, SE23 *2*	167	L2
Pearcroft Rd E11	96	G4
Peardon St SW8	146	D5
Peareswood Gdns, Stan	69	P2
Pearfield Rd SE23	167	R5
Pearl Cl E6	116	G11
Pearl Rd E17	78	A6
Pearl St E1	131	K1
Pearman St SE1	27	L8
Pears Rd, Houns	139	T6
Pearscroft Ct SW6	145	K2
Pearscroft Rd SW6	145	K2
Pearse St SE15	36	J12
Pearson Ms, SW4 *3*	146	H6
Pearson St E2	13	L2
Pearsons Av, SE14 *1*	150	A1
Peartree Av, SW17 *5*	163	M5
Peartree Gdns, Dag	100	C9

Name	No.	Ref
Peartree Gdns, Rom	83	R3
Peartree La E1	113	M14
Peartree Rd, Enf	44	C6
Peartree Way SE10	133	N7
Peary Pl E2	113	M5
Peatfield Cl, Sid	171	S5
Pebble Way W3	124	D1
Pebworth Rd, Har	86	G4
Peckarmans Wd SE26	166	G5
Peckett Sq N5	93	S8
Peckford Pl SW9	147	P4
Peckham Gro SE15	36	J14
Peckham High St SE15	148	G2
Peckham Hill St SE15	130	G14
Peckham Pk Rd SE15	37	T13
Peckham Rd SE5	148	E1
Peckham Rd SE15	148	E1
Peckham Rye SE15	148	H6
Peckham Rye SE22	148	H7
Pecks Yd E1	21	M1
Peckwater St NW5	92	E10
Pedlars Wk N7	93	K11
Pedley Rd, Dag	100	E2
Pedley St E1	13	P11
Pedro St E5	95	P6
Pedworth Gdns, SE16 *1*	131	L7
Peek Cres SW19	162	B9
Peel Cl E4	62	C4
Peel Cl N9	60	H5
Peel Dr NW9	71	M6
Peel Dr, Ilf	80	D5
Peel Gro E2	113	L4
Peel Pas W8	126	G2
Peel Pl, Ilf	80	C4
Peel Prec NW6	108	G4
Peel Rd E18	79	L2
Peel Rd NW6	108	F5
Peel Rd, Har	68	E6
Peel Rd, Orp	203	M9
Peel Rd, Wem	87	N5
Peel St W8	126	G2
Peerless St EC1	12	C8
Pegamoid Rd N18	61	L6
Pegasus Cl N16	93	U8
Pegasus Pl, SE11 *1*	35	K9
Pegasus Way N11	58	C11
Pegg Rd, Houns *1*	120	G13
Pegley Gdns SE12	169	P3
Pegwell St SE18	135	R13
Pekin Cl, E14 *1*	114	B12
Pekin St E14	114	B12
Peldon Ct, Rich	141	U8
Pelham Av, Bark	117	S2
Pelham Cl SE5	148	D5
Pelham Cres SW7	31	N3
Pelham Pl SW7	31	N3
Pelham Rd E18	79	R5
Pelham Rd N15	76	E8
Pelham Rd N22	75	N4
Pelham Rd SW19	162	H14
Pelham Rd, Beck	185	M3
Pelham Rd, Bexh	155	P6
Pelham Rd, Ilf	99	P4
Pelham St SW7	31	M2
Pelican Est SE15	148	E2
Pelican Pas, E1 *6*	113	L7
Pelican Wk, SW9 *22*	147	R8
Pelier St SE17	36	A10
Pelinore Rd SE6	168	J4
Pellant Rd SW6	126	D13
Pellatt Gro N22	75	N2
Pellatt Rd SE22	148	F10
Pellatt Rd, Wem	87	P3
Pellerin Rd N16	94	D9
Pelling St E14	114	A11
Pellipar Cl N13	59	N6
Pellipar Gdns SE18	134	E9
Pelly Rd E13	115	P3
Pelter St E2	13	M6
Pelton Rd SE10	132	J9
Pembar Av E17	77	R6
Pember Rd NW10	108	A6

Name	No.	Ref
Pemberley Chase (West Ewell), Epsom	192	D9
Pemberton Gdns N19	92	F5
Pemberton Gdns, Rom	82	J10
Pemberton Rd N4	75	P10
Pemberton Rd, E Mol	175	U8
Pemberton Row EC4	19	L6
Pemberton Ter N19	92	F5
Pembridge Av, Twick	157	L2
Pembridge Cres W11	108	G13
Pembridge Gdns W2	108	G14
Pembridge Ms W11	108	G13
Pembridge Pl W2	108	H13
Pembridge Rd W11	108	G14
Pembridge Sq W2	108	H14
Pembridge Vil W2	108	G13
Pembridge Vil W11	108	G13
Pembroke Av, Enf	45	K1
Pembroke Av, Har	68	H5
Pembroke Av, Pnr	84	H1
Pembroke Av, Surb	178	C10
Pembroke Cl SW1	24	E7
Pembroke Gdns W8	126	F7
Pembroke Gdns, Dag	101	R6
Pembroke Gdns Cl W8	126	F6
Pembroke Ms E3	113	S5
Pembroke Ms, N10 *2*	74	B1
Pembroke Ms, W8 *6*	126	G6
Pembroke Pl W8	126	G6
Pembroke Pl, Edg	54	B14
Pembroke Pl, Islw	140	B3
Pembroke Rd E6	116	E9
Pembroke Rd E17	78	C10
Pembroke Rd N8	74	J7
Pembroke Rd N10	74	B1
Pembroke Rd N13	59	U6
Pembroke Rd N15	76	F9
Pembroke Rd SE25	184	C8
Pembroke Rd W8	126	G7
Pembroke Rd, Brom	187	U4
Pembroke Rd, Erith	137	U9
Pembroke Rd, Grnf	103	S7
Pembroke Rd, Ilf	99	T2
Pembroke Rd, Mitch	182	A4
Pembroke Rd, Wem	87	P6
Pembroke Sq W8	126	G6
Pembroke St N1	93	K14
Pembroke Studios W8	126	F7
Pembroke Vil W8	126	G6
Pembroke Vil, Rich	141	N8
Pembroke Wk W8	126	G7
Pembury Av, Wor Pk	179	P14
Pembury Cl, Brom	187	M13
Pembury Cres, Sid	172	J4
Pembury Pl E5	94	J9
Pembury Rd E5	94	J9
Pembury Rd N17	76	F3
Pembury Rd SE25	184	H8
Pembury Rd, Bexh	137	K13
Pemdevon Rd, Croy	183	P14
Pemell Cl E1	113	M7
Pempath Pl, Wem	87	N3
Penally Pl N1	112	B1
Penang St E1	131	K1
Penard Rd, Sthl	121	R5
Penarth St SE15	131	L11
Penates, Esher	190	A7
Penberth Rd SE6	168	F2
Penbury Rd, Sthl	121	L9
Pencombe Ms, W11 *10*	108	F13
Pencraig Way SE15	130	J12
Penda Rd, Erith	137	S13
Pendall Cl, Barn	41	S7
Pendarves Rd SW20	179	T2
Penda's Mead E9	95	S8
Pendennis Rd N17	76	A5
Pendennis Rd SW16	165	K7
Penderel Rd, Houns	139	P9
Penderry Ri SE6	168	G4

Name	No.	Ref
Penderyn Way N7	92	H7
Pendle Rd SW16	164	D11
Pendlestone Rd E17	78	C10
Pendragon Rd, Brom	169	N5
Pendragon Wk NW9	70	J11
Pendrell Rd SE4	149	R4
Pendrell St SE18	135	P12
Pendula Dr, Hayes	102	H8
Penerley Rd SE6	168	D2
Penfold Cl, Croy	197	P6
Penfold La, Bex	172	G3
Penfold Pl NW1	15	N2
Penfold Rd N9	61	N1
Penfold St NW1	7	L11
Penfold St NW8	7	L11
Penford Gdns SE9	152	A6
Penford St SE5	147	S3
Pengarth Rd, Bex	154	H10
Penge La SE20	167	M13
Penge Rd E13	115	T1
Penge Rd SE20	184	H5
Penge Rd SE25	184	H5
Penhall Rd SE7	134	A7
Penhill Rd, Bex	154	F12
Penhurst Rd, Ilf	65	K14
Penifather La, Grnf	104	B5
Peninsular Pk Rd SE7	133	P8
Penistone Rd SW16	164	J13
Penketh Dr, Har	86	A5
Penmon Rd SE2	136	B5
Penn Cl, Grnf	103	S4
Penn Cl, Har	69	L8
Penn Gdns, Chis	188	J3
Penn La, Bex	154	H10
Penn Rd N7	93	K9
Penn St N1	112	B2
Pennack Rd SE15	37	N12
Pennant Ms W8	30	A1
Pennant Ter E17	77	U3
Pennard Rd W12	125	T3
Pennards, The, Sun	174	F4
Penner Cl SW19	162	C4
Penners Gdns, Surb	177	S13
Pennethorne Cl E9	113	L2
Pennethorne Rd SE15	130	J14
Pennine Dr NW2	90	C3
Pennine La NW2	90	C3
Pennington Cl, SE27 *6*	166	B8
Pennington Dr N21	43	A9
Pennington St E1	21	U11
Pennington Way SE12	169	S4
Penniston Cl N17	75	T3
Penny Rd NW10	106	D5
Pennyfather La, Enf	43	U5
Pennyfields E14	114	A13
Pennyroyal Av E6	116	H12
Penpoll Rd E8	94	J11
Penpool La, Well	154	D6
Penrhyn Av E17	78	A2
Penrhyn Cres E4	78	B2
Penrhyn Cres SW14	142	F7
Penrhyn Gro E17	78	A2
Penrhyn Rd, Kings T	177	N6
Penrith Cl SW15	144	D10
Penrith Cl, Beck	186	C1
Penrith Pl SE27	165	R4
Penrith Rd N15	76	A9
Penrith Rd, N Mal	178	H7
Penrith Rd, Th Hth	183	U3
Penrith St SW16	164	F11
Penrose Av, Wat	50	H4
Penrose Ho SE17	35	U8
Penrose St SE17	35	U8
Penry St SE1	37	K4
Penryn St NW1	9	S2
Pensbury Pl SW8	146	F3
Pensbury St SW8	146	F3
Penscroft Gdns, Borwd	38	G7
Pensford Av, Rich	142	B3
Penshurst Av, Sid	154	D12
Penshurst Gdns, Edg	54	C10
Penshurst Grn, Brom	187	M10
Penshurst Rd E9	95	N14

Penshurst Rd N17	60	E14
Penshurst Rd, Bexh	155	M1
Penshurst Rd, Th Hth	183	R9
Penshurst Way, Sutt	194	H14
Pensilver Cl, Barn	41	S7
Penstemon Cl N3	56	H12
Penstock Footpath N22	75	L5
Pentelow Gdns, Felt	138	A11
Pentire Rd E17	78	G2
Pentland Av, Edg	54	D4
Pentland Cl NW11	90	C4
Pentland Gdns, SW18 *3*	145	L11
Pentland Pl, Nthlt	102	J2
Pentland St SW18	145	L11
Pentlands Cl, Mitch	182	C6
Pentlow St SW15	143	U5
Pentlow Way, Buck H	48	C14
Pentney Rd, E4 *5*	62	G2
Pentney Rd SW12	164	E1
Pentney Rd SW19	180	C1
Penton Gro, N1 *3*	11	K3
Penton Pl SE17	35	S5
Penton Ri WC1	10	G5
Penton St N1	10	J2
Pontonville Rd N1	10	I14
Pentridge St SE15	130	E14
Pentyre Av N18	60	A9
Penwerris Av, Islw	121	U14
Penwith Rd SW18	162	J3
Penwortham Rd SW16	164	E11
Penylan Pl, Edg	54	B14
Penywern Rd SW5	126	H9
Penzance Pl W11	126	C1
Penzance St W11	126	C1
Peony Gdns W12	107	N13
Peploe Rd NW6	108	B3
Pepper All, Loug	47	N2
Pepper Cl E6	116	F10
Pepper St E14	132	C5
Pepper St SE1	27	T5
Peppermead Sq SE13	150	B9
Peppermint Cl, Croy *1*	182	J13
Peppermint Pl, E11 *7*	96	J6
Pepys Cres, E16 *6*	133	P1
Pepys Cres, Barn	39	U9
Pepys Ri, Orp	203	U2
Pepys Rd SE14	149	P1
Pepys Rd SW20	179	T1
Pepys St EC3	21	K10
Perceval Av NW3	91	R9
Perch St E8	94	F8
Percheron Cl, Islw	140	G5
Percheron Rd, Borwd	38	G11
Percival Ct N17	60	E13
Percival Gdns, Rom	82	F11
Percival Rd SW14	142	E8
Percival Rd, Enf	44	F7
Percival Rd, Orp	203	K4
Percival St EC1	11	R8
Percival Way, Epsom	192	G8
Percy Circ, WC1 *5*	10	H6
Percy Gdns, Enf	45	P9
Percy Gdns, Islw	140	H5
Percy Gdns, Wor Pk	192	J1
Percy Ms W1	17	R4
Percy Rd E11	78	J13
Percy Rd E16	115	K9
Percy Rd N12	57	L9
Percy Rd N21	43	U14
Percy Rd SE20	185	N2
Percy Rd SE25	184	F9
Percy Rd W12	125	P3
Percy Rd, Bexh	155	K4
Percy Rd, Hmptn	157	N13
Percy Rd, Ilf	82	A13
Percy Rd, Islw	140	H7
Percy Rd, Mitch	182	A14
Percy Rd, Rom	83	S5
Percy Rd, Twick	157	S3
Percy St W1	17	R4
Percy Way, Twick	157	T1
Percy Yd WC1	10	G6
Peregrine Cl NW10	88	H10
Peregrine Ct SW16	165	L7
Peregrine Ct, Well	153	T2
Peregrine Gdns, Croy	199	R3
Peregrine Way SW19	161	T13
Perham Rd W14	126	D10
Peridot St E6	116	D9
Perifield SE21	165	U2
Perimeade Rd, Grnf	105	M3
Periton Rd SE9	152	A8
Perivale Gdns W13	104	J7
Perivale Gra, Grnf	104	G5
Perivale Ind Pk, Grnf	104	J3
Perivale La, Grnf	104	G5
Perivale New Business Cen, Grnf	105	K3
Perkin Cl, Wem	86	J9
Perkin's Rents SW1	25	S10
Perkins Rd, Ilf	81	N9
Perkins Sq SE1	28	B2
Perks Cl SE3	150	J4
Perpins Rd SE9	153	R12
Perran Rd SW2	165	R2
Perran Wk, Brent	123	R10
Perren St NW5	92	C11
Perrers Rd W6	125	R7
Perrin Rd, Wem	86	H7
Perrins Ct, NW3 *6*	91	M8
Perrins La NW3	91	M8
Perrins Wk NW3	91	M8
Perrin's Wk NW3	91	M8
Perrott St SE18	135	M7
Perry Av W3	106	H11
Perry Ct N15	76	C11
Perry Gdns N9	60	B5
Perry Garth, Nthlt	102	F1
Perry Hall Rd, Orp	189	U12
Perry Hill SE6	167	T4
Perry How, Wor Pk	193	L1
Perry Mead, Enf	43	S3
Perry Ri SE23	167	R6
Perry Rd, Dag	119	M8
Perry St, Chis	171	R12
Perry Vale SE23	167	M3
Perryfield Way NW9	71	M12
Perryfield Way, Rich	159	K4
Perrymans Fm Rd. Ilf	81	N11
Perrymead St SW6	144	H2
Perryn Rd SE16	130	J5
Perryn Rd W3	106	H14
Perrys Pl W1	17	R5
Persant Rd SE6	168	J5
Perseverance Pl SW9	129	P14
Perseverance Pl, Rich	141	R6
Pershore Cl, Ilf	81	K9
Pershore Gro, Cars	181	P12
Pert Cl N10	58	C12
Perth Av NW9	70	H14
Perth Av, Hayes	102	F7
Perth Cl SW20	179	N3
Perth Rd E10	95	S2
Perth Rd E13	115	R4
Perth Rd N4	93	N2
Perth Rd N22	75	R1
Perth Rd, Bark	117	P2
Perth Rd, Beck	186	E4
Perth Rd, Ilf	80	H11
Perth Ter, Ilf	81	M14
Perwell Av, Har	85	M2
Perwell Ct, Har	85	M2
Peter Av NW10	89	R14
Peter James Business Cen, Hayes	120	M4
Peter St W1	17	R9
Peterboat Cl SE10	133	K7
Peterborough Gdns, Ilf	80	D13
Peterborough Ms SW6	144	G3
Peterborough Rd E10	78	F10
Peterborough Rd SW6	144	H5
Peterborough Rd, Cars	181	R11
Peterborough Rd, Har	86	E1
Peterborough Vil, SW6 *3*	144	J1
Petergate SW11	145	M7
Peters Cl, Dag	100	G1
Peters Cl, Stan	53	N11
Peters Cl, Well	153	S3
Peters Hill EC4	19	T8
Peters Path SE26	166	J7
Petersfield Cl N18	59	T10
Petersfield Ri SW15	161	R1
Petersfield Rd W3	124	F3
Petersham Cl, Rich	159	P3
Petersham Cl, Sutt	194	F10
Petersham Dr, Orp	189	U4
Petersham Gdns, Orp	189	U4
Petersham La SW7	22	F10
Petersham Ms SW7	22	F10
Petersham Pl SW7	22	F10
Petersham Rd, Rich	141	R12
Peterstone Rd SE2	136	D4
Peterstow Cl SW19	162	D3
Peterwood Way, Croy	197	L3
Petherton Rd N5	93	U10
Petley Rd W6	125	U12
Peto Pl NW1	8	J10
Peto St N, E16 *4*	115	L13
Petrie Cl NW2	90	D11
Pett St SE18	134	C7
Petticoat La E1	21	K4
Petticoat Sq E1	21	L5
Pettits Pl, Dag	101	N10
Pettits Rd, Dag	101	N10
Pettiward Cl, SW15 *9*	143	T7
Pettman Cres SE28	135	N6
Petts Hill, Nthlt	85	S10
Petts Wd Rd, Orp	201	T1
Pettsgrove Av, Wem	87	M9
Petty France SW1	25	P9
Petworth Cl, Nthlt	85	M13
Petworth Gdns, SW20 *1*	179	R5
Petworth Rd N12	57	S10
Petworth Rd, Bexh	155	N10
Petworth St SW11	145	S1
Petyt Pl, SW3 *3*	31	N12
Petyward SW3	31	R4
Pevensey Av N11	58	G10
Pevensey Av, Enf	44	B3
Pevensey Cl, Islw	121	T14
Pevensey Rd E7	97	M7
Pevensey Rd SW17	163	N8
Pevensey Rd, Felt	156	J2
Peverel E6	116	G11
Peveret Cl N11	58	C9
Peveril Dr, Tedd	158	B9
Pewsey Cl E4	62	A10
Peyton Pl, SE10 *6*	132	E13
Pharaoh Cl, Mitch *3*	181	T13
Pheasant Cl E16	115	P11
Phelp St SE17	36	D9
Phene St SW3	31	R10
Philbeach Gdns SW5	126	G9
Philchurch Pl E1	21	T8
Philimore Cl SE18	135	S10
Philip Gdns, Croy	199	T3
Philip La N15	115	N7
Philip St E13	115	N7
Philip Wk SE15	148	M8
Philipot Path SE9	152	E12
Philippa Gdns SE9	152	A3
Philips Cl, Cars	196	A2
Phillimore Gdns NW10	107	T1
Phillimore Gdns W8	126	G4
Phillimore Gdns Cl, W8 *4*	126	G5
Phillimore Pl W8	126	G4
Phillimore Wk W8	126	G5
Phillipp St N1	112	D2
Philpot La EC3	20	G10
Philpot Sq SW6	144	J6
Philpot St E1	113	K11
Phineas Pett Rd SE9	152	C5
Phipp St EC2	12	H10
Phipps Br Rd SW19	181	M3
Phipps Br Rd, Mitch	181	N5
Phipp's Ms SW1	32	H1
Phoebeth Rd SE4	150	B9
Phoenix Cl E8	112	E1
Phoenix Cl, W Wick	200	H3
Phoenix Dr, Kes	202	B6
Phoenix Pk, Brent	123	P9
Phoenix Pl WC1	10	H10
Phoenix Rd NW1	9	R5
Phoenix Rd SE20	167	M12
Phoenix St, WC2 *8*	17	U7
Phoenix Way, Houns	120	G12
Phoenix Wf SE10	133	L3
Phoenix Wf Rd, SE1 *2*	29	N7
Phyllis Av, N Mal	179	S9
Physic Pl SW3	31	U10
Picardy Manorway, Belv	137	S6
Picardy Rd, Belv	137	P7
Picardy St, Belv	137	P6
Piccadilly W1	17	P12
Piccadilly Circ W1	17	R11
Pickard St EC1	11	S5
Pickering Av E6	116	H4
Pickering Cl, E9 *5*	95	N13
Pickering Gdns, Croy	184	F11
Pickering Ms W2	14	C6
Pickering St, N1 *5*	111	S1
Pickets Cl, Bushey	52	B1
Pickets St SW12	146	C13
Pickett Cft, Stan	69	N2
Picketts Lock La N9	61	M3
Pickford Cl, Bexh	154	J4
Pickford La, Bexh	155	K3
Pickford Rd, Bexh	154	J6
Pickfords Wf N1	11	T3
Pickhurst Grn, Brom	187	L13
Pickhurst La, Brom	187	K11
Pickhurst La, W Wick	201	L1
Pickhurst Mead, Brom	187	L14
Pickhurst Pk, Brom	187	L10
Pickhurst Ri, W Wick	186	F14
Pickwick Cl, Houns *2*	139	K10
Pickwick Ms N18	60	D8
Pickwick Pl, Har	68	C14
Pickwick Rd SE21	148	B13
Pickwick St, SE1 *8*	27	U7
Pickwick Way, Chis	171	M11
Pickworth Cl, SW8 *5*	129	K14
Picton Pl W1	16	F7
Picton Pl, Surb	192	A2
Picton St SE5	130	A14
Piedmont Rd SE18	135	P10
Pier Head W1	130	J2
Pier Rd E16	134	F3
Pier Rd, Felt	138	C9
Pier St E14	132	F7
Pier Ter SW18	145	K7
Pier Way SE28	135	N5
Piermont Grn SE22	148	J10
Piermont Pl, Brom	188	C3
Piermont Rd SE22	148	J10
Pierrepoint Rd W3	106	D14
Pierrepoint Row, N1 *1*	11	N1
Pigeon La, Hmptn	157	P8
Pigott St E14	114	A12
Pike Cl, Brom	169	R10
Pike Rd NW7	54	H7
Pikes End, Pnr	66	D8
Pikestone Cl, Hayes	102	J8
Pilgrim Cl, Mord	181	K13
Pilgrim Hill SE27	165	T7
Pilgrim St EC4	19	R8
Pilgrimage St SE1	28	C8
Pilgrims Cl N13	59	M8
Pilgrims Cl, Nthlt	85	U10

Name	Page	Grid
Pilgrims Ct SE3	151	P1
Pilgrim's La NW3	91	P8
Pilgrims Pl, NW3 10	91	N8
Pilgrims Ri, Barn	41	S9
Pilgrims Way, E6 7	116	D1
Pilgrims Way N19	92	G3
Pilgrims Way, S Croy	198	F10
Pilgrim's Way, Wem	88	C2
Pilkington Rd SE15	148	J4
Pilkington Rd, Orp	203	L5
Pilsdon Cl SW19	162	A2
Piltdown Rd, Wat	50	G7
Pimlico Rd SW1	32	E5
Pimlico Wk N1	12	H5
Pinchbeck Rd, Orp	203	U11
Pinchin St E1	21	T9
Pincott Pl SE4	149	P6
Pincott Rd SW19	181	L1
Pincott Rd, Bexh	155	P9
Pindar St EC2	20	G1
Pindock Ms W9	6	D11
Pine Av E15	96	H9
Pine Av, W Wick	200	D1
Pine Cl E10	96	C4
Pine Cl N14	42	F14
Pine Cl, N19 12	92	E4
Pine Cl, SE20 1	185	L1
Pine Cl, Stan	52	J7
Pine Coombe, Croy	199	P8
Pine Gdns, Ruis	84	D2
Pine Gdns, Surb	178	B11
Pine Glade, Orp	202	E7
Pine Gro N4	93	K3
Pine Gro N20	56	G2
Pine Gro SW19	162	E10
Pine Ms NW10	108	A3
Pine Rd N11	58	A3
Pine Rd NW2	90	A7
Pine St EC1	11	K9
Pine Tree Cl, Houns	138	C1
Pine Wk, Brom	169	U14
Pine Wk, Surb	178	B11
Pine Wd, Sun	174	B1
Pineapple Ct, SW1 1	25	M9
Pinecrest Gdns, Orp	203	K8
Pinefield Cl E14	114	A13
Pinehurst Wk, Orp 2	203	R1
Pinelands Cl, SE3 2	133	M14
Pinemartin Cl NW2	89	T5
Pines, The N14	42	E9
Pines, The, Sun	174	B8
Pines, The, Wdf Grn	63	M5
Pines Rd, Brom	188	C4
Pinewood Av, Pnr	51	R12
Pinewood Av, Sid	171	S2
Pinewood Cl, Borwd	38	G2
Pinewood Cl, Croy	199	R6
Pinewood Cl, Nthwd	50	C10
Pinewood Cl, Orp	203	P3
Pinewood Cl, Pnr	51	R12
Pinewood Dr, Orp	203	R9
Pinewood Gro W5	105	M12
Pinewood Rd SE2	136	G11
Pinewood Rd, Brom	187	P7
Pinewood Rd, Felt	156	D5
Pinfold Rd SW16	164	J7
Pinkcoat Cl, Felt 6	156	C6
Pinkerton Pl, SW16 1	164	G8
Pinkham Way N11	58	B12
Pinley Gdns, Dag	118	C1
Pinnacle Hill, Bexh	155	S6
Pinnacle Hill N, Bexh	155	S8
Pinnell Pl SE9	152	B8
Pinnell Rd SE9	152	B8
Pinner Ct, Pnr	67	N7
Pinner Grn, Pnr	66	F4
Pinner Gro, Pnr	67	K8
Pinner Hill, Pnr	66	E1
Pinner Hill Rd, Pnr	66	E3
Pinner Pk, Pnr	67	N2
Pinner Pk Av, Har	67	T4
Pinner Pk Gdns, Har	67	U4
Pinner Rd, Har	67	T11
Pinner Rd, Nthwd	66	B3
Pinner Rd, Pnr	67	M7
Pinner Vw, Har	67	T11
Pintail Cl, E6 14	116	C10
Pintail Rd, Wdf Grn	63	S13
Pintail Way, Hayes	102	G9
Pinto Cl, Borwd	38	G11
Pinto Way SE3	151	R7
Pioneer St SE15	148	G1
Pioneer Way W12	107	S12
Pioneers Ind Pk, Croy	196	J1
Piper Cl N7	93	L10
Piper Rd, Kings T	178	A5
Piper's Gdns, Croy	185	R13
Pipers Grn NW9	70	F10
Pipers Grn La, Edg	53	S6
Pipewell Rd, Cars	81	R11
Pippin Cl NW2	89	R5
Pippin Cl, Croy	199	T1
Piquet Rd SE20	185	L4
Pirbright Cres, Croy	200	F12
Pirbright Rd SW18	162	F1
Pirie Cl SE5	148	B5
Pirie St E16	133	S2
Pitcairn Cl, Rom	83	P7
Pitcairn Rd, Mitch	163	T13
Pitchford St E15	96	H14
Pitfield Cres SE28	136	A2
Pitfield Est N1	12	F6
Pitfield St N1	12	G7
Pitfield Way NW10	88	E11
Pitfield Way, Enf	45	L1
Pitfold Cl SE12	151	P12
Pitfold Rd SE12	151	N13
Pitlake, Croy	197	S3
Pitman St SE5	35	T14
Pitsea Pl, E1 9	113	P12
Pitsea St E1	113	P12
Pitshanger La W5	105	K8
Pitshanger Pk W13	105	L6
Pitt Cres SW19	162	J7
Pitt Rd, Croy	183	U10
Pitt Rd, Orp	203	M8
Pitt Rd, Th Hth	183	U10
Pitt St W8	126	H3
Pittman Gdns, Ilf	99	M10
Pitt's Head Ms W1	24	F3
Pittsmead Av, Brom	187	N14
Pittville Gdns SE25	184	G5
Pixley St E14	113	U11
Place Fm Av, Orp	203	P1
Plaistow Gro E15	115	L2
Plaistow Gro, Brom	169	R14
Plaistow La, Brom	169	P13
Plaistow Pk Rd E13	115	R3
Plaistow Rd E13	115	M2
Plaistow Rd E15	115	M2
Plane St SE26	166	J6
Plane Tree Cres, Felt	156	C5
Plantagenet Cl, Wor Pk	192	H7
Plantagenet Gdns, Rom	82	G14
Plantagenet Pl, Rom	82	H14
Plantagenet Rd, Barn	41	L7
Plantain Pl SE1	28	D6
Plantation, The SE3	151	P4
Plantation Wf SW11	145	M5
Plashet Gro E6	98	C13
Plashet Rd E13	115	P1
Plassy Rd SE6	150	D14
Platina St, EC2 1	12	F10
Plato Rd SW2	147	K8
Platt, The SW15	144	B6
Platt St NW1 9		S2
Platt's Eyot, Hmptn	175	P4
Platt's La NW3	90	H6
Platts Rd, Enf	45	M2
Plawsfield Rd, Beck	185	P1
Plaxtol Cl, Brom	187	U2
Plaxtol Rd, Erith	137	P13
Playfair St, W6 3	125	U10
Playfield Av, Rom	83	T1
Playfield Rd, Edg	70	F3
Playford Rd N4	93	N4
Playgreen Way SE6	168	A6
Playground Cl, Beck	185	P4
Playhouse Yd EC4	19	P8
Pleasance, The SW15	143	R8
Pleasance Rd SW15	143	R9
Pleasant Gro, Croy	199	U5
Pleasant Pl N1	93	S14
Pleasant Row, NW1 6	110	D2
Pleasant Vw Pl, Orp	203	L10
Pleasant Way, Wem	105	M4
Plender St NW1	110	E2
Pleshey Rd N7	92	G8
Plevna Cres N15	76	C11
Plevna Rd N9	60	H6
Plevna Rd, Hmptn	175	S2
Plevna St E14	132	E5
Pleydell Av SE19	166	F13
Pleydell Av W6	125	M6
Pleydell St, EC4 17	19	L7
Plimsoll Cl E14	114	C12
Plimsoll Rd N4	93	R5
Plough Ct EC3	20	F9
Plough La SE22	148	F12
Plough La SW17	163	L8
Plough La SW19	163	L8
Plough La, Tedd	158	G10
Plough La, Wall	196	J8
Plough La, Cl, Wall	196	J9
Plough Pl, EC4 3	19	L5
Plough Rd SW11	145	P7
Plough Rd, Epsom	192	H14
Plough St, E1 1	21	R6
Plough Ter SW11	145	P8
Plough Way SE16	131	P7
Plough Yd EC2	12	J11
Ploughmans Cl NW1	110	G1
Ploughmans End, Islw	140	B9
Plover Way SE16	131	S5
Plover Way, Hayes	102	G11
Plowman Cl N18	60	B10
Plowman Way, Dag	100	F1
Plum Garth, Brent	123	P8
Plum La SE18	135	L13
Plumbers Row E1	21	S4
Plumbridge St, SE10 7	150	E1
Plummer La, Mitch	181	T3
Plummer Rd SW4	146	G13
Plumpton Cl, Nthlt	85	N11
Plumpton Way, Cars	195	S5
Plumstead Common Rd SE18	134	J11
Plumstead High St SE18	135	R8
Plumstead Rd SE18	135	L7
Plumtree Cl, Dag	101	S12
Plumtree Cl, Wall	196	G13
Plumtree Ct EC4	19	N5
Plumtree Mead, Loug	48	H6
Plymouth Rd E16	115	N10
Plymouth Rd, Brom	187	R1
Plymouth Wf E14	132	G7
Plympton Av NW6	90	E14
Plympton Cl, Belv 3	136	J6
Plympton Pl, NW8 1	7	P11
Plympton Rd NW6	90	E14
Plympton St NW8	7	P11
Plymstock Rd, Well	136	F14
Pocklington Cl NW9	70	J3
Pocock St SE1	27	R6
Podmore Rd SW18	145	L8
Poets Rd N5	94	A9
Poets Way, Har 1	68	D8
Point Cl SE10	150	F1
Point Hill SE10	150	F1
Point of Thomas Path, E1 2	113	M14
Point Pl, Wem	88	C13
Point Pleasant SW18	144	G8
Pointalls Cl N3	73	L3
Pointer Cl SE28	118	G12
Pointers Cl E14	132	C9
Poland St W1	17	N7
Pole Cat All, Brom	201	M4
Pole Hill Rd E4	46	E14
Polebrook Rd SE3	151	U5
Polecroft La SE6	167	T4
Polesden Gdns SW20	179	R4
Polesworth Rd, Dag	100	H13
Pollard Cl E16	115	N13
Pollard Cl N7	93	M8
Pollard Rd N20	57	R4
Pollard Rd, Mord	181	P10
Pollard Row E2	13	U6
Pollard St E2	13	U7
Pollard Wk, Sid	172	F11
Pollards Cl, Loug	47	U10
Pollards Cres SW16	183	K6
Pollards Hill E SW16	183	M5
Pollards Hill N SW16	183	L5
Pollards Hill S SW16	183	L6
Pollards Hill W SW16	183	K6
Pollards Wd Rd SW16	183	K5
Pollen St W1	17	K8
Pollitt Dr NW8	7	L9
Polperro Cl, Orp	189	T12
Polsted Rd SE6	149	U14
Polthorne Est SE18	135	N7
Polthorne Gro SE18	135	M7
Polworth Rd SW16	164	J10
Polygon, The SW4	146	E7
Polygon Rd NW1	9	R4
Polytechnic St SE18	134	H7
Pomell Way E1	21	N5
Pomeroy St SE14	131	M14
Pomfret Rd, SE5 1	147	T5
Pomoja La N19	92	H4
Pond Cl, N12 4	57	S12
Pond Cl SE3	151	M4
Pond Cottage La, W Wick	200	B1
Pond Cotts SE21	166	D2
Pond Fld End, Loug	47	U13
Pond Hill Gdns, Sutt 4	194	C11
Pond Mead SE21	148	B11
Pond Path, Chis	171	K11
Pond Pl SW3	31	N4
Pond Rd E15	114	J3
Pond Rd SE3	151	M4
Pond Sq N6	92	B1
Pond St NW3	91	R9
Pond Way, Tedd	159	L12
Ponder St N7	93	L13
Ponders End Ind Est, Enf	45	T8
Pondfield Rd, Brom	201	K1
Pondfield Rd, Dag	101	R9
Pondfield Rd, Orp	203	K5
Pondwood Ri, Orp	189	R14
Ponler St E1	112	J12
Ponsard Rd NW10	107	R5
Ponsford St E9	95	M11
Ponsonby Pl SW1	33	U5
Ponsonby Rd, SW15 3	143	R13
Ponsonby Ter SW1	33	U5
Pont St SW1	24	B11
Pont St Ms SW1	23	T11
Pontefract Rd, Brom	169	M10
Ponton Rd SW8	33	T12
Pontypool Pl, SE1 1	27	N6
Pool Cl, Beck	168	B10
Pool Cl, W Mol	175	M10
Pool Ct SE6	168	B3
Pool Rd, Har	68	A14
Pool Rd, W Mol	175	L10
Poole Ct Rd, Houns 1	138	J3
Poole Rd E9	95	N12
Poole Rd, Epsom	192	G12
Poole St N1	112	A2
Pooles Bldgs EC1	10	J11
Pooles La SW10	127	L14
Pooles La, Dag	119	K4
Pooles Pk N4	93	N4
Poolmans St SE16	131	P3
Poolsford Rd NW9	71	K8
Poonah St E1	113	M12
Pope Cl SW19	163	P11

Street	Page	Grid
Pope Rd, Brom	188	A9
Pope St SE1	29	K8
Popes Av, Twick	158	D3
Popes Dr N3	72	H1
Popes Gro, Croy	199	T5
Popes Gro, Twick	158	F4
Popes La W5	123	U5
Popes Rd SW9	147	N7
Popham Cl, Felt	157	L6
Popham Rd N1	111	T2
Popham St N1	111	S1
Poplar Av, Mitch	181	U2
Poplar Av, Orp	203	K3
Poplar Av, Sthl	121	S5
Poplar Bath St, E14 *13*	114	D13
Poplar Business Pk E14	114	E14
Poplar Cl E9	95	T9
Poplar Cl, Pnr	66	H2
Poplar Ct SW19	162	H9
Poplar Cres, Epsom	192	E11
Poplar Fm Cl, Epsom	192	E12
Poplar Gdns, N Mal	178	H4
Poplar Gro N11	58	A12
Poplar Gro W6	125	U4
Poplar Gro, N Mal	178	H5
Poplar Gro, Wem	88	F6
Poplar High St E14	114	D14
Poplar Mt, Belv	137	S7
Poplar Pl SE28	118	E14
Poplar Pl W2	14	C10
Poplar Pl, Hayes	102	A14
Poplar Rd SE24	147	T7
Poplar Rd SW19	180	H3
Poplar Rd, Sutt	194	E1
Poplar Rd S SW19	180	H5
Poplar St, Rom	83	U8
Poplar Vw, Wem	87	P4
Poplar Wk SE24	147	T8
Poplar Wk, Croy	197	T3
Poplar Way, Felt	156	C6
Poplar Way, Ilf	81	M8
Poplars, The N14	42	D10
Poplars Av NW10	89	T12
Poplars Rd E17	78	D12
Poppins Ct EC4	19	N7
Poppleton Rd E11	79	K12
Poppy Cl, Wall	196	B1
Porch Way N20	57	T5
Porchester Cl SE5	148	A7
Porchester Gdns W2	14	C9
Porchester Gdns Ms W2	14	D8
Porchester Mead, Beck	168	B12
Porchester Ms W2	14	D6
Porchester Pl W2	15	R7
Porchester Rd W2	14	C5
Porchester Rd, Kings T	178	C4
Porchester Sq W2	14	C5
Porchester Ter W2	14	E9
Porchester Ter N W2	14	D5
Porcupine Cl SE9	170	D3
Porden Rd SW2	147	M8
Porlock Av, Har	85	U1
Porlock Rd W10	108	B8
Porlock Rd, Enf	44	E14
Porlock St SE1	28	D6
Porrington Cl, Chis	188	G1
Port Cres E13	115	R8
Portal Cl SE27	165	P5
Portal Cl, Ruis	84	B8
Portbury Cl, SE15 *1*	148	H2
Portcullis Lo Rd, Enf	44	A5
Portelet Rd E1	113	N6
Porten Rd W14	126	C6
Porter Rd E6	116	F11
Porter Sq N19	92	J2
Porter St SE1	28	A2
Porter St W1	16	C1
Porters Av, Dag	100	D11
Portersfield Rd, Enf	44	C8
Porteus Rd W2	14	H3
Portgate Cl W9	108	F7
Porthcawe Rd SE26	167	S8
Porthkerry Av, Well	154	B7
Portia Way E3	113	T8
Portinscale Rd SW15	144	D10
Portland Av N16	76	F14
Portland Av, N Mal	179	M13
Portland Av, Sid	154	B12
Portland Cl, Rom	82	J9
Portland Cres SE9	170	C4
Portland Cres, Grnf	103	S9
Portland Cres, Stan	69	P4
Portland Gdns N4	75	S15
Portland Gdns, Rom	82	H9
Portland Gro SW8	147	L1
Portland Ms, W1 *2*	17	P7
Portland Pl W1	16	J2
Portland Ri N4	93	T2
Portland Ri Est N4	93	T1
Portland Rd N15	76	E8
Portland Rd SE9	170	C4
Portland Rd SE25	184	J8
Portland Rd W11	126	D1
Portland Rd, Brom	169	T9
Portland Rd, Kings T	177	S6
Portland Rd, Mitch	181	S4
Portland Rd, Sthl	121	L5
Portland Sq E1	130	J1
Portland St SE17	36	C5
Portland Ter, Rich	141	N8
Portman Av SW14	142	G6
Portman Cl W1	16	C6
Portman Cl, Bexh	154	H6
Portman Dr, Wdf Grn	80	A4
Portman Gdns NW9	70	G4
Portman Gate NW1	7	R11
Portman Ms S W1	16	C8
Portman Pl E2	113	M6
Portman Rd, Kings T	177	U4
Portman Sq W1	16	C6
Portman St W1	16	C7
Portmeadow Wk SE2	136	G3
Portmeers Cl E17	78	A11
Portnall Rd W9	108	E5
Portobello Rd W10	108	C9
Portobello Rd W11	108	F13
Porton Ct, Surb	177	M11
Portpool La EC1	18	J1
Portree Cl N22	59	M14
Portree St E14	114	H11
Portsdown Av NW11	72	E12
Portsdown Ms NW11	72	F11
Portsea Ms W2	15	S7
Portsea Pl W2	15	S7
Portslade Rd SW8	146	E3
Portsmouth Av, T Ditt	176	G13
Portsmouth Ms, E16 *14*	133	S1
Portsmouth Rd SW15	143	S14
Portsmouth Rd, Kings T	177	N8
Portsmouth Rd, Surb	177	N8
Portsmouth St, WC2 *1*	18	F7
Portsoken St E1	21	M9
Portugal Gdns, Twick	157	T4
Portugal St WC2	18	F7
Portway E15	115	L1
Portway Gdns SE18	134	B14
Post La, Twick	158	A1
Post Office App E7	97	R10
Post Office Ct, EC3 *14*	20	E8
Post Office Way SW8	33	R13
Post Rd, Sthl	121	R5
Postern Grn, Enf	43	P4
Postmill Cl, Croy	199	N6
Postway Ms, Ilf	99	K5
Potier St SE1	28	F11
Pott St E2	113	K6
Potter Cl, Mitch	182	D4
Potter St, Nthwd	66	B2
Potter St, Pnr	66	D1
Potter St Hill, Pnr	50	C13
Potterne Cl, SW19 *2*	144	B13
Potters Cl, Croy	199	S2
Potters Cl, Loug	48	D4
Potters Gro, N Mal	178	F8
Potters Hts Cl, Pnr	50	C14
Potters La SW16	164	G11
Potters La, Barn	40	H8
Potters Rd SW6	145	L4
Potters Rd, Barn	41	K7
Pottery La W11	108	C14
Pottery Rd, Bex	173	U4
Pottery Rd, Brent	123	S11
Pottery St, SE16 *3*	130	J4
Poulett Gdns, Twick	158	G2
Poulett Rd E6	116	E3
Poulters Wk, Kes	202	B9
Poulton Av, Sutt	195	P6
Poulton Cl E8	94	J11
Poultry EC2	20	C7
Pound Cl, Orp	203	P4
Pound Cl, Surb	191	L1
Pound Ct Dr, Orp	203	P4
Pound La NW10	89	N12
Pound Pk Rd SE7	134	A8
Pound Pl SE9	152	G11
Pound St, Cars	195	T9
Poundfield Rd, Loug	48	H9
Pountney Rd SW11	146	A5
Poverest Rd, Orp	189	U9
Powder Mill La, Twick	157	P2
Powell Cl, Chess	191	N10
Powell Cl, Edg	53	T11
Powell Cl, Wall	196	H13
Powell Gdns, Dag	101	N8
Powell Rd E5	95	K6
Powell Rd, Buck H	47	U14
Powell's Wk W4	125	K12
Power Rd W4	124	C8
Powers Ct, Twick	141	N13
Powerscroft Rd E5	95	M7
Powerscroft Rd, Sid	172	E12
Powis Gdns NW11	72	E14
Powis Gdns W11	108	F11
Powis Ms W11	108	F11
Powis Pl WC1	10	D12
Powis Rd E3	114	D6
Powis Sq W11	108	F11
Powis St SE18	134	H6
Powis Ter W11	108	F11
Powlett Pl NW1	92	C12
Pownall Gdns, Houns	139	S8
Pownall Rd E8	112	G2
Pownall Rd, Houns	139	S7
Powster Rd, Brom	169	P9
Powys Cl, Bexh	136	H12
Powys La N13	58	J9
Powys La N14	58	J8
Poynders Gdns SW4	146	F13
Poynders Rd SW4	146	F13
Poynings Rd N19	92	E5
Poynings Way N12	56	G10
Poyntell Cres, Chis	189	P1
Poynter Rd, Enf	44	G10
Poynton Rd N17	76	H3
Poyntz Rd, SW11 *5*	145	T4
Poyser St E2	113	K4
Praed Ms W2	15	L6
Praed St W2	15	K7
Pragel St E13	115	S4
Pragnell Rd SE12	169	R3
Prague Rd SW2	146	J10
Prah Rd N4	93	P4
Prairie St SW8	146	B4
Pratt Ms, NW1 *1*	110	E2
Pratt St NW1	110	E2
Pratt Wk SE11	34	G1
Prayle Gro NW2	90	A1
Prebend Gdns W4	125	L7
Prebend Gdns W6	125	L7
Prebend St N1	111	T2
Precinct Rd, Hayes	102	B14
Premier Cor W9	108	E4
Premier Pk NW10	106	D2
Premiere Pl, E14 *1*	114	A14
Prendergast Rd SE3	151	K5
Prentis Rd SW16	164	H7
Prentiss Ct SE7	134	A8
Presburg Rd, N Mal	179	K9
Prescelly Pl, Edg	69	U2
Prescot St E1	21	P9
Prescott Av, Orp	188	J12
Prescott Cl, SW16	164	J13
Prescott Grn, Loug	49	L5
Prescott Pl SW4	146	G6
Presentation Ms SW2	165	M3
President Dr E1	130	J1
President St EC1	11	T6
Press Rd NW10	88	H5
Prestage Way E14	114	F13
Prestbury Rd E7	97	U13
Prestbury Sq SE9	170	F7
Prested Rd, SW11 *3*	145	R7
Prestige Way, NW4 *1*	71	U9
Preston Av E4	62	G12
Preston Cl SE1	36	G2
Preston Cl, Twick	158	C5
Preston Dr E11	79	T10
Preston Dr, Bexh	154	H2
Preston Dr, Epsom	193	K11
Preston Gdns, NW10 *2*	89	K12
Preston Gdns, Ilf	80	D12
Preston Hill, Har	69	S13
Preston Pl NW2	89	P11
Preston Pl, Rich	141	S9
Preston Rd E11	79	K12
Preston Rd SE19	165	S11
Preston Rd SW20	161	M14
Preston Rd, Har	87	S5
Preston Rd, Wem	69	S14
Preston Waye, Har	87	R1
Prestons Rd E14	132	F3
Prestons Rd, Brom	201	N5
Prestwick Cl, Sthl	120	J9
Prestwick Rd, Wat	50	G9
Prestwood Av, Har	69	K8
Prestwood Cl SE18	136	A13
Prestwood Cl, Har	69	K8
Prestwood Gdns, Croy	183	T13
Prestwood St, N1 *1*	12	A4
Pretoria Av E17	77	R8
Pretoria Cl N17	60	E13
Pretoria Cres E4	62	F2
Pretoria Rd E4	62	F2
Pretoria Rd E11	96	G2
Pretoria Rd E16	115	L6
Pretoria Rd N17	60	E12
Pretoria Rd SW16	164	D11
Pretoria Rd, Ilf	98	J9
Pretoria Rd, Rom	83	T9
Pretoria Rd N N18	60	E11
Prevost Rd N11	58	A3
Price Cl NW7	56	C11
Price Cl SW17	163	T6
Price Rd, Croy	197	S9
Price Way, Hmptn	157	K11
Price's Yd N1	111	M1
Pricklers Hill, Barn	41	K11
Priddy's Yd, Croy	197	T4
Prideaux Pl W3	106	H13
Prideaux Pl WC1	10	H6
Prideaux Rd, SW9 *1*	147	K5
Pridham Rd, Th Hth	184	A8
Priest Pk Av, Har	85	P3
Priestfield Rd SE23	167	S5
Priestlands Pk Rd, Sid	171	U5
Priestley Cl N16	76	F13
Priestley Gdns, Rom	82	C12
Priestley Rd, Mitch	182	B3
Priestley Way E17	77	N6
Priestley Way NW2	89	P1
Priests Br SW14	143	K6
Priests Br SW15	143	K6
Prima Rd SW9	35	K13
Primrose Av, Enf	44	B1
Primrose Av, Rom	82	C13

Name	Page	Grid
Primrose Cl SE6	168	F9
Primrose Cl, Har	85	L7
Primrose Cl, Wall	196	C1
Primrose Gdns NW3	91	S11
Primrose Gdns, Ruis	84	E9
Primrose Hill EC4	19	M8
Primrose Hill Ct NW3	91	T14
Primrose Hill Rd NW3	91	T14
Primrose Hill Studios, NW1 *4*	110	A1
Primrose La, Croy	199	N1
Primrose Ms, NW1 *9*	91	U14
Primrose Ms SE3	133	R14
Primrose Rd E10	96	C2
Primrose Rd E18	79	R4
Primrose Sq E9	95	M14
Primrose St EC2	20	H1
Primrose Wk, Epsom	193	M13
Primrose Way, Wem	105	N4
Primula St W12	107	N12
Prince Albert Rd NW1	7	R3
Prince Albert Rd NW8	7	R3
Prince Arthur Ms NW3	91	M8
Prince Arthur Rd NW3	91	M9
Prince Charles Dr NW4	71	T14
Prince Charles Rd SE3	151	L1
Prince Charles Way, Wall	196	C5
Prince Consort Dr, Chis	189	N2
Prince Consort Rd SW7	22	H9
Prince Edward Rd, E9 *1*	96	A12
Prince George Av N14	42	J10
Prince George Duke of Kent Ct, Chis *2*	171	N13
Prince George Rd N16	94	D8
Prince George's Av SW20	179	U3
Prince George's Rd SW19	181	P1
Prince Henry Rd SE7	134	B14
Prince Imperial Rd SE18	152	F1
Prince Imperial Rd, Chis	171	K14
Prince John Rd SE9	152	C10
Prince of Wales Cl, NW4 *3*	71	T7
Prince of Wales Dr SW8	128	C14
Prince of Wales Dr SW11	146	B1
Prince of Wales Gate SW7	23	N6
Prince of Wales Pas, NW1 *4*	9	M7
Prince of Wales Rd NW5	92	C12
Prince of Wales Rd SE3	151	M2
Prince of Wales Rd, Sutt	195	N4
Prince of Wales Ter W4	124	J9
Prince of Wales Ter W8	22	D7
Prince Regent La E13	115	S6
Prince Regent La E16	115	T10
Prince Regent Rd, Houns	139	T5
Prince Rd SE25	184	C9
Prince Rupert Rd SE9	152	E7
Prince St SE8	131	U11
Princedale Rd W11	126	D1
Princelet St E1	21	N2
Princes Av N3	72	H1
Princes Av N10	74	C6
Princes Av N13	59	N10
Princes Av N22	74	H1
Princes Av NW9	70	E6
Princes Av W3	124	B6
Princes Av, Cars	195	T14
Princes Av, Grnf	103	S11
Princes Av, Orp	189	R10
Princes Av, Surb	192	B3
Princes Av, Wdf Grn	63	S8
Princes Cl N4	93	S1
Princes Cl NW9	70	A7
Princes Cl, SW4 *1*	146	E6
Princes Cl, Edg	54	A10
Princes Cl, Sid	172	G5
Princes Cl, Tedd	158	A8
Princes Ct E1	113	K14
Princes Ct SE16	131	T6
Princes Ct, Wem	87	R9
Princes Dr, Har	68	C6
Princes Gdns SW7	23	M10
Princes Gdns W3	106	B10
Princes Gdns W5	105	L8
Princes Gate SW7	23	P7
Princes Gate Ct, SW7 *1*	23	L8
Princes Gate Ms SW7	23	M10
Princes La N10	74	C6
Princes Ms W2	14	A10
Princes Pk Av NW11	72	D9
Princes Pl SW1	25	N2
Princes Pl W11	126	C1
Princes Plain, Brom	202	D1
Princes Ri SE13	150	F4
Princes Riverside Rd SE16	131	N1
Princes Rd N18	61	L7
Princes Rd SE20	167	N12
Princes Rd SW14	142	H6
Princes Rd SW19	162	G12
Princes Rd W13	123	K1
Princes Rd, Buck H	63	T4
Princes Rd, Ilf	81	N7
Princes Rd, Kings T	160	A14
Princes Rd, Rich	141	T9
Princes Rd (Kew), Rich	141	U1
Princes Rd, Tedd	158	B8
Princes Sq W2	14	B9
Princes St EC2	20	D7
Princes St N17	60	D12
Princes St W1	17	K7
Princes St, Bexh	155	L7
Princes St, Sutt	195	N8
Princes Ter E13	115	S2
Princes Way SW19	162	C1
Princes Way, Buck H	63	T4
Princes Way, Croy	197	M10
Princes Way, Ruis	84	J7
Princes Way, W Wick	201	L7
Princes Yd, W11 *14*	126	D2
Princess Alice Way SE28	135	N3
Princess Av, Wem	87	S3
Princess Cres N4	93	S3
Princess May Rd N16	94	D8
Princess Ms, NW3 *2*	91	P11
Princess Par, Orp	202	A9
Princess Pk Manor N11	58	A10
Princess Rd NW1	110	A1
Princess Rd NW6	108	G4
Princess Rd, Croy	183	U11
Princess St SE1	27	R11
Princethorpe Rd SE26	167	N8
Princeton Ct, SW15 *2*	144	B6
Princeton St WC1	18	F3
Pringle Gdns SW16	164	F8
Print Village SE15	148	F4
Printer St, EC4 *9*	19	M6
Printers Inn Ct, EC4 *1*	19	K5
Printing Ho Yd, E2 *3*	13	K7
Priolo Rd SE7	133	T10
Prior Av, Sutt	195	R13
Prior Bolton St N1	93	S12
Prior Rd, Ilf	98	H5
Prior St SE10	132	E14
Prioress Rd SE27	165	R6
Prioress St SE1	28	F11
Priors Cft E17	77	T3
Priors Fld, Nthlt	85	K12
Priors Gdns, Ruis	84	F10
Priors Mead, Enf	44	C1
Priory, The SE3	151	M7
Priory Av E4	62	A5
Priory Av E17	78	A9
Priory Av N8	74	H7
Priory Av W4	125	K6
Priory Av, Orp	189	P11
Priory Av, Sutt	194	B8
Priory Av, Wem	86	F8
Priory Cl E4	61	U5
Priory Cl E18	79	N1
Priory Cl N3	72	F2
Priory Cl N14	42	D10
Priory Cl N20	40	E14
Priory Cl SW19	181	K1
Priory Cl, Beck	185	S6
Priory Cl, Chis	188	F2
Priory Cl, Hmptn	175	M1
Priory Cl, Hayes	102	D14
Priory Cl, Stan	52	F5
Priory Cl, Sun	156	B14
Priory Cl (Sudbury), Wem	86	F7
Priory Ct E17	77	T4
Priory Ct SW8	146	H2
Priory Ct, Bushey	51	U1
Priory Ct Est E17	77	U4
Priory Cres SE19	165	U14
Priory Cres, Sutt	194	B8
Priory Cres, Wem	86	G6
Priory Dr SE2	136	H10
Priory Dr, Stan	52	E5
Priory Fld Dr, Edg	54	D7
Priory Gdns N6	74	C12
Priory Gdns SE25	184	E8
Priory Gdns, SW13 *4*	143	L6
Priory Gdns, W4 *11*	125	K7
Priory Gdns, Hmptn	157	M14
Priory Gdns, Wem	86	G7
Priory Grn Est N1	10	G2
Priory Gro SW8	146	J2
Priory Hill, Wem	86	G7
Priory La SW15	143	L7
Priory La, W Mol	175	R8
Priory Ms SW8	146	J2
Priory Pk SE3	151	M6
Priory Pk Rd NW6	108	F1
Priory Pk Rd, Wem	86	G8
Priory Rd E6	116	A2
Priory Rd N8	74	G8
Priory Rd NW6	90	J14
Priory Rd SW19	163	N14
Priory Rd W4	124	G5
Priory Rd, Bark	99	N13
Priory Rd, Chess	191	R6
Priory Rd, Croy	183	N14
Priory Rd, Hmptn	157	N14
Priory Rd, Houns	139	U9
Priory Rd, Loug	48	D8
Priory Rd, Rich	124	A12
Priory Rd, Sutt	194	B8
Priory St E3	114	D5
Priory Ter NW6	108	J1
Priory Ter, Sun	156	B14
Priory Wk SW10	30	G7
Priory Way, Har	67	R7
Priory Way, Sthl	120	H6
Pritchard's Rd E2	13	U1
Priter Rd SE16	29	T11
Private Rd, Enf	44	C10
Probert Rd SW2	147	P9
Probyn Rd SW2	165	R3
Procter St WC1	18	E4
Proctor Cl, Mitch	182	A2
Proctors Cl, Felt	156	A1
Progress Business Pk, Croy	197	M4
Progress Way N22	75	N1
Progress Way, Croy	197	M3
Progress Way, Enf	44	H10
Promenade, The W4	143	K2
Promenade App Rd W4	124	J13
Prospect Business Pk, Loug	49	N8
Prospect Cl SE26	166	J7
Prospect Cl, Belv	137	P8
Prospect Cl, Houns	139	M2
Prospect Cl, Ruis	66	G14
Prospect Cotts, SW18 *3*	144	G8
Prospect Cres, Twick	139	T12
Prospect Hill E17	78	D7
Prospect Pl E1	131	L1
Prospect Pl N2	73	P7
Prospect Pl N17	60	D14
Prospect Pl, NW2 *1*	90	F5
Prospect Pl, NW3 *3*	91	L8
Prospect Pl, Brom *5*	187	R6
Prospect Pl, Rom	83	T4
Prospect Ring N2	73	P6
Prospect Rd NW2	90	F5
Prospect Rd, Barn	40	H8
Prospect Rd, Surb	177	L12
Prospect Rd, Wdf Grn	63	U11
Prospect St SE16	131	K5
Prospect Vale SE18	134	D7
Prospero Rd N19	92	G2
Protea Cl E16	115	L7
Prothero Gdns NW4	71	S9
Prothero Rd SW6	126	D13
Prout Gro NW10	89	K8
Prout Rd E5	95	K5
Providence Ct W1	16	E9
Providence Pl, Rom	83	L3
Providence Yd, E2 *1*	13	R5
Provident Ind Est, Hayes	120	A4
Provost Est N1	12	D5
Provost Rd NW3	91	U13
Provost St N1	12	D5
Prowse Av, Bushey	51	U3
Prowse Pl NW1	92	E13
Pruden Cl N14	58	F3
Prusom St E1	131	K1
Pryors, The NW3	91	P6
Pudding La EC3	20	F11
Pudding La, Chig	49	S13
Pudding Mill La E15	114	D2
Puddle Dock EC4	19	R9
Puffin Cl, Beck	185	N9
Pulborough Rd SW18	144	E13
Pulborough Way, Houns	138	E8
Pulford Rd N15	76	B11
Pulham Av N2	73	M7
Puller Rd, Barn	40	C5
Pulleyns Av E6	116	D5
Pullman Ct SW2	165	K2
Pullman Gdns SW15	143	U11
Pullman Pl SE9	152	D9
Pulross Rd SW9	147	L6
Pulteney Cl E3	113	T2
Pulteney Rd E18	79	R5
Pulteney Ter N1	111	M2
Pulton Pl SW6	126	G14
Puma Ct E1	21	M2
Pump All, Brent	123	P13
Pump Cl, Nthlt	103	P4
Pump Ct EC4	19	K8
Pump Hill, Loug	48	E4
Pump Ho Cl, Brom	187	L4
Pump La SE14	131	M13
Pump La, Hayes	120	C4
Pump Pail N, Croy	197	T6
Pump Pail S, Croy	197	T6

Name	No	Grid
Pumping Sta Rd W4	125	K13
Pundersons Gdns E2	113	K5
Punjab La, Sthl	121	L1
Purbeck Av, N Mal	179	M12
Purbeck Dr NW2	90	C3
Purbrook Est SE1	29	K8
Purbrook St SE1	29	K9
Purcell Cres SW6	126	B13
Purcell Rd, Grnf	103	R9
Purcell St N1	12	G2
Purcells Av, Edg	54	A9
Purchese St NW1	9	T3
Purdy St E3	114	C7
Purelake Ms SE13	150	G6
Purland Cl, Dag	101	L1
Purland Rd SE28	135	U4
Purleigh Av, Wdf Grn	64	D11
Purley Av NW2	90	D4
Purley Cl, Ilf	80	H4
Purley Pl N1	93	R13
Purley Rd N9	60	B5
Purley Rd, S Croy	198	A14
Purley Way, Croy	197	M1
Purneys Rd SE9	152	A7
Purrett Rd SE18	135	U10
Purser's Cross Rd SW6	144	F1
Pursewardens Cl W13	123	L1
Pursley Rd NW7	55	R13
Purves Rd NW10	107	U4
Putney Br SW6	144	C6
Putney Br SW15	144	C6
Putney Br App SW6	144	D5
Putney Br Rd SW15	144	D7
Putney Br Rd SW18	144	G8
Putney Common SW15	143	T5
Putney Gdns, Rom	82	D9
Putney Heath SW15	143	U12
Putney Heath La SW15	144	B12
Putney High St SW15	144	C7
Putney Hill SW15	144	B11
Putney Pk Av SW15	143	P7
Putney Pk La SW15	143	R7
Puttenham Cl, Wat	50	F5
Pycroft Way N9	60	F7
Pyecombe Cor N12	56	F8
Pylbrook Rd, Sutt	194	H6
Pylon Way, Croy	197	K2
Pym Cl, Barn	41	P10
Pymers Mead SE21	165	U1
Pymmes Cl N13	59	L10
Pymmes Cl N17	76	J2
Pymmes Gdns N N9	60	F6
Pymmes Gdns S N9	60	F6
Pymmes Grn Rd N11	58	D7
Pymmes Rd N13	59	K11
Pymms Brook Dr, Barn	41	R7
Pyne Rd, Surb	192	A2
Pynfolds SE16	130	J4
Pynham Cl SE2	136	C6
Pynnacles Cl, Stan	53	K9
Pyrland Rd N5	94	A9
Pyrland Rd, Rich	141	U11
Pyrles Grn, Loug	48	J2
Pyrles La, Loug	48	J2
Pyrmont Gro SE27	165	R6
Pyrmont Rd W4	124	B11
Pyrmont Rd, Ilf 1	99	M4
Pytchley Cres SE19	165	U12
Pytchley Rd SE22	148	D6

Q

Name	No	Grid
Quad Rd, Wem	87	P5
Quadrangle, The W2	15	N6
Quadrangle Ms, Stan	53	L13
Quadrant, The SW20	180	D1
Quadrant, The, Bexh	136	H14
Quadrant, The, Rich	141	P8
Quadrant, The, Sutt	195	L11
Quadrant Gro NW5	91	U10
Quadrant Rd, Rich 1	141	P8
Quadrant Rd, Th Hth	183	S7
Quaggy Wk SE3	151	N7
Quainton St NW10	88	G6
Quaker Ct E1	13	M12
Quaker La, Sthl	121	P5
Quaker St E1	13	N12
Quakers Course NW9	71	L2
Quakers La, Islw	140	H1
Quaker's Pl E7	98	A10
Quakers Wk N21	44	A11
Quality Ct WC2	18	J5
Quantock Dr, Wor Pk 3	193	U3
Quantock Gdns NW2	90	A3
Quarr Rd, Cars	181	P12
Quarrendon St SW6	144	H3
Quarry Pk Rd, Sutt	194	E11
Quarry Ri, Sutt	194	E11
Quarry Rd SW18	145	M11
Quarter Mile La E10	96	C8
Quarterdeck, The E14	132	A4
Quay W, Tedd	158	J9
Quebec Ms W1	16	A7
Quebec Rd, Hayes	102	E13
Quebec Rd, Ilf	81	L12
Quebec Way SE16	131	P4
Queen Adelaide Rd SE20	167	M12
Queen Alexandra's Ct SW19	162	E10
Queen Anne Av N15	76	E9
Queen Anne Av, Brom	187	M5
Queen Anne Dr, Esher	190	D14
Queen Anne Ms W1	16	J4
Queen Anne Rd E9	95	N12
Queen Anne St W1	16	G4
Queen Anne Ter, E1 2	113	K14
Queen Anne's Cl, Twick	158	B6
Queen Anne's Gdns W4	124	J6
Queen Annes Gdns W5	123	R4
Queen Annes Gdns, Enf	44	C11
Queen Anne's Gdns, Mitch	181	T5
Queen Anne's Gate SW1	25	S8
Queen Anne's Gate, Bexh 1	154	H6
Queen Annes Gro W4	124	J6
Queen Annes Gro W5	123	R3
Queen Annes Gro, Enf	44	C13
Queen Annes Pl, Enf	44	D11
Queen Caroline Est W6	125	U10
Queen Caroline St W6	125	U8
Queen Elizabeth Gdns, Mord 1	180	H8
Queen Elizabeth Rd E17	77	S6
Queen Elizabeth Rd, Kings T	177	T3
Queen Elizabeth St SE1	29	L5
Queen Elizabeth Wk SW13	143	S2
Queen Elizabeths Cl N16	94	A3
Queen Elizabeths Dr N14	58	J1
Queen Elizabeths Wk N16	94	A3
Queen Elizabeth's Wk, Wall	196	H7
Queen Margaret's Gro N1	94	C10
Queen Mary Av, Mord	180	A10
Queen Mary Cl, Surb	192	B6
Queen Mary Rd SE19	165	S11
Queen Mary's Av, Cars	195	T14
Queen of Denmark Ct SE16	131	T5
Queen Sq WC1	10	C12
Queen Sq Pl, WC1 3	10	C12
Queen St EC4	20	B10
Queen St N17	60	D12
Queen St W1	24	H2
Queen St, Bexh	155	L6
Queen St, Croy	197	T7
Queen St Pl EC4	20	B11
Queen Victoria Av, Wem	87	N13
Queen Victoria St EC4	19	P9
Queen Victoria Ter, E1 4	113	K14
Queenborough Gdns, Chis	171	N12
Queenborough Gdns, Ilf	80	H7
Queenhithe EC4	20	A10
Queens Acre, Sutt	194	C13
Queens Av N3	73	L1
Queens Av N10	74	B6
Queens Av N20	57	P4
Queen's Av N21	59	S2
Queens Av, Felt	156	E8
Queens Av, Grnf	103	S11
Queens Av, Stan	69	L5
Queens Av, Wdf Grn	63	S9
Queen's Circ SW8	128	C14
Queen's Circ SW11	128	C14
Queens Cl, Edg	54	A10
Queens Cl, Wall 5	196	C9
Queens Club Gdns W14	126	D11
Queens Ct SE23	167	K3
Queens Cres NW5	92	A12
Queens Cres, Rich	141	U9
Queens Dr E10	78	B14
Queens Dr N4	93	R3
Queens Dr W3	106	A12
Queens Dr W5	106	A12
Queens Dr, Surb	178	B12
Queens Dr, T Ditt	176	H13
Queen's Elm Sq, SW3 1	31	L7
Queens Gdns NW4	71	U10
Queens Gdns W2	14	F9
Queens Gdns W5	105	L9
Queen's Gdns, Houns	139	K1
Queen's Gate SW7	22	H8
Queen's Gate Gdns SW7	22	G12
Queen's Gate Gdns SW15	143	S7
Queen's Gate Ms SW7	22	G9
Queen's Gate Pl SW7	22	G11
Queen's Gate Pl Ms SW7	22	H12
Queen's Gate Ter SW7	22	F10
Queen's Gro NW8	109	N2
Queen's Gro Ms NW8	109	N2
Queens Gro Rd E4	62	H1
Queen's Head St N1	111	S2
Queens Head Yd, SE1 5	28	C4
Queens Ho, Tedd	158	E12
Queens La N10	74	C5
Queens Ms W2	14	C9
Queens Par, N11 2	57	T10
Queens Par W5	105	T12
Queens Par Cl N11	57	T10
Queens Pk Ct W10	108	B6
Queens Pas, Chis	171	K11
Queens Pl, Mord 2	180	H7
Queens Reach, E Mol	176	C7
Queens Ride SW13	143	P6
Queens Ride SW15	143	S5
Queen's Ride, Rich	160	E1
Queens Ri, Rich	141	T11
Queens Rd E11	78	H14
Queens Rd E13	115	S2
Queen's Rd E17	77	T12
Queens Rd N3	73	L2
Queens Rd N9	60	J5
Queen's Rd N11	58	J13
Queens Rd NW4	71	T10
Queen's Rd SE14	149	M2
Queen's Rd SE15	149	M2
Queens Rd SW14	142	H6
Queens Rd SW19	162	G11
Queens Rd W5	105	R11
Queens Rd, Bark	99	L12
Queens Rd, Barn	40	A6
Queens Rd, Beck	185	S4
Queens Rd, Brom	187	P3
Queens Rd, Buck H	63	S3
Queen's Rd, Chis	171	K11
Queen's Rd, Croy	183	S11
Queens Rd, Enf	44	D7
Queens Rd, Felt	156	D1
Queen's Rd, Hmptn	157	R8
Queen's Rd, Houns	139	R5
Queen's Rd, Kings T	160	B13
Queens Rd, Loug	48	D5
Queens Rd, Mitch	181	N5
Queens Rd, Mord	180	H7
Queens Rd, N Mal	179	M8
Queens Rd, Rich	141	T11
Queens Rd, Sthl	120	J4
Queen's Rd, Tedd	158	E12
Queen's Rd, T Ditt	176	F10
Queens Rd, Twick	158	G1
Queens Rd, Wall	196	C9
Queen's Rd, Well	154	C3
Queens Rd W E13	115	P3
Queen's Row SE17	36	C9
Queens Ter E13	115	S2
Queens Ter NW8	109	N2
Queens Ter, Islw	140	H7
Queens Ter Cotts, W7 1	122	D3
Queens Wk E4	62	G1
Queens Wk NW9	88	F3
Queens Wk SW1	25	M5
Queens Wk W5	105	L8
Queen's Wk, Har	68	C7
Queens Wk, Ruis	84	H8
Queen's Wk, The SE1	28	J2
Queens Way NW4	71	U9
Queens Way, Croy	197	M10
Queens Way, Felt	156	E8
Queens Well Av N20	57	S7
Queen's Wd Rd N10	74	C11
Queens Yd WC1	9	P12
Queensberry Ms W SW7	30	J2
Queensberry Pl SW7	30	J1
Queensberry Way SW7	31	K1
Queensborough Ms W2	14	E10
Queensborough Pas, W2 3	14	E10
Queensborough Studios, W2 1	14	E10
Queensborough Ter W2	14	D9
Queensbridge Pk, Islw	140	B11
Queensbridge Rd E2	112	F2
Queensbridge Rd E8	112	F1
Queensbury Rd NW9	70	G14
Queensbury Rd, Wem	105	U3
Queensbury Sta Par, Edg	70	A5
Queensbury St N1	93	U14

Queenscourt, Wem	87	S7
Queenscroft Rd	152	B11
SE9		
Queensdale Cres	126	B1
W11		
Queensdale Pl W11	126	C2
Queensdale Rd W11	126	B2
Queensdale Wk W11	126	C2
Queensdown Rd E5	94	J7
Queensferry Wk,	76	J8
N17 *3*		
Queensgate Gdns,	189	N2
Chis		
Queensgate Pl,	90	G14
NW6 *5*		
Queensland Av N18	59	U11
Queensland Av	180	J1
SW19		
Queensland Pl N7	93	N8
Queensland Rd N7	93	N8
Queensmead NW8	109	P1
Queensmead Rd,	187	L4
Brom		
Queensmere Cl	162	A5
SW19		
Queensmere Rd	162	A4
SW19		
Queensmill Rd SW6	126	A14
Queensthorpe Rd	167	N8
SE26		
Queenstown Rd	32	G12
SW8		
Queensville Rd	146	G14
SW12		
Queensway W2	14	C9
Queensway, Enf	45	K8
Queensway, Orp	189	M10
Queensway, Sun	174	C3
Queensway,	201	K7
W Wick		
Queenswood Av	78	E2
E17		
Queenswood Av,	157	R11
Hmptn		
Queenswood Av,	139	L3
Houns		
Queenswood Av,	183	P10
Th Hth		
Queenswood Av,	196	H8
Wall		
Queenswood Gdns	97	P2
E11		
Queenswood Pk N3	72	D3
Queenswood Rd	167	R6
SE23		
Queenswood Rd,	153	T11
Sid		
Quemerford Rd N7	93	L9
Quentin Pl,	151	K6
SE13 *2*		
Quentin Rd SE13	151	K6
Quernmore Cl,	169	N12
Brom		
Quernmore Rd N4	75	N12
Quernmore Rd,	169	N11
Brom		
Querrin St SW6	145	L4
Quex Ms NW6	108	H1
Quex Rd NW6	108	H1
Quick Pl, N1 *3*	111	R2
Quick Rd W4	124	J10
Quick St N1	11	P3
Quick St Ms N1	11	P3
Quicks Rd SW19	163	K13
Quickswood NW3	91	S13
Quiet Nook,	202	B6
Brom		
Quill La SW15	144	A7
Quill St N4	93	P5
Quill St W5	105	R5
Quilp St, SE1 *1*	27	U5
Quilter St E2	13	R6
Quilter St SE18	135	T9
Quinta Dr, Barn	39	T10
Quintin Av SW20	180	E2
Quinton Cl, Beck	186	F6
Quinton Cl, Houns	120	C13
Quinton Cl, Wall	196	C7
Quinton Rd, T Ditt	190	H1
Quinton St SW18	163	L4
Quixley St E14	114	G13
Quorn Rd SE22	148	D7

R

Rabbits Rd E12	98	D7
Rabournmead Dr,	85	K10
Nthlt		
Raby Rd, N Mal	178	H7
Raby St, E14 *8*	113	R11
Raccoon Way,	138	F4
Houns		
Rachel Cl, Ilf	81	N7
Rackham Cl, Well	154	C4
Rackham Ms,	164	F11
SW16 *1*		
Racton Rd SW6	126	G12
Radbourne Av W5	123	M7
Radbourne Cl E5	95	P7
Radbourne Cres E17	78	G4
Radbourne Rd	146	F14
SW12		
Radcliffe Av NW10	107	N3
Radcliffe Av, Enf *1*	43	U1
Radcliffe Ms,	157	U10
Hmptn *1*		
Radcliffe Rd N21	59	S1
Radcliffe Rd SE1	29	K10
Radcliffe Rd, Croy	198	E4
Radcliffe Rd, Har	68	G4
Radcliffe Sq SW15	144	B11
Radcliffe Way, Nthlt	102	G6
Radcot St SE11	35	M8
Raddington Rd,	108	D10
W10 *7*		
Radfield Way, Sid	153	P13
Radford Rd SE13	150	F11
Radford Way, Bark	117	T5
Radipole Rd SW6	144	E1
Radland Rd E16	115	M12
Radlet Av SE26	167	K4
Radlett Cl, E7 *1*	97	M11
Radlett Pl NW8	109	R1
Radley Av, Ilf	99	U8
Radley Ct SE16	131	P3
Radley Gdns, Har	69	S8
Radley Ms W8	22	A12
Radley Rd N17	76	D3
Radley's La E18	79	N4
Radleys Mead, Dag	101	R11
Radlix Rd E10	96	B2
Radnor Av, Har	68	C9
Radnor Av, Well	154	C9
Radnor Cl, Chis	171	S12
Radnor Cl, Mitch	183	K8
Radnor Cres SE18	136	A13
Radnor Cres, Ilf	80	E10
Radnor Gdns, Enf	44	D1
Radnor Gdns, Twick	158	E3
Radnor Ms W2	15	M8
Radnor Pl W2	15	N7
Radnor Rd NW6	108	C2
Radnor Rd SE15	37	S13
Radnor Rd, Har	68	C9
Radnor Rd, Twick	158	F3
Radnor St EC1	12	A8
Radnor Ter W14	126	E7
Radnor Wk SW3	31	S7
Radnor Wk, Croy	185	S12
Radnor Way NW10	106	C7
Radstock Av, Har	68	H6
Radstock St,	127	R14
SW11 *1*		
Raebarn Gdns, Barn	39	S9
Raeburn Av, Surb	178	C10
Raeburn Cl NW11	73	L11
Raeburn Cl, Kings T	159	N14
Raeburn Rd, Edg	70	A3
Raeburn Rd, Sid	153	S11
Raeburn St SW2	147	K8
Rafford Way, Brom	187	R4
Raft Rd SW18	144	H9
Raggleswood, Chis	188	H1
Raglan Gdns, Wat	139	L10
Raglan Ct SE12	151	N9
Raglan Ct, S Croy	197	S9
Raglan Ct, Wem	87	U7
Raglan Gdns, Wat	50	D1

Raglan Rd E17	78	F9
Raglan Rd SE18	135	L9
Raglan Rd, Belv	137	M8
Raglan Rd, Brom	187	U8
Raglan Rd, Enf	44	D13
Raglan St NW5	92	D11
Raglan Ter, Har	85	S8
Raglan Way, Nthlt	85	T11
Ragley Cl W3	124	E3
Raider Cl, Rom	83	R2
Railey Ms NW5	92	E9
Railshead Rd, Islw	140	J7
Railton Rd SE24	147	P8
Railway App N4	75	P12
Railway App SE1	28	E3
Railway App, Har	68	E7
Railway App, Twick	140	G14
Railway App, Wall	196	D10
Railway Av SE16	131	M3
Railway Ms, E3 *1*	114	A6
Railway Ms W10	108	D11
Railway Pas, Tedd	158	G11
Railway Pl, Belv	137	P6
Railway Ri SE22	148	D7
Railway Rd, Tedd	158	E8
Railway Side SW13	143	K5
Railway St N1	10	C3
Railway St, Rom	100	E1
Railway Ter SE13	150	C9
Railway Ter, Felt	156	B2
Rainborough Cl	88	E11
NW10		
Rainbow Av E14	132	C9
Rainbow St SE5	36	H14
Raine St E1	131	K1
Rainham Cl SE9	153	P11
Rainham Cl SW11	145	S11
Rainham Rd NW10	107	U6
Rainham Rd N, Dag	101	R4
Rainham Rd S, Dag	101	S8
Rainhill Way E3	114	C6
Rainsborough Av	131	R8
SE8		
Rainsford Cl, Stan	53	L8
Rainsford Rd NW10	106	C5
Rainsford St W2	15	N5
Rainton Rd SE7	133	P9
Rainville Rd W6	125	U12
Raisins Hill, Pnr	66	D6
Raith Av N14	58	G6
Raleana Rd,	132	F1
E14 *11*		
Raleigh Av, Hayes	102	C10
Raleigh Av, Wall	196	G7
Raleigh Cl NW4	71	T9
Raleigh Cl, Pnr	66	H13
Raleigh Ct, Wall	196	D12
Raleigh Dr N20	57	S6
Raleigh Dr, Esher	190	B10
Raleigh Dr, Surb	192	F1
Raleigh Gdns SW2	147	L11
Raleigh Gdns, Mitch	181	T5
Raleigh Ms, Orp *8*	203	U10
Raleigh Rd N8	75	N7
Raleigh Rd SE20	167	N13
Raleigh Rd, Enf	44	A8
Raleigh Rd, Rich	141	U6
Raleigh Rd, Sthl	120	J9
Raleigh St N1	111	S2
Raleigh Way N14	58	H1
Raleigh Way, Felt	156	E9
Ralph Ct W2	14	C6
Ralph Perring Ct,	186	B7
Beck		
Ralston St SW3	31	U8
Ralston Way, Wat	50	G4
Ram Pas, Kings T	177	N4
Ram Pl E9	95	L11
Ram St SW18	144	J10
Rama Cl SW16	164	J14
Rama Ct, Har	86	D4
Ramac Way SE7	133	R8
Rambler Cl SW16	164	E8
Rame Cl SW17	164	A10
Ramilles Cl SW2	147	K11
Ramilles Pl W1	17	M7
Ramillies Rd NW7	55	K4
Ramillies Rd W4	124	H6
Ramillies Rd, Sid	154	C11
Ramillies St W1	17	M7

Rampart St, E1 *7*	112	J11
Rampayne St SW1	33	S5
Rampton Cl E4	62	A5
Rams Gro, Rom	83	K7
Ramsay Ms SW3	31	N9
Ramsay Pl, Har	86	C1
Ramsay Rd E7	97	L7
Ramsay Rd W3	124	F5
Ramscroft Cl N9	44	C14
Ramsdale Rd SW17	164	B10
Ramsden Rd N11	57	U10
Ramsden Rd SW12	146	A12
Ramsey Cl NW9	71	M12
Ramsey Cl, Grnf	86	A9
Ramsey Ms N4	93	S5
Ramsey Rd, Th Hth	183	M11
Ramsey St E2	13	T9
Ramsey Way N14	42	F14
Ramsgate Cl,	133	R2
E16 *19*		
Ramsgate St E8	94	F11
Ramsgill App, Ilf	81	T8
Ramsgill Dr, Ilf	81	T9
Ramulis Dr, Hayes	102	H8
Ramus Wd Av, Orp	203	R10
Rancliffe Gdns SE9	152	B8
Rancliffe Rd E6	116	D4
Randall Av NW2	89	K4
Randall Cl SW11	145	R1
Randall Cl, Erith	137	U12
Randall Pl SE10	132	E13
Randall Rd SE11	34	E4
Randall Row SE11	34	E4
Randell's Rd N1	111	K1
Randle Rd, Rich	159	M8
Randlesdown Rd	168	A7
SE6		
Randolph App,	115	U12
E16 *12*		
Randolph Av W9	6	G10
Randolph Cl, Bexh	155	T5
Randolph Cl,	160	F10
Kings T		
Randolph Cres W9	6	F11
Randolph Gdns	6	A3
NW6		
Randolph Gro, Rom	82	E10
Randolph Ms W9	6	G12
Randolph Rd E17	78	D9
Randolph Rd W9	6	F11
Randolph Rd, Sthl	121	L3
Randolph St NW1	92	F14
Randon Cl, Har	67	S3
Ranelagh Av SW6	144	E5
Ranelagh Av SW13	143	P4
Ranelagh Cl, Edg	54	A7
Ranelagh Dr, Edg	54	A7
Ranelagh Dr, Twick	141	K9
Ranelagh Gdns E11	79	T9
Ranelagh Gdns SW6	144	E5
Ranelagh Gdns W4	124	E13
Ranelagh Gdns W6	125	M6
Ranelagh Gdns, Ilf	98	G1
Ranelagh Gro SW1	32	F5
Ranelagh Ms W5	123	P3
Ranelagh Pl, N Mal	178	J9
Ranelagh Rd E6	116	G2
Ranelagh Rd E11	96	J7
Ranelagh Rd E15	115	L3
Ranelagh Rd N17	76	D5
Ranelagh Rd N22	75	L2
Ranelagh Rd NW10	107	L4
Ranelagh Rd SW1	33	N7
Ranelagh Rd SW5	123	P3
Ranelagh Rd, Sthl	120	H2
Ranelagh Rd, Wem	87	P11
Ranfurly Rd, Sutt	194	H3
Rangefield Rd, Brom	168	J9
Rangemoor Rd N15	76	F9
Rangers Rd E4	47	L14
Rangers Rd, Loug	47	R12
Rangers Sq SE10	150	G1
Rangeworth Pl, Sid	171	U5
Rankin Cl NW9	71	K6
Ranleigh Gdns,	137	M13
Bexh		
Ranmere St	164	D1
SW12 *7*		
Ranmoor Cl, Har	68	B8
Ranmoor Gdns, Har	68	B8

Name	Page	Grid
Ranmore Av, Croy	198	F6
Rannoch Cl, Edg	54	D4
Rannoch Rd W6	125	U12
Rannock Av NW9	70	H14
Ranskill Rd, Borwd	38	A2
Ransom Rd, SE7 *3*	133	U9
Ransom Wk, SE7 *1*	133	U8
Ranston St NW1	15	P1
Ranulf Rd NW2	90	F7
Ranwell Cl, E3 *2*	113	T2
Ranwell St, E3 *3*	113	T2
Ranworth Rd N9	61	L4
Ranyard Cl, Chess	191	T6
Raphael Dr, T Ditt	176	F14
Raphael St SW7	23	T8
Rashleigh St, SW8 *9*	146	D4
Rasper Rd N20	57	M4
Rastell Av SW2	164	G3
Ratcliff Rd E7	97	T10
Ratcliffe Cl SE12	151	N14
Ratcliffe Cross St, E1 *8*	113	P12
Ratcliffe La E14	113	R12
Ratcliffe Orchard, E1 *3*	113	P13
Rathbone Pl W1	17	R6
Rathbone St E16	115	L11
Rathbone St W1	17	P4
Rathcoole Av N8	75	M9
Rathcoole Gdns N8	75	M9
Rathfern Rd SE6	167	U2
Rathgar Av W13	123	K2
Rathgar Cl N3	72	E3
Rathgar Rd, SW9 *4*	147	S5
Rathmell Dr SW4	146	G12
Rathmore Rd SE7	133	R9
Rattray Rd SW2	147	N8
Raul Rd SE15	148	H3
Raveley St NW5	92	E8
Raven Cl NW9	71	K4
Raven Rd E18	79	T3
Raven Row E1	113	K9
Ravenet St SW11	146	C2
Ravenfield Rd SW17	163	U6
Ravenhill Rd E13	115	T3
Ravenna Rd SW15	144	B9
Ravenoak Way, Chig	65	R10
Ravenor Pk Rd, Grnf	103	S5
Ravens Cl, Brom	187	M5
Ravens Cl, Enf	44	C4
Ravens Ms SE12	151	N8
Ravens Way SE12	151	N9
Ravensbourne Av, Beck	168	H14
Ravensbourne Av, Brom	168	G13
Ravensbourne Gdns W13	104	J10
Ravensbourne Gdns, Ilf	80	H1
Ravensbourne Pk SE6	150	A13
Ravensbourne Pk Cres SE6	149	U13
Ravensbourne Pl SE13	150	D3
Ravensbourne Rd SE6	167	T1
Ravensbourne Rd, Brom	187	N5
Ravensbourne Rd, Twick	141	L11
Ravensbury Av, Mord	181	M10
Ravensbury Gro, Mitch	181	N8
Ravensbury La, Mitch	181	N8
Ravensbury Path, Mitch	181	N7
Ravensbury Rd SW18	162	J3
Ravensbury Ter SW18	163	K2
Ravenscar Rd, Brom	168	J8
Ravenscar Rd, Surb	191	U3
Ravenscourt Av W6	125	P8
Ravenscourt Gdns W6	125	N7
Ravenscourt Pk W6	125	P7
Ravenscourt Pl W6	125	R8
Ravenscourt Rd W6	125	R7
Ravenscourt Sq W6	125	N6
Ravenscraig Rd N11	58	E8
Ravenscroft Av NW11	72	E13
Ravenscroft Av, Wem	69	T14
Ravenscroft Cl E16	115	N9
Ravenscroft Cres SE9	170	E6
Ravenscroft Pk, Barn	40	B7
Ravenscroft Rd E16	115	P9
Ravenscroft Rd W4	124	F7
Ravenscroft Rd, Beck	185	N2
Ravenscroft St E2	13	P4
Ravensdale Av N12	57	M8
Ravensdale Gdns SE19	166	B14
Ravensdale Gdns, Houns	138	J5
Ravensdale Rd N16	76	F13
Ravensdale Rd, Houns	138	J5
Ravensdon St SE11	35	L7
Ravensfield Cl, Dag	100	H7
Ravensfield Gdns, Epsom	193	K9
Ravenshaw St NW6	90	F10
Ravenshill, Chis	188	J2
Ravenshurst Av NW4	71	T7
Ravenside Cl N18	61	N10
Ravenside Retail Pk N18	61	N10
Ravenslea Rd SW12	145	U14
Ravensmead Rd, Brom	168	H14
Ravensmede Way W4	125	M8
Ravenstone SE17	36	J7
Ravenstone Rd N8	75	N6
Ravenstone Rd, NW9 *5*	71	M12
Ravenstone St SW12	164	B2
Ravenswood, Bex	172	J1
Ravenswood Av, Surb	191	U4
Ravenswood Av, W Wick	200	E2
Ravenswood Ct, Kings T	160	D12
Ravenswood Cres, Har	85	L3
Ravenswood Cres, W Wick	200	E1
Ravenswood Gdns, Islw	140	D1
Ravenswood Pk, Nthwd	50	A12
Ravenswood Rd E17	78	D8
Ravenswood Rd SW12	146	D14
Ravenswood Rd, Croy	197	R6
Ravensworth Rd NW10	107	S3
Ravensworth Rd SE9	170	E7
Ravent Rd SE11	34	G2
Ravey St EC2	12	H9
Ravine Gro SE18	135	R12
Rawlings Cl, Orp	203	U9
Rawlings St SW3	31	T2
Rawlins Cl N3	72	C5
Rawlins Cl, S Croy	199	S14
Rawnsley Av, Mitch	181	P8
Rawson St SW11	146	B2
Rawsthorne Cl, E16 *4*	134	E2
Rawstone Wk E13	115	P3
Rawstorne Pl, EC1 *4*	11	N6
Rawstorne St EC1	11	N6
Ray Cl, Chess	191	M12
Ray Gdns, Bark	118	A4
Ray Gdns, Stan	53	K9
Ray Lo Rd, Wdf Grn	63	U11
Ray Massey Way, E6 *3*	116	D1
Ray Rd, W Mol	175	R9
Ray St, EC1 *9*	11	L11
Ray St Br, EC1 *8*	11	M11
Raydean Rd, Barn	40	J10
Raydon St N19	92	D4
Raydons Gdns, Dag	101	K8
Raydons Rd, Dag	101	K9
Rayfield Cl, Brom	188	C12
Rayford Av SE12	151	M14
Rayleas Cl SE18	152	J2
Rayleigh Av, Tedd	158	D12
Rayleigh Cl N13	60	A5
Rayleigh Ct, Kings T	177	U3
Rayleigh Ri, S Croy	198	D12
Rayleigh Rd E16	133	S1
Rayleigh Rd N13	59	U5
Rayleigh Rd SW19	180	E1
Rayleigh Rd, Wdf Grn	63	T12
Raymead Av, Th Hth	183	P9
Raymere Gdns SE18	135	P13
Raymond Av E18	79	L5
Raymond Av W13	122	H8
Raymond Bldgs WC1	18	G2
Raymond Cl SE26	167	L9
Raymond Rd E13	97	T14
Raymond Rd SW19	162	D12
Raymond Rd, Beck	185	R8
Raymond Rd, Ilf	81	N13
Raymond Way, Esher	190	H12
Raymouth Rd SE16	131	K7
Rayne Ct E18	79	M7
Rayners Cl, Wem	87	N9
Rayners Ct, Har	85	N2
Rayners Cres, Nthlt	102	C5
Rayners Gdns, Nthlt	102	C5
Rayners La, Har	85	R4
Rayners La, Pnr	67	M14
Rayners Rd SW15	144	C10
Raynes Av E11	79	U14
Raynham Av N18	60	H11
Raynham Rd N18	60	G9
Raynham Rd W6	125	R7
Raynham Ter N18	60	H10
Raynor Cl, Sthl	121	L2
Raynor Pl N1	93	U14
Raynton Cl, Har	85	K1
Rays Av N18	61	L8
Rays Rd N18	61	L8
Rays Rd, W Wick	186	F14
Reachview Cl, NW1 *1*	92	F14
Read Cl, T Ditt	176	G14
Reading La E8	94	J12
Reading Rd, Nthlt	85	S9
Reading Rd, Sutt	195	M10
Reading Way NW7	56	C10
Reads Cl, Ilf *2*	98	J5
Reapers Cl NW1	110	G1
Reapers Way, Islw *2*	140	A9
Reardon Ct N21	59	T3
Reardon Path E1	131	K2
Reardon St E1	130	J1
Reaston St SE14	131	N13
Reckitt Rd W4	124	J10
Record St SE15	131	L11
Recovery St SW17	180	H3
Recreation Av, Rom	83	U10
Recreation Rd SE26	167	N7
Recreation Rd, Brom	187	L3
Recreation Rd, Sid	171	S5
Recreation Rd, Sthl	120	J7
Recreation Way, Mitch	182	J6
Rector St N1	111	T2
Rectory Cl E4	62	A5
Rectory Cl N3	72	F2
Rectory Cl SW20	179	T5
Rectory Cl, Sid	172	C8
Rectory Cl, Stan	53	K10
Rectory Cl, Surb	191	K2
Rectory Cres E11	79	T11
Rectory Fld Cres SE7	133	T13
Rectory Gdns N8	74	J7
Rectory Gdns SW4	146	E5
Rectory Gdns, Nthlt	103	M1
Rectory Grn, Beck	185	U2
Rectory Gro SW4	146	E5
Rectory Gro, Croy	197	R4
Rectory Gro, Hmptn	157	M8
Rectory La SW17	164	A10
Rectory La, Edg	54	B11
Rectory La, Loug	49	L7
Rectory La, Sid	172	F8
Rectory La, Stan	52	J10
Rectory La, Surb	191	K1
Rectory La, Wall	196	F7
Rectory Orchard SW19	162	D8
Rectory Pk Av, Nthlt	103	L5
Rectory Pl SE18	134	G7
Rectory Rd E12	98	F10
Rectory Rd E17	78	C6
Rectory Rd N16	94	F6
Rectory Rd SW13	143	P3
Rectory Rd W3	124	D1
Rectory Rd, Beck	186	A2
Rectory Rd, Dag	101	P12
Rectory Rd, Hayes	102	A12
Rectory Rd, Houns	138	D2
Rectory Rd, Kes	202	B14
Rectory Rd, Sthl	121	L6
Rectory Rd, Sutt	194	J6
Rectory Sq E1	113	P9
Reculver Ms N18	60	H8
Reculver Rd SE16	131	N9
Red Anchor Cl, SW3 *2*	31	N11
Red Barracks Rd SE18	134	F8
Red Cedars Rd, Orp	189	R14
Red Hill, Chis	170	J10
Red Ho La, Bexh	154	H8
Red La, Esher	190	G11
Red Lion Cl SE17	36	C10
Red Lion Ct, EC4 *8*	19	L7
Red Lion Hill, N2 *3*	73	N4
Red Lion La SE18	134	G14
Red Lion Pl SE18	152	G2
Red Lion Rd, Surb	192	A3
Red Lion Row SE17	36	B10
Red Lion Sq WC1	18	E3
Red Lion St WC1	18	F3
Red Lion St, Rich	141	P9
Red Lion Yd W1	24	F2
Red Lo Rd, W Wick	186	G12
Red Oak Cl, Orp	203	K5
Red Path E9	95	T11
Red Post Hill SE21	148	B10
Red Post Hill SE24	148	A8
Redan Pl W2	14	B8
Redan Ter SE5	147	S3
Redberry Gro SE26	167	L5
Redbourne Av N3	72	H1
Redbridge Enterprise Cen, Ilf	99	M3
Redbridge Gdns SE5	130	D14
Redbridge La E, Ilf	80	B11
Redbridge La W E11	79	S12
Redburn St SW3	31	T9
Redcar Cl, Nthlt	85	R10
Redcar St SE5	129	T14
Redcastle Cl E1	113	L13
Redchurch St E2	13	M10
Redcliffe Gdns SW5	30	C8
Redcliffe Gdns SW10	30	C8
Redcliffe Gdns, Ilf	98	G1
Redcliffe Ms SW10	30	D8
Redcliffe Pl SW10	30	E11
Redcliffe Rd SW10	30	D8
Redcliffe Sq SW10	30	D8
Redcliffe St SW10	30	C9
Redclose Av, Mord	180	G10
Redclyffe Rd E6	115	U2
Redcroft Rd, Sthl	103	T13

Redcross Way SE1 28 A5
Reddings, The NW7 55 L6
Reddings Cl NW7 55 M7
Reddins Rd SE15 37 R12
Reddons Rd, Beck 167 R14
Rede Pl W2 108 H12
Redesdale Gdns, 122 G14
Islw
Redesdale St SW3 31 S9
Redfern Av, Houns 139 N14
Redfern Rd NW10 89 K14
Redfern Rd SE6 150 F14
Redfield La SW5 126 H7
Redfield Ms, 126 H7
SW5 2
Redford Av, Th Hth 183 M8
Redford Av, Wall 196 J13
Redgate Dr, Brom 201 R4
Redgate Ter SW15 144 C11
Redgrave Cl, Croy 184 F12
Redgrave Rd SW15 144 B6
Redhill Dr, Edg 70 D4
Redhill St NW1 8 J4
Redhouse Rd, Croy 182 G11
Redington Gdns 90 J7
NW3
Redington Rd NW3 90 J7
Redland Gdns, 175 M8
W Mol
Redlands Ct, Brom 169 M13
Redlands Rd, Enf 45 R1
Redlands Way SW2 147 L14
Redleaf Cl, Belv 137 N12
Redlees Cl, Islw 144 A12
Redman Cl, Nthlt 102 E4
Redman's Rd E1 113 M9
Redmead La E1 29 S3
Redmore Rd W6 125 R7
Redpoll Way, Erith 136 H5
Redriff Est SE16 131 T5
Redriff Rd SE16 131 R5
Redriff Rd, Rom 83 S4
Redriffe Rd E13 115 M2
Redroofs Cl, Beck 186 C1
Redruth Cl N22 59 L14
Redruth Rd, E9 3 113 M1
Redstart Cl E6 116 C9
Redstart Cl, 131 R13
SE14 8
Redston Rd N8 74 G7
Redvers Rd N22 75 N3
Redvers St, N1 2 13 K5
Redwald Rd E5 95 P8
Redway Dr, Twick 139 U13
Redwing Path, 115 P2
SE28 1
Redwood Cl N14 42 H14
Redwood Cl SE16 131 S2
Redwood Cl, Sid 154 A14
Redwood Cl, Wat 50 F7
Redwood Est, Houns 120 D12
Redwood Gdns E4 46 C12
Redwood Ms, 146 D5
SW4 13
Redwood Wk, Surb 191 P2
Redwood Way, Barn 40 A9
Redwoods SW15 161 N2
Redwoods Cl, 63 R4
Buck H
Reece Ms SW7 30 J2
Reed Av, Orp 203 R6
Reed Cl E16 115 N10
Reed Cl SE12 151 P10
Reed Rd N17 76 F4
Reede Gdns, Dag 101 R10
Reede Rd, Dag 101 N11
Reede Way, Dag 101 R11
Reedham Cl N17 76 J7
Reedham St SE15 148 G4
Reedholm Vil N16 94 B7
Reedworth St SE11 35 L3
Reenglass Rd, Stan 53 P7
Rees Dr, Stan 53 R7
Rees Gdns, Croy 184 F12
Rees St N1 111 U2
Reesland Cl E12 98 G10
Reets Fm Cl NW9 71 K11
Reeves Av NW9 70 G14
Reeves Cor, 197 S4
Croy 2

Reeves Ms W1 16 D12
Reeves Rd E3 114 C7
Reeves Rd SE18 134 J12
Reform Row N17 76 F3
Reform St SW11 145 U3
Regal Cl E1 21 U2
Regal Cl W5 105 P10
Regal Ct N18 60 F9
Regal Cres, Wall 196 C5
Regal Dr N11 58 C10
Regal Pl E3 113 U6
Regal Way, Har 69 S13
Regan Way N1 12 H3
Regency Cl W5 105 S12
Regency Cl, Chig 65 M10
Regency Cl, 157 M9
Hmptn 2
Regency Cres NW4 72 B4
Regency Lo, Buck H 64 B3
Regency Ms, 89 P12
NW10 1
Regency Ms, Beck 186 E1
Regency Ms, 140 C10
Islw 1
Regency Pl SW1 33 S1
Regency St SW1 33 T3
Regency Wk, Croy 185 T12
Regency Way, Bexh 154 H6
Regent Cl N12 57 M10
Regent Cl, Har 69 R11
Regent Cl, Houns 138 D2
Regent Gdns, Ilf 82 A12
Regent Pl SW19 163 K10
Regent Pl, W1 5 17 N10
Regent Pl, Croy 198 E1
Regent Rd SE24 147 R11
Regent Rd, Surb 177 U10
Regent Sq E3 114 C6
Regent Sq WC1 10 C8
Regent Sq, Belv 137 R7
Regent St NW10 108 B6
Regent St SW1 17 R12
Regent St W1 17 K6
Regent St W4 124 B10
Regents Av N13 59 N10
Regents Br Gdns 34 D13
SW8
Regents Cl, S Croy 198 D11
Regents Dr, Kes 202 A9
Regents Ms NW8 6 H2
Regent's Pk NW1 8 C3
Regent's Pk Est NW1 9 L7
Regents Pk Rd N3 72 F6
Regents Pk Rd NW1 109 U1
Regents Pk Ter NW1 110 C1
Regent's Pl NW1 9 M9
Regent's Pl SE3 151 N3
Regents Row E8 112 G2
Regina Cl, Barn 40 A6
Regina Rd N4 93 L1
Regina Rd SE25 184 H6
Regina Rd W13 122 H2
Regina Rd, Sthl 120 J8
Regina Ter W13 122 J2
Reginald Rd E7 97 N12
Reginald Rd SE8 132 A14
Reginald Sq SE8 132 B14
Regis Pl SW2 147 L8
Regis Rd NW5 92 D10
Regnart Bldgs, 9 P8
NW1 1
Reid Cl, Pnr 66 B7
Reidhaven Rd SE18 135 R7
Reigate Av, Sutt 194 H2
Reigate Rd, Brom 169 M5
Reigate Rd, Ilf 1 99 T4
Reigate Way, Wall 197 K9
Reighton Rd E5 94 H5
Relay Rd W12 107 U14
Relf Rd SE15 148 H5
Relko Gdns, Sutt 195 P9
Relton Ms SW7 23 R9
Rembrandt Cl E14 132 G6
Rembrandt Cl SW1 32 D4
Rembrandt Rd, 193 M11
Epsom
Rembrandt Rd SE13 150 J8
Rembrandt Rd, Edg 70 B2
Remington Rd E6 116 C11
Remington Rd N15 76 B11

Remington St N1 11 S4
Remnant St WC2 18 E5
Rempstone Ms, 12 E2
N1 2
Remus Rd E3 96 A14
Rendle Cl, Croy 1 184 G10
Rendlesham Rd E5 94 H6
Rendlesham Rd, Enf 43 S1
Renforth St SE16 131 M4
Renfrew Cl E6 116 G12
Renfrew Rd SE11 35 N3
Renfrew Rd, Houns 138 H3
Renfrew Rd, Kings T 160 D13
Renmuir St SW17 163 U12
Rennell St SE13 150 E6
Renness Rd E17 77 S6
Rennets Cl SE9 153 R9
Rennets Wd Rd SE9 153 P10
Rennie Est SE16 131 K8
Rennie St SE1 27 N2
Renown Cl, Croy 197 S2
Renown Cl, Rom 83 P1
Rensburg Rd E17 77 P10
Renshaw Cl, 137 M11
Belv 4
Renters Av NW4 71 U12
Renwick Ind Est, 118 C2
Bark
Renwick Rd, Bark 118 D8
Repens Way, Hayes 102 H8
Rephidim St, 28 G12
SE1 1
Replingham Rd 162 F1
SW18
Reporton Rd SW6 144 D1
Repository Rd SE18 134 F10
Repton Av, Wem 87 L8
Repton Av, Cars 195 R10
Repton Ct, Beck 186 D1
Repton Gro, Ilf 80 F2
Repton Rd, Har 69 U8
Repton St E14 113 S11
Repulse Cl, Rom 83 R1
Reservoir Cl, Th Hth 184 A7
Reservoir Rd N14 42 E10
Reservoir Rd SE4 149 R4
Resolution Wk SE18 134 E5
Restell Cl SE3 133 K11
Restmor Way, Wall 196 B3
Reston Pl SW7 22 F8
Restons Cres SE9 153 P11
Restormel Cl, Houns 139 P9
Retcar Pl N19 92 D3
Retford St N1 13 K4
Retingham Way E4 62 D4
Retreat, The NW9 70 G9
Retreat, The, 143 K6
SW14 6
Retreat, The, Har 67 P14
Retreat, The, Surb 177 T12
Retreat, The, Th Hth 184 A7
Retreat, The, Wor Pk 193 S4
Retreat Cl, Har 69 M9
Retreat Pl E9 95 M12
Retreat Rd, Rich 141 N9
Reveley Sq, 131 S4
SE16 3
Revell Ri SE18 135 T12
Revell Rd, Kings T 178 D2
Revell Rd, Sutt 194 E11
Revelon Rd SE4 149 R6
Revelstoke Rd SW18 162 G4
Reventlow Rd SE9 171 L2
Reverdy Rd SE1 37 R3
Reverend Cl, Har 85 R5
Revesby Rd, Cars 181 R12
Review Rd NW2 89 L4
Review Rd, Dag 119 R2
Rewell St, SW6 1 127 L14
Rewley Rd, Cars 181 N12
Rex Pl W1 24 E1
Reydon Av E11 79 T11
Reynard Cl SE4 2 149 S6
Reynard Cl, Brom 188 F5
Reynard Dr SE19 166 E14
Reynardson Rd N17 59 U14
Reynolds Av E12 98 H10
Reynolds Av, Chess 191 N14
Reynolds Av, Rom 82 F13
Reynolds Cl NW11 72 J14

Reynolds Cl SW19 181 P2
Reynolds Cl, Cars 195 U2
Reynolds Ct, 97 M5
E11 3
Reynolds Ct, Rom 82 G6
Reynolds Dr, Edg 69 U5
Reynolds Pl SE3 133 S13
Reynolds Pl, Rich 141 T12
Reynolds Rd SE15 149 M9
Reynolds Rd W4 124 F5
Reynolds Rd, Hayes 102 F8
Reynolds Rd, N Mal 178 H13
Reynolds Way, Croy 198 D7
Rheidol Ms N1 11 T1
Rheidol Ter N1 11 S1
Rheola Cl N17 76 F2
Rhoda St E2 13 N9
Rhodes Av N22 74 E2
Rhodes Moorhouse 180 H12
Ct, Mord
Rhodes St, N7 2 93 M10
Rhodesia Rd E11 96 H3
Rhodesia Rd SW9 147 K4
Rhodeswell Rd E14 113 S9
Rhodrons Av, Chess 191 R9
Rhondda Gro E3 113 S6
Rhyl Rd, Grnf 104 F3
Rhyl St NW5 92 B11
Rhys Av N11 58 H13
Rialto Rd, Mitch 182 B3
Ribble Cl, 63 U11
Wdf Grn 1
Ribblesdale Av N11 58 A11
Ribblesdale Av, 85 R12
Nthlt
Ribblesdale Rd N8 75 M8
Ribblesdale Rd 164 C12
SW16
Ribchester Av, Grnf 104 F5
Ribston Cl, Brom 202 E2
Ricardo St E14 114 C12
Ricards Rd SW19 162 F9
Rich La SW5 30 A7
Rich St E14 113 U13
Richard Cl SE18 134 D7
Richard Foster Cl 77 T13
E17
Richard Ho Dr E16 116 B12
Richard St E1 112 J12
Richards Av, Rom 83 U11
Richards Cl, Har 68 G10
Richards Pl E17 78 B6
Richards Pl SW3 31 S1
Richardson Cl, 112 E1
E8 2
Richardson Rd E15 114 J3
Richardson's Ms, 9 L11
W1 3
Richbell Pl, WC1 1 18 F1
Richborne Ter SW8 34 G14
Richborough Rd 90 B8
NW2
Richens Cl, Houns 140 A4
Riches Rd, Ilf 99 L4
Richford Rd E15 115 L1
Richford St W6 125 T4
Richlands Av, Epsom 193 P8
Richmond Av E4 62 G10
Richmond Av N1 111 M1
Richmond Av NW10 89 T12
Richmond Av SW20 180 D2
Richmond Br, Rich 141 N11
Richmond Br, Twick 141 N11
Richmond Bldgs, 17 R8
W1 1
Richmond Cl E17 77 U11
Richmond Cl, Borwd 38 H9
Richmond Cres E4 62 G9
Richmond Cres N1 111 M1
Richmond Cres N9 60 H1
Richmond Gdns 71 P9
NW4
Richmond Gdns, 52 E13
Har
Richmond Grn, Croy 197 K6
Richmond Gro N1 93 R14
Richmond Gro, Surb 177 T12
Richmond Hill, Rich 141 N11
Richmond Hill Ct, 141 R11
Rich

Richmond Ms W1	17	S8
Richmond Pk, Kings T	160	C4
Richmond Pk, Rich	160	C4
Richmond Pk Rd SW14	142	G8
Richmond Pk Rd, Kings T	159	S14
Richmond Pl SE18	135	M8
Richmond Rd E4	62	G1
Richmond Rd E7	97	S9
Richmond Rd E8	94	J12
Richmond Rd E11	96	G3
Richmond Rd, N2 2	73	L4
Richmond Rd N11	58	J12
Richmond Rd N15	76	C12
Richmond Rd SW20	179	R2
Richmond Rd W5	123	R3
Richmond Rd, Barn	41	K10
Richmond Rd, Croy	197	K5
Richmond Rd, Ilf	99	L5
Richmond Rd, Islw	140	H6
Richmond Rd, Kings T	159	P9
Richmond Rd, Th Hth	183	S7
Richmond Rd, Twick	141	K13
Richmond St E13	115	P4
Richmond Ter SW1	26	B5
Richmond Way E11	97	N3
Richmond Way W12	126	B4
Richmond Way W14	126	B5
Richmount Gdns SE3	151	P6
Rick Roberts Way E15	114	F2
Rickard Cl NW4	71	R8
Rickard Cl SW2	165	N1
Rickards Cl, Surb	191	R2
Rickett St SW6	126	H11
Rickman St, E1 15	113	M7
Rickmansworth Rd, Pnr	66	D3
Rickthorne Rd N19	92	J4
Rickyard Path, SE9	152	D7
Ridding La, Grnf	86	E10
Riddons Rd SE12	169	U6
Ride, The, Brent	123	K9
Ride, The, Enf	45	M6
Hideout St SE18	134	E8
Rider Cl, Sid	153	R11
Ridgdale St E3	114	B4
Ridge, The, Bex	155	M13
Ridge, The, Orp	203	P4
Ridge, The, Surb	178	A10
Ridge, The, Twick	140	A13
Ridge Av N21	43	U13
Ridge Cl NW4	72	B4
Ridge Cl NW9	70	H8
Ridge Cl SE28	135	P3
Ridge Crest, Enf	43	M1
Ridge Hill NW11	90	D1
Ridge Rd N8	75	M12
Ridge Rd N21	60	A1
Ridge Rd NW2	90	F5
Ridge Rd, Mitch	164	D13
Ridge Rd, Sutt	194	F2
Ridge Way, Felt	156	J6
Ridgebrook Rd SE3	151	U6
Ridgecroft Cl, Bex	173	T2
Ridgemont Gdns, Edg	54	F8
Ridgemount Av, Croy	199	P3
Ridgemount Gdns, Enf	43	P4
Ridgeview Cl, Barn	40	A12
Ridgeview Rd N20	57	L5
Ridgeway, Brom	201	N3
Ridgeway, Wdf Grn	63	U8
Ridgeway, The E4	62	D3
Ridgeway, The N3	56	J14
Ridgeway, The N11	57	T8
Ridgeway, The N14	59	K3
Ridgeway, The NW7	56	A10
Ridgeway, The NW9	70	J8
Ridgeway, The NW11	90	E1

Ridgeway, The W3	124	B5
Ridgeway, The, Enf	197	M6
Ridgeway, The, Enf	43	R4
Ridgeway, The, Har	67	L9
Ridgeway, The (Kenton), Har	69	L12
Ridgeway, The, Ruis	67	R12
Ridgeway, The, Stan	53	L12
Ridgeway Av, Barn	41	T11
Ridgeway Cres, Orp	203	S6
Ridgeway Cres Gdns, Orp	203	S4
Ridgeway Dr, Brom	169	S7
Ridgeway E, Sid	153	T9
Ridgeway Gdns N6	74	F13
Ridgeway Gdns, Ilf	80	D9
Ridgeway Rd SW9	147	R6
Ridgeway Rd, Islw	140	D1
Ridgeway Rd N, Islw	122	C13
Ridgeway W, Sid	153	S9
Ridgewell Cl N1	111	U1
Ridgewell Cl SE26	167	T8
Ridgewell Cl, Dag	119	S1
Ridgmount Gdns WC1	17	S1
Ridgmount Pl WC1	17	S2
Ridgmount Rd SW18	145	K10
Ridgmount St WC1	17	S1
Ridgway SW19	162	C11
Ridgway, The, Sutt	195	P14
Ridgway Gdns SW19	162	A13
Ridgway Pl SW19	162	C12
Ridgwell Rd E16	115	U9
Riding, The NW11	72	E14
Riding Ho St W1	17	L4
Ridings, The W5	105	U8
Ridings, The, Sun	174	A2
Ridings, The, Surb	178	B10
Ridings Av N21	43	S8
Ridings Cl N6	74	F14
Ridley Av W13	122	J6
Ridley Rd E7	97	T7
Ridley Rd E8	94	E10
Ridley Rd NW10	107	P3
Ridley Rd SW19	162	J13
Ridley Rd, Brom	187	M5
Ridley Rd, Well	154	C2
Ridsdale Rd SE20	184	J1
Riefield Rd SE9	153	M8
Riesco Dr, Croy	199	M12
Riffel Rd NW2	89	T10
Rifle Pl SE11	35	L9
Rifle Pl W11	126	B1
Rifle St E14	114	D10
Rigault Rd SW6	144	D4
Rigby Cl, Croy	197	N5
Rigby Ms, Ilf	98	H4
Rigden St E14	114	C12
Rigeley Rd NW10	107	P5
Rigg App E10	95	P2
Rigge Pl SW4	146	H8
Riggindale Rd SW16	164	G9
Riley Rd SE1	29	L9
Riley St SW10	31	K13
Rinaldo Rd SW12	146	C14
Ring, The W2	109	R13
Ring Cl, Brom	169	S13
Ring Rd W12	125	T1
Ringcroft St N7	93	N10
Ringers Rd, Brom	187	N5
Ringford Rd SW18	144	F11
Ringlet Cl E16	115	R11
Ringlewell Cl, Enf	44	J3
Ringmer Av SW6	144	D2
Ringmer Gdns N19	93	K3
Ringmer Pl N21	44	A10
Ringmer Way, Brom	188	D9
Ringmore Ri SE23	149	K13
Ringslade Rd N22	75	L3
Ringstead Rd SE6	150	D13
Ringstead Rd, Sutt	195	P8
Ringway N11	58	E12
Ringway, Sthl	122	J10
Ringwold Cl, Beck	167	R14
Ringwood Av N2	73	U5
Ringwood Av, Croy	183	K13

Ringwood Cl, Pnr	66	F6
Ringwood Gdns, E14 8	132	B7
Ringwood Gdns SW15	161	P3
Ringwood Rd E17	77	T11
Ringwood Way N21	43	R14
Ringwood Way, Hmptn	157	P8
Ripley Cl, Brom	188	E9
Ripley Cl, Croy	200	E12
Ripley Gdns SW14	142	H5
Ripley Gdns, Sutt	195	L8
Ripley Ms E11	78	J12
Ripley Rd E16	115	T11
Ripley Rd, Belv	137	N7
Ripley Rd, Enf	43	T1
Ripley Rd, Hmptn	157	N13
Ripley Rd, Ilf	99	T4
Ripley Vil W5	105	M12
Riplington Ct, SW15 1	143	P13
Ripon Cl, Nthlt	85	P10
Ripon Gdns, Chess	191	M9
Ripon Gdns, Ilf	80	C13
Ripon Rd N9	45	K14
Ripon Rd N17	76	A6
Ripon Rd SE18	134	J12
Ripon Way, Borwd	38	H9
Rippersley Rd, Well	154	A2
Ripple Rd, Bark	99	M14
Ripple Rd, Dag	118	C2
Rippleside Commercial Est, Bark	118	E3
Ripplevale Gro N1	93	M14
Rippolson Rd SE18	135	T9
Risborough Dr, Wor Pk	179	P13
Risborough St, SE1 2	27	S5
Risdon St SE16	131	M4
Rise, The N11	79	N9
Rise, The N13	59	P8
Rise, The NW7	55	M12
Rise, The NW10	88	H7
Rise, The, Bex	154	E14
Rise, The, Buck H	48	B14
Rise, The, Edg	54	C9
Rise, The, Grnf	86	G10
Risedale Rd, Bexh	155	T5
Riseldine Rd SE23	149	R12
Risinghill St N1	10	H2
Risingholme Cl, Har	68	D2
Risingholme Rd, Har	68	C3
Risings, The E17	78	H7
Risley Av N17	76	A2
Rita Rd SW8	34	E13
Ritches Rd N15	75	T9
Ritchie Rd, Croy	185	K12
Ritchie St N1	11	L1
Ritchings Av E17	77	R7
Ritherdon Rd SW17	164	B4
Ritson Rd E8	94	G11
Ritter St SE18	134	G12
Rivaz Pl E9	95	M11
Rivenhall Gdns E18	79	L7
River Av N13	59	R5
River Av, T Ditt	176	H13
River Bank N21	43	T14
River Bank, E Mol	176	C6
River Bank, T Ditt	176	F10
River Bank, W Mol	174	J4
River Barge Cl E14	132	F4
River Brent Business Pk W7	122	D6
River Cl E11	79	T11
River Cl, Sthl	121	U3
River Cl, Surb	177	N9
River Crane Wk, Felt	156	H1
River Crane Wk, Houns	156	H1
River Crane Way, Felt 4	157	M4
River Front, Enf	44	B6
River Gdns, Cars	196	A4
River Gdns, Felt	138	D8
River Gro Pk, Beck	185	U2
River La, Rich	159	P1

River Pk Gdns, Brom	168	H13
River Pk Rd N22	75	M3
River Pl N1	93	T14
River Reach, Tedd	159	M10
River Rd, Bark	117	S4
River Rd, Buck H	64	C1
River Rd Business Pk, Bark	117	T6
River St EC1	11	K6
River Ter W6	125	T10
River Wk, Walt	174	B11
River Way, Epsom	192	H10
River Way, Loug	48	G11
River Way, Twick	157	R4
Riverbank Way, Brent	123	L11
Rivercourt Rd W6	125	R8
Riverdale Dr SW18	162	J2
Riverdale Gdns, Twick	141	M11
Riverdale Rd SE18	135	T9
Riverdale Rd, Bex	155	L12
Riverdale Rd, Erith	137	S10
Riverdale Rd, Felt	157	K7
Riverdale Rd, Twick	141	M11
Riverdene, Edg	54	F7
Riverdene Rd, Ilf	98	H6
Riverhead Cl E17	77	N3
Rivermead, E Mol	175	T5
Rivermead Cl, Tedd	159	K10
Rivermead Ct SW6	144	E6
Rivermeads Av, Twick	157	P5
Rivernook Cl, Walt	174	F10
Riversdale Rd N5	93	T6
Riversdale Rd, T Ditt	176	G10
Riversfield Rd, Enf	44	C5
Riverside NW4	71	R13
Riverside SE7	133	S6
Riverside, Twick	158	J1
Riverside, The, E Mol		
Riverside Av, E Mol	176	B10
Riverside Business Cen SW18	145	K14
Riverside Cl E5	95	M3
Riverside Cl W7	104	D8
Riverside Cl, Kings T	177	P7
Riverside Cl, Wall	196	C6
Riverside Ct E4	46	C12
Riverside Ct SW8	33	T10
Riverside Dr NW11	72	C11
Riverside Dr W4	142	J1
Riverside Dr, Mitch	181	S9
Riverside Dr, Rich	159	K4
Riverside Gdns N3	72	C6
Riverside Gdns W6	125	S9
Riverside Gdns, Enf	43	U4
Riverside Gdns, Wem	105	S4
Riverside Ind Est, Bark	118	B5
Riverside Ind Est, Enf	45	R12
Riverside Rd E15	114	F4
Riverside Rd N15	76	H11
Riverside Rd SW17	163	K7
Riverside Rd, Sid	173	K4
Riverside Wk SE1	26	F5
Riverside Wk, Bex	154	H13
Riverside Wk, Islw	140	D6
Riverside Wk, Loug	49	K11
Riverton Cl W9	108	F6
Riverview Gdns SW13	125	S11
Riverview Gdns, Twick	158	F4
Riverview Gro W4	124	D12
Riverview Pk SE6	168	A3
Riverview Rd W4	124	D12
Riverview Rd, Epsom	192	F7
Riverway N13	59	N9
Riverwood La, Chis	189	N2
Rivington Av, Wdf Grn	80	A3
Rivington Ct NW10	107	N2
Rivington Cres NW7	55	L14
Rivington Pl EC2	12	J7
Rivington St EC2	12	H8

Rivington Wk E8	112	H1
Rivulet Rd N17	59	T13
Rixon St, N7 **2**	93	N6
Rixsen Rd E12	98	D10
Roach Rd E3	96	B13
Roads Pl N19	93	K3
Roan St SE10	132	E12
Robb Rd, Stan	52	H12
Robert Cl W9	6	H11
Robert Adam St W1	16	D5
Robert Cl, Chig	65	U9
Robert Dashwood Way SE17	35	T3
Robert Keen Cl, SE15 **2**	148	H2
Robert Lowe Cl SE14	131	P13
Robert Owen Ho SW6	144	B1
Robert St E16	134	J2
Robert St NW1	9	K7
Robert St SE18	135	N8
Robert St, WC2 **10**	18	C12
Robert St, Croy	197	U5
Roberta St E2	13	T7
Roberton Dr, Brom	187	U2
Roberts Cl SE9	171	N2
Roberts Cl, Pnr	66	D10
Roberts Cl, Sutt	194	B13
Roberts Ms SW1	24	D11
Robert's Pl, EC1 **5**	11	L10
Roberts Rd E17	78	C1
Roberts Rd, NW7 **1**	56	C11
Roberts Rd, Belv	137	P10
Robertsbridge Rd, Cars	181	M14
Robertson Rd E15	114	F1
Robertson St SW8	146	D4
Robeson St E3	113	U8
Robeson Way, Borwd	38	F1
Robin Cl NW7	54	J5
Robin Cl, Hmptn	157	K10
Robin Ct, SE16 **3**	37	R1
Robin Cres E6	116	B9
Robin Gro N6	92	A3
Robin Gro, Brent	123	M12
Robin Gro, Har	69	U12
Robin Hill Dr, Chis	170	D11
Robin Hood Dr, Har	52	E14
Robin Hood La E14	114	F13
Robin Hood La SW15	160	J7
Robin Hood La, Bexh	155	K9
Robin Hood La, Sutt	194	H9
Robin Hood Rd SW19	161	R9
Robin Hood Way SW15	161	K9
Robin Hood Way SW20	161	K9
Robin Hood Way, Grnf	86	F11
Robina Cl, Bexh	154	H7
Robinhood Cl, Mitch	182	F6
Robinhood La, Mitch	182	F6
Robinia Cl, Ilf	65	R11
Robinia Cres E10	96	B4
Robins Cl SE12	169	T6
Robins Gro, W Wick	201	N6
Robinscroft Ms, SE10 **6**	150	D2
Robinson Cres, Bushey	51	T2
Robinson Rd E2	113	L4
Robinson Rd SW17	163	R12
Robinson Rd, Dag	101	N7
Robinson St SW3	31	T10
Robinsons Cl W13	104	H10
Robinwood Pl SW15	160	H7
Robsart St SW9	147	M3
Robson Av NW10	89	P14
Robson Cl, E6 **24**	116	C11
Robson Cl, Enf	43	R4
Robson Rd SE27	165	T5
Roch Av, Edg	69	U3
Rochdale Rd E17	78	A13
Rochdale Rd SE2	136	C8
Roche Rd SW16	183	L2
Roche Wk, Cars	181	N12
Rochelle Cl SW11	145	N8
Rochelle St E2	13	M8
Rochester Av E13	115	T2
Rochester Av, Brom	187	S4
Rochester Av, Felt	156	A4
Rochester Cl SW16	165	K14
Rochester Cl, Enf	44	D2
Rochester Cl, Sid **2**	154	C11
Rochester Dr, Bex	155	P11
Rochester Dr, Pnr	66	G9
Rochester Gdns, Croy	198	D5
Rochester Gdns, Ilf	80	E14
Rochester Ms NW1	92	E13
Rochester Pl NW1	92	F13
Rochester Rd NW1	92	E12
Rochester Rd, Cars	195	U7
Rochester Row SW1	33	P2
Rochester Sq NW1	92	F13
Rochester St SW1	25	R12
Rochester Ter NW1	92	E12
Rochester Wk, SE1 **1**	28	C2
Rochester Way SE3	151	S2
Rochester Way SE9	152	E6
Rochester Way Relief Rd SE3	151	S2
Rochester Way Relief Rd SE9	152	F9
Rochford Av, Loug	49	L5
Rochford Av, Rom	82	E9
Rochford Cl E6	116	A3
Rochford Grn, Loug	49	L5
Rochford St NW5	91	U9
Rochford Wk E8	94	H13
Rochford Way, Croy	182	J12
Rock Av SW14	142	H6
Rock Gdns, Dag	101	R10
Rock Gro Way SE16	37	U1
Rock Hill SE26	166	E8
Rock St N4	93	P4
Rockbourne Rd SE23	167	N2
Rockells Pl SE22	149	K12
Rockford Av, Grnf	104	J4
Rockhall Rd NW2	90	A8
Rockhampton Cl, SE27 **2**	165	P7
Rockhampton Rd SE27	165	N7
Rockhampton Rd, S Croy	198	C12
Rockingham Cl SW15	143	L7
Rockingham Est SE1	28	A11
Rockingham St SE1	27	U11
Rockland Rd SW15	144	D8
Rocklands Dr, Stan	69	K4
Rockley Rd W14	126	A3
Rockmount Rd SE18	135	U10
Rockmount Rd SE19	166	B12
Rocks La SW13	143	P5
Rockware Av, Grnf	104	C1
Rockways, Barn	39	M12
Rockwell Gdns SE19	166	D9
Rockwell Rd, Dag	101	R10
Rockwood Pl, W12 **1**	125	U3
Rocliffe St N1	11	R3
Rocombe Cres, SE23 **1**	149	L14
Rocque La SE3	151	M5
Rodborough Rd NW11	90	G1
Roden Ct N6	74	G13
Roden Gdns, Croy	184	C12
Roden St N7	93	L6
Roden St, Ilf	98	H6
Rodenhurst Rd SW4	146	G11
Roderick Rd NW3	91	U8
Roding Av, Wdf Grn	64	D13
Roding Gdns, Loug	48	D11
Roding La, Buck H	64	B2
Roding La, Chig	64	G3
Roding La N, Wdf Grn	80	B4
Roding La S, Ilf	80	A7
Roding La S, Wdf Grn	80	B5
Roding Ms E1	29	U1
Roding Rd E5	95	R9
Roding Rd E6	116	J9
Roding Rd, Loug	48	F11
Roding Trd Est, Bark	98	J14
Roding Vw, Buck H	64	B1
Rodings, The, Wdf Grn	63	U11
Rodmarton St W1	16	B4
Rodmell Cl, Hayes	102	J8
Rodmell Slope N12	56	F9
Rodmere St SE10	133	K10
Rodmill La SW2	147	K14
Rodney Cl, Croy	197	S2
Rodney Cl, N Mal	178	J9
Rodney Cl, Pnr	66	J13
Rodney Ct W9	6	H9
Rodney Gdns, Pnr	66	D9
Rodney Gdns, W Wick	201	P7
Rodney Pl E17	77	S3
Rodney Pl SE17	36	B1
Rodney Pl SW19	181	L1
Rodney Rd E11	79	R8
Rodney Rd SE17	36	C3
Rodney Rd, Mitch	181	R4
Rodney Rd, N Mal	178	J9
Rodney Rd, Twick	139	N12
Rodney St N1	10	G2
Rodney Way, Rom	83	P2
Rodway Rd SW15	143	P13
Rodway Rd, Brom	169	R14
Rodwell Cl, Ruis	66	E14
Rodwell Pl, Edg	54	A12
Rodwell Rd SE22	148	F11
Roe End NW9	70	E7
Roe Grn NW9	70	F9
Roe La NW9	70	D7
Roe Way, Wall	197	K13
Roebourne Way E16	134	G3
Roebuck Cl, Felt	156	C7
Roebuck La, N17 **1**	60	F12
Roebuck La, Buck H	47	T14
Roebuck Rd, Chess	192	A9
Roedean Av, Enf	45	L1
Roedean Cl, Enf	45	L1
Roedean Cres SW15	142	J11
Roehampton Cl SW15	143	N8
Roehampton Dr, Chis	171	M12
Roehampton Gate SW15	142	J11
Roehampton High St SW15	143	P13
Roehampton La SW15	143	N8
Roehampton Vale SW15	161	L5
Roffey St E14	132	E4
Roger St WC1	10	G12
Rogers Gdns, Dag	101	P10
Rogers Rd E16	115	M11
Rogers Rd SW17	163	P7
Rogers Rd, Dag	101	P10
Rojack Rd SE23	167	N2
Rokeby Gdns, Wdf Grn	79	P1
Rokeby Pl SW20	161	S13
Rokeby Rd SE4	149	T3
Rokeby St E15	114	J1
Rokesby Cl, Well	153	P3
Rokesby Pl, Wem	87	N10
Rokesly Av N8	74	J9
Roland Gdns SW7	30	H5
Roland Ms, E1 **5**	113	N9
Roland Rd E17	78	G8
Roland Way SE17	36	E8
Roland Way SW7	30	G5
Roland Way, Wor Pk	193	M3
Roles Gro, Rom	82	H7
Rolfe Cl, Barn	41	S8
Rolinsden Way, Kes	202	B8
Roll Gdns, Ilf	80	H10
Rollesby Rd, Chess	192	A12
Rollesby Way SE28	118	E12
Rolleston Av, Orp	189	K12
Rolleston Cl, Orp	189	K13
Rolleston Rd, S Croy	198	A14
Rollins St SE15	131	M11
Rollit Cres, Houns	139	P9
Rollit St N7	93	N9
Rolls Bldgs EC4	19	K6
Rolls Pk Av E4	62	B10
Rolls Pk Rd E4	62	C10
Rolls Rd SE1	37	N5
Rollscourt Av SE24	147	T9
Rolt St SE8	131	S11
Rolvenden Gdns, Brom	170	A14
Rolvenden Pl N17	60	H14
Roma Read Cl, SW15 **4**	143	R14
Roma Rd E17	77	S6
Roman Cl, Felt	138	E10
Roman Ind Est, Croy	184	C13
Roman Ri SE19	166	B11
Roman Rd E2	113	L6
Roman Rd E3	113	R4
Roman Rd E6	116	B8
Roman Rd N10	58	C14
Roman Rd NW2	89	U5
Roman Rd W4	125	L7
Roman Rd, Ilf	99	K11
Roman Sq SE28	136	B2
Roman Way N7	93	M12
Roman Way, Croy	197	S3
Roman Way, Enf	44	F9
Romanfield Rd SW2	147	M14
Romanhurst Av, Brom	187	K8
Romanhurst Gdns, Brom	186	J8
Romany Gdns, E17 **1**	77	R2
Romany Gdns, Sutt	180	G14
Romany Ri, Orp	203	M2
Romberg Rd SW17	164	A6
Romborough Gdns SE13	150	E9
Romborough Way SE13	150	E9
Romero Cl, SW9 **3**	147	M5
Romero Sq SE3	151	T8
Romeyn Rd SW16	165	M6
Romford Rd E7	97	P11
Romford Rd E12	98	B9
Romford Rd E15	97	K12
Romford St E1	21	U4
Romilly Dr, Wat	51	K7
Romilly Rd N4	93	R4
Romilly St W1	17	T9
Rommany Rd SE27	166	A8
Romney Cl N17	76	J1
Romney Cl NW11	91	L2
Romney Cl SE14	131	M14
Romney Cl, Chess	191	R8
Romney Cl, Har	67	P13
Romney Dr, Brom	170	A14
Romney Dr, Har	67	P13
Romney Gdns, Bexh	155	M1
Romney Ms W1	16	C1
Romney Rd SE10	132	G11
Romney Rd, N Mal	178	H12
Romney St SW1	25	U12
Romola Rd SE24	165	R1
Romsey Cl, Orp	203	K7
Romsey Gdns, Dag	118	H1
Romsey Rd W13	104	H14
Romsey Rd, Dag	118	H1
Ron Leighton Way E6	116	D1
Rona Rd NW3	92	A8
Ronald Av E15	115	K6
Ronald Cl, Beck	185	U8
Ronald St, E1 **11**	113	M12
Ronalds Rd N5	93	P10
Ronalds Rd, Brom	187	P1
Ronaldstone Rd, Sid	153	S11
Ronart St, Har	68	F5
Rondu Rd NW2	90	C9
Ronelean Rd, Surb	191	T5
Ronver Rd SE12	169	M11
Rood La EC3	20	G10
Rookby Ct, N21 **1**	59	S3
Rooke Way SE10	133	L9

Name	Page	Grid
Rookeries Cl, Felt	156	E6
Rookery Cl NW9	71	L9
Rookery Cres, Dag	101	S14
Rookery Dr, Chis	188	G1
Rookery La, Brom	188	A11
Rookery Rd SW4	146	E7
Rookery Way NW9	71	L10
Rookfield Av N10	74	E7
Rookfield Cl N10	74	E7
Rookstone Rd SW17	163	T10
Rookwood Av, Loug	49	M5
Rookwood Av, N Mal	179	N8
Rookwood Av, Wall	196	G7
Rookwood Gdns E4	63	L3
Rookwood Gdns, Loug	49	M6
Rookwood Rd N16	76	F13
Rootes Dr W10	108	A8
Rope St SE16	131	S6
Rope Wk, Sun	174	E5
Rope Wk Gdns E1	21	U6
Rope Yd Rails SE18	134	J6
Ropemaker Rd SE16	131	R4
Ropemaker St EC2	20	D2
Ropemakers Flds, E14 *10*	113	T14
Roper La SE1	29	K7
Roper St SE9	152	F10
Roper Way, Mitch *4*	182	B3
Ropers Av E4	62	E10
Ropery St E3	113	T8
Ropley St E2	13	R4
Rosa Alba Ms N5	93	T7
Rosaline Rd SW6	126	D14
Rosamond St SE26	166	J6
Rosamun St, Sthl	121	K8
Rosamund Cl, S Croy	198	B8
Rosary Cl, Houns	139	K3
Rosary Gdns SW7	30	G4
Rosaville Rd SW6	126	E14
Roscoe St EC1	12	B11
Roscoff Cl, Edg	70	E1
Rose All SE1	28	A1
Rose & Crown Yd, SW1 *3*	25	P3
Rose Av E18	79	S4
Rose Av, Mitch	181	U1
Rose Av, Mord	181	M9
Rose Bates Dr NW9	70	A8
Rose Ct SE26	166	J4
Rose Ct, Pnr	66	E5
Rose Dale, Orp	203	K3
Rose End, Wor Pk	194	A2
Rose Gdn Cl, Edg	53	S11
Rose Gdns W5	123	P5
Rose Gdns, Felt	156	A4
Rose Gdns, Sthl	103	P8
Rose Glen NW9	70	G7
Rose Hill, Sutt	195	K2
Rose La, Rom	82	H5
Rose Lawn, Bushey	51	U2
Rose Sq SW3	31	L5
Rose St, WC2 *6*	18	B10
Rose Wk, Surb	178	D9
Rose Wk, W Wick	200	F4
Rose Way SE12	151	N10
Rose Way, Edg	54	F7
Roseacre Cl W13	104	J9
Roseacre Rd, Well	154	D6
Rosebank SE20	166	J13
Rosebank Av, Wem	86	E8
Rosebank Cl N12	57	R8
Rosebank Cl, Tedd	158	H12
Rosebank Gdns E3	13	S4
Rosebank Gro E17	77	T6
Rosebank Rd E17	78	B12
Rosebank Rd W7	122	D4
Rosebank Vil E17	78	A8
Rosebank Wk SE18	134	D7
Rosebank Way W3	106	G11
Roseberry Gdns N4	75	S11
Roseberry Gdns, Orp	203	R6
Roseberry Pl E8	94	E12
Roseberry St SE16	130	J8
Rosebery Av E12	98	E11
Rosebery Av EC1	10	J11
Rosebery Av N17	76	H3
Rosebery Av, Har	85	L7
Rosebery Av, N Mal	179	L4
Rosebery Av, Sid	153	R13
Rosebery Av, Th Hth	183	U3
Rosebery Cl, Mord	180	A12
Rosebery Gdns N8	74	J10
Rosebery Gdns W13	104	H11
Rosebery Gdns, Sutt	195	K7
Rosebery Ms N10	74	E3
Rosebery Ms, SW2 *1*	146	J11
Rosebery Rd N9	60	G5
Rosebery Rd N10	74	E3
Rosebery Rd SW2	146	J11
Rosebery Rd, Houns	139	U10
Rosebery Rd, Kings T	178	C4
Rosebery Rd, Sutt	194	F12
Rosebery Sq EC1	10	J11
Rosebery Sq, Kings T	178	B4
Rosebine Av, Twick	140	B14
Rosebury Rd SW6	145	K4
Rosecourt Rd, Croy	183	L12
Rosecroft Av NW3	90	H5
Rosecroft Gdns NW2	89	N6
Rosecroft Gdns, Twick	158	B1
Rosecroft Rd, Sthl	103	P8
Rosecroft Wk, Pnr	66	H10
Rosecroft Wk, Wem	87	P10
Rosedale Cl SE2	136	C5
Rosedale Cl W7	122	E4
Rosedale Cl, Stan	53	K12
Rosedale Ct, N5 *1*	93	R8
Rosedale Gdns, Dag	100	C14
Rosedale Rd E7	97	U10
Rosedale Rd, Dag	100	C14
Rosedale Rd, Epsom	193	N9
Rosedale Rd, Rich	141	R7
Rosedale Rd, Rom	83	U5
Rosedene NW6	108	B1
Rosedene Av SW16	165	M6
Rosedene Av, Croy	183	K13
Rosedene Av, Grnf	103	P5
Rosedene Av, Mord	180	H9
Rosedene Gdns, Ilf	80	H7
Rosedene Ter E10	96	D3
Rosedew Rd W6	126	A12
Rosefield Cl, Cars *1*	195	S9
Rosefield Gdns E14	114	A13
Rosehart Ms, W11 *7*	108	G12
Rosehatch Av, Rom	82	H6
Roseheath Rd, Houns	139	L9
Rosehill, Esher	190	G12
Rosehill, Hmptn	175	P2
Rosehill Av, Sutt	195	L1
Rosehill Gdns, Grnf	86	E10
Rosehill Gdns, Sutt	195	K3
Rosehill Pk W, Sutt	195	L3
Rosehill Rd SW18	145	L11
Roseland Cl N17	60	B13
Roseleigh Av N5	93	S8
Roseleigh Cl, Twick	141	N12
Rosemary Av N3	73	K3
Rosemary Av N9	60	J2
Rosemary Av, Enf	44	B1
Rosemary Av, Houns	138	H4
Rosemary Av, W Mol	175	N6
Rosemary Cl, Croy *5*	182	J12
Rosemary Dr E14	114	G12
Rosemary Dr, Ilf	80	B10
Rosemary Gdns, Chess	191	R8
Rosemary Gdns, Dag	101	M2
Rosemary La SW14	142	F5
Rosemary Rd SE15	37	N14
Rosemary Rd SW17	163	K6
Rosemary Rd, Well	153	U2
Rosemary St N1	112	A1
Rosemead NW9	71	M13
Rosemead Av, Mitch	182	F5
Rosemead Av, Wem	87	S10
Rosemont Av N12	57	L11
Rosemont Rd NW3	91	L11
Rosemont Rd W3	106	C14
Rosemont Rd, N Mal	178	E5
Rosemont Rd, Rich	141	S12
Rosemont Rd, Wem	105	R2
Rosemoor St SW3	31	T3
Rosemount Cl, Wdf Grn	64	E12
Rosemount Dr, Brom	188	E7
Rosemount Rd W13	104	H11
Rosenau Cres SW11	145	S2
Rosenau Rd SW11	145	S1
Rosendale Rd SE21	165	U12
Rosendale Rd SE24	147	T14
Roseneath Av N21	59	R1
Roseneath Rd SW11	146	A11
Roseneath Wk, Enf	44	C8
Rosens Wk, Edg	54	D6
Rosenthal Rd SE6	150	D12
Rosenthorpe Rd SE15	149	N9
Roserton St, E14 *1*	132	E4
Roses, The, Croy	185	N11
Roses, The, Wdf Grn	63	M13
Rosethorn Cl SW12	146	G14
Rosetta Cl, SW8 *2*	129	K14
Roseveare Rd SE12	169	U7
Roseville Av, Houns	139	N10
Roseville Rd, Hayes	120	A9
Rosevine Rd SW20	179	T2
Roseway SE21	148	B12
Rosewell Cl SE20	166	J14
Rosewood, Esher	190	G3
Rosewood, Grnf	86	G10
Rosewood Cl, Sid	172	E5
Rosewood Ct, Brom	187	U1
Rosewood Ct, Rom	82	E9
Rosewood Gdns SE13	150	E3
Rosewood Gro, Sutt	195	M3
Rosewood Sq, W12 *1*	107	N12
Rosher Cl E15	96	G14
Rosina St E9	95	N10
Roskell Rd SW15	144	A6
Roslin Rd W3	124	D5
Roslin Way, Brom	169	P10
Roslyn Cl, Mitch	181	N3
Roslyn Rd N15	76	B9
Rosmead Rd W11	108	D13
Rosoman Pl EC1	11	L9
Rosoman St, EC1 *1*	11	L8
Ross Av NW7	56	D10
Ross Av, Dag	101	L3
Ross Cl, Har	51	U13
Ross Cl SW15	144	A13
Ross Par, Wall	196	D11
Ross Rd SE25	184	C5
Ross Rd, Twick	155	T2
Ross Rd, Wall	196	E10
Ross Way SE9	152	D5
Rossall Cres NW10	105	T6
Rossdale, Sutt	195	S9
Rossdale Dr N9	45	L12
Rossdale Dr NW9	88	E1
Rossdale Rd SW15	143	U7
Rosse Ms SE3	151	R1
Rossendale St E5	94	J3
Rossendale Way NW1	92	F14
Rossetti Rd SE16	130	J9
Rossignol Gdns, Cars	196	A4
Rossindel Rd, Houns	139	N9
Rossington St E5	94	H4
Rossiter Flds, Barn	40	E11
Rossiter Rd SW12	164	D2
Rossland Cl, Bexh	155	R9
Rosslyn Av E4	63	L3
Rosslyn Av SW13	143	K6
Rosslyn Av, Barn	41	R12
Rosslyn Av, Dag	83	M14
Rosslyn Av, Felt	138	B12
Rosslyn Cl, W Wick	201	L5
Rosslyn Cres, Har	68	E8
Rosslyn Cres, Wem	87	R7
Rosslyn Hill NW3	91	P8
Rosslyn Ms NW3	91	P9
Rosslyn Rd E17	78	E8
Rosslyn Rd, Bark	99	N13
Rosslyn Rd, Twick	141	L12
Rossmore Rd NW1	7	R10
Rosswood Gdns, Wall *2*	196	E11
Rostella Rd SW17	163	P8
Rostrevor Av N15	76	E12
Rostrevor Gdns, Sthl	121	K10
Rostrevor Ms, SW6 *1*	144	E2
Rostrevor Rd SW6	144	E1
Rostrevor Rd SW19	162	G10
Rotary St SE1	27	P9
Rothbury Gdns, Islw	122	H14
Rothbury Rd E9	95	U13
Rothbury Wk N17	60	H14
Rotherfield Rd, Cars	196	B8
Rotherfield St N1	93	U14
Rotherhill Av SW16	164	H12
Rotherhithe New Rd SE16	130	J10
Rotherhithe Old Rd SE16	131	N7
Rotherhithe St SE16	131	M3
Rotherhithe Tunnel E1	131	M2
Rotherhithe Tunnel App E14	113	P13
Rotherhithe Tunnel App SE16	131	L4
Rothermere Rd, Croy	197	M10
Rotherwick Hill W5	105	U8
Rotherwick Rd NW11	72	G14
Rotherwood Cl SW20	180	C1
Rotherwood Rd SW15	144	A5
Rothery St, N1 *4*	111	R1
Rothery Ter SW9	35	N14
Rothesay Av SW20	180	D3
Rothesay Av, Grnf	86	A11
Rothesay Av, Rich	142	C7
Rothesay Rd SE25	184	B8
Rothsay Rd E7	97	T13
Rothsay St SE1	28	G10
Rothschild Rd W4	124	E6
Rothschild St SE27	165	S8
Rothwell Gdns, Dag	118	F1
Rothwell Rd, Dag	118	E1
Rothwell St NW1	109	U1
Rotten Row NW1	24	C5
Rotten Row SW7	23	N5
Rotterdam Dr E14	132	F6
Rouel Rd SE16	29	R11
Rougemont Av, Mord	180	G12
Round Gro, Croy	185	P14
Round Hill SE26	167	L4
Roundaway Rd, Ilf	80	E3
Roundel Cl SE4	149	T8
Roundhay Cl SE23	167	N4
Roundhill Dr, Enf	43	L8
Roundmead Av, Loug	48	H5
Roundmead Cl, Loug	48	G5
Roundtable Rd, Brom	169	M5
Roundtree Rd, Wem	86	D3
Roundway, The N17	75	U1
Roundway, The, Esher	190	F11
Roundwood, Chis	188	J3
Roundwood Rd NW10	89	L12
Rounton Rd E3	114	B7
Roupell Rd SW2	165	M1
Roupell St SE1	27	L4
Rous Rd, Buck H	64	C2
Rousden St NW1	92	F14
Rouse Gdns SE21	166	D7
Routemaster Cl E13	115	R4

Routh Rd SW18	145	R14
Routh St E6	116	F10
Routledge Cl N19	92	H2
Rover Av, Ilf	65	T12
Rowallan Rd SW6	126	C14
Rowan Av E4	61	U11
Rowan Cl SW16	182	F2
Rowan Cl W5	123	S4
Rowan Cl, Ilf	99	N10
Rowan Cl, N Mal	178	J4
Rowan Cl, Stan	52	E11
Rowan Cl, Wem	86	H6
Rowan Cres SW16	182	F2
Rowan Dr NW9	71	N6
Rowan Gdns, Croy 6	198	F5
Rowan Rd SW16	182	F4
Rowan Rd W6	126	A8
Rowan Rd, Bexh	155	K6
Rowan Rd, Brent	123	K14
Rowan Ter, W6 1	126	A7
Rowan Wk N2	73	M11
Rowan Wk, N19 8	92	E4
Rowan Wk, Barn	40	J9
Rowan Wk, Brom	202	E5
Rowan Way, Rom	82	F6
Rowans, The N13	59	T6
Rowans Way, Loug	48	F7
Rowantree Cl N21	60	B1
Rowantree Rd N21	60	B1
Rowantree Rd, Enf	43	R3
Rowanwood Av, Sid	172	A1
Rowben Cl N20	56	J1
Rowberry Cl, SW6 4	125	U14
Rowcross St SE1	37	M6
Rowdell Rd, Nthlt	103	N1
Rowden Rd E4	62	B12
Rowden Rd, Beck	185	S1
Rowden Rd, Epsom	192	D8
Rowditch La SW11	146	A3
Rowdon Av NW10	89	S13
Rowdowns Rd, Dag	119	M1
Rowe Gdns, Bark	117	U3
Rowe La E9	95	L9
Rowe Wk, Har	85	P5
Rowena Cres SW11	145	S4
Rowfant Rd SW17	164	A2
Rowhill Rd E5	95	K8
Rowington Cl W2	14	B1
Rowland Av, Har	69	M6
Rowland Ct E16	115	L7
Rowland Cres, Chig	65	R8
Rowland Hill Av N17	59	U13
Rowland Hill St NW3	91	S9
Rowland Way, SW19 3	181	K1
Rowlands Av, Pnr	51	R12
Rowlands Cl N6	74	A12
Rowlands Cl NW7	55	N14
Rowlands Rd, Dag	101	M4
Rowley Av, Sid	154	D14
Rowley Cl, Wem	87	U14
Rowley Gdns N4	75	T13
Rowley Grn Rd, Barn	39	N10
Rowley Ind Pk W3	124	D5
Rowley La, Barn	39	K7
Rowley Rd N15	75	T9
Rowley Way NW8	109	L1
Rowlls Rd, Kings T	177	U5
Rowney Gdns, Dag	100	E12
Rowney Rd, Dag	100	D12
Rowntree Clifford Cl E13	115	R7
Rowntree Rd, Twick	158	C1
Rowse Cl E15	114	F1
Rowsley Av NW4	71	T5
Rowstock Gdns N7	92	H10
Rowton Rd SE18	135	M13
Roxborough Av, Har	68	B13
Roxborough Av, Islw	122	F14
Roxborough Pk, Har	68	C13
Roxborough Rd, Har	68	B11
Roxbourne Cl, Nthlt	84	H12
Roxburgh Rd SE27	165	R9
Roxby Pl, SW6 1	126	H11
Roxeth Grn Av, Har	85	T3
Roxeth Gro, Har	85	S7
Roxeth Hill, Har	86	B3
Roxley Rd SE13	150	D11
Roxton Gdns, Croy	200	A10
Roxwell Rd W12	125	N3
Roxwell Rd, Bark	118	B4
Roxwell Trd Pk E10	77	P14
Roxwell Way, Wdf Grn	63	U13
Roxy Av, Rom	82	E13
Roy Gdns, Ilf	81	S8
Roy Gro, Hmptn	157	R11
Roy Sq E14	113	T13
Royal Albert Dock E16	116	F14
Royal Albert Way E16	116	B13
Royal Arc, W1 1	17	L12
Royal Av SW3	31	U6
Royal Av, Wor Pk	193	K4
Royal Circ SE27	165	P5
Royal Cl N16	94	D2
Royal Cl, Ilf	82	A13
Royal Cl, Wor Pk	192	J3
Royal College St NW1	92	F14
Royal Ct SE16	131	T5
Royal Cres W11	126	B2
Royal Cres, Ruis	84	J6
Royal Cres Ms W11	126	B2
Royal Docks Rd E6	117	K12
Royal Dr N11	58	A10
Royal Ex EC3	20	E8
Royal Ex Av, EC3 10	20	F7
Royal Ex Bldgs EC3	20	F7
Royal Gdns W7	122	G6
Royal Hill SE10	132	E14
Royal Hospital Rd SW3	31	T10
Royal London Est, The N17	60	H12
Royal Ms, The SW1	24	J9
Royal Mint Ct EC3	21	N11
Royal Mint Pl, E1 2	21	P10
Royal Mint St E1	21	P10
Royal Mt Ct, Twick	158	D5
Royal Naval Pl, SE14 14	131	T13
Royal Oak Pl SE22	149	K11
Royal Oak Rd, E8 5	94	J11
Royal Oak Rd, Bexh	155	M9
Royal Opera Arc SW1	25	S1
Royal Orchard Cl SW18	144	C13
Royal Par SE3	151	L4
Royal Par W5	105	S6
Royal Par, Chis	171	M14
Royal Par Ms, Chis	171	M14
Royal Pl SE10	132	F14
Royal Rd E16	116	A12
Royal Rd SE17	35	N10
Royal Rd, Sid	172	G5
Royal Rd, Tedd	158	B9
Royal Route, Wem	87	U8
Royal St SE1	26	G9
Royal Victor Pl E3	113	P4
Royal Victoria Dock E16	115	S14
Royal Victoria Pl, E16 13	133	R1
Royal Wk, Wall 3	196	C5
Royal Windsor Ct, Surb	192	B2
Royalty Ms, W1 2	17	S8
Roycraft Av, Bark	117	T4
Roycraft Cl, Bark	117	T3
Roycroft Cl E18	79	R2
Roycroft Cl SW2	165	P2
Roydene Rd SE18	135	R11
Roydon Cl, Loug	48	D14
Roydon St, SW11 5	146	C1
Royle Cres W13	104	G8
Royston Av E4	62	B10
Royston Av, Sutt	195	P5
Royston Av, Wall	196	H7
Royston Cl, Houns	138	C1
Royston Ct SE24	147	U12
Royston Ct, Rich	141	U1
Royston Ct, Surb	192	B4
Royston Gdns, Ilf	80	A12
Royston Gro, Pnr	51	M12
Royston Par, Ilf	80	A12
Royston Pk Rd, Pnr	51	M11
Royston Rd SE20	185	N2
Royston Rd, Rich	141	S10
Royston St E2	113	M4
Roystons, The, Surb	178	C9
Rozel Rd SW4	146	E4
Rubastic Rd, Sthl	120	D5
Rubens Rd, Nthlt	102	F3
Rubens St SE6	167	U4
Ruberoid Rd, Enf	45	T5
Ruby Ms E17	78	A6
Ruby Rd E17	78	A5
Ruby St SE15	130	J11
Ruby Triangle SE15	130	J11
Ruckholt Cl E10	96	D6
Ruckholt Rd E10	96	C7
Rucklidge Av NW10	107	M3
Rudall Cres NW3	91	N7
Ruddington Cl E5	95	R7
Ruddstreet Cl SE18	135	K8
Rudland Rd, Bexh	155	S6
Rudloe Rd SW12	146	E13
Rudolf Pl SW8	34	C11
Rudolph Ct SE22	148	H13
Rudolph Rd E13	115	M4
Rudolph Rd NW6	108	H4
Rudyard Gro NW7	54	F11
Ruffetts, The, S Croy	199	K13
Ruffetts Cl, S Croy	198	J13
Rufford Cl, Har	68	H12
Rufford St N1	111	K1
Rufus Cl, Ruis	84	J6
Rufus St, N1 7	12	H7
Rugby Av N9	60	F1
Rugby Av, Grnf	86	B11
Rugby Av, Wem	87	K9
Rugby Cl, Har	68	C8
Rugby Gdns, Dag	100	E12
Rugby Rd NW9	70	C7
Rugby Rd W4	124	J4
Rugby Rd, Dag	100	C12
Rugby Rd, Twick	140	D11
Rugby St WC1	10	F12
Rugg St, E14 2	114	A13
Ruislip Cl, Grnf	103	R7
Ruislip Rd, Grnf	103	T7
Ruislip Rd, Nthlt	102	H4
Ruislip Rd, Sthl	103	P6
Ruislip Rd E W13	104	D8
Ruislip Rd E W13	104	F7
Ruislip Rd E, Grnf	103	U8
Ruislip St SW17	163	U7
Rum Cl E1	113	L14
Rumbold Rd SW6	127	K14
Rumsey Cl, Hmptn	157	L11
Rumsey Rd SW9	147	M5
Runbury Circle NW9	88	H3
Runcorn Cl N17	76	J8
Runcorn Pl, W11 2	108	C13
Rundell Cres NW4	71	R10
Runes Cl, Mitch	181	P8
Runnel Fld, Har	86	D6
Running Horse Yd, Brent 4	123	S11
Runnymede SW19	181	N2
Runnymede Cl, Twick	139	S12
Runnymede Ct, Croy 4	198	E4
Runnymede Cres SW16	182	H1
Runnymede Gdns, Grnf	104	C4
Runnymede Gdns, Twick	139	S13
Runnymede Rd, Twick	139	S12
Runway, The, Ruis	84	D9
Rupack St, SE16 3	131	L4
Rupert Av, Wem	87	S10
Rupert Ct, W Mol 7	175	P7
Rupert Gdns SW9	147	S4
Rupert Rd N19	92	H5
Rupert Rd NW6	108	F4
Rupert Rd W4	125	K6
Rupert St W1	17	S10
Rural Way SW16	164	D13
Ruscoe Rd E16	115	M11
Rush Grn Gdns, Rom	101	U1
Rush Grn Rd, Rom	101	T2
Rush Gro St SE18	134	F8
Rush Hill Ms, SW11 3	146	B6
Rush Hill Rd SW11	146	B6
Rusham Rd SW12	145	U12
Rushbrook Cres E17	77	U2
Rushbrook Rd SE9	171	L4
Rushcroft Rd E4	62	C13
Rushcroft Rd SW2	147	N8
Rushden Cl SE19	166	B14
Rushden Gdns NW7	55	U11
Rushden Gdns, Ilf	80	G5
Rushdene SE2	136	G6
Rushdene Av, Barn	41	S14
Rushdene Cl, Nthlt	102	E4
Rushdene Cres, Nthlt	102	D4
Rushdene Rd, Pnr	66	G11
Rushen Wk, Cars 2	195	P1
Rushett Cl, T Ditt	190	J1
Rushett Rd, T Ditt	176	J14
Rushey Cl, N Mal	178	G8
Rushey Grn SE6	150	D13
Rushey Hill, Enf	43	L8
Rushey Mead SE4	150	B10
Rushford Rd SE4	149	U12
Rushgrove Av NW9	71	L8
Rushley Cl, Kes	202	B7
Rushmead, E2 4	112	J6
Rushmead, Rich	159	K6
Rushmead Cl, Croy	198	E7
Rushmere Pl SW19	162	B10
Rushmoor Cl, Pnr	66	D8
Rushmore Cl, Brom	188	C6
Rushmore Cres, E5 5	95	N7
Rushmore Rd E5	95	L7
Rusholme Av, Dag	101	N6
Rusholme Gro SE19	166	D9
Rusholme Rd SW15	144	C12
Rushout Av, Har	68	J12
Rushton St N1	12	E2
Rushworth Gdns NW4	71	P6
Rushworth St SE1	27	R7
Rushy Meadow La, Cars	195	S4
Ruskin Av E12	98	D11
Ruskin Av, Rich	124	B14
Ruskin Av, Well	154	A4
Ruskin Cl NW11	72	J11
Ruskin Dr, Orp	203	R5
Ruskin Dr, Well	154	A5
Ruskin Dr, Wor Pk	193	T3
Ruskin Gdns W5	105	M7
Ruskin Gdns, Har	69	U8
Ruskin Gro, Well	154	A4
Ruskin Pk Ho SE5	148	B5
Ruskin Rd N17	76	E1
Ruskin Rd, Belv	137	N8
Ruskin Rd, Cars	196	A9
Ruskin Rd, Croy	197	S3
Ruskin Rd, Islw	140	E6
Ruskin Rd, Sthl	102	J14
Ruskin Wk N9	60	G3
Ruskin Wk SE24	147	U10
Ruskin Wk, Brom	188	E11
Ruskin Way SW19	181	N2
Rusland Av, Orp	203	N5
Rusland Pk Rd, Har	68	C8
Rusper Cl NW2	89	U6
Rusper Cl, Stan	53	M8
Rusper Rd N22	75	T5
Rusper Rd, Dag	100	F12
Russell Av N22	75	T8
Russell Cl NW10	88	E13
Russell Cl SE7	133	T14
Russell Cl, W4 6	125	L12
Russell Cl, Beck	186	D5
Russell Cl, Bexh	155	N7
Russell Cl, Ruis	84	F3
Russell Cl SW1	25	N3

Russell Gdns N20	57	S3
Russell Gdns NW11	72	D12
Russell Gdns W14	126	C5
Russell Gdns, Rich	159	L4
Russell Gdns Ms W14	126	C5
Russell Gro NW7	54	J9
Russell Gro SW9	129	P14
Russell Kerr Cl W4	124	F14
Russell La N20	57	S3
Russell Mead, Har	68	F1
Russell Pl, SE16 *7*	131	R6
Russell Rd E4	61	T8
Russell Rd E10	78	C12
Russell Rd E16	115	P11
Russell Rd E17	77	T6
Russell Rd N8	74	H11
Russell Rd N13	59	L11
Russell Rd N15	76	C10
Russell Rd N20	57	R3
Russell Rd NW9	71	M11
Russell Rd SW19	162	G13
Russell Rd, Buck H	63	S2
Russell Rd, Mitch	181	S5
Russell Rd, Nthlt	85	U9
Russell Rd, Twick *2*	140	E12
Russell Rd, Walt	174	B12
Russell Sq WC1	18	A2
Russell St WC2	18	D9
Russell Way, Sutt	194	H9
Russell's Footpath SW16	165	K9
Russet Dr, Croy	199	S1
Russets Cl E4	62	G7
Russett Way SE13	150	D3
Russia Ct, EC2 *4*	20	B7
Russia Dock Rd SE16	131	S2
Russia La E2	113	L3
Russia Row EC2	20	B7
Russia Wk SE16	131	R4
Rust Sq SE5	36	C13
Rusthall Av W4	124	H6
Rusthall Cl, Croy	185	L11
Rusthall Av SW16	164	D13
Rustic Pl, Wem *1*	87	N7
Rustic Wk, E16 *4*	115	R11
Rustington Wk, Mord	180	F13
Ruston Av, Surb	178	C14
Ruston Gdns N14	42	B12
Ruston Ms W11	108	C12
Ruston Rd SE18	134	C6
Ruston St E3	13	U1
Rutford Rd SW16	164	J9
Ruth Cl, Stan	69	T7
Rutherford Cl, Borwd	38	F3
Rutherford Cl, Sutt	195	N11
Rutherford St SW1	33	S1
Rutherford Way, Bushey	52	B2
Rutherford Way, Wem	88	B7
Rutherglen Rd SE2	136	A11
Rutherwyke Cl, Epsom	193	P11
Ruthin Cl NW9	70	J11
Ruthin Rd SE3	133	N11
Ruthven St, E9 *4*	113	N1
Rutland Av, Sid	154	B13
Rutland Cl SW14	142	D5
Rutland Cl, Bex	163	R13
Rutland Cl, SW19 *3*		
Rutland Cl, Bex	172	G3
Rutland Cl, Chess	191	U11
Rutland Ct, Enf	45	L10
Rutland Dr, Mord	180	G13
Rutland Dr, Rich	159	R1
Rutland Gdns N4	75	S11
Rutland Gdns SW7	23	R7
Rutland Gdns W13	104	G10
Rutland Gdns, Croy	198	D8
Rutland Gdns, Dag	100	E9
Rutland Gdns Ms, SW7 *3*	23	R8
Rutland Gate SW7	23	P6
Rutland Gate, Belv	137	R10
Rutland Gate, Brom	187	M8
Rutland Gate Ms SW7	23	P8
Rutland Gro W6	125	S9
Rutland Ms NW8	109	K2
Rutland Ms E, SW7 *1*	23	R9
Rutland Ms S, SW7 *2*	23	P10
Rutland Pk NW2	89	U12
Rutland Pk SE6	167	U4
Rutland Pl EC1	19	S1
Rutland Pl, Bushey	52	B1
Rutland Rd E7	98	A13
Rutland Rd E9	113	M1
Rutland Rd E11	79	S9
Rutland Rd E17	78	B11
Rutland Rd SW19	163	R13
Rutland Rd, Har	67	U11
Rutland Rd, Ilf	99	K6
Rutland Rd, Sthl	103	N10
Rutland Rd, Twick	158	A4
Rutland St SW7	23	R10
Rutland Wk SE6	167	U4
Rutley Cl SE17	35	N10
Rutlish Rd SW19	180	G1
Rutter Gdns, Mitch	181	M8
Rutts, The, Bushey	52	B1
Rutts Ter SE14	149	M2
Ruvigny Gdns SW15	144	B5
Ruxley Cl, Epsom	192	D9
Ruxley Cl, Sid	172	H12
Ruxley Cor Ind Est, Sid	172	G12
Ruxley Cres, Esher	190	J12
Ruxley La, Epsom	192	D11
Ruxley Ms, Epsom	192	D9
Ruxley Ridge, Esher	190	H14
Ryalls Ct N20	57	U6
Ryan Cl SE3	151	T7
Ryan Cl, Ruis	84	C2
Ryan Dr, Brent	122	H12
Ryarsh Cres, Orp	203	S8
Rycott Path, SE22 *1*	148	G13
Rycroft Way N17	76	F6
Ryculff Sq SE3	151	M3
Rydal Cl NW4	72	C2
Rydal Cres, Grnf	105	L5
Rydal Dr, Bexh	155	M3
Rydal Dr, W Wick	201	K3
Rydal Gdns NW9	71	K9
Rydal Gdns SW15	160	J9
Rydal Gdns, Houns	109	S13
Rydal Gdns, Wem	87	M1
Rydal Rd SW16	164	G8
Rydal Way, Enf	45	M11
Rydal Way, Ruis	84	E8
Ryde Pl, Twick	141	M11
Ryde Vale Rd SW12	164	E3
Ryder Cl, Brom	169	S10
Ryder Dr SE16	130	J10
Ryder Ms, E9 *4*	95	M10
Ryder St SW1	25	N2
Ryder Yd SW1	25	N1
Ryders Ter NW8	6	E2
Rydon St, N1 *5*	111	U1
Rydons Cl SE9	152	C5
Rydston Cl N7	93	K13
Rye, The N14	42	F13
Rye Cl, Bex	155	S11
Rye Hill Pk SE15	149	L8
Rye La SE15	148	G2
Rye Pas SE15	148	H5
Rye Rd SE15	149	N8
Rye Wk SW15	144	A10
Rye Way, Edg	53	U11
Ryecotes Mead SE21	166	D1
Ryecroft Av, Ilf	80	J3
Ryecroft Av, Twick	157	S1
Ryecroft Cres, Barn	39	S10
Ryecroft Rd SE13	150	F9
Ryecroft Rd SW16	165	P11
Ryecroft Rd, Orp	189	N12
Ryecroft St SW6	144	J2
Ryedale SE22	148	J11
Ryefield Cres, Nthwd	66	B4
Ryefield Path, SW15 *7*	161	P1
Ryefield Rd SE19	165	U12
Ryelands Cres SE12	151	T12
Ryfold Rd SW19	162	G5
Ryhope Rd N11	58	D7
Ryland Rd NW5	92	C11
Rylandes Rd NW2	89	N5
Rylett Cres W12	125	M5
Rylett Rd W12	125	M5
Rylston Rd N13	60	A6
Rylston Rd SW6	126	E12
Rymer Rd, Croy	184	D14
Rymer St SE24	147	S11
Rymill St E16	134	G2
Rysbrack St SW3	23	U9
Rythe Ct, T Ditt	176	H14
Rythe Rd, Esher	190	B10

S

Sabbarton St, E16 *4*	115	L12
Sabella Ct, E3 *11*	113	S3
Sabine Rd SW11	145	U5
Sable Cl, Houns	138	F5
Sable St N1	93	S13
Sach Rd E5	95	K3
Sackville Av, Brom	201	N1
Sackville Cl, Har	86	A6
Sackville Est SW16	165	K6
Sackville Gdns, Ilf	98	E2
Sackville Rd, Sutt	194	G14
Sackville St W1	17	N11
Saddle Yd, W1 *2*	24	G1
Saddlers Cl, Borwd *2*	38	G11
Saddlers Ms, Wem	86	F7
Saddlers Path, Borwd *1*	38	G10
Saddlescombe Way N12	56	G10
Sadler Cl, Mitch	181	T4
Sadlers Ride, W Mol	175	T4
Saffron Av E14	114	G13
Saffron Cl NW11	72	E10
Saffron Cl, Croy	182	J12
Saffron Hill EC1	19	M1
Saffron Rd, Rom	83	U3
Saffron St EC1	19	M1
Saffron Way, Surb	191	P2
Sage Cl E6	116	E10
Sage St E1	113	L13
Sage Way WC1	10	F7
Saigasso Cl, E16 *2*	116	A12
Sail St SE11	34	H1
Sainfoin Rd SW17	164	B4
Sainsbury Rd SE19	166	C9
St. Agatha's Dr, Kings T	159	U12
St. Agathas Gro, Cars	195	T1
St. Agnes Cl E9	113	L2
St. Agnes Pl SE11	35	N11
St. Aidan's Rd SE22	148	J11
St. Aidans Rd W13	123	K4
St. Alban's Av E6	116	G5
St. Alban's Av W4	124	G6
St. Albans Av, Felt	156	H9
St. Albans Cl NW11	90	H2
St. Albans Cres N22	75	N2
St. Alban's, Cres, Wdf Grn	63	N14
St. Alban's Gdns, Tedd	148	H9
St. Albans Gro W8	22	C9
St. Alban's Gro, Cars	181	S14
St. Albans La NW11	90	G1
St. Albans Ms W2	15	U1
St. Alban's Pl N1	111	R2
St. Albans Rd NW5	92	B5
St. Albans Rd NW10	106	J2
St. Albans Rd, Barn	40	C4
St. Albans Rd, Ilf	99	T2
St. Alban's Rd, Kings T	159	S12
St. Alban's Rd, Sutt	194	E8
St. Alban's Rd, Wdf Grn	63	N14
St. Albans St SW1	17	S12
St. Albans Ter W6	126	C11
St. Alfege Pas SE10	132	E12
St. Alfege Rd SE7	134	B11
St. Alphage Gdns EC2	20	B3
St. Alphage Wk, Edg	70	F3
St. Alphege Rd N9	45	L13
St. Alphonsus Rd SW4	146	F8
St. Amunds Cl SE6	168	B7
St. Andrew St EC4	19	M4
St. Andrews Av, Wem	86	G7
St. Andrew's Cl N12	57	L7
St. Andrews Cl NW2	89	R6
St. Andrews Cl, SE16 *11*	131	K10
St. Andrew's Cl, Islw	140	C1
St. Andrews Cl, Ruis	84	G4
St. Andrews Cl, Stan	69	M3
St. Andrew's Ct SW18	163	L3
St. Andrews Dr, Stan	69	M1
St. Andrew's Gro N16	94	B1
St. Andrew's Hill EC4	19	R9
St. Andrew's Ms N16	94	C1
St. Andrews Ms, SE3 *2*	133	N13
St. Andrews Pl NW1	8	J10
St. Andrews Rd E11	78	J12
St. Andrews Rd E13	115	R6
St. Andrews Rd E17	77	P4
St. Andrews Rd N9	45	M14
St. Andrews Rd NW9	88	G2
St. Andrews Rd NW10	89	S12
St. Andrews Rd NW11	72	E12
St. Andrews Rd W3	107	K12
St. Andrews Rd W7	122	C4
St. Andrews Rd W14	126	D11
St. Andrews Rd, Cars	195	S5
St. Andrews Rd, Croy *2*	197	U7
St. Andrews Rd, Enf	44	B6
St. Andrews Rd, Ilf	80	F14
St. Andrews Rd, Sid	172	H6
St. Andrews Rd, Surb	177	P11
St. Andrews Rd, Wat	50	G5
St. Andrews Sq, W11 *12*	108	C12
St. Andrew's Sq, Surb	177	N11
St. Andrews Way E3	114	C8
St. Anna Rd, Barn	40	B9
St. Anne St, E14 *10*	113	U12
St. Anne's Cl N6	92	B5
St. Anne's Cl, Wat	50	F8
St. Annes Gdns NW10	105	T5
St. Annes Pas E14	113	T12
St. Annes Rd E11	96	G3
St. Annes Rd, Wem	87	P9
St. Anne's Rd, E14 *11*	113	U12
St. Ann's, Bark	117	M2
St. Ann's Cres SW18	145	L11
St. Ann's Gdns, NW5 *1*	92	A11
St. Ann's Hill SW18	145	K10
St. Ann's La SW1	25	T10
St. Ann's Pk Rd SW18	145	L12
St. Ann's Pas SW13	143	K5
St. Anns Rd N9	60	F3

St. Ann's Rd N15	76	C11
St. Ann's Rd SW13	143	L2
St. Anns Rd W11	108	B14
St. Ann's Rd, Bark 1	117	M1
St. Ann's Rd, Har	68	D11
St. Ann's St SW1	25	U10
St. Anns Ter NW8	7	L2
St. Anns Vil W11	126	B1
St. Anns Way, S Croy	197	S12
St. Anselm's Pl, W1 2	16	G9
St. Anthonys Av, Wdf Grn	63	T12
St. Anthonys Cl E1	29	S2
St. Anthonys Cl, SW17 4	163	R4
St. Antony's Rd E7	97	R13
St. Arvans Cl, Croy	198	D5
St. Asaph Rd SE4	149	P5
St. Aubyn's Av SW19	162	E9
St. Aubyns Av, Houns	139	N10
St. Aubyns Cl, Orp	203	U5
St. Aubyns Gdns, Orp	203	U4
St. Aubyn's Rd, SE19 5	166	E12
St. Audrey Av, Bexh	155	P3
St. Augustine's Av W5	105	S4
St. Augustines Av, Brom	188	C9
St. Augustine's Av, S Croy	197	T12
St. Augustines Av, Wem	87	S5
St. Augustine's Path N5	93	S9
St. Augustines Rd NW1	92	G13
St. Augustine's Rd, Belv	137	M7
St. Austell Cl, Edg	69	U4
St. Austell Rd SE13	150	F3
St. Awdry's Rd, Bark	99	N14
St. Barnabas Cl, SE22 2	148	D9
St. Barnabas Cl, Beck	186	E4
St. Barnabas Ct, Har	67	U1
St. Barnabas Gdns, W Mol	175	N9
St. Barnabas Rd E17	78	A11
St. Barnabas Rd, Mitch	164	A13
St. Barnabas Rd, Sutt	195	N9
St. Barnabas Rd, Wdf Grn	79	S1
St. Barnabas St SW1	32	F5
St. Barnabas Ter E9	95	N10
St. Barnabas Vil, SW8 1	147	K1
St. Bartholomews Cl SE26	167	L7
St. Bartholomew's Rd E6	116	E3
St. Benedict's Cl, SW17 1	164	A9
St. Benet's Cl, SW17 5	163	S4
St. Benet's Gro, Cars	181	L14
St. Benet's Pl, EC3 3	20	F9
St. Bernards, Croy	198	D6
St. Bernard's Cl SE27	166	A7
St. Bernard's Rd E6	116	B2
St. Blaise Av, Brom	187	R3
St. Botolph St EC3	21	L6
St. Bride St EC4	19	N6
St. Brides Av, Edg	69	T2
St. Brides Cl, Erith	136	H3
St. Catherines Cl, SW17 6	163	S4

St. Catherines Dr, SE14 9	149	P4
St. Catherine's Ms SW3	31	T2
St. Catherines Rd E4	62	B4
St. Chads Cl, Surb	177	M14
St. Chad's Gdns, Rom	82	J13
St. Chad's Pl WC1	10	D5
St. Chad's Rd, Rom	82	J12
St. Chad's St WC1	10	C6
St. Charles Pl, W10 3	108	C10
St. Charles Sq W10	108	C9
St. Christopher's Cl, Islw	140	C1
St. Christopher's Dr, Hayes	102	C13
St. Christophers Gdns, Th Hth 1	183	N6
St. Christophers Ms, Wall	196	E9
St. Clair Dr, Wor Pk	193	R6
St. Clair Rd E13	115	S4
St. Clair's Rd, Croy	198	C4
St. Clare Cl, Ilf	80	E4
St. Clare St EC3	21	M8
St. Clements Ct, EC4 1	20	F9
St. Clements Hts SE26	166	G6
St. Clement's La WC2	18	G7
St. Clements St N7	93	N13
St. Cloud Rd SE27	165	U7
St. Crispins Cl NW3	91	S8
St. Crispins Cl, Sthl	103	M11
St. Cross St EC1	19	L1
St. Cuthberts Gdns, Pnr	51	M13
St. Cuthberts Rd N13	59	P11
St. Cuthberts Rd NW2	90	E11
St. Cyprian's St SW17	163	T8
St. Davids Cl, SE16 7	131	K10
St. Davids Cl, Wem	88	E6
St. David's Cl, W Wick	186	C14
St. Davids Dr, Edg	69	T2
St. Davids Pl NW4	71	R13
St. Davids Sq E14	132	D9
St. Denis Rd SE27	166	A7
St. Dionis Rd SW6	144	F3
St. Donatts Rd SE14	149	T2
St. Dunstans Av W3	106	G13
St. Dunstans Gdns W3	106	G13
St. Dunstan's Hill EC3	20	H11
St. Dunstan's Hill, Sutt	194	E7
St. Dunstan's La EC3	20	G11
St. Dunstan's La, Beck	186	E11
St. Dunstan's Rd E7	97	S11
St. Dunstan's Rd SE25	184	F7
St. Dunstans Rd W6	126	A10
St. Dunstans Rd W7	122	D4
St. Dunstans Rd, Houns	138	E4
St. Edmunds Cl NW8	109	T2
St. Edmunds Cl, SW17 2	163	R3
St. Edmunds Cl, Erith	136	H3
St. Edmunds Dr, Stan	68	G1
St. Edmund's La, Twick	139	S13
St. Edmunds Rd N9	44	G13
St. Edmunds Rd, Ilf	80	F12
St. Edmunds Sq, SW13 1	125	T12
St. Edmunds Ter NW8	109	S2

St. Edwards Cl NW11	72	G12
St. Egberts Way E4	62	E1
St. Elmo Rd W12	125	M3
St. Elmos Rd SE16	131	R4
St. Erkenwald Ms, Bark 2	117	N1
St. Erkenwald Rd, Bark	99	N14
St. Ermin's Hill SW1	25	R9
St. Ervans Rd W10	108	D9
St. Faiths Cl, Enf	43	U1
St. Faith's Rd SE21	165	S2
St. Fillans Rd SE6	168	F1
St. Francis Cl, Orp	189	S12
St. Francis Cl, Wat	50	D2
St. Francis Rd SE22	148	D7
St. Francis Way, Ilf	99	R8
St. Frideswides Ms, E14 6	114	E12
St. Gabriel's Cl E11	97	R3
St. Gabriels Rd NW2	90	A10
St. George St W1	17	K8
St. Georges Av E7	97	S13
St. Georges Av N7	92	G7
St. Georges Av NW9	70	F7
St. George's Av W5	123	N3
St. Georges Av, Sthl	103	L14
St. Georges Circ SE1	27	N9
St. Georges Cl, NW11 1	72	E11
St. Georges Cl, Wem	86	G6
St. Georges Ct E6	116	E7
St. Georges Ct EC4	19	P6
St. George's Dr SW1	33	K5
St. Georges Dr, Wat	50	J6
St. Georges Flds W2	15	R8
St. George's Gdns, Surb	192	C3
St. Georges Gro SW17	163	P5
St. Georges Gro Est SW17	163	P5
St. Georges Ind Est, Kings T	159	P9
St. Georges Ms, NW1 2	91	U14
St. Georges Pl, Twick 4	158	H1
St. Georges Rd E7	97	R12
St. Georges Rd E10	96	F5
St. Georges Rd N9	60	H5
St. Georges Rd N13	59	L5
St. Georges Rd NW11	72	E11
St. Georges Rd SE1	27	M10
St. George's Rd SW19	162	E12
St. Georges Rd W4	124	J4
St. Georges Rd W7	122	E2
St. George's Rd, Beck	186	C2
St. Georges Rd, Brom	188	E4
St. George's Rd, Dag	100	J9
St. George's Rd, Felt	156	H8
St. Georges Rd, Ilf	80	E13
St. Georges Rd, Kings T	160	A14
St. George's Rd, Mitch	182	C5
St. George's Rd, Orp	189	P11
St. George's Rd, Rich	141	U6
St. George's Rd, Sid	172	H11
St. Georges Rd, Twick	141	K10
St. Georges Rd, Wall	196	C9
St. Georges Rd W, Brom	188	D2
St. Georges Sq E7	97	S13
St. Georges Sq, E14 1	113	R13
St. Georges Sq SE8	131	T7
St. George's Sq SW1	33	R7

St. George's Sq Ms SW1	33	S8
St. Georges Ter NW1	91	U14
St. Georges Wk, Croy	197	U5
St. Georges Way SE15	36	J12
St. Gerards Cl SW4	146	E10
St. German's Pl SE3	151	N2
St. Germans Rd SE23	167	R1
St. Giles Av, Dag	101	S13
St. Giles Cl, Dag	101	S13
St. Giles Cl, Orp	203	N9
St. Giles High St WC2	17	U6
St. Giles Pas WC2	17	U7
St. Giles Rd SE5	148	C1
St. Gothard Rd SE27	166	A7
St. Gregory Cl, Ruis	84	E7
St. Helena Rd SE16	131	N8
St. Helena St WC1	11	K6
St. Helens Cres SW16	183	L2
St. Helens Gdns W10	108	A10
St. Helens Pl EC3	20	H6
St. Helens Rd SW16	183	L2
St. Helen's Rd W13	123	L1
St. Helens Rd, Erith	136	H4
St. Helens Rd, Ilf	80	F12
St. Helier Av, Mord	181	L12
St. Heliers Av, Houns	139	N10
St. Heliers Rd E10	78	E12
St. Hildas Cl NW6	90	B14
St. Hildas Cl SW17	163	R3
St. Hilda's Rd SW13	125	R11
St. Hughe's Cl, SW17 3	163	S3
St. Hughs Rd SE20	166	J14
St. James Av N20	57	R6
St. James Av W13	122	H2
St. James Av, Sutt	194	G9
St. James Cl N20	57	R6
St. James Cl E18	135	L9
St. James Cl, Barn	41	P7
St. James Cl, N Mal	179	L10
St. James Cl, Ruis	84	F3
St. James Gdns, Wem	87	P14
St. James Gro SW11	145	T3
St. James Ms E14	132	F6
St. James Ms E17	77	S10
St. James Rd E15	97	L9
St. James Rd N9	60	J4
St. James Rd, Cars	195	S5
St. James Rd, Kings T	177	P4
St. James Rd, Mitch	164	A14
St. James Rd, Surb	177	P11
St. James Rd, Sutt	194	G9
St. James St W6	125	T10
St. James Way, Sid	173	K10
St. James's SE14	149	S1
St. James's Av E2	113	M3
St. James's Av, Beck	185	R6
St. James's Av, Hmptn	157	T9
St. James's Cl SW17	163	T3
St. James's Cotts, Rich 4	141	P9
St. James's Ct SW1	25	N10
St. James's Cres SW9	147	P5
St. James's Dr SW12	163	T1
St. James's Dr SW17	163	T1
St. James's Gdns W11	126	C1
St. James's La N10	74	D7
St. James's Mkt, SW1 8	17	S12
St. James's Palace SW1	25	N5

St. James's Pk SW1   25   R5
St. James's Pk, Croy   183   T13
St. James's Pas EC3   21   K7
St. James's Pl SW1   25   M3
St. James's Rd SE1   37   U8
St. James's Rd SE16   29   T9
St. James's Rd, Croy   183   S14
St. James's Rd, Hmptn   157   T8
St. James's Row, EC1 **3**   11   N10
St. James's Sq SW1   25   R2
St. James's St E17   77   S9
St. James's St SW1   25   M2
St. James's Ter NW8   7   T1
St. James's Ter Ms NW8   109   T2
St. James's Wk EC1   11   N10
St. Joans Rd N9   60   F2
St. John Fisher Rd, Erith   136   J5
St. John St EC1   11   R12
St. Johns Av N11   57   U10
St. John's Av NW10   107   L1
St. John's Av SW15   144   C9
St. John's Ch Rd, E9 **1**   95   L10
St. Johns Cl N14   42   F11
St. John's Cl, SW6 **5**   126   G13
St. John's Cl, Wem   87   R9
St. John's Cotts, SE20 **3**   167   M13
St. Johns Cotts, Rich **2**   141   R6
St. John's Ct, Buck H   63   S2
St. John's Ct, Islw   140   E4
St. John's Cres SW9   147   N5
St. Johns Dr SW18   162   J1
St. John's Est N1   12   F3
St. John's Est SE1   29   L6
St. John's Gdns W11   108   E14
St. Johns Gro N19   92   F4
St. Johns Gro, SW13 **1**   143   L3
St. John's Hill SW11   145   R7
St. John's Hill Gro SW11   145   N8
St. John's La EC1   11   P12
St. John's Ms W11   108   G12
St. John's Pk SE3   133   M14
St. John's Pas, SW19 **1**   162   C12
St. John's Pl EC1   11   N12
St. Johns Rd E4   62   D7
St. John's Rd E6   116   D2
St. Johns Rd E16   115   N11
St. John's Rd E17   78   D3
St. John's Rd N15   76   C12
St. Johns Rd NW11   72   F12
St. John's Rd SE20   167   M13
St. Johns Rd SW11   145   S7
St. Johns Rd SW19   162   C13
St. John's Rd, Bark   117   R2
St. John's Rd, Cars   195   S5
St. Johns Rd, Croy   197   S5
St. Johns Rd, E Mol   176   B8
St. John's Rd, Felt   157   K8
St. John's Rd, Har   68   E11
St. John's Rd, Ilf   81   R13
St. John's Rd, Islw   140   D3
St. John's Rd, Kings T   177   M3
St. Johns Rd, Loug   48   E4
St. John's Rd, N Mal   178   E6
St. John's Rd, Orp   189   P12
St. Johns Rd, Rich   141   R7
St. John's Rd, Sid   172   C7
St. Johns Rd, Sthl   120   J6
St. John's Rd, Sutt   194   H4
St. John's Rd, Well   154   C6
St. John's Rd, Wem   87   R8
St. Johns Sq EC1   11   P12
St. Johns Ter E7   97   S11
St. Johns Ter SE18   135   M11
St. Johns Ter W10   108   B7
St. Johns Vale SE8   150   B4

St. Johns Vil N19   92   G3
St. John's Vil, W8 **8**   22   C12
St. Johns Way N19   92   G2
St. John's Wd Ct, NW8 **1**   7   L8
St. John's Wd High St NW8   7   N3
St. John's Wd Pk NW8   91   P14
St. John's Wd Rd NW8   7   K8
St. John's Wd Ter NW8   7   N2
St. Josephs Cl W10   108   D10
St. Joseph's Cl, Orp **2**   203   T7
St. Joseph's Ct SE7   133   S12
St. Josephs Dr, Sthl   121   K2
St. Joseph's Gro NW4   71   R8
St. Josephs Rd N9   45   K14
St. Joseph's Vale SE3   150   H4
St. Jude St N16   94   D10
St. Jude's Rd E2   113   K4
St. Julian's Cl SW16   165   N8
St. Julian's Fm Rd SE27   165   P8
St. Julian's Rd NW6   108   F1
St. Katharines Prec, NW1 **2**   8   G2
St. Katharine's Way E1   29   N1
St. Katherines Rd, Erith   136   H3
St. Katherine's Wk, W11 **5**   126   B1
St. Keverne Rd SE9   170   D7
St. Kilda Rd W13   122   H3
St. Kilda Rd, Orp   203   U1
St. Kilda's Rd N16   94   B2
St. Kilda's Rd, Har   68   C11
St. Kitts Ter SE19   166   C9
St. Laurence Cl NW6   108   B2
St. Lawrence Cl, Edg   53   T13
St. Lawrence Dr, Pnr   66   D11
St. Lawrence St, E14 **9**   132   F1
St. Lawrence Ter W10   108   C10
St. Lawrence Way SW9   147   P3
St. Leonards Av E4   62   J11
St. Leonards Av, Har   69   L9
St. Leonard's Cl, Well   154   B6
St. Leonards Ct N1   12   F5
St. Leonard's Gdns, Houns   138   J1
St. Leonards Gdns, Ilf   99   L10
St. Leonards Ri, Orp   203   R8
St. Leonards Rd E14   114   E10
St. Leonards Rd NW10   106   H8
St. Leonard's Rd SW14   142   D6
St. Leonards Rd W13   105   L13
St. Leonards Rd, Croy **5**   197   R6
St. Leonards Rd, Esher   190   F12
St. Leonard's Rd, Surb   177   N10
St. Leonards Rd, T Ditt   176   G13
St. Leonards Sq NW5   92   B12
St. Leonard's Sq, Surb **1**   177   N10
St. Leonards St E3   114   D5
St. Leonard's Ter SW3   31   U7
St. Leonards Wk SW16   165   L14
St. Loo Av SW3   31   S10

St. Louis Rd SE27   165   U8
St. Loy's Rd N17   76   D4
St. Lucia Dr E15   115   L1
St. Luke's Av SW4   146   G7
St. Luke's Av, Ilf   99   K9
St. Luke's Cl SE25   185   K11
St. Luke's Est EC1   12   C8
St. Lukes Ms W11   108   E11
St. Lukes Pas, Kings T   177   T1
St. Lukes Rd W11   108   F10
St. Lukes Sq E16   115   M12
St. Luke's St SW3   31   P5
St. Luke's Yd W9   108   E4
St. Malo Av N9   61   L5
St. Margarets, Bark   117   N1
St. Margarets Av N15   75   R7
St. Margarets Av N20   57   L3
St. Margarets Av, Har   85   T5
St. Margarets Av, Sid   171   P5
St. Margaret's Av, Sutt   194   D6
St. Margaret's Ct SE1   28   B4
St. Margarets Cres SW15   143   S10
St. Margaret's Dr, Twick   140   J9
St. Margaret's Gro, E11 **1**   97   L5
St. Margarets Gro SE18   135   L11
St. Margarets Gro, Twick   140   H11
St. Margarets La W8   22   A11
St. Margarets Pas SE13   150   J6
St. Margarets Rd E12   97   U4
St. Margaret's Rd N17   76   C5
St. Margaret's Rd NW10   107   T5
St. Margarets Rd SE4   149   T7
St. Margarets Rd W7   122   C4
St. Margarets Rd, Edg   54   C10
St. Margarets Rd, Islw   141   K12
St. Margarets Rd, Twick   141   K12
St. Margarets Sq SE4   149   U8
St. Margaret's St SW1   26   B8
St. Margaret's Ter SE18   135   L10
St. Mark St E1   21   P7
St. Marks Cl SE10   132   E14
St. Marks Cl W11   108   C12
St. Mark's Cl, Barn   40   J6
St. Marks Cres NW1   110   B1
St. Mark's Gro SW10   30   D12
St. Mark's Hill, Surb   177   R11
St. Mark's Pl, SW19 **3**   162   E11
St. Marks Pl W11   108   D12
St. Marks Ri E8   94   F9
St. Marks Rd, Brom **3**   184   H7
St. Mark's Rd W5   123   N2
St. Marks Rd W7   123   S1
St. Marks Rd W10   108   B11
St. Marks Rd W11   108   C12
St. Marks Rd, Brom **3**   187   R6
St. Marks Rd, Enf   44   F10
St. Marks Rd, Mitch   181   U4
St. Mark's Rd, Tedd   159   K13
St. Marks Sq, NW1 **1**   110   A2
St. Martins Av E6   116   A4
St. Martins Cl NW1   110   E1

St. Martins Cl, Enf   44   J1
St. Martins Cl, Erith   136   H3
St. Martin's Cl, Wat   50   F8
St. Martins Est SW2   165   P2
St. Martin's La WC2   18   A10
St. Martin's Pl WC2   18   A11
St. Martins Rd N9   60   J4
St. Martin's Rd SW9   147   L3
St. Martin's St WC2   17   U12
St. Martins Way SW17   163   L6
St. Martin's-le-Grand EC1   19   T6
St. Mary Abbots Pl, W8 **2**   126   F6
St. Mary Abbots Ter W14   126   F6
St. Mary at Hill EC3   20   G11
St. Mary Av, Wall   196   B6
St. Mary Axe EC3   20   H7
St. Mary Rd E17   78   B8
St. Mary St SE18   134   F7
St. Marychurch St, SE16 **2**   131   L3
St. Marys, Bark   117   N2
St. Marys App E12   98   F9
St. Marys Av E11   79   S12
St. Mary's Av N3   72   D3
St. Mary's Av, Brom   187   K6
St. Mary's Av, Tedd   158   E12
St. Mary's Av Cen, Sthl   121   R8
St. Mary's Av N, Sthl   121   R8
St. Mary's Av S, Sthl   121   R8
St. Marys Cl, Chess   191   T13
St. Marys Cl, Epsom   193   M14
St. Mary's Cl, Sun **1**   174   A7
St. Marys Ct E6   116   E7
St. Mary's Ct SE7   134   A13
St. Mary's Cres NW4   71   R5
St. Marys Cres, Islw   122   B13
St. Mary's Gdns SE11   35   L2
St. Mary's Gate W8   22   A12
St. Mary's Gro N1   93   S12
St. Mary's Gro SW13   143   R6
St. Mary's Gro W4   124   D11
St. Mary's Gro, Rich   141   U7
St. Marys Mans W2   14   J1
St. Marys Ms NW6   90   J14
St. Marys Path N1   111   R1
St. Mary's Pl W5   123   N3
St. Mary's Pl W8   22   C11
St. Marys Rd E10   96   F4
St. Marys Rd E13   115   R3
St. Marys Rd N8   75   K7
St. Marys Rd N9   61   M1
St. Marys Rd NW10   107   K1
St. Marys Rd NW11   72   C13
St. Marys Rd SE15   149   L2
St. Marys Rd SE25   184   C6
St. Mary's Rd (Wimbledon) SW19   162   D9
St. Mary's Rd W5   123   N3
St. Mary's Rd, Barn   41   T14
St. Mary's Rd, Bex   173   U2
St. Marys Rd, E Mol   176   A9
St. Mary's Rd, Ilf   99   M4
St. Marys Rd, Surb   177   P11
St. Mary's Rd (Long Ditton), Surb   177   M14
St. Mary's Rd, Wor Pk   193   K4
St. Marys Sq W2   14   J2
St. Marys Ter W2   14   J2
St. Mary's Vw, Har   69   L9
St. Mary's Wk SE11   35   M2
St. Mary's Way, Chig   64   G9
St. Matthew St SW1   25   S11
St. Matthew's Av, Surb   191   S1
St. Matthew's Dr, Brom   188   E5

St. Matthew's Rd SW2	147	M10
St. Matthews Rd W5	123	R2
St. Matthew's Row E2	13	S8
St. Matthias Cl NW9	71	L9
St. Maur Rd SW6	144	F1
St. Merryn Cl SE18	135	P13
St. Michaels Av N9	45	L13
St. Michael's Av, Wem	88	B11
St. Michaels Cl, E16 *9*	116	A10
St. Michael's Cl N3	72	E4
St. Michael's Cl N12	57	R9
St. Michaels Cl, Brom	188	C5
St. Michaels Cl, Erith *1*	136	H3
St. Michaels Cl, Wor Pk	193	L4
St. Michaels Cres, Pnr	67	K11
St. Michaels Gdns, W10 *4*	108	C10
St. Michaels Rd NW2	89	T7
St. Michael's Rd SW9	147	L3
St. Michaels Rd, Croy	197	U2
St. Michaels Rd, Wall	196	E11
St. Michaels Rd, Well	154	C6
St. Michaels St W2	15	N4
St. Michaels Ter N22	75	K2
St. Mildred's Ct, EC2 *12*	20	D7
St. Mildreds Rd SE12	151	L13
St. Nicholas Glebe SW17	164	A10
St. Nicholas Rd SE18	135	U9
St. Nicholas Rd, Sutt	195	K10
St. Nicholas Rd, T Ditt	176	E12
St. Nicholas St, SE8 *4*	150	A2
St. Nicholas Way, Sutt	194	J8
St. Nicolas La, Chis	188	D2
St. Ninian's Ct N20	57	T6
St. Norbert Grn SE4	149	S7
St. Norbert Rd SE4	149	R7
St. Olaf's Rd SW6	126	D14
St. Olave's Est SE1	29	K5
St. Olaves Rd E6	116	G1
St. Olave's Wk SW16	182	G4
St. Olav's Sq SE16	131	L5
St. Oswald's Pl SE11	34	F6
St. Oswald's Rd SW16	183	R1
St. Oswulf St SW1	33	U3
St. Pancras Way NW1	92	F14
St. Paul St N1	111	T2
St. Paul's Av NW2	89	T11
St. Paul's Av SE16	131	P1
St. Pauls Av, Har	69	T8
St. Paul's Chyd EC4	19	S7
St. Paul's Cl SE7	134	A10
St. Paul's Cl W5	123	T3
St. Paul's Cl, Cars	195	R1
St. Pauls Cl, Chess	191	P8
St. Paul's Cl, Houns	139	L4
St. Pauls Cray Rd, Chis	189	R3
St. Paul's Cres NW1	92	H13
St. Pauls Dr E15	96	G10
St. Paul's Ms, NW1 *4*	92	H13
St. Paul's Pl N1	94	A11
St. Pauls Ri N13	59	R11
St. Paul's Rd N1	93	S11
St. Paul's Rd N17	76	H1
St. Paul's Rd, Bark	117	L2
St. Paul's Rd, Brent	123	N12
St. Paul's Rd, Erith	137	T14
St. Paul's Rd, Rich	141	T6
St. Paul's Rd, Th Hth	183	U6
St. Paul's Shrubbery N1	94	A11
St. Pauls Sq, Brom	187	N3
St. Paul's Ter SE17	35	R9
St. Paul's Way E3	113	T10
St. Paul's Way E14	113	T10
St. Paul's Way N3	56	J14
St. Pauls Wd Hill, Orp	189	S4
St. Peter's Av, E2 *2*	13	T4
St. Peter's Av E17	78	J7
St. Peters Av N18	60	H8
St. Peter's Cl E2	13	T4
St. Peters Cl, SW17 *1*	163	R3
St. Peter's Cl, Barn	39	S10
St. Peters Cl, Bushey	52	A1
St. Peter's Cl, Chis	171	N14
St. Peters Cl, Ilf	81	S8
St. Peter's Cl, Ruis	84	G3
St. Peter's Ct NW4	71	U9
St. Peters Ct SE3	151	M9
St. Peters Ct SE4	149	U4
St. Peters Ct, W Mol	175	P7
St. Peter's Gdns SE27	165	N6
St. Peter's Gro W6	125	N8
St. Peter's Pl W9	6	A11
St. Peters Rd N9	61	K1
St. Peter's Rd W6	125	N9
St. Peter's Rd, Croy	198	A8
St. Peters Rd, Kings T *1*	178	A4
St. Peters Rd, Sthl	103	N10
St. Peters Rd, Twick	141	K9
St. Peter's Rd, W Mol	175	P7
St. Peter's Sq, E2 *1*	13	T4
St. Peter's Sq W6	125	N9
St. Peters St N1	11	S1
St. Peter's St, S Croy	198	B9
St. Peters Ter SW6 *15*	126	D14
St. Peter's Vil W6	125	N8
St. Peter's Way N1	94	D14
St. Peters Way W5	105	P10
St. Petersburgh Ms W2	14	B10
St. Petersburgh Pl W2	14	B10
St. Philip Sq, SW8 *6*	146	C3
St. Philip St SW8	146	C4
St. Philip's Av, Wor Pk	193	S3
St. Philip's Rd E8	94	G12
St. Philips Rd, Surb	177	P11
St. Philip's Way N1	111	U2
St. Quentin Rd, Well	153	U5
St. Quintin Av W10	107	U10
St. Quintin Gdns W10	107	U10
St. Quintin Rd E13	115	R4
St. Raphael's Way NW10	88	F10
St. Regis Cl N10	74	C3
St. Ronans Cres, Wdf Grn	63	N13
St. Rule St SW8	146	E3
St. Saviour's Est SE1	29	L9
St. Saviour's Rd SW2	147	L10
St. Saviours Rd, Croy	183	T12
St. Silas Pl NW5	92	A12
St. Silas St Est NW5	92	A11
St. Simon's Av SW15	143	U9
St. Stephens Av E17	78	E10
St. Stephens Av W12	125	S3
St. Stephens Av W13	104	H11
St. Stephens Cl NW8	109	S2
St. Stephens Cl, Sthl	103	N10
St. Stephens Cres, W2 *4*	108	H11
St. Stephens Cres, Th Hth	183	N6
St. Stephens Gdns, SW15 *2*	144	E9
St. Stephens Gdns W2	108	H10
St. Stephens Gdns, Twick	141	L12
St. Stephens Gro, SE13 *1*	150	F5
St. Stephens Ms, W2 *2*	108	H10
St. Stephen's Rd E3	113	T3
St. Stephens Rd E6	97	U14
St. Stephen's Rd, E17 *3*	78	D10
St. Stephens Rd W13	105	K11
St. Stephen's Rd, Barn	40	A9
St. Stephens Rd, Houns	139	P10
St. Stephens Ter SW8	129	L14
St. Stephen's Wk, SW7 *1*	30	F1
St. Swithin's La EC4	20	D9
St. Swithun's Rd SE13	150	G10
St. Thomas' Cl, Surb	191	U1
St. Thomas Ct, Bex	155	N13
St. Thomas Dr, Orp	203	M2
St. Thomas' Dr, Pnr	67	L2
St. Thomas Gdns, Ilf	99	L10
St. Thomas Pl NW1	92	H13
St. Thomas Rd E16	115	N11
St. Thomas Rd N14	42	H14
St. Thomas' Rd W4	124	E12
St. Thomas Rd, Belv	137	T4
St. Thomas St SE1	28	F4
St. Thomas's Gdns NW5	92	A11
St. Thomas's Pl E9	95	L13
St. Thomas's Rd N4	93	P4
St. Thomas's Rd NW10	107	K1
St. Thomas's Sq E9	95	K13
St. Thomas's Way SW6	126	E13
St. Timothy's Ms, Brom *3*	187	R2
St. Ursula Gro, Pnr	66	H10
St. Ursula Rd, Sthl	103	P11
St. Vincent Cl SE27	165	S9
St. Vincent Rd, Twick	139	T12
St. Vincent St W1	16	E4
St. Wilfrids Cl, Barn	41	R9
St. Wilfrids Rd, Barn	41	P9
St. Winefride's Av E12	98	F10
St. Winifreds Cl, Chig	65	M10
St. Winifred's Rd, Tedd	159	K11
Saints Cl SE27	165	R7
Saints Dr E7	98	A9
Salamanca Pl SE1	34	E4
Salamanca St SE1	34	E4
Salamander Cl, Kings T	159	M9
Salcombe Dr, Mord	194	B1
Salcombe Dr, Rom	83	M12
Salcombe Gdns NW7	55	U12
Salcombe Pk, Loug	48	B9
Salcombe Rd E17	77	U13
Salcombe Rd, N16 *4*	94	D9
Salcombe Way, Ruis	84	A4
Salcott Rd SW11	145	S10
Salcott Rd, Croy	197	K6
Sale Pl W2	15	N4
Sale St E2	13	T9
Salehurst Cl, Har	69	S9
Salehurst Rd SE4	149	T12
Salem Pl, Croy	197	T6
Salem Rd W2	14	C9
Salford Rd SW2	164	H2
Salhouse Cl, SE28 *2*	118	E12
Salisbury Av N3	72	E5
Salisbury Av, Bark	99	N13
Salisbury Av, Sutt	194	F12
Salisbury Cl SE17	36	D2
Salisbury Cl, Wor Pk	193	L5
Salisbury Ct EC4	19	N8
Salisbury Gdns SW19	162	D14
Salisbury Gdns, Buck H *1*	64	A3
Salisbury Hall Gdns E4	62	B12
Salisbury Ms, SW6 *14*	126	E14
Salisbury Pl SW9	129	S14
Salisbury Pl W1	15	U2
Salisbury Rd E4	62	B6
Salisbury Rd E7	97	N12
Salisbury Rd E10	96	F4
Salisbury Rd E12	98	B9
Salisbury Rd E17	78	E10
Salisbury Rd N4	75	S10
Salisbury Rd N9	60	G5
Salisbury Rd N22	75	R3
Salisbury Rd SE25	184	H12
Salisbury Rd SW19	162	D13
Salisbury Rd W13	122	J4
Salisbury Rd, Barn	40	C6
Salisbury Rd, Bex	173	N1
Salisbury Rd, Brom	188	C9
Salisbury Rd, Cars	195	U11
Salisbury Rd, Dag	101	S12
Salisbury Rd, Felt	156	F2
Salisbury Rd, Har	68	B9
Salisbury Rd, Houns	138	F6
Salisbury Rd, Ilf	99	S3
Salisbury Rd, N Mal	178	H5
Salisbury Rd, Pnr	66	A8
Salisbury Rd, Rich	141	S7
Salisbury Rd, Sthl	121	K7
Salisbury Rd, Wor Pk	193	L5
Salisbury Sq, EC4 *5*	19	M8
Salisbury St NW8	7	N11
Salisbury St W3	124	F3
Salisbury Ter SE15	149	M5
Salisbury Wk N19	92	E3
Salix Cl, Sun	156	C14
Salliesfield, Twick	140	B12
Salmen Rd E13	115	M4
Salmon La E14	113	S11
Salmon Rd, Belv	137	P10
Salmon St, E14 *9*	113	T11
Salmon St NW9	88	E3
Salmons Rd N9	60	G1
Salmons Rd, Chess	191	P11
Salomons Rd, E13 *10*	115	T9
Salop Rd E17	77	P11
Saltash Cl, Sutt	194	B8
Saltash Rd, Ilf	65	N13
Saltash Rd, Well	154	F1
Saltcoats Rd W4	124	J4
Saltcroft Cl, Wem	88	C1
Salter Cl, Har	85	M6
Salter Rd SE16	131	N2
Salter St E14	114	A13
Salter St NW10	107	N6
Salterford Rd SW17	164	A11
Salters Hall Ct, EC4 *4*	20	D9
Salters Hill SE19	166	B10
Salters Rd E17	78	H8
Salters Rd W10	108	A8

Salterton Rd N7	93	L6
Saltley Cl E6	116	D11
Saltoun Rd SW2	147	N8
Saltram Cl N15	76	F7
Saltram Cres W9	108	F5
Saltwell St E14	114	B13
Salusbury Rd NW6	108	E4
Salutation Rd SE10	133	K7
Salvia Gdns, Grnf	104	G3
Salvin Rd SW15	144	A6
Salway Cl, Wdf Grn	63	N14
Salway Pl, E15 *4*	96	H12
Salway Rd E15	96	H12
Sam Bartram Cl SE7	133	U9
Samantha Cl E17	77	T13
Sambruck Ms SE6	168	D3
Samels Ct W6	125	N9
Samford St NW8	7	N11
Samos Rd SE20	185	K3
Sampson Av, Barn	40	B10
Sampson Cl, Belv *6*	136	J6
Sampson St E1	29	U3
Samson St E13	115	T4
Samuel Cl E8	112	F1
Samuel Cl SE14	131	N12
Samuel Cl SE18	134	D7
Samuel Gray Gdns, Kings T	177	P1
Samuel Johnson Cl SW16	165	M7
Samuel Lewis Trust Dws SW3	31	P4
Samuel Lewis Trust Dws SW6	126	H13
Samuel St SE15	37	M14
Samuel St SE18	134	E7
Samuels Cl W6	125	N9
Sancroft Cl NW2	89	S6
Sancroft Rd, Har	68	G4
Sancroft St SE11	34	H5
Sanctuary, The, SW1 *1*	25	U8
Sanctuary, The, Bex	154	G12
Sanctuary, The, Mord	180	K11
Sanctuary St SE1	28	A7
Sandal Rd N18	60	G10
Sandal Rd, N Mal	178	J9
Sandal St E15	114	J1
Sandale Cl N16	94	A6
Sandall Cl W5	105	S7
Sandall Rd NW5	92	F12
Sandall Rd W5	105	R7
Sandalwood Cl E1	113	R8
Sandalwood Rd, Felt	156	D5
Sandbach Pl SE18	135	L8
Sandbourne Av SW19	180	J5
Sandbourne Rd SE4	149	R3
Sandbrook Cl NW7	54	H11
Sandbrook Rd N16	94	C6
Sandby Grn SE9	152	D6
Sandcroft Cl N13	59	R11
Sandell St SE1	27	K5
Sanders Cl, Hmptn	157	T10
Sanders La NW7	56	A13
Sanderson Cl NW5	92	C8
Sanderstead Av NW2	90	C4
Sanderstead Cl, SW12 *1*	146	F13
Sanderstead Rd E10	95	S1
Sanderstead Rd, S Croy	198	A14
Sandfield Gdns, Th Hth	183	S5
Sandfield Pas, Th Hth	183	T5
Sandfield Rd, Th Hth	183	S5
Sandford Av N22	59	T14
Sandford Av, Loug	49	L6
Sandford Cl E6	116	E7
Sandford Ct N16	94	C1
Sandford Rd E6	116	E5
Sandford Rd, Bexh	155	K7
Sandford Rd, Brom	187	P7
Sandford St, SW6 *13*	127	K14
Sandgate Cl, Rom	83	U13
Sandgate La SW18	163	R2
Sandgate Rd, Well	136	E13
Sandgate St SE15	130	J11
Sandhills, Wall	196	H7
Sandhurst Av, Har	67	S12
Sandhurst Av, Surb	178	C13
Sandhurst Cl NW9	70	A5
Sandhurst Dr, Ilf	99	U8
Sandhurst Rd N9	45	M12
Sandhurst Rd NW9	70	A6
Sandhurst Rd SE6	168	F1
Sandhurst Rd, Bex	154	G10
Sandhurst Rd, Sid	171	U6
Sandhurst Way, S Croy	198	D14
Sandiford Rd, Sutt	194	E3
Sandiland Cres, Brom	201	M3
Sandilands, Croy	198	G5
Sandilands Rd SW6	144	J2
Sandison St SE15	148	F5
Sandland St WC1	18	G3
Sandling Ri SE9	170	G6
Sandlings, The, N22	75	P4
Sandlings Cl, SE15 *9*	148	J1
Sandmere Rd SW4	146	J7
Sandon Cl, Esher	176	B14
Sandown Av, Dag	101	T12
Sandown Cl, Houns	138	B2
Sandown Rd SE25	184	J9
Sandown Way, Nthlt	85	K11
Sandpiper Cl E17	77	P1
Sandpiper Cl SE16	131	T2
Sandpit Pl SE7	134	D9
Sandpit Rd, Brom	168	J10
Sandpits Rd, Croy	199	N7
Sandpits Rd, Rich	159	P3
Sandra Cl N22	75	T2
Sandra Cl, Houns	139	S10
Sandridge Cl, Har	68	D7
Sandridge St, N19 *2*	92	F3
Sandringham Av SW20	180	D3
Sandringham Cl SW19	162	B1
Sandringham Cl, Enf	44	D3
Sandringham Cl, Ilf	81	M5
Sandringham Ct, W9 *2*	6	G8
Sandringham Cres, Har	85	P4
Sandringham Dr, Well	153	R4
Sandringham Gdns N8	75	K11
Sandringham Gdns N12	57	N11
Sandringham Gdns, Hours	138	B1
Sandringham Gdns, Ilf	81	M5
Sandringham Rd E7	97	T10
Sandringham Rd E8	94	G10
Sandringham Rd E10	78	G12
Sandringham Rd N22	75	T5
Sandringham Rd NW2	89	R11
Sandringham Rd NW11	72	C14
Sandringham Rd, Bark	99	T12
Sandringham Rd, Brom	169	P10
Sandringham Rd, Nthlt	85	P13
Sandringham Rd, Th Hth	183	U10
Sandringham Rd, Wor Pk	193	P5
Sandrock Pl, Croy	199	P7
Sandrock Rd SE13	150	B5
Sand's End La SW6	145	K1
Sands Way, Wdf Grn	64	E12
Sandstone Pl N19	92	D3
Sandstone Rd SE12	169	R4
Sandtoft Rd SE7	133	R11
Sandwell Cres NW6	90	H11
Sandwich St WC1	10	A7
Sandwick Cl NW7	55	P13
Sandy Bury, Orp	203	P6
Sandy Hill Av SE18	135	K10
Sandy Hill Rd SE18	134	J9
Sandy La, Har	69	T12
Sandy La, Kings T	177	L1
Sandy La, Mitch	182	B1
Sandy La, Nthwd	50	B10
Sandy La, Rich	159	M4
Sandy La, Sid	172	H13
Sandy La, Sutt	194	D13
Sandy La, Tedd	158	G13
Sandy La, Walt	174	E12
Sandy La Est, Rich	159	N4
Sandy La N, Wall	196	H10
Sandy La S, Wall	196	G12
Sandy Ridge, Chis	170	G11
Sandy Rd NW3	91	K3
Sandy Way, Croy	199	T5
Sandycombe Rd, Felt	156	B2
Sandycombe Rd, Rich	142	A2
Sandycoombe Rd, Twick	141	L12
Sandycroft SE2	136	A11
Sandyhill Rd, Ilf	98	J7
Sandymount Av, Stan	53	M10
Sandy's Row, E1 *4*	21	K3
Sanford La, N16 *2*	94	E4
Sanford St SE14	131	R12
Sanford Ter N16	94	F4
Sanford Wk SE14	131	R12
Sanger Av, Chess	191	T9
Sangley Rd SE6	150	F14
Sangley Rd SE25	184	D7
Sangora Rd SW11	145	P8
Sans Wk EC1	11	N10
Sansom Rd E11	97	K4
Sansom St SE5	130	B14
Santley St SW4	147	L7
Santos Rd SW18	144	G9
Sapcote Trd Cen NW10	89	M11
Saperton Wk SE11	34	G1
Saphora Cl, Orp	203	P9
Sapphire Cl E6	116	F11
Sapphire Cl, Dag	100	F1
Sapphire Rd SE8	131	S8
Sara Ct, Beck	186	D2
Saracen Cl, Croy	184	B11
Saracen St E14	114	B12
Sarah St N1	13	K6
Saratoga Rd E5	95	M7
Sardinia St WC2	18	F7
Sarita Cl, Har	68	A3
Sarjant Path, SW19 *3*	162	B4
Sark Cl, Houns	121	P14
Sark Wk E16	115	S11
Sarnesfield Rd, Enf *2*	44	A6
Sarre Rd NW2	90	E9
Sarsen Av, Houns	139	M3
Sarsfeld Rd SW12	163	U2
Sarsfield Rd, Grnf	105	K3
Sartor Rd SE15	149	N8
Sarum Ter E3	113	S8
Satanita Cl E16	116	A10
Satchell Mead NW9	71	L1
Satchwell Rd E2	13	R8
Sauls Grn, E11 *9*	97	K5
Saunders Cl, E14 *11*	113	U14
Saunders Ness Rd E14	132	F9
Saunders Rd SE18	135	T9
Saunders St SE11	34	J3
Saunders Way SE28	118	C14
Saunderton Rd, Wem	87	K10
Savage Gdns E6	116	F12
Savage Gdns EC3	21	K9
Savernake Rd N9	44	H12
Savernake Rd NW3	92	A8
Savery Dr, Surb	177	L13
Savile Cl, N Mal	179	K10
Savile Cl, T Ditt	190	F1
Savile Gdns, Croy	198	F4
Savile Row W1	17	L10
Savill Gdns SW20	179	P5
Savill Row, Wdf Grn	63	M11
Saville Rd E16	134	D2
Saville Rd W4	124	G6
Saville Rd, Rom	83	L12
Saville Rd, Twick	158	F2
Saville Row, Brom	201	M2
Saville Row, Enf	45	N4
Savona Cl SW19	162	C13
Savona Est SW8	128	E14
Savona St SW8	128	E14
Savoy Bldgs, WC2 *5*	18	E11
Savoy Cl E15	114	J1
Savoy Cl, Edg	54	A9
Savoy Ct WC2	18	D11
Savoy Hill WC2	18	E11
Savoy Pl WC2	18	D12
Savoy Row, WC2 *6*	18	E11
Savoy Steps, WC2 *4*	18	E11
Savoy St WC2	18	E10
Savoy Way WC2	18	E11
Sawbill Cl, Hayes	102	G10
Sawkins Cl SW19	162	B4
Sawley Rd W12	125	P1
Sawtry Cl, Cars	181	R14
Sawyer Cl N9	60	G4
Sawyer St SE1	27	T5
Sawyers Cl, Dag	101	T11
Sawyer's Hill, Rich	142	E13
Sawyers Lawn W13	104	G12
Saxby Rd SW2	146	J13
Saxham Rd, Bark *1*	117	T2
Saxlingham Rd E4	62	H6
Saxon Av, Felt	157	M4
Saxon Cl E17	78	A13
Saxon Cl, Surb	177	P12
Saxon Dr W3	106	C10
Saxon Rd E3	113	T4
Saxon Rd E6	116	D8
Saxon Rd N22	75	S1
Saxon Rd SE25	184	B10
Saxon Rd, Brom	169	M14
Saxon Rd, Ilf	99	K11
Saxon Rd, Sthl	103	K14
Saxon Rd, Wem	88	E6
Saxon Wk, Sid	172	E10
Saxon Way N14	42	G11
Saxonbury Av, Sun	174	E4
Saxonbury Cl, Mitch	181	N6
Saxonbury Gdns, Surb	191	M1
Saxonfield Cl SW2	147	M14
Saxton Cl SE13	150	H6
Sayers Wk, Rich *1*	141	T13
Sayes Ct St SE8	131	U11
Sayesbury La N18	60	H10
Scadbury Pk, Chis	171	T12
Scads Hill Cl, Orp	189	T12
Scala St W1	17	P3
Scales Rd N17	76	F5
Scampston Ms, W10 *4*	108	B12
Scandrett St E1	130	J2
Scarborough Rd E11	96	G1
Scarborough Rd N4	75	P14
Scarborough Rd N9	45	L13
Scarborough St E1	21	P8
Scarbrook Rd, Croy	197	T6
Scarle Rd, Wem	87	P12
Scarlet Rd SE6	168	J5
Scarsbrook Rd SE3	152	A5
Scarsdale Pl W8	22	A10
Scarsdale Rd, Har	85	T6
Scarsdale Vil W8	126	H6
Scarth Rd SW13	143	M5
Scawen Cl, Cars	196	A7
Scawen Rd SE8	131	R10

Scawfell St E2	13	P3
Scaynes Link N12	56	G9
Sceaux Est SE5	148	D1
Sceaux Gdns SE5	148	F1
Sceptre Rd E2	113	L6
Scholars Rd E4	62	F2
Scholars Rd SW12	164	E1
Scholefield Rd N19	92	H3
Schonfeld Sq N16	94	A3
School Ho La, Tedd	159	K14
School La SE23	167	K4
School La,	177	M2
Kings T		
School La, Pnr	66	J7
School La, Surb	191	U2
School La, Well	154	D5
School Pas, Kings T	177	U4
School Pas, Sthl	121	M1
School Rd E12	98	E8
School Rd NW10	106	H8
School Rd, Chis	189	M1
School Rd, Dag	119	P1
School Rd, E Mol	176	A8
School Rd, Hmptn	157	T11
School Rd, Houns	139	U5
School Rd,	177	M2
Kings T 2		
School Rd Av,	157	T11
Hmptn		
School Wk, Sun	174	A6
School Way N12	57	M7
School Way, Dag	100	D5
Schoolbell Ms E3	113	S4
Schoolhouse Gdns,	48	J7
Loug		
Schoolhouse La E1	113	N13
Schoolway N12	57	P11
Schooner Cl E14	132	G6
Schooner Cl,	131	N3
SE16 9		
Schubert Rd SW15	144	F9
Sclater St E1	13	N10
Scoble Pl N16	94	F8
Scoles Cres SW2	165	R1
Scoresby St SE1	27	P4
Scorton Av, Grnf	104	G3
Scot Gro, Pnr	50	H13
Scotch Common	104	H9
W13		
Scoter Cl, Wdf Grn	63	S13
Scotia Rd SW2	147	N14
Scotland Grn N17	76	F3
Scotland Grn Rd,	45	P10
Enf		
Scotland Grn Rd N,	45	P8
Enf		
Scotland Pl,	26	B3
SW1 3		
Scotland Rd, Buck H	63	U2
Scotsdale Cl, Orp	189	S8
Scotsdale Cl, Sutt	194	D13
Scotsdale Rd SE12	151	S10
Scotswood St,	11	M10
EC1 6		
Scotswood Wk N17	60	H13
Scott Cl SW16	183	L2
Scott Cl, Epsom	192	F9
Scott Cres, Har	85	R2
Scott Ellis Gdns	6	J8
NW8		
Scott Fm Cl, T Ditt	190	J1
Scott Gdns, Houns	120	G13
Scott Lidgett Cres	29	T8
SE16		
Scott Russell Pl,	132	C9
E14 10		
Scott St E1	112	J8
Scott Trimmer	139	K3
Way, Houns		
Scottes La, Dag	100	G1
Scotts Av, Brom	186	H3
Scotts Dr, Hmptn	157	R13
Scotts Fm Rd,	192	F11
Epsom		
Scotts La, Brom	186	G6
Scotts Rd E10	96	E2
Scotts Rd W12	125	S4
Scotts Rd, Brom	169	N14
Scotts Rd, Sthl	120	H5
Scott's Yd EC4	20	D9
Scottwell Dr NW9	71	M9
Scoulding Rd E16	115	M11
Scouler St, E14 1	114	G14
Scout App NW10	88	J7
Scout Way NW7	54	H7
Scovell Rd SE1	27	T8
Scrattons Ter, Bark	118	H3
Scriven St E8	112	F1
Scrooby St SE6	150	C12
Scrubs La NW10	107	S9
Scrubs La W10	107	P6
Scrutton Cl SW12	146	H14
Scrutton St EC2	12	G11
Scudamore La NW9	70	E7
Scutari Rd SE22	149	L10
Scylla Rd SE15	148	J5
Seabright St, E2 5	112	J6
Seabrook Dr,	200	J4
W Wick		
Seabrook Gdns, Rom	83	P14
Seabrook Rd, Dag	100	G5
Seacole Cl W3	106	H10
Seacourt Rd SE2	136	G3
Seacroft Gdns, Wat	50	G6
Seafield Rd N11	58	G8
Seaford Rd E17	78	C6
Seaford Rd N15	76	C9
Seaford Rd W13	122	J2
Seaford Rd, Enf	44	D7
Seaford St WC1	10	D8
Seaforth Av, N Mal	179	R9
Seaforth Cres N5	93	U9
Seaforth Gdns N21	43	M14
Seaforth Gdns,	193	M8
Epsom		
Seaforth Gdns,	63	U10
Wdf Grn		
Seaforth Pl,	25	P10
SW1 4		
Seagrave Rd SW6	126	H12
Seagry Rd E11	79	R13
Seal St E8	94	F8
Searle Pl N4	93	M2
Searles Cl SW11	127	S14
Searles Rd SE1	36	E1
Sears St SE5	36	D14
Seasprite Cl, Nthlt	102	H5
Seaton Av, Ilf	99	S9
Seaton Cl, E13 5	115	P8
Seaton Cl SE11	35	N5
Seaton Cl SW15	161	S1
Seaton Cl, Twick	140	A12
Seaton Gdns, Ruis	84	A5
Seaton Rd, Mitch	181	R4
Seaton Rd, Twick	139	U12
Seaton Rd, Well	136	E14
Seaton Rd, Wem	105	R3
Seaton St N18	60	H10
Sebastian St EC1	11	R7
Sebastopol Rd N9	60	H7
Sebbon St N1	93	S14
Sebergham Gro	55	P13
NW7		
Sebert Rd E7	97	R9
Sebright Pas, E2 3	13	U3
Sebright Rd, Barn	40	B5
Secker Cres, Har	67	T2
Secker St SE1	27	K3
Second Av E12	98	D8
Second Av E13	115	N5
Second Av E17	78	B9
Second Av N18	61	L7
Second Av NW4	72	A7
Second Av SW14	142	J5
Second Av W3	125	L1
Second Av W10	108	D7
Second Av, Dag	119	R2
Second Av, Enf	44	E10
Second Av, Rom	82	F9
Second Av, Walt	174	D12
Second Av, Wem	87	P3
Second Cl, W Mol	175	T7
Second Cross Rd,	158	C3
Twick		
Second Way, Wem	88	B8
Sedan Way SE17	36	G5
Sedcombe Cl, Sid	172	D8
Sedcote Rd, Enf	45	N9
Sedding St,	32	C2
SW1 2		
Seddon Rd, Mord	181	N10
Seddon St WC1	10	G8
Sedge Rd N17	61	L13
Sedgebrook Rd SE3	152	B4
Sedgecombe Av,	69	L10
Har		
Sedgeford Rd W12	125	M1
Sedgehill Rd SE6	168	B9
Sedgemere Av N2	73	M6
Sedgemere Rd SE2	136	F6
Sedgemoor Dr, Dag	101	P7
Sedgeway SE6	169	L2
Sedgewood Cl, Brom	187	L13
Sedgmoor Pl SE5	130	D14
Sedgwick Rd E10	96	E4
Sedgwick St E9	95	N10
Sedleigh Rd SW18	144	F11
Sedlescombe Rd	126	G12
SW6		
Sedley Ri, Loug	48	F3
Sedum Cl NW9	70	D10
Seeley Dr SE21	166	D7
Seelig Av NW9	71	N14
Seely Rd SW17	164	A11
Seething La EC3	21	K10
Seething Wells La,	177	M12
Surb		
Sefton Av NW7	54	G10
Sefton Av, Har	68	B2
Sefton Cl, Orp	189	T8
Sefton Rd, Croy	198	H2
Sefton Rd, Orp	189	T8
Sefton St SW15	143	U4
Segal Cl SE23	149	S14
Sekforde St EC1	11	N11
Sekhon Ter, Felt	157	N5
Selan Gdns, Hayes	102	C10
Selbie Av NW10	89	L10
Selborne Av E12	98	G7
Selborne Av, Bex	172	J1
Selborne Gdns	71	P7
NW4		
Selborne Gdns,	104	G2
Grnf		
Selborne Rd E17	78	A9
Selborne Rd N14	58	J5
Selborne Rd N22	75	L2
Selborne Rd,	148	A3
SE5 9		
Selborne Rd, Croy	198	E6
Selborne Rd, Ilf	98	G4
Selborne Rd, N Mal	178	J4
Selborne Rd, Sid	172	C8
Selborne Wk E17	77	U8
Selbourne Av, Surb	191	U4
Selby Chase, Ruis	84	C4
Selby Cl, E6 19	116	C10
Selby Cl, Chess	191	R13
Selby Gdns, Sthl	103	N8
Selby Grn, Cars	181	S13
Selby Rd E11	97	K6
Selby Rd E13	115	S9
Selby Rd N17	60	C12
Selby Rd SE20	184	H4
Selby Rd W5	105	K7
Selby Rd, Cars	181	S13
Selby St E1	13	U12
Selden Rd SE15	149	M4
Selhurst Cl SW19	162	A2
Selhurst New Rd	184	C11
SE25		
Selhurst Pl SE25	184	C12
Selhurst Rd N9	60	B5
Selhurst Rd SE25	184	C9
Selinas La, Dag	83	K14
Selkirk Rd SW17	163	S8
Selkirk Rd, Twick	157	T3
Sellers Cl, Borwd	38	F2
Sellers Hall Cl N3	56	G14
Sellincourt Rd SW17	163	T11
Sellindge Cl, Beck	167	U14
Sellon Ms SE11	34	G3
Sellons Av NW10	107	M2
Sellwood Dr, Barn	39	K4
Selsdon Av, S Croy	198	B11
Selsdon Cl, Rom	83	T1
Selsdon Cl, Surb	177	S9
Selsdon Pk Rd,	199	S14
S Croy		
Selsdon Rd E11	79	P13
Selsdon Rd E13	115	U2
Selsdon Rd NW2	89	M4
Selsdon Rd SE27	165	R6
Selsdon Rd, S Croy	198	A9
Selsdon Way E14	132	D6
Selsea Pl, N16 3	94	D9
Selsey Cres, Well	154	G1
Selsey St E14	114	A9
Selvage La NW7	54	G8
Selway Cl, Pnr	66	C7
Selwood Pl SW7	30	J6
Selwood Rd, Chess	191	N8
Selwood Rd, Croy	198	J3
Selwood Rd, Sutt	194	F1
Selwood Ter SW7	31	K6
Selworthy Cl E11	79	N10
Selworthy Rd SE6	167	T5
Selwyn Av E4	62	E12
Selwyn Av, Ilf	81	S11
Selwyn Av, Rich	141	S6
Selwyn Cl, Houns	139	K6
Selwyn Ct SE3	151	L5
Selwyn Cres, Well	154	C7
Selwyn Rd E3	113	T4
Selwyn Rd E13	115	R1
Selwyn Rd NW10	88	H14
Selwyn Rd, N Mal	178	G9
Semley Gate, E9 4	95	U11
Semley Pl SW1	32	F3
Semley Rd SW16	183	K3
Senate St, SE15 7	149	M4
Seneca Rd, Th Hth	183	T8
Senga Rd, Wall	196	A2
Senhouse Rd, Sutt	194	A6
Senior St W2	14	B2
Senlac Rd SE12	169	R2
Sennen Rd, Enf	44	E13
Sennen Wk, SE9 2	170	D5
Senrab St E1	113	N11
Sentinel Cl, Nthlt	103	K7
Sentinel Sq NW4	71	U8
September Way,	53	K12
Stan		
Sequoia Cl, Bushey	52	A2
Sequoia Gdns, Orp	189	U14
Sequoia Pk, Pnr	51	R11
Serbin Cl E10	78	F14
Serjeants Inn,	19	L8
EC4 18		
Serle St WC2	18	H6
Serpentine Rd W2	23	T3
Serviden Dr, Brom	188	A1
Setchell Rd SE1	37	M2
Setchell Way SE1	37	L1
Seth St, SE16 6	131	M4
Seton Gdns, Dag	100	F14
Settle Rd E13	115	N3
Settles St E1	21	U5
Settrington Rd SW6	144	J4
Seven Acres, Cars	195	R4
Seven Acres, Nthwd	50	B11
Seven Kings Rd, Ilf	99	T2
Seven Sisters Rd N4	93	M5
Seven Sisters Rd N7	93	M5
Seven Sisters Rd	93	M5
N15		
Sevenoaks Cl, Bexh	155	T7
Sevenoaks Rd SE4	149	S11
Sevenoaks Rd, Orp	203	U6
Sevenoaks Rd	203	T14
(Green St Grn),		
Orp		
Sevenoaks Way, Sid	172	E14
Seventh Av E12	98	E7
Severn Dr, Esher	190	H4
Severn Way NW10	89	L10
Severnake Cl E14	132	B7
Severus Rd SW11	145	S7
Seville Ms N1	94	C14
Seville St SW1	24	A7
Sevington Rd NW4	71	R11
Sevington St W9	6	A11
Seward Rd W7	122	G3
Seward Rd, Beck	185	P4
Seward St EC1	11	T8
Sewardstone Gdns	46	C10
E4		
Sewardstone Rd E2	113	L3
Sewardstone Rd E4	46	C12

Name	No.	Ref
Sewardstone Rd, Wal Abb	46	E2
Sewdley St E5	95	N7
Sewell Rd SE2	136	A5
Sewell St E13	115	P5
Sextant Av E14	132	G7
Seymour Av N17	76	H3
Seymour Av, Mord	180	B13
Seymour Cl, E Mol	175	T9
Seymour Cl, Loug	48	D11
Seymour Cl, Pnr	67	L1
Seymour Ct E4	63	L3
Seymour Dr, Brom	202	F2
Seymour Gdns SE4	149	R5
Seymour Gdns, Felt	156	E7
Seymour Gdns, Ilf	98	E2
Seymour Gdns, Ruis	84	H1
Seymour Gdns, Surb	177	U10
Seymour Gdns, Twick	140	J14
Seymour Ms W1	16	D6
Seymour Pl, SE25 7	184	J8
Seymour Pl W1	15	T5
Seymour Rd E4	62	C1
Seymour Rd E6	116	A2
Seymour Rd E10	95	T1
Seymour Rd N3	57	K13
Seymour Rd N8	75	R10
Seymour Rd N9	61	K4
Seymour Rd SW18	144	F12
Seymour Rd SW19	162	B5
Seymour Rd W4	124	F7
Seymour Rd, Cars 7	196	A9
Seymour Rd, E Mol	175	T9
Seymour Rd, Hmptn	157	U9
Seymour Rd, Kings T	177	N1
Seymour Rd, Mitch	182	A14
Seymour St W1	15	U8
Seymour St W2	15	T8
Seymour Ter SE20	184	J2
Seymour Vil SE20	184	H2
Seymour Wk SW10	30	F9
Seymours, The, Loug	48	G2
Seyssel St E14	132	F7
Shaa Rd W3	106	H14
Shacklegate La, Tedd	158	C8
Shackleton Cl SE23	167	K4
Shackleton Rd, Sthl	103	M14
Shacklewell Grn E8	94	F8
Shacklewell La E8	94	F9
Shacklewell Rd N16	94	F8
Shacklewell Row E8	94	F8
Shacklewell St E2	13	N9
Shad Thames SE1	29	N4
Shadbolt Av E4	61	R10
Shadbolt Cl, Wor Pk	193	M4
Shadwell Dr, Nthlt	103	L5
Shadwell Gdns E1	113	L13
Shadwell Pierhead E1	113	M14
Shaef Way, Tedd	158	H13
Shafter Rd, Dag	101	T11
Shaftesbury, Loug	48	B6
Shaftesbury Av W1	17	S10
Shaftesbury Av WC2	17	S10
Shaftesbury Av, Barn	41	L6
Shaftesbury Av, Enf	45	M4
Shaftesbury Av, Felt	138	B12
Shaftesbury Av, Har	85	S1
Shaftesbury Av (Kenton), Har	69	R13
Shaftesbury Av, Sthl	121	N6
Shaftesbury Circle, Har	85	T2
Shaftesbury Gdns NW10	107	K7
Shaftesbury Ms, SW4 1	146	E9
Shaftesbury Ms, W8 5	126	H6
Shaftesbury Rd, E4 3	62	H1
Shaftesbury Rd E7	97	T14
Shaftesbury Rd E10	96	B2
Shaftesbury Rd E17	78	C11
Shaftesbury Rd N18	60	D11
Shaftesbury Rd N19	92	J1
Shaftesbury Rd, Beck	185	U3
Shaftesbury Rd, Cars	181	P13
Shaftesbury Rd, Rich	141	R6
Shaftesbury St N1	12	B3
Shaftesbury Way, Twick	158	B5
Shaftesbury Waye, Hayes	102	E10
Shaftesburys, The, Bark	117	L3
Shafto Ms SW1	23	U12
Shafton Rd E9	113	P1
Shakespeare Av N11	58	F9
Shakespeare Av NW10	106	F1
Shakespeare Av, Felt	138	A12
Shakespeare Av, Hayes	102	D8
Shakespeare Cres E12	98	F12
Shakespeare Cres NW10	106	G2
Shakespeare Dr, Har	69	U12
Shakespeare Gdns N2	73	T8
Shakespeare Rd E17	77	P4
Shakespeare Rd N3	72	G1
Shakespeare Rd NW7	55	M8
Shakespeare Rd SE24	147	S8
Shakespeare Rd W3	124	F1
Shakespeare Rd W7	104	F12
Shakespeare Rd, Bexh	154	J1
Shakespeare Sq, Ilf	65	K12
Shakespeare Way, Felt	156	E8
Shakspeare Wk N16	94	C8
Shalcomb St SW10	30	H12
Shaldon Dr, Mord	180	C9
Shaldon Dr, Ruis	84	E5
Shaldon Rd, Edg	69	T2
Shalfleet Dr W10	108	A13
Shalford Cl, Orp	203	L8
Shalimar Gdns W3	106	E13
Shalimar Rd W3	106	E13
Shallons Rd SE9	170	J7
Shalston Vil, Surb 3	177	T12
Shalstone Rd SW14	142	D5
Shamrock Rd, Croy	183	L11
Shamrock St SW4	146	F5
Shamrock Way N14	58	D1
Shand St SE1	28	H5
Shandon Rd SW4	146	F11
Shandy St E1	113	P8
Shanklin Gdns, Wat	50	E8
Shanklin Rd N8	74	H10
Shanklin Rd N15	76	H8
Shannon Cl NW2	90	B5
Shannon Cl, Sthl	120	H9
Shannon Gro SW9	147	M7
Shannon Pl NW8	7	R2
Shannon Way, Beck	168	C12
Shap Cres, Cars	195	T1
Shapland Way N13	59	M9
Shardcroft Av SE24	147	S10
Shardeloes Rd SE14	149	T3
Sharland Cl, Th Hth	183	P11
Sharman Ct, Sid	172	A8
Sharnbrooke Cl, Well	154	E6
Sharon Cl, Surb	191	M1
Sharon Gdns E9	113	L1
Sharon Rd W4	124	G10
Sharon Rd, Enf	45	R3
Sharpe Cl, W7 1	104	F10
Sharpleshall St, NW1 8	91	U14
Sharpness Cl, Hayes	102	J9
Sharratt St SE15	131	M11
Sharsted St SE17	35	N8
Shaw Av, Bark	118	J3
Shaw Cl SE28	136	D2
Shaw Dr, Walt	174	F14
Shaw Gdns, Bark	118	J3
Shaw Rd SE22	148	D8
Shaw Rd, Brom	169	L6
Shaw Rd, Enf	45	N2
Shaw Sq E17	77	S2
Shaw Way, Wall	196	J13
Shawbrooke Rd SE9	152	A9
Shawbury Rd SE22	148	F9
Shawfield Pk, Brom	188	A3
Shawfield St SW3	31	S7
Shawford Ct SW15	143	P14
Shawford Rd, Epsom	192	G11
Shaws Cotts SE23	167	R5
Shearing Dr, Cars	181	M13
Shearling Way N7	93	K11
Shearman Rd SE3	151	L7
Shearwater Way, Hayes	102	G11
Sheaveshill Av NW9	70	J8
Sheen Common Dr, Rich	142	B8
Sheen Ct, Rich	142	B7
Sheen Ct Rd, Rich	142	B7
Sheen Gate Gdns SW14	142	E7
Sheen Gro N1	111	N1
Sheen La SW14	142	F5
Sheen Pk, Rich	141	T8
Sheen Rd, Orp	189	U8
Sheen Rd, Rich	141	R9
Sheen Way, Wall	197	L9
Sheen Wd SW14	142	E9
Sheendale Rd, Rich	141	T7
Sheenewood SE26	167	K8
Sheep La E8	112	J2
Sheep Wk Ms SW19	162	B11
Sheepcote Cl, Houns	120	B14
Sheepcote La SW11	145	U4
Sheepcote Rd, Har	68	F11
Sheepcotes Rd, Rom	82	J7
Sheephouse Way, N Mal	178	J14
Sheerwater Rd E16	116	A9
Sheffield St WC2	18	F7
Sheffield Ter W8	126	G2
Shefton Ri, Nthwd	50	B13
Shelbourne Cl, Pnr	67	L6
Shelbourne Rd N17	76	J2
Shelburne Rd N7	93	M7
Shelbury Cl, Sid	172	A6
Shelbury Rd SE22	149	K10
Sheldon Av N6	73	S13
Sheldon Av, Ilf	80	J3
Sheldon Cl SE12	151	R10
Sheldon Cl SE20	185	K1
Sheldon Rd N18	60	D8
Sheldon Rd NW2	90	B8
Sheldon Rd, Bexh	155	L2
Sheldon Rd, Dag	100	J13
Sheldon St, Croy	197	T6
Sheldrake Cl E16	134	E2
Sheldrake Pl W8	126	F3
Sheldrick Cl SW19	181	N3
Shelduck Cl E15	97	M9
Sheldwich Ter, Brom	188	C11
Shelford Pl N16	94	A6
Shelford Ri SE19	166	E14
Shelford Rd, Barn	39	U11
Shelgate Rd SW11	145	T9
Shell Cl, Brom	188	E12
Shell Rd SE13	150	C6
Shellduck Cl NW9	70	J3
Shelley Av E12	98	D12
Shelley Av, Grnf	104	A5
Shelley Cl SE15	149	K3
Shelley Cl, Edg	54	A8
Shelley Cl, Grnf	104	A6
Shelley Cl, Hayes	102	B9
Shelley Cl, Orp	203	S5
Shelley Cres, Houns	138	G3
Shelley Cres, Sthl	103	M12
Shelley Dr, Well	153	S2
Shelley Gdns, Wem	87	L4
Shelley Gro, Loug	48	E8
Shelley Way SW19	163	N11
Shellness Rd E5	94	J9
Shellwood Rd SW11	145	T4
Shelmerdine Cl E3	114	A9
Shelton Rd SW19	180	H1
Shelton St WC2	18	B8
Shenfield Rd, Wdf Grn	63	R14
Shenfield St N1	12	J4
Shenley Rd SE5	148	D2
Shenley Rd, Borwd	38	A7
Shenley Rd, Houns	139	K2
Shepherd Mkt, W1 1	24	H3
Shepherd St W1	24	G3
Shepherdess Pl, N1 4	12	B6
Shepherdess Wk N1	12	A2
Shepherds Bush Grn W12	125	U3
Shepherds Bush Mkt W12	125	T4
Shepherds Bush Pl W12	126	A3
Shepherds Bush Rd W6	125	U6
Shepherds Cl N6	74	D12
Shepherds Cl, Orp	203	T6
Shepherds Cl, Rom	82	G9
Shepherds Ct W12	126	A3
Shepherds Grn, Chis	171	P13
Shepherds Hill N6	74	C12
Shepherds La, E9 1	95	N11
Shepherds Pl, W1 1	16	D10
Shepherds Wk NW2	89	N3
Shepherds Wk NW3	91	N9
Shepherds Wk, Bushey	52	B3
Shepherds Way, S Croy	199	N14
Shepley Cl, Cars	196	A5
Sheppard Cl, Kings T 2	177	S8
Sheppard Dr SE16	130	J9
Sheppard St E16	115	M7
Shepperton Cl, Borwd	38	G2
Shepperton Rd N1	112	A1
Shepperton Rd, Orp	189	M12
Sheppey Gdns, Dag	100	F13
Sheppey Rd, Dag	100	C13
Sherard Rd SE9	152	D9
Sheraton Business Cen, Grnf	105	K4
Sheraton St W1	17	R7
Sherborne Av, Enf	45	L3
Sherborne Av, Sthl	121	N7
Sherborne Cl, Hayes	102	E11
Sherborne Cres, Cars	181	R13
Sherborne Gdns NW9	70	A6
Sherborne Gdns W13	105	K10
Sherborne La EC4	20	D9
Sherborne Rd, Chess	191	R9
Sherborne Rd, Orp	189	T9
Sherborne Rd, Sutt	194	G3
Sherborne St N1	112	A1
Sherboro Rd N15	76	E11
Sherbrook Gdns N21	43	S13
Sherbrooke Cl, Bexh	155	N7
Sherbrooke Rd SW6	126	E13
Shere Cl, Chess	191	P9
Shere Rd, Ilf	80	H9
Sheredan Rd E4	62	J10
Sherfield Gdns SW15	143	L12
Sheridan Ct, Houns 3	139	K10
Sheridan Cres, Chis	188	J3

Name	Page	Grid
Sheridan Gdns, Har	69	N12
Sheridan Pl SW13	143	L4
Sheridan Pl, Hmptn	175	S1
Sheridan Rd E7	97	M6
Sheridan Rd E12	98	D10
Sheridan Rd SW19	180	F2
Sheridan Rd, Belv	137	N7
Sheridan Rd, Bexh	154	J5
Sheridan Rd, Rich	159	L6
Sheridan St, E1 *13*	113	K12
Sheridan Wk NW11	72	G11
Sheridan Wk, Cars *4*	195	T10
Sheridan Way, Beck	185	T2
Sheringham Av E12	98	F7
Sheringham Av N14	42	H11
Sheringham Av, Felt	156	A5
Sheringham Av, Rom	83	U12
Sheringham Av, Twick	157	M2
Sheringham Dr, Bark	99	U9
Sheringham Rd N7	93	M11
Sheringham Rd SE20	185	K5
Sherington Av, Pnr	51	P13
Sherington Rd SE7	133	R12
Sherland Rd, Twick	158	F1
Sherlies Av, Orp	203	S4
Sherlock Ms W1	16	C2
Sherman Rd, Brom	187	P2
Shernhall St E17	78	F10
Sherrard Rd E7	97	T11
Sherrard Rd E12	98	B10
Sherrards Way, Barn	40	J12
Sherrick Grn Rd NW10	89	R10
Sherriff Rd NW6	90	H12
Sherrin Rd E10	96	B7
Sherringham Av N17	76	G3
Sherrock Gdns NW4	71	R7
Sherry Ms, Bark	99	P13
Sherwin Rd SE14	149	N2
Sherwood Av E18	79	R6
Sherwood Av SW16	164	G14
Sherwood Av, Grnf	86	D11
Sherwood Av, Hayes	102	C7
Sherwood Cl, SW13 *1*	143	S6
Sherwood Cl W13	122	J2
Sherwood Cl, Bex	154	F12
Sherwood Gdns E14	132	B7
Sherwood Gdns SE16	37	U7
Sherwood Gdns, Bark	99	N13
Sherwood Pk Av, Sid	154	C12
Sherwood Pk Rd, Mitch	182	G7
Sherwood Pk Rd, Sutt	194	H9
Sherwood Rd NW4	71	U5
Sherwood Rd SW19	162	F14
Sherwood Rd, Croy	184	J14
Sherwood Rd, Hmptn	157	T9
Sherwood Rd, Har	85	T4
Sherwood Rd, Ilf	81	N8
Sherwood Rd, Well	153	R4
Sherwood St N20	57	M5
Sherwood St W1	17	P10
Sherwood Ter, N20 *2*	57	N5
Sherwood Way, W Wick	200	D4
Shetland Cl, Borwd	38	G11
Shetland Rd E3	113	U3
Shield Dr, Brent	122	J11
Shieldhall St SE2	136	E7
Shifford Path SE23	167	P5
Shillibeer Pl W1	15	S2
Shillibeer Wk, Chig	65	T6
Shillingford St N1	93	S14
Shinfield St W12	107	T11
Shinglewell Rd, Erith	137	N13
Shinners Cl SE25	184	G9
Ship & Mermaid Row SE1	28	G6
Ship La SW14	142	F5
Ship St SE8	150	A1
Ship Yd E14	132	C9
Shipka Rd SW12	164	C1
Shipman Rd E16	115	S12
Shipman Rd SE23	167	P4
Shipton Cl, Dag	100	G5
Shipton St E2	13	P5
Shipwright Rd SE16	131	R4
Shirburn Cl SE23	149	M14
Shire Ct, Epsom	193	M13
Shire Horse Way, Islw	140	F5
Shirebrook Rd SE3	152	B5
Shirehall Cl NW4	72	A11
Shirehall Gdns NW4	72	A11
Shirehall La NW4	72	A11
Shirehall Pk NW4	72	B12
Shires, The, Rich	159	S8
Shirland Ms W9	108	F6
Shirland Rd W9	6	C11
Shirley Av, Bex	172	G1
Shirley Av, Croy	199	L2
Shirley Av, Sutt	195	R7
Shirley Ch Rd, Croy	199	N5
Shirley Cl E17	78	D9
Shirley Cl, Houns	139	T10
Shirley Ct, Croy	199	N6
Shirley Cres, Beck	185	R8
Shirley Dr, Houns	139	T10
Shirley Gdns W7	122	F1
Shirley Gdns, Bark	99	R11
Shirley Gro N9	45	N14
Shirley Gro SW11	146	B5
Shirley Hills Rd, Croy	199	N7
Shirley Ho Dr SE7	133	T13
Shirley Oaks Rd, Croy	199	N2
Shirley Pk Rd, Croy	199	K1
Shirley Rd E15	97	K13
Shirley Rd W4	124	H4
Shirley Rd, Croy	185	K14
Shirley Rd, Enf	43	T6
Shirley Rd, Sid	171	R6
Shirley St E16	115	L11
Shirley Way, Croy	199	S5
Shirlock Rd NW3	91	U8
Shobden Rd N17	76	A2
Shobroke Cl NW2	89	T5
Shoe La EC4	19	N6
Shoebury Rd E6	98	F13
Shoot Up Hill NW2	90	D11
Shooters Av, Har	69	N7
Shooter's Hill SE18	152	H2
Shooter's Hill, Well	152	H2
Shooter's Hill Rd SE3	151	M1
Shooter's Hill Rd SE10	150	H2
Shooter's Hill Rd SE18	152	B1
Shooters Rd, Enf	43	R1
Shore Cl, Felt	138	A14
Shore Cl, Hmptn	157	K10
Shore Gro, Felt	157	N4
Shore Pl E9	95	L14
Shore Rd E9	95	L14
Shoreditch High St E1	13	K8
Shoreham Cl, SW18 *10*	144	J9
Shoreham Cl, Bex	172	H2
Shoreham Cl, Croy	185	L11
Shoreham Way, Brom	187	N12
Shorncliffe Rd SE1	37	L6
Shorndean St SE6	168	F1
Shorne Cl, Sid *5*	154	D11
Shornefield Cl, Brom	188	G5
Shornells Way SE2	136	E9
Shorrolds Rd SW6	126	F13
Short Hedges, Houns	139	P2
Short Hill, Har *1*	86	C2
Short Path SE18	134	J11
Short Rd E11	96	J3
Short Rd E15	114	G1
Short Rd W4	124	J11
Short St NW4	71	U8
Short St SE1	27	M5
Short Wall E15	114	F5
Short Way SE9	152	C6
Short Way, Twick	139	U14
Shortcroft Rd, Epsom	193	M13
Shortcrofts Rd, Dag	101	L11
Shorter St E1	21	M10
Shortgate N12	56	F7
Shortlands W6	126	A8
Shortlands Cl N18	60	B6
Shortlands Cl, Belv	137	L6
Shortlands Gdns, Brom	187	K3
Shortlands Gro, Brom	186	H5
Shortlands Rd E10	78	C13
Shortlands Rd, Brom	186	H6
Shortlands Rd, Kings T	159	U14
Shorts Cft NW9	70	D7
Shorts Gdns WC2	18	A7
Shorts Rd, Cars	195	S8
Shortway N12	57	S11
Shotfield, Wall	196	D11
Shott Cl, Sutt *6*	195	M9
Shottendane Rd SW6	144	G1
Shottery Cl SE9	170	D5
Shottfield Av SW14	142	J7
Shoulder of Mutton All, E14 *8*	113	S13
Shouldham St W1	15	S4
Showers Way, Hayes	120	B2
Shrapnel Cl SE18	134	D13
Shrapnel Rd SE9	152	E6
Shrewsbury Av SW14	142	F8
Shrewsbury Av, Har	69	S7
Shrewsbury Cl, Surb	191	R3
Shrewsbury Cres NW10	106	H2
Shrewsbury La SE18	152	J2
Shrewsbury Ms, W2 *3*	108	G10
Shrewsbury Rd E7	98	A10
Shrewsbury Rd N11	58	G11
Shrewsbury Rd W2	108	G10
Shrewsbury Rd, Beck	185	S5
Shrewsbury Rd, Cars	181	S13
Shrewsbury St W10	107	U8
Shrewsbury St, Islw *1*	140	H6
Shrewton Rd SW17	163	U13
Shroffold Rd, Brom	169	K7
Shropshire Cl, Mitch	183	K8
Shropshire Pl WC1	17	R1
Shropshire Rd N22	59	L13
Shroton St NW1	15	R1
Shrubberies, The E18	79	P3
Shrubberies, The, Chig	65	L10
Shrubbery Cl, N1 *3*	111	U2
Shrubbery Gdns N21	43	S14
Shrubbery Rd N9	60	G6
Shrubbery Rd SW16	164	J2
Shrubbery Rd, Sthl	121	N1
Shrubland Gro, Wor Pk	193	T6
Shrubland Rd E8	112	F1
Shrubland Rd E10	78	B13
Shrubland Rd E17	78	A10
Shrublands Av, Croy	200	A7
Shrublands Cl N20	57	P2
Shrublands Cl, SE26 *6*	167	L6
Shrublands Cl, Chig	65	L11
Shrubsall Cl SE9	170	D1
Shurland Av, Barn	41	P12
Shurland Gdns, SE15 *2*	37	N14
Shurlock Dr, Orp	203	L7
Shuttle Cl, Sid	153	T14
Shuttle St E1	13	R12
Shuttlemead, Bex	155	L13
Shuttleworth Rd SW11	145	R3
Sibella Rd SW4	146	G4
Sibley Cl, Bexh	155	K10
Sibley Gro E12	98	D13
Sibthorpe Rd SE12	151	S13
Sibton Rd, Cars	181	R13
Sidbury St SW6	144	C1
Sidcup Bypass, Chis	171	P6
Sidcup Bypass, Orp	172	G14
Sidcup Bypass, Sid	172	A11
Sidcup High St, Sid	172	B7
Sidcup Hill, Sid	172	D9
Sidcup Hill Gdns, Sid	172	E10
Sidcup Pl, Sid	172	A9
Sidcup Rd SE9	151	U14
Sidcup Rd SE12	151	S10
Sidcup Technology Cen, Sid	172	G10
Siddeley Dr, Houns	138	J4
Siddons La NW1	8	A11
Siddons Rd N17	76	G2
Siddons Rd SE23	167	R4
Siddons Rd, Croy	197	P5
Side Rd E17	77	T9
Sidewood Rd SE9	171	N1
Sidford Pl SE1	26	H11
Sidings, The E11	96	F1
Sidings, The, Loug	48	C11
Sidings Ms N7	93	N7
Sidmouth Av, Islw	140	C3
Sidmouth Cl, Wat	50	C4
Sidmouth Dr, Ruis	84	A6
Sidmouth Rd E10	96	E5
Sidmouth Rd NW2	89	U14
Sidmouth Rd SE15	148	F1
Sidmouth Rd, Well	136	E14
Sidmouth St WC1	10	D8
Sidney Av N13	59	M10
Sidney Elson Way, E6 *3*	116	G4
Sidney Gdns, Brent	123	N11
Sidney Gro EC1	11	P4
Sidney Rd E7	97	P6
Sidney Rd N22	59	L13
Sidney Rd SE25	184	G9
Sidney Rd SW9	147	M4
Sidney Rd, Beck	185	R3
Sidney Rd, Har	67	U6
Sidney Rd, Twick	140	J12
Sidney Rd, Walt	174	B14
Sidney Sq E1	113	L10
Sidney St E1	113	L11
Sidworth St E8	95	K14
Siebert Rd SE3	133	P12
Siemens Rd SE18	134	B6
Sigdon Rd E8	94	H10
Sigers, The, Pnr	66	D11
Signmakers Yd, NW1 *9*	110	D2
Sigrist Sq, Kings T	177	S2
Silbury Av, Mitch	181	R2
Silbury St, N1 *3*	12	D6
Silchester Rd W10	108	B12
Silecroft Rd, Bexh	155	P2
Silesia Bldgs E8	95	K13
Silex St SE1	27	R7
Silk Cl SE12	151	N10
Silk Mills Path SE13	150	E4
Silk St EC2	20	B2
Silkfield Rd NW9	71	K9
Silkmills Sq E9	95	U11
Silkstream Rd, Edg	70	F2
Silsoe Rd N22	75	M4
Silver Birch Av E4	61	U11
Silver Birch Cl N11	58	A12
Silver Birch Cl SE28	136	A2
Silver Birch Gdns E6	116	E8
Silver Birch Ms, Ilf *2*	65	M12
Silver Cl SE14	131	R14

Silver Cl, Har	52	A13
Silver Cres W4	124	C8
Silver Jubilee Way, Houns	138	C4
Silver Pl, W1 *4*	17	P9
Silver Rd W12	108	A14
Silver Spring Cl, Erith	137	S11
Silver St N18	60	C8
Silver St, Enf	44	B6
Silver Wk SE16	131	T2
Silver Way, Rom	83	R6
Silverbirch Wk NW3	92	A12
Silvercliffe Gdns, Barn	41	R8
Silverdale SE26	167	M8
Silverdale, Enf	43	K8
Silverdale Av, Ilf *1*	81	T10
Silverdale Cl W7	122	D1
Silverdale Cl, Nthlt	85	L10
Silverdale Cl, Sutt	194	E7
Silverdale Dr SE9	170	C4
Silverdale Dr, Sun	174	C3
Silverdale Gdns, Hayes	120	B3
Silverdale Rd E4	62	G12
Silverdale Rd, Bexh	155	R4
Silverdale Rd, Hayes	120	A4
Silverdale Rd (Petts Wd), Orp	189	M8
Silverhall St, Islw	140	H5
Silverholme Cl, Har	69	P14
Silverland St E16	134	F2
Silverleigh Rd, Th Hth	183	L8
Silvermere Rd SE6	150	C12
Silverston Way, Stan	53	M12
Silverthorn Gdns E4	62	B3
Silverthorne Rd SW8	146	D3
Silverton Rd W6	126	A12
Silvertown Way E16	115	L11
Silvertree La, Grnf	104	A5
Silverwood Cl, Beck	168	A13
Silvester Rd SE22	148	F10
Silvester St SE1	28	B7
Silvocea Way E14	114	H12
Silwood Est SE16	131	M8
Silwood St SE16	131	M0
Simla Cl SE14	131	R12
Simmil Rd, Esher	190	C10
Simmons Cl N20	57	S2
Simmons Cl, Chess	191	M13
Simmons La E4	62	H4
Simmons Rd SE18	134	J9
Simmons Way N20	57	S3
Simms Cl, Cars	195	R4
Simms Rd SE1	37	T3
Simnel Rd SE12	151	R13
Simon Cl, W11 *11*	108	F13
Simonds Rd E10	96	B3
Simone Cl, Brom	188	B2
Simons Wk E15	96	H10
Simpson Cl, N21 *3*	43	K9
Simpson Dr W3	106	H11
Simpson Rd, Houns	139	M12
Simpson Rd, Rich	159	L7
Simpson St SW11	145	R3
Simpsons Rd E14	114	C14
Simpsons Rd, Brom *2*	187	P6
Simrose Ct, SW18 *5*	144	H10
Sims Wk SE3	151	L8
Sinclair Ct, Beck	168	B14
Sinclair Gdns W14	126	B4
Sinclair Gro NW11	72	B2
Sinclair Rd E4	61	S10
Sinclair Rd W14	126	C5
Sinclare Cl, Enf	44	F1
Singapore Rd W13	122	G1
Singer St EC2	12	F8
Singleton Cl SW17	163	T13
Singleton Cl, Croy *2*	183	T13
Singleton Rd, Dag	101	M10
Singleton Scarp N12	56	G9
Sinnott Rd E17	77	P1
Sion Rd, Twick	158	J1
Sir Alexander Cl W3	125	L1
Sir Alexander Rd W3	125	L1
Sir Cyril Black Way SW19	162	G13
Sir Thomas More Est SW3	31	M11
Sirdar Rd N22	75	S5
Sirdar Rd W11	108	B14
Sirdar Rd, Mitch	164	A12
Sirius Rd, Nthwd	50	A10
Sise La EC4	20	C8
Siskin Cl, Borwd	38	B7
Sisley Rd, Bark	117	T1
Sispara Gdns SW18	144	E11
Sissinghurst Rd, Croy *2*	184	H13
Sister Mabel's Way SE15	37	R14
Sisters Av SW11	145	U6
Sistova Rd SW12	164	D1
Sisulu Pl SW9	147	P5
Sittingbourne Av, Enf	44	B12
Sitwell Gro, Stan	52	E10
Siverst Cl, Nthlt	85	S12
Siviter Way, Dag	101	R13
Siward Rd N17	76	A2
Siward Rd SW17	163	L5
Siward Rd, Brom	187	S6
Six Acres Est N4	93	N4
Six Bridges Trd Est SE1	37	T8
Sixth Av E12	98	E8
Sixth Av W10	108	C6
Sixth Cross Rd, Twick	157	U6
Skardu Rd NW2	90	C9
Skeena Hill SW18	144	D14
Skeffington Rd E6	116	E1
Skelbrook St SW18	163	K3
Skelgill Rd SW15	144	E8
Skelley Rd E15	96	J4
Skelton Cl, E8 *13*	94	F12
Skelton Rd E7	97	P12
Skeltons La E10	78	D14
Skelwith Rd W6	125	U12
Skerne Rd, Kings T	177	R1
Sketchley Gdns SE16	131	N9
Sketty Rd, Enf	44	F6
Skiers St E15	114	J2
Skiffington Cl SW2	165	P1
Skinner Rd, E2 *16*	113	K3
Skinner Pl, SW1 *4*	32	D3
Skinner St EC1	11	M9
Skinners La EC4	20	B10
Skinners La, Houns	139	R1
Skinner's Row SE10	150	C1
Skipsey Av E6	116	F6
Skipton Cl, N11 *8*	58	A11
Skipworth Rd E9	113	M1
Sky Peals Rd, Wdf Grn	78	G1
Slade, The SE18	135	R12
Sladebrook Rd SE3	152	B5
Sladedale Rd SE18	135	R10
Slades Cl, Enf	43	N5
Slades Dr, Chis	171	L6
Slades Gdns, Enf	43	N5
Slades Hill, Enf	43	N5
Slades Ri, Enf	43	N5
Slagrove Pl SE13	150	C9
Slaidburn St SW10	30	G12
Slaithwaite Rd SE13	150	F8
Slaney Pl, N7 *4*	93	N9
Slater Cl, SE18 *5*	134	H9
Slattery Rd, Felt	156	F2
Sleaford Grn, Mat	50	G5
Sleaford St SW8	33	M14
Slievemore Cl, SW4 *2*	146	H6
Slingsby Pl, WC2 *4*	18	A9
Slippers Pl SE16	131	K5
Sloane Av SW3	31	S3
Sloane Ct E SW3	32	C5
Sloane Ct W SW3	32	C6
Sloane Gdns SW1	32	C3
Sloane Gdns, Orp *1*	203	L5
Sloane Sq SW1	32	B3
Sloane St SW1	32	B1
Sloane Ter SW1	32	C2
Sloane Wk, Croy	185	T11
Slocum Cl, SE28 *1*	118	E14
Slough La NW9	70	E10
Sly St, E1 *6*	112	J12
Smallberry Av, Islw	140	F3
Smallbrook Ms W2	14	J8
Smalley Cl N16	94	E4
Smallwood Rd SW17	163	N8
Smardale Rd, SW18 *1*	145	L9
Smarden Cl, Belv	137	N9
Smarden Gro, SE9 *1*	170	E7
Smart St E2	113	N5
Smarts La, Loug	48	C8
Smarts Pl N18	60	G10
Smart's Pl, WC2 *4*	18	C6
Smeaton Cl, Chess	191	M13
Smeaton Rd SW18	144	G14
Smeaton Rd, Wdf Grn	64	F10
Smeaton St E1	130	J1
Smedley St SW4	146	H3
Smedley St SW8	146	H3
Smeed Rd E3	96	A14
Smiles Pl SE13	150	E3
Smith Cl SE16	131	N2
Smith Sq SW1	26	A11
Smith St SW3	31	U7
Smith St, Surb	177	T12
Smith Ter SW3	31	T7
Smithfield St EC1	19	P4
Smithies Ct, E15 *4*	96	E9
Smithies Rd SE2	136	C7
Smith's Ct, W1 *4*	17	R10
Smiths Fm Est, Nthlt	103	P3
Smiths Yd, SW18 *1*	163	L3
Smith's Yd, Croy	197	U5
Smithson Rd N17	76	A1
Smithwood Cl SW19	162	C2
Smithy St E1	113	M9
Smock Wk, Croy	183	U12
Smokehouse Yd, EC1 *3*	19	R1
Smugglers Way SW18	145	K8
Smyrks Rd SE17	36	J7
Smyrna Rd NW6	90	G14
Smythe St E14	114	D13
Snakes La, Barn	42	E8
Snakes La E, Wdf Grn	63	T11
Snakes La W, Wdf Grn	63	N10
Snaresbrook Dr, Stan	53	P8
Snaresbrook Rd E11	78	J8
Snarsgate St W10	107	T10
Sneath Av NW11	72	E13
Snells Pk N18	60	F11
Sneyd Rd NW2	89	T8
Snow Hill EC1	19	N4
Snow Hill Ct, EC1 *1*	19	R5
Snowberry Cl E15	96	H8
Snowbury Rd, SW6 *10*	145	K4
Snowden St EC2	12	G12
Snowdon Dr NW9	70	J11
Snowdown Cl SE20	185	M2
Snowdrop Cl, Hmptn *3*	157	N11
Snowsfields SE1	28	E5
Snowshill Rd E12	98	C9
Snowy Fielder Waye, Islw	140	J4
Soames St SE15	148	E6
Soames Wk, N Mal	178	J2
Socket La, Brom	187	R12
Soho Sq W1	17	S6
Soho St W1	17	S6
Sojourner Truth Cl, E8 *8*	95	K12
Solander Gdns, E1 *1*	113	L13
Solebay St E1	113	R8
Solent Ri E13	115	N6
Solent Rd NW6	90	G10
Soley Ms WC1	10	J5
Solna Av SW15	143	T10
Solna Rd N21	44	A14
Solomon Av N9	60	G7
Solomon's Pas SE15	149	K7
Solon New Rd SW4	146	J7
Solon Rd SW2	147	K7
Solway Cl, E8 *12*	94	F12
Solway Cl, Houns	139	K5
Solway Rd N22	75	R1
Solway Rd SE22	148	G7
Somaford Gro, Barn	41	P11
Somali Rd NW2	90	E8
Somerby Rd, Bark	99	N13
Somercoates Cl, Barn	41	S6
Somerfield Rd N4	93	R4
Somerford Cl, Pnr	66	A8
Somerford Gro N16	94	E8
Somerford Gro, N17 *1*	60	H14
Somerford St E1	112	J8
Somerford Way SE16	131	R4
Somerhill Av, Sid	154	C14
Somerhill Rd, Well	154	D3
Somerleyton Pas, SW9 *14*	147	N8
Somerleyton Rd SW9	147	P7
Somers Cl, NW1 *3*	9	S2
Somers Cres W2	15	N7
Somers Ms W2	15	N7
Somers Pl SW2	147	L13
Somers Rd E17	77	U8
Somers Rd SW2	147	L12
Somersby Gdns, Ilf	80	E9
Somerset Av SW20	179	R3
Somerset Av, Chess	191	N7
Somerset Av, Well	153	U9
Somerset Cl N17	76	A3
Somerset Cl, N Mal	179	K11
Somerset Cl, Wdf Grn	79	P1
Somerset Est SW11	145	P1
Somerset Gdns N6	74	B14
Somerset Gdns N17	60	D13
Somerset Gdns SE13	150	C4
Somerset Gdns SW16	183	M5
Somerset Gdns, Tedd	158	D9
Somerset Rd E17	78	A10
Somerset Rd N17	76	F6
Somerset Rd N18	60	E9
Somerset Rd, NW4 *1*	71	T8
Somerset Rd SW19	162	C7
Somerset Rd W4	124	G5
Somerset Rd W13	123	K2
Somerset Rd, Barn	41	L9
Somerset Rd, Brent	123	M12
Somerset Rd, Har	67	T11
Somerset Rd, Kings T	177	U4
Somerset Rd, Sthl	103	M11
Somerset Rd, Tedd	158	D9
Somerset Sq W14	126	D4
Somerset Waye, Houns	120	J12
Somersham Rd, Bexh	155	K4
Somerton Av, Rich	142	C6
Somerton Rd NW2	90	C6
Somerton Rd SE15	149	K7
Somertrees Av SE12	169	R4
Somervell Rd, Har	85	L9
Somerville Av SW13	125	S12
Somerville Rd SE20	167	P13
Somerville Rd, Rom	82	F11

Sonderburg Rd N7	93	M4
Sondes St SE17	36	D9
Sonia Ct, Har	68	E13
Sonia Gdns N12	57	L7
Sonia Gdns NW10	89	L8
Sonia Gdns, Houns	121	N14
Sonning Gdns, Hmptn	157	K12
Sonning Rd SE25	184	G12
Soper Cl E4	61	U9
Sophia Rd E10	96	C1
Sophia Rd E16	115	R11
Sophia Sq, SE16 *6*	113	R14
Sopwith Av, Chess	191	S10
Sopwith Cl, Kings T	159	U9
Sopwith Rd, Houns	120	F13
Sopwith Way SW8	32	H13
Sopwith Way, Kings T	177	R2
Sorrel Cl SE28	136	B2
Sorrel Gdns E6	116	C9
Sorrel La, E14 *1*	114	H12
Sorrell Cl SE14	131	R13
Sorrento Rd, Sutt	194	H6
Sotheby Rd N5	93	T7
Sotheran Cl, E8 *4*	112	H1
Sotheron Rd, SW6 *14*	127	K14
Soudan Rd SW11	145	T2
Souldern Rd, W14 *6*	126	B6
South Access Rd E17	77	R13
South Acre NW9	71	L3
South Africa Rd W12	107	S14
South Audley St W1	16	E11
South Av E4	46	D13
South Av, Cars	196	A14
South Av, Rich	142	A3
South Av, Sthl	103	L14
South Av Gdns, Sthl	103	L14
South Bank, Chis	171	K6
South Bank, Surb	177	R11
South Bank Ter, Surb	177	S12
South Birkbeck Rd E11	96	H6
South Black Lion La, W6 *6*	125	N9
South Bolton Gdns SW5	30	D6
South Carriage Dr SW1	24	C6
South Carriage Dr SW7	23	M7
South Cl N6	74	C11
South Cl, Barn	40	E6
South Cl, Bexh	154	G8
South Cl, Dag	119	P2
South Cl, Pnr	67	M14
South Cl, Twick	157	P5
South Colonnade E14	132	B1
South Countess Rd E17	77	T5
South Cres E16	114	G8
South Cres WC1	17	S3
South Cross Rd, Ilf	81	L9
South Croxted Rd SE21	166	B6
South Dene NW7	54	H6
South Dr, Orp	203	S9
South Ealing Rd W5	123	N7
South Eastern Av N9	60	E5
South Eaton Pl SW1	32	E2
South Eden Pk Rd, Beck	186	C11
South Edwardes Sq W8	126	G6
South End W8	22	B9
South End, Croy	197	U7
South End Cl NW3	91	S8
South End Grn, NW3 *3*	91	S8
South End Rd NW3	91	R7
South End Row W8	22	C10
South Esk Rd E7	97	U12

South Gipsy Rd, Well	154	G5
South Glade, The, Bex	173	L1
South Gro E17	77	T10
South Gro N6	92	B1
South Gro N15	76	B10
South Hill, Chis	170	E12
South Hill Av, Har	86	C6
South Hill Gro, Har	86	D7
South Hill Pk NW3	91	R8
South Hill Pk Gdns NW3	91	S7
South Hill Rd, Brom	186	J7
South Huxley N18	60	A10
South Island Pl SW9	129	M14
South Lambeth Pl SW8	34	D9
South Lambeth Rd SW8	34	C12
South La, Kings T	177	P5
South La, N Mal	178	G8
South La W, N Mal	178	G7
South Lo Av, Mitch	182	J7
South Lo Cres, Enf	42	H7
South Lo Dr N14	42	J10
South Mead NW9	71	M2
South Mead, Epsom	193	K13
South Meadows, Wem	87	T9
South Molton La W1	16	G8
South Molton Rd E16	115	P11
South Molton St W1	16	G8
South Norwood Hill SE25	184	D4
South Oak Rd SW16	165	M7
South Par SW3	31	L6
South Par W4	124	G7
South Pk SW6	144	H4
South Pk Cres SE6	169	L1
South Pk Cres, Ilf	99	P5
South Pk Dr, Bark	99	R9
South Pk Dr, Ilf	99	R4
South Pk Gro, N Mal	178	E8
South Pk Hill Rd, S Croy	198	B9
South Pk Ms SW6	144	J5
South Pk Rd SW19	163	K12
South Pk Rd, Ilf	99	P5
South Pk Ter, Ilf	99	R6
South Pk Way, Ruis	84	F11
South Penge Pk Est SE20	184	J3
South Pl EC2	20	E3
South Pl, Enf	45	M9
South Pl, Surb	177	T13
South Pl Ms, EC2 *1*	20	E3
South Ri Way SE18	135	N9
South Rd N9	60	H1
South Rd SE23	167	N3
South Rd SW19	163	M12
South Rd W5	123	P7
South Rd, Edg	70	D1
South Rd, Felt	156	H10
South Rd, Hmptn	157	K12
South Rd (Chadwell Heath), Rom *1*	82	E10
South Rd (Little Heath), Rom	82	J11
South Rd, Sthl	121	L3
South Rd, Twick	158	B6
South Row SE3	151	M3
South Sea St SE16	131	T5
South Side W6	125	L6
South Sq NW11	72	H11
South Sq WC1	18	J3
South St W1	24	E1
South St, Brom	187	P3
South St, Enf	45	N10
South St, Islw	140	G5
South St, Rain	119	U4
South Tenter St E1	21	P9
South Ter SW7	31	N1
South Ter, Surb	177	S11
South Vale SE19	166	C12
South Vale, Har	86	D7

South Vw, Brom	187	S3
South Vw Dr E18	79	S6
South Vw Rd N8	74	H6
South Vw Rd, Loug	48	F11
South Vw Rd, Pnr	50	D12
South Vil NW1	92	H12
South Wk, W Wick	200	J6
South Way N9	61	M3
South Way, N11 *1*	58	E12
South Way, Brom	187	N13
South Way, Croy	199	S6
South Way, Har	67	P8
South Way, Wem	87	U9
South W India Dock Entrance E14	132	F3
South Western Rd, Twick	140	H11
South Wf Rd W2	15	L5
South Woodford to Barking Relief Rd E11	80	C13
South Woodford to Barking Relief Rd E12	98	G5
South Woodford to Barking Relief Rd E18	80	C13
South Woodford to Barking Relief Rd, Bark	116	J1
South Woodford to Barking Relief Rd, Ilf	80	C13
South Worple Av, SW14 *3*	143	K6
South Worple Way SW14	142	J6
Southacre Way, Pnr	66	E1
Southall La, Houns	120	D11
Southall La, Sthl	120	E8
Southall Pl SE1	28	D7
Southam St W10	108	D8
Southampton Bldgs WC2	18	J4
Southampton Gdns, Mitch *3*	182	J9
Southampton Ms E16	133	R1
Southampton Pl WC1	18	D4
Southampton Rd NW5	91	U10
Southampton Row WC1	18	C1
Southampton St WC2	18	C10
Southampton Way SE5	36	F14
Southbank, T Ditt	176	J13
Southborough Cl, Surb	191	P1
Southborough La, Brom	188	F10
Southborough Rd E9	113	M1
Southborough Rd, Brom	188	D6
Southborough Rd, Surb	191	R1
Southbourne, Brom	187	N14
Southbourne Av NW9	70	F4
Southbourne Cl, Pnr	67	K13
Southbourne Cres NW4	72	C7
Southbourne Gdns SE12	151	R9
Southbourne Gdns, Ilf	99	L10
Southbourne Gdns, Ruis	84	C2
Southbridge Pl, Croy	197	T7
Southbridge Rd, Croy	197	T7
Southbridge Way, Sthl	121	K4
Southbrook Ms SE12	151	M11
Southbrook Rd SE12	151	L11
Southbrook Rd SW16	183	K1

Southbury Av, Enf	44	G8
Southbury Rd, Enf	44	C6
Southchurch Rd E6	116	F4
Southcombe St, W14 *3*	126	C7
Southcote Av, Surb	178	C14
Southcote Rd E17	77	P9
Southcote Rd N19	92	E7
Southcote Rd SE25	185	K11
Southcroft Av, Well	153	S5
Southcroft Av, W Wick	200	E4
Southcroft Rd SW16	164	C12
Southcroft Rd SW17	164	A11
Southcroft Rd, Orp	203	S5
Southdale, Chig	65	P11
Southdean Gdns SW19	162	E3
Southdown Av W7	122	G6
Southdown Cres, Har	85	S2
Southdown Cres, Ilf	81	R9
Southdown Dr SW20	162	A14
Southdown Rd SW20	180	B2
Southend Cl SE9	152	J11
Southend Cres SE9	152	J12
Southend La SE6	167	U8
Southend La SE26	167	U8
Southend Rd E4	61	T12
Southend Rd E6	98	E13
Southend Rd E17	78	D1
Southend Rd E18	79	N2
Southend Rd, Beck	168	B13
Southend Rd, Wdf Grn	80	A4
Southern Av SE25	184	F6
Southern Av, Felt	156	A1
Southern Dr, Loug	48	E12
Southern Gro E3	113	T7
Southern Rd E13	115	S4
Southern Rd N2	73	T7
Southern Row W10	108	C8
Southern St N1	10	F2
Southern Way, Rom	83	P11
Southerngate Way SE14	131	R13
Southernhay, Loug	48	A9
Southerton Rd W6	125	T6
Southey Ms, E16 *12*	133	R1
Southey Rd N15	76	C9
Southey Rd SW9	147	N1
Southey Rd SW19	162	H13
Southey St SE20	167	N13
Southfield, Barn	40	A12
Southfield Cotts W7	122	F4
Southfield Gdns, Twick	158	E7
Southfield Pk, Har	67	R8
Southfield Rd N17	76	D4
Southfield Rd W4	124	J5
Southfield Rd, Enf	45	K11
Southfields NW4	71	P4
Southfields, E Mol	176	C11
Southfields Ct SW19	162	D2
Southfields Pas, SW18 *13*	144	G12
Southfields Rd SW18	144	G11
Southfleet Rd, Orp	203	S7
Southgate Circ N14	58	G1
Southgate Gro N1	94	B14
Southgate Rd N1	94	B13
Southholme Cl, SE19 *2*	184	D1
Southill La, Pnr	66	C8
Southill Rd, Chis	170	E13
Southill St E14	114	D12
Southland Rd SE18	135	U13
Southland Way, Houns	140	A9
Southlands Av, Orp	203	R8
Southlands Dr SW19	162	A4
Southlands Gro, Brom	188	C6
Southlands Rd, Brom	188	A8
Southly Cl, Sutt	194	G6

Name	Page	Ref
Southmead Rd SW19	162	C1
Southmont Rd, Esher	190	D4
Southmoor Way E9	95	U11
Southold Ri SE9	170	F6
Southolm St SW11	146	C2
Southover N12	56	H7
Southover, Brom	169	N10
Southport Rd SE18	135	P8
Southridge Pl SW20	162	A14
Southsea Rd, Kings T	177	R7
Southside Common SW19	161	U12
Southspring, Sid	153	P14
Southvale Rd SE3	151	K4
Southview Cl SW17	164	A10
Southview Cl, Bex	155	L12
Southview Cres, Ilf	80	J12
Southview Gdns, Wall	196	F14
Southview Rd, Brom	168	H7
Southville SW8	146	H1
Southville Rd, T Ditt	176	J14
Southwark Br EC4	20	A12
Southwark Br SE1	20	A12
Southwark Br Rd SE1	27	S8
Southwark Gro SE1	27	T3
Southwark Pk Est SE16	131	K7
Southwark Pk Rd SE16	37	R2
Southwark Pl, Brom	188	E6
Southwark St SE1	27	R2
Southwater Cl E14	113	T11
Southwater Cl, Beck	168	C13
Southway N20	56	H4
Southway NW11	72	J11
Southway SW20	180	A8
Southway, Wall	196	F8
Southwell Av, Nthlt	85	P11
Southwell Gdns SW7	22	F12
Southwell Gro Rd E11	96	J4
Southwell Rd SE5	147	T5
Southwell Rd, Croy	183	N12
Southwell Rd, Har	69	P11
Southwest Rd E11	96	H1
Southwick Ms W2	15	M6
Southwick Pl W2	15	N8
Southwick St W2	15	N6
Southwold Dr, Bark	100	A9
Southwold Rd E5	95	L4
Southwold Rd, Bex	155	R12
Southwood Av N6	74	C13
Southwood Av, Kings T	178	F1
Southwood Cl, Brom	188	F7
Southwood Cl, Wor Pk	194	A2
Southwood Dr, Surb	178	F14
Southwood Gdns, Esher	190	G6
Southwood Gdns, Ilf	80	J8
Southwood La N6	74	B13
Southwood Lawn Rd N6	74	C13
Southwood Rd SE9	171	K3
Southwood Rd SE28	136	C2
Sovereign Cl E1	113	K14
Sovereign Cl W5	105	L9
Sovereign Ct, Brom	188	E11
Sovereign Ct, W Mol	175	M7
Sovereign Cres SE16	113	R14
Sovereign Gro, Wem	87	N6
Sovereign Ms E2	13	L2
Sovereign Pk NW10	106	D7
Sovereign Rd, Bark	118	E5
Sowerby Cl SE9	152	D10
Spa Cl SE25	184	C2
Spa Grn Est EC1	11	N6
Spa Hill SE19	184	A1
Spa Rd SE16	29	S10
Space Waye, Felt	138	B9
Spafield St, EC1 1	11	K9
Spalding Rd NW4	71	U12
Spalding Rd SW17	164	C10
Spanby Rd E3	114	B8
Spaniards Cl NW11	91	M1
Spaniards End NW3	91	N1
Spaniards Rd NW3	91	M4
Spanish Pl W1	16	E5
Spanish Rd SW18	145	M9
Spareleaze Hill, Loug	48	E8
Sparkbridge Rd, Har	68	D8
Sparks Cl W3	106	G12
Sparks Cl, Dag	100	H3
Sparks Cl, Hmptn	157	K11
Sparrow Cl, Hmptn	156	J11
Sparrow Dr, Orp	203	M1
Sparrow Fm Dr, Felt	138	F14
Sparrow Fm Rd, Epsom	193	R8
Sparrow Grn, Dag	101	R5
Sparrows La SE9	153	M14
Sparsholt Rd N19	93	L1
Sparsholt Rd, Bark	117	R2
Sparta St SE10	150	D2
Spear Ms SW5	126	H8
Spearman St SE18	134	H12
Spearpoint Gdns, Ilf	81	T8
Spears Rd N19	92	J2
Speart La, Houns	120	J14
Spedan Cl NW3	91	K6
Speedwell St, SE8 14	132	A14
Speedy Pl WC1	10	B7
Speer Rd, T Ditt	176	E11
Speirs Cl, N Mal	179	M11
Speke Rd, Th Hth	184	A4
Spekehill SE9	170	F6
Speldhurst Cl, Brom	187	N10
Speldhurst Rd E9	95	N14
Speldhurst Rd W4	124	H5
Spelman St E1	21	R3
Spence Cl, SE16 5	131	T4
Spencer Av N13	59	L12
Spencer Av, Hayes	102	A10
Spencer Cl N3	72	G3
Spencer Cl NW10	105	U5
Spencer Cl, Orp	203	S4
Spencer Cl, Wdf Grn	63	U10
Spencer Dr N2	73	M11
Spencer Gdns SE9	152	E9
Spencer Gdns SW14	142	E9
Spencer Hill SW19	162	C12
Spencer Hill Rd SW19	162	D13
Spencer Ms, SW8 2	147	L2
Spencer Ms W6	126	C11
Spencer Pk SW18	145	P10
Spencer Pl, Croy	188	B13
Spencer Ri NW5	92	D7
Spencer Rd E6	116	B1
Spencer Rd E17	78	E2
Spencer Rd N8	75	L9
Spencer Rd N11	58	C7
Spencer Rd N17	76	H2
Spencer Rd SW18	145	P8
Spencer Rd SW20	179	S2
Spencer Rd W3	124	F1
Spencer Rd W4	124	F14
Spencer Rd, Brom	169	K14
Spencer Rd, E Mol	175	U9
Spencer Rd, Har	68	D4
Spencer Rd, Ilf	99	U1
Spencer Rd, Islw	140	A1
Spencer Rd, Mitch	182	B5
Spencer Rd (Beddington Cor), Mitch	182	A14
Spencer Rd, S Croy	198	D9
Spencer Rd, Twick	158	D5
Spencer Rd, Wem	87	L3
Spencer St EC1	11	P7
Spencer St, Sthl	120	G4
Spencer Wk SW15	144	A7
Spenser Gro N16	94	C8
Spenser Rd SE24	147	R10
Spenser St SW1	25	N10
Spensley Wk N16	94	B5
Speranza St SE18	135	T9
Sperling Rd N17	76	D4
Spert St, E14 2	113	R13
Spey St E14	114	E10
Speydale N14	42	E12
Spezia Rd NW10	107	N3
Spicer Cl SW9	147	S3
Spicer Cl, Walt	174	E11
Spice's Yd, Croy 4	197	U7
Spigurnell Rd N17	76	A2
Spikes Br Rd, Sthl	103	K12
Spilsby Cl NW9	71	K3
Spindle Cl SE18	134	D6
Spindlewood Gdns, Croy	198	C7
Spindrift Av E14	132	B8
Spinel Cl SE18	135	U10
Spinnells Rd, Har	85	L1
Spinney, The N21	43	N13
Spinney, The SW16	164	G5
Spinney, The, Barn	41	K4
Spinney, The, Sid	172	J9
Spinney, The, Stan	53	S8
Spinney, The, Sun	174	B1
Spinney, The, Sutt	193	U8
Spinney, The, Wem	86	G6
Spinney Cl, N Mal	178	J9
Spinney Dr, Felt	138	J9
Spinney Gdns SE19	166	E10
Spinney Gdns, Dag	101	K9
Spinney Oak, Brom	188	D3
Spinneys, The, Brom	188	E3
Spital Sq E1	21	K1
Spital St E1	21	R1
Spital Yd, E1 1	21	K1
Spitfire Est, Houns	120	E10
Spitfire Way, Houns	120	E9
Spode Wk, NW6 2	91	K10
Spondon Rd N15	76	G8
Spoonbill Way, Hayes	102	H10
Spooner Wk, Wall	196	H9
Sportsbank St SE6	150	E14
Spottons Gro N17	75	T1
Spout Hill, Croy	200	A9
Spratt Hall Rd E11	79	P11
Spray La, Twick	140	C11
Spray St SE18	135	K7
Spreighton Rd, W Mol	175	S8
Sprimont Pl SW3	31	T5
Spring Br Ms, W5 2	105	N13
Spring Br Rd W5	105	N13
Spring Cl, Barn	40	A9
Spring Cl, Borwd	38	B2
Spring Cl, Dag	100	H1
Spring Cl La, Sutt 6	194	D11
Spring Dr, Pnr	66	B11
Spring Gdns SW1	25	A2
Spring Gdns, Rom	83	T11
Spring Gdns, Wall 1	196	E10
Spring Gdns, W Mol	175	T9
Spring Gdns, Wdf Grn	63	T13
Spring Gdns Ind Est, Rom	83	T11
Spring Gro, SE19 9	166	E13
Spring Gro W4	124	A10
Spring Gro, Hmptn	175	R2
Spring Gro, Loug	48	B11
Spring Gro, Mitch	182	B2
Spring Gro Cres, Houns	139	T1
Spring Gro Rd, Houns	139	S2
Spring Gro Rd, Islw	140	C2
Spring Gro Rd, Rich	141	T9
Spring Hill E5	76	H14
Spring Hill SE26	167	M8
Spring Lake, Stan	52	J7
Spring La E5	95	K1
Spring La N10	74	A5
Spring La SE25	184	J12
Spring Ms W1	16	B2
Spring Pk Av, Croy	199	P4
Spring Pk Dr N4	93	T1
Spring Pk Rd, Croy	199	P4
Spring Pas SW15	144	A5
Spring Path NW3	91	N9
Spring Pl NW5	92	C10
Spring St W2	15	K8
Spring Ter, Rich	141	R9
Spring Vale, Bexh	155	S7
Spring Vil Rd, Edg	54	A13
Spring Wk E1	21	S2
Springall St SE15	131	K14
Springbank N21	43	L12
Springbank Rd SE13	150	J12
Springbourne Ct, Beck	186	F1
Springcroft Av N2	73	T7
Springdale Rd N16	94	A8
Springfield E5	94	J1
Springfield, Bushey	52	A1
Springfield Av N10	74	E6
Springfield Av SW20	180	E5
Springfield Av, Hmptn	157	R11
Springfield Cl N12	56	J10
Springfield Cl, Stan	52	H5
Springfield Dr, Ilf	81	M12
Springfield Gdns E5	95	K2
Springfield Gdns NW9	70	H9
Springfield Gdns, Brom	188	F8
Springfield Gdns, Ruis	84	D2
Springfield Gdns, W Wick	200	D3
Springfield Gdns, Wdf Grn	63	U13
Springfield Gro SE7	133	T12
Springfield La NW6	108	H2
Springfield Mt NW9	70	J9
Springfield Pl, N Mal	178	E7
Springfield Ri SE26	166	J6
Springfield Rd E4	62	J1
Springfield Rd E6	98	F13
Springfield Rd E15	115	K5
Springfield Rd E17	77	T11
Springfield Rd N11	58	D10
Springfield Rd N15	76	G7
Springfield Rd NW8	109	L2
Springfield Rd SE26	167	K10
Springfield Rd SW19	162	F10
Springfield Rd W7	122	D1
Springfield Rd, Bexh	155	S6
Springfield Rd, Brom	188	E8
Springfield Rd, Har	68	C11
Springfield Rd, Hayes	102	F14
Springfield Rd, Kings T	177	S6
Springfield Rd, Tedd	158	G10
Springfield Rd, Th Hth	183	T1
Springfield Rd, Twick	157	P1
Springfield Rd, Wall	196	C10
Springfield Rd, Well	154	C5
Springfield Wk NW6	108	J2
Springhill Cl SE5	148	B6
Springhurst Cl, Croy	199	T7
Springpark Dr, Beck	186	F5
Springpond Rd, Dag	101	K9
Springrice Rd SE13	150	F11
Springvale Av, Brent	123	P9
Springvale Est W14	126	B6
Springvale Ter W14	126	B6
Springwater Cl SE18	152	G2
Springway, Har	68	A13
Springwell Av NW10	107	M2
Springwell Cl SW16	165	M8
Springwell Ct, Houns 2	138	H3
Springwell Rd SW16	165	N8
Springwell Rd, Houns	138	H1
Springwood Cres, Edg	54	D3

Name	Page	Grid
Sprowston Ms E7	97	N11
Sprowston Rd E7	97	P10
Spruce Ct W5	123	S5
Spruce Hills Rd E17	78	D4
Sprucedale Gdns, Croy	199	P7
Sprules Rd SE4	149	R4
Spur Rd N15	76	A7
Spur Rd SE1	27	K6
Spur Rd SW1	25	M7
Spur Rd, Bark	117	L4
Spur Rd, Edg	53	S7
Spur Rd, Felt	138	D9
Spur Rd, Islw	122	J14
Spur Rd Est, Edg	53	T7
Spurfield, W Mol	175	R6
Spurgeon Av SE19	184	A1
Spurgeon Rd SE19	184	A1
Spurgeon St SE1	28	C11
Spurling Rd SE22	148	F8
Spurling Rd, Dag	101	M11
Spurstowe Rd E8	94	J10
Spurstowe Ter, E8 3	94	J10
Square, The W6	125	U10
Square, The, Cars	196	A9
Square, The, Ilf	80	G14
Square, The, Rich	141	P9
Square, The, Wdf Grn	63	M10
Square Rigger Row, SW11 4	145	M5
Squarey St SW17	163	M6
Squires Ct SW19	162	G7
Squires La N3	73	M1
Squires Mt NW3	91	N6
Squires Wd Dr, Chis	170	E14
Squirrel Cl, Houns	138	F4
Squirrel Ms W13	104	F14
Squirrels, The SE13	150	G6
Squirrels, The, Pnr	67	M6
Squirrels Cl N12	57	L7
Squirrels Grn, Wor Pk	193	M3
Squirrels La, Buck H	64	B6
Squirries St E2	13	T6
Stable Cl, Nthlt	103	N3
Stable Way, W10 3	107	U12
Stable Yd SW1	25	M5
Stable Yd SW9	147	M4
Stable Yd, SW15 1	143	U5
Stable Yd Rd SW1	25	N4
Stables, The, Buck H	47	U14
Stables End, Orp	203	M6
Stables Ms SE27	165	U10
Stables Way SE11	35	K6
Stacey Av N18	61	L8
Stacey Cl E10	78	G10
Stacey St N7	93	N6
Stacey St WC2	17	U7
Stackhouse St, SW3 1	23	U9
Stadium Rd NW2	71	T14
Stadium Rd SE18	134	E13
Stadium St SW10	127	M14
Stadium Way, Wem	87	U8
Staff St EC1	12	E8
Staffa Rd E10	95	R1
Stafford Cl E17	77	U12
Stafford Cl N14	42	E10
Stafford Cl NW6	108	G6
Stafford Cl, Sutt	194	D11
Stafford Ct W8	126	G5
Stafford Cross, Croy	197	M9
Stafford Gdns, Croy	197	M9
Stafford Pl SW1	25	L9
Stafford Pl, Rich	141	T13
Stafford Rd E3	113	T4
Stafford Rd E7	98	A12
Stafford Rd NW6	108	G5
Stafford Rd, Croy	197	N8
Stafford Rd, Har	67	U1
Stafford Rd, N Mal	178	E5
Stafford Rd, Sid	171	S7
Stafford Rd, Wall	196	E12
Stafford St, W1 1	25	L1
Stafford Ter W8	126	G5

Name	Page	Grid
Staffordshire St SE15	148	H1
Stag Cl, Edg	70	E3
Stag La NW9	70	E8
Stag La SW15	161	M4
Stag La, Buck H	63	R3
Stag La, Edg	70	D4
Stag Pl SW1	25	M10
Staggart Grn, Chig	65	U11
Stags Way, Islw	122	E12
Stainbank Rd, Mitch	182	C5
Stainby Rd N15	76	F7
Stainer St SE1	28	F4
Staines Av, Sutt	194	B4
Staines Rd, Houns	139	P6
Staines Rd, Ilf	99	M9
Staines Rd, Twick	157	R5
Staines Rd E, Sun	174	E2
Staines Wk, Sid	172	F11
Stainforth Rd E17	78	B8
Stainforth Rd, Ilf	81	P13
Staining La EC2	20	A5
Stainmore Cl, Chis	189	P1
Stainsbury St, E2 5	113	M4
Stainsby Pl E14	114	A11
Stainsby Rd E14	114	A11
Stainton Rd SE6	150	G13
Stainton Rd, Enf	45	M1
Stalbridge St NW1	15	R1
Stalham St SE16	131	K6
Stambourne Way SE19	166	D14
Stambourne Way, W Wick	200	F5
Stamford Brook Av W6	125	M6
Stamford Brook Rd W6	125	L6
Stamford Cl N15	76	G8
Stamford Cl, Har	52	D13
Stamford Cl, Sthl	103	N14
Stamford Ct W6	125	M7
Stamford Dr, Brom	187	M8
Stamford Gdns, Dag	100	E14
Stamford Gro E N16	94	G1
Stamford Gro W N16	94	G1
Stamford Hill N16	94	E1
Stamford Hill Est N16	94	E1
Stamford Rd E6	116	C1
Stamford Rd N1	94	D13
Stamford Rd N15	76	G9
Stamford Rd, Dag	100	D14
Stamford St SE1	27	L2
Stamp Pl E2	13	M5
Stanard Cl N16	76	D13
Stanborough Cl, Hmptn 1	157	L11
Stanborough Rd, Houns	140	B5
Stanbridge Pl N21	59	S3
Stanbridge Rd SW15	143	U5
Stanbrook Rd SE2	136	C4
Stanbury Rd SE15	149	K2
Stancroft NW9	70	J8
Standard Ind Est E16	134	F3
Standard Pl EC2	12	J7
Standard Rd NW10	106	F7
Standard Rd, Belv	137	N10
Standard Rd, Bexh	155	K8
Standard Rd, Houns	139	K6
Standen Rd SW18	144	F14
Standfield Rd, Dag	101	P10
Standish Rd W6	125	N8
Stane Cl SW19	163	K14
Stane Way SE18	134	C14
Stanfield Rd, E3 8	113	S4
Stanford Cl, Hmptn	157	M11
Stanford Cl, Rom	83	R11
Stanford Cl, Wdf Grn	64	D10
Stanford Pl SE17	36	H3
Stanford Rd N11	57	U9
Stanford Rd SW16	182	G3
Stanford Rd W8	22	C10
Stanford St SW1	33	R3
Stanford Way SW16	182	G4

Name	Page	Grid
Stangate Cres, Borwd	38	J9
Stangate Gdns, Stan	53	K8
Stanger Rd SE25	184	H8
Stanhope Av N3	72	F5
Stanhope Av, Brom	201	M1
Stanhope Av, Har	68	A2
Stanhope Gdns N4	75	S11
Stanhope Gdns N6	74	E12
Stanhope Gdns NW7	55	L10
Stanhope Gdns SW7	30	H1
Stanhope Gdns, Dag	101	L5
Stanhope Gdns, Ilf	98	E2
Stanhope Gate W1	24	F2
Stanhope Gro, Beck	185	U9
Stanhope Ms E SW7	30	H1
Stanhope Ms S SW7	30	G3
Stanhope Ms W SW7	30	G1
Stanhope Par NW1	9	L5
Stanhope Pk Rd, Grnf	103	U7
Stanhope Pl W2	15	T8
Stanhope Rd E17	78	C9
Stanhope Rd N6	74	E12
Stanhope Rd N12	57	M10
Stanhope Rd, Barn	40	A11
Stanhope Rd, Bexh	155	K3
Stanhope Rd, Cars	196	A14
Stanhope Rd, Croy	198	C6
Stanhope Rd, Dag	101	L4
Stanhope Rd, Grnf	103	U9
Stanhope Rd, Sid	172	A7
Stanhope Row, W1 4	24	G3
Stanhope St NW1	9	L7
Stanhope Ter W2	15	L10
Stanier Cl W14	126	F10
Stanlake Ms W12	125	T2
Stanlake Rd W12	125	T2
Stanlake Vil W12	125	T2
Stanley Av, Bark	117	T4
Stanley Av, Beck	186	F5
Stanley Av, Dag	101	M1
Stanley Av, Grnf	103	T2
Stanley Av, N Mal	179	N9
Stanley Av, Wem	87	S14
Stanley Cl SW8	34	E12
Stanley Cl, Wem	87	R14
Stanley Cres W11	108	E13
Stanley Gdns NW2	89	U10
Stanley Gdns W3	124	J2
Stanley Gdns W11	108	F13
Stanley Gdns, Mitch	164	A12
Stanley Gdns, Wall	196	E12
Stanley Gdns Ms, W11 6	108	F13
Stanley Gdns Rd, Tedd	158	C9
Stanley Gro SW8	146	B4
Stanley Gro, Croy	183	N12
Stanley Pk Dr, Wem	87	T14
Stanley Pk Rd, Cars	196	A13
Stanley Pk Rd, Wall	196	C12
Stanley Pas NW1	10	A3
Stanley Rd E4	62	H1
Stanley Rd E10	78	C12
Stanley Rd E12	98	C10
Stanley Rd E15	114	G2
Stanley Rd E18	79	M2
Stanley Rd N2	73	P6
Stanley Rd N9	60	E2
Stanley Rd N10	58	C14
Stanley Rd N11	58	G10
Stanley Rd N15	75	S8
Stanley Rd, NW9 2	71	N13
Stanley Rd SW14	142	C8
Stanley Rd SW19	162	H13
Stanley Rd W3	124	E5
Stanley Rd, Brom	187	T7
Stanley Rd, Cars	196	A14
Stanley Rd, Croy	183	N13
Stanley Rd, Enf	44	D6
Stanley Rd, Har	85	T4
Stanley Rd, Houns	139	T7
Stanley Rd, Ilf	99	N4
Stanley Rd, Mitch	164	A13
Stanley Rd, Mord	180	H7

Name	Page	Grid
Stanley Rd, Nthwd	66	B2
Stanley Rd, Sid	172	B6
Stanley Rd, Sthl	102	J14
Stanley Rd, Sutt	194	J13
Stanley Rd, Tedd	158	D10
Stanley Rd, Twick	158	B6
Stanley Rd, Wem 1	87	U11
Stanley St SE8	131	U14
Stanley Ter N19	92	J4
Stanleycroft Cl, Islw	140	C2
Stanmer St SW11	145	S3
Stanmore Gdns, Rich	141	U6
Stanmore Gdns, Sutt	195	L6
Stanmore Hall, Stan	52	J6
Stanmore Hill, Stan	53	K8
Stanmore Pk, Stan	52	J11
Stanmore Rd E11	97	L1
Stanmore Rd N15	75	S7
Stanmore Rd, Belv	137	U7
Stanmore Rd, Rich	141	T5
Stanmore St N1	111	L1
Stanmore Ter, Beck 3	186	B3
Stanmore Way, Loug	48	G1
Stannard Ms, E8 3	94	G11
Stannard Rd E8	94	G11
Stannary Pl SE11	35	L8
Stannary St SE11	35	L9
Stannet Way, Wall	196	E7
Stannington Path, Borwd 1	38	A1
Stansfeld Rd E6	116	B10
Stansfield Rd SW9	147	M5
Stansfield Rd, Houns	138	D4
Stansgate Rd, Dag	101	N4
Stanstead Cl, Brom	187	M11
Stanstead Gro, SE6 2	167	U1
Stanstead Manor, Sutt	194	H11
Stanstead Rd E11	79	R9
Stanstead Rd SE6	167	U1
Stanstead Rd SE23	167	N1
Stansted Cres, Bex	172	G2
Stanswood Gdns, SE5	130	D14
Stanthorpe Cl SW16	164	J9
Stanthorpe Rd SW16	164	J9
Stanton Av, Tedd	158	C11
Stanton Cl, Epsom	192	C10
Stanton Cl, Wor Pk	194	A2
Stanton Rd, SE26 1	167	T8
Stanton Rd SW13	143	L2
Stanton Rd SW20	180	A2
Stanton Rd, Croy	183	T14
Stanton Sq SE26	167	T7
Stanton Way SE26	167	T7
Stanway Cl, Chig	65	S9
Stanway Gdns, Edg	54	E11
Stanway St N1	12	J3
Stanwick Rd W14	126	E8
Stanworth St SE1	29	M8
Stanwyck Dr, Chig	65	M9
Stapenhill Rd, Wem	86	J5
Staple Inn Bldgs, WC1 1	18	J4
Staple St SE1	28	E8
Staplefield Cl SW2	165	K1
Staplefield Cl, Pnr	50	J13
Stapleford Av, Ilf	81	S10
Stapleford Cl E4	62	E6
Stapleford Cl SW19	144	C14
Stapleford Cl, Kings T	178	B4
Stapleford Rd, Wem	87	N13
Stapleford Way, Bark	118	D5
Staplehurst Rd SE13	150	J10
Staplehurst Rd, Cars	195	R14
Staples Cl SE16	131	R1
Staples Cor NW2	89	S2

Name	Page	Grid
Staples Cor Business Pk NW2	89	R2
Staples Rd, Loug	48	C6
Stapleton Gdns, Croy	197	P9
Stapleton Hall Rd N4	75	M14
Stapleton Rd SW17	164	A5
Stapleton Rd, Bexh	137	M13
Stapleton Rd, Orp	203	T6
Stapley Rd, Belv	137	N10
Stapylton Rd, Barn	40	C6
Star & Garter Hill, Rich	159	S1
Star La E16	114	J8
Star Pl E1	21	R12
Star Rd W14	126	E11
Star Rd, Islw	140	B4
Star St E16	115	M9
Star St W2	15	N5
Star Yd WC2	18	J6
Starboard Way E14	132	B5
Starch Ho La, Ilf	81	N3
Starcross St NW1	9	N8
Starfield Rd W12	125	N4
Starling Cl, Buck H	63	P2
Starling Cl, Pnr	66	F5
Starling Ms SE28	135	P4
Starmans Cl, Dag	119	K1
Starts Cl, Orp	202	H10
Starts Hill Av, Orp	203	K9
Starts Hill Rd, Orp	203	K8
State Fm Av, Orp	203	K8
Statham Gro N16	94	A6
Statham Gro N18	60	C9
Station App E7	97	R8
Station App (Snaresbrook) E11	79	N9
Station App N11	58	C9
Station App (Woodside Pk) N12	56	J8
Station App (Stoke Newington) N16	94	E3
Station App NW10	107	L5
Station App SE1	26	H8
Station App (Mottingham) SE9	170	E2
Station App (Sydenham), SE26 2	167	M8
Station App SW6	144	D5
Station App SW16	164	H9
Station App W7	122	D1
Station App, Barn	41	M8
Station App, Bex	173	P1
Station App, Bexh	155	K4
Station App (Barnehurst), Bexh	155	T4
Station App, Brom	201	N2
Station App, Buck H	64	A7
Station App, Chis	188	G2
Station App (Elmstead Wds), Chis	170	D12
Station App (Stoneleigh), Epsom	193	N10
Station App (Hinchley Wd), Esher	190	E5
Station App, Grnf	86	A14
Station App, Hmptn	175	P1
Station App, Har	68	D13
Station App, Kings T	178	B2
Station App, Loug	48	D10
Station App (Debden), Loug	49	L8
Station App, Orp	203	T3
Station App, Pnr	66	J7
Station App, Rich	142	A1
Station App, Ruis	84	D10
Station App, Sun	174	A1
Station App (Cheam), Sutt	194	D13
Station App (Carpenders Pk), Wat	50	H5
Station App, Well	154	A4
Station App, Wem	87	K11
Station App N, Sid	172	B4
Station App Rd W4	124	F13
Station Av, SW9 5	147	S5
Station Av, N Mal	179	K6
Station Av, Rich	142	A1
Station Cl N3	72	H2
Station Cl (Woodside Pk) N12	56	J8
Station Cl, Hmptn	175	R1
Station Cres N15	76	A8
Station Cres SE3	133	N10
Station Cres, Wem	87	K11
Station Est, Beck	185	P7
Station Est Rd, Felt	156	C1
Station Garage Ms, SW16 2	164	H12
Station Gdns W4	124	F14
Station Gro, Wem	87	S11
Station Hill, Brom	201	N3
Station Ho Ms N9	60	G7
Station Par E11	79	N9
Station Par, N14 1	58	G2
Station Par NW2	89	U11
Station Par W3	106	B11
Station Par, Bark	99	M13
Station Par, Felt	138	C14
Station Par, Rich 2	142	A2
Station Pas E18	79	R4
Station Pl N4	93	P3
Station Ri SE27	165	R3
Station Rd (Chingford) E4	62	H1
Station Rd E7	97	N7
Station Rd E12	98	C8
Station Rd E17	77	S11
Station Rd N3	72	H3
Station Rd N11	58	C10
Station Rd N17	76	H6
Station Rd N19	92	F6
Station Rd N21	59	R1
Station Rd N22	75	M3
Station Rd NW4	71	P11
Station Rd NW7	55	K11
Station Rd NW10	107	L4
Station Rd SE13	150	E5
Station Rd SE20	167	L12
Station Rd (Norwood Junct) SE25	184	F7
Station Rd SW13	143	N5
Station Rd SW19	181	M1
Station Rd SW5	105	T12
Station Rd (Hanwell) W7	122	D1
Station Rd, Barn	40	J9
Station Rd, Belv	137	P6
Station Rd, Bexh	155	K5
Station Rd, Borwd	38	A7
Station Rd, Brent	123	M11
Station Rd, Brom	187	P2
Station Rd (Shortlands), Brom	187	K3
Station Rd, Cars	195	U7
Station Rd, Chess	191	S10
Station Rd, Chig	65	K6
Station Rd (East Croydon), Croy	198	B3
Station Rd (West Croydon), Croy	197	T2
Station Rd, Edg	54	B11
Station Rd, Esher	190	A3
Station Rd (Claygate), Esher	190	B10
Station Rd, Hmptn	175	R2
Station Rd, Har	68	E13
Station Rd (North Harrow), Har	67	R9
Station Rd, Houns	139	R8
Station Rd, Ilf	98	J5
Station Rd (Barkingside), Ilf	81	P6
Station Rd, Kings T	178	A2
Station Rd (Hampton Wick), Kings T	177	M1
Station Rd, Loug	48	C8
Station Rd (Motspur Pk), N Mal	179	R10
Station Rd, Orp	203	U4
Station Rd (Chadwell Heath), Rom	82	G14
Station Rd, Sid	172	A6
Station Rd, Sun	156	A14
Station Rd, Tedd	158	G11
Station Rd, T Ditt	176	F13
Station Rd, Twick	158	F1
Station Rd, W Wick	200	F2
Station Rd N, Belv	137	R6
Station Sq (Petts Wd), Orp	189	M10
Station St E15	96	G13
Station St, E16 1	134	J2
Station Ter NW10	108	A4
Station Ter SE5	147	U1
Station Vw, Grnf	104	A1
Station Way (Roding Valley), Buck H	63	U7
Station Way (Claygate), Esher	190	C11
Station Way (Cheam), Sutt	194	D12
Station Yd, Twick	140	G14
Staunton Rd, Kings T	159	T13
Staunton St SE8	131	U11
Stave Yd Rd SE16	131	R2
Staveley Cl, E9 2	95	M9
Staveley Cl N7	93	K8
Staveley Cl SE15	149	L1
Staveley Gdns W4	142	H1
Staveley Rd W4	124	F12
Staverton Rd NW2	89	T13
Stavordale Rd N5	93	P7
Stavordale Rd, Cars	181	M14
Stayner's Rd E1	113	N7
Stayton Rd, Sutt	194	H5
Stead St SE17	36	C4
Steadfast Rd, Kings T	177	P2
Stean St E8	112	E1
Stebbing Way, Bark	118	B4
Stebondale St E14	132	F8
Stedham Pl, WC1 5	18	A5
Steedman St SE17	35	T3
Steeds Rd N10	73	U2
Steeds Way, Loug	48	D5
Steele Rd E11	96	J7
Steele Rd N17	76	D5
Steele Rd NW10	106	F4
Steele Rd W4	124	F6
Steele Rd, Islw	140	H8
Steele Wk, Erith	137	P12
Steeles Ms N NW3	91	T12
Steeles Ms S NW3	91	U12
Steeles Rd NW3	91	T12
Steel's La E1	113	M12
Steep Cl, Orp	203	U11
Steep Hill SW16	164	H6
Steep Hill, Croy	198	C7
Steeple Cl SW6	144	D4
Steeple Cl SW19	162	D9
Steeplestone Cl N18	59	T9
Steerforth St SW18	163	K4
Steers Mead, Mitch	181	T1
Steers Way SE16	131	S4
Stella Rd SW17	163	U11
Stellman Cl E5	94	G6
Stembridge Rd SE20	184	J4
Stephan Cl, E8 5	112	H1
Stephen Cl, Orp	203	T6
Stephen Ms W1	17	R4
Stephen Rd, Bexh	155	U6
Stephen St W1	17	S4
Stephendale Rd SW6	145	K3
Stephen's Rd E15	115	K2
Stephenson Rd E17	77	R10
Stephenson Rd W7	104	E1
Stephenson Rd, Twick	139	N13
Stephenson St E16	114	J8
Stephenson St NW10	107	K6
Stephenson Way NW1	9	P9
Stepney Causeway E1	113	N12
Stepney Grn E1	113	N9
Stepney High St E1	113	P10
Stepney Way E1	112	J10
Sterling Av, Edg	53	U7
Sterling Av, Pnr	66	J14
Sterling Cl, Pnr	84	H1
Sterling Gdns SE14	131	R12
Sterling Ind Est, Dag	101	S8
Sterling Pl W5	123	R8
Sterling Rd, Enf	44	A1
Sterling St SW7	23	M8
Sterling Way N18	60	D9
Sterndale Rd W14	126	A6
Sterne St W12	126	A3
Sternhall La SE15	148	H5
Sternhold Av SW2	164	G3
Sterry Cres, Dag	101	N9
Sterry Dr, Epsom	192	J7
Sterry Dr, T Ditt	176	D12
Sterry Gdns, Dag	101	N11
Sterry Rd, Bark	117	T1
Sterry Rd, Dag	101	N10
Sterry St SE1	28	C8
Steucers La SE23	167	S1
Steve Biko La SE6	168	B8
Steve Biko Rd N7	93	N6
Steve Biko Way, Houns	139	P6
Stevedale Rd, Well	154	F4
Stevedore St E1	130	J1
Stevenage Rd E6	98	G12
Stevenage Rd SW6	126	A14
Stevens Av E9	95	M11
Stevens Cl, Beck	168	B12
Stevens Cl, Hmptn	157	L11
Stevens Cl, Pnr	66	E10
Stevens Grn, Bushey	51	U2
Stevens La, Esher	190	H12
Stevens Rd, Dag	100	D5
Stevens St SE1	29	K9
Stevens Way, Chig	65	S8
Stevenson Cl, Barn	41	P12
Stevenson Cres SE16	37	U6
Steventon Rd W12	107	M14
Stew La EC4	19	U10
Steward St E1	21	K2
Stewards Holte Wk N11	58	C8
Stewart Cl NW9	70	F12
Stewart Cl, Chis	171	K9
Stewart Cl, Hmptn	157	K11
Stewart Rd E15	96	G8
Stewart St E14	132	F4
Stewart's Gro SW3	31	N5
Stewart's Rd SW8	128	E14
Stewartsby Cl N18	59	T10
Steyne Rd W3	124	D1
Steyning Gro SE9	170	E8
Steyning Way, Houns	138	E7
Steynings Way N12	56	G10
Steynton Av, Bex	172	H7
Stickland Rd, Belv	137	P7
Stickleton Cl, Grnf	103	R6
Stile Hall Gdns W4	124	A10
Stile Path, Sun	174	B6
Stilecroft Gdns, Wem	86	J6
Stiles Cl, Brom	188	F11
Stiles Cl, Erith	137	S10
Stillingfleet Rd SW13	125	P12
Stillington St SW1	33	N1
Stillness Rd SE23	149	S12
Stilton Cres NW10	88	F14
Stipularis Dr, Hayes	102	H8
Stirling Cl SW16	182	F2
Stirling Cor, Barn	38	H11
Stirling Cor, Borwd	38	H11
Stirling Gro, Houns	139	U4
Stirling Rd E13	115	R4
Stirling Rd E17	77	R5
Stirling Rd N17	76	G2
Stirling Rd N22	75	R1
Stirling Rd SW9	146	J4
Stirling Rd W3	124	D5
Stirling Rd, Har	68	E5

Stirling Rd, Hayes	102	C14
Stirling Rd, Twick	139	P14
Stirling Rd Path, E17 *8*	77	R5
Stirling Wk, N Mal	178	E9
Stirling Wk, Surb	178	C11
Stirling Way, Borwd	38	H10
Stirling Way, Croy	182	J13
Stiven Cres, Har	85	L6
Stock Orchard Cres N7	93	L8
Stock Orchard St N7	93	L8
Stock St E13	115	N4
Stockbury Rd, Croy	185	L11
Stockdale Rd, Dag	101	L3
Stockdove Way, Grnf	104	E5
Stockfield Rd SW16	165	M5
Stockfield Rd, Esher	190	C9
Stockholm Rd SE16	131	M10
Stockholm Way E1	29	S2
Stockhurst Cl SW15	144	A4
Stockingswater La, Enf	45	S4
Stockport Rd SW16	182	G2
Stocks Pl E14	113	U13
Stocksfield Rd E17	78	F6
Stockton Gdns N17	59	T14
Stockton Gdns NW7	54	H5
Stockton Rd N17	59	T14
Stockton Rd N18	60	J11
Stockwell Av SW9	147	M6
Stockwell Cl, Brom	187	R4
Stockwell Gdns SW9	147	L2
Stockwell Gdns Est SW9	147	K3
Stockwell Grn SW9	147	L4
Stockwell La SW9	147	L4
Stockwell Ms, SW9 *6*	147	L4
Stockwell Pk Cres SW9	147	M3
Stockwell Pk Est SW9	147	M4
Stockwell Pk Rd SW9	147	L2
Stockwell Pk Wk SW9	147	M5
Stockwell Rd SW9	147	L3
Stockwell St SE10	132	F12
Stockwell Ter, SW9 *4*	147	L2
Stodart Rd SE20	185	L1
Stofield Gdns SE9	170	A5
Stoford Cl SW19	144	C14
Stoke Newington Ch St N16	94	A6
Stoke Newington Common N16	94	F5
Stoke Newington High St N16	94	E6
Stoke Newington Rd N16	94	E8
Stoke Pl NW10	107	L5
Stoke Rd, Kings T	160	F13
Stokenchurch St SW6	144	J2
Stokes Rd E6	116	C7
Stokes Rd, Croy	185	P12
Stokesby Rd, Chess	191	T12
Stokesley St W12	107	M11
Stoll Cl NW2	89	U6
Stoms Path SE6	168	B9
Stonard Rd N13	59	P5
Stonard Rd, Dag	100	D9
Stonards Hill, Loug	48	E11
Stondon Pk SE23	149	R12
Stondon Wk E6	116	B3
Stone Bldgs WC2	18	H4
Stone Cl SW4	146	F4
Stone Cl, Dag	101	M4
Stone Hall Gdns W8	22	B11
Stone Hall Pl, W8 *9*	22	B11
Stone Hall Rd N21	43	M13
Stone Pk Av, Beck	186	B7
Stone Pl, Wor Pk	193	P3
Stone Rd, Brom	187	M9
Stone St, Croy	197	N10
Stonebanks, Walt	174	A13
Stonebridge Pk NW10	88	G13
Stonebridge Rd N15	76	D10
Stonebridge Way, Wem	88	D11
Stonechat Sq, E6 *13*	116	D9
Stonecot Cl, Sutt	194	D2
Stonecot Hill, Sutt	194	D1
Stonecroft Cl, Barn	39	S8
Stonecroft Rd, Erith	137	T14
Stonecroft Way, Croy	183	K13
Stonecutter St EC4	19	N5
Stonefield Cl, Bexh	155	N6
Stonefield Cl, Ruis	84	J9
Stonefield St N1	111	P1
Stonefield Way, SE7 *4*	134	B13
Stonefield Way, Ruis	84	H9
Stonegrove, Edg	53	T10
Stonegrove Est, Edg	53	T8
Stonegrove Gdns, Edg	53	S9
Stonehall Av, Ilf	80	C12
Stoneham Rd N11	58	F10
Stonehill Cl SW14	142	G9
Stonehill Grn, Dart	173	U13
Stonehill Rd SW14	142	F9
Stonehill Rd, W4 *4*	124	B10
Stonehill Wds Caravan Pk, Sid	173	S11
Stonehills Ct SE21	166	D5
Stonehorse Rd, Enf	45	M9
Stoneleigh Av, Enf	45	K1
Stoneleigh Av, Wor Pk	193	P7
Stoneleigh Bdy, Epsom	193	N10
Stoneleigh Cres, Epsom	193	M9
Stoneleigh Pk Av, Croy	185	P11
Stoneleigh Pk Rd, Epsom	193	M10
Stoneleigh Pl W11	108	B14
Stoneleigh Rd N17	76	F5
Stoneleigh Rd, Cars	181	R13
Stoneleigh Rd, Ilf	80	E6
Stoneleigh St W11	108	B13
Stoneleigh Ter N19	92	D3
Stonells Rd SW11	145	U10
Stonemasons Cl N15	76	B7
Stonenest St, N4 *3*	93	M2
Stones End St SE1	27	U8
Stonewall E6	116	G10
Stoney All SE18	152	H4
Stoney La E1	21	L6
Stoney La, SE19 *4*	166	E12
Stoney St SE1	28	C2
Stoneyard La, E14 *12*	114	C14
Stoneycroft Cl SE12	151	M13
Stoneycroft Rd, Wdf Grn	64	C11
Stoneydeep, Tedd *1*	158	H8
Stoneydown E17	77	R7
Stoneydown Av E17	77	R7
Stoneyfields Gdns, Edg	54	G8
Stoneyfields La, Edg	54	F8
Stonhouse St SW4	146	G6
Stonor Rd W14	126	E8
Stony Path, Loug	48	F3
Stopes St SE15	130	F14
Stopford Rd E13	115	P1
Stopford Rd SE17	35	S7
Store Rd E16	134	G3
Store St E15	96	H10
Store St WC1	17	S3
Storers Quay E14	132	G8
Storey Rd E17	77	U8
Storey Rd N6	73	U11
Storey St E16	134	H2
Storey's Gate SW1	25	U7
Stories Ms SE5	148	C4
Stories Rd SE5	148	C5
Stork Rd E7	97	M12
Storks Rd SE16	29	U11
Storksmead Rd, Edg	54	J13
Stormont Rd N6	73	T13
Stormont Rd SW11	146	A7
Stormont Way, Chess	191	M10
Storrington Rd, Croy	198	F1
Story St, N1 *6*	93	L14
Stothard St E1	113	M7
Stott Cl SW18	145	P11
Stoughton Av, Sutt	194	B9
Stoughton Cl SE11	34	G3
Stoughton Cl, SW15 *8*	161	P1
Stour Av, Sthl	121	P6
Stour Cl, Kes	201	U8
Stour Rd E3	96	A14
Stour Rd, Dag	101	P4
Stourcliffe St W1	15	T7
Stourhead Cl SW19	144	B13
Stourhead Gdns SW20	179	P5
Stourton Av, Felt	157	L7
Stow Cres E17	61	S14
Stowage SE8	132	C12
Stowe Pl N15	76	D6
Stowe Rd W12	125	R3
Stowting Rd, Orp	203	R7
Stox Mead, Har	68	A2
Stracey Rd E7	97	P8
Stracey Rd NW10	106	H2
Strachan Pl SW19	161	U12
Stradbroke Dr, Chig	64	J11
Stradbroke Gro, Buck H	64	A2
Stradbroke Gro, Ilf	80	C5
Stradbroke Pk, Chig	64	J12
Stradbroke Rd N5	93	U8
Stradbrook Cl, Har	85	L6
Stradella Rd SE24	147	T11
Strafford Av, Ilf	80	H3
Strafford Rd W3	124	E4
Strafford Rd, Barn	40	C5
Strafford Rd, Houns	139	M6
Strafford Rd, Twick	140	H14
Strafford St E14	132	A3
Strahan Rd E3	113	R5
Straight, The, Sthl	120	H4
Straightsmouth SE10	132	E13
Strait Rd E6	116	C13
Straker's Rd SE15	148	J8
Strand WC2	18	C11
Strand on the Grn W4	124	A11
Strand Pl N18	60	C8
Strand Sch App W4	124	B11
Strandfield Cl SE18	135	S9
Strangways Ter W14	126	E5
Stranraer Way N1	93	K14
Strasburg Rd SW11	146	C2
Stratfield Pk Cl N21	43	R13
Stratfield Rd, Borwd	38	B4
Stratford Av W8	22	A12
Stratford Cl, Bark	100	A14
Stratford Cl, Dag *1*	101	T13
Stratford Ct, N Mal *4*	178	G7
Stratford Ho Av, Brom	188	D5
Stratford Pl W1	16	G7
Stratford Rd E13	115	M2
Stratford Rd NW4	72	A8
Stratford Rd W8	126	H6
Stratford Rd, Hayes	102	C7
Stratford Rd, Sthl	120	J8
Stratford Rd, Th Hth	183	P7
Stratford Vil NW1	92	F13
Strath Ter SW11	145	R8
Strathan Cl SW18	144	D12
Strathaven Rd SE12	151	S11
Strathblaine Rd SW11	145	P8
Strathbrook Rd SW16	165	L14
Strathcona Rd, Wem	87	N3
Strathdale SW16	165	M9
Strathdon Dr SW17	163	N5
Strathearn Av, Twick	157	T1
Strathearn Pl W2	15	N9
Strathearn Rd SW19	162	H8
Strathearn Rd, Sutt	194	H9
Stratheden Par SE3	133	N14
Stratheden Rd SE3	133	N14
Strathfield Gdns, Bark	99	P12
Strathleven Rd SW2	147	K9
Strathmore Gdns N3	72	J2
Strathmore Gdns, W8 *9*	126	H1
Strathmore Gdns, Edg	70	C3
Strathmore Rd SW19	162	H5
Strathmore Rd, Croy	183	U14
Strathmore Rd, Tedd	158	C7
Strathnairn St SE1	37	T3
Strathray Gdns NW3	91	R12
Strathville Rd SW18	162	J3
Strathyre Av SW16	183	N6
Stratton Cl SW19	180	G3
Stratton Cl, Bexh	155	K5
Stratton Cl, Edg	53	U12
Stratton Cl, Houns	139	N2
Stratton Dr, Bark	99	T10
Stratton Gdns, Sthl	103	M11
Stratton Rd SW19	180	G4
Stratton Rd, Bexh	155	K6
Stratton St W1	25	K1
Strattondale St E14	132	E5
Strauss Rd W4	124	H4
Strawberry Hill, Twick	158	E6
Strawberry Hill Cl, Twick	158	E7
Strawberry Hill Rd, Twick	158	E5
Strawberry La, Cars	196	A5
Strawberry Vale N2	73	N2
Strawberry Vale, Twick	158	G6
Streakes Fld Rd NW2	89	P3
Stream La, Edg	54	C10
Streamdale SE2	136	B12
Streamside Cl N9	60	E2
Streamside Cl, Brom	187	P7
Streamway, Belv	137	N11
Streatfield Av E6	116	E1
Streatfield Rd, Har	69	L6
Streatham Cl SW16	165	K5
Streatham Common N SW16	165	K10
Streatham Common S SW16	165	K12
Streatham Ct SW16	164	J5
Streatham High Rd SW16	164	J6
Streatham Hill SW2	165	K3
Streatham Pl SW2	146	J14
Streatham Rd SW16	182	B1
Streatham Rd, Mitch	182	B1
Streatham St, WC1 *5*	18	A4
Streatham Vale SW16	164	G14
Streathbourne Rd SW17	164	B5
Streatley Pl NW3	91	M7
Streatley Rd NW6	90	E14
Streeters La, Wall	196	H6
Streetfield Ms, SE3 *1*	151	P5
Streimer Rd E15	114	J13
Strelley Way W3	106	J13
Stretton Rd, Croy	184	D14
Stretton Rd, Rich	159	L4
Strickland Row SW18	145	N14

Strickland St SE8	150	B3
Strickland Way, Orp	203	T7
Stride Rd E13	115	M4
Strode CI N10	58	B13
Strode Rd E7	97	P7
Strode Rd N17	76	D4
Strode Rd NW10	89	P12
Strode Rd SW6	126	B13
Strone Rd E7	97	T12
Strone Rd E12	98	C11
Strone Way, Hayes	102	J8
Strongbow Cres SE9	152	E9
Strongbow Rd SE9	152	F9
Strongbridge CI, Har	85	P1
Stronsa Rd W12	125	L3
Stroud Cres SW15	161	N5
Stroud Fld, Nthlt	84	J12
Stroud Gate, Har	85	S8
Stroud Grn Gdns, Croy	185	L13
Stroud Grn Rd N4	93	N2
Stroud Grn Way, Croy	185	L12
Stroud Rd SE25	184	H12
Stroud Rd SW19	162	G5
Stroudes CI, Wor Pk	179	K14
Stroudley Wk E3	114	C5
Strouds CI (Chadwell Heath), Rom	82	C9
Strouts PI, E2 1	13	M5
Strutton Grd SW1	25	S10
Strype St E1	21	L4
Stuart Av NW9	71	N14
Stuart Av W5	123	U2
Stuart Av, Brom	201	N1
Stuart Av, Har	85	L6
Stuart Cres N22	75	M2
Stuart Cres, Croy	199	U6
Stuart Evans CI, Well	154	E5
Stuart Gro, Tedd	158	D9
Stuart PI, Mitch	181	T1
Stuart Rd NW6	108	G6
Stuart Rd SE15	149	M8
Stuart Rd SW19	162	G5
Stuart Rd W3	124	E1
Stuart Rd, Bark	99	T14
Stuart Rd, Barn	41	S14
Stuart Rd, Har	68	F6
Stuart Rd, Rich	159	K4
Stuart Rd, Th Hth	183	U7
Stuart Rd, Well	154	D1
Stubbs Dr SE16	130	J9
Stubbs Way, SW19 3	181	N2
Stucley PI, NW1 6	92	D14
Stucley Rd, Houns	121	T14
Studd St N1	111	R1
Studdridge St SW6	144	H3
Studholme Ct NW3	90	H8
Studholme St SE15	130	J14
Studio Ct, Borwd	38	F4
Studio PI SW1	24	B7
Studio Way, Borwd	38	F4
Studland CI, Sid	171	U6
Studland Rd SE26	167	N10
Studland Rd W7	104	B11
Studland Rd, Kings T	159	S12
Studland St W6	125	R8
Studley Av E4	62	G13
Studley CI E5	95	R10
Studley Ct, Sid	172	D9
Studley Dr, Ilf	80	B12
Studley Est SW4	146	J2
Studley Gra Rd W7	122	D4
Studley Rd E7	97	R12
Studley Rd SW4	147	K3
Studley Rd, Dag	100	H14
Stukeley Rd E7	97	S14
Stukeley St WC2	18	C5
Stumps Hill La, Beck	168	B12
Sturdy Rd SE15	148	J4
Sturge Av E17	78	D3
Sturge St SE1	27	T6
Sturgeon Rd SE17	35	T8
Sturges Fld, Chis	171	N12
Sturgess Av NW4	71	R13

Sturminster CI, Hayes	102	D11
Sturrock CI N15	76	A8
Sturry St E14	114	C12
Sturt St N1	12	A4
Stutfield St E1	21	U8
Styles Gdns SW9	147	S5
Styles Way, Beck	186	F8
Sudbourne Rd SW2	147	L9
Sudbrook Gdns, Rich	159	P6
Sudbrook La, Rich	159	R3
Sudbrooke Rd SW12	145	U12
Sudbury Av, Wem	87	M6
Sudbury Ct Dr, Har	86	F6
Sudbury Ct Rd, Har	86	G6
Sudbury Cres, Brom	169	N10
Sudbury Cres, Wem	86	J9
Sudbury Cft, Wem	86	F7
Sudbury Gdns, Croy	198	D7
Sudbury Hts Av, Grnf	86	F9
Sudbury Hill, Har	86	E5
Sudbury Hill CI, Wem	86	F6
Sudbury Rd, Bark	99	U9
Sudeley St N1	11	R3
Sudlow Rd SW18	144	H9
Sudrey St SE1	27	T7
Suez Av, Grnf	104	F3
Suez Rd, Enf	45	S7
Suffield Rd E4	62	D6
Suffield Rd N15	76	E9
Suffield Rd SE20	185	L4
Suffolk CI, Borwd	38	G10
Suffolk Ct E10	78	B14
Suffolk Ct, Ilf	81	S11
Suffolk Ct, Surb	177	P11
Suffolk La EC4	20	D10
Suffolk Pk Rd E17	77	S7
Suffolk PI SW1	25	T1
Suffolk Rd E13	115	M6
Suffolk Rd N15	76	B11
Suffolk Rd NW10	89	K13
Suffolk Rd SE25	184	F7
Suffolk Rd SW13	125	M14
Suffolk Rd, Bark	99	P14
Suffolk Rd, Dag	101	T9
Suffolk Rd, Enf	45	K10
Suffolk Rd, Har	67	M11
Suffolk Rd, Ilf	81	S11
Suffolk Rd, Sid	172	E11
Suffolk Rd, Wor Pk	193	M3
Suffolk St E7	97	N9
Suffolk St SW1	17	T12
Sugar Ho La E15	114	E4
Sugar Loaf Wk E2	113	L5
Sugar Quay Wk EC3	20	J12
Sugden Rd SW11	146	A7
Sugden Rd, T Ditt	190	J2
Sugden Way, Bark	117	U3
Sulgrave Gdns, W6 3	125	U4
Sulgrave Rd W6	125	U5
Sulina Rd SW2	146	J14
Sulivan Ct SW6	144	G4
Sulivan Rd SW6	144	H6
Sullivan Av E16	116	A9
Sullivan CI SW11	145	R5
Sullivan CI, W Mol 4	175	P5
Sullivan Rd SE11	35	M1
Sultan Rd E11	79	R8
Sultan St SE5	35	U14
Sultan St, Beck	185	P3
Sumatra Rd NW6	90	H11
Sumburgh Rd SW12	146	B11
Summer Av, E Mol	176	C10
Summer Gdns, E Mol	176	C9
Summer Hill, Borwd	38	A10
Summer Hill, Chis	188	H3
Summer Hill Vil, Chis	188	H2
Summer Rd, E Mol	176	C9
Summer Rd, T Ditt	176	F11
Summer St EC1	11	K11
Summer Trees, Sun	174	C1
Summercourt Rd E1	113	M11
Summerene CI, SW16 4	164	F13

Summerfield Av NW6	108	D3
Summerfield La, Surb	191	N4
Summerfield Rd W5	105	K7
Summerfield Rd, Loug	48	A12
Summerfield St SE12	151	M14
Summerfields Av N12	57	S11
Summerhill CI, Orp	203	R6
Summerhill Gro, Enf	44	C12
Summerhill Rd N15	76	B7
Summerhill Way, Mitch 2	182	B2
Summerhouse Av, Houns	138	J1
Summerhouse Rd N16	94	D4
Summerland Gdns N10	74	D6
Summerlands Av W3	106	E14
Summerlee Av N2	73	T7
Summerlee Gdns N2	73	T7
Summerley St SW18	163	K3
Summers CI, Sutt 3	194	H14
Summers CI, Wem	88	C1
Summers La N12	57	N13
Summers Row N12	57	S11
Summersby Rd N6	74	C11
Summerstown SW17	163	L7
Summerton Way SE28	118	H12
Summerville Gdns, Sutt	194	E12
Summerwood Rd, Islw	140	E10
Summit, The, Loug	48	F1
Summit Av NW9	70	H9
Summit CI N14	58	E3
Summit CI NW9	70	H8
Summit CI, Edg	54	B14
Summit Dr, Wdf Grn	80	B3
Summit Est N16	76	G14
Summit Rd E17	78	U8
Summit Rd, Nthlt	85	P14
Summit Way N14	58	D3
Summit Way SE19	166	D14
Sumner Av SE15	148	F1
Sumner CI, Orp	203	L7
Sumner Est SE15	130	F14
Sumner Gdns, Croy 3	197	P1
Sumner PI SW7	31	L4
Sumner PI Ms SW7	31	L3
Sumner Rd SE15	37	N11
Sumner Rd, Croy	197	R1
Sumner Rd, Har	67	U13
Sumner Rd S, Croy	197	P2
Sumner St SE1	27	T2
Sumpter CI NW3	91	M11
Sun All, Rich 5	141	R8
Sun Ct EC3	20	F7
Sun La SE3	133	S14
Sun Pas SE16	29	S10
Sun Rd W14	126	E10
Sun St EC2	20	F2
Sun St Pas EC2	20	H4
Sun Wk E1	21	R12
Sunbeam Cres W10	107	U8
Sunbeam Rd NW10	106	G8
Sunbury Av NW7	54	G9
Sunbury Av SW14	142	H8
Sunbury Ct, Sun	174	G5
Sunbury Ct Island, Sun	174	G5
Sunbury Ct Ms, Sun	174	G4
Sunbury Ct Rd, Sun	174	F3
Sunbury Gdns NW7	54	G9
Sunbury La SW11	145	P1
Sunbury La, Walt	174	B11
Sunbury Lock Ait, Walt	174	C7

Sunbury Rd, Sutt	194	B5
Sunbury St SE18	134	F6
Sunbury Way, Felt	156	E9
Suncroft PI SE26	167	L5
Sunderland Ct SE22	148	H14
Sunderland Mt SE23	167	P3
Sunderland Rd SE23	167	P1
Sunderland Rd W5	123	N5
Sunderland Ter W2	14	A6
Sunderland Way E12	98	B3
Sundew Av W12	107	N14
Sundial Av SE25	184	E5
Sundorne Rd SE7	133	T10
Sundridge Av, Brom	188	A2
Sundridge Av, Chis	170	C13
Sundridge Av, Well	153	P4
Sundridge PI, Croy 4	198	G1
Sundridge Rd, Croy	184	F14
Sunfields PI SE3	133	R13
Sunland Av, Bexh	155	K8
Sunleigh Rd, Wem	105	R1
Sunley Gdns, Grnf	104	G2
Sunlight CI SW19	163	L12
Sunlight Sq E2	113	K6
Sunmead Rd, Sun	174	A5
Sunna Gdns, Sun	174	D3
Sunningdale N14	58	H9
Sunningdale Av W3	107	K13
Sunningdale Av, Bark	117	N1
Sunningdale Av, Felt	156	J4
Sunningdale Av, Ruis	84	F1
Sunningdale CI, SE16 3	130	J10
Sunningdale CI SE28	118	J12
Sunningdale CI, Stan	52	H12
Sunningdale CI, Surb	191	S3
Sunningdale Gdns NW9	70	E10
Sunningdale Rd, Brom	188	C8
Sunningdale Rd, Sutt	194	F7
Sunningfields Cres NW4	71	S4
Sunningfields Rd NW4	71	S5
Sunninghill Rd SE13	150	C4
Sunny Bank SE25	184	H6
Sunny Cres NW10	88	E14
Sunny Gdns Rd NW4	71	T5
Sunny Hill NW4	71	R6
Sunny Nook Gdns, S Croy	198	B11
Sunny Rd, The, Enf	45	P2
Sunny Vw NW9	70	H9
Sunny Way N12	57	R13
Sunnycroft Rd SE25	184	G6
Sunnycroft Rd, Houns	139	R3
Sunnydale, Orp	202	H4
Sunnydale Gdns NW7	54	H11
Sunnydale Rd SE12	151	R9
Sunnydene Av E4	62	H9
Sunnydene Av, Ruis	84	A2
Sunnydene Gdns, Wem	87	L12
Sunnydene St SE26	167	R8
Sunnyfield NW7	55	L7
Sunnyhill CI E5	95	R7
Sunnyhill Rd SW16	165	K8
Sunnyhurst CI, Sutt	194	H5
Sunnymead Av, Mitch	182	G5
Sunnymead Rd NW9	70	G13
Sunnymead Rd SW15	143	R10
Sunnymede Dr, Ilf	80	J8
Sunnyside NW2	90	F5

Sunnyside SW19	162	C11
Sunnyside, Walt	174	E10
Sunnyside Dr E4	46	F14
Sunnyside Pas SW19	162	C12
Sunnyside Pl, SW19 2	162	C12
Sunnyside Rd E10	96	A1
Sunnyside Rd N19	74	G14
Sunnyside Rd W5	123	N2
Sunnyside Rd, Ilf	99	N7
Sunnyside Rd,Tedd	158	B8
Sunnyside Rd E N9	60	G6
Sunnyside Rd N N9	60	G6
Sunnyside Rd S N9	60	F6
Sunray Av SE24	148	A8
Sunray Av, Brom	188	D11
Sunray Av, Surb	192	D3
Sunrise Cl, Felt	157	L6
Sunset Av E4	62	D1
Sunset Av, Wdf Grn	63	L7
Sunset Gdns SE25	184	E3
Sunset Rd SE5	147	U7
Sunset Rd SE28	136	A3
Sunset Vw, Barn	40	C4
Sunshine Way, Mitch	181	T3
Superior Dr, Orp 3	203	T12
Surbiton Ct, Surb	177	M11
Surbiton Cres, Kings T	177	R9
Surbiton Hall Cl, Kings T	177	R8
Surbiton Hill Pk, Surb	178	C9
Surbiton Hill Rd, Surb	177	S9
Surbiton Rd, Kings T	177	R7
Surlingham Cl SE28	118	G12
Surma Cl E1	112	H8
Surr St N7	92	J10
Surrendale Pl W9	108	H8
Surrey Canal Rd SE14	131	M11
Surrey Canal Rd SE15	131	M11
Surrey Cres W4	124	B9
Surrey Gdns N4	75	T12
Surrey Gro SE17	36	H7
Surrey Gro, Sutt	195	N5
Surrey La SW11	145	R2
Surrey La Est SW11	145	R1
Surrey Lo SE1	26	J11
Surrey Ms SE27	166	C8
Surrey Mt SE23	167	K2
Surrey Quays Rd SE16	131	M5
Surrey Rd SE15	149	N9
Surrey Rd, Bark	99	R14
Surrey Rd, Dag	101	S9
Surrey Rd, Har	67	T10
Surrey Rd, W Wick	200	D2
Surrey Row SE1	27	P6
Surrey Sq SE17	36	H5
Surrey St E13	115	S6
Surrey St WC2	18	G9
Surrey St, Croy	197	T5
Surrey Ter SE17	36	J5
Surrey Water Rd SE16	131	P2
Surridge Gdns SE19	166	A12
Susan Cl, Rom	83	T6
Susan Rd SE3	151	S4
Susan Wd, Chis	188	H1
Susannah St E14	114	D12
Sussex Av, Islw	140	C6
Sussex Cl N19	92	J3
Sussex Cl, Ilf	80	E11
Sussex Cl, N Mal	179	K7
Sussex Cl, Twick 3	141	K11
Sussex Cres, Nthlt	85	N11
Sussex Gdns N4	75	T10
Sussex Gdns N6	73	T9
Sussex Gdns W2	15	L7
Sussex Gdns, Chess	191	N11
Sussex Ms E W2	15	M8
Sussex Ms W W2	15	L10
Sussex Pl NW1	7	U10
Sussex Pl W2	15	M8
Sussex Pl W6	125	T9
Sussex Pl, Erith	137	R13
Sussex Pl, N Mal	179	K7
Sussex Ring N12	56	H10
Sussex Rd E6	116	H2
Sussex Rd, Cars	195	T12
Sussex Rd, Erith	137	R13
Sussex Rd, Har	67	S10
Sussex Rd, Mitch 4	182	J9
Sussex Rd, N Mal	179	K7
Sussex Rd, Sid	172	D9
Sussex Rd, S Croy	198	B11
Sussex Rd, Sthl	120	H5
Sussex Rd, W Wick	200	D2
Sussex Sq W2	15	L9
Sussex St E13	115	S6
Sussex St SW1	33	K6
Sussex Wk SW9	147	R7
Sussex Way N7	73	U7
Sussex Way N19	92	J2
Sussex Way, Barn	42	B9
Sutcliffe Cl NW11	73	K9
Sutcliffe Rd SE18	135	S12
Sutcliffe Rd, Well	154	F3
Sutherland Av W9	6	D10
Sutherland Av W13	104	J12
Sutherland Av, Hayes	120	A7
Sutherland Av, Orp	189	T11
Sutherland Av, Well	153	R8
Sutherland Cl, Barn	40	D8
Sutherland Ct NW9	70	C8
Sutherland Dr, SW19 4	181	N2
Sutherland Gdns SW14	143	K6
Sutherland Gdns, Wor Pk	179	R14
Sutherland Gro SW18	144	E12
Sutherland Gro, Tedd	158	D10
Sutherland Pl W2	108	G11
Sutherland Rd E17	77	R5
Sutherland Rd N9	60	H1
Sutherland Rd N17	60	H14
Sutherland Rd W4	124	J11
Sutherland Rd W13	104	H12
Sutherland Rd, Belv	137	P5
Sutherland Rd, Croy	183	P14
Sutherland Rd, Enf	45	N11
Sutherland Rd, Sthl	103	L12
Sutherland Rd Path, E17 7	77	P5
Sutherland Row SW1	32	J6
Sutherland Sq SE17	35	U8
Sutherland St SW1	33	K7
Sutherland Wk SE17	36	A8
Sutlej Rd SE7	133	U13
Sutterton St N7	93	L12
Sutton Cl, Beck	186	D2
Sutton Cl, Loug	48	D13
Sutton Cl, Pnr	66	B10
Sutton Common Rd, Sutt	194	G2
Sutton Ct W4	124	F11
Sutton Ct Rd E13	115	T5
Sutton Ct Rd W4	124	F10
Sutton Ct Rd, Sutt	195	L11
Sutton Cres, Barn	40	B9
Sutton Dene, Houns	139	R2
Sutton Est SW3	31	R5
Sutton Est W10	107	T9
Sutton Est, The N1	93	R4
Sutton Gdns, Bark 2	117	S3
Sutton Gdns, Croy	184	F10
Sutton Gro, Sutt	195	P9
Sutton Hall Rd, Houns	121	N14
Sutton La, Houns	139	M4
Sutton La N W4	124	E10
Sutton La S, W4 1	124	E11
Sutton Pk Rd, Sutt	195	K11
Sutton Pl E9	95	L10
Sutton Rd E13	115	M7
Sutton Rd E17	77	P2
Sutton Rd N10	74	A2
Sutton Rd, Bark	117	S3
Sutton Rd, Houns	139	P1
Sutton Row W1	17	T6
Sutton Sq E9	95	L10
Sutton Sq, Houns	139	M1
Sutton St E1	113	L12
Sutton Way W10	107	T9
Sutton Way, Houns	139	M1
Sutton's Way EC1	12	B12
Swaby Rd SW18	163	M4
Swaffield Rd SW18	145	L13
Swain Cl SW16	164	C12
Swain Rd, Th Hth	183	U9
Swains La N6	92	B5
Swains Rd SW17	163	T13
Swainson Rd W3	125	L3
Swaledale Cl, N11 4	58	B11
Swallands Rd SE6	168	B6
Swallow Cl SE14	149	N2
Swallow Cl, Bushey	51	T1
Swallow Dr, NW10 2	88	H11
Swallow Dr, Nthlt	103	N3
Swallow Gdns SW16	164	G9
Swallow Pl, W1 2	17	K7
Swallow St E6	116	D9
Swallow St W1	17	N12
Swallowfield Rd SE7	133	S10
Swan App E6	116	C10
Swan Cl E17	77	R1
Swan Cl, Croy	184	C13
Swan Cl, Felt	157	K8
Swan Dr NW9	70	J3
Swan La EC4	20	E11
Swan La N20	57	L5
Swan La, Loug	47	U13
Swan Mead SE1	28	H12
Swan Path, E10 1	96	E2
Swan Pl SW13	143	M3
Swan Rd SE16	131	M3
Swan Rd SE18	134	B6
Swan Rd, Felt	156	J9
Swan Rd, Sthl	103	R11
Swan St SE1	28	B8
Swan St, Islw	140	J5
Swan Wk SW3	31	U10
Swan Way, Enf	45	N3
Swan Yd N1	93	R12
Swanage Rd E4	62	F14
Swanage Rd SW18	145	M12
Swanage Waye, Hayes	121	F12
Swanbridge Rd, Bexh	155	P2
Swandon Way SW18	145	K8
Swanfield St E2	13	M7
Swanley Rd, Well	154	F2
Swanscombe Rd W4	125	K9
Swanscombe Rd W11	126	B1
Swansea Rd, Enf	45	L7
Swanshope, Loug	49	K3
Swansland Gdns, E17 2	77	R1
Swanston Path, Wat	50	F5
Swanton Gdns SW19	162	B1
Swanton Rd, Erith	137	R13
Swanwick Cl SW15	143	M13
Swaton Rd E3	114	B8
Swaylands Rd, Belv	137	P12
Swaythling Cl N18	61	K7
Sweden Gate SE16	131	R6
Swedenborg Gdns E1	21	U10
Sweeney Cres SE1	29	N8
Sweet Briar Grn N9	60	E6
Sweet Briar Gro N9	60	E6
Sweet Briar Wk N18	60	E8
Sweetmans Av, Pnr	66	E6
Sweets Way N20	57	N4
Swete St E13	115	P4
Sweyn Pl SE3	151	P4
Swift Cl E17	61	H14
Swift Cl, Har	85	R3
Swift Rd, Felt	157	K6
Swift Rd, Sthl	121	N5
Swift St SW6	144	E1
Swiftsden Way, Brom	169	K11
Swinbrook Rd W10	108	D9
Swinburne Ct SE5	147	U7
Swinburne Cres, Croy	185	L12
Swinburne Rd SW15	143	P8
Swinderby Rd, Wem	87	R12
Swindon Cl, Ilf	99	S3
Swindon St W12	125	T1
Swinfield Cl, Felt	156	J7
Swinford Gdns SW9	147	R5
Swingate La SE18	135	S11
Swinnerton St E9	95	R10
Swinton Cl, Wem	88	D2
Swinton Pl, WC1 2	10	F6
Swinton St WC1	10	F6
Swires Shaw, Kes	202	B8
Swiss Ter NW6	91	N13
Swithland Gdns SE9	170	G7
Swyncombe Av W5	123	K8
Swynford Gdns NW4	71	P7
Sybil Ms N4	75	S12
Sybil Phoenix Cl SE8	131	P9
Sybourn St E17	77	U14
Sycamore Av W5	123	P5
Sycamore Av, Sid	153	U11
Sycamore Cl E16	114	J8
Sycamore Cl N9	60	G7
Sycamore Cl SE9	170	C3
Sycamore Cl, Barn	41	P11
Sycamore Cl, Cars	195	T8
Sycamore Cl, Felt	156	B6
Sycamore Cl, Loug	49	K4
Sycamore Cl, Nthlt	103	K2
Sycamore Ct, Surb 1	177	S13
Sycamore Gdns W6	125	S4
Sycamore Gdns, Mitch	181	P4
Sycamore Gro NW9	70	F14
Sycamore Gro SE6	150	E12
Sycamore Gro SE20	166	H14
Sycamore Gro, N Mal	178	J5
Sycamore Hill N11	58	B11
Sycamore Ms SW4	146	E6
Sycamore Rd SW19	161	T12
Sycamore St, EC1 11	11	T11
Sycamore Way, Tedd	159	M11
Sycamore Way, Th Hth	183	N9
Sydenham Av N21	43	L9
Sydenham Av SE26	167	K10
Sydenham Cotts, SE12 1	169	T4
Sydenham Hill SE23	166	J2
Sydenham Hill SE26	166	J4
Sydenham Hill Est SE26	166	H6
Sydenham Pk SE26	167	M5
Sydenham Pk Rd SE26	167	L5
Sydenham Ri SE23	166	J3
Sydenham Rd SE26	167	S8
Sydenham Rd, Croy	184	B12
Sydmons Ct SE23	149	L13
Sydner Ms N16	94	E7
Sydner Rd N16	94	F7
Sydney Cl SW3	31	M4
Sydney Gro NW4	71	T10
Sydney Ms SW3	31	M4
Sydney Pl SW7	31	M3
Sydney Rd, E11 2	79	S12
Sydney Rd N8	75	N7
Sydney Rd N10	74	B2
Sydney Rd SE2	136	G6
Sydney Rd SW20	180	B3
Sydney Rd W13	122	H3
Sydney Rd, Bexh	154	H8
Sydney Rd, Enf	44	B7
Sydney Rd, Felt	156	B2
Sydney Rd, Ilf	81	L4
Sydney Rd, Rich	141	S8

Street	No.	Ref	Street	No.	Ref	Street	No.	Ref	Street	No.	Ref
Sydney Rd, Sid	171	S8	Talbot Rd, Dag	101	M12	Tantallon Rd SW12	164	A1	Taviton St WC1	9	S9
Sydney Rd, Sutt	194	H8	Talbot Rd, Har	68	F4	Tantony Gro, Rom	82	H6	Tavy Cl SE11	35	M5
Sydney Rd, Tedd	158	E10	Talbot Rd, Islw	140	H7	Tanworth Gdns, Pnr	66	D4	Tawney Rd SE28	118	C14
Sydney Rd, Wdf Grn	63	N8	Talbot Rd, Sthl	121	K7	Tanyard La, Bex	173	P1	Tawny Cl W13	122	J1
Sydney St SW3	31	N4	Talbot Rd, Th Hth	184	B8	Tanza Rd NW3	91	T7	Tawny Cl, Felt 4	156	B5
Sylvan Av N3	72	H3	Talbot Rd, Twick	158	E1	Tapestry Cl, Sutt	194	J14	Tawny Way SE16	131	P7
Sylvan Av N22	59	N13	Talbot Rd, Wem	87	P10	Taplow SE17	36	G7	Tayben Av, Twick	140	D12
Sylvan Av NW7	55	L11	Talbot Sq W2	15	L7	Taplow Rd N13	59	U8	Taybridge Rd SW11	146	B8
Sylvan Av, Rom	83	M11	Talbot Wk W11	108	C12	Taplow St N1	12	A4	Tayburn Cl E14	114	E11
Sylvan Est SE19	184	F2	Talbot Yd SE1	28	D4	Tapp St E1	112	J7	Taylor Av, Rich	142	C3
Sylvan Gdns, Surb	191	N1	Talfourd Pl SE15	148	E2	Tappesfield Rd SE15	149	L5	Taylor Cl N17	60	G13
Sylvan Gro NW2	90	B8	Talfourd Rd SE15	148	E2	Tapster St, Barn	40	E6	Taylor Cl, Hmptn	157	U9
Sylvan Gro SE15	131	K12	Talgarth Rd W6	125	U9	Tarbert Rd SE22	148	D9	Taylor Cl, Houns	139	U2
Sylvan Hill SE19	184	D1	Talgarth Rd W14	126	C9	Tariff Cres SE8	131	T7	Taylor Cl, Orp 3	203	T7
Sylvan Rd E7	97	R11	Talgarth Wk NW9	70	J10	Tariff Rd N17	60	H12	Taylor Ct, E15 2	96	E9
Sylvan Rd E11	79	N9	Talisman Cl, Ilf	100	D1	Tarleton Gdns SE23	167	K2	Taylor Rd, Mitch	163	S14
Sylvan Rd E17	78	A9	Talisman Sq SE26	166	G7	Tarling Cl, Sid	172	D6	Taylor Rd, Wall	196	F5
Sylvan Rd SE19	184	E2	Talisman Way, Wem	87	T5	Tarling Rd E16	115	M12	Taylors Bldgs SE18	135	K7
Sylvan Rd, Ilf	99	L4	Tall Elms Cl, Brom	187	L9	Tarling Rd N2	73	M3	Taylors Cl, Sid	171	T7
Sylvan Wk, Brom	188	E6	Tall Trees SW16	183	L6	Tarling St E1	113	L12	Taylors Grn W3	106	J11
Sylvan Way, Dag	100	C6	Tallack Cl, Har	52	D14	Tarling St Est E1	113	L12	Taylors La NW10	88	J13
Sylvan Way, W Wick	201	K8	Tallack Rd E10	95	U1	Tarn St SE1	27	T11	Taylors La SE26	166	J7
Sylverdale Rd, Croy	197	R5	Tallis Cl E16	115	R12	Tarnbank, Enf	43	K9	Taylors La, Barn	40	E1
Sylvester Av, Chis	170	E12	Tallis Gro SE7	133	S11	Tarnwood Pk SE9	170	E1	Taymount Ri SE23	167	L3
Sylvester Rd E8	95	K11	Tallis St EC4	19	M9	Tarragon Cl SE14	131	R13	Tayport Cl N1	93	K14
Sylvester Rd, E17 2	77	U13	Tallis Vw NW10	88	H11	Tarragon Gro SE26	167	N11	Tayside Dr, Edg	54	C5
Sylvester Rd N2	72	M3	Tally Ho Cor N12	57	M9	Tarrant Pl W1	15	T3	Taywood Rd, Nthlt	103	M6
Sylvester Rd, Wem	87	M9	Talma Gdns, Twick	140	C12	Tarrington Cl SW16	164	G6	Teak Cl SE16	131	92
Sylvestrus Cl, Kings T	178	B2	Talma Rd SW2	147	P8	Tarry La SE8	131	R7	Teal Cl E16	116	A10
Sylvia Av, Pnr	51	L12	Talmage Cl SE23	149	M14	Tarver Rd SE17	35	S6	Teale St E2	13	T2
Sylvia Gdns, Wem	88	C13	Talman Gro, Stan	53	N11	Tarves Way SE10	132	D13	Tealing Dr, Epsom	192	G8
Symes Ms, NW1 1	9	L1	Talwin St E3	114	D6	Tash Pl N11	58	D9	Teasel Cl, Croy 4	199	N1
Symons St SW3	32	A3	Tamar Cl E3	113	U2	Tasker Rd NW3	91	T10	Teasel Way E15	114	J5
Syon Gate Way, Brent	122	H13	Tamar Sq, Wdf Grn	63	S12	Tasman Rd SW9	147	K6	Tebworth Rd N17	60	E14
Syon La, Islw	122	J14	Tamar St SE7	134	C6	Tasman Wk E16	116	A12	Teck Cl, Islw	140	H4
Syon Pk Gdns, Islw	122	E13	Tamar Way N17	76	G5	Tasmania Ter N18	59	U11	Tedder Cl, Chess	191	M11
Syon Vista, Rich	141	R1	Tamarisk Sq W12	107	M14	Tasso Rd W6	126	C11	Tedder Rd, S Croy	199	N14
			Tamesis Gdns, Wor Pk	192	J3	Tatam Rd NW10	88	F13	Teddington Lock, Tedd	158	J8
T			Tamian Way, Houns	138	F8	Tate & Lyle Jetty E16	134	C4	Teddington Pk, Tedd	158	F9
			Tamworth Av, Wdf Grn	63	K11	Tate Rd E16	134	D2	Teddington Pk Rd, Tedd	158	F8
Tabard Gdn Est SE1	28	F8	Tamworth Pk, Mitch	182	D6	Tate Rd, Sutt	194	G10	Tedworth Gdns SW3	31	T8
Tabard St SE1	28	C7	Tamworth Pl, Croy 3	197	T4	Tatnell Rd SE23	149	R12	Tedworth Sq SW3	31	T8
Tabernacle Av, E13 4	115	N8	Tamworth Rd, Croy	197	T3	Tattersall Cl SE9	152	D9	Tee, The W3	106	J11
Tabernacle St EC2	12	F10	Tamworth St SW6	126	G11	Tatton Cres N16	76	F13	Tees Av, Grnf	104	D3
Tableer Av SW4	146	F9	Tancred Rd N4	75	R12	Tatum St SE17	36	F3	Teesdale Av, Islw	140	H2
Tabley Rd N7	92	J7	Tandridge Dr, Orp	203	P1	Tauheed Cl N4	93	T3	Teesdale Cl E2	13	U3
Tabor Gdns, Sutt	194	E12	Tandridge Pl, Orp 1	203	P1	Taunton Av SW20	179	R4	Teesdale Gdns SE25	184	C3
Tabor Gro SW19	162	D13	Tanfield Av NW2	89	M5	Taunton Av, Houns	139	T3	Teesdale Gdns, Islw	140	H2
Tabor Rd W6	125	S6	Tanfield Rd, Croy	197	T7	Taunton Cl, Ilf	65	U12	Teesdale Rd E11	79	L12
Tachbrook St SW1	33	T7	Tangier Rd, Rich	142	C7	Taunton Cl, Sutt	194	G2	Teesdale St E2	112	J4
Tachbrook Ms SW1	33	M2	Tangle Tree Cl N3	73	K4	Taunton Dr N2	73	M4	Teesdale Yd E2	13	U2
Tachbrook Rd, Sthl	120	H7	Tanglebury Cl, Brom	188	D7	Taunton Dr, Enf	43	N5	Teevan Cl, Croy 3	184	H14
Tachbrook St SW1	33	N3	Tanglewood Cl, Croy	199	M5	Taunton Ms NW1	7	U12	Teevan Rd, Croy	184	H14
Tack Ms SE4	150	A5	Tanglewood Cl, Stan	52	C4	Taunton Pl NW1	7	T10	Teignmouth Cl SW4	146	G8
Tadema Rd SW10	127	M13	Tanglewood Way, Felt	156	C7	Taunton Rd SE12	151	K10	Teignmouth Cl, Edg	69	U3
Tadmor St W12	126	A2	Tangley Gro SW15	143	M13	Taunton Rd, Grnf	103	S1	Teignmouth Gdns, Grnf	104	G4
Tadworth Av, N Mal	179	L8	Tangley Pk Rd, Hmptn	157	M10	Taunton Way, Stan	69	S4	Teignmouth Rd NW2	90	C11
Tadworth Rd NW2	89	N4	Tangmere Gdns, Nthlt	102	F4	Tavern Cl, Cars	181	R14	Teignmouth Rd, Well	154	E3
Taeping St E14	132	C7	Tangmere Gro, Kings T	159	N9	Tavern La SW9	147	P3	Telegraph Hill NW3	90	J5
Taffy's How, Mitch	181	S4	Tangmere Way NW9	71	K3	Taverner Sq N5	93	T8	Telegraph La, Esher	190	F11
Taft Way E3	114	D5	Tankerton Rd, Surb	191	U3	Taverners Way E4	62	J1	Telegraph Ms, Ilf	100	B1
Tagg's Island, Hmptn	176	A4	Tankerton St WC1	10	C7	Tavistock Av E17	77	P6	Telegraph Pl E14	132	C7
Tailworth St, E1 1	21	R3	Tankerville Rd SW16	164	J13	Tavistock Av, Grnf	104	H4	Telegraph Rd SW15	143	S13
Tait Rd, Croy	184	C13	Tankridge Rd NW2	89	S4	Tavistock Cl N16	94	D10	Telegraph St, EC2 8	20	D6
Talacre Rd NW5	92	B11	Tanner St SE1	28	J7	Tavistock Cres W11	108	E10	Telemann Sq SE3	151	S6
Talbot Av N2	73	N6	Tanner St, Bark	99	L12	Tavistock Cres, Mitch	182	J8	Telephone Pl, SW6 18	126	F11
Talbot Cl N15	76	E8	Tanners Cl, Walt	174	D12	Tavistock Gdns, Ilf	99	S8	Telfer Cl W3	134	E3
Talbot Ct EC3	20	F10	Tanners End La N18	60	D8	Tavistock Gate, Croy	198	A1	Telferscot Rd SW12	164	G1
Talbot Cres NW4	71	P10	Tanners Hill SE8	150	A2	Tavistock Gro, Croy	184	A14	Telford Av SW2	164	G2
Talbot Gdns, Ilf	100	A3	Tanners La, Ilf	81	M6	Tavistock Ms E18	79	P6	Telford Cl E17	77	S12
Talbot Pl SE3	150	J3	Tannery Cl, Beck	185	N9	Tavistock Pl E18	79	P7	Telford Cl, SE19 7	166	E12
Talbot Rd E6	116	G3	Tannery Cl, Dag	101	R5	Tavistock Pl N14	42	C12	Telford Dr, Walt	174	E13
Talbot Rd E7	97	N7	Tannington Ter N5	93	P6	Tavistock Pl WC1	10	A10	Telford Rd N11	58	F10
Talbot Rd N6	74	A12	Tannsfeld Rd SE26	167	N9	Tavistock Rd E7	97	L7	Telford Rd NW9	71	N12
Talbot Rd N15	76	F8	Tansley Cl N7	92	H10	Tavistock Rd E15	97	L12	Telford Rd SE9	171	N14
Talbot Rd N22	74	F2	Tanswell Est SE1	27	L7	Tavistock Rd E18	79	N6	Telford Rd W10	108	C9
Talbot Rd SE22	148	D7	Tanswell St SE1	27	K7	Tavistock Rd N4	76	A12	Telford Rd, Sthl	103	R12
Talbot Rd W2	108	H11	Tansy Cl E6	116	H12	Tavistock Rd NW10	107	L3	Telford Rd, Twick	139	N13
Talbot Rd W11	108	E12	Tant Av E16	115	L11	Tavistock Rd W11	108	E10	Telford Ter SW1	33	L8
Talbot Rd W13	122	G1				Tavistock Rd, Brom	187	M7	Telford Way W3	106	E3
Talbot Rd, Cars	196	A9				Tavistock Rd, Cars	195	P2	Telford Way, Hayes	102	J10
						Tavistock Rd, Croy	198	A1	Telfords Yd E1	21	T11
						Tavistock Rd, Edg	70	A1	Telham Rd E6	116	G4
						Tavistock Rd, Well	154	E1			
						Tavistock Sq WC1	9	U10			
						Tavistock St WC2	18	D10			
						Tavistock Ter N19	92	H5			
						Tavistock Wk, Cars	195	P1			

Tell Gro SE22	148	E8	Tennyson Av E12	98	C13	Thackeray CI SW19	162	B13
Tellson Av SE18	152	C1	Tennyson Av NW9	70	E6	Thackeray CI, Har	85	P2
Telscombe CI, Orp	203	S4	Tennyson Av,	179	T9	Thackeray CI, Islw	140	H4
Temeraire St SE16	131	M4	N Mal			Thackeray Dr, Rom	82	C14
Temperley Rd SW12	146	B13	Tennyson Av, Twick	158	F2	Thackeray Rd E6	116	B3
Templar Dr SE28	118	H12	Tennyson CI, Enf	45	N10	Thackeray Rd SW8	146	C4
Templar PI, Hmptn	157	N12	Tennyson CI, Well	153	S2	Thackeray St W8	22	C8
Templar St SE5	147	S3	Tennyson Rd E10	96	D2	Thackrah CI N2	73	M4
Templars Av NW11	72	F12	Tennyson Rd E15	96	J13	Thakeham CI SE26	166	J8
Templars Cres N3	72	G4	Tennyson Rd E17	77	U11	Thalia CI SE10	132	H11
Templars Dr, Har	52	A12	Tennyson Rd NW6	108	E1	Thame Rd SE16	131	P3
Temple EC4	111	N13	Tennyson Rd NW7	55	N9	Thames Av SW10	145	N1
Temple Av EC4	19	M9	Tennyson Rd SE20	167	P13	Thames Av, Dag	119	P9
Temple Av N20	41	N14	Tennyson Rd SW19	163	L11	Thames Av, Grnf	104	E4
Temple Av, Croy	199	T5	Tennyson Rd W7	104	E14	Thames Bank SW14	142	F4
Temple Av, Dag	101	N1	Tennyson Rd, Houns	139	T3	Thames Circle, x	132	B7
Temple CI E11	78	J13	Tennyson St SW8	146	C4	Wdf 3		
Temple CI, N3 1	72	E4	Tensing Rd, Sthl	121	N5	Thames CI, Hmptn	175	S3
Temple CI SE28	135	M5	Tent Peg La, Orp	189	L9	Thames Ditton	176	G11
Temple Fortune	72	G10	Tent St E1	112	J7	Island, T Ditt		
Hill NW11			Tentelow La, Sthl	121	S6	Thames Gateway,	119	L4
Temple Fortune La	72	G11	Tenter Grd E1	21	L3	Dag		
NW11			Tenter Pas, E1 5	21	N8	Thames Meadow,	175	P4
Temple Gdns NW11	72	E11	Tenterden CI NW4	72	A5	W Mol		
Temple Gdns, Dag	100	G5	Tenterden CI,	170	E7	Thames Path SE1	19	N12
Temple Gro NW11	72	G11	SE9 2			Thames Path SE7	133	T6
Temple Gro, Enf	43	S5	Tenterden Dr NW4	72	B6	Thames Rd E16	134	A2
Temple La EC4	19	L8	Tenterden Gdns	72	A6	Thames Rd W4	124	B11
Temple Mead CI,	52	J12	NW4			Thames Rd, Bark	117	S5
Stan			Tenterden Gdns,	184	H13	Thames Side,	177	P2
Temple Mill La E15	96	C7	Croy 1			Kings T		
Temple PI WC2	18	H10	Tenterden Gro NW4	72	A6	Thames St SE10	132	D11
Temple Rd E6	116	C1	Tenterden Rd N17	60	E14	Thames St, Hmptn	175	S2
Temple Rd N8	75	L8	Tenterden Rd, Croy	184	H13	Thames St, Kings T	177	P3
Temple Rd NW2	89	U7	Tenterden Rd, Dag	101	L3	Thames St, Sun	174	E5
Temple Rd W4	124	E6	Tenterden St W1	16	J8	Thames Village W4	142	E1
Temple Rd W5	123	N6	Teredo St SE16	131	P6	Thames Wf E16	133	L1
Temple Rd, Croy	198	A8	Terence Ct, Belv 3	137	M11	Thamesbank PI	118	F11
Temple Rd, Houns	139	S7	Teresa Ms E17	78	B7	SE28		
Temple Rd, Rich	141	U5	Terling CI E11	97	L5	Thamesgate CI, Rich	159	K8
Temple Sheen	142	D8	Terling Rd, Dag	101	N3	Thameshill Av, Rom	83	U4
SW14			Terminus PI SW1	25	K12	Thameside, Tedd	159	N13
Temple Sheen Rd	142	D8	Terrace, The E4	62	J6	Thameside Ind Est	134	C3
SW14			Terrace, The NW6	108	G1	E16		
Temple St E2	112	J4	Terrace, The SW3	143	K4	Thameside Wk SE28	118	E12
Temple W Ms SE11	27	P11	Terrace, The, Har	86	J1	Thamesmead,	174	B13
Templecombe Rd E9	113	L1	Terrace, The,	63	N11	Walt 1		
Templecombe	180	C10	Wdf Grn			Thamesmead	137	S4
Way, Mord			Terrace Gdns SW13	143	L3	Spine Rd, Belv		
Templehof Av NW2	89	T1	Terrace La, Rich	141	S12	Thamesmere Dr	118	B13
Templeman Rd W7	104	F10	Terrace Rd E9	95	M13	SE28		
Templemead CI W3	106	J12	Terrace Rd E13	115	P2	Thamesvale CI,	139	P4
Templeton Av E4	62	B7	Terrace Rd, Walt	174	C13	Houns		
Templeton CI SE19	184	B2	Terrace Wk, Dag	101	K10	Thane Vil N7	93	M5
Templeton PI SW5	126	H8	Terrapin Rd SW17	164	D5	Thanescroft Gdns,	198	D6
Templeton Rd N15	76	A11	Terrick Rd N22	75	K2	Croy		
Templewood W13	105	K9	Terrick St W12	107	S12	Thanet Dr, Kes	202	B6
Templewood Av	90	J6	Terrilands, Pnr	67	L6	Thanet PI, Croy	197	U7
NW3			Terront Rd N15	75	T9	Thanet Rd, Bex	155	P14
Templewood Gdns	90	J6	Tessa Sanderson	146	D5	Thanet St WC1	10	A7
NW3			PI, SW8 17			Thanington Ct SE9	153	R11
Tempsford Av,	38	H7	Tessa Sanderson	86	B9	Thant CI E10	96	D6
Borwd			Way, Grnf 4			Tharp Rd, Wall	196	G10
Tempsford CI, Enf	43	T6	Testerton Wk W11	108	B13	Thatcham Gdns N20	41	M14
Temsford CI, Har	67	T3	Tetbury PI N1	111	R2	Thatchers CI, Loug	49	L4
Tenbury CI E7	98	A10	Tetcott Rd SW10	127	L14	Thatchers Way, Islw	140	A10
Tenbury Ct,	164	H1	Tetherdown N10	74	B5	Thatches Gro, Rom	82	J7
SW2 2			Tetty Way, Brom	187	N3	Thavies Inn,	19	M5
Tenby Av, Har	68	J4	Teversham La SW8	147	K1	EC1 4		
Tenby CI N15	76	F8	Teviot CI, Well	154	D1	Thaxted PI,	162	A14
Tenby CI, Rom	82	J12	Teviot St E14	114	E9	SW20 3		
Tenby Gdns, Nthlt	85	N12	Tewkesbury Av	149	K14	Thaxted Rd SE9	171	L4
Tenby Rd E17	77	R9	SE23			Thaxted Rd, Buck H	48	C14
Tenby Rd, Edg	69	U2	Tewkesbury Av, Pnr	67	K10	Thaxton Rd W14	126	F11
Tenby Rd, Enf	45	L7	Tewkesbury CI,	76	B11	Thayer St W1	16	E4
Tenby Rd, Rom	83	K12	N15 3			Thayers Fm Rd,	185	S2
Tenby Rd, Well	154	G1	Tewkesbury CI,	48	C11	Beck		
Tench St E1	130	J2	Loug			Theatre St SW11	145	U6
Tenda Rd SE16	130	J8	Tewkesbury Gdns	70	C5	Theberton St N1	111	P1
Tendring Way, Rom	82	E9	NW9			Theed St SE1	27	K3
Tenham Av SW2	164	G2	Tewkesbury Rd N15	76	A12	Thelma Gdns SE3	152	C1
Tenison Way SE1	26	H4	Tewkesbury Rd W13	104	G14	Thelma Gro, Tedd	158	G11
Tenniel CI W2	14	E9	Tewkesbury Rd,	195	P1	Theobald Cres, Har	67	S2
Tennis Ct La, E Mol	176	E6	Cars			Theobald Rd E17	77	U13
Tennis St SE1	28	C6	Tewkesbury Ter N11	58	G11	Theobald Rd, Croy	197	R3
Tennison Av, Borwd	38	C9	Tewson Rd SE18	135	S9	Theobald St SE1	28	D12
Tennison Rd SE25	184	E9	Teynham Av, Enf	44	B11	Theobalds Av N12	57	L8
Tenniswood Rd, Enf	44	E2	Teynham Grn, Brom	187	N9	Theobald's Rd WC1	18	F2
Tennyson Av E11	79	P14	Teynton Ter N17	75	U2	Theodore Rd SE13	150	G11
			Thackeray Av N17	76	G3			

Therapia La, Croy	183	K12
Therapia Rd SE22	149	L11
Theresa Rd W6	125	N8
Thermopylae Gate	132	D8
E14		
Theseus Wk, N1 4	11	S4
Thesiger Rd SE20	167	P13
Thessaly Rd SW8	128	E14
Thetford CI N13	59	S12
Thetford Gdns, Dag	100	H14
Thetford Rd, Dag	118	H1
Thetford Rd, N Mal	178	H10
Theydon Gro,	63	T12
Wdf Grn		
Theydon Pk Rd, Epp	49	R2
Theydon Rd E5	95	L3
Theydon St E17	77	T13
Thicket Cres, Sutt	195	M8
Thicket Gro,	166	G13
SE20 3		
Thicket Gro, Dag	100	F11
Thicket Rd SE20	166	J12
Thicket Rd, Sutt	195	M7
Third Av E12	98	D8
Third Av E13	115	P5
Third Av E17	78	B9
Third Av W3	125	L2
Third Av W10	108	D7
Third Av, Dag	119	R2
Third Av, Enf	44	F9
Third Av, Rom	82	F11
Third Av, Wem	87	N3
Third CI, W Mol	175	S7
Third Cross Rd,	158	B3
Twick		
Third Way, Wem	88	Q8
Thirleby Rd SW1	25	N11
Thirleby Rd, Edg	70	G1
Thirlmere Av, Grnf	105	L5
Thirlmere Gdns,	87	N1
Wem		
Thirlmere Ri, Brom	169	L12
Thirlmere Rd N10	74	D2
Thirlmere Rd SW16	164	G8
Thirlmere Rd, Bexh	155	T2
Thirsk CI, Nthlt	85	P11
Thirsk Rd SE25	184	B7
Thirsk Rd SW11	146	A6
Thirsk Rd, Mitch	164	A13
Thistle Gro SW10	30	H7
Thistle Mead, Loug	48	H6
Thistlebrook SE2	136	E5
Thistlebrook Ind	136	E5
Est SE2		
Thistlecroft Gdns,	69	N2
Stan		
Thistledene, T Ditt	176	D11
Thistledene Av, Har	85	K6
Thistlemead, Chis	188	H3
Thistlewaite Rd E5	95	K6
Thistlewood CI N7	93	M3
Thistleworth CI,	122	A13
Islw		
Thistley CI, N12 1	57	S11
Thomas a'Beckett	86	F7
CI, Wem		
Thomas Baines Rd	145	P6
SW11		
Thomas Darby Ct,	108	C12
W11 13		
Thomas Dean Rd	167	T8
SE26		
Thomas Dinwiddy	169	S4
Rd, SE12 1		
Thomas Doyle St	27	R10
SE1		
Thomas La SE6	150	B14
Thomas More St E1	21	R12
Thomas More Way	73	L5
N2		
Thomas PI, W8 5	22	B12
Thomas Rd E14	114	A10
Thomas St SE18	134	J7
Thomas Wall CI,	194	J9
Sutt 2		
Thompson Av, Rich	142	B5
Thompson CI, Ilf	99	M4
Thompson Rd SE22	148	F11
Thompson Rd, Dag	101	M6
Thompson's Av SE5	35	U13

Name	Page	Grid
Thompson's La, Loug	47	M1
Thomson Cres, Croy	197	N1
Thomson Rd, Har	68	D5
Thorburn Sq SE1	37	S3
Thorburn Way SW19	181	M2
Thoresby St N1	12	A6
Thorkhill Gdns, T Ditt	190	H1
Thorkhill Rd, T Ditt	176	J13
Thorn Av, Bushey	51	U2
Thorn Cl, Brom	188	H11
Thorn Cl, Nthlt	103	M5
Thornaby Gdns N18	60	H11
Thornbury Av, Islw	122	A14
Thornbury Gdns, Borwd	38	F8
Thornbury Rd SW2	146	J12
Thornbury Rd, Islw	140	B1
Thornbury Sq N6	92	E1
Thornby Rd E5	95	L6
Thorncliffe Rd SW2	146	J12
Thorncliffe Rd, Sthl	121	L9
Thorncombe Rd SE22	148	D9
Thorncroft Rd, Sutt	194	J8
Thorncroft St SW8	128	J14
Thorndean St SW18	163	L4
Thorndene Av N11	58	A2
Thorndike Av, Nthlt	102	G2
Thorndike Cl SW10	30	F14
Thorndike St SW1	33	R4
Thorndon Cl, Orp	189	U3
Thorndon Gdns, Epsom	193	K8
Thorndon Rd, Orp	189	U3
Thorndyke Ct, Pnr	51	M12
Thorne Cl E11	96	J7
Thorne Cl E16	115	N11
Thorne Cl, Erith	137	T11
Thorne Pas SW13	143	K4
Thorne Rd SW8	128	J14
Thorne St E16	115	M11
Thorne St SW13	143	K5
Thorneloe Gdns, Croy	197	P10
Thornes Cl, Beck	186	E6
Thornet Wd Rd, Brom	188	G6
Thorney Cres SW11	127	P14
Thorney Hedge Rd W4	124	C8
Thorney St SW1	34	B1
Thorneycroft Cl, Walt	174	E11
Thornfield Av NW7	72	C1
Thornfield Rd W12	125	S3
Thornford Rd SE13	150	F10
Thorngate Rd W9	108	H7
Thorngrove Rd E13	115	S1
Thornham Gro E15	96	G10
Thornham St SE10	132	D12
Thornhaugh St WC1	9	U12
Thornhill Av SE18	135	S13
Thornhill Av, Surb	191	S4
Thornhill Br Wf N1	111	L2
Thornhill Cres N1	93	L14
Thornhill Gdns E10	96	D4
Thornhill Gdns, Bark	99	S13
Thornhill Gro N1	93	M14
Thornhill Rd E10	96	C4
Thornhill Rd N1	93	N14
Thornhill Rd, Croy	183	U14
Thornhill Rd, Surb	191	T3
Thornhill Sq N1	93	M14
Thornlaw Rd SE27	165	R8
Thornley Cl N17	60	H13
Thornley Dr, Har	85	S4
Thornley Pl, SE10 *3*	132	J10
Thornsbeach Rd SE6	168	F2
Thornsett Pl SE20	184	J4
Thornsett Rd SE20	184	J4
Thornsett Rd SW18	163	K3
Thornside, Edg	54	B12
Thornton Av SW2	164	H2
Thornton Av W4	125	K8
Thornton Av, Croy	183	L12
Thornton Cl SW20	180	A9
Thornton Dene, Beck	186	B3
Thornton Gdns SW12	164	G1
Thornton Gro, Pnr	51	N12
Thornton Hill SW19	162	C13
Thornton Pl W1	16	A2
Thornton Rd E11	96	H3
Thornton Rd N18	61	M6
Thornton Rd SW12	146	G14
Thornton Rd SW14	142	G6
Thornton Rd SW19	162	B12
Thornton Rd, Barn	40	C6
Thornton Rd, Belv	137	R7
Thornton Rd, Brom	169	P9
Thornton Rd, Cars	181	S14
Thornton Rd, Croy	183	M12
Thornton Rd, Ilf	98	J8
Thornton Rd, Th Hth	183	M11
Thornton Rd E, SW19 *2*	162	B12
Thornton Rd Retail Pk, Croy	183	L11
Thornton Row, Th Hth *3*	183	P9
Thornton St SW9	147	N3
Thornton Way NW11	73	K10
Thorntree Rd SE7	134	B10
Thornville Gro, Mitch	181	M3
Thornville St SE8	150	A2
Thornwood Cl E18	79	S3
Thornwood Rd SE13	150	J10
Thorogood Gdns E15	97	K10
Thorold Rd N22	59	K13
Thorold Rd, Ilf	99	L2
Thorparch Rd SW8	146	H1
Thorpe Cl, Orp	203	S4
Thorpe Cres E17	77	U3
Thorpe Hall Rd E17	78	F2
Thorpe Rd E6	116	E2
Thorpe Rd E7	97	M7
Thorpe Rd E17	78	E3
Thorpe Rd N15	76	D12
Thorpe Rd, Bark	99	N13
Thorpe Rd, Kings T	159	S13
Thorpebank Rd W12	125	P1
Thorpedale Gdns, Ilf	80	H7
Thorpedale Rd N4	93	K3
Thorpewood Av SE26	167	K4
Thorsden Way SE19	166	C8
Thorverton Rd NW2	90	C6
Thoydon Rd E3	113	R4
Thrale Rd SW16	164	E9
Thrale St SE1	28	A3
Thrawl St E1	21	N3
Threadneedle St EC2	20	E7
Three Colt St E14	113	U13
Three Colts Cor, E2 *2*	13	R11
Three Colts La E2	113	K7
Three Cors, Bexh	155	S4
Three Cups Yd, WC1 *5*	18	G3
Three Kings Rd, Mitch	182	A5
Three Kings Yd W1	16	G9
Three Mill La E3	114	E5
Three Oak La SE1	29	M6
Threshers Pl, W11 *4*	108	C13
Thriffwood SE26	167	M6
Thrift Fm La, Borwd	38	E3
Thrigby Rd, Chess	191	U12
Throckmorten Rd E16	115	S12
Throgmorton Av EC2	20	E6
Throgmorton St EC2	20	E6
Throwley Cl SE2	136	E5
Throwley Rd, Sutt	195	K10
Throwley Way, Sutt	195	K9
Thrupp Cl, Mitch	182	D4
Thrush Grn, Har	67	N8
Thrush St SE17	35	T6
Thunderer Rd, Dag	119	K8
Thurbarn Rd SE6	168	C9
Thurland Rd SE16	29	S10
Thurlby Cl, Har	68	G12
Thurlby Cl, Wdf Grn	64	E10
Thurlby Rd SE27	165	P8
Thurlby Rd, Wem	87	P12
Thurleigh Av SW12	146	B11
Thurleigh Rd SW12	145	T13
Thurleston Av, Mord	180	C9
Thurlestone Av N12	57	T11
Thurlestone Av, Ilf	99	T8
Thurlestone Rd SE27	165	P7
Thurloe Cl SW7	31	N1
Thurloe Pl SW7	31	M1
Thurloe Pl Ms, SW7 *1*	31	L1
Thurloe Sq SW7	31	N1
Thurloe St SW7	31	L2
Thurlow Cl E4	62	E11
Thurlow Gdns, Ilf	65	P12
Thurlow Gdns, Wem	87	P10
Thurlow Hill SE21	165	T2
Thurlow Pk Rd SE21	165	T3
Thurlow Rd NW3	91	N9
Thurlow Rd W7	122	G4
Thurlow St SE17	36	F5
Thurlow Ter NW5 *3*	92	A10
Thurlstone Rd, Ruis	84	A5
Thurnby Ct, Twick	158	D5
Thursland Rd, Sid	172	J10
Thursley Cres, Croy	200	F14
Thursley Gdns SW19	162	B4
Thursley Rd SE9	170	E6
Thurso St SW17	163	N7
Thurstan Rd SW20	161	R13
Thurston Rd SE13	150	D4
Thurston Rd, Sthl	103	M12
Thurtle Rd E2	13	N1
Thwaite Cl, Erith	137	T12
Thyer Cl, Orp	203	L8
Thyra Gro N12	57	K12
Tibbatts Rd E3	114	C7
Tibbenham Wk, E13 *3*	115	M4
Tibberton Sq, N1 *6*	93	T14
Tibbets Cl SW19	162	A2
Tibbet's Cor SW15	143	U14
Tibbet's Ride SW15	144	A13
Tiber Gdns N1	111	K2
Ticehurst Cl, Orp	172	B14
Ticehurst Rd SE23	167	S4
Tickford Cl SE2	136	E3
Tidal Basin Rd E16	115	M13
Tidenham Gdns, Croy	198	D5
Tideswell Rd SW15	143	U9
Tideswell Rd, Croy	200	A5
Tideway Cl, Rich	159	K8
Tidey St E3	114	B9
Tidford Rd, Well	153	U3
Tidworth Rd E3	114	A7
Tiepigs La, Brom	201	K3
Tiepigs La, W Wick	201	K3
Tierney Rd SW2	164	J1
Tiger La, Brom	187	R7
Tiger Way E5	94	J7
Tilbrook Rd SE3	151	U6
Tilbury Cl, SE15 *1*	37	N13
Tilbury Rd E6	116	F4
Tilbury Rd E10	78	E14
Tildesley Rd SW15	143	T11
Tile Fm Rd, Orp	203	P6
Tile Kiln La N6	92	E1
Tile Kiln La N13	59	T9
Tile Kiln La, Bex	173	T3
Tile Yd E14	113	U12
Tilehurst Rd SW18	163	N2
Tilehurst Rd, Sutt	194	C10
Tileyard Rd N7	92	J13
Tilford Av, Croy	200	F14
Tilford Gdns SW19	162	A2
Tilia Cl, Sutt	194	F9
Tilia Rd E5	95	K8
Tiller Rd E14	132	B5
Tillett Cl NW10	88	E12
Tillett Sq, SE16 *2*	131	S4
Tillett Way E2	13	S6
Tilling Rd NW2	71	U14
Tilling Way, Wem	87	P5
Tillingbourne Gdns N3	72	F6
Tillingbourne Way, N3 *1*	72	F7
Tillingham Way N12	56	H7
Tillman St E1	113	K12
Tilloch St, N1 *4*	93	L14
Tillotson Rd N9	60	E3
Tillotson Rd, Har	51	S14
Tillotson Rd, Ilf	80	G13
Tilney Ct EC1	12	B10
Tilney Dr, Buck H	63	P3
Tilney Gdns N1	94	B12
Tilney Rd, Dag	101	M12
Tilney Rd, Sthl	120	E7
Tilney St W1	24	F7
Tilson Gdns SW2	146	J13
Tilson Rd N17	76	H2
Tilt Yd App SE9	152	E12
Tilton St SW6	126	F13
Tiltwood, The W3	106	F13
Timber Cl, Chis	188	H3
Timber Mill Way SW4	146	G5
Timber Pond Rd SE16	131	P2
Timber St, EC1 *8*	11	U10
Timbercroft, Epsom	192	J7
Timbercroft La SE18	135	R12
Timberdene NW4	72	B3
Timberdene Av, Ilf	81	K2
Timberland Rd E1	113	K12
Timberwharf Rd N16	76	H11
Time Sq E8	94	E10
Times Sq, Sutt	195	K9
Timothy Cl SW4	146	E9
Timothy Cl, Bexh	154	J9
Timothy Rd E3	113	T10
Timsbury Wk SW15	161	P1
Tindal St SW9	147	R1
Tinderbox All SW14	142	H5
Tine Rd, Chig	65	S9
Tinsley Rd E1	113	M9
Tintagel Cres SE22	148	E7
Tintagel Dr, Stan	53	P8
Tintern Av NW9	70	D6
Tintern Cl SW15	144	C10
Tintern Cl SW19	163	L13
Tintern Gdns N14	43	K13
Tintern Rd N22	75	T2
Tintern Rd, Cars	195	P2
Tintern St SW4	147	K7
Tintern Way, Har	85	S2
Tinto Rd E16	115	P8
Tinwell Ms, Borwd	38	F9
Tinworth St SE11	34	D5
Tippetts Cl, Enf	43	U2
Tipthorpe Rd, SW11 *1*	146	A6
Tipton Dr, Croy	198	D7
Tiptree Cl E4	62	E6
Tiptree Cres, Ilf	80	H5
Tiptree Dr, Enf	44	B8
Tiptree Est, Ilf	80	H5
Tiptree Rd, Ruis	84	D7
Tirlemont Rd, S Croy	197	T13
Tirrell Rd, Croy	183	T12
Tisbury Rd SW16	182	J4
Tisdall Pl SE17	36	F4
Titchborne Row W2	15	R7
Titchfield Rd NW8	109	T3
Titchfield Rd, Cars	195	P1
Titchfield Wk, Cars *1*	181	P14
Titchwell Rd SW18	145	N14
Tite, St SW3	32	A9
Tithe Barn Cl, Kings T	177	T2
Tithe Barn Way, Nthlt	102	D5
Tithe Cl NW7	71	N1
Tithe Cl, Walt	174	D12
Tithe Fm Av, Har	85	N5
Tithe Fm Cl, Har	85	N5
Tithe Wk NW7	71	N1

Name	Page	Ref
Titley Cl E4	62	A10
Titmuss Av SE28	118	D14
Titmuss St W12	125	S4
Tiverton Av, Ilf	80	G5
Tiverton Dr SE9	171	L1
Tiverton Rd N15	76	A12
Tiverton Rd N18	60	C10
Tiverton Rd NW10	108	B2
Tiverton Rd, Edg	69	T4
Tiverton Rd, Houns	139	T3
Tiverton Rd, Ruis	84	B5
Tiverton Rd, Th Hth 2	183	N9
Tiverton Rd, Wem	105	S3
Tiverton St SE1	27	T11
Tiverton Way, Chess	191	M10
Tivoli Ct, SE16 10	131	T3
Tivoli Gdns SE18	134	C7
Tivoli Rd N8	74	G10
Tivoli Rd SE27	165	T9
Tivoli Rd, Houns	138	J8
Toad La, Houns	139	L7
Tobago St, E14 1	132	A3
Tobin Cl NW3	91	S13
Toby La E1	113	R8
Toby Way, Surb	192	C4
Token Yd SW15	144	C7
Tokenhouse Yd EC2	20	D6
Tokyngton Av, Wem	87	U12
Toland Sq SW15	143	N10
Tolcarne Dr, Pnr	66	D5
Toley Av, Wem	69	S14
Tollbridge Cl W10	108	D7
Tollesbury Gdns, Ilf	81	N5
Tollet St E1	113	N7
Tollgate Dr SE21	166	D4
Tollgate Gdns NW6	6	A1
Tollgate Rd E6	116	C10
Tollgate Rd E16	115	U10
Tollhouse Way, N19 1	92	F3
Tollington Pk N4	93	L3
Tollington Pl N4	93	L3
Tollington Rd N7	93	L7
Tollington Way N7	92	J5
Tolmers Sq NW1	9	N9
Tolpuddle Av, E13 1	115	T2
Tolpuddle St N1	11	K1
Tolsford Rd E5	95	K10
Tolson Rd, Islw	140	G6
Tolverne Rd SW20	179	T2
Tolworth Cl, Surb	192	C2
Tolworth Gdns, Rom	82	H9
Tolworth Pk Rd, Surb	191	T3
Tolworth Rd, Surb	191	T4
Tom Coombs Cl SE9	152	D7
Tom Cribb Rd SE28	135	M6
Tom Gros Cl, E15 6	96	H10
Tom Hood Cl, E15 8	96	H10
Tom Jenkinson Rd, E16 17	133	R1
Tom Mann Cl, Bark	117	S2
Tom Nolan Cl E15	115	K4
Tom Smith Cl SE10	132	J11
Tomlins Gro E3	114	B5
Tomlins Orchard, Bark	117	L2
Tomlins Ter, E14 2		
Tomlinson Cl E2	13	N8
Tomlinson Cl W4	124	C9
Tompion St EC1	11	P8
Tomswood Ct, Ilf	81	M2
Tomswood Hill, Ilf	81	M2
Tomswood Rd, Chig	64	H11
Tonbridge Cres, Har	69	R7
Tonbridge Rd, W Mol	175	K8
Tonbridge St WC1	10	B6
Tonfield Rd, Sutt	194	E1
Tonge Cl, Beck	186	B9
Tonsley Hill SW18	145	K9
Tonsley Pl SW18	145	K9
Tonsley Rd SW18	145	K9
Tonsley St SW18	145	K9
Tonstall Rd, Mitch	182	A3
Tony Cannell Ms E3	113	T6
Tooke Cl, Pnr	66	J1
Took's Ct EC4	19	K5
Tooley St SE1	28	E2
Toorack Rd, Har	68	B3
Tooting Bec Gdns SW16	164	H7
Tooting Bec Rd SW16	164	F7
Tooting Bec Rd SW17	164	A5
Tooting Gro SW17	163	R9
Tooting High St SW17	163	R10
Tootswood Rd, Brom	187	K8
Top Ho Ri E4	46	G14
Top Pk, Beck	186	J9
Topcliffe Dr, Orp	203	N8
Topham Sq N17	75	U1
Topham St, EC1 3	11	K10
Topiary Sq, Rich	141	T5
Topley St SE9	151	U7
Topp Wk NW2	89	T4
Topsfield Cl N8	74	H10
Topsfield Rd N8	74	J9
Topsham Rd SW17	164	A6
Tor Gdns W8	126	G3
Tor Rd, Well	154	F1
Torbay Rd NW6	90	E14
Torbay Rd, Har	85	K5
Torbay St, NW1 7	92	D13
Torbitt Way, Ilf	81	T9
Torbridge Cl, Edg	53	S14
Torbrook Cl, Bex	155	K11
Torcross Dr SE23	167	L4
Torcross Rd, Ruis	84	D6
Tormead Cl, Sutt	194	H11
Tormount Rd SE18	135	R11
Toronto Av E12	98	E7
Toronto Rd E11	96	H7
Toronto Rd, Ilf	99	K1
Torquay Gdns, Ilf	80	B7
Torquay St W2	14	A3
Torr Rd SE20	167	N14
Torre Wk, Cars	195	R1
Torrens Rd E15	97	L11
Torrens Rd SW2	147	L9
Torrens Sq E15	97	L11
Torrens St EC1	11	N3
Torriano Av NW5	92	G10
Torriano Cotts NW5	92	F10
Torriano Ms NW5	92	F9
Torridge Gdns SE15	149	L7
Torridge Rd, Th Hth	183	S9
Torridon Rd SE6	168	H2
Torridon Rd SE13	150	J13
Torrington Av N12	57	P9
Torrington Cl N12	57	N8
Torrington Cl, Esher	190	D12
Torrington Dr, Har	85	R7
Torrington Dr, Loug	49	M7
Torrington Gdns N11	58	F12
Torrington Gdns, Grnf	105	L1
Torrington Gdns, Loug	49	M7
Torrington Gro N12	57	R9
Torrington Pk N12	57	M9
Torrington Pl E1	29	U3
Torrington Pl WC1	17	R1
Torrington Rd E18	79	P6
Torrington Rd, Dag	101	M1
Torrington Rd, Esher	190	D11
Torrington Rd, Grnf	105	L2
Torrington Rd, Ruis	84	A5
Torrington Sq WC1	9	T12
Torrington Sq, Croy 6	184	A14
Torrington Way, Mord	180	G13
Torver Rd, Har	68	C8
Torver Way, Orp	203	N5
Torwood Rd SW15	143	P10
Tothill St SW1	25	S8
Totnes Rd, Well	136	D14
Totnes Wk N2	73	P8
Tottan Ter E1	113	P11
Tottenhall Rd N13	59	N11
Tottenham Ct Rd W1	9	P12
Tottenham Grn E N15	76	E7
Tottenham La N8	75	K10
Tottenham Ms W1	17	N2
Tottenham Rd N1	94	C12
Tottenham St W1	17	N3
Totterdown St SW17	163	U9
Totteridge Common N20	55	U2
Totteridge Grn N20	56	G4
Totteridge La N20	57	K2
Totteridge Village N20	56	F3
Totternhoe Cl, Har	69	M10
Totton Rd, Th Hth	183	P6
Toulmin St SE1	27	U7
Toulon St, SE5 1	129	T14
Tournay Rd SW6	126	F13
Toussaint Wk, SE16 5	29	U10
Tovil Cl SE20	184	H3
Towcester Rd E3	114	D8
Tower Br E1	130	E2
Tower Br SE1	130	E2
Tower Br App E1	29	M1
Tower Br Rd SE1	28	H10
Tower Cl NW3	91	P9
Tower Cl SE20	166	J13
Tower Cl, Ilf	65	K12
Tower Cl, Orp	203	U4
Tower Ct, WC2 14	17	U9
Tower Gdns, Esher	190	H14
Tower Gdns Rd N17	76	A2
Tower Hamlets Rd E7	97	M8
Tower Hamlets Rd E17	78	B6
Tower Hill EC3	21	K12
Tower La, Wem	87	N5
Tower Ms E17	78	B8
Tower Mill Rd SE15	36	G12
Tower Pier EC3	29	K1
Tower Pl EC3	20	J12
Tower Ri, Rich	141	R6
Tower Rd NW10	89	N13
Tower Rd, Belv	137	U8
Tower Rd, Bexh	155	P7
Tower Rd, Orp	203	U5
Tower Rd, Twick	158	E5
Tower Royal, EC4 2	20	B9
Tower St WC2	18	A8
Tower Ter N22	75	L3
Tower Vw, Croy	185	P14
Towers Pl, Rich	141	R9
Towers Rd, Pnr	66	J1
Towers Rd, Sthl	103	P7
Towfield Rd, Felt	157	L3
Town, The, Enf	44	B6
Town Ct Path N4	93	U1
Town Fld Way, Islw 2	140	H4
Town Hall App Rd N15	76	E7
Town Hall Av W4	124	G9
Town Hall Rd SW11	145	U6
Town Meadow, Brent	123	P13
Town Quay, Bark	117	K2
Town Rd N9	60	J4
Towncourt Cres, Orp	189	M9
Towncourt La, Orp	189	N12
Towney Mead, Nthlt	103	L4
Townholm Cres W7	122	E5
Townley Ct E15	97	L12
Townley Rd SE22	148	D10
Townley Rd, Bexh	155	M10
Townley St SE17	36	C5
Townmead Rd SW6	145	L3
Townmead Rd, Rich	142	D3
Townsend Av N14	58	H7
Townsend Ind Est NW10	106	G3
Townsend La NW9	70	H14
Townsend Rd N15	76	E10
Townsend Rd, Sthl	120	J2
Townsend St SE17	36	F3
Townsend Yd N6	92	B1
Townshend Cl, Sid	172	D12
Townshend Est NW8 7		P1
Townshend Rd NW8	109	R2
Townshend Rd, Chis	170	J10
Townshend Rd, Rich	141	T8
Townshend Ter, Rich	141	T8
Townson Av, Nthlt	102	B4
Townson Way, Nthlt	102	C4
Towpath Wk E9	95	T9
Towpath Way, Croy	184	E11
Towton Rd SE27	165	T4
Toynbee Cl, Chis	171	K8
Toynbee Rd SW20	180	C1
Toynbee St E1	21	M3
Toyne Way N6	73	U11
Tracey Av NW2	89	T9
Tracy Ct, Stan	53	L14
Trade Cl N13	59	N8
Trader Rd E6	116	J12
Tradescant Rd SW8	129	K14
Trading Est Rd NW10	106	E8
Trafalgar Av N17	60	C12
Trafalgar Av SE15	37	N9
Trafalgar Av, Wor Pk	194	B2
Trafalgar Business Cen, Bark	117	U7
Trafalgar Cl, SE16 1	131	R7
Trafalgar Gdns E1	113	P9
Trafalgar Gdns W8	22	B10
Trafalgar Gro SE10	132	H11
Trafalgar Pl E11	79	P8
Trafalgar Pl N18	60	G10
Trafalgar Rd SE10	132	J10
Trafalgar Rd SW19	163	K13
Trafalgar Rd, Twick	158	B4
Trafalgar Sq SW1	25	U1
Trafalgar Sq WC2	25	U1
Trafalgar St SE17	36	D6
Trafalgar Ter, Har	86	C1
Trafalgar Way E14	132	E1
Trafalgar Way, Croy	197	M3
Trafford Cl E15	96	D9
Trafford Cl, Ilf	65	U12
Trafford Rd, Th Hth	183	M9
Tramway Av E15	96	J13
Tramway Av N9	45	K13
Tramway Path, Mitch	181	T9
Tranby Pl E9	95	P9
Tranley Ms, NW3 2	91	S8
Tranmere Rd N9	44	E14
Tranmere Rd SW18	163	L2
Tranmere Rd, Twick	139	S13
Tranquil Vale SE3	151	K4
Transay Wk N1	93	A11
Transept St NW1	15	R3
Transmere Cl, Orp	189	M12
Transmere Rd, Orp	189	M12
Transom Cl, SE16 3	131	S7
Transom Sq E14	132	C9
Transport Av, Brent	122	J11
Tranton Rd SE16	29	U10
Traps Hill, Loug	48	E7
Traps La, N Mal	160	J14
Travellers Way, Houns	138	F3
Travers Cl E17	77	P1
Travers Rd N7	93	N5
Treacy Cl, Bushey	51	U3
Treadgold St W11	108	B13
Treadway St E2	112	J4
Treaty St N1	111	L2
Trebeck St W1	24	H2
Trebovir Rd SW5	126	H9
Treby St E3	113	T8
Trecastle Way N7	92	H8
Tredegar Ms E3	113	T5
Tredegar Rd E3	113	T4
Tredegar Rd N11	58	H14
Tredegar Sq E3	113	T5
Tredegar Ter E3	113	T5
Trederwen Rd E8	112	H1
Tredown Rd SE26	167	M10
Tredwell Cl SW2	165	M4

Tredwell Cl, Brom	188	C7	Trevor Cl, Barn	41	P11	Trojan Way, Croy	197	M5
Tredwell Rd SE27	165	R8	Trevor Cl, Brom	187	M14	Troon Cl, SE16 10	131	K9
Tree Cl, Rich	159	P2	Trevor Cl, Har	52	F13	Troon St E1	113	R11
Tree Rd E16	115	T19	Trevor Cl, Islw	140	F9	Trosley Rd, Belv	137	N12
Treen Av SW13	143	K6	Trevor Gdns, Edg	70	G1	Trossachs Rd SE22	148	D9
Treetops Cl SE2	137	K9	Trevor Gdns, Nthlt	102	E4	Trothy Rd SE1	37	T2
Treeview Cl, SE19 1	184	D1	Trevor Gdns, Ruis	84	A7	Trott Rd N10	58	A14
Treewall Gdns, Brom	169	R8	Trevor Pl SW7	23	S7	Trott St SW11	145	P2
Trefgarne Rd, Dag	101	N4	Trevor Rd SW19	162	D14	Trotwood, Chig	65	P11
Trefil Wk N7	93	K7	Trevor Rd, Edg	70	H2	Troughton Rd SE7	133	S9
Trefoil Rd SW18	145	M10	Trevor Rd, Wdf Grn	63	P13	Troutbeck Rd SE14	149	R1
Tregaron Av N8	75	K12	Trevor Sq SW7	23	T8	Trouville Rd SW4	146	E12
Tregaron Gdns, N Mal	179	K7	Trevor St SW7	23	S7	Trowbridge Rd E9	95	U12
Tregarvon Rd SW11	146	B7	Trevose Rd E17	78	G2	Trowlock Av, Tedd	159	M11
Tregenna Av, Har	85	N7	Trevose Way, Wat	50	E5	Trowlock Island, Tedd	159	N10
Tregenna Cl N14	42	F10	Trewenna Dr, Chess	191	P9	Trowlock Way, Tedd	159	N12
Tregenna Ct, Har	85	P7	Trewince Rd SW20	179	U2	Troy Ct SE18	135	K8
Trego Rd E9	95	U13	Trewint St SW18	163	L4	Troy Rd SE19	166	B12
Tregothnan Rd SW9	147	K5	Trewsbury Rd SE26	167	P9	Troy Town SE15	148	H6
Tregunter Rd SW10	30	E8	Triandra Way, Hayes	102	H9	Trubshaw Rd, Sthl 3	121	R5
Trehearn Rd, Ilf	65	N13	Triangle, The, Kings T	178	E4	Truesdale Rd E6	116	F12
Trehern Rd SW14	142	H6	Triangle Ct E16	116	A9	Trulock Rd N17	60	H13
Treherne Ct SW17	164	B7	Triangle Pas, Barn	41	M8	Truman Cl, Edg	54	D13
Trehurst St E5	95	R9	Triangle Pl SW4	146	G8	Truman's Rd N16	94	D9
Trelawn Rd E10	96	F6	Triangle Rd E8	112	J1	Trump St, EC2 5	20	B7
Trelawn Rd SW2	147	N9	Trident St SE16	131	P7	Trumpers Way W7	122	E6
Trelawney Cl E17	78	D8	Trident Way, Sthl	120	D5	Trumpington Rd E7	97	L7
Trelawney Est E9	95	L11	Trig La EC4	19	U10	Trundle St, SE1 7	27	U6
Trelawney Rd, Ilf	65	N14	Trigon Rd SW8	34	H13	Trundlers Way, Bushey	52	C1
Treloar Gdns SE19	166	A12	Trilby Rd SE23	167	P3	Trundleys Rd SE8	131	P9
Tremadoc Rd SW4	146	H7	Trim St SE14	131	T12	Trundleys Ter SE8	131	P8
Tremaine Cl SE4	150	A4	Trimmer Wk, Brent 1	123	R11	Truro Gdns, Ilf	80	D14
Tremaine Rd SE20	185	K4				Truro Rd E17	77	U8
Trematon Pl, Tedd	159	M13	Trinder Gdns N19	93	K1	Truro Rd N22	59	L14
Tremlett Gro N19	92	E5	Trinder Rd N19	93	K1	Truro St NW5	92	A12
Tremlett Ms N19	92	E5	Trinder Rd, Barn	39	U9	Truslove Rd SE27	165	P9
Trenance Gdns, Ilf	100	A5	Tring Av W5	123	U3	Trussley Rd W6	125	T6
Trenchard Av, Ruis	84	C8	Tring Av, Sthl	103	M11	Trust Wk SE21	165	S1
Trenchard Cl, Stan	52	H11	Tring Av, Wem	88	A12	Tryfan Cl, Ilf	80	B9
Trenchard St SE10	132	H10	Tring Cl, Ilf	81	N10	Tryon St SW3	31	U5
Trenholde St SW8	34	B12	Trinidad St, E14 13	113	U13	Trystings Cl, Esher	190	H11
Trenholme Cl, SE20 4	167	K13	Trinity Av N2	73	N6	Tuam Rd SE18	135	N12
Trenholme Rd SE20	166	J13	Trinity Av, Enf	44	F11	Tubbenden Cl, Orp	203	R5
Trenholme Ter SE20	166	J13	Trinity Buoy Wf E14	115	L14	Tubbenden Dr, Orp	203	P7
Trenmar Gdns NW10	107	R5	Trinity Ch Pas SW13	125	S12	Tubbenden La, Orp	203	S5
Trent Av W5	123	M5	Trinity Ch Rd SW13	125	S12	Tubbenden La S, Orp	203	N9
Trent Gdns N14	42	D12	Trinity Cl CO	94	F11	Tubbs Rd NW10	107	M4
Trent Rd SW2	147	L10	Trinity Cl E11	96	J3	Tudor Av, Hmptn	157	P12
Trent Rd, Buck H	63	R2	Trinity Cl SE13	150	G8	Tudor Av, Wor Pk	193	R6
Trent Way, Wor Pk	193	T5	Trinity Cl, Brom	202	C2	Tudor Cl N6	74	E14
Trentbridge Cl, Ilf	65	T12	Trinity Cl, Houns	139	K7	Tudor Cl NW3	91	R10
Trentham St SW18	162	G1	Trinity Cotts, Rich	141	U6	Tudor Cl NW7	55	P12
Trentwood Side, Enf	43	L5	Trinity Ct N1	112	C1	Tudor Cl NW9	88	F3
Treport St SW18	145	K13	Trinity Ct SE7	134	A8	Tudor Cl SW2	147	L12
Tresco Cl, Brom	168	J12	Trinity Cres SW17	163	U4	Tudor Cl, Chess	191	S9
Tresco Gdns, Ilf	100	A4	Trinity Gdns SW9	147	L7	Tudor Cl, Chig	64	H7
Tresco Rd SE15	149	K7	Trinity Gro SE10	150	E1	Tudor Cl, Chis	188	F2
Trescoe Gdns, Har	67	K14	Trinity Ms SE20	185	K2	Tudor Cl, Pnr	66	B10
Tresham Cres NW8	7	P9	Trinity Ms W10	108	B11	Tudor Cl, Sutt	194	B10
Tresham Rd, Bark	99	T14	Trinity Path SE26	167	L6	Tudor Cl, Wall	196	F14
Tresilian Av N21	43	L9	Trinity Pl, Bexh	155	L7	Tudor Cl, Wdf Grn	63	S9
Tressell Cl N1	93	S14	Trinity Ri SW2	147	R14	Tudor Ct E17	77	S13
Tressillian Cres SE4	150	A5	Trinity Rd N2	73	N5	Tudor Ct, Felt	156	E7
Tressillian Rd SE4	149	U7	Trinity Rd N22	75	L1	Tudor Ct N, Wem	88	B10
Trestis Cl, Hayes	102	H8	Trinity Rd SW17	163	U4	Tudor Ct S, Wem	88	B10
Treswell Rd, Dag	119	K1	Trinity Rd SW18	145	L8	Tudor Cres, Enf	43	S1
Tretawn Gdns NW7	55	K7	Trinity Rd SW19	162	H11	Tudor Cres, Ilf	65	L11
Tretawn Pk NW7	55	K7	Trinity Rd, Ilf	81	L5	Tudor Dr, Kings T	159	P9
Trevanion Rd W14	126	D9	Trinity Rd, Rich	141	U6	Tudor Dr, Mord	179	B12
Treve Av, Har	68	A14	Trinity Rd, Sthl	120	J2	Tudor Est NW10	106	C4
Trevelyan Av E12	98	F8	Trinity Sq EC3	21	K11	Tudor Gdns NW9	88	F4
Trevelyan Cres, Har	69	P13	Trinity St E16	115	M10	Tudor Gdns, SW13 5	143	K6
Trevelyan Gdns NW10	107	T2	Trinity St SE1	28	A8	Tudor Gdns W3	106	B10
Trevelyan Rd E15	97	L8	Trinity St, Enf	43	T3	Tudor Gdns, Twick	158	F1
Trevelyan Rd SW17	163	S11	Trinity Wk NW3	91	M12	Tudor Gdns, W Wick	200	E6
Treveris St SE1	27	P3	Trinity Way E4	61	U12	Tudor Gro E9	95	L14
Treverton St W10	108	B8	Trinity Way W3	107	K14	Tudor Gro N20	57	R5
Treves Cl N21	43	L9	Trio Pl SE1	28	A8	Tudor Pl W1	17	S5
Treville St SW15	143	R13	Tristan Sq SE3	151	K6	Tudor Pl, Mitch	163	S14
Treviso Rd, SE23 5	167	P3	Tristram Cl E17	78	H5	Tudor Rd E4	62	D11
Trevithick St, SE8 6	132	A11	Tristram Rd, Brom	169	M7	Tudor Rd E6	115	U2
Trevone Gdns, Pnr	67	K11	Triton Sq NW1	9	L10	Tudor Rd E9	95	L14
			Tritton Av, Croy	197	K7	Tudor Rd N9	45	K14
			Tritton Rd SE21	166	A6	Tudor Rd SE19	166	E13
			Triumph Rd E6	116	F11	Tudor Rd SE25	185	K10
						Tudor Rd, Bark	117	T1
						Tudor Rd, Barn	40	J5
						Tudor Rd, Beck	186	D6
						Tudor Rd, Hmptn	157	P14
						Tudor Rd, Har	68	B3
						Tudor Rd, Houns	140	A7
						Tudor Rd, Kings T	160	A14
						Tudor Rd, Pnr	66	F4
						Tudor Rd, Sthl	102	J14
						Tudor St EC4	19	L9
						Tudor Wk, Bex	155	K11
						Tudor Way N14	58	H1
						Tudor Way W3	124	A4
						Tudor Way, Orp	189	N11
						Tudor Well Cl, Stan	53	K10
						Tudway Rd SE3	151	T8
						Tufnell Pk Rd N7	92	J6
						Tufnell Pk Rd N19	92	E7
						Tufter Rd, Chig	65	T10
						Tufton Gdns, W Mol	175	S4
						Tufton Rd E4	62	A8
						Tufton St SW1	26	A11
						Tugboat St SE28	135	R3
						Tugela Rd, Croy	184	A12
						Tugela St SE6	167	U4
						Tugmutton Cl, Orp 3	203	K8
						Tuilerie St E2	13	S2
						Tulip Cl E6	116	E10
						Tulip Cl, Croy	199	N2
						Tulip Cl, Hmptn	157	M11
						Tulip Cl, Sthl	121	U3
						Tulip Ct, Pnr	66	E5
						Tulip Gdns, Ilf	98	J11
						Tull St, Mitch	181	T14
						Tulse Cl, Beck	186	E6
						Tulse Hill SW2	147	N11
						Tulse Hill Est SW2	147	N12
						Tulsemere Rd SE27	165	U3
						Tumbling Bay, Walt	174	A11
						Tummons Gdns SE25	184	D3
						Tuncombe Rd, N18 1	60	C7
						Tunis Rd W12	125	S1
						Tunley Rd NW10	106	J1
						Tunley Rd SW17	164	A2
						Tunmarsh La E13	115	T5
						Tunnan Leys E6	116	H11
						Tunnel Av SE10	132	H4
						Tunnel Gdns N11	58	F13
						Tunnel Rd SE16	131	L3
						Tunstall Cl, Orp	203	S7
						Tunstall Rd SW9	147	M7
						Tunstall Rd, Croy	198	D2
						Tunstall Wk, Brent 2	123	R11
						Tunstock Way, Belv	137	K6
						Tunworth Cl NW9	70	F12
						Tunworth Cres SW15	143	L12
						Tupelo Rd E10	96	C4
						Turenne Cl SW18	145	M8
						Turin Rd N9	45	L14
						Turin St E2	13	R7
						Turkey Oak Cl SE19	184	C1
						Turk's Head Yd EC1	19	N1
						Turks Row SW3	32	B6
						Turle Rd N4	93	L3
						Turle Rd SW16	182	J3
						Turlewray Cl N4	93	L2
						Turley Cl E15	115	K2
						Turnagain La, EC4 2	19	N5
						Turnage Rd, Dag	100	J2
						Turnberry Cl NW4	72	B3
						Turnberry Cl, SE16 8	131	K10
						Turnberry Ct, Wat	50	E6
						Turnberry Quay E14	132	D6
						Turnberry Way, Orp	203	P1
						Turnbury Cl SE28	118	H12
						Turnchapel Ms, SW4 12	146	C6
						Turner Av N15	76	C8
						Turner Av, Mitch	181	T1
						Turner Av, Twick	157	U5
						Turner Cl NW11	73	K12
						Turner Cl, Wem	87	N11
						Turner Dr NW11	72	J12

Turner Rd E17	78	E6
Turner Rd, Edg	69	U5
Turner Rd, N Mal	178	H13
Turner St E1	112	J10
Turner St E16	115	L12
Turners Meadow	185	T2
Way, Beck		
Turners Rd E3	113	T10
Turners Way, Croy	197	N4
Turners Wd NW11	91	L1
Turneville Rd W14	126	E11
Turney Rd SE21	147	U14
Turnham Grn Ter	124	J7
W4		
Turnham Grn Ter	124	J8
Ms, W4 *4*		
Turnham Rd SE4	149	R9
Turnmill St EC1	11	M12
Turnpike Cl SE8	131	U13
Turnpike La N8	75	N6
Turnpike La, Sutt	195	M10
Turnpike Link, Croy	198	D4
Turnpike Way, Islw	140	G2
Turnpin La SE10	132	F12
Turnstone Cl E13	115	N5
Turnstone Cl,	71	K3
NW9 *3*		
Turpentine La SW1	32	J7
Turpin Way N19	92	G2
Turpin Way, Wall	196	D13
Turpington Cl, Brom	188	C12
Turpington La, Brom	188	C13
Turpins La, Wdf Grn	64	F10
Turquand St SE17	36	B4
Turret Gro SW4	146	E5
Turton Rd, Wem	87	R10
Turville St, E2 *3*	13	M9
Tuscan Rd SE18	135	P10
Tuskar St SE10	132	J10
Tustin Est SE15	131	L12
Tuttlebee La, Buck H	63	P3
Tweedale Ct,	96	E9
E15 *1*		
Tweeddale Rd, Cars	195	N1
Tweedmouth Rd E13	115	R4
Tweedy Cl, Enf	44	E10
Tweedy Rd, Brom	187	N2
Tweezer's All,	18	J9
WC2 *3*		
Twelvetrees Cres E3	114	E7
Twentyman Cl,	63	P9
Wdf Grn		
Twickenham Br,	141	L10
Rich		
Twickenham Br,	141	L10
Twick		
Twickenham Cl,	197	L6
Croy *4*		
Twickenham Gdns,	86	G9
Grnf		
Twickenham Gdns,	52	C14
Har		
Twickenham Rd E11	96	G3
Twickenham Rd,	157	M6
Felt		
Twickenham Rd,	141	M8
Rich		
Twickenham Rd,	158	H9
Tedd		
Twickenham Trd	140	E11
Est, Twick		
Twig Folly Cl E2	113	P4
Twilley St SW18	144	J14
Twin Tumps Way	118	A14
SE28		
Twine Cl, Bark	118	C5
Twine Ct E1	113	L13
Twineham Grn N12	56	H7
Twining Av, Twick	157	U5
Twinn Rd NW7	56	D11
Twisden Rd NW5	92	C7
Twybridge Way	88	F14
NW10		
Twycross Ms SE10	133	K8
Twyford Abbey Rd	106	B4
NW10		
Twyford Av N2	73	U5
Twyford Av W3	106	B14
Twyford Cres W3	124	B1

Twyford Rd, Cars	195	N1
Twyford Rd, Har	67	R14
Twyford Rd, Ilf	99	L9
Twyford St N1	111	L1
Tyas Rd E16	115	L8
Tybenham Rd SW19	180	G5
Tyberry Rd, Enf	45	K5
Tyburn La, Har	68	D13
Tyburn Way W1	16	A9
Tycehurst Hill, Loug	48	E8
Tye La, Orp	203	M10
Tyers Est SE1	28	H6
Tyers Gate SE1	28	H6
Tyers St SE11	34	F5
Tyers Ter SE11	34	F7
Tyeshurst Cl SE2	137	K10
Tylecroft Rd SW16	183	K3
Tylehurst Gdns, Ilf	99	L9
Tyler Cl E2	13	M1
Tyler St SE10	133	K10
Tylers Cl, Loug	48	C13
Tylers Gate, Har	69	S12
Tylers Path, Cars	195	U7
Tylney Av SE19	166	E9
Tylney Rd E7	97	T7
Tylney Rd, Brom	188	A4
Tynan Cl, Felt	156	B1
Tyndale Ct E14	132	C8
Tyndale La N1	93	R13
Tyndale Ter N1	93	R13
Tyndall Rd E10	96	E4
Tyndall Rd, Well	153	U6
Tyne St, E1 *6*	21	N6
Tyneham Rd SW11	146	B4
Tynemouth Cl E6	116	J12
Tynemouth Rd N15	76	F8
Tynemouth Rd SE18	135	T9
Tynemouth Rd,	164	A13
Mitch		
Tynemouth St SW6	145	L3
Type St E2	113	N4
Tyrawley Rd SW6	144	J1
Tyrell Cl, Har	86	D7
Tyrell Ct, Cars	195	U7
Tyrols Rd SE23	167	P1
Tyron Way, Sid	171	T9
Tyrone Rd E6	116	F4
Tyrrel Way NW9	71	M13
Tyrrell Av, Well	154	C10
Tyrrell Rd SE22	148	H8
Tyrrell Sq, Mitch	181	R2
Tyrwhitt Rd SE4	150	B5
Tysoe St EC1	11	L8
Tyson Rd SE23	149	M14
Tyssen Pas E8	94	E11
Tyssen Rd N16	94	E5
Tyssen St E8	94	F11
Tyssen St N1	12	J3
Tytherton Rd N19	92	G6

U

Uamvar St E14	114	D9
Uckfield Gro, Mitch	182	B1
Udall St SW1	33	P3
Udney Pk Rd, Tedd	158	H10
Uffington Rd NW10	107	P1
Uffington Rd SE27	165	P7
Ufford Cl, Har	51	S14
Ufford Rd, Har	51	S14
Ufford St SE1	27	M6
Ufton Gro N1	94	B13
Ufton Rd N1	94	B14
Uhura Sq, N16 *4*	94	D6
Ujima Ct SW16	165	K7
Ullathorne Rd SW16	164	E8
Ulleswater Rd N14	59	K6
Ullin St E14	114	E10
Ullswater Cl SW15	160	H8
Ullswater Cl, Brom	169	K12
Ullswater Ct, Har	67	N14
Ullswater Cres	160	H7
SW15		
Ullswater Rd SE27	165	R4
Ullswater Rd SW13	125	N14
Ulster Gdns N13	59	T7
Ulster Pl NW1	8	G11
Ulster Ter NW1	8	F11

Ulundi Rd SE3	133	K12
Ulva Rd, SW15 *10*	144	B8
Ulverscroft Rd SE22	148	F10
Ulverston Rd E17	78	G3
Ulverstone Rd,	165	R4
SE27 *1*		
Ulysses Rd NW6	90	F9
Umberston St E1	112	H11
Umbria St SW15	143	P12
Umfreville Rd N4	75	R12
Undercliff Rd SE13	150	B5
Underhill, Barn	40	G9
Underhill Rd SE22	148	G10
Underhill St NW1	110	D2
Underne Av N14	58	D4
Undershaft EC3	20	H7
Undershaw Rd,	169	L6
Brom		
Underwood, Croy	200	E10
Underwood, The	170	F4
SE9		
Underwood Rd E1	13	S12
Underwood Rd E4	62	D9
Underwood Rd,	63	U14
Wdf Grn		
Underwood Row,	12	B5
N1 *3*		
Underwood St N1	12	B5
Undine Rd E14	132	D7
Undine St SW17	163	T9
Uneeda Dr, Grnf	104	B1
Union Cl E11	96	H7
Union Cotts, E15 *7*	97	K13
Union Ct EC2	20	G5
Union Dr E1	113	R7
Union Gro SW8	146	G3
Union Rd N11	58	H11
Union Rd SW4	146	H4
Union Rd SW8	146	H4
Union Rd, Brom	188	B9
Union Rd, Croy	183	U13
Union Rd, Nthlt	103	P4
Union Rd, Wem	87	R11
Union Sq N1	111	T2
Union St E15	114	F2
Union St SE1	27	S4
Union St, Barn	40	D6
Union St, Kings T	177	P4
Union Wk E2	13	K5
Unity Cl NW10	89	N12
Unity Cl SE19	165	T10
Unity Way SE18	134	A5
University Cl,	55	L14
NW7 *2*		
University Gdns,	155	M13
Bex		
University Pl, Erith	137	T14
University Rd SW19	163	P12
University St WC1	9	P11
University Way E16	116	H14
Unwin Cl SE15	37	R12
Unwin Rd SW7	23	L10
Unwin Rd, Islw	140	D6
Upbrook Ms W2	14	G8
Upcerne Rd SW10	127	M14
Upchurch Cl,	167	K14
SE20 *6*		
Upcroft Av, Edg	54	E9
Updale Rd, Sid	171	T7
Upfield, Croy	198	J5
Upfield Rd W7	104	E9
Uphall Rd, Ilf	99	K10
Upham Pk Rd W4	125	K7
Uphill Dr NW7	55	K9
Uphill Dr NW9	70	F10
Uphill Gro NW7	55	K7
Uphill Rd NW7	55	K8
Upland Ms SE22	148	G9
Upland Rd E13	115	N7
Upland Rd SE22	148	H9
Upland Rd, Bexh	155	L6
Upland Rd, S Croy	198	A10
Upland Rd, Sutt	195	P14
Uplands, Beck	186	A4
Uplands, The, Loug	48	E6
Uplands, The, Ruis	66	B14
Uplands Av E17	77	P4
Uplands Business	77	N5
Pk E17		
Uplands Cl SW14	142	D10

Uplands End,	64	C13
Wdf Grn		
Uplands Pk Rd, Enf	43	P4
Uplands Rd N8	75	M10
Uplands Rd, Barn	58	B2
Uplands Rd, Rom	82	G6
Uplands Rd,	64	C14
Wdf Grn		
Uplands Way N21	43	N9
Upney La, Bark	99	S10
Upnor Way SE17	37	K6
Uppark Dr, Ilf	81	M11
Upper Abbey Rd,	137	M7
Belv		
Upper Addison	126	C3
Gdns W14		
Upper Belgrave St	24	F9
SW1		
Upper Berkeley St	15	U7
W1		
Upper Beulah Hill	184	C1
SE19		
Upper Brighton Rd,	177	R13
Surb		
Upper Brockley Rd	149	T5
SE4		
Upper Brook St W1	16	C11
Upper Butts, Brent	123	N12
Upper Cavendish	72	G5
Av N3		
Upper Cheyne Row	31	P10
SW3		
Upper Clapton Rd	94	J3
E5		
Upper Elmers End	185	S10
Rd, Beck		
Upper Fm Rd,	175	M8
W Mol		
Upper Grn E, Mitch	181	T4
Upper Grn W, Mitch	181	T4
Upper Grosvenor	16	C11
St W1		
Upper Grotto Rd,	158	E3
Twick		
Upper Grd SE1	26	H2
Upper Grd SE25	184	D7
Upper Gro Rd, Belv	137	L11
Upper Ham Rd,	159	P7
Kings T		
Upper Ham Rd, Rich	159	P7
Upper Harley St	8	G11
NW1		
Upper Hitch, Wat	51	K2
Upper Holly Hill	137	S9
Rd, Belv		
Upper James St,	17	N10
W1 *4*		
Upper John St W1	17	N10
Upper Mall W6	125	P9
Upper Marsh SE1	26	G9
Upper Montagu St	15	U2
W1		
Upper Mulgrave	194	D14
Rd, Sutt		
Upper N St E14	114	B12
Upper Palace Rd,	175	U6
E Mol		
Upper Pk, Loug	48	A9
Upper Pk Rd N11	58	D10
Upper Pk Rd NW3	91	T10
Upper Pk Rd, Belv	137	R8
Upper Pk Rd, Brom	187	S1
Upper Pk Rd,	160	A12
Kings T		
Upper Phillimore	126	C9
Gdns W8		
Upper Richmond	144	C9
Rd SW15		
Upper Richmond	142	E7
Rd W SW14		
Upper Richmond	142	B8
Rd W, Rich		
Upper Rd E13	115	N5
Upper Rd, Wall	196	H10
Upper St. Martin's	18	A9
La, WC2 *8*		
Upper Selsdon Rd,	198	D14
S Croy		
Upper Sheridan	137	N7
Rd, Belv		

Upper Shirley Rd, 199 M4
Croy
Upper St N1 11 M2
Upper Sunbury Rd, 175 M2
Hmptn
Upper Sutton La, 139 N1
Houns
Upper Tachbrook 33 N2
St SW1
Upper Tail, Wat 51 K6
Upper Teddington 159 L14
Rd, Kings T
Upper Ter, NW3 *1* 91 L6
Upper Thames St 19 T10
EC4
Upper Tollington 93 N1
Pk N4
Upper Tooting Pk 163 U3
SW17
Upper Tooting Rd 163 T7
SW17
Upper Town Rd, 103 R8
Grnf
Upper Tulse Hill 147 L13
SW2
Upper Vernon Rd, 195 N9
Sutt
Upper 78 G7
Walthamstow Rd
E17
Upper Wickham 154 C4
La, Well
Upper Wimpole St 16 F1
W1
Upper Woburn Pl 9 T9
WC1
Upperton Rd, Sid 171 U9
Upperton Rd E E13 115 U5
Upperton Rd W E13 115 T6
Uppingham Av, Stan 69 M5
Upsdell Av N13 59 N11
Upstall St SE5 147 S2
Upton Av E7 97 P13
Upton Cl, Bex 155 M11
Upton Dene, Sutt 194 J14
Upton Gdns, Har 69 K10
Upton La E7 97 P13
Upton Pk Rd E7 97 R14
Upton Rd N18 60 H9
Upton Rd SE18 135 M12
Upton Rd, Bex 155 L11
Upton Rd, Bexh 154 J7
Upton Rd, Houns 139 P6
Upton Rd, Th Hth 184 A3
Upton Rd S, Bex 155 M12
Upway N12 57 R13
Upwood Rd SE12 151 N11
Upwood Rd SW16 183 K2
Urlwin St SE5 36 A11
Urlwin Wk SW9 147 P2
Urmston Dr SW19 162 C1
Ursula Ms N4 93 S2
Ursula St SW11 145 R2
Urswick Gdns, Dag 100 J14
Urswick Rd E9 95 L9
Urswick Rd, Dag 100 H14
Usborne Ms SW8 34 G14
Usher Rd E3 113 U3
Usk Rd SW11 145 M7
Usk St E2 113 N5
Utopia Village NW1 110 A1
Uvedale Rd, Dag 101 P5
Uvedale Rd, Enf 44 A9
Uverdale Rd SW10 127 M14
Uxbridge Rd W3 124 D2
Uxbridge Rd W5 105 S14
Uxbridge Rd W7 122 E2
Uxbridge Rd W12 125 T2
Uxbridge Rd W13 105 L14
Uxbridge Rd, Felt 156 G3
Uxbridge Rd, Hmptn 157 S12
Uxbridge Rd, Har 51 U13
Uxbridge Rd, Hayes 102 F13
Uxbridge Rd, 177 P8
Kings T
Uxbridge Rd, Pnr 51 P13
Uxbridge Rd, Sthl 122 E2
Uxbridge Rd, Stan 52 E11
Uxbridge St W8 126 G1
Uxendon Cres, Wem 87 S1

Uxendon Hill, Wem 87 T1

V

Valan Leas, Brom 187 K6
Valance Av E4 63 L2
Vale, The N10 74 A1
Vale, The N14 42 H14
Vale, The NW11 90 B5
Vale, The SW3 31 L9
Vale, The W3 124 J2
Vale, The, Croy 199 P4
Vale, The, Felt 138 D11
Vale, The, Houns 120 J12
Vale, The, Ruis 84 F7
Vale, The, Sun 156 B11
Vale, The, Wdf Grn 63 P14
Vale Av, Borwd 38 C9
Vale Cl W9 6 F6
Vale Cl, Orp 202 H7
Vale Ct W9 6 F7
Vale Cres SW15 161 K6
Vale Cft, Pnr 66 J9
Vale Dr, Barn 40 F8
Vale End SE22 148 E7
Vale Gro N4 75 T13
Vale Gro W3 124 H3
Vale La W3 106 A10
Vale of Health NW3 91 M5
Vale Ri NW11 90 F1
Vale Rd E7 97 R11
Vale Rd N4 75 T13
Vale Rd, Brom 188 G3
Vale Rd, Epsom 193 M7
Vale Rd, Mitch 182 G7
Vale Rd, Sutt 194 J7
Vale Rd, Wor Pk 193 M6
Vale Rd N, Surb 191 S3
Vale Rd S, Surb 191 S4
Vale Row N5 93 S5
Vale Royal N7 92 J14
Vale St SE27 166 A6
Vale Ter N4 75 T12
Valence Av, Dag 100 G4
Valence Circ, Dag 100 H7
Valence Wd Rd, Dag 100 H6
Valencia Rd, Stan 53 M8
Valentia Pl SW9 147 P7
Valentine Av, Bex 172 J3
Valentine Ct SE23 167 N4
Valentine Pl SE1 27 N6
Valentine Rd E9 95 N12
Valentine Rd, Har 85 S6
Valentine Row SE1 27 N7
Valentines Rd, Ilf 98 J2
Valerian Way E15 115 K5
Valeswood Rd, Brom 169 L10
Valetta Gro E13 115 N3
Valetta Rd W3 125 L3
Valette St E9 95 K11
Valiant Cl, Nthlt 102 H5
Valiant Cl, Rom 83 R3
Valiant Way E6 116 E9
Vallance Rd E1 21 U1
Vallance Rd E2 13 T8
Vallance Rd N22 74 E3
Vallentin Rd E17 78 E7
Valley Av N12 57 P8
Valley Cl, Loug 48 E11
Valley Dr NW9 70 B11
Valley Flds Cres, 43 N3
Enf
Valley Gdns SW19 163 P13
Valley Gdns, Wem 87 T13
Valley Gro SE7 133 U9
Valley Hill, Loug 48 D13
Valley Link Ind Est, 45 R11
Enf
Valley Ms, Twick 158 F3
Valley Rd SW16 165 L10
Valley Rd, Brom 187 K4
Valley Side E4 62 B2
Valley Vw, Barn 40 C11
Valley Wk, Croy 199 M3
Valleyfield Rd SW16 165 M9
Valliere Rd NW10 107 P5
Valliers Wd Rd, Sid 171 P2
Vallis Way W13 104 G9

Vallis Way, Chess 191 N8
Valmar Rd SE5 147 U2
Valnay St SW17 163 T9
Valognes Av E17 77 R1
Valonia Gdns SW18 144 F11
Vambery Rd SE18 135 L11
Van Dyck Av, N Mal 178 H13
Vanbrough Cres, 102 F2
Nthlt
Vanbrugh Cl, 116 A10
E16 *4*
Vanbrugh Dr, Walt 174 E11
Vanbrugh Flds SE3 133 L13
Vanbrugh Hill SE3 133 L11
Vanbrugh Hill SE10 133 L11
Vanbrugh Pk SE3 133 L14
Vanbrugh Pk Rd SE3 133 M13
Vanbrugh Pk Rd W 133 L13
SE3
Vanbrugh Rd W4 124 H5
Vanbrugh Ter SE3 151 M1
Vanburgh Cl, Orp 203 R1
Vancouver Rd SE23 167 S3
Vancouver Rd, Edg 70 C1
Vancouver Rd, 102 C7
Hayes
Vancouver Rd, Rich 159 M8
Vanderbilt Rd SW18 163 L1
Vandome Cl E16 115 R12
Vandon Pas, 25 P9
SW1 *3*
Vandon St SW1 25 P9
Vandy St EC2 12 G12
Vandyke Cl SW15 144 B13
Vandyke Cross SE9 152 C10
Vane Cl NW3 91 N8
Vane Cl, Har 69 T12
Vane St SW1 33 P1
Vanessa Cl, Belv 137 P9
Vanguard Cl E16 115 R10
Vanguard Cl, Croy 197 R2
Vanguard Cl, Rom 83 R4
Vanguard St SE8 151 P1
Vanguard Way, 196 J14
Wall
Vanneck Sq SW15 143 P10
Vanoc Gdns, Brom 169 N7
Vansittart Rd E7 97 M7
Vansittart St, 131 S12
SE14 *10*
Vanston Pl SW6 126 G13
Vant Rd SW17 163 U10
Vantage Ms, 132 F2
E14 *15*
Varcoe Rd SE16 131 K10
Varden St E1 112 J11
Vardens Rd SW11 145 P8
Vardon Cl N3 72 D1
Vardon Cl W3 106 H11
Varley Par NW9 71 K8
Varley Rd E16 115 S11
Varley Way, Mitch 181 P4
Varna Rd SW6 126 D13
Varna Rd, Hmptn 175 R2
Varndell St NW1 9 L6
Varsity Dr, Twick 140 D10
Varsity Row SW14 142 E4
Vartry Rd N15 76 C12
Vassall Rd SW9 129 P14
Vauban Est SE16 29 P12
Vauban St SE16 29 P11
Vaughan Av NW4 71 P9
Vaughan Av W6 125 M7
Vaughan Gdns, Ilf 80 F14
Vaughan Rd E15 97 L12
Vaughan Rd SE5 147 T5
Vaughan Rd, Har 67 U13
Vaughan Rd, T Ditt 176 J13
Vaughan Rd, Well 153 U4
Vaughan St SE16 131 T4
Vaughan Way E1 21 S11
Vaughan Williams 132 A14
Cl, SE8 *10*
Vauxhall Br SE1 34 A7
Vauxhall Br SW1 34 A7
Vauxhall Br Rd SW1 33 N2
Vauxhall Gdns, 197 U12
S Croy
Vauxhall Gdns Est 34 G7
SE11

Vauxhall Gro SW8 34 E9
Vauxhall St SE11 34 G5
Vauxhall Wk SE11 34 E5
Vawdrey Cl E1 113 L8
Veals Mead, Mitch 181 S1
Vectis Gdns, 164 C12
SW17 *3*
Vectis Rd SW17 164 C12
Veda Rd SE13 150 B8
Velde Way, 148 D9
SE22 *3*
Veldene Way, Har 85 L6
Vellum Dr, Cars 196 A6
Venables Cl, Dag 101 S7
Venables St NW8 7 L12
Vencourt Pl W6 125 P9
Venetia Rd N4 75 R12
Venetia Rd W5 123 N4
Venetian Rd SE5 147 U4
Venn St SW4 146 H5
Venner Rd SE26 167 M10
Ventnor Av, Stan 69 K2
Ventnor Dr N20 56 J5
Ventnor Gdns, Bark 99 R11
Ventnor Rd SE14 131 P14
Ventnor Rd, Sutt 195 K14
Venture Cl, Bex 154 J13
Venue St E14 114 D9
Venus Rd SE18 134 E6
Vera Av N21 43 N10
Vera Lynn Cl, E7 *5* 97 P8
Vera Rd SW6 144 D2
Verbena Cl E16 115 L7
Verbena Gdns W6 125 N9
Verdant La SE6 169 K1
Verdayne Av, Croy 199 P3
Verdun Rd SE18 136 A12
Verdun Rd SW13 125 N13
Vere Rd, Loug 49 L7
Vere St W1 16 H7
Vereker Dr, Sun 174 B5
Vereker Rd W14 126 D10
Verity Cl W11 108 C12
Vermeer Gdns SE15 149 L8
Vermont Cl, Enf 43 S7
Vermont Rd SE19 166 B12
Vermont Rd SW18 145 K11
Vermont Rd, Sutt 194 J5
Verney Gdns, Dag 100 J8
Verney Rd SE16 37 U9
Verney Rd, Dag 101 K9
Verney St NW10 88 G6
Verney Way SE16 130 J10
Vernham Rd SE18 135 L12
Vernon Av E12 98 E8
Vernon Av SW20 180 A3
Vernon Av, Wdf Grn 63 R13
Vernon Cl, Epsom 192 F12
Vernon Ct, Stan 68 J1
Vernon Cres, Barn 42 A11
Vernon Dr, Stan 68 H1
Vernon Ms, E17 *5* 77 U8
Vernon Ms, 126 D8
W14 *2*
Vernon Pl WC1 18 D3
Vernon Ri WC1 10 G5
Vernon Ri, Grnf 86 A10
Vernon Rd E3 113 U4
Vernon Rd E11 97 K2
Vernon Rd E15 97 K13
Vernon Rd E17 77 U9
Vernon Rd N8 75 P6
Vernon Rd SW14 142 G6
Vernon Rd, Ilf 99 T2
Vernon Rd, Sutt 195 M9
Vernon Sq, WC1 *1* 10 G5
Vernon St W14 126 C8
Vernon Yd W11 108 E12
Veroan Rd, Bexh 154 J3
Verona Dr, Surb 191 S5
Verona Rd E7 97 P13
Veronica Gdns 182 E2
SW16
Veronica Rd SW17 164 C14
Veronique Gdns, Ilf 81 L9
Verran Rd SW12 146 C14
Versailles Rd SE20 166 G14
Verulam Av E17 77 T12
Verulam Bldgs WC1 18 H1
Verulam Rd, Grnf 103 P7

Name	Page	Grid
Verulam St WC1	18	J2
Verwood Dr, Barn	41	T6
Verwood Rd, Har	67	T4
Vespan Rd W12	125	N3
Vesta Rd SE4	149	R4
Vestris Rd SE23	167	P3
Vestry Ms SE5	148	C2
Vestry Rd E17	78	C8
Vestry Rd SE5	148	D3
Vestry St N1	12	D6
Vevey St SE6	167	T4
Veysey Gdns, Dag	101	N5
Viaduct Pl E2	112	J6
Viaduct St E2	112	J6
Vian St SE13	150	D5
Vibart Gdns SW2	147	M14
Vicarage Av SE3	133	P14
Vicarage Cl, Erith	137	U12
Vicarage Cl, Nthlt	85	M14
Vicarage Cl, Wor Pk	192	J2
Vicarage Cres SW11	145	N2
Vicarage Dr SW14	142	G9
Vicarage Dr, Bark	99	M14
Vicarage Dr, Beck	186	A2
Vicarage Fm Rd, Houns	139	K1
Vicarage Flds, Walt	174	E12
Vicarage Gdns, W8 5	126	H2
Vicarage Gdns, Mitch	181	R6
Vicarage Gate W8	22	A5
Vicarage Gro SE5	148	B1
Vicarage La E6	116	F5
Vicarage La E15	97	L13
Vicarage La, Chig	65	M3
Vicarage La, Ilf	99	N2
Vicarage Pk SE18	135	M10
Vicarage Path N8	74	J13
Vicarage Rd E10	96	D2
Vicarage Rd E15	97	L13
Vicarage Rd N17	76	G1
Vicarage Rd NW4	71	P12
Vicarage Rd SE18	135	M10
Vicarage Rd SW14	142	G9
Vicarage Rd, Bex	173	S2
Vicarage Rd, Croy	197	P5
Vicarage Rd, Dag	101	R12
Vicarage Rd, Kings T	177	P3
Vicarage Rd (Hampton Wick), Kings T	177	L1
Vicarage Rd, Sutt	194	J7
Vicarage Rd, Tedd	158	G9
Vicarage Rd, Twick	158	D3
Vicarage Rd (Whitton), Twick	139	T12
Vicarage Rd, Wdf Grn	64	D14
Vicarage Way NW10	88	H6
Vicarage Way, Har	67	P13
Vicars Br Cl, Wem	105	R3
Vicars Cl E9	113	L2
Vicars Cl E15	115	N1
Vicars Cl, Enf	44	D4
Vicars Hill SE13	150	C7
Vicars Moor La N21	43	R14
Vicars Oak Rd SE19	166	D11
Vicars Rd NW5	92	A9
Vicars Wk, Dag	100	D6
Viceroy Cl N2	73	R6
Viceroy Ct NW8	7	R2
Viceroy Rd SW8	146	J1
Vickers Way, Houns	139	K10
Victor Gro, Wem	87	S13
Victor Rd NW10	107	R5
Victor Rd SE20	167	P13
Victor Rd, Har	67	U6
Victor Rd, Tedd	158	C8
Victor Vil N9	60	B5
Victoria Av E6	116	A1
Victoria Av EC2	21	K4
Victoria Av N3	72	F2
Victoria Av, Barn	41	P8
Victoria Av, Houns	139	N9
Victoria Av, Wall	196	B6
Victoria Av, Wem	88	D10
Victoria Av, W Mol	175	P5
Victoria Cl, Barn	41	P8
Victoria Cl, W Mol 1	175	P5
Victoria Cotts, Bark	141	U2
Victoria Ct, Wem	88	B11
Victoria Cres N15	76	C10
Victoria Cres SE19	166	C11
Victoria Cres, SW19 4	162	F13
Victoria Dock Rd E16	115	L12
Victoria Dr SW19	144	A14
Victoria Embk EC4	19	R10
Victoria Embk SW1	26	C6
Victoria Embk WC2	18	G11
Victoria Gdns, W11 2	126	G1
Victoria Gdns, Houns	138	J1
Victoria Gro N12	57	N9
Victoria Gro W8	22	E9
Victoria Gro Ms, W2 17	108	H14
Victoria Ind Est NW10	107	K6
Victoria La, Barn	40	E7
Victoria Ms NW6	108	G1
Victoria Ms, SW4 16	146	C7
Victoria Ms SW18	163	M2
Victoria Pk E9	113	S1
Victoria Pk Rd E9	113	L2
Victoria Pk Sq E2	113	L5
Victoria Pl, Rich 5	141	P9
Victoria Retail Pk, Ruis	84	H9
Victoria Ri SW4	146	C6
Victoria Rd E4	63	K1
Victoria Rd E11	96	J7
Victoria Rd E13	115	N4
Victoria Rd E17	78	E4
Victoria Rd E18	79	R4
Victoria Rd N4	75	M14
Victoria Rd N9	60	G5
Victoria Rd N15	76	G8
Victoria Rd N18	60	F8
Victoria Rd N22	74	F2
Victoria Rd NW4	71	U8
Victoria Rd NW6	108	E3
Victoria Rd NW7	55	L9
Victoria Rd NW10	106	J8
Victoria Rd SW14	142	G5
Victoria Rd W3	106	G9
Victoria Rd W5	105	K10
Victoria Rd W8	22	E8
Victoria Rd, Bark	99	K11
Victoria Rd, Barn	41	P9
Victoria Rd, Bexh	155	N8
Victoria Rd, Brom	188	B10
Victoria Rd, Buck H	64	A3
Victoria Rd, Bushey	51	R1
Victoria Rd, Chis	170	H10
Victoria Rd, Dag	101	S9
Victoria Rd, Felt	156	C2
Victoria Rd, Kings T	177	U4
Victoria Rd, Mitch	163	T14
Victoria Rd, Ruis	84	C5
Victoria Rd, Sid	171	U6
Victoria Rd, Sthl	121	L6
Victoria Rd, Surb	177	P12
Victoria Rd, Sutt	195	N10
Victoria Rd, Tedd	158	G12
Victoria Rd, Twick	140	J13
Victoria Sq SW1	24	J10
Victoria Sta SW1	33	K1
Victoria St E15	96	J13
Victoria St SW1	25	P10
Victoria St, Belv	137	M10
Victoria Ter N4	93	N1
Victoria Ter, Har	86	C2
Victoria Vil, Rich	141	U6
Victoria Way SE7	133	R9
Victoria Wf E14	113	S14
Victorian Gro N16	94	D6
Victorian Rd N16	94	D6
Victors Dr, Hmptn	157	K12
Victors Way, Barn	40	E6
Victory Av, Mord	181	M9
Victory Business Cen, Islw	140	F6
Victory Pl E14	113	S13
Victory Pl SE17	36	B2
Victory Pl SE19	166	D12
Victory Rd E11	79	R7
Victory Rd SW19	163	L13
Victory Rd Ms, SW19 5	163	L14
Victory Wk SE8	150	A1
Victory Way SE16	131	S4
Victory Way, Houns	120	E10
Victory Way, Rom	83	R3
Vidler Cl, Chess 5	191	M12
Vienna Cl, Ilf	80	B5
View, The SE2	137	K9
View Cl N6	73	U13
View Cl, Chig	65	N10
View Cl, Har	68	A7
View Rd N6	73	U12
Viewfield Cl, Har	69	R14
Viewfield Rd SW18	144	F12
Viewfield Rd, Bex	172	E1
Viewland Rd SE18	135	T10
Viga Rd N21	43	P11
Vigilant Cl SE26	166	G8
Vignoles Rd, Rom	83	P13
Vigo St W1	17	M11
Viking Cl, E3 9	113	S4
Viking Ct, SW6 2	126	H12
Viking Gdns E6	116	C8
Viking Pl E10	95	U2
Viking Rd, Sthl	103	K13
Viking Way, Erith	137	U6
Villa Rd SW9	147	N5
Villa St SE17	36	E8
Villacourt Rd SE18	136	A13
Village, The SE7	133	U11
Village Arc, E4 6	62	H1
Village Cl E4	62	F10
Village Hts, Wdf Grn	63	M10
Village Ms NW9	88	G3
Village Pk Cl, Enf	44	C11
Village Rd N3	72	C3
Village Rd, Enf	44	B12
Village Row, Sutt	194	G13
Village Way NW10	88	H7
Village Way SE21	148	A11
Village Way, Beck	186	A4
Village Way, Pnr	67	K13
Village Way E, Har	67	M14
Villas Rd SE18	135	M8
Villiers Av, Surb	177	T9
Villiers Av, Twick	157	M2
Villiers Cl E10	96	B3
Villiers Cl, Surb	177	U7
Villiers Path, Surb	177	S9
Villiers Rd NW2	89	N11
Villiers Rd, Beck	185	P4
Villiers Rd, Islw	140	C3
Villiers Rd, Kings T	177	T7
Villiers Rd, Sthl	121	M2
Villiers St WC2	26	C1
Vincam Cl, Twick	139	P13
Vince St EC1	12	E8
Vincent Av, Surb	192	D2
Vincent Cl SE16	131	R4
Vincent Cl, Barn	40	A5
Vincent Cl, Brom	187	S8
Vincent Cl, Ilf	65	M12
Vincent Cl, Sid	171	R2
Vincent Gdns NW2	89	M5
Vincent Ms E3	114	A4
Vincent Rd E4	62	H12
Vincent Rd N15	75	T7
Vincent Rd N22	75	P3
Vincent Rd SE18	135	K8
Vincent Rd W3	124	E5
Vincent Rd, Croy	184	D14
Vincent Rd, Dag	100	J14
Vincent Rd, Houns	138	G4
Vincent Rd, Islw	140	A2
Vincent Rd, Kings T	178	B5
Vincent Rd, Wem	87	U14
Vincent Row, Hmptn	157	T10
Vincent Sq SW1	33	N1
Vincent St E16	115	M10
Vincent St SW1	33	T2
Vincent Ter N1	11	P2
Vine Cl, Surb	177	U11
Vine Cl, Sutt	195	L6
Vine Ct E1	21	U3
Vine Ct, Har	69	S11
Vine Gdns, Ilf	99	L9
Vine Hill EC1	11	K12
Vine La SE1	28	J4
Vine Pl, Houns	139	R7
Vine Rd E15	97	L13
Vine Rd SW13	143	M5
Vine Rd, E Mol	175	U7
Vine Rd, Orp	203	U12
Vine Sq W14	126	F10
Vine St EC3	21	M10
Vine St W1	17	N12
Vine St, Rom	83	U8
Vine St Br EC1	11	M12
Vine Yd, SE1 6	28	A7
Vinegar All E17	78	D8
Vinegar St, E1 10	130	J1
Vinegar Yd, SE1 1	28	G5
Viner Cl, Walt	174	E12
Vineries, The N14	42	F16
Vineries, The, Enf	44	D5
Vineries Bank NW7	55	S9
Vineries Cl, Dag	101	N11
Vines Av N3	72	J1
Viney Rd SE13	150	D6
Vineyard, The, Rich	141	P10
Vineyard Av NW7	56	C14
Vineyard Cl SE6	168	A2
Vineyard Gro N3	73	K2
Vineyard Hill Rd SW19	162	G8
Vineyard Path SW14	142	G5
Vineyard Rd, Felt	156	A5
Vineyard Row, Kings T	177	L1
Vineyard Wk, EC1 2	11	K10
Vining St, SW9 9	147	P7
Vintry Ms, E17 1	78	A8
Viola Av SE2	136	C8
Viola Av, Felt	138	E12
Viola Sq W12	107	M13
Violet Cl E16	115	K8
Violet Gdns, Croy	197	R10
Violet Hill NW8	6	F4
Violet La, Croy	197	S8
Violet Rd E3	114	C8
Violet Rd E17	78	B12
Violet Rd E18	79	R3
Violet St E2	113	K6
Virgil Pl W1	15	T3
Virgil St SE1	26	H10
Virginia Cl, N Mal 1	178	E7
Virginia Gdns, Ilf	81	M4
Virginia Rd E2	13	L7
Virginia Rd, Th Hth	183	S1
Virginia St E1	21	T1
Virginia Wk SW2	147	M12
Viscount Cl N11	58	B10
Viscount Dr E6	116	E9
Viscount Gro, Nthlt	102	H6
Viscount St EC1	11	U12
Vista, The SE9	152	B13
Vista Av, Enf	45	N4
Vista Dr, Ilf	80	B10
Vista Way, Har	71	R10
Vivian Av NW4	71	R10
Vivian Av, Wem	88	D11
Vivian Cl, Wat	50	B3
Vivian Gdns, Wat	50	B2
Vivian Gdns, Wem	88	A10
Vivian Rd E3	113	R3
Vivian Sq SE15	148	E3
Vivian Way N2	73	P9
Vivien Cl, Chess	191	R13
Vivienne Cl, Twick	141	N12
Voce Rd SE18	135	P14
Voewood Cl, N Mal	193	F11
Volta Way, Croy	197	L1
Voltaire Rd SW4	146	D8
Voluntary Pl E11	79	N11
Vorley Rd N19	92	C12
Voss St E2	13	T8
Voss St SW16	165	K12
Voyagers Cl SE28	118	F7
Vulcan Cl, Wall	197	L13
Vulcan Gate, Enf	43	P4
Vulcan Rd SE4	149	T3

Vulcan Sq E14	132	B8
Vulcan Ter SE4	149	T3
Vulcan Way N7	93	M11
Vyne, The, Bexh	155	S6
Vyner Rd W3	106	H14
Vyner St E2	113	K2
Vyse Cl, Barn	39	T8

W

Wadding St SE17	36	C3
Waddington Cl, Enf	44	D8
Waddington Rd E15	96	H10
Waddington St E15	96	H11
Waddington Way SE19	165	U14
Waddon Cl, Croy	197	P5
Waddon Ct Rd, Croy	197	N6
Waddon Marsh Way, Croy	197	M2
Waddon New Rd, Croy	197	N5
Waddon Pk Av, Croy	197	N7
Waddon Rd, Croy	197	P5
Waddon Way, Croy	197	S12
Wades Gro N21	43	P14
Wades Hill N21	43	P13
Wades La, Tedd	158	G10
Wades Ms N21	43	P14
Wades Pl E14	114	C13
Wadeson St E2	113	K3
Wadeville Av, Rom	83	L13
Wadeville Cl, Belv	137	P11
Wadham Av E17	62	D14
Wadham Gdns NW3	91	R14
Wadham Gdns, Grnf	86	C10
Wadham Rd E17	62	C14
Wadham Rd SW15	144	D8
Wadhurst Cl SE20	184	J4
Wadhurst Rd SW8	146	E1
Wadhurst Rd W4	124	G6
Wadley Rd E11	78	J13
Wadsworth Business Cen, Grnf	105	L3
Wadsworth Cl, Enf	45	N10
Wadsworth Cl, Grnf	105	L4
Wadsworth Rd, Grnf	105	K3
Wager St E3	113	J8
Waghorn Rd E13	115	T2
Waghorn Rd, Har	69	P6
Waghorn St SE15	148	G5
Wagner St SE15	131	L13
Wagtail Cl NW9	70	J3
Waights Ct, Kings T	177	S1
Wainfleet Av, Rom	83	U4
Wainford Cl, SW19 4	162	B1
Wainwright Gro, Islw	140	B8
Waite Davies Rd SE12	151	M14
Waite St SE15	37	M9
Wakefield Gdns, Ilf	166	C14
Wakefield Gdns SE19	80	C12
Wakefield Ms, WC1 1	10	C8
Wakefield Rd N11	58	H10
Wakefield Rd N15	76	F9
Wakefield Rd, Rich	141	P10
Wakefield St E6	116	C2
Wakefield St N18	60	G10
Wakefield St WC1	10	D9
Wakeham St N1	94	A12
Wakehams Hill, Pnr	67	L6
Wakehurst Rd SW11	145	U9
Wakelin Rd E15	114	J3
Wakeling Rd W7	104	E10
Wakeling St E14 6	113	R12
Wakeman Rd NW10	107	U5
Wakemans Hill Av NW9	70	H9
Wakering Rd, Bark	99	L12
Wakerley Cl, E6 8	116	F12
Wakley St EC1	11	P5

Walberswick St, SW8 1	129	K14
Walbrook EC4	20	C9
Walburgh St E1	112	J12
Walcorde Av SE17	36	A4
Walcot Rd, Enf	45	T3
Walcot Sq SE11	35	L1
Walcott St, SW1 8	33	P2
Waldair Ct E16	134	J3
Waldair Wf E16	135	K3
Waldeck Gro SE27	165	R6
Waldeck Rd N15	75	S7
Waldeck Rd SW14	142	F5
Waldeck Rd W4	124	B11
Waldeck Rd W13	105	K12
Waldegrave Av, Tedd 2	158	F10
Waldegrave Gdns, Twick	158	E4
Waldegrave Pk, Twick	158	F7
Waldegrave Rd N8	75	P6
Waldegrave Rd SE19	166	F14
Waldegrave Rd W5	105	T12
Waldegrave Rd, Brom	188	D8
Waldegrave Rd, Dag	100	C4
Waldegrave Rd, Tedd	158	E9
Waldegrave Rd, Twick	158	E6
Waldegrove, Croy	198	E6
Waldemar Av SW6	144	D2
Waldemar Av W13	123	L2
Waldemar Rd SW19	162	G9
Walden Av N13	59	U7
Walden Av, Chis	170	F8
Walden Cl, Belv	137	L9
Walden Gdns, Th Hth	183	M7
Walden Rd, N17 2	76	A2
Walden Rd, Chis	170	E11
Walden St E1	112	J11
Walden Way NW7	56	B12
Walden Way, Ilf	65	R13
Waldenshaw Rd SE23	167	L2
Waldo Cl SW4	146	F9
Waldo Pl, Mitch	163	S14
Waldo Rd NW10	107	P5
Waldo Rd, Brom	188	A6
Waldram Cres SE23	167	M2
Waldram Pk Rd SE23	167	N2
Waldram Pl, SE23 2	167	M3
Waldrist Way, Erith	137	M4
Waldron Gdns, Brom	186	H6
Waldron Ms SW3	31	M10
Waldron Rd SW18	163	L5
Waldron Rd, Har	86	C2
Waldronhyrst, S Croy	197	S8
Waldrons, The, Croy	197	S8
Waldrons Path, S Croy	197	T8
Waldstock Rd SE28	118	B14
Waleran Cl, Stan	52	F10
Walerand Rd SE13	150	F4
Wales Av, Cars	195	T10
Wales Cl SE15	130	J13
Wales Fm Rd W3	106	G10
Waley St, E1 13	113	P9
Walfield Av N20	41	K13
Walford Rd N16	94	D7
Walfrey Gdns, Dag	101	K13
Walham Gro SW6	126	G13
Walham Ri SW19	162	C11
Walham Yd, SW6 4	126	G13
Walkden Rd, Chis	170	H9
Walker Cl N11	58	F8
Walker Cl SE18	135	L7
Walker Cl W7	122	C2
Walker Cl, Hmptn	157	L11
Walkers Ct E8	94	G11
Walkers Pl, SW15 4	144	C7

Walkerscroft Mead SE21	165	U2
Walks, The N2	73	P5
Wall End Rd E6	98	G14
Wall St N1	94	B12
Wallace Cl SE28	118	H14
Wallace Cres, Cars	195	T9
Wallace Rd N1	93	U11
Wallbutton Rd SE4	149	R4
Wallcote Av NW2	90	A1
Waller Dr, Nthwd	66	A3
Waller Rd SE14	149	N3
Wallers Cl, Dag	119	K2
Wallers Cl, Wdf Grn	64	E11
Wallers Hoppit, Loug	48	D4
Wallflower St W12	107	M14
Wallgrave Rd SW5	30	A2
Wallingford Av W10	108	A10
Wallington Rd, Ilf	81	U13
Wallis All, SE1 5	28	A6
Wallis Cl SW11	145	N6
Wallis Ms, N22 2	75	N5
Wallis Rd E9	96	A12
Wallis Rd, Sthl	103	R11
Wallis's Cotts SW2	146	J14
Wallorton Gdns SW14	142	H7
Wallwood Rd E11	78	H14
Wallwood St E14	113	U10
Walm La NW2	90	B10
Walmer Cl E4	62	C4
Walmer Cl, Orp	203	N8
Walmer Cl, Rom	83	S4
Walmer Gdns W13	122	H5
Walmer Pl W1	15	T2
Walmer Rd W10	107	U12
Walmer Rd W11	108	C13
Walmer St W1	15	T2
Walmer Ter SE18	135	N7
Walmgate Rd, Grnf	104	J2
Walmington Fold N12	56	G11
Walnut Cl, SE8 4	131	U12
Walnut Cl, Cars	195	T10
Walnut Cl, Ilf	81	M7
Walnut Gdns E15	96	J9
Walnut Gro, Enf	44	B10
Walnut Ms, Sutt	195	L13
Walnut Rd E10	96	B4
Walnut Tree Av. Mitch 1	181	S5
Walnut Tree Cl SW13	143	M1
Walnut Tree Cl, Chis	189	M1
Walnut Tree Rd SE10	133	K10
Walnut Tree Rd, Brent	123	R11
Walnut Tree Rd, Dag	100	H4
Walnut Tree Rd, Houns	121	M12
Walnut Tree Wk SE11	34	J1
Walnut Way, Buck H	64	A6
Walnut Way, Ruis	84	E11
Walpole Av, Rich	141	T4
Walpole Cl W13	123	L3
Walpole Cl, Pnr	51	N12
Walpole Cres, Tedd	158	E10
Walpole Gdns W4	124	E9
Walpole Gdns, Twick	158	D4
Walpole Ms NW8	109	N2
Walpole Pk W5	123	M2
Walpole Pl, Tedd	158	E10
Walpole Rd E6	97	U14
Walpole Rd E17	77	S7
Walpole Rd E18	79	L2
Walpole Rd (Downhills Way) N17	75	U5
Walpole Rd (Lordship La) N17	75	U3
Walpole Rd SW19	163	P12
Walpole Rd, Brom	188	B9
Walpole Rd, Croy	198	A3
Walpole Rd, Surb	177	R13
Walpole Rd, Tedd	158	E10
Walpole Rd, Twick	158	C4

Walpole St SW3	31	U5
Walrond Av, Wem	87	S10
Walsham Cl N16	94	G1
Walsham Cl SE28	118	G13
Walsham Rd SE14	149	N3
Walsham Rd, Felt	138	D13
Walsingham Gdns, Epsom	193	L9
Walsingham Pk, Chis	189	M3
Walsingham Pl SW11	146	B11
Walsingham Rd E5	94	H5
Walsingham Rd, W13 1	122	G1
Walsingham Rd, Enf	44	A8
Walsingham Rd, Mitch	181	U9
Walsingham Wk, Belv	137	P11
Walt Whitman Cl, SE24 17	147	S7
Walter Rodney Cl E6	98	F12
Walter St E2	113	N6
Walter St, Kings T	177	S2
Walter Ter E1	113	P11
Walter Wk, Edg	54	F12
Walters Rd SE25	184	D8
Walters Rd, Enf	45	M9
Walters Way SE23	149	N12
Walters Yd, Brom	187	N3
Walterton Rd W9	108	F8
Waltham Av NW9	70	B11
Waltham Dr, Edg	70	B4
Waltham Pk Way E17	78	A1
Waltham Rd, Cars	181	P14
Waltham Rd, Sthl	120	J6
Waltham Rd, Wdf Grn	64	C11
Waltham Way E4	61	T6
Walthamstow Av E4	62	B14
Walthamstow Business Cen E17	78	E4
Walthouse Av N17	76	A2
Walthouse Gdns N17	76	A1
Walton Av, Har	85	M8
Walton Av, N Mal	179	L8
Walton Av, Sutt	194	E5
Walton Cl, E5 4	95	P6
Walton Cl NW2	89	C4
Walton Cl SW8	34	C14
Walton Cl, Har	68	B7
Walton Cres, Har	85	M7
Walton Dr NW10	88	H11
Walton Dr, Har	68	B8
Walton Gdns W3	106	D10
Walton Gdns, Wem	87	R3
Walton Pl SW3	23	T11
Walton Rd E12	98	G8
Walton Rd E13	115	T3
Walton Rd, N15 2	76	F9
Walton Rd, E Mol	176	A8
Walton Rd, Har	68	B7
Walton Rd, Sid	172	E6
Walton Rd, Walt	174	J9
Walton Rd, W Mol	175	N7
Walton St SW3	31	R1
Walton St, Enf	44	A1
Walton Way W3	106	D10
Walton Way, Mitch	182	E7
Walworth Pl SE17	36	B7
Walworth Rd SE1	35	U4
Walworth Rd SE17	35	U4
Walwyn Av, Brom	188	A6
Wanborough Dr SW15	161	R1
Wanderer, Bark	118	D5
Wandle Bank SW19	163	N13
Wandle Bank, Croy	196	J6
Wandle Ct, Epsom	192	E8
Wandle Ct Gdns, Croy	196	J7
Wandle Rd SW17	163	S3
Wandle Rd, Croy	197	U6
Wandle Rd (Waddon), Croy	197	K6
Wandle Rd, Mord	181	M8
Wandle Rd, Wall	196	C4
Wandle Side, Croy	197	M6

Name	Page	Grid
Wandle Side, Wall	196	C5
Wandle Way SW18	162	J1
Wandle Way, Mitch	181	T9
Wandon Rd SW6	127	K14
Wandsworth Br SW6	145	K6
Wandsworth Br SW18	145	K6
Wandsworth Br Rd SW6	144	J3
Wandsworth Common SW12	145	N9
Wandsworth Common W Side SW18	145	M10
Wandsworth High St SW18	144	H10
Wandsworth Plain, SW18 *9*	144	J9
Wandsworth Rd SW8	34	B10
Wangey Rd, Rom	82	G13
Wanless Rd SE24	147	T6
Wanley Rd SE5	148	B7
Wanlip Rd E13	115	S7
Wannock Gdns, Ilf	65	K13
Wansbeck Rd E9	96	A13
Wansdown Pl, SW6 *1*	30	A14
Wansey St SE17	36	A3
Wansford Pk, Borwd	38	J8
Wansford Rd, Wdf Grn	79	T1
Wanstead Cl, Brom	187	U3
Wanstead La, Ilf	80	B12
Wanstead Pk E11	79	U14
Wanstead Pk Av E12	98	A3
Wanstead Pk Rd, Ilf	98	D1
Wanstead Pl E11	79	P11
Wanstead Rd, Brom	187	T4
Wansunt Rd, Bex	173	U1
Wantage Rd SE12	151	L10
Wantz Rd, Dag	101	R8
Wapping Dock St, E1 *12*	131	K2
Wapping High St E1	29	T3
Wapping La E1	131	K1
Wapping Wall E1	131	L1
Warbank La, Kings T	161	L14
Warbeck Rd W12	125	S3
Warberry Rd N22	75	L3
Warboys App, Kings T *1*	160	D11
Warboys Cres E4	62	F10
Warboys Rd, Kings T	160	D11
Warburton Cl, N1 *1*	94	C11
Warburton Cl, Har	52	A11
Warburton Rd, E8 *8*	113	K1
Warburton Rd, Twick	157	R1
Warburton St, E8 *18*	112	J1
Warburton Ter E17	78	D3
Ward Cl, S Croy	198	C10
Ward Rd, E15 *1*	114	G1
Ward Rd N19	92	E6
Wardalls Gro SE14	131	M13
Wardell Cl NW7	55	K14
Wardell Fld NW9	71	K1
Warden Av, Har	85	L2
Warden Rd NW5	92	B11
Wardens Fld Cl, Orp	203	S11
Wardens Gro SE1	27	U4
Wardle St E9	95	N10
Wardley St SW18	145	K14
Wardo Av SW6	144	C1
Wardour Ms W1	17	P7
Wardour St W1	17	S10
Wards Rd, Ilf	81	N13
Ware Pt Dr SE28	135	P3
Wareham Cl, Houns	139	R7
Waremead Rd, Ilf	80	J9
Warenford Way, Borwd	38	A2
Warfield Rd NW10	108	A6
Warfield Rd, Hmptn	175	R1
Wargrave Av N15	76	F11
Wargrave Rd, Har	85	T6
Warham Rd N4	75	P10
Warham Rd, Har	68	E3
Warham Rd, S Croy	197	S9
Warham St SE5	35	R14
Waring Cl, Orp	203	U11
Waring Dr, Orp	203	U11
Waring Rd, Sid	172	E11
Waring St SE27	165	T7
Warkworth Gdns, Islw	122	G13
Warkworth Rd N17	60	B14
Warland Rd SE18	135	R14
Warley Av, Dag	83	M14
Warley Av, Hayes	102	A11
Warley Rd N9	61	L3
Warley Rd, Hayes	102	A11
Warley Rd, Ilf	80	H1
Warley Rd, Wdf Grn	63	R14
Warley St E2	113	N5
Warlingham Rd, Th Hth	183	R8
Warlock Rd W9	108	G7
Warlters Cl N7	93	K7
Warlters Rd N7	93	K7
Warltersville Rd N19	74	J14
Warmington Cl, E5 *1*	95	N5
Warmington Rd SE24	147	U11
Warmington St, E13 *3*	115	P7
Warminster Gdns SE25	184	G4
Warminster Rd SE25	184	F4
Warminster Way, Mitch	182	D2
Warndon St, SE16 *4*	131	M8
Warne Pl, Sid *6*	154	D11
Warneford Rd, Har	69	P6
Warneford St E9	113	K1
Warner Av, Sutt	194	C3
Warner Cl E15	97	K10
Warner Cl NW9	71	M13
Warner Cl, Hmptn	157	M10
Warner Pl E2	13	T5
Warner Rd E17	77	S8
Warner Rd N8	74	G7
Warner Rd SE5	147	U2
Warner Rd, Brom	169	M14
Warner St EC1	11	K11
Warner Yd, EC1 *11*	11	K11
Warners Cl, Wdf Grn	63	N9
Warners La, Kings T	159	N8
Warners Path, Wdf Grn	63	N10
Warnford Rd, Orp	203	U10
Warnham Ct Rd, Cars	195	T13
Warnham Rd N12	57	R10
Warple Ms W3	124	J3
Warple Way W3	124	J3
Warren, The E12	98	D7
Warren, The, Hayes	102	B12
Warren, The, Houns	121	L14
Warren, The, Wor Pk	192	H7
Warren Av, E10 *5*	96	G5
Warren Av, Brom	168	J13
Warren Av, Orp	203	T9
Warren Av, Rich	142	C7
Warren Av, S Croy	199	N14
Warren Cl N9	45	N14
Warren Cl SE21	147	T14
Warren Cl, Hayes	102	E10
Warren Cl, Wem	87	P3
Warren Ct, Chig	65	P8
Warren Cres N9	44	F14
Warren Cutting, Kings T	160	G13
Warren Dr, Grnf	103	S7
Warren Dr, Ruis	66	G14
Warren Dr, The E11	79	T14
Warren Dr N, Surb	192	C2
Warren Dr S, Surb	192	E2
Warren Footpath, Twick	141	P12
Warren Gro, Borwd	38	H8
Warren Hill, Loug	47	T12
Warren La SE18	134	J6
Warren La, Stan	52	F5
Warren Ms W1	9	L11
Warren Pk, Kings T	160	G12
Warren Pk Rd, Sutt	195	P11
Warren Pond Rd E4	63	L1
Warren Ri, N Mal	178	H1
Warren Rd E4	62	E3
Warren Rd E10	96	F5
Warren Rd E11	97	U1
Warren Rd NW2	89	M4
Warren Rd SW19	163	R12
Warren Rd, Bexh	155	N9
Warren Rd, Brom	201	N3
Warren Rd, Bushey	51	U2
Warren Rd, Croy	198	D1
Warren Rd, Ilf	81	N9
Warren Rd, Kings T	160	E11
Warren Rd, Orp	203	U9
Warren Rd, Sid	172	E6
Warren Rd, Twick	139	U12
Warren St W1	9	L11
Warren Ter, Rom	82	H8
Warren Wk SE7	133	U11
Warren Way NW7	56	D11
Warren Wd Cl, Brom	201	M4
Warrender Rd N19	92	F6
Warrender Way, Ruis	66	A13
Warrens Shawe La, Edg	54	D3
Warriner Dr N9	60	G6
Warriner Gdns SW11	146	A2
Warrington Cres W9	6	E10
Warrington Gdns W9	6	E12
Warrington Pl, E14 *10*	132	F1
Warrington Rd, Croy	197	R6
Warrington Rd, Dag	100	H3
Warrington Rd, Har	68	C10
Warrington Rd, Rich *8*	141	P10
Warrington Sq, Dag	100	H4
Warrior Sq E12	98	G7
Warsaw Cl, Ruis *1*	84	D12
Warsdale Dr, NW9 *1*	70	H10
Warspite Rd SE18	134	C5
Warton Rd E15	114	F1
Warwall E6	116	J11
Warwick Av W2	14	F1
Warwick Av W9	6	C11
Warwick Av, Edg	54	D6
Warwick Av, Har	85	L8
Warwick Cl, Barn	41	P9
Warwick Cl, Bex	155	M14
Warwick Cl, Hmptn	157	T13
Warwick Ct SE15	148	H4
Warwick Ct WC1	18	H3
Warwick Cres W2	14	F2
Warwick Dene W5	123	S2
Warwick Dr SW15	143	R6
Warwick Est W2	14	C3
Warwick Gdns N4	75	T10
Warwick Gdns W14	126	F7
Warwick Gdns, Ilf	99	K2
Warwick Gdns, T Ditt	176	E10
Warwick Gro E5	94	J2
Warwick Gro, Surb	177	T13
Warwick Ho St SW1	25	T2
Warwick La EC4	19	S7
Warwick Pl W5	123	P3
Warwick Pl W9	14	E1
Warwick Pl N SW1	33	L4
Warwick Rd E4	62	A9
Warwick Rd E11	79	S9
Warwick Rd E12	98	C10
Warwick Rd E15	97	M12
Warwick Rd E17	77	T3
Warwick Rd N11	58	H11
Warwick Rd N18	60	D8
Warwick Rd SE20	185	K5
Warwick Rd SW5	126	H9
Warwick Rd W5	123	S2
Warwick Rd W14	126	E7
Warwick Rd, Barn	40	J8
Warwick Rd, Borwd	38	G5
Warwick Rd, Houns	138	D5
Warwick Rd, Kings T	177	M1
Warwick Rd, N Mal	178	E5
Warwick Rd, Sid	172	C10
Warwick Rd, Sthl	121	M6
Warwick Rd, Sutt	195	L8
Warwick Rd, T Ditt	176	E10
Warwick Rd, Th Hth	183	N6
Warwick Rd, Twick	158	D1
Warwick Rd, Well	154	E5
Warwick Row SW1	25	K11
Warwick Sq EC4	19	R6
Warwick Sq SW1	33	L4
Warwick Sq Ms SW1	33	L4
Warwick St W1	17	N10
Warwick Ter SE18	135	P11
Warwick Way SW1	33	M3
Warwick Yd EC1	12	A11
Warwickshire Path SE8	131	U13
Washington Av E12	98	D7
Washington Cl E3	114	E11
Washington Rd E6	97	U14
Washington Rd, E18 *2*	79	M3
Washington Rd SW13	125	P13
Washington Rd, Kings T	178	A4
Washington Rd, Wor Pk	193	R3
Wastdale Rd SE23	167	F5
Wat Tyler Rd SE3	150	F3
Wat Tyler Rd SE10	150	F3
Watchfield Ct W4	124	F9
Watcombe Cotts, Rich	124	B12
Watcombe Rd SE25	184	J9
Water Gdns, Stan	53	K12
Water La E15	97	K11
Water La N9	60	J1
Water La NW1	92	D14
Water La SE14	131	M14
Water La, Ilf	99	S6
Water La, Kings T	177	P2
Water La, Rich	141	N10
Water La, Sid	173	L4
Water La, Twick	158	H1
Water Lily Cl, Sthl *3*	121	U3
Water Ms SE15	149	L7
Water Rd, Wem	105	U2
Water St, WC2 *3*	18	H9
Water Twr Hill, Croy	198	B7
Waterbank Rd SE6	168	D6
Waterbeach Rd, Dag	100	F11
Waterbrook La NW4	71	U10
Watercress Pl, N1 *14*	94	D14
Waterdale Rd SE2	136	A12
Waterden Rd E15	96	C11
Waterer Ri, Wall	196	H12
Waterfall Cl N14	58	E5
Waterfall Cotts SW19	163	P11
Waterfall Rd N11	58	D8
Waterfall Rd N14	58	F5
Waterfall Rd, SW19 *4*	163	P11
Waterfall Ter SW17	163	R11
Waterfield Cl SE28	136	C1
Waterfield Cl, Belv	137	P5
Waterfield Gdns SE25	184	C9
Waterford Rd SW6	126	J14
Watergardens, The, Kings T	160	F12
Watergate, EC4 *2*	19	N9
Watergate, The, Wat	50	H3
Watergate St SE8	132	A11
Watergate Wk, WC2 *12*	18	C12
Waterhall Av E4	62	J7
Waterhall Cl E17	77	P1
Waterhouse Cl E16	116	A9
Waterhouse Cl NW3	91	P9
Waterhouse Cl W6	126	B9
Waterhouse Sq EC1	19	K4

Name	Page	Grid
Waterloo Br SE1	18	F11
Waterloo Br WC2	18	F11
Waterloo Cl E9	95	M9
Waterloo Est E2	113	L3
Waterloo Gdns E2	113	L3
Waterloo Pas NW6	90	F14
Waterloo Pl SW1	25	S2
Waterloo Pl (Kew), Rich	124	A12
Waterloo Rd E6	97	U14
Waterloo Rd, E7 *1*	97	M9
Waterloo Rd E10	78	A14
Waterloo Rd NW2	89	P3
Waterloo Rd SE1	26	J4
Waterloo Rd, Ilf	81	L3
Waterloo Rd, Sutt	195	N9
Waterloo Ter N1	93	R14
Waterlow Rd N19	92	E2
Waterman St SW15	144	B6
Waterman Way E1	130	J1
Waterman's Cl, Kings T *1*	159	R14
Watermans Wk SE16	131	R4
Watermead La, Cars	181	U12
Watermead Rd SE6	168	E7
Watermead Way N17	76	J5
Watermeadow La SW6	145	L4
Watermen's Sq, SE20 *2*	167	M13
Watermill Cl, Rich	159	L6
Watermill La N18	60	C9
Watermill Way SW19	181	M1
Watermill Way, Felt	157	M4
Watermint Quay N16	76	H13
Waters Gdns, Dag	101	N10
Waters Pl SW15	143	U4
Waters Rd SE6	169	K5
Waters Rd, Kings T	178	C4
Waters Sq, Kings T	178	C5
Watersedge, Epsom	192	E8
Watersfield Way, Edg	53	P13
Waterside Cl E3	113	T1
Waterside Cl SE16	29	T8
Waterside Cl, Bark	100	A8
Waterside Cl, Nthlt	103	M5
Waterside Cl, Surb	191	S3
Waterside Dr, Walt	174	C10
Waterside Pl NW1	110	B1
Waterside Pt SW11	127	S13
Waterside Rd, Sthl	121	N5
Waterside Trd Cen W7	122	D5
Waterside Way SW17	163	M8
Watersmeet Way SE28	118	F12
Waterson St E2	13	K6
Watersplash Cl, Kings T	177	R5
Watersplash La, Hayes	120	B7
Watersplash La, Houns	120	C10
Waterworks La E5	95	N4
Waterworks Rd SW2	147	L11
Waterworks Yd, Croy *8*	197	T5
Watery La SW20	180	E3
Watery La, Nthlt	102	F4
Watery La, Sid	172	D12
Wates Way, Mitch	181	U12
Wateville Rd N17	75	U2
Watford Cl SW11	145	S1
Watford Rd E16	115	P10
Watford Rd, Har	86	H5
Watford Rd, Wem	86	J7
Watford Way NW4	71	R9
Watford Way NW7	71	P3
Watkin Rd, Wem	88	C6
Watkinson Rd N7	93	L11
Watling Av, Edg	70	G1
Watling Ct, EC4 *6*	20	A8
Watling Fm Cl, Stan	53	L1
Watling Gdns NW2	90	D11
Watling St EC4	20	A8
Watling St, SE15 *1*	36	J12
Watling St, Bexh	155	T8
Watlings Cl, Croy	185	R11
Watlington Gro SE26	167	R9
Watney Mkt E1	113	K12
Watney Rd SW14	142	E4
Watney St E1	113	K12
Watneys Rd, Mitch	182	G10
Watson Av E6	98	G13
Watson Av, Sutt	194	C3
Watson Cl N16	94	B9
Watson Cl SW19	163	S12
Watson St E13	115	R3
Watson's Ms W1	15	R4
Watsons Rd N22	75	M3
Watson's St SE8	132	A14
Watsons Yd NW2	89	M3
Wattisfield Rd E5	95	L5
Watts Gro E3	114	C9
Watts La, Chis	189	L1
Watts La, Tedd	158	G9
Watts Rd, T Ditt	176	G13
Watts St E1	131	K1
Watts St, SE15 *2*	148	F1
Watto Way SW7	23	L10
Wauthier Cl N13	59	R9
Wavel Ms N8	74	H8
Wavel Ms NW6	90	J14
Wavel Pl SE26	166	F8
Wavell Dr, Sid	153	S11
Wavendon Av W4	124	G10
Waveney Av SE15	149	K7
Waveney Cl E1	29	T2
Waverley Av E4	61	T8
Waverley Av E17	78	G6
Waverley Av, Surb	178	D11
Waverley Av, Sutt	195	K4
Waverley Av, Twick	157	P2
Waverley Av, Wem	87	U10
Waverley Cl E18	79	T2
Waverley Cl, Brom	188	A10
Waverley Cl, W Mol	175	P10
Waverley Cres SE18	135	N11
Waverley Gdns E6	116	D10
Waverley Gdns NW10	105	T5
Waverley Gdns, Bark	117	R4
Waverley Gdns, Ilf	81	M4
Waverley Gdns, Nthwd	66	A2
Waverley Gro N3	72	C5
Waverley Ind Est, Har	68	A6
Waverley Pl N4	93	S2
Waverley Pl NW8 *6*	6	J2
Waverley Rd E17	78	F6
Waverley Rd E18	79	T2
Waverley Rd N8	74	H12
Waverley Rd N17	60	J13
Waverley Rd SE18	135	M9
Waverley Rd SE25	184	J7
Waverley Rd, Enf	43	S7
Waverley Rd, Epsom	193	R10
Waverley Rd, Har	67	K14
Waverley Rd, Sthl	103	P13
Waverley Vil, N17 *3*	76	F4
Waverley Wk W2	108	H9
Waverley Way, Cars	195	S12
Waverton Rd SW18	145	L14
Waverton St W1	24	F1
Wavertree Rd E18	79	P3
Wavertree Rd SW2	165	L2
Waxlow Cres, Sthl	103	N11
Waxlow Rd NW10	106	F3
Waxwell Cl, Pnr	66	H4
Waxwell La, Pnr	66	H4
Waxwell Ter, SE1 *1*	26	G8
Waye Av, Houns	138	B1
Wayfarer Rd, Nthlt	102	J6
Wayfield Link SE9	153	P12
Wayford St SW11	145	S4
Wayland Av E8	94	H10
Waylands Mead, Beck	186	D2
Wayleave, The SE28	118	D14
Waylett Pl SE27	165	S5
Waylett Pl, Wem	87	N7
Wayne Cl, Orp	203	T6
Waynflete Av, Croy	197	R6
Waynflete Sq, W10 *1*	108	A13
Waynflete St SW18	163	L3
Wayside NW11	90	D2
Wayside SW14	142	F9
Wayside, Croy	200	D12
Wayside Cl N14	42	F11
Wayside Commercial Est, Bark	118	A3
Wayside Ct, Twick	141	L11
Wayside Ct, Wem	88	A6
Wayside Gdns, SE9 *3*	170	F8
Wayside Gdns, Dag	101	N9
Wayside Gro SE9	170	E8
Wayside Ms, Ilf	80	H10
Weald, The, Chis	170	F11
Weald Cl SE16	130	J9
Weald Cl, Brom	202	C3
Weald La, Har	68	A3
Weald Ri, Har	68	E1
Weald Way, Rom	83	R12
Wooldstone Rd, Sutt	104	F4
Wealdwood Gdns, Pnr	51	R11
Weale Rd E4	62	H5
Wear Pl E2	112	J5
Weardale Gdns, Enf	44	B1
Weardale Rd SE13	150	H8
Wearside Rd SE13	150	D8
Weatherley Cl E3	113	U9
Weaver Cl E6	116	J13
Weaver St E1	13	S11
Weaver Wk SE27	165	S8
Weavers Cl, Islw	140	D7
Weavers Ter SW6	126	H12
Weavers Way NW1	110	G1
Webb Cl W10	107	T8
Webb Est E5	76	H14
Webb Gdns E13	115	P7
Webb Pl NW10	107	L6
Webb Rd SE3	133	L12
Webb St SE1	28	H11
Webber Row SE1	27	L9
Webber St SE1	27	L6
Webbs Rd SW11	145	U10
Webbs Rd, Hayes	102	B5
Webbscroft Rd, Dag	101	R7
Webster Gdns W5	123	P2
Webster Rd E11	96	F6
Webster Rd SE16	29	U11
Wedderburn Rd NW3	91	P10
Wedderburn Rd, Bark	117	R1
Wedgwood Way SE19	165	T12
Wedlake St, W10 *2*	108	D7
Wedmore Av, Ilf	80	G1
Wedmore Gdns N19	92	G5
Wedmore Ms N19	92	H5
Wedmore Rd, Grnf	104	B6
Wedmore St N19	92	H5
Weech Rd NW6	90	G8
Weedington Rd NW5	92	B10
Weekley Sq, SW11 *13*	145	P6
Weigall Rd SE12	151	P8
Weighhouse St W1	16	F9
Weighton Rd SE20	184	J3
Weighton Rd, Har	68	B1
Weihurst Gdns, Sutt	195	P10
Weimar St SW15	144	C6
Weir Hall Av N18	60	B11
Weir Hall Gdns N18	60	A9
Weir Hall Rd N17	60	B12
Weir Hall Rd N18	60	B12
Weir Rd SW12	146	F14
Weir Rd SW19	163	K5
Weir Rd, Bex	155	R14
Weir Rd, Walt	174	B12
Weirdale Av N20	57	T3
Weir's Pas NW1	9	U6
Weiss Rd SW15	144	A6
Welbeck Av, Brom	169	P8
Welbeck Av, Hayes	102	C7
Welbeck Av, Sid	172	B1
Welbeck Cl N12	57	N9
Welbeck Cl, Borwd	38	A5
Welbeck Cl, Epsom	193	N14
Welbeck Cl, N Mal	179	L9
Welbeck Rd E6	116	A5
Welbeck Rd, Barn	41	P11
Welbeck Rd, Cars	195	S1
Welbeck Rd, Har	85	R1
Welbeck Rd, Sutt	195	P3
Welbeck St W1	16	G6
Welbeck Way W1	16	G5
Welby St SE5	147	S2
Welch Pl, Pnr	66	E2
Weld Pl N11	58	D10
Weldon Cl, Ruis	84	D12
Weldon Dr, W Mol	175	L7
Welfare Rd E15	97	K13
Welford Cl, E5 *3*	95	P6
Welford Pl SW19	162	D8
Welham Rd SW16	164	D11
Welham Rd SW17	164	B10
Welhouse Rd, Cars	195	R2
Well App, Barn	39	U9
Well Cl SW16	165	M8
Well Cl, Ruis	84	J6
Well Cottage Cl E11	79	T13
Well Ct EC4	20	B8
Well Ct SW16	165	M8
Well Gro N20	57	M1
Well Hall Par SE9	152	E8
Well Hall Rd SE9	152	E6
Well La SW14	142	E9
Well Pas NW3	91	N6
Well Rd NW3	91	N6
Well Rd, Barn	39	U9
Well St E9	95	L14
Well St E15	96	J11
Well Wk NW3	91	N6
Wellacre Rd, Har	69	K11
Wellan Cl, Sid	154	C10
Welland Gdns, Grnf	104	E4
Welland Ms E1	29	U1
Welland St SE10	132	E11
Wellands Cl, Brom	188	B2
Wellbrook Rd, Orp	202	H7
Wellclose Sq E1	21	T10
Wellclose St, E1 *1*	21	T11
Welldon Cres, Har	68	G5
Weller St SE1	27	U6
Weller's Ct N1	10	A3
Wellesley Av W6	125	R6
Wellesley Ct W9	6	F6
Wellesley Ct Rd, Croy *5*	198	A4
Wellesley Cres, Twick	158	C4
Wellesley Gro, Croy	198	A3
Wellesley Pk Ms, Enf *1*	43	S3
Wellesley Pl NW1	9	S7
Wellesley Rd E11	79	P9
Wellesley Rd E17	78	A1
Wellesley Rd N22	75	N3
Wellesley Rd NW5	92	A10
Wellesley Rd W4	124	D9
Wellesley Rd, Croy	197	U2
Wellesley Rd, Har	68	C10
Wellesley Rd, Ilf	195	M11
Wellesley Rd, Sutt	195	M11
Wellesley Rd, Twick	158	B5
Wellesley St E1	113	N10
Wellesley Ter N1	12	A5
Wellfield Av N10	72	H13
Wellfield Rd SW16	165	K8
Wellfield Wk SW16	165	M9
Wellfields, Loug	48	H5
Wellfit St, SE24 *6*	147	S6
Wellgarth, Grnf	86	J11
Wellgarth Rd NW11	71	U9
Wellhouse La, Barn	40	A8
Wellhouse Rd, Beck	186	A4
Welling High St, Well	154	C5
Welling Way SE9	153	N6

Name	Page	Grid
Welling Way, Well	153	N6
Wellington Av E4	62	B4
Wellington Av N9	61	K5
Wellington Av N15	76	F11
Wellington Av, Houns	139	N9
Wellington Av, Pnr	67	L1
Wellington Av, Sid	154	B11
Wellington Av, Wor Pk	193	T6
Wellington Bldgs SW1	32	F8
Wellington Cl, SE14 5	149	N2
Wellington Cl W11	108	G12
Wellington Cl, Dag	101	U13
Wellington Cl, Wat	51	L5
Wellington Ct NW8	7	L3
Wellington Cres, N Mal	178	F6
Wellington Dr, Dag	101	U14
Wellington Gdns SE7	133	T10
Wellington Gdns, Twick	158	A2
Wellington Gro, SE10 9	132	G14
Wellington Ms SE7	133	T11
Wellington Ms SE22	148	H7
Wellington Pk Est NW2	89	N3
Wellington Pas E11	79	P9
Wellington Pl N2	73	S9
Wellington Pl NW8	7	N4
Wellington Rd E6	116	F3
Wellington Rd E7	97	M8
Wellington Rd E10	95	R1
Wellington Rd E11	79	P9
Wellington Rd E17	77	S7
Wellington Rd NW8	7	M4
Wellington Rd, NW10 1	108	B6
Wellington Rd SW19	162	H4
Wellington Rd W5	123	L6
Wellington Rd, Belv	137	M9
Wellington Rd, Bex	154	G10
Wellington Rd, Brom	187	U8
Wellington Rd, Croy	183	S14
Wellington Rd, Enf	44	D14
Wellington Rd, Hmptn	158	A7
Wellington Rd, Har	68	C5
Wellington Rd, Pnr	67	L1
Wellington Rd, Twick	158	A7
Wellington Rd N, Houns	139	L5
Wellington Rd S, Houns	139	M8
Wellington Row E2	13	R6
Wellington Sq SW3	31	U6
Wellington St SE18	134	G8
Wellington St WC2	18	E9
Wellington St, Bark	117	M1
Wellington Ter, E1 8	130	J1
Wellington Ter, Har	86	B2
Wellington Way E3	114	A6
Wellmeadow Rd SE6	151	K14
Wellmeadow Rd SE13	150	J12
Wellmeadow Rd W7	122	G7
Wellow Wk, Cars	195	P2
Wells, The N14	42	H14
Wells Cl, Nthlt	102	F5
Wells Dr NW9	88	G2
Wells Gdns, Dag	101	R10
Wells Gdns, Ilf	80	D13
Wells Ho Rd NW10	106	J9
Wells Ms W1	17	N5
Wells Pk Rd SE26	166	G6
Wells Ri NW8	109	T2
Wells Rd W12	125	T4
Wells Rd, Brom	188	F3
Wells Sq, WC1 4	10	F7
Wells St W1	17	M4
Wells Ter N4	93	N3
Wells Way SE5	36	G12
Wells Way SW7	22	J10
Wells Yd, N7 5	93	N9
Wellside Cl, Barn	39	U8
Wellsmoor Gdns, Brom	188	G5
Wellsprings Cres, Wem	88	D5
Wellstead Av N9	45	N14
Wellstead Rd E6	116	G4
Wellwood Rd, Ilf	100	A1
Welsford St SE1	37	R4
Welsh Cl E13	115	N6
Welshpool St E8	112	H1
Weltje Rd W6	125	P9
Welton Rd SE18	135	R14
Welwyn St E2	113	M5
Wembley Commercial Cen, Wem	87	N4
Wembley Hill Rd, Wem	87	U9
Wembley Pk Business Cen, Wem	88	D6
Wembley Pk Dr, Wem	87	T6
Wembley Rd, Hmptn	175	N1
Wembley Way, Wem	88	D11
Wemborough Rd, Stan	53	M14
Wembury Rd N6	74	D13
Wemyss Rd SE3	151	L4
Wendela Ct, Har	86	C5
Wendell Rd W12	125	L4
Wendle Ct SW8	34	B11
Wendling Rd, Sutt	195	N2
Wendon St, E3 4	113	U1
Wendover SE17	36	G6
Wendover Cl, Hayes 3	102	J7
Wendover Dr, N Mal	179	M12
Wendover Rd NW10	107	L3
Wendover Rd SE9	152	B6
Wendover Rd, Brom	187	S6
Wendover Way, Well	154	B9
Wendy Cl, Enf	44	F11
Wendy Way, Wem	105	S2
Wenlock Gdns, NW4 4	71	P8
Wenlock Rd N1	12	A3
Wenlock Rd, Edg	54	D13
Wenlock St N1	12	C3
Wennington Rd E3	113	P4
Wensley Av, Wdf Grn	63	N13
Wensley Cl SE9	152	E12
Wensley Rd N18	60	J11
Wensleydale Av, Ilf	80	D4
Wensleydale Gdns, Hmptn	157	R14
Wensleydale Pas, Hmptn	175	P1
Wensleydale Rd, Hmptn	157	P13
Wentland Cl SE6	168	H4
Wentland Rd SE6	168	H4
Wentworth Av N3	56	H14
Wentworth Cl N3	56	J13
Wentworth Cl SE28	118	H11
Wentworth Cl, Brom 1	201	N3
Wentworth Cl, Mord	180	G13
Wentworth Cl, Orp	203	R9
Wentworth Cres, SE15	130	H14
Wentworth Dr, Pnr	66	A9
Wentworth Gdns N13	59	R7
Wentworth Hill, Wem	87	T1
Wentworth Ms, E3 1	113	S7
Wentworth Pk N3	56	H14
Wentworth Pl, Stan	52	H12
Wentworth Rd E12	98	B8
Wentworth Rd NW11	72	E12
Wentworth Rd, Barn	40	B5
Wentworth Rd, Croy	183	N14
Wentworth Rd, Sthl	120	G8
Wentworth St E1	21	N4
Wentworth Way, Pnr	66	J8
Wenvoe Av, Bexh	155	R3
Wernbrook St SE18	135	M11
Werndee Rd SE25	184	H8
Werneth Hall Rd, Ilf	80	F6
Werrington St NW1	9	P3
Werter Rd SW15	144	C8
Wesley Av E16	133	R1
Wesley Av, Houns	139	L3
Wesley Av NW10	106	G5
Wesley Cl N7	93	M4
Wesley Cl SE17	35	R4
Wesley Cl, Har	85	U3
Wesley Rd E10	78	E14
Wesley Rd NW10	88	F14
Wesley Rd, Hayes	102	B13
Wesley St W1	16	F3
Wesleyan Pl NW5	92	C8
Wessex Av SW19	180	H4
Wessex Cl, Ilf	81	S11
Wessex Cl, Kings T	178	C2
Wessex Dr, Pnr	51	K13
Wessex Gdns NW11	90	C1
Wessex La, Grnf	104	B4
Wessex St E2	113	M6
Wessex Way NW11	90	C1
West App, Orp	189	M10
West Arbour St E1	113	N11
West Av E17	78	C8
West Av N3	56	G12
West Av NW4	72	A9
West Av, Pnr	67	L13
West Av, Sthl	103	L13
West Av, Wall	197	K10
West Av Rd E17	78	B8
West Bank N16	76	C14
West Bank, Bark	117	K1
West Bank, Enf	43	T4
West Barnes La, SW20	179	S4
West Barnes La, N Mal	179	R6
West Carriage Dr W2	23	M4
West Cen St WC1	18	B5
West Chantry, Har	67	R1
West Cl N9	60	F5
West Cl, Barn	39	S10
West Cl (Cockfosters), Barn	42	B8
West Cl, Grnf	103	U4
West Cl, Wem	87	U2
West Common Rd, Brom	201	P3
West Common Rd, Kes	201	S7
West Cotts NW6	90	H10
West Ct SE18	134	F14
West Ct, Wem	87	L4
West Cromwell Rd SW5	126	E9
West Cromwell Rd W14	126	E9
West Cross Cen, Brent	122	J12
West Cross Route W10	108	A14
West Cross Route W11	108	A14
West Cross Way, Brent	122	J12
West Dene, Sutt 3	194	C11
West Dr SW16	164	C8
West Dr, Har	52	A12
West Dr Gdns, Har	52	A12
West Eaton Pl SW1	32	C1
West Eaton Pl Ms, SW1	32	C1
West Ella Rd NW10	88	J14
West End Av E10	78	F10
West End Av, Pnr	66	H8
West End Ct, Pnr	66	H8
West End Gdns, Nthlt	102	F4
West End La NW6	108	H1
West End La, Barn	40	B7
West End La, Pnr	66	H9
West End Rd, Nthlt	84	D11
West End Rd, Ruis	84	E13
West End Rd, Sthl	120	J2
West Gdn Pl W2	15	R7
West Gdns E1	113	K14
West Gdns, SW17	163	R11
West Gate W5	105	R5
West Grn Pl, Grnf	104	B1
West Grn Rd N15	75	S7
West Gro SE10	150	G1
West Gro, Wdf Grn	63	U10
West Halkin St SW1	24	C10
West Hall Rd, Rich	142	C2
West Hallowes SE9	170	B1
West Ham La E15	96	H13
West Ham Pk E7	97	N14
West Hampstead Ms NW6	90	J12
West Harding St, EC4 7	19	L6
West Heath Av NW11	90	H1
West Heath Cl NW3	90	H5
West Heath Dr NW11	90	H2
West Heath Gdns NW3	90	G4
West Heath Rd NW3	90	J5
West Heath Rd SE2	136	G12
West Hendon Bdy NW9	71	P14
West Hill SW15	144	C12
West Hill SW18	144	G10
West Hill, Har	86	C3
West Hill, Wem	87	U1
West Hill Ct N6	92	A5
West Hill Pk N6	91	U3
West Hill Rd SW18	144	G12
West Hill Way N20	56	J2
West Holme, Erith	155	U11
West Ho Cl SW19	162	C1
West India Av E14	132	A1
West India Dock Rd E14	113	U12
West Kentish Town Est NW5	92	B11
West La SE16	130	J4
West Lo Av W3	124	A2
West Mead, Epsom	192	J12
West Mead, Ruis	84	E7
West Mersea Cl, E16 18	133	R2
West Ms N17	60	J12
West Ms SW1	33	L4
West Oak, Beck	186	G2
West Pk SE9	170	D2
West Pk Av, Rich	142	B1
West Pk Cl, Houns	121	L12
West Pk Cl, Rom	82	H10
West Pk Rd, Sthl	121	U2
West Parkside SE10	133	K4
West Pier E1	130	J2
West Pl SW19	161	T9
West Poultry Av EC1	19	P3
West Quarters W12	107	N12
West Quay Dr, Hayes	102	J10
West Ridge Gdns, Grnf	103	T4
West Rd E15	115	M2
West Rd N17	60	J12
West Rd SW3	32	A8
West Rd SW4	146	H9
West Rd W5	105	R9
West Rd, Barn	58	A1
West Rd, Kings T	178	F1
West Rd (Chadwell Heath), Rom	82	H11
West Row W10	108	C7
West Sheen Vale, Rich	141	T7
West Side Common SW19	161	U10
West Smithfield EC1	19	P4
West Sq SE11	27	N12
West St E2	113	K4
West St E11	96	J5
West St, E17 4	78	D10
West St WC2	17	U8

Name	Pg	Ref
West St, Bexh	155	L7
West St, Brent	123	L12
West St, Brom	187	N3
West St, Cars	195	T6
West St, Croy	197	U7
West St, Har	86	B1
West St, Sutt	194	J9
West St La, Cars	195	T8
West Temple Sheen SW14	142	D9
West Tenter St E1	21	N8
West Twrs, Pnr	66	G11
West Vw NW4	71	T7
West Vw, Loug	48	F6
West Wk W5	105	R10
West Wk, Barn	58	A1
West Wk, Hayes	120	A2
West Walkway, The, Sutt *3*	194	J10
West Warwick Pl SW1	33	K4
West Way N18	60	A8
West Way NW10	88	H6
West Way, Croy	199	R4
West Way, Edg	54	D11
West Way, Houns	139	L1
West Way, Pnr	66	G7
West Way, W Wick	186	J12
West Way Gdns, Croy	199	P4
West Woodside, Bex	173	K1
Westacott Cl N19	92	H2
Westall Rd, Loug	49	K5
Westbank Rd, Hmptn	157	T12
Westbeech Rd N22	75	P5
Westbere Dr, Stan	53	P9
Westbere Rd NW2	90	D9
Westbourne Av W3	106	G12
Westbourne Av, Sutt	194	C3
Westbourne Br W2	14	E4
Westbourne Cl, Hayes	102	D7
Westbourne Cres W2	14	J9
Westbourne Cres Ms, W2 *1*	14	J9
Westbourne Dr SE23	167	N3
Westbourne Gdns W2	14	A5
Westbourne Gro W2	108	J12
Westbourne Gro W11	108	F12
Westbourne Gro Ms, W11 *6*	108	G12
Westbourne Gro Ter W2	14	B6
Westbourne Pk Ms, W2 *1*	14	B6
Westbourne Pk Pas, W2 *1*	108	H9
Westbourne Pk Rd W2	14	A5
Westbourne Pk Rd W11	108	H11
Westbourne Pk Vil W2	108	H10
Westbourne Pl N9	61	K5
Westbourne Rd N7	93	N12
Westbourne Rd SE26	167	N11
Westbourne Rd, Bexh	136	J13
Westbourne Rd, Croy	184	E12
Westbourne St W2	14	J8
Westbourne Ter W2	14	H7
Westbourne Ter Ms W2	14	F5
Westbourne Ter Rd W2	14	E3
Westbridge Rd SW11	145	R1
Westbrook Av, Hmptn	157	L13
Westbrook Cl, Barn	41	P6
Westbrook Cres, Barn	41	N6
Westbrook Rd SE3	151	P2
Westbrook Rd, Houns	121	M13
Westbrook Rd, Th Hth	184	A2
Westbrook Sq, Barn	41	N5
Westbrooke Cres, Well	154	F5
Westbrooke Rd, Sid	171	P4
Westbrooke Rd, Well	154	E5
Westbury Av N22	75	R5
Westbury Av, Esher	190	E11
Westbury Av, Sthl	103	N7
Westbury Av, Wem	87	R13
Westbury Cl, Ruis	66	A13
Westbury Gro N12	56	H11
Westbury La, Buck H	63	T3
Westbury Lo Cl, Pnr	66	H6
Westbury Pl, Brent	123	P11
Westbury Rd E7	97	S10
Westbury Rd E17	78	A7
Westbury Rd N11	58	J12
Westbury Rd N12	56	H11
Westbury Rd SE20	185	N2
Westbury Rd W5	105	R12
Westbury Rd, Bark	117	N1
Westbury Rd, Beck	185	35
Westbury Rd, Brom	188	B1
Westbury Rd, Buck H	63	T3
Westbury Rd, Croy	184	A12
Westbury Rd, Felt	156	H2
Westbury Rd, Ilf	98	G4
Westbury Rd, N Mal	178	J9
Westbury Rd, Wem	87	S13
Westbury St SW8	146	E4
Westbury Ter E7	97	S11
Westchester Dr NW4	72	A5
Westcombe Av, Croy	183	L13
Westcombe Dr, Barn	40	G9
Westcombe Hill SE3	133	P12
Westcombe Hill SE10	133	P12
Westcombe Pk Rd SE3	133	L12
Westcoombe Av SW20	179	M2
Westcote Rd SW16	164	F10
Westcott Cl, N15 *3*	76	E11
Westcott Cl, Brom	188	D9
Westcott Cres W7	104	E10
Westcott Rd SE17	35	R9
Westcourt, Sun	174	D4
Westcroft Cl NW2	90	D8
Westcroft Gdns, Mord	180	E6
Westcroft Rd, Cars	196	B8
Westcroft Rd, Wall	196	B8
Westcroft Sq W6	125	M7
Westcroft Way NW2	90	C7
Westdale Rd SE18 *5*	134	J11
Westdale Rd SE18	135	K11
Westdean Av SE12	169	S2
Westdean Cl, SW18 *15*	145	K11
Westdown Rd E15	96	E7
Westdown Rd SE6	150	A14
Westerdale Rd SE10	133	N10
Westerfield Rd N15	76	E9
Westergate Rd SE2	137	K11
Westerham Av N9	60	C6
Westerham Dr, Sid	154	D11
Westerham Rd E10	78	C12
Westerham Rd, Kes	202	C7
Westerley Cres SE26	167	U10
Westerley Ware, Rich *2*	124	A12
Western Av NW11	72	B12
Western Av W3	106	J13
Western Av W5	106	F9
Western Av, Grnf	105	M5
Western Av, Nthlt	84	J14
Western Av, Ruis	84	J14
Western Ct, N3 *1*	56	H12
Western Gdns W5	106	A13
Western Gateway E16	115	P14
Western La SW12	146	A13
Western Pl, SE16 *7*	131	M3
Western Rd E13	115	T3
Western Rd E17	78	F10
Western Rd N2	73	T7
Western Rd N22	75	L4
Western Rd NW10	106	E7
Western Rd SW9	147	P6
Western Rd SW19	181	R2
Western Rd W5	105	P14
Western Rd, Mitch	181	R2
Western Rd, Sthl	120	J6
Western Rd, Sutt	194	G10
Western Trd Est NW10	106	E7
Western Way SE28	135	S3
Western Way, Barn	40	H12
Westernville Gdns, Ilf	81	L13
Westferry Circ E14	131	U1
Westferry Rd E14	114	A14
Westfield, Loug	48	A9
Westfield Cl NW9	70	F6
Westfield Cl SW10	127	L14
Westfield Cl, Enf	46	R6
Westfield Cl, Sutt	194	E7
Westfield Dr, Har	69	P8
Westfield Gdns, Har	69	P8
Westfield La, Har	69	N8
Westfield Pk, Pnr	51	M13
Westfield Pk Dr, Wdf Grn	64	D12
Westfield Rd NW7	54	J6
Westfield Rd W13	122	H2
Westfield Rd, Beck	185	T3
Westfield Rd, Bexh	155	U5
Westfield Rd, Croy	197	R3
Westfield Rd, Dag	101	K8
Westfield Rd, Mitch	181	S4
Westfield Rd, Surb	177	N10
Westfield Rd, Sutt	194	E7
Westfield Rd, Walt	175	K14
Westfield St SE18	134	B6
Westfield Way E1	113	R6
Westfields SW13	143	L5
Westfields Av SW13	143	K5
Westfields Rd W3	106	D10
Westgate Rd SE25	184	J8
Westgate Rd, Beck	186	U3
Westgate St E8	112	J1
Westgate Ter SW10	30	C9
Westglade Ct, Har	69	N9
Westgrove La SE10	150	F1
Westhay Gdns SW14	142	D9
Westholm NW11	72	J8
Westholme, Orp	189	S14
Westholme Gdns, Ruis	84	A1
Westhorne Av SE9	151	T11
Westhorne Av SE12	151	R12
Westhorpe Gdns NW4	71	U6
Westhorpe Rd SW15	143	U6
Westhurst Dr, Chis	171	K9
Westlake Cl N13	59	N5
Westlake Cl, Hayes	102	J8
Westlake Rd, Wem	87	P4
Westland Dr, Brom	201	L4
Westland Pl N1	12	C6
Westlands Cl, Hayes	120	A7
Westlands Ter SW12 *3*	146	E12
Westlea Rd W7	122	J5
Westleigh Av SW15	144	A10
Westleigh Dr, Brom	188	C2
Westleigh Gdns, Edg	70	B2
Westmead SW15	143	R12
Westmead Rd, Sutt	195	R8
Westmede, Chig	65	M11
Westmere Dr NW7	54	G5
Westminster Av, Th Hth	183	R3
Westminster Br SE1	26	C7
Westminster Br SW1	26	C7
Westminster Br Rd SE1	26	J9
Westminster Cl, Felt	156	A1
Westminster Cl, Ilf	81	N4
Westminster Cl, Tedd	158	G9
Westminster Dr N13	58	J10
Westminster Gdns E4	63	K2
Westminster Gdns, Bark	117	R4
Westminster Gdns, Ilf	81	M4
Westminster Rd N9	61	K2
Westminster Rd W7	122	D2
Westminster Rd, Sutt	195	N3
Westmoat Cl, Beck	168	E14
Westmont Rd, Esher	190	D4
Westmoor Gdns, Enf	45	N3
Westmoor Rd, Enf	45	N3
Westmoor St SE7	134	A6
Westmoreland Av, Well	153	S6
Westmoreland Pl SW1	32	J7
Westmoreland Pl W5	105	N9
Westmoreland Rd NW9	69	U7
Westmoreland Rd SE17	36	C10
Westmoreland Rd SW13	143	M1
Westmoreland Rd, Brom	187	K9
Westmoreland St W1	16	F3
Westmoreland Ter SW1	32	J7
Westmorland Cl E12	98	B3
Westmorland Cl, Twick *2*	141	K11
Westmorland Rd E17	78	B12
Westmorland Rd, Har	67	S10
Westmorland Ter, SE20 *7*	167	K14
Westmorland Way, Mitch	182	H8
Westmount Rd SE9	152	F4
Westoe Rd N9	61	K4
Weston Av, T Ditt	176	C14
Weston Av, W Mol	175	L7
Weston Dr, Stan	69	K2
Weston Gdns, Islw	140	B2
Weston Grn, Dag	101	L7
Weston Grn, T Ditt	190	D1
Weston Grn Rd, Esher	190	B2
Weston Grn Rd, T Ditt	176	D14
Weston Gro, Brom	187	M1
Weston Pk N8	75	M10
Weston Pk, Kings T	177	R3
Weston Pk, T Ditt	190	D2
Weston Pk Cl, T Ditt *4*	190	C2
Weston Ri WC1	10	G4
Weston Rd W4	124	E6
Weston Rd, Brom	169	M14
Weston Rd, Dag	101	K7
Weston Rd, Enf	44	B2
Weston Rd, T Ditt	190	C2
Weston St SE1	35	L5
Weston Wk, E8 *12*	95	K14
Westover Hill NW3	90	H4
Westover Rd SW18	145	M12
Westow Hill SE19	166	D12
Westow St SE19	166	D12
Westpoint Trd Est W3	106	C8
Westpole Av, Barn	42	D9
Westport Rd E13	115	R8
Westport St E1	113	P11
Westrow SW15	143	U11
Westrow Dr, Bark	100	A8
Westrow Gdns, Ilf	99	U5

Westside NW4	71	R3
Westvale Ms W3	125	K2
Westview Cl NW10	89	L9
Westview Cl W7	104	C11
Westview Cl W10	107	U11
Westview Cres N9	44	C14
Westview Dr, Wdf Grn	80	A3
Westville Rd W12	125	P3
Westville Rd, T Ditt	176	H14
Westward Rd E4	61	S10
Westward Way, Har	69	R12
Westway SW20	179	S7
Westway W2	14	A3
Westway W9	108	G9
Westway W10	108	B12
Westway W12	107	M13
Westway, Orp	189	N10
Westway Cl SW20	179	S6
Westways, Epsom	193	M8
Westwell Rd SW16	164	J12
Westwell Rd App, SW16 1	164	J12
Westwick Gdns SW14	126	A4
Westwick Gdns, Houns	138	D3
Westwood Av SE19	183	U1
Westwood Av, Har	85	S8
Westwood Cl, Brom	188	B5
Westwood Gdns SW13	143	L6
Westwood Hill SE26	166	J8
Westwood La, Sid	154	A10
Westwood La, Well	153	T6
Westwood Pk SE23	149	K14
Westwood Rd E16	133	R1
Westwood Rd SW13	143	L6
Westwood Rd, Ilf	99	U1
Wetheral Dr, Stan	69	L3
Wetherby Cl, Nthlt	85	R11
Wetherby Gdns SW5	30	E4
Wetherby Ms, SW5 2	30	C6
Wetherby Pl SW7	30	F3
Wetherby Rd, Enf	43	U1
Wetherby Way, Chess	191	S13
Wetherden St E17	77	T14
Wetherell Rd E9	113	P1
Wetherill Rd N10	74	B2
Wexford Rd SW12	145	T14
Wey Ct, Epsom	192	F8
Weybourne St SW18	163	L4
Weybridge Ct, SE16 1	37	U7
Weybridge Rd, Th Hth	183	P8
Weydown Cl SW19	162	C2
Weyhill Rd E1	21	T6
Weylond Rd, Dag	101	L6
Weyman Rd SE3	151	U1
Weymouth Av NW7	54	J9
Weymouth Av W5	123	M5
Weymouth Cl E6	116	J12
Weymouth Ct, Sutt	194	H13
Weymouth Ms W1	16	H2
Weymouth St W1	16	G2
Weymouth Ter E2	13	N2
Weymouth Wk, Stan	52	G12
Whadcote St N4	93	N4
Whalebone Av, Rom	83	L11
Whalebone Ct EC2	20	D5
Whalebone Gro, Rom	83	L11
Whalebone La E15	97	K14
Whalebone La N, Rom	83	K10
Whalebone La S, Dag	83	L14
Whalebone La S, Rom	83	L14
Wharf La, Twick	158	G2
Wharf Pl E2	112	H2
Wharf Rd E15	114	G1
Wharf Rd N1	11	U3
Wharf Rd, Enf	45	S11
Wharf St E16	114	J10
Wharfdale Rd N1	10	D2
Wharfedale Gdns, Th Hth	183	L7
Wharfedale St SW10	30	B7
Wharfside Rd E16	114	J11
Wharncliffe Dr, Sthl	122	B1
Wharncliffe Gdns SE25	184	C4
Wharncliffe Rd SE25	184	C4
Wharton Cl NW10	89	K11
Wharton Rd, Brom	187	R2
Wharton St WC1	10	G7
Whateley Rd SE20	167	P13
Whateley Rd SE22	148	F10
Whatley Av SW20	180	D4
Whatman Rd SE23	149	P14
Wheat Sheaf Cl E14	132	C7
Wheatfield Way, Kings T	177	R4
Wheatfields, E6 1	116	J11
Wheatfields, Enf	45	R2
Wheathill Rd SE20	184	J5
Wheatlands, Houns	121	N12
Wheatlands Rd, SW17 1	164	A5
Wheatley Cl NW4	71	P4
Wheatley Cres, Hayes	102	A13
Wheatley Gdns N9	60	C4
Wheatley Rd, Islw	140	E6
Wheatley St, W1 3	16	F3
Wheatley's Ait, Sun	174	B9
Wheatsheaf Cl, Nthlt	84	J10
Wheatsheaf La SW6	125	U13
Wheatsheaf La SW8	34	B14
Wheatsheaf Ter, SW6 17	126	F14
Wheatstone Cl, Mitch 2	181	R1
Wheatstone Rd, W10 6	108	D9
Wheel Fm Dr, Dag	101	U5
Wheeler Cl, Wdf Grn	64	E10
Wheelers Cross, Bark	117	N3
Wheelock Cl, Erith	137	S14
Wheelwright St N7	93	L13
Whelan Way, Wall	196	H6
Wheler St E1	13	L11
Whellock Rd W4	124	J5
Whenman Av, Bex	173	U4
Whernside Cl SE28	118	F14
Whetstone Cl N20	57	N3
Whetstone Pk WC2	18	F5
Whetstone Rd SE3	151	U3
Whewell Rd N19	93	K4
Whichcote St, SE1 1	18	B4
Whidborne Cl, SE8 2	150	B4
Whidborne St WC1	10	C7
Whimbrel Cl SE28	118	E13
Whimbrel Way, Hayes 3	102	G10
Whinchat Rd SE28	135	P5
Whinfell Cl SW16	164	G9
Whinyates Rd SE9	152	C6
Whipps Cross Rd E11	79	K11
Whiskin St EC1	11	M8
Whisperwood Cl, Har	52	D14
Whistler Gdns, Edg	69	U4
Whistler Ms, SE15 3	130	F14
Whistler St N5	93	R9
Whistlers Av SW11	127	P14
Whiston Rd E2	112	E3
Whitakers Way, Loug	48	F1
Whitbread Cl N17	76	G1
Whitbread Rd SE4	149	S8
Whitburn Rd SE13	150	D8
Whitby Av NW10	106	C5
Whitby Gdns NW9	70	B5
Whitby Gdns, Sutt 1	195	N3
Whitby Rd SE18	134	E7
Whitby Rd, Har	85	T6
Whitby Rd, Ruis	84	C5
Whitby Rd, Sutt	195	N3
Whitby St E1	13	M10
Whitcher Cl, SE14 2	131	R12
Whitcher Pl NW1	92	F12
Whitchurch Av, Edg	53	T14
Whitchurch Cl, Edg	53	T11
Whitchurch Gdns, Edg	53	T12
Whitchurch La, Edg	54	A13
Whitchurch Rd W11	108	B13
Whitcomb St WC2	17	T11
White Acre NW9	71	K3
White Bear Pl, NW3 9	91	N7
White Br Av, Mitch 1	181	P6
White Butts Rd, Ruis	84	H6
White Ch La E1	21	R5
White Ch Pas, E1 2	21	R5
White City Cl W12	107	T14
White City Est W12	107	R13
White City Rd W12	107	S13
White Conduit St, N1 6	11	L2
White Craig Cl, Pnr	51	P10
White Gdns, Dag	101	N11
White Hart La N17	59	S13
White Hart La N22	75	M1
White Hart La NW10	89	L11
White Hart La SW13	143	K5
White Hart La, Rom	83	R4
White Hart Rd SE18	135	S8
White Hart Slip, Brom 5	187	P3
White Hart St SE11	35	M5
White Hart Yd SE1	28	D3
White Heron Ms, Tedd	158	F11
White Horse Hill, Chis	170	G8
White Horse La E1	113	P9
White Horse Ms, SE1 4	27	M9
White Horse Rd E1	113	R12
White Horse Rd E6	116	F5
White Horse St W1	24	H3
White Horse Yd EC2	20	C5
White Ho Dr, Stan	53	M8
White Kennett St E1	21	K5
White Lion Ct, EC3 11	20	F7
White Lion Hill EC4	19	S10
White Lion St N1	11	K3
White Lo SE19	165	S13
White Lo Cl N2	73	P12
White Lo Cl, Sutt	195	M13
White Oak Dr, Beck	186	F4
White Oak Gdns, Sid	153	U14
White Orchards N20	40	E14
White Orchards, Stan	52	G10
White Post La E9	95	U13
White Post St, SE15 5	131	M13
White Rd E15	97	K13
White St, Sthl	120	H4
White Swan Ms, W4 1	124	J11
Whiteadder Way E14	132	D7
Whitear Wk E15	96	H11
Whitebarn La, Dag	119	P1
Whitebeam Av, Brom	188	G12
Whitebeam Cl SW9	129	M14
Whitechapel High St E1	21	N6
Whitechapel Rd E1	21	T4
Whitecote Rd, Sthl	103	S12
Whitecroft Cl, Beck	186	G7
Whitecroft Way, Beck	186	G7
Whitecross St EC1	12	B11
Whitefield Av NW2	71	U14
Whitefield Cl SW15	144	D12
Whitefoot La, Brom	168	F7
Whitefoot Ter, Brom	169	L5
Whitefriars Av, Har	68	C4
Whitefriars Dr, Har	68	B3
Whitefriars St EC4	19	M8
Whitegate Gdns, Har	52	E13
Whitehall SW1	26	A3
Whitehall Ct SW1	26	B3
Whitehall Cres, Chess	191	P9
Whitehall Gdns E4	62	J2
Whitehall Gdns SW1	26	B4
Whitehall Gdns W3	124	B2
Whitehall Gdns W4	124	D11
Whitehall La, Buck H	63	N4
Whitehall Pk N19	92	F1
Whitehall Pk Rd W4	124	D12
Whitehall Pl E7	97	P9
Whitehall Pl SW1	26	B3
Whitehall Pl, Wall 4	196	C8
Whitehall Rd E4	63	K3
Whitehall Rd W7	122	G4
Whitehall Rd, Brom	188	B9
Whitehall Rd, Har	68	C13
Whitehall Rd, Th Hth	183	N10
Whitehall Rd, Wdf Grn	63	N4
Whitehall St N17	60	E14
Whitehaven Cl, Brom	187	N7
Whitehaven St NW8	7	P12
Whitehead Cl N18	60	B9
Whitehead Cl SW18	145	L14
Whitehead's Gro SW3	31	S4
Whitehills Rd, Loug	48	H6
Whitehorse La SE25	184	B7
Whitehorse Rd, Croy	183	U14
Whitehorse Rd, Th Hth	184	A10
Whitehouse Av, Borwd	38	C7
Whitehouse La, Enf	43	U1
Whitehouse Way N14	58	D4
Whiteledges W13	105	L11
Whitelegg Rd E13	115	M4
Whiteley Rd SE19	166	B9
Whiteleys Cotts W14	126	F8
Whiteleys Way, Felt	157	N5
Whiteoaks La, Grnf	104	B4
Whites Av, Ilf	81	R11
Whites Grds SE1	28	J7
Whites Grds Est SE1	28	J6
White's Row E1	21	L3
White's Sq, SW4 9	146	H8
Whitestile Rd, Brent	123	M9
Whitestone La NW3	91	M5
Whitestone Wk NW3	91	L5
Whitethorn Gdns, Croy	199	K3
Whitethorn Gdns, Enf	44	A9
Whitethorn St E3	114	B9
Whitewebbs Way, Orp	189	U2
Whitfield Pl W1	9	M11
Whitfield Rd E6	97	U14
Whitfield Rd SE3	150	H2
Whitfield Rd, Bexh	137	L13
Whitfield St W1	9	M11
Whitford Gdns, Mitch	181	U5
Whitgift Av, S Croy	197	T10
Whitgift Cen, Croy	197	U3
Whitgift St SE11	34	F2
Whitgift St, Croy	197	T6
Whiting Av, Bark	99	K14
Whitings Rd, Barn	39	U10
Whitings Way E6	116	G9
Whitland Rd, Cars	195	P2
Whitley Rd N17	76	B4
Whitlock Dr SW19	144	D14
Whitman Rd E3	113	R6
Whitmead Cl, S Croy	198	C11
Whitmore Cl N11	58	D10
Whitmore Est N1	112	D2
Whitmore Gdns NW10	107	T3
Whitmore Rd N1	112	C2
Whitmore Rd, Beck	185	U5
Whitmore Rd, Har	67	S14

Whitnell Way SW15	144	A10
Whitney Av, Ilf	80	A8
Whitney Rd E10	78	C13
Whitney Wk, Sid	172	J12
Whitstable Cl, Beck	185	T2
Whitstable Pl, Croy	197	U8
Whitta Rd E12	98	B7
Whittaker Av, Rich	141	N10
Whittaker Rd, E6 *1*	98	A14
Whittaker Rd, Sutt	194	E5
Whittaker St SW1	32	D4
Whittell Gdns SE26	167	L6
Whittingstall Rd SW6	144	F2
Whittington Av EC3	20	G8
Whittington Ct N2	73	T10
Whittington Ms, N12 *1*	57	M7
Whittington Rd N22	59	K12
Whittington Way, Pnr	67	K10
Whittle Cl E17	77	S12
Whittle Cl, Sthl	103	R11
Whittle Rd, Houns	120	F14
Whittle Rd, Sthl *1*	121	R4
Whittlebury Cl, Cars	195	U13
Whittlesea Cl, Har	51	T14
Whittlesea Path, Har	67	T1
Whittlesea Rd, Har	67	T1
Whittlesey St SE1	27	K4
Whitton Av E, Grnf	86	B10
Whitton Av W, Grnf	86	B10
Whitton Av W, Nthlt	85	S9
Whitton Cl, Grnf	87	K12
Whitton Dene, Houns	139	S11
Whitton Dene, Islw	140	C10
Whitton Dr, Grnf	86	H11
Whitton Manor Rd, Islw	139	U10
Whitton Rd, Houns	139	S7
Whitton Rd, Twick	140	F13
Whitton Wk E3	114	A5
Whitton Waye, Houns	139	P12
Whitwell Rd E13	115	N6
Whitworth Pl SE18	135	K8
Whitworth Rd SE18	134	H13
Whitworth Rd SE25	184	E7
Whitworth St SE10	133	K9
Whorlton Rd SE15	148	J6
Whymark Av N22	75	P5
Whytecroft, Houns	120	H14
Whyteville Rd E7	97	R11
Wick La E3	114	B3
Wick Rd E9	95	N12
Wick Rd, Tedd	159	L14
Wick Sq, E9 *1*	95	T11
Wickers Oake SE19	166	E8
Wickersley Rd SW11	146	B4
Wicket, The, Croy	200	A10
Wicket Rd, Grnf	104	G5
Wickets Way, Ilf	65	U11
Wickford St E1	113	L7
Wickford Way E17	77	N7
Wickham Av, Croy	199	R3
Wickham Av, Sutt	193	T9
Wickham Chase, W Wick	187	K13
Wickham Cl, Enf	45	K5
Wickham Cl, N Mal	179	L10
Wickham Ct Rd, W Wick	200	F3
Wickham Cres, W Wick	200	F3
Wickham Gdns SE4	149	T6
Wickham La SE2	136	B12
Wickham La, Well	136	B12
Wickham Ms SE4	149	U4
Wickham Rd E4	62	E13
Wickham Rd SE4	149	T6
Wickham Rd, Beck	186	B2
Wickham Rd, Croy	199	N4
Wickham Rd, Har	68	A4
Wickham St SE11	34	F6
Wickham St, Well	153	S3
Wickham Way, Beck	186	B6
Wickliffe Av N3	72	C4
Wickliffe Gdns, Wem	88	B3
Wicklow St WC1	10	E6
Wicks Cl SE9	170	A7
Wickwood St SE5	147	S4
Widdecombe Av, Har	84	J4
Widdenham Rd N7	93	L8
Widdin St E15	96	H14
Wide Way, Mitch	182	H6
Widecombe Gdns, Ilf	80	D7
Widecombe Rd SE9	170	D6
Widecombe Way N2	73	N8
Widegate St, E1 *3*	21	K3
Widenham Ct, Pnr	66	E10
Widgeon Cl E16	115	R11
Widley Rd W9	108	H6
Widmore Lo Rd, Brom	188	A4
Widmore Rd, Brom	187	S2
Wieland Rd, Nthwd	50	A13
Wigeon Path SE28	135	P5
Wigeon Way, Hayes	102	H11
Wiggins Mead NW9	55	L14
Wigginton Av, Wem	88	B12
Wightman Rd N4	75	P11
Wightman Rd N8	75	N7
Wigley Rd, Felt	156	H3
Wigmore Pl W1	16	H5
Wigmore Rd, Cars	195	R3
Wigmore St W1	16	E6
Wigmore Wk, Cars	195	P3
Wigram Rd E11	79	T11
Wigram Sq E17	78	F5
Wigston Cl N18	60	C10
Wigston Rd E13	115	R7
Wigton Gdns, Stan	69	R2
Wigton Pl, SE11 *4*	35	L7
Wigton Rd E17	77	U1
Wilberforce Rd N4	93	S5
Wilberforce Rd NW9	71	N11
Wilberforce Way SW19	162	A11
Wilbraham Pl SW1	32	C2
Wilbury Way N18	60	A10
Wilby Ms W11	126	F1
Wilcox Cl SW8	34	C14
Wilcox Cl, Borwd	38	E2
Wilcox Pl, SW1 *5*	25	P11
Wilcox Rd SW8	34	B14
Wilcox Rd, Sutt	194	J8
Wilcox Rd, Tedd	158	B7
Wild Ct WC2	18	E6
Wild Goose Dr SE14	149	M2
Wild Hatch NW11	72	H12
Wild St WC2	18	D7
Wildcroft Gdns, Edg	53	N12
Wildcroft Rd SW15	143	U13
Wilde Cl E8	112	G1
Wilde Pl N13	59	R11
Wilde Pl SW18	145	P14
Wilde Rd, Erith	137	R14
Wilder Cl, Ruis	84	C2
Wilderness, The, E Mol	175	T10
Wilderness, The, Hmptn	157	S8
Wilderness Rd, Chis	171	K13
Wilderton Rd N16	76	D14
Wildfell Rd SE6	150	C13
Wild's Rents SE1	28	G10
Wildwood Cl SE12	151	M13
Wildwood Gro NW3	91	L2
Wildwood Ri NW11	91	L2
Wildwood Rd NW11	91	L2
Wildwood Ter NW3	91	L2
Wilford Cl, Enf	44	A6
Wilfred Owen Cl, SW19 *2*	163	L11
Wilfred St SW1	25	M9
Wilfrid Gdns W3	106	E9
Wilkes Rd, Brent *6*	123	R12
Wilkes St E1	21	N2
Wilkin St NW5	92	C11
Wilkins Cl, Mitch	181	S1
Wilkinson Rd E16	115	U11
Wilkinson St SW8	129	L14
Wilkinson Way W4	124	G3
Wilks Gdns, Croy	199	S2
Wilks Pl N1	12	J3
Will Crooks Gdns SE9	152	A7
Willan Rd N17	76	B4
Willan Wall, E16 *1*	115	L13
Willard St SW8	146	C5
Willcocks Cl, Chess	191	S6
Willcott Rd W3	124	C2
Willen Fld Rd NW10	106	E4
Willenhall Av, Barn	41	L12
Willenhall Rd SE18	134	J10
Willersley Av, Orp	203	P5
Willersley Av, Sid	153	U14
Willersley Cl, Sid	171	T1
Willes Rd NW5	92	D11
Willesden La NW2	90	A12
Willesden La NW6	108	E1
Willett Cl, Nthlt *5*	102	F5
Willett Cl, Orp	189	R11
Willett Pl, Th Hth *1*	183	N9
Willett Rd, Th Hth	183	N9
Willett Way, Orp	189	R10
William Barefoot Dr SE9	170	H5
William Bonney Est, SW4 *7*	146	H8
William Booth Rd SE20	184	H1
William Carey Way, Har	68	D12
William Cl N2	73	P4
William Cl, Rom	83	U2
William Cl, Sthl	121	U3
William Dyce Ms, SW16 *2*	164	H8
William Ellis Way, SE16 *2*	29	U11
William IV St WC2	18	A12
William Gdns SW15	143	S9
William Guy Gdns E3	114	D6
William Margrie Cl, SE15 *8*	148	H3
William Ms SW1	24	B7
William Morley Cl E6	116	A1
William Morris Cl E17	77	T5
William Morris Way SW6	145	L5
William Pl, E3 *14*	113	T3
William Rd NW1	9	L8
William Rd SW19	162	D14
William Rd, Sutt	195	M9
William Sq, SE16 *7*	113	S14
William St E10	78	D12
William St N17	60	F13
William St SW1	24	B7
William St, Bark	99	L13
William St, Cars	195	T6
Williams Av E17	77	T2
Williams Bldgs, E2 *5*	113	L7
Williams Cl N8	74	H12
Williams Gro N22	75	N1
Williams Gro, Surb	177	L13
William's La SW14	142	E4
Williams La, Mord	181	M10
Williams Rd W13	122	H1
Williams Rd, Sthl	120	J8
Williams Ter, Croy	197	P11
Williamson Cl, SE10 *6*	133	L9
Williamson Rd N4	75	S12
Williamson St N7	93	K8
Williamson Way NW7	56	D11
Willifield Way NW11	72	G9
Willingale Cl, Loug	49	M4
Willingale Cl, Wdf Grn	64	A12
Willingale Rd, Loug	49	N4
Willingdon Rd N22	75	R4
Willingham Cl NW5	92	E9
Willingham Ter NW5	92	F10
Willingham Way, Kings T	178	A5
Willington Rd SW9	146	J6
Willis Av, Sutt	195	R12
Willis Rd E15	115	L2
Willis Rd, Croy	183	U13
Willis Rd, Erith	137	U7
Willis St E14	114	D12
Willmore End SW19	180	J2
Willoughby Av, Croy	197	L8
Willoughby Gro N17	60	J13
Willoughby La N17	61	K12
Willoughby Ms, SW4 *14*	146	C7
Willoughby Pk Rd N17	60	J13
Willoughby Pas, E14 *5*	132	A1
Willoughby Rd N8	75	P7
Willoughby Rd NW3	91	N8
Willoughby Rd, Kings T	177	U1
Willoughby Rd, Twick	141	M11
Willoughby St, WC1 *4*	18	A4
Willoughby Way SE7	133	R7
Willow Av SW13	143	M4
Willow Av, Sid	154	A11
Willow Bank SW6	144	D5
Willow Bank, Rich	159	K5
Willow Br Rd N1	93	T12
Willow Business Cen, Mitch	181	U11
Willow Cl, Bex	155	L12
Willow Cl, Brent	123	M12
Willow Cl, Brom	188	F10
Willow Cl, Buck H	64	A5
Willow Cl, Th Hth	183	R11
Willow Cotts, Mitch	182	G6
Willow Cotts, Rich *3*	124	A12
Willow Ct, EC2 *5*	12	G9
Willow Ct, Edg	53	S7
Willow Dene, Pnr	66	G3
Willow Dr, Barn	40	C8
Willow End N20	56	G4
Willow End, Nthwd	50	A12
Willow End, Surb	191	S1
Willow Fm La SW15	143	S5
Willow Gdns, Houns	139	N2
Willow Gro, Chis	170	J12
Willow La, Mitch	181	U10
Willow Mt, Croy *3*	198	D6
Willow Pl SW1	33	N1
Willow Rd NW3	91	P7
Willow Rd W5	123	S4
Willow Rd, Enf	44	C6
Willow Rd, N Mal	178	E7
Willow Rd, Rom	83	K11
Willow Rd, Wall	196	D13
Willow St E4	46	G14
Willow St EC2	12	G9
Willow St, Rom	83	U8
Willow Tree Cl, E3 *1*	113	S2
Willow Tree Cl SW18	163	K2
Willow Tree Cl, Hayes	102	F8
Willow Tree La, Hayes	102	F8
Willow Tree Wk, Brom	187	S2
Willow Vale W12	125	P1
Willow Vale, Chis	170	J12
Willow Vw SW19	181	N2
Willow Wk E17	77	T9
Willow Wk N2	73	N4
Willow Wk N15	75	S7
Willow Wk N21	43	L12
Willow Wk SE1	37	L2
Willow Wk, Orp	202	J6
Willow Wk, Sutt	194	F5
Willow Way N3	56	J14
Willow Way SE26	167	L6
Willow Way, W11 *3*	108	B14
Willow Way, Epsom	192	H11
Willow Way, Sun	174	B8
Willow Way, Twick	157	R4

Name	Page	Grid
Willow Way, Wem	86	H6
Willow Wd Cres SE25	184	C11
Willowbrook Rd SE15	37	P13
Willowbrook Rd, Sthl	121	N6
Willowcourt Av, Har	69	K10
Willowdene N6	73	U13
Willowdene Cl, Twick	139	T13
Willowhayne Av, Walt	174	C14
Willowhayne Gdns, Wor Pk	193	U6
Willowmead Cl W5	105	N9
Willows, The, Buck H	64	B6
Willows, The, Esher	190	C12
Willows Av, Mord	181	K10
Willows Cl, Pnr	66	E3
Willowtree Way, Th Hth	183	P1
Willrose Cres SE2	136	D9
Wills Cres, Houns	139	R11
Wills Gro NW7	55	R9
Wilman Gro E8	94	H13
Wilmar Gdns, W Wick	200	C1
Wilmer Cl, Kings T	159	U10
Wilmer Cres, Kings T	159	U10
Wilmer Gdns N1	112	C2
Wilmer Lea Cl E15	96	G14
Wilmer Way N14	58	H9
Wilmington Av W4	124	G14
Wilmington Gdns, Bark	99	P12
Wilmington Sq WC1	11	K8
Wilmington St WC1	11	K7
Wilmot Cl N2	73	M3
Wilmot Cl, SE15 *4*	130	G14
Wilmot Pl NW1	92	E13
Wilmot Pl W7	122	D2
Wilmot Rd E10	96	C4
Wilmot Rd N17	76	A5
Wilmot Rd, Cars *5*	195	T9
Wilmot St E2	112	J7
Wilmount St SE18	134	J8
Wilna Rd SW18	145	L14
Wilsham St W11	126	C1
Wilshaw St SE14	150	A1
Wilsmere Dr, Har	52	D13
Wilsmere Dr, Nthlt	85	K11
Wilson Av, Mitch	163	S14
Wilson Cl, S Croy *6*	198	A9
Wilson Cl, Wem	69	U13
Wilson Dr, Wem	69	T13
Wilson Gdns, Har	67	T13
Wilson Gro SE16	130	J4
Wilson Rd E6	116	A5
Wilson Rd SE5	148	C2
Wilson Rd, Chess	191	T11
Wilson Rd, Ilf	80	F14
Wilson St E17	78	E9
Wilson St EC2	20	F2
Wilson St N21	43	P14
Wilsons Pl E14	113	T12
Wilsons Rd, W6 *4*	126	B9
Wilstone Cl, Hayes	102	J7
Wilthorne Gdns, Dag	101	S13
Wilton Av W4	125	K10
Wilton Cres SW1	24	D8
Wilton Cres SW19	180	E1
Wilton Gdns, W Mol	175	P6
Wilton Gro SW19	180	F1
Wilton Gro, N Mal	179	L11
Wilton Ms SW1	24	F9
Wilton Par, Felt	156	B3
Wilton Pk Ct SE18	134	G14
Wilton Pl SW1	24	C7
Wilton Rd N10	74	A3
Wilton Rd SE2	136	F7
Wilton Rd SW1	25	L12
Wilton Rd SW19	163	S13
Wilton Rd, Barn	41	T7
Wilton Rd, Houns	138	G5
Wilton Rd, Ilf	98	J7
Wilton Row SW1	24	D7
Wilton Sq N1	112	A1
Wilton St SW1	24	G10
Wilton Ter SW1	24	D9
Wilton Vil, N1 *6*	112	A2
Wilton Way E8	94	H12
Wiltshire Cl NW7	55	L9
Wiltshire Cl SW3	31	T2
Wiltshire Gdns N4	75	T12
Wiltshire Gdns, Twick	157	U2
Wiltshire La, Pnr	66	B8
Wiltshire Rd SW9	147	P6
Wiltshire Rd, Th Hth	183	P6
Wiltshire Row N1	112	A2
Wilverley Cres, N Mal	179	K12
Wimbart Rd SW2	147	M13
Wimbledon Br SW19	162	E12
Wimbledon Common SW19	161	P7
Wimbledon Hill Rd SW19	162	D11
Wimbledon Pk SW19	162	F5
Wimbledon Pk Est SW19	162	E2
Wimbledon Pk Rd SW18	144	G12
Wimbledon Pk Rd SW19	162	D4
Wimbledon Pk Side SW19	162	A2
Wimbledon Rd SW17	163	M7
Wimbledon Sta SW19	162	F12
Wimbolt St E2	13	S5
Wimborne Av, Hayes	102	D11
Wimborne Av, Sthl	121	N8
Wimborne Cl SE12	151	L10
Wimborne Cl, Buck H	63	S4
Wimborne Cl, Wor Pk	193	U2
Wimborne Dr NW9	70	B5
Wimborne Dr, Pnr	66	H13
Wimborne Gdns W13	105	K11
Wimborne Rd N9	60	G3
Wimborne Rd N17	76	D3
Wimborne Way, Beck	185	P6
Wimbourne Av, Orp	189	U7
Wimbourne St N1	12	C2
Wimpole Cl, Brom	187	T7
Wimpole Cl, Kings T	177	U4
Wimpole Ms W1	16	G2
Wimpole St W1	16	H6
Wimshurst Cl, Croy	196	J1
Winans Wk SW9	147	N4
Wincanton Cres, Nthlt	85	P9
Wincanton Gdns, Ilf	80	J4
Wincanton Rd SW18	144	F13
Winchcomb Gdns SE9	152	B6
Winchcombe Rd, Cars	181	P14
Winchelsea Av, Bexh	137	L14
Winchelsea Cl SW15	144	A10
Winchelsea Rd E7	97	N7
Winchelsea Rd N17	76	D6
Winchelsea Rd NW10	106	H2
Winchelsey Ri, S Croy	198	E11
Winchendon Rd SW6	126	E14
Winchendon Rd, Tedd	158	B8
Winchester Av NW6	108	D1
Winchester Av NW9	70	A6
Winchester Av, Houns	121	M11
Winchester Cl E6	116	E12
Winchester Cl SE17	35	R3
Winchester Cl, Brom	187	L6
Winchester Cl, Enf	44	C10
Winchester Cl, Kings T	160	D13
Winchester Dr, Pnr	66	G9
Winchester Ms NW3	91	P13
Winchester Pk, Brom	187	L6
Winchester Pl, E8 *6*	94	E10
Winchester Pl N6	92	D1
Winchester Rd E4	62	F14
Winchester Rd N6	92	D1
Winchester Rd N9	60	G4
Winchester Rd NW3	91	P13
Winchester Rd, Bexh	154	G3
Winchester Rd, Brom	187	L6
Winchester Rd, Felt	157	L5
Winchester Rd, Har	69	S7
Winchester Rd, Ilf	99	N5
Winchester Rd, Twick	140	J11
Winchester Sq SE1	28	C2
Winchester St SW1	33	K6
Winchester St W3	124	F3
Winchester Wk SE1	28	C2
Winchfield Cl, Har	69	M10
Winchfield Rd SE26	167	S9
Winchilsea Cres, W Mol	175	T4
Winchmore Hill Rd N14	58	H1
Winchmore Hill Rd N21	43	L13
Winckley Cl, Har	69	U9
Wincott St SE11	35	L3
Wincrofts Dr SE9	153	N7
Windall Cl SE19	184	G1
Windborough Rd, Cars	196	A13
Windermere Av N3	72	G6
Windermere Av NW6	108	D2
Windermere Av SW19	180	J5
Windermere Av, Har	69	L14
Windermere Av, Ruis	66	F14
Windermere Av, Wem	87	M2
Windermere Cl, Orp	202	J5
Windermere Ct SW13	125	M12
Windermere Gdns, Ilf	80	D10
Windermere Gro, Wem *1*	87	M2
Windermere Rd N10	74	C2
Windermere Rd, N19 *4*	92	F3
Windermere Rd SW15	160	J8
Windermere Rd SW16	182	G2
Windermere Rd W5	123	L5
Windermere Rd, Bexh	155	T3
Windermere Rd, Croy	198	F1
Windermere Rd, Sthl	103	M9
Windermere Rd, W Wick	200	J3
Winders Rd SW11	145	R4
Windfield Cl SE26	167	N8
Windham Rd, Rich	141	U5
Winding Way, Dag	100	F5
Winding Way, Har	86	C7
Windlass Pl SE8	131	S8
Windlesham Gro SW19	162	A1
Windley Cl SE23	167	L3
Windmill Av, Sthl	121	U3
Windmill Cl, SE1 *1*	37	U2
Windmill Cl, SE13 *2*	150	F3
Windmill Cl, Surb	177	L14
Windmill Dr SW4	146	D9
Windmill Dr, Kes	201	U8
Windmill Gdns, Enf	43	N5
Windmill Gro, Croy	183	T12
Windmill Hill NW3	91	L6
Windmill Hill, Enf	43	S6
Windmill La E15	96	H11
Windmill La, Barn	39	M11
Windmill La, Bushey	52	D1
Windmill La, Grnf	103	T8
Windmill La, Islw	122	D10
Windmill La, Sthl	121	U4
Windmill La, Surb	177	L14
Windmill Ms, W4 *2*	124	J8
Windmill Pas, W4 *1*	124	J8
Windmill Ri, Kings T	160	C13
Windmill Rd N18	60	B8
Windmill Rd SW18	145	N11
Windmill Rd SW19	161	S2
Windmill Rd W4	124	J8
Windmill Rd W5	123	M9
Windmill Rd, Brent	123	N10
Windmill Rd, Croy	183	T10
Windmill Rd, Hmptn	157	S10
Windmill Rd, Mitch	182	E9
Windmill Row, SE11 *3*	35	K7
Windmill St W1	17	R3
Windmill St, Bushey	52	C1
Windmill Wk SE1	27	L4
Windover Av NW9	70	H7
Windrose Cl SE16	131	N3
Windrush Cl, SW11 *15*	145	N7
Windrush Cl W4	142	E1
Windrush La SE23	167	N5
Windsock Cl, SE16 *4*	131	T7
Windsor Av E17	77	S3
Windsor Av SW19	181	M2
Windsor Av, Edg	54	C7
Windsor Av, N Mal	178	F10
Windsor Av, Sutt	194	E6
Windsor Av, W Mol	175	P5
Windsor Cl N3	72	D4
Windsor Cl SE27	165	T8
Windsor Cl, Borwd	38	A1
Windsor Cl, Brent	122	J12
Windsor Cl, Chis	171	K9
Windsor Cl, Har	85	P6
Windsor Cl, Nthwd	66	A3
Windsor Ct N14	42	E14
Windsor Ct, Sun	156	A13
Windsor Cres, Har	85	N6
Windsor Cres, Wem	88	C5
Windsor Dr, Barn	41	T11
Windsor Gdns W9	108	G9
Windsor Gdns, Croy	197	K6
Windsor Gro SE27	165	T8
Windsor Pl SW1	25	N12
Windsor Rd E4	62	C7
Windsor Rd E7	97	R10
Windsor Rd E10	96	D4
Windsor Rd E11	97	P3
Windsor Rd N3	72	D4
Windsor Rd N7	93	K6
Windsor Rd N13	59	P6
Windsor Rd N17	76	H4
Windsor Rd NW2	89	R11
Windsor Rd W5	105	R14
Windsor Rd, Barn	40	B11
Windsor Rd, Bexh	154	A3
Windsor Rd, Dag	101	K6
Windsor Rd, Har	68	A2
Windsor Rd, Houns	138	D3
Windsor Rd, Ilf	99	K7
Windsor Rd, Kings T	159	S14
Windsor Rd, Rich	141	U4
Windsor Rd, Sthl	121	L5
Windsor Rd, Sun	156	A12
Windsor Rd, Tedd	158	B9
Windsor Rd, Th Hth	183	S4
Windsor Rd, Wor Pk	193	T4
Windsor St N1	111	S1
Windsor Ter N1	12	A5
Windsor Wk SE5	148	B4
Windsor Way W14	126	B7
Windsor Wf E9	95	U10
Windsors, The, Buck H	64	C3

Name	No.	Ref	Name	No.	Ref	Name	No.	Ref	Name	No.	Ref
Windspoint Dr, SE15 3	130	J12	Winterborne Av, Orp	203	P6	Wolffe Gdns, E15 3	97	L12	Wood Vale Est SE23	149	K13
Windus Rd N16	94	F2	Winterbourne Rd SE6	167	U1	Wolffram Cl SE13	150	J9	Wood Way, Orp	202	H3
Windus Wk N16	94	F2	Winterbourne Rd, Dag	100	E4	Wolfington Rd SE27	165	R7	Wood Wf SE10	132	D11
Windy Ridge, Brom	188	C2	Winterbourne Rd, Th Hth	183	N7	Wolftencroft Cl SW11	145	P5	Woodall Cl E14	114	D13
Windyridge Cl SW19	162	B9	Winterbrook Rd SE24	147	T11	Wollaston Cl SE1	35	T2	Woodall Rd, Enf	45	P12
Wine Cl E1	113	L14	Winterburn Cl N11	58	A11	Wolmer Cl, Edg	54	C7	Woodbank Rd, Brom	169	L6
Wine Office Ct EC4	19	M6	Winterfold Cl SW19	162	C3	Wolmer Gdns, Edg	54	B6	Woodbastwick Rd SE26	167	P10
Winery La, Kings T	177	T5	Wintergreen Cl, E6 10	116	C9	Wolseley Av SW19	162	G4	Woodberry Av N21	59	P3
Winford Par, Sthl 2	103	R12	Winters Rd, T Ditt	177	K13	Wolseley Gdns W4	124	D11	Woodberry Av, Har	67	S8
Winforton St SE10	150	E1	Winterstoke Rd SE6	167	U1	Wolseley Rd E7	97	S13	Woodberry Cl, Sun	156	A13
Winfrith Rd SW18	145	L14	Winterton Pl, SW10 1	30	H10	Wolseley Rd N8	74	G10	Woodberry Cres N10	74	C5
Wingate Cres, Croy	182	J11	Winterwell Rd SW2	147	K9	Wolseley Rd N22	54	C12	Woodberry Down N4	75	T14
Wingate Rd W6	125	R5	Winthorpe Rd SW15	144	D8	Wolseley Rd W4	124	F7	Woodberry Down Est N4	75	T13
Wingate Rd, Ilf	99	K9	Winthrop St E1	112	J9	Wolseley Rd, Har	68	D5	Woodberry Gdns N12	57	L12
Wingate Rd, Sid	172	E10	Winthrop Wk, Wem 1	87	R6	Wolseley Rd, Mitch	182	A14	Woodberry Gro N4	75	T14
Wingate Trd Est N17	60	G13	Winton Av N11	58	F14	Wolseley St SE1	29	R7	Woodberry Gro N12	57	L11
Wingfield Ms, SE15 1	148	G5	Winton Cl N9	45	N14	Wolsey Av E6	116	H6	Woodberry Way E4	46	F14
Wingfield Rd, E15 2	96	J8	Winton Gdns, Edg	53	U13	Wolsey Av E17	77	U6	Woodberry Way N12	57	L12
Wingfield Rd E17	78	D9	Winton Rd, Orp	202	J8	Wolsey Av, T Ditt	176	E10	Woodbine Cl, Twick	158	A5
Wingfield Rd, Kings T	160	A11	Winton Way SW16	165	P10	Wolsey Cl SW20	161	R13	Woodbine Gro SE20	167	K14
Wingfield St SE15	148	G5	Wisbeach Rd, Croy	184	B9	Wolsey Cl, Houns	139	T8	Woodbine La, Wor Pk 5	193	T5
Wingfield Way, Ruis	84	C11	Wisdons Cl, Dag	101	S2	Wolsey Cl, Sthl	121	T5	Woodbine Pl E11	79	R11
Wingford Rd SW2	146	J12	Wise La NW7	55	S12	Wolsey Cl, Kings T	178	D2	Woodbine Rd, Sid	171	R1
Wingmore Rd SE24	147	T6	Wise Rd E15	114	G2	Wolsey Cl, Wor Pk	193	N7	Woodbine Ter E9	95	M11
Wingrave Rd W6	125	U12	Wiseman Rd E10	96	A3	Wolsey Cres, Mord	180	D13	Woodbines Av, Kings T	177	P6
Wingrove Rd SE6	169	K4	Wiseton Rd SW17	163	S1	Wolsey Dr, Kings T	159	R10	Woodborough Rd SW15	143	R8
Wings Cl, Sutt	194	H8	Wishart Rd SE3	152	A2	Wolsey Gdns, Ilf	65	K12	Woodbourne Av SW16	164	H6
Winifred Gro SW11	145	U7	Wisley Rd SW11	146	A10	Wolsey Gro, Edg	54	H13	Woodbourne Dr, Esher	190	E11
Winifred Pl, N12 2	57	M9	Wisley Rd, Orp	172	C13	Wolsey Ms NW5	92	E11	Woodbourne Gdns, Wall	196	D13
Winifred Rd SW19	180	H1	Wisteria Cl NW7	55	L11	Wolsey Ms, Orp	203	U10	Woodbridge Cl N7	93	M4
Winifred Rd, Dag	101	K3	Wisteria Cl, Ilf	98	J10	Wolsey Rd N1	94	B10	Woodbridge Cl NW2	89	P5
Winifred Rd, Hmptn	157	N8	Wisteria Cl, Orp	203	K3	Wolsey Rd, E Mol	176	B7	Woodbridge Ct, Wdf Grn	64	D14
Winifred St E16	134	F2	Wisteria Rd SE13	150	G8	Wolsey Rd, Enf	45	K4	Woodbridge Rd, Bark	99	T10
Winifred Ter, E13 5	115	N4	Witan St E2	113	K6	Wolsey Rd, Hmptn	157	S11	Woodbridge St EC1	11	N9
Winkfield Rd E13	115	R4	Witham Cl, Loug	48	D11	Wolsey St E1	113	L10	Woodbrook Rd SE2	136	B12
Winkfield Rd N22	75	P1	Witham Rd SE20	185	L5	Wolsey Way, Chess	192	B9	Woodburn Cl NW4	72	B10
Winkley St, E2 14	112	J4	Witham Rd W13	122	H1	Wolstonbury N12	56	G10	Woodbury Cl E11	79	R8
Winlaton Rd, Brom	168	H8	Witham Rd, Dag	101	P10	Wolvercote Rd SE2	136	G4	Woodbury Cl, Croy	190	F4
Winmill Rd, Dag	101	L6	Witham Rd, Islw	140	B2	Wolverley St, E2 2	112	J6	Woodbury Hill, Loug	48	D4
Winn Common Rd SE18	135	S11	Witherby Cl, Croy	198	D9	Wolverton SE17	36	G6	Woodbury Hollow, Loug	48	D4
Winn Rd SE12	169	R1	Witherington Rd N5	93	P10	Wolverton Av, Kings T	178	B1	Woodbury Pk Rd W13	104	J8
Winnett St W1	17	S9	Withers Cl, Chess 3	191	M12	Wolverton Gdns W5	105	U14	Woodbury Rd E17	78	C7
Winnington Cl N2	73	N11	Withers Mead NW9	71	L1	Wolverton Gdns W6	126	A7	Woodbury St SW17	163	S10
Winnington Rd N2	73	N14	Witherston Way SE9	170	G4	Wolverton Rd, Stan	53	K12	Woodchester Sq W2	14	A1
Winnipeg Dr, Orp	203	T12	Withy Mead E4	62	H6	Wolverton Way N14	42	F10	Woodchurch Cl, Sid	171	P6
Winns Av E17	77	T5	Withycombe Rd SW19	144	A14	Wolves La N13	59	R11	Woodchurch Dr, Brom	170	A14
Winns Ms N15	76	D8	Witley Cres, Croy	200	E12	Wolves La N22	59	P14	Woodchurch Rd NW6	90	H14
Winns Ter E17	78	A4	Witley Gdns, Sthl	121	L7	Womersley Rd N8	75	L12	Woodclyffe Dr, Chis	188	H3
Winsbeach E17	78	G4	Witley Rd N19	92	F4	Wonford Cl, Kings T	179	K1	Woodcock Ct, Har	69	N14
Winscombe Cres W5	105	N8	Witney Cl, Pnr	51	M11	Wontner Cl, N1 4	93	T14	Woodcock Dell Av, Har	69	N14
Winscombe St N19	92	D5	Witney Path SE23	167	P5	Wontner Rd SW17	163	U3	Woodcock Hill, Har	69	M13
Winscombe Way, Stan	52	H9	Wittenham Way E4	62	H5	Wood Cl E2	13	S9	Woodcocks E16	115	U10
Winsford Rd SE6	167	U5	Wittering Cl, Kings T	159	N10	Wood Cl NW9	70	H14	Woodcombe Cres SE23	167	M1
Winsford Ter N18	60	A9	Wittersham Rd, Brom	169	L10	Wood Cl, Har	68	A14	Woodcote Av NW7	55	U11
Winsham Gro SW11	146	A10	Wivenhoe Cl SE15	148	J5	Wood Dr, Chis	170	C11	Woodcote Av, Th Hth	183	R8
Winslade Rd SW2	147	K9	Wivenhoe Ct, Houns	139	M7	Wood End Av, Har	85	T7	Woodcote Av, Wall	196	D14
Winsland Ms W2	15	K6	Wivenhoe Rd, Bark	118	B3	Wood End Cl, Nthlt	86	B9	Woodcote Cl, Enf	45	M11
Winsland St W2	15	K6	Wiverton Rd SE26	167	M11	Wood End Gdns, Nthlt	85	U9	Woodcote Cl, Kings T	159	U10
Winsley St W1	17	M6	Wix Rd, Dag	118	H1	Wood End La, Nthlt	85	T10	Woodcote Dr, Orp	203	P1
Winslow SE17	36	H7	Wixs La SW4	146	C6	Wood End Rd, Har	86	B8	Woodcote Ms, Wall	196	D11
Winslow Cl, NW10 2	88	J6	Woburn Cl SE28	118	H12	Wood End Way, Nthlt	85	U9	Woodcote Pl SE27 8	165	S9
Winslow Cl, Pnr	66	D11	Woburn Cl SW19	163	M12	Wood La N6	74	C11	Woodcote Rd E11	79	S13
Winslow Gro E4	62	J4	Woburn Pl WC1	9	U10	Wood La NW9	88	H1	Woodcote Rd, Wall	196	E13
Winslow Rd W6	125	U11	Woburn Rd, Cars	195	R2	Wood La W12	107	U14	Woodcroft N21	59	N2
Winslow Way, Felt	156	J6	Woburn Rd, Croy	197	U1	Wood La, Dag	100	G7	Woodcroft SE9	170	F5
Winsor Ter E6	116	H10	Woburn Sq WC1	9	T11	Wood La, Islw	122	D11	Woodcroft, Grnf	86	H11
Winstanley Est SW11	145	P5	Woburn Wk, WC1 2	9	U8	Wood La, Stan	53	K4	Woodcroft Av NW7	55	K13
Winstanley Rd SW11	145	P6	Wodehouse Av SE5	148	E1	Wood La, Wdf Grn	63	L9			
Winstead Gdns, Dag	101	U9	Woffington Cl, Kings T	177	L1	Wood Lo Gdns, Brom	170	C14			
Winston Av NW9	70	J14	Woking Cl SW15	143	M7	Wood Lo La, W Wick	200	F5			
Winston Cl, Har	52	E12	Woldham Pl, Brom	187	T7	Wood Retreat SE18	135	N13			
Winston Cl, Rom	83	S8	Woldham Rd, Brom	187	T7	Wood Ride, Barn	41	N1			
Winston Ct, Har	51	R14	Wolds Dr, Orp	202	G7	Wood Ride, Orp	189	R8			
Winston Rd N16	94	B8	Wolfe Cl, Brom	187	P11	Wood Ri, Pnr	66	A10			
Winston Way, Ilf	98	J5	Wolfe Cl, Hayes	102	C6	Wood St E16	115	S12			
Winstre Rd, Borwd	38	B2	Wolfe Cres SE7	134	A9	Wood St E17	78	G8			
Winter Av E6	116	D2	Wolfe Cres SE16	131	P4	Wood St EC2	20	A7			
Winter Box Wk, Rich	141	T8	Wolferton Rd E12	98	F8	Wood St W4	125	K10			
						Wood St, Barn	40	A7			
						Wood St, Kings T	177	P2			
						Wood St, Mitch	182	A14			
						Wood Vale N10	74	E10			
						Wood Vale SE23	148	J14			

Woodcroft Av, Stan	68	F1
Woodcroft Ms SE8	131	R8
Woodcroft Rd, Th Hth	183	R11
Woodedge Cl E4	63	L1
Woodend SE19	165	T11
Woodend, Sutt	195	L4
Woodend Gdns, Enf	42	J8
Woodend Rd E17	78	E3
Wooder Gdns E7	97	M8
Wooderson Cl SE25	184	C8
Woodfall Av, Barn	40	F9
Woodfall Rd N4	93	N3
Woodfall St SW3	31	U7
Woodfarrs SE5	148	B8
Woodfield Av NW9	71	K8
Woodfield Av SW16	164	G5
Woodfield Av W5	105	N8
Woodfield Av, Cars	196	A12
Woodfield Av, Wem	87	M6
Woodfield Cl SE19	165	U13
Woodfield Cl, Enf	44	C8
Woodfield Cres W5	105	M8
Woodfield Dr, Barn	58	A1
Woodfield Gdns, W9 10	108	F9
Woodfield Gdns, N Mal	179	L9
Woodfield Gro SW16	164	H5
Woodfield La SW16	164	G5
Woodfield Pl W9	108	F8
Woodfield Rd W5	105	M8
Woodfield Rd W9	108	F9
Woodfield Rd, Houns	138	D3
Woodfield Way N11	58	G13
Woodford Av, Ilf	80	F9
Woodford Av, Wdf Grn	80	C5
Woodford Br Rd, Ilf	80	B6
Woodford Cres, Pnr	66	C4
Woodford New Rd E17	78	J6
Woodford New Rd E18	79	K1
Woodford New Rd, Wdf Grn	79	K1
Woodford Pl, Wem	87	R2
Woodford Rd E7	97	R7
Woodford Rd E18	79	N7
Woodford Trd Est, Wdf Grn	80	A5
Woodgate Av, Chess	191	N10
Woodgate Cres, Nthwd	50	B12
Woodgate Dr SW16	164	G13
Woodger Rd W12	125	U4
Woodget Cl, E6 27	116	C11
Woodgrange Av N12	57	N12
Woodgrange Av W5	124	A1
Woodgrange Av, Enf	44	H11
Woodgrange Av, Har	69	M9
Woodgrange Cl, Har	69	N9
Woodgrange Gdns, Enf	44	H11
Woodgrange Rd E7	97	P9
Woodhall Av SE21	166	E5
Woodhall Av, Pnr	66	J3
Woodhall Dr SE21	166	E5
Woodhall Dr, Pnr	66	H1
Woodhall Gate, Pnr	50	H14
Woodhall La, Wat	50	H6
Woodhall Rd, Pnr	50	G12
Woodham Ct E18	79	L8
Woodham Rd SE6	168	E5
Woodhatch Cl, E6 17	116	C10
Woodhaven Gdns, Ilf	81	L7
Woodhayes Rd SW19	161	T13
Woodhead Dr, Orp	203	S5
Woodheyes Rd NW10	88	H10
Woodhill SE18	134	D8
Woodhill Cres, Har	69	N12
Woodhouse Av, Grnf	104	F3
Woodhouse Cl, Grnf	104	E3
Woodhouse Eaves, Nthwd	50	A10
Woodhouse Gro E12	98	C12
Woodhouse Rd E11	97	L5
Woodhouse Rd N12	57	N11
Woodhurst Av, Orp	189	L11
Woodhurst Rd SE2	136	B8
Woodhurst Rd W3	106	F14
Woodington Cl SE9	152	G11
Woodison St E3	113	S8
Woodknoll Dr, Chis	188	E2
Woodland App, Grnf 1	86	H11
Woodland Cl NW9	70	F11
Woodland Cl, SE19 2	166	D11
Woodland Cl, Epsom	193	K12
Woodland Cl, Wdf Grn	63	R5
Woodland Cres, SE10 1	132	J11
Woodland Cres SE16	131	N4
Woodland Gdns N10	74	C9
Woodland Gdns, Islw	140	C5
Woodland Gro SE10	132	J10
Woodland Hill SE19	166	D11
Woodland Ri N10	74	C8
Woodland Ri, Grnf	86	H12
Woodland Rd E4	62	F2
Woodland Rd N11	58	C9
Woodland Rd SE19	166	E10
Woodland Rd, Loug	48	C6
Woodland Rd, Th Hth	183	P8
Woodland St, E8 10	94	E11
Woodland Ter SE7	134	C8
Woodland Wk NW3	91	S9
Woodland Wk, Brom	168	J7
Woodland Way N21	59	N4
Woodland Way NW7	55	K11
Woodland Way SE2	136	G8
Woodland Way, Croy	199	R1
Woodland Way, Mitch	164	B13
Woodland Way, Mord	180	F8
Woodland Way, Orp	189	M9
Woodland Way, Surb	192	D3
Woodland Way, W Wick	200	E6
Woodland Way, Wdf Grn	63	R5
Woodlands NW11	72	C11
Woodlands SW20	179	U8
Woodlands, Har	67	N8
Woodlands, The N14	58	D2
Woodlands, The SE13	150	H13
Woodlands, The SE19	165	U14
Woodlands, The, Islw	140	E4
Woodlands Av E11	97	R2
Woodlands Av N3	73	L1
Woodlands Av W3	124	D2
Woodlands Av, N Mal	178	F2
Woodlands Av, Rom	82	J13
Woodlands Av, Ruis	84	F2
Woodlands Av, Sid	171	S1
Woodlands Av, Wor Pk	193	N3
Woodlands Cl NW11	72	C10
Woodlands Cl, Borwd	38	D7
Woodlands Cl, Brom	188	E4
Woodlands Cl, Esher	190	F14
Woodlands Dr, Stan	52	F12
Woodlands Dr, Sun	174	F3
Woodlands Gro, Islw	140	D4
Woodlands Pk, Bex	173	U7
Woodlands Pk Rd N15	75	T9
Woodlands Pk Rd SE10	132	J11
Woodlands Rd E11	96	J3
Woodlands Rd E17	78	F5
Woodlands Rd N9	61	L1
Woodlands Rd SW13	143	L6
Woodlands Rd, Bexh	155	K5
Woodlands Rd, Brom	188	D4
Woodlands Rd, Enf	44	A1
Woodlands Rd, Har	68	E9
Woodlands Rd, Ilf	99	L5
Woodlands Rd, Islw	140	D4
Woodlands Rd, Sthl	120	H2
Woodlands Rd, Surb	177	H13
Woodlands St SE13	150	H13
Woodlands Way SW15	144	E9
Woodlawn Cl SW15	144	E10
Woodlawn Cres, Twick	157	R3
Woodlawn Dr, Felt	156	H4
Woodlawn Rd SW6	126	A14
Woodlea Dr, Brom	187	K10
Woodlea Rd N16	94	C5
Woodleigh Av N12	57	S11
Woodleigh Gdns SW16	165	K6
Woodley Cl, SW17 5	163	U13
Woodley La, Cars	195	P5
Woodman La E4	46	J10
Woodman Path, Ilf	65	S11
Woodman St E16	134	H2
Woodmans Gro, NW10 1	89	M9
Woodmans Ms W12	107	S10
Woodmansterne Rd SW16	164	F14
Woodmere SE9	152	E14
Woodmere Av, Croy	185	R14
Woodmere Cl, SW11 2	146	B5
Woodmere Cl, Croy	185	P14
Woodmere Gdns, Croy	185	N14
Woodmere Way, Beck	186	G9
Woodnook Rd SW16	164	D9
Woodpecker Cl N9	44	J11
Woodpecker Cl, Bushey	51	T2
Woodpecker Cl, Har	68	E1
Woodpecker Rd SE14	131	R12
Woodpecker Rd SE28	118	E14
Woodquest Av SE24	147	T10
Woodridge Cl, Enf	43	P2
Woodridings Av, Pnr	67	M1
Woodridings Cl, Pnr	51	K14
Woodriffe Rd E11	78	H13
Woodrow SE18	134	E8
Woodrow Cl, Grnf	87	K14
Woodrow Ct N17	61	K14
Woodrush Cl, SE14 7	131	R13
Woodrush Way, Rom	82	G8
Woods, The, Nthwd	50	B9
Woods Ms W1	16	C10
Woods Pl SE1	28	J11
Woods Rd SE15	148	J2
Woodseer St E1	21	R1
Woodsford Sq W14	126	D3
Woodshire Rd, Dag	101	S6
Woodside NW11	72	H9
Woodside SW19	162	E11
Woodside, Buck H	63	T4
Woodside Av N6	73	T9
Woodside Av N10	74	B8
Woodside Av N12	57	L7
Woodside Av SE25	184	J11
Woodside Av, Chis	171	L10
Woodside Av, Esher	176	C14
Woodside Av, Wem	105	S1
Woodside Cl, Stan	52	J9
Woodside Cl, Surb	178	E14
Woodside Cl, Wem	105	S1
Woodside Ct N12	57	K8
Woodside Ct Rd, Croy	184	H14
Woodside Cres, Sid	171	S5
Woodside End, Wem	105	S2
Woodside Gdns E4	62	D10
Woodside Gdns N17	76	D4
Woodside Gra Rd N12	57	K8
Woodside Grn SE25	184	H12
Woodside Gro N12	57	L6
Woodside La N12	57	L6
Woodside La, Bex	154	F11
Woodside Ms, SE22 8	148	E11
Woodside Pk SE25	184	H11
Woodside Pk Av E17	78	G8
Woodside Pk Rd N12	57	K8
Woodside Pl, Wem	105	S1
Woodside Rd E13	115	T7
Woodside Rd N22	59	N13
Woodside Rd SE25	184	J12
Woodside Rd, Brom	188	C9
Woodside Rd, Kings T	159	R14
Woodside Rd, N Mal	178	H4
Woodside Rd, Sid	171	S6
Woodside Rd, Sutt	195	L6
Woodside Rd, Wdf Grn	63	N7
Woodside Way, Croy	185	L12
Woodside Way, Mitch	182	D2
Woodsome Rd NW5	92	B6
Woodspring Rd SW19	162	D3
Woodstead Gro, Edg	53	S12
Woodstock Av NW11	72	C14
Woodstock Av W13	122	H5
Woodstock Av, Islw	140	G9
Woodstock Av, Sthl	103	M6
Woodstock Av, Sutt	180	E14
Woodstock Cl, Bex	173	L1
Woodstock Cl, Stan	69	S4
Woodstock Ct SE12	151	N12
Woodstock Cres N9	44	J11
Woodstock Gdns, Beck	186	D1
Woodstock Gdns, Ilf	100	A3
Woodstock Gro W12	126	B3
Woodstock La N, Surb	191	L3
Woodstock La S, Chess	191	K8
Woodstock La S, Esher	191	L6
Woodstock Ms, W1 4	16	F7
Woodstock Ri, Sutt	180	E14
Woodstock Rd E7	97	T13
Woodstock Rd E17	78	G3
Woodstock Rd N4	93	P2
Woodstock Rd NW11	72	E14
Woodstock Rd W4	125	K6
Woodstock Rd, Cars	196	B9
Woodstock Rd, Croy	198	A6
Woodstock Rd, Wem	87	T14
Woodstock St, E16 3	115	L11
Woodstock St W1	16	H8
Woodstock Ter E14	114	D13
Woodstock Way, Mitch	182	D3
Woodstone Av, Epsom	193	P10
Woodsyre SE26	166	F7
Woodthorpe Rd SW15	143	S8
Woodtree Cl NW4	71	U3
Woodvale Av SE25	184	E4
Woodvale Way NW11	90	B5
Woodview Av E4	62	E7

Woodview Cl N4	75	S13
Woodview Cl SW15	160	G7
Woodville SE3	151	S1
Woodville Cl SE12	151	N9
Woodville Cl, Tedd	158	G8
Woodville Gdns, NW11 1	72	B13
Woodville Gdns W5	105	S11
Woodville Gdns, Ilf	80	J6
Woodville Gro, Well	154	B5
Woodville Rd E11	97	M1
Woodville Rd E17	77	S8
Woodville Rd E18	79	S4
Woodville Rd N16	94	C9
Woodville Rd NW6	108	F3
Woodville Rd NW11	72	C13
Woodville Rd W5	105	P12
Woodville Rd, Barn	40	J7
Woodville Rd, Mord	180	G7
Woodville Rd, Rich	159	K5
Woodville Rd, Th Hth	184	A6
Woodville St SE18	134	D8
Woodward Av NW4	71	P10
Woodward Cl, Esher	190	F12
Woodward Gdns, Dag	100	E13
Woodward Gdns, Stan	52	F13
Woodward Rd, Dag	100	C14
Woodwarde Rd SE22	148	E12
Woodway Cres, Har	68	H11
Woodwell St, SW18 2	145	M9
Woodyard Cl NW5	92	B10
Woodyard La SE21	148	C14
Woodyates Rd SE12	151	N12
Wool Rd SW20	161	S13
Woolacombe Rd SE3	151	T3
Wooler St SE17	36	D7
Woolf Cl SE28	136	C2
Woollaston Rd N4	75	R12
Woolmead Av NW9	71	N14
Woolmer Gdns N18	60	H10
Woolmer Rd N18	60	H10
Woolmore St E14	114	E13
Woolneigh St, SW6 2	144	J5
Woolstaplers Way SE16	37	R1
Woolston Cl E17	77	N3
Woolstone Rd SE23	167	S4
Woolwich Ch St SE18	134	D6
Woolwich Common SE18	134	G12
Woolwich Ferry Pier E16	134	G4
Woolwich Foot Tunnel E16	134	G4
Woolwich Foot Tunnel SE18	134	G4
Woolwich Garrison SE18	134	E11
Woolwich High St SE18	134	G6
Woolwich Manor Way E6	116	G8
Woolwich Manor Way E16	134	J3
Woolwich New Rd SE18	134	H10
Woolwich Rd SE2	136	G11
Woolwich Rd SE7	133	R9
Woolwich Rd SE10	133	L9
Woolwich Rd, Belv	137	M9
Woolwich Rd, Bexh	155	N6
Wooster Gdns, E14 4	114	G15
Wooster Ms, Har	67	U6
Wooster Pl SE1	36	F1
Wootton Gro N3	72	H2
Wootton St SE1	27	L4
Worbeck Rd E16	185	K3
Worcester Av N17	60	G13
Worcester Cl, NW2 1	89	R5
Worcester Cl, Croy	200	A4
Worcester Cl, Mitch	182	B4
Worcester Cres NW7	54	J5
Worcester Cres, Wdf Grn	63	T8
Worcester Dr W4	125	K4
Worcester Gdns, Grnf	85	U12
Worcester Gdns, Ilf	80	D13
Worcester Gdns, Wor Pk	193	K5
Worcester Ms, NW6 3	91	K11
Worcester Pk Rd, Wor Pk	192	G6
Worcester Rd E12	98	E6
Worcester Rd E17	77	P3
Worcester Rd SW19	162	F10
Worcester Rd, Sutt	195	K12
Wordsworth Av E12	98	C12
Wordsworth Av E18	79	M5
Wordsworth Av, Grnf	104	A5
Wordsworth Dr, Sutt	193	U7
Wordsworth Rd N16	94	D8
Wordsworth Rd, SE1 2	37	N4
Wordsworth Rd SE20	167	N13
Wordsworth Rd, Hmptn	157	L8
Wordsworth Rd, Wall	196	F12
Wordsworth Rd, Well	153	S2
Wordsworth Wk NW11	72	G8
Worfield St SW11	127	S14
Worgan St SE11	34	F6
Worgan St SE16	131	P7
Worland Rd E15	97	K13
World's End Est SW10	30	J14
Worlds End La N21	43	M10
Worlds End La, Enf	43	M7
Worlds End La, Orp	203	T12
World's End Pas, SW10 1	31	K13
Worlidge St W6	125	T9
Worlingham Rd SE22	148	F7
Wormholt Rd W12	125	N1
Wormwood St EC2	20	G5
Wornington Rd W10	108	C8
Woronzow Rd NW8	109	R2
Worple Av SW19	162	B14
Worple Av, Islw	140	G9
Worple Cl, Har	85	M1
Worple Rd SW19	179	U3
Worple Rd SW20	179	T3
Worple Rd, Islw	140	H7
Worple Rd Ms SW19	162	E11
Worple St SW14	142	H5
Worple Way, Har	85	L1
Worple Way, Rich	141	S9
Worship St EC2	12	E12
Worslade Rd SW17	163	N8
Worsley Br Rd SE26	167	U9
Worsley Br Rd, Beck	168	B12
Worsley Rd E11	96	J7
Worsopp Dr SW4	146	F9
Worth Cl, Orp	203	S7
Worthfield Cl, Epsom	192	H14
Worthing Cl E15	115	K2
Worthing Rd, Houns	121	L12
Worthington Cl, Mitch	182	D7
Worthington Rd, Surb	191	T2
Worthy Down Ct, SE18 7	134	G14
Wortley Rd E6	98	A14
Wortley Rd, Croy	183	N13
Worton Gdns, Islw	140	A3
Worton Hall Ind Est, Islw	140	C7
Worton Rd, Islw	140	F6
Worton Way, Houns	140	A3
Worton Way, Islw	140	A3
Wotton Rd NW2	89	T6
Wotton Rd SE8	131	U12
Wouldham Rd E16	115	L11
Wragby Rd E11	97	K6
Wrampling Pl N9	60	H2
Wrangthorn Wk, Croy 2	197	N8
Wray Av, Ilf	80	H6
Wray Cres N4	93	K3
Wrayfield Rd, Sutt	194	B6
Wraysbury Cl, Houns	139	K10
Wrekin Rd SE18	135	M13
Wren Av NW2	89	U9
Wren Av, Sthl	121	M7
Wren Cl E16	115	M11
Wren Cl N9	61	N2
Wren Cres, Bushey	51	T1
Wren Gdns, Dag	100	H9
Wren Landing, E14 7	132	B1
Wren Path SE28	135	P5
Wren Rd SE5	148	A2
Wren Rd, Dag	100	G9
Wren Rd, Sid	172	E7
Wren St WC1	10	C9
Wrentham Av NW10	108	A3
Wrenthorpe Rd, Brom	168	J8
Wrenwood Way, Pnr	66	D7
Wrexham Rd E3	114	B4
Wricklemarsh Rd SE3	151	S2
Wrigglesworth St SE14	131	N13
Wright Rd, N1 4	94	D11
Wright Rd, Houns	120	F13
Wrights All SW19	161	U12
Wrights Cl SE13	150	G8
Wrights Cl, Dag	101	R6
Wrights La W8	22	A9
Wrights Pl, NW10 1	88	F11
Wrights Rd E3	113	T3
Wrights Rd SE25	184	D5
Wrights Row, Wall	196	C8
Wrights Wk, SW14 1	142	G5
Wrigley Cl E4	62	H10
Wrotham Cl NW1	92	F14
Wrotham Rd, W13 1	123	L1
Wrotham Rd, Barn	40	C4
Wrotham Rd, Well	154	E2
Wroths Path, Loug	48	F2
Wrottesley Rd NW10	107	P3
Wrottesley Rd SE18	135	L12
Wroughton Rd SW11	145	U11
Wroughton Ter, NW4 3	71	S7
Wroxall Rd, Dag	100	F11
Wroxham Gdns N11	58	F14
Wroxham Rd SE28	118	G13
Wroxton Rd SE15	149	K4
Wrythe Grn, Cars 5	195	T6
Wrythe Grn Rd, Cars	195	T6
Wrythe La, Cars	195	M1
Wulfstan St W12	107	L11
Wyatt Cl SE16	131	T4
Wyatt Cl, Felt	156	G2
Wyatt Cl, Hayes	102	B10
Wyatt Dr SW13	125	T13
Wyatt Pk Rd SW2	165	L3
Wyatt Rd E7	97	P12
Wyatt Rd N5	93	T5
Wyatts La E17	78	E6
Wybert St, NW1 1	9	K9
Wyborne Way NW10	88	E13
Wyburn Av, Barn	40	E5
Wych Elm Pas, KingsT 2	159	T14
Wyche Gro, S Croy	198	A14
Wycherley Cl SE3	133	L13
Wycherley Cres, Barn	40	J11
Wychwood Av, Edg	53	N12
Wychwood Av, Th Hth	183	T5
Wychwood Cl, Edg	53	N12
Wychwood Cl, Sun	156	A12
Wychwood End, N6 1	74	F13
Wychwood Gdns, Ilf	80	F8
Wychwood Way, SE19 2	166	B11
Wyclif St EC1	11	N8
Wycliffe Cl, Well	153	T2
Wycliffe Rd SW11	146	B4
Wycliffe Rd SW19	163	K12
Wycombe Gdns NW11	90	G3
Wycombe Pl SW18	145	L11
Wycombe Rd N17	76	H2
Wycombe Rd, Ilf	80	F10
Wycombe Rd, Wem	106	B1
Wydehurst Rd, Croy	184	H13
Wydell Cl, Mord	180	A12
Wydeville Manor Rd SE12	169	R7
Wye Cl, Orp	189	T13
Wye St SW11	145	P4
Wyemead Cres E4	62	J3
Wyevale Cl, Pnr	66	A6
Wyfields, Ilf	81	K2
Wyfold Rd SW6	144	C1
Wyhill Wk, Dag	101	T12
Wyke Cl, Islw	122	F12
Wyke Gdns W7	122	G6
Wyke Rd E3	96	A14
Wyke Rd SW20	179	U3
Wykeham Av, Dag	100	F11
Wykeham Grn, Dag	100	F11
Wykeham Hill, Wem	87	T1
Wykeham Ri N20	56	D1
Wykeham Rd NW4	71	T9
Wykeham Rd, Har	68	J7
Wyld Way, Wem	88	C11
Wyldes Cl NW11	91	L2
Wyleu St SE23	149	R13
Wylie Rd, Sthl	121	P5
Wyllen Cl E1	113	L8
Wylo Dr, Barn	39	N11
Wymering Rd W9	108	H6
Wymond St SW15	143	U5
Wynan Rd E14	132	C9
Wynash Gdns, Cars	195	T10
Wyncham Av, Sid	171	S1
Wynchgate N14	58	H1
Wynchgate N21	43	K14
Wynchgate, Har	52	D13
Wyncroft Cl, Brom	188	E6
Wyndale Av NW9	70	B11
Wyndcliff Rd SE7	133	S12
Wyndcroft Cl, Enf	43	R6
Wyndham Cl, Orp	203	L2
Wyndham Cl, Sutt 2	194	H14
Wyndham Cres N19	92	E6
Wyndham Cres, Houns	139	N11
Wyndham Est SE5	36	A13
Wyndham Ms W1	15	U4
Wyndham Pl W1	15	U3
Wyndham Rd E6	98	A14
Wyndham Rd SE5	129	T14
Wyndham Rd W13	122	J5
Wyndham Rd, Barn	57	T2
Wyndham Rd, KingsT	159	U13
Wyndham St W1	15	T2
Wyneham Rd SE24	148	A10
Wynell Rd SE23	167	P5
Wynford Pl, Belv	137	N11
Wynford Rd N1	10	G1
Wynford Way SE9	170	F5
Wynlie Gdns, Pnr	66	D4
Wynn Br Cl, Wdf Grn	80	A1
Wynndale Rd E18	79	R1
Wynne Rd SW9	147	N4
Wynns Av, Sid	153	U10
Wynnstay Gdns W8	126	H5

Wynter St SW11	145	M7
Wynton Gdns SE25	184	E9
Wynton Pl W3	106	C11
Wynyard Ter SE11	34	H6
Wynyatt St EC1	11	N7
Wyre Gro, Edg	54	D6
Wyre Gro, Hayes	120	A8
Wyresdale Cres, Grnf	104	F5
Wythburn Pl W1	15	U7
Wythens Wk SE9	152	J11
Wythenshawe Rd, Dag	101	P6
Wythes Cl, Brom	188	E3
Wythes Rd E16	134	C2
Wythfield Rd SE9	152	E11
Wyvenhoe Rd, Har	85	T6
Wyvil Est SW8	34	B13
Wyvil Rd SW8	34	B12
Wyvis St E14	114	D9

Y

Yabsley St E14	132	F1
Yalding Rd SE16	37	R1
Yale Cl, Houns	139	L9
Yarborough Rd, SW19 2	181	N2
Yardley Cl E4	46	D10
Yardley La E4	46	D10
Yardley St WC1	10	J8
Yarmouth Cres N17	76	J9
Yarmouth Pl W1	24	H3
Yarnfield Sq SE15	148	H2
Yarnton Way SE2	136	G4
Yarnton Way, Erith	136	J4
Yarrow Cres E6	116	C9
Yateley St SE18	134	B6
Yates Ct NW2	90	B12
Yeading Av, Har	84	J2
Yeading Fork, Hayes	102	E9
Yeading Gdns, Hayes	102	C10
Yeading La, Hayes	102	C12
Yeading La, Nthlt	102	G4
Yeames Cl W13	104	G12
Yeate St N1	94	A14
Yeatman Rd N6	73	U12

Yeats Cl NW10	88	J11
Yeend Cl, W Mol	175	P7
Yeldham Rd W6	126	A10
Yellow Hammer Ct, NW9 2	71	K3
Yelverton Rd SW11	145	P4
Yenston Cl, Mord	180	H12
Yeo St E3	114	C9
Yeoman Cl E6	116	J13
Yeoman Cl SE27	165	R6
Yeoman Rd, Nthlt	85	K13
Yeoman St SE8	131	R7
Yeomans Acre, Ruis	66	A11
Yeoman's Row SW3	23	R11
Yeomans Way, Enf	45	K4
Yeomans Yd, E1 1	21	P9
Yeomen Way, Ilf	65	L11
Yeovil Cl, Orp	203	R3
Yeovilton Pl, Kings T	159	M9
Yerbury Rd N19	92	H5
Yester Dr, Chis	170	D14
Yester Pk, Chis	170	F12
Yester Rd, Chis	170	D14
Yew Cl, Buck H	64	B3
Yew Gro NW2	90	B8
Yew Tree Cl N21	43	N14
Yew Tree Cl, Well	154	A2
Yew Tree Cl, Wor Pk	193	K1
Yew Tree Gdns (Chadwell Heath), Rom	83	K9
Yew Tree Rd W12	107	M13
Yew Tree Wk, Houns	139	M10
Yew Wk, Har	86	C1
Yewdale Cl, Brom	169	K12
Yewfield Rd NW10	89	L12
Yewtree Cl N22	74	E2
Yewtree Cl, Har	67	R8
Yewtree Rd, Beck	185	T5
Yoakley Rd N16	94	C3
Yoke Cl N7	93	K11
Yolande Gdns SE9	152	C10
Yonge Pk N4	93	N5
York Av SW14	142	F9
York Av W7	122	D1
York Av, Sid	171	T4
York Av, Stan	69	K3
York Br NW1	8	D10

York Bldgs, WC2 11	18	C12
York Cl E6	116	E12
York Cl, W7 1	122	D1
York Cl, Mord	180	J7
York Cres, Borwd	38	G4
York Cres, Loug	48	D6
York Gate N14	42	J13
York Gate NW1	8	D11
York Gro SE15	149	L2
York Hill SE27	165	R5
York Hill, Loug	48	D5
York Hill Est SE27	165	R5
York Ho Pl W8	22	B5
York Ms NW5	92	D10
York Ms, Ilf	98	H5
York Par, Brent	123	N9
York Pl SW11	145	N5
York Pl, Dag	101	T11
York Pl, Ilf	98	J4
York Ri NW5	92	C6
York Ri, Orp	203	S3
York Rd E4	62	A9
York Rd E7	97	N12
York Rd E10	96	E6
York Rd E17	77	P10
York Rd N11	58	H11
York Rd N18	60	J11
York Rd N21	44	A14
York Rd SE1	26	G6
York Rd SW11	145	P4
York Rd SW18	145	M7
York Rd SW19	163	L11
York Rd W3	106	F11
York Rd W5	123	M6
York Rd, Barn	41	N9
York Rd, Brent	123	N10
York Rd, Croy	183	P13
York Rd, Houns	139	R5
York Rd, Ilf	98	H5
York Rd, Kings T	159	U14
York Rd, Nthwd	66	A4
York Rd, Rich 4	141	T9
York Rd, Sutt	194	G11
York Rd, Tedd	158	C8
York Sq, E14 7	113	R12
York St W1	16	A2
York St, Bark	117	L2
York St, Mitch	182	A14
York St, Twick	158	H1

York Ter, Erith	155	T1
York Ter E NW1	8	E11
York Ter W NW1	8	C12
York Way N1	111	K3
York Way N7	92	H11
York Way N20	57	T5
York Way, Borwd	38	G4
York Way, Chess	191	R13
York Way, Felt	157	L5
York Way Ct N1	111	K2
Yorkland Av, Well	153	T6
Yorkshire Cl N16	94	D6
Yorkshire Gdns N18	60	J10
Yorkshire Grey Pl NW3	91	M8
Yorkshire Grey Yd, WC1 3	18	E3
Yorkshire Rd E14	113	R12
Yorkshire Rd, Mitch	182	J8
Yorkton St E2	13	R3
Young Rd E16	115	T10
Young St W8	22	B7
Youngmans Cl, Enf	43	T1
Young's Bldgs, EC1 6	12	A10
Youngs Rd, Ilf	81	N11
Yoxley App, Ilf	81	M11
Yoxley Dr, Ilf	81	M11
Yukon Rd SW12	146	D13
Yuletide Cl NW10	88	J12
Yunus Khan Cl E17	78	B10

Z

Zampa Rd SE16	131	L10
Zander Ct, E2 5	13	U5
Zangwill Rd SE3	152	B1
Zealand Rd E3	113	R3
Zennor Rd SW12	164	E1
Zenoria St SE22	148	E8
Zermatt Rd, Th Hth	183	T8
Zetland St E14	114	E10
Zion Pl, Th Hth	184	A8
Zion Rd, Th Hth	184	A8
Zoar St SE1	27	T2
Zoffany St N19	92	H3